8 M - 531

Compiled and published by Kennedy Publications
publishers of **Consultants News, Executive Recruiter News**
Directory of Executive Recruiters, Directory of Management Consultants
and **Directory of Outplacement Firms**
Templeton Road, Fitzwilliam, N.H. 03447
(603) 585-6544, FAX 585-9555

Library of Congress Catalog Card Number 73-642226
ISBN #0-916654-72-9

Price $39.95

Publisher's Note . . .

This publication is much more than just an up-to-date listing of executive recruiters: it is designed as a companion to people interested in changing jobs, and also as a guide to organizations seeking professional assistance in filling key posts. It has become the commanding reference in this field.

For this reason you'll find a goodly amount of text explaining the search business: advice on resumes, hints on working with recruiters, do's & don'ts, etc.

The office listings and cross-indexes, of course, are the "heart" of the publication, and this 21st edition is further evidence of our commitment to produce the very best listing of executive recruiters at the lowest possible price. We include the names of key principals at each firm (over 5000 of them, fully cross-indexed). We also asked each firm to provide a 10-word self-description for further clarification and positioning.

We invest thousands of dollars every year to update and improve this directory, and we sincerely appreciate the response it has received in the marketplace. Mentioned regularly by researchers and writers covering the executive job market, this directory is quite possibly the most widely circulated such volume in the world today.

You might be interested to know that, while two-thirds of the sales are to individuals interested in a job change, the other third has been to hiring organizations trying to find a recruiting firm. In recent years we have acknowledged this organizational interest with a Corporate Edition while continuing the Personal Edition.

We welcome user comments and suggestions: tell us how this directory works for you . . . and how we can improve it. (Please remember that recruiters don't like to be telephoned or faxed, and this is why we don't include their numbers in this Personal Edition.)

Remember, too, that the price of this publication is kept as low as possible as a service to individuals who need it.

For this reason—as stated elsewhere—we cannot condone—without permission or payment of an appropriate fee—**commercial** use (i.e. by an organization selling something to recruiters or copying into a data base for sale in whole or in part to individuals or organizations).

James H. Kennedy
Editor & Publisher

Kathleen Kennedy Burke
Director of Research

Foreword

Every effort has been made to obtain up-to-date and reliable information. We assume no responsibility, however, for errors or omissions and reserve the right to include or eliminate listings and otherwise edit the list based on our judgment as to what is useful to our customers.

Let us add, too, that one's chances of getting a new job as a result of sending a resume to a recruiter are rather slim. Many do connect, however, and some job-changers have used this directory several times over the years. We continue to feel, therefore, that following this course is a worthwhile element in the total job-change program.

Published annually since 1971

21st edition, 1991

Note: Each edition is carefully updated and obsoletes the preceding one. SEND FOR THE NEW EDITION RATHER THAN USE THIS COPY AFTER 1992.

Table of Contents

FOR CLIENTS

LISTINGS

APPENDIX

About This Directory

Designed to function as a **workbook** as well as a continuing reference, this listing of over 2300 firms and offices is admittedly a compromise. There are many more firms or individuals offering "executive search" service, but some are too small or too regional to warrant listing, others offer counseling or other services for which the individual must pay, still others we simply haven't found yet.

To our knowledge, all of the firms in this directory are compensated by management to locate executives. (If any operate the other way, we would like to know so their names can be deleted.)

We do not intentionally list firms that charge any fee to the individual.

Locally you can supplement this information by looking in the Yellow Pages under the following headings: Management Consultants; Executive Search Consultants; Personnel Consultants. Remember, however, that the telephone company is not very discriminating in its policy of allowing businesses to select categories for listing! An "Executive Search" firm that is also listed under "Employment Agencies" is probably the latter. Check with the Better Business Bureau or Chamber of Commerce for reference.

Turnover in this business is high; new firms are constantly being formed, partnerships dissolve, addresses change. **Using a current directory pays for itself in time and postage savings alone.**

Specialist vs Generalist Recruiters

Most executive recruiters do not specialize, believing that their techniques are universally applicable. (Too, specialization can become a dead-end street for the recruiting firm that ethically follows the rules forbidding recruiting from clients.)

Many recruiters, however, do specialize: some in a single industry (e.g., textiles), some in a single functional area (e.g., training.)

Most of the firms listed in this directory classified themselves as generalists or specialists. Generalists checked "Most" at the top of the list of Functions and/or Industries. Specialists were allowed to select up to five specialties from each listing. In addition, those firms viewing themselves as both generalists and specialists were allowed to check both "Most" and up to five specialties.

Importance of Professional Affiliations

There is only one accrediting organization for executive search firms: the Association of Executive Search Consultants (AESC). It has about 100 members.

Membership in AESC is indicated first under "Professional Affiliations" in the basic listing of each search firm.

Listees were invited to name additional affiliations that they considered to be significant, and these are given after the AESC designation . . . i.e.

<table>
<tr><td align="center">AESC</td><td align="center">ASPA, APA, etc.</td></tr>
<tr><td align="center">♠</td><td align="center">♠</td></tr>
<tr><td>indicative of a commitment
to professionalism in
executive recruiting</td><td>possibly indicative of
professional competence or
skill in a specific field</td></tr>
</table>

Note that some listees have included "professional" affiliations that are relatively meaningless. (Some, for example, proudly mentioned membership in American Management Association, but such references have been mercifully deleted: to our knowledge AMA's admission requirements do not equate with professional recognition in any accrediting sense).

Because we don't know enough about other professional bodies, however, we've allowed most of the claimed memberships to stand. Users of this directory familiar with specific industries or areas of technical/functional expertise can get added insight into each consulting firm by judging the "Other Professional Affiliations" it has claimed.

Professional Association

AESC
ASSOCIATION OF EXECUTIVE SEARCH CONSULTANTS, INC.

The following information is from the Association of Executive Search Consultants.

AESC was organized in 1959 as the Association of Executive Recruiting Consultants. It brought together leading consultants who, for the first time, established standards of ethical practice for their profession. Today, AESC membership identifies the consultant who is not only pledged to these high standards, but who is also recognized by professional peers (many of them competitors) as having the highest competence and integrity.

The client engaging an executive recruiting consultant will find that AESC's Code of Ethics and Professional Practice Guidelines assures him of a confidential clientconsultant relationship as with a banker, lawyer, or accountant.

CODE OF ETHICS EFFECTIVE 1984

I. Professionalism
Executive search consulting is a professional endeavor. A profession is characterized by the objectivity, integrity and thoroughness of its practitioners. Members will maintain the highest standards of professional work and behavior so that their actions reflect favorably on the Association, its members, their clients and candidates. In this endeavor, members will serve their clients in a professional manner, including the performance of at least the following services before proposing any candidates:

A. Meetings with the client to develop understanding of the client's organization and needs and the position to be filled;

B. Written documentation outlining the position description, scope and character of the services to be provided;

C. Thorough independent research on the nature and needs of the client organization;

D. Comprehensive search for qualified candidates;

E. Thorough evaluation of potential candidates, including in-depth personal interviews, verification of credentials, and careful assessment of the individual's strengths and weaknesses, in order to provide an adequate basis for independent and expert recommendations to the client; and

F. Either before or after presentation of a candidate, but prior to final selection by the client, performance of comprehensive reference checking.

Any practices that do not embody the above process cannot be objective, are adverse to the client's best interest, undermine independent judgment, tend to bring disrepute to the profession, and are in violation of this code.

II. Qualifications
Members will accept only those assignments that they are qualified to undertake on the basis of full knowledge of the client situation and the professional competence and capacity of the consultants involved. Assignments accepted will be based on a comprehensive written document outlining the scope and character of the services to be provided.

III. Client Relationship
Members will, in each assignment undertaken, define, preferably in writing, what constitutes "the client organization." The member will not recruit or cause to be recruited any person from the defined client organization for a period of two years after the completion of such assignment unless the member firm and client agree in writing to an exception. The member will disclose to the client limitations arising through service to other clients that may affect the scope of the search assignment. In the event that a client retains a member to conduct a search and any other firm has already been retained by the client, the member shall assure that its retention is fully disclosed to such other previously retained firms.

IV. Confidentiality
Members shall regard as totally confidential all information concerning the business affairs of their clients and of candidates.

V. Promotion Activities
Members will conduct all firm promotion, public relations and new business activities in a manner that involves no representations, express or implied, that are false, deceptive, unsubstantiated, or that otherwise have a capacity to mislead.

VI. Promotion of Competition

It is the policy of AESC and its members to promote free and fair competition in the provision of executive search consulting services. Neither AESC nor any member will engage in any unlawful restraint of trade, unfair method of competition, or other violation of the antitrust laws.

PROFESSIONAL PRACTICE GUIDELINES

AESC requires that any search conducted by a member firm result from a business relationship between the hiring organization and the member firm, and otherwise conform to the principles set forth in the Code of Ethics and the following guidelines.

Guarantees of Placement

Executive search is a specialized form of management consulting that may or may not result in the placement of an executive. Accordingly, in order to avoid misleading the client, proposals and presentations should not guarantee placement as the inevitable conclusion of a search assignment.

Resume Floating & Executive Referral

AESC member firms are retained to fill bona-fide executive vacancies. Therefore, consultants shall not volunteer resumes in the absence of a specific search unless:

1. the client has asked them to do so and;
2. there is an ongoing and current retainer-based client relationship where such transmittals have been contractually promised or contemplated.

Clearly, resumes should not be presented to non-clients. However, source lists of potential candidates and of summary backgrounds may be transmitted as part of the process of defining the search and/or competing for an assignment. Such source lists are permissible only if the individuals are not represented as qualified candidates, nor that they have been interviewed for this specific assignment, and that their confidentiality has been protected.

Transmittal of a resume on behalf of a friend or business acquaintance as a courtesy without any future client expectation takes advantage of the consultant/client relationship and is discouraged.

Misrepresentation

Telephone sourcing techniques that involve falsehood regarding the identity of the caller or the purpose of the call are unethical.

Members shall assure that their professional and research staffs understand and comply with this provision and that any subcontractors employed by the search firm are similarly compliant.

Client and Candidate Communications

Relationships among the search firm, its clients and its candidates should be characterized by honesty, objectivity, accuracy and an appropriate sense of urgency.

The progress of the assignment shall be communicated by frank, timely communications and periodic reports.

When it becomes apparent that no candidates can be presented that meet the specifications or if the length of the search will differ considerably from that originally anticipated, the client should be advised promptly and offered alternative courses of action. If the client is unlikely to benefit from the continuation of the assignment, cancellation should be recommended.

During the interview phase, the client, the position, and the candidate shall be presented as honestly and factually as possible.

Where the client characterizes his organization falsely or withholds relevant information from candidates which could tend to mislead candidates, the search firm, if not able to rectify the situation, should withdraw from the assignment.

Where the candidate misleads the client or the search consultant regarding his or her qualifications, the client shall be advised and the candidate rejected unless client, candidate and consultant agree that the candidacy should continue following disclosure of the facts.

Prospects and candidates shall be kept advised in a timely fashion of the status and disposition of their candidacies.

Candidates shall not be presented for client interviews without prior interviews in person by the search consultant nor recommended for employment without reference checks.

Firm Advertising

AESC firms may advertise. Any such advertising shall be conducted in a professional manner in conformity with Federal, state and local laws and regulations.

Public Relations

Articles and interviews with the media shall be conducted with dignity and discretion so as to reflect favorably upon the AESC, the client and the executive search profession. Client and/or candidate approval shall be obtained before external discussion of specific assignments.

Position Advertising

Advertising as a mechanism for filling a position is generally discouraged.

When advertising is used because conventional search techniques are ineffective or if dictated by law or practice, the client shall be advised in advance and his approval secured.

Fees

The written documentation outlining the scope and character of the engagement shall specify the fees to be charged for the services rendered and the basis of the expenses to be reimbursed.

As the executive search consultant is retained and paid scby the client to be completely objective in the evaluation of candidates, under no circumstances shall a member firm accept payment for counseling or assisting an individual to find employment.

Conflict of Interest

Any business or personal relationships between search consultant and candidate that might affect, or appear to affect, the consultant's objectivity in evaluating the candidate should be disclosed to the client before presentation of the candidate.

Non-Discrimination

AESC members affirm without reservation the principles of equal opportunity in employment. As a matter of policy and practice, member organizations of the AESC do not and will not discriminate against qualified candidates for any unlawful reasons, including race, religion, gender, national origin, age, or disability. AESC members encourage and anticipate that their clients will also comply with non-discrimination policies and practices.

For more information and a list of member firms, send $25 to:
Association of Executive Search Consultants
230 Park Avenue
New York, New York 10169
(212) 949-9556

International Association of Corporate & Professional Recruiters, Inc.

IACPR

Founded by leading corporate human resource executives and key people from respected management recruitment firms, the International Association of Corporate and Professional Recruiters is a forum for its members. The organization is dedicated to developing and promoting standards and ethical practices in the identification, recruitment, evaluation and referral of candidates for executive and professional positions in the United States and abroad.

Our Mission Statement:

Through the effective partnership of its members, the mission of the IACPR is to provide all constituents with the highest level of executive resources by providing leadership to the executive recruiting profession and to business organizations, on current and emerging issues relevant to executive recruiting and related areas of human resource management.

Our Purposes:

To develop and promote standards and ethical practices in the identification, recruitment, evaluation and referral of candidates for executive and professional positions.

To provide a format through which members may exchange ideas and information and generally aid one another in conducting executive recruitment.

To enhance the professional status and importance of executive recruitment.

To promote personal acquaintanceships among executive recruiting professionals.

To sponsor and conduct conferences, meetings and symposia designed to inform members and other interested parties of legislative developments, current research, problem issues and practices relating to the executive recruitment profession.

POLICIES & GUIDELINES OF THE ASSOCIATION

Section 1. Membership Criteria

Membership in IACPR is limited to senior-level Human Resources executives and retained executive search consultants, whose current or primary responsibilities include executive search and who have at least ten years of relevant business experience. At the time of application for membership, the candidate must currently have responsibility for assigning or conducting searches for executive personnel. Individuals are only admitted or retained as members of IACPR if their personal recruiting practices, and/or the recruiting practices of individuals under their direction, include all of the actions listed below before candidates are proposed:

- Meet with the client or hiring manager to develop an understanding of the open position and of the person needed to fill it.
- Develop written specifications for approval.
- Conduct comprehensive research for qualified candidates.
- Evaluate potential candidates through in-depth personal interviews.
- Perform comprehensive reference checking.

IACPR takes the position that the above items are always necessary to the conduct of a professional search whether performed internally by corporate staff or externally by search consultants. All candidates are to be sponsored by four professional references, two of whom are current members of the Association.

Section 2. Professional Recruiting Guidelines

A. Purpose
To develop, establish and promote ethical standards and practices among the IACPR membership.

B. Privileged Information
It is vital to the executive search process that exchange of information between the search firm and the company be held in confidence. The Executive Search Consultants must have access to sensitive information such as organizational strengths and weaknesses, marketing plans, new product developments and strategic plans in order to set the benchmarks for qualifying candidates. The use of such information for any other purpose is prohibited. Similarly, company representatives must treat information from a search firm with confidentiality such as candidate profiles, search strategies, search firm policies and procedures, and data gleaned through candidate interviews.

C. Defined Limits
Executive Search Consultants will agree with the client what constitutes the "client organization" and will not recruit nor cause to be recruited any person

from the defined organization for a mutually agreed upon period after the completion of an assignment for the client organization. Search firms are obliged to notify a prospective client in advance of any companies appropriate to the search that will not be used due to prior client obligations.

D. Reference Checking
A feeling of trust must be preserved and cultivated between an Executive Search Consultant and a potential candidate. Reference checking without the knowledge and permission of the candidate, while sometimes expedient, is nevertheless a disservice to the candidate, unprofessional and is also unlawful.

E. Discrimination
No members of IACPR will permit candidate discrimination based on age, sex, religion, race or country of origin or handicap, except when addressing an imbalance by affirmative action.

F. Professional Conduct
Each member of IACPR assumes responsibility for maintaining ethical standards and projecting an image of professionalism. Members should refrain from making derogatory comments that adversely affect the interest of the Association or individual members or which conflicts with the purpose and standards of the Association.

Section 3. Professional Recruiting Commitment to Candidates

- A candidate will be informed by the Executive Search Consultant of the role of the search firm in the assignment, the nature of the engagement, and how the search process is likely to evolve.
- A candidate has the right to accurate information from the search consultant and/or corporate recruiter, negative as well as positive, about the position, company, hiring executive, and business conditions.
- A candidate can expect confidentiality and discretion at all times. Specific information obtained by the search consultant during discussions with the candidate may not be disclosed to the client if the candidate specifically so requests.
- A candidate must be made aware, however, that the Executive Search Consultant can choose not to present a candidate based on a judgment that the candidate is not qualified or appropriate for the position.
- A candidate will be told by the Executive Search Consultant and/or corporate recruiter the title, specifications of the position, reporting relationship, location, background of the company, and responsibilities of the position prior to a first interview with the hiring executive.
- A candidate will be kept informed of the status of his or her potential candidacy on a timely and candid basis by the search consultant or corporate recruiter.

- A candidate should expect that the Executive Search Consultant and/or corporate recruiter, or another company executive will not check references without the candidate's approval or do anything that might otherwise jeopardize the candidate's present position.

- A candidate should be informed of the fact, when appropriate, that an offer may be contingent upon successful completion of reference checks, special testing or any other conditions of employment.

- A candidate should expect that an Executive Search Consultant and/or corporate recruiter will objectively communicate his opinion of the impact on the individual's career of joining the company in the specified position.

- A candidate who is not ultimately offered the position can expect that all files will be kept confidential by the Executive Search Consultant and/or corporate client. Resumes will not be sent to another client or elsewhere in the organization without the candidate's prior approval.

- A candidate will be informed promptly by the Executive Search Consultant and/or corporate recruiter of the client's selection decision.

- A candidate should expect to continue to communicate with the Executive Search Consultant and/or corporate recruiter for at least six months after joining the company to ensure that any adjustment problems on either side are properly handled.

For more information, contact
International Association of Corporate and Professional Recruiters, Inc.
4000 Woodstone Way
Louisville, KY 40241
(502) 228-4500

Key to "Other" Professional Affiliations

Note: This list includes most of the professional associations referenced in the text, and some of these are more meaningful and more legitimate than others. Additional information (headquarters, membership requirements) on most of these organizations can be found in Gale Research's **Encyclopedia of Associations**.

AAA	Amer. Acad. of Act./Am. Arbritration Assoc./Am. Arch. Assoc.
AAAI	American Assn for Artificial Intelligence
AAAS	American Association of the Advancement of Science
AACC	American Association of Clinical Chemists
AAEL	American Association of of Equipment Lessors
AAF	American Advertising Federation
AAFA	American Association of Finance & Accounting
AAFRC	American Association of Fund-Raising Counsel
AAHC	American Association of Hospital/Healthcare Consultants
AAHE	American Association for Higher Education
AAMA	Amer Apparel Mfg Assoc/Amer Acad of Med Admn/Asian Amer Mfg Assoc
AAMD	American Academy of Medical Directors
AAPA	Amer Assoc of Public Administration/Amer Acad of Physician Assistants
AAPC	American Association of Professional Consultants
AAPG	American Association of Petroleum Geologists
AAPS	American Association of Pharmaceutical Scientists
AASA	American Association of School Administrators
AATCC	American Association of Textile Chemists and Colorists
AATT	American Association of Textile Technologists
AAUP	American Association of University Professors
ABA	American Banking Association or American Bar Association
ABC	Assoc Builders & Contractors/Assoc of Biotechnology Companies
ACA	American Compensation Assoc./American Correctional Assoc.
ACE	American Council on Education
ACEP	American College of Emergency Physicians
ACF	American Culinary Federation
ACG	Association for Corporate Growth
ACHE	American College of Healthcare Executives
ACI	American Concrete Institute
ACM	Association for Computing Machinery
ACME	Association of Consulting Management Engineers
ACNY	Advertising Club of New York

ACOG	American College of Obstetrics and Gynenocology
ACPE	American College of Physician Executives
ACS	American Chemical Society, American Ceramic Society
ACT	American College of Toxicology
ACerS	American Ceramic Society
ADAPSO	Association of Data Processing Service Organizations
ADC	Art Directors Club
ADPA	American Defense Preparedness Association
AEA	American Economic Association/American Electronics Assoc.
AED	Associated Equipment Distributors
AERC	Association of Executive Recruiting Consultants
AESC	Association of Executive Search Consultants
AFA	AirForce Association
AFCEA	Armed Forces Communications and Electronics Association
AFPE	American Foundation for Pharmaceutical Education
AFS	American Foundrymen's Society
AFSMI	Association of Field Service Managers International
AGA	American Gas Association/Association of Government Accountants
AGC	Associated General Contractors of America
AGE	Association of Energy Engineers
AGPA	American Group Practice Association
AHA	American Hospital Association
AHMA	American Hotel and Motel Association
AHRC	American Human Resources Council
AHRSP	Association of Human Resource Systems Professionals
AHS	American Helicopter Society
AI	Appraisal Institute
AIA	American Institute of Architects
AIAA	American Institute of Aeronautics and Astronautics
AIC	American Institute of Chemists
AICE	American Institute of Chemical Engineers
AICHE	American Institute of Chemical Engineers
AICPA	American Institute of Certified Public Accountants
AIEF	Advertising Industry Emergency Fund
AIGA	American Institute of Graphic Arts
AIHA	American Industrial Hygiene Associations
AIIE	American Institute of Industrial Engineers
AIIM	Association of Information and Image Management
AIME	American Institute of Mining Metallurgical & Pet. Engineers
AIMT	Association for Integrated Manufacturing Technology
AIP	American Institute of Planners/American Institute of Physics
AIPG	American Institute of Professional Geologists
AISI	American Iron and Steel Institute
AIUM	American Institute for Ultrasound in Medicine
AIWF	American Institute of Wine & Food
AJA	American Jail Association
ALA	American Library Association
AM	Academy of Management
AMA	American Medical/American Marketing/American Mgmt. Assoc.
AMBAE	Association of MBA Executives
AMC	American Mining Congress or Assoc. of Managing Consultants
AME	Association for Manufacturing Excellence
AMI	American Meat Institute

AMS	Administrative Management Society
AMWA	American Medical Writers Association
ANA	Association of Naval Aviation
ANS	American Nuclear Society
AOC	Association of Old Crows (Electronic Defense Group)
AOTA	American Occupational Therapy Association
APA	American Psychological/Planning/Payroll Association
APAA	Automotive Parts and Accessories Association
APACS	Association of Physician Assistants in Cardiovascular Surgery
APC	American Pension Conference, Assoc. of Personal Consultants
APCC	Association of Professional Computer Consultants
APCNY	Association of Personnel Consultants of New York
API	American Petroleum Institute
APICS	American Production and Inventory Control Society
APPAC	Association of Professional Placement Agencies and Consultan
APS	Academy of Pharmaceutical Sciences/American Purchasing Society
APTA	Amer Public Transit Association/Amer Physical Therapy Association
APhA	American Pharmaceutical Association
ARA	American Restaurant Association
ASA	American Scientific/Statistical Assoc./Amer. Society of Appraisers
ASAC	American Society of Agricultural Consultants
ASAE	American Society of Association Executives
ASCA	Arizona Search Consultants Association
ASCE	American Society of Civil Engineers
ASHE	American Society for Hospital Engineering
ASHHRA	American Society for Healthcare Human Resources Admin.
ASHRM	American Society of Hospital Risk Mgrs/Human Resources Mgmt.
ASIS	American Society for Industrial Security/Information Science
ASJA	American Society of Journalists and Authors
ASM	Assoc. for Sys. Mgmt./Amer. Soc. for Microbiol/Soc. of Metal
ASMC	American Society for Management Consultants
ASME	American Society of Mechanical/Metallurgical Engineers
ASMS	American Society for Mass Spectrometry
ASNT	American Society for Nondestructive Testing
ASPA	American Society of Personnel Administration
ASQC	American Society for Quality Control
ASSC	Association Search and Selection Consultancies
ASSE	American Society of Safety Engineers
ASTA	American Seed Trade Association
ASTD	American Society for Training & Development
ASTL	American Society of Transportation & Logistics
ASTM	American Society of Testing Materials
ASWA	American Society of Women Accountants
ASWCPA	American Society of Women CPA's
ATA	American Trucking Association/American Telemarketing Assoc.
ATLA	American Trial Lawyers Association
ATMA	American Textile Machinery Association
ATMI	American Textile Manufacturers Institute
AUSA	Association of United States Army
AVS	American Vacuum Society

AWBO	Association of Women Business Owners
AWC	Association for Women in Computing
AWMA	Air and Waste Management Association
AWWA	American Water Works Association
BCPA	British Columbia Psychological Associatiom
BCS	Boston/British Computer Society
BCUN	Business Council for the United Nations
BDPA	Black Data Processing Assoc.
BIA	Building Institute/Industry of America
BIC	Business Industry Council
BMA	Biomedical Marketing/Bank Marketing/Business Marketing Assoc
BOMA	Building Owners and Managers Association
BPAA	Business/Professional Advertising Association
BPS	British Psychological Society/BioPhysical Society
CACI	Chicago/Colorado Association of Commerce and Industry
CACPA	California Association of CPA's
CADM	Chicago Association of Direct Marketing
CAHMA	California Hotel and Motel Association
CAI	Community Association Institute
CAMC	Canadian Association of Management Consultants
CAPC	Calif./Connecticut/Colorado Assoc. of Personnel Consultants
CASA	Computer & Automated Systems Association
CASE	Council for Advancement and Support of Education
CBA	Consumer Bankers Assn./California Bankers/Bar Association
CBIA	Connecticut Business and Industry Association
CCA	Chicago Compensation Association
CDA	Commercial Development Associaton
CDMA	Canadian Direct Marketing Association
CERA	California Executive Recruiters Association
CEW	Cosmetic Executive Women
CHA	Catholic Health Association
CIMA	Construction Industry Manufacturers Association
CIPCA	Cogeneration: Independent Power Coalition of America
CLA	California Libraries Association
CLM	Council of Logistics Management
CMA	Colorado Mining Association or Chemical Manufacturers Assoc.
CMRA	Chem. Market Research Assoc./Chemical Management and Resorce Assco.
CONRO	Consultants Roundtable
CPA	Canadian Psychological Association
CPC	College Placement Council
CPDG	Chicagoland Pharmaceutival Discussion Group
CPPA	Calif. Professional Placement Association
CPPQ	Corporation of Psychology, Province of Quebec
CRA	California Restaurant Association
CRS	Controlled Release Society
CSA	Communications Security Association
CSCPA	California Society of CPA's
CSH	Cornell Society of Hotelmen
CSI	Computer Search International or Computer Security Institute
CUPA	College and University Personnel Association

DAPC	Dayton Association Personnel Consultants
DCAT	Drug Chemical and Allied Trades Association
DIA	Drug Information Association
DMA	Direct Marketing Association
DMCG	Direct Marketing Creative Guild
DMCNY	Direct Marketing Club of NY
DMCSC	Direct Marketing Club of Southern California
DMI	Design Management Institute
DPMA	Data Processing Management Association
DSA	Direct Selling Association
EDMA	European Direct Marketing Association
EDPAA	EDP Auditors Association
EIA	Electronic Industry Association
EMA	Employment Management Association
EMI	Equipment Manufacturers Institute
EMMA	Emerging Medical Manufacturers Association
ESD	Engineers Society of Detroit
FAF	Financial Analyst Federation
FAPC	Florida Association of Personnel Consultants
FEI	Financial Executives Institute
FIN	First Interview Network
FIPC	First International Group of Personnel Consultants
FMA	Fulfillment Management Association/Fabricators Manufacturers Assoc.
FMG	Financial Managers Society
FMI	Food Marketing Institute
FPA	Flexible Packaging Association
FPRS	Forest Products Research Society
FPS	Fluid Power Society
FSN	Financial Search Network
GAPC	Georgia Associaton of Personnel Consultants
GCAPC	Greater Cleveland Association of Personnel Consultants
GHA	Group Health Association
GHAA	Group Health Association of America
GMRA	Grocery Manufacturers Representative Association
HAAPC	Houston Area Association of Personnel Consultants
HESS	Houston Engineering & Scientific Society
HFMA	Hospital/Healthcare Financial Management Associaton
HFS	Human Factors Society
HIMSS	Healthcare Information and Management Systems Society
HMAI	Hotel/Motel Association of Illinois
HMCRI	Hazardous Materials Control Research Institute
HRA	Human Resource Association
HRMA	Human Resources Management Association
HRMAC	Human Resource Management Association of Chicago
HRP	Human Resource Planning Society
HRPS	Human Resource Planning Society
HRSP	Human Resources Systems Professionals
HSMA	Hotel Sales Managers Assoc., Hotel Sales & Marketing Assoc.
IAAO	International Association of Assessing Officers
IABC	International Association of Business Communicators

IACPR	International Assoc. of Corporate & Professional Recruiters
IAER	Illinois Association Execuitve Recruiters
IAFP	International Association of Financial Planners
IAGAC	International Association of Graphic Arts Consultants
IAHA	International Association of Hospitality Accountants
IAP	Illinois Assoc. of Personnel Consultants
IAPC	Illinois/Indiana/Iowa Association of Personnel Consultants
IAPW	International Association for Personnel Women
IBA	Institute of Business Appraisers/Illinois Bankers Assoc.
IBRT	International Bankers Roundtable
ICI	Investment Company Institute
ICMA	Int'l. City Management Assoc./Institute of Certified Management Acct
ICMCC	Inst. of Cert. Management Consultants of Canada
ICPA	Inter-City Personnel Associates
ICPM	Institute of Certified Professional Managers
ICSA	International Customer Service Association
ICSC	International Council of Shopping Centers
IDSA	Industrial Designers Society of America
IEEE	Institute of Electronic and Electrical Engineers
IERA	Illinois Executive Recruiters Association
IESC	Illinois Executive Search Consultants
IFA	International Franchise Association
IFAI	Industrial Fabrics Association International
IFG	International Fashion Group
IFMA	Int'l. Facility Management/Foodservice Manufacturers Assoc.
IFSEA	International Food Service Executives Association
IFT	Institute of Food Technology/Int'l. Foundation for Timesharing
IIA	Institute of Internal Auditors/ Information Industry Assoc.
IIE	Institute of Industrial Engineers
IMA	Institute of Management Accounting
IMC	Institute of Management Consultants
IMCO	Institute of Management Consultants of Ontario
IMD	International Management Development
IMESC	Illinois Management and Executive Search Consultants
IMRT	International Management Roundtable
INS	Insurance National Search
IOPP	Institute of Packaging Professionals
IPA	Illinois Psychological Assoc. or Inter-City Personnel Assoc.
IPAC	Industrial Psychological Association of Chicago
IPCCNY	Independent Personnel Consultants of Central New York
IPMA	Internatonal Personnel Management Assciation
IPMI	International Precision Metals Institute
IPRA	International Public Relations Association
IPT	Institute of Property Taxation
IRA	Illinois Restaurant Association
IREM	Institute of Real Estate Management
IRTS	International Radio and Television Society
ISA	Instrument Society of America & Int'l. Search Associates
ISCPA	Illinois Society of CPA's
ISHM	International Society for Hybrid Microelectronics
ISP&SM	International Society for Planning & Strategic Management
ISPA	Institute for Science and Public Affairs
ISPE	International Society of Pharmaceutical Engineers
ISSA	Int'l. Sanitary Supply Assoc./ Info. Systems Security Assoc.

ITE	Institute of Transportation Engineers
ITEA	International Test and Evaluation association
ITPA	Independent Telephone Pioneers Association
JAS	Japan America Society
JS	Japan Society
KTA	Knitted Textile Association
LOMA	Life Office Management Association
MAAPC	Mid-Atlantic Association of Personnel Consultants
MAHRC	Minn. Association of Human Resource Consultants
MAPC	MA.,MN.,or MI. Association of Personnel Consultants
MAPRC	Maryland Association of Professional Recruitment Consultants
MBA	Mortgage Bankers Association
MESA	Minority Executive Search Association
MGMA	Medical Group Management Association
MHA	Massachusetts Hospital Association
MHRPG	Midwest Human Resources Planners Group
MORS	Military Operations Research Society
MPPC	Massachusetts Professional Placement Consultants
MSPC	Midwest Society of Professional Consultants
NAA	National Association of Accountants
NABA	National Association of Black Accountants
NABE	National Association of Business Econcomists
NABIS	National Association of Business & Industrial Saleswomen
NACCB	National Assoc of Computer or Contract Consulting Businesses
NACD	National Association of Corporate Directors
NACE	National Association of Catering Executives
NACORE	National Association of Corporate Real Estate Executives
NACUBO	National Association of College and University Business Officers
NAER	National Association of Executive Recruiters
NAFBR	National Association of Food and Beverage Recruiters
NAFE	National Association for Female Executives
NAHB	National Association of Home Builders
NAHD	National Association of Hospital Development
NAHR	National Association for Healthcare Recruitment
NAIOP	National Association of Industrial Office Parks
NAIS	National Association of Independent Schools
NALSC	National Association of Legal Search Consultants
NAMA	National Automatic Merchandising Assoc./Nat'l. Agri-Marketing Assoc.
NAPC	National/Nebraska Association of Personnel Consultants
NAPM	National Association for Purchasing Management
NAPPH	National Association of Private Psychiatric Hospitals
NAPR	National Association of Physician Recruiters
NARI	National Association of the Remodeling Industry
NASCP	North American Society for Corporate Planning
NASP	National Association of School Psychologists
NATA	North American Telecommunications Association
NATS	National Association of Temporary Services

NAWBO	National Association of Women Business Owners
NBN	National Banking Network
NBNS	National Banking Network Systems
NCA	National Computer Association/National Club Association
NCAPC	North Carolina Association of Personnel Consultants
NCHCM	National College of Health Care Marketing
NCHRC	Northern California Human Resource Council
NCPA	North Carolina Psyc. Assoc.
NCPDM	National Council of Physical Distribution Management
NCTA	National Cable Television Assoc.
NEA	National Employment Association
NEAIHC	New England Association of Independent Healthcare Consultants
NEDMA	New England Direct Marketing Association
NEHRA	Northeast Human Resource Association
NEHRMG	New England Human Resource Management Group
NEN	National Environmental Network
NFIB	National Federation of Independent Business
NFPA	Nat'l Fluid Power Assoc/Nat'l Fed. of Paralegal Assn.
NHAPC	New Hampshire Association of Personnel Consultants
NHIF	National Head Injury Foundation
NIIA	Northern Illinois Industrial Association
NIRA	National Insurance Recruiters Association
NIRI	National Investor Relations Institute
NJACP	New Jersey Association of Personnel Consultants
NJAPC	New Jersey Association of Personnel Consultants
NJAWBO	New Jersey Association of Women Business Owners
NKMA	National Knitwear Manufacturers Assoc.
NL	Navy League
NMHC	National Multi Housing Councel
NNEAPC	Northern New England Association of Personnel Consultants
NOMDA	National Office Machine Dealers Association
NPA	National Personnel Associates
NPC	National Association of Personnel Consultants
NRA	National Restaurant/National Rehabilitation Association
NRF	National Retail Federation
NRMA	National Retail Merchants Association
NSC	National Safety Council
NSFRE	National Society of Fund Raising Executives
NSPE	National Society of Professional Engineers
NWWA	National Water Well Association
NYABE	New York Association of Business Economists
NYBA	New York Biotechnology Association
NYHRP	New York Human Resource Planners
NYPMA	New York Personnel Management Association
NYSBA	New York State Bar Association
NYSSA	New York Society of Security Analysts
OAPC	Ohio/Oregon/Oklahoma Association Personnel Consultants
ODN	Organization Development Network
ONS	Oncocogy Nursing Society
OPA	Ontario Psychological Association
ORSA	Operations Research Society Of America
ORTHO	American OrthoPsychiatric Association
OSA	Optical Society of America

PA	Proprietory Association
PAC	Pharmaceutical Advertising Council
PAPC	Pennsylvania/Pittsburgh Association of Personnel Consultants
PAPER	Pulp & Paper Executive Recruiters
PATCA	Professional and Technical Consultants Association
PDA	Parenteral Drug Association
PEI	Planning Executives Institute
PERC	Professional Employment Research Council
PF	Planning Forum
PI	Packaging Institute
PIA	Printing Industries America
PIMA	Paper Industry Management Association
PIRA	Personnel and Industrial Relations Association
PMA	Performance Management Association
PMAA	Promotion Marketing Association of America
PMI	Project Management Institute
PRSA	Public Relations Society of America
PS	Protein Society
PSMA	Professional Services Management Association
RAPS	Regulatory Affairs Professionals Society
RESSI	Real Estate Securities and Syndication Institute
RI	Robotics International /Rotary International
RIMS	Risk & Insurance Management Society
RMA	Rubber Manufacturers Association
RR	Research Roundtable
SAE	Society of Automotive Engineers
SAM	Society for Advanceent of Management
SAME	Society of American Military Engineers
SAMPE	Society for Advancement of Material & Process Engineering
SBANE	Smaller Business Association of New England
SBSB	Small Business Service Bureau
SCAPS	South Carolina Association of Personnel Services
SCC	Society of Cosmetic Chemists
SCVPA	Santa Clara Valley Personnel Association
SDA	Soap and Detergent Association
SEGD	Society of Environmental Graphic Designers
SEMA	Specialty Equipment Market Association
SEMI	Semiconductor Equipment & Materials Institute
SERC	Society of Executive Recruiting Consultants, Inc.
SFFI	San Francisco Fashion Industries
SFM	Society for Foodservice Management
SHARP	Society for Human Resources and Personnel
SHPM	Society of Hospital Planning and Marketing
SHRM	Society for Human Resource Management
SHRP	Society for Human Resourse Professionals
SIM	Society for Information Management
SLA	Special Libraries Association
SME	Society of Manufacturing Engineers/Sales & Marketing Executives
SMEI	Sales and Marketing Executives International
SMIS	Society for Management Information Systems
SMPF	Strategic Planning & Management Forum
SMPS	The Society for Marketing Professional Services
SMTA	Surface Mount Technology Association

SPA	Software Publishers Assoc; Soc. for Personality Assessment
SPE	Society for Petroleum, Plastics, or Professional Engineers
SPI	Society of the Plastics Industry
SPIE	Society for Photo Optical And Instrumentation Engineers
SRA	Society for Risk Analysis
SSP	Society of Satellite Professionals
SSPI	Society of Satellite Professionals Intl
STLE	Society of Troboligist and Lubrication Engineers
TAPC	Texas or Tennessee Association Personnel Consultants
TAPPI	Technical Association for Pulp & Paper Industry
TI	Toastmanster International
TIMS	The Institute of Management Sciences
TMA	Turnaround Management Association/Training Media Association
TMS	Minerals, Metals And Materials Society
TPF	The Planning Forum
TSPE	Texas Society of Professional Engineers
TTRA	Travel & Tourism Research Association
UC	The Underfashion Club
UDI	Urban Development Institute
ULI	Urban Land Institute
USCBC	U.S.-China Business Council
USTA	United States Telecommunications Association
VAPS	Virginia Association of Personnel Services
WAI	Wire Association International
WAPC	Wisconsin Association of Personnel Consultants
WCPA	Western College Placement Association
WDRG	Women Direct Response Group
WERC	Warehouse Education Research Council
WHRM	Women in Human Resource Management
WIP	Women in Production
WPCF	Water Pollution Control Fed.
WPCFA	Water Pollution Control Federation
WTCA	World Trade Centers Assoc.

The Lexicon of Executive Recruiting

A Glossary of Terms Used in the Professional Process of Searching for Executives

Compiled and published by Executive Recruiter News, the confidential newsletter of the executive search profession.

Annual Retainer. A form of volume discounting of executive search services. Client agrees to pay so much a month, quarter or year, thereby establishing a credit account against which specific placements are billed. Encourages long-term relationships for greater efficency, lower marketing costs, improved client service.

Appraisal Interview. See EVALUATION OF CANDIDATES.

Association of Executive Search Consultants (AESC). Organized in 1959 as the Association of Executive Recruiting Consultants, Inc., this association brought together leading executive search consultants who established strict requirements for membership and standards of ethical practice for their professional field. AESC membership identifies the consultant who is not only pledged to these high standards but who is also accredited by his professional peers to conduct his practice with professional competence and integrity. The association's office is at 230 Park Avenue, New York, NY 10169.

Blockages. Places where recruiters cannot look for candidates to fill a position. Usually refers to corporations that are "off-limits" because they are, or recently have been, clients of the search firm. See OFF LIMITS POLICY.

Body-Snatcher. See HEADHUNTER.

Boutique.   An executive search firm that specializes in one or more relatively narrow niches in contrast to presenting a generalist image.

Bundling.   Relatively new term describing the talents required in today's "super executive" who is brought in to replace two or three others and is expected to reflect a "bundling" of all their attributes. Bad for search in that there are fewer jobs to fill, but good because super-execs are scarce & hard to find, requiring professional search.

Candidate.   A person who survives extensive screening, reference-checking, and interviewing and is to be presented to the client for the position to be filled.

Candidate Blockages.   Candidates who may not be considered for a position because they are active candidates in another search.

Candidate Reports.   Summaries prepared on each final candidate that usually include a complete employment history, personal biographical data, appraisal of qualifications, and initial reference information. Data is verified and submitted to the client for examination prior to the first meeting with the candidate. Where possible, search consultants prefer to make their presentation in person so as to permit maximum exchange of ideas and information.

Career Counselors.   Firms or individuals offering services to individuals. Some are legitimate but many are not. Some have been forced out of business by state Attorneys General for failure to meet promises: many have been investigated. (Be wary of claims in blaring ads in *Wall Street Journal, N.Y. Times,* etc.)
   Services can include psychological testing, resume preparation, interview training, job-search planning, etc. Fees can run from modest to $10,000! Read fine print in contracts and check with legal counsel before making a down payment or signing anything. Dealing with a small, local counselor on a 1-1 basis is usually best and least expensive. Extreme caution is advised.

Client.   Organization sponsoring and paying the recruiter for a search.

Client Anonymity.   One of the principal reasons for using executive search. Client identity is usually not revealed to prospective candidates until well along in the process, except in general terms.

Client Block.   See OFF LIMITS POLICY.

Code of Ethics. Every profession has found it necessary to establish a code of ethics as a part of the process of self-discipline, and to protect the interests of clients and assure them of fair treatment.

A code of professional ethics helps the practitioner determine the propriety of his conduct in his professional relationships. It indicates the kind of professional posture the practitioner must develop and maintain if he is to succeed. It gives the clients and potential clients a basis for feeling confident that the professional person desires to serve them well, and places services ahead of financial reward. It gives clients assurance that the professional person will do his work in conformity with professional standards of competence, independence, and integrity.

The AESC Code of Ethics is followed by many executive recruiting consultants in North America.

Compensation Package. Total compensation can include various elements other than salary for senior executives: typically a mix of deferred income, incentive bonus, profit-sharing, stock options, tax shelters (or some type of compensation that permits estate-building), thrift plans, pension plans, life insurance, health insurance, long-term disability insurance, dental insurance, tuition assistance, payment for personal and family medical and dental expenses, cars, club memberships, loans, joining bonus, and other perquisites (including, increasingly, some form of hiring bonus).

Completion Rate. Percentage of retained searches that result in a hire. Estimated to be as low as 60%, claimed by some to be 100% (be wary of the latter: no one is perfect, and the imponderables/intangibles in a search are many). Greatly affected by client lassitude in interviewing and following up with candidates, changes (written and subtle) in job specifications, internal client politics, organizational changes, etc. . . . as well as by recruiter performance and effectiveness.

Confidential Search. There are times when it is important for the client to conduct confidential searches. When secrecy is necessary, it is virtually impossible to handle a search from within the organization. For example, a company may want to introduce a whole new line of products or acquire a new product or company before competitors learn about it. In such cases, a recruiter can work effectively on its behalf without disclosing its identity until the final stages of the search. The company can make its selection and announce its plans after the new executive is on board.

Keeping a search totally confidential requires considerable discipline and skill on the part of both client and recruiter. Once the client has been identified to the top two or three candidates, both the client and the recruiter must be ready and able to move fast to make a final decision and a public announcement. This is the only way to avoid possible leaks, and it requires careful coordination.

"Con-tainer" Search. Fee arrangement that combines elements of retainer and contingency methods of payment. Usually involves an initiation payment and progress payment(s) that may not be refundable, with a "success" or "completion" portion due only on actual hiring.

Contingency Search. The search consultant who uses the contingent fee approach must fill the position before his fee is paid by the client, and this can change the entire rationale of the assignment.

There is a strong tendency for some recruiters who conduct contingency searches to spend as little time as possible on a search, to refer as many candidates as possible, or to compromise standards by referring mediocre or marginal candidates to the client.

On the other hand, a minority of contingency recruiters visit their clients, interview their candidates, conduct reference checks and otherwise differ from their retainer counterparts only in mechanics of payment.

Dehiring. See OUTPLACEMENT.

Directory of Executive Recruiters. Listing published by Kennedy Publications since 1971. Thousands of names and addresses, with salary minimums and areas of specialty (indexed by management function, industry and geography). Updated annually.

Employment Agency. Employment agencies normally limit their efforts to representing individuals who are actively looking for new employment opportunities within the local area. When an organization contacts an agency to fill a specific job opening, the agency usually reviews its files for applications from people with appropriate backgrounds and may place ads in local newspapers to attract additional applicants.

Employment agencies often try to place their applicants in any of a large number of local organizations because they are paid by the individual applicant or employer only if a placement is made. They make the majority of their placements in the lower salary ranges. Their payment is a fee based on the employee's starting salary.

Their fees may be regulated by the state, and frequently follow the pattern of a 5 percent minimum plus 1 percent for each $1,000 of the annual salary of the individual employed, up to a maximum of 20-30 percent. Some states also permit an advance fee or charge to the individual who lists himself with an employment agency. The line between Fee Paid Employment Agency and Contingency Recruiter is sometimes very difficult to draw.

Employment Agreement. When the client organization and candidate have agreed on terms of employment, it is usually important to put these into writing as a protection to both parties. The employment agreement may take the form of a formal agreement or letter to the new executive spelling out everything discussed and agreed upon: job specifications, reporting relationships, base salary, benefits, moving costs, etc. The executive will then reply, either by telephone or letter, and the deal will be settled.

Equal Opportunity Act. An Equal Employment Opportunity Commission was established in Washington, D.C. in 1964 to prevent employment discrimination. (The Roosevelt Administration established a similar organization to prevent such discrimination during World War II.) Although the law demands that women and other minority employees be considered for executive positions at various levels, most organizations, for example, lack candidates with both the education and experience required for such positions. Consequently, a growing number of these organizations must look outside for qualified individuals from the relatively small pool of qualified middle and top managers. To help such companies some search firms have set up special departments to recruit such executives. Others specialize in this field.

Evaluation of Candidates. At a convenient time and place, the recruiter interviews the prospective candidate to verify the original information gathered during the process of sourcing and researching, to examine his background in depth, and to determine if the personal chemistry will be appropriate.

These appraisal interviews develop an in-depth picture of each candidate: his employment background, business philosophy, career objectives, potential, and personality characteristics. Education and employment are verified, and a reference investigation is made of past performance. From the group of prospective candidates evaluated, several of the best qualified are selected for introduction to the client. During this phase of an engagement, the recruiter's breadth of background, depth of insight, and sound judgment are critical.

Evaluation of Executive Recruiter. What benchmarks should the client use in evaluating the recruiter's performance over a period of time? They include professionalism, results, adequate communications, realistic costs, proper staffing of assignments, and timing of assignments.

Executive Assimilation Process. The process of integrating the new executive into the organization. See SHAKEDOWN EXERCISE.

Executive Clearing House. These are information centers whose basic function is to bring together employers and candidates for positions on an informational basis. They collect information from two sources: individuals interested in a position, and employers or their search consultants seeking executives to fill specific positions. The information concerning the person and the position is classified and put into a mechanized or computerized retrieval system. Both the individual and the employer are expected to share the cost of these information centers. Companies may pay either a standard amount per position or per year, or a placement fee if and when they employ a person referred by the Clearing House. Some of these have been computerized into Job Banks or Registries of one sort or another. Caution is advised.

Executive Recruiting. The service performed for a fee by independent and objective persons or a group of consultants organized as a firm or similar entity. Executive recruiters help managers of client organizations identify and appraise executives well-qualified to fill specific management positions in commerce, industry, government, and the nonprofit field. Their fees are paid by the organizations that retain them.

This highly specialized area of the management consulting profession started as a normal service rendered by general management consulting firms. Executive recruiting has experienced rapid growth since the end of World War II, both in the United States and abroad. There are hundreds of consultants (most of whom refer to themselves as "firms") that handle executive search either as a specialty or in conjunction with other forms of consulting work.

Executive recruiting firms, also known as executive search consultants, generally bill their clients monthly as the search progresses and deduct these payments from the total fee, frequently up to 35 percent of the first year's total compensation. Some may use other methods of billing such as a regular per diem, or a flat fee, plus out-of-pocket expenses.

The true role of the executive recruiting consultant is not that of a glorified pirate, body-snatcher, headhunter, or any other erroneous label frequently applied to him or her.

Executive recruiting consultants are usually willing to receive resumes from executives seeking new job opportunities, but they are not in a position to help executives find jobs.

Executive Referral. Euphemism for RESUME FLOATING to former or present client.

Executive Search. Synonym for EXECUTIVE RECRUITING, although some feel strongly that "search" better describes the process and identifies its major thrust.

Expenses. Additions to the search fee intended to compensate the recruiter for out-of-pocket payments incurred specifically for a given search (i.e. telephone calls, special directories or subscriptions, candidate & recruiter travel, etc.). An item to be carefully monitored by the diligent client, as some search firms tend to "make money" on expenses (double-billing for travel involving two clients, for example). Other firms attempt to recover ordinary administrative expenses. A variable item on the search firm's invoice, but bears watching & documentation of over 15-20% of the fee.

Fair Credit Reporting Acts. Legislation to amend general business law regarding procedures for securing information about individuals seeking commercial credit, loans, jobs, etc. Also covers the confidentiality, accuracy, relevancy, and proper utilization of such information. Can affect the reference-checking aspect of executive recruiting significantly. Regulations vary widely from state to state.

Fallout. Term popularly used to describe the following condition: after a placement has been made (or during the assignment), the client decides to hire one or more additional candidates who were surfaced and recommended by the recruiter. Some search firms demand full fee for each such additional hire; others will not accept a fee. Most frequently a matter of negotiation dependent on the time frame, client relations, etc. See PLACEMENT, MULTIPLE.

Fee. The total fee paid by the client to an executive recruiter for a search assignment. Most recruiters these days charge clients 30 to 33 percent of first year's total compensation for the executive hired, plus out-of-pocket expenses. Thus, if the new executive is paid $50,000 base salary and no bonus or incentive, the client's fee would be about $15,000 regardless of the billing method, plus 10 to 25 percent of the professional fee for out-of-pocket expenses. Retainer recruiters are paid for their services whether or not a placement is made. See METHODS OF BILLING, FRONT END RETAINER, INVOICING ARRANGEMENT and REIMBURSABLE EXPENSES.

Front-End Retainer. During the course of a search, clients are invoiced monthly for agreed-upon fees, plus out-of-pocket expenses. These monthly installments generally range from one-third to one-fourth of the total fee involved. They are sometimes called "front-end retainers" and are credited toward the total fee when the individual is employed. Usually a final billing for any remaining fee is rendered at that time. Retainer recruiters require a payment before commencing a search. This is also called a "front-end retainer."

Greenlighting. When companies merge, this is the signal given to the manager to start looking, because his counterpart in the other company will assume his role for the combined firm.

Guarantee. Promise by the search firm to replace a failed candidate within a certain period of time (usually one year), especially if caused by negligence on the recruiter's part. Search is usually reinstated for expenses only.

Handwriting Analysis. (Graphology) A controversial selection technique pioneered in Germany and in occasional use elsewhere as another tool to help predict candidate performance and fit.

Headhunter. Formerly pejorative term for executive recruiter, still only passively accepted by professionals in the field . . . currently used more in a jocular and light-hearted sense than critically . . . even voiced occasionally by some headhunters themselves! (Other labels, far less in evidence today, have included "body-snatcher," "pirate," etc.)

Hiring Bonus. A one-time payment originally intended to compensate a joining executive for extra expenses occasioned by a major move. Now viewed somewhat more broadly, though not quite like a professional ball-player's "signing bonus," nonethless the comparison had been made! The concept includes, for example, recompense for "lost" bonuses at the company the executive is leaving. It can also be a device to compensate for lower salary scales in the hiring company. A hiring or joining bonus, then, is whatever it takes—in addition to total compensation—to convince the candidate to join. The amount can range from a few thousand to over a million dollars, sometimes paid half on joining and half six months later.

Interview. Another word for both preliminary and appraisal interviews which are conducted for the purpose of assessing prospective candidates.

Interview, Stress. This is a Nazi-like technique once promoted by a recruiter in New York City as applicable in executive recruiting. Through it, the prospective candidate is bludgeoned with insulting remarks until he finally loses his temper, thus presumably revealing his true inner self. Few (if any) recruiters use such techniques.

Invoicing Arrangement. Regardless of the type of fee structure used by the recruiter, the client should understand the invoicing arrangement in advance. Many recruiters require a payment before commencing the search. Others will do much of the preliminary work involved in a search before sending the first invoice. Invoices for professional fees and out-of-pocket expenses may be payable monthly for three to four months or may require payment at certain periods during the search, usually with the final payment upon completion of the search.

Job Counselors. See CAREER COUNSELORS and OUTPLACEMENT.

Job Description. This describes the client position to be filled and outlines the desired characteristics and experience that the executive being sought should possess. When approved by the client, the "specs" become the guidelines for the search.

Leaving Money on the Table. Outside search consultant's lament when placed executive gets higher first-year compensation than was estimated and fee was fixed, not percentage.

Length of Recruiting Assignment. The average recruiting assignment takes three to four months from the initial meeting with the client until the candidate is finally selected. Once a new executive is selected, it may take two to four weeks or more before he or she actually reports to work. An assignment may take as little as a month or two if everything goes right, but this is rare. On the other hand, a search may take six months to a year. When it lasts that long, chances are that the position was impossible to fill, the specifications were changed, the client was not available to meet candidates or didn't really want to fill the position, the recruiter miscalculated, or something else out of the ordinary happened.

Licensing. Many years ago, when immigrant laborers were taken advantage of by unethical employment agencies, most states enacted legislation to protect individuals by licensing and control of such agencies. Thus employment agencies are licensed today; executive recruiters are generally not. As employment agencies move into fee-paid and retainer work, the line becomes more difficult to draw. Many states now write specific exemptions for executive recruiters, citing salary minimums and the fact that the individual does not pay a fee.

Lobbing. Following a shootout, the losing firm "lobs" a resume to the client, showing the kind of candidate the losing firm would have recruited had it been given the assignment.

Methods of Billing. The most commonly used methods of calculating the professional fees charged for executive search services are:

- A fixed percentage fee, usually 30 to 33 percent of the first year's agreed-upon total compensation of the executive recruited.
- A flat fee, fixed in advance on the basis of estimated time and difficulty of the search.
- A retainer fee for professional services over a stated period of time.
- A straight time formula, based on actual time spent on the search, but sometimes governed by an agreed-to-maximum.
- A per-diem or hourly fee for any candidate appraised and recommended by the recruiter and hired by the client.

In addition to the fee, there are also expenses. These are mainly for travel and communications, and they will vary, depending on the complexity of the search and the distances between client, recruiter, and candidates. It is customary for clients to pay for candidates' travel to interviews. See FEE and REIMBURSABLE EXPENSES.

Off Limits Policy.   A key issue in executive search. Refers to the recruiter agreeing not to approach executives in the client organization. Factors are definition of "client" and time: the whole corporation (e.g., General Motors) or the division the search was done for (Chevrolet), or some even more specific entity (Truck Division, Northeast Region) . . . and for one year, two, three?

Some large firms say they can't "afford" a strict Off Limits policy because it reduces the universe from which they can draw and gets extremely complicated ("client" served by the San Francisco or Zurich office, how significant a client, etc.). Small firms magnanimously offer "full" worldwide client protection because it doesn't really affect their business.

Whether this is an ethical or trade practice or business issue, it is extremely important to have it fully and mutually understood—preferably in writing—at the outset of a search assignment.

Outplacement.   When executives are fired or dropped by various kinds of organizations today, they are often referred to outplacement consultants. These specialized consultants help them and analyze their skills and abilities and counsel them on how to prepare resumes and find new careers. Outplacement consultants work for and are always paid by the firing organization. A few serve both companies and displaced executives, and there is in such circumstances a potential conflict of interest. The Association of Executive Search Consultants (AESC) bars its members from offering outplacement services for the same reason.

Person Specification.   A synonym for JOB DESCRIPTION.

Personal Chemistry. There is a rough analogy between mixing chemicals and mixing executives at the top level. By combining executives an organization can achieve synergy, or neutralization, or can produce explosions. The daily newspapers verify this chemical analogy as it operates in the executive suite.

The search for a new executive is part of a process of organization change, often with traumatic implications. Preparing for this change and tackling the inherent integration problems are essential if the needs of the individual and group are to be met.

In their evaluation of prospective candidates, professional recruiters try hard to determine whether the personal chemistry will be appropriate. A few recruiters help clients integrate new executives into the organization on as firm a footing as possible by means of formal programs. Interpersonal breakdowns can create enormous organizational cost, and it is important to anticipate and head them off.

Pirate. See HEADHUNTER.

Placement. The act of an executive recruiter in filling a client position.

Placement, Multiple. When a recruiter is searching for a top level executive, he or she frequently interviews candidates who are not exactly right for the position, but who may be of interest to the client for another position. When the client fills a secondary opening with a candidate presented to him for the primary position, it is called a secondary or multiple placement. This happens often enough so that the recruiter should spell out the details in his confirmation letter before commencing the search. Some recruiters charge a full fee, others reduce their fee for a secondary placement because their research effort time devoted to the placement has been absorbed by the primary search. See FALLOUT.

Privacy. An infrequently used synonym for confidential search. It is also used to refer to the various privacy acts and legislation protecting the individual.

Professional Practice Guidelines. These are standards of good practice for the guidance of executive recruiters. They make for equitable and satisfactory client relationships and contribute to success in recruiting. (See the AESC Code of Ethics and Professional Practice Guidelines for specific standards of good practice.)

Progress Payments.   Monthly payments made to the recruiter by the client for agreed-upon fees, plus out-of-pocket expenses, during the course of the search. Frequently cited as a key difference between Contingency and Retainer Search.

Proposals, Letters of Agreement and Contracts.   Each recruiting assignment should have as its base point a formal written instrument (usually a letter of agreement or proposal) between the recruiter and the client: it should accurately describe the terms of the assignment. Unwritten agreements often lead to misunderstandings and dissatisfaction on the part of one or both of the parties. The written agreement should be specific on all pertinent points: job or position specifications, responsibilities of each party, amount of fee, method of payment, time limits involved, and any other pertinent points of agreement.

Psychological Testing.   Professional search consultants develop their own evaluation methods. Formal psychological evaluation is almost always left to the client's discretion. If a client has doubts about the fitness of a candidate, psychological evaluation may be indicated. But it is not likely that the search consultant will use psychological testing as part of its own selection process.

Ratcheting.   The temptation faced by retainer recruiters charging on a percentage basis: the higher the salary at which the candidate is hired, the higher the fee (even a hint of conflict of interest in such instances is eliminated when charged on fixed-fee basis).

Records Maintenance.   Professional recruiters have clear policies known to their staffs regarding the retention of records and coding in compliance with existing laws and regulations on Federal and state levels, together with the spirit of the various privacy acts and legislation protecting the individual.

Recruiting Costs.   See FEE and METHODS OF BILLING.

Recruitment Advertising.   Professional recruiters feel that advertising with regard to a particular assignment should be done judiciously, and only with the approval of the client. It should state the position clearly and be used with discretion. Absolute honesty in statements and actions should be observed in the text of the advertisement.

   In Europe and Canada, advertising is commonly used in the executive search process. Sometimes this is called Executive Selection; at other times the terms are interchangeable.

References. Persons to whom a recruiter refers for testimony as to a candidate's character, background, abilities, etc.

Executive recruiters usually take references proffered by candidates only as a starting point. They then confidentially seek out former superiors, subordinates, peers, colleagues, vendors, suppliers, etc., to get an independent and objective evaluation of the candidate. See below.

Reference Checking. After intensive interviews with the candidates (but before introduction to the client) the recruiter will begin to check references. Initially the recruiter will be limited to references provided by the candidates themselves. These are likely to be favorable. However, from these references the recruiter will obtain others (known in recruiting as second-generation references) who will be more likely to provide a more objective picture of the candidates. These references include such persons as social contacts, professors, business associates, and former roommates.

This initial checking of references is a delicate area and must be done with prudence. It is vital that the candidate not be embarrassed or have his current job jeopardized as a result of these checks. In addition, the client often wants the search to remain confidential at this stage.

For these reasons, it is customary to defer an in-depth development of reference information until mutuality of interest has been determined.

Reference investigation and reporting should be conducted with the candidate's prior knowledge; within the spirit and intent of applicable Federal and/or state laws and regulations; with persons considered knowledgeable about the candidate and whose information can be cross-checked for objectivity and reliability; and with respect for the personal and professional privacy of all parties concerned. References today are rarely in writing, usually in the form of telephone notes.

Referral Service. Most large banks in metropolitan areas provide a referral service for executives, especially in financial and general management fields. They provide this service at no cost to their customers, and the executives are generally seeking a new position. Often, banks will recommend executives for senior positions if their particular skills will strengthen the customer's position. Large law firms sometimes provide a referral service to their clients. Trade associations and professional organizations also refer names of members who are actively in the job market at no cost to job seekers or interested companies. In addition, placement offices of most universities offer a free referral service, and many graduate schools of business help place their alumni.

Reimbursable Expenses. All recruiters incur out-of-pocket expenses in their day-to-day search activities. Typically, there are travel expenses for both recruiter and candidate, related costs for hotels, meals, long-distance telephone calls, printing and other related costs. Some recruiters charge for their reimbursable expenses at cost while others may add a service charge. Some charge for secretarial, research and other support services while other recruiters absorb part or all of the expenses.

Reimbursable expenses may run from 10 percent to 25 percent of the professional fee or more, depending on such factors as length of assignment, location of client and the majority of candidates, number of offices used by the recruiter, and salary range of the position being filled. International searches covering several countries obviously incur higher expenses.

Replacement Guarantee.   See GUARANTEE.

Research.   The foundation of professional recruiting is research. All well-established recruiting consultants maintain research facilities to develop background information about industries, companies, and key executives. In a rapidly changing business environment, constant research is the principal guarantee against superficial or haphazard research work.

Resource.   Someone who can possibly recommend a candidate for a specific opening.

Resume.   A brief account of personal and educational experience and qualification of a job applicant. The resume is the first formal contact between a company and a potential employee, and in some ways it is the most critical. Personnel officers in most major corporations can usually give only 20 to 30 seconds of attention for each of the many resumes they see everyday. So, to make the best impression, an applicant's resume must be constructed in such a way that it provides the most pertinent information about him or her in the simplest and most easily digestible form. The information should be brief, complete, and easily accessible.

Resume Floating.   Frowned-upon practice of sending resumes to a potential hiring organization without a contractual search assignment, in hope of a "hit" . . . banned by AESC as "inappropriate."

Retained Search.   Retained search is one in which a client retains a recruiter to identify and appraise executives well-qualified to fill a specific management position. An initial downpayment is followed by progress payments, and the full fee may have been paid before the position is actually filled.

Retainer.   A retainer fee (usually paid monthly) for professional services for an agreed-upon period of time.

Rusing. Using subterfuge to obtain information, typically posing as editor or researcher or personal friend to get information on executive names, titles, etc., in research phase . . . banned by AESC as unethical. See UNETHICAL RESEARCH.

Search Process, The. The task of identifying and appraising well-qualified executives is painstaking and time-consuming and must be governed by an orderly approach consisting of several major steps or phases if it is to be successful. These steps represent the broad phases of a typical search assignment and identify the major areas of activity involved in the work that recruiters do for clients.

These steps are interrelated and interdependent, but they are often adapted and modified by search consultants as they work out their own approaches to client engagements. The professional search process does not depend on luck, shortcuts, or gimmicks, but on a step-by-step procedure whereby a list of potentially suitable executives is reduced to several uniquely qualified candidates. In outline form, the successful search consultant must: meet with the client to discuss the engagement in depth; develop a strategy or search plan; review files and previous search assignments; contact candidates and evaluate them; check references and participate in negotiations; and follow-up with the client and executive to see how things are going.

The aim is not merely to produce qualified candidates (which is relatively easy) but the very best candidates.

Second Generation Reference. See REFERENCE CHECKING.

Shakedown Exercise. This exercise or process sometimes involves getting the new executive and his or her boss together in a one or two-day session with a behavioral psychologist before the new executive reports to work. It is based on the premise that the end of the search process is only the beginning of the more rigorous, more critical process of integration into the new organization. In these sessions each nails down precisely what each is expecting of the other. The purpose of the shakedown exercise is to bridge the gap between promise and performance. This approach, with its emphasis on behavioral science techniques, is not yet common practice in recruiting.

Shootout. Popular term for competition that finds several search firms making new-business presentations to a potential client. Increasingly used—to the recruiter's chagrin—by sophisticated, cost-conscious or short-sighted clients who sometimes fail to see the value in long-term professional relationships.

Source. Person or organization that can suggest possible candidates to a recruiter during a search.

Specialist vs Generalist. Increasingly, clients demand a certain amount of industry or functional knowledge from the executive recruiter. Exclusive practices have sprung up in banking, healthcare, training, hi-tech, finance, etc. Yet there is always the demand, in addition (especially at higher executive levels), for the generalist viewpoint. How else, for example, can an executive with consumer products marketing experience in soft drinks be found for the personal computer company that has decided it needs this type of leadership?

Some industries lend themselves to recruiter specialization, i.e., those with a large number of non-competing units nationally (banks, hospitals). Others, with a high concentration of firms (automobiles, for example) do not lend themselves to specialization. The determinant is adherence to a professional Off Limits policy. See OFF LIMITS.

Stalking Horse. A candidate submitted relatively early to test, confirm and fine-tune specifications. Not a uniform practice and frowned upon by some as unfair to the candidate.

Stick Rate. Term somtimes used to describe effectiveness of executive-position matches, whether through search or otherwise ... no real statistics yet on whether searched executives last longer in new posts. Not to be confused, however, with success rate (i.e., underperformers can sometimes stay in the job for along time!).

Super-Executive. Manager who combines the talents and experience of the two or three people he or she is replacing. See BUNDLING.

Suspect. A person identified in a preliminary way as a possible candidate to fill a search assignment.

Total Compensation. See COMPENSATION PACKAGE.

Types of Executive Recruiters. These include independent individual recruiters and recruiting firms, executive recruiting divisions of management consultant firms and certified public accounting firms, and internal recruiting departments in companies.

Unbundling. Separating the key elements of full search and offering them individually, i.e., research, interviewing, etc., sometimes "demanded" by aggressive clients, sometimes offered aggressively by entrepreneurial recruiters seeking additional revenues.

Unethical Research. Certain practices, such as phone-sourcing and "research" techniques which involve misrepresenting the caller or purpose of the call, are unprofessional and are not tolerated by professional recruiters regardless of whether they are employed by subcontractors or the search consultant himself. Such practices undermine client confidence in the integrity and professional reliability of recruiters. See RUSING.

Available in booklet form. An option is also offered for customizing the booklet with an individual firm's logo and message on the back cover. Call or write:
Consultants Bookstore, 21 Templeton Road, Fitzwilliam, NH
03447. (603) 585-6544

For Candidates

A Word to Executives Open to Change . . .

Remember that executive recruiters are paid by management and must be so oriented. They rarely interview unless with a specific job in mind, and most do not even acknowledge resumes. If you're lucky enough to have qualifications matching a recruiter's current assignment, however, the road to an interview can be almost instantaneous.

A few cautions:

- **Don't telephone to follow up:** This is a waste of your time and an annoyance to the recruiter.
- **Don't walk in and expect an interview.**
- **Don't attempt to fool anyone on present or expected salary level.** These experts have a way of zeroing in on the truth. Frankness and honesty is the best policy.

While some recruiters file over-the-transom resumes, most don't. **So repeat in six months if you are still in the market.** And don't take any listed salary minimums too literally—merely use as a general guide.

One last word: the recruiter as a professional must respect the confidence of your situation. This is automatic. If you have any doubts, don't venture out. There is always a remote possibility of a slip-up, but this is a chance you have to take once you have decided to test the market or make a change.

GOOD LUCK!

Planning Your Career Search: The Four Major Strategies

by James F. Mohar

There are four, and only four, major search strategies, and each can be used at any time during the job-changing process:

1. Contact executive search firms.
2. Network with family, friends, acquaintances and business contacts.
3. Contact "target firms" of potential interest.
4. Reply to position available listings in newspapers, association and university publications, etc.

Warning: Don't just jump into the process and "get busy": it's extremely important to take time out for planning. Your search will probably take longer than you think—and what worked for someone else may not work for you—so if one, two, or three of the four search strategies are eliminated from consideration at the outset, a potentially career-making opportunity could be choked off.

It makes sense to consider using all four strategies and, if possible, concurrently, during the search process. Each one may produce interviews and, eventually, an offer.

The use of the four search strategies, and the balance it provides, is similar to the concept of financial asset diversification. Investment advisors point to portfolio diversification as a technique to provide balance between return and risk. In much the same way, using all four search strategies simultaneously helps uncover employment opportunities that otherwise would be missed.

1. CONTACT EXECUTIVE SEARCH FIRMS

There's no better ego stroke than to be "found" by a recruiter conducting a search on behalf of a corporate client.

But you can't wait for the telephone to ring: contact search firms directly. Unless you know the recruiter personally, the most effective method is to send a well-worded one-page cover letter with your resume.

Advantages

- *Quick Hit*—A resume reaching the right recruiter at the right time can result in an immediate interview. Timing and candidate/client compatibility relative to the position being filled are the crucial factors.
- *Shelf Life*—More so than any other strategy, contacting executive search firms may lead to residual benefits. Although some of the larger search firms may get hundreds of unsolicited resumes a week, the advent of computerized data entry and retrieval has permitted candidate credential retention at volumes far greater than in the old, strictly "hard copy" days. It's not unusual for a recruiter with a well-organized system to initiate contact with a candidate months, or even years, after the initial mailing.
- *Validation*—Passing the recruiter's screening process, and being presented on the slate of proposed candidates, permits you to compete on "a level playing field" with your opponents. Also, chances are that you can avoid— or at least have minimal contact with—the firm's human resources department, an organization typically better at screening out candidates than screening them in.

Disadvantages

- *Timing*—If a recruiter isn't currently working on a search assignment compatible with your background, objectives, salary level, or even location when you're actively seeking a new position, there is no match. Unfortunately, this probability is extremely high at the time of your particular mailing. Somewhere, of course, an executive search firm probably is conducting an assignment matching your career objective and skills. But which one? The remedy is to contact as many search firms as possible.
- *Pain in the Butt Stuff*—Usually, a carefully crafted letter and professionally prepared resume are expected to generate one of three responses from a recruiter. First, a telephone call (the ideal) suggesting that ". . . your credentials appear to be an excellent match with a current assignment. Let's meet." Second, a polite acknowledgement letter and third, no response.

    Here are two other response derivatives which, if occurring with any frequency, will test your patience:
    - *Sourcing*—The recruiter calls, and after your heart skips a beat or two in anticipation, you learn the purpose of the contact is for the recruiter to tap into your network of business associates to fill a search for which you're not qualified.

The best response is to be cooperative. Even though your immediate interests as a potential candidate are not being served, you may be in a position to help both the recruiter and a colleague who, even if not actively searching, may find an excellent new career position through your unselfish efforts. The recruiter will remember, too. And the next time, it may be your turn.

— *Forms*—Very few retainer firms, but approximately 5-10 percent of the contingency firms, will reply to your cover letter/resume by mailing back to you their "form." The implication is that, if the potential candidate devotes the necessary time and effort to complete the form (between 30 and 90 minutes, depending on length) the search firm will be in a better position to help place the candidate as an appropriate client search assignment materializes. If the form is simple and short (seldom the case), fine . . . go ahead and fill it out. After receiving your dozenth form over a two-month period, however, you'll probably change your mind. And, why not? The probability of a "fill out my form first" search firm submitting you as a candidate is no greater than that of a recruiter not wasting your time with administrative nonsense.

2. NETWORK

The purpose of networking is to tap into the people you know, asking them to either make you aware of available positions consistent with your professional objective and background, or to introduce you to their contacts who may be in a similar position to advance your search and, eventually, placement. This strategy takes the old saying "It's not what you know, it's who you know" one step further: "It's not just who you know, it's who you know who knows whom you should get to know."

Networking can serve one of two basic purposes, and the second purpose sometimes has a hidden agenda: a) to gather information about a function or industry you're not familiar with, to help you to determine the feasibility of making such a switch, and b) to plug into a position, probably unadvertised, for which you are qualified.

The "hidden agenda" may come into play here. Remember that networking isn't interviewing. The premise for the network meeting is normally to obtain advice and direction from the contact agreeing to meet with you in the first place so an opening line such as, "I'd like to work with your firm. When can we meet?" isn't likely to be received favorably. Still, it's realistic to expect that, sooner or later, networking will result in your meeting with a decision-maker, in an excellent firm, with whom develops that highly desirable quality of "personal chemistry." Your hidden agenda, then, is to sell yourself as if you were actually being interviewed ... understanding, of course, that your contact must initiate the first step of soliciting your candidacy with the firm.

The fundamental theory of networking is to request your contact to provide you the names of two to three contacts with whom you may also meet to discuss your career aspirations. If successful, the networking campaign progresses geometrically and, ideally, only ends upon completing the search for a new position.

Advantages

- *Differentiation*—The best cover letter and resume can't sell you like you can sell yourself. Networking is the only strategy of the four that, from the start, permits eye-to-eye contact.
- *Creativity*—A properly managed meeting, and the give-and-take dialogue that ensues, can easily spawn creative ideas on the part of your contact that wouldn't materialize from only a 30-second reading of your resume.
- *No competition*—You're not just one of a dozen candidates being interviewed for the same position this week.

Disadvantages

- *Timing*—The probability of scheduling a meeting is governed by the vagaries of ongoing business and personal commitments, so you must balance perseverance with good judgment.
- *Concentric, Weakening Circles*—Normally, you'll make the biggest "splash" with those who are closest, e.g., family, friends, acquaintances and personal business contacts. The further you extend beyond your inner circle, the less likely you are to be met with meaningful help.
- *Time Consumptive*—Be prepared to spend a lot of time networking if that's your strategy of choice, because it *will* chew up this valuable resource. Unless you're within walking distance to a network contact, or at least a short drive, figure that the combination of a one-hour meeting and round-trip commuting can take as much as a half-day.

3. CONTACT TARGET FIRMS

No matter how extensive your list of personal contacts, or how adept you become at networking, you simply won't be able to meet decision-makers at every firm you find appealing. The next best alternative? Write directly to the firms, sending a one-page cover letter and your resume. Be sure to say why you're leaving (keep it positive) and outline your career objectives. Other important elements:

- *Value Statement*—Although a well-prepared resume outlines responsibilities and accomplishments, a one-paragraph synopsis of your value to the prospective employer in the cover letter serves as a "grabber." After all, the foremost question in the prospective employer's mind is "What can this person do for me?" If the cover letter doesn't stimulate adequate interest, the resume may never get read.

■ *Compensation*—Salary, bonus, and "soft dollar" compensation (e.g., deferred, 401(k), stock options, etc.) don't all have to be mentioned in the cover letter. Simply stating your compensation range over the last several years, however, gives the reader insight into your affordability. Omitting this information, however, risks their assuming your financial profile is out of sync with their structure.

■ *Call for Action*—Put the ball in their court by asking them to contact you (the soft sell), or risk being called pushy (not all bad) by saying you'll be calling soon for an appointment.

Advantages

■ *Differentiation*—As with networking, writing to target firms enables you to present your unique credentials to the decision-maker of your choice ... assuming your contact actually reads the cover letter/resume. Most do.

■ *No Competition*—While any given target firm, at any given time, probably isn't in a position to hire you, you're not competing with others. The advantage is getting your foot in the door before a recruiter is given a search assignment or before the firm decides to run a position available ad in a newspaper.

■ *Selectivity*—You can write to whomever you choose and at any time. If the initial mailing is rejected or unanswered, the option is always open to contact the same individual at a later date or, if appropriate, another decision-maker.

Disadvantages

■ *Not Read*—There is no guarantee your recipient will actually read your letter and resume—and there are no absolute antidotes for this problem—but two tactics can minimize your being ignored.

First, you always have the option of making a follow-up phone call within 30 days of the mailing.

Second, writing to executives just below the top echelon, i.e., those who don't appear on every mailing list, may get attention simply because their in-baskets aren't as filled as those of the target firm's chairman, president, and C.F.O.

■ *Timing/Volume*—There is no way to anticipate which target firms may have a need for your services as you undertake a mailing campaign, so the remedy is to generate volume. Target firm letters result in interviews less than five percent of the time and, unless your function is in high demand ... and unless your credentials and accomplishments are impeccable ... and, and, and ... the number is closer to one-two percent.

Getting an interview is not the same as getting a job offer. Figure that, at least, approximately 6-10 interviews are necessary to generate one or two offers.

All these numbers suggest it will take a target firm letter campaign of about 1,000 to materialize in only a few offers, and that's if you stay in your career field. If a career field switch is attempted, plan on boosting the number of letters to 2,000-3,000.

- *Shelf Life*—Target firm letters customarily have a very short shelf life. Either your recipient is interested or not.
- *Geography*—Overcoming the timing problem is hard enough to do without superimposing the geographical barrier, but there are two ways to minimize this difficulty. First, focus out-of-town target firm letters on your current employer's direct competitors, those organizations which presumably would have the most interest in your specific industry experience. Second, assuming you want to relocate to a specific city, evaluate whether your interest is strong enough to warrant your paying the associated travel expenses.

4. REPLY TO POSITION LISTINGS

Position listings tend to be discounted, as if answering an ad is an admission we're looking for a new job (which we are) or replying to an ad is beneath our dignity (which it's not). If those two psychological barriers can be surpassed, the third bias, "It doesn't work," is a favorite of many, and is equally invalid. The fact is, position listings do work. Admittedly, this fourth major strategy may not be as sophisticated, market research-oriented or "refined" as the other three, but its unsexy nature shouldn't disguise the probability that, comparing effort expended vs. results, answering ads holds its own.

Three primary sources to consult for position listings:

- *The Wall Street Journal*—especially Tuesdays. If you're interested in nationwide listings, the *WSJ* also publishes aggregated positions available in its *National Business Employment Weekly*.
- *Local Newspapers*—Particularly in large metropolitan areas, position listings appear daily. Sunday editions usually feature the largest number of these advertisements.
- *Other*—Certain professional and trade organizations, as well as some colleges/universities, publish position listings in periodic magazines and newsletters. Not all do, of course, but it's worth investigating.

Advantages

- *Easy*—An ad response is relatively easy and doesn't absorb a lot of time.
- *Timing/Defined Need*—By its very placement, a position listing announces a defined staffing need, and a need now. No mass mailings to target firms or executive recruiters here. No time-consuming hours in arranging and meeting network contacts either. If you believe a "fit" exists, a single mail piece and a trip to the nearest mailbox is all it takes.

Disadvantages

- *Competition*—Face it. This strategy screams for competition. But if your functional qualifications, industry experience and salary are compatible with the specifications presented in the ad, you may find the competition isn't so stiff after all.
- *Singular Transaction*—Of the four major search strategies, responding to a position listing typically has the shortest shelf life. In fact, it's probably fair to say there is no shelf life: your reply is either classified a "go" or "no go."

There is no magic formula for changing employers effectively. But, pursuing each of the four major career search strategies, combined with persevering hard work, luck, and faith, will make the process less imperfect.

Mr. Mohar is a management consultant from Naperville, Illinois, specializing in strategy implementation. He is a former job search candidate and wrote this article from his own experience.

A Basic Approach to Job Changing

Twelve steps to guide you from self-appraisal to negotiating offers

by William E. Gould

Statistics indicate that executives typically change jobs five to six times in their business lives. There are many reasons to change, ranging from the need to generate more income to the avoidance of career plateauing and burnout. Whatever the reason, the following is a basic 12-step plan for changing jobs that will help you maximize opportunities while minimizing risks.

Step 1: Do a thorough self-appraisal. It is essential to find out everything about that itch that says, "I've got to look around." To determine what's bothering you, analyze your job, yourself and your needs. Questions to consider are: What do I like about my current job? What don't I like about it? What is the culture of my current environment?

In addition, you should ask: What is my personality? How do others perceive me? Is my style autocratic or participative? What are the characteristics of a "perfect environment" for me?

And finally, you must say: What kind of community do I want to live in? What schools, recreation, and social life must be a part of that community? What is my and my family's tolerance for travel? Do I want to commute to my job? If so, how long and by what mode?

Step 2: Analyze the effects of a job change on your spouse, your children and yourself. It is essential to share your thoughts with your family. Handled improperly, you can become an unpopular person in the household at a time when you need complete family support.

If your spouse is working and you change cities, will your spouse be able to find a new job? Or, if your spouse stops working, can you stand the loss of one income while one of you conducts a job search?

How will relocating affect your children? If they are in high school, will your daughter, who is just becoming her own person, be able to handle a move? Is your son going to land that quarterback position in a new school?

And finally, are you psychologically prepared to pull up old and trusted roots, move to a new company and start all over again as a new person on the block?

Step 3: Prepare a resume. There are hundreds of formats to choose from. The key to resume writing is to give the reader a brief outline of your business life and education without telling your life story. Save the details for the personal interview.

Don't include your job objective. A cover letter tailored to a particular job or company should mention your objective. Remember, everything you send out gives a signal about you. Invest in quality paper and typesetting. Make it look like an executive resume.

Step 4: Prepare a target list of companies that best suits your needs. Researching companies takes time and you will find it difficult to fit this into your everyday schedule. Nevertheless, you must have this list in front of you before talking to anyone.

Step 5: Determine your target acceptance date. It takes a minimum of three months to conduct a job campaign. Select a date for accepting an offer that is at *least* 12 weeks from the time you begin looking. You need enough time to develop options.

The timing of your search strategy is critical. Corporations tend to hire during two periods: February through June and September through November. Backing up at least three months from the middle of the cycles, the best times to begin the process of changing jobs are in January and July.

If you are pressured to accept an offer before your targeted date, tell the company that you need a certain amount of time to explore opportunities and that you will make your decision by a specific date. Emphasize that you are not out of a job, that this is one of the most important decisions in life and that you want to make the right choice.

Offers typically come 9 to 12 weeks into your search. However, you must discipline yourself not to accept before you have reviewed enough opportunities. In this way, you can be sure to make the right decision.

Step 6: To minimize the risk of exposure within your company, put the word out among a few trusted friends who may know of opportunities.

This is the least risky approach. It will be 8 to 12 weeks before word begins to filter back to your organization. Remember also that this approach is the one least likely to yield that ideal opportunity as the probability of your friends being in a target company is low.

Step 7: Put the word out with executive search consultants. This keeps your risk of exposure to a minimum while expanding your outreach.

In selecting search firms, you can contact the Association of Executive Search Consultants, Inc. in Greenwich, CT, whose member firms subscribe to a professional code of ethics, assuring you of strict confidentiality. In addition, Kennedy Publications in Fitzwilliam, NH, publishes *The Directory of Executive Recruiters.* Either source can provide a comprehensive listing of professional recruiters.

At each firm you contact, request a 15 or 20 minute get-acquainted visit. This meeting puts your face in their file. Don't be offended, however, if the executive search firm will not see you. It just means they probably don't have an assignment that is appropriate to your background. Search firms are busy focusing on their clients' needs and cannot have time to see everyone who contacts them.

Nevertheless, every firm is interested in knowing the availability of good people. So make a follow-up call to reinforce your original contact. The risk of exposure from an executive search firm is low.

Once you begin to meet prospective employers, expect word to get back to your company in four to six weeks. Prepare for the possibility of discovery and immediate dismissal. Remember, it takes longer to find a job without a job, especially if you are more than 50 years old.

Step 8: When your intentions are fully public, pull out the stops. Use your college alumni records and your association membership lists and cross-reference these people with your original target list. Use annual reports, 10K's, every lead you can think of.

The most effective and rewarding way of gaining entry is through a recommendation by someone. Try to find introductions into target companies where you don't have firsthand acquaintances. Call your contact and explain why you would like to be introduced to the firm.

Step 9: When you have an interview at the ideal target company, approach it as a learning experience. It's a chance to learn about yourself, the job opportunity and the person interviewing you.

Get rid of your anger, if you have any. Negative exhortations about your current situation work against you. Let off steam before the interview, and get your defenses under control. Relax, be positive, and be open, honest and candid.

Listen carefully to interviewers. Be open to their sequence of questions and, above all, don't try to control the interview. Your resume answers basic historical questions, but you should expect to answer certain inevitable questions, such as: what are your strengths and weaknesses and what is your management style? Never attempt to sell an idealized concept of who you should be; sell yourself by being yourself.

Always be candid about your salary, bonus and perks, titles, responsibilities and college degrees. Be truthful, as someone will check this information.

Feel free to go on the offensive and ask the questions you want answered. Why is the position open? What happened in the past in this area? Will you be blocked? Is the boss' temperament a problem?

It is important to ask about company politics. Is the job in the corporate mainstream? Where is it likely to lead? What is the future strategy of the corporation? How will it affect your particular area?

Step 10: After several interviews, rank your options and choose the finalist.   Go back for as many repeat visits as you need to really get to know those companies. Don't hesitate to investigate them thoroughly; they are going to investigate you!

Step 11: Negotiate your terms.   Timing is very important in negotiations. If they conclude too quickly, you probably neglected some issues. On the other hand, if negotiations go on and on, the potential employer may start to cool, and you risk having the offer withdrawn.

Therefore, ask important questions early in the negotiation process to avoid nitpicking in the latter stages; look into: state and local taxes, living costs, mortgage differential (most companies now make up the difference between your existing rate and the new rate on your current base from two to five years) and moving costs.

In addition, learn what pre-tax benefits are available, such as cars (an important perk today that can be worth $8,000 to $10,000 in income), club memberships and medical insurance. Find out about incentive compensation, performance share programs and stock options, and explore profit sharing, pension plans, and of course, your starting salary. Minimum switching premiums today are running between 10% and 20%. Where in the salary range for the position are you? Will you experience salary compression by coming in at the top half of the top quartile with this new company? Investigate bonuses. What is the range? How many years in the past 10 have they been paid out?

Don't overlook vacations. Regardless of stated "policy," if a company wants you badly enough, they often can compromise. It's tough to go backward.

Step 12: When you have negotiated several offers, and your target date has arrived, you have to make a decision. Listen to your instincts: they are important. Listen to what your family says; their instincts are superb! They know you best and will pick up signals you may not discern. Before making any final decision, look into local living conditions, schools, etc., with your family. Ideally, have an interview dinner on their turf with all other spouses present. They can be revealing. You will learn the company's values and norms.

Your new employer is going to require references. You should be thinking of several past superiors, peers and subordinates who can be contacted. It is in your best interest to delay this until the last possible moment. When someone in your office is called for a reference, your intention to leave the company is completely exposed. During the negotiation stage, have several relatively "safe" references of people who will respect a confidence. Save the last references for the time when you have a firm offer.

Finally, enjoy the rewards that come from the challenges of change.

William E. Gould is managing director of Gould & McCoy, Inc., a New York based executive search firm, and was president of the Association of Executive Search Consultants in Greenwich, Conn.

When Is the Time Right to Change Jobs?

by Frederick Hornberger

Today's job market is rich with opportunity. You can see signs of it everywhere. . . . A friend accepts an exciting new position. . . . Neighbors leave for that once-in-a-lifetime promotion. . . . Hot executives dominate the news. It's enough to make you wonder—why don't the opportunities you want knock at your office door?

Is it time to change jobs?

That's a difficult decision. A new job, after all, might bring you higher pay, more authority, greater responsibility, a better chance for advancement—even a pleasanter atmosphere. On the other hand, maybe the boss is right: you're just not ready for promotion. Maybe your current salary is the best you can expect. Maybe you'll be branded as an opportunist, and lose that bigger opportunity down the road. Perhaps just looking for the "right opportunity" will cost you the job you have.

Changing jobs is a difficult decision *if* you have no career plan to guide you. You're liable to worry through each move, with good reason. You may take a job that looks promising, but leads nowhere. By contrast, with a sound career plan, you'll know how to find the right jobs and when to take them.

A Two-Step, Sure-Fire Plan

The following is a proven career planning method. We have recommended it—and seen it work—countless times. At a glance, this advice may read like elementary common sense. It is, but don't be fooled. Developing your career plan will demand discipline, self-searching and extra effort. And it will be worth it. The ultimate result will be that position you thought you could only dream about.

To improve your career, decide on a career goal. Then, develop a "job plan" for reaching that goal. These two steps let you—not fate alone—control your advancement.

Your career goal should be a specific position in a specific industry. For example, you might wish to be an executive editor of a technical publications company or the chief engineer of a major auto parts manufacturer.

Your job plan will have two elements. Your long-term plan will be a list of all the jobs you must hold to reach your career goal. This plan should include not only job titles but all the skills and experience you'll need for each post. Your short-term job plan will list the skills and experience you'll need to move the next rung up your ladder.

For most of us, there is no shortcut around this planning process. Only with a goal can you know when you've arrived. Only with a plan can you be confident that you will arrive on schedule, or at all.

To choose a fitting goal, you must honestly assess your experience, skills, interests, strengths, weaknesses, enthusiasms and aversions. If you find self-assessment difficult, have a close friend help you, or consult a career counselor. Once you have a clear picture of how you best operate, you can select a career goal that conforms to your character.

Questions, Questions

You must understand the day-to-day reality of the post to which you aspire. Research is paramount here. Spend time at the library. Read relevant books and magazines. Talk to executive recruiters; they know what it takes to flourish in a given role. As you begin to clarify your goal, interview people who have achieved it. Find out if you really want their responsibilities and hard work. (Either way, it's best to know beforehand!)

To begin establishing your job plan, ask your role models how they rose to their present position. Chart their career histories and consider the composite result a very rough road map. You can't follow their advice verbatim because the trail to your goal is always shifting slightly. For example, foreign languages may become important as your business or industry becomes more international. You may need expertise in a process or technology that didn't exist when your mentors were at your stage.

Therefore, be sure to ask your interviewees two additional questions: What qualifications will your successor be expected to have? What knowledge did you lack—but wish you had—when you began this job?

As you begin to see the path to your goal, interview people who hold the jobs along your way. The better you understand what lies ahead, the better you can meet the challenge.

Acting on the Plan

When you're ready to act on your plan, timing becomes paramount. You should seek each new job as soon as you are prepared to succeed in it. Moving

No Goal? No Plan? Not Much Satisfaction

These two true stories from my personnel consultancy illustrate the costs of haphazard career management. I have changed the names, but the facts are true.

Jim Peters dreams of becoming a sales manager for a national construction firm. For five years, he's been a salesman for a Georgia-based construction firm. He sees no opportunity to advance, feels underpaid and thinks he's learned all he can from his boss.

Quietly, Jim talks to a few local firms hiring salespeople with his level of experience. A local architectural firm offers him a job with a better salary. The prospect of a new boss, new work environment and the opportunity for advancement excite Jim. He accepts the offer, and the new firm makes him feel welcome.

But four years later, the bloom is off the rose. The new job turns out to have little chance of advancement. Jim's boss is fine, but the work is difficult and different from what Jim was accustomed to. Worst of all, the 10 percent raise Jim engineered by job-hopping was also paid to his successor at his former employer. Jim feels ready to change jobs again.

This time, he vows to view any new job realistically. He has heard that Washington, D.C., is one of the hottest building markets, so he decides to hunt for work there. Given his disenchantment with architectural sales, he opts to return to construction sales. But he finds no firm willing to raise his salary because he is coming from the more limited field of architectural sales. One firm convinces Jim to take the same pay for the chance to re-enter construction sales. After all, there will be plenty of opportunity for advancement later.

Jim moves his family to the D.C. area—and one more disappointment. His hoped-for promotion never materializes. Jim chases one rainbow after another until he retires as a franchise co-owner (with his brother-in-law) of a fast-food restaurant.

Bill Doyle is a civil engineer who graduates with top honors from a good school. He dreams of heading a design team for one of the top engineering firms in America, designing luxury hotels.

Unfortunately, the career guidance department at his alma mater is unable to bring any hot civil engineering recruiters to campus, and Bill receives no responses to the resumes he sends out cold. The most lucrative offer he gets upon graduation is from a local power company. He accepts.

Three years later, Bill hears of the exceptional salaries civil engineers are earning in the Texas oil fields. He forwards his resume to a major oil firm and gets back an offer at 25 percent higher pay, which he delightedly takes.

Five years later, Bill is laid off in an oil downturn. Because layoffs are so extensive, he is out of work for six months. He finally lands a job designing pulp and paper plants—for a 20 percent cut in pay.

Eventually, Bill retires as a designer on a team in which he designs rather boring motels for a national chain.

You've got to know what you want and how to get there. Otherwise, you won't.

before you have the skills and confidence can be disastrous to your career and your company. Besides, there is no need to move too soon or too high just because an outstanding opportunity comes prematurely. There are always opportunities for outstanding talent.

Likewise, there is no career benefit in staying on your present job once you're truly prepared for a better one. Loyalty and stagnation are two different things! As soon as you're ready for more responsibility, seek it.

As you advance, keep abreast of changes in your industry. Changing regulations, technology and business conditions have the potential to change both your path and your destination. Remain flexible, then, and periodically review your plans and goal.

Keep a High Profile

Your reputation within your industry is highly influential in gaining interviews and securing new positions. Never assume that doing good work is enough. It's simply a good start. The best way to develop your reputation (and keep up with the job market) is to become active in your trade association. Serve on a committee in your area of interest. Write articles for your association journal and for your area's business page. Speak when invited. These initiatives advertise your commitment to your field.

Cultivate a network of successful people within your industry. Make it clear that you respect their attainment and want to emulate them. Most people will be flattered, and happy to help. This network will be your early warning system regarding the best openings, which are rarely advertised or made public.

If you have the choice, it is better to remain employed and learn about openings through your network than to quit your job and sleuth full-time. Your attractiveness as a successful employee is worth far more than extra hours to shop.

To review, effective career management requires a goal, a plan and good timing. Choose a goal which is worthwhile yet attainable. Develop a plan based on thorough, up-to-date industry knowledge. Seek your next job as soon as you have the skill and confidence to advance.

Do these things consistently and well, and you will realize your true potential in your career.

Frederick Hornberger, CPC, is president of Hornberger Management Company, a Wilmington, Delaware-based executive search firm.

The Seven Most Common Blunders Made by Executives on Their Resumes and Cover Letters

1. **Don't be informal.** Don't start your cover letter with the words: "Good morning" or "How are you today?" Don't address the executive recruiter by his or her first name in your letter. Don't begin your letter with "Can we talk?"
2. **Don't use colored paper** such as chartreuse, orange, brown or gray. Besides giving the wrong impression, they don't xerox well and sooner or later, your resume, if it is of interest to a company, will have to be copied.
3. **Don't include a picture.** In the '40s or '50s, this practice was popular. Today, it's passe and gives the impression that you're old-fashioned. In any case, please don't send an 8½ by 11 glossy. Even if you have movie star good looks, it has little impact on the search firm in determining your suitability for a job.
4. **Don't use gimmicks.** While they work well for people looking for jobs in the advertising industry, they work against you for corporate posts. Don't tape a nickel or a dollar bill on your cover letter; don't send your resume in a file folder labeled with your name.
5. **Watch your language.** Don't start your cover letter with a bang, i.e., "Are you looking for a marketing superstar?" It's better to err on the boring side than to be too promotional. Don't hype your letter with terms like, "I'm a young 57" or "I'm a high-powered executive."

6. **Leave out personal information.** No one is interested in your wife's maiden name (unless it's DuPont), your children's names and ages, when you graduated high school, or your religion.
7. **Don't send too much material.** Don't send your present company's annual report; don't turn your resume into a book-length project and don't send references. If a search firm or other employer needs that sort of back-up, you're probably on the verge of getting the job.

Source: Battalia and Associates, a New York-based executive search firm that is a member of the Euram Consultants Group, Ltd., with offices in England, Scotland, France, West Germany and Sweden.

A Job-Seeking Executive's Guide to Executive Search

by Don Baiocchi

What should high-level executives in the job market know about the retained executive search process? The following guide attempts to address the question.

Executives in or approaching the 6-figure compensation range should first know how retained search works. Put quite simply, there are 10 steps:

1. **Situation Analysis.** Client and search consultant review industry, company, and position to determine requirements and compensation level of candidates.

2. **Position Specification.** Consultant (or client) prepares description of the position's relationships, responsibilities, and requirements for agreement before search begins.

3. **Research.** Consultant defines the universe of target companies and individuals. Consultant and consulting firm research department then retrieve and review appropriate individual and company files.

4. **Field Search.** Consultant and research associate contact sources and prospects to qualify prospects for personal interviews. This is mostly telephone screening but may be in person as well.

5. **Consultant Interview.** Consultant interviews prospects and evaluates them relative to the position specifications. With qualified executives, consultant stimulates interest in the position.

6. **Presentation of Candidates.** Consultant presents written reports and comparative analysis to the client on the most qualified candidates.

7. **Client Interview.** Client and candidate mutually explore attractiveness and suitability.

8. **Negotiation.** Consultant assists client in discussions leading to acceptance by the preferred candidate of client's employment offer.
9. **Reference Report.** Consultant investigates candidate's history through inquiry of former and (maybe) present associates and verifies academic credentials.
10. **Assimilation into Organization.** Consultant follows up with both client and the new executive to assure successful adjustment.

The Initial Contact with Executive Search

In order for the job-seeker to get into the executive search process, it is necessary to send a cover letter and resume to the retained executive search firms.

Many books have been written on what to say in cover letters and how to write resumes, so we will not go into this in much detail. What the cover letter should communicate, though, is the function(s) and maybe industry (industries) targeted, the present cash compensation, and the attitude toward relocating. The search consultant needs to have all of this information in order to properly evaluate the fit with any particular search. The individual's file is created and retrieved on the basis of function, industry, and compensation.

The resume should adequately describe the employer, reporting relationship, and the responsibilities. And it must emphasize key accomplishments in terms of specific actions taken and results achieved.

Where should the cover letter and resume be sent? Our view is that if there are no geographic preferences or restrictions (and sometimes even if there are), the materrials should be sent to the entire 1000-plus list of retained firms and each and every one of their offices, as listed in *The Directory of Executive Recruiters.*

Many outplacement consultants advise sending a "national" mailing to 200-300 retained search firms and almost no one sends to each and every office of each and every firm.

The claim is that this restricted mailing covers a significant percentage of the searches outstanding at any time. They also claim that most of the firms have one centralized processing office so why send 10 letters to 10 different offices when they will all converge at one place anyway. And, besides, handling all these resumes irritates the search firm to boot. Finally, others frequently send this restricted mailing to a specific search consultant.

Let's take these differences one at a time. Our mailing to all 1000 firms (there are about 300 additional offices to bring the total to a 1300+ piece mailing) rather than to just 200-300 firms is done because we do not want to concede the percentage that would not be covered. The percentage varies because the search community is a highly dynamic one. But we believe that the additional cost is justified because, at the time of any given mailing, the probability of a "quick match" increases by 30% to 50%. Why concede 1 of 2 or 3 quick matches?

Okay, why do we send the material to each and every office when we know each of the 10 (or whatever number) eventually works its way to one central processing office. The reason is that when new searches begin in the "outer" offices, the researchers and consultants who process the incoming resumes "pick-off" the "quick matches." Mailing to each office gets our client's materials into the right hands early in the process. This is important because of the significant temptation for the consultant/researcher to cut-off the retrieval process after 25 or 50 or 75 promising matches are found. Since it takes from a few days to a few months for a resume to work itself into the search firm's internal research and retrieval system, if we did not send to the "outer" offices, our client may get into the system in the central office too late.

Another key aspect: Executive search is very much a relationship business. The implication relevant here is that a California or New York recruiter with a client relationship in Chicago may get a search for a position in Chicago. Since the first step in Research (Step 3) is to check the internal file system, it may pay to have the candidate's material in the California or New York search firm files.

Finally, why do we mail to a firm or an office of a firm and not to a specific recruiter? The reason is to expedite processing to get the material into the system as quickly as possible, so it can be retrieved by all of the firm's recruiters at all of their offices. If the material is sent to a specific recruiter, he or she may be traveling or on vacation for a week or two. Or he or she may set it aside "temporarily" (thinking of a possible search to be discussed the following week or month). Or, worst yet, when I was in search I was frequently guilty of putting a resume on the side "temporarily" only to find it on the bottom of some stack in a remote corner of my office 6 months later. In the meantime, my "friend" was mumbling, "What is wrong with that SOB (Sweet Old Baiocchi, of course) and his associates? Why haven't they contacted me in all these months?" The answer is the resume never got into the retrieval system.

Additionally, we want the job-seeker to use his or her contacts, especially with a search consultant. So after we have sent the general mailing, we have the job-seeker send a personal mailing to known consultants. In that letter, the consultant is advised that the Research Department may already have created a file based on the previous general mailing.

Networking with the Search Community

Should there be an effort to personally network with the search consultant? The answer is "yes" if the job-seeker is a friend of the consultant or a former client, prospect, candidate, or successful candidate (i.e., a placement). The answer may be "yes" if the job-seeker has a friend who is willing to call the consultant and prevail upon him or her to see the job-seeker.

Barring that, though, what about it? This is a sticky issue and there is considerable controversy both in the search community and in the outplacement community. Nevertheless, I do not think many of my search friends would take exception to the basis for the "yes" and "maybe" situations depicted in the preceding paragraph.

On the search side of the issue is the following principle: Search consultants serve their clients by finding qualified candidates for their clients' positions and not by finding appropriate positions for qualified candidates. On the job-seeker side is the following principle: Job-seekers are qualified candidates for some position, somewhere, and need advice and counsel from, and interface with, as many informed parties as possible to find these positions.

Hence, the above principles depict that the search consultants represent the demand side of the equation and the job-seekers the supply side. Historically, my effort has been to try to determine the appropriate way to bridge the demand and the supply. Barring the client-friend-prospect-candidate-successful candidate relationship, I generally recommend building the bridge via the written material and not pushing the networking.

On the other hand, when the job-seeker is an outplacement candidate in my program and I believe he or she has unique and particularly attractive characteristics, I try to identify those search consultants who would benefit "somewhat" from a personal contact. When I say "somewhat" I mean that I recognize that the primary benefit is to my outplacement client but that the consultant would also gain something.

What might the "something" be? Well, for example, if my candidate is a consumer products president, or a bank president, or a chief financial officer, or a human resources officer, I try to determine which search consultants frequently work in these functions and industries. Back in my search days, I devoted one-half day a week to meeting job-seekers in those categories (plus a few others). The potential for new business down the road was not great, but it helped to keep me current in my areas of search expertise. Also, I was adding to an ever-expanding network of new sources and prospects—and ultimately a few new clients.

So, I believe that outplacement counselors should not encourage every job-seeker to see as many search consultants as possible. But I also believe that consultants should selectively see a few job-seekers.

A recently noted phenomenon in my outplacement practice is what I call "negative selection." In other words, despite my comments, some of my candidates list search consultants and their firms as ones that they will not use in the future because of an unwillingness to see them in their time of need. While the consultants can justify their position on the principle previously stated, those consultants who are willing to go out of their way occasionally are gaining a potential future competitive advantage.

The Process and Its Impact

The executive search process is one that is sometimes difficult to understand by someone who has never done, or been a significant user of search work.

For example, based on Steps 1 and 2, a list of "must have, preferred, desired" experiences and characteristics may be developed and agreed to by the client and search consultant. The "must have, preferred, desired" requirements may not make sense to anyone not intimately familiar with the particular specification. Also, the set of "must have, preferred, desired" requirements may be the starting point, but, a few months after candidates are identified, the requirements may be loosened.

So when a search consultant or researcher initially calls (Step 4), a job-seeker may be disappointed that no follow-up is intended because the job-seeker has only 4 of the 5 "must have" experiences. Even if the one missing is the least significant of the five, if the consultant or researcher thinks there will be candidates with all five "must haves" to interview (Step 5), he or she may pass. This may be particularly disappointing to the job-seeker who believes that if given a personal interview, "I could sell the fact that my 4 of 5 are better than anyone else's 5 of 5." While this may be true, the consultant or researcher is literally sticking to the specification, at least at that point of the search.

One other troublesome aspect to the job-seeker is when the search consultant will not disclose the identity of the client. In many instances, this is justified. Some valid reasons include: (1) the incumbent is not aware that a search for a replacement is being conducted; (2) the position may have strategic implications and the client does not want to disclose the strategy until the last minute; (3) the client has a complex issue or problem that would take considerable time or effort to fully disclose so limited disclosure is based on a "need to know."

Yet another frequent occurrence is when a job-seeker says that he or she has had two recruiters call. The first described the situation and then probed the job-seeker's background. It was left that the job-seeker would hear from the consultant in a few weeks. The second did the same but wanted to meet that afternoon. The job-seeker typically sees the second consultant as much more decisive and aggressive in pursuing the client's interest than the first. At that point, I invariably explain that in the second instance the search had probably proceeded through Step 8 (Negotiation) or 9 (Referencing) and the second consultant was looking for a quick match due to recycling back to Step 5 for the second time. The first consultant was probably in Step 4 and was looking for the first time for candidates to go through and beyond Step 5.

Communication Problems and Frustrations

One of the often frustrating things to the job-seeker at Step 4 (Field Search) is that the search consultant or researcher will not immediately decide if there will be a face-to-face interview. More often than not, the consultant or researcher will simply say that, at this point, the job-seeker is a "possibility." The decision to interview will be made in a few weeks, depending on the quality and quantity of the prospects identified.

At this point, the job-seeker may be genuinely interested and even excited. But the next move is at the search consultant/researcher's option, not the job-seeker's. So the job-seeker starts counting the days—and counts—and counts. And then wonders what happened. So he or she calls or writes the consultant/researcher. No response. No return phone calls. No letter advising the status. Another "rejection" for the job-seeker. But this is even more frustrating because the job-seeker has no idea why there was no follow-up. Did the consultant lose the file? Did it fall through the cracks? Did the consultant learn something negative about the job-seeker from another source? Did the spec change? Did the client decide that the experience was wrong? No answers.

This same frustration for the job-seeker may also happen after Step 5 (Consultant Interview), Step 6 (Presentation of Candidate), or Step 7 (Client Interview). After the interview has taken place with either or both the search consultant or client executives, there may not be any feedback to the job-seeker. As incredible as this may seem, i.e., that neither the consultant nor the client will follow-up, it is a frequent, everyday occurrence. Even after a job-seeker travels to a company for interviews, meets several executives, sends an expense reimbursement letter to either the consultant or company, receives a reimbursement check (more often than not with no note or, if with a note, it simply says the job-seeker will be hearing from someone soon), there may be no follow-up.

This failure to communicate is extremely frustrating. While there are many search consultants who appropriately and regularly do follow-up and keep their candidates informed, there are many who do not. As you can imagine, the reaction on the part of the job-seeker is very negative toward the company, the consultant and the search firm. This is a real opportunity for consultants and their clients to gain a competitive advantage simply by demonstrating common courtesy and professionalism.

Rationale for Leaving

One of the first things we do in outplacement counseling is develop a statement explaining why the executive is leaving his or her employer. We call this a "rationale for leaving." It is designed to explain the circumstances underlying the separation of the executive. The words are carefully chosen because they are the words that the job-seeker will use in the marketplace and the words that the appropriate executives of the former employer will use when called as a reference by a potential employer. Hence, we draft the "rationale for leaving" and review it with the job-seeker's former superior and maybe the human resources contact or other appropriate executives.

This can be a delicate balancing act. As outplacement counselors, we are the job-seeker's confidant and advocate. Yet our own reputation for honesty is also on the line. We are careful to phrase the statement as positively as possible and yet avoid any deception or fraud; there is a built-in checkpoint in that executives of the former employer must also sign-off on the statement.

Some search consultants are troubled by the "rationale for leaving." They want "total candor" in this instance. I believe that what they get from our "rationales for leaving" is "total candor most positively stated." And I ask the consultant this question: If they were in the job-seeker's shoes, would they do anything differently? Would they not choose their words carefully and try to be as positive as possible?

Interview Training

A similar situation involves interview training. With some of our job-seekers (but not all), we give intensive interview training. This is done with the objective of having our job-seeker invited back for a second round. The training is done not to deceive but to show the interviewee how to avoid the "knock-out factors" that skilled interviewers use to reduce the number of candidates to a workable "short list." We tell the job-seeker that "total candor" is appropriate for the second and later rounds but inappropriate for the first.

Our search consultant friends tell us that the ideal is for them to interview our job-seeker before they have had the in-depth interview training but that the job-seeker should have the training before they meet with the consultant's client to make the most positive presentation possible.

Some search consultants and their clients have complained about the ethics of interview training. They believe that it distorts the truth and hence is a deceptive practice. We believe that there is a potential for deception, but that the training is appropriate and non-deceptive if done professionally. We draw the parallel with the public relations aspects of most companies. We view interview training as "personal public relations." There also is a strong parallel with sales training. The interview training we provide contains significant elements of professional sales training. Indeed, many senior executives with whom we work have had significant sales training and experience and need little, if any, interview training.

Search Firm Blockage and End-Arounds

Two closely related concerns that job-seekers have are blockages at search firms and the perceived need to go around the search firm and go directly to their client.

"Search firm blockage" is a different twist of the "client blockage" that search firms have. "Client blockage" arises from the ethics of not searching executives out of companies for whom the search firm has worked in a retained search capacity within the past 24 months (or some similar guideline). "Search firm blockage" from the job-seeker's perspective arises when the job-seeker is locked out of other appropriate searches within the same search firm.

Many search firms follow the practice that a job-seeker may be a candidate on only one client search at a time. Doesn't this seem reasonable?

But a problem may arise when the job-seeker is a candidate on Search A with the XYZ Search Company. Search A is put on hold—for any of a number of valid reasons—but Search A is not cancelled. So the job-seeker is technically still a candidate for Search A and will be until the "hold" is lifted or the search is cancelled. In the meantime, XYZ also has Search B, C, and so on—all searches that the job-seeker would fit, except for the "blockage" from being considered because there is still the question of candidacy on Search A.

Now the job-seeker has a dilemma. He or she hears about searches B and C and hears that the XYZ Search Company is also doing them. If the job-seeker withdraws from Search A, he or she may then pursue Search B or Search C through XYZ. Alternatively, the job-seeker can stand pat on Search A and attempt to go directly to the B or C company and not through XYZ. Even another choice is to withdraw from Search A, ask XYZ about B and C, become a candidate on B or C through XYZ, and then go directly to the company (B or C) on the other search.

Of course, by doing an "end-around" on XYZ to Company B and/or C, the job-seeker runs the risk of having XYZ "blackball" the job-seeker from any and all searches. On several occasions, the decision to stay or withdraw as a candidate on a search that was put on "hold" was based on determining the probability of the search firm having other appropriate searches.

From an outplacement counselor's perspective, we believe that a job-seeker should be simultaneously considered for any number of searches within a given search firm. By definition, a job-seeker is doing an active job search campaign. To put the job-seeker on "hold" with Client A and be blocked from consideration for searches B and C simultaneously is without benefit to the job-seeker or B and C.

But we do recognize that this creates competition among clients A, B, and C. Hence, the dilemma. The realities are that because Client A cannot go forward with the job-seeker's candidacy at the time—for any reason—it is unreasonable to expect an active job-seeker to wait for "if and when" to happen. This may be different for a candidate who is gainfully employed and, we believe, both the client company and the search firm should recognize the difference.

The "fit" is another reason that the job-seeker should be considered for all appropriate searches within a given search firm at any specific time. The fit with Client A may be "average" whereas the fit with Client B may be "outstanding." If Client A's search got there one day ahead of Client B's, is it fair to both Client B and the job-seeker to be "blocked" from each other? We think not. Yet we see it all the time—unfortunately. Again, a rigid application of an inappropriate policy. Inappropriate because it considers only Client A's perspective, not clients' B, C, D, etc., much less the job-seekers'.

Also, try as much as we can, we cannot always prevent an "end-around" by the job-seeker going directly to the client. The aggressive job-seeker is going to do it frequently, regardless of what we say. And we have frequently seen client companies get upset with their search firm for "missing" such a strong candidate. On the other hand, we hasten to add that we know that it is appropriate for the search consultant to "close-out" consideration of new candidates at some point, so we do understand the dilemma that is posed both for the search firm and the job-seeker.

The Successful Candidate

The executive search process is a key bridge between executive supply and demand. Statistics generally available and from our own practice indicate that about 50% of the new employer placements over $200,000 are through the executive search process. It behooves both the job-seeker/outplacement consultant looking for a new opportunity and the search consultant to work together knowledgeably and respectfully. Let's all do what we can to make that happen!

Don Baiocchi of Baiocchi/Rinker & Associates in Chicago is a former executive search consultant now practicing corporate outplacement and management consulting. His text appeared originally in Baiocchi's Bulletin.

Understanding Executive Search: A Candidate's Perspective

by J. Larry Tyler

Executive search firms are growing and becoming increasingly involved in the process of hiring executives. As a potential candidate, you need to learn some of the new rules for dealing with these firms. If you can appreciate the differences between firms, you'll operate with more realistic expectations and gain more control over the hiring process.

Executive search firms developed after World War II when an expanding economy caused shortages of skilled labor. A "middle man" was needed to facilitate employment. In many of these early agencies, the applicant paid the employment fee (*Applicant Paid Fee* or *APF*). Today, APF firms are unheard of in healthcare and viewed as an anachronism in the search business.

From APFs there sprang up a new kind of agency. In contingency search, the employer paid the fee, but only if a hire was made. The fee was therefore "contingent" upon placement of a candidate. At about the same time, another fee arrangement evolved. Focusing on the senior executive level, these agencies took a consulting approach to employment. An executive search firm was engaged exclusively to seek candidates for an employer and a fee was paid during the course of the search. In other words, these firms were "retained," giving birth to the term, "retained search."

In today's environment, there are both contingency and retained firms. On a dollar volume basis, they divide up the employment market fairly equally. But while the results of contingency and retained search are the same (someone gets hired), their approaches are different. Because these firms vary in both approach and payment, you'll need to adjust your expectations and how you deal with them. *Figure 1* notes some of the major differences.

Figure 1

RETAINER	CONTINGENCY
■ Fee paid by employer during the search regardless of results	■ Fee contingent on placement
■ Exclusive assignment with client	■ Probably not exclusive
■ Out-of-pocket expenses paid by client to search firm	■ No out-of-pocket expenses paid
■ Survey visit to client	■ No survey visit
■ Contract	■ Contingency contract
■ Salary ranges 50K+	■ 20-100K salary range, but may go higher
■ Not in business to get you a job	■ Wants to get you hired
■ Provides comprehensive report on candidate: resume, references, interview	■ Often forwards resume and brief references only
■ Limited number of opportunities offered to a candidate	■ Exposure to many opportunities
■ Confidentiality generally assumed	■ Confidentiality could be at risk
■ Presents 3 to 5 candidates on average	■ Sends numerous candidates
■ May present you to only one client at a time	■ Will freely circulate your resume
■ Smooth closing negotiations and one-year guarantee over fee payment	■ Potential conflicts between firms or firms and clients

Retainer Firms

Your primary advantages in working with a retained firm are:

■ Exclusivity on a job opportunity.
■ A thorough selection process.
■ Full information on the work setting.
■ Protected confidentiality.

The process begins when the search consultant visits the client's organization for a site survey. In this phase, the consultant interviews executives to develop a candidate profile and secures information for prospective candidates such as community background, annual reports and job descriptions. In addition, the consultant establishes a compensation range for the position, plans the search schedule, sets target dates, and most important, gains a sense of the organization's dynamics and management style. It's easy to see why employers who enter into this exhaustive process are usually serious about filling a position.

Recruitment begins with networks in the profession. Consultants identify candidates from target organizations and professional groups such as the American College of Healthcare Executives, state hospital associations and graduate programs in health services administration. Through advertising and direct mail, consultants seek out executives to participate in the process or to offer referrals to other executives.

When you receive a call from a retained search consultant, expect to hear a brief description about the opportunity as well as specifications for the candidate such as years of experience, educational qualifications and specific technical skills. If there's a strong match between the opportunity and your background, the consultant will request your resume and then check references and verify degrees and certifications.

If you seem like an exceptionally good fit, the consultant will arrange to interview you in more depth. Be aware that during this initial screening process, the consultant is trying to produce three to five candidates who meet the client's needs. Expect to receive regular feedback on your standing in the search process, but be assertive about asking questions and be generous in supplying information about yourself, including your special needs for making a move.

If you change your mind about the position, extend the courtesy of dropping out early. It's best for everyone involved: you, the client, the consultant and the other candidates. If you wait until the last minute to drop out, you may not get a second chance.

About six to eight weeks into the engagement, the consultant will send candidate reports of the finalists to the client, including references and interview notes. The client will then decide to interview the finalists or request additional candidates from the consultant.

The retained search approach offers several advantages:

1. Before meeting the client personally, you're introduced through a comprehensive and objective package. Your candidacy is given a fair chance, and even if the client decides on someone else, the consultant offers you feedback that's useful for future interviews.

2. If you're selected to interview with the client, the search consultant sticks with you through the process of first and second interviews, community tours and compensation negotiations.

3. If you're hired, a retained search firm also offers a one-year guarantee on your success. In other words, if you leave or are terminated within a year, the search firm will conduct another search at no charge. However cynical that may seem, it adds a boost to your move because the client is assured of satisfaction.

4. Through retained search, you received an expert recommendation for a high-level position, but preclude the chance of being presented for several positions at once or having a recruiter "campaign" for you.

It's best to work with a number of retained search firms, keeping your file updated and establishing contacts over time. But be sure to be as selective as the firms are and narrow down your choices of positions, locations and compensation. The consultant will wonder if you appear too eager for too many types of positions. Even if you're not actively looking and just want to stay abreast of the career market and keep your options open, relationships with several retained search firms are a good idea.

When you send your resume to a retained search firm, you'll usually receive some sort of acknowledgement. If the organization has more than one office, be sure to send a copy to the head of each office. Once you make the initial contact, it may be some time before you receive a response, but don't get discouraged. Remember that retainer firms work on fewer searches so your activity with any one firm may be limited. However, when activity does occur, it will usually be meaningful and substantial.

Contingency Firms

Contingency firms can give you lots of exposure and their approach usually works well for junior, middle and unemployed executives. If you're in senior management, the method can still work if the listing is legitimate and if it offers an excellent opportunity with an organization you wouldn't otherwise have contacted. Contingency firms sometimes have "exclusives" with a client, but more often they don't. So be careful about offering them permission to use your resume.

Contingency search differs from retained search because contingency firms don't have contracts or expenses paid by the client. Site surveys, extensive candidate screening and follow-through are impossible under this system. Of course, this doesn't mean that the process is any less effective; it's just different.

If you get a call from a contingency recruiter, you can expect a brief description of the opportunity but usually no exact identification of the position. This is because the contingency recruiter has to protect the listing from candidates who may try to go directly to the employer or from having the opening fed to other agencies.

Once the contingency recruiter has your resume, you'll hear as much information as possible under the circumstances. But you'll probably need to look out for yourself in researching the employer and evaluating whether your qualifications fit the opportunity. The contingency recruiter typically guarantees candidates for only 90 days, so there's a tendency to take a chance and send your resume out to many employers.

If you're local, the recruiter may want to help market your candidacy. Although you might be offered numerous interviews, take care to invest your time only in strong opportunities. Contingency recruiters are enthusiastic advocates and often their motto is, "When in doubt, send em out!" It's up to you to look after your interests and avoid being cajoled into a string of dead-end meetings.

If you find a listing that interests you, keep in mind that you may be on your own during the interviewing process and in final negotiations. It will be far more challenging to feel at ease with your potential employer than if you were working through retained search.

The best way to qualify a recruiter is to ask these questions:

1. Do you have an exclusive?
2. Can you reveal the full information on the client?
3. Will I be notified before my resume is sent to your client?
4. Do you operate on a contingency fee or retainer basis?
5. What is your screening process—interviews, references, etc.?

Asking these questions will help you determine what kind of recruiter you're dealing with. At that point, you can tailor your expectations and act accordingly.

Healthcare executives can easily confuse executive search firms with outplacement/career counseling firms. Outplacement firms are in business to coach you on getting a job. Although they don't guarantee job placement, these firms have an important role in the job search process. For a fee that's typically 15 percent of your compensation, they help you develop a resume, practice interviewing on videotape, identify career goals through vocational testing and build a network of contacts. If you haven't been in the job market for many years or if you left your last employer under traumatic circumstances, you might be a good candidate for outplacement counseling.

Your first and best line of action in career development is your own network. The majority of positions are still filled through personal contacts well before any search firm has made a proposal. You don't necessarily need representation or advocacy from search firms. A high profile in the profession, a strong track record of accomplishments and an extensive network of industry contacts will make you desirable and accessible to employers and search firms. Rest assured: Your head will be hunted. Just keep in mind that search firms augment your own efforts; they don't replace them.

If you haven't been exposed to executive search firms and don't know where to seek them out, you might want to take a look at the classified sections of trade publications. Another excellent source is the *Directory of Executive Recruiters* from Kennedy Publications.

J. Larry Tyler is president of Tyler & Company in Atlanta, Georgia. Tyler & Company consults nationally in executive search, physician search and human resources consulting. Mr. Tyler is a member of the American College of Healthcare Executives and a credential member of the American Association of Healthcare Consultants.

Reprinted by permission of *Healthcare Executive*, published by the American College of Healthcare Executives, Chicago. © 1989

Attracting the Aid of An Executive Recruiter

Be helpful, meet as many as possible and follow up

by Perri Capell

Some job hunters think of executive recruiters as elite corporate agents in touch with the most desirable job openings. With one call to a recruiter, they think, an unhappy executive can take his pick of promising new jobs.

Not so. Recruiting firms won't find you a job. They're paid to find candidates with specific credentials to match current openings. Most people they contact are successfully employed.

They may recommend you if your credentials are ideal, but it's a long shot. Some recruiters say they discard 80% of the resumes they receive, purge the remainder within six months and only take calls from referred job seekers. Still, it's important to enlist recruiters' support during a job search since they may recommend you for an opening. But if they're so picky, how do you get their attention?

Start Right Away

Start by developing relationships with recruiters early in your career. Always be pleasant and helpful when a recruiter calls, says Chuck Sweet, president of A. T. Kearney Executive Search in Chicago. He says most savvy executives cultivate friendships with recruiters because they know it can boost their careers. As evidence of this growing recognition, search firm executives are invited to graduate business schools to speak to and develop relationships with M.B.A. students, Mr. Sweet says.

"Anytime you have an opportunity to meet a recruiter in person, you should do it, even if you're happily employed," Mr. Sweet says. "Always treat that person well because it can have a long-standing effect on your career."

Helping recruiters uncover information about another candidate or a company is a smart move. Such friendly dealings can cement a relationship for life, recruiters say. And, if you're asked to consider an undesirable job, meet the recruiter anyway to reinforce the relationship, Mr. Sweet says. "Then when an appropriate opportunity arrives, you'll be one of the people the recruiter thinks of," he says.

Personal referrals are another good way to make contacts, says Gordie Grand, managing director and deputy office manager of Russell Reynolds Associates in New York. "If you're looking for a job and you send a resume in blind, chances are it isn't going to get very far," says Mr. Grand. "But if someone calls and says I know this guy and he's really good, we'll see if we're working on anything they might fit."

Seek out recruiters at conferences, trade shows and other industry functions, recommends David Lambert, senior vice president and principal of Garofolo, Curtiss & Co. in Ardmore, Pa. "That's the best time to buttonhole a recruiter," says Mr. Lambert. "I go to display our services and also to make contacts with potential candidates. I couldn't see everyone who sends me a resume, but I'm usually available at these functions."

Increase Your Odds

Make contact with recruiters at as many firms as possible. The more firms you contact, the greater your chances of fitting a current search opportunity, says James Kennedy, publisher of the Directory of Executive Recruiters. "We recommend being as broad as possible (in contacting recruiters) since statistically there's such a slight chance that a recruiter will have an opening that fits you," Mr. Kennedy says.

Identify firms that specialize in your field or industry by networking. If you're an employed senior executive, you may want to work only with retained search firms, which are hired by client companies to fill a position and are paid regardless of their success. They have minimum salary requirements for candidates and refrain from sending your resume to specific companies by request, says Mr. Lambert.

Contingency search firms are paid only if a candidate they represent is hired. They normally work on positions paying less than $100,000 annually, and may send an executive's resume to numerous companies, which can endanger confidentiality, Mr. Kennedy says.

"If you're a high level person, you want to be more cautious," he says. "If you're right on the line as far as salary levels for retainer firms, then you might selectively contact some contingency firms."

Never send your resume in blind to a search firm. If you don't have a referral, keep networking until you obtain the name of an executive who specializes in your area. A last resort is to ask the research department of a major firm for the name of an appropriate person to contact.

No Grammatical Mistakes

Make sure your resume is impeccable and shows a progression of increasing responsibility before sending it to a search firm. Add a three-paragraph cover letter stating your intentions, says Mr. Sweet.

"We can shoot through 100 resumes in an hour," he says. "What we're looking for is a record of accomplishments. Where you'll get eliminated is if a search person has to delve into the resume in detail to see what you've done and where you've done it."

Research departments at large firms normally make initial cuts on resumes, eliminating those which indicate salary requirements below the minimum or objectives that don't match those of typical searches. Grammatical mistakes also are anathemas, says Mr. Sweet.

Remaining resumes are then compared to the requirements of current searches. A. T. Kearney receives about 800 resumes weekly, half of them at its Chicago office. About 20% "that make sense" are stored for about six months and the remainder are discarded, Mr. Sweet says.

After sending a resume, don't take it personally if you aren't contacted for an interview. Even if your credentials are fine, the firm might not have anything that suits your talents. Mr. Sweet suggests resubmitting your resume a few months later because by then, the firm will have new assignments which may match your qualifications. "Another misconception is that if you send your resume to our Chicago office, it's being circulated at our other offices," he says. "You should contact our other offices as well."

Recruiters say they don't mind if you follow up your resume with a phone call, as long as you don't expect much. "Phone calls are a pain in the neck to any search firm but they never hurt," says Mr. Sweet. "If you're trying to find a job, you have to be pretty selfish and take whatever steps you can."

Still, try not to be too pushy, says Mr. Lambert. "When a search firm says they'll get back to you, that's what they mean," he says. "You don't want to make a pest of yourself."

Check Credentials

If you're contacted about a job, ask plenty of questions to ensure the firm is reliable, says Ron Weber, president of Weber Executive Search in Huntington, N.Y. Ask the recruiter how he knows you, what his track record is in placing others and what the hiring company is like. If he can't divulge the company's name, ask about it size, location and product.

Expect to be asked a lot of questions, but realize you don't have to answer them until you know more about the search firm, Mr. Weber says. "I'm amazed at the kind of questions people answer without knowing who they're talking to over the phone," he says. "It's just good business to find out who you're dealing with."

If you don't want the job, say so politely and ask to be remembered if something more promising turns up. Recruiters don't like being misled and it can embarrass them with clients if you say at the last minute you're not interested, says Mr. Lambert. Candidates' credentials are checked extensively and "if you stretch the truth, it will be found out," he adds.

Be patient about the hiring process if you're a final candidate for a job. Recruiters can't force a company to hire you and frequently are frustrated by indecisive hiring managers who can't decide whom they want, Mr. Weber says. It's not unusual for a candidate who survives an initial screening to wait six or seven weeks to meet the final hiring manager, he adds.

"We have to introduce people with different backgrounds to help clients find out who they're really looking for," he says. "A highly motivated candidate can go crazy by the weeks and months of screenings."

Ms. Capell is associate editor of the National Business Employment Weekly.

How to Enlist the Support of an Executive Recruiter

by Tony Lee

Sending an unsolicited resume makes sense if you qualify

Executive search firms carry a mystique that often deters jobhunting managers from making unsolicited contact. Candidates tend to believe that recruiters are too inaccessible or specialized to have interest in a resume that arrives over the transom. Such a belief couldn't be more wrong, say recruiters.

Almost every reputable search firm saves the resumes it receives from job hunters. The advent of computerized record keeping allows firms to categorize arriving resumes by industry, specialty, location and compensation level, and retain them indefinitely. In the event that a person's qualifications closely match the needs of a client company, chances are good the candidate will be contacted, recruiters say.

"If you have the right qualifications at the right time, it makes sense to contact search firms because it's possible you could be brought into the loop of a search," says Paul R. Ray Jr., president of recruiters Paul R. Ray & Co., based in Fort Worth, Texas. "My philosophy is, nothing ventured, nothing gained."

Alfonso Duarte agrees, saying the economics of contacting recruiters are particularly sound. "Every avenue should be explored and since it only costs 25 cents for a stamp, it's worth sending a resume to us," says the vice president of Korn/Ferry International in New York, the nation's largest search firm.

Do You Earn Enough?

To be sure, not every resume mailed to a recruiter is entered into the firm's data base. The criteria for inclusion are strict throughout the industry, with a large percentage of unsolicited resumes weeded out each day. Salary level is the biggest hurdle.

"We cull unsolicited resumes for our data base by salary first, with $75,000 as the minimum accepted level," says Mr. Duarte, who estimates that his firm receives 1,000 resumes a week, 300 of those at its New York office. While the salary level is lower at some Korn/Ferry offices in other parts of the country, Mr. Duarte says managers earning below $75,000 annually should concentrate on reaching contingency rather than retained search firms. (Retained search firms are hired by client companies to fill a specific opening and are paid regardless of their success. Contingency search firms are paid only if the candidate they represent is hired.)

The next hurdle faced by job hunters is how their resumes and cover letters are viewed by each firm's research department, which is where most unsolicited resumes are forwarded. Correspondence that's poorly written, full of typographical errors or unconventional in format or style is eliminated immediately from consideration, says David Richardson, executive vice president of Chicago-based recruiters DHR International.

"Assuming that a person is at the right salary level, we contact about 10%" of the job hunters who submit resumes, "unless they've given a half-hearted effort in their letter and resume," says Mr. Richardson, whose firm recently incorporated the Chicago offices of Boyden International. A poorly conceived resume or cover letter demonstrates a lack of effort and ability and is justification enough for throwing it away, he says.

A resistance to relocating is another barrier that excludes some candidates from consideration. Few recruiters limit their clients to one geographic area. By sending your resume to a recruiter, therefore, you implicitly acknowledge your willingness to move for the right opportunity, says Mr. Ray in Fort Worth. His advice to job hunters: "Think seriously about whether you'd relocate and under what circumstances before becoming involved in a search."

When trying to set an effective strategy for contacting search firms, applicants should follow a few guidelines, recruiters say. First, call recruiters who may have contacted you in the past. Even if you rebuffed their advances before, you aren't necessarily eliminated from future consideration. Next, talk to co-workers and other managers in your industry. "Ask if they've ever been contacted and get the names of specific recruiters for you to write to," says Mr. Ray.

If your network doesn't turn up a recruiter's name, you're left to choose between two approaches: rifle and shotgun. "Candidates who feel they're in the senior-level national or international job market should take a broad approach and contact all of the largest search firms. Those are the types of positions they specialize in," says James H. Kennedy, a Fitzwilliam, N.H.-based consultant and publisher.

"It's awfully hard for an individual to find out which recruiter specializes in the cat food industry at Heidrick & Struggles in Chicago, for example. Therefore, they should use a shotgun rather than a rifle approach when sending resumes and try to hit as many search firms as possible," says Mr. Kennedy, whose publications include Executive Recruiter News, a monthly newsletter and the annual Directory of Executive Recruiters.

Middle managers, on the other hand, and senior staff specialists typically have better luck contacting smaller, more specialized search firms. "The top 100 firms by and large are generalists. They're relationship-oriented not industry-oriented," says Mr. Richardson in Chicago. "Of those, the top 40 receive material from every possible source: outplacement firms, universities, senior executives." By focusing on smaller firms, he says, you increase the odds of being called and receiving personalized attention if you match a client's needs.

A Matter of Contention

Whatever size of search firm you decide to target, how you get your resume into the right hands is a matter of contention. Some firms actively discourage follow-up telephone calls while others advocate a personal follow-up. "To zero in on the right person to contact, it's a hell of a good idea to call each firm and ask who specializes in your industry," says Mr. Richardson. "You might get the name of a research director, from whom you can find out if there's one person or one office that handles more searches in your field," he says.

Paul Ray Jr. hopes few job hunters adopt this strategy. "It's a hassle to have people follow up by phone. We receive from 500 to 1,000 resumes a week, and we'd be on the phone all the time" if even a small percentage tried to call, he says.

If your efforts to enlist a recruiter's support are successful, Mr. Ray offers a checklist of points to be considered that can make your relationship with the search firm more effective. Those include:

- Remember that the primary objective of a retained search firm is to serve the client, not the candidate.
- Be candid up-front concerning your background, education and salary level. Those facts will be verified later on.
- If a position isn't of interest to you, say so immediately and ask to be kept in mind when a better match arises. You will be called when that occurs, he says.
- Ask about the firm's past business experience working in your industry or function before agreeing to interview.
- Ask for specific job information about responsibilities, exposure to top management, company culture and the compensation package, but realize that not all information can be divulged during the early stages of a search.

■ If you aren't invited to interview, understand that it isn't a reflection on you personally. It's probably just not the right situation for you in this case, Mr. Ray says.

Tony Lee is editor of the National Business Employment Weekly.

This article is reprinted by permission of the National Business Employment Weekly, © 1989, Dow Jones & Co., Inc., 1989. All rights reserved. For subscription information, call 1-800-JOB-HUNT.

How to Work Productively with Executive Recruiters

It's unlikely that you'll land a new position by contacting search firms, but it's worth a try

by Gabrielle Solomon

Hopeful job hunters flood executive recruiters' offices with thousands of resumes daily. Yet few truly understand how search firms operate or how to work with them productively.

Many candidates think recruiting firms will find them jobs. If they don't receive a reply after sending a resume, they become resentful. They believe search consultants have the power to whisk favorites directly into plum positions, so they go to great lengths to land in-person interviews. Such misconceptions waste job hunters' and recruiters' time.

In reality, recruiting firms are paid by hiring companies to find the best candidates for specific job openings. Even recruiters who like you and think you're extraordinarily talented can't find you a job unless you happen to match one of their assignments. Therefore, the chance that you'll be selected is slim at best.

"You could be a water-walker, but if I don't have a position for a water-walker, I can't get you in," says Dan Shepherd, principal of Sweeney Shepherd Bueschel Provus Harbert & Mummert Inc., a Chicago-based retained search firm.

How the Process Works

That doesn't mean you should ignore search firms completely. Getting to know recruiters can boost your career, even if there's no immediate payoff. And it's always possible that your resume will land on a recruiter's desk just when he or she is looking for someone with your skills.

Typically, an unsolicited resume that arrives at a search firm is scanned to see whether it matches any current assignments. If it doesn't but looks promising, it will be entered into the firm's data base, which is searched at the outset of any new assignments. Depending on the size of the firm and to whom it's addressed, an unsolicited resume will be reviewed by either a search consultant or a member of the research department. It's often worth the extra effort to address your resume to an individual search consultant, say recruiters.

"If someone digs out my name, I pay more attention to that correspondent," says Mr. Shepherd, whose firm receives about 2,000 unsolicited resumes a week. His six-person office processes resumes quickly, with consultants spending an average of 10 seconds on each application. If critical information isn't in the cover letter, "we just toss it," says Mr. Shepherd. "We're making snap decisions."

Since job hunters have so little time to make an impression on recruiters, cover letters should be "short and sweet," Mr. Shepherd says. The first paragraph should explain why the person is corresponding (i.e., they were recently laid off, they're looking for a new challenge, they're considering a career change). The next paragraph should state any preferences as to industry, function or geography. The final paragraph should state current or most recent base salary, bonus and perquisites. Compensation is "life's little report card, and we grade that way," says Mr. Shepherd.

When sending a resume to a recruiter, don't experiment with functional or other nontraditional formats. Information that recruiters look for about particular company or industry affiliations, reporting responsibilities, job descriptions and significant accomplishments is best highlighted in a standard reverse-chronological resume, recruiters say.

Particularly qualified job hunters may get special attention. John Lynch, chairman of Lynch & Co., an Orange, Calif., retained search firm, says when he receives a superior resume, he discusses it at the next staff meeting to make sure his co-workers are aware of the candidate.

Anxious job seekers often call search firms to make sure their resumes arrived and to press for a little extra attention. However, such calls are unnecessary, recruiters say.

"If I have a need for your skills, I won't just beat a path to your door, I'll beat your door down," says Mr. Shepherd.

Still, the chances that your resume will be "the one" are meager at best. People who send unsolicited resumes account for maybe three top candidates out of 50 or more annual assignments, says Ted Muendel, president of Marlar International, a retained firm based in Annapolis, Md. More often, candidates who send unsolicited resumes are contacted for more information, a process called "sourcing," he says.

Opportunities to act as a source shouldn't be neglected, recruiters say. It makes sense to get to know search consultants before you ever need one.

"We like people who cooperate with us," says Mr. Shepherd. "People are immature or off-base if they think impressing us won't pay off in the long run."

Even if you aren't interested in changing jobs, try to help recruiters when they call, advises Mr. Shepherd, who adds that he records and files information about everyone he contacts during a search. His notes include observations such as whether a person was articulate, helpful, crisp or rude.

To impress recruiters who call, try to position yourself as a good source of information, advises David Lord, managing editor of Fitzwilliam, N.H.-based Kennedy Publications, which publishes "The Directory of Executive Recruiters." Describe your background and experiences and note that you'll keep them in mind if you hear of a potential search assignment at your company, he suggests.

In your efforts to get on recruiters' good sides, however, don't pretend to know people whom you don't, says Mr. Lord. Such statements will only backfire later. Honesty is critical to your relationship with recruiters.

"Any lack of truthfulness will totally destroy your credibility," says Dick Kern, managing partner of the New York office of Heidrick & Struggles Inc., a Chicago-based retained firm. "If you're not sure you want to make a job change, say that. If you have problems in your background or have been fired, be honest with the recruiter. It will come out somewhere."

Similarly, if a recruiter calls you about a position you're truly interested in, don't play hard to get, says Mr. Lord.

"Be honest about your interest without being coy," he says, and mention from the beginning any possible roadblocks. If there's no way you'll relocate to California, make that clear at the start.

Don't let enthusiasm get in the way of good judgment, though. If a recruiter calls from a firm you've never heard of, check out the firm before spilling your guts. Make some excuse to get off the phone and do a little research before calling back. Then see whether the firm is listed in recruiting firm directories and affiliated with an association that has professional practice standards, such as the Association of Executive Search Consultants in New York. Also, request literature on the firm, ask what types of searches the recruiter has completed in your field and whether he or she has a specific assignment or is just fishing.

Who to Contact

If you rarely get calls from recruiters, think about initiating contact. Try sending several reputable firms a letter indicating that you've noticed they recruit people in your field and that you'd be happy to be a source, says Mr. Lord.

If you're unemployed and haven't made many recruiter contacts, you'll have to take a more direct approach. Some career counselors advise mailing a re-

---

What They're Really Saying

Translating what recruiters tell you isn't always easy. The following glossary should help:

"I can't identify who our client is, but if I could, you'd see it as a big plus."
Translation: "I want to whet your appetite with a description of the job before telling you the company because you've probably never heard of it."

"You were referred to me by a colleague of yours who asked me not to use his name."
Translation: "This is a cold call and I don't know you from Adam."

"Our client is still actively considering your candidacy."
Translation: "They're not sure what they want and I've got to come up with someone better than you."

"You have an inside track on this position and I have a good feeling about your chances."
Translation: "I hope you hang in there because you're my fall-back position if the No. 1 candidate takes a hike."

Source: Allerton/Heinze & Partners Inc., Chicago

---

sume to every branch of every U.S. search firm, thus increasing the chances that you'll match a current assignment.

When making your list, note the difference between contingency and retained search firms. Retained firms are given exclusive assignments and are paid whether or not their searches result in a placement. They tend to work on high-level executive searches, with minimum annual salaries ranging from $50,000 to $100,000+. Contingency firms tend to be more accessible to professionals and mid-level executives. They're paid only if they place a candidate, so they may float your resume to see if any companies are interested in your skills.

If your salary is $75,000 or more, or confidentiality is a factor, you may want to approach retained firms, says Mr. Lord. If not, you'll likely have more luck with contingency firms.

If you're currently employed, maintaining confidentiality is critical. Recruiters say that most larger, reputable contingency firms will respect your request for confidentiality, but accidents can happen. Contingency firms sometimes send packets of resumes to potential clients, and by some fluke, "your resume could end up on your boss's desk," says Mr. Shepherd.

In any event, Mr. Lord doesn't think that inundating recruiting firms with your resume is the wisest job-search strategy. Instead, job seekers should conduct research to determine which firms are most likely to have appropriate assignments, then send resumes only to firms on their target list, he says. A general manager for a consumer products company earning between $50,000 and $75,000 annually may have several hundred contingency firms on his list, he says, while a senior executive for a high-tech firm may need to contact only a few dozen.

"The higher the salary range, the more selective you want to be," says Mr. Lord, adding that the search firm's location is irrelevant. "West Coast firms have East Coast clients and vice versa."

Once you've sent a resume, keep the recruiter apprised whenever you find a new job or earn a promotion, says Rick Richardson, a director with SpencerStuart & Associates' Stamford, Conn., office. Some recruiting firms keep promising resumes in data bases for as long as five years. If you keep your information updated, they'll be able to contact you should appropriate positions come along.

Mr. Richardson recommends that job hunters also develop a target list of potential employers. "I wish more people would spend more time developing their markets," says Mr. Richardson. "It's a lot more effective than just blindly calling search firms."

Gabrielle Solomon is a staff writer for the National Business Employment Weekly.

---

13 Tips on Responding to Executive Recruiters

by James H. Kennedy

1. Have a clear career game plan & job-changing mind-set before you get the call. (This includes always having an up-to-date resume.)
2. Be open but cautious.
3. Ask questions to help you determine the recruiter's legitimacy, credibility, reputation & modus operandi (i.e. contingency or retainer, exclusive assignment or not, professional affiliations, office location).
4. Never stretch the truth: about job experience, education, income, etc.
5. Bow out early if you're really not interested: offer to be a resource if not a candidate.
6. Do your homework on the client organization, once identified. (The recruiter should provide basic material such as the Annual Report, but go beyond to clippings, trade publication stories, etc.)
7. Don't play hard to get. Keep appointments, return calls, cooperate.
8. Sign the reference-checking authorization if presented: it proves you have nothing to hide.
9. Cover yourself at work: despite all precautions and confidentiality, slip-ups sometimes occur. Tell your superiors you're always getting calls from recruiters, but that it doesn't mean you're looking.
10. Don't cultivate an offer just to get leverage where you are: such short-term, self-serving strategy usually backfires.
11. Of 200 "suspects" uncovered in initial research, perhaps 50 will make the first cut, 5 will be finalists, 1 will get the job. Don't take it personally: the search process aims for a perfect fit, and it's probably in your best interests anyway.
12. Don't burn your bridges: with the recruiter or with your present employer.

13. Let the recruiter run interference for you: on salary & benefits & perks. While compensated by the hiring organization, the search consultant can be your advocate, too, and has a stake in your success.

James H. Kennedy is founder, editor and publisher of Executive Recruiter News.

Executive Recruiting: An Inside Perspective

What search firms can and cannot do for you

by Paul R. Ray, Jr.

You receive a phone call from someone who identifies himself as an executive recruiter. He tells you he's working for a client to locate a key executive. Although he won't reveal the company's name, he describes the position in general terms, the salary range and the region of the country where the company is located.

If you are a competent, successful achiever, there is a good chance you will receive this type of call some time in your career. Knowing how executive search works can help you make the most of what may be an opportunity to advance your career, salary and personal satisfaction.

What happens next depends on the type of recruiting firm handling the search. "Contingency" search firms conduct the bulk of their searches for jobs in the $35,000 to $75,000 range, although some searches exceed the $100,000 level. These firms receive a fee of 20% to 33% of the candidate's first year salary only if they succeed in making the placement.

In order to save costs, contingency firms will frequently interview a candidate only over the phone. No face-to-face meeting is scheduled. Instead, if the recruiter thinks the candidate is qualified, he will send the prospect directly to the hiring company for the next interview.

"Executive" search firms typically handle searches above the $60,000 salary level and are retained by the client on an exclusive, fee-paid basis. They usually receive one-third of the first year's cash compensation and are paid for their efforts even if no successful placement is made. Often referred to as "retainer" firms, these recruiters operate as the hiring company's alter ego, conducting only a handful of searches at any given time. They will always interview a candidate in person before sending him or her to meet directly with the company.

The search process begins when a company identifies a management or staff position that it wants to fill from the outside. The first task of the executive search firm is to discuss the position to get a clear understanding of exactly what the company wants. Initially, specific position requirements are defined, such as working experience and educational background. Then, more subjective qualities are considered, such as personal style, ability to communicate and self-confidence.

The recruiter begins the search by phoning his contacts to seek referrals for the position. These contacts include key people in the industry who the recruiter has met or dealt with in other searches. He also draws upon the internal research capabilities of his firm to generate a list of potential prospects. Speed is essential, and top search firms can usually present a qualified candidate to a company within 30 days.

Your phone call will be one of several that a recruiter makes to establish a prospect pool. From the recruiter's perspective, the primary purpose of the call is to identify you as a potential candidate and determine such basic background information as your career history, education and interest in the position.

Some Caveats.   To protect yourself from possible misuse of personal information, you should establish the identity of the recruiter, his company's experience and the types of clients he has. This is especially important if you're currently employed. Ask about his company's policy on confidentiality. If he will not reveal the name of his client, insist that you likewise don't want your name mentioned to anyone until you've decided whether you're seriously interested in the position. Don't send your resume unless your are comfortable that it will be treated with confidentiality.

Occasionally, a prospect has been embarrassed to find his or her resume turn up in undesirable places because a firm has circulated it to attract interest. Ask the recruiter whether he's conducting the search on an exclusive basis. Retainer firms call you for a specific position and will grant you, as a candidate, the same level of confidentiality they grant the client.

If the position interests you and you feel you are qualified to handle it, tell the recruiter. If relocation would be a problem, however, now is the time to bow out.

Within three weeks after the search begins, the recruiter hopes to have a good selection of prospects. He will choose those who most closely match the client position specification and will schedule a personal interview with them.

The executive recruiter will arrange to meet you at a mutually convenient location, often an airport. Lasting approximately two hours, this meeting typically gives the recruiter the opportunity to tell you who his client is and establish an in-depth candidate profile. It also gives him a chance to evaluate personal chemistry factors that can be critical to the company's acceptance or rejection of a candidate.

Expect questions concerning your personal management philosophy and ability to relocate and adapt to a new community. The recruiter will probe to determine your involvement in and responsibility for your stated professional achievements. He will also observe your thought process, level of confidence and professional polish.

Be sure to question the recruiter extensively concerning the client company's style and culture. Ask his candid opinon on the pros and cons of the position and the organization. Ask about reporting relationships. Even though it is true that his primary responsibility is to the client, it serves his best long-term interests to give you a realistic picture of the situation so you won't be surprised later.

The Final Stages.   Although the recruiter is probably considering three to five candidates for the position he will present each one to his client as soon as he is convinced a good fit exists. The next step is up to the hiring company. If the company invites you for an interview, you can expect to spend a half-day on your first visit, longer on a second interview. Occasionally both you and your spouse will be asked to make a third trip to the client location before an offer is made.

Once both you and the company have expressed interest in each other, the search firm will conduct in-depth reference checks.

Even though you have accepted an offer and are settled in your new position, you should not have heard the last of the search firm. A good recruiter will follow up with his clients about six to 12 months after placing them to make sure the fit is right and all parties are content.

Executive Recruiter Checklist

1. Keep in mind that although a search firm will do its best to accommodate your interest, its primary objective is finding a qualified candidate for their client.
2. Be candid with the recruiter concerning your background, education and salary level. He can verify these facts at a later stage.
3. If you have no interest in the position or feel you would not be a suitable candidate, ask the recruiter to keep you in mind if something should develop in the future. If the search firm has a candidate inventory system, ask if your background can be included in it.
4. Relocation often proves to be the stumbling block in a successful match. You should think seriously about where you would consider relocating and under what circumstances.

5. Query the recruiter on his search procedures, his experience in the business and how his firm is compensated for its services. It can tell you a lot about how you will be treated in the ensuing steps of the search.

6. Always communicate your professional and personal requirements to the recruiter when you meet in person. Some areas you should discuss include job responsibilities, the authority level of the position and its relationship in the overall organization, its degree of exposure to top management, opportunities for advancement, the "culture" of the company and the compensation package, including the company's relocation policy.

7. If you are not invited for a personal interview either with the search firm or the client, don't interpret it as your professional inadequacy. Often, there are several individuals who are better qualified or who have the "chemistry" the position requires. If you have been upfront about your background and requirements, you are likely to be called again.

Paul R. Ray, Jr., is president of Paul R. Ray & Co., an international executive recruiting firm headquartered in Fort Worth, Texas.

Conventional Retainer Search vs Contingency Recruiting

Conventional executive recruiters view themselves as professionals and argue that they should be paid whether or not they are successful in filling a position. (Like the doctors who earn fees whether or not the patient dies and lawyers who similarly are paid whether or not successful for their clients). This is called "retainer" or "retained" search. Clients pay a portion of the fee to initiate the search, then most or all of the remainder over the next 60 or 90 days regardless of progress on the search itself.

Contingency search, however, incorporates a different way of charging the hiring organization: no fee is due until the candidate is actually hired.

The Association of Executive Search Consultants goes as far as legally advisable to bar contingency work by its member firms (though the definition of "contingency" gets pretty convoluted at times.)

Contingency recruiters argue that payment for performance is the American Way, and that they are **not** under pressure to submit dozens of candidates or push a particular one to increase chances of a "hit."

Actually, there's something to be said on both sides . . . and **the executive seeking maximum exposure should certainly be in touch with all possible recruiters. Remember that neither conventional nor contingency recruiters ever charge the individual: all fees are assumed by the hiring organization.**

Contingency Recruiters

They may provide your next job if you're looking to earn between $30,000 and $70,000 a year

by David Diamond

In the employment field, contingency recruiters are a misunderstood lot. They aren't employment agencies, those ubiquitous folks who are in the business of finding candidates jobs, mostly under $40,000 a year. Nor are they traditional executive recruiters, the "headhunters" who are retained by a corporate client to track down the best candidate for a vacant senior- level position.

Unlike employment agencies, contingency recruiters usually represent jobs in the $30,000 to $70,000 range and the fee is always paid by the corporation that enlisted their services. But unlike traditional "retainer" executive reruiters that get paid whether they fill a job or not, "contingency" recruiters get paid only when the position is filled.

The distinction is partly a matter of semantics, but it has created the longest-running debate in the employment field, one that job seekers should understand. Knowing how to use contingency recruiters could be the key to finding a new job.

Since contingency recruiters are compensated only after the client offers and the candidate accepts, critics claim they are likely to be insensitive to the needs of both, haphazardly distributing unsolicited resumes on the chance that a match, no matter how imperfect, will be made. A contingency recruiter might take your resume and distribute it without ever interviewing you. "They can't bother to spend too much time with interviews. It's a business of paper shuffling," says Alan Stern, chairman of the National Association of Corporate and Professional Recruiters, a 400-member trade group that doesn't accept firms unless they interview candidates.

But on their own behalf, contingency firms say candidates benefit from the compensation structure that makes contingency types more aggressive than the more exclusive retainer firms. "A retainer firm is paid regardless of results, so they will take a resume and file it away until they have an active assignment that calls for the individual. A contingency firm will actively market the person. In other words, call up companies for you," says Robert Mulberger, spokesman for the National Association of Personnel Consultants, a 1,750- member trade group with contingency operations in the majority.

On one point, both sides generally agree: For most job seekers in the $30,000 to $70,000 range, contingency recruiters are more approachable than are retainer recruiters.

The numbers make contingency recruiters a force to be carefully considered. In terms of billings, they comprise roughly half the $2 billion recruiting industry, according to James H. Kennedy. The profession's self-appointed industry watchdog, Mr. Kennedy segregates contingency recruiters from retainer recruiters in his annual directory and he uniformly excludes them from his list of the 50 leading U.S. executive recruiters.

Kenneth Cole, author of *The Headhunter Strategy: How to Make it Work for You,* and publisher of *Recruiting and Search Report Newsletter,* a competing directory of recruiters, is even-handed in his assessment of contingency recruiters. "Many of the 'experts' in the field will say that because a contingency recruiter always takes his best shot, he'll only present the top candidate," says Mr. Cole.

He cautions job seekers to distinguish between a hardworking recruiter and an overzealous one, however. He points to the subgroup of "bucketshop" contingency recruiters who earn their fee on the law of averages by sending out hundreds of unsolicited copies of a candidate's resume. Horror stories abound. Even contingency recruiters such as Arthur Adams, president of Arthur Adams and Associates in Worthington, Ohio, warn of contingency firms that have destroyed a candidate's confidentiality—and possibly cost them a job—by mass mailing a resume to the candidate's employer. "Some contingency firms are notorious for spraying a resume all over the place," he says. Adds Mr. Kennedy: "They might just blow your cover."

The bottom line for job hunters is to get their resumes into the appropriate employer's hands. To that end, says Mr. Adams, "It would behoove jobhunters to send their resumes to both contingency and retainer firms on the chances that one is working on an assignment that will fit them." The question is: How to keep from getting burned?

Mr. Kennedy suggests using contingency recruiters the same as you would a retainer recruiter but "with a little more caution." If your job requires a recruiter with an industry or position specialty, obviously you want one who fits your needs. Through a directory you can build a list of suitable firms. Narrow the list by consulting with colleagues, members of the human resources department of companies for which you would like to work, or others who would have dealt with contingency recruiters and be able to offer some advice. David McAllister, president of the Atlanta-based McAllister Group, a contingency recruiter, says, "If you are in sales, call up a major buyer you deal with. Ask him which contingency recruiters have approached him and what they're good for."

Once you select recruiters, send resumes and follow up with a telephone call about a week later. Some contingency firms prefer to hear from you before you send a resume. "Call us first. We probably can save you 25 cents [if you fail to conform to the firm's specialty profile] or we might have something right away," says Mr. McAllister. "Expediency is important."

When you make the initial telephone contact with a recruiter, contingency or retained, beware of anyone who comes across as having instant answers. Warns Mr. Cole, "That's someone who would say 'You're the perfect guy for the job,' but who has never met you. A bad sign is a recruiter who doesn't even want to meet you. I encourage every job hunter to make the same judgmental choice they would with any other business relationship. Ask yourself: Is the person persuasive and assertive without being overbearing, obnoxious and know-it-all?"

Find out if the recruiter belongs to a professional organization in both the personnel field and the industry of specialty. "If he or she works in the restaurant industry and belongs to the Restaurant Industry Association, that's some indication of professionalism. It's better than nothing," says Mr. Kennedy. Adds Mr. Cole: "Is the recruiter well-respected in his or her area of specialty or expertise? Obviously, the best tie to a recruiter is someone else's recommendation, someone who knows the recruiter professionally. The top recruiters are probably paranoid about their reputation," he says.

Finding the perfect job is partly a numbers game; winning often depends on getting your resume before as many potential employers as possible. Exposure is crucial. Because contingency recruiters are known to hustle—and because they ordinarily are required to work with more hiring organizations at any one time than are retainer recruiters—job seekers could be in better hands with a contingency firm.

But it's crucial that you select recruiters with impeccable reputations in your industry—and ones with whom you feel the most comfortable. Tell them if you don't want your resume distributed wholesale. Tell them if you don't feel comfortable having them represent you before even interviewing you.

And don't get too hung up on the contingency/retainer split, regardless of the heated emotions it evokes among employment professionals. Fact is, as the employment industry grows, the line of demarcation is eroding a bit. "Even retainer recruiters are constantly 'identifying' the contingency line," says industry guru Mr. Kennedy. "Sometimes the final portion of the fee is only due on actual hiring. It's like being a little bit pregnant."

Mr. Diamond writes frequently on management and business issues from Philadelphia.

How should you assess an executive recruiter who contacts you . . . or one with whom you initiate the contact?

1. Beware of phony firms: never pay any money, not even a "registration" fee. Legitimate recruiters never, but never, charge the individual.

2. Don't expect an instant interview or even super-courteous treatment. Recruiters owe their allegiance—and their time—to the hiring organizations who pay their fees.

3. Ask if the recruiter has a specific assignment or is just fishing . . . and act accordingly: A low-level contingency recruiter might be tempted to troll your availability & blow your cover. Retainer recruiters don't "float" resumes.

4. Cover yourself at your present job. Tell your employer from Day 1 that you're frequently called by recruiters and that talking with them doesn't mean you're disloyal. This will give you more flexibility & few sleepless nights when you really are "looking."

5. Don't play games with legitimate recruiters on your career objectives, salary, etc. . . . but don't spill your guts to everyone who calls you by phone. It's a good sign if the recruiter wants a personal interview: it's in your best interests to cooperate.

6. You can sometimes judge a book by its cover. Visit the recruiter's office & get brochures, reprints, etc., describing the firm . . . and judge for yourself. (**Note:** too-fancy offices can be a negative signal, too, as hundreds burned by career counselors can attest.)

Avoid These Mistakes When Dealing With Your Executive Recruiter

by James Kennedy

1. Floating a typeset resume complete with picture and reference quote from Sister Mary Loretta in fifth grade. Keep it simple. A typewritten page or two in standard format is just fine.
2. Phoning: "Did you get my resume?" Even if you're lucky enough to get through to the recruiter, he's immediately sorry he took the call, because he thought it was the other Mr. Barofsky (a current client).
3. Phoning 60 days later: "What's up: got anything for me yet?" Your slim chance of ever getting referred just went down the drain.
4. Saying that Jim Kennedy gave you his name and suggested you write or call. I sell some 250,000 copies (or some such ridiculous number) of the Directory of Executive Recruiters, so this ploy doesn't work either.
5. Lying about your age, education, job title, salary, etc. Little White Lies can turn into Big Black Clouds that come back to haunt you, even after hiring!
6. Missing an interview date. Miss your grandmother's funeral if necessary, but never an interview set up by your faithful headhunter . . . because then you're history.
7. Failing to take the recruiter's advice on appropriate dress. White-on-white shirts and Nehru jackets may still be fine in Kankakee, but never on Sunday in Silicon Valley.
8. Refusing to take the recruiter's call after you get the job. Next time you're on the beach he won't return your calls, either!

9. Asking: "What did you think of my resume?" Get advice from your first boss or wife (may be the same person), or from Aunt Alice the English teacher, but don't expect the recruiter to be your personal career counselor.

10. Expecting too much. Remember that the recruiter is paid by the other side and is really interested in you only if you can be converted into a bank deposit. Don't expect him to return your calls or give you an interview (but expose yourself to enough and you'll get some action.)

James H. Kennedy is founder, editor and publisher of Executive Recruiter News.

What You as a Candidate Should Know

by Robert W. Dingman

You have indicated an interest in discussing a position I am seeking to fill for a client firm. That makes you a "candidate" in the lexicon of the search consultant. Let me clarify what this process entails and what you can expect from me (and from all ethical recruiters). This explanation is intended to provide information of my responsibility to both you and my client. I would not want you to be confused about what comes next.

First, I am retained by the client firm, never paid by a candidate, on only a retainer-fee basis versus a contingent-fee arrangement. I will be paid whether you or the other candidates are hired or not. Consequently, even though you are a candidate I am not primarily serving your interests. Even if I believe you are "perfect" for the position we are discussing, I have a responsibility to my client to present a panel of well qualified candidates; so you will have a built in competition from my efforts. Overwhelmingly, my search assignments are successfully completed, so there are minimal financial reasons for me to pressure you or the client to make a match. Lastly, like most search firms, my fees are usually based on a percentage of the first year's cash compensation of the person selected. This means that if you were able to negotiate a higher figure with my client, it is to my financial advantage, but you should know that I will never assist you to raise that amount. If the client requests it, I will serve as an intermediary in salary negotiations, but my function is only to help reduce communication problems.

If I request references from you there are things you should know about what will ensue. I do not want references who are likely to let the word out that you are being considered for a position and then have this complicate your current work situation. The worst professional blunder I can make is to be indiscreet and compromise your employment somehow. I take this responsibility very seriously, so please give me names of people who will be discreet.

Why do I need to check references, anyhow? The knowledge I gain is essential if both your interests and those of the client are to be served well, and reference checking is that tool for gathering that information. Neither I, nor anyone, has the ability to interview an executive and know fully the strengths and limitations of that person.

Ideally, I like to get views of a candidate from superiors, peers and subordinates. If we continue our discussions to the point where you are a "finalist" whom I present to the client, I will at some point feel free to discreetly contact references other than the ones you named. My responsibility to my client requires that I document your achievements. It is professionally embarrassing for me to have a client find out information such as a candidate misstatement, whether it involves compensation, professional achievements, reason for termination, pertinent personal data, degrees or employment dates. Material misrepresentations make it very difficult for me to present such a candidate because of concern about veracity.

A last comment on referencing. You will never hear from me what your references said about you. The data I collect is sacrosanct and is shared only with the client, *if* I present you. Naturally, if I present you as a finalist your references must have, on balance, been supportive of you. Conversely, if you are *not* presented it would be unwise to assume that it was due to poor references because so many other factors are involved. Because I am a one-man firm no one else gets into my files, and reference material obviously does not go to other offices or staff people. This assures confidentiality.

I will be as candid with you in our dealings as the situation allows. If my candor is sometimes at the expense of being sensitive and tactful, please forgive me. I will not string you along if things are not going to move forward. You have honored me with your time and interest, and candor is the very least I owe you. When the search is completed I will let you know who was selected. If the client met you and you were not selected, I will feed back to you any information that I am free to share that might be useful to you in future interviews.

Each of us has only one career, and a mistake in changing jobs can prove disruptive and harmful. I covenant with you that if we get to the "short strokes" with a client, I will tell you all the negatives I know about the client organization and personnel, as well as the positive things that recruiters always point out. I take seriously the responsibility of possibly shaping the future direction of your career.

If any of these comments raise questions for you, or something is not acceptable to you in what I have spelled out, let's discuss it. Please excuse me if this sounds formidable, because it really isn't and perhaps you understood how it all works. However, not everyone does and it is important for every candidate to be fully informed.

Robert W. Dingman of Robert W. Dingman Co., Westlake Village, Calif. wrote this and gives a copy to every candidate.

Some Thoughts on Resumes

A resume is as essential to a job search as wings are to a bird: it's impossible to fly without it. But whether you call it an essential evil or whatever, it must be a mirror image (albeit a bit polished) of its subject. Embellishment leads to jail (or at least disappointment): shyness or sloppiness errs in the other direction.

Show me a person who can't distill a lifetime onto two pages and I'll show you a scatterbrain or an egomaniac.

Printers' resumes—and maybe a few others in the creative arena—are appropriately printed. For all the rest, neat typing does it.

COMMENT: A resume is like a snowflake: highly individualized & painfully short-lived ... but best used in large quantities. The statistical chances of a few resumes producing results are so miniscule as to justify mass distribution to all likely targets, in most cases.

A Recruiter's Do's and Don'ts of Resume Writing

by William G. Hetzel

Your resume is your most important marketing tool. Yet even if yours is flawless, employers and search consultants who receive it in the mail probably won't invite you to interview.

Most search consultants receive up to 300 unsolicited resumes weekly. They won't see a candidate unless his or her credentials match the requirements of a current assignment. But if your resume confirms that you fit an employer's needs, you may receive a screening call.

Obtaining this initial call is the strategic purpose of your resume. The rest is up to you and your persuasive powers. Impress the phone interviewer and you may proceed to personal interviews, reference checks and perhaps psychological testing. If you survive this round, you stand a good chance of landing the job.

When contacting executive recruiters, remember that you're one of hundreds and take steps to ensure that your resume gets read. The following are some helpful do's and don'ts of resume preparation.

Make your resume easy to read. Use a traditional reverse-chronological format of company, job title and dates for each position. Recruiters have limited time. If an initial scan shows you fit an opening, they'll re-read it in depth. Chronological resumes are easier to scan than functional resumes, which make it difficult to match dates with positions.

Keep the length to two or three pages. One page doesn't provide enough detail for search consultants. Three pages or more are hard to scan. A resume in letter form, with only prose paragraphs, is a waste of time and postage.

Professionalize your resume's appearance. Have it printed on a good grade of white or off-white colored paper with plenty of white space. Avoid provocative shades such as bright yellow or hot pink unless you're an interior designer.

Quantify your responsibilities and achievements. Accomplishments backed up with percent increases and dollar amounts are always more convincing than statements without supporting figures.

Use action words. Exciting verbs connote an active, achievement-oriented individual. Substitute verbs for adjectives and adverbs. Say you "led," "increased," "directed" or "introduced."

Include a brief cover letter. Use printed letterhead if possible and state your present compensation. If your most recent salary was $100,000, you shouldn't be contacted for a $200,000 position and vice versa.

Never make misleading or inaccurate statements about yourself. Any competent recruiter eventually will learn the truth and never consider you again. If you're a manager, don't say you're a director or vice president. Your past titles and education will be verified.

One candidate claimed undergraduate degrees from the University of Michigan and an M.B.A. from Wayne State University. A background check revealed he never attended those schools and held no degrees. Another candidate used his brother's more impressive educational background and work experience. He, too, was caught.

Eliminate unnecessary information. Don't state a job objective. Instead, let your work history illustrate your skills. Don't include annual reports, authored articles or a photograph. Save them for the interview.

Avoid weak language. Don't use gerunds (words ending in "ing") such as "developing," "increasing" or "delegating." They rarely make a strong impression.

Don't expect a follow-up interview. Just because you sent your resume doesn't mean you'll be interviewed. Only known candidates or those referred by known executives receive courtesy interviews. Recruiters are just too busy to see everyone.

By applying these do's and don'ts to your resume, you're ready to begin contacting recruiters.

William G. Hetzel is president of William Hetzel Associates Inc., a Schaumburg, Illinois-based executive search firm.

How to Write a Resume Recruiters Will Read

Answer four critical questions and don't be cute or most search firms will discard your correspondence

by Ann S. Barry

Every year, tens of thousands of job seekers send their resumes to executive search firms expecting to be plucked from unemployment or dismal jobs, interviewed and found new opportunities. Instead, they're deeply disappointed by the lack of response.

Recruiters are equally frustrated by the sheer volume of "write-ins," follow-up phone calls and misunderstandings about what they can do for individual job seekers.

To start, many candidates don't realize that search firms—both retainer and contingency—work for client companies, not for individual job seekers. Retained recruiters are hired on an exclusive basis by client companies to find executives for senior-level positions. Such firms are paid between 30% and 35% of total compensation in retainer fees regardless of whether the job is filled.

Leading retainer firms normally fill positions starting at $75,000, with the average position paying about $150,000. Contingency-based recruiters handle assignments starting at the lower middle-management levels, and are paid only if a successful placement is made. Many specialize in certain industries or functions, but their assignments aren't always exclusive.

Both large and small firms are inundated with unsolicited resumes. Still, most recruiters read each one hoping to find candidates to fill their most difficult assignment or to file for future use. Most can scan a resume in 30 to 60 seconds, discarding those that don't immediately answer pertinent questions. If they see a match with current assignments or future needs, they'll review the resume more carefully.

To guard against your resume getting pitched, make sure you know what recruiters are looking for. If you're struggling to put your entire career down on paper, the good news is that the straightforward, reverse-chronological resume is the best way to convey this information. New or untraditional styles of writing and formatting resumes often only detract from your background and cause recruiters to stop reading. But if your resume answers the following questions, it's likely to be read:

1. **What do you do for a living?** Put this on the first page, and describe your job fully if the title is deceptive. Make sure there's no room for confusion. One candidate who sent his resume to a leading firm listed 18 skills ranging from marketing and accounting to closed-loop control under a "Background Summary" section on the first page, followed by 10 accomplishments over a 16-year period. On the second page, he listed the titles of previous jobs, but they didn't relate to the first page's list. With such a broad range of skills and accomplishments, the firm didn't know whether to slot the executive as a vice president of marketing or project engineering.

2. **What company are you with?** Always include your employer, since company identity is a key factor in evaluating credentials, and job content is meaningless unless it's related to a specific company. Even if your employer is a client of the search firm, recruiters will maintain your confidentiality.

    If you're unemployed, state your last employer. In today's economy, being unemployed isn't viewed negatively. If the company isn't well-known or is a unit of a bigger organization, include a brief explanation of its business. "I get frustrated when resumes neglect to give information on a division of a much larger company," says Kathleen M. Shea, president of The Penn Partners Inc., a Philadelphia-based executive search firm. "It's impossible to know what every company does and it doesn't help get the attention of the recruiter."

3. **What's your industry and functional expertise?** For certain types of positions, especially line management spots, specific industry knowledge is often a critical specification. For staff positions, industry knowledge may be less important than special skills or experience. An otherwise excellent resume sent by a vice president of operations to a major search firm failed to mention his company's product and manufacturing technologies. Thus, the firm was unable to match his qualifications against current assignments.

4. **What is the size of your organization?** Search firms always want to know the size of your most recent company, group, department and staff since many specifications relate to those factors. For example, one company was unwilling to consider candidates who had managed fewer than 700 people for a top operations job. In another case, a $10 million

company only wanted managers with small-company experience because it assumed few large-company executives could make the cultural adjustment.

Don't be Cute

Gimmicks designed to make your resume stand out frequently backfire. I've been sent money, videotapes, fancy (and expensive) packaging, including some snappy all-black presentations and accordion brochures. The most memorable had a full-length photo of the candidate on the front and a photo of his back on the back. The only attention a gimmicky resume gets is to be circulated as the weirdest submission of the week. Plain white or light cream business-sized quality paper with black type is just fine and easy on the eyes. The idea is to convey a professional image no matter what your earnings level.

Remember that your resume is an introduction to a longer dialogue, probably first on the phone and then in person. Therefore, it need not tell all. However, limiting resumes to one page is useful advice only for new graduates or the chairman of the board. In fact, a logical and concise three-page resume can be easier to read than two pages with no white space and miniature print. Five pages is too long.

Make sure your resume can stand alone and makes a strong first impression. When faced with reading thousands of resumes (it's not unusual for a medium-sized search firm to receive 10,000 per year), overworked recruiters skim for the meat. This often means reading a resume before a cover letter, then returning to the letter for information on salary, relocation preferences, the reason for sending the resume and so forth.

Functional and other resume formats can obscure or skew the key facts. As a result, the cover letter doesn't get read since the recruiter has already rejected the resume. Letters sent without a resume are usually a waste of time.

Many "how-to" books stress focusing on accomplishments and using action-oriented verbs. These are nice, but after reading thousands, even hundreds, of resumes, it's hard to understand why the economy is in such bad shape given all the wonderful things everyone has achieved. When accomplishments are the focus of a resume, the context in which they were achieved is lost. One regional sales manager who contacted a recruiting firm listed impressive accomplishments, but didn't mention his industry, company or territory size. He could have been selling soap or nuclear generators, and calling on purchasing agents or CEOs. Without enough information to properly evaluate his credentials or code him into a computer retrieval system, the firm discarded his resume.

"I prefer resumes that include accomplishments under the specific position rather than a separate list," says Mary Tynes, a search consultant at Russell

Reynolds Associates Inc. in New York. "You get an immediate understanding of the person and his or her track record."

Follow the Rules

The following are seven "Golden Rules" of resume writing that can help you avoid severe mistakes:

Rule 1. Write your own resume. Professionally written resumes often seem "canned" and lack believability. If you aren't a good writer, ask someone else to edit and proofread it carefully.

Rule 2. Strive for clarity in your writing, and format your resume clearly. The acid test is whether someone who knows nothing about your industry or function can get a basic understanding of what you do for a living in 30 seconds. Don't use company abbreviations, acronyms and jargon.

Rule 3. Give your audience enough information so that your credentials can be evaluated against basic specifications. If you're in marketing or sales, what are the channels of distribution and the target markets? If in plant management, indicate the current technologies and whether it's a unionized operation.

Rule 4. Limit personal information to marital status, family and meaningful outside activities. Mention your participation in professional committees, awards and senior-level nonprofit or community work. However, "enjoy scuba diving, sailing, running and travel" only gives the impression that you have little time for work. Save personal interests for a face-to-face meeting.

Rule 5. Never misstate your educational credentials or inflate your degrees. Practically all search firms verify the college education and professional accreditation of candidates submitted to clients. If you misrepresent this information, you'll be dropped from further consideration. If you're ashamed about your lack of degree, go back to school.

Rule 6. Don't clutter your resume with meaningless verbiage. For example, "Health: Excellent" (has anyone ever said their health was poor?), "References Available Upon Request" and the inevitable paragraph on "Career Objectives." Many search-firm assignments are too unique to be listed as a career objective, but they're still terrific jobs. Be careful about the summary of qualifications section; a laundry list of "excellent skills in . . ." doesn't rate much attention.

Rule 7. Don't include attachments, articles and brochures. These can be discussed in an interview and shouldn't be sent with your resume. Never send photographs.

A well-written resume won't guarantee gaining a position through a search firm, but it's the first step in what could be a productive relationship. By following these suggestions, you may find yourself talking to a recruiter sooner than you think.

Ann S. Barry, a human resources professional, writes on career issues from New York. She formerly was vice president of research for Handy Associates, a New York management consulting and executive search firm.

The 13 Most Critical Interviewing Mistakes

Preparation, dress and decorum are important concerns

by Edmund R. Hergenrather

The number of job candidates who disqualify themselves in interviews by their lack of basic executive etiquette is amazing. Most simply assume that the position is theirs for the taking. That kind of arrogant attitude is hard to miss and rarely ingratiating.

The most important strategy for interviewees to remember is that nothing should be taken for granted. Every meeting deserves thorough preparation and careful attention to detail, even if the position doesn't appear to be a close match. "Winging it" is seen for what it is: a waste of everyone's time.

People who succeed as executive and corporate recruiters do so by making hunches with their head and heart. Job candidates who know before the interview what recruiters want to see will minimize unpleasant surprises on both sides of the desk. As an extra bonus, recruiters will appreciate their ability to streamline the process.

To increase your chances of making a lasting impression that will lead to a job offer, remember to apply the 13 following tenets of good interviewing:

1. **Always confirm your appointment and never be late.**
   Calling the interviewer's secretary one day early to confirm time and place is more than just courteous: it's proper business behavior. Schedules change frequently and meetings can be forgotten. And it's certainly better to have interviewers thankful that you called in advance, sparing them from embarrassment.

2. **Arrive prepared.**
   Learn as much as you can (within reason) about the

company's history, products, markets, competitors, direction, culture and problems. Your local library should have much of this information in its reference department. At appropriate points in the interview, interject a piece of information that reflects your preparation. It will be noted and remembered.

3. **Dress appropriately.**
This should go without saying, yet a surprising number of interviewees (particularly those living in warm climates) show up in attire better suited for the golf course, such as plaid trousers and sport shirts. Find out how company executives dress and, no pun intended, follow suit.

4. **Never invite your spouse or a friend along on the interview.**
Again, this should be obvious, but judging from several recent incidents, it isn't. One well-qualified candidate for a $125,000-a-year position as vice president of finance at an agricultural products company brought his wife along on an interview. At first, she waited in the outer office. But after our meeting, he was most anxious for me to meet her. His reasoning: "My wife is very important to me when making career decisions." I mentioned this incident to the client company, his potential employer, who decided against the candidate because of his poor judgment and lack of self-confidence.

Unless specifically invited to meet the employer, spouses or friends should be left at home. Otherwise, their presence is apt to send a strange signal, i.e., "I can't make decisions on my own," or "Let's hurry this up. My friend is waiting."

5. **Don't smoke unless invited.**
Many companies have adopted non-smoking policies and avoid hiring smokers in an attempt to reduce health care costs. Even if you're invited to smoke, it's best to decline (unless the employer is a tobacco manufacturer, of course).

6. **Don't monopolize the conversation, even if the recruiter doesn't say much.**
Too many candidates see interviews as an opportunity to sell, sell, sell. Instead, listen closely to how the interviewer defines each question before launching into an answer. Try also to get a feel for the interviewer's personality before asking questions so you know the best way to phrase them.

One bright, articulate nuclear engineering manager was well qualified for a vice president of technology position at a Berkeley, Calif., firm. Unfortunately, the client company and I agreed that he talked more than he listened. The candidate was ultimately rejected in favor of someone who listened intently and asked concise, intelligent questions, but otherwise spoke very little. Obviously, the first candidate may have had better luck if the job was in sales or public relations.

7. Show enthusiasm at every step of the process.

Try to register an honest degree of excitement at the prospect of joining the hiring company. If the position isn't for you, say so. But if the open position looks like a perfect fit, don't show a poker face in hopes of boosting the salary offer later. The offer won't come if you appear disinterested.

8. Don't offer solutions to the employer's apparent problems.

Be careful about suggesting new ideas to age-old corporate obstacles during an interview. You risk sounding arrogant and uninformed. And if your great idea has been tried in the past and failed, you can cripple your candidacy. If pressed for a new idea, you might respond by asking. "Have you tried so-and-so or this idea?"

9. Never lie or overstate your past areas of responsibility.

In a rush to fill a position, Seiko Epson Corp. once hired a training manager at $60,000-a-year without completing a reference check. When they had time to verify his records, they discovered that he had failed to disclose a recent job that he had held for just three months. The offer was rescinded.

When your references are checked, little lies, exaggerations and embellishments will be uncovered. In 99% of the cases, your candidacy will be terminated if this occurs. The exception is a legitimate misunderstanding, such as your stating a previous salary of $55,000 (including bonuses) when the company says you earned $50,000 (excluding bonuses).

To check the accuracy of your stated areas of responsibility, many corporate and executive recruiters will ask you (or one of your references) to explain or draw an organizational chart of your former employer. If it doesn't mesh with your claims, be prepared for detailed questioning.

10. Don't reveal the amount of money you hope to earn in the new position.

An extremely able human resources manager was hired recently by a large industrial products distributor in Southern California. His starting salary was considerably less than what he had earned in his last position because he unwisely stated his desired salary range, and the company president offered him a position at the lowest end of the range. If the candidate had kept his mouth closed, he doubtless would have received an offer $5,000 to $10,000 higher. Eager to land a new job, he accepted the lower salary in hopes that he would make up the difference after 12 months or so.

11. **Never accept a job offer at the first interview.**

    Even though you may fit the position perfectly and are excited by the challenge, talk it over with your family and sleep on it before accepting. Once you say "I accept," backing out is possible only at the risk of ruining your reputation. Have you asked about travel, benefits, new projects, reporting relationships, etc.?

12. **Don't play hard to get.**

    Seldom does this tactic work. Aloofness is usually mistaken for a strong lack of interest.

    The best qualified applicant we saw for a $175,000-a-year general manager's position with a paper manufacturer knew he was the favored candidate. But he played games too long. He asked for a number of minor benefits, and requested too much time "to think it over and talk about it with my wife." The client soured and withdrew the offer. The number two candidate, who originally showed strong interest and needed just the weekend to decide, landed the position.

13. **Don't make unreasonable relocation requests.**

    Aside from the moving of personal goods, house-hunting trip reimbursements and home-selling assistance, don't expect carte blanche treatment from the hiring company. You can ask for help in moving your boat or your daughter's horse, but don't demand it.

One Southern California subcontracting company was considering a high-tech engineer from New England. This fellow fancied himself as some kind of backyard Tarzan. His animal kingdom included two tigers, a few small bears, large snakes and an assortment of other beasts typically found in zoos. The estimated cost of putting his menagerie on wheels was triple the normal amount spent relocating a new employee. His insistence on being reimbursed for this expense cost him the position.

Interviews are often lost on dumb mistakes. Take steps to make sure you emerge as the smart candidate.

Mr. Hergenrather is chairman of Hergenrather & Co., an executive search firm based in Solvang, Calif. A 37-year veteran of executive search, Mr. Hergenrather has been honored as one of the founding fathers of the profession by the Association of Executive Search Consultants.

---

5 Steps to Evaluate a Job Offer Before Accepting

by James H. Lane

Employers shouldn't be the only ones asking for references during the job hunting process.

Job candidates should carefully evaluate the "credentials" of prospective employers as well.

Too many employment disasters occur because individuals do not do their homework before accepting a new position. When a company makes a job offer, there's risk on both sides, but it's far greater for the candidate than for the company, especially if the position involves relocation.

To avoid taking the wrong career step, job candidates should research five key areas before saying "yes":

1. **Talk with Current Employees.** Try to meet employees at all levels: your peers, prospective boss, and subordinates. Make a special effort to spend ample time with the boss, in a social environment as well as in the office. The higher the job level, the more important the "chemistry" and the more subjective the hiring process.

2. **Check Customer References.** Don't be shy quizzing customers about their satisfaction with the company's product or service; why they selected the firm as a vendor; strengths and weakness from a customer's perspective; as well as projections about their business relationship in the future.

3. **Financial Stability of the Company.** If the firm is publicly held, the company should be willing to provide certain information at your request. Depending on the seniority of the position, it may be advisable to get a professional financial opinion, especially in the case of a privately owned operation. Other good sources of financial information include investors, whether venture capital or banks, and vendors. (If they don't pay on time, there's a good chance your paychecks may not be predictable!)

4. **The Work Environment.** Make sure you see where you'll be working and get a clear picture of the available resources, including the professional/clerical support necessary to do the job.
5. **Organizational Expectations.** Understanding and adapting to the "corporate culture" is critical, especially at executive levels. The new boss management style, level of expectations and communications approach will be important factors in determining your success on the job.

Don't overlook these points, but remember to sell yourself first, get the offer, and THEN ask the tough questions.

For individuals who find themselves in a new situation that looks like a mismatch, start looking immediately. The longer you stay in the "wrong" job, the more you damage your employment credentials. A brief stay with a company is easier to explain in your next interview than a series of one or two-year stints.

James H. Lane is president of the outplacement division of Costello & Company, a Massachusetts management consulting firm specializing in human resources.

What Not to Do After Getting Fired

There's no reason to panic or launch into a job search

by Dennis M. Buckmaster

Until recently, getting fired usually didn't surprise the manager who received the pink slip. There were warnings, a steady decline in productivity, lost sales or some other signal that the end was coming. By then, the manager often had reconciled himself that a job hunt was in order.

Rampant mergers, takeovers and reorganizations have changed all that. Almost every salaried employee is suspect during a period of upheaval, and it's just as likely that you, your boss or even the company's president will be left out after the dust settles.

Examples abound of people who were told to pack their desks and sign up for outplacement counseling. In Texas, about 60 bank presidents became obsolete after First RepublicBank Corp.—the newly created holding company following the merger of RepublicBank and InterFirst Corp.—converted most of its statewide banks into branches. And at the Hamilton Standard division of United Technologies Corp., more than 1,000 salaried employees are being asked to leave as part of a corporate restructuring.

Given that career change can happen quickly and without warning, it's important for all managers to know how to proceed when the bottom falls out. It's even more important, however, to know how *not* to proceed. The following seven guidelines identify steps that laid-off managers should avoid at all costs. Each is fraught with peril and can only confuse and frustrate everyone involved in the search.

1. **Don't panic.** It's impossible not to feel concern and apprehension after losing a job. But panicking rarely is warranted and never is helpful. Few people are

terminated because they're "bad." At worst, they were in jobs that weren't compatible with their skills or goals. That doesn't make them bad people, and in fact offers them a chance to find a better match at another employer.

Panic is spawned by runaway fear. One of my clients recently shared a thought that put fear into perspective. "Fear is the perverted use of imagination." An unexpected push into the job market can bring visions of lost savings, rejection, family pressures and month after month of unsuccessful job hunting. Instead of letting these thoughts take hold, adopt the opposite outlook. Imagine a short job hunt, numerous interviews, interested employers, a supportive family and the chance to work in a much better job. With a positive strategy such as this, the odds of everything working to your benefit are greatly enhanced.

2. **Don't feel guilty, depressed or ashamed about being unemployed.** Almost everyone in the business world today has experienced or will experience unemployment in their careers. Guilt is a negative emotion that drains your energy and enthusiasm. It's easily read by prospective employers, who can't help but let your guilt alter their perception of you.

Don't play games with yourself or your family. One client of mine felt so ashamed about his termination (which clearly came because of a business downturn) that he pretended to go to work every morning for weeks so that his neighbors wouldn't suspect his situation. His guilt practically immobilized his job search. Even when he generated interviews, his guilt dissuaded employers from taking a chance on him.

3. **Don't carry residual anger toward your ex-employer or former boss.** No one likes to be around "victims." And certainly no company will hire someone with a chip on his or her shoulder.

A controller at a major electronics manufacturer recently was fired because of the intense anger he showed in his daily dealings. When the end arrived, he was so angry that it took me almost five hours to calm him down. He wanted to know the name of an attorney who handled wrongful discharge cases. He paced back and forth, pounded on desks and walls, shouted, called names, blamed everyone for his condition and was generally outraged. At 34, he was convinced they had ruined his career.

This man's anger not only cost him his job, but killed any hope of positive references. Even his friends were afraid to help him. Until he learns to move ahead with his life and forget the past, this former controller's resentment and anger will cause him to miss numerous opportunities.

4. **Don't neglect your family or friends.** Many people feel that changing jobs is a burden they should carry alone. Conducting a job search is just another one of life's challenges. Keep a rational perspective and remember that it's only a matter of time before you find employment.

   One interesting trend is the growing number of spouses who work together in a job hunt. Harry, a retired Coast Guard officer, and his wife Ann, for example, compiled a list of several hundred potential employers in just three afternoons. Ann helped with the mechanics of his mailings, became an excellent interview coach and, because she was in on every development, was a terrific sounding board for Harry's job offers. The two agree that their bond as husband and wife was strengthened by their chance to work together on an important project.

5. **Don't "crash" into the market until you're ready.** Calling on employers, filling out applications, applying to ads and visiting agencies is a mistake if you're not fully prepared. Some people, however, feel they must apply their aggressive, at-work behavior to get something done.

   Peter, formerly a senior manager at a large manufacturing company, says in retrospect that he shouldn't have tried to land a new position immediately after losing his previous job. Instead of researching the market and updating his resume, he reverted to office behavior and began networking at a frenzied pace.

   Peter was sure that his previous position, title and company affiliation were all he needed to land another post. Developing job search skills, he thought, was something only lower- to mid-level managers worried about. Senior executives like him could rebound on a handshake.

   After just three weeks, Peter had worn out several friends with referral interviews and had wasted the time of several potentially valuable job contacts by requesting nothing more than informational interviews. Once he accepted that there are no short cuts when conducting a job search, he took 10 days to research his industry and function. With this foundation, he soon landed numerous interviews and job offers weren't far behind.

6. **Don't let pride interfere with getting outside help.** Some people, especially men, hate to admit to a weakness. Somewhere they've developed an attitude that the ability to find a job without anyone's assistance is a measure of their worth. Actually, finding help when unemployed is common in today's job market. Few people were ever trained in job hunting, and even if they were 20 or 30 years ago, the job market is radically different today.

7. **Don't allow financial pressures to blind your decision process.** Obviously, this isn't a good time to buy a luxury car. But don't be afraid to spend money on needed resources. Postage, printing, travel and new

clothes will be necessary expenses. You also may need resume writing help, secretarial support, an answering service or career counseling. Many of these costs are tax-deductible and inexpensive in comparision to the extra month or more you may spend looking because you greatly limited your job hunting expenses.

If your situation causes financial hardship, communicate with your creditors. Most will cooperate by reducing your payments if you keep them informed of your progress. Don't slack off just because you received a comfortable severance package or profitsharing payout. That money should be used to get you back on your feet. It isn't intended to become a retirement nestegg, unless, of course, you're ready to retire.

Mr. Buckmaster is co-founder of Career Improvement Group, a Seattlebased counseling firm.

How to Keep From Getting Conned

Most firms and consultants are legitimate, but here's what to do if you're not sure

by John Artise

A 41-year-old executive, recently the victim of a corporate downsizing, walks into the plush, professional-looking office of a newly established "career marketing" firm. He is greeted congenially by the receptionist, who, with a contrived British accent, offers him a cup of coffee. Taking a seat in the waiting area, he is presented with a swank brochure of the firm's players, replete with photographs and lengthy, erudite biographies.

He notices there are no other clients waiting. In a span of 30 minutes, not a phone rings, not a soul appears at the front door and no one is seen passing between the many offices. He thinks this is rather strange, but he's so desperate for career help, the thought passes quickly.

Just then, a middle-aged man, small in stature, comes out to greet him.

"Mr. Williams? How do you do? Please come in and let's chat." He loosens his tie and adopts the demeanor of a funeral director consoling the bereaved. "I usually don't see clients on Wednesdays, but because of the urgent nature of your call, I decided to come in today.

"I understand that your company is terminating a lot of people," he says, continuing. "Yes, it seems that's going around quite a bit these days. I have hundreds of executives in your position, all about your age, too—some even older. It's a real shame."

After a couple of seconds of silence, the 41-year-old executive responds anxiously, "Well, can you help me?"

"Oh, sure, I've helped thousands. In fact, (he reaches into a drawer for a pile of letters) these are testimonials from some of my recent clients. You can look at them if you like."

"No, that's OK. Where do we begin? I need another job fast."

"Well, that's what I like. A man of purpose and commitment. With that attitude, you should land another job in practically no time. But, you have to follow a definite plan which I will outline for you. You can't deviate from it, or it won't work. Understand?"

"Sure."

The consultant pulls a program outline from his drawer along with a lengthy contract. He now switches to a selling mode which sounds rehearsed.

"There are 12 stages in this program. You can't skip stages. We do everything for you: resumes, letters, mailings. We even call prospective employers to set up interviews for you. The way we've planned it, you hardly have to do anything on your own. How's that?"

"That sounds great! What's the cost of the program?"

"First, I need a retainer of $950 which, by the way, isn't refundable. Then, as the contract stipulates, you pay in biweekly installments of $600 per stage. Should there be a need for more counseling, which I don't think will be needed, after the twelfth stage, the rate drops to $500 for each additional stage. This cost is reasonable when you consider all of the wasted time and lost job opportunities if you were to do this on your own. And what's a few thousand dollars now in order to land a $60,000-a-year job?"

The executive, appearing quite relieved and excited about the prospects, responds, "You're right. I'm sure glad I came to see you. Where do I sign?"

The Market Is Right

This scenerio takes place all too frequently. The rash of corporate downsizings has dumped thousands of ex-employees into the market and spurred their still-employed colleagues to start looking for safer havens. The result is a flood of people entering the job market—and the rise of con artists who prey on the most vulnerable.

These charlatans, in the guise of "career marketers," go after individuals who are forced to pay for their services themselves because their companies have refused or couldn't afford to offer outplacement assistance.

Often, incomplete services are provided by these so-called "career marketers" at exorbitant prices. Or, they string the clients along indefinitely by making false promises that raise expectations and keep their prey on the hook and paying.

Let me emphasize, most corporate outplacement firms are honest, reputable, ethical and able to do a very professional job for their clients. Outplacement firms contract directly with the corporations from which the counselees are referred, so no individual pays out of pocket.

Additionally, there are many competent, reputable and ethical career counselors who provide services for individuals at much lower costs than the "career marketing" firms.

But there are, unfortunately, some disreputable and unethical independents and established firms that prey on unsuspecting, traumatized and desperate individuals. They are the ones I take aim at.

In the mid 1970's, during the time I researched the job interviewing process, I decided to visit several of the widely advertised retail "career marketing" firms. I usually wore casual attire and presented a weak or "says nothing" resume. I purposely acted both ignorant of the job market and desperate to get a high-paying job. Needless to say, they saw a customer coming and gave me a sales pitch for snake oil rather than useful career counseling. From what my counseling clients tell me, the come-on hasn't changed. I can't tell you how many of my clients were tempted to sign on the dotted line and spend thousands of dollars.

Some Guidelines

I'm sorry to say, almost as many came to me too late, when they had already signed the contract and paid high retainer fees. As far as seeking legal remedies, few managed to win any of the long, drawn-out cases. If some did win, only a percentage of their money was returned.

"Let the buyer beware" is an expression that should be heeded. If you're the victim of a company layoff and are in dire need of career counseling, here are some guidelines to follow:

When meeting with an independent consultant or a representative of a firm, ask,

1. **"Are the services flexible?"**
   That is, can you choose whatever you need, instead of going through the entire track? If you really need only a resume written, why should you spend money on other unnecessary services?
2. **"How long have you been in business?"**
   Get an idea of how new to the industry this person or firm is. How much experience can they boast?
3. **"May I call a couple of your current or former clients? Can you provide a list?"**
   This is a good question to ask to check references. But slick con artists will already have prepared a list of colleagues and friends who will easily vouch for them. I remember one firm I checked on several years ago. When I asked this question the consultant provided me with a loose-leaf binder of testimonials from satisfied "customers." They looked official, indeed. I later found out they were fictitious names with the ad-

dresses and phone numbers of colleagues known to the firm. They were warned of my calling them.

A better idea is to check with the Better Business Bureau in your area to inquire about any complaints against the firm. This is harder to do, however, with independent consultants, unless they are incorporated and registered with the state in which they practice. Even then, the BBB desn't always receive all consumer complaints.

4. "How much of the job hunting will I have to do myself?"

Be wary of the "leave the driving to us" concept which these "consultants" try to promote. *No one can get a job for you.* You will have to do most of the work when composing letters, calling employers and, of course, interviewing. The consultant can show you how to approach these processes correctly.

5. "How long will this process take?"

Are they operating within a reasonable time frame? After all, you're spending a lot of money and want to be connected with a new position as soon as possible to justify your investment.

The consultant's response should be realistic and honest. While no one can give you the exact day or month of when you will be offered a job, watch out for answers such as, "Oh, as long as it takes. We'll stick with you all the way." (By that time you will have paid for a full program and then some.) Or, "About six weeks for people with your background. That's the rule around here." They're getting off the hook by telling you what the "average" search time is. If it takes longer for you, then they say that you're one of the exceptions to the rule and need a little more help.

6. "If I decide to terminate the process in midstream, how much of my money is refundable?"

This is important. *Read the contract carefully before signing.*

If you're confused by the sales pitch, just say that you want to think it over before proceeding. It's worth getting the advice of a good lawyer who is familiar with contracts.

I remember one client who signed a contract with an independent career counselor. She didn't read the "fine print" which stated that all fees were refundable except[cf1] for reasons of personal disatissfaction with the service and unpredictable fluctuations in the job market. My client's lawsuit against the counselor was futile.

7. "Do you schedule interviews for me?"

This is an excellent question. The con artists, hungry to make the sale, will invariably say, "Sure. That can be arranged. Especially after we prepare you for the interview."

I will never forget a career marketing firm (now out of business) I investigated about 10 years ago. They promised every client (especially the desperate ones) to have employment interviews arranged for them with major Fortune 500 companies. One of their customers told me in the waiting room, "Boy, I can't wait. They're setting up an interview for me right here with a big oil company."

When I asked him the name of the company, I was very surprised. "Why would a company so well known come here to interview people for job openings?" I asked myself. Well, I later found out that the so-called interviewer was both a friend of the firm and a former employee of the big oil company. They were just putting the unsuspecting soul through the motions, making him feel that he was actually making progress.

After the interview, they said that the interviewer really liked him, but that he needed to make a stronger presentation. As a result, he was convinced to pay for additional interview training sessions.

Before making a commitment of any sort, shop around and compare services. If you're not sure what to look for in a good career consultant, here's a list of qualities which he or she must display:

1. Up-to-date knowledge of the job market and the psychology of the hiring process.
2. A good track record of assisting clients in their job reconnection.
3. An ability to listen closely and motivate clients to action.
4. Offers reliable advice and information and is accessible to the client when needed.
5. A genuine concern and empathy for the client's situation.
6. Is a coach and mentor, especially in interview training, networking and career/lifeplanning.
7. Carefully monitors the client's progress.
8. Is flexible and tailors the program to the client's immediate needs.
9. Sees the client through to the job offer.
10. Exhibits qualities which the client might emulate.

Mr. Artise is a human resources and outplacement consultant in New York City.

When Offered a Good Job, Should You Tell Your Boss?

by Mortimer R. Feinberg & Bruce Serlen

Being in demand can be a mixed blessing. Suppose you are urged by a recruiter or a credible employment agency to become a candidate for a position at a highly regarded competitor. Besides having anxieties about your qualifications for the new job, or whether it would be an advantageous career move, you are particularly uneasy about how (or whether) to broach the subject with your present employer. This is made difficult if you enjoy a close and mutually supportive relationship with your present employer, or with your boss in particular.

If you do submit your resume and begin the interview process, you have no way of being certain word won't get back to your present company. Confidentiality is supposedly guaranteed, but is it? The number of key players in many industries is limited, and those players network.

In light of this, you might decide to keep your predicament to yourself. The alternative is to take your boss into your confidence, figuring it is better to tell him now than wait for him to hear it through the grapevine or accidentally over lunch.

Either way, you still may be open to charges of disloyalty. And if you don't get the new job, or decide in the end that it isn't quite what you wanted, you may find you have jeopardized a bright future at your present company.

How then to proceed? It can be a painful quandry that requires subtle judgment calls. Consider these guidelines:

- **Read the corporate culture.** Is the company environment responsive to people or is it more rigid and formalized? How extensive is the career-development effort within the firm? If other executives have been recruited out of the firm, how has their departure been viewed?

In some companies, people come and go with regularity. In others, anyone who leaves immediately becomes a nonperson. "Be sensitive to these cultural signs," says Karl Eller, chairman of Circle K Corp., a national retailer based in Phoenix. Then, if you eventually accept an offer, you won't be shocked if you get an unpleasant farewell.

- **Enter negotiations cautiously.** As you begin discussions with the employment agency or recruiter, remember you're entitled to ask how many other candidates are being considered and where you stand in the ranking. James Wesley Jr., president of Summit Communications Group in Atlanta, notes that "recruiters can cast a fairly wide net on many searches."

Ask, too, about the expected time frame for completing the search. Some searches can drag on four to six months. If any of the responses you are given don't ring true, it may be a sign the situation is too precarious for you.

- **Touch base on your present job performance.** Request a career discussion with your boss, separate from your regular performance reviews. If this raises any eyebrows, simply explain that you've had a "rush of career anxiety." You need to know your boss's honest and candid estimation of your prospects. Make no mention at this point of any possible job offer. Whatever input you receive, store it in your mind while you consider whether to proceed further.

- **Realize you may not be able to turn back.** If you decide in your own mind that you do not want to leave your present position, be wary of going beyond preliminary discussions with the agency. Once you throw your hat in the ring, it may become increasingly difficult to extract yourself from the process unscathed.

- **Act when an offer is imminent.** Now is the time to raise the subject with your present boss. Don't go in, however, unless you are mentally prepared to accept the other company's offer and resign. Remember, this is not a negotiation ploy, especially as it concerns your present compensation. Senior management at one broadcasting company meets with employees to discuss outside offers, though the cultural ground rules stipulate that salary shouldn't be an issue.

Can you have a candid, open disucssion with your boss at this point? "Yes," says Carl Dargene, chief executive officer of Amcore Financial Inc. in Rockford, Ill., "if your prior relationship has been solid and you act sincerely."

"I appreciate people consulting me," agrees William Schwartz, chief executive of Capital Cable in St. Louis. "And in reviewing their career prospects at the company, it sometimes becomes clear they should pursue the other opportunity."

Other chief executives, however, aren't nearly as sanguine. To their minds, any broaching of another offer can poison their relationship with the employee, possibly permanently. The person is no longer considered a team player. The ground shifts. He or she suddenly represents a risk to the organization. "Sure you can have an 'honest' talk with your boss, but it'll be your last," says John Kelly, president of Kelhan Ltd., a marketing promotion company in New York. So know your boss's attitude well before you act.

■ **Don't count on counteroffers.** In a recent survey, the search firm of Boyden International reported that of 450 managers who changed positions during a 36-month period, 39 received counteroffers. Of these, 27 decided to remain. Their fate, however, was none too rosy. Of the 27 who stayed, 25 were gone within 18 months, having been fired or opting to resign voluntarily!

Why is the outlook on counteroffers so bleak? The company may have felt blackmailed and only waited until a more advantageous moment to act. The last thing a company wants to do is cave in to one employee's demands. "It can then find itself in a virtual bidding war where everyone is attempting the same strategy," says Dennis Bottorff, vice chairman and chief operating officer of Sovran Financial Corp. in Norfolk, VA.

Then, too, deep down the employee may still have unresolved feelings about his or her long-term tenure and ends up leaving within a short time anyway.

Mr. Feinberg is chairman of BFS Psychgological Associates in New York. Mr. Serlin writes on management subjects from New York.

For Clients

For Organizations Seeking Search Assistance . . .

Don't look for bargains: you pretty much get what you pay for. But there are enough ways of charging to warrant talking with several firms before you sign up initially. Once satisfied, however, let such a firm continue to serve you rather than shop each time.

The cost may seem high—and is—but internal costs on a do-it-yourself basis can mount, too; and insiders are rarely as effective as the experts.

Beware of firms that charge the individual, too, even though under a separate company name. And don't expect full search services if you find a recruiter who agrees to be paid only if you hire one of his candidates (contingency).

Check the Code of Ethics to which members of the Association of Executive Search Consultants must adhere—and use it as a guide in your dealings with any search firm.

EDITOR'S NOTE: This is the Personal Edition, *The Directory of Executive Recruiters*. We also publish a Corporate Edition with much more information on each firm.

ADVICE TO HIRING ORGANIZATIONS

What You Should Know About "Headhunters" and How to Use Them

Look upon a professional executive search as an investment in improving the quality of your managerial and technical horsepower

by James H. Kennedy

The next time you have an important managerial or technical slot to fill in your company, consider putting an executive search firm to work for you. "I can't afford it," you might say. An executive search may certainly seem to be expensive (at a fee of 30% of the first year's compensation plus out-of-pocket incidental expenses, this works out to around $25,000 for a $75,000 job).

What you really can't afford, however, is to make a selection mistake, or to settle for less than the best available. What sense does it make to "save" a headhunter's fee and wind up hiring someone who makes a few $100,000 mistakes, or who puts in a day's work and looks the part, but doesn't really share your values or your motivation?

Here's What A Search Firm Can Do For You That You Can't Do For Yourself:

- Cast a wider net to increase your chances of finding a superior person.
- Preserve confidentiality, if it's important.
- Evaluate candidates objectively.
- Get reference-givers to really open up.
- Advise on compensation levels and packages.

You won't get this kind of service from your banker or your lawyer or accountant or your college alumni office or any of the other people you might turn to for suggestions.

Matchmaking: A Team Effort. I think the term "matchmaker" is much more appropriate than "headhunter." A good recruiter spends more time on the potential fit than on digging up candidates, more time reference-checking than running ads or telephoning prospects. True, executive search is widely accepted by the corporate giants, but it's even more important for smaller companies, where one hiring mistake can have disastrous results.

Filling an important post, however, isn't a task that you can farm out entirely to anyone, not even the most competent retainer-based executive search firm. The very best executive search is done on a teamwork basis, insiders working hand in hand with professionals and sharing information, reactions, expectations, and disappointments.

An Unofficial Definition of Executive Search

Executive search/recruiting is a specialized branch of management consulting in which outside professionals are authorized by organizations to identify, attract and refer qualified candidates for important executive, managerial and technical positions. This usually confidential process involves research, seach, and evaluation based on clear understanding of position and person specifications, and it is always employer-paid.

---

10 Questions to Ask in Selecting A Search Firm. As a recruiter, Roger Williams points out in *How To Evaluate, Select and Work With Executive Recruiters* (*Consultants News* '81), picking competent professionals in this field can be quite a challenge:

"Since there are no laws or regulatory agencies at this time to certify or license executive recruiters, it may be difficult for you to identify legitimate practitioners. There is a professional organization—Association of Executive Recruiting Consultants, Inc.—but many firms are not members. Lack of membership in AERC does not imply that a recruitment consultant is not highly qualified. The fact remains, however, that anyone can hang out a shingle and represent himself as an executive search or recruitment consultant. Therefore, the same caution should be exercised in selecting a recruiter as you employ in looking for a doctor, lawyer, banker, or anyone else in whom you place your confidence."

Here are some key questions to ask of a firm you're considering using:

- **Are you really an executive recruiter?** Or are you basically an employment agency? Would I find you under employment agencies in the Yellow Pages? How long have you been in business, and what are your credentials?

- **Do you operate on a contingency or retainer basis—and why?** You can't expect the same level of service from a firm where total income rests on contingency.

  While some of these firms do excellent work, many tend to refer a plethora of candidates in hopes that one will stick. They can't afford to do interviewing and reference-checking on every candidate they handle.

- **How does your firm match our needs?** You don't need the world-wide resources of a big international firm for a local or regional search. Many quality searchers operate regionally, or within a given industry, or among certain functional specialties (training directors, for example).

- **How much do you charge?** Don't be satisfied with "25-33% plus expenses." Ask percentage of what? Guaranteed first-year income? Salary and guaranteed bonus? If there are progress payments, is the final portion contingent on any actual hiring?

- **Who'll do the work?** Are you dealing with a PR person or the person doing the actual work? Through how many levels will our work be filtered? Some search firms have research departments. In others, the recruiter does everything (there's a case for each approach).

- **What guarantees do you offer?** Most searchers won't recruit people from client organizations for a year or two. Does this mean your whole company, this division, or what? What if the new person doesn't work out? Will the recruiter find a replacement at no cost, or for expenses only?

- **What is your expense reimbursement policy? Out-of-pocket only? Is there a mark-up on research or administrative expenses? How much detail will be on the invoice?** (A recent *Executive Recruiter News* survey showed expenses averaging 16 percent of the fee.)

- **What are the ethical guidelines?** If you don't really care ("Just find me the right guy: I don't care how"), be prepared: the same techniques may be used *against* you. Posing as a reporter to get the name of your Product Manager is illegal and immoral.

  Ask to see the code of ethics and professional practices of the Association of Executive Search Consultants. Compare it to your recruiter's policies.

- **What's your hidden agenda?** How much of your business is search? Do you really just want to get your foot in the door to sell us outplacement or management consulting or accounting/auditing services?

■ **For whom have you done similar work?** While search is a confidential service, beware of the firm that hides totally behind this veil. Insist on talking to someone (locally or far away) for whom the firm has worked.

Asking these questions will help you pick the firm that is best for you, and it will also further your understanding of the executive search process.

When Things Go Wrong. Despite all precautions in selecting and working with executive recruiters, problems are bound to arise, especially when dealing in such an unscientific area. Veteran recruiter A. Robert Taylor (*How To Select And Use An Executive Search Firm*, McGraw-Hill, '84) cites 13 complaints most frequently voiced by organizations that retain executive search firms:

1. The consultant does not understand our requirement.
2. The consultant fails to understand the human chemistry in our organization.
3. The consultant is obviously overloaded.
4. The consultant has not conducted a thorough search.
5. The consultant was arrogant.
6. The consultant inflated the compensation package.
7. The consultant failed to check the candidate's background thoroughly.
8. The consultant was of little help during the negotiations with the candidate.
9. The consultant ignored us after the candidate accepted our offer.
10. The consultant tried to overcharge us.
11. A search firm recruited one of our executives after we had become a client of theirs.
12. The search took far too long.
13. The firm presented only one really good candidate.

Some Facts About Executive Search Firms

by A. Robert Taylor

If you have not already had extensive experience in retaining executive search firms, this chapter will help you to make the decision on whether to retain one for your particular executive vacany problem. Brief answers are provided to questions most often asked about executive search. The subsequent chapters in this book cover these answers more thoroughly.

A. Why has the executive search profession grown so extensively?
There are several reasons. Probably the predominant one is the maturing of management as a professional function. This development brought about a realization that the success of an organization depends largely on the quality and performance of its managers. The organization with the best executives is most likely to move ahead of its competitors. Therefore, ways had to be found to develop the best from within and recruit the best from outside.

A second reason is the gradual understanding that executive search firms are the main means of bringing about better utilization of scarce executive talent. There is no way that a frustrated executive can advertise his desire for a bigger job that does not exist for him in his present organization. Nor can companies and other organizations usually broadcast their confidential executive requirements. Search firms become the much needed instruments for bringing underutilized executives into organizations in which their talents could be more effectively applied.

Another reason is confidentiality. The organization may not want the decision to be known either internally or within the business community. Under those circumstances a third party must do the searching, protecting the identity of the organization.

A fourth reason for the growth of the executive search profession is that the costliness of errors in executive selection became increasingly evident. The wrong man may hinder or even cripple the organization for years. The time required to indoctrinate an executive into a new position, give him sufficient time to demonstrate his effectiveness, the agonizing, time-consuming decision to replace him, and the costly internal or external recruiting process all over again have taught some hard lessons. Such events led to the recognition of the need for professional assistance in finding the right man for the position.

A fifth reason is that experience with executive search in turn brought about a better understanding of the special skills needed to find and bring into the organization the right executive for the vacant position. Among these are the definition of the true needs of the organization and the kind of executive most likely to fulfill them; a realistic appraisal of the difficulty in finding the right man and what it will cost to attract him; the ability to thoroughly search out the very best candidates regardless of where they may be or how invisible they are; the infrastructure and experience required to evaluate more than a hundred prospective candidates and select the two or three who would be the best performers; counseling the organization on handling candidates from the first telephone contact through the interviews and all of the other steps until the executive is in place; the especially useful role of a professional third party in negotiations between organization and candidate that are often difficult and complex; the special abilities needed to conduct confidential and delicate inquiries into the candidate's record, qualifications, and reputation in a way that will not create embarrassment for anyone yet leave no stone unturned; the ability to counsel the selected candidate in extricating himself smoothly from his present organization and community and in establishing himself in his new position; the ability to smooth out any problems for either the organization or the new executive during the beginning phase of their new relationship.

A sixth reason is the realization of the importance of an objective, independent, unbiased third party role in helping management to make critical executive staffing decisions. There is growing acceptance of the fact that organizations are often too strongly influenced by their own personal preferences, prejudices, habits, and preconceptions.

A seventh reason is that in conjunction with the growing professionalism of the management function, the need for more profound candidate specifications became evident. This development, in turn, made it necessary to search more broadly and deeply to find the best executive to meet these specifications.

B. How did the executive search function develop from the beginning to the present?
Prior to the existence of executive search firms, executive recruitment was conducted informally through personal contacts including bankers, lawyers, public accounting firms, management consulting firms, and the old boy net-

work. Then came the provision, by some management consulting and public accounting firms, of executive recruitment services in the United States. The next development was the establishment, usually by people who already had some experience with these organizations, of small executive search firms. Some of these early firms grew into multi-office operations.

The multinational clients of search firms in the United States began to ask for professional services in staffing their overseas operations. At first, there were attempts to provide these services from the U.S., but it soon became evident that only by having qualified executive search consultants in overseas locations, could the same service standards be maintained.

When the first executive search service actively began in Europe, European companies and executives were certain that only American companies and candidates would be involved. Their opinion was that European culture systems would not accept the idea of executives being systematically moved from one company to another. However, as U.S. search firms became more active in Europe, they began moving European and British executives into U.S. multinationals to replace American expatriates and to meet their growing requirements. European and British companies soon realized that they too could not achieve their growth and diversification objectives nor be competitive without the help of executive search firms. As demand for these services increased, European and British search firms also evolved.

In Latin America, in the Asia Pacific regions and later, in South Africa, the history of executive search has been similar to the developments in Europe and the United Kingdom. At first, it was the U.S. multinationals that demanded services in these areas, especially as they sought to replace American expatriates with local national or thirdcountry national executives. South of the U.S. border, Mexico was the first country in which international executive search services began. Subsequently, Brazil, Argentina, Venezuela, and Colombia became bases for international executive search offices. The sequence in Asia Pacific was Hong Kong, Australia, Japan, and Singapore.

Local companies in all of these areas were at first slow to utilize executive search services. They doubted that a foreign firm could help them with their local staffing, and they were unaccustomed to paying for such services which, in their eyes, had usually been provided free of charge by their banks, law offices, friends, and acquaintances.

Today, with the exception of Japan, the continuing substantial growth rate of executive search services outside the U.S.A. is occurring because they are being increasingly utilized by national firms.

Consultants with growing search firms everywhere left, in some cases, to start their own operations. Today, there are a few large firms with billings in excess of $10 million dollars per year, several medium-sized and scores of small firms. The large firms have their own practices outside the United States.

The medium-sized firms have mostly made agreements with foreign search firms. Some foreign search firms have offices in the U.S.

C. Efforts to strengthen professionalism.

During the later 1950s, leaders in the executive search profession in the United States decided that the time had arrived to establish a professional association. There were two basic reasons. State legislatures began to move in the direction of applying the same regulations to executive search firms as they had already done to employment agencies which, of course, offer an entirely different service. This would have imposed conditions that would have made it impossible for executive search firms to continue to function, such as government access to confidential files and regulation of service charges.

The other basic reason for the emergence of a professional association was that the necessity to set up standards became apparent if executive search was to gain recognition as an established profession. Accordingly, the Association of Executive Recruiting Consultants was organized. The name has since been changed to the Association of Executive Search Consultants (AESC). Today it is a well-known professional organization. The AESC has developed and published a code of ethics and professional practice guidelines [see page 4]. Firms that are members must adhere to the code and practices. Firms that apply for membership must prove that their policies and practices are in accordance with the standards required by AESC.

There are now over 60 member firms. Recently, the AESC Board decided to consider applications for membership from search firms whose operations are entirely or mostly outside the United States.

There are some search firms that have decided against membership in AESC but that maintain at least the same professional standards as do AESC members.

D. How are search firms organized and how do they function?

Search firms are usually mainly owned and controlled by their founders, until the founder either retires or dies and the often difficult transition is made to ownership and control by the next generation. The few firms that are broadly held usually did not start out that way. Some users of executive search believe that broadly held firms may be more inclined to function as a team.

Another important factor in the organization of search firms is the method of compensation of the consultants. In some firms, the consultant's compensation is determined entirely or largely by the amount of billings that he individually earns for the firm through bringing in clients and assignments and through working on assignments. This system motivates individual consultants. It sometimes leads to overloading and lack of teamwork.

The other method of compensating consultants is judgmental. They are paid salaries and allocated bonuses based on the judgments of their peers and superiors with regard to their contribution to the overall firm's performance. This system, in theory, reduces the tendency to overload and increases the likelihood of good team work. However, in either case, the performance of the firm is heavily influenced by the quality of the consultants and the effectiveness of management.

Some firms staff themselves with bright young executives, usually with graduate business degrees. Others prefer more mature, proven, senior-level executives. Between these two extremes are firms in which the younger executives are supervised and encouraged to develop by the more senior members of the firm, similar to the practices of major accounting and law firms.

Some firms use their "heavy hitters" to sell their services and monitor the work, leaving the search work to less experienced associates. In other firms, the man who brings in the work often handles the resulting assignment. There are, of course, many combinations of these practices, and this is particularly true when searches have to be conducted outside the country in which the assignment is taken.

There are large firms that have specialists for specific industries and functions. There are small firms that specialize. There are generalist firms that have demonstrated their ability to handle all functions and all industries.

E. How do executive search firms charge for their services?

Executive search firms usually base their service charges on the annual compensation applicable to the position to be filled. There are numerous executive recruiters who offer their services on a contingent basis, i.e., the client pays only if an executive is placed. However, the firms that are considered to be the most professional charge retainers from the outset of their work for their clients. These retainers are credited against the final basic service charge or a total charge based upon time expended on the assignment. The basic service charges usually range from 30% to 33$^1/_3$% of the annual compensation. Some firms charge 35% or more for international assignments requiring searching in more than one country. Such expenses as long-distance phone charges, meals with sources and prospective candidates, and travel to interview candidates and meet with clients are added to the billings.

There are a variety of practices in charging the retainers. Some firms charge $^1/_3$ of the estimated basic charge at the outset of the work, another $^1/_3$ part way through the assignment, and the final $^1/_3$ when the assignment is successfully completed. Others charge $^1/_5$ of the estimated basic charge at the outset plus $^1/_5$ per month. Most firms do not continue charging retainers if the work goes beyond the estimated time frame unless the delays are due to major changes in specifications or inability of the client to meet interview schedules.

Some firms, instead of expressing the basic charge in terms of percentage of the annual compensation, will quote a fixed amount based upon their estimate of the difficulty and the amount of work that will be required. Usually these fixed basic charges approximate the percentages charged by those firms that apply the 30% or 33¹/₃% or 35% system.

Multi-country searches are the most difficult to manage and are the most costly to search firms. Although many firms claim that they will conduct a thorough search in several countries for an international assignment, the truth is that they cannot afford to do this for a normal basic charge. Unless the client is willing to pay for extensive searching on a multi-country basis, the search firm is forced to compromise in order to avoid heavy losses on the assignment.

How is a search conducted?

The effective conduct of an executive search involves a number of fundamental steps. The first one, of course, is a thorough understanding and agreement between client and search firm of the organization, the position, and the specifications for the executive required to fill it. This information should be spelled out in writing.

The next step is research, conducted by the search firm's research department or by the consultant or both. The purpose of the research is to develop as much information as is needed on prospective candidates and sources of information throughout related companies, industries, functions, and geographic areas to enable the consultant to conduct such a thorough search that he can be confident that he is presenting to his client the two or three best candidates who can be found.

Based upon the research data, the consultant contacts scores of sources and prospective candidates, screens many of the prospects by telephone, and interviews those who are both interested and appear promising. The consultant should be in close contact with the client throughout the course of his search. Jointly with his client, they decide upon those two or three candidates who should be interviewed by the client.

The next step is presenting the candidates to the client, sometimes in person and always with well written documentation.

The next phase is negotiation with the selected candidate, the consultant acting as an objective professional third party. Then comes the resignation by the candidate after careful counseling by the consultant.

The consultant stays in close touch with candidate and client until the candidate is on board and for some time afterwards to help to ensure that any problems that may arise are successfully resolved.

Prior to recommending candidates, the consultant will have commenced checking on their backgrounds and reputations. Despite the difficulty of obtaining reliable information on an executive who is currently employed and whose candidacy must be kept secret, the consultant must obtain enough information about him to ensure that the client will not have any major un-pleasant surprises later on regarding the candidate's past.

For most assignments, it is advisable to allow 45 days from the commence-ment of the search until the two or three candidates are formally presented to the client. More time for the search is usually needed when more than one country is involved. The period from presentation of candidates until the selected candidate is on board is influenced by many variables. Ideally, the interviews of candidates by the client plus the selection and negotiation process should take no more than a month, and the candidate should require no more than another month to extricate himself from his current position. Of course, contractual agreements between employer and executive sometimes result in a longer notice period.

F. How many executive search assignments are successful?
The one major underlying cause for the failure of executive search assignments is the lack of a sufficently close partnership between search firm and client. To succeed, they must work closely together as a team. Failures will occur if the search firm does not carry out all of the steps thoroughly and professionally, and if the client does not provide the necessary information, handle candidates skillfully, conduct interviews promptly, and make decisions without delay. In fact, there is a direct relationship between the passage of time from the start of an assignment and the likelihood of failure.

Approximately 25% of all executive search assignments may not be com-pleted successfully for reasons beyond the control of the search firm. Among these reasons are an unexpected change in the client organization structure, a sudden decision to promote from within because a previous internal candidate has changed his mind, or a change in the availability of an outside candidate who was previously under consideration.

What happens if an executive who has been placed by a search firm is terminated?

The fact is that the search firm has already expended the professional man-hours, has completed the assignment, and has been paid accordingly. As is true with other professions such as investment banking, law, and general man-agement consulting, if the subsequent events bring negative results, the client is not entitled to any form of reimbursement. However, if the executive is terminated within twelve months of placement and if the reason for termi-nation is clearly not the fault of the client, some search firms will make a special arrangement to replace the executive and bill the client for a partial service charge plus expenses.

G. What kinds of assignments are executive search firms most successful in completing?
The answer is that most kinds of upper-level executive search assignments can be successfully handled by a good search firm. If the search involves other

countries, the firm should have proven experience in those countries. Success or failure is not governed so much by the kind of assignment but more on the selection of the right search firm and the establishment of a close working partnership between client and search firm.

H. What is the present state of the executive search profession?

In the United States, there are a large number of executive search firms. To an increasing extent the responsibility for selecting search firms and overseeing their relationships with organizations has been delegated to senior personnel executives. Many of these personnel executives are thoroughly knowledgeable and highly selective.

Whereas many years ago only one search firm might be invited to discuss a confidential assignment, today it is not uncommon to have three or more search firms invited to make competitive presentations on a specific assignment.

To an increasing extent, these knowledgeable personnel executives have established detailed criteria for monitoring and assessing the performance of search firms. The line executives who are involved with the search participate in these assessments.

Concurrently, search firms are becoming more sophisticated. They are making increasing use of electronic data processing and are improving their research capability.

Executive search is not yet as well established as a profession as are law, banking, architecture, and engineering. But there are growing indications that executive search consultants, especially the more sophisticated ones, are now viewed as equally essential to the success of an enterprise as are the lawyers, the bankers, and the CPAs.

A good executive search firms can usually overcome most of the problems that make creative executive staffing so difficult. The professional executive search organization will more than justify its cost by being able to do well that which the organization cannot do as well itself.

I. What is the future outlook for the executive search profession?

During the next few years, we will probably see the continuing emergence of a few major strong executive search firms with worldwide coverage. Some smaller firms may well disappear as competition increases.

There will be increasing use made of electronic data processing and telecommunications. The next major area that is ripe for a breakthrough is in improving the ability of search firms to assess executives and predict their behavior and performance in relation to their client's needs.

How to Be A Good Client

Or Ten Ways to Improve Your Chances of Getting The Best Candidate For Your Job

by Jacques C. Nordeman

In any service business, especially the search business, the key to being a good client (and ensuring a successful search) is to develop a relationship with a firm that is based on three elements: trust, chemistry, and professional respect. If any of these important elements are missing, the relationship is doomed from the start. Consequently, to assure the greatest probability of success, the client should look for the key elements that enhance the trust, chemistry, and professional respect between themselves and the search firm.

First, one must understand the search process. The more one understands the process, the greater the contribution he/she can make in working closely with the search firm and in getting the most out of the collaboration.

During each step of the process, it is important for the search firm to understand the client and his/her needs, and for a client to understand the process and to work closely with the individuals assigned to the search in a positive and supportive manner. A "good client" improves the chances of a successful search effort.

The following is a list of ten key practices which, if carried out during a search, will go a long way toward your becoming a good client:

1. **Pick the search firm, and team within the firm, best suited for the position you are trying to fill.**
   The key point here is that there are as many differences between firms as there are among individuals working on the assignments. In selecting the firm, a good client should have done his/her homework to make sure the firm and individual selected is the right one. Ask the right questions, reference

thoroughly and attain a rapport with the search team. In making the final selection, as in picking a doctor, you, the client, should feel comfortable in listening to their guidance and counsel. If this trust and comfort level are not there, the search is off to a bad start.

2. **Make sure you have chosen the proper *client* team for the assignment as well, and that you have their understanding and commitment to the particular assignment before you begin.**

Since searches are done by individuals, by groups, and by committees, it is hard to generalize about what the ideal composition of a client search team should be. Clearly important are: including individuals who will be importantly affected by the recruitment; ensuring that there is a consensus on the need to go outside for the position in the first place, and that there is a good understanding among all interested parties on the needs of the search and a commitment to undertake a search effort.

3. **Organize and manage your search team to use them more productively.**

Make sure the decision makers (i.e., client team) represent all major constituencies involved with the position.

Ensure that the decision-making group is in agreement on the objectives of the position.

Ask the search firm to identify any differences of opinion among the selection committee (i.e., the client team) and bring those executives together to work out a single point of view on the objectives of the position and on the specifications of the ideal person.

Make sure the search committee works well as a team; i.e., that its members are able to communicate, work together, and reason; have developed a friendly, open, trusting relationship with each other; and that they display an enthusiasm about the position that will be conveyed to candidates.

Make sure the search committee is not too large or, if large, agree to accomplish a great deal through a smaller sub-committee.

The ideal size for a search committee is five to seven people. Realize that the composition, level, number, and geographical proximity of the search committee will affect the process, as well as the results.

4. **Do your homework before you meet with the search firm. Although this is not always possible, a lot of time can be saved if internal discussions are held and conclusions are reached before you meet with the search firm.**

While a good search firm will help you crystalize your thinking, focus on key issues, and very often raise issues you have not thought about, the greater the preparation on your part, the better the results will be. Some of the key issues to consider are:

- Gain a consensus on the long- and short-term expectations for the job. Put another way, what will this individual have to do to be successful? Be explicit about priorities.
- Think through key organizational issues related to the position, i.e., the reporting and working relationships of the individual, the number of people he or she will manage, who the individual will have to work most closely with, etc.
- Understand the critical dimensions or key issues of the job. These will determine whether the candidate succeeds or fails. Get agreement on these issues.
- Be as explicit as you can in relation to the chemistry and culture of the organization.
- Think about the possible issues that could undermine the search effort from being successful, e.g., reporting relationships (straight line, dotted line), style differences, unrealistic expectations among members of the search committee, etc. Being sensitive to an agenda in a search effort can very often highlight potential problems in the beginning, allowing the search to proceed smoothly during later stages.

5. **Do not hide information. Be thorough, honest, and very direct in describing the good and bad aspects of the situation.**
   Think through both the positive elements of the position, as well as the negative aspects. You are better served to get these on the table at the beginning, rather than have them surface during the process.

   Be forthright in pointing out the pluses and minuses of the job early on; otherwise, if candidates are exposed to negatives too late in the search process, they can lose confidence in the entire situation. The best search is one which has no surprises and where there is an open and candid dialogue between company, recruiter, and candidate.

6. **Make sure there is a good understanding of expectations between you and the search firm. This relates to both the specifications of the assignment and the expectations of the process.**
   Set expectations that are realistic, yet establish high standards in evaluating candidates. Do not compromise your standards, nevertheless, be sensitive to feedback from the search firm. Assume, until proven otherwise, that they will normally have a better perspective of the outside market than you do.

   Develop a good understanding of what the individual must do to be successful in the new position and what could cause him/her to fail.

Think through the ideal specifications of the job and understand the trade-offs between requirements you *must* have and those you *would like* to have.

7. **Take advantage of the expertise the search firm brings to the assignment. A good search firm will be more than an introducer of candidates. They should be able to advise you on all key issues relating to your search.**

Get their input on critical issues where perspective on the market, organization, compensation, or other factors can assist you in formulating your own guidelines for the position.

Listen carefully to what the search professional is saying, as it might affect the particular methodology and a specific market process that is most effective for your particular search.

Follow the search firm's advice.

Do not be rigid in your thinking. Keep an open mind and be receptive to ways of solving the position at hand by modifying your original thinking as it relates to how the position is organized or the qualifications of the individual.

8. **Once the search process has started, make sure it keeps moving.**

Understand that good candidates are perishable.

Realize that an internal process of communication and timely feedback among the decision-making executives is as important as regular feedback to the search firm.

9. **Be responsive to the need for regular communication and feedback throughout all stages of the recruitment process.**

Feedback both ways is very important. It is the responsibility of the search firm to advise of their progress, problems or idiosyncrasies encountered in the marketplace. It is also important that you provide them with all relevant comments and concerns on the part of the client team as soon as you know about them.

Give the search firm immediate and consistent feedback as it relates to particular candidates.

Find time to have periodic reviews with the search team. Make yourself available for meetings, particularly the critical ones: i.e., at the beginning of the search, during the search when candidates are being interviewed, and at the end of the search.

10. **Realize that the best recruitments are those where there is a feeling of partnership and a close involvement during every stage of the process between you, the candidates, and the search firm.**

Keep tight security over all of the prospects in the search process. Some of the best candidates will not come forward if they believe their candidacy will become known. This is particularly important in the later stages of the search when all constituencies must be part of the decision-making process and when a candidate is most exposed.

After the search is completed and candidate hired, be sensitive to your new executive's "check-in" period.

Give your search firm feedback on the initial progress of the new recruit.

In summary, the way to ensure a successful outcome of a search is to develop a collaborative, frank, and open relationship with the search firm. Understand the many ways in which a good search firm can help you, take advantage of their input, and be receptive to their recommendations.

Jacques C. Nordeman is chairman of Nordeman Grimm, Inc.,
N.Y.C., a firm specializing in recruiting senior and middle
management executives.

Reprinted from "Aiming High on a Small Budget: Executive
Searches & the Nonprofit Sector;" a collection of papers prepared by
the Effective Sector Leadership/Management Program of
INDEPENDENT SECTOR. © INDEPENDENT SECTOR 1986.

Retainer Recruiting Firms, A to Z

Firms in this section are retained by the hiring entity and paid at least a portion of their fee immediately to initiate the search.

Full street addresses for all U.S., Canada and Mexico locations, when known.

Network membership, international affiliations and branches identified by name followed by city.

Indexes for functions and industries immediately follow these retainer listings. Geographic and key principals indexes for both sections begin on page 689.

See page 393 for a parallel A to Z listing of firms charging on a contingency basis all or part of the time.

A la Carte Int'l., Inc.
1120 Laskin Rd.
Virginia Beach, Virginia 23451
Salary Minimum: $60,000
Key Contact: Michael Romaniw

Functions: 01.3 02.1 05.3 05.4 11.2
Industries: B.10 D.10
Professional Affiliations: AMI, FMI, IFMA,
    IFT, NAER, NRA
Description: Executive search; marketing, sales,
    environmental, technical & operational
    disciplines for food mfg.

The Abbott Group
530 College Pkwy., Ste. N
Annapolis, Maryland 21401
Salary Minimum: $85,000
Key Contact: Peter Darby Abbott
George McFadden
D. Clarke Havener
Vickie Moore

International Branches:
London

Functions: 01.0 02.0 04.0 05.0 09.0
Industries: B.00 D.00 D.E0 D.H0 L.00
Professional Affiliations: ACS, AFCEA, ASAE,
    IEEE, SPIE, TMS
Description: Small, highly personalized senior
    level executive search and management
    consulting firm

Actuaries & Assoc.
576 Lakeside Circle
Ft. Lauderdale, Florida 33326
Salary Minimum: $35,000
Key Contact: Mark W. Safford

Functions: 01.0 05.0 10.0
Industries: H.10 H.I0
Description: Our search & recruitment services
    involve all actuarial & banking related
    occupations

Adams & Assoc. Int'l
978 Hampton Park
Barrington, Illinois 60010
Salary Minimum: $75,000
Key Contact: Adam Zak

International Branches:
Berlin, Frankfurt, London, Paris, Warsaw

Functions: Most + 01.2 01.3 02.0
Industries: Most
Professional Affiliations: AICPA
Description: Specialists for international
    management recruiting with European-
    American contact network

Jeffrey C. Adams & Co., Inc.
50 Fremont St., Ste. 2210
San Francisco, California 94105
Salary Minimum: $50,000
Key Contact: Jeffrey C. Adams

Functions: 01.0 02.0 05.0 06.0 08.0
Industries: Most + B.0W D.00 D.H0 D.I0
    G.00
Professional Affiliations: CERA
Description: Generalist search firm with a
    diverse client base

Advanced Executive Resources
4610 44th St.
Grand Rapids, Michigan 49512
Salary Minimum: $45,000
Key Contact: Michael D. Harvey

Functions: Most + 01.0 02.0 03.0 05.0 11.5
Industries: D.12 D.E0 D.H0 G.00 I.10
Description: Specialize in manufacturing
    professionals & mgmt (furniture, retail &
    electronics industries)

The Advisory Group, Inc.
19925 Stevens Creek Blvd., Ste. 112
Cupertino, California 95014
Salary Minimum: $70,000
Key Contact: George Vaccaro

Functions: Most
Industries: D.00 D.18 D.24
Description: 20 year old retained search
    consultancy serving San Francisco Bay
    Area

Aim Executive Consulting Services

35000 Chardon Rd., Ste. 425
Willoughby Hills, Ohio 44094
Salary Minimum: $70,000
Key Contact: John ₁hornton
Eric Peterson
Gary Gallagher

Branches:
6605 W. Central Ave., Ste. 250
Toledo, Ohio 43617
Key Contact: Kim Davis

Functions: Most + 02.0 05.4 08.0 09.0 11.1
Industries: Most + D.00 D.22 I.14 I.18
Description: Highly professional executive
search firm, known for performance &
timely work

J.R. Akin & Co.

183 Sherman St.
Fairfield, Connecticut 06430
Salary Minimum: $75,000
Key Contact: J.R. Akin
Frank Rico
George H. Orgelman
Barbara Dobbins

Functions: 01.2 02.0 03.0 05.3 06.0
Industries: D.H0
Professional Affiliations: AESC, IACPR
Description: Personalized & responsive in high
technology, aerospace, packaged goods &
financial services

Alexander Ross Inc.

280 Madison Ave.
New York, New York 10016
Salary Minimum: $60,000
Key Contact: Ben Lichtenstein
Paula Marks
Nicholas J. D'Ambrosio

Functions: 06.0 06.1 06.2 11.1
Industries: Most
Professional Affiliations: IACPR
Description: Search practice dedicated solely to
human resource functions

Allerton Heneghan & O'Neill

208 S. LaSalle St., Ste. 766
Chicago, Illinois 60604
Salary Minimum: $75,000
Key Contact: Donald Allerton
Donald A. Heneghan
James P. O'Neill
Byron R. Foster
Rachel L. Roche

Functions: Most + 11.2
Industries: Most
Professional Affiliations: IACPR, ASHHRA,
EMA, HRMAC, HRPS
Description: National firm retained for senior
executive searches in most industries &
functions

Alwyn Assoc., Inc.

P.O. Box 757
Southport, Connecticut 06490
Key Contact: Arthur P. D'Elia

Functions: Most + 01.0 06.0 08.0 08.2
Industries: H.10 H.11 H.R0 I.20 I.21
Professional Affiliations: IACPR
Description: All searches are conducted by the
principal of our firm

Peter W. Ambler Co.

14643 Dallas Pkwy., Ste. 537
Dallas, Texas 75240
Salary Minimum: $50,000
Key Contact: Peter W. Ambler

Functions: Most + 01.0 02.0
Industries: B.00 D.00 D.D0 D.H0 G.00
Description: Handles search assignments over
$50,000 per yearly salary

American Executive Management, Inc.

30 Federal St.
Salem, Massachusetts 01970
Salary Minimum: $70,000
Key Contact: E. J. Cloutier
S. K. Okun
S. Smith

Functions: 01.0 02.3 05.0 06.0 11.6
Industries: B.00 B.0W C.00 D.00 D.I0
Professional Affiliations: AICHE, ASME, IEEE,
   IMC, ISA, PMI, SME
Description: Top management consulting and
   leading small international search firm—
   large corporations

Affiliates/Other Offices:
International Business Corporation, Tokyo
Kellerhas, Crameri & Partner, Zurich

American Executive Search Services, Inc.

7045 ViaValverde
San Jose, California 95135
Salary Minimum: $75,000
Key Contact: Donald F. Tischer

Functions: Most + 01.0 02.0 05.0 08.0 09.0
Industries: Most + D.00 D.D0 D.H0
Description: Generalist plus special high
   technology management requirements,
   management evaluation

International Branches:
Copenhagen, Hertfordshire, Toorak

American Group Practice, Inc.

420 Madison Ave., 7th Fl.
New York, New York 10017
Salary Minimum: $60,000
Key Contact: Ralph Herz, Jr.

Functions: 11.1
Industries: I.14 I.15
Professional Affiliations: ACPE, AGPA, AHA,
   AMA, CHA, GHA, MGMA
Description: Retainer search for practicing
   physicians, physician executives sr-level
   healthcare execs

Ames & Ames

P.O. Box 7404
Menlo Park, California 94026
Salary Minimum: $75,000
Key Contact: Andrew P. Ames

Functions: Most
Industries: D.00 D.18 D.25 D.H0
Description: Executive search, nationwide,
   since 1981

Andcor Human Resources

600 S. Highway 169, Ste. 1150
Minneapolis, Minnesota 55426
Key Contact: Dennis Anderson
Kieran Folliard
E. Thomas Mitchell

Functions: Most
Industries: Most
Professional Affiliations: MAHRC, NAPC
Description: A comprehensive human resource
   consulting & staffing firm

Anders Incorporated

P.O. Box 20429
Cleveland, Ohio 44120
Salary Minimum: $60,000
Key Contact: Kenneth J. Anderson

Functions: 01.2 04.0 09.2 11.3
Industries: D.I0 I.12 I.13 I.14 I.15
Description: Concern for quality, timely
   service, with highest professional ethics

Anderson Bradshaw Assoc., Inc.

1225 N. Loop West, Ste. 820
Houston, Texas 77008
Salary Minimum: $60,000
Key Contact: Robert W. Anderson
John W. Bradshaw

Functions: Most + 09.2 09.3 09.7 11.5 11.6
Industries: Most + B.00 B.0W C.00 D.H0 J.13
Description: General practice firm/domestic &
   international senior level assignments

The Andre Group, Inc.
460 N. Gulph Rd., Ste. 410
King of Prussia, Pennsylvania 19406
Salary Minimum: $50,000
Key Contact: Richard Andre

Functions: 06.0 06.1 06.2
Industries: Most
Professional Affiliations: IACPR, ACA, ASTD,
EMA, HRPS, NEHRA, ODN, SHRM
Description: Specialists in recruitment & search
of human resource professionals
nationwide

Annapolis Consulting Group
1099 Winterson Rd.
Linthicum, Maryland 21090
Salary Minimum: $65,000
Key Contact: Ronald J. Lindner
Thomas J. McMahon

Functions: 01.0 02.0 04.0 09.0 09.1
Industries: B.00 B.0W D.00 D.H0 D.I0
Professional Affiliations: ACM, AMA, IEEE,
OSA
Description: Offering the only appropriate
guarantee in the executive search industry

Anthony Executive Search
P.O. Box 320
Dublin, NH 03444
Salary Minimum: $60,000
Key Contact: Charles H. Anthony

Functions: Most
Industries: H.00
Professional Affiliations: IACPR

Argus National, Inc.
98 Mill Plain Rd., Ste. 301
Danbury, Connecticut 06811-5148
Salary Minimum: $50,000
Key Contact: Constance Gruen
Ronald J Guido

Functions: 01.0 02.0 03.0 05.0 08.0
Industries: Most + D.00 H.00 H.10 H.R0
Description: Management search & recruitment
designed for one company

Ariail & Assoc.
210 Friendly Ave., Ste. 200
Greensboro, North Carolina 27401
Salary Minimum: $65,000
Key Contact: Randolph C. Ariail

Functions: 01.0 01.2 02.0 03.0 04.0
Industries: D.12
Description: Retained executive search serving
furniture manufacturing & their suppliers

Armitage Assoc.
95 King St. E., Ste. 300
Toronto, Ontario M5C 1G4 Canada
Salary Minimum: $60,000
Key Contact: John D. Armitage
Karen Wood

Functions: Most
Industries: Most
Description: Boutique specializing in mid to
senior level assignments

William B. Arnold Assoc., Inc.
600 S. Cherry St., Ste. 1105
Denver, Colorado 80222
Salary Minimum: $50,000
Key Contact: William B. Arnold
Sheridan J. Arnold

Functions: Most + 01.0 02.0 08.0 11.3 11.6
Industries: Most
Description: Founded 1964, high performance
retained search firm-Rocky Mountain
focus

Artgo, Inc.
547 Hanna Bldg.
Cleveland, Ohio 44115
Salary Minimum: $40,000
Key Contact: Arthur D. Baldwin, II

Functions: Most
Industries: Most
Description: Executive search for special
corporate needs

Ashworth Consultants, Inc.
53 Fulton St.
Boston, Massachusetts 02109-1401
Salary Minimum: $75,000
Key Contact: Robert I. Ash

Functions: Most
Industries: Most
Description: Compensation, management &
search consulting to the threshold
companies

Ast/Bryant
51 Locust Ave., Ste. 304
New Canaan, Connecticut 06840
Salary Minimum: $60,000
Key Contact: Steven T. Ast

Functions: 11.4
Industries: I.12 I.13 I.14
Description: Specializing in development
(fund-raising) for non-profit organizations
nationwide

Branches:
2800 28th St., Ste. 321
Santa Monica, California 90405
Key Contact: Christopher P. Bryant

Atlantic Search
21 Charles St., Ste. 203
Westport, Connecticut 06880
Salary Minimum: $60,000
Key Contact: Don R. Davis
Timothy Davis

Functions: Most
Industries: H.I0
Description: All lines of insurance & financial
services, both domestic & international

Aubin Int'l. Inc.
281 Winter St.
Waltham, Massachusetts 02154
Salary Minimum: $90,000
Key Contact: Richard E. Aubin
Juli Ann Reynolds

Functions: Most + 01.0 05.4 09.0 11.3
Industries: D.15 H.12 I.14 I.16 J.13
Professional Affiliations: IACPR, AEA, EMA,
SEMI
Description: Executive management consulting
& worldwide search for high technology
companies

International Branches:
London, Paris

Auerbach Assoc.
30 Hillside Terrace
Belmont, Massachusetts 02178
Key Contact: Judith A. Auerbach
Margot S. Lansing
Gale Batchelder

Functions: 01.0 01.1 01.2 11.2 11.4
Industries: I.12 I.13 I.14 I.17 K.00
Description: Executive search & organizational
development for colleges/universities,
public sector & non-profit

Affiliates/Other Offices:
The Landmark Consulting Group Inc., Toronto

BDO Seidman
1430 Broadway
New York, New York 10018-3305
Salary Minimum: $70,000
Key Contact: Bernard J. Ryan
Donna Filipkowski

Functions: Most + 01.2 02.0 06.0 08.0 09.0
Industries: Most + D.11 D.13 G.00 H.10
H.R0
Description: Executive search, compensation,
performance, eval. incentives, training &
benefits services

Branches:
1900 Ave. of the Stars
Los Angeles, California 90067
Key Contact: Sidar Wieder

99 Monroe Ave., N.W.
Grand Rapids, Michigan 49503-2603
Key Contact: John Sullivan

Two Plaza E.
330 E. Kilbourn Ave.
Milwaukee, Wisconsin 53202-3143
Key Contact: Jim Heller

Babson, Moore & Wilcox

809 Gleneagles Court, Suite #102
Baltimore, Maryland 21204
Salary Minimum: $50,000
Key Contact: Chuck Haines
Bryan E. Mooney
Chris Brown
John Moore
Sue Ann Hudson

Functions: Most + 06.0 08.0 10.0 11.5
Industries: Most + B.0W D.00 D.H0 H.00
H.I0
Professional Affiliations: ASPA, EMA, TMA
Description: Quality retainer based executive
search for mid & upper management

The Badger Group

4125 Blackhawk Plaza Circle, Ste. 270
Danville, California 94506
Salary Minimum: $90,000
Key Contact: Fred Badger

Functions: Most + 01.0 02.0 05.0 08.0 09.0
Industries: D.24 D.E0 D.H0 H.00 J.00
Professional Affiliations: CERA
Description: Senior executives for high
technology companies & large MIS
organizations

Baldwin Associates, Inc.

39 Locust Ave.
New Canaan, Connecticut 06840
Salary Minimum: $90,000
Key Contact: Max M. Baldwin
Marsha L. Shannon

Functions: Most
Industries: D.15 D.24 D.H0 I.00 J.00
Description: Specialize in senior executive
assignments across most industries &
functions

Ballantyne & Assoc.

P.O. Box 810
Moss Beach, California 94038
Salary Minimum: $55,000
Key Contact: Tom Ballantyne

Functions: 05.0 05.1 11.2 11.4
Industries: D.10 D.16 D.18 D.24 I.00
Professional Affiliations: CERA
Description: Specializing in the search for
marketing & advertising management
professionals nationwide

Ballos & Co., Inc.

415 Speedwell Ave.
Morris Plains, New Jersey 07950
Salary Minimum: $80,000
Key Contact: Constantine J. Ballos
H.P. Ballos

Functions: Most + 01.0 02.0 03.0 04.0 05.0
Industries: Most + D.00 D.10 D.13 D.15 D.18
Professional Affiliations: CDA, CMRA, DCAT,
TAPPI
Description: Effective, ethical, professional
search firm with high percentage repeat
business

James Bangert & Assoc., Inc.

1212 E. Wayzata Blvd.
Wayzata, Minnesota 55391
Salary Minimum: $50,000
Key Contact: James Bangert

Functions: Most + 02.0 05.0 08.0 09.0 09.7
Industries: Most + D.00 D.H0 D.I0 H.I0 I.00
Professional Affiliations: AEA, EMMA,
NCHCM
Description: Executive search consultants with
experience in all management disciplines

Barger & Sargeant, Inc.

1 Bicentennial Sq., Ste. 3
Concord, New Hampshire 03301
Salary Minimum: $75,000
Key Contact: H. Carter Barger

Functions: Most + 01.0 01.1 02.0 05.5 08.0
Industries: Most + D.00 G.00 H.10 H.I0 I.14
Professional Affiliations: AESC, IACPR
Description: Twice selected in top 50 US
search firms by ERN

J.W. Barleycorn & Assoc.

1614 Lancaster Ave.
Reynoldsburg, Ohio 43068-2639
Salary Minimum: $50,000
Key Contact: James M. Barleycorn
Susan Erwin

Functions: Most + 01.0 02.0 05.0 06.0 08.0
Industries: Most + D.00 I.14 I.15 I.17
Description: Specializing in small & medium
size companies

Barnes, Walters & Assoc., Inc.

1110 N. Old World Third St., Ste. 510
Milwaukee, Wisconsin 53203-1102
Salary Minimum: $40,000
Key Contact: Richard E. Barnes
William F. Walters
Donald Hucko
Timothy Pappas
Kenneth J. Battani

Functions: Most
Industries: Most + D.00 I.14
Professional Affiliations: IACPR, IMC
Description: Practice dedicated to retained
executive search consulting; national client
base

Nathan Barry Assoc., Inc.

301 Union Wharf
Boston, Massachusetts 02109
Salary Minimum: $100,000
Key Contact: Nathan Barry

Functions: 01.0 02.0 04.0 05.0 08.0
Industries: D.17 D.18 D.25 D.I0 I.14
Description: Prime focus is helping
management/investors build/grow client
company

Bartholdi & Co.

70 Walnut St.
Wellesley, Massachusetts 02181
Salary Minimum: $85,000
Key Contact: Theodore G. Bartholdi, Sr.

Functions: 01.0 04.0
Industries: Most + D.H0
Description: Senior level search & consulting
firm specializing in venture capital,
telecommunications & hi-tech

Branches:
3000 Sand Hill Rd., Bldg. 3
Menlo Park, California 94025
Key Contact: Theodore G. Bartholdi, Jr.

P.O. Box 2547
Avon, Colorado 81620
Key Contact: Peter P. Gombrecht

Barton Raben, Inc.

Three Riverway, Ste. 910
Houston, Texas 77056
Salary Minimum: $50,000
Key Contact: Gary Barton
Steve Raben
John Freud
W. Randall Lowry

Functions: Most + 01.0 05.0 08.0 09.0
Industries: B.00 D.00 H.10 I.00 J.13
Description: Retainer firm with a national
practice covering most industries and
functions

Barton Sans Int'l.

551 5th Ave.
New York, New York 10017
Salary Minimum: $60,000
Key Contact: Gerard Sans
Ann Leubert

Industries: C.00 H.R0
Description: Our goal is to recruit the best
possible individuals for every assignment
we undertake

Branches:
P.O. Box 10315
Phoenix, Arizona 85064
Key Contact: Robert Rawson

Bason Assoc., Inc.

401 Crescent Ave.
Cincinnati, Ohio 45215
Salary Minimum: $40,000
Key Contact: Maurice L. Bason
Robert L. Fancher
L. Christine Visnich

Functions: Most + 01.0 02.0 05.0 08.0 11.6
Industries: Most
Professional Affiliations: IACPR, AMA, SPE
Description: Generalists for dynamic smaller
business units (1-1000 employees)

Battalia Winston Int'l., Inc.

275 Madison Ave.
New York, New York 10016
Salary Minimum: $75,000
Key Contact: O. William Battalia
Dale Winston
Terence M. Gallagher
Spencer H. Sanders
Jo Bennett
Laurie Atkins
Sarah Adin
Stacy Kalmus

Functions: Most + 01.0 02.0 03.0 05.0 06.0
Industries: Most + D.10 D.13 D.18 D.24 H.10
Professional Affiliations: AESC, IACPR
Description: A long established & well
respected domestic & international
executive search firm

Networks:
Euram Consultants Group
Abo, Oslo, Kopenhamn, Stockholm, Toronto, Malmo, Paris, Edinburgh, Scotland, Wiesbaden,
London, Goteborg

Martin H. Bauman Assoc., Inc.

410 Park Ave., Ste. 1600
New York, New York 10022
Salary Minimum: $70,000
Key Contact: Martin H. Bauman
Virginia Jerman
Arlene Van Valkenburg
Michael Martinolich
Audrey Hellinger

Functions: Most + 01.0 03.0 05.0 06.0 08.0
Industries: Most + D.00 E.00 F.00 H.00 I.00
Professional Affiliations: AESC, IACPR,
NAPM, SHRM
Description: Our main service is executive
recruitment; secondary service is
assessment

The Baxter Group

11 Amber Sky Dr.
Rancho Palos Verdes, California 90274
Salary Minimum: $50,000
Key Contact: Chet Bayliss
Edna English

Functions: 01.5 08.0
Industries: H.10 I.17
Professional Affiliations: CERA
Description: Financial retainer firm—all
positions within savings and loans, banks
and mortgage companies

Beall & Co., Inc.

535 Colonial Park Dr.
Roswell, Georgia 30075
Salary Minimum: $75,000
Key Contact: Charles P. Beall
Dennis A. Desmond
Carleton A. Palmer
Wayne F. Carmichael

Functions: Most
Industries: Most
Professional Affiliations: ADAPSO, AEA, AMA

Branches:
1317 F St. NW, Ste. 400
Washington, District of Columbia 20004
Key Contact: Jordan V. Christo

The Beam Group
1424 Chestnut St., Ste. 500
Philadelphia, Pennsylvania 19102
Salary Minimum: $60,000
Key Contact: Russell A. Glicksman
Brian Ginty

Branches:
600 3rd St.
New York, New York 10016
Key Contact: Rick Evans
Al Swann

Functions: Most + 05.0 05.5 05.6 06.0 10.0
Industries: Most + D.00 H.00 H.10 H.I0 J.00
Description: Retained executive search firm
emphasizing client satisfaction

Becker, Norton & Co.
4088 Alpha Dr., Alpha Bldg.
Allison Park, Pennsylvania 15101
Salary Minimum: $60,000
Key Contact: Robert C. Becker
William K. Gray

Functions: Most + 01.0 02.0 05.0 06.0 08.0
Industries: Most + C.00 D.22 H.00 H.I0
Professional Affiliations: APA, ASPA
Description: A strong regional firm with
capability of conducting national searches

Beech Preger & Partners, Ltd.
110 Bloor St. W., Ste. 300
Toronto, Ontario M5S 2W7 Canada
Salary Minimum: $60,000
Key Contact: G. A. Preger
Lisa M. Beech

Functions: Most
Industries: Most
Description: A leading independent executive
search firm in Canada—all industries &
functions

Richard Beers & Assoc., Ltd.
600 Plum Tree Rd.
Barrington Hills, Illinois 60010
Salary Minimum: $70,000
Key Contact: Richard W. Beers

Functions: Most
Industries: Most
Description: Executive search consultants
serving broad range of corporations-all
functions

Nelson Bell & Partners Inc.
245 Park Ave., Ste. 3301
New York, New York 10167
Salary Minimum: $100,000
Key Contact: Nelson C. Bell
Vivian Wishingrad

Functions: 01.1 01.2 05.0 08.0 08.2
Industries: H.00 H.10 H.11 H.12
Description: A practice focused upon financial
services serving a select client base

Joy Reed Belt & Assoc., Inc.
P.O. Box 18446
Oklahoma City, Oklahoma 73154
Salary Minimum: $40,000
Key Contact: Joy Reed Belt
Charlotte Day-Berry
Robert L. Spinks

Functions: Most + 01.0 02.0 03.0 05.0 06.0
Industries: Most + B.00 C.00 D.00 E.00 F.00
Description: A human resources consulting
firm specializing in executive search

Belvedere Partners
432 Golden Gate Ave.
Belvedere, California 94920
Salary Minimum: $75,000
Key Contact: Mollie Paul Collins

Functions: 01.0 01.1 01.2 11.2 11.4
Industries: I.00 I.12 I.13 I.14
Professional Affiliations: CERA
Description: Recruiting senior management for
not-for-profit organizations

Bennett Search & Consulting Co.
570 Bald Eagle Dr.
Naples, Florida 33941
Salary Minimum: $40,000
Key Contact: Robert C. Bennett, Jr.

Functions: 01.0 04.0 05.0 06.0 08.0
Industries: Most + D.13 D.22 D.24 D.26 I.14
Description: Heavy concentration in hi-tech,
healthcare, manufacturing, MIS & retail

Benton Schneider & Assoc.

3030 Warrenville Rd., Ste. 330
Lisle, Illinois 60532
Key Contact: Laddie J. Polz
Robert P. Podgorski
Steve Mamikonian

Branches:
1425 Greenway, Ste. 525
Irving, Texas 75038
Key Contact: Christopher Raymond

Functions: Most + 03.1 06.0 07.0 09.7 10.0
Professional Affiliations: APICS, CLM, EMA, SHRM
Description: Assess needs, define program, implement solutions to recruitment situations

Richard T. Bergsund Assoc.

30 El Portal, Ste. 106
Sausalito, California 94965
Salary Minimum: $75,000
Key Contact: Richard T. Bergsund
Joan R. Bergsund

Affiliates/Other Offices:
Avery Crafts Assoc., Ltd., New York
Dutton Executive Search, London

Professional Affiliations: CERA
Description: We provide specialized expertise in senior level insurance executive search

The Berman Consulting Group

209 14th St., Ste. 307
Atlanta, Georgia 30309
Key Contact: Fred Berman
Robert Berman

International Branches:
Moscow

Functions: Most
Industries: C.00 D.24 D.E0 D.H0
Description: CAD/CAM, ATE, health care, telecommunications, construction

Bertrand, Ross & Assoc., Inc.

6300 N. River Rd., Ste. 102
Rosemont, Illinois 60018
Salary Minimum: $50,000
Key Contact: Thomas R. Bertrand
Robert F. Ross
Frank Davis
Carl A. Johnson

Functions: Most
Industries: Most
Description: Retained searches for middle management positions

Elliott J. Berv & Assoc.

2 City Ctr., Ste. 401
Portland, Maine 04101-0244
Salary Minimum: $50,000
Key Contact: Elliott J. Berv

Branches:
160 State St.
Boston, Massachusetts 02116

Description: Provides executive search & human resource consulting services in Northeast

116 S. River Rd.
Bedford, New Hampshire 03102

Bialecki Inc.

780 3rd. Ave., Ste. 4203
New York, New York 10017
Salary Minimum: $150,000
Key Contact: Linda Bialecki

Functions: 08.2
Industries: H.00 H.10 H.11
Professional Affiliations: AESC
Description: Specialized finance searches for investment banks and financial service clients

Bialla & Assoc., Inc.
4000 Bridgeway, Ste. 201
Sausalito, California 94965
Salary Minimum: $80,000
Key Contact: Vito Bialla
Don Wright
H. Scott Thomson
Lisa Murphy

Functions: 01.0 05.0 05.1 05.3 05.5
Industries: D.10 D.16 H.10 I.10 J.10
Description: Specialists in consumer goods marketing, advertising & senior management

Paul J. Biestek Assoc., Inc.
O'Hare E. Office Bldg.
9501 W. Devon Ave., Ste. 300
Rosemont, Illinois 60018
Salary Minimum: $50,000
Key Contact: Paul J. Biestek

Functions: Most
Industries: Most
Professional Affiliations: AESC, IACPR
Description: Small retained firm with 15 years experience

Billington & Assoc., Inc.
3250 Wilshire Blvd., Ste. 900
Los Angeles, California 90010
Salary Minimum: $50,000
Key Contact: Brian J. Billington

Functions: Most + 08.0
Industries: Most
Professional Affiliations: CERA
Description: Middle management recruitment with finance & administration specialty

Billington, Fox & Ellis, Inc.
20 N. Wacker Dr., Ste. 3850
Chicago, Illinois 60606-3182
Salary Minimum: $60,000
Key Contact: W. H. Billington
J. Thomas Kenny
Fred D. Harms

Functions: Most
Industries: Most
Description: Founded in 1964, each staff member has over twelve years of recruiting

BioQuest Inc.
100 Spear St.
San Francisco, California 94105
Salary Minimum: $50,000
Key Contact: Roger J. Anderson
Craig Lambert
H. Jurgen Weber

Functions: 01.0 02.0 04.0 05.0
Industries: D.17 D.18 D.I0 I.16
Description: Executive search specific to the healthcare product/service industry

Deborah Bishop & Assoc.
1070 Marina Village Pkwy., Ste. 203
Alameda, California 94501
Salary Minimum: $85,000
Key Contact: Deborah Bishop

Functions: 01.0 01.1 03.0 04.0 05.0
Industries: D.H0
Professional Affiliations: CAPC
Description: We specialize in high-tech industry; Retained search only

Bishop Assoc.
708 Third Ave., 22nd Fl.
New York, New York 10017
Salary Minimum: $75,000
Key Contact: Susan K. Bishop
Claire Burns
Mary E. Matthews

Functions: Most + 01.0 05.0 06.0 08.0 09.7
Industries: I.11 J.10 J.11 J.12 J.13
Professional Affiliations: AESC, NCTA
Description: Specialists in media, entertainment & telecommunications

The Blackman Kallick Search Division
300 S. Riverside Plz., Ste. 660
Chicago, Illinois 60606
Salary Minimum: $40,000
Key Contact: Gary M. Wolfson

Functions: Most + 01.1 02.0 08.0 09.0 11.0
Industries: Most + D.00 D.H0 G.00 I.10 I.17
Description: Broad based middle management specialist in developing custom tailored search

Blackshaw, Olmstead & Atwood

3414 Peachtree Rd., NE
736 Monarch Plz.
Atlanta, Georgia 30326
Salary Minimum: $70,000
Key Contact: Brian Blackshaw
George T. Olmstead
Calvin W. Atwood

Branches:
60 Arch St.
Greenwich, Connecticut 06830
Key Contact: John P. Lynch, III

Functions: Most
Industries: Most
Professional Affiliations: IACPR
Description: BO&A is a retainer-only,
   generalist firm, specializing in upper
   management

Blake, Hansen & Nye, Ltd.

1155 Connecticut Ave. N.W.
Ste. 300
Washington, District of Columbia 20036
Salary Minimum: $65,000
Key Contact: David S. Nye

Branches:
215 W. 78th St., Ste. 4A
New York, New York 10023
Key Contact: Jeri E. Schmidt

Functions: Most
Industries: Most
Professional Affiliations: IACPR, ADPA,
   AFCEA, SHRM
Description: Board member, officer & senior
   executive search consulting since 1974

Blanchard, Zufall & Assoc.

P.O. Box 66815
Scotts Valley, California 95066
Salary Minimum: $75,000
Key Contact: Ross L. Blanchard
Robert B. Zufall

Functions: Most
Industries: D.00 D.H0 H.00 H.I0 H.R0
Professional Affiliations: ASPA, NAER
Description: Performance oriented, retained
   search firm

Blaney Executive Search

97 Lowell Rd.
Concord, Massachusetts 01742
Salary Minimum: $80,000
Key Contact: John A. Blaney

Functions: Most + 01.0 04.0 05.0 09.0 11.3
Industries: D.24 D.25 D.H0 D.I0 H.12
Description: Small firm providing quality
   search services to high technology and
   venture capital organizations

Blau Kaptain Schroeder

12 Roszel Rd., Ste. C-101
Princeton, New Jersey 08540
Salary Minimum: $75,000
Key Contact: John Kaptain
Gene Mancino

Branches:
1702 FirsTier Bank Bldg.
Lincoln, Nebraska 65808
Key Contact: Lee Schroeder

Functions: Most + 01.0 01.2 02.1 04.0 05.0
Industries: D.10 D.17 D.18 H.12 I.16
Description: Retainer firm specializing in the
   health care industry

Blendow & Johnson Inc.

445 Greenbrier Rd.
Half Moon Bay, California 94019
Salary Minimum: $60,000
Key Contact: Bart A. Colucci

Functions: Most
Industries: D.00 D.I0 I.14 I.15 I.16
Description: Medical technology assignments in
   pharmaceuticals, biotech., diagnostics
   devices & instrumentation

Blendow, Crowley & Oliver, Inc.
629 Fifth Ave.
Pelham, New York 10803-1248
Salary Minimum: $60,000
Key Contact: Lawrence P. Crowley
Ronald H. Oliver
Thomas E. Wheeler

Functions: Most + 01.0 02.4 04.0 11.3
Industries: D.13 D.17 D.18 D.D0 D.I0
Description: In business twenty-four years;
    managed by executive search professionals

Affiliates/Other Offices:
Life Science Network, Inc., San Francisco

Block & Assoc.
20 Sunnyside Ave., Ste. A 332
Mill Valley, California 94941
Salary Minimum: $90,000
Key Contact: Randall T. Block

Functions: Most
Industries: D.H0 I.21
Professional Affiliations: AAMA, CERA
Description: We recruit senior executives in
    the high tech industry

Marc-Paul Bloome Ltd.
10 East End Ave., 7th Fl.
New York, New York 10021-1106
Salary Minimum: $50,000
Key Contact: Marc Bloome

Functions: 01.2 02.4 05.4
Industries: D.22 D.E0 I.14
Description: Specialize in corporations
    changing industries, cultures or
    management styles

Blum & Co.
P.O. Box 128
Nashotah, Wisconsin 53058
Salary Minimum: $40,000
Key Contact: D. L. Buzz Blum

Functions: Most
Industries: Most
Description: Results oriented firm serving local
    & international clients

The Blunt Co., Inc.
1400 N. Woodward, Ste. 230
Bloomfield Hills, Michigan 48304-2854
Salary Minimum: $60,000
Key Contact: John W. Blunt
Miles Blunt

Functions: Most
Industries: Most + D.00 D.22 D.23 E.00
Professional Affiliations: ACG, AMA
Description: Management consulting firm
    specializing in director-level executive
    search

Boardroom Planning & Consulting Group
24 Fort Salonga Rd.
Centerport, New York 11721
Salary Minimum: $85,000
Key Contact: Justin Thompson
James P. Waldron
James Tsivitis

Functions: 01.0 05.0 05.3 05.4
Industries: D.11 D.12 D.13 D.24
Description: Specialists in senior management
    for corporations competing in
    international trade

International Branches:
Amsterdam

Boettcher Assoc.
120 Bishops Way, Ste. 126
Brookfield, Wisconsin 53005
Salary Minimum: $50,000
Key Contact: Jack W. Boettcher

Functions: Most
Industries: Most
Description: National generalist executive
    search firm in all areas with consulting in
    human resource areas

John C. Boone & Co.
1807 Henley St.
Glenview, Illinois 60025
Salary Minimum: $45,000
Key Contact: John C. Boone

Functions: Most + 02.0 05.0 06.0 08.0 11.6
Industries: Most + D.00
Description: Over 20 years executive search
  experience in multi-disciplines & diverse
  industries

The Borton Wallace Co.
22 Broad St.
Asheville, North Carolina 28801
Salary Minimum: $50,000
Key Contact: Murray B. Parker

Functions: 02.0 04.0 11.3 11.5
Industries: D.00 D.13 D.15 D.20 D.D0
Professional Affiliations: NAER, SME, TAPPI
Description: Most functions within polymeric,
  paper, nonwoven & vertically integrated
  industries

Botrie Assoc.
8 King St. E., 15th Fl.
Toronto, Ontario M5C 1B5 Canada
Salary Minimum: $50,000
Key Contact: James Botrie
Nicholas Williams

Functions: Most
Description: A research based organization
  with a 96% success rate

Affiliates/Other Offices:
Clarke Henning & Beldam Ltd., Toronto

Bowden & Co., Inc.
5000 Rockside Rd., Ste. 120
Cleveland, Ohio 44131
Salary Minimum: $80,000
Key Contact: Otis H. Bowden, II
Harrison R. Magee
Chester W. Dickey

Functions: Most + 01.0 02.0 05.0 08.0 10.0
Industries: Most + D.00 D.E0 D.H0 H.00
  H.I0
Professional Affiliations: AESC, AMA, SAE
Description: Quality match productive results
  is our hallmark throughout North
  America

Peter Newell Bowen
P.O. Box 9
Glen Rock, Pennsylvania 17327
Salary Minimum: $65,000
Key Contact: Peter Newell Bowen

Functions: 01.2 01.3 11.0 11.3 11.6
Industries: D.15 D.E0 D.H0 I.14 K.10
Professional Affiliations: IACPR
Description: Independent search geared to
  optimum response to client requirements

Bowker, Brown & Co.
2451 Brickell Ave.
Miami, Florida 33129
Salary Minimum: $75,000
Key Contact: Gordon R. Bowker

Functions: 01.2 01.3 03.3
Industries: D.23 E.00
Description: Executive search & consulting to
  track transportation & corporate logistics
  departments

Dr. Will G. Bowman, Inc.
330 E. 75th St., Ste. 35-B
New York, New York 10021
Salary Minimum: $75,000
Key Contact: Will G. Bowman

Functions: 04.0 08.2 09.0 11.2 11.3
Industries: D.E0 D.H0 H.11
Professional Affiliations: NAER
Description: Recruiting brokers for Wall Street
  & multi-degreed engineers for high
  technology

Boyden Latin America S.A. de C.V.

Paseo de la Reforma-509, 11th Fl.
Mexico City, Mexico 06500 DF Mexico
Salary Minimum: $20,000
Key Contact: Alberto Rivas

Functions: Most
Industries: Most
Professional Affiliations: AESC
Description: Boyden-A reputation built for leadership in executive search

Boyden World Corp.

375 Park Ave., 10th Fl.
New York, New York 10152
Salary Minimum: $75,000
Key Contact: Leonard J. Clark, Jr.
William E. Goodman, IV
Leeda P. Marting

Functions: Most
Industries: Most
Professional Affiliations: AESC

Branches:
275 Battery St., Ste. 420
Embarcadero Center West Tower
San Francisco, California 94111
Key Contact: Putney Westerfield
Lynne Koll Martin
Julia C. Hirsch
Frederick J. Greene
Jennifer C. Hardie
Ronald T. Yamamoto
Rebecca M. Rucker-Eatherly

55 Madison Ave.
Morristown, New Jersey 07960-7354
Key Contact: Peter R. Schmidt
George V. Malone
Normand W. Green
James C. Burris
Franklin J. Barbosa
Gordon T. Sulcer

15951 Los Gatos Blvd.
Los Gatos, California 95030
Key Contact: Charles Splaine

625 Stanwix St., Ste. 2405
Allegheny Twr.
Pittsburgh, Pennsylvania 15222
Key Contact: Malcolm MacGregor
E. Wade Close, Jr.
Thomas F. Faught
Robert L. Kirkpatrick

1290 E. Main St.
Stamford, Connecticut 06902-3555
Key Contact: Paul C. Richardson

2 Prudential Pl.
180 N. Stetson Ave., Ste. 5050
Chicago, Illinois 60601
Key Contact: Richard A. McCallister
Janet L. Fischer
Trina D. Gordon
James M. Gross
John S. Gude

364 Elwood Ave.
Hawthorne, New York 10532-1239
Key Contact: Richard Foy

The Younge Richmond Centre
151 Yonge St., Ste. 1210
Toronto, Ontario Canada M5C 2W7

60 William St.
Wellesley, Massachusetts 02181
Key Contact: Joseph Onstott
Patricia Campbell

Paseo de la Reforma-509, 11th Fl.
Mexico City, Mexico 06500 DF Mexico
Key Contact: Alberto Rivas

International Branches:
Amsterdam, Bad Homburg-v.d.H., Bangkok, Bogota, Bombay, Bremen, Brussels, Budapest,
Chemnitz, Copenhagen, Geneva, Helsinki, Hong Kong, Johannesburg, Kuala Lumpur, Lisbon,
London, Madrid, Milan, Oslo, Paris, Rome, Sao Paulo, Seoul, Singapore, Stockholm, Sydney,
Taipei, Tokyo, Toronto, Valencia, Vienna, Warsaw

The Bradbury Management Group

22462 Salem Ave., Ste. 100
Cupertino, California 95014
Salary Minimum: $70,000
Key Contact: Paul W. Bradbury, Jr.
Peter D. Lang

Functions: 01.1
Industries: B.0W D.00 D.H0 J.00
Professional Affiliations: CERA, EMA, ISA, SEMI
Description: Specializing in microcomputer, peripheral, semi-conductor & environmental consulting industries

Brady Assoc. Int'l., Inc.

310 Madison Ave., Ste. 423
New York, New York 10017
Salary Minimum: $50,000
Key Contact: Robert E. Brady
Susan E. Harbers

Functions: Most + 11.2 11.5
Industries: B.00 B.0W H.00
Professional Affiliations: AGA, NYSSA
Description: Executive recruiters for banks, investment banks, utilities & energy companies

The Brand Co., Inc.

8402 Red Bay Court
Vero Beach, Florida 32963
Salary Minimum: $50,000
Key Contact: J. Brand Spangenberg

Functions: Most + 01.0 02.0 05.0 06.0 08.0
Industries: Most + B.00 D.00 D.D0 D.H0 I.00
Professional Affiliations: AESC
Description: Generalist retainer search firm with prominent credentials & nationwide capabilities

Branches:
15 Plantation Dr., NE
Atlanta, Georgia 30324

Brandywine Consulting Group

818 Kimberly Ln.
West Chester, Pennsylvania 19382
Salary Minimum: $60,000
Key Contact: Richard H. Beatty

Functions: Most + 01.2 01.3 02.0 04.0 05.0
Industries: Most + B.0W D.13 D.15 D.18
Professional Affiliations: EMA, SHRM
Description: Broad-based practice; strong in chemicals, paper, packaging, pharmaceuticals & consumer products

Brault & Assoc., Ltd.

11703 Bowman Green Dr.
Reston, Virginia 22090
Salary Minimum: $70,000
Key Contact: J-P. Brault

Functions: Most + 04.0 08.0 09.0 11.1
Industries: B.00 D.H0 H.00 I.00 J.00
Description: Executive search with practices in high tech, banking/finance, energy & environmental.

Brentwood Int'l.

9841 Airport Blvd., Ste. 420
Los Angeles, California 90045
Salary Minimum: $50,000
Key Contact: James Keenan
Douglas Frankel
Marilyn Bennett
David Whittinghill
Michelle Curtis
Jamie Patterson
Susan Cole-Hill
Cynthia Whittaker

Functions: Most
Industries: Most + D.00 D.E0 D.H0 H.00 I.00
Description: Exclusively executive search specializing in high technology, financial, public sector

Bricker & Assoc., Inc.

625 North Michigan Ave.
Ste. 1800
Chicago, Illinois 60611
Salary Minimum: $50,000
Key Contact: Betsy S. Tomlinson
Deborah A. Bricker

Functions: Most
Industries: Most
Description: Management consulting & generalist executive search firm

Brissenden, McFarland, Wagoner & Fuccella, Inc.

One Canterbury Green
Stamford, Connecticut 06901
Salary Minimum: $75,000
Key Contact: Richard M. McFarland
Robert E. Wagoner
John M. Foster

Functions: Most + 01.0 02.0 04.0 05.0 09.0
Industries: Most + B.00 D.00 D.H0 D.I0 I.00
Professional Affiliations: AESC
Description: Mgmt positions; utilities,
  chemicals, electronics, healthcare,
  manufacturing & telecommunications

Branches:
Mack Bridgewater 1
721 Route 202-206
Bridgewater, New Jersey 08807
Key Contact: Hoke Brissenden
Carl J. Fuccella
John R. Reynolds

F.J. Bruckner & Co.

12620 E. 86th St., N.
Owasso, Oklahoma 74055
Salary Minimum: $50,000
Key Contact: Frank Bruckner

Functions: Most
Industries: C.00
Description: Retained search; construction
  industry; branch/general management,
  senior staff

Bryce, Haultain & Assoc.

1 St. Clair Ave. E., 10th Fl.
Toronto, Ontario M4T 2V7 Canada
Salary Minimum: $55,000
Key Contact: Ross Finlay
Don Phaneuf

Functions: Most + 01.2 01.3 01.4 02.2 05.1
Industries: Most + B.0W D.00 D.H0 I.00 J.00
Description: Industry-sponsored executive
  search & relocation-counselling firm

Affiliates/Other Offices:
Technical Service Council, Calgary
Technical Service Council, Cambridge
Technical Service Council, Edmonton
Technical Service Council, Montreal
Technical Service Council, Oakville
Technical Service Council, Toronto
Technical Service Council, Vancouver
Technical Service Council, Winnipeg

Charles Buck & Assoc., Inc.

501 Madison Ave.
New York, New York 10022
Salary Minimum: $85,000
Key Contact: Charles A. Buck, Jr.

Functions: 01.0 05.0 05.1 05.2 06.0
Industries: Most
Description: A small, quality search firm
  specializing in marketing, communications
  & general management

International Branches:
London

Bullis & Co., Inc.

120 Quintara St.
San Francisco, California 94116
Salary Minimum: $75,000
Key Contact: Richard J. Bullis

Functions: Most + 01.0 02.0 05.0 08.0 09.0
Industries: Most + D.00 D.H0 D.I0 H.00 I.00
Description: All functional areas, high tech,
  healthcare, banking, finance & misc

Burke, O'Brien & Bishop Assoc., Inc.

1000 Herrontown Rd.
Princeton, New Jersey 08540
Salary Minimum: $100,000
Key Contact: James F. Bishop

Functions: Most
Industries: Most
Description: Most functional areas with
  emphasis on general management, finance,
  marketing & human resources

Thomas Burnham Co.

3151 Airway, Ste. R1
Costa Mesa, California 92626
Salary Minimum: $75,000
Key Contact: Thomas Burnham

Functions: Most + 01.2 02.0 05.0 06.0 08.0
Professional Affiliations: IACPR
Description: Generalist firm serving broad
  sector of industry. National in scope-
  extensive Pacific Rim expertise

Joseph R. Burns & Assoc., Inc.

2 Shunpike Rd.
Madison, New Jersey 07940
Salary Minimum: $70,000
Key Contact: Joseph R. Burns

Functions: Most
Industries: Most
Professional Affiliations: IACPR
Description: Retainer based executive search
  firm

Busch Int'l.

One First St., Ste. 4
Los Altos, California 94022
Salary Minimum: $75,000
Key Contact: Jack Busch
Kathy Kraemer
Walter Wong
Ed Sermone

Functions: Most
Industries: D.H0 D.I0 H.12
Description: Busch Int'l. specializes in high
  technology and life sciences exclusively

Business Search America

2120 Lebanon Rd.
Lawrenceville, Georgia 30243
Salary Minimum: $50,000
Key Contact: Martin Smith
Emma Smith

Functions: 02.5 05.6
Industries: Most
Description: Specialists in quality professionals
  as part of our consulting practice

Butterfass/Pepe Assoc., Inc.

171 Madison Ave., Ste. 910
New York, New York 10016
Salary Minimum: $50,000
Key Contact: Stanley W. Butterfass
Leonida R. Pepe
Deirdre MacCallan

Functions: 04.0 08.2 11.2
Industries: D.18 H.00 H.I0 H.R0 J.00
Professional Affiliations: IACPR, ACG
Description: Boutique search firm—specialties
  include: fixed income, private placement,
  M&A

Buzhardt Assoc.

1385 Narrow Gauge Rd.
Bolton, Mississippi 39041
Salary Minimum: $60,000
Key Contact: J.F. Buzhardt

Functions: 01.0 02.0 05.0 06.0 08.0
Industries: D.00 F.00 G.00 H.00
Description: Recruiting & evaluating the top
  management team for emerging
  organizations

T. Byrnes & Co., Inc.

9 E. 45th St., Ste. 907
New York, New York 10017
Salary Minimum: $50,000
Key Contact: Barbara Byrnes

Functions: 01.0 05.0 06.0 08.0 11.1
Industries: C.00 D.00 G.00 H.R0 I.00
Description: Specialized executive search for
  hospitality/leisure industry

Byron Leonard Int'l., Inc.

2659 Townsgate Rd., Ste 207
Westlake Village, California 91361
Salary Minimum: $60,000
Key Contact: Byron G. Contorinis
Leonard M. Linton
Stephen M. Wolf
Gary D. Bernard

Functions: 01.0 02.0 05.0 09.0 11.0
Industries: D.00 D.H0 D.I0 E.00 H.00
Professional Affiliations: IACPR, CERA, IEEE
Description: Established firm emphasizing
  "custom candidate fit", disciplined
  methodology,exceptional research

CEO'S Only
1865 Caminito Ascua
La Jolla, California 92037
Salary Minimum: $150,000
Key Contact: Gary Sutton

Functions: 01.0
Description: Place CEO's, period. Resumes not
    accepted

CSI Inc.
P.O. Box 16262
Phoenix, Arizona 85011-6262
Salary Minimum: $50,000
Key Contact: Robert F. Graham

Functions: Most + 11.3
Industries: D.E0 D.H0
Professional Affiliations: IACPR, ADPA, AOC,
    ASCA, IEEE
Description: Executive & technical search for
    the electronics industry

Robert Caldwell & Assoc.
12021 Wilshire Blvd., Ste. 650
Los Angeles, California 90025
Salary Minimum: $100,000
Key Contact: Robert Caldwell

Functions: Most
Industries: Most
Professional Affiliations: IACPR
Description: National firm specializing in
    difficult to fill executive positions

The Caldwell Partners Int'l.
64 Prince Arthur Ave.
Toronto, Ontario M5R 1B4 Canada
Salary Minimum: $60,000
Key Contact: Judy Keen
Kelly A. Blair
C. Douglas Caldwell
Ralph A. Chauvin
George P. Delaney
Robert D. Elhart
Anne M. Fawcett
Clarke H. Jackson
Kevin R. McBurney
Patrick O'Callaghan
Ronald D. Charles
Christopher J. Laubitz
Francis W. H. Brunelle
Joseph M. B. Beaupre
Jean Raymond
L. Grant Spitz
Margaret Pelton
Robert Sutton
Martha Evans
Ernest Yin
Sharon Kucherepa
Theresa Paine
Don Prior
Nicole Faure
Mary O'Neill

Functions: Most
Industries: Most
Professional Affiliations: AESC
Description: Leading Canadian executive
    search firm

Branches:
400-3rd. Ave. S.W.
Calgary, Alberta T2P 4H2 Canada

1840 Sherbrooke St., W.
Montreal, Quebec H3A 1E4 Canada

999 W. Hastings St., Ste. 750
Vancouver, British Columbia V6C 2W2
    Canada

Networks:
Amrop Int'l.
Amsterdam, Atlanta, Auckland, Berlin, Brussels, Buenos Aires, Chicago, Cleveland, Copenhagen, Dallas, Dublin, Dusseldorf, Frankfurt, Garza Garcia, Goteberg, Hamburg, Helsinki, Hong Kong, Houston, Johannesburg, Kuala Lumpur, Lisbon, London, Madrid, Melbourne, Mexico City, Milan, Munich, New York, Paris, Queretaro, Rome, Sao Paulo, Singapore, Stockholm, Sydney, Taipei, Tampa, Zurich

Lee Calhoon & Co., Inc.

P.O. Box 201
Birchrunville, Pennsylvania 19421
Salary Minimum: $50,000
Key Contact: Lee Calhoon
Karen McCloskey
Pat Calhoon

Functions: 01.0 04.0 05.0 09.0 10.0
Industries: H.I0 I.14 I.15 I.18 L.00
Description: Specialists in insurance, benefits, managed care and information systems for all functions

Branches:
33 Bedford St., Ste. 17
Lexington, Massachusetts 02173-4430
Key Contact: Geoffrey Fitzgerald

P.O. Box 399
St. Peters, Pennsylvania 19470
Key Contact: Abby Mayes
Tara McCabe

21 Lodge St.
Albany, New York 12207
Key Contact: Pamela S. Leone

Callan Assoc., Ltd.

1550 Spring Rd.
Oak Brook, Illinois 60521
Salary Minimum: $100,000
Key Contact: Robert M. Callan
Elizabeth Callan Beaudin
Marianne Callan Ray
Marie Owen

Functions: Most + 01.0 02.0 04.0 05.0 06.0
Industries: Most
Professional Affiliations: IACPR, IMESC
Description: A firm of experienced, close knit consultants dedicated to recruiting exceptional management

Cambridge Group Ltd.-Exec. Search Div.

830 Post Rd. E.
Westport, Connecticut 06880
Salary Minimum: $80,000
Key Contact: Michael Salvangwo

Functions: 09.0
Industries: Most
Description: Specialized data processing, technical support, telecommunications & information services search

Cambridge Management Planning

2323 Yonge St., Ste. 203
Toronto, Ontario M4P 2C9 Canada
Salary Minimum: $55,000
Key Contact: Graham Carver
Carl Campa
Robert Graham

Functions: Most
Industries: Most
Description: Executive search-middle to senior searches for a wide range of corporations

Robert Campbell & Assoc.

18 S. Michigan Ave.
Chicago, Illinois 60603-3202
Salary Minimum: $250,000
Key Contact: Robert Campbell
Richard J. Hill
Angus Putgorney MacGregor
Jill Christy
Ricki Clark

Functions: 01.0 01.2
Industries: Most
Description: Senior management assignments across wide spectrum of industry & not-for-profit organizations

CanMed Consultants Inc.
62 Queen St. S.
Mississauga, Ontario L5M 1K4 Canada
Salary Minimum: $50,000
Key Contact: Marc C. Raheja

Functions: Most
Industries: D.18 D.I0 I.14 I.15
Professional Affiliations: IMCO, NAPR
Description: International consultants to
executives & professionals in the
healthcare sector

Canny, Bowen Inc.
200 Park Ave., 49th Fl.
New York, New York 10166
Salary Minimum: $110,000
Key Contact: Carl W. Menk
David R. Peasback
Theodore J. Erikson
Jeffrey G. Neuberth
Amy F. Bragg
William K. Sur
John A. Coleman
Mary Rose Conboy

Functions: Most + 01.0 01.2 03.1 05.0 06.0
Industries: Most + B.0W D.I0 E.00 H.00 I.17
Professional Affiliations: AESC
Description: Specialize in senior executive
search

Branches:
101 Federal St.
Boston, Massachusetts 02110
Key Contact: W. Allen Moorhead

Affiliates/Other Offices:
J. Friisberg & Partners, Copenhagen
J. Friisberg & Partners, Frankfurt
J. Friisberg & Partners, Helsinki
J. Friisberg & Partners, Lausanne
J. Friisberg & Partners, London
J. Friisberg & Partners, Milan
J. Friisberg & Partners, Oslo
J. Friisberg & Partners, Paris

Cardwell Group
1991 Crocker Rd., Ste. 220
Cleveland, Ohio 44145
Salary Minimum: $75,000
Key Contact: James W. Cardwell

Functions: 01.0 01.1 01.2 01.3
Industries: Most + D.26 H.10 I.14 I.15
Professional Affiliations: IACPR, NACD
Description: We use an organizational
development consulting approach

Career Plus Executive Search
23926 B DeVille Way
Malibu, California 90265
Salary Minimum: $60,000
Key Contact: Thomas Myers

Functions: 01.1 05.2 05.3 05.4 08.0
Industries: B.0W D.00 D.E0 D.H0 H.00
Description: Search for technical sales
managers & marketing, general
management, executives in electronics

L.L. Carey & Assoc., Inc.
840 Port Walk Pl.
Redwood City, California 94065
Key Contact: Linda L. Carey
Lynne Peaks

Functions: Most
Industries: D.17 D.18 D.I0 H.12 I.14
Description: Specializing in hi-technology &
healthcare technology; project & team
building orientation

Carpenter, Shackleton & Co.

Civic Opera Bldg.
20 N. Wacker Dr., Ste. 3119
Chicago, Illinois 60606-3101
Key Contact: George M. Shackleton
Eric G. Carpenter
Yoshiaki Satoh
Beverly L. Turbak
Louise Rodriguez

Functions: Most + 11.2 11.4 11.5 11.6
Industries: Most
Description: Specialize in recruiting for
    Chicago area clients for all functions

Carris, Jackowitz Assoc.

201 E. 79th St.
New York, New York 10021
Salary Minimum: $70,000
Key Contact: S. Joseph Carris

Branches:
Box 54
Andover, New Jersey 07821
Key Contact: Ronald N. Jackowitz

Functions: Most
Industries: Most

M.L. Carter & Assoc., Inc.

3347 W. Hospital Ave.
Atlanta, Georgia 30341
Salary Minimum: $45,000
Key Contact: Minor L. Carter
Donald E. Dearwent

Functions: Most + 09.0 10.0
Industries: Most + I.14 I.15
Description: Executive search & management
    systems consulting for healthcare industry

Cascadia Group Int'l.

620 SW Fifth Ave., Ste. 1225
Portland, Oregon 97204-1426
Salary Minimum: $40,000
Key Contact: Gail L. Woodworth
Gail Martwick

Functions: 01.0 02.0 03.0 05.0 09.0
Industries: B.00 D.00 D.25 D.D0
Description: Fortune 500 experience, discipline
    & professionalism

Caswell/Winters & Assoc., Inc.

11400 W. Lake Park Dr.
Milwaukee, Wisconsin 53224
Key Contact: David G. Caswell

Functions: 11.0
Industries: I.14 I.15
Professional Affiliations: NAPR
Description: Physician, allied health & health
    care administration search-all specialities

Catalyx Group, Inc.

4 Park Ave., Ste. 11J
New York, New York 10016
Salary Minimum: $70,000
Key Contact: Lawrence Poster

Functions: Most + 01.0 02.0 04.0 05.0 08.0
Industries: Most + D.17 D.18 D.H0 D.I0
    H.12
Professional Affiliations: ABC
Description: Geoglobal capability recruiting
    exceptional senior executives & seasoned
    entrepreneurs

Michael J. Cavanaugh & Assoc.

1250 Bay St., Ste. 400
Toronto, Ontario M5R 2B1 Canada
Salary Minimum: $70,000
Key Contact: Michael Cavanaugh
Dana Stehr

Functions: 01.0 02.0 06.0 08.0 09.0
Industries: D.24 D.E0 D.H0 I.14
Description: One of Canada's most experienced
    recruiters in aerospace

Cejka & Co.
222 S. Central, Ste. 400
St. Louis, Missouri 63105
Salary Minimum: $60,000
Key Contact: Susan Cejka
Robert Hardy
James Schmidt
Michael Taylor
Wiley C. Smith

Functions: 01.0 05.0 07.0 08.0 09.0
Industries: D.18 D.E0 E.00 H.I0 I.14
Description: We live up to our promises

Challenger & Hunt
7777 Bonhomme Ave., Ste. 1385
St. Louis, Missouri 63105
Salary Minimum: $60,000
Key Contact: Joseph T. Farrell
Ken Williams
Dan Ingram
Michael W. Wright

Industries: I.15
Professional Affiliations: NAPR
Description: National retainer based physician
search firm

David Chambers & Assoc., Inc.
6 East 43rd St.
New York, New York 10017
Salary Minimum: $75,000
Key Contact: David E. Chambers
Gene M. Tate
Peter Murphy

Functions: Most
Industries: Most
Description: 18 year old generalist search firm
with over 80% repeat business each year

International Branches:
Frankfurt, London, Paris

Joseph Chandler & Assoc., Inc.
905 W. Hillgrove Ave., Ste. 4
La Grange, Illinois 60525
Salary Minimum: $60,000
Key Contact: Joseph J. Chandler

Functions: Most
Industries: Most
Professional Affiliations: IACPR
Description: Well established generalist
working nationwide

Chandler & Rozner Assoc.
4726 Howard Ave.
Western Springs, Illinois 60558-1721
Salary Minimum: $50,000
Key Contact: John Rozner
Barbara Murphy
Daniel J. Rozner

Functions: Most
Industries: D.00 D.D0 D.H0 E.00 I.00
Description: Thirty years human resource
officer experience, Fortune 500 companies

Chanko-Ward, Ltd.
2 West 45th St.
New York, New York 10036
Salary Minimum: $60,000
Key Contact: Jim Chanko
Dick Ward

Functions: 01.4 06.0 08.0 09.0
Industries: B.00
Description: Selection & identification of
financial, accounting, planning & MIS
professionals

Chartwell Partners Int'l., Inc.
275 Battery St., Ste. 2180
Embarcadero Center West Tower
San Francisco, California 94111-3305
Salary Minimum: $75,000
Key Contact: David M. deWilde
Stuart H. Sadick
Peter V. Hall
Louis C. Burnett

Functions: 01.2 01.4 05.0 08.0 11.1
Industries: H.00 H.10 H.11 H.I0 H.R0
Description: National practice concentrating in
financial services, technology & real estate

Chase Partners

111 Richmond St., W, Ste. 308
Toronto, Ontario M5H 2G4 Canada
Salary Minimum: $50,000
Key Contact: John S. Harrison

Functions: Most
Industries: Most
Description: Integrating human resource
  planning & executive search consulting

Chase-Owens Assoc., Inc.

1218 Chestnut St., Ste. 603
Philadelphia, Pennsylvania 19107
Salary Minimum: $45,000
Key Contact: Ralph Owen

Functions: Most + 05.3 05.4 09.4 09.7
Industries: Most + D.10 D.24 D.H0 J.13
Professional Affiliations: IACPR, ACA, ASPA,
  EMA
Description: High tech specialists directed by
  former corporate human resource
  professionals

Chestnut Hill Partners, Inc.

20 William St.
Wellesley Hills, Massachusetts 02181
Salary Minimum: $80,000
Key Contact: Steven M. Garfinkle

Functions: Most
Industries: Most
Professional Affiliations: IACPR
Description: Concentrations include high
  technology, industrial products, financial
  services, venture capital

Affiliates/Other Offices:
Insight Consultants, Dublin
Insight Consultants, London

Chicago Research Group, Inc.

272 E. Deerpath Rd., Ste. 200
Lake Forest, Illinois 60045
Salary Minimum: $65,000
Key Contact: Deborah Marshall
Robert Ross

Functions: Most
Industries: Most
Description: Provide the highest quality
  business research in the industry

China Human Resources Group

29 Airpark Rd.
Princeton, New Jersey 08540
Salary Minimum: $30,000
Key Contact: Christine Casati

Functions: Most + 01.0 02.0 05.0 06.0 08.0
Industries: Most
Professional Affiliations: NAPC, USCBC
Description: We meet the growing demand for
  experienced mgmt. talent in the People's
  Republic of China

International Branches:
Shanghai

Chrisman & Co., Inc.

350 S. Figueroa St., Ste. 550
Los Angeles, California 90071
Salary Minimum: $60,000
Key Contact: Timothy Chrisman

Functions: Most
Industries: H.00 H.I0 H.R0 I.00 K.00
Description: Board member, middle & upper
  echelon executive searches, nationally

Branches:
1180 E. Shaw Ave., Ste. 122
Fresno, California 93710
Key Contact: Paul S. Williams

Christenson & Hutchison

466 Southern Blvd.
Chatham, New Jersey 07928
Salary Minimum: $80,000
Key Contact: H. Alan Christenson
William K. Hutchison

Functions: Most
Industries: Most
Professional Affiliations: AESC, IACPR
Description: Partners manage all assignments,
recruit all disciplines, nationwide practice

Christian & Timbers, Inc.

30050 Chagrin Blvd., Ste. 300
Cleveland, Ohio 44124
Salary Minimum: $75,000
Key Contact: Jeffrey E. Christian

Functions: Most + 01.2 02.0 04.0 05.0 09.0
Industries: Most + B.0W D.10 D.18 D.24
D.H0
Description: Specializing in building fast
growth & high technology companies

Branches:
1250 Oakmead Pkwy., Ste. 210
Sunnyvale, California 94088
Key Contact: Hiram French

70 Walnut St.
Wellesley, Massachusetts 02181

Christopher-Patrick & Assoc.

24200 Chagrin Blvd.
Beachwood, Ohio 44122
Salary Minimum: $50,000
Key Contact: John R. Donnelly
John P. Ludwick
George M. Miller

Functions: 02.0 06.0 09.0 11.2 11.5
Industries: A.00 C.00 D.D0 D.H0 K.00
Description: Automotive OEM, aftermarkets,
aerospace, high tech research from middle
management—president

Jack Clarey Assoc., Inc.

1200 Shermer Rd., Ste. 108
Northbrook, Illinois 60062
Salary Minimum: $90,000
Key Contact: J. Douglas Andrews
Jack R. Clarey

Functions: Most + 01.0 02.0 05.0 06.0 08.0
Industries: Most + D.00 I.00
Professional Affiliations: AESC, IACPR
Description: Small generalist firm; assignments
conducted only by experienced principals

Claveloux, McCaffrey, McInerney, Inc.

P.O. Box 101
Green Farms, Connecticut 06436
Salary Minimum: $60,000
Key Contact: Denis Claveloux
Ellen McInerney

Functions: Most + 04.0 05.0 08.0 09.0
Industries: Most + B.0W D.00 D.18 D.19
D.H0
Professional Affiliations: IACPR
Description: Small, personal, flexible

Clemo, Evans & Co., Inc.

33 River St.
Chagrin Falls, Ohio 44022
Salary Minimum: $70,000
Key Contact: James A. Clemo

Functions: Most + 01.1 01.2 02.0 05.0 08.0
Industries: Most
Description: Our firm does the senior level
searches for the clients we serve

Dean M. Coe Assoc.

303 Congress St., Ste. 600-A
Boston, Massachusetts 02210
Salary Minimum: $75,000
Key Contact: Dean M Coe

Functions: 01.2
Industries: H.R0
Professional Affiliations: BOMA, IFMA,
IREM, NACORE, NAIOP
Description: Executive search & recruitment,
specializing in real estate asset, portfolio &
property mgmt.

Branches:
32 Pine St.
Sandwich, Massachusetts 02563

Coelyn Miller Phillip & Assoc.

1400 Fashion Island Blvd., Ste. 300
San Mateo, California 94404
Salary Minimum: $50,000
Key Contact: John R. Phillip
Ronald H. Coelyn

Functions: Most + 11.3
Industries: Most + D.I0 I.00 I.14 I.16 I.20
Professional Affiliations: CERA
Description: Client-driven, specializing in mid
to upper level management requirements

Cole Human Resource Services

148 Great Hills Rd.
Short Hills, New Jersey 07078
Salary Minimum: $60,000
Key Contact: Charlotte L. Cole
Alan Leighton

Functions: Most
Industries: Most
Description: On-site executive recruitment &
search consultants to smaller & mid-size
companies

Cole, Warren & Long, Inc.

2 Penn Center Plz., Ste. 1020
Philadelphia, Pennsylvania 19102
Salary Minimum: $60,000
Key Contact: Ronald Cole
Lloyd W. Spangler
Richard Warren

Functions: Most
Industries: Most
Professional Affiliations: AAA, ACA, ACG,
ASPA, IACPR, IMC, WTCA
Description: An executive search & general
management consulting firm servicing
nationwide clients

J. Kevin Coleman & Assoc., Inc.

2609 E. Colorado Blvd., P.O. Box 70474
Pasadena, California 91117
Salary Minimum: $60,000
Key Contact: J. Kevin Coleman

Functions: 01.0 02.0 04.0 08.0 11.5
Industries: B.0W C.00 D.00 D.E0 D.H0
Professional Affiliations: IACPR, CERA
Description: Executive search services for
financial, high technology &
environmental companies

Coleman Lew & Assoc., Inc.

326 W. Tenth St.
Charlotte, North Carolina 28202
Key Contact: Charles E. Lew
Kenneth D. Carrick, Jr.
Ann N. Whitlock

Functions: Most
Industries: Most
Professional Affiliations: IACPR
Description: Generalist search firm, expertise
in food industry, all functions- national
clients

W. Hoyt Colton Assoc., Inc.

67 Wall St.
New York, New York 10005
Salary Minimum: $75,000
Key Contact: W. Hoyt Colton

Functions: Most
Industries: Most
Description: Completely satisfying our client's
staffing requirements-our corporate/
consultants commitment

Colton Bernard Inc.

417 Spruce St.
San Francisco, California 94118
Salary Minimum: $75,000
Key Contact: Harry Bernard
Roy C. Colton

Functions: Most
Industries: D.11
Professional Affiliations: AAA, AAMA, NAER,
SFFI
Description: Full srvc. marketing, information,
organizational & management recruiting
for the apparel industry

Branches:
50 W. 34th St., Ste. 18A8
New York, New York 10001
Key Contact: Myron I. Blumenfeld

Comann Assoc., Inc.
3033 S. Parker Rd., Ste. 200
Aurora, Colorado 80014
Salary Minimum: $50,000
Key Contact: R. Kent Comann

Functions: Most
Industries: A.00
Professional Affiliations: AIME, AMC, CMA
Description: Executive search devoted
   exclusively to the mining & mineral
   industry

The Communications Search Group
708 Third Ave.
New York, New York 10017
Salary Minimum: $50,000
Key Contact: William A. Lydgate
Tom Burke
Jack Fitzgerald

Functions: 05.0 05.7
Industries: J.00 J.10
Professional Affiliations: IABC, PRSA
Description: Business confined to
   communications public relations, public
   affairs, marketing

Compass Group Ltd.
401 S. Woodward, Ste. 362
Birmingham, Michigan 48009
Salary Minimum: $60,000
Key Contact: Paul Czamanske
Katherine Slaughter
Peter Czamanski

Functions: 01.0 02.0 03.0 05.0 06.0
Industries: Most + D.22 D.23 D.25 D.H0 I.10
Professional Affiliations: AESC, AIAG, IMC
Description: Emphasis in automotive,
   manufacturing, high-tech & service
   industries; international in scope

Branches:
Two Mid America Plz., Ste. 800
Oakbrook Terrace, Illinois 60181
Key Contact: Jerold L. Lipe

Computer Professionals
3601 Algonquin Rd., Ste. 129
Rolling Meadows, Illinois 60008
Salary Minimum: $50,000
Key Contact: Kevin Hogan

Functions: Most
Industries: Most
Description: Executive search/management
   consulting firm specialized in the
   computer industry

Conard Assoc., Inc.
76 Northeastern Blvd., Ste. 29
Nashua, New Hampshire 03062
Salary Minimum: $60,000
Key Contact: Rodney J. Conard

Functions: Most + 01.0 02.6 05.0 06.0 08.0
Industries: Most
Professional Affiliations: IACPR
Description: Emphasis on small to mid-sized
   companies; consultative team-building
   approach

Conex Inc.
919 Third Ave., 18th Fl.
New York, New York 10022
Salary Minimum: $65,000
Key Contact: Fred Siegel
Ann Marie Pizzariello
James Schwab

Functions: Most + 01.0 06.0 07.0 08.0 11.1
Industries: Most
Description: Generalist firm with broad
   domestic & international client base

Branches:
1801 Ave. of the Stars, Ste. 640
Los Angeles, California 90067
Key Contact: Richard A. Farago

Joseph Conley & Assoc., Inc.
625 N. Michigan Ave.
Chicago, Illinois 60611
Salary Minimum: $80,000
Key Contact: Joseph R. Conley

Functions: Most + 01.0 02.0 05.0 06.0 08.0
Industries: Most + B.00 D.00 D.10 D.22 H.00
Professional Affiliations: IACPR
Description: Assist clients in business problem-solving. Specialists in matching personal chemistries

Conley Assoc., Inc.
31191 W. Beaver Lake Rd.
Hartland, Wisconsin 53029
Salary Minimum: $50,000
Key Contact: Gordon Housfeld

Functions: Most + 01.0 02.0 05.0 06.0 08.0
Industries: Most
Description: National generalist executive search firm with 45 years experience serving $50-500,000 salary range

Robert Connelly & Assoc., Inc.
P.O. Box 24028
Minneapolis, Minnesota 55424
Salary Minimum: $40,000
Key Contact: Robert F. Olsen

Functions: 07.3 11.5 11.6
Industries: B.0W B.10 C.00 H.R0 L.00
Description: Specializing in architectural/engineering, real estate, construction & environmental industries

Branches:
5949 Sherry Ln., Ste 82J
Dallas, Texas 75225
Key Contact: Sandra Henoch

Walter V. Connor Int'l., Inc.
2 E. Read St., Ste. 100
Baltimore, Maryland 21202-2470
Salary Minimum: $75,000
Key Contact: Timothy C. McNamara
Jon P. Miller
Hugh A. Mallon III
Erika Bogar

Functions: Most
Industries: D.00 D.I0 E.00 H.00 I.00
Description: Each assignment based on original research & direct principal management

Conrey Interamericana
Prado Sur 240
Mexico City, Mexico DF 11000 Mexico
Salary Minimum: $40,000
Key Contact: Craig J. Dudley
Luis Lesama
Adriana Hobbs

Functions: Most
Industries: Most
Description: Our professional staff combines more than 30 years recruiting experience

Philip Conway Management
320 Hampton Place
Hinsdale, Illinois 60521
Salary Minimum: $60,000
Key Contact: Philip A. Conway

Functions: Most + 01.0 02.0 05.0 05.4 08.0
Industries: Most
Description: Specialists in the recruitment of senior & middle managers

Grant Cooper & Assoc., Inc.
795 Office Pkwy., Ste. 117
St. Louis, Missouri 63141
Salary Minimum: $50,000
Key Contact: Stephen H. Loeb
J. Dale Meier
William Tunney
Linda Bearman

Functions: Most + 01.0 02.0 05.0 06.0 08.0
Industries: D.00 G.00 H.00 I.00 J.00
Professional Affiliations: AHA, AMS, ASPA, ASTD, EMA, IACPR
Description: Generalist searches in mid- to upper-level assignments, also consulting in related areas

The Cooper Executive Search Group, Inc.

P.O. Box 28
Delafield, Wisconsin 53018
Salary Minimum: $50,000
Key Contact: Robert M. Cooper

Functions: Most
Industries: Most
Professional Affiliations: IACPR
Description: Full service firm with particular
strengths in transitional & middle market
companies

Coopers & Lybrand Consulting Group

145 King St. W.
Toronto, Ontario M5H 1V8 Canada
Salary Minimum: $50,000
Key Contact: Jo Ann Compton

Functions: Most
Industries: Most
Description: One of the largest international
accounting & management consulting
firms

Branches:
255 5th Ave., S.W.
Calgary, Alberta T2P 3G6 Canada
Key Contact: Andy Celmainis

1111 W. Hastings St.
Vancouver, British Columbia V6E 3R2
Canada
Key Contact: Rick Roberts

1170 Peel St.
Montreal, Quebec H3B 4T2 Canada
Key Contact: Michael Goodman

Coopers & Lybrand, Management Consulting Services

203 N. La Salle
Chicago, Illinois 60601
Salary Minimum: $60,000
Key Contact: Bob Murphy

Functions: Most + 01.0 01.1 01.2 01.3
Industries: Most + D.00 H.00 H.IO I.00
Professional Affiliations: IACPR, AICPA,
SHRP
Description: Executive search, organizational
planning and human resources consulting
services

Branches:
Ten Almaden Blvd., Ste. 1600
San Jose, California 95113
Key Contact: Steve Goveia

400 Renaissance Ctr.
Detroit, Michigan 48243
Key Contact: Jerry Habelmann

Cornell Int'l.

36 Winchip Rd.
Summit, New Jersey 07901
Salary Minimum: $75,000
Key Contact: H. Arthur Cornell
Marcia H. Cornell

Functions: 07.0 08.0
Industries: H.10 H.11
Description: A specialist firm in international
trading & finance

Corporate Environment Ltd.

P.O. Box 798
Crystal Lake, Illinois 60014-0798
Salary Minimum: $40,000
Key Contact: Tom McDermott

Functions: Most + 01.0 02.0 04.0 05.0 11.5
Industries: Most + B.00 B.0W D.00 H.00 I.00
Description: Specialty-environmental industry,
process capital equipment/services &
banking: general industrial

The Corporate Source Group

1 Cranberry Hill
Lexington, Massachusetts 02173
Key Contact: Dana Willis
Carolyn Culbreth

Functions: 01.0 03.2 05.1 08.0 09.0
Industries: D.18 D.E0 H.00 H.R0 J.10
Professional Affiliations: IACPR, NEHRA
Description: Specializing in targeted search for
difficult assignments. Performance
guaranteed

Washington, District of Columbia
Tampa, Florida

The Corporate Staff

400 S. El Camino Real, Ste. 780
San Mateo, California 94402
Salary Minimum: $50,000
Key Contact: Stephen T. Pickford

Functions: Most
Industries: Most
Professional Affiliations: CERA
Description: Personalized executive search
service. Also offer search for interim
executives

Corporate Staffing Group

Penns Court, 350 S. Main St.
Bldg. 213
Doylestown, Pennsylvania 18901
Salary Minimum: $45,000
Key Contact: C.D. Baker
L. B. Carey

Functions: 01.0 04.0 05.0 09.2 09.4
Industries: D.24 D.H0 J.00 J.13
Professional Affiliations: AFCEA, ISA, NATA,
USTA
Description: Marketing, engineering, executive
management, & technology search in the
telephone industry

The Corrigan Group

15135 Sunset Blvd., Ste. 201
Los Angeles, California 90272
Salary Minimum: $70,000
Key Contact: Gerald F. Corrigan

Functions: Most + 01.0 05.0 06.0 08.0 11.1
Industries: Most
Professional Affiliations: IACPR
Description: Professional search firm with
broad industry and functional recruitment
experience

Edmond J. Corry & Co., Inc.

637 Wyckoff Ave., Ste. 121
Wyckoff, New Jersey 07481
Salary Minimum: $100,000
Key Contact: Edmond J. Corry

Functions: Most
Industries: Most
Description: Highly personalized, research
based, with enviable reputation for
durable placements

Counsel Search Co.

124 N. Summit St., Ste. 305
Ft. Industry Sq.
Toledo, Ohio 43604
Key Contact: William M. Falvey

Functions: 01.5
Industries: Most
Description: Attorney recruitment only

The Crosby Group, Inc.

One Northbrook Place
5 Revere Dr., Ste. 200
Northbrook, Illinois 60062
Salary Minimum: $75,000
Key Contact: Elizabeth Langan
George W. Crosby

Functions: Most
Industries: Most
Professional Affiliations: ACA, HRMAC,
MSPC, NIIA
Description: H.R. consultants engaged in
search, compensation, employee relations,
organizational issues, etc.

Crowder & Company

877 S. Adams, Ste. 301
Birmingham, Michigan 48009
Salary Minimum: $60,000
Key Contact: Edward W. Crowder
Sherry L. Serpa
Nancy J. Turnquist

Functions: Most
Industries: D.00 D.H0 E.00 H.00 I.00
Professional Affiliations: ACG, BMA, SMPF
Description: Results-oriented firm committed
to the effective recruitment of leading
executives

M.J. Curran & Assoc., Inc.
75 State St., Ste. 2130
Boston, Massachusetts 02109
Salary Minimum: $75,000
Key Contact: Martin Curran

Functions: 01.0 02.0 06.0 08.0 09.0
Industries: D.00 D.H0 D.I0 H.00 I.00
Professional Affiliations: IACPR, DMA,
    NEHRA
Description: Senior level executives positions
    for growth industries & turnarounds

Curran Partners
224 Pearsall Pl.
Bridgeport, Connecticut 06605
Key Contact: Michael N. Curran

Functions: Most
Industries: Most
Description: Executive search service

Curry, Telleri Group, Inc.
86 N. Main St.
Milltown, New Jersey 08850
Salary Minimum: $40,000
Key Contact: Michael J. Curry
Frank C. Telleri

Functions: Most + 02.0 04.0 06.0 09.0 11.5
Industries: Most + D.00 D.15 D.18 D.20 D.I0
Professional Affiliations: ACS, AICHE, CDA,
    IEEE, SPE
Description: Nationwide executive search for
    chemical, plastics, pharmaceutical,
    electronic

The Curtiss Group, Inc.
2600 Military Trail
Boca Raton, Florida 33431
Salary Minimum: $60,000
Key Contact: William E. Frank, Jr.
Robert L. Beatty
John A. Farrell
Conrad P. Lee

Functions: Most
Industries: Most
Description: Executive search consultants,
    based in Florida, with international
    clientele

Peter Cusack & Partners, Inc.
30 Rockefeller Plz., Ste. 3314
New York, New York 10112
Salary Minimum: $75,000
Key Contact: Peter Cusack
Glenna Q. McNally

Functions: Most
Industries: Most
Description: Generalist firm with primary focus
    on corporate management disciplines

D E G Co., Inc.
30961 Agoura Rd., Ste. 227
Westlake Village, California 91361
Salary Minimum: $50,000
Key Contact: David E. Grumney

Functions: Most
Industries: D.14
Professional Affiliations: PIA
Description: Executive recruitment for the
    domestic printing and graphic arts
    industry

D'Aries Five Enterprises
P.O. Box 440667
Aurora, Colorado 80044-0667
Salary Minimum: $50,000
Key Contact: Delores Fritz

Functions: 01.5
Industries: Most
Description: A combined human resources
    service company

DCS Assoc., Inc.
11 Calle Medico, Ste. 2
Santa Fe, New Mexico 87501
Salary Minimum: $75,000
Key Contact: David Silver
Alan Fleischauer

Functions: 04.0 06.0
Industries: D.18 I.14 I.15 I.16
Description: Specialists in human resources,
    physicians & scientists for research

International Branches:
Rome

DHR Int'l., Inc.

10 S. Riverside Plz., Ste. 1650
Chicago, Illinois 60606
Salary Minimum: $50,000
Key Contact: David H. Hoffmann
Warren K. Hendriks, Jr.
Donna M. Skunda
William F. Kanzer
A. De Vries
P. DeMay
A. Ochota
H. Huette
Jim Coffou

Functions: Most
Industries: Most
Description: Generalist firm with specialty
practices and national & international
coverage

Branches:
1801 Avenue of the Stars, Ste. 640
Los Angeles, California 90067

2810 E. Oakland Park Blvd. Ste 304
Ft. Lauderdale, Florida 33306
Key Contact: Victor P. Viglino

248 Lorraine Ave.
Upper Montclair, New Jersey 07043
Key Contact: Rainette Bannon

International Branches:
London, San Juan

80 Park Ave.
New York, New York 10016
Key Contact: David M Richardson

5215 N. O'Connor, Ste 200
Irving, Texas 75039
Key Contact: Dorothy M. Billingsly
Jeff J. Dandurand

The DLR Group, Inc.

310 Madison Ave., Ste. 320
New York, New York 10017
Salary Minimum: $50,000
Key Contact: Daniel Lee Roberts
Marc S. Gouran

Functions: Most
Industries: H.I0 I.14 I.15 I.21
Professional Affiliations: GHAA
Description: Practices in the personnel services
industry & the managed healthcare/group
insurance industry

Dahl-Morrow Int'l.

12110 Sunset Hills Rd., Ste. 450
Reston, Virginia 22091
Salary Minimum: $100,000
Key Contact: Barbara Steinem

Functions: Most + 01.0 05.0 08.0 09.0
Industries: Most
Description: Provider of retained search &
interim assignments worldwide

Branches:
562011 Arbor Club Way
Boca Raton, Florida 33433
Key Contact: Kit Stelika

Marge Dana Assoc.

4 Lynn Ct.
East Haven, Connecticut 06512
Salary Minimum: $75,000
Key Contact: Marge Dana
Cynthia Darcy

Functions: Most + 01.0 02.0 05.0 08.0
Industries: Most + B.0W D.00 H.00 I.00
Description: A full service, nationwide firm
serving small to Fortune 100 clients

Danforth Group

21 Locust Ave.
New Canaan, Connecticut 06840
Salary Minimum: $80,000
Key Contact: A. Edwards Danforth

Functions: Most
Industries: H.00 H.I0 H.R0
Description: Banking, capital markets,
corporate finance and insurance nationally
and internationally

Alfred Daniels & Assoc.
5795 Waverly Ave.
La Jolla, California 92037
Salary Minimum: $50,000
Key Contact: Alfred Daniels
Lynn Scullion Reisfeld

Functions: 01.0 04.0 05.0 08.0 11.0
Industries: B.00 D.I0 H.00 H.R0 I.17
Description: Worldwide searches for American,
European, & Asian commercial &
investment banks

The Dartmouth Group
1200 Broadway, 7D-8D
New York, New York 10001
Salary Minimum: $50,000
Key Contact: Herbert F. Storfer
Nancy I. Johnson

Functions: 01.2 02.0 03.0 04.0 05.2
Industries: D.16 D.17 D.18 D.D0 I.16
Description: A highly professional, specialized
executive search firm offering focused,
personal service

William N. Davis & Assoc., Inc.
105 W. Market St.
P.O. Box 615
Sandusky, Ohio 44871-0615
Salary Minimum: $50,000
Key Contact: William N. Davis
William Wolfis
Monica Capizzi

Functions: Most
Industries: Most
Professional Affiliations: EMA
Description: Executive search, professional staff
& consulting to nearly every industry

John J. Davis & Assoc., Inc.
P.O. Box G
Short Hills, New Jersey 07078
Salary Minimum: $85,000
Key Contact: John J. Davis
John D. Simon
Jack P. Long
Jack Shea

Functions: 01.4 09.1 09.3 09.4 09.7
Industries: Most
Description: A retainer executive search
organization with a practice in
information systems management

Affiliates/Other Offices:
H.M. Long Int'l., Ltd., New York

Davis & Company
455 E. Eisenhower Pkwy.
Ste. 411
Ann Arbor, Michigan 48108
Salary Minimum: $50,000
Key Contact: G. Gordon Davis

Functions: Most
Industries: Most
Description: Generalist firm serving a limited
clientele for maximum effectiveness

Charles E. Day & Assoc., Inc.
1919 W. Stadium Blvd.
Ann Arbor, Michigan 48104
Salary Minimum: $50,000
Key Contact: Charles E. Day
Stanley B. Hone

Functions: Most + 01.0 02.0 04.0 05.0 08.0
Industries: Most + D.00 D.23 D.E0 D.H0
Professional Affiliations: AHS, ASM, ESD,
ISHM, SAE, SME
Description: Primarily engaged in
transportation, foundry, machine tool,
aerospace & related mfg. activities

De Funiak & Edwards
10207 Old Hunt Rd.
Vienna, Virginia 22181
Salary Minimum: $50,000
Key Contact: William S. De Funiak
Randolph J. Edwards

Functions: 01.0 09.3 11.1
Industries: H.I0
Professional Affiliations: NAER
Description: National practice specializing in
insurance information systems &
administration

Branches:
211 W. Chicago Ave., Ste 116
Hinsdale, Illinois 60521

DeHayes Consulting Group
3300 Douglas Blvd., #385
Roseville, California 95661-3829
Salary Minimum: $70,000
Key Contact: A. James De Hayes
Steve Rekedal
Joe Villa
Vicki Munoz

Functions: Most + 01.0 02.0 05.0 08.0 10.0
Industries: Most + D.00 H.00 H.I0 I.00
Professional Affiliations: CERA
Description: Middle & senior management
 search on general industry basis

Branches:
191 Post Rd. W.
Westport, Connecticut 06880
Key Contact: Oscar Scofield

100 Allentown Pkwy., Ste. 218
Allen, Texas 75002
Key Contact: Robert A. Fryer

Deane, Howard & Simon, Inc.
81 Wethersfield Ave.
Hartford, Connecticut 06114
Salary Minimum: $125,000
Key Contact: Robert A. Simon

Functions: Most
Industries: Most + D.00 D.H0 H.00 H.I0
 H.R0
Professional Affiliations: AESC, IACPR,
 SHRM
Description: High quality boutique with
 significant research & documentation skills

Branches:
102 Via Teresa
Los Gatos, California 95030
Key Contact: Howard D. Nitchke

Thorndike Deland Assoc.
275 Madison, 13th Fl.
New York, New York 10016
Salary Minimum: $75,000
Key Contact: Howard Bratches
J. Carideo
Thorndike Deland
L. Hoyda
Dennis Devere
Sheila Pianin

Functions: Most
Industries: Most
Professional Affiliations: AESC, NRMA
Description: Specialize in retailing, consumer
 goods & services & industrial search

Networks:
Greenwich International Group
London, Paris, Milan, Madrid, Brussels

Denney & Co., Inc.
Three Gateway Ctr., 16 N.
Pittsburgh, Pennsylvania 15222
Salary Minimum: $125,000
Key Contact: Thomas L. Denney
John W. Thornton
Arthur W. Gregg
Alexander M. Laughlin

Functions: Most
Industries: Most
Professional Affiliations: AESC
Description: Since 1972, consultants in
 executive search and acquisition search

Development Search Specialists
W1072 First National Bank Bldg.
St. Paul, Minnesota 55101-1312
Salary Minimum: $50,000
Key Contact: Fred J. Lauerman

Functions: 11.4
Industries: I.12 I.13
Professional Affiliations: CASE, NSFRE
Description: Senior-level nonprofit fundraising
 executives

Deven Assoc., Int'l., Inc.
1 Claridge Dr.
Verona, New Jersey 07044
Salary Minimum: $75,000
Key Contact: John P. DiVenuto
Peter T. Maher
Paul A. Verstraete

Branches:
18662 MacArthur Blvd., Ste. 200
Irvine, California 92715

International Branches:
Birmingham, Frankfurt, London

Affiliates/Other Offices:
Daniel Porte Consultants, Paris la Defense
Harper & Lynch, Madrid
Selectra Group Conseil Int'l., Pointe-Claire

Functions: Most
Industries: Most
Professional Affiliations: IACPR, IMC
Description: Medium sized multi-office
    international search practice and client
    base, generalists

15250 Ventura Blvd., Ste. 1108
Sherman Oaks, California 91403
Key Contact: Paul A. Verstraete

1 Dag Hammarskjold Plz.
New York, New York 10017

DiMarchi Partners
1225 17th St.
Denver, Colorado 80202
Salary Minimum: $45,000
Key Contact: Paul DiMarchi
Lynn Jordan
Woody Daroca
Carolyn Sherman

Functions: Most + 01.0 02.0 05.0 08.0 09.0
Industries: Most + D.00 G.00 H.00 H.I0 I.00
Professional Affiliations: IACPR
Description: Generalist firm, national scope,
    searches for "key contributors"

Dieckmann & Assoc., Ltd.
75 E. Wacker Dr., Ste. 1800
Chicago, Illinois 60601
Salary Minimum: $60,000
Key Contact: Ralph E. Dieckmann
James F. McSherry
Kathleen M. Miller
Susan C. Khoury
Terence N. Burns

Affiliates/Other Offices:
Bragg & Co., Melbourne
Clive & Stokes Int'l., London
Executive Access Limited, Wanchai
Executive Resources, Ltd., Johannesburg
Hansar-Exsel Ltd., Athens
Hansar Int'l., S.A., Brussels
Hommes & Enterprises, Paris
P.A.R. Assoc., Inc., Boston
Ten Bokkel Huinink b.v., Utrecht
Youngs & Co., Dallas
Zay & Company, Atlanta

Functions: Most + 01.0 02.0 05.0 06.0 08.0
Industries: Most + D.00 D.D0 H.00 H.I0 I.00
Professional Affiliations: AESC, IACPR, EMA,
    HRMAC, ISA
Description: Small, internationally affiliated,
    highly professional generalist practice

Robert W. Dingman Co., Inc.
32131 W. Lindero Canyon Rd.
Westlake Village, California 91361
Salary Minimum: $75,000
Key Contact: Robert W. Dingman
Bruce Dingman

Functions: 01.0 02.0 05.0 06.0 08.0
Industries: D.00 D.E0 D.H0 I.00 I.10
Professional Affiliations: AESC, IACPR, CERA
Description: Senior management level searches
    in most industries & functions

R. J. Dishaw & Assoc.

5440 Harvest Hill Rd., Ste. 125
Dallas, Texas 75230
Salary Minimum: $50,000
Key Contact: Raymond J. Dishaw
Robert Buster

Functions: Most
Industries: Most
Description: A generalist firm specializing in
quality service

Diversified Health Search

2005 Market St., Ste. 3300
One Commerce Sq.
Philadelphia, Pennsylvania 19103
Salary Minimum: $60,000
Key Contact: Judith M. Von Seldeneck
L. Wood Von Seldeneck, Jr.
Claire W. Gargalli

Functions: Most
Industries: I.14 I.15
Professional Affiliations: IACPR
Description: National executive search
consultants specializing in the healthcare
industry

Diversified Search, Inc.

2005 Market St., Ste. 3300
One Commerce Sq.
Philadelphia, Pennsylvania 19103
Salary Minimum: $75,000
Key Contact: Judith M. Von Seldeneck
L. Wood Von Seldeneck, Jr.
Claire W. Gargalli

Functions: Most
Industries: Most
Professional Affiliations: AESC, IACPR
Description: Diversified executive search firm,
founded 1971, serving regional & national
clients

The Domann Organization

One Sansome St., Ste. 1900
Citicorp Ctr.
San Francisco, California 94104
Salary Minimum: $50,000
Key Contact: William A. Domann, Jr.

Functions: 01.2 02.1 03.2 05.3 11.3
Industries: D.17 D.18 D.I0
Description: Specialists in all medical products
and services industries

Donahue/Bales Assoc.

303 W. Madison, Ste. 1150
Chicago, Illinois 60606
Salary Minimum: $60,000
Key Contact: E.M. Donahue
L. Patrick Bales

Affiliates/Other Offices:
Associates In Executive Search, Ltd., Surrey

Functions: Most + 01.0 02.0 05.0 08.0 09.0
Industries: Most + D.00 D.E0 D.H0 H.00 I.00
Professional Affiliations: IMESC
Description: General practice encompasses
most functional areas

Dougan-McKinley-Strain

The Phoenix Twr., 33rd Fl.
3200 Southwest Fwy.
Houston, Texas 77027-7526
Key Contact: James M. McKinley
Lee Strain

International Branches:
London

Branches:
16800 Imperial Valley Dr., Ste. 220
Houston, Texas 77060
Key Contact: David W. Dougan

Functions: Most + 01.0 02.0 04.0 06.0 08.0
Industries: B.00 B.0W C.00 D.15 H.00
Description: International firm conducting
senior executive and board of directors
searches

Drew Assoc. Int'l.
77 Park St.
Montclair, New Jersey 07042
Salary Minimum: $60,000
Key Contact: Robert R. Detore
Mary Ellen Scaturro
Charles Vevier
Dr. Reginald K. Jenkins
Michael Coon

Functions: 10.0 11.1 11.2 11.3 11.4
Industries: I.13 I.14 I.15 I.16 I.21
Professional Affiliations: NAPR
Description: Consultants to the health care
industry for executive, physician & foreign
nurse selection

Dromeshauser Assoc.
20 William St., Ste. 215
Wellesley, Massachusetts 02181
Salary Minimum: $80,000
Key Contact: Peter Dromeshauser

Functions: 01.0 02.0 05.0 09.0
Industries: D.24 D.25 J.00
Description: Hi tech & senior management;
computers, software & hardware,
communications & information services

Affiliates/Other Offices:
Mather & Co., Mill Valley

Duggan & Company
10050 N. Wolfe Rd., Ste. 270
Cupertino, California 95014
Salary Minimum: $100,000
Key Contact: Edward J. Duggan

Functions: Most + 01.0 01.1 01.2 09.2
Industries: D.24 D.H0 J.13
Description: Searches are limited to senior
executives for high technology companies

The Duncan Group Inc.
341 Madison Ave., 18th Fl.
New York, New York 10017
Salary Minimum: $25,000
Key Contact: Melba J. Duncan

Functions: Most
Industries: Most + B.00 H.10
Description: Recruitment of executive
secretaries, administrative assistants &
office administrators

Michael S. Dunford, Inc.
478 Pennsylvania Ave., Ste. 301
Glen Ellyn, Illinois 60137
Salary Minimum: $150,000
Key Contact: Michael S. Dunford

Functions: 01.0 04.0 05.0 09.0 11.4
Industries: D.00 D.H0 H.00 H.I0 I.00
Description: Generalist firm focusing on
executive level positions over $150,000

S.R. Dunlap & Assoc., Inc.
100 W. Long Lake Rd., Ste.112
Bloomfield Hills, Michigan 48304
Salary Minimum: $50,000
Key Contact: Stanley R. Dunlap

Functions: Most
Industries: Most
Description: Medium-sized professional
generalist firm, basically Midwest clients

Dupuis & Ryden, P.C.
124 E. Fourth St.
Flint, Michigan 48502
Salary Minimum: $30,000
Key Contact: Nancy Rosevear
Linda Holloway

Functions: 01.0 02.0 05.0 06.0 08.0
Industries: C.00 D.00 F.00 I.00 J.00
Description: Public accounting & consulting
firm-90 person firm-59 year history

Branches:
100 W. Big Beaver Rd., Ste. 350
Troy, Michigan 48084

North Towne Professional Ctr.
14165 N. Fenton Rd.
Fenton, Michigan 48430
Key Contact: Kim Virkler

C. A. Durakis Assoc., Inc.
1 Post Rd.
Fairfield, Connecticut 06430
Salary Minimum: $80,000
Key Contact: Charles A. Durakis, Sr.
John F. Corbani
Charles Durakis, Jr.

Branches:
Center Park
4041 Powder Mill Rd., Ste. 300
Calverton, Maryland 20705

Functions: Most
Industries: Most
Description: General practice searches; senior executive & middle management—all industries

Lynn Dwigans & Co.
1610 Lawrence Rd.
Danville, California 94506
Salary Minimum: $60,000
Key Contact: Lynn Dwigans

Functions: 07.0 08.0 08.1 08.2 08.3
Industries: D.00 D.10 D.24 D.H0
Description: Retained firm specializing in the recruitment of financial, MIS & adminstrative executives

Dwyer Consulting Group, Inc.
303 E. 57th St.
New York, New York 10022
Salary Minimum: $75,000
Key Contact: Gilbert E. Dwyer

Affiliates/Other Offices:
Cameron Consulting Group, San Francisco

Functions: Most + 01.0 02.0 04.0 08.0 11.3
Industries: Most + D.10 D.18 D.20 D.I0 I.00
Description: A broad and general executive recruiting & consulting practice

EFL Assoc.
7101 College Blvd., Ste. 550
Overland Park, Kansas 66210-1891
Salary Minimum: $50,000
Key Contact: Peter K. Lemke
Harold D. Brannan
Evelyn C. Davis
Karen S. Barnes

Branches:
5271 S. Quebec, Ste. 110
Denver, Colorado 80111
Key Contact: Jeffrey K. Riley

Functions: Most
Industries: Most
Professional Affiliations: ASPA, ASTD
Description: Executive search, outplacement & psychological testing for diverse client base

ESP Management Services, Inc.
P.O. Box 14
Rockville Centre
New York, New York 11571
Salary Minimum: $60,000
Key Contact: John Foehl

Functions: 01.2 01.3 05.0 06.0 08.0
Industries: H.00 H.10 H.I0 H.R0 I.21
Description: Independent retainer search firm specializing in financial services

Earley Kielty & Assoc., Inc.
2 Pennsylvania Pl.
New York, New York 10121
Salary Minimum: $50,000
Key Contact: John L. Kielty, III
Martin R. Levine
Eugene Hersman
Jay Stirling

Functions: Most
Industries: Most
Professional Affiliations: IACPR, AICPA, ASPA, NAA
Description: Executive search firm specializing in financial & general management, MIS & human resources

Branches:
One Landmark Sq., Ste. 801
Stamford, Connecticut 06901
Key Contact: Frank E. Jones

Bert H. Early Assoc., Inc.
55 E. Monroe St., Ste. 4530
Chicago, Illinois 60603-5805
Salary Minimum: $75,000
Key Contact: Bert Early
B. Tucker Olson

Functions: 01.5
Industries: Most
Description: Corporate and law firm retainer
search for senior lawyers

Eastman & Beaudine, Inc.
1370 One Galleria Twr.
13355 Noel Rd., LB-31
Dallas, Texas 75240
Salary Minimum: $60,000
Key Contact: Robert E. Beaudine
Frank R. Beaudine

Functions: Most
Industries: Most
Description: Consultants to management in
executive selection

Branches:
1117 Perimeter Center W., Ste. 500E
Atlanta, Georgia 30338
Key Contact: Frank R. Beaudine, Jr.

Ebbert Assoc.
1625 Paine Ct.
Claremont, California 91711
Salary Minimum: $50,000
Key Contact: Duane Ebbert

Functions: Most + 01.3 02.0 02.1 04.0 08.0
Industries: D.00 D.H0
Professional Affiliations: IMC
Description: Regional search generalist
covering Southern California

Educational Management Network
Box 792
Nantucket, Massachusetts 02554
Key Contact: Nancy Archer-Martin
Evelyn Danforth
Binth Rustad
Mimi Young
Nancy Critchell
Helen Seager

Functions: 01.2 08.2 09.3 11.2 11.4
Industries: I.13 J.10 L.00
Professional Affiliations: ACE, CASE
Description: Executive search & human
resources consulting in education & not-
for-profit community

Bruce Edwards & Associates, Inc.
1 University Pl., Ste. 210
Durham, North Carolina 27707
Salary Minimum: $50,000
Key Contact: Bruce Edwards

Functions: Most
Industries: Most
Description: Retained generalist executive &
professional search firm

Effective Search, Inc.
7811 N. Alpine, Ste. 210
Rockford, Illinois 61111
Salary Minimum: $40,000
Key Contact: John A. Cain
Gordon C. Quimby
Philip W. Devoir

Functions: Most + 01.0 02.0 04.0 05.0 08.0
Industries: Most + D.00 D.22 D.24 D.E0
D.H0
Professional Affiliations: ASM, FMA, SME
Description: Specializing in management
positions for all functional areas requiring
technical degrees

Branches:
3601 Algonquin Rd., Ste. 207
Rolling Meadows, Illinois 61008
Key Contact: Chris A. Anderson

Egan & Assoc.
White House Ctr., 128 S. Sixth Ave.
West Bend, Wisconsin 53095
Salary Minimum: $55,000
Key Contact: Daniel K. Egan
John J. Kuhn
Joy V. Massar

Eggleston Consulting Int'l.
5 Concourse Pkwy, Ste 3100
Atlanta, Georgia 30328
Salary Minimum: $100,000
Key Contact: G. Dudley Eggleston

William J. Elam & Assoc.
434 Greentree Ct.
Lincoln, Nebraska 68505-2438
Salary Minimum: $75,000
Key Contact: William J. Elam, Jr.
Renee A. Lengeling

The Elliott Company
400 W. Cummings Park, Ste. 2750
Woburn, Massachusetts 01801
Salary Minimum: $70,000
Key Contact: Roger S. Elliott

Elliott, Pfisterer, Chinetti Assoc., Inc.
333 W. Wacker Dr., Ste 2600
Chicago, Illinois 60606
Salary Minimum: $100,000
Key Contact: Peter J. Chinetti
John G. Elliott

David M. Ellner Assoc.
2 Penn Plaza, Ste. 1500
New York, New York 10121
Salary Minimum: $50,000
Key Contact: David M. Ellner

The Elson Group, Inc.
510 Lake Cook Rd., Ste. 350
Deerfield, Illinois 60015
Salary Minimum: $40,000
Key Contact: John B. Elson

402 Wood Dr., Ste. 102
Philadelphia, Pennsylvania 19422
Key Contact: Craig Toedtman

Functions: Most
Industries: Most
Description: Perform executive searches on a retainer basis only—no contingency work performed

Functions: Most
Industries: H.R0
Professional Affiliations: ICSC, NAIOP, ULI
Description: Specialize in real estate exclusively retained search in all functional areas

Functions: Most + 02.0 04.0 05.0 09.0 10.0
Industries: D.18 D.23 D.I0 H.I0 I.14
Professional Affiliations: APAA
Description: Professionals out of industry-focus on automotive & pharmaceuticals industries

Functions: Most + 01.0 05.0 06.0 08.0 11.0
Industries: Most + D.00 I.00 L.00
Description: Multinational retained practice broadly spread by clients & project activity

Functions: Most + 06.1 06.2
Industries: Most
Professional Affiliations: APA
Description: Our practice is focused on executive search, managerial & executive assessment & OD

Functions: Most + 02.0 04.0 05.0 08.0 09.0
Industries: D.00 H.00 H.I0 H.R0 J.11
Description: Executive search services tailored to the small & medium sized organization

Functions: Most + 02.0 03.0 05.0 08.0 11.0
Industries: Most + D.00 D.D0 H.00 I.00 K.00
Description: Search for manufacturing/distribution; financial services & general assignments

Elwell & Assoc., Inc.

301 E. Liberty, Ste. 535
Ann Arbor, Michigan 48104
Salary Minimum: $75,000
Key Contact: Richard F. Elwell
David A. Gilmore

Functions: Most
Industries: Most
Professional Affiliations: AESC
Description: A generalist firm serving multiple
industries & disciplines nationwide

Emmons Assoc., Inc.

226 Lost District Dr.
New Canaan, Connecticut 06840
Salary Minimum: $100,000
Key Contact: William F. Emmons

Functions: Most
Industries: Most + D.24
Description: Serve manufacturers & users of
computer and communications products
& services

Empire International

1147 Lancaster Ave.
Berwyn, Pennsylvania 19312
Salary Minimum: $50,000
Key Contact: Charles V. Combe, II
M.J. Stanford
R. Loprete
Donald B. Lynch
Steve D. Neri

Functions: Most
Industries: D.15 D.20 D.21 D.H0 L.00
Professional Affiliations: ACS, CMA, IPMI,
ISHM, SPIE
Description: Clients in chemicals/precious
metals/electronics/ceramics/medical/
biotechnology/environmental

George Enns Partners Inc.

70 University Ave., Ste. 410
P.O. Box 14
Toronto, Ontario M5J 2M4 Canada
Salary Minimum: $80,000
Key Contact: George Enns
Roy Miller
Alan Burns

Functions: Most
Industries: Most
Professional Affiliations: AESC
Description: Experienced cnslt. firm serving the
sr. executive search requirements of org.
across Canada

Mary R. Erickson & Assoc.

8300 Norman Center Dr., Ste. 545
Minneapolis, Minnesota 55437
Salary Minimum: $70,000
Key Contact: Mary R. Erickson

Functions: Most
Industries: Most
Description: Generalist firm serving senior
management in executive acquisition &
organizational consulting

Erlanger Assoc.

2 Pickwick Plz.
Greenwich, Connecticut 06830
Salary Minimum: $100,000
Key Contact: Richard A. Erlanger
Catherine A. Porter

Branches:
777 S. Flagler Dr.
8th Fl., West Tower
West Palm Beach, Florida 33401

Functions: Most + 01.0 02.0 05.0
Industries: Most + D.00 D.D0 D.H0 D.I0
H.00
Description: Focus on searches for line
executives in buyouts & turnarounds

Erwin Assoc.

2021 Midwest Rd., Ste. 200
Oak Brook, Illinois 60521
Salary Minimum: $75,000
Key Contact: John T. Cizek
Ronald R. Erwin

Functions: 01.2 02.2 02.4 03.1 05.4
Industries: Most
Description: Generalist firm serving
manufacturing & service businesses -
special competence in metal working

Euromedica USA
6964 Hill Ct., The Pinery
Parker, Colorado 80134
Salary Minimum: $50,000
Key Contact: Sarah Carr

Functions: 01.0 02.1 04.0 05.0 11.3
Industries: D.17 D.18 I.14 I.15 I.16
Professional Affiliations: ASSC
Description: International executive search in healthcare industry, specializing in European issues

International Branches:
Brussels, London, Paris, Wiesbaden

Excelsior Services Group Inc.
1010 Wayne Ave., Ste. 520
Silver Spring, Maryland 20910
Salary Minimum: $30,000
Key Contact: Will Phillips
W. Juan McAlister

Functions: Most + 01.0 05.0 06.0 11.0 11.6
Industries: Most + D.E0 D.H0 J.00 K.00
Professional Affiliations: BDPA
Description: We provide staffing solutions to industry & government

Branches:
3110 Vickers Dr.
P.O. Box 2572
Colorado Springs, Colorado 80918
Key Contact: Wendell Phillips

ExecuCounsel Management Consultants Inc.
1235 Bay St., Ste. 500
Toronto, Ontario M5R 3K4 Canada
Salary Minimum: $70,000
Key Contact: Dick Marty

Functions: Most + 01.0 02.0 05.0 06.0 08.0
Industries: Most
Description: Specialist in senior executive & CEO recruitment; leader in healthcare/ hospital sector

Executive Appointments Ltd., Int'l.
1100 Jorie Blvd., Ste. 215
Oak Brook, Illinois 60521
Salary Minimum: $60,000
Key Contact: Kenneth L. Moss
Susan M. Blazek

Functions: 01.0 02.0 05.0 08.0 09.0
Industries: D.00 D.10 D.18 D.24 I.14
Description: A general management firm committed to excellence, ethics & results

Branches:
263 Center Ave.
Westwood, New Jersey 07675
Key Contact: Jay M. Fink

Affiliates/Other Offices:
Ober & Company, Los Angeles

Executive Management Systems, Inc.
9191 Towne Centre Dr., Ste. 105
San Diego, California 92122
Salary Minimum: $60,000
Key Contact: Paul X. Bouzan
Lincoln R. Ward

Functions: Most + 01.2 01.5 11.4 11.5
Industries: Most
Description: General industrial search practice; hi-tech, engineering, legal, finance/ banking, biotechnology

Executive Manning Corp.
3000 NE 30th Place, Ste. 405
Ft. Lauderdale, Florida 33306
Salary Minimum: $100,000
Key Contact: Richard L. Hertan
William A. Hertan

Functions: Most
Industries: Most
Description: Services cover entire range of personnel consulting & recruitment

Executive Profiles Inc.
17 Sword St.
Toronto, Ontario M5A 3N3 Canada
Salary Minimum: $65,000
Key Contact: Marnie Keith-Murray

Functions: 05.5 11.5 11.6
Industries: I.13
Professional Affiliations: ICMCC
Description: Specializing in environment,
      engineering & direct marketing recruiting
      in Canada

Executive Quest
6342 Forest Hill Blvd., Ste. 336
West Palm Beach, Florida 33415
Salary Minimum: $50,000
Key Contact: David Lance
Alice R. Lance

Functions: Most + 01.2 01.3 06.0
Industries: I.14
Professional Affiliations: ASHHRA, SHRM
Description: Healthcare/hospitals; we blend
      organization analysis & human chemisty;
      reasonable & effective

Executive Resource Group
29 Oakhurst Rd.
Cape Elizabeth, Maine 04107
Salary Minimum: $50,000
Key Contact: Sibyl Masquelier

Functions: Most
Industries: D.00 D.D0 D.E0 D.H0 J.11
Description: Speed, thoroughness,
      confidentiality & economy in executive
      search

Executive Search Inc.
5401 Gamble Dr., Ste. 275
Parkdale One
Minneapolis, Minnesota 55416
Salary Minimum: $50,000
Key Contact: James G. Gresham
Nanette Wiley

Functions: Most
Industries: Most
Description: Provide exacting search &
      evaluation for upper management
      positions

Raymond L. Extract & Assoc.
20501 Ventura Blvd., Ste. 112
Woodland Hills, California 91364
Salary Minimum: $60,000
Key Contact: Raymond L. Extract

Functions: Most
Industries: Most
Description: Broad range of executive search
      services primarily for California clients

FGI
1593 Spring Hill Rd., Ste. 410
Vienna, Virginia 22182
Salary Minimum: $50,000
Key Contact: Fred C. Gloss

Functions: 01.2 04.0 05.2
Industries: D.E0 D.H0 J.13
Professional Affiliations: ADPA, AFA, AFCEA,
      AIAA, AOC, ITEA, MORS, SSPI
Description: Specialty: national defense/
      security, aerospace, telecommunications,
      & high technology industries

Fagan & Co.
Robb Rd., P.O. Box 611
Ligonier, Pennsylvania 15658
Salary Minimum: $50,000
Key Contact: Stephanie L. Bronder
Charles A. Fagan, III
Alfred N. Pilz

Functions: Most + 01.0 02.0 05.0 11.4
Industries: Most + D.00 D.H0 H.00 I.00
Description: Executive search & consulting
      services for American & European clients

Fairfaxx Management Assoc.
100B East Ave.
Norwalk, Connecticut 06851
Salary Minimum: $75,000
Key Contact: Jeffrey Thomas

Description: Executive search, domestic &
      international

Hill Fallon & Assoc.

712 Whistler Dr.
Arlington, Texas 76006
Salary Minimum: $50,000
Key Contact: Hillman O. Fallon

Functions: Most + 02.0 06.0 08.0
Industries: D.00 G.00 H.00 H.I0
Professional Affiliations: ASTD, HRPS, SERC
Description: Quiet, confidential firm known for ability to identify upper quartile performers

Leon A. Farley Assoc.

468 Jackson St.
San Francisco, California 94111
Salary Minimum: $100,000
Key Contact: Creighton E. Barton
Leon A. Farley
Patricia L. Wilson

Functions: Most + 01.0 02.0 05.0 08.0
Industries: Most
Professional Affiliations: AESC, IACPR, CERA
Description: Senior level searches in the U.S., Canada, Hong Kong, U.K., Europe & Australia

Networks:
Penrhyn Partners Int'l.
Hong Kong, London, Long Beach, Melbourne VIC, New York, Toronto

Farrell & Phin, Inc.

845 Third Ave.
New York, New York 10022
Salary Minimum: $50,000
Key Contact: Frank J. Farrell, Jr.
Jane G. Phin

Functions: Most
Industries: D.14 J.11
Description: Generalist firm-special expertise in infor/media

James Farris Assoc.

4900 Richmond Square, Ste. 201
Oklahoma City, Oklahoma 73118
Salary Minimum: $40,000
Key Contact: James W. Farris

Functions: Most
Industries: Most
Description: Executive search & consulting services for mid to top level

George Fee Assoc., Inc.

345 N. Canal St., Ste. 308
Chicago, Illinois 60606
Salary Minimum: $75,000
Key Contact: Richard C. Quaintance

Functions: Most + 01.0 01.2 06.0 08.0 11.5
Industries: Most + B.0W D.00 D.H0 H.00 I.17
Description: Recruit attorneys for law firms corporate law departments

James Feerst & Assoc., Inc.

One Northfield Plz., Ste. 330
Northfield, Illinois 60093
Salary Minimum: $40,000
Key Contact: James E. Feerst

Functions: Most + 01.0 02.0 04.0 05.0
Industries: D.17 D.18 D.I0 I.15 I.16
Description: Search leader in pharmaceuticals, biotechnology, diagnostics & medical devices

Fenwick Partners

57 Bedford St., Ste. 101
Lexington, Massachusetts 02173
Salary Minimum: $75,000
Key Contact: Pamela Kostka

Functions: Most + 01.0 02.0 05.0 09.0 11.5
Industries: B.0W D.24 D.25 D.H0 J.13
Professional Affiliations: AESC, ACG, EMA, NEHRA
Description: Top quality, multi-specialty firm with clients & international affiliates

Affiliates/Other Offices:
Kieffer, Ford, & Hadelman, Ltd., Oak Brook
Kors Montgomery Int'l., Houston
Baker-Harris & Partners, Ltd., Toronto
Civitas Int'l. GmbH, Munich
IMCA Group, Tokyo
Jamieson Scott Executive Search, London
Technology Consulting S.R.C., Milan

Finnegan Assoc.

P.O. Box 1183
Palos Verdes Estates, California 90274-1938
Salary Minimum: $90,000
Key Contact: Richard Finnegan

Functions: Most + 01.0 02.0 04.0 05.0 08.0
Industries: D.E0 D.H0 D.I0 H.00 K.00
Description: A national & international
    management consulting/executive search
    firm

Fiordalis Assoc., Inc.

600 Crown Oak Ctr. Dr.
Longwood, Florida 32750
Salary Minimum: $75,000
Key Contact: Stuart Clark Fiordalis

Functions: Most + 01.0 05.0 06.0 08.0
Industries: I.14 I.15
Description: Retainer only, concentrating on
    senior assignments in healthcare &
    physician management

First Colorado Consulting Group, Inc.

10730 E. Bethany Dr, Ste 309
Aurora, Colorado 80014
Salary Minimum: $35,000
Key Contact: Daniel J. Kerstein
Michael J. Zabinski

Functions: Most + 02.1 06.0 11.3
Industries: Most + D.00 D.H0 H.00
Professional Affiliations: ASTD, SHRM
Description: Executive search/human resource
    consulting

Howard Fischer Assoc., Inc.

1530 Chestnut St., Ste. 800
Philadelphia, Pennsylvania 19102
Salary Minimum: $75,000
Key Contact: Howard M. Fischer

Functions: 01.0 02.0 03.0 04.0 05.0
Industries: Most
Professional Affiliations: IACPR, NACD
Description: Executive search generalist
    headquartered in the Delaware Valley

Fisher Personnel Management Services

1219 Morningside Drive
Manhattan Beach, California 90266
Salary Minimum: $50,000
Key Contact: Neal Fisher

Functions: 01.0 02.0 03.0 05.0 09.0
Industries: D.22 D.23 D.24 D.E0 D.H0
Professional Affiliations: IACPR, CERA
Description: Services the aerospace, aircraft,
    electronics, computer & trucking
    manufacturing companies

Fleming Energy Group

One Landmark Sq., Ste. 805
Stamford, Connecticut 06901
Salary Minimum: $60,000
Key Contact: Robert L. Burr, Jr.

Functions: Most
Industries: B.00 B.0W
Professional Affiliations: AGA, AGE, ANS,
    ASCE, ASME, IEEE, ISA
Description: Executive recruitment within the
    utility & energy related industries

Fogec Consultants

400 N. Executive Dr., Ste. 455
Brookfield, Wisconsin 53005
Salary Minimum: $40,000
Key Contact: Thomas G. Fogec

Functions: Most + 01.0 02.0 05.0 06.0 08.0
Industries: Most + B.00 D.00 H.10 I.14 J.11
Professional Affiliations: EMA, PIRA, SHRM
Description: Specialize in executive, managerial
    & professional positions across industry
    lines

J. H. Folger Company
17 Kenneth Rd.
Marblehead, Massachusetts 01945
Salary Minimum: $60,000
Key Contact: J.H. Folger

Functions: Most
Industries: Most
Professional Affiliations: AAA, IMC
Description: Upper & middle echelon executive search & board members

L.W. Foote Co.
110-110th Ave. NE, Ste. 680
Bellevue, Washington 98004
Salary Minimum: $70,000
Key Contact: Lee Foote

Functions: Most
Industries: Most

D.E. Foster & Partners, L.P.
345 Park Ave., 40 Fl.
New York, New York 10154
Salary Minimum: $60,000
Key Contact: Dwight E. Foster
Joan Higbee

Functions: Most
Industries: Most
Description: A generalist firm that provides a worldwide service to a wide array of disciplines

Branches:
3001 Summer St., Stamford Sq.
Stamford, Connecticut 06905
Key Contact: G. Charles Roy

90 S. Seventh St.
4200 Norwest Center
Minneapolis, Minnesota 55402
Key Contact: Robert Lyngen

2001 M St., NW
Washington, District of Columbia 20036
Key Contact: Dann P. Stringer

Thanksgiving Tower, Ste. 1400
1601 Elm Street
Dallas, Texas 75201
Key Contact: J. Richard Davis

Affiliates/Other Offices:
KPMG Klynveld Adviseurs voor Personeel Management, Utrecht
KPMG Cofror Management, Courbevoie
KPMG Peat Marwick Consultants S.N.C., Milan
KPMG Peat Marwick McLintock Management Consultants, London
PEAT, Int'l. Consultants S.A., Zurich
PMM Management Consultants GmbH, Frankfurt

Stephen Fox Assoc. Inc.
4712 N. Sabath
McHenry, Illinois 60050
Salary Minimum: $50,000
Key Contact: Stephen Fox

Functions: Most + 02.0 03.0 04.0 05.0 06.0
Industries: D.00 D.15 D.19 D.E0 D.H0
Professional Affiliations: IMESC
Description: Industrial manufacturers-functions usually mfg., engineering, marketing, quality control & finance

Fox Hill Assoc., Ltd.
250 Regency Ct.
Waukesha, Wisconsin 53186
Key Contact: Charles E. Jack, III

Functions: 11.0
Industries: I.15
Professional Affiliations: NAPR
Description: Physician recruitment firm serving clients nationwide since 1976

Foy, Schneid & Daniel, Inc.
509 Madison Ave., Ste 1400
New York, New York 10022
Salary Minimum: $60,000
Key Contact: James C. Foy
Beverly R. Daniel

Functions: 01.0 02.0 05.0 06.0 08.0
Industries: Most
Description: Professional executive search practice with targeted experience in most industries

Francis & Assoc.

6923 Vista Dr.
West Des Moines, Iowa 50265
Salary Minimum: $50,000
Key Contact: Dwaine Francis
N. Kay Francis

Functions: Most
Industries: Most
Description: Very professional firm, known for high quality & timely work

Gerald Frisch Assoc., Inc.

380 Madison Ave., Ste. 503
New York, New York 10017
Salary Minimum: $70,000
Key Contact: Gerald Frisch

Functions: Most + 02.5 05.0 06.0 08.0 09.0
Industries: Most + J.00
Professional Affiliations: IBRT, IMRT
Description: Offering the exclusive GFA planned executive search system

Fulton, Longshore & Assoc., Inc.

527 Plymouth Rd., Ste. 410
Plymouth Meeting, Pennsylvania 19462
Salary Minimum: $50,000
Key Contact: A. A. Fulton
George F. Longshore

Functions: 01.1 06.1 11.0
Industries: I.14 I.15
Professional Affiliations: AHA, AMA, AOHA, COTH, NAPR
Description: Professional search firm, professional search assignments in service industries

Furlong—Gates, Inc.

26540 Agoura Rd.
Calabasas, California 91302
Salary Minimum: $60,000
Key Contact: Edward Gates

Functions: Most
Industries: D.24 D.25
Professional Affiliations: AEA, CERA
Description: Oldest retained search firm serving the electronic industry exclusively

Branches:
2465 E. Bayshore Rd.
Palo Alto, California 94303
Key Contact: James W. Furlong

The Furman Group, Ltd.

5 E. 22nd St., Ste. 24C
New York, New York 10010
Salary Minimum: $50,000
Key Contact: Barbara Furman

Functions: 01.0 08.0
Industries: D.26 H.00 H.10 H.11
Professional Affiliations: IACPR, APA
Description: Financial management for manufacturing & financial service companies

GKR Int'l.

200 Galleria Pkwy., Ste. 630
Atlanta, Georgia 30339
Salary Minimum: $75,000
Key Contact: Charles J. Chalk
Colin S. Brady
Sherry Wileman
David W. Gallagher

Description: General executive search firm with in-depth experience in senior level recruitment

Branches:
10 S. La Salle St., Ste. 3505
Chicago, Illinois 60603
Key Contact: John Montgomery
Kenneth Daubensteck

342 Madison Ave., Ste. 1010
New York, New York 10173
Key Contact: Alan M. Johnson
Donald M. Fordyce

International Branches:
Bath, Dusseldorf, Frankfurt, Hong Kong, Leeds, London, Madrid, Manchester, Milan, Paris, Tokyo

GSW Consulting Group, Inc.
4550 Kearny Villa Rd., Ste. 112
San Diego, California 92123
Salary Minimum: $60,000
Key Contact: Joel M. Winitz
Marla B. Winitz

Functions: Most + 01.0 02.0 08.0 11.5
Industries: B.0W D.00 D.H0 D.I0
Professional Affiliations: IMC
Description: Provide executive search,
executive compensation & organization
consulting to senior management

Gaffney Management Consultants
121 Fairfield Way, Ste. 260
Bloomingdale, Illinois 60108-1559
Salary Minimum: $50,000
Key Contact: William Gaffney
Larry Yeisley

Functions: Most + 01.0 02.0 03.0 05.0 06.0
Industries: Most + A.00 D.00 D.E0 D.H0
K.00
Description: Executive search firm functioning
as extension of client company

Jay Gaines & Co.
598 Madison Ave.
New York, New York 10022
Salary Minimum: $125,000
Key Contact: Jay Gaines
Tarin Anwar

Functions: 01.0 08.0 09.0 09.4 11.1
Industries: H.00 H.10 H.11 I.21 J.13
Professional Affiliations: AESC
Description: Key management assignments-
financial srvcs, info industry, management
consulting, info technology

W.N. Garbarini & Assoc.
961 Cherokee Court
Westfield, New Jersey 07090
Salary Minimum: $60,000
Key Contact: William N. Garbarini
Linda Lauchiere

Functions: Most + 01.0 05.0 06.0 08.0 09.0
Industries: Most + D.00 D.H0 G.00 I.00
Description: Boutique general search firm with
unique personalized service approach

Gardiner Stone Hunter Int'l., Inc.
70 East 55th St., Heron Tower
New York, New York 10022
Salary Minimum: $125,000
Key Contact: E. Nicholas P. Gardiner
Robert Stone
Henry J. Scherck

Functions: Most
Industries: D.10 D.15 H.00 I.16 J.00
Professional Affiliations: AESC
Description: Specialists in cross-border searches
in specific industries & financial services

Branches:
One International Pl.
Boston, Massachusetts 02110
Key Contact: Durant A. Hunter

Allan Gardner & Assoc., Inc.
221 Nathaniel Ave.
Cherry Hill, New Jersey 08003
Salary Minimum: $60,000
Key Contact: Allan E. Gardner

Functions: Most + 01.0 05.0 08.0 11.1 11.5
Industries: Most + D.00 H.00 I.14 I.16
Description: Practitioner emphasizing sales,
finance, consulting & general mgmt. across
industry lines

Gardner-Ross Assoc., Inc.
300 Madison Ave.
New York, New York 10017
Salary Minimum: $75,000
Key Contact: Marvin Gardner
Elsa Ross
Al Griffin

Functions: Most + 01.0 02.0 03.0 05.0 09.0
Industries: Most + D.00 D.D0 J.00 J.11 J.13
Professional Affiliations: NAPC
Description: We are a generalist firm with
several specialties; packaging, magazine
publishing & graphic arts

Garland Assoc.
912 Calle Cortita
Santa Barbara, California 93109
Salary Minimum: $45,000
Key Contact: R. Darryl Garland

Functions: Most
Industries: Most
Description: Since 1979, exclusive, discreet &
highly ethical service oriented firm

Garofolo, Curtiss, Lambert & MacLean
326 W. Lancaster Ave.
Ardmore, Pennsylvania 19003
Salary Minimum: $60,000
Key Contact: Burton A. MacLean
Frank Garofolo
Elizabeth Allen
David H. Lambert
Joshua C. Thompson
William Wilson
Jean M. Caulfield

Functions: Most + 01.0 08.0 11.0 11.4
Industries: Most + H.00 I.13 I.14 I.15
Professional Affiliations: AESC, AHA, NAPR
Description: Generalist firm serving business,
education & not-for-profit organizations

The Gedge Group
P.O. Box 990
Ft. Montgomery, New York 10922
Salary Minimum: $50,000
Key Contact: Albert C. Gedge

Functions: Most + 01.0 04.0 05.0 11.0
Industries: Most + D.15 D.18 D.19 D.20
D.D0
Professional Affiliations: NAER
Description: Specialized in the adhesives,
coatings, sealants & related industries

Geneva Group Int'l.
4 Embarcadero Ctr., Ste. 3400
San Francisco, California 94111
Salary Minimum: $70,000
Key Contact: Igor M. Sill

Functions: 05.0 05.4 11.6
Industries: D.H0 D.I0
Professional Affiliations: CERA
Description: Senior level marketing, sales &
engineering professionals for high tech. &
software companies

Branches:
124 University Ave., Ste. 300
Palo Alto, California 94301
Key Contact: J. Michael Kennedy

7091 Orchard Lake Rd., Ste. 260
West Bloomfield, Michigan 48322
Key Contact: Craig Bassin

Genovese & Co.
455 Otter Creek, NE
Atlanta, Georgia 30328
Salary Minimum: $75,000
Key Contact: Donald P. Genovese

Functions: Most + 01.0 02.0 03.0 08.0 09.0
Industries: Most + B.00 B.0W D.H0 G.00
H.00
Professional Affiliations: CERA
Description: Small, high quality firm with
emphasis in EDP systems & financial
searches

Affiliates/Other Offices:
Jeffrey C. Adams & Co., Inc., San Francisco
Telford & Co., Inc., Newport Beach

John D. Gibbons & Assoc., Inc.
100 Oxford Dr., Ste. 812
Monroeville, Pennsylvania 15146
Salary Minimum: $80,000
Key Contact: John Gibbons

Functions: 01.0 01.1 01.2 01.3
Industries: H.R0
Professional Affiliations: BOMA, IREM,
NAIOP
Description: Executive search firm operating
exclusively in the real estate industry

Gibson & Co., Inc.

675 Ridge Rd.
West Bend, Wisconsin 53095
Salary Minimum: $100,000
Key Contact: Bruce Gibson

Branches:
P.O. Box 1547
Monterey, California 93942

Functions: Most
Industries: Most
Description: Principal has 23 years of
   experience in officer level executive search

N.W. Gibson Int'l.

5900 Wilshire Blvd., Ste. 760
Los Angeles, California 90036
Salary Minimum: $100,000
Key Contact: Nelson W. Gibson
J.S. Webb
Johanna Gibson

International Branches:
Dusseldorf, Zurich

Functions: 01.0 02.0 05.0 08.0 09.0
Industries: D.00 D.E0 D.H0 H.00 I.00
Professional Affiliations: CERA
Description: All industries & functions-some
   emphasis commercial & aerospace high
   technology

Gilbert & Van Campen Int'l.

420 Lexington Ave., Ste. 1624-27
New York, New York 10170
Salary Minimum: $100,000
Key Contact: Jerry Gilbert
Stephen B. Van Campen
Thomas Schneider
Tina Hill
Gloria Takacs
Robert Merse
Laura Pearle

Branches:
Conference Ctr., Box 393
393 Lake Shore Dr.
Mountain Lakes, New Jersey 07046

International Branches:
London, Stockholm

Functions: Most
Industries: Most
Professional Affiliations: IACPR, AMA, ASTD,
   EMA, HRPS, NACD, NYPMA
Description: Worldwide executive recruiting &
   selection. Organization building &
   management consulting

Gilbert Tweed Assoc., Inc.

630 Third Ave.
New York, New York 10017
Salary Minimum: $60,000
Key Contact: Achilles Perry
Barbara Talabisco
Frances Costa
Lynn Tendler Bignell
Janet Tweed
Thomas E. Battles
Marjorie J. Marks
Zenia Weber

Branches:
3411 Silverside Rd., 100 Hagley Bldg.
Wilmington, Delaware 19810
Key Contact: Patricia Hoffmeir
Robert E. Templin
Donald J. Roberts

Functions: Most + 02.0 05.0
Industries: Most + D.00 D.15 D.24 D.D0 I.14
Professional Affiliations: IACPR, AAMA, ACE,
   ACG, ACHE, ACS, AHA, AMA, APTA,
   ASPA, DSA, IAPW, IMC
Description: Generalist practice other services:
   relosearch, spouse search, insearch &
   organizational profiles

33 Boston Post Rd. W, Ste. 270
Marlborough, Massachusetts 01752
Key Contact: Deb Germaine
Rick Wacholz

155 Prospect Ave.
West Orange, New Jersey 07052
Key Contact: Stephanie Pinson
John A. Ebeling

Box 1248
Pittsford, Vermont 05763
Key Contact: J. Alvin Wakefield
Networks:
International Executive Search Associates
Brussels, Frankfurt, Gothenburg, Lausanne,
London, Madrid, Milan, Paris, Vienna

Howard Gilmore & Assoc.

15 Chelsea Ct.
Beachwood, Ohio 44122
Salary Minimum: $25,000
Key Contact: Howard A. Gilmore

Functions: Most + 01.2 01.3 05.2 05.4 11.1
Industries: D.15 D.19 D.22
Description: Search & outplacement services in
the sales, marketing, management areas

Gleason & Assoc.

8208 Melrose Dr., Ste. 210
Pine Ridge II
Lenexa, Kansas 66214
Salary Minimum: $40,000
Key Contact: Kenneth R. Gleason

Functions: Most
Industries: Most
Description: Generalists with an unmatched
record for success in the industry

Branches:
9891 Broken Land Pky., Ste 300
Columbia, Maryland 21046
Key Contact: John Gnall

602 Cottingham Dr.
Allison Park, Pennsylvania 15101
Key Contact: Pamela G. McDonald

12444 Powerscourt Dr., Ste 300
St. Louis, Missouri 63131
Key Contact: Carl Poslosky

9300 Forest Point Cir., Ste 100
Manassas, Virginia 22110
Key Contact: John Camastra

Global Resources Group

3655 Nobel Dr., Ste. 400
San Diego, California 92122
Salary Minimum: $75,000
Key Contact: Donn E. Bleau

Functions: 06.0 06.1 10.0 11.1
Industries: H.I0 I.14 I.15 I.21
Description: A search firm that is
knowledgeable, ethical & professional
which produces timely results

Glou Int'l., Inc.

687 Highland Ave.
Needham, Massachusetts 02194-2232
Salary Minimum: $60,000
Key Contact: Alan Glou

Functions: Most
Industries: Most + D.00 D.E0 H.10 I.00 L.00
Professional Affiliations: IACPR, AEA, SBANE
Description: Retained executive search for
small & large domestic/international firms
since 1960

The Gobbell Co.

1001 Dove St., Ste.190
Newport Beach, California 92660
Salary Minimum: $70,000
Key Contact: John J. Gobbell

Functions: Most
Industries: Most
Professional Affiliations: CERA
Description: Retained only: specialize hi-tech,
entertainment, financial services, health
care

H. L. Goehring & Assoc., Inc.

1250 W. Dorothy Ln., Ste. 204
Dayton, Ohio 45409
Salary Minimum: $40,000
Key Contact: Hal Goehring

Functions: Most + 01.2 01.3 02.0 06.0
Industries: D.14 D.22 D.H0 I.14 I.15
Professional Affiliations: ASTD, IAGAC, PIA,
SHRM
Description: Executive search/management,
servicing broad base of industries, all
functions, nationwide

Fred J. Goldsmith Assoc.
14056 Margate St.
Van Nuys, California 91401
Salary Minimum: $50,000

Functions: 01.4 02.0 05.0 06.0 08.0
Industries: B.00 D.00 D.10 E.00 I.00
Professional Affiliations: ASPA, EMA, PIRA
Description: Transportation, computer,
consumer products, distribution, oil,
exploration & food services

The Goodrich & Sherwood Co.
521 Fifth Ave.
New York, New York 10175
Salary Minimum: $60,000
Key Contact: Andrew Sherwood
Richard A. Miners

Functions: 01.0 02.0 05.0 06.0 08.0
Industries: D.00 D.10
Professional Affiliations: HRPA, IACPR
Description: Upper middle top management
search

Branches:
Merritt Seven Corporate Pk.
501 Penthouse
Norwalk, Connecticut 06851
Key Contact: Richard E. Spann

666 Plainsboro Rd.
P.O. Box 7405
Princeton, New Jersey 08543
Key Contact: William H. Heald

6 Century Drive
Parsippany, New Jersey 07054
Key Contact: Larry Shelfield

250 Mill St.
Rochester, New York 14614
Key Contact: Cornelius J. Murphy

B. Goodwin, Ltd.
88 Beach Rd., P.O. Box 537
Fairfield, Connecticut 06430
Salary Minimum: $50,000
Key Contact: Herbert L. Barkin

Functions: Most + 01.0 02.0 04.0 05.0
Industries: Most + D.00 F.00 I.11
Description: A generalist firm serving multiple
industries & disciplines nationwide

Gordon/Tyler
2220 Brandywine St.
Philadelphia, Pennsylvania 19130
Salary Minimum: $50,000
Key Contact: Fern Polaski

Functions: 02.1 02.5 03.4 04.0
Industries: D.00 D.10 D.16 D.18 D.D0
Description: Specialists in R & D, technical
services & engineering for consumer
package goods companies

Goss & Assoc., Inc.
5225 Katy Freeway, Ste. 250
Houston, Texas 77007-2251
Key Contact: Stanley B. Goss
Susan Waller
Bonnie Monych
Susan Watern

Functions: Most
Industries: Most
Professional Affiliations: NBN, TAPC
Description: Specialize in executive placement
& recruitment consulting for a wide
variety of industries

Gossage Regan Assoc.
25 W. 43rd St., Ste. 812
New York, New York 10036
Salary Minimum: $40,000
Key Contact: Wayne Gossage
Muriel Regan
Keith Doms
James Humphry, III

Functions: 11.0
Industries: Most + I.12
Professional Affiliations: ALA, ASIS, SLA
Description: Executive recruitment for
corporate, academic & public libraries &
information centers

Gould & McCoy, Inc.
551 Madison Ave.
New York, New York 10022
Salary Minimum: $75,000
Key Contact: William E. Gould
Millington F. McCoy
Susan L. Chadick
Joan Higbee

Affiliates/Other Offices:
Berndtson Int'l. S.A., Barcelona
Berndtson Int'l. S.A., Brussels
Berndtson Int'l. ApS, Copenhagen
Berndtson Int'l. GmbH, Frankfurt
Berndtson Int'l. S.A., Geneva
Berndtson Int'l. A/S, Helsinki
Berndtson Int'l. Ltd., London
Berndtson Int'l. Ltd., Madrid
Berndtson Int'l. Srl, Milan
Berndtson Int'l. A/S, Oslo
Berndtson Int'l. Sarl, Paris
Berndtson Int'l. AB, Stockholm

Functions: Most
Industries: Most + D.00 I.00 L.00
Professional Affiliations: AESC, IACPR
Description: Generalist senior level executive
search firm

Graham & Co.
34 Sycamore Ave., Bldg. 2E
Little Silver, New Jersey 07739
Salary Minimum: $50,000
Key Contact: Harold Scott
James Gray
Harold Murnane

Functions: Most
Industries: Most
Description: General search—emphasis in
manufacturing, marketing, employee
relations & general management

International Branches:
Adelaide, Amsterdam, Barcelona, Brussels, Dusseldorf, Goteborg, London, Milan, Paris, Tokyo

Robert Graham Assoc., Inc.
Wellington Sq., 580 Thames St.
Newport, Rhode Island 02840
Salary Minimum: $75,000
Key Contact: Robert W. Graham

Functions: Most + 01.2 02.0 05.0 06.0 08.0
Industries: Most
Description: Upper level corp. mgmt.
concentration-financial, manufacturing,
HR & management consulting

Granger, Counts & Assoc.
728 Trade Sq., W.
Troy, Ohio 45373
Salary Minimum: $30,000
Key Contact: Robert L. Counts

Functions: Most
Industries: Most
Professional Affiliations: SME
Description: Highly responsive search firm for
management, professional & technical
personnel

A. Davis Grant & Co.
1 Ronson Rd.
Iselin, New Jersey 08830
Salary Minimum: $40,000
Key Contact: Allan D. Grossman
Lynn Lewis

Functions: 09.0 09.1 09.3 09.4 09.7
Industries: Most
Professional Affiliations: IACPR
Description: Executive recruiting firm
dedicated exclusively to information
systems & technology professionals

Grantham & Co., Inc.
207 Providence Rd.
Chapel Hill, North Carolina 27514
Salary Minimum: $60,000
Key Contact: John D. Grantham

Functions: Most + 01.0 02.0 05.0 06.0 08.0
Industries: Most + D.00 D.D0 D.E0 E.00 I.00
Description: Small, high quality, highly
responsive generalist serving North
America

Annie Gray Assoc., Inc.
201 S. Central, Ste. 310
Clayton, Missouri 63105
Salary Minimum: $45,000
Key Contact: Annie Gray

Functions: Most + 01.1 01.2 01.3 05.1
Industries: D.10 D.D0 F.00
Professional Affiliations: ASPA, EMA, IACPR
Description: Boutique firm enjoying success
with high level, different assignmentsthan
sales & D.P.

Paul C. Green & Assoc. Ltd.
P.O. Box 1448
Green Valley, Arizona 85622
Salary Minimum: $50,000
Key Contact: Carole J. Green
Paul C. Green

Functions: Most + 08.0 10.0
Industries: H.00 H.I0
Professional Affiliations: IAFP
Description: Executive search to CEO's of
financial services organizations-primarily
insurance & brokerages

Greger Assoc.
2828 Donald Douglas Loop N.
Santa Monica, California 90405
Salary Minimum: $100,000
Key Contact: Kenneth R. Greger

Functions: 01.0 01.2 05.0 08.0
Industries: D.H0 H.00 H.R0 I.10 I.11
Professional Affiliations: CERA, CSCPA
Description: Retained only, top management-
hospitality/leisure specialty; $100,000+

Griffith & Werner, Inc.
8370 W. Flagler St., Ste. 209
Miami, Florida 33144
Salary Minimum: $75,000
Key Contact: Warland Griffith, III

Functions: Most + 05.0 06.0 08.0 09.0 11.2
Industries: D.10 D.18 D.24 H.R0 I.14
Professional Affiliations: JAS
Description: Senior level executive & upper
management search consulting services.

Jack Groban & Assoc.
445 S. Figueroa St., Ste. 3030
Los Angeles, California 90071
Salary Minimum: $75,000
Key Contact: Jack L. Groban

Functions: Most
Industries: Most
Professional Affiliations: IACPR
Description: Founder 20 years in search,
former director—California Executive
Recruiters Association

Robert Grossberg & Assoc.
1100 Sorie Blvd., Ste. 215
Oak Brook, Illinois 60521
Salary Minimum: $45,000
Key Contact: Robert M. Grossberg

Functions: 01.0 02.0 03.0 05.0 08.0
Industries: D.00 D.14 D.22 E.00 I.00
Professional Affiliations: IACPR, EMA,
SHRM, SHRP
Description: A human resource consulting
practice specializing in executive search

Grover & Assoc.
1310 Hickory Ridge
Worthington, Ohio 43235
Salary Minimum: $70,000
Key Contact: James R. Grover

Functions: Most
Industries: Most + B.0W D.15 D.18 D.19
D.20
Professional Affiliations: ACS, SHRM
Description: Since 1973, serving the process
industries: chemicals, pharmaceutical,
minerals & metals

Guidry, East, Barnes & Bono, Inc.
19506 Eastex Frwy., Ste. 301
Humble, Texas 77338
Salary Minimum: $50,000
Key Contact: Robert G. East
Jim Guidry
Greg Barnes
Susan Bono

Functions: 06.0 08.0
Industries: D.I0 I.14 I.15 I.16
Professional Affiliations: ACHE, AHA, TAPC
Description: Executive & physician search,
healthcare specialty

Gundersen Brenner, Inc.
137 Fifth Ave., 5th Fl.
New York, New York 10010
Salary Minimum: $75,000
Key Contact: Steven G. Gundersen
Roberta Brenner

Professional Affiliations: IACPR, AMA, CEW,
NYHRP, PMAA
Description: Boutique dedicated to quality/
service specializing in marketing/
marketing services & general mgmt.

Branches:
74 W. Long Lake Rd.
Bloomfield Hills, Michigan 48304
Key Contact: John Bissell

Gustin Partners, Ltd.
The Ware Mill
Newton Lower Falls, Massachusetts 02162-
1452
Salary Minimum: $100,000
Key Contact: Frank A. Juska
Vivian C. Brocard

Functions: Most
Industries: D.24 I.18 J.13
Description: Worldwide executive search for
high technology, specializing in software &
systems integration

Gutreuter & Assoc.
703 Schooner Ln.
Elk Grove Village, Illinois 60007
Salary Minimum: $40,000
Key Contact: William E. Gutreuter

Functions: Most + 02.1 05.4 09.7
Industries: D.24 J.13
Description: We specialize in searches in the
computer, office equipment &
telecommunications industry

William Guy & Assoc., Inc.
1880 Century Park E., 2nd Fl.
Century City, California 90067
Salary Minimum: $50,000
Key Contact: C. William Guy

Functions: Most
Industries: Most
Description: Cornerstone World Headquarters;
board level & upper/middle echelon
executive searches

Gynn Assoc., Inc.
3001 N. Rocky Point Dr. E.
Ste. 340
Tampa, Florida 33607
Salary Minimum: $50,000
Key Contact: Walter T. Gynn
Margaret A. Gynn

Professional Affiliations: ICSC, NAIOP, ULI
Description: Human resource consultants
exclusively representing the real estate
development industry

Affiliates/Other Offices:
Dillon & Taras Partners, Los Angeles
McBride Assoc., New York
Taras Assoc., Inc., Atlanta

HRD Consultants, Inc.
60 Walnut Ave.
Clark, New Jersey 07066
Salary Minimum: $80,000
Key Contact: Marcia Glatman

Functions: 06.0 06.1 06.2
Industries: Most
Professional Affiliations: IACPR, ACA, ASTD,
HRPS, NAFE, ODN, SHRM
Description: A retainer firm that specializes in
the placement of executive level human
resource professionals

Hackett & Co.
48 W. 10th St.
New York, New York 10011
Salary Minimum: $100,000
Key Contact: K.J. Hackett
R.C. Plazza

Functions: 06.0
Industries: Most + H.10 H.11 L.00
Professional Affiliations: ASPA, JS
Description: Generalist boutique with emphasis
on investment banking, securities &
human resources

Affiliates/Other Offices:
The Executive Source, New York

Haddad Assoc.
97 Lowell Rd., P.O. Box 594
Concord, Massachusetts 01742
Salary Minimum: $50,000
Key Contact: Ronald J. Haddad

Functions: Most + 11.0 11.1 11.4 11.5
Industries: Most + B.0W C.00 D.H0 H.R0
Description: Retained executive search, general
practice; emphasis in consulting industries

Hadley Lockwood, Inc.
199 Water St., 22nd Fl.
New York, New York 10038
Salary Minimum: $75,000
Key Contact: Irwin Brandon
David Hart

Functions: 01.0 05.0
Industries: H.00 H.10 H.11 H.12
Description: Executive search & consulting for
financial & investment industry

Halbrecht Lieberman Assoc., Inc.
1200 Summer St.
Stamford, Connecticut 06905
Salary Minimum: $65,000
Key Contact: Herb Halbrecht
Beverly Lieberman

Functions: 09.0
Industries: Most
Professional Affiliations: AESC, ORSA, SIM,
TIMS
Description: Specialists-information
management & technology all industries

Halden & Assoc.
8711 E. Pinnacle Peak Rd., Box 328
Scottsdale, Arizona 85255
Salary Minimum: $50,000
Key Contact: Kermit W. Halden

Functions: Most
Industries: G.00 I.10
Description: Heavy retail experience in our
firm-merchandising, finance, MIS, sales
promo, presentation, personnel

Haley Assoc., Inc.
526 Ramona St.
Palo Alto, California 94301
Salary Minimum: $90,000
Key Contact: Timothy Haley

Functions: 01.0 04.0 05.0 05.4
Industries: D.H0 D.I0 H.12 J.13
Description: CEO/vice president search for
venture financed high technology
companies

Halstead & Assoc.
7515 Greenville Ave.
Dallas, Texas 75231
Salary Minimum: $80,000
Key Contact: Frederick A. Halstead

Functions: Most
Industries: Most
Description: Identify & recruit people who best
meet the needs of our clients

The Halyburton Co., Inc.
6201 Fairview Rd., Ste. 200
Charlotte, North Carolina 28210
Salary Minimum: $50,000
Key Contact: Robert R. Halyburton

Functions: Most
Industries: Most + B.10 C.00 D.12 D.14 K.00
Professional Affiliations: IACPR
Description: Specialties include the contract &
residential furniture industries

The Hamilton Group
8500 Leesburg Pike, Ste. 7300
Vienna, Virginia 22182
Salary Minimum: $100,000
Key Contact: James B. Lawrence
Ronald T. Boguski

Functions: 01.0 02.0 05.2 09.0 11.1
Industries: D.24 D.E0 D.H0 D.I0 I.18
Description: Partners conduct president/CEO
and senior executive management
assignments

Hamlin Assoc.
2450-8 W. Bayshore Rd.
Palo Alto, California 94303
Salary Minimum: $40,000
Key Contact: Harry Hamlin

Industries: D.24 D.H0 J.00 J.13
Description: Engineers, programmers,
marketing & sales professionals for high
tech industry.

R. C. Handel Assoc. Inc.
117 New London Turnpike
Glastonbury, Connecticut 06033
Salary Minimum: $50,000
Key Contact: Richard C. Handel, Jr.

Functions: Most + 02.0 05.0 08.0 10.0
Industries: Most + D.00 H.I0
Description: Provide management search &
human resource consulting to client
companies

W.L. Handler & Assoc.
100 Cumberland Circle, Ste. 1290
Atlanta, Georgia 30339
Salary Minimum: $45,000
Key Contact: William L. Handler
Harold Massey, Jr.

Functions: Most + 02.0 05.0 06.0 09.0
Industries: Most + D.00 G.00 H.00 I.00
Description: Retained assignments middle &
senior management & technical-all
disciplines

Handy HRM
250 Park Ave.
New York, New York 10177
Salary Minimum: $100,000
Key Contact: J. Gerald Simmons
John M. Bondur
Richard K. Phillips
James R. Clovis, Jr.
Chester A. Hopkins
William F. Emmons, Jr.
Franklin Key Brown
Francis J. Burns
Marc D. Lewis
Patrick Brennan

International Branches:
Paris

Functions: 01.0 05.0 06.0 08.0 09.0
Industries: B.0W D.D0 D.H0 H.00 J.00
Description: Search & executive compensation
consulting

Hans & Assoc., Inc.
3408-D West Denton
Phoenix, Arizona 85017-2834
Salary Minimum: $25,000
Key Contact: Hans R. Schacke

Functions: 01.0 02.0 05.0 08.0 11.0
Industries: D.00 H.00 I.10 I.11 I.14
Professional Affiliations: AAPC, AHMA, ARA,
HSMA
Description: Specializing in executive search &
recruiting for hotel/resort/restaurant/
leisure/healthcare

Hansen Group, Ltd.
1920 Bayshore Dr.
Englewood, Florida 34223
Salary Minimum: $70,000
Key Contact: Ty E. Hansen

Functions: 01.1 01.2 01.3 11.0
Industries: D.23 D.25 D.E0 D.H0 E.00
Professional Affiliations: ADPA, AFCEA,
    ANA, AOC, IACPR
Description: Specialists in aerospace, aviation
    & defense since 1974

Hansen Management Search Co.
1442 S. Fern Dr.
Mt. Prospect, Illinois 60056
Salary Minimum: $35,000
Key Contact: H. Jack Hansen
Joan D. Hansen

Functions: 01.3 02.0 03.0 07.0
Industries: D.00 D.E0 E.00 H.10 I.14
Description: Confine search to middle
    management positions

Hanzel & Co., Inc.
6 E. 39th St.
New York, New York 10016
Salary Minimum: $80,000
Key Contact: Bruce S. Hanzel
Robert T. Anderson

Functions: 01.2
Industries: H.10 H.11 H.12
Description: Primary concentration in line
    functions of investment and commercial
    banking

Harreus & Assoc., Inc.
600 Montgomery St., 35th Fl.
San Francisco, California 94111
Salary Minimum: $50,000
Key Contact: Charles F. Harreus

Functions: 05.0 05.1 05.2
Industries: D.10 D.16 J.00 J.10
Professional Affiliations: CERA
Description: Specializing in consumer products
    & services, marketing & advertising

Harris Heery & Assoc., Inc.
One Norwalk W., 40 Richards Ave.
Norwalk, Connecticut 06854
Salary Minimum: $50,000
Key Contact: William J. Heery
Andrew S. Harris
Linda Leonard

Functions: 01.0 05.0
Industries: D.00 H.I0 I.00
Description: A specialized recruiting firm for
    consumer goods & service companies

Hartman, Barnette & Assoc.
P.O. Box 7966
Charlottesville, Virginia 22906
Salary Minimum: $70,000
Key Contact: Robert J. Hartman

Functions: Most
Industries: D.17 D.18 D.I0 H.12 J.10
Description: Pharmaceuticals, diagnostics, drug
    delivery, medical devices,
    bipharmaceuticals, biotechnology

Branches:
P.O. Box 414
Highlands, New Jersey 07732
Key Contact: Fred A. Barnette
Linda Linton

Harvard Aimes Group
6 Holcomb St., P.O. Box 16006
West Haven, Connecticut 06516
Salary Minimum: $40,000
Key Contact: James J. Gunther

Functions: 10.0
Industries: Most
Professional Affiliations: CAPC, NAPC
Description: Specialize exclusively in corporate
    risk management recruiting-client retained
    only

Hauft Mark Assoc., Inc.

1219 Morningside Dr.
Manhattan Beach, California 90266
Key Contact: John L. Mark
Neil E. Hauft

Functions: Most
Industries: Most + B.0W D.00 E.00 I.00 J.00
Professional Affiliations: IACPR
Description: Specialists in identifying
    candidates who are complimentary with
    client's style

The Hawkins Co.

5410 Wilshire Blvd., Ste. 715
Los Angeles, California 90036
Salary Minimum: $40,000
Key Contact: William D. Hawkins
W. J. Moore

Functions: 01.0 01.1 06.0 08.0 11.2
Industries: J.10 J.11 J.12 J.13 K.00
Description: Retained search firm specializing
    in minority recruitment

Hayden Group, Inc.

10 High St.
Boston, Massachusetts 02110
Salary Minimum: $100,000
Key Contact: James A. Hayden
Robert E. Hawley

Functions: 01.0 01.2 06.0 08.0 09.0
Industries: Most + H.00 H.10 H.I0
Description: Senior management, middle
    management & board members—financial
    services specialists

Hayman & Co.

2101 Skyway Tower
Dallas, Texas 75201
Salary Minimum: $60,000
Key Contact: Thomas C. Hayman

Functions: Most
Industries: Most

Health Industry Consultants, Inc.

9250 East Costilla Ave., Ste. 600
Englewood, Colorado 80112
Salary Minimum: $55,000
Key Contact: Jon K. Fitzgerald

Functions: 01.0 02.0 04.0 05.0 11.3
Industries: D.18 D.25 D.I0
Description: Medical products, biotechnology
    management & senior technical

F. P. Healy & Co., Inc.

230 Park Ave., Ste. 232
New York, New York 10169
Salary Minimum: $50,000
Key Contact: Frank P. Healy

Functions: Most
Industries: Most
Professional Affiliations: AMA, EMA, IACPR
Description: Executive search, all industries

Heath/Norton Assoc., Inc.

545 Eighth Ave., 7th Fl.
New York, New York 10018
Salary Minimum: $65,000
Key Contact: Richard S. Stoller
Alan H. Gross
Robert Kleinman
Richard Rosenow

Functions: Most + 01.0 02.0 05.0 05.4
Industries: Most + D.00 D.D0 D.H0 D.I0
Description: Retainer firm specializing in sales,
    marketing, engineering, manufacturing &
    general management

R. W. Hebel Assoc.

4821 Spicewood Springs Rd., Ste. 102
Austin, Texas 78759
Salary Minimum: $100,000
Key Contact: Robert W. Hebel
Robert L. Golding

Functions: 01.1 02.1 04.0 05.0 06.0
Industries: D.17 D.18 D.I0 I.16 J.00
Description: Retainer search firm specializing
    in healthcare executive recruitment

Heffelfinger Assoc., Inc.
470 Washington St.
Chestnut Green
Norwood, Massachusetts 02062
Salary Minimum: $80,000
Key Contact: Thomas V. Heffelfinger

International Branches:
London

Functions: 01.4 04.0 05.0 09.0 11.6
Industries: Most + D.24 D.H0 J.00
Description: Founded in 1965, specialize in
   computer/communication industry, both
   vendor/user

Hegarty & Co.
680 N. Lake Shore Dr. Twrs., Ste 2045
Chicago, Illinois 60611
Salary Minimum: $80,000
Key Contact: Robert Allen
Robert J. Hegarty

Functions: Most
Industries: Most
Description: Executive search firm with
   expertise and successes in most industries

The Heidrick Partners, Inc.
20 N. Wacker Dr., Ste. 2850
Chicago, Illinois 60606
Salary Minimum: $90,000
Key Contact: Robert L. Heidrick
Gardner W. Heidrick
Theodore W. Seweloh
H. Richard Collins
John R. Berry
L. Eugene Williams

Functions: Most + 01.0 01.1 02.0 05.0 08.0
Industries: Most + B.00 D.00 H.00 H.R0 I.00
Professional Affiliations: AESC
Description: Board and executive search
   consultants

Heidrick and Struggles, Inc.
125 S. Wacker Dr., Ste. 2800
Chicago, Illinois 60606-4590
Salary Minimum: $60,000
Key Contact: Robert E. Hallagan
Gerard R. Roche
P. Frederick Kahn

Functions: Most
Industries: Most
Professional Affiliations: AESC
Description: Board member, upper & middle
   echelon executive searches

Branches:
300 S. Grand Ave., Ste. 2400
Los Angeles, California 90071
Key Contact: Thomas M. Mitchell

285 Peachtree Ctr. Ave.
Ste. 2100
Atlanta, Georgia 30303
Key Contact: Patrick S. Pittard

Four Embarcadero Ctr.
San Francisco, California 94111
Key Contact: Conrad E. Prusak

One Post Office Sq.
Boston, Massachusetts 02109
Key Contact: Robert E. Hallagan

2740 Sand Hill Rd.
Menlo Park, California 94025
Key Contact: David B. Kixmiller

245 Park Ave
New York, New York 10167-0152
Key Contact: Brenda L. Ruello

104 Field Point Rd.
Greenwich, Connecticut 06830
Key Contact: Ray P. Foote, Jr.

1100 Superior Ave., Ste. 930
Cleveland, Ohio 44114
Key Contact: Stuart M. Schreiber

2000 K Street, N.W., Ste. 610
Washington, District of Columbia 20006
Key Contact: Eugene M. Rackley

1999 Bryan St., Ste. 1919
Dallas, Texas 75201
Key Contact: R. William Funk

76 S. Laura St., Ste 2110
Jacksonville, Florida 32202
Key Contact: Charles R. Hoskins

1 Place Ville Marie, Ste. 2400
Montreal, Quebec H3B 3M9 Canada
Key Contact: Bruce F. G. Ward

National Bank Bldg.
150 York St., P.O.Box 500
Toronto, Ontario M5H 3A9 Canada
Key Contact: Paul Michaelis

International Branches:
Barcelona, Brussels, Dusseldorf, Frankfurt/Main 71, Helsinki, London, Madrid, Munich, Paris, Stockholm, Sydney, Tokyo

Helfer Executive Consultants
628 Harpeth Trace Dr.
P.O. Box 50239
Nashville, Tennessee 37205-0239
Salary Minimum: $40,000
Key Contact: Frederick W. Helfer

Functions: Most + 01.0 02.0 03.0 04.0 05.0
Industries: B.0W C.00 D.00 D.E0 H.00
Description: Managerial, professional & technical positions for Mid-South client base

G.W. Henn & Co.
85 East Gay St., Ste. 1007
Columbus, Ohio 43215
Salary Minimum: $80,000
Key Contact: George W. Henn, Jr.

Functions: Most
Industries: Most
Description: General recruiting practice focusing on senior management positions—all industries

Henning & Assoc.
323 E. Matilija St., Ste. 205
Ojai, California 93023
Salary Minimum: $50,000
Key Contact: John I. Henning

Functions: 01.2 01.3 02.4 05.2 05.4
Industries: D.10
Description: Search firm specializing primarily in food & beverage fields

Henry Michaels & Assoc.
1450 American Ln., Ste. 1400
Schaumburg, Illinois 60173-4989
Salary Minimum: $60,000
Key Contact: H. Michael Kocmond

Functions: 01.2 01.4 05.4 09.0 09.2
Industries: D.H0 I.18
Description: Specializing in the recruitment of data processing sales & marketing personnel

Hergenrather & Co.
1559 Pacific Coast Hwy., Ste. 662
Hermosa Beach, California 90254
Salary Minimum: $60,000
Key Contact: Richard A. Hergenrather
Robert S. Putnam

Functions: Most + 01.0 02.0 05.0 06.0 09.0
Industries: Most + B.00 D.00 D.H0 I.00 J.00
Professional Affiliations: CERA
Description: Conduct searches in every functional area & most industries

Branches:
3125 Riley Rd., P.O. Box 1100
Solvang, California 93463
Key Contact: Ed Hergenrather

Hersher Assoc., Ltd.
3000 Dundee Rd., Ste. 314
Northbrook, Illinois 60062
Salary Minimum: $50,000
Key Contact: Betsy S. Hersher
Linda B. Hodges

Functions: 01.0 03.0 05.0 08.0 09.0
Industries: I.14
Professional Affiliations: ACHE, HFMA, HIMSS
Description: Exclusively healthcare, the CIO experts

Stanley Herz & Co.

300 Broad St., Ste. 502
Stamford, Connecticut 06901
Salary Minimum: $60,000
Key Contact: Stanley Herz

Functions: 01.0 08.0 09.0
Industries: Most
Professional Affiliations: IACPR
Description: Executive search; specialty is
finance & information systems, clients are
regional

William Hetzel Assoc., Inc.

Williamsburg Village
1601 Colonial Pkwy.
Inverness, Illinois 60067
Salary Minimum: $75,000
Key Contact: William G. Hetzel
Karen M. Ross

Functions: Most
Industries: Most
Professional Affiliations: IACPR, ABA, ASPA,
ASTD, IMESC
Description: Successful search specialists at
senior management levels.

Higdon, Joys & Mingle, Inc.

375 Park Ave., 16th Fl.
The Seagram Bldg.
New York, New York 10152
Salary Minimum: $150,000
Key Contact: Larry D. Mingle
David S. Joys
Henry G. Higdon

Functions: Most + 01.0 05.0 06.0 08.0 11.0
Industries: Most
Professional Affiliations: AESC
Description: High level search consulting for
senior decision makers in various
industries

Affiliates/Other Offices:
Jouve & Associes, Paris
MacLennan & Partners Ltd., London

Higgins Assoc., Inc.

108 Wilmot Rd.
Deerfield, Illinois 60015
Salary Minimum: $70,000
Key Contact: John B. Higgins
Roger W. Van Dyke

Functions: Most
Professional Affiliations: IACPR
Description: Retainer fee, generalist search firm

The Hindman Co.

2000 Warrington Way
Browenton Place, Ste. 110
Louisville, Kentucky 40222
Salary Minimum: $50,000
Key Contact: Neil C. Hindman
Harold B. Berry
Robert J. Noll
Ted K. Ellis
Jack L. Reid

Functions: Most + 01.0 02.0 03.0 05.0 06.0
Industries: Most + C.00 D.00 D.E0 D.H0 J.00
Description: Worldwide; emphasize
manufacturing/industrial, transportation,
communications & finance

International Branches:
Lausanne, London

Hite Executive Search

P.O. Box 43217
Cleveland, Ohio 44143-0217
Salary Minimum: $50,000
Key Contact: William A. Hite, III
John P. Proudfit
Lauren R. Pacini
Marilyn A. Chornan

Functions: Most + 01.0 02.0 05.0 08.0 11.0
Industries: Most + B.0W D.00 D.H0 D.I0 I.00
Description: Middle & senior level
management specialist

Hockett Assoc., Inc.

3000 Sand Hill Rd., Bldg. 2-185
Menlo Park, California 94025
Salary Minimum: $85,000
Key Contact: Bill Hockett

Functions: Most + 01.0 02.0 04.0 05.0 08.0
Industries: Most + D.18 D.24 D.H0 D.I0 J.13
Professional Affiliations: CERA
Description: Senior management search for life
   sciences, technology and other companies

Hodge-Cronin & Assoc., Inc.

9575 W. Higgins Rd., Ste. 503
Rosemont, Illinois 60018
Salary Minimum: $75,000
Key Contact: Kathleen A. Cronin
Richard J. Cronin

Functions: Most + 04.0 05.0 06.0 08.0 09.7
Industries: C.00 D.00 D.D0 D.H0 H.I0
Professional Affiliations: IACPR
Description: Has worked in most industries/
   disciplines, international

Networks:
International Independent Consultants (IIC)
Amstelveen, Frankfurt, Hamburg, London, Madrid, Milan, Oslo, Paris, San Francisco, Singapore,
Stockholm, Toronto, Vedbaek, Vienna, Zurich

Hogan Assoc.

112 Southwyck, Ste. PH
Chagrin Falls, Ohio 44022-4106
Salary Minimum: $60,000
Key Contact: Lawrence Hogan
Marilyn Gallagher

Functions: 01.0 02.0 05.0 08.0 11.0
Industries: D.19 D.22 D.23 D.25 H.12
Professional Affiliations: NFPA, NSPE, SME,
   SPE, SPI
Description: Acquisitions & mergers, CNC,
   motion control, plastics & capital
   equipment

Harvey Hohauser & Assoc.

5600 New King St., Ste. 355
Troy, Michigan 48098
Salary Minimum: $60,000
Key Contact: Harvey Hohauser
Hubert Price, Jr.

Functions: Most
Industries: Most + D.00 H.00 I.00 I.15
Description: Management consultants
   specializing in executive recruitment

Richard D. Holbrook Assoc.

Security Mutual Bldg.
80 Exchange St., Ste. 317
Binghamton, New York 13901
Salary Minimum: $50,000
Key Contact: Richard D. Holbrook

Functions: Most
Industries: Most
Description: Responsive firm with a quality,
   solutions-oriented approach to executive
   search

Holland, McFadzean & Assoc., Inc.

2901 Tasman Dr., Ste. 204
Santa Clara, California 95054
Salary Minimum: $75,000
Key Contact: James A. McFadzean

Functions: 01.0 02.0 04.0 05.0 09.0
Industries: D.24 D.H0 H.12 I.18 J.13
Description: Retained search firm specializes in
   high technology senior management
   searches

Holland Rusk & Assoc.

750 N. Orleans St., Ste. 401
Chicago, Illinois 60610
Salary Minimum: $60,000
Key Contact: Susan R. Holland
Mitchell Watkins

Functions: Most + 01.0 02.0 08.0 11.0 11.2
Industries: Most + B.00 C.00 D.00 E.00 I.17
Professional Affiliations: EMA
Description: Small, highly professional
   generalist practice of national and
   international scope

The Hollins Group, Inc.
225 W. Wacker Dr., Ste. 2125
Chicago, Illinois 60606-1229
Salary Minimum: $60,000
Key Contact: Lawrence I. Hollins
Mary Jo Zaksas

Functions: Most + 11.2
Industries: Most
Professional Affiliations: HRMAC
Description: Provide executive search
consulting to various industries &
functional disciplines

Holohan Group, Ltd.
12218 Manchester Rd., Ste. B
St. Louis, Missouri 63131
Salary Minimum: $60,000
Key Contact: Barth A. Holohan, Jr.
Marie Falbo Holohan
Erwin H. Peters
Margaret O. Pautler
K. Wayne Ratts

Functions: Most + 04.0 05.0 09.0 11.2 11.3
Industries: Most + A.00 D.15 D.17 D.18 D.I0
Description: Quality executive selection/
recruitment management consulting firm,
all industries/functions

Holt Pearson & Caldwell, Inc.
23F Main St.
Tiburon, California 94920
Salary Minimum: $80,000
Key Contact: John R. Pearson
William R. Caldwell
John A. Farnsworth

Functions: Most
Industries: Most + H.00
Description: Senior level search with emphasis
on financial sector & marketing

J.B. Homer Assoc. Inc.
521 Fifth Ave.
New York, New York 10175
Salary Minimum: $60,000
Key Contact: Judy B. Homer

Functions: 01.0 06.0 08.0 09.0 09.7
Industries: Most + D.00 H.00 H.I0 J.00
Professional Affiliations: NAA, NYPMA,
SMIS, WHRM
Description: Specialize in finance &
accounting, management info systems,
human resources-all mgmt levels

R. H. Horton Int'l.
30 Tower Ln.
Avon, Connecticut 06001
Salary Minimum: $100,000
Key Contact: Robert H. Horton
C. Edward Snyder
John C. Fischer
James J. Klauck
Joanna B. Miller
Dale E. Smith

Functions: Most
Industries: Most
Description: Seasoned operating executives
experienced in manufacturing, marketing,
finance, H-R/benefits

Branches:
785 S. Orange Grove Blvd., Ste. 5
Pasadena, California 91105
Key Contact: C. Edward Snyder

International Branches:
Birmingham, London

Houtz, Strawn Assoc.
5000 Plaza on the Lake, # 320
Austin, Texas 78746
Salary Minimum: $110,000
Key Contact: William M. Strawn
Kenneth H. Houtz

Functions: 01.2 11.0 11.3
Industries: D.18 D.I0 H.12 I.16
Description: Senior level assignments with
pharmaceutical & medical device
companies, health care corporations

William C. Houze & Co.

48249 Vista De Nopal
La Quinta, California 92253
Salary Minimum: $90,000
Key Contact: William C. Houze
Geoffry Houze

Functions: Most
Industries: D.00 D.E0 D.H0 D.I0 I.00
Professional Affiliations: AESC, AAUP, AFA,
    AFCEA, AOC, SAE
Description: All searches performed with care,
    in compliance with AESC standards

Branches:
Del Amo Financial Center
21535 Hawthorne Blvd., Ste. 209
Torrance, California 90503

Affiliates/Other Offices:
Dennis & Gemmill Ltd., London

Houze, Shourds & Montgomery, Inc.

Greater LA World Trade Ctr.
One World Trade
Long Beach, California 90831-1840
Salary Minimum: $90,000
Key Contact: James Montgomery
Mary Shourds

Functions: Most
Industries: Most
Professional Affiliations: AESC, IACPR,
    WTCA
Description: A highly professional generalist
    firm with a national practice

Networks:
Penrhyn Partners Int'l.
Hong Kong, London, Melbourne, New York, San Francisco, Toronto

Randall Howard & Assoc., Inc.

5353 Flowering Peach Dr.
Memphis, Tennessee 38115-5947
Salary Minimum: $50,000
Key Contact: Randall C. Howard

Functions: Most
Industries: Most
Professional Affiliations: DPMA, NAA, NAPC
Description: Since 1970, specialized search
    assignments for financial & corporate
    management professionals

Howard-Sloan Communications Search

353 Lexington Ave.
New York, New York 10016
Salary Minimum: $60,000
Key Contact: Edward R. Koller, Jr.
Karen Danziger

Functions: 05.1 05.4 05.7
Industries: J.00 J.11
Professional Affiliations: BPAA, DMA, IIA
Description: Search & consulting in magazine
    & book publ., direct mktg., public
    relations/info. indus. field

Robert Howe & Assoc.

35 Glenlake Pkwy., Ste. 164
Atlanta, Georgia 30328
Salary Minimum: $50,000
Key Contact: Robert W. Hamill
K. Michael Bidaman
Kathy E. Cullen

Functions: Most + 01.3 02.0 04.0 05.0 08.0
Industries: Most + D.11 D.15 I.10 I.14 I.15
Description: Representing small to large firms
    in mid-upper level positions

Howe, McMahon & Assoc., Inc.

2 Radnor Corp. Ctr., Ste. 250
Radnor, Pennsylvania 19087
Salary Minimum: $70,000
Key Contact: Edward R. Howe, Jr.
Norman E. McMahon

Functions: Most
Industries: Most
Professional Affiliations: IACPR
Description: Serves corporations headquartered
    in the Delaware valley & nationwide

Howe-Lewis Int'l.

525 University Ave., Ste. 825
Palo Alto, California 94301
Salary Minimum: $80,000
Key Contact: John C. Taylor
Daphne Lewis

Branches:
200 W. 57th St., Ste. 605
New York, New York 10019
Key Contact: Anita Howe-Waxman
Annette Pfister

International Branches:
Lausanne, Sydney

Functions: Most
Professional Affiliations: AESC
Description: Total healthcare focus-senior
management, medical & scientific
executives

Howe-Weaver, Inc.

P.O. Box 584
Barrington, Illinois 60011
Salary Minimum: $60,000
Key Contact: W. Lawrence Howe
Charlene R. Krafski
John T. Weaver

Functions: 10.0
Industries: H.I0
Description: Executive search in the insurance
& financial services industries

Arnold Huberman Assoc., Inc.

51 E. 25th St., Ste. 501
New York, New York 10010
Key Contact: Arnold Huberman

Affiliates/Other Offices:
Bird & Co., London
Shulman-Alexander Inc., Palo Alto
Shulman-Alexander Inc., San Francisco

Functions: 05.7 11.4
Industries: I.11
Description: Specialists in recruiting for public
relations/corporate communications
professionals

Huff Assoc.

500 Bay Ave., N., Ste. B
Ocean City, New Jersey 08226
Salary Minimum: $45,000
Key Contact: William Z. Huff
Margaret L. Huff

Functions: Most + 02.0 04.0 11.3 11.6
Industries: Most + D.00 D.H0 I.10 I.14 I.15
Description: Results-oriented, budget-
conscience & functionally broad
throughout multifarious industries

Hughes & Assoc., Inc.

P.O. Box 440848
Aurora, Colorado 80044
Salary Minimum: $35,000
Key Contact: A.J. Bud Hughes

Functions: 01.0 02.0 03.0 05.0 06.0
Industries: Most
Description: A management consulting firm
that provides guaranteed results in search

M.J. Hughes Int'l., Inc.

100 Shoreline Hwy., Ste. B-140
Mill Valley, California 94941
Salary Minimum: $100,000
Key Contact: Michele J. Hughes

Functions: Most
Industries: Most
Description: Management consultants
specializing in executive search at the
most senior level

Human Resource Technologies, Inc.

3158 Des Plaines Ave.. Ste. 125
Des Plaines, Illinois 60018
Salary Minimum: $35,000
Key Contact: Rick Sondhi

Functions: Most + 11.1 11.2 11.3 11.5 11.6
Industries: Most
Description: Consultants specializing in
retained professional search &
employment support services

The Human Resource Consulting Group, Inc.
165 S. Union Blvd., Ste. 456
Lakewood, Colorado 80228-2211
Salary Minimum: $50,000
Key Contact: Joseph L. Zaccaro

Functions: Most + 01.0 02.5 05.0 06.0 08.0
Industries: Most + D.00 D.H0 I.14 J.00 J.13
Description: A national executive search
    practice with highly experienced business
    executives

Branches:
3 Wallace Ct., Ste. 8A
Lexington, Massachusetts 02173
Key Contact: Daniel D. Cantor

Human Resource Research Inc.
747 Main St., Ste. 222
Concord, Massachusetts 01742
Salary Minimum: $45,000
Key Contact: Claudia B. Liebesny
Irene M. Miller

Functions: 01.0 04.0 05.0 09.2 09.3
Industries: D.18 D.24 D.H0 D.I0 K.10
Description: Specialized individual contributor
    & managerial professionals, mainly high
    technology

Human Resource Services, Inc.
1700 Lincoln, Ste. 3700
Denver, Colorado 80203
Salary Minimum: $75,000
Key Contact: William K. Zinke

Functions: 01.0 01.5 05.0 06.0 08.0
Industries: Most
Description: We provide search plus range of
    other HR-related consulting services

Human Resources, Inc.
7 James St.
Providence, Rhode Island 02903
Salary Minimum: $90,000
Key Contact: Albert L. Richard, Jr.

Functions: 01.0 02.0 05.0 08.0 09.0
Industries: D.00 D.22 D.H0 I.18 J.13
Professional Affiliations: AESC
Description: Information services, computer,
    communications, software mfg., general
    technology & quality

William Humphreys & Assoc., Inc.
4261 Sherwoodtowne Blvd., Ste. 301
Mississauga, Ontario L4Z 1Y5 Canada
Salary Minimum: $50,000
Key Contact: William M. Humphreys
Margaret H. Robison
Scott W. Humphreys

Functions: 01.0 01.1 05.0 05.1 09.7
Industries: D.D0 E.00 H.10 H.12 J.00
Description: Direct sourcing (no advertising)
    executive search client base: Canada,
    United States, United Kingdom

The Hunt Co.
274 Madison Ave.
New York, New York 10016
Salary Minimum: $75,000
Key Contact: Bridgford H. Hunt

Functions: Most
Industries: Most
Description: Maintain confidential
    relationships with clients before, during &
    after the assignment

Hunter Int'l., Inc.
129 Good Hill Rd.
Oxford, Connecticut 06478-1542
Salary Minimum: $75,000
Key Contact: Ron Kelly
William Ryan

Functions: Most + 01.0 05.0 06.0 08.0 10.0
Industries: Most + D.00 D.18 H.I0 I.00
Description: Generalist practice with emphasis
    in major business disciplines

Jack Hurst & Assoc., Inc.
500 N. Central, Ste. 201
Plano, Texas 75074
Salary Minimum: $60,000
Key Contact: Jack K. Hurst
Kenneth N. Hurst

Functions: Most + 01.0 02.0 05.0 08.0
Industries: Most + D.00
Description: Focus on manufacturing industries
    at director level & above

Hutchinson Resources International
183 Beach 121st St.
Belle Harbor, New York 11694
Salary Minimum: $50,000
Key Contact: Loretta M. Hutchinson

Functions: Most + 01.0 02.0 04.0 05.0 08.0
Industries: Most + B.0W D.00 D.I0 H.00 I.00
Professional Affiliations: NAFE, RR, SLA
Description: High quality provider of research
  services & discounted executive search
  services

Huxtable Assoc., Inc.
P.O. Box 4069
St. Peters, Missouri 63376
Salary Minimum: $40,000
Key Contact: Carroll G. Huxtable
Fulton L. Huxtable

Functions: Most
Industries: Most
Description: Consultants to management on
  executive evaluation & selection since
  1971

Hyde Danforth & Co.
5950 Berkshire Ln., Ste. 1600
Dallas, Texas 75225
Salary Minimum: $50,000
Key Contact: W. Michael Danforth
W. Jerry Hyde

Functions: Most
Industries: Most
Description: Oldest independent firm in Dallas-
  generalists serving industry, law &
  academia

The Hyde Group, Inc.
209 Palmer Point, River Rd.
Cos Cob, Connecticut 06807
Salary Minimum: $70,000
Key Contact: Anne P. Hyde

Functions: 01.0 05.0 06.0 11.1 11.2
Industries: Most
Description: Specialize: HR including training
  & development, leadership, organization
  change & exec development

Hyman, Mackenzie & Partners, Inc.
3650 Victoria Park Ave., Ste. 203
Willowdale, Ontario M2H 3P7 Canada
Salary Minimum: $45,000
Key Contact: Curtis D. Hyman

Functions: 06.2
Industries: C.00 D.12 H.00 I.00
Professional Affiliations: ICSC, NACORE, UDI
Description: Retainer based, research oriented,
  professional search group, internationally
  associated

International Branches:
Bangkok, Singapore

John Imber Assoc., Ltd.
3601 Algonquin Rd., Ste. 129
Rolling Meadows, Illinois 60008
Salary Minimum: $35,000
Key Contact: John Imber

Functions: Most
Industries: Most
Professional Affiliations: IMESC
Description: Professional recruitment since
  1962

Ingram, Inc.
430 Park Ave.
New York, New York 10022
Salary Minimum: $100,000
Key Contact: D. John Ingram
G. Thomas Aydelotte
D. Kyle Felt
James B. King

Functions: Most + 01.0 05.0 06.0 10.0
Industries: Most + D.00 H.I0 I.00 J.00
Description: Senior management, board of
  director search consultants- most
  industries, functions

Inmark Executive Search
252 Autumn Chase Dr.
Annapolis, Maryland 21401
Salary Minimum: $45,000
Key Contact: R. Bronson Turner

Functions: Most
Industries: Most
Description: Mid to upper level executives &
  engineers in Mid Atlantic region

Innkeeper's Management Corp.

14 E. 60th St., Ste. 1210
New York, New York 10022
Salary Minimum: $60,000
Key Contact: Herbert Regehly

Functions: 01.0 05.0 06.0 08.0
Industries: I.10 I.11
Professional Affiliations: AHMA, CSH, HSMA
Description: 27 year hospitality industry
    related retained search firm for senior
    positions

Inside Management Assoc.

24 East 38th St.
New York, New York 10016
Salary Minimum: $50,000
Key Contact: Paul D. Steinberg
W. Neail Behringer
Charles J. Seitz
John P. Gilmore

Functions: Most + 02.0 05.0 06.0 08.0 09.0
Industries: Most + B.0W D.E0 G.00 I.00 J.00
Description: Experienced business professionals
    providing executive search/general
    management consulting

Branches:
15 Boulder Brook Rd.
Greenwich, Connecticut 06830

106 Peninsula Dr.
Babylon, New York 11702

The Interface Group, Ltd.

1025 Thomas Jefferson St., NW, Ste. 410
East Lobby
Washington, District of Columbia 20007
Salary Minimum: $75,000
Key Contact: William H. Marumoto
S. Hope Johnson

Functions: Most + 01.0 05.0 06.0 07.0 08.0
Industries: H.00 H.I0 I.12 J.00 K.00
Professional Affiliations: AESC, IACPR
Description: Retainer-based executive search
    firm specializing in recruiting for
    management

The Interim Management Corp.(IMCOR)

475 Park Ave. S., 33rd Fl.
New York, New York 10016
Salary Minimum: $75,000
Key Contact: John A. Thompson
Marshall M. Jeanes

Functions: 01.0 02.0 03.0 05.0 06.0
Industries: Most
Professional Affiliations: IACPR
Description: IMCOR places executives into
    interim or temporary assignments

Branches:
23133 Hawthorne Blvd.
Republic Bank Bldg., Ste. 311
Torrance, California 90505
Key Contact: Michael J. Hagerthy

60 Guernsey Ave.
Stamford, Connecticut 06901
Key Contact: David L. Thorpe
Bruce M. Clark

International Management Advisors, Inc.

516 Fifth Ave., Ste. 701
New York, New York 10036-7501
Salary Minimum: $60,000
Key Contact: Constance W. Klages
R. James Lotz, Jr.
Daniel J. O'Connor
Paul J. Harbaugh, Jr.
Henri J.P. Manassero
Michael D. Pedalino

Functions: Most
Industries: Most
Professional Affiliations: IACPR, ISA
Description: Quality, medium size generalist
    firm serving multinational & national
    organizations

Branches:
75 E. Wacker Dr.
Chicago, Illinois 60601

International Branches:
Athens, Brussels, Kowloon, London, Melbourne, Milano, Paris, Stockholm, Utrecht, Zurich

International Management Services Inc.
6300 N. River Rd., Ste. 102
Rosemont, Illinois 60018
Salary Minimum: $50,000
Key Contact: Carl A. Johnson
Byron T. Garoufalis
James P. Barry
James M. Barz
Frank Davis
Ken Duffy

Functions: Most
Industries: Most
Description: Retained search and management
  consulting in mostly technology based
  industries

Jeffrey Irving Assoc., Inc.
216 S. Payne St.
Alexandria, Virginia 22314
Salary Minimum: $75,000
Key Contact: Jeffrey J. Irving

Functions: Most + 01.0 05.0 06.0 08.0 09.0
Industries: Most + D.00 D.H0 H.00 I.00 J.00
Professional Affiliations: APA
Description: Diversified client-centered middle
  and senior level executive search

Isaacson, Miller, Inc.
105 Chauncy St., 8th Fl.
Boston, Massachusetts 02111
Salary Minimum: $50,000
Key Contact: John Isaacson
Arnie Miller

Functions: Most + 11.2 11.4 11.5
Industries: B.0W E.00 I.12 I.14 K.00
Professional Affiliations: APTA, MHA
Description: A national, retained search firm,
  completing 100-150 senior executive
  searches per year

Branches:
1233 20th St. NW, Ste. 202
The Lion Bldg.
Washington, District of Columbia 20036
Key Contact: Tom Goodwin

JDavid Assoc., Inc.
24 Crest Dr., N.
Cresskill, New Jersey 07626
Salary Minimum: $75,000
Key Contact: Joe D. Tuschman

Functions: Most
Industries: Most
Professional Affiliations: IACPR
Description: Retained search within most
  disciplines & a variety of industries

JM & Co.
P.O. Box 285
Wayne, Pennsylvania 19087
Salary Minimum: $50,000
Key Contact: John C. Marshall
John D. Hildebrand
Robert A. Sargent
George T. Corrigan
Philip L. Byrnes
Robert B. Hobbs

Functions: 01.0 02.0 03.0 04.0 05.0
Industries: D.13 D.14 D.15 D.19 D.D0
Description: Provide confidentiality, detailed
  recruiting, thoroughness and
  professionalism

Jablo Partners
P.O. Box 795549
Dallas, Texas 75379-5549
Salary Minimum: $60,000
Key Contact: Steven A. Jablo
Marilyn B. Polan

Industries: Most
Description: Highly personal, professional &
  discreet service

Jackson & Coker

115 Perimeter Ctr. Pl., Ste. 380
Atlanta, Georgia 30346
Key Contact: Kay Slayden
Joe Carson

Industries: I.14 I.15
Description: Placing physicians in hospitals,
group practices, HMO's & other
healthcare settings nationwide

Jahrling & Co.

P.O. Box 1223
Morristown, New Jersey 07962-1223
Salary Minimum: $60,000
Key Contact: Walter F. Jahrling

Functions: Most
Industries: Most
Professional Affiliations: IACPR
Description: A professional firm that offers
personalized service

Jakobs & Assoc. Int'l.

79 Burda Ave.
New City, New York 10956
Salary Minimum: $75,000
Key Contact: Nancy M. Jakobs
Frederick H. Jakobs

Functions: Most
Industries: Most
Description: Executive search, compensation &
human resources consulting services to
diverse industries

Pendleton James & Assoc., Inc.

200 Park Ave., Ste. 3706
New York, New York 10166
Salary Minimum: $100,000
Key Contact: E. Pendleton James

Functions: Most
Industries: Most
Description: Senior management level searches

Michael James & Co., Inc.

3000 Langford Rd., Bldg. 400
Norcross, Georgia 30071
Salary Minimum: $50,000
Key Contact: M. James Soutouras

Functions: Most
Industries: D.00 D.E0 D.H0 E.00 J.13
Description: Aircraft, aerospace,
telecommunications, high tech industries:
senior mgmt. & technical positions

James, Layton Int'l., Inc.

2 N. Riverside Plz., Ste. 2323
Chicago, Illinois 60606
Salary Minimum: $50,000
Key Contact: James G. Aslaksen
Bernard L. Layton
Timothy W. O'Donnell
Andrew J. Lane
Margaret B. Mulligan

Functions: Most
Industries: Most + C.00 D.15 D.18 D.19 D.I0
Professional Affiliations: AACC, AICHE, ASM,
ISPE, SPE
Description: Specialists in chemicals, plastics,
medical, pharmaceuticals & construction
industries

January Management Group

172 E. State St.
Columbus, Ohio 43215
Salary Minimum: $50,000
Key Contact: Bruce M. Bastoky

Functions: Most + 01.0 02.0 03.0 06.0
Industries: Most + D.00 F.00 G.00 H.R0
Professional Affiliations: IACPR, ASTD,
SHRM
Description: Generalist firm staffed by former
human resources executives

Jender & Company

800 W. 5th Ave., Ste. 205B
Naperville, Illinois 60563
Salary Minimum: $50,000
Key Contact: Jesse Jender
Timothy Gaffney

Functions: Most + 01.0 02.0 03.0 04.0 05.0
Industries: B.0W D.00 D.D0 D.E0 D.H0
Professional Affiliations: EMA
Description: Specialize: all functional areas for
any company manufacturing a product

John & Powers, Inc.

12935 N. Forty Dr., Ste. 214
St. Louis, Missouri 63141
Salary Minimum: $75,000
Key Contact: Harold A. John

Functions: Most
Industries: Most
Description: Consulting firm which specializes in executive search to all industries

Johnson & Assoc., Inc.

101 First St., Ste. 282
Los Altos, California 94022
Salary Minimum: $50,000
Key Contact: Cheri Johnson

Functions: Most
Industries: B.10 D.24 D.25 D.H0 D.I0
Professional Affiliations: CERA, NAER, NCHRC
Description: Search specialists primarily hi-tech, artificial intelligence, bio-medical instrumentation

John H. Johnson & Assoc., Inc.

332 S. Michigan Ave., Ste. 1201
Chicago, Illinois 60604
Salary Minimum: $50,000
Key Contact: John H. Johnson

Functions: Most + 02.0 04.0 05.0 11.5
Industries: Most + C.00 D.00 D.E0 D.H0
Description: Professional retainer based executive search for all industries/functional areas

L.J. Johnson & Co.

2705 Lowell Rd.
Ann Arbor, Michigan 48103-2249
Salary Minimum: $40,000
Key Contact: L.J. Johnson

Functions: Most + 02.0 04.0 06.0 09.0 11.1
Industries: Most + D.00 D.E0 D.H0 H.00 J.00
Professional Affiliations: FEI
Description: Top management, technical management, MIS, financial, sales & high technology

Ronald S. Johnson Assoc., Inc.

11661 San Vicente Blvd.
Los Angeles, California 90049
Salary Minimum: $90,000
Key Contact: Ronald S. Johnson
Pat Kriste

Functions: Most + 01.1 01.2 04.0 05.0 11.5
Industries: B.0W D.00 D.H0 D.I0 H.12
Professional Affiliations: CERA
Description: Senior management recruiting for medium to high technology & environmental areas

Johnson Smith & Knisely Inc.

475 Fifth Ave., 14th Fl.
New York, New York 10017
Salary Minimum: $75,000
Key Contact: Kendall A. Elsom, Jr.
Debbie Erder
Susan Goodman
Maureen Kelleher
Gary I. Klein
Gary Knisely
Ruth Loomis
Anthony W.G. Lord
William Maher
John W. Malcom
Joel Millonzi, M.D.
Freda Mindlin
Vincent S. Morgan
Barbara Pickens
Carrie Loomis Pryor
F. Clawson Smith
James Theodore
Paula Weiner
Jeffrey Zwiff

Functions: Most + 01.0 05.0 06.0 08.0 09.0
Industries: D.10 G.00 I.10 I.12 J.11
Professional Affiliations: AESC, ACG, NYHRP
Description: An internationally recognized, research-based generalist firm with strong market niches

International Branches:
Dusseldorf, Frankfurt, Hamburg, London, Lund, Malmo, Milan, Munchen, Paris, Zurich

Networks:
Accord Group
Hong Kong, London, Lund, Milan, Paris

Jordan-Sitter Assoc.

14074 Nacogdoches, Ste. 323
San Antonio, Texas 78247
Salary Minimum: $35,000
Key Contact: William P. Sitter

Functions: Most + 01.0 02.0 04.0 05.0 06.0
Industries: A.00 C.00 D.22 D.23
Professional Affiliations: AED, CIMA, EMI, ICPM, SERC
Description: All functions of construction equipment manufacturers & dealers on retained basis

Inge Judd Assoc.

120 E. 36th St.
New York, New York 10016
Salary Minimum: $100,000
Key Contact: Inge Judd
Gene Judd

Functions: Most + 05.0 05.1 05.5 06.0 11.1
Industries: B.0W I.11 J.00 J.12
Description: Specialist in consumer goods, consumer financial services & direct marketing

Jim Just & Assoc.

P.O. Box 946
Safety Harbor, Florida 34695-0946
Salary Minimum: $35,000
Key Contact: Jim Just
Debra A. Just

Functions: Most
Industries: D.11 D.12 D.21 G.00
Description: Broad range of consulting services to the apparel, home furnishings & textile industries

L. E. Justice Consulting Assoc.

960 Ponderosa Ln.
Barrington, Illinois 60010-5800
Salary Minimum: $50,000
Key Contact: Larry E. Justice
Ginger L. Justice

Functions: 01.0 02.0 03.0 05.0 06.0
Industries: D.00 D.10 D.11 D.12 D.19
Professional Affiliations: AMA, APICS
Description: Executive search, professional placement & mgmt. consulting services to manufacturing industry

K/N Int'l.

1150 Post Rd.
Fairfield, Connecticut 06430
Salary Minimum: $60,000
Key Contact: Edgar F. Newman
Edward J. Kuzma

Functions: 01.0 02.0 05.0 08.0 09.7
Industries: D.H0 D.I0 H.10 I.14 I.15
Description: Recruit in all functional areas for
our multi-national client base

George Kaludis Assoc., Inc.

2505 Hillsboro Rd., Ste. 302
Nashville, Tennessee 37212
Salary Minimum: $50,000
Key Contact: G.J. Posner

Functions: Most
Industries: I.12 I.13 J.13 K.00
Professional Affiliations: AAHE, CUPA,
NACUBO
Description: Specialize in recruiting senior
administrators for colleges, universities &
non-profit organizations

Gary Kaplan & Assoc.

201 S. Lake Ave., Ste. 600
Pasadena, California 91101
Salary Minimum: $50,000
Key Contact: Gary Kaplan
Walter B. McNichols
Timothy C. Alders
Laurence Broe
Christine Montagna
Kristine M. Anderson

Functions: Most + 01.0 06.0 08.0 09.0 11.4
Industries: Most + D.00 D.H0 H.00 I.00 J.00
Professional Affiliations: IACPR, ACA, CERA,
EMA, SHRM
Description: General search practice

Karam Group Int'l.

821 Seventeenth St., Ste 620
Denver, Colorado 80202
Salary Minimum: $60,000
Key Contact: Richard P. Karam

Functions: Most + 01.0 01.1 01.2 01.3
Industries: Most
Description: Provides retained executive search
& selection services

Howard Karr & Assoc., Inc.

1777 Borel Pl., Ste. 408
San Mateo, California 94402
Salary Minimum: $70,000
Key Contact: Nancy Tilley Bush
Howard L. Karr

Functions: 01.0 06.0 08.0
Industries: Most
Professional Affiliations: AESC, CERA
Description: Specializing in senior financial &
administrative searches

Allan Karson Assoc., Inc.

8200 Blvd. East
North Bergen, New Jersey 07047
Salary Minimum: $100,000
Key Contact: Allan Karson

Functions: 01.2 01.3 04.0 05.0 09.0
Industries: D.24 D.H0 I.18 J.13
Description: Senior management positions in
high technology

Martin Kartin & Co., Inc.

211 E. 70th St.
New York, New York 10021
Salary Minimum: $50,000
Key Contact: Martin C. Kartin

Functions: Most
Industries: D.10 D.11 D.16 D.18 G.00
Description: Individualized custom service.
Consumer products specialists

Keane Assoc.

676 Commonwealth Ave.
Newton, Massachusetts 02159
Salary Minimum: $75,000
Key Contact: Kevin Keane
Janet Britcher

Industries: D.24 D.H0 J.13
Professional Affiliations: SHRM
Description: All searches conducted by
principals

A.T. Kearney Executive Search
222 S. Riverside Plz.
Chicago, Illinois 60606
Salary Minimum: $60,000
Key Contact: Charles W. Sweet
Paul W. Schmidt

Branches:
6930 E. First St.
Scottsdale, Arizona 85251
Key Contact: Jill S. Faber

Biltmore Tower
500 S. Grand Ave.
Los Angeles, California 90071
Key Contact: Norman B. Keider

1 Lagoon Dr., Ste. 220
Redwood City, California 94065
Key Contact: Carl Olsen

One Tabor Ctr., Ste. 1300
1200 17th St.
Denver, Colorado 80202
Key Contact: Patricia S. Cook

4 Landmark Sq., Ste. 302
Stamford, Connecticut 06901
Key Contact: Mark McMahon

Miami Center, Suite 3180
201 South Biscayne Boulevard
Miami, Florida 33131
Key Contact: John T. Mestepey

1100 Abernathy Rd., Ste 900
Atlanta, Georgia 30328-5603
Key Contact: Norman F. Mitchell

Functions: Most
Industries: Most
Professional Affiliations: AESC
Description: Broad line firm serving most
    industries & all functions

8500 Normandale Lake Blvd., Ste. 1730
Minneapolis, Minnesota 55437
Key Contact: Don A. Hykes

875 Third Ave.
New York, New York 10022
Key Contact: Mark McMahon

1111 Superior, Ste 900
Cleveland, Ohio 44114
Key Contact: Lewis F. Lenkaitis

500 N. Akard St., Ste. 4170
Lincoln Plz.
Dallas, Texas 75201
Key Contact: Rocky Johnson

5599 San Felipe, Ste. 760
Sonat Twr. B
Houston, Texas 77056
Key Contact: Bruce F. Brownson

225 Reinekers Ln.
Alexandria, Virginia 22314
Key Contact: Roger I. Sekera

Box 10, Suite 2314, 20 Queen Street West
Toronto, Ontario M5H-3R3 Canada
Key Contact: Sandra Fowler

International Branches:
Amsterdam, Brussels, Dusseldorf, London, Madrid, Neuilly-sur-Seine

Affiliates/Other Offices:
Frieze & Assoc. Pty. Ltd., Melbourne
Frieze & Assoc. Pty. Ltd., Sydney

Kellogg Consulting Group
13000 Sawgrass Village Cir., #6
Ponte Vedra Beach, Florida 32082
Salary Minimum: $30,000
Key Contact: William M. Flemister, Jr.
Buddy Holt
Michael White
Kristin Grant

Functions: Most + 02.0 09.0
Industries: B.0W D.00 D.E0 I.00 I.14
Description: Firm specializing in healthcare,
    data processing, & engineering/
    manufacturing & finance/banking

M. Scott Kemp & Assoc., Inc.
44 E. Long Lake Rd., Ste. 145
Bloomfield Hills, Michigan 48304-2322
Salary Minimum: $75,000
Key Contact: Scott Kemp
Jean Lacey
Mark Boyer

Functions: Most + 02.0 03.0 04.0 05.0 09.0
Industries: Most + D.00 D.D0 D.H0 E.00
    H.00
Description: Experienced consultants working
    on senior management searches-retainer
    only

Kendro & Assoc.

11512 N. Port Washington Rd.
P.O. Box 68
Mequon, Wisconsin 53092
Salary Minimum: $30,000
Key Contact: Richard J. Kendro
Barbara A. Kendro

Functions: Most
Industries: Most
Professional Affiliations: ASPA
Description: Serving clients nationwide in most functions & industries with expertise in heat transfer

Kennedy & Co.

20 N. Wacker Drive, Ste. 2507
Chicago, Illinois 60606
Salary Minimum: $60,000
Key Contact: Thomas J. Moran
Alan P. Hanley
Thomas Peterson
Diane Dombeck

Functions: Most
Industries: Most
Description: Specialized practice to the financial services industry

Kenny, Kindler, Hunt & Howe

1 Dag Hammarskjold Plz.
New York, New York 10017
Salary Minimum: $100,000
Key Contact: James E. Hunt
Roger M. Kenny
Peter A. Kindler
William S. Howe

Functions: Most
Industries: Most
Professional Affiliations: AESC, IACPR, NACD
Description: Skilled veterans who practice their craft at the highest levels

Affiliates/Other Offices:
Delta Management Consultants, Dusseldorf
Delta Management Consultants, Frankfurt
Delta Management Consultants, Hamburg
Delta Management Consultants, Melbourne
Delta Management Consultants, Munich
Delta Management Consultants, Paris
Delta Management Consultants, Zurich
Delectus Chefsrekrytering AB, Malmo
Delectus Chefsrekrytering AB, Stockholm
Saxton Bampfylde Int'l. plc, London

Kensington Management Consultants, Inc.

25 Third St.
Stamford, Connecticut 06905
Salary Minimum: $40,000
Key Contact: Ann M. Fimmano
Seymour J. Sindeband

Functions: Most + 01.0 04.0 08.0 09.0 09.7
Industries: Most + D.E0 I.00 J.13 K.00
Description: Broad range of executive search & general management consulting

Branches:
25 S. Bemiston Ave., Ste. 212
St. Louis, Missouri 63105
Key Contact: Gerald Fimmano

International Branches:
London

Melvin Kent & Assoc., Inc.

88 E. Broad. St.
Columbus, Ohio 43215
Salary Minimum: $60,000
Key Contact: Melvin Kent

Functions: Most + 05.4 10.0 11.4 11.5
Industries: Most + B.0W D.H0 G.00 I.11 J.00
Description: Senior level sales searches for small to mid size clients

D. F. Kerry & Assoc.
1113 S. Third St.
Philadelphia, Pennsylvania 19147
Salary Minimum: $50,000
Key Contact: Donald F. Kerry

Functions: 01.1 01.2 01.3 02.4
Industries: A.00 B.00 B.0W D.22
Professional Affiliations: AIME, AMC
Description: Executive recruiting & executive
   outplacement

Kieffer, Ford, & Hadelman, Ltd.
2015 Spring Rd., Ste. 510
Oak Brook, Illinois 60521
Salary Minimum: $85,000
Key Contact: J. Daniel Ford
Jordan M. Hadelman
Michael C. Kieffer
Michael F. Doody

Functions: Most
Industries: I.00
Professional Affiliations: AESC
Description: Provide executive search at senior
   management level; concentrate in health
   care industry

Branches:
1100 Town & Country Rd., Ste. 1340
Orange, California 92668
Key Contact: Richard A. Swan

2301 E. Lamar Blvd., Ste. 464
Arlington, Texas 76000
Key Contact: Marvene M. Eastham

Affiliates/Other Offices:
Fenwick Partners, Lexington
Kors Montgomery Int'l., Houston
Civitas Int'l. GmbH, Munich
Jamieson Scott Executive Search, London
Technology Consulting S.R.C., Milan

Kincannon & Reed
8607 Westwood Center Dr.
Vienna, Virginia 22182
Salary Minimum: $75,000
Key Contact: Kelly Kincannon

Functions: Most
Industries: A.00 D.10 D.15 D.I0
Professional Affiliations: AESC, AAAS, ACS,
   ASTA, IACPR
Description: We provide international
   executive search services in biotechnology,
   food & agribusiness

The Kinlin Co., Inc.
6 Union St.
Natick, Massachusetts 01760
Salary Minimum: $50,000
Key Contact: Ellen C. Kinlin
Markey Burke

Functions: Most
Industries: Most
Professional Affiliations: NEHRA
Description: Generalist firm with focus on
   middle to senior management $50,000–
   $250,000

Richard Kinser & Assoc.
919 Third Ave., Ste. 2140
New York, New York 10022
Salary Minimum: $75,000
Key Contact: Richard Kinser
Lois Evans

Functions: Most + 01.0 05.0 06.0 08.0
Industries: Most + J.00
Professional Affiliations: AESC, IACPR
Description: Professional, experienced search
   for senior & middle management &
   boards

Kirby & Assoc.
1323 SE 4th Ave.
Ft. Lauderdale, Florida 33316
Salary Minimum: $60,000
Key Contact: Richard L. Kirby
A. Ashley McGinnis
C.E. Wilcoxen
Janet C. Kayan

Functions: Most
Industries: Most
Professional Affiliations: IACPR
Description: Specializing in hospitality,
   banking, travel, financial services &
   environmental

Kirkman & Searing

8000 Towers Crescent Dr., Ste. 560
Vienna, Virginia 22182
Salary Minimum: $70,000
Key Contact: J. Michael Kirkman
James M. Searing

Functions: Most
Industries: D.17 D.H0 H.10 I.14 J.13
Description: Generalist focusing in technology, healthcare & financial services

Kishbaugh Associates

2 Elm Sq., Musgrove Bldg.
Andover, Massachusetts 01810
Salary Minimum: $75,000
Key Contact: Herbert S. Kishbaugh
Douglas G. Walker

Functions: Most + 01.0 02.0 04.0 05.0 06.0
Industries: Most
Professional Affiliations: NEHRA
Description: Senior management search firm providing quality full service client support

Kittleman & Assoc.

300 S. Wacker Dr.
Chicago, Illinois 60606
Salary Minimum: $40,000
Key Contact: James M. Kittleman
Richard M. King
Jeanne M. Halvorsen

Functions: 01.1 05.5 06.2 08.1 11.4
Industries: I.12 I.13 I.14
Description: Executive search & management consulting exclusively for non-profit organizations

Jonah Kleinstein Assoc., Inc.

1270 Ave of the Americas
New York, New York 10020
Salary Minimum: $60,000
Key Contact: Jonah A. Kleinstein

Functions: Most + 02.0 05.0 06.0 08.0 11.5
Industries: Most + B.0W D.00 H.00 I.00 I.16
Description: Our unique approach enables us to present candidates to clients within 3-4 weeks

Kline Consulting, Inc.

250 Park Ave. S., Ste. 5000A
New York, New York 10003-1459
Salary Minimum: $75,000
Key Contact: Ellen K. Couch
Linda Kline

Functions: Most + 05.0 06.0 08.0 09.0 11.1
Industries: Most + D.00 D.H0 D.I0 H.00 I.16
Professional Affiliations: ACA, ASPA, ASTD, PF
Description: Professional personalized service; broad-based expertise in mid-upper management searches

Knapp Consultants

184 Old Ridgefield Rd.
Wilton, Connecticut 06897
Salary Minimum: $90,000
Key Contact: Ronald A. Knapp

Functions: Most
Industries: B.00 D.00 D.E0 D.H0
Professional Affiliations: IACPR
Description: Specialize in aerospace, high technology, electronics & general manufacturing industries

Koehler & Co.

700 N. Pilgrim Pkwy., Ste. 104
Elm Grove, Wisconsin 53122
Salary Minimum: $60,000
Key Contact: Jack Koehler

Functions: Most + 01.0 02.0 05.0
Industries: Most + D.00
Description: Conduct searches in all disciplines for technology & manufacturing oriented clients

T. J. Koellhoffer & Assoc.

The Campus Bldg., 1250 Rte. 28
Box 5362
North Branch, New Jersey 08876
Salary Minimum: $50,000
Key Contact: Thomas J. Koellhoffer

Functions: 01.0 04.0 05.0 09.2 09.4
Industries: D.13 D.E0 D.H0 J.12 K.10
Professional Affiliations: ASPA, ASQC
Description: Aerospace, info. processing, telecommunications, research/ development & biomedical electronics

Branches:
RD. 1
Ft. Plain, New York 13339
Key Contact: Robert W. Ritz

Fred Koffler Assoc.

942 Greenfield Rd.
Woodmere, New York 11598
Salary Minimum: $50,000
Key Contact: Fred Koffler

Functions: Most
Industries: Most
Description: Nationwide executive search firm specializing in senior management positions

Kolden & Assoc., Ltd.

20 N. Tower Rd., Ste. 12A
Oak Brook, Illinois 60521
Salary Minimum: $50,000
Key Contact: John A. Kolden

Functions: Most
Industries: Most
Professional Affiliations: IAER
Description: Mid to upper management recruiting

Koontz, Jeffries & Assoc., Inc.

383 Main St.
Chatham, New Jersey 07928
Salary Minimum: $70,000
Key Contact: Donald N. Koontz
Carlyle Newell

Functions: 01.0 02.0 03.0 04.0 05.0
Industries: D.00 D.H0 D.I0 I.00 J.00
Professional Affiliations: IACPR
Description: National generalist firm; written performance guaranteed; written off-limits policy

Korn/Ferry Int'l.

237 Park Ave.
New York, New York 10017
Salary Minimum: $75,000
Key Contact: Richard M. Ferry

Functions: Most
Industries: Most
Professional Affiliations: AESC

Branches:
100 E. Wardlow
Long Beach, California 90807
Key Contact: Jane Hurd

The Transamerica Pyramid
600 Montgomery St., 31st Flr.
San Francisco, California 94111
Key Contact: Buzz Schulte
Ted Ward

1800 Century Park East
Ste. 900
Los Angeles, California 90067

One Landmark Sq.
Stamford, Connecticut 06901
Key Contact: Michael Rottblatt

601 S. Figueroa, Ste. 1900
Los Angeles, California 90017
Key Contact: Bob Rollo

Presidential Plaza
900 19th St., N.W.
Washington, District of Columbia 20006
Key Contact: Ron Walker

Embarcadero Corp. Ctr.
2483 E. Bayshore Rd., Ste. 101
Palo Alto, California 94303
Key Contact: Michael Helft

1300 Dove St., Ste. 300
Newport Beach, California 92660
Key Contact: Elliot Gordon

233 Peachtree St., N.E.
Ste. 701
Atlanta, Georgia 30303
Key Contact: Tom Hall

120 S. Riverside Plaza
Ste. 918
Chicago, Illinois 60606
Key Contact: Michael Boxberger

101 Federal St., 24th Flr.
Boston, Massachusetts 02110
Key Contact: John Sullivan

2508 IDS Center, 80 S. 8th St.
Minneapolis, Minnesota 55402
Key Contact: Allan Raymond

Eaton Center
1111 Superior Ave.
Cleveland, Ohio 44114
Key Contact: Jim Herget

3950 Lincoln Plz.
500 N. Akard St.
Dallas, Texas 75201
Key Contact: Richard Hardison

1100 Milam Bldg., Ste. 3400
Houston, Texas 77002
Key Contact: Gerald Griffin

First Interstate Ctr.
1201 Third Ave., Ste. 2120
Seattle, Washington 98101
Key Contact: Ed Blecksmith

40 King St. W., Ste. 1814
Scotia Plaza, P.O. Box 118
Toronto, Ontario M5H 3YZ Canada
Key Contact: Sid Humphreys

Montes Urales
641 Lomas de Chapultepec
Mexico City, Mexico DF11000 Mexico
Key Contact: Horacio McCoy

Daniel Zambrano
525 Col. Chepe Vera
Monterrey, Nuevo Leon Mexico
Key Contact: Juan Llaguno

International Branches:
Amsterdam, Bangkok, Brussels, Budapest, Buenos Aires, Chacao, Copenhagen, Frankfurt, Geneva, Hato Rey, Hong Kong, Kuala Lumpur, London, Madrid, Melbourne, Milan, Paris, Rome, Sao Paulo, Singapore, Sydney, Tokyo, Zurich

Korn/Ferry, Int'l., S.A. de C.V.
Montes Urales 641
Mexico City, Mexico DF 11000 Mexico
Salary Minimum: $50,000
Key Contact: Horacio McCoy
Manuel Papayanopulos
Thurston R. Hamer
Maria Elena Valdez
Fernando Tello

Branches:
Daniel Zambrano 525
Col. Chepe Vera
Monterrey, Nuevo Leon Mexico
Key Contact: Juan F. Llaguno

Functions: Most
Industries: Most
Professional Affiliations: ARIOAC
Description: By far Mexico's leading & largest executive search firm

Kors Montgomery Int'l.
1980 Post Oak Blvd., Ste. 2280
Houston, Texas 77056
Salary Minimum: $100,000
Key Contact: R. Paul Kors

Functions: Most
Industries: Most + B.00 D.15
Description: Search firm with a global reach, concentrating on technology, energy, chemicals & ntrl. resources

Affiliates/Other Offices:
Fenwick Partners, Lexington
Kieffer, Ford, & Hadelman, Ltd., Oak Brook
Baker-Harris & Partners, Ltd., Toronto
Technology Consulting S.R.C., Milan
Civitas Int'l. GmbH, Munich
IMCA Group, Tokyo

Kostmayer Assoc., Inc.
40 N. Tulane St.
Princeton, New Jersey 08540
Salary Minimum: $100,000
Key Contact: Roger Kostmayer

Branches:
1410 Harper House,
Village of Cross Keys
Baltimore, Maryland 21210
Key Contact: Roger C. Kostmayer

Functions: Most
Industries: H.00 H.10 H.11 H.12 H.I0
Professional Affiliations: IACPR
Description: Financial services, insurance,
mutual funds-all line & staff functions

The J. Kovach Group, Inc.
Gateway Twrs., Ste. 2710
Pittsburgh, Pennsylvania 15222
Salary Minimum: $50,000
Key Contact: Jerry Kovach

Functions: 01.0 05.0 07.0 08.0
Industries: C.00 H.R0 I.14
Professional Affiliations: AHA, ICSC, IREM,
MBA, NAIOP, ULI
Description: Specialize exclusively in real
estate, healthcare & construction
industries—national clientele

J. Krauss Assoc.
29 Polly Drive
Huntington, New York 11743
Salary Minimum: $35,000
Key Contact: Jack Krauss

Functions: Most + 01.0 02.0 05.0
Industries: Most + D.00
Professional Affiliations: NAPC
Description: Domestic/international executive
search, assessment & outplacement of
mid-upper management

Krauthamer & Assoc.
5530 Wisconsin Ave., Ste. 1110
Chevy Chase, Maryland 20815
Salary Minimum: $75,000
Key Contact: Gary L. Krauthamer
Ellen S. Dorfman

Functions: Most
Industries: B.00 D.00 D.E0 E.00 H.00
Description: Transportation, aerospace,
financial svs, power, manufacturing,
infrastructure & healthcare

Kremple & Meade, Inc.
23440 Civic Center Way, Ste. 100
Malibu, California 90265
Salary Minimum: $75,000
Key Contact: Jeannette Clemens
Thomas M. Meade

Functions: Most + 01.1 02.0 03.0 04.0 05.0
Industries: D.14 D.D0 D.E0 D.H0 H.10
Description: National firm engaged for senior
executive searches in various industries

D.A. Kreuter Assoc., Inc.
1700 Walnut St., Ste. 1121
Philadelphia, Pennsylvania 19103
Salary Minimum: $50,000
Key Contact: Daniel A. Kreuter
Joel Harrison
Brian A. Kilcullen

Functions: Most + 01.2 05.0 10.0
Industries: H.00 H.I0 I.14
Professional Affiliations: IACPR, ICI
Description: National executive search
consultants for the diversified/financial
services sector

Ira W. Krinsky & Assoc.
600 Westgate St.
Pasadena, California 91103
Key Contact: Ira W. Krinsky
Paula Carabelli

Functions: 01.0 01.1 01.2 11.0 11.4
Industries: I.12 I.13 I.14 K.00
Professional Affiliations: AASA, ACE, CERA,
NAIS
Description: Client-retained, non-contingent
executive search firm specializing in
education

Kuehne & Co., Inc.
180 N. LaSalle St., Ste. 2920
Chicago, Illinois 60601
Salary Minimum: $50,000
Key Contact: Kenneth H. Kuehne

Functions: Most
Industries: Most
Description: Executive recruiting & human
resources management consulting

John Kuhn & Assoc.
12065 W. Janesville Rd.
P.O. Box 214
Hales Corners, Wisconsin 53130
Salary Minimum: $50,000
Key Contact: John J. Kuhn

Functions: Most
Industries: Most + D.12 D.13 D.18 D.19 D.21
Description: A small retainer firm dedicated to
excellence in executive search

Paul Kull & Co.
121 Center Grove Rd.
Randolph, New Jersey 07869
Salary Minimum: $40,000
Key Contact: Paul Kull

Functions: 01.0 02.0 04.0 05.0 09.0
Industries: B.0W D.00 D.D0 D.H0 D.I0
Description: High technology, multidisciplinary
searches-electronics, hardware/software,
energy

Kunzer Assoc., Ltd.
2001 Spring Rd.
Oak Brook, Illinois 60521
Salary Minimum: $50,000
Key Contact: William J. Kunzer
Diane S. Kunzer

Functions: Most + 01.0 02.0 04.0 05.0 08.0
Industries: Most + D.00 D.D0 D.H0 G.00
I.00
Professional Affiliations: IACPR
Description: Provide executive search services
for domestic & international organizations

John Kurosky & Assoc.
3 Corporate Park Dr., Ste 210
Irvine, California 92714
Salary Minimum: $50,000
Key Contact: John Kurosky

Functions: 01.0 02.0 03.0 04.0 05.0
Industries: Most + B.00 D.00 D.H0 D.I0
Description: High technology oriented
executive search, all disciplines, middle/
senior management

L O R Personnel Div.
418 Wall St.
Princeton, New Jersey 08540
Salary Minimum: $35,000
Key Contact: Joan Aller
M. Don Lyons
V. G. Rogers

Functions: 01.0 02.0 05.0 08.0 11.0
Industries: A.00 D.00 D.I0 H.00 I.00
Professional Affiliations: MAAPC, NAPC,
NJAPC
Description: Small; executive recruiters all
disciplines; $35k up; manufacturing &
financial industries

Marvin Laba & Assoc.
6255 Sunset Blvd., Ste. 2000
Los Angeles, California 90028
Salary Minimum: $35,000
Key Contact: Marvin Laba

Functions: 01.0 05.0 06.0 08.0 09.0
Industries: D.00 F.00 G.00 H.00 J.00
Description: Specialists in department,
specialty & mass retailers & the vendors
who supply them

Laguzza Assoc., Ltd.
810 Seventh Ave.
New York, New York 10017
Salary Minimum: $75,000
Key Contact: John Laguzza

Functions: 01.0 08.0
Industries: A.00
Description: Specializing in financial functions

Networks:
ACES (Associated Consultants in Executive Search)
Brussels, London, Lyon, Milan, Paris, Wiesbaden

Lamalie Assoc., Inc.

489 Fifth Ave.
New York, New York 10017
Salary Minimum: $75,000
Key Contact: John F. Johnson
Anthony B. Cashen

Functions: Most
Industries: Most
Professional Affiliations: AESC, EMA, HRPS, IACPR
Description: Search practice spanning most industries, with emphasis on senior management

Branches:
13920 North Dale Mabry
Tampa, Florida 33618
Key Contact: Jack P. Wissman

1375 E. Ninth St., Ste. 1320
One Cleveland Ctr.
Cleveland, Ohio 44114
Key Contact: John F. Johnson
Charles E. Wallace, Jr.

3340 Peachtree Rd., NE
Tower Pl.
Atlanta, Georgia 30326
Key Contact: Michael S. Reeder

1601 Elm St., Thanksgiving Twr.
Dallas, Texas 75201
Key Contact: Robert L. Pearson

123 N. Wacker Dr., #950
Chicago, Illinois 60606
Key Contact: John T. Gardner

1301 McKinney St., Ste. 3520
Chevron Tower
Houston, Texas 77010
Key Contact: Arthur Newman
William A. Clarey, II

Networks:
AMROP International
Amsterdam, Auckland, Berlin, Brussels,
Buenos Aires, Calgary, Copenhagen, Dublin,
Dusseldorf, Frankfurt, Garza Garcia,
Gothenburg, Hamburg, Helsinki, Hong Kong,
Johannesburg, Kuala Lumpur, Lisbon, Madrid,
Melbourne, Mexico City, Milan, Montreal,
Munich, Paris, Queretaro, Sao Paulo,
Singapore, Stockholm, Sydney, Taipei,
Toronto, Vancouver, Zurich

The Landmark Consulting Group Inc.

155 University Ave., Ste 206
Toronto, Ontario M5H 3B7 Canada
Key Contact: James Lundy
Janet Wright

Functions: 01.2 11.4
Industries: I.12 I.13 I.14 K.00
Description: Specialize in senior-level searches in the public & not-for-profit sectors

Affiliates/Other Offices:
Auerbach Assoc., Belmont

Langer Assoc., Inc.

188 East Post Rd.
White Plains, New York 10601
Salary Minimum: $75,000
Key Contact: Joel A. Langer

Functions: Most + 01.0 05.0 06.0 08.0 09.0
Industries: Most + D.00 D.10 D.18 I.00 J.11
Description: Retainer search firm with focus on difficult to fill executive positions

Lansky Assoc.

5895 Friars Rd., Ste. 5206
San Diego, California 92110
Salary Minimum: $40,000
Key Contact: Loren Lansky

Functions: 01.0 01.1 01.2 01.3 08.0
Industries: H.00 H.10 H.11 H.12 J.10
Professional Affiliations: ICSC
Description: Retained executive search & management consulting within the shopping center industry

Lawrence L. Lapham, Inc.

80 Park Ave., Ste. 3K
New York, New York 10016
Salary Minimum: $50,000
Key Contact: Lawrence L. Lapham

Functions: Most + 01.0 02.0 03.0 04.0 05.0
Industries: Most + D.00 D.D0 D.H0 E.00
   F.00
Professional Affiliations: AESC

Larkin & Co.

582 Market, Ste. 1115
San Francisco, California 94104
Salary Minimum: $70,000
Key Contact: Dick Larkin

Functions: Most + 01.2 02.5 05.2 09.7 11.5
Industries: B.0W D.E0 D.H0 I.00 J.00
Professional Affiliations: CERA
Description: Strong orientation to marketing &
   general management

Larsen & Lee, Inc.

7101 Wisconsin Ave.
Bethesda, Maryland 20814
Salary Minimum: $60,000
Key Contact: Jospeh J. Lee

Functions: Most + 08.0 08.4 11.2 11.5
Industries: Most
Description: Tax & financial executive search
   for CPA-firm & corporate clients,
   environmental & minority

Larsen Int'l., Inc.

7200 Wisconsin Ave., Ste. 702
Bethesda, Maryland 20814
Salary Minimum: $60,000
Key Contact: Edward Bitar
Wyche Bonnot
Martha Seitz
Robert C. Hanawalt

Functions: 01.0 08.4 11.6
Industries: C.00 H.10 I.19
Professional Affiliations: ASME, AWWA,
   IEEE, PSMA, SMPS
Description: Specializing in architectural/
   engineering, design/construct & public
   accounting areas

Larson & Stephanian

31877 Del Obispo, Ste. 213
San Juan Capistrano, California 92675
Salary Minimum: $50,000
Key Contact: Paul W. Larson
Armand Stephanian

Functions: Most + 01.0 02.0 04.0 05.0
Industries: D.17 D.18 D.I0 I.14
Description: Specialists in medical device,
   medical diagnostics, biotechnology &
   health care providers

Lasher Assoc.

1200 S. Pine Island Rd., Ste 370
Ft. Lauderdale, Florida 33324
Salary Minimum: $50,000
Key Contact: Charles M. Lasher

Functions: Most + 02.0 04.0 05.0 08.0
Industries: Most + D.00 D.H0 I.00 J.00
Description: Serving major corporations to
   emerging companies commited to quality
   performance

Michael Latas & Assoc., Inc.

1311 Lindbergh Plaza Ctr.
St. Louis, Missouri 63132
Salary Minimum: $40,000
Key Contact: Michael Latas
Gary Jesberg
Richard Latas
Violetta Dupman

Functions: Most
Industries: Most + C.00 D.00 G.00 H.R0
Description: All areas of construction,
   construction engineering, retail &
   manufacturing nationally

Branches:
P.O. Box 4503
Youngstown, Ohio 44515
Key Contact: Samuel Rusnov

Lauer Consulting Services, Inc.

3180 N. Lake Shore Dr., Ste. 13A
Chicago, Illinois 60657
Salary Minimum: $50,000
Key Contact: Peter H. Lauer
Therese A. Lauer

Functions: Most + 02.0 02.4 03.0 05.0 08.0
Industries: B.0W B.10 D.19 H.12 I.13
Professional Affiliations: AICPA, AMA, ISCPA
Description: Principal has 20+ years in
retainer search; 20 in industry

Lauer, Sbarbaro Assoc., Inc.

30 N. LaSalle St., Ste. 4030
Chicago, Illinois 60602
Salary Minimum: $50,000
Key Contact: Richard D. Sbarbaro
William J. Yacullo
Robert A. Mayer
Linda A. Dainis

Functions: Most + 02.0 05.0 06.0 08.0 09.0
Industries: Most + D.00 G.00 H.00 I.00
Professional Affiliations: AESC, IACPR, AMA,
ASPA, HRMAC, IERA
Description: Generalist firm operating
nationwide in the $50,000 to $500,000
range

Networks:
EMA Partners Int'l.
Amsterdam, Barcelona, Berlin, Bologna, Brussels, Caracas, Coral Gables, Dublin, Frankfurt,
London, Madrid, Miami, Milan, New York, Paris, Singapore, Turin, Verona, Washington

Lawrence-Leiter & Co.

427 W. 12th St.
Kansas City, Missouri 64105
Salary Minimum: $50,000
Key Contact: Wm B. Beeson

Functions: Most
Professional Affiliations: IMC
Description: Generalist management
consulting/human resources firm-seach
focus association executives

Lee & Burgess Assoc., Inc.

4501 College Blvd., Ste. 200
Leawood, Kansas 66211
Salary Minimum: $35,000
Key Contact: Michael C. Haughton
Theodore P. Richmond

Functions: Most + 01.0 02.0 05.0 06.0 08.0
Industries: Most + B.0W D.00 H.00 H.I0 I.00
Professional Affiliations: SHRM
Description: Specialize in human resources
management consulting & executive
search

Branches:
1401 17th St., Ste. 580
Denver, Colorado 80202
Key Contact: Ed Ryer

473 N. Kirkwood Rd., Ste. 200
St. Louis, Missouri 63122
Key Contact: Bruce Coonam

J. E. Lessner Assoc., Inc.

2143 East Newark Rd.
Lapeer, Michigan 48446
Salary Minimum: $50,000
Key Contact: Jack Lessner
Mary Ann Lessner
Lori Thomas

Functions: Most
Industries: B.00 D.00 D.D0 I.14 K.10
Description: Perform executive searches,
organizational development &
outplacement activities

Levin & Assoc.

3000 Sand Hill Rd., Bldg. 3, Ste. 110
Menlo Park, California 94025
Salary Minimum: $40,000
Key Contact: Becky Levin
Danelle Storm

Functions: Most
Industries: D.15 D.17 D.18 D.I0 I.16
Professional Affiliations: AACC, NAER
Description: Executive & technical recruiting/
consulting services for the healthcare
industries

The Lieberman Group
1140 Ave. of the Americas, 9th Fl.
New York, New York 10036
Salary Minimum: $75,000
Key Contact: Carole S. Lieberman

Functions: 01.0 02.0 03.0 05.0 06.0
Industries: Most
Professional Affiliations: IACPR
Description: Full service firm: large company
expertise, small company attention,
flexibility

Locke & Assoc.
2160 Charlotte Plaza
Charlotte, North Carolina 28244
Salary Minimum: $50,000
Key Contact: M. Fred Locke, Jr.

Functions: Most + 01.0 02.0 05.0 08.0 11.0
Industries: Most + B.00 C.00 D.00 H.00 I.00
Professional Affiliations: AESC
Description: Engineering & construction,
manufacturing, financial & service
industries-all disciplines

Branches:
4144 Carmichael Rd., Ste. 20
Montgomery, Alabama 36106
Key Contact: Glen O. Pruitt

The Lockridge Group, Inc.
P.O. Box 2658
Des Plaines, Illinois 60017-2658
Salary Minimum: $75,000
Key Contact: David Tannenbaum

Functions: Most
Industries: D.00
Description: Clientele limited to manufacturing
& distributing firms-all functional areas

J.P. Logan & Co., Inc.
101 E. 52nd St., 36th Fl.
New York, New York 10022
Salary Minimum: $100,000
Key Contact: James P. Logan, III

Functions: Most
Industries: Most
Description: Consultants to management in
executive selection

The Logan Group, Inc.
8816 Manchester #190
St. Louis, Missouri 63144
Key Contact: Brian Ryan

Functions: Most + 01.0 02.0 05.0 06.0 09.0
Industries: Most + D.00 D.E0 D.H0 I.00 J.00
Professional Affiliations: BPAA, EMA
Description: National/int'l. firm engaged in
quality search & surveys-activity tailored
to clients' needs

H.M. Long Int'l., Ltd.
237 Park Ave., Park Ave. Atrium
New York, New York 10017
Salary Minimum: $100,000
Key Contact: Helga Long

Functions: Most + 01.0 01.2 04.0 05.0
Industries: Most + D.10 D.13 D.18 D.I0 H.10
Professional Affiliations: IACPR
Description: We specialize in global, multi-
country senior executive search services

Branches:
35 Sebonac Rd.
Southampton, New York 11968
Key Contact: Robert Van Olst

Lovejoy & Lovejoy
90 Corona, Ste. 1407
Denver, Colorado 80218
Salary Minimum: $100,000
Key Contact: Alan K. Lovejoy
Ralph F. Lovejoy

Functions: Most + 01.0
Industries: Most
Professional Affiliations: NABIS
Description: Practice confined to search &
selection of company presidents and
presidents-to-be

Lowderman & Haney, Inc.
3939 Roswell Rd. NE, Ste. 100
Marietta, Georgia 30062
Salary Minimum: $50,000
Key Contact: J. Don Haney
William H. Lowderman

Functions: Most
Industries: I.14 I.15
Description: Healthcare executive & physician
search firm

Robert Lowell Int'l.
12200 Park Central Dr., Ste 120
Dallas, Texas 75251
Salary Minimum: $60,000
Key Contact: Robert M. Bryza
Lowell Foster
Frank D. Goushas
Emanuel Pearlman

Functions: Most
Industries: B.00 D.00 D.E0 D.H0 E.00
Description: Executive search, physician
recruitment & specialized management
consulting services

The John Lucht Consultancy Inc.
The Olympic Twr.
641 Fifth Ave.
New York, New York 10022
Salary Minimum: $120,000
Key Contact: John Lucht

Functions: Most + 01.0 05.0 06.0 08.0 09.0
Industries: Most + D.00 G.00 H.00 H.I0 J.00
Professional Affiliations: AESC, IACPR
Description: Outstanding generalist firm-CEO's
& senior management-all industries and
functions

The Lumsden Co., Inc.
1300 Grove Ave., Ste. 201
Barrington, Illinois 60010
Salary Minimum: $70,000
Key Contact: Roy S. Lumsden

Functions: Most + 01.0 02.0 05.0 06.0 08.0
Industries: Most + D.00 H.00 H.10 I.13 I.17
Description: A full service practice,
emphasizing quality & service to clients

Lund & Assoc., Inc.
1520 W. Cameron Ave., Ste. 160
West Covina, California 91790
Salary Minimum: $50,000
Key Contact: J. Kenneth Lund

Functions: Most + 02.0 04.0 05.0 11.3 11.5
Industries: B.00 B.0W C.00 D.00 D.H0
Description: Serve high technology & other
technology-driven industries

Lynch & Co.
3857 Birch St., Ste. 131
Newport Beach, California 92660
Salary Minimum: $50,000
Key Contact: John W. Lynch
Thomas B. Birch
Theodore P. Lynch
Edward A. Stearn

Functions: Most
Industries: C.00 D.E0 H.I0 H.R0
Description: Search for managers & key
technical specialists

Branches:
1940 W. Orangewood Ave., Ste. 110
Orange, California 92668

P.J. Lynch Assoc.
P.O. Box 967
Ridgefield, Connecticut 06877
Salary Minimum: $65,000
Key Contact: Patrick J. Lynch
Mary Wyton
Arlene Heissan

Functions: 01.0 05.0 06.0 08.0 11.0
Industries: Most
Description: Senior management assignment &
recruiting-specialty in information
products industry

Lynch Miller Moore, Inc.

10 S. Wacker Dr., Ste. 2935
Chicago, Illinois 60606
Salary Minimum: $75,000
Key Contact: Michael C. Lynch
Michael R. Miller
David S. Moore
Richard G. Hypes, Jr.
Daniel M. O'Hara

Functions: Most + 01.0 02.0 08.0 09.0
Industries: Most + D.00 D.H0 D.I0 H.00
Description: Retainer based firm specializing in senior assignments on national basis

MCC Assoc.

10 Wood Duck Ct.
Hackettstown, New Jersey 07840
Salary Minimum: $50,000
Key Contact: Daniel P. McConnell

Functions: Most + 01.0 02.0 05.0 08.0 09.0
Industries: Most + D.00 D.18 D.H0 I.15
Professional Affiliations: ASPA
Description: Quality human resources consulting, executive & management recruiting services

MD Resources, Inc.

9360 Sunset Dr., Ste. 250
Miami, Florida 33173
Salary Minimum: $80,000
Key Contact: Judith E. Berger
Stephen G. Schoen
Martin H. Osinski
Pat Wall

Functions: 11.0
Industries: I.00 I.14 I.15
Professional Affiliations: AAMD, ACHE, AGPA, AHA, AMA, MGMA, NAPR
Description: Leaders in retained search for physicians & healthcare executives, nationwide

Branches:
12774 Flat Meadow Ln.
Herndon, Virginia 22071
Key Contact: Michael E. Kurtz

720 Olive Way, Ste. 1625
Seattle, Washington 98101

META/MAT, Ltd.

120 Wood Ave. S., Ste. 300
Iselin, New Jersey 08830
Salary Minimum: $75,000
Key Contact: Fred Kopff
Andrew Borkin
Lesley C. Tischio

Functions: Most + 02.0 05.0 06.0 08.0 09.0
Industries: Most + D.00 D.H0 H.00 I.00
Professional Affiliations: IACPR, SHRM
Description: Unusual depth & breadth of knowledge in finance, high technology & consumer products businesses

Branches:
237 Park Ave., 21st Fl.
New York, New York 10017

M/J/A Partners

1100 Jorie Blvd., Ste. 215
Oak Brook, Illinois 60521
Salary Minimum: $65,000
Key Contact: Manuel J. Alves
Sue Mitchell

Functions: Most + 01.0 02.0 05.0 06.0 08.0
Professional Affiliations: IACPR, AMC, EMA, IMC

The Macdonald Group, Inc.

301 Rte. 17, Ste. 800
Rutherford, New Jersey 07070
Key Contact: G. William Macdonald

Functions: Most
Industries: Most + D.00 D.I0 H.00
Professional Affiliations: IACPR
Description: National practice generalist

Robert Madigan Assoc., Inc.
122 East 42nd St., Ste. 800
New York, New York 10168
Salary Minimum: $60,000
Key Contact: Robert M. Madigan

Functions: Most + 05.0 08.0 09.0 09.7
Industries: Most + D.00 H.00 H.10 J.00 J.13
Description: General practice across most
    management disciplines

The Madison Group
342 Madison Ave., Ste. 1060
New York, New York 10017
Salary Minimum: $75,000
Key Contact: David Soloway

Functions: Most
Industries: Most + B.0W D.H0 D.I0 H.00
Professional Affiliations: IACPR
Description: Commitment to providing quality
    service to a manageable number of clients

R.J. Maglio & Assoc., Inc.
P.O. Box 915858
Longwood, Florida 32791-5858
Salary Minimum: $55,000
Key Contact: Dick Maglio
Chris Petrie

Functions: 06.0 06.1 06.2
Industries: Most
Professional Affiliations: IACPR, SHRM
Description: Specializes in mid & senior level
    human resources management

Maglio & Co., Inc.
450 N. Sunnyslope Rd.
Brookfield, Wisconsin 53005
Salary Minimum: $30,000
Key Contact: Charles J. Maglio
Alan Konetzki
Vicki Burbach

Functions: Most
Industries: Most + I.14 I.15
Professional Affiliations: AHA, APICS, ASPA,
    NAPR, SHPM
Description: Retainer based executive search
    firm serving clients nationwide

Maiorino & Weston Assoc., Inc.
90 Grove St., Ste. 205
The Executive Pavilion
Ridgefield, Connecticut 06877
Salary Minimum: $50,000
Key Contact: Robert V. Maiorino

Functions: 01.3 02.4 05.0 06.0 08.0
Industries: D.00 F.00 H.10 H.12 I.00
Description: Generalist with concentration in
    marketing & sales management, both
    domestic & international

Maly & Assoc.
P.O. Box 55
Mill Valley, California 94941
Salary Minimum: $75,000
Key Contact: Anna Mae Maly

Functions: 06.0 06.1 11.3 11.5 11.6
Industries: B.00 B.0W B.10 C.00 D.I0
Professional Affiliations: CPC, EMA, NCHRC,
    SHRM, WCPA
Description: Design, implement & evaluate in-
    house recruiting programs

Management Advisors of Princeton, Inc.
301 N. Harrison St., Ste. 483
Princeton, New Jersey 08540
Salary Minimum: $60,000
Key Contact: Arthur M. Currier
Robert Greiff

Functions: Most
Industries: Most
Description: Large research staff—computerized

Management Catalysts
P.O. Box 70
Ship Bottom, New Jersey 08008
Key Contact: J.R. Stockton
N.O. Boyd

Functions: 02.1 02.5 03.4 04.0 11.3
Industries: D.10 D.15 D.16 D.18 D.I0
Professional Affiliations: ACS, ASM, IFT
Description: Technical leadership in food,
    drug, chemical and allied industries

Management Resources Int'l.

160 E. 88th St., Ste. 12G
New York, New York 10028
Salary Minimum: $25,000
Key Contact: F. J. Rotundo

Functions: Most
Industries: Most
Description: Search assignments conducted for Fortune 500, banking, financial & institutions

Management Science Assoc.

MSA Bldg., Ste. 300
4801 Cliff Ave.
Independence, Missouri 64055
Salary Minimum: $50,000
Key Contact: Jane Cook

Functions: Most + 01.2 06.0 11.4
Industries: I.14
Description: Represent client hospitals in retained searches for executives in hospital administration

F. L. Mannix & Co., Inc.

10 Village Rd.
Weston, Massachusetts 02193
Salary Minimum: $30,000
Key Contact: Francis L. Mannix

Functions: Most + 01.0 05.0 06.0 08.0
Industries: Most + D.19 D.24 D.25 D.E0 J.12
Professional Affiliations: IACPR, AAA, IMC
Description: Middle and upper management & hard to find technologist searches

Mark Stanley & Co.

Two Alhambra Plz., Ste. 1106
Coral Gables, Florida 33134
Salary Minimum: $80,000
Key Contact: John H. Ramsey
Dianne D. Railton
Paul S. Weller, Jr.
Raymond A. Parker

Functions: Most
Industries: Most
Professional Affiliations: AESC
Description: Senior management, all industries, Int'l, LBO investment groups & financial services

Networks:
EMA Partners Int'l.
Amsterdam, Barcelona, Berlin, Bologna, Brussels, Caracas, Dublin, Frankfurt, London, Madrid, Milan, Paris, Singapore, Turin, Verona, Vienna

Marks & Co., Inc.

324 Main Ave., #364
Norwalk, Connecticut 06851
Salary Minimum: $50,000
Key Contact: Sharon Marks
Whitney Reese

Functions: 01.4 09.1
Industries: Most
Description: National primary practice in EDP audit, data security, general audit

Brad Marks Int'l.

1888 Century Park E, Ste. 1040
Los Angeles, California 90067
Salary Minimum: $60,000
Key Contact: Brad Marks
Leslie Hollingsworth

Functions: Most
Industries: I.00 I.11 J.00 J.10 J.11 J.12
Description: Executive exclusively for the recruitment across all functions

Affiliates/Other Offices:
Peter Clark/Julia Curphey, London

Marlar Int'l. Inc.

410 Severn Ave., Ste. 403
Annapolis, Maryland 21403
Salary Minimum: $60,000
Key Contact: H. Edward Muendel

Functions: Most + 01.0 02.0 04.0 08.0 11.3
Industries: Most + B.0W D.00 D.I0 H.00 I.00
Professional Affiliations: IACPR, BCUN
Description: International executive search practice with 13 offices in 9 countries

Branches:
10880 Wilshire Blvd., Ste. 1010
Los Angeles, California 90024
Key Contact: Edward J. Savage

4590 McArthur Blvd., Ste. 550
Newport Beach, California 92660
Key Contact: Donald E. Parker

International Branches:
Amsterdam, Gothenburg, Guildford, London, Munich, Paris, Sydney, Vedbaek

Affiliates/Other Offices:
Dalmar, S.A., Madrid

575 Madison Ave.
New York, New York 10022

Marling Inc.
8283 Riverside Dr. P.O. Box 95
Dublin, Ohio 43017
Salary Minimum: $50,000
Key Contact: Richard A. Marling

Functions: Most
Industries: Most
Description: Generalist firm—national scope—
50k & up

The Marlow Group
149 Benvenue St., P.O. Box 707
Wellesley, Massachusetts 02181
Salary Minimum: $50,000
Key Contact: Paul M. Jones

Functions: 05.4 05.6 09.0 09.7 11.5
Industries: B.0W D.24 D.H0 D.I0 J.13
Description: Generalist-emphasis on sales &
marketing

Marra/Pizzi Assoc., Inc.
Millburn Esplanade
Millburn, New Jersey 07041
Salary Minimum: $60,000
Key Contact: John V. Marra, Jr.
Don Pizzi
Elaine Burfield

Functions: Most + 01.0 05.0 08.0 09.0 11.1
Industries: D.00 D.H0 D.I0 H.00 I.00
Professional Affiliations: IACPR, AICPA,
AMA, HRP, ISA, NAHB, SHRM, SIM
Description: Ability to deliver the
sophistication of a large firm without any
loss of personalized service

Branches:
2777 Summer St.
Stamford, Connecticut 06905
Key Contact: Donald A. Lotufo

Marshall Consultants, Inc.
360 E. 65th St.
New York, New York 10021
Salary Minimum: $25,000
Key Contact: Larry Marshall
Hugh McCandless

Functions: 05.1 05.7
Industries: Most
Professional Affiliations: IACPR, IABC, IPRA,
NIRI, PRSA
Description: 25 years experience searching for
communications, public relations &
advertising executives

Branches:
Box 1749
Seattle, Washington 98111
Key Contact: Judith Cushman

C.R. Martin & Assoc.
33 N. Dearborn St., Ste. 1500
Chicago, Illinois 60602
Key Contact: C. Robert Martin

Functions: 01.0 01.1 11.0 11.4
Industries: Most
Professional Affiliations: IMESC, NACD
Description: Director recruitment-corporate &
advisory boards

J. Martin & Assoc.
10820 Holman Ave., Ste. 103
Los Angeles, California 90024
Salary Minimum: $70,000
Key Contact: Judy R. Martin

Functions: Most + 01.0 01.2 01.3 05.0 09.0
Industries: D.24 D.H0
Description: Executive search-hi-tech,
   electronics, venture capital, upper mgmt
   positions, all disciplines

George R. Martin
P.O. Box 673
Doylestown, Pennsylvania 18901
Salary Minimum: $50,000
Key Contact: George R. Martin

Functions: Most
Industries: B.0W D.00 D.15 D.18 D.I0
Description: Marketing, sales, engineering,
   R&D & operations functions represent
   ninety percent of assignments

The Martin Group
1981 N. Broadway, Ste. 430
Walnut Creek, California 94596
Salary Minimum: $75,000
Key Contact: Lois G. Martin
Timothy P. Martin

Functions: Most + 01.0 02.0 06.0 08.0 09.0
Industries: Most
Professional Affiliations: CERA
Description: Specialists in general mgmt,
   finance, MIS, human resources,
   manufacturing, warehousing & dist.

Martin Mirtz Morice, Inc.
One Dock St., 3rd Fl.
Stamford, Connecticut 06902
Salary Minimum: $70,000
Key Contact: Robert F. Martin
P. John Mirtz
James L. Morice

Functions: Most
Industries: Most + D.00 D.H0 H.00 H.I0 I.00
Professional Affiliations: AESC
Description: Executive search/consulting firm
   serving clients worldwide

Maschal/Connors Inc.
115 N. Bay Ave., P. O. Box 1301
Beach Haven, New Jersey 08008
Salary Minimum: $100,000
Key Contact: Chuck Maschal
Jennifer Mancini

Functions: Most
Industries: D.00 D.22 D.23 D.24 D.25
Professional Affiliations: IACPR, NAER
Description: All functions for manufacturers in
   specified industries

Bruce Massey & Partners Inc.
330 Bay St., Ste. 1104
Toronto, Ontario M5H 2S8 Canada
Salary Minimum: $75,000
Key Contact: R. Bruce Massey
Wayne B. Perry

Functions: 01.0 01.2 02.0 03.0 04.0
Industries: B.0W D.00 D.E0 H.00 H.I0
Professional Affiliations: IACPR
Description: Senior management recruiting
   firm servicing clients nationally &
   internationally

Affiliates/Other Offices:
Charles Belle Isle Inc., Montreal

Matte & Company, Inc.
124 W. Putnam Ave., 2nd Fl.
Greenwich, Connecticut 06830
Salary Minimum: $70,000
Key Contact: Norman E. Matte

Functions: 01.0 02.0 05.0 08.0 11.5
Industries: B.0W D.00 H.00 H.I0 I.10
Professional Affiliations: IACPR
Description: Consulting services in the areas of
   exec. search & mgmt. assessment for
   multinational corporations

International Branches:
London

Gayle L. Mattson & Assoc.

2363 E. Stadium Blvd.
Ann Arbor, Michigan 48104
Salary Minimum: $50,000
Key Contact: Gayle L. Mattson

Functions: Most + 01.0 02.0 04.0 05.0 06.0
Industries: Most + D.00 D.22 E.00 I.00
Professional Affiliations: AFS, SAE
Description: National & international search;
metals, materials & manufacturing, all
levels

Mazza & Riley, Inc.

45 William St., Ste. 270
Wellesley Hills, Massachusetts 02181
Salary Minimum: $90,000
Key Contact: David B. Mazza
Elizabeth Riley

Functions: 01.0 01.2 05.0 08.0
Industries: Most
Description: Senior level: venture capital, high
tech, consumer areas, communications

The Mazzitelli Group, Ltd.

603 E. Lake St., Ste. 200K
Wayzata, Minnesota 55391
Key Contact: Teresa Mazzitelli

Functions: 01.0 01.2 02.0 02.4 05.0
Industries: D.00 D.13 D.14 D.18 J.00
Professional Affiliations: IACPR, NAWBO,
SMEI
Description: Generalist retainer search firm

McBride Assoc., Inc.

1511 K St., NW
Washington, District of Columbia 20005
Salary Minimum: $120,000
Key Contact: Jonathan E. McBride

Functions: Most + 01.0 05.0 06.0 08.0
Industries: Most + D.00 D.18 D.24 H.00 H.I0
Professional Affiliations: AESC, IACPR
Description: Discreet, comprehensive,
thorough, small; specialize in select high-
level assignments

McCooe & Assoc., Inc.

1250 E. Ridgewood Ave.
Ridgewood, New Jersey 07450
Key Contact: John J. McCooe
Sean J. McCooe

Functions: Most
Industries: B.10 D.12 D.13 D.15 D.21
Professional Affiliations: ACA, AIIE, AMA,
ASTD, EMA, IMC, RAPS, TAPPI
Description: Specializes in management
recruiting, management consulting &
organization development

McCormack & Farrow

695 Town Center Dr., Ste. 660
Costa Mesa, California 92626
Salary Minimum: $65,000
Key Contact: Jerry M. Farrow
Joseph A. McCormack

Functions: Most + 01.0 02.0 04.0 05.0 08.0
Industries: Most + D.00 D.H0 H.00 I.12 I.14
Professional Affiliations: AESC, CERA
Description: Retained search for senior &
middle management executives

McCullough Assoc.

6 Commerce Dr., Ste. 2000
Cranford, New Jersey 07016
Salary Minimum: $50,000
Key Contact: Kenneth D. McCullough

Functions: Most
Industries: Most + D.00
Professional Affiliations: IACPR
Description: 20 years experience; quality
approach

McDonald Assoc.

1290 N. Western Ave., #209
Lake Forest, Illinois 60045-1257
Salary Minimum: $50,000
Key Contact: Stanleigh B. McDonald
Scott A. McDonald
Jack A. Gillum

Functions: 01.0 06.0 11.0 11.1 11.6
Industries: B.00 C.00 D.00 H.R0 I.00
Professional Affiliations: ACA, ASPA, ASTD,
CCA, EMA, HRMAC, ISP&SM
Description: Retainer executive search/career
transition & outplacement

Branches:
1225 Live Oak Ct., Ste. 301
Ft. Collins, Colorado 80525

P.O. Box 905
110 Lafayette Rd.
North Hampton, New Hampshire 03862
Key Contact: Scott A. McDonald

McDonald/Long Assoc., Inc.
670 White Plains Rd.
Scarsdale, New York 10583
Salary Minimum: $75,000
Key Contact: Edwin C. McDonald
William G. Long

Functions: Most + 01.0 02.0 06.0 08.0 10.0
Industries: Most + D.00 H.00 H.I0 I.00 J.00
Description: Senior level search with specialty in corporate financial banking & insurance

McFeely Wackerle Shulman
20 N. Wacker Dr., Ste. 3110
Chicago, Illinois 60606
Salary Minimum: $150,000
Key Contact: Frederick W. Wackerle
Clarence E. McFeely

Functions: 01.0 11.1
Industries: Most
Professional Affiliations: AESC
Description: Generalist practice concentrating on senior executive level positions; CEO, COO

Branches:
425 California St.
San Francisco, California 94104
Key Contact: Mel Shulman

Robert E. McGrath & Assoc.
One Landmark Sq., Ste. 805
Stamford, Connecticut 06901
Salary Minimum: $65,000
Key Contact: Robert E. McGrath

Functions: 01.0 02.0 03.0 04.0 09.0
Industries: B.00 D.11 D.13 D.15 D.18
Professional Affiliations: IACPR, ISPE, PIMA, TAPPI
Description: Firm specializes in paper, pulp, nonwovens & pharmaceuticals

McKeen Melancon & Co.
P.O. Box 850143
Richardson, Texas 75085-0143
Salary Minimum: $60,000
Key Contact: James J. McKeen
S. L. Nyvall

Functions: 01.0 02.0 04.0 09.0 11.3
Industries: D.00 D.H0
Professional Affiliations: ASPA, ASTD, HRPS
Description: Engineering & technology mgmt. specialists-semi conductor, electronic systems,computer/peripherals

McMahon & Dee, Inc.
6111 Peachtree Dunwoody Rd.
Atlanta, Georgia 30328
Salary Minimum: $75,000
Key Contact: William Vincent Dee
Arthur H. McMahon
Robert J. Sweet
Ralph Wright

Functions: Most
Industries: Most
Professional Affiliations: AFCEA, AIAA, AIMT, AME, EIA, IEEE, PF, SAE, SME
Description: Twelve-year record of improving clients' competitiveness through executive search

Branches:
8777 Via De Ventura, Ste. 100
Scottsdale, Arizona 85258
Key Contact: William Franquement

32 Amelia
North Caldwell, New Jersey 07006
Key Contact: Stephan J. Lovett

McManners Assoc., Inc.
245 E. 63rd St.
New York, New York 10021
Salary Minimum: $100,000
Key Contact: Donald E. McManners
David S. Johnson
Pat Kent

Functions: Most + 01.0 02.0 04.0 05.0 06.0
Industries: Most + D.00 D.E0 D.H0 D.I0 E.00
Professional Affiliations: IACPR, EMA
Description: Senior level searches conducted,
all functions, strong candidate/industry
research capability

McNichol Assoc.
600 Chestnut St., Ste 1031
Philadelphia, Pennsylvania 19106
Salary Minimum: $60,000
Key Contact: John McNichol

Functions: Most + 11.0 11.5 11.6
Industries: Most + B.0W B.10 C.00
Professional Affiliations: IACPR, ASSE, IFMA,
ISPE, PMI, PSMA, SAME, SMPS
Description: Design/technical management
personnel for A/E consulting,
construction, institutional & industry

Jon McRae & Assoc., Inc.
300 Galleria Pkwy., Ste. 400
Atlanta, Georgia 30339
Key Contact: Jon McRae

Functions: 01.0 08.0 11.4
Industries: I.12 I.13
Professional Affiliations: ACE, CASE,
NACUBO, NSFRE
Description: A boutique firm serving higher
education & other non-profits

McSherry & Assoc.
7465 W. Cashew Dr.
Orland Park, Illinois 60462
Salary Minimum: $50,000
Key Contact: John P. McSherry

Functions: Most + 02.2 05.4 07.4 08.1 11.1
Industries: Most + D.26 I.14 I.18 I.19 J.13
Professional Affiliations: IACPR, AFSMI,
ASPA, CACI, HRMA
Description: Adept at speciality searches and
newly created position(s) searches

James Mead & Co.
164 Kings Hwy N.
Westport, Connecticut 06880
Salary Minimum: $70,000
Key Contact: James D. Mead
Laura T. Putnam

Functions: Most + 01.0 05.0 05.4
Industries: D.10 D.11 D.13 D.16 I.10
Description: Personalized search in consumer
package goods & related industries

Meder & Assoc.
111 Pfingsten Rd., Ste 319
Deerfield, Illinois 60015
Key Contact: Peter F. Meder

Functions: Most
Industries: D.00 D.10 H.00 H.R0 I.19
Description: Management consultants
specializing in executive search

Martin H. Meisel Assoc., Inc.
55 E. 87th St.
New York, New York 10128
Salary Minimum: $75,000
Key Contact: Martin H. Meisel
Norman Metzger

Functions: 01.2 06.0 06.1 06.2 08.0
Industries: H.00 I.14 I.15 I.19 I.21
Description: Research built search firm—
emphasis presently in medical and health
care fields

Meng, Finseth & Assoc., Inc.

Del Amo Executive Plz.
3868 Carson St., Ste. 112
Torrance, California 90503
Salary Minimum: $50,000
Key Contact: Cameron E. Meng
Carl L. Finseth
Charles M. Meng
Marlene M. Rafferty

Functions: Most
Industries: Most
Professional Affiliations: CERA
Description: Retainer search firm established
1970, serving broad range clientele-public
& private sector

Menzel, Robinson, Baldwin, Inc.

550 W. Campus Dr.
Arlington Heights, Illinois 60004
Salary Minimum: $60,000
Key Contact: Keith R. Baldwin
Gerald D. Menzel
Sharon K. Dahl

Functions: Most
Industries: Most
Professional Affiliations: IACPR, IERA
Description: Strong in sourcing and recognizing
exceptional talent, holistic interview &
evaluation

Mercedes & Co., Inc.

98 N. Washington St., Ste. 102
Boston, Massachusetts 02114
Salary Minimum: $100,000
Key Contact: Linda Mercedes Correia
Linda Mikula
Rebecca M. Deignan

Functions: Most
Industries: D.18 D.24 D.H0 D.I0 I.14
Description: Personal & responsive practice-
specialization: biotechnology,
pharmaceutical, software & hi-tech

The Mercer Group, Inc.

990 Hammond Dr., Ste. 510
One Lakeside Commons
Atlanta, Georgia 30328
Salary Minimum: $40,000
Key Contact: James L. Mercer

Functions: Most
Industries: K.00
Description: Limited to public & private sector
management consulting & public sector
executive search

Messett Assoc., Inc.

9350 S. Dixie Hwy., Ste. 970
Miami, Florida 33156
Salary Minimum: $75,000
Key Contact: William J. Messett, III
Alexander Young

Affiliates/Other Offices:
Int'l. Executive Search, Inc., Bangkok
Int'l. Executive Search, Inc., Hong Kong
Int'l. Executive Search, Inc., London
Int'l. Executive Search, Inc., Sao Paulo
Int'l. Executive Search, Inc., Singapore

Functions: Most + 01.0 02.0 05.0 06.0 08.0
Industries: Most
Description: We undertake top level executive
searches & mergers & acquisitions
worldwide; an IES partner

Michael Assoc.

613 Poplar Ave.
Elmhurst, Illinois 60126
Salary Minimum: $30,000
Key Contact: Michael S. Golding

Functions: 01.0 02.0 03.0 06.0 07.0
Industries: D.00
Professional Affiliations: IACPR
Description: Searches for manufacturing
management, engineering & technical
supervisors

The Neil Michael Group, Inc.
305 Madison Ave., Ste. 902
New York, New York 10165
Salary Minimum: $50,000
Key Contact: James Manuso
Alfred Middleton
Neil M. Solomon
Howard Glazer
Emile Hiesiger

International Branches:
London

Functions: Most + 01.0 02.0 04.0 05.0 08.0
Industries: D.00 D.H0 D.I0 I.00 I.16
Professional Affiliations: ABC, IMC, RAPS
Description: Retainer search firm with
  emphasis in healthcare and biotechnology-
  international

E.J. Michaels, Ltd.
1865 Palmer Ave., Ste. 101
Larchmont, New York 10538
Key Contact: Phillip E. Jacobs, Ph.D.

Functions: 11.4
Industries: I.14 I.15
Professional Affiliations: NAPR
Description: Healthcare specialization, special
  expertise in physician recruiting

Million & Assoc., Inc.
Carew Tower, Ste. 1831
Cincinnati, Ohio 45202
Salary Minimum: $40,000
Key Contact: Ken Million
Kim Kramer

Functions: Most
Industries: Most
Description: Executive search and recruitment
  in all fields of endeavor

Herbert Mines Assoc., Inc.
399 Park Ave., 27th Fl.
New York, New York 10022
Salary Minimum: $75,000
Key Contact: Herbert Mines
Lorna Pokart
Elaine Gilbert
Jane Vergari
Linda Pettibone
Howard Gross
Robert Nielsen

Functions: 01.0 02.0 05.0 06.0 08.0
Industries: D.10 D.11 D.16 F.00 G.00
Professional Affiliations: AESC, NRMA
Description: Search for senior mgmt. for retail,
  fashion mfg., cosmetics, consumer
  products & direct marketing

Jay Mitchell & Co.
501 Madison Ave.
New York, New York 10022
Salary Minimum: $60,000
Key Contact: Michael Mitchell
Edith Lord Young

Functions: 01.0 04.0
Industries: H.R0
Description: Executive search consultants to
  the institutional real estate community

Mitchell, Larsen & Zilliacus
523 W. 6th St., Ste. 1228
Los Angeles, California 90014
Salary Minimum: $50,000
Key Contact: Richard F. Larsen
Patrick W. Zilliacus

Branches:
599 Lexington Ave., 23rd Fl.
New York, New York 10022
Key Contact: Allen E. Parmenter

Functions: Most + 01.1 01.2 02.0 05.0 08.0
Industries: Most
Description: High level, general management
  retainer based recruiting firm

Networks:
Transearch Int'l.
Barcelona, Brussels, Budapest, Cologne, Copenhagen, Dusseldorf, Essen, Frankfurt, Gothenburg, Hamburg, Helsinki, Hilversum, Kent, Leeds, Lisbon, London, Milan, Munich, Oslo, Paris, Stockholm, Stuttgart, Vienna, Warsaw

Mitchell/Wolfson, Assoc.

2345 Waukegan Rd., Ste. N-190
Bannockburn, Illinois 60015
Salary Minimum: $100,000
Key Contact: Robert H. Wolfson

Functions: 06.1 10.0
Industries: H.10 H.I0
Professional Affiliations: ACA, LOMA
Description: Work is primarily in insurance and financial areas on a national basis

Montenido Assoc.

481 Cold Canyon Rd.
Calabasas, California 91302
Salary Minimum: $50,000
Key Contact: Stephen M. Wolf

Functions: 01.4 05.0 09.0 11.1
Industries: D.24 D.H0 H.00 I.17 I.18
Professional Affiliations: CERA
Description: Management searches for the computer hardware/software & financial services industries

Thomas R. Moore Executive Search

Parkway Central Plaza
611 Ryan Plaza Dr., Ste. 700
Arlington, Texas 76011
Salary Minimum: $40,000
Key Contact: Thomas R. Moore

Functions: 11.0 11.4
Industries: I.12 I.13 I.14
Professional Affiliations: AAFRC, CASE, NAHD, NSFRE
Description: Specialize in senior development personnel for gift-supported institutions

Morgan/Webber

4 Carman Mill Rd.
Massapequa, New York 11758
Salary Minimum: $50,000
Key Contact: Steven M. Lavender

Functions: 01.0 02.0 03.0 05.0 09.0
Industries: Most + D.19 D.22 D.D0 D.I0
Professional Affiliations: IACPR
Description: Generalist- strong in operations, technology, DOD, turn-arounds, material science, finance, start ups

Moriarty/Fox, Inc.

20 N. Wacker Dr., Ste. 2410
Chicago, Illinois 60606
Salary Minimum: $75,000
Key Contact: Philip S.J. Moriarty

Functions: Most + 01.0 02.0 05.0 06.0 08.0
Industries: Most + D.00 D.10 I.00
Description: Senior managers—all functions, all industries, close partnership with clients

Morris & Berger

201 S. Lake Ave., Ste. 700
Pasadena, California 91101
Salary Minimum: $50,000
Key Contact: Kristine A. Morris
Jay V. Berger

Functions: Most
Industries: Most
Professional Affiliations: CERA
Description: Retained generalist executive search firm

R.C. Morton & Assoc. Inc.

230 S. Bemiston, Ste. 1212
St. Louis, Missouri 63105
Salary Minimum: $50,000
Key Contact: R. C. Morton
John F. Truex

Functions: Most + 01.0 02.0 04.0 05.0 06.0
Industries: Most + A.00 D.00 D.D0 D.I0 I.00
Description: Upper level retained search encompassing most all functions & industries

Edwin Mruk & Partners
675 Third Ave., Ste. 1804
New York, New York 10017
Salary Minimum: $100,000
Key Contact: Edwin S. Mruk
Finian I. Lennon
Bernard E. Brooks

Branches:
75 Second Ave.
Needham, Massachusetts 02194-2800
Networks:
EMA Partners Int'l.
Amsterdam, Barcelona, Berlin, Bologna,
Brussels, Caracas, Chicago, Dublin, Frankfurt,
London, Madrid, Miami, Milan, Paris,
Singapore, Turin, Verona, Vienna, Washington

Functions: Most + 01.1 01.2 01.3 01.4 02.0
Industries: Most
Professional Affiliations: IMC
Description: Director and executive search
consultants

Paul Mueller & Assoc., Inc.
P.O. Box 37694
Raleigh, North Carolina 27627
Salary Minimum: $60,000
Key Contact: Paul M. Mueller

Functions: Most + 01.0 02.0 03.0 05.0 08.0
Industries: Most + D.00 D.E0 E.00 F.00 I.00
Professional Affiliations: IACPR, CLM
Description: Provides high quality executive
search services for corporate clients
nationwide

The Mulshine Co., Inc.
2517 Rte. 35, Ste. D-201
Manasquan, New Jersey 08736
Salary Minimum: $50,000
Key Contact: Michael A. Mulshine
Michael G. Mulshine

Functions: 01.0 02.0 02.1 03.4 04.0
Industries: D.10 D.15 D.16 D.18 D.D0
Professional Affiliations: NAER
Description: Senior & middle level in R&D,
packaging, engineering & manufacturing

R. F. Mulvaney & Assoc., Inc.
222 S. Meramec, Ste. 201
St. Louis, Missouri 63105-3514
Salary Minimum: $60,000
Key Contact: Ronald F. Mulvaney
John Green

Functions: 01.2 02.4 11.6
Industries: Most + I.14
Description: Specialists in non metropolitan
executive search in manufacturing &
service industries

Munroe, Curry & Bond Assoc.
43 North Main St.
P.O. Box 1299
Medford, New Jersey 08055
Salary Minimum: $50,000
Key Contact: Barbara Czubek
T. David Cole
Michael P. Harkins
Louise M. Milnes
Kevin Graham

Functions: Most
Industries: Most
Professional Affiliations: ASME, ASPA, BMA,
IEEE
Description: Creative firm established 1975—
also offers management consulting

P. J. Murphy & Assoc., Inc.
735 N. Water St.
Milwaukee, Wisconsin 53202
Salary Minimum: $50,000
Key Contact: Patrick J. Murphy
Craig S. Zaffrann
James F. Zahradka
Jeanne M. Filo

Functions: Most + 01.0 02.0 05.0 06.0 08.0
Industries: Most
Description: Established firm, retainer only-
considerable work with boards

Robert Murphy Assoc.

230 Park Ave.
New York, New York 10169
Salary Minimum: $65,000
Key Contact: Robert Murphy
Thomas Cook
Rita Dreyfus
Paul Hill
John Murray

Functions: Most + 02.0 03.0 04.0 05.0 06.0
Industries: Most + B.00 B.0W D.00 D.D0
D.E0
Description: Specialists in recruiting senior &
middle management for major corprations

NDI Services

42112 Crestview
Northville, Michigan 48167
Salary Minimum: $45,000
Key Contact: David Kosteva

Functions: 01.0 03.0 06.0 08.0
Industries: I.14
Professional Affiliations: AAHC, ASHHRA,
HFMA, NAPM
Description: Human resources consulting &
executive search services

Nadzam, Lusk & Assoc., Inc.

3211 Scott Blvd., Ste. 205
Santa Clara, California 95054
Salary Minimum: $90,000
Key Contact: Theodore E. Lusk
Richard J. Nadzam

Functions: Most + 01.0 02.0 04.0 05.0 09.0
Industries: B.00 C.00 D.00 D.E0 D.H0
Professional Affiliations: AESC, IACPR, CERA
Description: Search & consulting, national &
international, primarily in high technology

Nagler & Co., Inc.

65 William St.
Wellesley Hills, Massachusetts 02181
Salary Minimum: $60,000
Key Contact: Leon G. Nagler

Functions: Most
Industries: Most
Professional Affiliations: IACPR, ABA, IMESC,
SHRM
Description: Senior level search practice across
most industries & functions

Affiliates/Other Offices:
William Hetzel Assoc., Inc., Inverness

Barry Nathanson Assoc.

40 Cutter Mill Rd.
Great Neck, New York 11021
Salary Minimum: $100,000
Key Contact: Barry F. Nathanson

Functions: Most
Industries: Most
Description: Worldwide executive search firm

National Restaurant Search, Inc.

1834 Walden Office Sq., Ste.150
Schaumburg, Illinois 60173
Salary Minimum: $50,000
Key Contact: John W. Chitvanni

Functions: Most
Industries: I.10 I.11
Professional Affiliations: IRA
Description: Management positions related to
the restaurant/hospitality industry

Newell Assoc.

89 Devonshire Rd.
New Rochelle, New York 10804
Salary Minimum: $50,000
Key Contact: Donald Pierce Newell

Functions: Most + 01.0 02.0 04.0 08.0 11.2
Industries: Most + D.12 E.00 H.10 H.R0
Description: Senior mgmt (G.M's-all
functions)-particular specialty investment
banking

Newpher & Co., Inc.
2215 York Rd., Ste. 214
Oak Brook, Illinois 60521
Salary Minimum: $70,000
Key Contact: James A. Newpher
Marjorie K. Siemandel

Affiliates/Other Offices:
Arn Associates, Geneva
Lyrd Mark Birdwood, London

Functions: Most + 02.0 03.0 04.0 08.0
Industries: Most
Professional Affiliations: IACPR, EMA, IESC,
SHRM
Description: Executive search at senior levels-
organization planning & analysis

Nicholaou & Co.
15308 Treetop Dr.
Orland Park, Illinois 60462-4616
Salary Minimum: $50,000
Key Contact: Jean Nicholaou

Functions: Most
Industries: Most
Description: Personalized search service, mid
to upper management-nationwide

Nicholson & Assoc., Inc.
230 Park Ave.
New York, New York 10169
Salary Minimum: $50,000
Key Contact: Constantine Nicholson

Functions: Most
Industries: Most + G.00 H.00 H.10 H.11
Professional Affiliations: IACPR
Description: Management recruiters & custom
training program design & delivery

The Niemond Corp.
P.O. Box 4106
San Marcos, California 92069
Salary Minimum: $100,000
Key Contact: Wesley E. Niemond
Nancy A. Niemond

Functions: Most + 01.0 02.0 04.0 05.0 09.0
Industries: D.00 D.24 D.25 D.E0 D.H0
Professional Affiliations: ADPA, AFCEA,
AUSA
Description: Principal has 20 years of
nationwide retained executive search
experience

W.D. Nolte & Company
6 Middlesex Rd.
Darien, Connecticut 06820
Salary Minimum: $60,000
Key Contact: William D. Nolte, Jr.

Functions: Most + 11.0 11.1
Industries: Most
Professional Affiliations: IACPR
Description: Over 20 years as a consultant-
flexible approaches to problem solving

Nordeman Grimm, Inc.
717 Fifth Ave.
New York, New York 10022
Salary Minimum: $75,000
Key Contact: Peter G. Grimm
Jacques C. Nordeman

Branches:
150 N. Michigan Ave.
Chicago, Illinois 60601
Key Contact: Lawrence F. Nein
Ted Martin

Professional Affiliations: AESC
Description: Specialists in recruiting
exceptional senior executives

Affiliates/Other Offices:
Euro Contact Consulting & Handels Ges.m.b.H., Warsaw
H. Neumann Int'l., Amsterdam
H. Neumann Int'l., Berlin 30
H. Neumann Int'l., Budapest
H. Neumann Int'l., Copenhagen K
H. Neumann Int'l., Dusseldorf 30

H. Neumann Int'l., Frankfurt
H. Neumann Int'l., Madrid
H. Neumann Int'l., Milan
H. Neumann Int'l., Munich
H. Neumann Int'l., Paris
H. Neumann Int'l., Prague
H. Neuman Int'l., Strasbourg
H. Neumann Int'l., Vienna
H. Neumann Int'l., Zurich
Odgers & Company, Ltd., London

Norman Broadbent Int'l., Inc.
200 Park Ave.
New York, New York 10166
Salary Minimum: $100,000
Key Contact: William B. Clemens, Jr.
Jeffrey G. Bell
Claudia L. Kelly
Norbert A. Gottenberg
Bruce J. Robertson

Functions: Most + 01.0 05.0 08.0 09.0 10.0
Industries: Most + D.18
Professional Affiliations: AESC, IACPR
Description: Executive search activity focused on sr. line & staff requirements within consumer/financial

Branches:
100 Prospect St., 2nd Fl.
South Bldg.
Stamford, Connecticut 06901
Networks:
The International Search Partnership
Barcelona, Dusseldorf, Milan, Paris, Stockholm, Sydney, Toronto, Vedbaek, Zurich

International Branches:
Hong Kong, London

Paul Norsell & Assoc., Inc.
P.O. Box 4113
Woodland Hills, California 91365-4113
Salary Minimum: $100,000
Key Contact: Paul E. Norsell

Functions: 01.0 02.0 04.0 05.0 08.0
Industries: Most + D.00 D.H0 D.I0 H.00 J.13
Professional Affiliations: CERA, IEEE, NAA
Description: Serve corporate & institutional business clients on a national basis

Northern Consultants Inc.
P.O. Box 220
17 Western Ave.
Hampden, Maine 04444
Salary Minimum: $50,000
Key Contact: James D. Brown
Alta C. Brown

Functions: Most + 01.0 02.0 04.0 05.0
Industries: Most + D.D0 I.14
Professional Affiliations: IMC, SPE
Description: Specialize in search & operational audits: plastics, packaging, machinery & health care

Norton & Assoc., Inc.
600 Colonial Park Dr.
Roswell, Georgia 30075
Salary Minimum: $60,000
Key Contact: James B. Norton, III
Lance J. Richards

Functions: Most + 08.2
Industries: D.E0 D.H0 H.00 H.I0 I.10
Description: Banking/financial services; hospitality/leisure services

Richard E. Nosky & Assoc.
2525 E. Arizona Biltmore Cir., Ste. 124
Phoenix, Arizona 85016
Salary Minimum: $60,000
Key Contact: Richard E. Nosky
Marti J. Cizek

Functions: 01.0 02.0 05.0 06.0 09.0
Industries: Most + D.00 D.I0
Professional Affiliations: AESC
Description: Emphasis in utilities, electronics, high technology, banking & manufacturing

Branches:
261 Montair Dr.
Danville, California 94525

C. J. Noty & Assoc.

332 S. Michigan Ave.
Chicago, Illinois 60604
Salary Minimum: $50,000
Key Contact: Richard E. Nicholsen
Charles Noty

Functions: Most
Industries: Most
Professional Affiliations: APA, ASTD, IPA, IPAC, SHRM, TIMS
Description: Personnel selection & research, industrial/organizational psychology

Nuessle, Kurdziel & Weiss, Inc.

5 Penn Center Plaza
Philadelphia, Pennsylvania 19103
Salary Minimum: $50,000
Key Contact: John F. Kurdziel
Warren G. Nuessle
Gerald E. Weiss

Functions: Most
Industries: Most
Description: Assignments most areas, emphasis on general management, finance, human resources & marketing

Nursing Technomics

814 Sunset Hollow Rd.
West Chester, Pennsylvania 19380
Salary Minimum: $50,000
Key Contact: Joan I. McCrea

Functions: Most + 01.0 01.4
Industries: I.14
Description: Specializing in executive search for executive nurses

O'Brien & Co., Inc.

1127 Euclid Ave., Ste. 375
Cleveland, Ohio 44115
Salary Minimum: $70,000
Key Contact: Tim O'Brien

Functions: Most + 01.4 02.4 06.0 08.0 09.0
Industries: D.22 D.23 D.24 I.14 I.19
Description: All functions of senior managers & executives for manufacturing, healthcare & retail organizations

O'Callaghan, Honey & Assoc., Inc.

400, 400 5th Ave. SW
Calgary, Alberta T2P 0L6 Canada
Salary Minimum: $75,000
Key Contact: T. K. O'Callaghan
W. M. M. Honey
K. C. Coe, M.D.

Functions: Most + 01.0 06.0 08.0 09.0 09.7
Industries: B.00 E.00 H.00 H.R0 I.00
Description: Calgary's most experienced executive search consultants serving domestic/int'l. clientele

Networks:
Alliance Int'l.
Montreal, Toronto, Vancouver

O'Connor, O'Connor, Lordi, Ltd.

707 Grant St., Ste. 2727, Gulf Tower
Pittsburgh, Pennsylvania 15219-1908
Salary Minimum: $60,000
Key Contact: Thomas F. O'Connor
Richard E. Brown

Functions: Most
Industries: Most
Description: Custom tailored executive recruiting program for middle to upper echelon executives

John O'Keefe & Assoc., Inc.

P.O. Box 1092—10 Sasco Hill Rd.
Southport, Connecticut 06490
Salary Minimum: $50,000
Key Contact: Kathy O'Keefe
John O'Keefe
Kevin Keating
Tom Wilczynski
Gene Sullivan
Diane Sweeney
Eric Bosch

Branches:
4238 163rd Ave., S.E.
Bellevue, Washington 98004
Key Contact: Jack O'Keefe

Functions: 01.4 05.2 05.3 05.5
Industries: Most
Professional Affiliations: FMI, PA
Description: Specialize in the consumer package goods industry & high tech management

O'Rourke Co., Inc.

4100 International Plz.
Tower II, Ste. 612
Ft. Worth, Texas 76109
Salary Minimum: $40,000
Key Contact: Dennis M. O'Rourke
Patti Cox
Lee Leonhart
Rachel Whisenant

Branches:
260 Hearthstone
Boise, Idaho 83616
Key Contact: Chrystine Eiguren Brassey
Andrew L. Brassey

Functions: Most + 02.0 05.0 06.0 08.0
Industries: Most + D.13
Description: Executive search/management consulting firm with broad industrial experience

O'Shea, Divine & Co.

610 Newport Center Dr., Ste. 490
Newport Beach, California 92660
Salary Minimum: $60,000
Key Contact: Robert S. Divine
Timothy J. O'Shea

Functions: Most + 01.0 02.0 05.0 08.0 09.0
Industries: Most
Professional Affiliations: NACD, SIM
Description: General management & most function searches conducted by experienced principals

Dennis P. O'Toole & Assoc. Inc.

1865 Palmer Ave., Ste. 210
Larchmont, New York 10538
Salary Minimum: $70,000
Key Contact: Dennis P. O'Toole

Functions: Most + 01.0 05.0 06.0 08.0 11.0
Industries: Most + E.00 I.00 I.10 I.11 I.12
Description: Executive & middle management search in the hospitality industry

O'Toole & Company

1047 Forest
Oak Park, Illinois 60302
Salary Minimum: $60,000
Key Contact: William R. O'Toole

Functions: Most + 01.0 02.0 05.0 06.0 08.0
Industries: Most + D.00 H.00
Description: Professional & experienced search for senior & middle management

Ober & Company

11777 San Vicente Blvd.
Ste. 755
Los Angeles, California 90049
Salary Minimum: $65,000
Key Contact: Lynn W. Ober

Functions: Most + 01.0 02.0 05.0 06.0 08.0
Industries: Most + B.0W D.00 D.E0 H.00 I.00
Professional Affiliations: CERA
Description: Retained executive search consulting practice in most industries & functions

Affiliates/Other Offices:
Executive Appointments Ltd., Int'l., Oak Brook
Executive Appointments Ltd., Int'l., Westwood

Oberlander & Co., Inc.
223 E. State St., P.O. Box 789
Geneva, Illinois 60134
Salary Minimum: $50,000
Key Contact: Howard I. Oberlander

Functions: Most
Industries: Most
Description: Specialize in providing
    professional, confidential guidance in
    management selection area

The Odessa Group
523 W. 6th St., Ste. 807
Los Angeles, California 90014
Salary Minimum: $75,000
Key Contact: Phillip Eastman
Odessa J. Felactu
Kathleen E. Rexrode

Functions: Most
Industries: Most
Description: Enhance client organizations'
    profits & competitiveness through
    executive search

The Ogdon Partnership
375 Park Ave.
New York, New York 10152-0175
Salary Minimum: $75,000
Key Contact: Thomas H. Ogdon
Forest C. Meade, Jr.
Richard E. Linde

Functions: Most
Industries: Most
Professional Affiliations: IACPR
Description: General recruiting; specializations:
    marketing, publishing, financial svcs.,
    venture management

Affiliates/Other Offices:
The Butterfield Partnership Ltd., London
Francois Carn & Associes, Paris
George Enns Partners Inc., Toronto
John Lucas Pty. Limited, Sydney

Oliver & Rozner Assoc., Inc.
598 Madison Ave.
New York, New York 10022
Salary Minimum: $75,000
Key Contact: Burton L. Rozner

Functions: Most
Industries: Most + D.00 D.E0 D.H0
Professional Affiliations: AESC
Description: Top tiers of management; hard-to-
    find specialists

Robert Olivier & Assoc., Inc.
50 Broad. St.
New York, New York 10004
Salary Minimum: $80,000
Key Contact: Mark A. Gronet

Functions: 01.1 08.0
Industries: H.00 H.10 H.11 H.12
Description: Representing the financial service
    industry for over 20 years

The Onstott Group
60 William St.
Wellesley, Massachusetts 02181
Salary Minimum: $50,000
Key Contact: Patricia A. Campbell
Joseph E. Onstott
Frederick H. Stephens

Functions: Most + 05.0 09.0
Industries: J.00
Professional Affiliations: AESC
Description: Broad based firm operating
    nationally in executive recruiting

Oppedisano & Co., Inc.
370 Lexington Ave., Ste. 1200
New York, New York 10017
Key Contact: Edward A. Oppedisano
Thomas C. Lincoln

Functions: Most
Industries: H.00 H.11
Professional Affiliations: IACPR
Description: Our firm consults exclusively to
    the investment management industry

Organization Resources Inc.
63 Atlantic Ave., Boston Harbor
Boston, Massachusetts 02110
Salary Minimum: $70,000
Key Contact: John R. Kris
Peter T. Austin
John C. Jay
Alfred J. LaGreca

Functions: Most
Industries: Most + I.12
Professional Affiliations: IACPR, ASPA,
   SBANE
Description: General management consulting
   firm—65% search

Orion Consulting, Inc.
115 Rte. 46, Bldg. B, Ste. 13/14
Mountain Lakes, New Jersey 07046
Salary Minimum: $45,000
Key Contact: James V. Dromsky

Functions: Most + 01.0 02.0 03.0 05.0 06.0
Industries: Most
Professional Affiliations: AERC, NAPC
Description: Retained executive search
   assignments for manufacturing & service
   clients

Ott & Hansen, Inc.
136 S. Oak Knoll, Ste. 300
Pasadena, California 91101
Salary Minimum: $70,000
Key Contact: David G. Hansen
George W. Ott

Functions: 01.0 02.0 03.0 08.0 09.0
Industries: C.00 D.00 D.E0 H.R0 I.00
Professional Affiliations: CERA
Description: Offers complete partner
   involvement & excellent placement
   percentage for senior & hard-to-fill

Robert Ottke Assoc.
P.O. Box 7553
Newport Beach, California 92660
Salary Minimum: $40,000
Key Contact: Robert C. Ottke

Functions: Most
Industries: Most + B.00 D.18 D.19 D.20 D.24
Description: General executive search-special
   emphasis healthcare, medical,
   pharmaceutical & high tech

Overton Group
10140 N. Port Washington Rd.
Mequon, Wisconsin 53092
Salary Minimum: $75,000
Key Contact: Justin V. Strom
Larry T. Slauter

Functions: 01.1 01.2 02.4 05.0 06.0
Industries: Most + D.00
Professional Affiliations: IACPR, EMA
Description: Boutique firm offering tailored
   recruitment services

P.A.R. Assoc., Inc.
27 State St.
Boston, Massachusetts 02109-2706
Salary Minimum: $80,000
Key Contact: Peter A. Rabinowitz
Marcie R. Nothnagel

Functions: 01.0 05.0 06.0 08.0 11.4
Industries: Most + D.00 H.00 H.10 I.00 I.12
Professional Affiliations: ISA
Description: Focus: healthcare, non-profits:
   academia, arts, professional services, mfg.
   & general management

The PAR Group—Paul A. Reaume, Ltd.
100 Waukegan Rd., Ste. 200
Lake Bluff, Illinois 60044
Salary Minimum: $45,000
Key Contact: Paul A. Reaume
Gerald R. Plock
James C. Lyons

Functions: 01.0 11.0 11.4 11.5
Industries: E.00 I.00 I.12 K.00
Professional Affiliations: ASPA, ICMA, IPMA
Description: Searches for government, not-for-
   profit & related organizations, nationally

Branches:
175 Derby St., Ste 7
Hingham, Massachusetts 02043
Key Contact: Richard T. Bennett

Affiliates/Other Offices:
Karam Group Int'l., Denver

PCD Partners

7 Wynnewood Rd.
Wynnewood, Pennsylvania 19096
Salary Minimum: $60,000
Key Contact: James Pappas
Michael S. Landes

Functions: Most
Industries: Most
Description: Generalist firm operating
nationally-marketing, manufacturing &
finance-all areas

G.S. Page Inc.

5956 Sherry Ln., Ste. 1601
Dallas, Texas 75225
Salary Minimum: $80,000
Key Contact: Schuyler Page

Functions: Most + 01.4 08.0 09.3 09.4 11.5
Industries: Most + B.0W H.00 H.10 H.I0 J.00
Description: Established firm providing a full
range of national search & selection
services

Page-Wheatcroft & Co. Ltd.

2401 Turtle Creek Blvd., Ste. 2700
The White House
Dallas, Texas 75219
Salary Minimum: $100,000
Key Contact: Stephen J. L. Page

Functions: Most + 01.0 05.0 09.0 11.1
Industries: Most + H.00 I.00 I.17 I.18
Description: Senior level executive search
practice with expertise in all industries

John Paisios Ltd.

2211 York Rd.
Oak Brook, Illinois 60521
Salary Minimum: $50,000
Key Contact: John P. Paisios

Functions: Most
Industries: Most
Professional Affiliations: APA
Description: Human resources consulting firm
with emphasis on organizational planning,
staffing & exec. search

Kirk Palmer & Assoc., Inc.

6 E. 43rd St., Ste. 2004
New York, New York 10017
Salary Minimum: $50,000
Key Contact: Kirk Palmer

Functions: Most + 01.0 02.1 03.1 05.1 06.0
Industries: D.11 F.00 G.00
Description: Recognized authorities in the
retail & apparel industries.

Palmer Assoc., Inc.

54 West Shore Dr.
Pennington, New Jersey 08534
Salary Minimum: $50,000
Key Contact: John C. Palmer
Margot E. Palmer

Functions: Most + 01.0 02.0 04.0 05.0 08.0
Industries: D.17 D.18 D.25 D.I0 I.16
Description: Special focus in medical
diagnostics, pharmaceuticals, biotechology,
lab instrumentation

Jim Parham & Assoc., Inc.

5146 Colbert Rd.
Lakeland, Florida 33813-4010
Salary Minimum: $35,000
Key Contact: Jim Parham
Dave George

Functions: 05.2 05.4 06.0 06.2 10.0
Industries: E.00
Professional Affiliations: ASPA
Description: Executive search for
transportation (motor freight) &
distribution firms

Frank Parillo & Assoc.

1801 E. Heim Ave., Ste. 200
Orange, California 92665
Salary Minimum: $50,000
Key Contact: Frank Parillo

Functions: 05.7
Industries: J.00
Description: Specialists in medical diagnostics,
medical device & biotechnology middle &
senior management

D.P. Parker & Assoc., Inc.
55 William St.
Wellesley, Massachusetts 02181
Salary Minimum: $60,000
Key Contact: David P. Parker

Functions: 02.0 04.0 05.0 11.3
Industries: B.00 B.0W D.15 D.E0 D.H0
Description: R&D/engineering/technology management & senior individual contributors

Parker, Sholl & Gordon, Inc.
440 Totten Pond Rd.
Boston, Massachusetts 02154
Salary Minimum: $65,000
Key Contact: Calvin K. Sholl
Raymond C. Gordon

Functions: Most
Industries: Most
Professional Affiliations: AESC, IACPR, IMC
Description: Successful search activity since 1962

Michael W. Parres & Assoc.
21 Kercheval, Ste. 200
Grosse Pointe Farms, Michigan 48236
Salary Minimum: $50,000
Key Contact: Mike Parres

Functions: Most + 02.0 03.0 05.0 06.0 08.0
Industries: D.00 D.22 D.23
Description: Conduct searches for most disciplines in auto /truck/aerospace industries

Parsons Assoc. Inc.
601 Forest Ave.
Glen Ellyn, Illinois 60137
Salary Minimum: $50,000
Key Contact: Sue N. Parsons

Functions: Most + 01.3 02.4 05.4 06.0 09.0
Industries: Most + D.10 D.12 D.14 D.19 D.22
Professional Affiliations: HRMAC, IAPW, NAWBO
Description: Specialize in recruiting & selection of highly talented middle management executives

Pasini & Co.
2021 Midwest Rd., Ste. 200
Oak Brook, Illinois 60521
Salary Minimum: $50,000
Key Contact: Raymond J. Pasini

Functions: Most
Industries: Most
Description: Emphasizes personal service

Patton, Perry & Sproull Inc.
112 S. Tryon St.
Ste. 500
Charlotte, North Carolina 28202
Salary Minimum: $50,000
Key Contact: Mitchell Patton
Robin Perry
J. William Sproull

Functions: Most + 01.0 02.0 05.0 10.0
Industries: Most
Professional Affiliations: AESC
Description: Generalists—offering nationwide, personalized, professional consulting to selected clientele

Peat Marwick Stevenson & Kellogg
2300 Yonge St.
Toronto, Ontario M4P 1G2 Canada
Salary Minimum: $60,000
Key Contact: James A. Parr
William Berlet
Robert E. McMonagle
Heather Connelly
Ronald Dulhanty
Kathy Dempster
Alan Small

Functions: Most
Industries: Most
Professional Affiliations: IACPR, CAMC

Branches:
255 5th Ave. S.W., Ste. 2200
Calgary, Alberta T2P 3G6 Canada
Key Contact: Gordon Sivertsen
Merv Manthey

Canada Trust Tower, Ste. 2610
10104-103 ave.
Edmonton, Alberta T5J 0H8 Canada
Key Contact: Allan Jacobson

P.O. Box 10472 Pacific Centre
500-777 Dunsmuir St.
Vancouver, British Columbia V7Y IK5
    Canada
Key Contact: Anne Moore
Larry Sowa

1200-447 Portage Ave.
Winnipeg, Manitoba R3B 3H5 Canada
Key Contact: Emmet McMullan

100 New Tower St., Ste. 800
Cabot Place
St. John's, Newfoundland AIC IJ3 Canada
Key Contact: Lloyd Powell

The Peck Consultancy
17 West 54th St.
New York, New York 10019
Salary Minimum: $75,000
Key Contact: David W. Peck, Jr.

Peeney Assoc., Inc.
141 South Ave.
Fanwood, New Jersey 07023
Salary Minimum: $50,000
Key Contact: James D. Peeney

People Management Northeast, Inc.
10 Station St.
Simsbury, Connecticut 06070
Salary Minimum: $60,000
Key Contact: Steven Darter

Branches:
1117 Permiter Ctr. W, Ste. 307
Atlanta, Georgia 30338
Key Contact: Mike Taylor

100 Portland Ave., Ste. 225
Minneapolis, Minnesota 55401
Key Contact: Robert Stevenson
Richard Chant

#1507, Purdy's Wharf Twr. I
1959 Upper Water St.
Halifax, Nova Scotia B3J 3N2 Canada
Key Contact: Kenneth A.H. Hubbard

706-101 Frederick St.
Kitchener, Ontario N2H 6R2 Canada
Key Contact: Michael R. Follett

112 Kent St., 21st Fl.
Ottawa, Ontario K1P 5W6 Canada
Key Contact: Garry Reid
Judith Wightman

220 Dundas St. 7th Floor
London, Ontario N6A IH3 Canada
Key Contact: W. Allan Methven

3400 de Maisonneuve Blvd., West
Ste. 1400
Montreal, Quebec H3Z 3B8 Canada
Barbara Shore

1000 Canada Trust Bldg.
1801 Hamilton St.
Regina, Saskatchewan S4P-4B4 Canada
Key Contact: John Sinclair

Functions: Most
Industries: Most
Professional Affiliations: IACPR
Description: Executive search for profit & not-
    for-profit institutions

Functions: Most + 01.0 02.0 05.0 06.0 08.0
Industries: Most + D.00 D.22 D.23 H.10
Professional Affiliations: IACPR
Description: Specialists in automotive,
    machine tool, financial, health care/health
    services

Functions: Most + 01.0 01.2 02.0 05.0 08.0
Industries: D.00 D.H0 H.00 H.I0 I.14
Professional Affiliations: IACPR
Description: Extensive experience within
    insurance, financial services,
    manufacturing & technical organizations

R. H. Perry & Assoc., Inc.
2607 31st St., NW
Washington, District of Columbia 20008
Key Contact: R. H. Perry
Neil A. Stein

Functions: Most
Industries: Most
Professional Affiliations: AMBAE
Description: Search & personnel consulting
 firm based in Washington, DC

Perry-D'Amico & Assoc.
P.O. Box 671
Half Moon Bay, California 94019
Salary Minimum: $50,000
Key Contact: Len Perry

Functions: Most + 02.4 02.5 03.0 05.0 06.0
Industries: Most + D.17 D.I0 I.14 I.21
Description: Healthcare manufacturing research
 & service-med to high tech
 manufacturing—all functions

Barry Persky & Co., Inc.
301 Merritt 7 Corporate Park
Norwalk, Connecticut 06851
Salary Minimum: $50,000
Key Contact: Barry Persky
David M. Cochran
Thomas J. Naglieri
Walter M. Nagle

Functions: Most + 11.3 11.5 11.6
Industries: Most + B.00 B.0W B.10 C.00 J.11
Professional Affiliations: IACPR, EMA
Description: Recruiting services utilized by
 broad sector of industry since 1971

Personnel Assoc.
4000 Long Beach Blvd., Ste. 260
Long Beach, California 90807
Salary Minimum: $30,000
Key Contact: Roger Lubin

Functions: 01.0 06.0 07.0 08.0
Industries: K.00
Description: Specializing in recruitment, search
 & selection of professionals at the mid to
 senior mgmt. levels

Branches:
405 14th St., Ste. 152
Oakland, California 94612
Key Contact: Sheryl Lindquist

The Personnel Laboratory
733 Summer St.
Stamford, Connecticut 06901
Salary Minimum: $15,000
Key Contact: Irene Salese
Joanna Steinberg
King Whitney, Jr.

Description: Primarily consultants on
 personnel selection; search as an ancillary
 activity

Richard Peterson & Assoc., Inc.
5064 Roswell Rd., Ste. C-201
Atlanta, Georgia 30342
Salary Minimum: $40,000
Key Contact: Richard A. Peterson

Functions: Most
Industries: H.10 H.I0 H.R0 I.17
Description: Executive search for financial
 services, legal, manufacturing

Peterson Consulting/W.P., Inc.
2525 Cabot Dr., Ste. 300
Lisle, Illinois 60532
Salary Minimum: $40,000
Key Contact: Don Peterson
Pat Peterson
Mike Peterson

Functions: 01.4 08.0 09.0 09.2 10.0
Industries: D.H0 H.00 H.10 H.I0 I.18
Description: Data processing specializing in
 senior positions sales, management,
 financial & vendors

Pflueger & Company
901 Dove St., Ste. 210
Newport Beach, California 92660
Salary Minimum: $75,000
Key Contact: Andrew P. Pflueger

Functions: Most
Industries: Most
Professional Affiliations: CERA
Description: Generalist firm with emphasis on high-tech environment

Phillips Group of Companies
200 Bay St., P.O. Box 3
Royal Bank Plaza
Toronto, Ontario M5J 2J1 Canada
Salary Minimum: $65,000
Key Contact: G. Michael Wolkensperg

Functions: 01.0 01.2 02.4 06.0 08.2
Industries: A.00 D.18 D.22 G.00 K.00
Description: In the practice of executive search & succession dynamics

Branches:
4350 La Jolla Village Dr., 3rd Fl.
San Diego, California 92122
Key Contact: David Valley

Place de Ville, Tower B, Ste. 1880
112 Kent St.
Ottawa, Ontario KlP 5P2 Canada
Key Contact: Pierre Lefebure

1 Place Ville Marie, Ste. 2736
Montreal, Quebec H3B 4G4 Canada
Key Contact: Camille Morin-Tutsch

Physician Executive Management Center
4014 Gunn Hwy., Ste. 160
Tampa, Florida 33624
Salary Minimum: $85,000
Key Contact: David R. Kirschman
Jennifer R. Grebenschikoff

Industries: I.14 I.15
Professional Affiliations: AAHC, NAPR
Description: Only national executive search firm specializing in physician executives

Physician Services of America
2000 Warrington Way
Browenton Pl., Ste. 250
Louisville, Kentucky 40222
Key Contact: John E. Hill
R. Lynn Cook

Industries: I.15
Professional Affiliations: MGMA, NAPR
Description: Full service physician recruitment-physician consulting-medical director search

Picard & Co., Inc.
101 Park Ave.
New York, New York 10178
Key Contact: Lee H. Walton
Robert A. Flohr
Daniel A. Picard
Georgina Lichtenstein

Functions: 05.0 06.0 08.3 11.1
Industries: Most + D.H0
Professional Affiliations: IACPR
Description: Strategic planning, corporate consulting, financial services, high technology

Pierce & Assoc., Inc.
8102 Club Court
Austin, Texas 78759
Salary Minimum: $50,000
Key Contact: Douglas F. Pierce

Functions: Most
Industries: Most
Description: In business for 20 years-all management areas

Pierce Assoc.
100 Drakes Landing Rd., #300
Greenbrae, California 94904
Salary Minimum: $60,000
Key Contact: Richard Pierce

Functions: 01.0 01.2 05.0 09.0 09.2
Industries: D.H0 H.12 J.13
Professional Affiliations: CERA
Description: Specializing in computer related high tech industry

Pierce Assoc.

151 New Park Ave.
Hartford, Connecticut 06106
Salary Minimum: $75,000
Key Contact: Austin P. Gillis

Functions: Most + 01.0 02.0 03.0 05.0 09.0
Industries: Most + D.00 D.15 D.19 D.22
D.H0
Description: Generalist firm dedicated to
providing quality service to quality clients

Martin Pierce Inc.

2206 Sexton Dr., Ste. 100
Arlington, Texas 76015
Salary Minimum: $75,000
Key Contact: Martin J. Pierce
William C. Pierce

Functions: Most + 01.0 06.0 08.0 09.0 10.0
Industries: Most
Professional Affiliations: AICPA
Description: Concentrating in VP finance,
controller, treasurer & corporate planning

Pinsker & Co., Inc.

P.O. Box 3269
Saratoga, California 95070
Salary Minimum: $75,000
Key Contact: Richard J. Pinsker

Functions: Most
Industries: Most + D.00 G.00 L.00
Professional Affiliations: IMC
Description: Executive selection consultants;
searches conducted on a retainer hourly
basis

Rene Plessner Assoc., Inc.

375 Park Ave.
New York, New York 10152
Salary Minimum: $75,000
Key Contact: Rene Plessner
Maxine Martens

Functions: Most + 01.0 05.0 05.1 05.4 05.5
Description: A 2 person boutique-
entrepreneurial-cosmetics, fashion related

R.L. Plimpton Assoc.

7800 E. Union Ave., Ste. 440
Denver, Colorado 80237
Salary Minimum: $45,000
Key Contact: Ralph L. Plimpton
James L. Anderson

Functions: Most + 01.0 02.0 05.0 08.0
Industries: Most + B.00 D.00 D.H0
Description: General management, financial,
high technology, manufacturing &
marketing

Plummer & Assoc., Inc.

50 Myano Ln., Ste. 36
Stamford, Connecticut 06902
Salary Minimum: $100,000
Key Contact: John Plummer

Functions: Most + 01.0 02.0 03.0 05.0 06.0
Industries: D.00 F.00 G.00 I.10 I.11
Description: Specializes in CEO/COO/senior
officers for retail & consumer industries

Pocrass Assoc.

16760 Stagg St., Unit 218
Van Nuys, California 91406
Salary Minimum: $75,000
Key Contact: Nancy Gilmore
Richard D. Pocrass

Functions: Most + 01.0 05.0 09.0
Industries: D.24 D.H0 H.10 I.18 J.13
Professional Affiliations: CERA, PIRA, SHRM
Description: Clients include computer
companies, financial institutions & other
high technology firms

Poirier, Hoevel & Co.

12400 Wilshire Blvd., Ste. 1250
Los Angeles, California 90025
Salary Minimum: $75,000
Key Contact: Michael J. Hoevel
Roland L. Poirier

Functions: Most
Industries: Most
Professional Affiliations: CERA
Description: California based professional
firm—national & international Fortune
1000 client base

Polson & Co., Inc.
1115 Second Ave. S, Ste. 600
Minneapolis, Minnesota 55403
Salary Minimum: $60,000
Key Contact: Shirley S. Norman
Christopher C. Polson

Functions: Most + 02.2 02.4 02.5 08.0 09.0
Industries: D.00 D.H0 H.10 J.00 J.13
Professional Affiliations: IACPR
Description: Full service, retainer fee, executive
    search firm; generalist

David Powell, Inc.
2995 Woodside Rd., Ste. 150
Woodside, California 94062
Salary Minimum: $100,000
Key Contact: David Powell
Jean Bagileo
Bill Wraith
Christine Seaver
Mike Scott
David Powell, Jr.

Functions: Most + 01.0 02.0 05.0 08.0 09.0
Industries: Most + D.00 D.H0 H.00 I.00 I.18
Description: Officer-level assignments for
    emerging high technology co's., CEO,
    marketing, sales & finance

Pre-Search, Inc.
6421 North Hamlin Ave.
Lincolnwood, Illinois 60645
Salary Minimum: $35,000
Key Contact: Joel Yaseen

Functions: Most
Industries: Most
Professional Affiliations: ASPA, EMA, SHRM
Description: Generalist firm serving most
    industries & disciplines

Predictor Systems Corp.
2659 Townsgate Rd., Ste. 100
Westlake Village, California 91361
Salary Minimum: $50,000
Key Contact: Larry A. Dillon
Helen Schultz

Branches:
31 Hansen Ct.
Moraga, California 94556

Functions: Most + 01.2 01.3 05.3 05.4 09.7
Industries: Most
Professional Affiliations: AEA
Description: Evaluation system utilizing
    behavioral science with video & computer
    technology

Preng & Assoc., Inc.
2925 Briarpark Dr., Ste. 1111
Houston, Texas 77042
Salary Minimum: $60,000
Key Contact: David E. Preng
Richard J. Preng
Ginger L. Napier

International Branches:
London

Functions: Most
Industries: B.00 B.0W C.00 D.00 D.H0
Professional Affiliations: AESC
Description: Worldwide executive search

Prior Martech Assoc.
700 112th Ave., NE, Ste. 203
Bellevue, Washington 98004-5106
Salary Minimum: $35,000
Key Contact: Paul R. Meyer

Branches:
The Bank of California Twr., Ste. 1000
707 SW Washington St.
Portland, Oregon 97205-3536
Key Contact: Donald R. Walker

Functions: Most
Industries: Most
Professional Affiliations: IMC
Description: Executive recruiting specializing in
    top management positions

QVS Int'l.

1640-21 Powers Ferry Rd.
Atlanta, Georgia 30067
Salary Minimum: $50,000
Key Contact: B. V. Cooper

Functions: Most + 01.0 05.0 11.3 11.5
Industries: Most + B.0W D.13 D.14 D.26
Description: International generalist firm.
  Emphasis of foreign firms operating in
  U.S.

Quaintance Assoc., Inc.

345 N. Canal St., Ste. 308
Chicago, Illinois 60606
Salary Minimum: $75,000
Key Contact: Richard C. Quaintance

Functions: Most + 02.0 05.0 06.0 08.0 11.5
Industries: Most + B.00 B.0W D.H0 I.13 J.00
Description: General business—middle & upper
  management, all industries, all functions

Quigley Assoc., Inc.

345 83rd St., Ste. B
Burr Ridge, Illinois 60521
Salary Minimum: $45,000
Key Contact: John E. Quigley

Industries: I.14 I.15
Description: Quality retainer executive search
  firm serving the healthcare field
  exclusively

L. J. Quinn & Assoc., Inc.

2 N. Lake Dr., Ste. 230
Pasadena, California 91101
Salary Minimum: $60,000
Key Contact: Leonard J. Quinn

Functions: Most
Industries: Most

Branches:
122 E. 42nd St., 17th Fl.
New York, New York 10168
Key Contact: Cy Callahan

Quinn Bailey & Morgan

345 W. Lancaster Ave., Ste. 30
Haverford, Pennsylvania 19041
Salary Minimum: $75,000
Key Contact: John Burns

Functions: Most + 01.0 02.0 05.0 08.0 09.0
Industries: Most + D.00 D.H0 H.00 I.00 J.00
Description: Partner led executive retainer
  search for mid & upper management

RG International

1379 Morris Ave., Ste. 203
Union, New Jersey 07083
Salary Minimum: $50,000
Key Contact: William D. MacKenzie

Functions: Most
Industries: Most
Description: An experienced search firm for
  middle & upper management positions

RIC Corp.

2001 Racquet Club Dr.
Palm City, Florida 34990
Salary Minimum: $50,000
Key Contact: R. Thomas Welch
C.M. Breder
Kathleen A. O'Neill

Functions: Most + 01.0 02.0 04.0 05.0
Industries: Most + B.00 D.00 D.H0 I.00
Description: Highly regarded small firm
  specializing in management, technical,
  sales & excecutive

Branches:
P.O. Box 14807
North Palm Beach, Florida 33408

8787 Southside Blvd., Ste. 1003
Jacksonville, Florida 32256
Key Contact: Carl Knapp

RZL Y Asociados, S.C.

Amberes #4—2nd & 3rd Fl.
Col. Juarez
Mexico City, Mexico DF 06600 Mexico
Salary Minimum: $60,000
Key Contact: Carlos A. Rojas
Josue P. Marroquin
Ma. Elena Juarez
Jose Luis Laguna

Functions: Most
Industries: Most
Description: Multinational, multilingual,
multicultural, all disciplines, private &
public sectors

Branches:
Edificio Losoles
Av. Lazaro Cardenas 2400 Pte., P.D. 2
Garza Garcia, Nuevo Leon 66270 Mexico
Key Contact: Jose G. Carrillo

Calz. de Los Arcos No. 62-205
Colonia Carretas
Queretaro, Queretaro 76050 Mexico

Rafey & Company

70 Walnut St.
Wellesley, Massachusetts 02181
Salary Minimum: $85,000
Key Contact: Andrew M. Rafey
Carol Knipper
Douglas C. Peck

Functions: Most + 01.0 01.1 05.0 08.0 09.0
Industries: Most + D.E0 D.H0 G.00
Description: Senior level firm with over 15
years of combined experience—emphasis:
venture capital community

Raines Int'l. Inc.

1180 Ave. of the Americas, Ste. 1830
New York, New York 10036
Salary Minimum: $50,000
Key Contact: Bruce R. Raines
Allen A. Geller
Henry Martin
John A. Castellani
Louise M. Young

Functions: Most + 06.0 08.0 09.0 11.1 11.2
Industries: Most + D.10 H.00 H.I0 H.R0 I.17
Professional Affiliations: IACPR
Description: International generalist firm
specializing in middle to upper
management executives

Walter Raleigh & Assoc.

161 Mansfield Ave.
Darien, Connecticut 06820
Salary Minimum: $80,000
Key Contact: Walter Raleigh

Functions: 01.0 01.1 01.2 05.2 05.4
Industries: D.00
Description: Senior management & executives
reporting directly to senior management,
plus board of directors

Ramming & Assoc., Inc.

3 Thackery Lane
Cherry Hill, New Jersey 08003-1925
Salary Minimum: $50,000
Key Contact: George Ramming

Functions: 01.0
Industries: Most
Description: All industries

Ramsey & Beirne Assoc., Inc.

500 Executive Blvd.
Ossining-on-Hudson, New York 10562
Salary Minimum: $80,000
Key Contact: David M. Beirne
Charles E. Ramsey
Alan B. Seiler
Mark Bradley

Functions: 01.0 09.0
Industries: D.00 D.24 D.H0 J.00 J.13
Description: Nationwide, senior level
consulting firm exclusively in the high
technology industry

Rand Assoc.
9 Hampden St.
Springfield, Massachusetts 01103
Key Contact: Rand W. Gesing

Functions: Most + 01.0 02.0 03.0 05.0 06.0
Industries: Most + D.00 D.H0 H.00 H.I0
Description: Generalist with a concentration with manufacturing & financial services firms

Randell-Heiken, Inc.
60 E. 42nd. St., Ste. 2005
New York, New York 10165
Key Contact: James W. Randell, Jr.
Barbara E. Heiken

Functions: 06.0 06.1 06.2 11.1
Industries: Most
Professional Affiliations: IACPR, ASTD, HRPS
Description: Search specializing in human resources, strategic planning & marketing

The Rankin Group, Ltd.
P.O. Box 1120
Lake Geneva, Wisconsin 53147
Salary Minimum: $50,000
Key Contact: Jeffrey A. Rankin
M. J. Rankin

Functions: 01.0 05.0 11.0
Industries: H.10 H.12 L.00
Description: Recruit Sr. & mid mgmt candidates for trust, private banking investments & family office mgmt

Paul Ray & Carre Orban Int'l.
301 Commerce St., Ste. 2300
Ft. Worth, Texas 76102
Salary Minimum: $90,000
Key Contact: Paul R. Ray, Sr.
Paul R. Ray, Jr.
Reece Pettigrew
Sharon Voros

Functions: Most + 01.0 01.2
Industries: Most
Professional Affiliations: AESC
Description: International firm specializing in executive search & management audit services

Branches:
2029 Century Park E.
Ste. 1000
Los Angeles, California 90067
Key Contact: David B. Radden

825 Third Ave., 22nd Floor
New York, New York 10022
Key Contact: Jacques P. Andre

1 Ravinia Dr., Ste. 1240
Atlanta, Georgia 30346
Key Contact: Paul D. McKinnis

2170 North Twr., Plaza of the Americas
700 N. Pearl, Lock Box 373
Dallas, Texas 75201

10 S. Riverside Plaza, Ste. 720
Chicago, Illinois 60606-3709
Key Contact: Andrew E. Weidener

301 Commerce St., Ste. 2300
Ft. Worth, Texas 76102
Key Contact: Breck Ray

Allen Ctr., 150 Allen Rd.
Liberty Corner, New Jersey 07938
Key Contact: Kenneth M. Clark

4801 Woodway, Ste. 300E
Houston, Texas 77056

International Branches:
Amsterdam, Barcelona, Brussels, Dusseldorf, Frankfurt, Geneva, Gothenburg, London, Luxembourg, Madrid, Milan, Munich, Oslo, Paris, Rome, Stockholm, Tokyo, Zeist, Zurich

Redden & Assoc.
35 N. Lake Ave., Ste. 800
Pasadena, California 91101
Salary Minimum: $50,000
Key Contact: Daniel J. Redden

Functions: Most
Industries: Most + D.00 D.D0 F.00 I.00
Description: Executive search & organizational development services offered by small, focused team

Redden & McGrath Assoc., Inc.

2 Overhill Rd.
Scarsdale, New York 10583
Salary Minimum: $50,000
Key Contact: Mary Redden
Laura McGrath Faller

Functions: 05.0 05.1 05.3 05.5
Industries: D.00 I.00 J.11
Description: Specializing in marketing,
marketing research, sales promotion &
direct marketing

Reddick and Co., Int'l.

5500 Interstate North Pkwy.
Ste. 500
Atlanta, Georgia 30328
Salary Minimum: $60,000
Key Contact: David C. Reddick
Frank D. Strickland

Functions: Most + 01.0 02.0 05.0 08.0
Industries: B.0W D.10 D.H0 H.00 I.14
Description: Management consultants in
executive selection

International Branches:
London, Singapore

Reese Assoc.

10475 Perry Highway
Wexford, Pennsylvania 15090
Salary Minimum: $70,000
Key Contact: Charles D. Reese, Jr.

Functions: Most
Industries: D.15 D.22 D.26
Description: Retainer search firm specializing
in metals, metals fabricating, capital
equipment

The Regis Group, Ltd.

1501 Johnson Ferry Rd. N.E., Ste 200
Marietta, Georgia 30062
Salary Minimum: $40,000
Key Contact: Stephan W. Kirschner
Roger E. Chagnon
Kenneth D. Lee

Functions: Most + 01.0 02.0 05.0 11.2
Industries: Most + D.00 D.D0 D.H0 H.00
Description: Results oriented firm serving
retained clients with integrity/
confidentiality/professionalism

D.M. Rein & Co., Inc.

4599 Highway Nine, North
Howell Twp., New Jersey 07731
Salary Minimum: $75,000
Key Contact: David Rein
Jack Adler

Functions: Most + 01.0 01.1 01.2
Industries: Most
Description: Company recruits CEO's & top
management teams primarily catering to
venture capital-high tech

The Repovich—Reynolds Group

745 S. Marengo
Pasadena, California 91106
Salary Minimum: $60,000
Key Contact: Smooch S. Reynolds

Functions: 05.1 05.2 05.3 05.7
Industries: Most
Professional Affiliations: IACPR, NIRI, SHRM
Description: National firm specializing in filling
senior level communications positions

Research Alternatives, Inc.

6443 W. North Ave.
Oak Park, Illinois 60302
Salary Minimum: $25,000
Key Contact: Robert Kowalski

Functions: Most + 02.0 03.0 06.0 09.3 11.5
Industries: Most
Description: Professional services in personnel
recruiting & selection

Resource Network Inc.

6802 Madison Ave.
Indianapolis, Indiana 46227
Salary Minimum: $60,000
Key Contact: Donald Pergal

Functions: 01.0 02.0 04.0 06.0 11.3
Industries: B.0W D.00 D.H0 D.I0
Description: Wide experience in all
management of engineer products
companies

Resources for Management

30 Pine St.
Pittsburgh, Pennsylvania 15223
Salary Minimum: $40,000
Key Contact: Thomas T. Flannery

Functions: Most
Industries: Most
Description: Generalists—fees based on time
expended up to budgeted figures

The Revere Assoc., Inc.

3700 Ira Commons
Bath, Ohio 44210-0498
Salary Minimum: $50,000
Key Contact: Michael W. Fremon

Functions: Most + 01.0 04.0 05.0 11.3 11.6
Industries: Most + D.13 D.15 D.19 D.D0
Professional Affiliations: ACS, AICHE, ASPA,
SAE, SPE, TAPPI
Description: Professional search in all
disciplines

Russell Reynolds Assoc., Inc.

200 Park Ave.
New York, New York 10166
Salary Minimum: $100,000
Key Contact: Hobson Brown, Jr.
Peter Drummond-Hay
F. Nadherny
Russell S. Reynolds, Jr.
Gordon Grand, III

Functions: Most
Industries: Most
Professional Affiliations: AESC
Description: Executive search consultants

Branches:
333 S. Grand Ave., Ste. 4200
Los Angeles, California 90071
Key Contact: Harry L. Usher

200 S. Wacker Dr., Ste. 3600
Chicago, Illinois 60606
Key Contact: Charles W. Kepler

101 California St., Ste. 3140
San Francisco, California 94111
Key Contact: P. Anthony Price

45 School St., Old City Hall
Boston, Massachusetts 02108
Key Contact: Jack H. Vernon

4 Landmark Sq., Ste. 230
Stamford, Connecticut 06901
Key Contact: Thomas L. McLane

90 S. Seventh St.
3050 Norwest Ctr.
Minneapolis, Minnesota 55402
Key Contact: Stephen B. Parker

1850 K St., NW, Ste. 365
Washington, District of Columbia 20006
Key Contact: John W. Franklin, Jr.

2001 Ross Ave.
1900 Trammell Crow Ctr.
Dallas, Texas 75201
Key Contact: David N. Konker

50 Hurt Plz., Ste. 600
The Hurt Bldg.
Atlanta, Georgia 30303
Key Contact: Joseph T. Spence, Jr.

1000 Louisiana, Ste. 4800
First Interstate Bank Plz.
Houston, Texas 77002-5096
Key Contact: David A. Morris

International Branches:
Frankfurt, Hong Kong, London, Madrid, Melbourne, Milan, Paris, Singapore, Sydney, Tokyo

Sydney Reynolds Assoc., Inc.

342 Madison Ave., Ste. 2001
New York, New York 10017
Salary Minimum: $60,000
Key Contact: Sydney Reynolds
Ron DiCamillo
Betty Roffwarg

Functions: 02.0 03.0 04.0 06.0 11.2
Industries: B.00 D.00 D.18 D.E0 D.H0
Professional Affiliations: AME
Description: Specialists: senior management,
large turnkey projects, glass ceiling
initiatives

E.J. Rhodes Assoc.
Two W. 45th St.
New York, New York 10036
Salary Minimum: $60,000
Key Contact: Stephen Littman
Norman Zarkin
Barry Bova
Barry Wilder

Functions: Most + 01.0 08.0
Industries: Most + G.00 H.00 I.14 I.15
Professional Affiliations: IACPR
Description: International practice specialists in
finance, real estate, healthcare & retail

Marshall Rice Assoc.
40 Boulder Ave., P.O. Box 1485
Charlestown, Rhode Island 02813
Salary Minimum: $50,000
Key Contact: Marshall T. Rice
Alan L. Greener

Functions: 01.2 01.3 11.4
Industries: I.12 I.13
Description: A search firm serving the not-for-
profit sector exclusively

Affiliates/Other Offices:
Educational Management Network, Nantucket

Ridenour & Assoc.
400 E. Randolph St., #6B
Chicago, Illinois 60601-7329
Salary Minimum: $75,000
Key Contact: Suzanne S. Ridenour
Andrew S. Yoelin

Functions: 01.0 01.1 01.2 05.0 11.4
Industries: Most
Professional Affiliations: CADM, CDMA,
DMA, EDMA, NAWBO, WDRG
Description: Recruitment for direct marketing
& integrated communications
professionals

Rieser & Assoc., Inc.
130 S. Bemiston, Ste. 710
St. Louis, Missouri 63105
Salary Minimum: $75,000
Key Contact: John D. Rieser

Functions: Most + 01.0 02.0 05.0 06.0 08.0
Industries: Most + D.10 D.15 D.18 D.24 H.10
Professional Affiliations: SHRM
Description: Dedicated to personalized service,
comprehensive research & ethical search

Norman Roberts & Assoc., Inc.
12424 Wilshire Blvd., Ste. 850
Los Angeles, California 90025-1042
Salary Minimum: $60,000
Key Contact: Norman C. Roberts
Valerie S. Frank

Functions: Most + 01.0 06.0 08.0 09.0 11.0
Industries: Most + E.00 I.12 I.13 I.14 K.00
Professional Affiliations: CERA
Description: Nationwide specialists in public
sector/not-for-profit, healthcare, education

Roberts Ryan & Bentley
1099 Winterson Rd., Ste. 140
Airport Sq. #19
Linthicum, Maryland 21090
Salary Minimum: $60,000
Key Contact: Richard R. Cappe
Richard A. Dannenberg
Mark Lorenzetti

Functions: 01.0 05.0 08.0 09.0 10.0
Industries: D.H0 D.I0 H.00 H.I0
Professional Affiliations: IACPR
Description: Research based retained executive
search for mid & upper management

Roberts-Lund Assoc., Ltd.
366 Madison Ave.
New York, New York 10017
Salary Minimum: $75,000
Key Contact: Michael P. Iserson

Industries: H.10 H.11 H.12
Description: Retained firm for financial
institutions

Robertson, Spoerlein & Wengert

10 S. Riverside Plz.
Chicago, Illinois 60606
Salary Minimum: $60,000
Key Contact: George O. Robertson
Kent Spoerlein

Functions: Most + 01.0 02.0 05.0 05.4 08.0
Industries: D.00 D.22 H.00 H.10 H.I0
Description: Dedicated to the selection of professional executives for industry & commerce

Robertson-Surrette Ltd.

1583 Hollis St., 5th Fl.
Halifax, Nova Scotia B3J 1V4 Canada
Salary Minimum: $40,000
Key Contact: Ronald W. Robertson
Mark J. Surrette

Functions: Most
Industries: Most
Description: Atlantic Canada's largest recruiting firm specializing in middle to senior management

Bruce Robinson Assoc.

250 W. 57th St., Ste. 510
New York, New York 10107
Salary Minimum: $60,000
Key Contact: Bruce Robinson

Functions: Most
Industries: Most
Professional Affiliations: AESC
Description: Top flight minority & female executive search

Robison & McAulay

1350 First Citizens Plaza
128 S. Tryon St.
Charlotte, North Carolina 28202
Salary Minimum: $50,000
Key Contact: Stuart C. Hemingway, III
Ronald E. Infinger
A.L. McAulay, Jr.
John H. Robison
John H. Robison, IV

Functions: Most
Industries: Most
Professional Affiliations: AESC
Description: Serve all industries & professions

Robsham & Assoc.

66 Long Wharf
Boston, Massachusetts 02110
Salary Minimum: $50,000
Key Contact: Beverly H. Robsham

Functions: Most + 05.0 05.5 08.0
Industries: Most + D.00 I.00 K.00 L.00
Professional Affiliations: IACPR, DMA, SBANE
Description: Individualized search-small to medium sized corporations-mostly New England & CA Bay area

The Romark Group, Ltd.

205 E. Main St., Ste. 3-6
Huntington, New York 11743
Salary Minimum: $50,000
Key Contact: Roberta Vaccaro Salerno

Functions: 01.2 01.3 02.1 02.5 04.0
Industries: D.10 D.16 D.17 D.18 I.10
Professional Affiliations: ACS, AICHE, ASTM, IFT, NAER
Description: Management consulting firm specializing in recruitment & executive search

Romeo-Hudgins & Assoc. Ltd.

200 Lake Dr. E., Ste. 101
Woodlake Falls Corporate Park
Cherry Hill, New Jersey 08002
Salary Minimum: $50,000
Key Contact: Paul C. Romeo

Functions: 01.4 06.0 09.0 09.3 09.4
Industries: D.18
Professional Affiliations: ASPA, DPMA, EMA
Description: Executive search for pharmaceutical, information services & human resource management

Ropes Assoc., Inc.

333 N. New River Dr., E., Ste. 4000
Ft. Lauderdale, Florida 33301-2240
Salary Minimum: $70,000
Key Contact: John Ropes

Functions: Most
Industries: H.10 H.R0 I.10
Professional Affiliations: AESC, NAIOP, ULI
Description: Executive search; real estate-developers, builders, operators, financiers, financial institutions

Rourke, Bourbonnais Assoc., Ltd.

1130 Sherbrooke St., W
Penthouse II
Montreal, Quebec H3A 2M8 Canada
Salary Minimum: $60,000
Key Contact: Marianne Donaldson
Roger Lachance
Patrick W. Rourke

Functions: Most
Industries: Most
Description: Executive recruiting consultants—senior & middle management-general management, marketing & finance

Branches:
175 Bloor St., E
North Tower, Ste. 806
Toronto, Ontario M4W 3R8 Canada

David Rowe & Assoc., Inc.

515 W. Maple St.
Hinsdale, Illinois 60521
Key Contact: David E. Rowe
Carol E. Rozenboom

Functions: Most
Industries: I.14 I.15
Description: Conducts searches for all management levels with the healthcare industry

Rurak & Assoc., Inc

1350 Connecticut Ave., NW
Ste. 801
Washington, District of Columbia 20036
Salary Minimum: $100,000
Key Contact: Zbigniew T. Rurak
June M. Cartoon

Functions: Most
Industries: Most
Professional Affiliations: IACPR
Description: Counselors to senior management in executive search, selection & development

Rusher, Loscavio & Lo Presto

111 Maiden Ln., Ste. 460
San Francisco, California 94108
Salary Minimum: $75,000
Key Contact: J. Michael Loscavio
William H. Rusher, Jr.
M. Claire Pister

Functions: Most
Industries: Most
Professional Affiliations: CERA
Description: Assist growth-oriented companies in recruiting, developing & maintaining superior management teams

Branches:
2479 E. Bayshore Rd., Ste. 700
Palo Alto, California 94303
Key Contact: Robert L. Lo Presto
Art Pedroza

Charles Russ Assoc.

10983 Granada Ln.
Overland Park, Kansas 66211
Salary Minimum: $40,000
Key Contact: Charles F. Russ, Jr.
Dr. Richard Sanderson

Functions: Most
Industries: Most
Professional Affiliations: ABA
Description: Founded in 1972, we guarantee our searches for 1 full year

James Russell, Inc.

P.O. Box 427
Bloomington, Illinois 61702-0427
Salary Minimum: $50,000
Key Contact: Billy D. Adkisson

Functions: 01.0 05.0 08.0
Industries: I.14 I.15 I.16
Professional Affiliations: AAHC, ACHE,
    AGPA, MGMA, NAPR
Description: Physician search, executive search,
    healthcare consulting

Russell, Montgomery & Assoc.

101 Continental Pl., Ste. 105
Brentwood, Tennessee 37027
Salary Minimum: $30,000
Key Contact: Dennis M. Russell
William S. Montgomery

Functions: Most
Industries: Most
Description: Consultants specializing in
    executive search, corporate outplacement
    & employee appraisal

Branches:
310 Gallaher View Rd.
Ste. 123
Knoxville, Tennessee 37919
Key Contact: Thomas C. Prince, III

James J. Rust Executive Search

420 Lexington Ave.
New York, New York 10170
Salary Minimum: $75,000
Key Contact: James J. Rust

Functions: Most + 05.0 06.0 07.0 08.0 09.0
Industries: D.E0 E.00 H.00 I.00 J.13
Description: Broad industry & functionally
    based executive recruiter

Affiliates/Other Offices:
James J. Rust Executive Search, Brussels
James J. Rust Executive Search, Frankfurt
James J. Rust Executive Search, Helsinki
James J. Rust Executive Search, London
James J. Rust Executive Search, Milan
James J. Rust Executive Search, Paris

SRH Resource Group

72 Cummings Point Rd.
Stamford, Connecticut 06902
Salary Minimum: $75,000
Key Contact: Stanley R. Haladyna
Robert Martin
Gretta Hall

Functions: Most + 01.0 02.0 03.0 04.0 07.0
Industries: Most + D.10 D.15 D.16 D.18 D.I0
Professional Affiliations: IFT, SDA
Description: Senior level searches, mainly
    biotech, chemical, food & pharmaceutical
    industries

SS & A Executive Search Consultants

4350 E. Camelback Rd., Ste. B200
Phoenix, Arizona 85253
Salary Minimum: $40,000
Key Contact: Susan F. Shultz
Roger Vanderploeg

Functions: Most + 01.1 01.2 01.3 01.5 05.0
Industries: Most + A.00 H.00 I.17 J.00 K.00
Description: Retained firm, completing
    management, professional, international
    and board searches

Affiliates/Other Offices:
Morgan & Partners, Atnwerpen
Morgan & Partners, Brussels
Morgan & Partners, Harrow
Morgan & Partners, Helsinki
Morgan & Partners, Luxumbourg
Morgan & Partners, Malmo
Morgan & Partners, Madrid
Morgan & Partners, Milan
Morgan & Partners, Monte Carlo
Morgan & Partners, Paris

Saber Consultants, Inc.
5300 Hollister, Ste. 100
Houston, Texas 77040
Salary Minimum: $30,000
Key Contact: Steven E. LeMay
Michael C. Scharringhausen
Michael P. O'Leary

Functions: Most
Industries: Most
Professional Affiliations: HAAPC, NAPC,
   TAPC
Description: Executive search—All industries

Wilbur M. Sachtjen Assoc., Inc.
50 Main St., Ste. 1047
White Plains, New York 10606
Salary Minimum: $100,000
Key Contact: Wilbur M. Sachtjen

Functions: Most + 01.2 08.0
Industries: Most + H.00
Description: Senior management level searches,
   with specialty in financial services

Sage/Walters Ltd.
666 Fifth Ave.
New York, New York 10103
Salary Minimum: $100,000
Key Contact: Fred Sage

Industries: H.00 H.10 H.11 H.12
Description: Retainer based firm exclusively
   supporting the European investment
   banking community

Saley Partners Int'l.
WaterPark Place, 14th Floor
10 Bay St.
Toronto, Ontario M5J 2R8 Canada
Salary Minimum: $60,000
Key Contact: William W. Probert
W.C. Stewart

Functions: Most + 02.0 05.0 06.0 08.0
Industries: Most + D.00 H.00
Description: Executive search consultants to
   senior management serving corporations
   across Canada

Sampson, Neill & Wilkins Inc.
543 Valley Rd.
Upper Montclair, New Jersey 07043
Salary Minimum: $70,000
Key Contact: Martin C. Sampson, M.D.
Wellden C. Neill
Walter K. Wilkins
Robert J. Hodges

Functions: 01.0 01.1 04.0 05.0 11.5
Industries: D.18 D.I0 H.12 I.15 I.16
Description: Specializing in pharmaceutical,
   biomedical, biotechnology, health care &
   environmental indus.

International Branches:
London

Sandhurst Assoc.
4851 LBJ Freeway, Ste. 601
Dallas, Texas 75244
Salary Minimum: $50,000
Key Contact: James P. Demchak
Duane R. Goar
James N. Farrell
S. Scott Porter
Susan Procter
Judith McCall
Rayna Loeb

Functions: Most
Industries: Most
Description: Middle management through
   senior executive levels in most disciplines

Allan Sarn Assoc., Inc.
230 Park Ave., Ste. 1522
New York, New York 10169
Salary Minimum: $80,000
Key Contact: Allan G. Sarn

Functions: 06.0 06.1 06.2
Industries: Most + D.00 G.00 H.00
Professional Affiliations: IACPR, ACA, EMA,
   NYHRP, NYPMA
Description: Executive search consultants
   specializing exclusively in human
   resources

298 / DIRECTORY OF EXECUTIVE RECRUITERS

Sathe & Assoc., Inc.
5821 Cedar Lake Rd.
Minneapolis, Minnesota 55416
Salary Minimum: $50,000
Key Contact: Mark Sathe
Bill Dubbs
Arlene Clapp
Jim Brimeger

Functions: Most + 02.0 05.0 06.0 10.0 11.5
Industries: Most + B.0W D.00 H.I0 H.R0
   K.00
Professional Affiliations: IACPR
Description: Government, real estate,
   healthcare, insurance, manufacturing &
   banking

Savoy Partners, Ltd.
1899 L St. N.W., Ste 1001
Washington, District of Columbia 20036
Salary Minimum: $90,000
Key Contact: Robert J. Brudno

Functions: Most
Professional Affiliations: IACPR
Description: Independent, highly-regarded
   senior level executive search &
   management consulting firm

Schalekamp & Assoc., Inc.
7900 Xerxes Ave., S., Ste. 718
Minneapolis, Minnesota 55431
Salary Minimum: $30,000
Key Contact: Paul D. Schalekamp

Functions: 01.4 09.3 10.0
Industries: H.I0
Professional Affiliations: NAPC, NIRA
Description: Retained search specialists for the
   insurance industry

Schenkel & Company
P.O. Box 6416
Westlake Village, California 91359-6416
Salary Minimum: $50,000
Key Contact: Donald D. Schenkel

Functions: Most + 01.0
Industries: Most + I.00 I.14 J.00
Description: Organizational & executive search
   consulting for mid to executive level
   management

F. B. Schmidt Intl.
30423 Canwood Pl., Ste. 239
Agoura Hills, California 91301
Salary Minimum: $60,000
Key Contact: Frank B. Schmidt

Functions: 01.2 01.3 05.0 05.1 05.2
Industries: D.00 D.10 D.16 D.17 J.10
Professional Affiliations: AMA, CERA
Description: Exclusive recruitment specialists
   in consumer marketing management

The Schmitt Tolette Group
122 E. 42nd St., Ste. 1700
New York, New York 10168
Salary Minimum: $75,000
Key Contact: Thomas G. Schmitt
I.G. Skip Tolette

Functions: 01.0 05.0 06.0 08.0 09.0
Industries: H.00 I.11 J.00 J.11 J.12
Professional Affiliations: AESC
Description: Functional strength: information
   technology, sales & marketing, general
   management, finance & HR

Schuyler, Frye & Baker, Inc.
5600 Glenridge Dr., NE, Ste. 225
Glenridge Centre E.
Atlanta, Georgia 30342
Salary Minimum: $100,000
Key Contact: Lambert Schuyler, Jr.
Garland V. Frye
Jerry H. Baker
Sally A. McDowell

Functions: Most
Industries: Most + I.13
Professional Affiliations: AESC
Description: Senior management for: domestic
   & non-domestic companies higher
   education institutions

Affiliates/Other Offices:
Smith, Goerss & Ferneborg, Inc., San Francisco

Schwab-Carrese Assoc.

128 S. Tryon St., Ste. 1570
Charlotte, North Carolina 28202
Salary Minimum: $40,000
Key Contact: James K. Schwab
Godfrey G. Bennett, Jr.

Functions: Most
Industries: Most
Description: Executive search firm serving all
industries & professions

Schweichler Assoc., Inc.

100 Drake's Landing Rd.
Ste. 120
Greenbrae, California 94904
Salary Minimum: $100,000
Key Contact: Lee Schweichler
Ann Peckenpaugh
Colleen J. Richardson

Functions: 01.0 02.0 04.0 05.0 09.0
Industries: D.00 D.24 D.25 D.H0 J.00
Description: Recruit senior executives for start-
up & high growth companies

The Michael Scott Consulting Co., Inc.

119 W. 57th St., Penthouse
New York, New York 10019
Salary Minimum: $75,000
Key Contact: Victor A. Caleo
James Kerrs

Functions: Most + 10.0
Industries: Most
Description: General practitioner

J. Robert Scott

27 State St.
Boston, Massachusetts 02109
Salary Minimum: $80,000
Key Contact: William A. Holodnak
Bentley H. Beaver
Mary K. Morse

Functions: Most
Industries: Most + D.00 D.H0 D.I0 H.00 I.00
Professional Affiliations: IACPR
Description: Broad experience with an
emphasis on quality performance &
commitment to clients

Search Express

30050 Chagrin Blvd., Ste. 300
Cleveland, Ohio 44124
Salary Minimum: $30,000
Key Contact: Adam Kohn

Functions: Most + 01.0 02.0 04.0 05.0 11.5
Industries: Most + B.0W B.10 D.00 D.24
D.H0
Description: Specializing in executive search-
quality assistance for mid-level positions

Search Source, Inc.

2019 B Johnson Rd., P.O. Box 1161
Granite City, Illinois 62040
Salary Minimum: $30,000
Key Contact: James McKechan

Functions: Most
Industries: D.H0 J.00 J.12 J.13
Description: Broad range of recruiting for high-
tech fields

Seiden Assoc., Inc.

375 Park Ave.
New York, New York 10152
Salary Minimum: $100,000
Key Contact: Steven A. Seiden
Phoebe Eilenberg

Functions: Most + 01.0 02.0 05.0 06.0 08.0
Industries: Most
Professional Affiliations: IACPR
Description: Retainer firm specializing in CEOs
and executives who report to CEOs

Seitchik, Corwin & Seitchik Inc.

1830 Jackson St., Ste. C
San Francisco, California 94109
Key Contact: William Seitchik
Blade Corwin
Jack Seitchik

Functions: Most
Industries: D.11 G.00
Professional Affiliations: AAMA, IFAI,
NKMA, SFFI
Description: Specialize in apparel, textile,
footwear & needletrades industries

Branches:
330 E 38th St., Ste. 5P
New York, New York 10016

Robert Sellery Assoc., Ltd.
1155 Connecticut Ave. NW, Ste. 500
Washington, District of Columbia 20036
Key Contact: Robert A. Sellery, Jr.
Julia B. Randall

Functions: Most + 11.4
Industries: Most + I.12 I.13 I.14
Description: Full service executive recruiting
    firm based on 19 years of experience

Shaffer Consulting Group
2437 Grand Ave., Ste. 255
Ventura, California 93003
Salary Minimum: $75,000
Key Contact: Bradford W. Shaffer

Functions: 01.0 02.0 05.0 06.0 09.0
Industries: D.24 D.H0 D.I0 H.10 J.13
Professional Affiliations: IACPR
Description: Senior level searches across major
    functional units

M.B. Shattuck & Assoc., Inc.
100 Bush St., Ste. 501
San Francisco, California 94104
Salary Minimum: $75,000
Key Contact: M.B. Shattuck

Functions: Most + 01.0 02.0 03.0 04.0 05.0
Industries: Most + D.00 D.24 D.25 D.26
    D.H0
Professional Affiliations: AESC, IACPR, CERA
Description: Specialize in senior/upper middle
    management: high technology,
    manufacturing, health/medical, others

Networks:
International Independent Consultants (IIC)
Amstelveen, Bangkok, Frankfurt, Hamburg, Hong Kong, London, Milan, Oslo, Paris, Rosemont,
Singapore, Vedbaek, Vienna, Zurich

Kimball Shaw Assoc.
3 Pleasant St.
Hingham, Massachusetts 02043
Key Contact: Kimball Shaw

Functions: Most + 01.0 02.0 06.0 09.0 11.0
Industries: Most + D.00 I.00 I.14 I.15 I.18
Description: Fixed professional fee, guaranteed
    completion search services to most
    industries

Sheperd Bueschel & Provus, Inc.
One S. Wacker Dr., Ste. 2740
Chicago, Illinois 60606
Salary Minimum: $75,000
Key Contact: David A. Bueschel
Barbara L. Provus
Daniel M. Shepherd

Functions: Most
Industries: Most
Professional Affiliations: AESC, IACPR
Description: Senior & upper-middle
    management level searches for
    corporations, associations & ventures

Sherbrooke Assoc., Inc.
430 Lake Ave.
Colonia, New Jersey 07067
Salary Minimum: $40,000
Key Contact: William M. Levy
James D. Scanlon

Functions: Most
Industries: Most
Description: Recruiting generalists with a
    Northeast customer base

Sheridan Search
405 N. Wabash, Ste. 3310
Chicago, Illinois 60611
Salary Minimum: $100,000
Key Contact: John A. Sheridan

Functions: 06.2
Industries: B.00 D.H0 H.10 I.10 J.11
Professional Affiliations: IACPR
Description: The firm specializes in human
    resources search assignments

Branches:
27853 Berwick Dr.
Carmel, California 93923
Key Contact: David Wells

Michael Shirley Assoc.
10965 Granada Ln., Ste 102
Overland Park, Kansas 66211
Salary Minimum: $50,000
Key Contact: Michael R. Shirley

Functions: Most + 01.0 05.0 06.0 09.0
Industries: Most + I.00
Description: Generalists executive search &
senior level outplacement firm

Shoemaker & Assoc.
4720 Chamblee Dunwoody Rd.
Atlanta, Georgia 30338
Salary Minimum: $60,000
Key Contact: Larry Shoemaker

Functions: Most
Industries: Most + D.00 D.10 D.D0
Description: Broad range of executive search
activities, upper & middle management
levels

E.L. Shore & Assoc. Corp.
2 St. Clair Ave. East, Ste. 1201
Toronto, Ontario M4T 2T5 Canada
Salary Minimum: $60,000

Functions: Most
Industries: Most
Professional Affiliations: IACPR
Description: Specialists in retail, financial
services, manufacturing, health care &
automotive

The Shotland Group
6345 Balboa Blvd., Ste. 370
Encino, California 91316
Salary Minimum: $50,000
Key Contact: David R. Shotland

Functions: Most + 01.0 02.0 03.0 06.0
Industries: Most
Description: A generalist practice emphasizing
the recruitment of middle & upper level
management

W. Shryock & Co.
610 Newport Center Dr., Ste. 270
Newport Beach, California 92660
Salary Minimum: $75,000
Key Contact: William Shryock

Functions: Most
Industries: H.R0
Professional Affiliations: BIA, ICSC, NAIOP,
ULI
Description: Executive search services
exclusively to the real estate industry

John Sibbald Assoc., Inc.
8725 Higgins Rd.
Chicago, Illinois 60631
Salary Minimum: $60,000
Key Contact: John R. Sibbald
Carol S. Jeffers
Robert G. Southwell
Kathryn J. Costick
John B. Hunter, Jr.

Functions: Most + 01.0 02.0 05.0 06.0 08.0
Industries: Most + C.00 D.00 G.00 I.10 I.12
Professional Affiliations: NCA
Description: Generalist-highly personalized
service-senior searches only. Private club
division

Sievers & Assoc.
P.O. Box 50754
St. Paul, Minnesota 55150-0754
Salary Minimum: $35,000
Key Contact: Carl R. Sievers, III

Functions: Most + 01.0 08.0 11.0
Industries: Most + F.00 G.00 I.10 I.14
Description: General management, finance,
sales/marketing, physicians & related
healthcare professionals

Sigma Group Inc.

717 Seventeenth St., Ste. 1440
Denver, Colorado 80202-3314
Salary Minimum: $75,000
Key Contact: George L. Reisinger
Ronald R. Evans

Branches:
555 Clover Ln.
Boulder, Colorado 80303
Key Contact: W. M. Young

Functions: 01.0 02.0 05.0 08.0 09.0
Industries: B.00 D.00 D.H0 H.00 I.00
Professional Affiliations: ASPA, EMA
Description: Exclusively provides retained
executive search consulting service to
clients nationally

Daniel A. Silverstein Assoc. Inc.

5355 Town Ctr. Rd., Ste. 1001
Boca Raton, Florida 33486
Salary Minimum: $100,000
Key Contact: Daniel A. Silverstein

Functions: 01.0 01.1 01.2 04.0 05.0
Industries: D.17 D.18 D.I0 I.14 I.15
Description: Pharmaceuticals, bio-tech,
diagnostics, medical sevices, hospital
supplies & venture capital

C.W. Sink & Co., Inc.

16 N.E. Executive Park
Burlington, Massachusetts 01803
Salary Minimum: $70,000
Key Contact: Clifton W. Sink
Delese Hovey

Branches:
50 Airport Pkwy.
San Jose, California 95110

Functions: Most + 01.0 02.0 04.0 05.0 11.0
Industries: D.00 D.H0 I.00 J.00
Description: Recruiting all functions—emphasis
on voice & data communications,
hardware & software

5956 Sherry Ln., Ste. 600
Dallas, Texas 75225

Skott/Edwards Consultants

201 Rte. 17 N.
Rutherford, New Jersey 07070
Salary Minimum: $75,000
Key Contact: Skott B. Burkland

Affiliates/Other Offices:
B.D.C., London
William Kyle, Hong Kong
William Kyle, Taipei
William Kyle, Toyko
M.B. Shattuck & Assoc., Inc., San Francisco

Functions: 01.0 04.0 08.0 09.0 10.0
Industries: D.00 D.10 D.17 D.I0 H.12
Professional Affiliations: AESC, IACPR
Description: Expertise emphasizes healthcare,
pharmaceuticals, financial services venture
capital & high-tech

Slater & Assoc.

12221 Merit Dr., Ste. 1325
Dallas, Texas 75251
Salary Minimum: $125,000
Key Contact: Robert W. Slater

Functions: Most
Description: Senior level executive search

Slayton Int'l., Inc.

10 S. Riverside Plaza
Ste. 312
Chicago, Illinois 60606
Salary Minimum: $85,000
Key Contact: Richard C. Slayton
Vincent P. Schwartz
Elizabeth W. Souder
Richard S. Slayton

Functions: Most + 01.0 02.0 04.0 09.0 11.1
Industries: Most + D.00 D.22 D.23 D.H0 I.00
Professional Affiliations: IACPR, HRMA
Description: An IE & partner, dedicated to the
search for excellence worldwide

International Branches:
Bankok, Hong Kong, Toronto, Singapore

Sloane, Sloane & Mayne

41 Glasco Turnpike
Woodstock, New York 12498
Salary Minimum: $60,000
Key Contact: William G. Sloane

Functions: Most + 01.2 02.0 06.0 08.0 11.6
Industries: Most + B.0W B.10 D.00
Description: Full service firm staffed with
senior professional managers—results
guaranteed

Stephen R. Smith & Co., Inc.

P.O. Box 626
Naperville, Illinois 60566-0626
Salary Minimum: $50,000
Key Contact: Stephen R. Smith

Functions: Most
Industries: Most
Description: Broad & deep experience for 25
years—vp/director levels

Robert L. Smith & Co., Inc.

666 Fifth Ave., 37th Fl.
New York, New York 10103
Salary Minimum: $80,000
Key Contact: Robert L. Smith
Patricia L. Sawyer

Functions: Most + 01.0 05.0 06.0 09.0
Industries: Most + D.00 G.00 I.00 J.00
Professional Affiliations: AESC
Description: Senior management, most
functions in services & information-
intensive businesses

Networks:
Penrhyn Partners Int'l.
Long Beach, San Francisco, Toronto, Hong Kong, London, Melbourne

Howard W. Smith Assoc.

Old State House
P.O. Box 230877
Hartford, Connecticut 06123-0877
Salary Minimum: $60,000
Key Contact: Howard W. Smith

Functions: Most + 01.0 05.0 06.0 07.0 08.0
Industries: Most + H.00 H.10 H.I0 H.R0 I.00
Professional Affiliations: IACPR
Description: Search emphasizing investments,
real estate, financial services, mortgage
banking, marketing

Smith, Goerss & Ferneborg, Inc.

25 Ecker St., Ecker Sq.,
Ste. 850
San Francisco, California 94105
Salary Minimum: $60,000
Key Contact: John R. Ferneborg
Ronald G. Goerss
Ann E. Blackwell

Functions: Most
Industries: D.00 D.18 D.24 J.13
Professional Affiliations: AESC
Description: Multi-specialty firm serving broad
range of clients nationwide

Affiliates/Other Offices:
Schuyler, Frye & Baker, Inc., Atlanta

H.C. Smith Ltd.

20600 Chagrin Blvd., Ste. 400
Tower East
Cleveland, Ohio 44122
Salary Minimum: $70,000
Key Contact: Herbert C. Smith
Rebecca Ruben
Ralph S. Tyler

Branches:
2 Stanley Keyes Court
Rye, New York 10580
Key Contact: Naomi D'Agostino

Functions: Most + 01.1 01.2 01.3 11.2 11.4
Description: Quality generalist search,
recognized for ability to recruit minorities
& women, domest. & int'l.

Smith, Roth & Squires

200 Park Ave., Ste. 303 E.
New York, New York 10166
Salary Minimum: $45,000
Key Contact: Steven L. Smith
Ronald P. Roth
R. James Squires

Branches:
4350 Brownsboro Rd., Ste. 110
Louisville, Kentucky 40207
Key Contact: Robert J. Butler

Functions: Most
Industries: Most
Description: Executive search consultants for
all functional areas throughout the United
States

Smith Search, S.A.

Barranca del Muerto, No.472
Col. Alpes, Del. A. Obregon
Mexico City, Mexico DF 01010 Mexico
Salary Minimum: $60,000
Key Contact: John E. Smith, Jr.
Maria Elena Pardo
Cony Gutierrez Otero

Branches:
Av. San Ignacio No. 906
Zapopan
Guadalajara, Jalisco Mexico
Key Contact: Alejandro Gaxiola

Affiliates/Other Offices:
SpencerStuart, Chicago

Functions: Most
Industries: D.10 D.22 D.24 H.10 I.18
Description: Mexico's leading independent
executive search firm, affiliate of
SpencerStuart

Herman Smith Transearch Inc.

P.O. Box 255
Toronto-Dominion Ctr.
Toronto, Ontario M5K 1J5 Canada
Salary Minimum: $65,000
Key Contact: Herman M. Smith
Barbara Nelson
Glenn A. Wilkie
J. Michael Schoales

Functions: Most + 01.0 01.1 01.2
Industries: Most
Professional Affiliations: IACPR, TI
Description: International specialists in
recruitment, as well as recruitment
program design

A. William Smyth, Inc.

P.O. Box 380
Ross, California 94957
Salary Minimum: $60,000
Key Contact: William Smyth

Functions: Most + 01.2 01.3 05.0 08.0 08.1
Industries: D.16 F.00 I.10 I.11 J.10
Professional Affiliations: CERA

Sockwell & Anderson
1 Twelve Tryon Plz., Ste. 1500
Charlotte, North Carolina 28284
Salary Minimum: $50,000
Key Contact: Douglas K. Anderson
J. Edgar Sockwell, III

Functions: Most
Industries: D.12 D.14 H.00 H.10 H.R0
Professional Affiliations: AESC
Description: Executive search in economic
development, graphic arts, financial
services & real estate

Soltis Management Services
876 Brower Rd.
Radnor, Pennsylvania 19087
Salary Minimum: $60,000
Key Contact: Charles W. Soltis

Functions: Most + 01.0 02.0 06.0 08.0 11.5
Industries: B.0W D.00 H.00 H.R0 I.00
Description: A management consulting firm
specializing in executive search

SpencerStuart
55 E. 52nd St.
New York, New York 10055-1021
Salary Minimum: $75,000
Key Contact: Robert L. Benson
George J. Helmer
H. H. Humphrey
Denis B.K. Lyons
Leslie Maddin
E. Peter McLean
Thomas J. Neff
Nicholas S. Young
Thomas G. Hardy
Michael Castine
W. Davis Hawkins
Robert A. Damon

Functions: Most
Professional Affiliations: AESC
Description: Senior level executive & board of
director search consulting services

Branches:
400 S. Hope St., Ste. 2430
Los Angeles, California 90071-2825
Key Contact: John C. Westwater
Dennis Boyer
Karen Folsom
Anthony Pfannkuche
Stephen Unger

695 East Main St.
Financial Centre
Stamford, Connecticut 06901
Key Contact: H. James Krauser
David Arnold
Rick Richardson
Jack Lohnes
Thomas W. Wasson
Richard B. White
Edward C. Slowik
Dayton Ogden
Carlton W. Thompson

333 Bush Street, Ste 2500
San Francisco, California 94104-2161
Key Contact: Jeffrey W. Hodge
Joseph E. Griesedieck, Jr.
John Ware
E.C. Grayson

1201 W. Peachtree St.
One Atlantic Ctr., Ste. 3230
Atlanta, Georgia 30309
Key Contact: William B. Reeves
Gerald J. Bump
M. Evan Lindsay
Heath C. Boyer

3000 Sand Hill Rd.
Building 1, Ste. 275
Menlo Park, California 94025
Key Contact: Brad Stirn
Stephen Strain

401 N. Michigan Ave.
Chicago, Illinois 60611-4244
Key Contact: James J. Drury, III
Arthur J. Davidson
Paul W. Earle
J. Curtis Fee
Susan Hart
Joseph Kopsick
Christopher C. Nadherny
Jack Preschlack
Scott K. Shelton
Toni S. Smith
Gilbert R. Stenholm
Donald R. Utroska
Leonard H. Serwat

2005 Market St., Ste. 2350
Philadelphia, Pennsylvania 19103
Key Contact: Dennis C. Carey
David R. McCarthy
Kenneth L. Kring

1717 Main St., Ste. 5300
Dallas, Texas 75201-4605
Key Contact: O.D. Cruse
David C. Anderson
John W. Schroeder
Patrick W. Haragan
Ronald J. Zera

1111 Bagby, Ste. 1616
Houston, Texas 77002-2594
Key Contact: Louis J. Rieger
Joseph A. Collard
Jonathan A. Crystal
John A. Griffin

International Branches:
Amsterdam, Barcelona, Brussels, Cheshire, Dusseldorf, Frankfurt, Geneva, London, Madrid, Melbourne, Milan, Munich, Oslo, Paris, Sao Paulo, Stockholm, Stuttgart, Sydney, Tokyo, Zurich

Splaine & Assoc., Inc.
15951 Los Gatos Blvd., Ste. 13
Los Gatos, California 95032
Salary Minimum: $70,000
Key Contact: Charles Splaine

Functions: Most
Industries: B.0W D.H0 D.I0 H.00 J.00
Description: International search for broad spectrum of companies in all functions

Spriggs & Co., Inc.
1701 Lake Ave.,Ste. 265
Glenview, Illinois 60025
Salary Minimum: $50,000
Key Contact: Robert D. Spriggs

Functions: Most + 01.0 01.2
Industries: Most + D.00 D.10 D.14 D.15 D.22
Professional Affiliations: IACPR, IMESC
Description: Search & management consulting

M.H. Springer & Assoc.
5855 Topanga Canyon Blvd.
Ste. 230
Woodland Hills, California 91367
Salary Minimum: $75,000
Key Contact: Mark H. Springer
Gregory R. Neal

Functions: 11.0
Industries: H.00 H.10 H.11 H.12
Professional Affiliations: CERA
Description: Small retained firm specializing in financial services (banks, savings/loans, mortgage banking)

Stack Assoc.
51 Locust Ave.
New Canaan, Connecticut 06840
Salary Minimum: $75,000
Key Contact: J. William Stack, Jr.

Functions: Most + 01.1 01.2
Industries: Most
Description: Specialists in senior management positions in all industries worldwide

The Stamford Group Inc.
155 Sycamore St.
Glastonbury, Connecticut 06033
Salary Minimum: $40,000
Key Contact: William Peoples
Denice Peoples

Functions: Most
Industries: I.14 I.15 I.16
Professional Affiliations: AAPA, ACEP, ACOG, APACS, APTA, NAHR, NAPC, ONS
Description: Specializing in medical/technical positions through executive level, including physicians

Stanislaw & Assoc., Inc.
P.O. Box 589, 405 N. Calhoun
Brookfield, Wisconsin 53005
Salary Minimum: $60,000
Key Contact: Robert Stanislaw

Functions: Most + 01.0 02.0 05.0 06.0 08.0
Industries: D.00 D.19 D.24 D.H0
Description: Work nationally within certain
technologies & regionally within major
Fortune 500 firms

Staples Consulting Inc.
P.O. Box 63-6425
Margate, Florida 33063-6425
Salary Minimum: $80,000
Key Contact: Arthur B. Staples

Functions: Most + 01.1 01.2 01.3 01.5 06.0
Industries: Most + D.00 D.I0 H.00 H.I0 I.17
Professional Affiliations: IACPR, ASME, EMA
Description: Specializing in identifying &
evaluating executives since 1973, flat fee

Staub, Warmbold & Barkauskas, Inc.
555 Fifth Ave.
New York, New York 10017
Salary Minimum: $75,000
Key Contact: Robert A. Staub
Herman P. Warmbold
Richard Barkauskas

Functions: Most
Industries: Most
Professional Affiliations: IACPR

Lee Stephens & Assoc.
2168 Balboa Ave., Ste. 3
San Diego, California 92109
Salary Minimum: $100,000
Key Contact: Lee Stephens

Functions: Most + 08.0 09.0
Industries: Most + C.00 H.00 H.R0
Professional Affiliations: BOMA, ICSC, NAHB,
NAIOP
Description: Specializing in real estate
nationally since 1970; also finance, MIS/
telecommunications & healthcare

Stephens Assoc. Ltd.
88 N. Fifth St., P.O. Box 151114
Columbus, Ohio 43215
Salary Minimum: $70,000
Key Contact: Stephen A. Martinez
Lowell A. Gordon
Gretchen K. Snediker

Functions: Most
Industries: B.00 B.0W D.24 D.H0 J.00
Description: Emphasis in computer (HW, SW),
telecommunications, environmental,
financial, & research technology

Stern & Watson, Inc.
245 Fifth Ave., Ste. 1802
New York, New York 10016
Salary Minimum: $75,000
Key Contact: Leslie W. Stern
Hanan S. Watson
Susan E. Fein
Roxanne Duncan-Powell

Functions: 05.0 08.0 11.1
Industries: Most
Professional Affiliations: IACPR, ACG, AMA,
HRPS, NASCP
Description: Highly respected for quality,
creativity, selectivity, thoroughness and
performance

Michael Stern Assoc. Inc.
77 Bloor St., W., Ste. 1205
Toronto, Ontario M5S 1M2 Canada
Salary Minimum: $60,000
Key Contact: Michael Stern
David Sprague

Functions: Most
Industries: Most
Professional Affiliations: IACPR, AMA, IMCO
Description: Committed to superior results
with personal service

The Stevenson Group/SES
836 Farmington Ave., Ste. 223
West Hartford, Connecticut 06119
Salary Minimum: $70,000
Key Contact: James R. Johnston
William A. Rutledge
Earl E. Eisenbach

Functions: Most
Industries: Most
Professional Affiliations: IACPR, AMA, ASPA,
  ASTD, HRPS
Description: Insurance/financial srvc/
  pharmaceutical/cosmetics/chemical/
  electronics/education/consumer products

Branches:
9744 Wilshire Blvd., Ste. 205
Beverly Hills, California 90212
Key Contact: Simon C. Baitler

910 Sylvan Ave.
Englewood Cliffs, New Jersey 07632
Key Contact: Stephen M. Steinman
E. Theodore Lewis
Donald Harshman

S. K. Stewart & Assoc.
The Executive Bldg., Box 40110
Cincinnati, Ohio 45240
Salary Minimum: $50,000
Key Contact: Stephen K. Stewart

Functions: Most + 01.0 04.0 05.0 06.0 09.0
Industries: Most + D.00 D.H0 H.00 I.14 I.18
Description: General search practice,
  confidential, high integrity

Stewart, Stein & Scott, Ltd.
1000 Shelard Pkwy., Ste. 215
Minneapolis, Minnesota 55426
Salary Minimum: $60,000
Key Contact: Terry W. Stein
Karen R. Scott
Jeffrey O. Stewart

Functions: Most
Industries: Most
Description: Consultants to management in
  executive recruitment & selection

Stewart/Laurence Assoc., Inc.
P.O. Box 1156, Atrium Executive Park
Englishtown, New Jersey 07726
Salary Minimum: $50,000
Key Contact: Shelley Klein
Mel Stewart
Martin Wolff

Functions: 01.0 01.1 05.2 09.2 09.4
Industries: D.14 D.24 D.H0 I.18 J.13
Description: Professional recruitment on
  national level for all areas of high
  technology

Affiliates/Other Offices:
Gerd Hassler GmbH, Augsburg

Stimmel Search Division
460 Main St., P.O. Box 2258
Acton, Massachusetts 01720-0258
Salary Minimum: $60,000
Key Contact: A. Craig Stimmel
Bob Hines
Carol F. Stimmel
Glenn Cooper
Carol Andersen

Functions: Most
Professional Affiliations: NAPA, NOMDA
Description: Search specialists to the office
  products, computer, office supplies,
  furniture industries

International Branches:
Hanover, Hong Kong, London, Tokyo

Stone, Murphy & Olson

5500 Wayzata Blvd., Ste. 1020
The Colonnade
Minneapolis, Minnesota 55416
Salary Minimum: $50,000
Key Contact: Toni M. Barnum
Gary J. Murphy

Functions: Most + 02.0 05.0 06.0 08.0 10.0
Industries: Most + D.00 D.H0 H.10 H.11
H.I0
Description: Professional retainer search firm
engaged in general practice

Stoneham Assoc.

372 Bay St., Ste. 1900
Toronto, Ontario M5H 2W9 Canada
Salary Minimum: $150,000
Key Contact: Herbert E. C. Stoneham
Gary C. Taylor
David S. M. Williams
Glenn Headrick

Functions: Most
Industries: Most
Professional Affiliations: IACPR
Description: Recruitment of positions of
primary concern to the CEO

Stonehill Management Consultants, Inc.

521 Fifth Ave., Ste. 1765
New York, New York 10175
Salary Minimum: $50,000
Key Contact: Dee Drost
Gary J. Stevens

Functions: 05.2 11.0
Industries: Most
Professional Affiliations: NABE, PF
Description: Specialists in planning: corporate,
strategic, economic, marketing and
financial planning

Strategic Alternatives

3210 Alpine Rd.
Menlo Park, California 94025
Salary Minimum: $65,000
Key Contact: Alexander A. Salottolo
Ira M. Marks

Functions: 01.0 02.0 04.0 05.0 09.0
Industries: D.24 D.H0 I.18 J.00
Description: Senior management positions in
high technology companies in all functions

Strategic Search Corp.

645 N. Michigan Ave.
Chicago, Illinois 60611
Salary Minimum: $50,000
Key Contact: Scott R. Sargis

Functions: 02.0 02.1 02.4 04.0 11.3
Industries: D.10 D.15 D.18 D.19 D.I0
Professional Affiliations: ACS, SPE, SPI
Description: Technical specialists in chemical,
biochemical & allied industries

Strategic Staffing Concepts, Inc.

P.O. Box 2922
Darien, Illinois 60559-2922
Salary Minimum: $60,000
Key Contact: James K. Halerz

Functions: Most + 01.0 02.0 08.0 09.0 11.1
Industries: Most
Description: Executive search performed by
former Big Six consulting director

W. R. Strathmann Assoc.

150 Fifth Ave.
New York, New York 10011
Salary Minimum: $90,000
Key Contact: Winfried R. Strathmann

Functions: Most + 01.0 01.1 01.2
Industries: Most + H.00 H.10 H.11 H.I0
H.R0
Description: Firm specializes in recruiting for
the international business community in
the US

Straube Assoc., Inc.

Three Lakeside Circle
Andover, Massachusetts 01810
Salary Minimum: $60,000
Key Contact: Stan Straube
Kathy Kelley
Bill Marlow

Functions: Most
Industries: Most
Professional Affiliations: IACPR
Description: Generalists, servicing all
industries, client concentration in
Northeast

Stricker & Zagor

717 Fifth Ave.
New York, New York 10022
Salary Minimum: $90,000
Key Contact: Anne F. Keating
Richard J. Newman
Sidney G. Stricker, Jr.
Howard S. Zagor
Fred Schulte

Functions: Most + 01.0 02.0 05.0 06.0 08.0
Industries: Most + D.00 G.00 H.00 I.00 J.00
Description: Senior level executive search &
management consulting across wide
industry spectrum

Stuart, Wood Inc.

188 Broadway, P.O. Box 8675
Woodcliff Lake, New Jersey 07675
Salary Minimum: $75,000
Key Contact: Wallace Schneider

Functions: Most
Industries: Most
Professional Affiliations: IACPR
Description: Generalist competent in most
industries & all corporate disciplines

Studwell Assoc.

1327 Butterfield Rd., Ste. 606
Downers Grove, Illinois 60515-1005
Salary Minimum: $50,000
Key Contact: Jon L. Baker

Functions: Most + 01.0 02.0 04.0 05.0 09.0
Industries: Most + B.0W D.15 D.19 D.23
D.D0
Professional Affiliations: ACS, IEEE, NSPE,
NWWA, SAE, SPE, TAPPI, WPCFA
Description: Key management positions in all
functional areas, domestic & international

Branches:
P.O. Box 579
Apple Valley, California 92307
Key Contact: Barbara Bowen

P.O. Box 595
Professional Bldg.
Stevensville, Maryland 21666
Key Contact: John Huskin

P.O. Box 760
Hanover, Pennsylvania 17331-0760
Key Contact: John Huskin

Affiliates/Other Offices:
QVS Int'l., Atlanta

Joe Sullivan & Assoc., Inc.

44210 County Rd. 48
P.O. Box 612
Southold, New York 11971
Salary Minimum: $70,000
Key Contact: Joseph J. Sullivan, Jr.

Functions: Most
Industries: J.12
Professional Affiliations: IRTS
Description: Executive search & recruitment in
radio, television & cable television

Sullivan & Co.

20 Exchange Pl. 50th Floor
New York, New York 10005-3202
Salary Minimum: $100,000
Key Contact: Brian M. Sullivan
Brendan G. Burnett
Jory J. Marino

Functions: Most + 01.4 01.5 09.3 09.4 11.1
Industries: Most + H.10 H.11 H.I0 I.17
Description: Capital markets, investment
management, technology, legal, finance &
marketing search

Sullivan-Murphy Assoc.

6 Landmark Sq., Ste. 406
Stamford, Connecticut 06901
Salary Minimum: $80,000
Key Contact: R. Blair Murphy

Functions: Most + 01.0 01.1 01.2 01.3 05.0
Industries: Most
Description: Senior level executive & board of
director search consultant services

Branches:
5215 N. Ironwood Rd.
Milwaukee, Wisconsin 53217
Key Contact: Robert C. Sullivan

Sweeney Harbert & Mummert, Inc.
777 S. Harbour Island Blvd., Ste. 130
Tampa, Florida 33602
Salary Minimum: $75,000
Key Contact: Dennis D. Mummert
James W. Sweeney
David O. Harbert

Functions: Most
Industries: Most
Description: Specialists in senior-level
   executive search

Synergistics Assoc. Ltd.
320 N. Michigan Ave., Ste. 1803
Chicago, Illinois 60601
Salary Minimum: $70,000
Key Contact: Alvin J. Borenstine

Functions: 01.4 09.0 09.3 09.4 11.1
Industries: Most
Professional Affiliations: SIM
Description: Data processing executives &
   consultants, particularly CIO's, MIS
   directors

TASA, Inc.
750 Lexington Ave., Ste. 1800
New York, New York 10022-1291
Salary Minimum: $100,000
Key Contact: Klaus Jacobs
John McLaughlin
R. Fred Rijke
Christine Houston

Functions: Most
Industries: Most
Professional Affiliations: AESC
Description: Consultants to management on
   executive search, worldwide

Branches:
430 Cowper St. Ste. 219
Palo Alto, California 94301
Key Contact: Herman DeKesel

240 N. Washington Blvd., Ste. 322
Sarasota, Florida 34237
Key Contact: Richard L. Fleming

1428 Franklin St.
P.O. Box 604
Columbus, Indiana 47202
Key Contact: James E. Lloyd
Robert L. Piers

9300 Shelbyville Rd., Ste 1010
Hurstbourne Pl.
Louisville, Kentucky 40222
Key Contact: Edward R. Swartz

International Branches:
Barcelona, Bogota, Brussels, Buenos Aires, Caracas, Frankfurt, Hong Kong, Johannesburg, London,
Madrid, Melbourne, Mexico City, Milan, Milano, Munich, Paris, Sao Paulo, Seoul, Singapore,
Stockholm, Sydney, Tokyo, Vienna, Zurich

TEMCO—The Executive Mgmt. Cons. Org.
P.O. Box 303
Oconomowoc, Wisconsin 53066-0303
Salary Minimum: $30,000
Key Contact: Thomas E. Masson

Functions: Most
Industries: Most
Professional Affiliations: ASPA, PIRA
Description: Human resource management
   consultants with broad range of services

Tama Lucas Ltd.
300 E. 42nd St.
New York, New York 10017
Salary Minimum: $75,000
Key Contact: Phyllis E. Tama
Ellen Lucas

Functions: Most
Industries: F.00 G.00
Description: Experience, quality & personal
   service are our commitment to each client
   & candidate

Tanton/Mitchell Group

710-1050 W. Pender St.
Vancouver, British Columbia V6E 3S7 Canada
Salary Minimum: $60,000
Key Contact: Kyle Mitchell
John Tanton

Networks:
Alliance Int'l.
Calgary, Montreal, Toronto

Functions: Most
Industries: Most
Description: Provides executive & management
search services in Western Canada

Tarnow Int'l.

150 Morris Ave.
Springfield, New Jersey 07081
Salary Minimum: $60,000
Key Contact: Emil Vogel
A. Marc Auster
Karen L. Gordon

Functions: Most + 01.0 02.0 04.0 08.0 09.0
Industries: Most
Professional Affiliations: IACPR
Description: Broad range of industries and
disciplines in corporate community
worldwide

Carl J. Taylor & Co.

2501 Oak Lawn, Ste. 305
Dallas, Texas 75219
Salary Minimum: $50,000
Key Contact: Carl J. Taylor

Functions: Most + 04.0 08.0 09.0 11.1
Industries: Most
Description: Generalized practice concentrating
in financial, MIS, legal & professional
services

Taylor Search Assoc., Inc.

5601 Sheridan Rd.
Chicago, Illinois 60660
Salary Minimum: $45,000
Key Contact: M. Kent Taylor

Functions: 01.0 02.0 04.0 05.0 11.3
Industries: D.24 D.25 D.E0
Professional Affiliations: AMA, AVS, IEEE,
ISA
Description: Will locate specialized technical/
managerial talent in emerging, advanced
technologies

Tech > Mark Group

32123 Lindero Canyon Rd.
The Landing, Ste. 201
Westlake Village, California 91361
Salary Minimum: $80,000
Key Contact: Harry M. Croner
Jerry E. Knotts
William G. Thomas
W. Arthur Fredericks

Branches:
41865 Boardwalk, Ste. 214
Palm Desert, California 92260

Functions: 01.0 02.0 05.0 09.0
Industries: C.00 D.H0 D.I0 I.10 I.14
Description: Specialists in food & technology
company search for management

Tesar-Reynes, Inc.

500 N. Michigan Ave., Ste. 1300
Chicago, Illinois 60611
Salary Minimum: $30,000
Key Contact: Tony Reynes
Bob Tesar

Functions: Most + 05.1 05.2 05.3 05.5 11.2
Industries: Most
Description: One of the largest specialists in
marketing & communications
management

Thalatta Corp.

P.O. Box 76643
Atlanta, Georgia 30358
Salary Minimum: $40,000
Key Contact: Wallace G. Webb

Functions: Most
Industries: H.00 H.10 H.11 H.12
Professional Affiliations: ASPA
Description: A firm with in-depth skills in
recruiting, candidate assessment &
placement negotiation

Theobald & Assoc.

1750 Montgomery St.
San Francisco, California 94111
Salary Minimum: $70,000
Key Contact: David B. Theobald
Helen O. Troy

Functions: Most + 01.0 02.0 05.0 06.0 08.0
Industries: Most + D.00 D.H0 D.I0 H.00 I.00
Professional Affiliations: CERA
Description: Assignments on hourly basis
produces highly professional search
services for senior executives

Thomas Mangum Co.

930 Colorado Blvd.
Los Angeles, California 90041
Salary Minimum: $65,000
Key Contact: William T. Mangum
Maria Mangum
Carolyn Carter

Functions: Most + 01.0 02.0 03.0 04.0 09.0
Industries: Most + B.00 B.0W D.00 D.E0
D.H0
Professional Affiliations: IACPR, AIAA, AOC,
APICS, ASPA, ASQC, CERA, EMA,
IEEE, SAE, SME
Description: Perform service in executive
search, professional staffing & related
manpower consulting

Branches:
2469 Cahuilla Hills Rd.
Palm Springs, California 92264

Thomas, Richardson, Runden & Co. Inc.

9525 Katy Freeway, Ste. 212
Houston, Texas 77024-1487
Salary Minimum: $40,000
Key Contact: W. H. Thomas, III

Functions: Most
Industries: Most
Description: We are a retained search firm in
business for over 14 years at the same
location

Thomas-Pond

520 Speedwell Ave., Ste. 100
The Dayton Bldg.
Morris Plains, New Jersey 07950
Salary Minimum: $40,000
Key Contact: Lorraine M. Thomas

Functions: 01.0 08.0 09.0 10.0 11.0
Industries: Most
Professional Affiliations: IACPR
Description: Contract retained executive search
& other human resources consulting
services

Branches:
1532 Dunwoody Village Pkwy.
Ste. 200
Atlanta, Georgia 30338
Key Contact: Luke Greene

Affiliates/Other Offices:
Joseph Crisanti, Inc., Holmdel

Thomure Medsearch, Inc.

55 West Port Plz., Ste. 700
St. Louis, Missouri 63146
Salary Minimum: $18,000
Key Contact: Joseph E. Thomure
Tim Donohue

Industries: I.14 I.15
Professional Affiliations: NAPC, NAPR
Description: Physician search and practice
management firm; OB-GYN Practice
Services—subsidiary

Thorne, Brieger Assoc., Inc.

11 E. 44th St.
New York, New York 10017
Salary Minimum: $75,000
Key Contact: Steven M. Brieger
Mike Jacobs

Functions: Most
Industries: Most
Description: Skilled recruiters bringing a
consultant's approach to solving
organizational problems

Tierney Assoc., Inc.

51 Downing St.
Wilkes-Barre, Pennsylvania 18702
Salary Minimum: $40,000
Key Contact: George F. Tierney
Andrew D. Check
Thomas McGeehan

Functions: Most + 01.0 02.0 05.0 08.0
Industries: D.00 D.22 D.24 D.25 D.H0
Description: Profit/loss & middle management
expertise in all functional disciplines

Branches:
1025 Bedford Hills Dr.
Earleysville, Virginia 22936
Key Contact: David L. Ambruster

Tirocchi, Wright, Inc.

3301 El Camino Real, Ste. 200
Atherton, California 94027
Salary Minimum: $80,000
Key Contact: Fred Tirocchi
Paula G. Wright

Functions: Most
Industries: D.00 D.E0 D.H0
Description: Executive search-primary focus in
high-tech: systems, electronics & aerospace

Branches:
1661 E. Camelback, Ste. 250B
Phoenix, Arizona 85016

Torretto & Assoc., Inc.

P.O. Box 265, 307 Bridgeway
Sausalito, California 94966
Salary Minimum: $80,000
Key Contact: Mary Stoch
Richard Torretto

Functions: Most + 01.0 02.0 05.0 06.0 08.0
Industries: Most + B.0W D.00 D.D0 D.E0
G.00
Professional Affiliations: CERA, PI
Description: Firm concentrates on upper
middle & senior level management
searches

Trac One

239 Route 22 East
Green Brook, New Jersey 08812
Salary Minimum: $50,000
Key Contact: Thomas C. Wood

Functions: Most + 01.4 09.0 09.3 09.4
Industries: Most + I.18
Professional Affiliations: IACPR, DPMA
Description: Executive search firm specializing
in MIS professionals exclusively

Travis & Co., Inc.

325 Boston Post Rd.
Sudbury, Massachusetts 01776
Salary Minimum: $75,000
Key Contact: John A. Travis
Kevin Frary
John A. Fusco
J. Scott Lord

Functions: Most
Industries: Most + D.10 D.15 D.17 D.18 D.I0
Description: Broadly based retainer firm
established in 1978

Gilles Tremblay & Assoc.

1350, rue Sherbrooke ouest
#1600
Montreal, Quebec H3G 1J1 Canada
Salary Minimum: $50,000
Key Contact: Gilles Tremblay
Gilles Shink
Gab. Caloca
Marc Levasseur

Functions: Most
Industries: Most
Description: We do exclusively executive
   search; we do not advertise

Trout & Assoc., Inc.

4016 Magna Carta Rd.
Calabasas, California 91302-5678
Salary Minimum: $45,000
Key Contact: Thomas L. Trout

Functions: Most + 02.0 05.0 06.0 08.0 09.0
Industries: Most + D.00 D.E0 D.H0 H.00 I.00
Description: Human resources consulting
   specializing in executive search &
   outplacement services

Trowbridge & Co., Inc.

110 Cedar St.
Wellesley Hills, Massachusetts 02181
Salary Minimum: $75,000
Key Contact: Robert L. Trowbridge

Functions: Most
Industries: Most
Description: Most industries (including non-
   profit) & most functions

Tucker Assoc.

1015 Mercer Rd.
Princeton, New Jersey 08540
Salary Minimum: $75,000
Key Contact: John J. Tucker
Merlene K. Tucker

Functions: Most
Industries: Most + D.00 H.00 H.I0 I.00 J.00
Description: Generalist firm serving client co's.
   in insurance, securities, banking & related
   financial services

Michael Tucker Assoc.

17304 Preston Rd., Ste. 800
Dallas, Texas 75252
Salary Minimum: $65,000
Key Contact: Michael Tucker
Jim Henry
Marsha Murphy

Functions: Most + 01.0 05.0 05.4
Industries: D.17 D.18 D.I0 I.14 I.16
Description: Retained healthcare firm

The Thomas Tucker Co.

100 Drakes Landing Rd., Ste. 300
Greenbrae, California 94904
Salary Minimum: $100,000
Key Contact: Thomas A. Tucker
Jennifer M. Sheehan

Functions: Most
Industries: Most + D.00 D.H0 J.00
Description: Engaged in management selection
   since 1969

Tully & Birch, Inc.

Pillow Hill Rd., Box 250
Spring Grove, Illinois 60081-0250
Salary Minimum: $80,000
Key Contact: James Tully
John Birch

Functions: Most + 01.0 05.0
Industries: Most
Description: We cover all functional areas &
   many industries

K. W. Tunnell Co., Inc.

900 E. 8th Ave., Ste. 106
King of Prussia, Pennsylvania 19406-1324
Salary Minimum: $40,000
Key Contact: Arthur E. Murphy

Functions: Most
Industries: D.00 D.D0 D.E0 D.H0 J.00
Professional Affiliations: ACME
Description: Recruiting division of consulting
   firm focused on manufacturing &
   distribution services/operations

Tuttle, Neidhart, Semyan, Inc.
12655 N. Central Expy., Ste. 500
Dallas, Texas 75243
Salary Minimum: $80,000
Key Contact: John K. Semyan
Craig C. Neidhart
Donald E. Tuttle

Functions: 01.0 02.0 05.0 06.0 09.0
Industries: D.10 D.E0 D.H0 H.10 I.18
Description: Generalist firm with an emphasis
on high technology

Tyler & Co.
9040 Roswell Rd., Ste. 550
Atlanta, Georgia 30350
Salary Minimum: $60,000
Key Contact: J. Larry Tyler
Robin Walker
Marth Hauser

Functions: 01.2 01.3 11.4
Industries: I.14 I.15
Professional Affiliations: AAHC
Description: National searches for healthcare
management & physicians

The Ultimate Source
2147 Avy
Menlo Park, California 94025
Salary Minimum: $65,000
Key Contact: Jean M. Martin

Functions: Most
Industries: D.24 D.25
Description: Specializing in high technology
industries & human resource consulting

P. T. Unger Assoc.
8605 Westwood Ctr. Dr., Ste. 501
Vienna, Virginia 22182
Salary Minimum: $75,000
Key Contact: Paul T. Unger

Functions: Most + 06.0 09.0 09.4 09.7
Industries: B.0W D.24 D.E0 D.H0 J.13
Professional Affiliations: IACPR, SSP
Description: Broad specialty:
telecommunications, information,
aerospace, defense electronics & emerging
tech

Universal Executive Search, Inc.
307 N. Michigan Ave., Ste. 305
Chicago, Illinois 60601
Salary Minimum: $50,000
Key Contact: Arlene M. Margolis

Functions: Most + 01.0 05.0 06.0 08.0
Industries: Most
Professional Affiliations: EMA
Description: Generalist practice emphasizing
excellence in service & results

Valletta Ritson & Co.
250 Mill St.
Rochester, New York 14614
Salary Minimum: $50,000
Key Contact: Steve Ritson

Functions: Most + 01.0 04.0 11.2
Industries: D.00
Description: Executive search focusing on
management & technology driven
professionals

Branches:
139 Grand Ave.
Johnson City, New York 13760
Key Contact: Frank L. Valletta

6115 Creekhaven
Cleveland, Ohio 44130

Peter Van Leer & Assoc.
1212 E. Wayzata Blvd.
Wayzata, Minnesota 55391
Salary Minimum: $50,000
Key Contact: Peter Van Leer

Functions: 10.0
Industries: H.I0
Description: Retainer search specialized in
insurance industry

VanMaldegiam Assoc., Inc.
555 Pierce Rd., Ste. 255
Itasca, Illinois 60143
Salary Minimum: $60,000
Key Contact: Norman E. VanMaldegiam

Functions: Most + 01.0 02.0 05.0 06.0 08.0
Industries: Most + D.00 D.H0 H.00 I.00
Professional Affiliations: IACPR, IMESC, NIIA
Description: Small, owner operated, MBA, 20
plus years retainer executive search
experience

VanReypen Enterprises, Ltd.
3100 Monroe Ave.
Rochester, New York 14618
Salary Minimum: $40,000
Key Contact: Robert D. VanReypen
Shirley VanReypen

Functions: Most
Industries: Most
Professional Affiliations: AMA, DSA
Description: International executive recruiters
with expertise recruiting middle/senior
management executives

John Velcamp & Assoc.
3333 Bowers Ave., Ste. 130
Santa Clara, California 95054
Salary Minimum: $90,000
Key Contact: John Velcamp
Bernie Ditter
Marcia Abrahamsen

Functions: Most + 01.0 02.0 04.0 05.0 06.0
Industries: D.24 D.25 D.26 D.H0 J.00
Professional Affiliations: ISA
Description: A service-oriented high technology
search firm for emerging companies

Venture Management
2995 Woodside Rd., Ste. 400-384
Woodside, California 94062
Salary Minimum: $120,000
Key Contact: Kathryn C. Gould

Functions: 01.2 02.0 04.0 05.0
Industries: D.H0 J.13
Description: Recruit CEO's/vice presidents for
venture capital funded technology
companies

Venture Resources, Inc.
999 Baker Way, Ste. 200
San Mateo, California 94404
Salary Minimum: $100,000
Key Contact: Jerome J. Brown
Kevin Pert
Cindy Lantis
Jessie Dennis

Functions: 04.0 05.0 08.2 09.0 11.0
Industries: D.24 H.12 I.14 I.16 J.00
Description: CEO, VP level placement, venture
based, high technology start-up companies

Verkamp-Joyce Assoc., Inc.
Westwood of Lisle
2443 Warrenville Rd., Ste. 600
Lisle, Illinois 60532
Salary Minimum: $80,000
Key Contact: Sheila M. Joyce
J. Frank Verkamp

Functions: Most + 02.0 03.0 04.0 06.0 11.2
Industries: Most + D.00 D.10 D.16 D.18 D.24
Professional Affiliations: IACPR, IMESC
Description: Upper/mid level searches for
every major industry throughout the U.S.-
specialty is manufacturing

VideoFields, Ltd.
21 Charles St., 203
Westport, Connecticut 06880
Salary Minimum: $35,000
Key Contact: Timothy J. Davis

Functions: Most + 05.7
Industries: I.11 J.10 J.12
Description: Providing seasoned professionals
to the highest end of television

Villareal & Assoc., Inc.
427 S. Boston, Ste. 215
Tulsa, Oklahoma 74103
Salary Minimum: $40,000
Key Contact: Morey Villareal

Functions: Most
Industries: Most
Description: HR consulting specializing in
compensation, organization analysis &
executive search

The Viscusi Group, Inc.
38 E. 29th St.
New York, New York 10016
Salary Minimum: $75,000
Key Contact: Stephen P. Viscusi

Branches:
84 Sherman St.
Brickyard Office Pk.
Cambridge, Massachusetts 02140

Vista Resource Group
620 Newport Center Dr.
Newport Beach, California 92660
Salary Minimum: $75,000
Key Contact: Joseph A. Sasenick
Barbara Barr

Vlcek & Co., Inc.
620 Newport Ctr. Dr.
Ste. 1100
Newport Beach, California 92660
Salary Minimum: $60,000
Key Contact: Thomas J. Vlcek
Suzanne Galante

Voigt Assoc.
601 Skokie Rd., Ste. 301
Northbrook, Illinois 60062
Salary Minimum: $50,000
Key Contact: Raymond R. Voigt

Von Storch Assoc.
60 Arch St.
Greenwich, Connecticut 06830
Salary Minimum: $100,000
Key Contact: Peter Von Storch

WDI, Int'l.
Seven Office Park Dr., Ste. 748
Hilton Head, South Carolina 29928
Salary Minimum: $80,000
Key Contact: Jack W. Cumming
G.E. Waters

WTW Assoc., Inc.
675 Third Ave., Ste. 2808
New York, New York 10017
Salary Minimum: $60,000
Key Contact: Warren T. Wasp, Jr.
Jacqueline Mercedes
Nancy Lombardi
David W. Morris

Functions: 01.0 05.0 05.4 11.2 11.6
Industries: D.11 F.00 G.00 I.12
Description: Interior/furnishings, architectural
products industry, design, interim, graphic
& industrial

759 South Shore Dr.
Holland, Michigan 49423

Functions: 01.0 01.1 04.0 05.0 11.1
Industries: A.00 D.00 D.D0 D.I0 F.00
Professional Affiliations: CERA
Description: People & international/new
product strategies adding incremental
profit

Functions: Most
Industries: Most + D.00 D.10 H.00 I.00
Professional Affiliations: IACPR, CERA
Description: Specializing in mid to senior
management searches for consumer
related companies

Functions: Most
Industries: D.17 D.18 D.I0
Description: Search consultant since 1978;
serves biotechnology & pharmaceutical
industries exclusively

Functions: Most + 01.1 01.2 01.4
Industries: D.H0
Description: Retainer firm accepting general
management assignments for high
technology clients

Functions: 05.2
Industries: D.18 D.I0 I.16
Description: International consultancy
specializing in search, strategic planning &
investment banking

Functions: 01.0 05.0 06.0 08.0 09.0
Industries: D.00 D.H0 H.10 I.11 J.12
Professional Affiliations: IACPR
Description: Small generalist executive search
firm dedicated to providing quality service

The WalCar Partnership
Box 11160
Pittsburgh, Pennsylvania 15237
Salary Minimum: $45,000
Key Contact: Carl Takacs

Functions: 01.1 01.2 11.6
Industries: H.R0
Description: Real estate: construction, development, financial, acquisition/ syndication, commercial, residential

Walker Group, Inc.
5009 Excelsior Blvd., Ste. 100
Minneapolis, Minnesota 55416
Salary Minimum: $50,000
Key Contact: Walter G. Walker

Functions: Most
Industries: G.00 H.I0 J.10
Description: Specialize in retailing & insurance industry searches on a national basis

Albert J. Walsh & Assoc.
Continental Corp. Ctr.
P.O. Box 301
Newtown, Pennsylvania 18940
Salary Minimum: $60,000
Key Contact: Albert J. Walsh

Functions: Most + 01.0 04.0 05.2 05.4 09.0
Industries: Most + D.00 D.24 D.H0 I.14 I.18
Description: Generalist search plus recruiting for hard to find individual contributors

James L. Walsh & Assoc., Inc.
13629 Esworthy Rd., Ste. 201
Germantown, Maryland 20874
Salary Minimum: $60,000
Key Contact: James L. Walsh

Functions: 01.2 01.3 09.4 09.7 11.3
Industries: D.24 D.H0 J.00 J.12 J.13
Description: Executive searches in telecommunications, high technology electronics and other fields

J.D. Walsh & Co.
456 Lost District Dr.
New Canaan, Connecticut 06840
Salary Minimum: $50,000

Functions: Most + 01.0 05.0 07.0 09.7 11.1
Industries: Most
Description: Specialization within financial and information services industries

Ward Howell Int'l. Inc.
99 Park Ave., Ste. 2000
New York, New York 10016-1699
Salary Minimum: $75,000
Key Contact: Max M. Ulrich
Key Contact: Marcia P. Pryde
John H. Callen, Jr.
Stephen M. McPherson
G. Leslie Fabian
A. Donald Ikle
Robert W. Ankerson
Eleanor H. Raynolds
Vance A. Howe
Michael A. Tappan
George H. Haley
James K. Makrianes, Jr.
Robert E. Nahas

Functions: Most + 01.0 02.0 08.0 10.0 11.2
Industries: Most + B.0W D.00 H.00 H.I0 I.00
Professional Affiliations: AESC, IACPR
Description: Executive search firm concentrating on senior level search

Branches:
16255 Ventura Blvd., Ste 400
Encino, California 91436-2394
Key Contact: Neal L. Maslan
Dr. Martin B. Ross
Marilyn M. Terry

800 W. 6th St., Ste. 400
Pacific Financial Ctr.
Los Angeles, California 90017-2707
Key Contact: Paul J. Papanek
Fred J. Clayton
Francis J. Madden

One Landmark Sq., Ste. 1810
Stamford, Connecticut 06901
Key Contact: Linford E. Stiles
George G. Atkeson
K. Michael Blount
E. Kennedy Langstaff
Peter J.M. de Vries

3390 Peachtree Rd., N.E.
Atlanta, Georgia 30326
Key Contact: Ernest A. Taylor
J. David Morgan
William R. Robertson
Paul Light

1250 Grove Ave., Ste. 201
Barrington, Illinois 60010
Key Contact: Laurence R. Masse
Douglas M. Smith

20 N. Wacker Dr., Ste 2920
Chicago, Illinois 60606
Key Contact: Larry Poore
John T. Thomas
Laura P. Phelps

1601 Elm St., Thanksgiving Twr., Ste 900
Dallas, Texas 75201
Key Contact: David M. Westberry

1000 Louisiana St., Ste. 5570
First Interstate Bank Plz.
Houston, Texas 77002
Key Contact: David L. Witte

141 Adelaide St. W., Ste. 1800
Toronto, Ontario M5H 3L5 Canada
Key Contact: Hugh G. Illsley

Homero No 1933-11 Piso Polanco
Mexico City, Mexico DF 11560 Mexico
Key Contact: Marco Antonio Ibarra

International Branches:
Amsterdam, Auckland, Barcelona, Brussels, Budapest, Chacao, Copenhagen, Dusseldorf, Helsinki, Hong Kong, Jakarta, Lisbon, London, Madrid, Melbourne, Milan, Munich, Oslo, Paris, Prague, Salzburg, Sao Paulo, Singapore, Stockholm, Sydney, Tokyo, Vienna, Zurich

Ward Liebelt Assoc. Inc.
50 Riverside Ave.
Westport, Connecticut 06880
Salary Minimum: $70,000
Key Contact: Anthony C. Ward
Albert J. Liebelt

Functions: 01.0 02.0 05.0 05.4 09.0
Industries: D.10 D.16 D.19 D.24 H.00
Professional Affiliations: IACPR, DPMA, SME
Description: Consumer packaged goods, general management, marketing/sales management, MIS & manufacturing

Wargo & Co., Inc.
250 Regency Court
Waukesha, Wisconsin 53186
Salary Minimum: $50,000
Key Contact: James W. Peters

Functions: Most + 02.0 04.0 06.0 11.2 11.3
Industries: D.00 D.E0 D.H0 D.I0 J.00
Professional Affiliations: IACPR, HRPS
Description: Specialize in strategic staffing engagements for organizations in high growth

Warring & Assoc.
5673 Stetson Ct.
Anaheim Hills, California 92807
Salary Minimum: $150,000
Key Contact: J. T. Warring

Functions: 01.0 05.0 08.2 10.0 11.2
Industries: H.00 H.10 H.I0 I.14 I.15
Description: Senior officer/director search in insurance and diversified financial organizations

Branches:
85 Livingston Avenue, Third Floor
Roseland, New Jersey 07068
Key Contact: Leland T. Waggoner

2727 Allen Pkwy.
Houston, Texas 77019
Key Contact: Benjamin N. Woodson

Hilton N. Wasserman & Assoc. Inc.

98 Cuttermill Rd.
Great Neck, New York 11021
Salary Minimum: $40,000
Key Contact: Hilton N. Wasserman

Functions: Most + 01.0 02.0 05.0 08.0 09.0
Industries: Most
Description: Full range search activities-all
industries-all executive/administrative
functions

Harold Webb Assoc., Ltd.

545 Lincoln Ave., Ste. 6
Winnetka, Illinois 60093
Salary Minimum: $50,000
Key Contact: M. Donald Thomas
Kenneth Underwood

Industries: I.13 K.00
Description: Counsel to school boards for top
echelon positions in school district
administration

Branches:
860 18th Ave.
Salt Lake City, Utah 84103

Webb, Johnson & Klemmer, Inc.

280 Park Ave.
New York, New York 10017
Salary Minimum: $100,000
Key Contact: George H. Webb, Jr.
Robert J. M. Farrington, Jr.
John W. Johnson, Jr.
Raymond J. Klemmer
Russell Marks, Jr.

Functions: Most
Industries: Most

Weber Executive Search

205 E. Main St., Ste. 2-3A
Huntington, New York 11743
Salary Minimum: $60,000
Key Contact: Ronald R. Weber
Ronald W. Shepherd

Functions: Most
Industries: D.00 D.D0 F.00 G.00 I.10
Description: Search firm specializing in food &
beverage industry

Weir Executive Search Assoc., Inc.

2323 Yonge St., Ste. 706
Toronto, Ontario M4P 2C9 Canada
Salary Minimum: $60,000
Key Contact: Douglas S. Weir
Michael J. Marmur

Functions: 01.4 09.0 09.1 09.2 09.3
Industries: Most + D.H0 H.00 I.14 I.18 J.13
Description: Specialists in recruitment of
information systems & high technology
professionals

C. Weiss Assoc., Inc.

60 W. 57th St.
New York, New York 10019
Salary Minimum: $40,000
Key Contact: Cathy Weiss

Functions: 05.0 05.1 05.2 05.3 05.5
Industries: H.00 H.10 H.R0 J.10
Description: Specialty in domestic &
international recruiting for consumer
financial services

D. L. Weiss & Assoc.

18500 Von Karman Ave., Ste. 715
Irvine, California 92715
Salary Minimum: $100,000
Key Contact: David L. Weiss

Functions: Most + 01.0 02.0 05.0 08.0
Industries: Most + D.14 D.23 D.E0 D.H0
Professional Affiliations: IACPR
Description: Retained firm dealing mostly in
the automotive & manufacturing
industries

Wellington Management Group

117 S. 17th St., Ste. 1625
Philadelphia, Pennsylvania 19103
Salary Minimum: $60,000
Key Contact: Walter R. Romanchek
Robert Scott Campbell

Functions: Most + 01.0 04.0 05.0 09.7 11.3
Industries: D.15 D.17 D.18 D.I0 J.13
Professional Affiliations: IACPR
Description: Generalist firm; expertise in
telecommunications, chemical,
pharmaceutical & biotechnology indus.

The Wentworth Co., Inc.

479 W. 6th St., Ste. 211
The Arcade Bldg.
San Pedro, California 90731
Key Contact: John Wentworth

Functions: Most
Industries: Most
Professional Affiliations: IACPR, EMA
Description: On-site contract recruiting,
recruiting management & mid-range single
position searches

Werner Int'l., Inc.

111 W. 40th St.
New York, New York 10018
Salary Minimum: $75,000
Key Contact: Martin H. Rubenstein
Walter A. Croen
David Kanal

Functions: Most + 01.0 02.0 05.0 08.0
Industries: D.00 D.11 D.21 F.00 G.00
Professional Affiliations: AAMA, AATT,
ACME, ATMA, ATMI, KTA
Description: Extraordinarily skilled in
determination, recruitment, selection &
engagement of key execs

International Branches:
Brussels

Jude M. Werra & Assoc.

205 Bishop's Way, Ste. 226
Brookfield, Wisconsin 53005
Salary Minimum: $50,000
Key Contact: Jude M. Werra
Alan G. Wallskog

Functions: Most + 01.0 02.0 03.0 05.0 06.0
Industries: Most + D.10 D.22 D.23 D.D0 I.00
Professional Affiliations: AMA, AMC, ASTD,
IMC, MHRPG, SHRM, SME
Description: HR consultants-executive
transition counseling, succession planning
& performance management

Wesley Brown & Bartle Co., Inc.

152 Madison Ave.
New York, New York 10016
Salary Minimum: $50,000
Key Contact: Wesley Poriotis
Barbara Tucker
Tom Bartle
Sherry Dworsky

Functions: 05.0 05.7 06.1 09.0 11.2
Industries: Most
Professional Affiliations: AAA, APC, IABC,
NIRI, PRSA, SMPS
Description: Nat'l. mgmt. consulting firm
providing specialized executive search &
organizational consulting svcs.

Westcott Associates, Inc.

1000 N. Lake Shore Plz.
Chicago, Illinois 60611-1335
Key Contact: Robert F. Westcott

Functions: Most
Industries: Most
Description: Establish specific needs of client
organization, emphasize recruiting non job
seekers

Western Reserve Search Assoc.

843 Ghent Sq., Box 2510
Bath, Ohio 44210
Salary Minimum: $75,000
Key Contact: Darrell G. Robertson
Lee G. Trautvetter

Functions: Most
Industries: B.0W C.00 D.E0 H.10 I.20
Professional Affiliations: ACS, ASPA, IEEE,
SME, SPE, TAPPI
Description: Professional handling of difficult
searches in all disciplines & industries

Weston Consultants, Inc.
P.O. Box 216
Weston, Massachusetts 02193
Salary Minimum: $60,000
Key Contact: Edmund J. Walsh

Functions: Most
Industries: Most
Professional Affiliations: IEEE, IMC, SBANE
Description: Executive search & human
    resources management consulting services

Wheeler, Moore & Elam Co.
14800 Quorum Dr., Ste. 200
Dallas, Texas 75240
Salary Minimum: $50,000
Key Contact: Mark H. Moore, Ph.D.
William A. Wheeler
Robert W. Elam

Functions: Most
Industries: Most
Description: Comprehensive retained national
    search firm with in-depth research
    capabilities

K. L. Whitney & Co., Inc.
6 Aspen Dr.
North Caldwell, New Jersey 07006
Salary Minimum: $75,000
Key Contact: Kenneth L. Whitney, Jr.

Functions: 01.0 01.1 05.0 08.0 08.2
Industries: H.00 H.10
Professional Affiliations: IACPR
Description: Retainer search exclusively within
    the investment counseling community

Branches:
7 East 35th St.
New York, New York 10016
Key Contact: Kenneth Michaels
Jeri Cohen

The Whitney Group
12 E. 49th St., Tower 49
New York, New York 10017
Salary Minimum: $75,000
Key Contact: Gary S. Goldstein
Alicia C. Lazaro
Eugene Y. Shen
Joseph H. McCann, III
Russ D. Gerson
John W. Townsend
Kunihiko Watanabe

Functions: 08.2
Industries: H.00 H.10 H.11 H.I0 H.R0
Description: Specialist firm focused in financial
    services, investment banking, real estate &
    capital markets

International Branches:
London, Minato-Ku, Tokyo

Wilkins & Co.
1300 Grove Ave., Ste. 201
Barrington, Illinois 60010
Salary Minimum: $100,000
Key Contact: Edwin N. Wilkins

Functions: Most + 01.0 02.0 08.0 11.5
Industries: B.0W D.10 D.15 D.18
Professional Affiliations: AESC, IACPR
Description: Nationwide senior level practice,
    some emphasis in consumer goods,
    chemicals & environmental

Wilkinson & Ives
601 California St., Ste. 502
San Francisco, California 94108
Salary Minimum: $120,000
Key Contact: Suzanne Snyder

Functions: Most + 01.0 04.0 05.0 09.0
Industries: Most + A.00 D.10 D.24
Professional Affiliations: CERA
Description: Senior firm specializing in
    engagements at Board, CEO & first line of
    management levels

Donald Williams Assoc., Inc.

303 W. Madison
Chicago, Illinois 60606
Salary Minimum: $250,000
Key Contact: Donald C. Williams

Functions: 01.0 01.1 01.2 05.0 08.0
Industries: Most
Description: Specialize in critical director/
officer level assignments-broadly based
geographically

Branches:
4350 E. Camelback Rd.
Ste. 140E
Phoenix, Arizona 85018

Williams, Roth & Krueger, Inc.

20 N. Wacker Dr., Ste. 3450
Chicago, Illinois 60606
Salary Minimum: $75,000
Key Contact: Clarence F. Krueger
Robert J. Roth
Roger K. Williams
Andrew R. Zaleta

Functions: Most
Industries: Most
Description: Specialize in upper-middle &
senior level searches-all industries &
functions

Craig Williamson, Inc.

6701 Rockledge Dr., Ste. 250
Bethesda, Maryland 20817
Salary Minimum: $100,000
Key Contact: Craig Williamson

Functions: Most + 01.0 02.1 09.2 09.3 09.7
Industries: D.24 D.H0 J.00 J.13
Description: National searches for technology
related businesses seeking vp/director level
executives

William Willis Worldwide, Inc.

164 Mason St.
Greenwich, Connecticut 06830-6611
Salary Minimum: $85,000
Key Contact: William H. Willis, Jr.
Robert P. Mulligan

Functions: Most + 01.0 04.0 05.0 06.0 08.0
Industries: Most + D.10 D.16 D.18 D.I0 H.00
Professional Affiliations: AESC, IACPR
Description: International practice, hands-on,
personalized consultants to management
on executive selection

Networks:
World Search Group
Copenhagen, Corseaux/Vevey, Hong Kong, London, Melbourne, Milan, Oslo, Paris, Roma,
Stockholm

Duane I. Wilson Assoc., Inc.

954 N. Hunter Blvd.
Birmingham, Michigan 48009
Salary Minimum: $30,000
Key Contact: Duane I. Wilson

Functions: 01.0 02.0 05.0 08.0 11.0
Industries: D.00 D.19 D.22 D.23 D.26
Description: Executive search for small to
medium size companies

The Winchester Group

901 Mariners Island Blvd.
Ste. 405
San Mateo, California 94404
Salary Minimum: $60,000
Key Contact: J. Barry Ryan
Bart L. Main

Functions: Most
Industries: Most
Professional Affiliations: NCHRC
Description: Recruiting for all functions in all
industries since 1979

Winguth & Company

2180 Sand Hill Rd., Ste. 170
Menlo Park, California 94025
Salary Minimum: $60,000
Key Contact: Ed W. Winguth
Patrick D. Donahue

Functions: Most
Industries: Most
Professional Affiliations: IACPR, CERA, ISA
Description: Generalist practice; emerging
company specialists

Networks:
International Search Associates (ISA)
Toronto, Amsterdam, Athens, Atlanta, Bellevue, Boston, Brussels, Capetown, Chicago, Dallas,
Hong Kong, Johannesburg, Leeds, London, Melbourne, Paris, Stockholm, Tokyo

Richard Winn & Co.

Box 4714
Salem, Oregon 97302
Salary Minimum: $25,000
Key Contact: Richard Winn

Functions: Most
Industries: D.18 D.24 D.H0 I.18
Description: HR mgmt. consulting & search in
commercial electronics, computer &
semiconductor related industries

Witt Assoc. Inc.

1211 W. 22nd St., Ste. 512
Oak Brook, Illinois 60521
Salary Minimum: $50,000
Key Contact: John S. Lloyd
Mark M. Cox

Functions: 01.0
Industries: H.I0 I.14 I.15
Professional Affiliations: AESC
Description: Oldest & largest search firm
providing healthcare executives

Branches:
2030 Main St.
Irvine, California 92714
Key Contact: James W. Gauss

4800 Hampden Ln.
Bethesda, Maryland 20814
Key Contact: Kathleen Ballein

14755 Preston Rd.
Dallas, Texas 75240
Key Contact: Keith Southerland

Wojdula & Assoc.

700 Rayovac Dr., Ste. 204
Madison, Wisconsin 53711
Salary Minimum: $50,000
Key Contact: Andrew Wojdula
Donna M. Wojdula

Functions: Most + 11.2 11.4
Industries: Most
Professional Affiliations: IACPR
Description: Management consulting firm;
executive & management recruiting &
staffing services

S. R. Wolman Assoc., Inc.

133 E. 35th St.
New York, New York 10016
Salary Minimum: $50,000
Key Contact: Steve Wolman
Alan Bender
Nannette Willner

Functions: Most + 01.0 03.0 05.0 06.0 08.0
Industries: D.10 D.16 D.18 J.10 J.12
Description: Particular expertise in luxury
products, packaged goods, design &
international

Wood, Franchot Inc.

1550 Utica Ave., S., Ste. 425
Minneapolis, Minnesota 55416
Salary Minimum: $60,000
Key Contact: Michael D. Wood

Functions: Most
Industries: Most

Wood-Glavin, Inc.

8695 College Blvd., Ste. 260
Overland Park, Kansas 66210
Salary Minimum: $50,000
Key Contact: William M. Wood
James E. Glavin

Functions: Most
Industries: Most
Description: The principals personally handle
all assignments

Wood/Sprau/Tannura, Inc.
2 First National Plz., Ste. 400
20 S. Clark St.
Chicago, Illinois 60603
Salary Minimum: $70,000
Key Contact: Milton M. Wood
Roy A. Cowell
John W. Poracky
Paul W. Norman

Functions: Most + 08.0 09.0
Industries: Most
Description: Two retained search practices: (1)
senior executive generalist (2) information
technology

Dick Wray & Consultants
4962 El Camino Real #126
Los Altos, California 94022
Salary Minimum: $50,000
Key Contact: Dick Wray

Industries: G.00 H.R0 I.10 I.11
Description: Retained searches-for corporate
restaurant & retail business

Wytmar & Co., Inc.
400 E. Randolph Dr., Ste. 6B
Chicago, Illinois 60601
Salary Minimum: $60,000
Key Contact: R.J. Wytmar
Thomas H. Coulter

Functions: Most
Industries: Most
Professional Affiliations: APA, IMD
Description: Executive search for industry,
business, government & education

Affiliates/Other Offices:
A&C Analistas de Empresas & Consultores de Direction SA, Buenos Aires
AES Analyses Economiques et Sociales SA, Ecublens
Baumgartner & Partner GMBH, Stuttgart
Bohlin & Stromberg AB, Solna
Consultoria Gerencial Y Mercadotecnica, Caracas
Dapiran, Knight Australia Pty. ltd., Melbourne
Demanda, Sao Paulo
Groupe Bernard Julhiet, Levallois-Perret
IOR Consultores de Organizacion, SA, Barcelona
IRM Europe S.A.R.L, Paris
IRM Inc., Toyko
Lisberg Partnere A/S, Aaby hoj Aavhus
Lisberg Partnere A/S, Horsholm
Lisberg Partners A/S, Kolding
MLI Int'l. Consultants AS, Oslo
Markon Marketing Konsulenten BV, Utrecht
Mercurio Misura SRL, Milano
Veritas Consultants Inc., Toronto
Harold Whitehead & Partners Ltd., London
Whitehead Morris (Pty.) Ltd., Randburg
Wytmar & Co., Inc., Munchen
Wytmar & Co., Inc., Lisbon

Xagas & Assoc.
701 E. State St., Ste. 1
Geneva, Illinois 60134
Salary Minimum: $30,000
Key Contact: Steve Xagas

Functions: 01.2 02.3 02.5 02.6 11.2
Industries: D.18 D.19 D.22 D.23 D.24
Professional Affiliations: ASQC, IMESC, SME
Description: Vertical integration of select
industries with emphasis on recruitment
of QA/QC professionals

Yelverton & Co.
311 Miller Ave.
Mill Valley, California 94941
Salary Minimum: $75,000
Key Contact: Jack R. Yelverton

Functions: Most
Industries: Most

The Yorkshire Group, Ltd.
381 Elliot St.
Newton Upper Falls, Massachusetts 02164
Salary Minimum: $50,000
Key Contact: Michael P. Tornesello
David O. McGavern
Thomas Van Berkel

Functions: Most
Industries: H.00 H.I0 I.00 I.17
Professional Affiliations: SHRM
Description: Search services primarily to the
insurance industry.

Youngs & Co.
P.O. Box 515665
Dallas, Texas 75251-5665
Salary Minimum: $100,000
Key Contact: Donald L. Youngs
Judith A. Youngs

Functions: 01.0 08.0 09.0 11.1
Industries: B.00 D.00 D.H0 G.00 I.00
Professional Affiliations: AESC, IACPR
Description: Generalist firm with broad-based
international experience at senior levels

International Branches:
Amsterdam, Athens, Brussels, Buenos Aires, Capetown, Frankfurt, Guadalajara, Hong Kong,
Johannesburg, Leeds, London, Manchester, Melbourne, Mexico City, Milan, Paris, Santiago, Sao
Paulo, Stockholm, Toronto, Zurich

Steven Yungerberg Assoc., Inc.
1022 IDS Tower
Minneapolis, Minnesota 55402-2106
Salary Minimum: $50,000
Key Contact: Steven A. Yungerberg

Functions: Most
Industries: Most
Description: Management consulting firm
specializing in executive selection &
recruitment

Charles Zabriskie Assoc., Inc.
2366 Commonwealth Ave.
Newton, Massachusetts 02166
Salary Minimum: $50,000
Key Contact: Charles Zabriskie, Jr.

Functions: 05.0 06.0 08.0
Industries: B.00 D.00 D.E0 D.H0 H.00
Description: Successful recruiting of financial
executives-most aspects of commercial,
trust, retail & mortgage

The Zammataro Co.
P.O. Box 339
Hudson, Ohio 44236
Salary Minimum: $50,000
Key Contact: Frank A. Zammataro

Functions: Most + 01.0 02.0 05.0 08.0 11.6
Industries: Most + D.10 D.13 D.15 D.22
Description: A high quality generalist executive
search firm

Zay & Company
1360 Peachtree St., NE
2 Midtown Plz., Ste. 1740
Atlanta, Georgia 30309
Salary Minimum: $75,000
Key Contact: Thomas C. Zay
Thomas C. Zay, Jr.

Functions: 01.0 02.0 05.0 06.0 08.0
Industries: Most + A.00 C.00 D.00 I.00
Professional Affiliations: IACPR
Description: Non industry-specific retained
executive search services for corporate
clients

Affiliates/Other Offices:
Bragg & Co., Melbourne
Clive & Stokes Int'l., London
Dieckmann & Assoc., Ltd., Chicago
Executive Access Limited, Wanchai
Executive Resources, Ltd., Johannesburg
L.W. Foote Co., Washington
Hansar-Exsel Ltd., Athens
Hansar Int'l., S.A., Brussels
Hansar Int'l., Stockholm
Hommes & Enterprises, Paris
P.A.R. Assoc., Inc., Boston
Saley Partners Int'l., Toronto
Saley Partners Int'l., Toronto
Ten Bokkel Huinink b.v., Utrecht
Youngs & Co., Dallas
Winguth & Co., San Francisco

Egon Zehnder Int'l. Inc.

55 E. 59th St., 14th Flr.
New York, New York 10022
Salary Minimum: $80,000
Key Contact: A. Daniel Meiland
Fortunat F. Mueller-Maerki
Joel M. Kobleutz
Marc P. Schappell
T. Lee Pomeroy, II
Wendy W. Costikyan
Reynold H. Lewke
Peter K. Gonye

Functions: Most
Industries: Most
Description: Professional management
consulting in areas of search, mgmt.
appraisals, mergers/acquisitions

Branches:
300 S. Grand Ave., Ste. 2625
California Plz.
Los Angeles, California 90071
Key Contact: Stephen B. Ste. Marie
John P. Derning
John W. Chamberlain
George C. Fifield
S. Ross Brown

1201 W. Peachtree St., NE
3000 IBM Twr.
Atlanta, Georgia 30309
Key Contact: Richard C. Reagan
Samuel H. Pettway
Douglas W. Edwards
Joseph E. McCann, III

One First National Plz., Ste.3004
Chicago, Illinois 60603
Key Contact: Kai Lindholst
Gregory T. Carrott
Ronald O. Tracy
Kenneth W. Taylor
Patricia A. Prinz

Blvd. Manuel Avila Camacho 1
Desp. 406 Lomas de Chapultepec
Mexico City, Mexico DF 11000 Mexico

1 First Canadian Pl., Ste. 7070
Toronto, Ontario M5X 1C7 Canada
Key Contact: Tom Long
Jan J. Stewart

1 Place Ville-Marie, Ste. 3308
Montreal, Quebec H3B 3N2 Canada
Key Contact: Eric Boulvd
Johan Mady
Pierre Payette
Raymond Roy
J. Robert Swidler

International Branches:
Amsterdam, Barcelona, Berlin, Brussels, Buenos Aires, Copenhagen, Dusseldorf, Frankfurt,
Geneva, Hamburg, Helsinki, Hong Kong, Lisbon, London, Luxembourg, Lyon, Madrid,
Melbourne, Milan, Munich, Paris, Rome, Sao Paulo, Singapore, Sydney, Tokyo, Vienna, Zurich

Zingaro & Co.
4200 Green Cliffs Rd.
Austin, Texas 78746
Salary Minimum: $100,000
Key Contact: Ron Zingaro

Functions: 01.0 02.0 04.0 05.0 06.0
Industries: D.17 D.18 D.I0 I.14 I.16
Description: Search & selection of senior level
  management in healthcare

Michael D. Zinn & Assoc., Inc.
601 Ewing St., Ste. C-9
Princeton, New Jersey 08540
Salary Minimum: $75,000
Key Contact: Michael D. Zinn
Robert D. Hennessy

Functions: Most + 01.0 02.0 05.0 11.5
Industries: Most + B.0W D.00 D.H0 H.00
Description: Retainer firm distinguished by its
  strong commitment to client service

The Zivic Group, Inc.
611 Washington St., Ste. 2505
San Francisco, California 94111
Salary Minimum: $60,000
Key Contact: Janis M. Zivic
John G. Faubion

Functions: Most + 01.0 06.0 08.0 11.2 11.3
Industries: Most + D.I0 I.12 I.14
Professional Affiliations: IACPR, CERA
Description: Established generalist firm: health
  care, finance, non-profit; all functions

Branches:
550 N. Brand Blvd., Ste. 700
Glendale, California 91203

Zurick, Davis & Co.
10 State St.
Woburn, Massachusetts 01801
Salary Minimum: $60,000
Key Contact: Peter E. Davis
Jeffrey M. Zegas

Functions: Most
Industries: Most + D.00 H.00 I.00 I.14 I.15
Description: Nationwide practice serving
  healthcare, financial services,
  manufacturing & service clients

Retainer Firm Indexes

Contingency Indexes begin after the Contingency Section, page 605.

Basis of "Functions" Classification

The kernel of this coding system was developed by several parties including Jerome H. Fuchs, Glenn Van Doren and Kennedy Publications.

00.0 MOST

01.0 GENERAL MANAGEMENT
01.1 Directors
01.2 Senior management
01.3 Middle management
01.4 MIS-Management information systems
01.5 Legal

02.0 MANUFACTURING
02.1 Product development
02.2 Production engineering, planning, scheduling & control
02.3 Automation, robotics
02.4 Plant management
02.5 Quality
02.6 Productivity

03.0 MATERIALS MANAGEMENT
03.1 Purchasing, inventory management
03.2 Materials & requirement planning
03.3 Physical distribution, traffic & transportation, logistics
03.4 Packaging

04.0 RESEARCH & DEVELOPMENT

05.0 MARKETING
05.1 Advertising, sales promotion
05.2 Marketing strategy & organization
05.3 Marketing & product research, consumer marketing
05.4 Sales, sales management, sales training
05.5 Direct mail, marketing, telemarketing
05.6 Customer service
05.7 Public relations

06.0 HUMAN RESOURCE MANAGEMENT
06.1 Benefits, compensation planning
06.2 Personnel selection, placement & records

07.0 ADMINISTRATIVE SERVICES
07.1 Clerical work measurement, records retention & management
07.2 Forms design, order processing & fulfillment, systems & procedures
07.3 Office layout, space planning
07.4 Office management

08.0 FINANCE & ACCOUNTING
08.1 Budgeting, cost controls
08.2 Cash management, financing & management of funds, portfolios
08.3 Credit & collection
08.4 Taxes

09.0 INFORMATION TECHNOLOGY
09.1 Computer security, disaster recovery, EDP audit
09.2 Specific technologies, e.g. AI, image, fiber-optics
09.3 Systems analysis & design, development, implementation, training & support
09.4 Systems integration, including hardware/software services, evaluation & selection
09.5 Expert systems
09.6 Decision support
09.7 Telecommunications

10.0 INSURANCE/RISK MANAGEMENT

11.0 SPECIALIZED SERVICES
11.1 Management consultants
11.2 Minorities
11.3 Scientific/technical
11.4 Fund-raisers & other non-profit services
11.5 Environmental
11.6 Architectural/engineering

Retainer Cross-Index by Functions

00.0 MOST

Adams & Assoc. Int'l
Advanced Executive Resources
The Advisory Group, Inc.
Aim Executive Consulting Services
Allerton Heneghan & O'Neill
Alwyn Assoc., Inc.
Peter W. Ambler Co.
American Executive Search Services, Inc.
Ames & Ames
Andcor Human Resources
Anderson Bradshaw Assoc., Inc.
Anthony Executive Search
Armitage Assoc.
William B. Arnold Assoc., Inc.
Artgo, Inc.
Ashworth Consultants, Inc.
Atlantic Search
Aubin Int'l. Inc.
BDO Seidman
Babson, Moore & Wilcox
The Badger Group
Baldwin Associates, Inc.
Ballos & Co., Inc.
James Bangert & Assoc., Inc.
Barger & Sargeant, Inc.
J.W. Barleycorn & Assoc.
Barnes, Walters & Assoc., Inc.
Barton Raben, Inc.
Bason Assoc., Inc.
Battalia Winston Int'l., Inc.
Martin H. Bauman Assoc., Inc.
Beall & Co., Inc.
The Beam Group
Becker, Norton & Co.
Beech Preger & Partners, Ltd.
Richard Beers & Assoc., Ltd.
Joy Reed Belt & Assoc., Inc.
Benton Schneider & Assoc.
The Berman Consulting Group
Bertrand, Ross & Assoc., Inc.
Paul J. Biestek Assoc., Inc.
Billington & Assoc., Inc.
Billington, Fox & Ellis, Inc.
Bishop Assoc.
The Blackman Kallick Search Division
Blackshaw, Olmstead & Atwood
Blake, Hansen & Nye, Ltd.
Blanchard, Zufall & Assoc.
Blaney Executive Search

Blau Kaptain Schroeder
Blendow & Johnson Inc.
Blendow, Crowley & Oliver, Inc.
Block & Assoc.
Blum & Co.
The Blunt Co., Inc.
Boettcher Assoc.
John C. Boone & Co.
Botrie Assoc.
Bowden & Co., Inc.
Boyden Latin America S.A. de C.V.
Boyden World Corp.
Brady Assoc. Int'l., Inc.
The Brand Co., Inc.
Brandywine Consulting Group
Brault & Assoc., Ltd.
Brentwood Int'l.
Bricker & Assoc., Inc.
Brissenden, McFarland, Wagoner & Fuccella, Inc.
F.J. Bruckner & Co.
Bryce, Haultain & Assoc.
Bullis & Co., Inc.
Burke, O'Brien & Bishop Assoc., Inc.
Thomas Burnham Co.
Joseph R. Burns & Assoc., Inc.
Busch Int'l.
CSI Inc.
Robert Caldwell & Assoc.
The Caldwell Partners Int'l.
Callan Assoc., Ltd.
Cambridge Management Planning
CanMed Consultants Inc.
Canny, Bowen Inc.
L.L. Carey & Assoc., Inc.
Carpenter, Shackleton & Co.
Carris, Jackowitz Assoc.
M.L. Carter & Assoc., Inc.
Catalyx Group, Inc.
David Chambers & Assoc., Inc.
Joseph Chandler & Assoc., Inc.
Chandler & Rozner Assoc.
Chase Partners
Chase-Owens Assoc., Inc.
Chestnut Hill Partners, Inc.
Chicago Research Group, Inc.
China Human Resources Group
Chrisman & Co., Inc.
Christenson & Hutchison

00.0 MOST (Cont'd)

Christian & Timbers, Inc.
Jack Clarey Assoc., Inc.
Claveloux, McCaffrey, McInerney, Inc.
Clemo, Evans & Co., Inc.
Coelyn Miller Phillip & Assoc.
Cole Human Resource Services
Cole, Warren & Long, Inc.
Coleman Lew & Assoc., Inc.
W. Hoyt Colton Assoc., Inc.
Colton Bernard Inc.
Comann Assoc., Inc.
Compass Group Ltd.
Computer Professionals
Conard Assoc., Inc.
Conex Inc.
Joseph Conley & Assoc., Inc.
Conley Assoc., Inc.
Walter V. Connor Int'l., Inc.
Conrey Interamericana
Philip Conway Management
Grant Cooper & Assoc., Inc.
The Cooper Executive Search Group, Inc.
Coopers & Lybrand Consulting Group
Coopers & Lybrand, Management Consulting
  Services
Corporate Environment Ltd.
The Corporate Staff
The Corrigan Group
Edmond J. Corry & Co., Inc.
The Crosby Group, Inc.
Crowder & Company
Curran Partners
Curry, Telleri Group, Inc.
The Curtiss Group, Inc.
Peter Cusack & Partners, Inc.
D E G Co., Inc.
DHR Int'l., Inc.
The DLR Group, Inc.
Dahl-Morrow Int'l.
Marge Dana Assoc.
Danforth Group
William N. Davis & Assoc., Inc.
Davis & Company
Charles E. Day & Assoc., Inc.
DeHayes Consulting Group
Deane, Howard & Simon, Inc.
Thorndike Deland Assoc.
Denney & Co., Inc.
Deven Assoc., Int'l., Inc.
DiMarchi Partners
Dieckmann & Assoc., Ltd.
R. J. Dishaw & Assoc.
Diversified Health Search
Diversified Search, Inc.
Donahue/Bales Assoc.
Dougan-McKinley-Strain
Duggan & Company
The Duncan Group Inc.
S.R. Dunlap & Assoc., Inc.
C. A. Durakis Assoc., Inc.
Dwyer Consulting Group, Inc.

EFL Assoc.
Earley Kielty & Assoc., Inc.
Eastman & Beaudine, Inc.
Ebbert Assoc.
Bruce Edwards & Associates, Inc.
Effective Search, Inc.
Egan & Assoc.
Eggleston Consulting Int'l.
William J. Elam & Assoc.
The Elliott Company
Elliott, Pfisterer, Chinetti Assoc., Inc.
David M. Ellner Assoc.
The Elson Group, Inc.
Elwell & Assoc., Inc.
Emmons Assoc., Inc.
Empire International
George Enns Partners Inc.
Mary R. Erickson & Assoc.
Erlanger Assoc.
Excelsior Services Group Inc.
ExecuCounsel Management Consultants Inc.
Executive Management Systems, Inc.
Executive Manning Corp.
Executive Quest
Executive Resource Group
Executive Search Inc.
Raymond L. Extract & Assoc.
Fagan & Co.
Hill Fallon & Assoc.
Leon A. Farley Assoc.
Farrell & Phin, Inc.
James Farris Assoc.
George Fee Assoc., Inc.
James Feerst & Assoc., Inc.
Fenwick Partners
Finnegan Assoc.
Fiordalis Assoc., Inc.
First Colorado Consulting Group, Inc.
Fleming Energy Group
Fogec Consultants
J. H. Folger Company
L.W. Foote Co.
D.E. Foster & Partners, L.P.
Stephen Fox Assoc. Inc.
Francis & Assoc.
Gerald Frisch Assoc., Inc.
Furlong - Gates, Inc.
GSW Consulting Group, Inc.
Gaffney Management Consultants
W.N. Garbarini & Assoc.
Gardiner Stone Hunter Int'l., Inc.
Allan Gardner & Assoc., Inc.
Gardner-Ross Assoc., Inc.
Garland Assoc.
Garofolo, Curtiss, Lambert & MacLean
The Gedge Group
Genovese & Co.
Gibson & Co., Inc.
Gilbert & Van Campen Int'l.
Gilbert Tweed Assoc., Inc.
Howard Gilmore & Assoc.
Gleason & Assoc.
Glou Int'l., Inc.

00.0 MOST (Cont'd)

The Gobbell Co.
H. L. Goehring & Assoc., Inc.
B. Goodwin, Ltd.
Goss & Assoc., Inc.
Gould & McCoy, Inc.
Graham & Co.
Robert Graham Assoc., Inc.
Granger, Counts & Assoc.
Grantham & Co., Inc.
Annie Gray Assoc., Inc.
Paul C. Green & Assoc. Ltd.
Griffith & Werner, Inc.
Jack Groban & Assoc.
Grover & Assoc.
Gustin Partners, Ltd.
Gutreuter & Assoc.
William Guy & Assoc., Inc.
Haddad Assoc.
Halden & Assoc.
Halstead & Assoc.
The Halyburton Co., Inc.
R. C. Handel Assoc. Inc.
W.L. Handler & Assoc.
Hartman, Barnette & Assoc.
Hauft Mark Assoc., Inc.
Hayman & Co.
F. P. Healy & Co., Inc.
Heath/Norton Assoc., Inc.
Hegarty & Co.
The Heidrick Partners, Inc.
Heidrick and Struggles, Inc.
Helfer Executive Consultants
G.W. Henn & Co.
Hergenrather & Co.
William Hetzel Assoc., Inc.
Higdon, Joys & Mingle, Inc.
Higgins Assoc., Inc.
The Hindman Co.
Hite Executive Search
Hockett Assoc., Inc.
Hodge-Cronin & Assoc., Inc.
Harvey Hohauser & Assoc.
Richard D. Holbrook Assoc.
Holland Rusk & Assoc.
The Hollins Group, Inc.
Holohan Group, Ltd.
Holt Pearson & Caldwell, Inc.
R. H. Horton Int'l.
William C. Houze & Co.
Houze, Shourds & Montgomery, Inc.
Randall Howard & Assoc., Inc.
Robert Howe & Assoc.
Howe, McMahon & Assoc., Inc.
Howe-Lewis Int'l.
Huff Assoc.
M.J. Hughes Int'l., Inc.
Human Resource Technologies, Inc.
The Human Resource Consulting Group, Inc.
The Hunt Co.
Hunter Int'l., Inc.
Jack Hurst & Assoc., Inc.

Hutchinson Resources International
Huxtable Assoc., Inc.
Hyde Danforth & Co.
John Imber Assoc., Ltd.
Ingram, Inc.
Inmark Executive Search
Inside Management Assoc.
The Interface Group, Ltd.
International Management Services Inc.
International Management Advisors, Inc.
Jeffrey Irving Assoc., Inc.
Isaacson, Miller, Inc.
JDavid Assoc., Inc.
Jahrling & Co.
Jakobs & Assoc. Int'l.
Pendleton James & Assoc., Inc.
Michael James & Co., Inc.
James, Layton Int'l., Inc.
January Management Group
Jender & Company
John & Powers, Inc.
Johnson & Assoc., Inc.
John H. Johnson & Assoc., Inc.
L.J. Johnson & Co.
Ronald S. Johnson Assoc., Inc.
Johnson Smith & Knisely Inc.
Jordan-Sitter Assoc.
Inge Judd Assoc.
Jim Just & Assoc.
George Kaludis Assoc., Inc.
Gary Kaplan & Assoc.
Karam Group Int'l.
Martin Kartin & Co., Inc.
A.T. Kearney Executive Search
Kellogg Consulting Group
M. Scott Kemp & Assoc., Inc.
Kendro & Assoc.
Kennedy & Co.
Kenny, Kindler, Hunt & Howe
Kensington Management Consultants, Inc.
Melvin Kent & Assoc., Inc.
Kieffer, Ford, & Hadelman, Ltd.
Kincannon & Reed
The Kinlin Co., Inc.
Richard Kinser & Assoc.
Kirby & Assoc.
Kirkman & Searing
Kishbaugh Associates
Jonah Kleinstein Assoc., Inc.
Kline Consulting, Inc.
Knapp Consultants
Koehler & Co.
Fred Koffler Assoc.
Kolden & Assoc., Ltd.
Korn/Ferry, Int'l., S.A. de C.V.
Korn/Ferry, Int'l.
Kors Montgomery Int'l.
Kostmayer Assoc., Inc.
J. Krauss Assoc.
Krauthamer & Assoc.
Kremple & Meade, Inc.
D.A. Kreuter Assoc., Inc.
Kuehne & Co., Inc.

00.0 MOST (Cont'd)
John Kuhn & Assoc.
Kunzer Assoc., Ltd.
Lamalie Assoc., Inc.
Langer Assoc., Inc.
Lawrence L. Lapham, Inc.
Larkin & Co.
Larsen & Lee, Inc.
Larson & Stephanian
Lasher Assoc.
Michael Latas & Assoc., Inc.
Lauer Consulting Services, Inc.
Lauer, Sbarbaro Assoc., Inc.
Lee & Burgess Assoc., Inc.
J. E. Lessner Assoc., Inc.
Levin & Assoc.
Locke & Assoc.
The Lockridge Group, Inc.
J.P. Logan & Co., Inc.
The Logan Group, Inc.
H.M. Long Int'l., Ltd.
Lovejoy & Lovejoy
Lowderman & Haney, Inc.
Robert Lowell Int'l.
The John Lucht Consultancy Inc.
The Lumsden Co., Inc.
Lund & Assoc., Inc.
Lynch & Co.
Lynch Miller Moore, Inc.
MCC Assoc.
META/MAT, Ltd.
M/J/A Partners
The Macdonald Group, Inc.
Robert Madigan Assoc., Inc.
The Madison Group
Maglio & Co., Inc.
Management Advisors of Princeton, Inc.
Management Resources Int'l.
Management Science Assoc.
F. L. Mannix & Co., Inc.
Mark Stanley & Co.
Brad Marks Int'l.
Marlar Int'l. Inc.
Marling Inc.
Marra/Pizzi Assoc., Inc.
J. Martin & Assoc.
George R. Martin
The Martin Group
Martin Mirtz Morice, Inc.
Maschal/Connors Inc.
Gayle L. Mattson & Assoc.
McBride Assoc., Inc.
McCooe & Assoc., Inc.
McCormack & Farrow
McCullough Assoc.
McDonald/Long Assoc., Inc.
McMahon & Dee, Inc.
McManners Assoc., Inc.
McNichol Assoc.
McSherry & Assoc.
James Mead & Co.
Meder & Assoc.

Meng, Finseth & Assoc., Inc.
Menzel, Robinson, Baldwin, Inc.
Mercedes & Co., Inc.
The Mercer Group, Inc.
Messett Assoc., Inc.
The Neil Michael Group, Inc.
Million & Assoc., Inc.
Mitchell, Larsen & Zilliacus
Moriarty/Fox, Inc.
Morris & Berger
R.C. Morton & Assoc. Inc.
Edwin Mruk & Partners
Paul Mueller & Assoc., Inc.
Munroe, Curry & Bond Assoc.
P. J. Murphy & Assoc., Inc.
Robert Murphy Assoc.
Nadzam, Lusk & Assoc., Inc.
Nagler & Co., Inc.
Barry Nathanson Assoc.
National Restaurant Search, Inc.
Newell Assoc.
Newpher & Co., Inc.
Nicholaou & Co.
Nicholson & Assoc., Inc.
The Niemond Corp.
W.D. Nolte & Company
Norman Broadbent Int'l., Inc.
Northern Consultants Inc.
Norton & Assoc., Inc.
C. J. Noty & Assoc.
Nuessle, Kurdziel & Weiss, Inc.
Nursing Technomics
O'Brien & Co., Inc.
O'Callaghan, Honey & Assoc., Inc.
O'Connor, O'Connor, Lordi, Ltd.
O'Rourke Co., Inc.
O'Shea, Divine & Co.
Dennis P. O'Toole & Assoc. Inc.
O'Toole & Company
Ober & Company
Oberlander & Co., Inc.
The Odessa Group
The Ogdon Partnership
Oliver & Rozner Assoc., Inc.
The Onstott Group
Oppedisano & Co., Inc.
Organization Resources Inc.
Orion Consulting, Inc.
Robert Ottke Assoc.
PCD Partners
G.S. Page Inc.
Page-Wheatcroft & Co. Ltd.
John Paisios Ltd.
Kirk Palmer & Assoc., Inc.
Palmer Assoc., Inc.
Parker, Sholl & Gordon, Inc.
Michael W. Parres & Assoc.
Parsons Assoc. Inc.
Pasini & Co.
Patton, Perry & Sproull Inc.
Peat Marwick Stevenson & Kellogg
The Peck Consultancy
Peeney Assoc., Inc.

00.0 MOST (Cont'd)

People Management Northeast, Inc.
R. H. Perry & Assoc., Inc.
Perry-D'Amico & Assoc.
Barry Persky & Co., Inc.
Richard Peterson & Assoc., Inc.
Pflueger & Company
Pierce & Assoc., Inc.
Pierce Assoc.
Martin Pierce Inc.
Pinsker & Co., Inc.
Rene Plessner Assoc., Inc.
R.L. Plimpton Assoc.
Plummer & Assoc., Inc.
Pocrass Assoc.
Poirier, Hoevel & Co.
Polson & Co., Inc.
David Powell, Inc.
Pre-Search, Inc.
Predictor Systems Corp.
Preng & Assoc., Inc.
Prior Martech Assoc.
QVS Int'l.
Quaintance Assoc., Inc.
L. J. Quinn & Assoc., Inc.
Quinn Bailey & Morgan
RG International
RIC Corp.
RZL Y Asociados, S.C.
Rafey & Company
Raines Int'l. Inc.
Rand Assoc.
Paul Ray & Carre Orban Int'l.
Redden & Assoc.
Reddick and Co., Int'l.
Reese Assoc.
The Regis Group, Ltd.
D.M. Rein & Co., Inc.
Research Alternatives, Inc.
Resources for Management
The Revere Assoc., Inc.
Russell Reynolds Assoc., Inc.
E.J. Rhodes Assoc.
Rieser & Assoc., Inc.
Norman Roberts & Assoc., Inc.
Robertson, Spoerlein & Wengert
Robertson-Surrette Ltd.
Bruce Robinson Assoc.
Robison & McAulay
Robsham & Assoc.
Ropes Assoc., Inc.
Rourke, Bourbonnais Assoc., Ltd.
David Rowe & Assoc., Inc.
Rurak & Assoc., Inc
Rusher, Loscavio & Lo Presto
Charles Russ Assoc.
Russell, Montgomery & Assoc.
James J. Rust Executive Search
SRH Resource Group
SS & A Executive Search Consultants
Saber Consultants, Inc.
Wilbur M. Sachtjen Assoc., Inc.

Saley Partners Int'l.
Sandhurst Assoc.
Sathe & Assoc., Inc.
Savoy Partners, Ltd.
Schenkel & Company
Schuyler, Frye & Baker, Inc.
Schwab-Carrese Assoc.
The Michael Scott Consulting Co., Inc.
J. Robert Scott
Search Express
Search Source, Inc.
Seiden Assoc., Inc.
Seitchik, Corwin & Seitchik Inc.
Robert Sellery Assoc., Ltd.
M.B. Shattuck & Assoc., Inc.
Kimball Shaw Assoc.
Sherbrooke Assoc., Inc.
Michael Shirley Assoc.
Shoemaker & Assoc.
E.L. Shore & Assoc. Corp.
The Shotland Group
W. Shryock & Co.
John Sibbald Assoc., Inc.
Sievers & Assoc.
C.W. Sink & Co., Inc.
Slater & Assoc.
Slayton Int'l., Inc.
Sloane, Sloane & Mayne
Robert L. Smith & Co., Inc.
Stephen R. Smith & Co., Inc.
Howard W. Smith Assoc.
Smith, Goerss & Ferneborg, Inc.
H.C. Smith Ltd.
Smith, Roth & Squires
Smith Search, S.A.
Herman Smith Transearch Inc.
A. William Smyth, Inc.
Sockwell & Anderson
Soltis Management Services
SpencerStuart
Splaine & Assoc., Inc.
Spriggs & Co., Inc.
Stack Assoc.
The Stamford Group Inc.
Stanislaw & Assoc., Inc.
Staples Consulting Inc.
Staub, Warmbold & Barkauskas, Inc.
Lee Stephens & Assoc.
Stephens Assoc. Ltd.
Michael Stern Assoc. Inc.
The Stevenson Group/SES
S. K. Stewart & Assoc.
Stewart, Stein & Scott, Ltd.
Stimmel Search Division
Stone, Murphy & Olson
Stoneham Assoc.
Strategic Staffing Concepts, Inc.
W. R. Strathmann Assoc.
Straube Assoc., Inc.
Stricker & Zagor
Stuart, Wood Inc.
Studwell Assoc.
Joe Sullivan & Assoc., Inc.

00.0 MOST (Cont'd)

Sullivan & Co.
Sullivan-Murphy Assoc.
Sweeney Shepherd Bueschel Provus Harbert &
  Mummert, Inc.
TASA, Inc.
TEMCO - The Executive Mgmt. Cons. Org.
Tama Lucas Ltd.
Tanton/Mitchell Group
Tarnow Int'l.
Carl J. Taylor & Co.
Tesar-Reynes, Inc.
Thalatta Corp.
Theobald & Assoc.
Thomas Mangum Co.
Thomas, Richardson, Runden & Co. Inc.
Thorne, Brieger Assoc., Inc.
Tierney Assoc., Inc.
Tirocchi, Wright, Inc.
Torretto & Assoc., Inc.
Trac One
Travis & Co., Inc.
Gilles Tremblay & Assoc.
Trout & Assoc., Inc.
Trowbridge & Co., Inc.
Tucker Assoc.
Michael Tucker Assoc.
The Thomas Tucker Co.
Tully & Birch, Inc.
K. W. Tunnell Co., Inc.
The Ultimate Source
P. T. Unger Assoc.
Universal Executive Search, Inc.
Valletta Ritson & Co.
VanMaldegiam Assoc., Inc.
VanReypen Enterprises, Ltd.
John Velcamp & Assoc.
Verkamp-Joyce Assoc., Inc.
VideoFields, Ltd.
Villareal & Assoc., Inc.
Vlcek & Co., Inc.
Voigt Assoc.
Von Storch Assoc.
Walker Group, Inc.
Albert J. Walsh & Assoc.
J.D. Walsh & Co.
Ward Howell Int'l. Inc.
Wargo & Co., Inc.
Hilton N. Wasserman & Assoc. Inc.
Webb, Johnson & Klemmer, Inc.
Weber Executive Search
D. L. Weiss & Assoc.
Wellington Management Group
The Wentworth Co., Inc.
Werner Int'l., Inc.
Jude M. Werra & Assoc.
Westcott Associates, Inc.
Western Reserve Search Assoc.
Weston Consultants, Inc.
Wheeler, Moore & Elam Co.
Wilkins & Co.
Wilkinson & Ives

Williams, Roth & Krueger, Inc.
Craig Williamson, Inc.
William Willis Worldwide, Inc.
The Winchester Group
Winguth & Company
Richard Winn & Co.
Wojdula & Assoc.
S. R. Wolman Assoc., Inc.
Wood, Franchot Inc.
Wood-Glavin, Inc.
Wood/Sprau/Tannura, Inc.
Wytmar & Co., Inc.
Yelverton & Co.
The Yorkshire Group, Ltd.
Steven Yungerberg Assoc., Inc.
The Zammataro Co.
Egon Zehnder Int'l. Inc.
Michael D. Zinn & Assoc., Inc.
The Zivic Group, Inc.
Zurick, Davis & Co.

01.0 GENERAL MANAGEMENT

The Abbott Group
Actuaries & Assoc.
Jeffrey C. Adams & Co., Inc.
Advanced Executive Resources
Alwyn Assoc., Inc.
Peter W. Ambler Co.
American Executive Management, Inc.
American Executive Search Services, Inc.
Annapolis Consulting Group
Argus National, Inc.
Ariail & Assoc.
William B. Arnold Assoc., Inc.
Aubin Int'l. Inc.
Auerbach Assoc.
The Badger Group
Ballos & Co., Inc.
Barger & Sargeant, Inc.
J.W. Barleycorn & Assoc.
Nathan Barry Assoc., Inc.
Bartholdi & Co.
Barton Raben, Inc.
Bason Assoc., Inc.
Battalia Winston Int'l., Inc.
Martin H. Bauman Assoc., Inc.
Becker, Norton & Co.
Joy Reed Belt & Assoc., Inc.
Belvedere Partners
Bennett Search & Consulting Co.
Bialla & Assoc., Inc.
BioQuest Inc.
Deborah Bishop & Assoc.
Bishop Assoc.
Blaney Executive Search
Blau Kaptain Schroeder
Blendow, Crowley & Oliver, Inc.
Boardroom Planning & Consulting Group
Bowden & Co., Inc.
The Brand Co., Inc.
Brissenden, McFarland, Wagoner & Fuccella,
  Inc.

01.0 GENERAL MANAGEMENT (Cont'd)

Charles Buck & Assoc., Inc.
Bullis & Co., Inc.
Buzhardt Assoc.
T. Byrnes & Co., Inc.
Byron Leonard Int'l., Inc.
CEO'S Only
Lee Calhoon & Co., Inc.
Callan Assoc., Ltd.
Robert Campbell & Assoc.
Canny, Bowen Inc.
Cardwell Group
Cascadia Group Int'l.
Catalyx Group, Inc.
Michael J. Cavanaugh & Assoc.
Cejka & Co.
China Human Resources Group
Jack Clarey Assoc., Inc.
J. Kevin Coleman & Assoc., Inc.
Conard Assoc., Inc.
Conex Inc.
Joseph Conley & Assoc., Inc.
Conley Assoc., Inc.
Philip Conway Management
Grant Cooper & Assoc., Inc.
Coopers & Lybrand, Management Consulting
    Services
Corporate Environment Ltd.
The Corporate Source Group
Corporate Staffing Group
The Corrigan Group
M.J. Curran & Assoc., Inc.
Dahl-Morrow Int'l.
Marge Dana Assoc.
Alfred Daniels & Assoc.
Charles E. Day & Assoc., Inc.
De Funiak & Edwards
DeHayes Consulting Group
DiMarchi Partners
Dieckmann & Assoc., Ltd.
Robert W. Dingman Co., Inc.
Donahue/Bales Assoc.
Dougan-McKinley-Strain
Dromeshauser Assoc.
Duggan & Company
Michael S. Dunford, Inc.
Dupuis & Ryden, P.C.
Dwyer Consulting Group, Inc.
Effective Search, Inc.
The Elliott Company
Erlanger Assoc.
Euromedica USA
Excelsior Services Group Inc.
ExecuCounsel Management Consultants Inc.
Executive Appointments Ltd., Int'l.
Fagan & Co.
Leon A. Farley Assoc.
George Fee Assoc., Inc.
James Feerst & Assoc., Inc.
Fenwick Partners
Finnegan Assoc.

Fiordalis Assoc., Inc.
Howard Fischer Assoc., Inc.
Fisher Personnel Management Services
Fogec Consultants
Foy, Schneid & Daniel, Inc.
The Furman Group, Ltd.
GSW Consulting Group, Inc.
Gaffney Management Consultants
Jay Gaines & Co.
W.N. Garbarini & Assoc.
Allan Gardner & Assoc., Inc.
Gardner-Ross Assoc., Inc.
Garofolo, Curtiss, Lambert & MacLean
The Gedge Group
Genovese & Co.
John D. Gibbons & Assoc., Inc.
N.W. Gibson Int'l.
The Goodrich & Sherwood Co.
B. Goodwin, Ltd.
Grantham & Co., Inc.
Greger Assoc.
Robert Grossberg & Assoc.
Hadley Lockwood, Inc.
Haley Assoc., Inc.
The Hamilton Group
Handy HRM
Hans & Assoc., Inc.
Harris Heery & Assoc., Inc.
The Hawkins Co.
Hayden Group, Inc.
Health Industry Consultants, Inc.
Heath/Norton Assoc., Inc.
The Heidrick Partners, Inc.
Helfer Executive Consultants
Hergenrather & Co.
Hersher Assoc., Ltd.
Stanley Herz & Co.
Higdon, Joys & Mingle, Inc.
The Hindman Co.
Hite Executive Search
Hockett Assoc., Inc.
Hogan Assoc.
Holland, McFadzean & Assoc., Inc.
Holland Rusk & Assoc.
J.B. Homer Assoc. Inc.
Hughes & Assoc., Inc.
The Human Resource Consulting Group, Inc.
Human Resource Research Inc.
Human Resource Services, Inc.
Human Resources, Inc.
William Humphreys & Assoc., Inc.
Hunter Int'l., Inc.
Jack Hurst & Assoc., Inc.
Hutchinson Resources International
The Hyde Group, Inc.
Ingram, Inc.
Innkeeper's Management Corp.
The Interface Group, Ltd.
The Interim Management Corp.(IMCOR)
Jeffrey Irving Assoc., Inc.
JM & Co.
January Management Group
Jender & Company

01.0 GENERAL MANAGEMENT (Cont'd)

Johnson Smith & Knisely Inc.
Jordan-Sitter Assoc.
L. E. Justice Consulting Assoc.
K/N Int'l.
Gary Kaplan & Assoc.
Karam Group Int'l.
Howard Karr & Assoc., Inc.
Kensington Management Consultants, Inc.
Richard Kinser & Assoc.
Kishbaugh Associates
Koehler & Co.
T. J. Koellhoffer & Assoc.
Koontz, Jeffries & Assoc., Inc.
The J. Kovach Group, Inc.
J. Krauss Assoc.
Ira W. Krinsky & Assoc.
Paul Kull & Co.
Kunzer Assoc., Ltd.
John Kurosky & Assoc.
L O R Personnel Div.
Marvin Laba & Assoc.
Laguzza Assoc., Ltd.
Langer Assoc., Inc.
Lansky Assoc.
Lawrence L. Lapham, Inc.
Larsen Int'l., Inc.
Larson & Stephanian
Lee & Burgess Assoc., Inc.
The Lieberman Group
Locke & Assoc.
The Logan Group, Inc.
H.M. Long Int'l., Ltd.
Lovejoy & Lovejoy
The John Lucht Consultancy Inc.
The Lumsden Co., Inc.
P.J. Lynch Assoc.
Lynch Miller Moore, Inc.
MCC Assoc.
M/J/A Partners
F. L. Mannix & Co., Inc.
Marlar Int'l. Inc.
Marra/Pizzi Assoc., Inc.
J. Martin & Assoc.
C.R. Martin & Assoc.
The Martin Group
Bruce Massey & Partners Inc.
Matte & Company, Inc.
Gayle L. Mattson & Assoc.
Mazza & Riley, Inc.
The Mazzitelli Group, Ltd.
McBride Assoc., Inc.
McCormack & Farrow
McDonald Assoc.
McDonald/Long Assoc., Inc.
McFeely Wackerle Shulman
Robert E. McGrath & Assoc.
McKeen Melancon & Co.
McManners Assoc., Inc.
Jon McRae & Assoc., Inc.
James Mead & Co.

Messett Assoc., Inc.
Michael Assoc.
The Neil Michael Group, Inc.
Herbert Mines Assoc., Inc.
Jay Mitchell & Co.
Morgan/Webber
Moriarty/Fox, Inc.
R.C. Morton & Assoc. Inc.
Paul Mueller & Assoc., Inc.
The Mulshine Co., Inc.
P. J. Murphy & Assoc., Inc.
NDI Services
Nadzam, Lusk & Assoc., Inc.
Newell Assoc.
The Niemond Corp.
Norman Broadbent Int'l., Inc.
Paul Norsell & Assoc., Inc.
Northern Consultants Inc.
Richard E. Nosky & Assoc.
Nursing Technomics
O'Callaghan, Honey & Assoc., Inc.
O'Shea, Divine & Co.
Dennis P. O'Toole & Assoc. Inc.
O'Toole & Company
Ober & Company
Orion Consulting, Inc.
Ott & Hansen, Inc.
P.A.R. Assoc., Inc.
The PAR Group - Paul A. Reaume, Ltd.
Page-Wheatcroft & Co. Ltd.
Kirk Palmer & Assoc., Inc.
Palmer Assoc., Inc.
Patton, Perry & Sproull Inc.
Peeney Assoc., Inc.
People Management Northeast, Inc.
Personnel Assoc.
Phillips Group of Companies
Pierce Assoc.
Pierce Assoc.
Martin Pierce Inc.
Rene Plessner Assoc., Inc.
R.L. Plimpton Assoc.
Plummer & Assoc., Inc.
Pocrass Assoc.
David Powell, Inc.
QVS Int'l.
Quinn Bailey & Morgan
RIC Corp.
Rafey & Company
Walter Raleigh & Assoc.
Ramming & Assoc., Inc.
Ramsey & Beirne Assoc., Inc.
Rand Assoc.
The Rankin Group, Ltd.
Paul Ray & Carre Orban Int'l.
Reddick and Co., Int'l.
The Regis Group, Ltd.
D.M. Rein & Co., Inc.
Resource Network Inc.
The Revere Assoc., Inc.
E.J. Rhodes Assoc.
Ridenour & Assoc.
Rieser & Assoc., Inc.

01.1 DIRECTORS (Cont'd)

H.C. Smith Ltd.
Herman Smith Transearch Inc.
Stack Assoc.
Staples Consulting Inc.
Stewart/Laurence Assoc., Inc.
W. R. Strathmann Assoc.
Sullivan-Murphy Assoc.
Vista Resource Group
Von Storch Assoc.
The WalCar Partnership
K. L. Whitney & Co., Inc.
Donald Williams Assoc., Inc.

01.2 SENIOR MANAGEMENT

Adams & Assoc. Int'l
J.R. Akin & Co.
Anders Incorporated
Ariail & Assoc.
Auerbach Assoc.
BDO Seidman
Nelson Bell & Partners Inc.
Belvedere Partners
Blau Kaptain Schroeder
Marc-Paul Bloome Ltd.
Peter Newell Bowen
Bowker, Brown & Co.
Brandywine Consulting Group
Bryce, Haultain & Assoc.
Thomas Burnham Co.
Robert Campbell & Assoc.
Canny, Bowen Inc.
Cardwell Group
Chartwell Partners Int'l., Inc.
Christian & Timbers, Inc.
Clemo, Evans & Co., Inc.
Dean M. Coe Assoc.
Coopers & Lybrand, Management Consulting
   Services
The Dartmouth Group
The Domann Organization
Duggan & Company
ESP Management Services, Inc.
Educational Management Network
Erwin Assoc.
Executive Management Systems, Inc.
Executive Quest
FGI
George Fee Assoc., Inc.
John D. Gibbons & Assoc., Inc.
Howard Gilmore & Assoc.
H. L. Goehring & Assoc., Inc.
Robert Graham Assoc., Inc.
Annie Gray Assoc., Inc.
Greger Assoc.
Hansen Group, Ltd.
Hanzel & Co., Inc.
Hayden Group, Inc.
Henning & Assoc.
Henry Michaels & Assoc.
Houtz, Strawn Assoc.
Ronald S. Johnson Assoc., Inc.

Karam Group Int'l.
Allan Karson Assoc., Inc.
D. F. Kerry & Assoc.
D.A. Kreuter Assoc., Inc.
Ira W. Krinsky & Assoc.
The Landmark Consulting Group Inc.
Lansky Assoc.
Larkin & Co.
H.M. Long Int'l., Ltd.
Management Science Assoc.
J. Martin & Assoc.
Bruce Massey & Partners Inc.
Mazza & Riley, Inc.
The Mazzitelli Group, Ltd.
Martin H. Meisel Assoc., Inc.
Mitchell, Larsen & Zilliacus
Edwin Mruk & Partners
R. F. Mulvaney & Assoc., Inc.
Overton Group
People Management Northeast, Inc.
Phillips Group of Companies
Pierce Assoc.
Predictor Systems Corp.
Walter Raleigh & Assoc.
Paul Ray & Carre Orban Int'l.
D.M. Rein & Co., Inc.
Marshall Rice Assoc.
Ridenour & Assoc.
The Romark Group, Ltd.
SS & A Executive Search Consultants
Wilbur M. Sachtjen Assoc., Inc.
F. B. Schmidt Intl.
Daniel A. Silverstein Assoc. Inc.
Sloane, Sloane & Mayne
H.C. Smith Ltd.
Herman Smith Transearch Inc.
A. William Smyth, Inc.
Spriggs & Co., Inc.
Stack Assoc.
Staples Consulting Inc.
W. R. Strathmann Assoc.
Sullivan-Murphy Assoc.
Tyler & Co.
Venture Management
Von Storch Assoc.
The WalCar Partnership
James L. Walsh & Assoc., Inc.
Donald Williams Assoc., Inc.
Xagas & Assoc.

01.3 MIDDLE MANAGEMENT

A la Carte Int'l., Inc.
Adams & Assoc. Int'l
Peter Newell Bowen
Bowker, Brown & Co.
Brandywine Consulting Group
Bryce, Haultain & Assoc.
Cardwell Group
Coopers & Lybrand, Management Consulting
   Services
ESP Management Services, Inc.
Ebbert Assoc.

01.3 MIDDLE MANAGEMENT (Cont'd)

Executive Quest
John D. Gibbons & Assoc., Inc.
Howard Gilmore & Assoc.
H. L. Goehring & Assoc., Inc.
Annie Gray Assoc., Inc.
Hansen Group, Ltd.
Hansen Management Search Co.
Henning & Assoc.
Robert Howe & Assoc.
Karam Group Int'l.
Allan Karson Assoc., Inc.
D. F. Kerry & Assoc.
Lansky Assoc.
Maiorino & Weston Assoc., Inc.
J. Martin & Assoc.
Edwin Mruk & Partners
Parsons Assoc. Inc.
Predictor Systems Corp.
Marshall Rice Assoc.
The Romark Group, Ltd.
SS & A Executive Search Consultants
F. B. Schmidt Intl.
H.C. Smith Ltd.
A. William Smyth, Inc.
Staples Consulting Inc.
Sullivan-Murphy Assoc.
Tyler & Co.
James L. Walsh & Assoc., Inc.

01.4 MIS-MANAGEMENT INFORMATION SYSTEMS

Bryce, Haultain & Assoc.
Chanko-Ward, Ltd.
Chartwell Partners Int'l., Inc.
John J. Davis & Assoc., Inc.
Fred J. Goldsmith Assoc.
Heffelfinger Assoc., Inc.
Henry Michaels & Assoc.
Marks & Co., Inc.
Montenido Assoc.
Edwin Mruk & Partners
Nursing Technomics
O'Brien & Co., Inc.
John O'Keefe & Assoc., Inc.
G.S. Page Inc.
Peterson Consulting/W.P., Inc.
Romeo-Hudgins & Assoc. Ltd.
Schalekamp & Assoc., Inc.
Sullivan & Co.
Synergistics Assoc. Ltd.
Trac One
Von Storch Assoc.
Weir Executive Search Assoc., Inc.

01.5 LEGAL

The Baxter Group
Counsel Search Co.
D'Aries Five Enterprises
Bert H. Early Assoc., Inc.
Executive Management Systems, Inc.

Human Resource Services, Inc.
SS & A Executive Search Consultants
Staples Consulting Inc.
Sullivan & Co.

02.0 MANUFACTURING

The Abbott Group
Adams & Assoc. Int'l
Jeffrey C. Adams & Co., Inc.
Advanced Executive Resources
Aim Executive Consulting Services
J.R. Akin & Co.
Peter W. Ambler Co.
American Executive Search Services, Inc.
Annapolis Consulting Group
Argus National, Inc.
Ariail & Assoc.
William B. Arnold Assoc., Inc.
BDO Seidman
The Badger Group
Ballos & Co., Inc.
James Bangert & Assoc., Inc.
Barger & Sargeant, Inc.
J.W. Barleycorn & Assoc.
Nathan Barry Assoc., Inc.
Bason Assoc., Inc.
Battalia Winston Int'l., Inc.
Becker, Norton & Co.
Joy Reed Belt & Assoc., Inc.
BioQuest Inc.
The Blackman Kallick Search Division
John C. Boone & Co.
The Borton Wallace Co.
Bowden & Co., Inc.
The Brand Co., Inc.
Brandywine Consulting Group
Brissenden, McFarland, Wagoner & Fuccella, Inc.
Bullis & Co., Inc.
Thomas Burnham Co.
Buzhardt Assoc.
Byron Leonard Int'l., Inc.
Callan Assoc., Ltd.
Cascadia Group Int'l.
Catalyx Group, Inc.
Michael J. Cavanaugh & Assoc.
China Human Resources Group
Christian & Timbers, Inc.
Christopher-Patrick & Assoc.
Jack Clarey Assoc., Inc.
Clemo, Evans & Co., Inc.
J. Kevin Coleman & Assoc., Inc.
Joseph Conley & Assoc., Inc.
Conley Assoc., Inc.
Philip Conway Management
Grant Cooper & Assoc., Inc.
Corporate Environment Ltd.
M.J. Curran & Assoc., Inc.
Curry, Telleri Group, Inc.
Marge Dana Assoc.
The Dartmouth Group
Charles E. Day & Assoc., Inc.

02.0 MANUFACTURING (Cont'd)

DeHayes Consulting Group
DiMarchi Partners
Dieckmann & Assoc., Ltd.
Robert W. Dingman Co., Inc.
Donahue/Bales Assoc.
Dougan-McKinley-Strain
Dromeshauser Assoc.
Dupuis & Ryden, P.C.
Dwyer Consulting Group, Inc.
Ebbert Assoc.
Effective Search, Inc.
William J. Elam & Assoc.
David M. Ellner Assoc.
The Elson Group, Inc.
Erlanger Assoc.
ExecuCounsel Management Consultants Inc.
Executive Appointments Ltd., Int'l.
Fagan & Co.
Hill Fallon & Assoc.
Leon A. Farley Assoc.
James Feerst & Assoc., Inc.
Fenwick Partners
Finnegan Assoc.
Howard Fischer Assoc., Inc.
Fisher Personnel Management Services
Fogec Consultants
Stephen Fox Assoc. Inc.
Foy, Schneid & Daniel, Inc.
GSW Consulting Group, Inc.
Gaffney Management Consultants
Gardner-Ross Assoc., Inc.
Genovese & Co.
N.W. Gibson Int'l.
Gilbert Tweed Assoc., Inc.
H. L. Goehring & Assoc., Inc.
Fred J. Goldsmith Assoc.
The Goodrich & Sherwood Co.
B. Goodwin, Ltd.
Robert Graham Assoc., Inc.
Grantham & Co., Inc.
Robert Grossberg & Assoc.
The Hamilton Group
R. C. Handel Assoc. Inc.
W.L. Handler & Assoc.
Hans & Assoc., Inc.
Hansen Management Search Co.
Health Industry Consultants, Inc.
Heath/Norton Assoc., Inc.
The Heidrick Partners, Inc.
Helfer Executive Consultants
Hergenrather & Co.
The Hindman Co.
Hite Executive Search
Hockett Assoc., Inc.
Hogan Assoc.
Holland, McFadzean & Assoc., Inc.
Holland Rusk & Assoc.
Robert Howe & Assoc.
Huff Assoc.
Hughes & Assoc., Inc.
Human Resources, Inc.

Jack Hurst & Assoc., Inc.
Hutchinson Resources International
Inside Management Assoc.
The Interim Management Corp.(IMCOR)
JM & Co.
January Management Group
Jender & Company
John H. Johnson & Assoc., Inc.
L.J. Johnson & Co.
Jordan-Sitter Assoc.
L. E. Justice Consulting Assoc.
K/N Int'l.
Kellogg Consulting Group
M. Scott Kemp & Assoc., Inc.
Kishbaugh Associates
Jonah Kleinstein Assoc., Inc.
Koehler & Co.
Koontz, Jeffries & Assoc., Inc.
J. Krauss Assoc.
Kremple & Meade, Inc.
Paul Kull & Co.
Kunzer Assoc., Ltd.
John Kurosky & Assoc.
L O R Personnel Div.
Lawrence L. Lapham, Inc.
Larson & Stephanian
Lasher Assoc.
Lauer Consulting Services, Inc.
Lauer, Sbarbaro Assoc., Inc.
Lee & Burgess Assoc., Inc.
The Lieberman Group
Locke & Assoc.
The Logan Group, Inc.
The Lumsden Co., Inc.
Lund & Assoc., Inc.
Lynch Miller Moore, Inc.
MCC Assoc.
META/MAT, Ltd.
M/J/A Partners
Marlar Int'l. Inc.
The Martin Group
Bruce Massey & Partners Inc.
Matte & Company, Inc.
Gayle L. Mattson & Assoc.
The Mazzitelli Group, Ltd.
McCormack & Farrow
McDonald/Long Assoc., Inc.
Robert E. McGrath & Assoc.
McKeen Melancon & Co.
McManners Assoc., Inc.
Messett Assoc., Inc.
Michael Assoc.
The Neil Michael Group, Inc.
Herbert Mines Assoc., Inc.
Mitchell, Larsen & Zilliacus
Morgan/Webber
Moriarty/Fox, Inc.
R.C. Morton & Assoc. Inc.
Edwin Mruk & Partners
Paul Mueller & Assoc., Inc.
The Mulshine Co., Inc.
P. J. Murphy & Assoc., Inc.
Robert Murphy Assoc.

02.0 MANUFACTURING (Cont'd)

Nadzam, Lusk & Assoc., Inc.
Newell Assoc.
Newpher & Co., Inc.
The Niemond Corp.
Paul Norsell & Assoc., Inc.
Northern Consultants Inc.
Richard E. Nosky & Assoc.
O'Rourke Co., Inc.
O'Shea, Divine & Co.
O'Toole & Company
Ober & Company
Orion Consulting, Inc.
Ott & Hansen, Inc.
Palmer Assoc., Inc.
D.P. Parker & Assoc., Inc.
Michael W. Parres & Assoc.
Patton, Perry & Sproull Inc.
Peeney Assoc., Inc.
People Management Northeast, Inc.
Pierce Assoc.
R.L. Plimpton Assoc.
Plummer & Assoc., Inc.
David Powell, Inc.
Quaintance Assoc., Inc.
Quinn Bailey & Morgan
RIC Corp.
Rand Assoc.
Reddick and Co., Int'l.
The Regis Group, Ltd.
Research Alternatives, Inc.
Resource Network Inc.
Sydney Reynolds Assoc., Inc.
Rieser & Assoc., Inc.
Robertson, Spoerlein & Wengert
SRH Resource Group
Saley Partners Int'l.
Sathe & Assoc., Inc.
Schweichler Assoc., Inc.
Search Express
Seiden Assoc., Inc.
Shaffer Consulting Group
M.B. Shattuck & Assoc., Inc.
Kimball Shaw Assoc.
The Shotland Group
John Sibbald Assoc., Inc.
Sigma Group Inc.
C.W. Sink & Co., Inc.
Slayton Int'l., Inc.
Sloane, Sloane & Mayne
Soltis Management Services
Stanislaw & Assoc., Inc.
Stone, Murphy & Olson
Strategic Alternatives
Strategic Search Corp.
Strategic Staffing Concepts, Inc.
Stricker & Zagor
Studwell Assoc.
Tarnow Int'l.
Taylor Search Assoc., Inc.
Tech > Mark Group
Theobald & Assoc.

Thomas Mangum Co.
Tierney Assoc., Inc.
Torretto & Assoc., Inc.
Trout & Assoc., Inc.
Tuttle, Neidhart, Semyan, Inc.
VanMaldegiam Assoc., Inc.
John Velcamp & Assoc.
Venture Management
Verkamp-Joyce Assoc., Inc.
Ward Howell Int'l. Inc.
Ward Liebelt Assoc. Inc.
Wargo & Co., Inc.
Hilton N. Wasserman & Assoc. Inc.
D. L. Weiss & Assoc.
Werner Int'l., Inc.
Jude M. Werra & Assoc.
Wilkins & Co.
Duane I. Wilson Assoc., Inc.
The Zammataro Co.
Zay & Company
Zingaro & Co.
Michael D. Zinn & Assoc., Inc.

02.1 PRODUCT DEVELOPMENT

A la Carte Int'l., Inc.
Blau Kaptain Schroeder
The Domann Organization
Ebbert Assoc.
Euromedica USA
First Colorado Consulting Group, Inc.
Gordon/Tyler
Gutreuter & Assoc.
R. W. Hebel Assoc.
Management Catalysts
The Mulshine Co., Inc.
Kirk Palmer & Assoc., Inc.
The Romark Group, Ltd.
Strategic Search Corp.
Craig Williamson, Inc.

02.2 PRODUCTION ENGINEERING, PLANNING, SCHEDULING & CONTROL

Bryce, Haultain & Assoc.
Erwin Assoc.
McSherry & Assoc.
Polson & Co., Inc.

02.3 AUTOMATION, ROBOTICS

American Executive Management, Inc.
Xagas & Assoc.

02.4 PLANT MANAGEMENT

Blendow, Crowley & Oliver, Inc.
Marc-Paul Bloome Ltd.
Erwin Assoc.
Henning & Assoc.
D. F. Kerry & Assoc.
Lauer Consulting Services, Inc.
Maiorino & Weston Assoc., Inc.
The Mazzitelli Group, Ltd.
R. F. Mulvaney & Assoc., Inc.

02.4 PLANT MANAGEMENT (Cont'd)

O'Brien & Co., Inc.
Overton Group
Parsons Assoc. Inc.
Perry-D'Amico & Assoc.
Phillips Group of Companies
Polson & Co., Inc.
Strategic Search Corp.

02.5 QUALITY

Business Search America
Gerald Frisch Assoc., Inc.
Gordon/Tyler
The Human Resource Consulting Group, Inc.
Larkin & Co.
Management Catalysts
Perry-D'Amico & Assoc.
Polson & Co., Inc.
The Romark Group, Ltd.
Xagas & Assoc.

02.6 PRODUCTIVITY

Conard Assoc., Inc.
Xagas & Assoc.

03.0 MATERIALS MANAGEMENT

Advanced Executive Resources
J.R. Akin & Co.
Argus National, Inc.
Ariail & Assoc.
Ballos & Co., Inc.
Battalia Winston Int'l., Inc.
Martin H. Bauman Assoc., Inc.
Joy Reed Belt & Assoc., Inc.
Deborah Bishop & Assoc.
Cascadia Group Int'l.
The Dartmouth Group
The Elson Group, Inc.
Howard Fischer Assoc., Inc.
Fisher Personnel Management Services
Stephen Fox Assoc. Inc.
Gaffney Management Consultants
Gardner-Ross Assoc., Inc.
Genovese & Co.
Robert Grossberg & Assoc.
Hansen Management Search Co.
Helfer Executive Consultants
Hersher Assoc., Ltd.
The Hindman Co.
Hughes & Assoc., Inc.
The Interim Management Corp.(IMCOR)
JM & Co.
January Management Group
Jender & Company
L. E. Justice Consulting Assoc.
M. Scott Kemp & Assoc., Inc.
Koontz, Jeffries & Assoc., Inc.
Kremple & Meade, Inc.
John Kurosky & Assoc.
Lawrence L. Lapham, Inc.
Lauer Consulting Services, Inc.
The Lieberman Group

Bruce Massey & Partners Inc.
Robert E. McGrath & Assoc.
Michael Assoc.
Morgan/Webber
Paul Mueller & Assoc., Inc.
Robert Murphy Assoc.
NDI Services
Newpher & Co., Inc.
Orion Consulting, Inc.
Ott & Hansen, Inc.
Michael W. Parres & Assoc.
Perry-D'Amico & Assoc.
Pierce Assoc.
Plummer & Assoc., Inc.
Rand Assoc.
Research Alternatives, Inc.
Sydney Reynolds Assoc., Inc.
SRH Resource Group
M.B. Shattuck & Assoc., Inc.
The Shotland Group
Thomas Mangum Co.
Verkamp-Joyce Assoc., Inc.
Jude M. Werra & Assoc.
S. R. Wolman Assoc., Inc.

03.1 PURCHASING, INVENTORY MANAGEMENT

Benton Schneider & Assoc.
Canny, Bowen Inc.
Erwin Assoc.
Kirk Palmer & Assoc., Inc.

03.2 MATERIALS & REQUIREMENT PLANNING

The Corporate Source Group
The Domann Organization

03.3 PHYSICAL DISTRIBUTION, TRAFFIC & TRANSPORTATION, LOGISTICS

Bowker, Brown & Co.

03.4 PACKAGING

Gordon/Tyler
Management Catalysts
The Mulshine Co., Inc.

04.0 RESEARCH & DEVELOPMENT

The Abbott Group
Anders Incorporated
Annapolis Consulting Group
Ariail & Assoc.
Ballos & Co., Inc.
Nathan Barry Assoc., Inc.
Bartholdi & Co.
Bennett Search & Consulting Co.
BioQuest Inc.
Deborah Bishop & Assoc.
Blaney Executive Search
Blau Kaptain Schroeder
Blendow, Crowley & Oliver, Inc.

04.0 RESEARCH & DEVELOPMENT (Cont'd)

The Borton Wallace Co.
Dr. Will G. Bowman, Inc.
Brandywine Consulting Group
Brault & Assoc., Ltd.
Brissenden, McFarland, Wagoner & Fuccella, Inc.
Butterfass/Pepe Assoc., Inc.
Lee Calhoon & Co., Inc.
Callan Assoc., Ltd.
Catalyx Group, Inc.
Christian & Timbers, Inc.
Claveloux, McCaffrey, McInerney, Inc.
J. Kevin Coleman & Assoc., Inc.
Corporate Environment Ltd.
Corporate Staffing Group
Curry, Telleri Group, Inc.
DCS Assoc., Inc.
Alfred Daniels & Assoc.
The Dartmouth Group
Charles E. Day & Assoc., Inc.
Dougan-McKinley-Strain
Michael S. Dunford, Inc.
Dwyer Consulting Group, Inc.
Ebbert Assoc.
Effective Search, Inc.
William J. Elam & Assoc.
David M. Ellner Assoc.
Euromedica USA
FGI
James Feerst & Assoc., Inc.
Finnegan Assoc.
Howard Fischer Assoc., Inc.
Stephen Fox Assoc. Inc.
The Gedge Group
B. Goodwin, Ltd.
Gordon/Tyler
Haley Assoc., Inc.
Health Industry Consultants, Inc.
R. W. Hebel Assoc.
Heffelfinger Assoc., Inc.
Helfer Executive Consultants
Hockett Assoc., Inc.
Hodge-Cronin & Assoc., Inc.
Holland, McFadzean & Assoc., Inc.
Holohan Group, Ltd.
Robert Howe & Assoc.
Huff Assoc.
Human Resource Research Inc.
Hutchinson Resources International
JM & Co.
Jender & Company
John H. Johnson & Assoc., Inc.
L.J. Johnson & Co.
Ronald S. Johnson Assoc., Inc.
Jordan-Sitter Assoc.
Allan Karson Assoc., Inc.
M. Scott Kemp & Assoc., Inc.
Kensington Management Consultants, Inc.
Kishbaugh Associates
T. J. Koellhoffer & Assoc.

Koontz, Jeffries & Assoc., Inc.
Kremple & Meade, Inc.
Paul Kull & Co.
Kunzer Assoc., Ltd.
John Kurosky & Assoc.
Lawrence L. Lapham, Inc.
Larson & Stephanian
Lasher Assoc.
H.M. Long Int'l., Ltd.
Lund & Assoc., Inc.
Management Catalysts
Marlar Int'l. Inc.
Bruce Massey & Partners Inc.
Gayle L. Mattson & Assoc.
McCormack & Farrow
Robert E. McGrath & Assoc.
McKeen Melancon & Co.
McManners Assoc., Inc.
The Neil Michael Group, Inc.
Jay Mitchell & Co.
R.C. Morton & Assoc. Inc.
The Mulshine Co., Inc.
Robert Murphy Assoc.
Nadzam, Lusk & Assoc., Inc.
Newell Assoc.
Newpher & Co., Inc.
The Niemond Corp.
Paul Norsell & Assoc., Inc.
Northern Consultants Inc.
Palmer Assoc., Inc.
D.P. Parker & Assoc., Inc.
RIC Corp.
Resource Network Inc.
The Revere Assoc., Inc.
Sydney Reynolds Assoc., Inc.
The Romark Group, Ltd.
SRH Resource Group
Sampson, Neill & Wilkins Inc.
Schweichler Assoc., Inc.
Search Express
M.B. Shattuck & Assoc., Inc.
Daniel A. Silverstein Assoc. Inc.
C.W. Sink & Co., Inc.
Skott/Edwards Consultants
Slayton Int'l., Inc.
S. K. Stewart & Assoc.
Strategic Alternatives
Strategic Search Corp.
Studwell Assoc.
Tarnow Int'l.
Carl J. Taylor & Co.
Taylor Search Assoc., Inc.
Thomas Mangum Co.
Valletta Ritson & Co.
John Velcamp & Assoc.
Venture Management
Venture Resources, Inc.
Verkamp-Joyce Assoc., Inc.
Vista Resource Group
Albert J. Walsh & Assoc.
Wargo & Co., Inc.
Wellington Management Group
Wilkinson & Ives

04.0 RESEARCH & DEVELOPMENT (Cont'd)

William Willis Worldwide, Inc.
Zingaro & Co.

05.0 MARKETING

The Abbott Group
Actuaries & Assoc.
Jeffrey C. Adams & Co., Inc.
Advanced Executive Resources
American Executive Management, Inc.
American Executive Search Services, Inc.
Argus National, Inc.
The Badger Group
Ballantyne & Assoc.
Ballos & Co., Inc.
James Bangert & Assoc., Inc.
J.W. Barleycorn & Assoc.
Nathan Barry Assoc., Inc.
Barton Raben, Inc.
Bason Assoc., Inc.
Battalia Winston Int'l., Inc.
Martin H. Bauman Assoc., Inc.
The Beam Group
Becker, Norton & Co.
Nelson Bell & Partners Inc.
Joy Reed Belt & Assoc., Inc.
Bennett Search & Consulting Co.
Bialla & Assoc., Inc.
BioQuest Inc.
Deborah Bishop & Assoc.
Bishop Assoc.
Blaney Executive Search
Blau Kaptain Schroeder
Boardroom Planning & Consulting Group
John C. Boone & Co.
Bowden & Co., Inc.
The Brand Co., Inc.
Brandywine Consulting Group
Brissenden, McFarland, Wagoner & Fuccella, Inc.
Charles Buck & Assoc., Inc.
Bullis & Co., Inc.
Thomas Burnham Co.
Buzhardt Assoc.
T. Byrnes & Co., Inc.
Byron Leonard Int'l., Inc.
Lee Calhoon & Co., Inc.
Callan Assoc., Ltd.
Canny, Bowen Inc.
Cascadia Group Int'l.
Catalyx Group, Inc.
Cejka & Co.
Chartwell Partners Int'l., Inc.
China Human Resources Group
Christian & Timbers, Inc.
Jack Clarey Assoc., Inc.
Claveloux, McCaffrey, McInerney, Inc.
Clemo, Evans & Co., Inc.
The Communications Search Group
Conard Assoc., Inc.
Joseph Conley & Assoc., Inc.

Conley Assoc., Inc.
Philip Conway Management
Grant Cooper & Assoc., Inc.
Corporate Environment Ltd.
Corporate Staffing Group
The Corrigan Group
Dahl-Morrow Int'l.
Marge Dana Assoc.
Alfred Daniels & Assoc.
Charles E. Day & Assoc., Inc.
DeHayes Consulting Group
DiMarchi Partners
Dieckmann & Assoc., Ltd.
Robert W. Dingman Co., Inc.
Donahue/Bales Assoc.
Dromeshauser Assoc.
Michael S. Dunford, Inc.
Dupuis & Ryden, P.C.
ESP Management Services, Inc.
Effective Search, Inc.
William J. Elam & Assoc.
The Elliott Company
David M. Ellner Assoc.
The Elson Group, Inc.
Erlanger Assoc.
Euromedica USA
Excelsior Services Group Inc.
ExecuCounsel Management Consultants Inc.
Executive Appointments Ltd., Int'l.
Fagan & Co.
Leon A. Farley Assoc.
James Feerst & Assoc., Inc.
Fenwick Partners
Finnegan Assoc.
Fiordalis Assoc., Inc.
Howard Fischer Assoc., Inc.
Fisher Personnel Management Services
Fogec Consultants
Stephen Fox Assoc. Inc.
Foy, Schneid & Daniel, Inc.
Gerald Frisch Assoc., Inc.
Gaffney Management Consultants
W.N. Garbarini & Assoc.
Allan Gardner & Assoc., Inc.
Gardner-Ross Assoc., Inc.
The Gedge Group
Geneva Group Int'l.
N.W. Gibson Int'l.
Gilbert Tweed Assoc., Inc.
Fred J. Goldsmith Assoc.
The Goodrich & Sherwood Co.
B. Goodwin, Ltd.
Robert Graham Assoc., Inc.
Grantham & Co., Inc.
Greger Assoc.
Griffith & Werner, Inc.
Robert Grossberg & Assoc.
Hadley Lockwood, Inc.
Haley Assoc., Inc.
R. C. Handel Assoc. Inc.
W.L. Handler & Assoc.
Handy HRM
Hans & Assoc., Inc.

05.0 MARKETING (Cont'd)

Harreus & Assoc., Inc.
Harris Heery & Assoc., Inc.
Health Industry Consultants, Inc.
Heath/Norton Assoc., Inc.
R. W. Hebel Assoc.
Heffelfinger Assoc., Inc.
The Heidrick Partners, Inc.
Helfer Executive Consultants
Hergenrather & Co.
Hersher Assoc., Ltd.
Higdon, Joys & Mingle, Inc.
The Hindman Co.
Hite Executive Search
Hockett Assoc., Inc.
Hodge-Cronin & Assoc., Inc.
Hogan Assoc.
Holland, McFadzean & Assoc., Inc.
Holohan Group, Ltd.
Robert Howe & Assoc.
Hughes & Assoc., Inc.
The Human Resource Consulting Group, Inc.
Human Resource Research Inc.
Human Resource Services, Inc.
Human Resources, Inc.
William Humphreys & Assoc., Inc.
Hunter Int'l., Inc.
Jack Hurst & Assoc., Inc.
Hutchinson Resources International
The Hyde Group, Inc.
Ingram, Inc.
Innkeeper's Management Corp.
Inside Management Assoc.
The Interface Group, Ltd.
The Interim Management Corp.(IMCOR)
Jeffrey Irving Assoc., Inc.
JM & Co.
Jender & Company
John H. Johnson & Assoc., Inc.
Ronald S. Johnson Assoc., Inc.
Johnson Smith & Knisely Inc.
Jordan-Sitter Assoc.
Inge Judd Assoc.
L. E. Justice Consulting Assoc.
K/N Int'l.
Allan Karson Assoc., Inc.
M. Scott Kemp & Assoc., Inc.
Richard Kinser & Assoc.
Kishbaugh Associates
Jonah Kleinstein Assoc., Inc.
Kline Consulting, Inc.
Koehler & Co.
T. J. Koellhoffer & Assoc.
Koontz, Jeffries & Assoc., Inc.
The J. Kovach Group, Inc.
J. Krauss Assoc.
Kremple & Meade, Inc.
D.A. Kreuter Assoc., Inc.
Paul Kull & Co.
Kunzer Assoc., Ltd.
John Kurosky & Assoc.
L O R Personnel Div.

Marvin Laba & Assoc.
Langer Assoc., Inc.
Lawrence L. Lapham, Inc.
Larson & Stephanian
Lasher Assoc.
Lauer Consulting Services, Inc.
Lauer, Sbarbaro Assoc., Inc.
Lee & Burgess Assoc., Inc.
The Lieberman Group
Locke & Assoc.
The Logan Group, Inc.
H.M. Long Int'l., Ltd.
The John Lucht Consultancy Inc.
The Lumsden Co., Inc.
Lund & Assoc., Inc.
P.J. Lynch Assoc.
MCC Assoc.
META/MAT, Ltd.
M/J/A Partners
Robert Madigan Assoc., Inc.
Maiorino & Weston Assoc., Inc.
F. L. Mannix & Co., Inc.
Marra/Pizzi Assoc., Inc.
J. Martin & Assoc.
Matte & Company, Inc.
Gayle L. Mattson & Assoc.
Mazza & Riley, Inc.
The Mazzitelli Group, Ltd.
McBride Assoc., Inc.
McCormack & Farrow
McManners Assoc., Inc.
James Mead & Co.
Messett Assoc., Inc.
The Neil Michael Group, Inc.
Herbert Mines Assoc., Inc.
Mitchell, Larsen & Zilliacus
Montenido Assoc.
Morgan/Webber
Moriarty/Fox, Inc.
R.C. Morton & Assoc. Inc.
Paul Mueller & Assoc., Inc.
P. J. Murphy & Assoc., Inc.
Robert Murphy Assoc.
Nadzam, Lusk & Assoc., Inc.
The Niemond Corp.
Norman Broadbent Int'l., Inc.
Paul Norsell & Assoc., Inc.
Northern Consultants Inc.
Richard E. Nosky & Assoc.
O'Rourke Co., Inc.
O'Shea, Divine & Co.
Dennis P. O'Toole & Assoc. Inc.
O'Toole & Company
Ober & Company
The Onstott Group
Orion Consulting, Inc.
Overton Group
P.A.R. Assoc., Inc.
Page-Wheatcroft & Co. Ltd.
Palmer Assoc., Inc.
D.P. Parker & Assoc., Inc.
Michael W. Parres & Assoc.
Patton, Perry & Sproull Inc.

05.0 MARKETING (Cont'd)

Peeney Assoc., Inc.
People Management Northeast, Inc.
Perry-D'Amico & Assoc.
Picard & Co., Inc.
Pierce Assoc.
Pierce Assoc.
Rene Plessner Assoc., Inc.
R.L. Plimpton Assoc.
Plummer & Assoc., Inc.
Pocrass Assoc.
David Powell, Inc.
QVS Int'l.
Quaintance Assoc., Inc.
Quinn Bailey & Morgan
RIC Corp.
Rafey & Company
Rand Assoc.
The Rankin Group, Ltd.
Redden & McGrath Assoc., Inc.
Reddick and Co., Int'l.
The Regis Group, Ltd.
The Revere Assoc., Inc.
Ridenour & Assoc.
Rieser & Assoc., Inc.
Roberts Ryan & Bentley
Robertson, Spoerlein & Wengert
Robsham & Assoc.
James Russell, Inc.
James J. Rust Executive Search
SS & A Executive Search Consultants
Saley Partners Int'l.
Sampson, Neill & Wilkins Inc.
Sathe & Assoc., Inc.
F. B. Schmidt Intl.
The Schmitt Tolette Group
Schweichler Assoc., Inc.
Search Express
Seiden Assoc., Inc.
Shaffer Consulting Group
M.B. Shattuck & Assoc., Inc.
Michael Shirley Assoc.
John Sibbald Assoc., Inc.
Sigma Group Inc.
Daniel A. Silverstein Assoc. Inc.
C.W. Sink & Co., Inc.
Robert L. Smith & Co., Inc.
Howard W. Smith Assoc.
A. William Smyth, Inc.
Stanislaw & Assoc., Inc.
Stern & Watson, Inc.
S. K. Stewart & Assoc.
Stone, Murphy & Olson
Strategic Alternatives
Stricker & Zagor
Studwell Assoc.
Sullivan-Murphy Assoc.
Taylor Search Assoc., Inc.
Tech > Mark Group
Theobald & Assoc.
Tierney Assoc., Inc.
Torretto & Assoc., Inc.

Trout & Assoc., Inc.
Michael Tucker Assoc.
Tully & Birch, Inc.
Tuttle, Neidhart, Semyan, Inc.
Universal Executive Search, Inc.
VanMaldegiam Assoc., Inc.
John Velcamp & Assoc.
Venture Management
Venture Resources, Inc.
The Viscusi Group, Inc.
Vista Resource Group
WTW Assoc., Inc.
J.D. Walsh & Co.
Ward Liebelt Assoc. Inc.
Warring & Assoc.
Hilton N. Wasserman & Assoc. Inc.
D. L. Weiss & Assoc.
C. Weiss Assoc., Inc.
Wellington Management Group
Werner Int'l., Inc.
Jude M. Werra & Assoc.
Wesley Brown & Bartle Co., Inc.
K. L. Whitney & Co., Inc.
Wilkinson & Ives
Donald Williams Assoc., Inc.
William Willis Worldwide, Inc.
Duane I. Wilson Assoc., Inc.
S. R. Wolman Assoc., Inc.
Charles Zabriskie Assoc., Inc.
The Zammataro Co.
Zay & Company
Zingaro & Co.
Michael D. Zinn & Assoc., Inc.

05.1 ADVERTISING, SALES PROMOTION

Ballantyne & Assoc.
Bialla & Assoc., Inc.
Bryce, Haultain & Assoc.
Charles Buck & Assoc., Inc.
The Corporate Source Group
Annie Gray Assoc., Inc.
Harreus & Assoc., Inc.
Howard-Sloan Communications Search
William Humphreys & Assoc., Inc.
Inge Judd Assoc.
Marshall Consultants, Inc.
Kirk Palmer & Assoc., Inc.
Rene Plessner Assoc., Inc.
Redden & McGrath Assoc., Inc.
The Repovich - Reynolds Group
F. B. Schmidt Intl.
Tesar-Reynes, Inc.
C. Weiss Assoc., Inc.

05.2 MARKETING STRATEGY & ORGANIZATION

Charles Buck & Assoc., Inc.
Career Plus Executive Search
The Dartmouth Group
FGI
Howard Gilmore & Assoc.

05.2 MARKETING STRATEGY & ORGANIZATION (Cont'd)

The Hamilton Group
Harreus & Assoc., Inc.
Henning & Assoc.
Larkin & Co.
John O'Keefe & Assoc., Inc.
Jim Parham & Assoc., Inc.
Walter Raleigh & Assoc.
The Repovich - Reynolds Group
F. B. Schmidt Intl.
Stewart/Laurence Assoc., Inc.
Stonehill Management Consultants, Inc.
Tesar-Reynes, Inc.
WDI, Int'l.
Albert J. Walsh & Assoc.
C. Weiss Assoc., Inc.

05.3 MARKETING & PRODUCT RESEARCH, CONSUMER MARKETING

A la Carte Int'l., Inc.
J.R. Akin & Co.
Bialla & Assoc., Inc.
Boardroom Planning & Consulting Group
Career Plus Executive Search
Chase-Owens Assoc., Inc.
The Domann Organization
John O'Keefe & Assoc., Inc.
Predictor Systems Corp.
Redden & McGrath Assoc., Inc.
The Repovich - Reynolds Group
Tesar-Reynes, Inc.
C. Weiss Assoc., Inc.

05.4 SALES, SALES MANAGEMENT, SALES TRAINING

A la Carte Int'l., Inc.
Aim Executive Consulting Services
Aubin Int'l. Inc.
Marc-Paul Bloome Ltd.
Boardroom Planning & Consulting Group
Career Plus Executive Search
Chase-Owens Assoc., Inc.
Philip Conway Management
Erwin Assoc.
Geneva Group Int'l.
Howard Gilmore & Assoc.
Gutreuter & Assoc.
Haley Assoc., Inc.
Heath/Norton Assoc., Inc.
Henning & Assoc.
Henry Michaels & Assoc.
Howard-Sloan Communications Search
Melvin Kent & Assoc., Inc.
The Marlow Group
McSherry & Assoc.
James Mead & Co.
Jim Parham & Assoc., Inc.
Parsons Assoc. Inc.
Rene Plessner Assoc., Inc.

Predictor Systems Corp.
Walter Raleigh & Assoc.
Robertson, Spoerlein & Wengert
Michael Tucker Assoc.
The Viscusi Group, Inc.
Albert J. Walsh & Assoc.
Ward Liebelt Assoc. Inc.

05.5 DIRECT MAIL, MARKETING, TELEMARKETING

Barger & Sargeant, Inc.
The Beam Group
Bialla & Assoc., Inc.
Executive Profiles Inc.
Inge Judd Assoc.
Kittleman & Assoc.
John O'Keefe & Assoc., Inc.
Rene Plessner Assoc., Inc.
Redden & McGrath Assoc., Inc.
Robsham & Assoc.
Tesar-Reynes, Inc.
C. Weiss Assoc., Inc.

05.6 CUSTOMER SERVICE

The Beam Group
Business Search America
The Marlow Group

05.7 PUBLIC RELATIONS

The Communications Search Group
Howard-Sloan Communications Search
Arnold Huberman Assoc., Inc.
Marshall Consultants, Inc.
Frank Parillo & Assoc.
The Repovich - Reynolds Group
VideoFields, Ltd.
Wesley Brown & Bartle Co., Inc.

06.0 HUMAN RESOURCE MANAGEMENT

Jeffrey C. Adams & Co., Inc.
J.R. Akin & Co.
Alexander Ross Inc.
Alwyn Assoc., Inc.
American Executive Management, Inc.
The Andre Group, Inc.
BDO Seidman
Babson, Moore & Wilcox
J.W. Barleycorn & Assoc.
Battalia Winston Int'l., Inc.
Martin H. Bauman Assoc., Inc.
The Beam Group
Becker, Norton & Co.
Joy Reed Belt & Assoc., Inc.
Bennett Search & Consulting Co.
Benton Schneider & Assoc.
Bishop Assoc.
John C. Boone & Co.
The Brand Co., Inc.
Charles Buck & Assoc., Inc.
Thomas Burnham Co.
Buzhardt Assoc.

06.0 HUMAN RESOURCE MANAGEMENT (Cont'd)

T. Byrnes & Co., Inc.
Callan Assoc., Ltd.
Canny, Bowen Inc.
Michael J. Cavanaugh & Assoc.
Chanko-Ward, Ltd.
China Human Resources Group
Christopher-Patrick & Assoc.
Jack Clarey Assoc., Inc.
Conard Assoc., Inc.
Conex Inc.
Joseph Conley & Assoc., Inc.
Conley Assoc., Inc.
Grant Cooper & Assoc., Inc.
The Corrigan Group
M.J. Curran & Assoc., Inc.
Curry, Telleri Group, Inc.
DCS Assoc., Inc.
Dieckmann & Assoc., Ltd.
Robert W. Dingman Co., Inc.
Dougan-McKinley-Strain
Dupuis & Ryden, P.C.
ESP Management Services, Inc.
The Elliott Company
Excelsior Services Group Inc.
ExecuCounsel Management Consultants Inc.
Executive Quest
Hill Fallon & Assoc.
George Fee Assoc., Inc.
Fiordalis Assoc., Inc.
First Colorado Consulting Group, Inc.
Fogec Consultants
Stephen Fox Assoc. Inc.
Foy, Schneid & Daniel, Inc.
Gerald Frisch Assoc., Inc.
Gaffney Management Consultants
W.N. Garbarini & Assoc.
Global Resources Group
H. L. Goehring & Assoc., Inc.
Fred J. Goldsmith Assoc.
The Goodrich & Sherwood Co.
Robert Graham Assoc., Inc.
Grantham & Co., Inc.
Griffith & Werner, Inc.
Guidry, East, Barnes & Bono, Inc.
HRD Consultants, Inc.
Hackett & Co.
W.L. Handler & Assoc.
Handy HRM
The Hawkins Co.
Hayden Group, Inc.
R. W. Hebel Assoc.
Hergenrather & Co.
Higdon, Joys & Mingle, Inc.
The Hindman Co.
Hodge-Cronin & Assoc., Inc.
J.B. Homer Assoc. Inc.
Hughes & Assoc., Inc.
The Human Resource Consulting Group, Inc.
Human Resource Services, Inc.
Hunter Int'l., Inc.

The Hyde Group, Inc.
Ingram, Inc.
Innkeeper's Management Corp.
Inside Management Assoc.
The Interface Group, Ltd.
The Interim Management Corp.(IMCOR)
Jeffrey Irving Assoc., Inc.
January Management Group
L.J. Johnson & Co.
Johnson Smith & Knisely Inc.
Jordan-Sitter Assoc.
Inge Judd Assoc.
L. E. Justice Consulting Assoc.
Gary Kaplan & Assoc.
Howard Karr & Assoc., Inc.
Richard Kinser & Assoc.
Kishbaugh Associates
Jonah Kleinstein Assoc., Inc.
Kline Consulting, Inc.
Marvin Laba & Assoc.
Langer Assoc., Inc.
Lauer, Sbarbaro Assoc., Inc.
Lee & Burgess Assoc., Inc.
The Lieberman Group
The Logan Group, Inc.
The John Lucht Consultancy Inc.
The Lumsden Co., Inc.
P.J. Lynch Assoc.
META/MAT, Ltd.
M/J/A Partners
R.J. Maglio & Assoc., Inc.
Maiorino & Weston Assoc., Inc.
Maly & Assoc.
Management Science Assoc.
F. L. Mannix & Co., Inc.
The Martin Group
Gayle L. Mattson & Assoc.
McBride Assoc., Inc.
McDonald Assoc.
McDonald/Long Assoc., Inc.
McManners Assoc., Inc.
Martin H. Meisel Assoc., Inc.
Messett Assoc., Inc.
Michael Assoc.
Herbert Mines Assoc., Inc.
Moriarty/Fox, Inc.
R.C. Morton & Assoc. Inc.
P. J. Murphy & Assoc., Inc.
Robert Murphy Assoc.
NDI Services
Richard E. Nosky & Assoc.
O'Brien & Co., Inc.
O'Callaghan, Honey & Assoc., Inc.
O'Rourke Co., Inc.
Dennis P. O'Toole & Assoc. Inc.
O'Toole & Company
Ober & Company
Orion Consulting, Inc.
Overton Group
P.A.R. Assoc., Inc.
Kirk Palmer & Assoc., Inc.
Jim Parham & Assoc., Inc.
Michael W. Parres & Assoc.

08.0 FINANCE & ACCOUNTING (Cont'd)

J.W. Barleycorn & Assoc.
Nathan Barry Assoc., Inc.
Barton Raben, Inc.
Bason Assoc., Inc.
Martin H. Bauman Assoc., Inc.
The Baxter Group
Becker, Norton & Co.
Nelson Bell & Partners Inc.
Bennett Search & Consulting Co.
Billington & Assoc., Inc.
Bishop Assoc.
The Blackman Kallick Search Division
John C. Boone & Co.
Bowden & Co., Inc.
The Brand Co., Inc.
Brault & Assoc., Ltd.
Bullis & Co., Inc.
Thomas Burnham Co.
Buzhardt Assoc.
T. Byrnes & Co., Inc.
Career Plus Executive Search
Catalyx Group, Inc.
Michael J. Cavanaugh & Assoc.
Cejka & Co.
Chanko-Ward, Ltd.
Chartwell Partners Int'l., Inc.
China Human Resources Group
Jack Clarey Assoc., Inc.
Claveloux, McCaffrey, McInerney, Inc.
Clemo, Evans & Co., Inc.
J. Kevin Coleman & Assoc., Inc.
Conard Assoc., Inc.
Conex Inc.
Joseph Conley & Assoc., Inc.
Conley Assoc., Inc.
Philip Conway Management
Grant Cooper & Assoc., Inc.
Cornell Int'l.
The Corporate Source Group
The Corrigan Group
M.J. Curran & Assoc., Inc.
Dahl-Morrow Int'l.
Marge Dana Assoc.
Alfred Daniels & Assoc.
Charles E. Day & Assoc., Inc.
DeHayes Consulting Group
DiMarchi Partners
Dieckmann & Assoc., Ltd.
Robert W. Dingman Co., Inc.
Donahue/Bales Assoc.
Dougan-McKinley-Strain
Dupuis & Ryden, P.C.
Lynn Dwigans & Co.
Dwyer Consulting Group, Inc.
ESP Management Services, Inc.
Ebbert Assoc.
Effective Search, Inc.
The Elliott Company
David M. Ellner Assoc.
The Elson Group, Inc.

ExecuCounsel Management Consultants Inc.
Executive Appointments Ltd., Int'l.
Hill Fallon & Assoc.
Leon A. Farley Assoc.
George Fee Assoc., Inc.
Finnegan Assoc.
Fiordalis Assoc., Inc.
Fogec Consultants
Foy, Schneid & Daniel, Inc.
Gerald Frisch Assoc., Inc.
The Furman Group, Ltd.
GSW Consulting Group, Inc.
Jay Gaines & Co.
W.N. Garbarini & Assoc.
Allan Gardner & Assoc., Inc.
Garofolo, Curtiss, Lambert & MacLean
Genovese & Co.
N.W. Gibson Int'l.
Fred J. Goldsmith Assoc.
The Goodrich & Sherwood Co.
Robert Graham Assoc., Inc.
Grantham & Co., Inc.
Paul C. Green & Assoc. Ltd.
Greger Assoc.
Griffith & Werner, Inc.
Robert Grossberg & Assoc.
Guidry, East, Barnes & Bono, Inc.
R. C. Handel Assoc. Inc.
Handy HRM
Hans & Assoc., Inc.
The Hawkins Co.
Hayden Group, Inc.
The Heidrick Partners, Inc.
Hersher Assoc., Ltd.
Stanley Herz & Co.
Higdon, Joys & Mingle, Inc.
Hite Executive Search
Hockett Assoc., Inc.
Hodge-Cronin & Assoc., Inc.
Hogan Assoc.
Holland Rusk & Assoc.
J.B. Homer Assoc. Inc.
Robert Howe & Assoc.
The Human Resource Consulting Group, Inc.
Human Resource Services, Inc.
Human Resources, Inc.
Hunter Int'l., Inc.
Jack Hurst & Assoc., Inc.
Hutchinson Resources International
Innkeeper's Management Corp.
Inside Management Assoc.
The Interface Group, Ltd.
Jeffrey Irving Assoc., Inc.
Johnson Smith & Knisely Inc.
K/N Int'l.
Gary Kaplan & Assoc.
Howard Karr & Assoc., Inc.
Kensington Management Consultants, Inc.
Richard Kinser & Assoc.
Jonah Kleinstein Assoc., Inc.
Kline Consulting, Inc.
The J. Kovach Group, Inc.
Kunzer Assoc., Ltd.

08.0 FINANCE & ACCOUNTING (Cont'd)

L O R Personnel Div.
Marvin Laba & Assoc.
Laguzza Assoc., Ltd.
Langer Assoc., Inc.
Lansky Assoc.
Larsen & Lee, Inc.
Lasher Assoc.
Lauer Consulting Services, Inc.
Lauer, Sbarbaro Assoc., Inc.
Lee & Burgess Assoc., Inc.
Locke & Assoc.
The John Lucht Consultancy Inc.
The Lumsden Co., Inc.
P.J. Lynch Assoc.
Lynch Miller Moore, Inc.
MCC Assoc.
META/MAT, Ltd.
M/J/A Partners
Robert Madigan Assoc., Inc.
Maiorino & Weston Assoc., Inc.
F. L. Mannix & Co., Inc.
Marlar Int'l. Inc.
Marra/Pizzi Assoc., Inc.
The Martin Group
Matte & Company, Inc.
Mazza & Riley, Inc.
McBride Assoc., Inc.
McCormack & Farrow
McDonald/Long Assoc., Inc.
Jon McRae & Assoc., Inc.
Martin H. Meisel Assoc., Inc.
Messett Assoc., Inc.
The Neil Michael Group, Inc.
Herbert Mines Assoc., Inc.
Mitchell, Larsen & Zilliacus
Moriarty/Fox, Inc.
Paul Mueller & Assoc., Inc.
P. J. Murphy & Assoc., Inc.
NDI Services
Newell Assoc.
Newpher & Co., Inc.
Norman Broadbent Int'l., Inc.
Paul Norsell & Assoc., Inc.
O'Brien & Co., Inc.
O'Callaghan, Honey & Assoc., Inc.
O'Rourke Co., Inc.
O'Shea, Divine & Co.
Dennis P. O'Toole & Assoc. Inc.
O'Toole & Company
Ober & Company
Robert Olivier & Assoc., Inc.
Ott & Hansen, Inc.
P.A.R. Assoc., Inc.
G.S. Page Inc.
Palmer Assoc., Inc.
Michael W. Parres & Assoc.
Peeney Assoc., Inc.
People Management Northeast, Inc.
Personnel Assoc.
Peterson Consulting/W.P., Inc.

Martin Pierce Inc.
R.L. Plimpton Assoc.
Polson & Co., Inc.
David Powell, Inc.
Quaintance Assoc., Inc.
Quinn Bailey & Morgan
Rafey & Company
Raines Int'l. Inc.
Reddick and Co., Int'l.
E.J. Rhodes Assoc.
Rieser & Assoc., Inc.
Norman Roberts & Assoc., Inc.
Roberts Ryan & Bentley
Robertson, Spoerlein & Wengert
Robsham & Assoc.
James Russell, Inc.
James J. Rust Executive Search
Wilbur M. Sachtjen Assoc., Inc.
Saley Partners Int'l.
The Schmitt Tolette Group
Seiden Assoc., Inc.
John Sibbald Assoc., Inc.
Sievers & Assoc.
Sigma Group Inc.
Skott/Edwards Consultants
Sloane, Sloane & Mayne
Howard W. Smith Assoc.
A. William Smyth, Inc.
Soltis Management Services
Stanislaw & Assoc., Inc.
Lee Stephens & Assoc.
Stern & Watson, Inc.
Stone, Murphy & Olson
Strategic Staffing Concepts, Inc.
Stricker & Zagor
Tarnow Int'l.
Carl J. Taylor & Co.
Theobald & Assoc.
Thomas-Pond
Tierney Assoc., Inc.
Torretto & Assoc., Inc.
Trout & Assoc., Inc.
Universal Executive Search, Inc.
VanMaldegiam Assoc., Inc.
WTW Assoc., Inc.
Ward Howell Int'l. Inc.
Hilton N. Wasserman & Assoc. Inc.
D. L. Weiss & Assoc.
Werner Int'l., Inc.
K. L. Whitney & Co., Inc.
Wilkins & Co.
Donald Williams Assoc., Inc.
William Willis Worldwide, Inc.
Duane I. Wilson Assoc., Inc.
S. R. Wolman Assoc., Inc.
Wood/Sprau/Tannura, Inc.
Youngs & Co.
Charles Zabriskie Assoc., Inc.
The Zammataro Co.
Zay & Company
The Zivic Group, Inc.

08.1 BUDGETING, COST CONTROLS

Lynn Dwigans & Co.
Kittleman & Assoc.
McSherry & Assoc.
A. William Smyth, Inc.

08.2 CASH MANAGEMENT, FINANCING & MANAGEMENT OF FUNDS, PORTFOLIOS

Alwyn Assoc., Inc.
Nelson Bell & Partners Inc.
Bialecki Inc.
Dr. Will G. Bowman, Inc.
Butterfass/Pepe Assoc., Inc.
Lynn Dwigans & Co.
Educational Management Network
Norton & Assoc., Inc.
Phillips Group of Companies
Venture Resources, Inc.
Warring & Assoc.
K. L. Whitney & Co., Inc.
The Whitney Group

08.3 CREDIT & COLLECTION

Lynn Dwigans & Co.
Picard & Co., Inc.

08.4 TAXES

Larsen & Lee, Inc.
Larsen Int'l., Inc.

09.0 INFORMATION TECHNOLOGY

The Abbott Group
Aim Executive Consulting Services
American Executive Search Services, Inc.
Annapolis Consulting Group
Aubin Int'l. Inc.
BDO Seidman
The Badger Group
James Bangert & Assoc., Inc.
Barton Raben, Inc.
The Blackman Kallick Search Division
Blaney Executive Search
Dr. Will G. Bowman, Inc.
Brault & Assoc., Ltd.
Brissenden, McFarland, Wagoner & Fuccella, Inc.
Bullis & Co., Inc.
Byron Leonard Int'l., Inc.
Lee Calhoon & Co., Inc.
Cambridge Group Ltd.-Exec. Search Div.
M.L. Carter & Assoc., Inc.
Cascadia Group Int'l.
Michael J. Cavanaugh & Assoc.
Cejka & Co.
Chanko-Ward, Ltd.
Christian & Timbers, Inc.
Christopher-Patrick & Assoc.
Claveloux, McCaffrey, McInerney, Inc.
The Corporate Source Group

M.J. Curran & Assoc., Inc.
Curry, Telleri Group, Inc.
Dahl-Morrow Int'l.
DiMarchi Partners
Donahue/Bales Assoc.
Dromeshauser Assoc.
Michael S. Dunford, Inc.
William J. Elam & Assoc.
David M. Ellner Assoc.
Executive Appointments Ltd., Int'l.
Fenwick Partners
Fisher Personnel Management Services
Gerald Frisch Assoc., Inc.
Jay Gaines & Co.
W.N. Garbarini & Assoc.
Gardner-Ross Assoc., Inc.
Genovese & Co.
N.W. Gibson Int'l.
A. Davis Grant & Co.
Griffith & Werner, Inc.
Halbrecht Lieberman Assoc., Inc.
The Hamilton Group
W.L. Handler & Assoc.
Handy HRM
Hayden Group, Inc.
Heffelfinger Assoc., Inc.
Henry Michaels & Assoc.
Hergenrather & Co.
Hersher Assoc., Ltd.
Stanley Herz & Co.
Holland, McFadzean & Assoc., Inc.
Holohan Group, Ltd.
J.B. Homer Assoc. Inc.
Human Resources, Inc.
Inside Management Assoc.
Jeffrey Irving Assoc., Inc.
L.J. Johnson & Co.
Johnson Smith & Knisely Inc.
Gary Kaplan & Assoc.
Allan Karson Assoc., Inc.
Kellogg Consulting Group
M. Scott Kemp & Assoc., Inc.
Kensington Management Consultants, Inc.
Kline Consulting, Inc.
Paul Kull & Co.
Marvin Laba & Assoc.
Langer Assoc., Inc.
Lauer, Sbarbaro Assoc., Inc.
The Logan Group, Inc.
The John Lucht Consultancy Inc.
Lynch Miller Moore, Inc.
MCC Assoc.
META/MAT, Ltd.
Robert Madigan Assoc., Inc.
The Marlow Group
Marra/Pizzi Assoc., Inc.
J. Martin & Assoc.
The Martin Group
Robert E. McGrath & Assoc.
McKeen Melancon & Co.
Montenido Assoc.
Morgan/Webber
Nadzam, Lusk & Assoc., Inc.

09.0 INFORMATION TECHNOLOGY (Cont'd)

The Niemond Corp.
Norman Broadbent Int'l., Inc.
Richard E. Nosky & Assoc.
O'Brien & Co., Inc.
O'Callaghan, Honey & Assoc., Inc.
O'Shea, Divine & Co.
The Onstott Group
Ott & Hansen, Inc.
Page-Wheatcroft & Co. Ltd.
Parsons Assoc. Inc.
Peterson Consulting/W.P., Inc.
Pierce Assoc.
Pierce Assoc.
Martin Pierce Inc.
Pocrass Assoc.
Polson & Co., Inc.
David Powell, Inc.
Quinn Bailey & Morgan
Rafey & Company
Raines Int'l. Inc.
Ramsey & Beirne Assoc., Inc.
Norman Roberts & Assoc., Inc.
Roberts Ryan & Bentley
Romeo-Hudgins & Assoc. Ltd.
James J. Rust Executive Search
The Schmitt Tolette Group
Schweichler Assoc., Inc.
Shaffer Consulting Group
Kimball Shaw Assoc.
Michael Shirley Assoc.
Sigma Group Inc.
Skott/Edwards Consultants
Slayton Int'l., Inc.
Robert L. Smith & Co., Inc.
Lee Stephens & Assoc.
S. K. Stewart & Assoc.
Strategic Alternatives
Strategic Staffing Concepts, Inc.
Studwell Assoc.
Synergistics Assoc. Ltd.
Tarnow Int'l.
Carl J. Taylor & Co.
Tech > Mark Group
Thomas Mangum Co.
Thomas-Pond
Trac One
Trout & Assoc., Inc.
Tuttle, Neidhart, Semyan, Inc.
P. T. Unger Assoc.
Venture Resources, Inc.
WTW Assoc., Inc.
Albert J. Walsh & Assoc.
Ward Liebelt Assoc. Inc.
Hilton N. Wasserman & Assoc. Inc.
Weir Executive Search Assoc., Inc.
Wesley Brown & Bartle Co., Inc.
Wilkinson & Ives
Wood/Sprau/Tannura, Inc.
Youngs & Co.

09.1 COMPUTER SECURITY, DISASTER RECOVERY, EDP AUDIT

Annapolis Consulting Group
John J. Davis & Assoc., Inc.
A. Davis Grant & Co.
Marks & Co., Inc.
Weir Executive Search Assoc., Inc.

09.2 SPECIFIC TECHNOLOGIES, E.G. AI, IMAGE, FIBER-OPTICS

Anders Incorporated
Anderson Bradshaw Assoc., Inc.
Corporate Staffing Group
Duggan & Company
Henry Michaels & Assoc.
Human Resource Research Inc.
T. J. Koellhoffer & Assoc.
Peterson Consulting/W.P., Inc.
Pierce Assoc.
Stewart/Laurence Assoc., Inc.
Weir Executive Search Assoc., Inc.
Craig Williamson, Inc.

09.3 SYSTEMS ANALYSIS & DESIGN, DEVELOPMENT, IMPLEMENTATION, TRAINING & SUP

Anderson Bradshaw Assoc., Inc.
John J. Davis & Assoc., Inc.
De Funiak & Edwards
Educational Management Network
A. Davis Grant & Co.
Human Resource Research Inc.
G.S. Page Inc.
Research Alternatives, Inc.
Romeo-Hudgins & Assoc. Ltd.
Schalekamp & Assoc., Inc.
Sullivan & Co.
Synergistics Assoc. Ltd.
Trac One
Weir Executive Search Assoc., Inc.
Craig Williamson, Inc.

09.4 SYSTEMS INTEGRATION, INCLUDING HARDWARE/ SOFTWARE SERVICES, EVALUATION

Chase-Owens Assoc., Inc.
Corporate Staffing Group
John J. Davis & Assoc., Inc.
Jay Gaines & Co.
A. Davis Grant & Co.
T. J. Koellhoffer & Assoc.
G.S. Page Inc.
Romeo-Hudgins & Assoc. Ltd.
Stewart/Laurence Assoc., Inc.
Sullivan & Co.
Synergistics Assoc. Ltd.
Trac One
P. T. Unger Assoc.
James L. Walsh & Assoc., Inc.

09.7 TELECOMMUNICATIONS

Anderson Bradshaw Assoc., Inc.
James Bangert & Assoc., Inc.
Benton Schneider & Assoc.
Bishop Assoc.
Chase-Owens Assoc., Inc.
John J. Davis & Assoc., Inc.
A. Davis Grant & Co.
Gutreuter & Assoc.
Hodge-Cronin & Assoc., Inc.
J.B. Homer Assoc. Inc.
William Humphreys & Assoc., Inc.
K/N Int'l.
Kensington Management Consultants, Inc.
Larkin & Co.
Robert Madigan Assoc., Inc.
The Marlow Group
O'Callaghan, Honey & Assoc., Inc.
Predictor Systems Corp.
P. T. Unger Assoc.
James L. Walsh & Assoc., Inc.
J.D. Walsh & Co.
Wellington Management Group
Craig Williamson, Inc.

10.0 INSURANCE/RISK MANAGEMENT

Actuaries & Assoc.
Babson, Moore & Wilcox
The Beam Group
Benton Schneider & Assoc.
Bowden & Co., Inc.
Lee Calhoon & Co., Inc.
M.L. Carter & Assoc., Inc.
DeHayes Consulting Group
Drew Assoc. Int'l.
William J. Elam & Assoc.
Global Resources Group
Paul C. Green & Assoc. Ltd.
R. C. Handel Assoc. Inc.
Harvard Aimes Group
Howe-Weaver, Inc.
Hunter Int'l., Inc.
Ingram, Inc.
Melvin Kent & Assoc., Inc.
D.A. Kreuter Assoc., Inc.
McDonald/Long Assoc., Inc.
Mitchell/Wolfson, Assoc.
Norman Broadbent Int'l., Inc.
Jim Parham & Assoc., Inc.
Patton, Perry & Sproull Inc.
Peterson Consulting/W.P., Inc.
Martin Pierce Inc.
Roberts Ryan & Bentley
Sathe & Assoc., Inc.
Schalekamp & Assoc., Inc.
The Michael Scott Consulting Co., Inc.
Skott/Edwards Consultants
Stone, Murphy & Olson
Thomas-Pond
Peter Van Leer & Assoc.
Ward Howell Int'l. Inc.

Warring & Assoc.

11.0 SPECIALIZED SERVICES

The Blackman Kallick Search Division
Peter Newell Bowen
Byron Leonard Int'l., Inc.
Caswell/Winters & Assoc., Inc.
Alfred Daniels & Assoc.
The Elliott Company
The Elson Group, Inc.
Excelsior Services Group Inc.
Fox Hill Assoc., Ltd.
Fulton, Longshore & Assoc., Inc.
Garofolo, Curtiss, Lambert & MacLean
The Gedge Group
Gossage Regan Assoc.
Haddad Assoc.
Hans & Assoc., Inc.
Hansen Group, Ltd.
Higdon, Joys & Mingle, Inc.
Hite Executive Search
Hogan Assoc.
Holland Rusk & Assoc.
Houtz, Strawn Assoc.
Ira W. Krinsky & Assoc.
L O R Personnel Div.
Locke & Assoc.
P.J. Lynch Assoc.
MD Resources, Inc.
C.R. Martin & Assoc.
McDonald Assoc.
McNichol Assoc.
Thomas R. Moore Executive Search
W.D. Nolte & Company
Dennis P. O'Toole & Assoc. Inc.
The PAR Group - Paul A. Reaume, Ltd.
The Rankin Group, Ltd.
Norman Roberts & Assoc., Inc.
Kimball Shaw Assoc.
Sievers & Assoc.
C.W. Sink & Co., Inc.
M.H. Springer & Assoc.
Stonehill Management Consultants, Inc.
Thomas-Pond
Venture Resources, Inc.
Duane I. Wilson Assoc., Inc.

11.1 MANAGEMENT CONSULTANTS

Aim Executive Consulting Services
Alexander Ross Inc.
American Group Practice, Inc.
Brault & Assoc., Ltd.
T. Byrnes & Co., Inc.
Chartwell Partners Int'l., Inc.
Conex Inc.
The Corrigan Group
De Funiak & Edwards
Drew Assoc. Int'l.
Jay Gaines & Co.
Allan Gardner & Assoc., Inc.
Howard Gilmore & Assoc.

11.1 MANAGEMENT CONSULTANTS (Cont'd)

Global Resources Group
Haddad Assoc.
The Hamilton Group
Human Resource Technologies, Inc.
The Hyde Group, Inc.
L.J. Johnson & Co.
Inge Judd Assoc.
Kline Consulting, Inc.
Marra/Pizzi Assoc., Inc.
McDonald Assoc.
McFeely Wackerle Shulman
McSherry & Assoc.
Montenido Assoc.
W.D. Nolte & Company
Page-Wheatcroft & Co. Ltd.
Picard & Co., Inc.
Raines Int'l. Inc.
Randell-Heiken, Inc.
Slayton Int'l., Inc.
Stern & Watson, Inc.
Strategic Staffing Concepts, Inc.
Sullivan & Co.
Synergistics Assoc. Ltd.
Carl J. Taylor & Co.
Vista Resource Group
J.D. Walsh & Co.
Youngs & Co.

11.2 MINORITIES

A la Carte Int'l., Inc.
Allerton Heneghan & O'Neill
Auerbach Assoc.
Ballantyne & Assoc.
Belvedere Partners
Dr. Will G. Bowman, Inc.
Brady Assoc. Int'l., Inc.
Butterfass/Pepe Assoc., Inc.
Carpenter, Shackleton & Co.
Christopher-Patrick & Assoc.
Drew Assoc. Int'l.
Educational Management Network
Griffith & Werner, Inc.
The Hawkins Co.
Holland Rusk & Assoc.
The Hollins Group, Inc.
Holohan Group, Ltd.
Human Resource Technologies, Inc.
The Hyde Group, Inc.
Isaacson, Miller, Inc.
Larsen & Lee, Inc.
Newell Assoc.
Raines Int'l. Inc.
The Regis Group, Ltd.
Sydney Reynolds Assoc., Inc.
H.C. Smith Ltd.
Tesar-Reynes, Inc.
Valletta Ritson & Co.
Verkamp-Joyce Assoc., Inc.
The Viscusi Group, Inc.
Ward Howell Int'l. Inc.

Wargo & Co., Inc.
Warring & Assoc.
Wesley Brown & Bartle Co., Inc.
Wojdula & Assoc.
Xagas & Assoc.
The Zivic Group, Inc.

11.3 SCIENTIFIC/TECHNICAL

Anders Incorporated
William B. Arnold Assoc., Inc.
Aubin Int'l. Inc.
Blaney Executive Search
Blendow, Crowley & Oliver, Inc.
The Borton Wallace Co.
Peter Newell Bowen
Dr. Will G. Bowman, Inc.
CSI Inc.
Coelyn Miller Phillip & Assoc.
The Domann Organization
Drew Assoc. Int'l.
Dwyer Consulting Group, Inc.
Euromedica USA
First Colorado Consulting Group, Inc.
Health Industry Consultants, Inc.
Holohan Group, Ltd.
Houtz, Strawn Assoc.
Huff Assoc.
Human Resource Technologies, Inc.
Lund & Assoc., Inc.
Maly & Assoc.
Management Catalysts
Marlar Int'l. Inc.
McKeen Melancon & Co.
D.P. Parker & Assoc., Inc.
Barry Persky & Co., Inc.
QVS Int'l.
Resource Network Inc.
The Revere Assoc., Inc.
Strategic Search Corp.
Taylor Search Assoc., Inc.
James L. Walsh & Assoc., Inc.
Wargo & Co., Inc.
Wellington Management Group
The Zivic Group, Inc.

11.4 FUND-RAISERS & OTHER NON-PROFIT SERVICES

Ast/Bryant
Auerbach Assoc.
Ballantyne & Assoc.
Belvedere Partners
Carpenter, Shackleton & Co.
Development Search Specialists
Drew Assoc. Int'l.
Michael S. Dunford, Inc.
Educational Management Network
Executive Management Systems, Inc.
Fagan & Co.
Garofolo, Curtiss, Lambert & MacLean
Haddad Assoc.
Arnold Huberman Assoc., Inc.
Isaacson, Miller, Inc.

11.4 FUND-RAISERS & OTHER NON-PROFIT SERVICES (Cont'd)

Gary Kaplan & Assoc.
Melvin Kent & Assoc., Inc.
Kittleman & Assoc.
Ira W. Krinsky & Assoc.
The Landmark Consulting Group Inc.
Management Science Assoc.
C.R. Martin & Assoc.
Jon McRae & Assoc., Inc.
E.J. Michaels, Ltd.
Thomas R. Moore Executive Search
P.A.R. Assoc., Inc.
The PAR Group - Paul A. Reaume, Ltd.
Marshall Rice Assoc.
Ridenour & Assoc.
Robert Sellery Assoc., Ltd.
H.C. Smith Ltd.
Tyler & Co.
Wojdula & Assoc.

11.5 ENVIRONMENTAL

Advanced Executive Resources
Anderson Bradshaw Assoc., Inc.
Babson, Moore & Wilcox
The Borton Wallace Co.
Brady Assoc. Int'l., Inc.
Carpenter, Shackleton & Co.
Christopher-Patrick & Assoc.
J. Kevin Coleman & Assoc., Inc.
Robert Connelly & Assoc., Inc.
Corporate Environment Ltd.
Curry, Telleri Group, Inc.
Executive Management Systems, Inc.
Executive Profiles Inc.
George Fee Assoc., Inc.
Fenwick Partners
GSW Consulting Group, Inc.
Allan Gardner & Assoc., Inc.
Haddad Assoc.
Human Resource Technologies, Inc.
Isaacson, Miller, Inc.
John H. Johnson & Assoc., Inc.
Ronald S. Johnson Assoc., Inc.
Melvin Kent & Assoc., Inc.
Jonah Kleinstein Assoc., Inc.

Larkin & Co.
Larsen & Lee, Inc.
Lund & Assoc., Inc.
Maly & Assoc.
The Marlow Group
Matte & Company, Inc.
McNichol Assoc.
The PAR Group - Paul A. Reaume, Ltd.
G.S. Page Inc.
Barry Persky & Co., Inc.
QVS Int'l.
Quaintance Assoc., Inc.
Research Alternatives, Inc.
Sampson, Neill & Wilkins Inc.
Sathe & Assoc., Inc.
Search Express
Soltis Management Services
Wilkins & Co.
Michael D. Zinn & Assoc., Inc.

11.6 ARCHITECTURAL/ ENGINEERING

American Executive Management, Inc.
Anderson Bradshaw Assoc., Inc.
William B. Arnold Assoc., Inc.
Bason Assoc., Inc.
John C. Boone & Co.
Peter Newell Bowen
Carpenter, Shackleton & Co.
Robert Connelly & Assoc., Inc.
Excelsior Services Group Inc.
Executive Profiles Inc.
Geneva Group Int'l.
Heffelfinger Assoc., Inc.
Huff Assoc.
Human Resource Technologies, Inc.
Larsen Int'l., Inc.
Maly & Assoc.
McDonald Assoc.
McNichol Assoc.
R. F. Mulvaney & Assoc., Inc.
Barry Persky & Co., Inc.
The Revere Assoc., Inc.
Sloane, Sloane & Mayne
The Viscusi Group, Inc.
The WalCar Partnership
The Zammataro Co.

Basis of "Industries" Classification

This classification system is based on the U.S. Government's SIC code but has been customized and updated by Kennedy Publications to suit our users' needs.

0.00	**MOST**
A.00	**AGRICULTURE, FORESTRY, FISHING & MINING**
A.01	Specific:
B.00	**ENERGY/UTILITIES**
B.0W	**ENVIRONMENTAL SERVICES**
B.10	Hazardous waste, study, clean up
C.00	**CONSTRUCTION**
D.00	**MANUFACTURING**
D.10	Food, beverage, tobacco & kindred products
D.11	Textile, apparel, related products
D.12	Lumber, wood, furniture & fixtures
D.13	Paper & allied products
D.14	Printing & allied industry
D.15	Chemicals & allied products
D.16	Soap, perfume, cosmetics
D.17	Drugs
D.18	Pharmaceuticals, medical manufacturers
D.19	Plastics, rubber products
D.20	Paints, allied products, petroleum products
D.21	Leather, stone, glass, concrete, clay products
D.22	Primary metal industry, fabricated metal products, machinery, general industrial machinery & appliances
D.23	Transportation equipment including automobiles & other motor vehicles
D.24	Office machinery, computers, computer products, software, electronic & electrical equipment & components
D.25	Measuring/analyzing & controlling instruments & optical goods
D.26	Miscellaneous manufacturing industries

D.D0	**PACKAGING**
D.E0	**AEROSPACE**
D.H0	**HIGH TECH/ELECTRONICS**
D.I0	**BIOTECH/GENETIC ENGINEERING**
E.00	**TRANSPORTATION**
F.00	**WHOLESALE TRADE**
G.00	**RETAIL TRADE**
H.00	**FINANCE**
H.10	Banking, financial institutions, credit agencies
H.11	Securities & commodities brokers
H.12	Venture capital
H.I0	**INSURANCE**
H.R0	**REAL ESTATE**
I.00	**SERVICES**
I.10	Hospitality-including hotels, resorts, clubs, restaurants, food & beverage services
I.11	Entertainment, leisure, amusement, recreation, sports, travel
I.12	Museums, galleries, music/arts, libraries & information services, membership & other non-profits
I.13	Higher Education
I.14	Healthcare (except physicians; see I.15) to include administrators & practitioners-hospitals, nursing/personal care, clinics
I.15	Physicians
I.16	Pharmaceutical (other than manufacturing)
I.17	Legal
I.18	Computer Services
I.19	Accounting & miscellaneous business services
I.20	Equipment services, including leasing
I.21	Management & personnel services
J.00	**COMMUNICATIONS**
J.10	Advertising/public relations
J.11	Publishing, print media
J.12	TV, cable, motion pictures, video, radio
J.13	Telephone, telecommunications
K.00	**PUBLIC ADMINISTRATION/GOVERNMENT**
K.10	Defense
L.00	**NON-CLASSIFIABLE INDUSTRIES**

Retainer Cross-Index by Industries

0.00 MOST

Adams & Assoc. Int'l
Jeffrey C. Adams & Co., Inc.
Aim Executive Consulting Services
Alexander Ross Inc.
Allerton Heneghan & O'Neill
American Executive Search Services, Inc.
Andcor Human Resources
Anderson Bradshaw Assoc., Inc.
The Andre Group, Inc.
Argus National, Inc.
Armitage Assoc.
William B. Arnold Assoc., Inc.
Artgo, Inc.
Ashworth Consultants, Inc.
BDO Seidman
Babson, Moore & Wilcox
Ballos & Co., Inc.
James Bangert & Assoc., Inc.
Barger & Sargeant, Inc.
J.W. Barleycorn & Assoc.
Barnes, Walters & Assoc., Inc.
Bartholdi & Co.
Bason Assoc., Inc.
Battalia Winston Int'l., Inc.
Martin H. Bauman Assoc., Inc.
Beall & Co., Inc.
The Beam Group
Becker, Norton & Co.
Beech Preger & Partners, Ltd.
Richard Beers & Assoc., Ltd.
Joy Reed Belt & Assoc., Inc.
Bennett Search & Consulting Co.
Bertrand, Ross & Assoc., Inc.
Paul J. Biestek Assoc., Inc.
Billington & Assoc., Inc.
Billington, Fox & Ellis, Inc.
The Blackman Kallick Search Division
Blackshaw, Olmstead & Atwood
Blake, Hansen & Nye, Ltd.
Blum & Co.
The Blunt Co., Inc.
Boettcher Assoc.
John C. Boone & Co.
Bowden & Co., Inc.
Boyden Latin America S.A. de C.V.
Boyden World Corp.
The Brand Co., Inc.
Brandywine Consulting Group

Brentwood Int'l.
Bricker & Assoc., Inc.
Brissenden, McFarland, Wagoner & Fuccella, Inc.
Bryce, Haultain & Assoc.
Charles Buck & Assoc., Inc.
Bullis & Co., Inc.
Burke, O'Brien & Bishop Assoc., Inc.
Joseph R. Burns & Assoc., Inc.
Business Search America
Robert Caldwell & Assoc.
The Caldwell Partners Int'l.
Callan Assoc., Ltd.
Cambridge Group Ltd.-Exec. Search Div.
Cambridge Management Planning
Robert Campbell & Assoc.
Canny, Bowen Inc.
Cardwell Group
Carpenter, Shackleton & Co.
Carris, Jackowitz Assoc.
M.L. Carter & Assoc., Inc.
Catalyx Group, Inc.
David Chambers & Assoc., Inc.
Joseph Chandler & Assoc., Inc.
Chase Partners
Chase-Owens Assoc., Inc.
Chestnut Hill Partners, Inc.
Chicago Research Group, Inc.
China Human Resources Group
Christenson & Hutchison
Christian & Timbers, Inc.
Jack Clarey Assoc., Inc.
Claveloux, McCaffrey, McInerney, Inc.
Clemo, Evans & Co., Inc.
Coelyn Miller Phillip & Assoc.
Cole Human Resource Services
Cole, Warren & Long, Inc.
Coleman Lew & Assoc., Inc.
W. Hoyt Colton Assoc., Inc.
Compass Group Ltd.
Computer Professionals
Conard Assoc., Inc.
Conex Inc.
Joseph Conley & Assoc., Inc.
Conley Assoc., Inc.
Conrey Interamericana
Philip Conway Management
The Cooper Executive Search Group, Inc.
Coopers & Lybrand Consulting Group

0.00 MOST (Cont'd)

Coopers & Lybrand, Management Consulting Services
Corporate Environment Ltd.
The Corporate Staff
The Corrigan Group
Edmond J. Corry & Co., Inc.
Counsel Search Co.
The Crosby Group, Inc.
Curran Partners
Curry, Telleri Group, Inc.
The Curtiss Group, Inc.
Peter Cusack & Partners, Inc.
D'Aries Five Enterprises
DHR Int'l., Inc.
Dahl-Morrow Int'l.
Marge Dana Assoc.
John J. Davis & Assoc., Inc.
William N. Davis & Assoc., Inc.
Davis & Company
Charles E. Day & Assoc., Inc.
DeHayes Consulting Group
Deane, Howard & Simon, Inc.
Thorndike Deland Assoc.
Denney & Co., Inc.
Deven Assoc., Int'l., Inc.
DiMarchi Partners
Dieckmann & Assoc., Ltd.
R. J. Dishaw & Assoc.
Diversified Search, Inc.
Donahue/Bales Assoc.
The Duncan Group Inc.
S.R. Dunlap & Assoc., Inc.
C. A. Durakis Assoc., Inc.
Dwyer Consulting Group, Inc.
EFL Assoc.
Earley Kielty & Assoc., Inc.
Bert H. Early Assoc., Inc.
Eastman & Beaudine, Inc.
Bruce Edwards & Associates, Inc.
Effective Search, Inc.
Egan & Assoc.
The Elliott Company
Elliott, Pfisterer, Chinetti Assoc., Inc.
The Elson Group, Inc.
Elwell & Assoc., Inc.
Emmons Assoc., Inc.
George Enns Partners Inc.
Mary R. Erickson & Assoc.
Erlanger Assoc.
Erwin Assoc.
Excelsior Services Group Inc.
ExecuCounsel Management Consultants Inc.
Executive Management Systems, Inc.
Executive Manning Corp.
Executive Search Inc.
Raymond L. Extract & Assoc.
Fagan & Co.
Leon A. Farley Assoc.
James Farris Assoc.
George Fee Assoc., Inc.
First Colorado Consulting Group, Inc.

Howard Fischer Assoc., Inc.
Fogec Consultants
J. H. Folger Company
L.W. Foote Co.
D.E. Foster & Partners, L.P.
Foy, Schneid & Daniel, Inc.
Francis & Assoc.
Gerald Frisch Assoc., Inc.
Gaffney Management Consultants
W.N. Garbarini & Assoc.
Allan Gardner & Assoc., Inc.
Gardner-Ross Assoc., Inc.
Garland Assoc.
Garofolo, Curtiss, Lambert & MacLean
The Gedge Group
Genovese & Co.
Gibson & Co., Inc.
Gilbert & Van Campen Int'l.
Gilbert Tweed Assoc., Inc.
Gleason & Assoc.
Glou Int'l., Inc.
The Gobbell Co.
B. Goodwin, Ltd.
Goss & Assoc., Inc.
Gossage Regan Assoc.
Gould & McCoy, Inc.
Graham & Co.
Robert Graham Assoc., Inc.
Granger, Counts & Assoc.
A. Davis Grant & Co.
Grantham & Co., Inc.
Jack Groban & Assoc.
Grover & Assoc.
William Guy & Assoc., Inc.
HRD Consultants, Inc.
Hackett & Co.
Haddad Assoc.
Halbrecht Lieberman Assoc., Inc.
Halstead & Assoc.
The Halyburton Co., Inc.
R. C. Handel Assoc. Inc.
W.L. Handler & Assoc.
Harvard Aimes Group
Hauft Mark Assoc., Inc.
Hayden Group, Inc.
Hayman & Co.
F. P. Healy & Co., Inc.
Heath/Norton Assoc., Inc.
Heffelfinger Assoc., Inc.
Hegarty & Co.
The Heidrick Partners, Inc.
Heidrick and Struggles, Inc.
G.W. Henn & Co.
Hergenrather & Co.
Stanley Herz & Co.
William Hetzel Assoc., Inc.
Higdon, Joys & Mingle, Inc.
The Hindman Co.
Hite Executive Search
Hockett Assoc., Inc.
Harvey Hohauser & Assoc.
Richard D. Holbrook Assoc.
Holland Rusk & Assoc.

0.00 MOST (Cont'd)

The Hollins Group, Inc.
Holohan Group, Ltd.
Holt Pearson & Caldwell, Inc.
J.B. Homer Assoc. Inc.
R. H. Horton Int'l.
Houze, Shourds & Montgomery, Inc.
Randall Howard & Assoc., Inc.
Robert Howe & Assoc.
Howe, McMahon & Assoc., Inc.
Huff Assoc.
Hughes & Assoc., Inc.
M.J. Hughes Int'l., Inc.
Human Resource Technologies, Inc.
The Human Resource Consulting Group, Inc.
Human Resource Services, Inc.
The Hunt Co.
Hunter Int'l., Inc.
Jack Hurst & Assoc., Inc.
Hutchinson Resources International
Huxtable Assoc., Inc.
Hyde Danforth & Co.
The Hyde Group, Inc.
John Imber Assoc., Ltd.
Ingram, Inc.
Inmark Executive Search
Inside Management Assoc.
The Interim Management Corp.(IMCOR)
International Management Advisors, Inc.
International Management Services Inc.
Jeffrey Irving Assoc., Inc.
JDavid Assoc., Inc.
Jablo Partners
Jahrling & Co.
Jakobs & Assoc. Int'l.
Pendleton James & Assoc., Inc.
James, Layton Int'l., Inc.
January Management Group
John & Powers, Inc.
John H. Johnson & Assoc., Inc.
L.J. Johnson & Co.
Gary Kaplan & Assoc.
Karam Group Int'l.
Howard Karr & Assoc., Inc.
A.T. Kearney Executive Search
M. Scott Kemp & Assoc., Inc.
Kendro & Assoc.
Kennedy & Co.
Kenny, Kindler, Hunt & Howe
Kensington Management Consultants, Inc.
Melvin Kent & Assoc., Inc.
The Kinlin Co., Inc.
Richard Kinser & Assoc.
Kirby & Assoc.
Kishbaugh Associates
Jonah Kleinstein Assoc., Inc.
Kline Consulting, Inc.
Koehler & Co.
Fred Koffler Assoc.
Kolden & Assoc., Ltd.
Korn/Ferry Int'l.
Korn/Ferry, Int'l., S.A. de C.V.

Kors Montgomery Int'l.
J. Krauss Assoc.
Kuehne & Co., Inc.
John Kuhn & Assoc.
Kunzer Assoc., Ltd.
John Kurosky & Assoc.
Lamalie Assoc., Inc.
Langer Assoc., Inc.
Lawrence L. Lapham, Inc.
Larsen & Lee, Inc.
Lasher Assoc.
Michael Latas & Assoc., Inc.
Lauer, Sbarbaro Assoc., Inc.
Lee & Burgess Assoc., Inc.
The Lieberman Group
Locke & Assoc.
J.P. Logan & Co., Inc.
The Logan Group, Inc.
H.M. Long Int'l., Ltd.
Lovejoy & Lovejoy
The John Lucht Consultancy Inc.
The Lumsden Co., Inc.
P.J. Lynch Assoc.
Lynch Miller Moore, Inc.
MCC Assoc.
META/MAT, Ltd.
The Macdonald Group, Inc.
Robert Madigan Assoc., Inc.
The Madison Group
R.J. Maglio & Assoc., Inc.
Maglio & Co., Inc.
Management Advisors of Princeton, Inc.
Management Resources Int'l.
F. L. Mannix & Co., Inc.
Mark Stanley & Co
Marks & Co., Inc.
Marlar Int'l. Inc.
Marling Inc.
Marshall Consultants, Inc.
C.R. Martin & Assoc.
The Martin Group
Martin Mirtz Morice, Inc.
Gayle L. Mattson & Assoc.
Mazza & Riley, Inc.
McBride Assoc., Inc.
McCormack & Farrow
McCullough Assoc.
McDonald/Long Assoc., Inc.
McFeely Wackerle Shulman
McMahon & Dee, Inc.
McManners Assoc., Inc.
McNichol Assoc.
McSherry & Assoc.
Meng, Finseth & Assoc., Inc.
Menzel, Robinson, Baldwin, Inc.
Messett Assoc., Inc.
Million & Assoc., Inc.
Mitchell, Larsen & Zilliacus
Morgan/Webber
Moriarty/Fox, Inc.
Morris & Berger
R.C. Morton & Assoc. Inc.
Edwin Mruk & Partners

0.00 MOST (Cont'd)
Paul Mueller & Assoc., Inc.
R. F. Mulvaney & Assoc., Inc.
Munroe, Curry & Bond Assoc.
P. J. Murphy & Assoc., Inc.
Robert Murphy Assoc.
Nagler & Co., Inc.
Barry Nathanson Assoc.
Newell Assoc.
Newpher & Co., Inc.
Nicholaou & Co.
Nicholson & Assoc., Inc.
W.D. Nolte & Company
Norman Broadbent Int'l., Inc.
Paul Norsell & Assoc., Inc.
Northern Consultants Inc.
Richard E. Nosky & Assoc.
C. J. Noty & Assoc.
Nuessle, Kurdziel & Weiss, Inc.
O'Connor, O'Connor, Lordi, Ltd.
John O'Keefe & Assoc., Inc.
O'Rourke Co., Inc.
O'Shea, Divine & Co.
Dennis P. O'Toole & Assoc. Inc.
O'Toole & Company
Ober & Company
Oberlander & Co., Inc.
The Odessa Group
The Ogdon Partnership
Oliver & Rozner Assoc., Inc.
Organization Resources Inc.
Orion Consulting, Inc.
Robert Ottke Assoc.
Overton Group
P.A.R. Assoc., Inc.
PCD Partners
G.S. Page Inc.
Page-Wheatcroft & Co. Ltd.
John Paisios Ltd.
Parker, Sholl & Gordon, Inc.
Parsons Assoc. Inc.
Pasini & Co.
Patton, Perry & Sproull Inc.
Peat Marwick Stevenson & Kellogg
The Peck Consultancy
Peeney Assoc., Inc.
R. H. Perry & Assoc., Inc.
Perry-D'Amico & Assoc.
Barry Persky & Co., Inc.
Pflueger & Company
Picard & Co., Inc.
Pierce & Assoc., Inc.
Pierce Assoc.
Martin Pierce Inc.
Pinsker & Co., Inc.
R.L. Plimpton Assoc.
Poirier, Hoevel & Co.
David Powell, Inc.
Pre-Search, Inc.
Predictor Systems Corp.
Prior Martech Assoc.
QVS Int'l.

Quaintance Assoc., Inc.
L. J. Quinn & Assoc., Inc.
Quinn Bailey & Morgan
RG International
RIC Corp.
RZL Y Asociados, S.C.
Rafey & Company
Raines Int'l. Inc.
Ramming & Assoc., Inc.
Rand Assoc.
Randell-Heiken, Inc.
Paul Ray & Carre Orban Int'l.
Redden & Assoc.
The Regis Group, Ltd.
D.M. Rein & Co., Inc.
The Repovich - Reynolds Group
Research Alternatives, Inc.
Resources for Management
The Revere Assoc., Inc.
Russell Reynolds Assoc., Inc.
E.J. Rhodes Assoc.
Ridenour & Assoc.
Rieser & Assoc., Inc.
Norman Roberts & Assoc., Inc.
Robertson-Surrette Ltd.
Bruce Robinson Assoc.
Robison & McAulay
Robsham & Assoc.
Rourke, Bourbonnais Assoc., Ltd.
Rurak & Assoc., Inc
Rusher, Loscavio & Lo Presto
Charles Russ Assoc.
Russell, Montgomery & Assoc.
SRH Resource Group
SS & A Executive Search Consultants
Saber Consultants, Inc.
Wilbur M. Sachtjen Assoc., Inc.
Saley Partners Int'l.
Sandhurst Assoc.
Allan Sarn Assoc., Inc.
Sathe & Assoc., Inc.
Schenkel & Company
Schuyler, Frye & Baker, Inc.
Schwab-Carrese Assoc.
The Michael Scott Consulting Co., Inc.
J. Robert Scott
Search Express
Seiden Assoc., Inc.
Robert Sellery Assoc., Ltd.
M.B. Shattuck & Assoc., Inc.
Kimball Shaw Assoc.
Sherbrooke Assoc., Inc.
Michael Shirley Assoc.
Shoemaker & Assoc.
E.L. Shore & Assoc. Corp.
The Shotland Group
John Sibbald Assoc., Inc.
Sievers & Assoc.
Slayton Int'l., Inc.
Sloane, Sloane & Mayne
Stephen R. Smith & Co., Inc.
Robert L. Smith & Co., Inc.
Howard W. Smith Assoc.

0.00 MOST (Cont'd)

Smith, Roth & Squires
Herman Smith Transearch Inc.
Spriggs & Co., Inc.
Stack Assoc.
Staples Consulting Inc.
Staub, Warmbold & Barkauskas, Inc.
Lee Stephens & Assoc.
Stern & Watson, Inc.
Michael Stern Assoc. Inc.
The Stevenson Group/SES
S. K. Stewart & Assoc.
Stewart, Stein & Scott, Ltd.
Stone, Murphy & Olson
Stoneham Assoc.
Stonehill Management Consultants, Inc.
Strategic Staffing Concepts, Inc.
W. R. Strathmann Assoc.
Straube Assoc., Inc.
Stricker & Zagor
Stuart, Wood Inc.
Studwell Assoc.
Sullivan & Co.
Sullivan-Murphy Assoc.
Sweeney Shepherd Bueschel Provus Harbert &
   Mummert, Inc.
Synergistics Assoc. Ltd.
TASA, Inc.
TEMCO - The Executive Mgmt. Cons. Org.
Tanton/Mitchell Group
Tarnow Int'l.
Carl J. Taylor & Co.
Tesar-Reynes, Inc.
Theobald & Assoc.
Thomas Mangum Co.
Thomas, Richardson, Runden & Co. Inc.
Thomas-Pond
Thorne, Brieger Assoc., Inc.
Torretto & Assoc., Inc.
Trac One
Travis & Co., Inc.
Gilles Tremblay & Assoc.
Trout & Assoc., Inc.
Trowbridge & Co., Inc.
Tucker Assoc.
The Thomas Tucker Co.
Tully & Birch, Inc.
Universal Executive Search, Inc.
VanMaldegiam Assoc., Inc.
VanReypen Enterprises, Ltd.
Verkamp-Joyce Assoc., Inc.
Villareal & Assoc., Inc.
Vlcek & Co., Inc.
Albert J. Walsh & Assoc.
J.D. Walsh & Co.
Ward Howell Int'l. Inc.
Hilton N. Wasserman & Assoc. Inc.
Webb, Johnson & Klemmer, Inc.
Weir Executive Search Assoc., Inc.
D. L. Weiss & Assoc.
The Wentworth Co., Inc.
Jude M. Werra & Assoc.

Wesley Brown & Bartle Co., Inc.
Westcott Associates, Inc.
Weston Consultants, Inc.
Wheeler, Moore & Elam Co.
Wilkinson & Ives
Donald Williams Assoc., Inc.
Williams, Roth & Krueger, Inc.
William Willis Worldwide, Inc.
The Winchester Group
Winguth & Company
Wojdula & Assoc.
Wood, Franchot Inc.
Wood-Glavin, Inc.
Wood/Sprau/Tannura, Inc.
Wytmar & Co., Inc.
Yelverton & Co.
Steven Yungerberg Assoc., Inc.
The Zammataro Co.
Zay & Company
Egon Zehnder Int'l. Inc.
Michael D. Zinn & Assoc., Inc.
The Zivic Group, Inc.
Zurick, Davis & Co.

A.00 AGRICULTURE, FORESTRY, FISHING & MINING

Christopher-Patrick & Assoc.
Comann Assoc., Inc.
Gaffney Management Consultants
Holohan Group, Ltd.
Jordan-Sitter Assoc.
D. F. Kerry & Assoc.
Kincannon & Reed
L O R Personnel Div.
Laguzza Assoc., Ltd.
R.C. Morton & Assoc. Inc.
Phillips Group of Companies
SS & A Executive Search Consultants
Vista Resource Group
Wilkinson & Ives
Zay & Company

B.00 ENERGY/UTILITIES

The Abbott Group
Peter W. Ambler Co.
American Executive Management, Inc.
Anderson Bradshaw Assoc., Inc.
Annapolis Consulting Group
Barton Raben, Inc.
Joy Reed Belt & Assoc., Inc.
Brady Assoc. Int'l., Inc.
The Brand Co., Inc.
Brissenden, McFarland, Wagoner & Fuccella,
   Inc.
Cascadia Group Int'l.
Chanko-Ward, Ltd.
Joseph Conley & Assoc., Inc.
Corporate Environment Ltd.
Alfred Daniels & Assoc.
Dougan-McKinley-Strain
The Duncan Group Inc.
Fleming Energy Group

B.00 ENERGY/UTILITIES (Cont'd)

Fogec Consultants
Genovese & Co.
Fred J. Goldsmith Assoc.
The Heidrick Partners, Inc.
Hergenrather & Co.
Holland Rusk & Assoc.
D. F. Kerry & Assoc.
Knapp Consultants
Kors Montgomery Int'l.
Krauthamer & Assoc.
John Kurosky & Assoc.
J. E. Lessner Assoc., Inc.
Locke & Assoc.
Robert Lowell Int'l.
Lund & Assoc., Inc.
Maly & Assoc.
McDonald Assoc.
Robert E. McGrath & Assoc.
Robert Murphy Assoc.
Nadzam, Lusk & Assoc., Inc.
O'Callaghan, Honey & Assoc., Inc.
Robert Ottke Assoc.
D.P. Parker & Assoc., Inc.
Barry Persky & Co., Inc.
R.L. Plimpton Assoc.
Preng & Assoc., Inc.
Quaintance Assoc., Inc.
RIC Corp.
Sydney Reynolds Assoc., Inc.
Sheridan Search
Sigma Group Inc.
Stephens Assoc. Ltd.
Thomas Mangum Co.
Youngs & Co.
Charles Zabriskie Assoc., Inc.

B.0W ENVIRONMENTAL SERVICES

Jeffrey C. Adams & Co., Inc.
American Executive Management, Inc.
Anderson Bradshaw Assoc., Inc.
Annapolis Consulting Group
Babson, Moore & Wilcox
The Bradbury Management Group
Brady Assoc. Int'l., Inc.
Brandywine Consulting Group
Brault & Assoc., Ltd.
Bryce, Haultain & Assoc.
Canny, Bowen Inc.
Career Plus Executive Search
Christian & Timbers, Inc.
Claveloux, McCaffrey, McInerney, Inc.
J. Kevin Coleman & Assoc., Inc.
Robert Connelly & Assoc., Inc.
Corporate Environment Ltd.
Marge Dana Assoc.
Dougan-McKinley-Strain
George Fee Assoc., Inc.
Fenwick Partners
Fleming Energy Group
GSW Consulting Group, Inc.
Genovese & Co.

Grover & Assoc.
Haddad Assoc.
Handy HRM
Hauft Mark Assoc., Inc.
Helfer Executive Consultants
Hite Executive Search
Hutchinson Resources International
Inside Management Assoc.
Isaacson, Miller, Inc.
Jender & Company
Ronald S. Johnson Assoc., Inc.
Inge Judd Assoc.
Kellogg Consulting Group
Melvin Kent & Assoc., Inc.
D. F. Kerry & Assoc.
Jonah Kleinstein Assoc., Inc.
Paul Kull & Co.
Larkin & Co.
Lauer Consulting Services, Inc.
Lee & Burgess Assoc., Inc.
Lund & Assoc., Inc.
The Madison Group
Maly & Assoc.
Marlar Int'l. Inc.
The Marlow Group
George R. Martin
Bruce Massey & Partners Inc.
Matte & Company, Inc.
McNichol Assoc.
Robert Murphy Assoc.
Ober & Company
G.S. Page Inc.
D.P. Parker & Assoc., Inc.
Barry Persky & Co., Inc.
Preng & Assoc., Inc.
QVS Int'l.
Quaintance Assoc., Inc.
Reddick and Co., Int'l.
Resource Network Inc.
Sathe & Assoc., Inc.
Search Express
Sloane, Sloane & Mayne
Soltis Management Services
Splaine & Assoc., Inc.
Stephens Assoc. Ltd.
Studwell Assoc.
Thomas Mangum Co.
Torretto & Assoc., Inc.
P. T. Unger Assoc.
Ward Howell Int'l. Inc.
Western Reserve Search Assoc.
Wilkins & Co.
Michael D. Zinn & Assoc., Inc.

B.10 HAZARDOUS WASTE, STUDY, CLEAN UP

A la Carte Int'l., Inc.
Robert Connelly & Assoc., Inc.
The Halyburton Co., Inc.
Johnson & Assoc., Inc.
Lauer Consulting Services, Inc.
Maly & Assoc.

B.10 HAZARDOUS WASTE, STUDY, CLEAN UP (Cont'd)

McCooe & Assoc., Inc.
McNichol Assoc.
Barry Persky & Co., Inc.
Search Express
Sloane, Sloane & Mayne

C.00 CONSTRUCTION

American Executive Management, Inc.
Anderson Bradshaw Assoc., Inc.
Barton Sans Int'l.
Becker, Norton & Co.
Joy Reed Belt & Assoc., Inc.
The Berman Consulting Group
F.J. Bruckner & Co.
T. Byrnes & Co., Inc.
Christopher-Patrick & Assoc.
J. Kevin Coleman & Assoc., Inc.
Robert Connelly & Assoc., Inc.
Dougan-McKinley-Strain
Dupuis & Ryden, P.C.
Haddad Assoc.
The Halyburton Co., Inc.
Helfer Executive Consultants
The Hindman Co.
Hodge-Cronin & Assoc., Inc.
Holland Rusk & Assoc.
Hyman, Mackenzie & Partners, Inc.
James, Layton Int'l., Inc.
John H. Johnson & Assoc., Inc.
Jordan-Sitter Assoc.
The J. Kovach Group, Inc.
Larsen Int'l., Inc.
Michael Latas & Assoc., Inc.
Locke & Assoc.
Lund & Assoc., Inc.
Lynch & Co.
Maly & Assoc.
McDonald Assoc.
McNichol Assoc.
Nadzam, Lusk & Assoc., Inc.
Ott & Hansen, Inc.
Barry Persky & Co., Inc.
Preng & Assoc., Inc.
John Sibbald Assoc., Inc.
Lee Stephens & Assoc.
Tech > Mark Group
Western Reserve Search Assoc.
Zay & Company

D.00 MANUFACTURING

The Abbott Group
Jeffrey C. Adams & Co., Inc.
The Advisory Group, Inc.
Aim Executive Consulting Services
Peter W. Ambler Co.
American Executive Search Services, Inc.
American Executive Management, Inc.
Ames & Ames
Annapolis Consulting Group
Argus National, Inc.

Babson, Moore & Wilcox
Ballos & Co., Inc.
James Bangert & Assoc., Inc.
Barger & Sargeant, Inc.
J.W. Barleycorn & Assoc.
Barnes, Walters & Assoc., Inc.
Barton Raben, Inc.
Martin H. Bauman Assoc., Inc.
The Beam Group
Joy Reed Belt & Assoc., Inc.
The Blackman Kallick Search Division
Blanchard, Zufall & Assoc.
Blendow & Johnson Inc.
The Blunt Co., Inc.
John C. Boone & Co.
The Borton Wallace Co.
Bowden & Co., Inc.
The Bradbury Management Group
The Brand Co., Inc.
Brentwood Int'l.
Brissenden, McFarland, Wagoner & Fuccella, Inc.
Bryce, Haultain & Assoc.
Bullis & Co., Inc.
Buzhardt Assoc.
T. Byrnes & Co., Inc.
Byron Leonard Int'l., Inc.
Career Plus Executive Search
Cascadia Group Int'l.
Chandler & Rozner Assoc.
Jack Clarey Assoc., Inc.
Claveloux, McCaffrey, McInerney, Inc.
J. Kevin Coleman & Assoc., Inc.
Joseph Conley & Assoc., Inc.
Walter V. Connor Int'l., Inc.
Grant Cooper & Assoc., Inc.
Coopers & Lybrand, Management Consulting Services
Corporate Environment Ltd.
Crowder & Company
M.J. Curran & Assoc., Inc.
Curry, Telleri Group, Inc.
Marge Dana Assoc.
Charles E. Day & Assoc., Inc.
DeHayes Consulting Group
Deane, Howard & Simon, Inc.
DiMarchi Partners
Dieckmann & Assoc., Ltd.
Robert W. Dingman Co., Inc.
Donahue/Bales Assoc.
Michael S. Dunford, Inc.
Dupuis & Ryden, P.C.
Lynn Dwigans & Co.
Ebbert Assoc.
Effective Search, Inc.
The Elliott Company
David M. Ellner Assoc.
The Elson Group, Inc.
Erlanger Assoc.
Executive Appointments Ltd., Int'l.
Executive Resource Group
Fagan & Co.
Hill Fallon & Assoc.

D.00 MANUFACTURING (Cont'd)

George Fee Assoc., Inc.
First Colorado Consulting Group, Inc.
Fogec Consultants
Stephen Fox Assoc. Inc.
GSW Consulting Group, Inc.
Gaffney Management Consultants
W.N. Garbarini & Assoc.
Allan Gardner & Assoc., Inc.
Gardner-Ross Assoc., Inc.
N.W. Gibson Int'l.
Gilbert Tweed Assoc., Inc.
Glou Int'l., Inc.
Fred J. Goldsmith Assoc.
The Goodrich & Sherwood Co.
B. Goodwin, Ltd.
Gordon/Tyler
Gould & McCoy, Inc.
Grantham & Co., Inc.
Robert Grossberg & Assoc.
R. C. Handel Assoc. Inc.
W.L. Handler & Assoc.
Hans & Assoc., Inc.
Hansen Management Search Co.
Harris Heery & Assoc., Inc.
Hauft Mark Assoc., Inc.
Heath/Norton Assoc., Inc.
The Heidrick Partners, Inc.
Helfer Executive Consultants
Hergenrather & Co.
The Hindman Co.
Hite Executive Search
Hodge-Cronin & Assoc., Inc.
Harvey Hohauser & Assoc.
Holland Rusk & Assoc.
J.B. Homer Assoc. Inc.
William C. Houze & Co.
Huff Assoc.
The Human Resource Consulting Group, Inc.
Human Resources, Inc.
Hunter Int'l., Inc.
Jack Hurst & Assoc., Inc.
Hutchinson Resources International
Ingram, Inc.
Jeffrey Irving Assoc., Inc.
Michael James & Co., Inc.
January Management Group
Jender & Company
John H. Johnson & Assoc., Inc.
L.J. Johnson & Co.
Ronald S. Johnson Assoc., Inc.
L. E. Justice Consulting Assoc.
Gary Kaplan & Assoc.
Kellogg Consulting Group
M. Scott Kemp & Assoc., Inc.
Jonah Kleinstein Assoc., Inc.
Kline Consulting, Inc.
Knapp Consultants
Koehler & Co.
Koontz, Jeffries & Assoc., Inc.
J. Krauss Assoc.
Krauthamer & Assoc.

Paul Kull & Co.
Kunzer Assoc., Ltd.
John Kurosky & Assoc.
L O R Personnel Div.
Marvin Laba & Assoc.
Langer Assoc., Inc.
Lawrence L. Lapham, Inc.
Lasher Assoc.
Michael Latas & Assoc., Inc.
Lauer, Sbarbaro Assoc., Inc.
Lee & Burgess Assoc., Inc.
J. E. Lessner Assoc., Inc.
Locke & Assoc.
The Lockridge Group, Inc.
The Logan Group, Inc.
Robert Lowell Int'l.
The John Lucht Consultancy Inc.
The Lumsden Co., Inc.
Lund & Assoc., Inc.
Lynch Miller Moore, Inc.
MCC Assoc.
META/MAT, Ltd.
The Macdonald Group, Inc.
Robert Madigan Assoc., Inc.
Maiorino & Weston Assoc., Inc.
Marlar Int'l. Inc.
Marra/Pizzi Assoc., Inc.
George R. Martin
Martin Mirtz Morice, Inc.
Maschal/Connors Inc.
Bruce Massey & Partners Inc.
Matte & Company, Inc.
Gayle L. Mattson & Assoc.
The Mazzitelli Group, Ltd.
McBride Assoc., Inc.
McCormack & Farrow
McCullough Assoc.
McDonald Assoc.
McDonald/Long Assoc., Inc.
McKeen Melancon & Co.
McManners Assoc., Inc.
Meder & Assoc.
Michael Assoc.
The Neil Michael Group, Inc.
Moriarty/Fox, Inc.
R.C. Morton & Assoc. Inc.
Paul Mueller & Assoc., Inc.
Robert Murphy Assoc.
Nadzam, Lusk & Assoc., Inc.
The Niemond Corp.
Paul Norsell & Assoc., Inc.
Richard E. Nosky & Assoc.
O'Toole & Company
Ober & Company
Oliver & Rozner Assoc., Inc.
Ott & Hansen, Inc.
Overton Group
P.A.R. Assoc., Inc.
Michael W. Parres & Assoc.
Peeney Assoc., Inc.
People Management Northeast, Inc.
Pierce Assoc.
Pinsker & Co., Inc.

D.00 MANUFACTURING (Cont'd)

R.L. Plimpton Assoc.
Plummer & Assoc., Inc.
Polson & Co., Inc.
David Powell, Inc.
Preng & Assoc., Inc.
Quinn Bailey & Morgan
RIC Corp.
Walter Raleigh & Assoc.
Ramsey & Beirne Assoc., Inc.
Rand Assoc.
Redden & Assoc.
Redden & McGrath Assoc., Inc.
The Regis Group, Ltd.
Resource Network Inc.
Sydney Reynolds Assoc., Inc.
Robertson, Spoerlein & Wengert
Robsham & Assoc.
Saley Partners Int'l.
Allan Sarn Assoc., Inc.
Sathe & Assoc., Inc.
F. B. Schmidt Intl.
Schweichler Assoc., Inc.
J. Robert Scott
Search Express
M.B. Shattuck & Assoc., Inc.
Kimball Shaw Assoc.
Shoemaker & Assoc.
John Sibbald Assoc., Inc.
Sigma Group Inc.
C.W. Sink & Co., Inc.
Skott/Edwards Consultants
Slayton Int'l., Inc.
Sloane, Sloane & Mayne
Robert L. Smith & Co., Inc.
Smith, Goerss & Ferneborg, Inc.
Soltis Management Services
Spriggs & Co., Inc.
Stanislaw & Assoc., Inc.
Staples Consulting Inc.
S. K. Stewart & Assoc.
Stone, Murphy & Olson
Stricker & Zagor
Theobald & Assoc.
Thomas Mangum Co.
Tierney Assoc., Inc.
Tirocchi, Wright, Inc.
Torretto & Assoc., Inc.
Trout & Assoc., Inc.
Tucker Assoc.
The Thomas Tucker Co.
K. W. Tunnell Co., Inc.
Valletta Ritson & Co.
VanMaldegiam Assoc., Inc.
Verkamp-Joyce Assoc., Inc.
Vista Resource Group
Vlcek & Co., Inc.
WTW Assoc., Inc.
Albert J. Walsh & Assoc.
Ward Howell Int'l. Inc.
Wargo & Co., Inc.
Weber Executive Search

Werner Int'l., Inc.
Duane I. Wilson Assoc., Inc.
Youngs & Co.
Charles Zabriskie Assoc., Inc.
Zay & Company
Michael D. Zinn & Assoc., Inc.
Zurick, Davis & Co.

D.10 FOOD, BEVERAGE, TOBACCO & KINDRED PRODUCTS

A la Carte Int'l., Inc.
Ballantyne & Assoc.
Ballos & Co., Inc.
Battalia Winston Int'l., Inc.
Bialla & Assoc., Inc.
Blau Kaptain Schroeder
Chase-Owens Assoc., Inc.
Christian & Timbers, Inc.
Joseph Conley & Assoc., Inc.
Lynn Dwigans & Co.
Dwyer Consulting Group, Inc.
Executive Appointments Ltd., Int'l.
Gardiner Stone Hunter Int'l., Inc.
Fred J. Goldsmith Assoc.
The Goodrich & Sherwood Co.
Gordon/Tyler
Annie Gray Assoc., Inc.
Griffith & Werner, Inc.
Harreus & Assoc., Inc.
Henning & Assoc.
Johnson Smith & Knisely Inc.
L. E. Justice Consulting Assoc.
Martin Kartin & Co., Inc.
Kincannon & Reed
Langer Assoc., Inc.
H.M. Long Int'l., Ltd.
Management Catalysts
James Mead & Co.
Meder & Assoc.
Herbert Mines Assoc., Inc.
Moriarty/Fox, Inc.
The Mulshine Co., Inc.
Parsons Assoc. Inc.
Raines Int'l. Inc.
Reddick and Co., Int'l.
Rieser & Assoc., Inc.
The Romark Group, Ltd.
SRH Resource Group
F. B. Schmidt Intl.
Shoemaker & Assoc.
Skott/Edwards Consultants
Smith Search, S.A.
Spriggs & Co., Inc.
Strategic Search Corp.
Travis & Co., Inc.
Tuttle, Neidhart, Semyan, Inc.
Verkamp-Joyce Assoc., Inc.
Vlcek & Co., Inc.
Ward Liebelt Assoc. Inc.
Jude M. Werra & Assoc.
Wilkins & Co.
Wilkinson & Ives

D.10 FOOD, BEVERAGE, TOBACCO & KINDRED PRODUCTS (Cont'd)

William Willis Worldwide, Inc.
S. R. Wolman Assoc., Inc.
The Zammataro Co.

D.11 TEXTILE, APPAREL, RELATED PRODUCTS

BDO Seidman
Boardroom Planning & Consulting Group
Colton Bernard Inc.
Robert Howe & Assoc.
Jim Just & Assoc.
L. E. Justice Consulting Assoc.
Martin Kartin & Co., Inc.
Robert E. McGrath & Assoc.
James Mead & Co.
Herbert Mines Assoc., Inc.
Kirk Palmer & Assoc., Inc.
Seitchik, Corwin & Seitchik Inc.
The Viscusi Group, Inc.
Werner Int'l., Inc.

D.12 LUMBER, WOOD, FURNITURE & FIXTURES

Advanced Executive Resources
Ariail & Assoc.
Boardroom Planning & Consulting Group
The Halyburton Co., Inc.
Hyman, Mackenzie & Partners, Inc.
Jim Just & Assoc.
L. E. Justice Consulting Assoc.
John Kuhn & Assoc.
McCooe & Assoc., Inc.
Newell Assoc.
Parsons Assoc. Inc.
Sockwell & Anderson

D.13 PAPER & ALLIED PRODUCTS

BDO Seidman
Ballos & Co., Inc.
Battalia Winston Int'l., Inc.
Bennett Search & Consulting Co.
Blendow, Crowley & Oliver, Inc.
Boardroom Planning & Consulting Group
The Borton Wallace Co.
Brandywine Consulting Group
JM & Co.
T. J. Koellhoffer & Assoc.
John Kuhn & Assoc.
H.M. Long Int'l., Ltd.
The Mazzitelli Group, Ltd.
McCooe & Assoc., Inc.
Robert E. McGrath & Assoc.
James Mead & Co.
O'Rourke Co., Inc.
QVS Int'l.
The Revere Assoc., Inc.
The Zammataro Co.

D.14 PRINTING & ALLIED INDUSTRY

D E G Co., Inc.
Farrell & Phin, Inc.
H. L. Goehring & Assoc., Inc.
Robert Grossberg & Assoc.
The Halyburton Co., Inc.
JM & Co.
Kremple & Meade, Inc.
The Mazzitelli Group, Ltd.
Parsons Assoc. Inc.
QVS Int'l.
Sockwell & Anderson
Spriggs & Co., Inc.
Stewart/Laurence Assoc., Inc.
D. L. Weiss & Assoc.

D.15 CHEMICALS & ALLIED PRODUCTS

Aubin Int'l. Inc.
Baldwin Associates, Inc.
Ballos & Co., Inc.
The Borton Wallace Co.
Peter Newell Bowen
Brandywine Consulting Group
Curry, Telleri Group, Inc.
Dougan-McKinley-Strain
Empire International
Stephen Fox Assoc. Inc.
Gardiner Stone Hunter Int'l., Inc.
The Gedge Group
Gilbert Tweed Assoc., Inc.
Howard Gilmore & Assoc.
Grover & Assoc.
Holohan Group, Ltd.
Robert Howe & Assoc.
JM & Co.
James, Layton Int'l., Inc.
Kincannon & Reed
Kors Montgomery Int'l.
Levin & Assoc.
Management Catalysts
George R. Martin
McCooe & Assoc., Inc.
Robert E. McGrath & Assoc.
The Mulshine Co., Inc.
D.P. Parker & Assoc., Inc.
Pierce Assoc.
Reese Assoc.
The Revere Assoc., Inc.
Rieser & Assoc., Inc.
SRH Resource Group
Spriggs & Co., Inc.
Strategic Search Corp.
Studwell Assoc.
Travis & Co., Inc.
Wellington Management Group
Wilkins & Co.
The Zammataro Co.

D.16 SOAP, PERFUME, COSMETICS

Ballantyne & Assoc.
Bialla & Assoc., Inc.

D.16 SOAP, PERFUME, COSMETICS (Cont'd)

The Dartmouth Group
Gordon/Tyler
Harreus & Assoc., Inc.
Martin Kartin & Co., Inc.
Management Catalysts
James Mead & Co.
Herbert Mines Assoc., Inc.
The Mulshine Co., Inc.
The Romark Group, Ltd.
SRH Resource Group
F. B. Schmidt Intl.
A. William Smyth, Inc.
Verkamp-Joyce Assoc., Inc.
Ward Liebelt Assoc. Inc.
William Willis Worldwide, Inc.
S. R. Wolman Assoc., Inc.

D.17 DRUGS

Nathan Barry Assoc., Inc.
BioQuest Inc.
Blau Kaptain Schroeder
Blendow, Crowley & Oliver, Inc.
L.L. Carey & Assoc., Inc.
Catalyx Group, Inc.
The Dartmouth Group
The Domann Organization
Euromedica USA
James Feerst & Assoc., Inc.
Hartman, Barnette & Assoc.
R. W. Hebel Assoc.
Holohan Group, Ltd.
Kirkman & Searing
Larson & Stephanian
Levin & Assoc.
Palmer Assoc., Inc.
Perry-D'Amico & Assoc.
The Romark Group, Ltd.
F. B. Schmidt Intl.
Daniel A. Silverstein Assoc. Inc.
Skott/Edwards Consultants
Travis & Co., Inc.
Michael Tucker Assoc.
Voigt Assoc.
Wellington Management Group
Zingaro & Co.

D.18 PHARMACEUTICALS, MEDICAL MANUFACTURERS

The Advisory Group, Inc.
Ames & Ames
Ballantyne & Assoc.
Ballos & Co., Inc.
Nathan Barry Assoc., Inc.
Battalia Winston Int'l., Inc.
BioQuest Inc.
Blau Kaptain Schroeder
Blendow, Crowley & Oliver, Inc.
Brandywine Consulting Group
Butterfass/Pepe Assoc., Inc.
CanMed Consultants Inc.

L.L. Carey & Assoc., Inc.
Catalyx Group, Inc.
Cejka & Co.
Christian & Timbers, Inc.
Claveloux, McCaffrey, McInerney, Inc.
The Corporate Source Group
Curry, Telleri Group, Inc.
DCS Assoc., Inc.
The Dartmouth Group
The Domann Organization
Dwyer Consulting Group, Inc.
William J. Elam & Assoc.
Euromedica USA
Executive Appointments Ltd., Int'l.
James Feerst & Assoc., Inc.
The Gedge Group
Gordon/Tyler
Griffith & Werner, Inc.
Grover & Assoc.
Hartman, Barnette & Assoc.
Health Industry Consultants, Inc.
R. W. Hebel Assoc.
Hockett Assoc., Inc.
Holohan Group, Ltd.
Houtz, Strawn Assoc.
Human Resource Research Inc.
Hunter Int'l., Inc.
James, Layton Int'l., Inc.
Martin Kartin & Co., Inc.
John Kuhn & Assoc.
Langer Assoc., Inc.
Larson & Stephanian
Levin & Assoc.
H.M. Long Int'l., Ltd.
MCC Assoc.
Management Catalysts
George R. Martin
The Mazzitelli Group, Ltd.
McBride Assoc., Inc.
Robert E. McGrath & Assoc.
Mercedes & Co., Inc.
The Mulshine Co., Inc.
Norman Broadbent Int'l., Inc.
Robert Ottke Assoc.
Palmer Assoc., Inc.
Phillips Group of Companies
Sydney Reynolds Assoc., Inc.
Rieser & Assoc., Inc.
The Romark Group, Ltd.
Romeo-Hudgins & Assoc. Ltd.
SRH Resource Group
Sampson, Neill & Wilkins Inc.
Daniel A. Silverstein Assoc. Inc.
Smith, Goerss & Ferneborg, Inc.
Strategic Search Corp.
Travis & Co., Inc.
Michael Tucker Assoc.
Verkamp-Joyce Assoc., Inc.
Voigt Assoc.
WDI, Int'l.
Wellington Management Group
Wilkins & Co.
William Willis Worldwide, Inc.

D.18 PHARMACEUTICALS, MEDICAL MANUFACTURERS (Cont'd)
Richard Winn & Co.
S. R. Wolman Assoc., Inc.
Xagas & Assoc.
Zingaro & Co.

D.19 PLASTICS, RUBBER PRODUCTS
Claveloux, McCaffrey, McInerney, Inc.
Stephen Fox Assoc. Inc.
The Gedge Group
Howard Gilmore & Assoc.
Grover & Assoc.
Hogan Assoc.
JM & Co.
James, Layton Int'l., Inc.
L. E. Justice Consulting Assoc.
John Kuhn & Assoc.
Lauer Consulting Services, Inc.
F. L. Mannix & Co., Inc.
Morgan/Webber
Robert Ottke Assoc.
Parsons Assoc. Inc.
Pierce Assoc.
The Revere Assoc., Inc.
Stanislaw & Assoc., Inc.
Strategic Search Corp.
Studwell Assoc.
Ward Liebelt Assoc. Inc.
Duane I. Wilson Assoc., Inc.
Xagas & Assoc.

D.20 PAINTS, ALLIED PRODUCTS, PETROLEUM PRODUCTS
The Borton Wallace Co.
Curry, Telleri Group, Inc.
Dwyer Consulting Group, Inc.
Empire International
The Gedge Group
Grover & Assoc.
Robert Ottke Assoc.

D.21 LEATHER, STONE, GLASS, CONCRETE, CLAY PRODUCTS
Empire International
Jim Just & Assoc.
John Kuhn & Assoc.
McCooe & Assoc., Inc.
Werner Int'l., Inc.

D.22 PRIMARY METAL INDUSTRY, FABRICATED METAL PRODUCTS, MACHINERY, GENERAL
Aim Executive Consulting Services
Becker, Norton & Co.
Bennett Search & Consulting Co.
Marc-Paul Bloome Ltd.
The Blunt Co., Inc.
Compass Group Ltd.

Joseph Conley & Assoc., Inc.
Effective Search, Inc.
Fisher Personnel Management Services
Howard Gilmore & Assoc.
H. L. Goehring & Assoc., Inc.
Robert Grossberg & Assoc.
Hogan Assoc.
Human Resources, Inc.
Jordan-Sitter Assoc.
D. F. Kerry & Assoc.
Maschal/Connors Inc.
Gayle L. Mattson & Assoc.
Morgan/Webber
O'Brien & Co., Inc.
Michael W. Parres & Assoc.
Parsons Assoc. Inc.
Peeney Assoc., Inc.
Phillips Group of Companies
Pierce Assoc.
Reese Assoc.
Robertson, Spoerlein & Wengert
Slayton Int'l., Inc.
Smith Search, S.A.
Spriggs & Co., Inc.
Tierney Assoc., Inc.
Jude M. Werra & Assoc.
Duane I. Wilson Assoc., Inc.
Xagas & Assoc.
The Zammataro Co.

D.23 TRANSPORTATION EQUIPMENT INCLUDING AUTOMOBILES & OTHER MOTOR VEHICLES
The Blunt Co., Inc.
Bowker, Brown & Co.
Compass Group Ltd.
Charles E. Day & Assoc., Inc.
William J. Elam & Assoc.
Fisher Personnel Management Services
Hansen Group, Ltd.
Hogan Assoc.
Jordan-Sitter Assoc.
Maschal/Connors Inc.
O'Brien & Co., Inc.
Michael W. Parres & Assoc.
Peeney Assoc., Inc.
Slayton Int'l., Inc.
Studwell Assoc.
D. L. Weiss & Assoc.
Jude M. Werra & Assoc.
Duane I. Wilson Assoc., Inc.
Xagas & Assoc.

D.24 OFFICE MACHINERY, COMPUTERS, COMPUTER PRODUCTS, SOFTWARE, ELECTRONIC &
The Advisory Group, Inc.
The Badger Group
Baldwin Associates, Inc.
Ballantyne & Assoc.

D.24 OFFICE MACHINERY, COMPUTERS, COMPUTER PRODUCTS, SOFTWARE, ELECTRONIC & (Cont'd)

Battalia Winston Int'l., Inc.
Bennett Search & Consulting Co.
The Berman Consulting Group
Blaney Executive Search
Boardroom Planning & Consulting Group
Michael J. Cavanaugh & Assoc.
Chase-Owens Assoc., Inc.
Christian & Timbers, Inc.
Corporate Staffing Group
Dromeshauser Assoc.
Duggan & Company
Lynn Dwigans & Co.
Effective Search, Inc.
Emmons Assoc., Inc.
Executive Appointments Ltd., Int'l.
Fenwick Partners
Fisher Personnel Management Services
Furlong - Gates, Inc.
Gilbert Tweed Assoc., Inc.
Griffith & Werner, Inc.
Gustin Partners, Ltd.
Gutreuter & Assoc.
The Hamilton Group
Hamlin Assoc.
Heffelfinger Assoc., Inc.
Hockett Assoc., Inc.
Holland, McFadzean & Assoc., Inc.
Human Resource Research Inc.
Johnson & Assoc., Inc.
Allan Karson Assoc., Inc.
Keane Assoc.
F. L. Mannix & Co., Inc.
The Marlow Group
J. Martin & Assoc.
Maschal/Connors Inc.
McBride Assoc., Inc.
Mercedes & Co., Inc.
Montenido Assoc.
The Niemond Corp.
O'Brien & Co., Inc.
Robert Ottke Assoc.
Pocrass Assoc.
Ramsey & Beirne Assoc., Inc.
Rieser & Assoc., Inc.
Schweichler Assoc., Inc.
Search Express
Shaffer Consulting Group
M.B. Shattuck & Assoc., Inc.
Smith, Goerss & Ferneborg, Inc.
Smith Search, S.A.
Stanislaw & Assoc., Inc.
Stephens Assoc. Ltd.
Stewart/Laurence Assoc., Inc.
Strategic Alternatives
Taylor Search Assoc., Inc.
Tierney Assoc., Inc.
The Ultimate Source
P. T. Unger Assoc.

John Velcamp & Assoc.
Venture Resources, Inc.
Verkamp-Joyce Assoc., Inc.
James L. Walsh & Assoc., Inc.
Albert J. Walsh & Assoc.
Ward Liebelt Assoc. Inc.
Wilkinson & Ives
Craig Williamson, Inc.
Richard Winn & Co.
Xagas & Assoc.

D.25 MEASURING/ANALYZING & CONTROLLING INSTRUMENTS & OPTICAL GOODS

Ames & Ames
Nathan Barry Assoc., Inc.
Blaney Executive Search
Cascadia Group Int'l.
Dromeshauser Assoc.
Fenwick Partners
Furlong - Gates, Inc.
Hansen Group, Ltd.
Health Industry Consultants, Inc.
Hogan Assoc.
Johnson & Assoc., Inc.
F. L. Mannix & Co., Inc.
Maschal/Connors Inc.
The Niemond Corp.
Palmer Assoc., Inc.
Schweichler Assoc., Inc.
M.B. Shattuck & Assoc., Inc.
Taylor Search Assoc., Inc.
Tierney Assoc., Inc.
The Ultimate Source
John Velcamp & Assoc.

D.26 MISCELLANEOUS MANUFACTURING INDUSTRIES

Bennett Search & Consulting Co.
Cardwell Group
The Furman Group, Ltd.
McSherry & Assoc.
QVS Int'l.
Reese Assoc.
M.B. Shattuck & Assoc., Inc.
John Velcamp & Assoc.
Duane I. Wilson Assoc., Inc.

D.D0 PACKAGING

Peter W. Ambler Co.
American Executive Search Services, Inc.
Blendow, Crowley & Oliver, Inc.
The Borton Wallace Co.
The Brand Co., Inc.
Cascadia Group Int'l.
Chandler & Rozner Assoc.
Christopher-Patrick & Assoc.
The Dartmouth Group
Dieckmann & Assoc., Ltd.
The Elson Group, Inc.
Erlanger Assoc.
Executive Resource Group

D.D0 PACKAGING (Cont'd)

Gardner-Ross Assoc., Inc.
The Gedge Group
Gilbert Tweed Assoc., Inc.
Gordon/Tyler
Grantham & Co., Inc.
Annie Gray Assoc., Inc.
Handy HRM
Heath/Norton Assoc., Inc.
Hodge-Cronin & Assoc., Inc.
William Humphreys & Assoc., Inc.
JM & Co.
Jender & Company
M. Scott Kemp & Assoc., Inc.
Kremple & Meade, Inc.
Paul Kull & Co.
Kunzer Assoc., Ltd.
Lawrence L. Lapham, Inc.
J. E. Lessner Assoc., Inc.
Morgan/Webber
R.C. Morton & Assoc. Inc.
The Mulshine Co., Inc.
Robert Murphy Assoc.
Northern Consultants Inc.
Redden & Assoc.
The Regis Group, Ltd.
The Revere Assoc., Inc.
Shoemaker & Assoc.
Studwell Assoc.
Torretto & Assoc., Inc.
K. W. Tunnell Co., Inc.
Vista Resource Group
Weber Executive Search
Jude M. Werra & Assoc.

D.E0 AEROSPACE

The Abbott Group
Advanced Executive Resources
The Budger Group
The Berman Consulting Group
Marc-Paul Bloome Ltd.
Bowden & Co., Inc.
Peter Newell Bowen
Dr. Will G. Bowman, Inc.
Brentwood Int'l.
CSI Inc.
Career Plus Executive Search
Michael J. Cavanaugh & Assoc.
Cejka & Co.
J. Kevin Coleman & Assoc., Inc.
The Corporate Source Group
Charles E. Day & Assoc., Inc.
Robert W. Dingman Co., Inc.
Donahue/Bales Assoc.
Effective Search, Inc.
Excelsior Services Group Inc.
Executive Resource Group
FGI
Finnegan Assoc.
Fisher Personnel Management Services
Stephen Fox Assoc. Inc.
Gaffney Management Consultants

N.W. Gibson Int'l.
Glou Int'l., Inc.
Grantham & Co., Inc.
The Hamilton Group
Hansen Group, Ltd.
Hansen Management Search Co.
Helfer Executive Consultants
The Hindman Co.
William C. Houze & Co.
Inside Management Assoc.
Michael James & Co., Inc.
Jender & Company
John H. Johnson & Assoc., Inc.
L.J. Johnson & Co.
Kellogg Consulting Group
Kensington Management Consultants, Inc.
Knapp Consultants
T. J. Koellhoffer & Assoc.
Krauthamer & Assoc.
Kremple & Meade, Inc.
Larkin & Co.
The Logan Group, Inc.
Robert Lowell Int'l.
Lynch & Co.
F. L. Mannix & Co., Inc.
Bruce Massey & Partners Inc.
McManners Assoc., Inc.
Paul Mueller & Assoc., Inc.
Robert Murphy Assoc.
Nadzam, Lusk & Assoc., Inc.
The Niemond Corp.
Norton & Assoc., Inc.
Ober & Company
Oliver & Rozner Assoc., Inc.
Ott & Hansen, Inc.
D.P. Parker & Assoc., Inc.
Rafey & Company
Sydney Reynolds Assoc., Inc.
James J. Rust Executive Search
Taylor Search Assoc., Inc.
Thomas Mangum Co.
Tirocchi, Wright, Inc.
Torretto & Assoc., Inc.
Trout & Assoc., Inc.
K. W. Tunnell Co., Inc.
Tuttle, Neidhart, Semyan, Inc.
P. T. Unger Assoc.
Wargo & Co., Inc.
D. L. Weiss & Assoc.
Western Reserve Search Assoc.
Charles Zabriskie Assoc., Inc.

D.H0 HIGH TECH/ELECTRONICS

The Abbott Group
Jeffrey C. Adams & Co., Inc.
Advanced Executive Resources
J.R. Akin & Co.
Peter W. Ambler Co.
American Executive Search Services, Inc.
Ames & Ames
Anderson Bradshaw Assoc., Inc.
Annapolis Consulting Group

D.H0 HIGH TECH/ELECTRONICS (Cont'd)

Babson, Moore & Wilcox
The Badger Group
Baldwin Associates, Inc.
James Bangert & Assoc., Inc.
Bartholdi & Co.
The Berman Consulting Group
Deborah Bishop & Assoc.
The Blackman Kallick Search Division
Blanchard, Zufall & Assoc.
Blaney Executive Search
Block & Assoc.
Bowden & Co., Inc.
Peter Newell Bowen
Dr. Will G. Bowman, Inc.
The Bradbury Management Group
The Brand Co., Inc.
Brault & Assoc., Ltd.
Brentwood Int'l.
Brissenden, McFarland, Wagoner & Fuccella, Inc.
Bryce, Haultain & Assoc.
Bullis & Co., Inc.
Busch Int'l.
Byron Leonard Int'l., Inc.
CSI Inc.
Career Plus Executive Search
Catalyx Group, Inc.
Michael J. Cavanaugh & Assoc.
Chandler & Rozner Assoc.
Chase-Owens Assoc., Inc.
Christian & Timbers, Inc.
Christopher-Patrick & Assoc.
Claveloux, McCaffrey, McInerney, Inc.
J. Kevin Coleman & Assoc., Inc.
Compass Group Ltd.
Corporate Staffing Group
Crowder & Company
M.J. Curran & Assoc., Inc.
Charles E. Day & Assoc., Inc.
Deane, Howard & Simon, Inc.
Robert W. Dingman Co., Inc.
Donahue/Bales Assoc.
Duggan & Company
Michael S. Dunford, Inc.
Lynn Dwigans & Co.
Ebbert Assoc.
Effective Search, Inc.
Empire International
Erlanger Assoc.
Excelsior Services Group Inc.
Executive Resource Group
FGI
Fagan & Co.
George Fee Assoc., Inc.
Fenwick Partners
Finnegan Assoc.
First Colorado Consulting Group, Inc.
Fisher Personnel Management Services
Stephen Fox Assoc. Inc.
GSW Consulting Group, Inc.

Gaffney Management Consultants
W.N. Garbarini & Assoc.
Geneva Group Int'l.
Genovese & Co.
N.W. Gibson Int'l.
H. L. Goehring & Assoc., Inc.
Greger Assoc.
Haddad Assoc.
Haley Assoc., Inc.
The Hamilton Group
Hamlin Assoc.
Handy HRM
Hansen Group, Ltd.
Heath/Norton Assoc., Inc.
Heffelfinger Assoc., Inc.
Henry Michaels & Assoc.
Hergenrather & Co.
The Hindman Co.
Hite Executive Search
Hockett Assoc., Inc.
Hodge-Cronin & Assoc., Inc.
Holland, McFadzean & Assoc., Inc.
William C. Houze & Co.
Huff Assoc.
The Human Resource Consulting Group, Inc.
Human Resource Research Inc.
Human Resources, Inc.
Jeffrey Irving Assoc., Inc.
Michael James & Co., Inc.
Jender & Company
Johnson & Assoc., Inc.
John H. Johnson & Assoc., Inc.
L.J. Johnson & Co.
Ronald S. Johnson Assoc., Inc.
K/N Int'l.
Gary Kaplan & Assoc.
Allan Karson Assoc., Inc.
Keane Assoc.
M. Scott Kemp & Assoc., Inc.
Melvin Kent & Assoc., Inc.
Kirkman & Searing
Kline Consulting, Inc.
Knapp Consultants
T. J. Koellhoffer & Assoc.
Koontz, Jeffries & Assoc., Inc.
Kremple & Meade, Inc.
Paul Kull & Co.
Kunzer Assoc., Ltd.
John Kurosky & Assoc.
Lawrence L. Lapham, Inc.
Larkin & Co.
Lasher Assoc.
The Logan Group, Inc.
Robert Lowell Int'l.
Lund & Assoc., Inc.
Lynch Miller Moore, Inc.
MCC Assoc.
META/MAT, Ltd.
The Madison Group
The Marlow Group
Marra/Pizzi Assoc., Inc.
J. Martin & Assoc.
Martin Mirtz Morice, Inc.

D.H0 HIGH TECH/ELECTRONICS (Cont'd)

McCormack & Farrow
McKeen Melancon & Co.
McManners Assoc., Inc.
Mercedes & Co., Inc.
The Neil Michael Group, Inc.
Montenido Assoc.
Nadzam, Lusk & Assoc., Inc.
The Niemond Corp.
Paul Norsell & Assoc., Inc.
Norton & Assoc., Inc.
Oliver & Rozner Assoc., Inc.
D.P. Parker & Assoc., Inc.
People Management Northeast, Inc.
Peterson Consulting/W.P., Inc.
Picard & Co., Inc.
Pierce Assoc.
Pierce Assoc.
R.L. Plimpton Assoc.
Pocrass Assoc.
Polson & Co., Inc.
David Powell, Inc.
Preng & Assoc., Inc.
Quaintance Assoc., Inc.
Quinn Bailey & Morgan
RIC Corp.
Rafey & Company
Ramsey & Beirne Assoc., Inc.
Rand Assoc.
Reddick and Co., Int'l.
The Regis Group, Ltd.
Resource Network Inc.
Sydney Reynolds Assoc., Inc.
Roberts Ryan & Bentley
Schweichler Assoc., Inc.
J. Robert Scott
Search Express
Search Source, Inc.
Shaffer Consulting Group
M.B. Shattuck & Assoc., Inc.
Sheridan Search
Sigma Group Inc.
C.W. Sink & Co., Inc.
Slayton Int'l., Inc.
Splaine & Assoc., Inc.
Stanislaw & Assoc., Inc.
Stephens Assoc. Ltd.
S. K. Stewart & Assoc.
Stewart/Laurence Assoc., Inc.
Stone, Murphy & Olson
Strategic Alternatives
Tech > Mark Group
Theobald & Assoc.
Thomas Mangum Co.
Tierney Assoc., Inc.
Tirocchi, Wright, Inc.
Trout & Assoc., Inc.
The Thomas Tucker Co.
K. W. Tunnell Co., Inc.
Tuttle, Neidhart, Semyan, Inc.
P. T. Unger Assoc.

VanMaldegiam Assoc., Inc.
John Velcamp & Assoc.
Venture Management
Von Storch Assoc.
WTW Assoc., Inc.
James L. Walsh & Assoc., Inc.
Albert J. Walsh & Assoc.
Wargo & Co., Inc.
Weir Executive Search Assoc., Inc.
D. L. Weiss & Assoc.
Craig Williamson, Inc.
Richard Winn & Co.
Youngs & Co.
Charles Zabriskie Assoc., Inc.
Michael D. Zinn & Assoc., Inc.

D.I0 BIOTECH/GENETIC ENGINEERING

Jeffrey C. Adams & Co., Inc.
American Executive Management, Inc.
Anders Incorporated
Annapolis Consulting Group
James Bangert & Assoc., Inc.
Nathan Barry Assoc., Inc.
BioQuest Inc.
Blaney Executive Search
Blendow & Johnson Inc.
Blendow, Crowley & Oliver, Inc.
Brissenden, McFarland, Wagoner & Fuccella, Inc.
Bullis & Co., Inc.
Busch Int'l.
Byron Leonard Int'l., Inc.
CanMed Consultants Inc.
Canny, Bowen Inc.
L.L. Carey & Assoc., Inc.
Catalyx Group, Inc.
Coelyn Miller Phillip & Assoc.
Walter V. Connor Int'l., Inc.
M.J. Curran & Assoc., Inc.
Curry, Telleri Group, Inc.
Alfred Daniels & Assoc.
The Domann Organization
Dwyer Consulting Group, Inc.
William J. Elam & Assoc.
Erlanger Assoc.
James Feerst & Assoc., Inc.
Finnegan Assoc.
GSW Consulting Group, Inc.
Geneva Group Int'l.
Guidry, East, Barnes & Bono, Inc.
Haley Assoc., Inc.
The Hamilton Group
Hartman, Barnette & Assoc.
Health Industry Consultants, Inc.
Heath/Norton Assoc., Inc.
R. W. Hebel Assoc.
Hite Executive Search
Hockett Assoc., Inc.
Holohan Group, Ltd.
Houtz, Strawn Assoc.
William C. Houze & Co.

D.I0 BIOTECH/GENETIC ENGINEERING (Cont'd)

Human Resource Research Inc.
Hutchinson Resources International
James, Layton Int'l., Inc.
Johnson & Assoc., Inc.
Ronald S. Johnson Assoc., Inc.
K/N Int'l.
Kincannon & Reed
Kline Consulting, Inc.
Koontz, Jeffries & Assoc., Inc.
Paul Kull & Co.
John Kurosky & Assoc.
L O R Personnel Div.
Larson & Stephanian
Levin & Assoc.
H.M. Long Int'l., Ltd.
Lynch Miller Moore, Inc.
The Macdonald Group, Inc.
The Madison Group
Maly & Assoc.
Management Catalysts
Marlar Int'l. Inc.
The Marlow Group
Marra/Pizzi Assoc., Inc.
George R. Martin
McManners Assoc., Inc.
Mercedes & Co., Inc.
The Neil Michael Group, Inc.
Morgan/Webber
R.C. Morton & Assoc. Inc.
Paul Norsell & Assoc., Inc.
Richard E. Nosky & Assoc.
Palmer Assoc., Inc.
Perry-D'Amico & Assoc.
Resource Network Inc.
Roberts Ryan & Bentley
SRH Resource Group
Sampson, Neill & Wilkins Inc.
J. Robert Scott
Shaffer Consulting Group
Daniel A. Silverstein Assoc. Inc.
Skott/Edwards Consultants
Splaine & Assoc., Inc.
Staples Consulting Inc.
Strategic Search Corp.
Tech > Mark Group
Theobald & Assoc.
Travis & Co., Inc.
Michael Tucker Assoc.
Vista Resource Group
Voigt Assoc.
WDI, Int'l.
Wargo & Co., Inc.
Wellington Management Group
William Willis Worldwide, Inc.
Zingaro & Co.
The Zivic Group, Inc.

E.00 TRANSPORTATION

Martin H. Bauman Assoc., Inc.
Joy Reed Belt & Assoc., Inc.

The Blunt Co., Inc.
Bowker, Brown & Co.
Byron Leonard Int'l., Inc.
Canny, Bowen Inc.
Cejka & Co.
Chandler & Rozner Assoc.
Walter V. Connor Int'l., Inc.
Crowder & Company
Fred J. Goldsmith Assoc.
Grantham & Co., Inc.
Robert Grossberg & Assoc.
Hansen Group, Ltd.
Hansen Management Search Co.
Hauft Mark Assoc., Inc.
Holland Rusk & Assoc.
William Humphreys & Assoc., Inc.
Isaacson, Miller, Inc.
Michael James & Co., Inc.
M. Scott Kemp & Assoc., Inc.
Krauthamer & Assoc.
Lawrence L. Lapham, Inc.
Robert Lowell Int'l.
Gayle L. Mattson & Assoc.
McManners Assoc., Inc.
Paul Mueller & Assoc., Inc.
Newell Assoc.
O'Callaghan, Honey & Assoc., Inc.
Dennis P. O'Toole & Assoc. Inc.
The PAR Group - Paul A. Reaume, Ltd.
Jim Parham & Assoc., Inc.
Norman Roberts & Assoc., Inc.
James J. Rust Executive Search

F.00 WHOLESALE TRADE

Martin H. Bauman Assoc., Inc.
Joy Reed Belt & Assoc., Inc.
Buzhardt Assoc.
Dupuis & Ryden, P.C.
B. Goodwin, Ltd.
Annie Gray Assoc., Inc.
January Management Group
Marvin Laba & Assoc.
Lawrence L. Lapham, Inc.
Maiorino & Weston Assoc., Inc.
Herbert Mines Assoc., Inc.
Paul Mueller & Assoc., Inc.
Kirk Palmer & Assoc., Inc.
Plummer & Assoc., Inc.
Redden & Assoc.
Sievers & Assoc.
A. William Smyth, Inc.
Tama Lucas Ltd.
The Viscusi Group, Inc.
Vista Resource Group
Weber Executive Search
Werner Int'l., Inc.

G.00 RETAIL TRADE

Jeffrey C. Adams & Co., Inc.
Advanced Executive Resources
Peter W. Ambler Co.
BDO Seidman

G.00 RETAIL TRADE (Cont'd)

Barger & Sargeant, Inc.
The Blackman Kallick Search Division
Buzhardt Assoc.
T. Byrnes & Co., Inc.
Grant Cooper & Assoc., Inc.
DiMarchi Partners
Hill Fallon & Assoc.
W.N. Garbarini & Assoc.
Genovese & Co.
Halden & Assoc.
W.L. Handler & Assoc.
Inside Management Assoc.
January Management Group
Johnson Smith & Knisely Inc.
Jim Just & Assoc.
Martin Kartin & Co., Inc.
Melvin Kent & Assoc., Inc.
Kunzer Assoc., Ltd.
Marvin Laba & Assoc.
Michael Latas & Assoc., Inc.
Lauer, Sbarbaro Assoc., Inc.
The John Lucht Consultancy Inc.
Herbert Mines Assoc., Inc.
Nicholson & Assoc., Inc.
Kirk Palmer & Assoc., Inc.
Phillips Group of Companies
Pinsker & Co., Inc.
Plummer & Assoc., Inc.
Rafey & Company
E.J. Rhodes Assoc.
Allan Sarn Assoc., Inc.
Seitchik, Corwin & Seitchik Inc.
John Sibbald Assoc., Inc.
Sievers & Assoc.
Robert L. Smith & Co., Inc.
Stricker & Zagor
Tama Lucas Ltd.
Torretto & Assoc., Inc.
The Viscusi Group, Inc.
Walker Group, Inc.
Weber Executive Search
Werner Int'l., Inc.
Dick Wray & Consultants
Youngs & Co.

H.00 FINANCE

Anthony Executive Search
Argus National, Inc.
Babson, Moore & Wilcox
The Badger Group
Martin H. Bauman Assoc., Inc.
The Beam Group
Becker, Norton & Co.
Nelson Bell & Partners Inc.
Bialecki Inc.
Blanchard, Zufall & Assoc.
Bowden & Co., Inc.
Brady Assoc. Int'l., Inc.
Brault & Assoc., Ltd.
Brentwood Int'l.
Bullis & Co., Inc.
Butterfass/Pepe Assoc., Inc.

Buzhardt Assoc.
Byron Leonard Int'l., Inc.
Canny, Bowen Inc.
Career Plus Executive Search
Chartwell Partners Int'l., Inc.
Chrisman & Co., Inc.
Joseph Conley & Assoc., Inc.
Walter V. Connor Int'l., Inc.
Grant Cooper & Assoc., Inc.
Coopers & Lybrand, Management Consulting
  Services
Corporate Environment Ltd.
The Corporate Source Group
Crowder & Company
M.J. Curran & Assoc., Inc.
Marge Dana Assoc.
Danforth Group
Alfred Daniels & Assoc.
DeHayes Consulting Group
Deane, Howard & Simon, Inc.
DiMarchi Partners
Dieckmann & Assoc., Ltd.
Donahue/Bales Assoc.
Dougan-McKinley-Strain
Michael S. Dunford, Inc.
ESP Management Services, Inc.
David M. Ellner Assoc.
The Elson Group, Inc.
Erlanger Assoc.
Fagan & Co.
Hill Fallon & Assoc.
George Fee Assoc., Inc.
Finnegan Assoc.
First Colorado Consulting Group, Inc.
The Furman Group, Ltd.
Jay Gaines & Co.
Gardiner Stone Hunter Int'l., Inc.
Allan Gardner & Assoc., Inc.
Garofolo, Curtiss, Lambert & MacLean
Genovese & Co.
N.W. Gibson Int'l.
Paul C. Green & Assoc. Ltd.
Greger Assoc.
Hadley Lockwood, Inc.
W.L. Handler & Assoc.
Handy HRM
Hans & Assoc., Inc.
Hayden Group, Inc.
The Heidrick Partners, Inc.
Helfer Executive Consultants
Harvey Hohauser & Assoc.
Holt Pearson & Caldwell, Inc.
J.B. Homer Assoc. Inc.
Hutchinson Resources International
Hyman, Mackenzie & Partners, Inc.
The Interface Group, Ltd.
Jeffrey Irving Assoc., Inc.
L.J. Johnson & Co.
Gary Kaplan & Assoc.
M. Scott Kemp & Assoc., Inc.
Jonah Kleinstein Assoc., Inc.
Kline Consulting, Inc.
Kostmayer Assoc., Inc.

H.00 FINANCE (Cont'd)

Krauthamer & Assoc.
D.A. Kreuter Assoc., Inc.
L O R Personnel Div.
Marvin Laba & Assoc.
Lansky Assoc.
Lauer, Sbarbaro Assoc., Inc.
Lee & Burgess Assoc., Inc.
Locke & Assoc.
The John Lucht Consultancy Inc.
The Lumsden Co., Inc.
Lynch Miller Moore, Inc.
META/MAT, Ltd.
The Macdonald Group, Inc.
Robert Madigan Assoc., Inc.
The Madison Group
Marlar Int'l. Inc.
Marra/Pizzi Assoc., Inc.
Martin Mirtz Morice, Inc.
Bruce Massey & Partners Inc.
Matte & Company, Inc.
McBride Assoc., Inc.
McCormack & Farrow
McDonald/Long Assoc., Inc.
Meder & Assoc.
Martin H. Meisel Assoc., Inc.
Montenido Assoc.
Nicholson & Assoc., Inc.
Paul Norsell & Assoc., Inc.
Norton & Assoc., Inc.
O'Callaghan, Honey & Assoc., Inc.
O'Toole & Company
Ober & Company
Robert Olivier & Assoc., Inc.
Oppedisano & Co., Inc.
P.A.R. Assoc., Inc.
G.S. Page Inc.
Page-Wheatcroft & Co. Ltd.
People Management Northeast, Inc.
Peterson Consulting/W.P., Inc.
David Powell, Inc.
Quinn Bailey & Morgan
Raines Int'l. Inc.
Rand Assoc.
Reddick and Co., Int'l.
The Regis Group, Ltd.
E.J. Rhodes Assoc.
Roberts Ryan & Bentley
Robertson, Spoerlein & Wengert
James J. Rust Executive Search
SS & A Executive Search Consultants
Wilbur M. Sachtjen Assoc., Inc.
Sage/Walters Assoc.
Saley Partners Int'l.
Allan Sarn Assoc., Inc.
The Schmitt Tolette Group
J. Robert Scott
Sigma Group Inc.
Howard W. Smith Assoc.
Sockwell & Anderson
Soltis Management Services
Splaine & Assoc., Inc.

M.H. Springer & Assoc.
Staples Consulting Inc.
Lee Stephens & Assoc.
S. K. Stewart & Assoc.
W. R. Strathmann Assoc.
Stricker & Zagor
Thalatta Corp.
Theobald & Assoc.
Trout & Assoc., Inc.
Tucker Assoc.
VanMaldegiam Assoc., Inc.
Vlcek & Co., Inc.
Ward Howell Int'l. Inc.
Ward Liebelt Assoc. Inc.
Warring & Assoc.
Weir Executive Search Assoc., Inc.
C. Weiss Assoc., Inc.
K. L. Whitney & Co., Inc.
The Whitney Group
William Willis Worldwide, Inc.
The Yorkshire Group, Ltd.
Charles Zabriskie Assoc., Inc.
Michael D. Zinn & Assoc., Inc.
Zurick, Davis & Co.

H.10 BANKING, FINANCIAL INSTITUTIONS, CREDIT AGENCIES

Actuaries & Assoc.
Alwyn Assoc., Inc.
Argus National, Inc.
BDO Seidman
Barger & Sargeant, Inc.
Barton Raben, Inc.
Battalia Winston Int'l., Inc.
The Baxter Group
The Beam Group
Nelson Bell & Partners Inc.
Bialecki Inc.
Bialla & Assoc., Inc.
Cardwell Group
Chartwell Partners Int'l., Inc.
Cornell Int'l.
The Duncan Group Inc.
ESP Management Services, Inc.
Fogec Consultants
The Furman Group, Ltd.
Jay Gaines & Co.
Glou Int'l., Inc.
Hackett & Co.
Hadley Lockwood, Inc.
Hansen Management Search Co.
Hanzel & Co., Inc.
Hayden Group, Inc.
William Humphreys & Assoc., Inc.
K/N Int'l.
Kirkman & Searing
Kostmayer Assoc., Inc.
Kremple & Meade, Inc.
Lansky Assoc.
Larsen Int'l., Inc.
H.M. Long Int'l., Ltd.
The Lumsden Co., Inc.

H.10 BANKING, FINANCIAL INSTITUTIONS, CREDIT AGENCIES (Cont'd)

Robert Madigan Assoc., Inc.
Maiorino & Weston Assoc., Inc.
Mitchell/Wolfson, Assoc.
Newell Assoc.
Nicholson & Assoc., Inc.
Robert Olivier & Assoc., Inc.
P.A.R. Assoc., Inc.
G.S. Page Inc.
Peeney Assoc., Inc.
Richard Peterson & Assoc., Inc.
Peterson Consulting/W.P., Inc.
Pocrass Assoc.
Polson & Co., Inc.
The Rankin Group, Ltd.
Rieser & Assoc., Inc.
Roberts-Lund Assoc., Ltd.
Robertson, Spoerlein & Wengert
Ropes Assoc., Inc.
Sage/Walters Ltd.
Shaffer Consulting Group
Sheridan Search
Howard W. Smith Assoc.
Smith Search, S.A.
Sockwell & Anderson
M.H. Springer & Assoc.
Stone, Murphy & Olson
W. R. Strathmann Assoc.
Sullivan & Co.
Thalatta Corp.
Tuttle, Neidhart, Semyan, Inc.
WTW Assoc., Inc.
Warring & Assoc.
C. Weiss Assoc., Inc.
Western Reserve Search Assoc.
K. L. Whitney & Co., Inc.
The Whitney Group

H.11 SECURITIES & COMMODITIES BROKERS

Alwyn Assoc., Inc.
Nelson Bell & Partners Inc.
Bialecki Inc.
Dr. Will G. Bowman, Inc.
Chartwell Partners Int'l., Inc.
Cornell Int'l.
The Furman Group, Ltd.
Jay Gaines & Co.
Hackett & Co.
Hadley Lockwood, Inc.
Hanzel & Co., Inc.
Kostmayer Assoc., Inc.
Lansky Assoc.
Nicholson & Assoc., Inc.
Robert Olivier & Assoc., Inc.
Oppedisano & Co., Inc.
Roberts-Lund Assoc., Ltd.
Sage/Walters Ltd.
M.H. Springer & Assoc.
Stone, Murphy & Olson

W. R. Strathmann Assoc.
Sullivan & Co.
Thalatta Corp.
The Whitney Group

H.12 VENTURE CAPITAL

Aubin Int'l. Inc.
Nelson Bell & Partners Inc.
Blaney Executive Search
Blau Kaptain Schroeder
Busch Int'l.
L.L. Carey & Assoc., Inc.
Catalyx Group, Inc.
Hadley Lockwood, Inc.
Haley Assoc., Inc.
Hanzel & Co., Inc.
Hartman, Barnette & Assoc.
Hogan Assoc.
Holland, McFadzean & Assoc., Inc.
Houtz, Strawn Assoc.
William Humphreys & Assoc., Inc.
Ronald S. Johnson Assoc., Inc.
Kostmayer Assoc., Inc.
Lansky Assoc.
Lauer Consulting Services, Inc.
Maiorino & Weston Assoc., Inc.
Robert Olivier & Assoc., Inc.
Pierce Assoc.
The Rankin Group, Ltd.
Roberts-Lund Assoc., Ltd.
Sage/Walters Ltd.
Sampson, Neill & Wilkins Inc.
Skott/Edwards Consultants
M.H. Springer & Assoc.
Thalatta Corp.
Venture Resources, Inc.

H.I0 INSURANCE

Actuaries & Assoc.
Atlantic Search
Babson, Moore & Wilcox
James Bangert & Assoc., Inc.
Barger & Sargeant, Inc.
The Beam Group
Becker, Norton & Co.
Blanchard, Zufall & Assoc.
Bowden & Co., Inc.
Butterfass/Pepe Assoc., Inc.
Lee Calhoon & Co., Inc.
Cejka & Co.
Chartwell Partners Int'l., Inc.
Chrisman & Co., Inc.
Coopers & Lybrand, Management Consulting Services
The DLR Group, Inc.
Danforth Group
De Funiak & Edwards
DeHayes Consulting Group
Deane, Howard & Simon, Inc.
DiMarchi Partners
Dieckmann & Assoc., Ltd.
Michael S. Dunford, Inc.

H.I0 INSURANCE (Cont'd)

ESP Management Services, Inc.
William J. Elam & Assoc.
David M. Ellner Assoc.
Hill Fallon & Assoc.
Global Resources Group
Paul C. Green & Assoc. Ltd.
R. C. Handel Assoc. Inc.
Harris Heery & Assoc., Inc.
Hayden Group, Inc.
Hodge-Cronin & Assoc., Inc.
J.B. Homer Assoc. Inc.
Howe-Weaver, Inc.
Hunter Int'l., Inc.
Ingram, Inc.
The Interface Group, Ltd.
Kostmayer Assoc., Inc.
D.A. Kreuter Assoc., Inc.
Lee & Burgess Assoc., Inc.
The John Lucht Consultancy Inc.
Lynch & Co.
Martin Mirtz Morice, Inc.
Bruce Massey & Partners Inc.
Matte & Company, Inc.
McBride Assoc., Inc.
McDonald/Long Assoc., Inc.
Mitchell/Wolfson, Assoc.
Norton & Assoc., Inc.
G.S. Page Inc.
People Management Northeast, Inc.
Richard Peterson & Assoc., Inc.
Peterson Consulting/W.P., Inc.
Raines Int'l. Inc.
Rand Assoc.
Roberts Ryan & Bentley
Robertson, Spoerlein & Wengert
Sathe & Assoc., Inc.
Schalekamp & Assoc., Inc.
Howard W. Smith Assoc.
Staples Consulting Inc.
Stone, Murphy & Olson
W. R. Strathmann Assoc.
Sullivan & Co.
Tucker Assoc.
Peter Van Leer & Assoc.
Walker Group, Inc.
Ward Howell Int'l. Inc.
Warring & Assoc.
The Whitney Group
Witt Assoc. Inc.
The Yorkshire Group, Ltd.

H.R0 REAL ESTATE

Alwyn Assoc., Inc.
Argus National, Inc.
BDO Seidman
Barton Sans Int'l.
Blanchard, Zufall & Assoc.
Butterfass/Pepe Assoc., Inc.
T. Byrnes & Co., Inc.
Michael J. Cavanaugh & Assoc.
Chartwell Partners Int'l., Inc.

Chrisman & Co., Inc.
Dean M. Coe Assoc.
Robert Connelly & Assoc., Inc.
The Corporate Source Group
Danforth Group
Alfred Daniels & Assoc.
Deane, Howard & Simon, Inc.
ESP Management Services, Inc.
Eggleston Consulting Int'l.
David M. Ellner Assoc.
John D. Gibbons & Assoc., Inc.
Greger Assoc.
Griffith & Werner, Inc.
Haddad Assoc.
The Heidrick Partners, Inc.
January Management Group
The J. Kovach Group, Inc.
Michael Latas & Assoc., Inc.
Lynch & Co.
McDonald Assoc.
Meder & Assoc.
Jay Mitchell & Co.
Newell Assoc.
O'Callaghan, Honey & Assoc., Inc.
Ott & Hansen, Inc.
Richard Peterson & Assoc., Inc.
Raines Int'l. Inc.
Ropes Assoc., Inc.
Sathe & Assoc., Inc.
W. Shryock & Co.
Howard W. Smith Assoc.
Sockwell & Anderson
Soltis Management Services
Lee Stephens & Assoc.
W. R. Strathmann Assoc.
The WalCar Partnership
C. Weiss Assoc., Inc.
The Whitney Group
Dick Wray & Consultants

I.00 SERVICES

Baldwin Associates, Inc.
Ballantyne & Assoc.
James Bangert & Assoc., Inc.
Barton Raben, Inc.
Martin H. Bauman Assoc., Inc.
Belvedere Partners
The Brand Co., Inc.
Brault & Assoc., Ltd.
Brentwood Int'l.
Brissenden, McFarland, Wagoner & Fuccella, Inc.
Bryce, Haultain & Assoc.
Bullis & Co., Inc.
T. Byrnes & Co., Inc.
Chandler & Rozner Assoc.
Chrisman & Co., Inc.
Jack Clarey Assoc., Inc.
Coelyn Miller Phillip & Assoc.
Walter V. Connor Int'l., Inc.
Grant Cooper & Assoc., Inc.
Coopers & Lybrand, Management Consulting Services

I.00 SERVICES (Cont'd)

Corporate Environment Ltd.
Crowder & Company
M.J. Curran & Assoc., Inc.
Marge Dana Assoc.
DeHayes Consulting Group
DiMarchi Partners
Dieckmann & Assoc., Ltd.
Robert W. Dingman Co., Inc.
Donahue/Bales Assoc.
Michael S. Dunford, Inc.
Dupuis & Ryden, P.C.
Dwyer Consulting Group, Inc.
The Elliott Company
The Elson Group, Inc.
Fagan & Co.
W.N. Garbarini & Assoc.
N.W. Gibson Int'l.
Glou Int'l., Inc.
Fred J. Goldsmith Assoc.
Gould & McCoy, Inc.
Grantham & Co., Inc.
Robert Grossberg & Assoc.
W.L. Handler & Assoc.
Harris Heery & Assoc., Inc.
Hauft Mark Assoc., Inc.
The Heidrick Partners, Inc.
Hergenrather & Co.
Hite Executive Search
Harvey Hohauser & Assoc.
William C. Houze & Co.
Hunter Int'l., Inc.
Hutchinson Resources International
Hyman, Mackenzie & Partners, Inc.
Ingram, Inc.
Inside Management Assoc.
Jeffrey Irving Assoc., Inc.
Gary Kaplan & Assoc.
Kellogg Consulting Group
Kensington Management Consultants, Inc.
Kieffer, Ford, & Hadelman, Ltd.
Jonah Kleinstein Assoc., Inc.
Koontz, Jeffries & Assoc., Inc.
Kunzer Assoc., Ltd.
L O R Personnel Div.
Langer Assoc., Inc.
Larkin & Co.
Lasher Assoc.
Lauer, Sbarbaro Assoc., Inc.
Lee & Burgess Assoc., Inc.
Locke & Assoc.
The Logan Group, Inc.
MD Resources, Inc.
META/MAT, Ltd.
Maiorino & Weston Assoc., Inc.
Brad Marks Int'l.
Marlar Int'l. Inc.
Marra/Pizzi Assoc., Inc.
Martin Mirtz Morice, Inc.
Gayle L. Mattson & Assoc.
McDonald Assoc.
McDonald/Long Assoc., Inc.

The Neil Michael Group, Inc.
Moriarty/Fox, Inc.
R.C. Morton & Assoc. Inc.
Paul Mueller & Assoc., Inc.
O'Callaghan, Honey & Assoc., Inc.
Dennis P. O'Toole & Assoc. Inc.
Ober & Company
Ott & Hansen, Inc.
P.A.R. Assoc., Inc.
The PAR Group - Paul A. Reaume, Ltd.
Page-Wheatcroft & Co. Ltd.
David Powell, Inc.
Quinn Bailey & Morgan
RIC Corp.
Redden & Assoc.
Redden & McGrath Assoc., Inc.
Robsham & Assoc.
James J. Rust Executive Search
Schenkel & Company
J. Robert Scott
Kimball Shaw Assoc.
Michael Shirley Assoc.
Sigma Group Inc.
C.W. Sink & Co., Inc.
Slayton Int'l., Inc.
Robert L. Smith & Co., Inc.
Howard W. Smith Assoc.
Soltis Management Services
Stricker & Zagor
Theobald & Assoc.
Trout & Assoc., Inc.
Tucker Assoc.
VanMaldegiam Assoc., Inc.
Vlcek & Co., Inc.
Ward Howell Int'l. Inc.
Jude M. Werra & Assoc.
The Yorkshire Group, Ltd.
Youngs & Co.
Zay & Company
Zurick, Davis & Co.

I.10 HOSPITALITY-INCLUDING HOTELS, RESORTS, CLUBS, RESTAURANTS, FOOD & BEVE

Advanced Executive Resources
Bialla & Assoc., Inc.
The Blackman Kallick Search Division
Robert W. Dingman Co., Inc.
Greger Assoc.
Halden & Assoc.
Hans & Assoc., Inc.
Robert Howe & Assoc.
Huff Assoc.
Innkeeper's Management Corp.
Johnson Smith & Knisely Inc.
Matte & Company, Inc.
James Mead & Co.
National Restaurant Search, Inc.
Norton & Assoc., Inc.
Dennis P. O'Toole & Assoc. Inc.
Plummer & Assoc., Inc.
The Romark Group, Ltd.

I.14 HEALTHCARE (EXCEPT PHYSICIANS; SEE I.15) TO INCLUDE ADMINISTRATORS & P (Cont'd)

Executive Appointments Ltd., Int'l.
Executive Quest
Fiordalis Assoc., Inc.
Fogec Consultants
Fulton, Longshore & Assoc., Inc.
Allan Gardner & Assoc., Inc.
Garofolo, Curtiss, Lambert & MacLean
Gilbert Tweed Assoc., Inc.
Global Resources Group
H. L. Goehring & Assoc., Inc.
Griffith & Werner, Inc.
Guidry, East, Barnes & Bono, Inc.
Hans & Assoc., Inc.
Hansen Management Search Co.
Hersher Assoc., Ltd.
Robert Howe & Assoc.
Huff Assoc.
The Human Resource Consulting Group, Inc.
Isaacson, Miller, Inc.
Jackson & Coker
K/N Int'l.
Kellogg Consulting Group
Kirkman & Searing
Kittleman & Assoc.
The J. Kovach Group, Inc.
D.A. Kreuter Assoc., Inc.
Ira W. Krinsky & Assoc.
The Landmark Consulting Group Inc.
Larson & Stephanian
J. E. Lessner Assoc., Inc.
Lowderman & Haney, Inc.
MD Resources, Inc.
Maglio & Co., Inc.
Management Science Assoc.
McCormack & Farrow
McSherry & Assoc.
Martin H. Meisel Assoc., Inc.
Mercedes & Co., Inc.
E.J. Michaels, Ltd.
Thomas R. Moore Executive Search
R. F. Mulvaney & Assoc., Inc.
NDI Services
Northern Consultants Inc.
Nursing Technomics
O'Brien & Co., Inc.
People Management Northeast, Inc.
Perry-D'Amico & Assoc.
Physician Executive Management Center
Quigley Assoc., Inc.
Reddick and Co., Int'l.
E.J. Rhodes Assoc.
Norman Roberts & Assoc., Inc.
David Rowe & Assoc., Inc.
James Russell, Inc.
Schenkel & Company
Robert Sellery Assoc., Ltd.
Kimball Shaw Assoc.
Sievers & Assoc.

Daniel A. Silverstein Assoc. Inc.
The Stamford Group Inc.
S. K. Stewart & Assoc.
Tech > Mark Group
Thomure Medsearch, Inc.
Michael Tucker Assoc.
Tyler & Co.
Venture Resources, Inc.
Albert J. Walsh & Assoc.
Warring & Assoc.
Weir Executive Search Assoc., Inc.
Witt Assoc. Inc.
Zingaro & Co.
The Zivic Group, Inc.
Zurick, Davis & Co.

I.15 PHYSICIANS

American Group Practice, Inc.
Anders Incorporated
J.W. Barleycorn & Assoc.
Blendow & Johnson Inc.
Lee Calhoon & Co., Inc.
CanMed Consultants Inc.
Cardwell Group
M.L. Carter & Assoc., Inc.
Caswell/Winters & Assoc., Inc.
Challenger & Hunt
DCS Assoc., Inc.
The DLR Group, Inc.
Diversified Health Search
Drew Assoc. Int'l.
Euromedica USA
James Feerst & Assoc., Inc.
Fiordalis Assoc., Inc.
Fox Hill Assoc., Ltd.
Fulton, Longshore & Assoc., Inc.
Garofolo, Curtiss, Lambert & MacLean
Global Resources Group
H. L. Goehring & Assoc., Inc.
Guidry, East, Barnes & Bono, Inc.
Harvey Hohauser & Assoc.
Robert Howe & Assoc.
Huff Assoc.
Jackson & Coker
K/N Int'l.
Lowderman & Haney, Inc.
MCC Assoc.
MD Resources, Inc.
Maglio & Co., Inc.
Martin H. Meisel Assoc., Inc.
E.J. Michaels, Ltd.
Physician Executive Management Center
Physician Services of America
Quigley Assoc., Inc.
E.J. Rhodes Assoc.
David Rowe & Assoc., Inc.
James Russell, Inc.
Sampson, Neill & Wilkins Inc.
Kimball Shaw Assoc.
Daniel A. Silverstein Assoc. Inc.
The Stamford Group Inc.
Thomure Medsearch, Inc.

I.15 PHYSICIANS (Cont'd)

Tyler & Co.
Warring & Assoc.
Witt Assoc. Inc.
Zurick, Davis & Co.

I.16 PHARMACEUTICAL (OTHER THAN MANUFACTURING)

Aubin Int'l. Inc.
BioQuest Inc.
Blau Kaptain Schroeder
Blendow & Johnson Inc.
Coelyn Miller Phillip & Assoc.
DCS Assoc., Inc.
The Dartmouth Group
Drew Assoc. Int'l.
Euromedica USA
James Feerst & Assoc., Inc.
Gardiner Stone Hunter Int'l., Inc.
Allan Gardner & Assoc., Inc.
Guidry, East, Barnes & Bono, Inc.
R. W. Hebel Assoc.
Houtz, Strawn Assoc.
Jonah Kleinstein Assoc., Inc.
Kline Consulting, Inc.
Levin & Assoc.
The Neil Michael Group, Inc.
Palmer Assoc., Inc.
James Russell, Inc.
Sampson, Neill & Wilkins Inc.
The Stamford Group Inc.
Michael Tucker Assoc.
Venture Resources, Inc.
WDI, Int'l.
Zingaro & Co.

I.17 LEGAL

Auerbach Assoc.
J.W. Barleycorn & Assoc.
The Baxter Group
The Blackman Kallick Search Division
Canny, Bowen Inc.
Alfred Daniels & Assoc.
George Fee Assoc., Inc.
Holland Rusk & Assoc.
The Lumsden Co., Inc.
Montenido Assoc.
Page-Wheatcroft & Co. Ltd.
Richard Peterson & Assoc., Inc.
Raines Int'l. Inc.
SS & A Executive Search Consultants
Staples Consulting Inc.
Sullivan & Co.
The Yorkshire Group, Ltd.

I.18 COMPUTER SERVICES

Aim Executive Consulting Services
Lee Calhoon & Co., Inc.
Gustin Partners, Ltd.
The Hamilton Group
Henry Michaels & Assoc.
Holland, McFadzean & Assoc., Inc.

Human Resources, Inc.
Allan Karson Assoc., Inc.
McSherry & Assoc.
Montenido Assoc.
Page-Wheatcroft & Co. Ltd.
Peterson Consulting/W.P., Inc.
Pocrass Assoc.
David Powell, Inc.
Kimball Shaw Assoc.
Smith Search, S.A.
S. K. Stewart & Assoc.
Stewart/Laurence Assoc., Inc.
Strategic Alternatives
Trac One
Tuttle, Neidhart, Semyan, Inc.
Albert J. Walsh & Assoc.
Weir Executive Search Assoc., Inc.
Richard Winn & Co.

I.19 ACCOUNTING & MISCELLANEOUS BUSINESS SERVICES

Larsen Int'l., Inc.
McSherry & Assoc.
Meder & Assoc.
Martin H. Meisel Assoc., Inc.
O'Brien & Co., Inc.

I.20 EQUIPMENT SERVICES, INCLUDING LEASING

Alwyn Assoc., Inc.
Coelyn Miller Phillip & Assoc.
Western Reserve Search Assoc.

I.21 MANAGEMENT & PERSONNEL SERVICES

Alwyn Assoc., Inc.
Block & Assoc.
The DLR Group, Inc.
Drew Assoc. Int'l.
ESP Management Services, Inc.
Jay Gaines & Co.
Global Resources Group
Martin H. Meisel Assoc., Inc.
Perry-D'Amico & Assoc.

J.00 COMMUNICATIONS

The Badger Group
Baldwin Associates, Inc.
The Beam Group
The Bradbury Management Group
Brault & Assoc., Ltd.
Bryce, Haultain & Assoc.
Butterfass/Pepe Assoc., Inc.
The Communications Search Group
Grant Cooper & Assoc., Inc.
Corporate Staffing Group
Dromeshauser Assoc.
Dupuis & Ryden, P.C.
Excelsior Services Group Inc.
Gerald Frisch Assoc., Inc.
Gardiner Stone Hunter Int'l., Inc.

J.00 COMMUNICATIONS (Cont'd)

Gardner-Ross Assoc., Inc.
Hamlin Assoc.
Handy HRM
Harreus & Assoc., Inc.
Hauft Mark Assoc., Inc.
R. W. Hebel Assoc.
Heffelfinger Assoc., Inc.
Hergenrather & Co.
The Hindman Co.
J.B. Homer Assoc. Inc.
Howard-Sloan Communications Search
The Human Resource Consulting Group, Inc.
William Humphreys & Assoc., Inc.
Ingram, Inc.
Inside Management Assoc.
The Interface Group, Ltd.
Jeffrey Irving Assoc., Inc.
L.J. Johnson & Co.
Inge Judd Assoc.
Gary Kaplan & Assoc.
Melvin Kent & Assoc., Inc.
Richard Kinser & Assoc.
Koontz, Jeffries & Assoc., Inc.
Marvin Laba & Assoc.
Larkin & Co.
Lasher Assoc.
The Logan Group, Inc.
The John Lucht Consultancy Inc.
Robert Madigan Assoc., Inc.
Brad Marks Int'l.
The Mazzitelli Group, Ltd.
McDonald/Long Assoc., Inc.
The Onstott Group
G.S. Page Inc.
Frank Parillo & Assoc.
Polson & Co., Inc.
Quaintance Assoc., Inc.
Quinn Bailey & Morgan
Ramsey & Beirne Assoc., Inc.
SS & A Executive Search Consultants
Schenkel & Company
The Schmitt Tolette Group
Schweichler Assoc., Inc.
Search Source, Inc.
C.W. Sink & Co., Inc.
Robert L. Smith & Co., Inc.
Splaine & Assoc., Inc.
Stephens Assoc. Ltd.
Strategic Alternatives
Stricker & Zagor
Tucker Assoc.
The Thomas Tucker Co.
K. W. Tunnell Co., Inc.
John Velcamp & Assoc.
Venture Resources, Inc.
James L. Walsh & Assoc., Inc.
Wargo & Co., Inc.
Craig Williamson, Inc.

J.10 ADVERTISING/PUBLIC RELATIONS

Bialla & Assoc., Inc.
Bishop Assoc.

The Communications Search Group
The Corporate Source Group
Educational Management Network
Harreus & Assoc., Inc.
Hartman, Barnette & Assoc.
The Hawkins Co.
Lansky Assoc.
Brad Marks Int'l.
F. B. Schmidt Intl.
A. William Smyth, Inc.
VideoFields, Ltd.
Walker Group, Inc.
C. Weiss Assoc., Inc.
S. R. Wolman Assoc., Inc.

J.11 PUBLISHING, PRINT MEDIA

Bishop Assoc.
David M. Ellner Assoc.
Executive Resource Group
Farrell & Phin, Inc.
Fogec Consultants
Gardner-Ross Assoc., Inc.
The Hawkins Co.
Howard-Sloan Communications Search
Johnson Smith & Knisely Inc.
Inge Judd Assoc.
Langer Assoc., Inc.
Brad Marks Int'l.
Barry Persky & Co., Inc.
Redden & McGrath Assoc., Inc.
The Schmitt Tolette Group
Sheridan Search

J.12 TV, CABLE, MOTION PICTURES, VIDEO, RADIO

Bishop Assoc.
The Hawkins Co.
Inge Judd Assoc.
T. J. Koellhoffer & Assoc.
F. L. Mannix & Co., Inc.
Brad Marks Int'l.
The Schmitt Tolette Group
Search Source, Inc.
Joe Sullivan & Assoc., Inc.
VideoFields, Ltd.
WTW Assoc., Inc.
James L. Walsh & Assoc., Inc.
S. R. Wolman Assoc., Inc.

J.13 TELEPHONE, TELECOMMUNICATIONS

Anderson Bradshaw Assoc., Inc.
Aubin Int'l. Inc.
Barton Raben, Inc.
Bishop Assoc.
Chase-Owens Assoc., Inc.
Corporate Staffing Group
Duggan & Company
FGI
Fenwick Partners
Jay Gaines & Co.
Gardner-Ross Assoc., Inc.

J.13 TELEPHONE, TELECOMMUNICATIONS

Gustin Partners, Ltd.
Gutreuter & Assoc.
Haley Assoc., Inc.
Hamlin Assoc.
The Hawkins Co.
Hockett Assoc., Inc.
Holland, McFadzean & Assoc., Inc.
The Human Resource Consulting Group, Inc.
Human Resources, Inc.
Michael James & Co., Inc.
George Kaludis Assoc., Inc.
Allan Karson Assoc., Inc.
Keane Assoc.
Kensington Management Consultants, Inc.
Kirkman & Searing
Robert Madigan Assoc., Inc.
The Marlow Group
McSherry & Assoc.
Paul Norsell & Assoc., Inc.
Pierce Assoc.
Pocrass Assoc.
Polson & Co., Inc.
Ramsey & Beirne Assoc., Inc.
James J. Rust Executive Search
Search Source, Inc.
Shaffer Consulting Group
Smith, Goerss & Ferneborg, Inc.
Stewart/Laurence Assoc., Inc.
P. T. Unger Assoc.
Venture Management
James L. Walsh & Assoc., Inc.
Weir Executive Search Assoc., Inc.
Wellington Management Group
Craig Williamson, Inc.

K.00 PUBLIC ADMINISTRATION/ GOVERNMENT

Auerbach Assoc.
Chrisman & Co., Inc.
Christopher-Patrick & Assoc.

The Elson Group, Inc.
Excelsior Services Group Inc.
Finnegan Assoc.
Gaffney Management Consultants
The Halyburton Co., Inc.
The Hawkins Co.
The Interface Group, Ltd.
Isaacson, Miller, Inc.
George Kaludis Assoc., Inc.
Kensington Management Consultants, Inc.
Ira W. Krinsky & Assoc.
The Landmark Consulting Group Inc.
The Mercer Group, Inc.
The PAR Group - Paul A. Reaume, Ltd.
Personnel Assoc.
Phillips Group of Companies
Norman Roberts & Assoc., Inc.
Robsham & Assoc.
SS & A Executive Search Consultants
Sathe & Assoc., Inc.
Harold Webb Assoc., Ltd.

K.10 DEFENSE

Peter Newell Bowen
Human Resource Research Inc.
T. J. Koellhoffer & Assoc.
J. E. Lessner Assoc., Inc.

L.00 NON-CLASSIFIABLE INDUSTRIES

The Abbott Group
Lee Calhoon & Co., Inc.
Robert Connelly & Assoc., Inc.
Educational Management Network
The Elliott Company
Empire International
Glou Int'l., Inc.
Gould & McCoy, Inc.
Hackett & Co.
Pinsker & Co., Inc.
The Rankin Group, Ltd.
Robsham & Assoc.

Contingency Recruiters, A to Z

Agencies and other firms in executive recruiting operating **all** or **part** of the time on a fee-paid basis payable on placement. Percentages of retainer and contingency work vary; check with individual firms.

Also in this section: Firms that we couldn't put up front because they didn't respond to our questionaire, which included specific questions on degree of contingency operation.

Full street address for Canada and Mexico when known.

Network membership, international affiliations and branches identified by name followed by city.

Indexes for contingency functions, industries, geography and key principals immediately follow these listings.

A. D. & Assoc.

5589 Woodsong Dr., Ste. 100
Atlanta, Georgia 30338
Salary Minimum: $35,000
Key Contact: A. Dwight Hawksworth

Functions: Most + 05.0 05.4 08.0 09.0 09.7
Industries: Most + D.H0 H.00 I.00 I.19 J.13
Description: Professional group that recognizes human importance when filling professional positions

ACC Consultants, Inc.

P.O. Box 91240
Albuquerque, New Mexico 87199
Key Contact: Jerry Berger

Functions: 01.1 01.2 01.3 11.5
Industries: A.00 B.0W B.10 I.10
Description: Geologists, hydrogeologists, chemical/civil/environmental engineers, industrial hygienists

ACR Assoc.

26616 Heather Brook
El Toro, California 92630
Salary Minimum: $50,000
Key Contact: W. Jeff Hausheer, Ph.D.

Functions: 04.0 11.3
Industries: D.10 I.16
Professional Affiliations: AAPS, AMWA, ASA, ASQC, DIA, RAPS
Description: Specialists in pharmaceutical, biotechnology & medical device R & D positions

AGRI-associates

500 Nichols Rd.
Kansas City, Missouri 64112
Salary Minimum: $25,000
Key Contact: Glenn J. Person

Functions: 01.0 02.0 04.0 06.0 07.0
Industries: A.00
Description: Specialize in personnel search & recruiting for agribusiness

AJS Assoc.

34208 Aurora Rd., Ste. 193
Solon, Ohio 44139
Salary Minimum: $30,000
Key Contact: Richard A. Smith
Chuck Cotter

Functions: Most + 01.4 09.0
Industries: Most + D.00 I.00
Description: Computer software professional services & human resource services specialists

A.L.S. Group

104 Mt. Joy Road
Milford, New Jersey 08848
Salary Minimum: $35,000
Key Contact: Scott Lysenko
Lisa Lysenko

Functions: 08.2 08.3
Industries: H.00 H.10 H.11 H.12 H.R0
Professional Affiliations: MAAPC, NJAPC
Description: Specializing in corporate lending, commercial lending & investment banking

A.M.C.R., Inc.

55 South Miller Rd., Ste. 202
Akron, Ohio 44313
Salary Minimum: $30,000
Key Contact: Randall S. Caldwell
William R. Hinebaugh
Harvey M. Lipton

Functions: 01.0 02.0 04.0 05.0 06.0
Industries: Most + D.00 D.16 D.19 D.D0
Professional Affiliations: IACPR, ACS, NAER, NAPC, NPA, OAPC, RMA, SHRM, SPE, STLE
Description: Executive search, contingency recruiting, employee relations consulting & outplacement firm

APA Search, Inc.

271 Madison Ave., Ste. 605
New York, New York 10016
Key Contact: Howard Kesten

Functions: Most + 02.0 02.2 03.0 03.1 05.0
Industries: D.00 D.20 D.22 E.00 I.20
Professional Affiliations: AIA, NAPC, SEMA
Description: A search firm handling all divisions of the automotive industry

ARJay & Assoc.

875 Walnut St., Ste. 150
Cary, North Carolina 27511
Salary Minimum: $30,000
Key Contact: Ronald T. Jones
Russell E. Miller

Functions: 01.0 02.0 03.0 04.0 05.0
Industries: B.00 D.22 D.24 D.H0
Professional Affiliations: NAPC
Description: Technical recruiting & executive search for engineers, scientists & management professionals

Abacus Consultants

1777 S. Harrison, Ste. 404
Denver, Colorado 80210
Salary Minimum: $30,000
Key Contact: Stephen J. Kukoy
Sandra M. Kukoy

Functions: 01.4 09.1 09.3 09.4 09.7
Industries: D.00 D.H0 H.00 H.I0 I.18
Professional Affiliations: NCA
Description: A well known & respected search firm specializing in MIS & accounting

Abbott, James & Oliver

644 N. Santa Cruz Ave., Ste. 13
Los Gatos, California 95030
Salary Minimum: $30,000
Key Contact: K. James Pond

Functions: 09.2 09.3 09.4 09.7
Industries: D.H0
Professional Affiliations: NAPC
Description: Technical search: upper level, engineers scientists, sales, marketing, manufacturing

Aberdeen Assoc.

25 Huntington Ave.
Boston, Massachusetts 02116
Salary Minimum: $45,000
Key Contact: Robert McLeish

Functions: 01.3 02.3 05.4 11.6
Industries: B.00 C.00 D.25
Description: Specializing in the building automation, HVAC & energy service industry

Abraham & London Ltd.

51 Sugar Hollow Rd.
Danbury, Connecticut 06810
Salary Minimum: $30,000
Key Contact: Todd Scott
William Bowen

Functions: 05.0 09.2 09.4 09.7
Industries: D.18 D.H0 D.I0 I.18 J.13
Professional Affiliations: CAPC, FIN, NAPC
Description: Middle management—executive level appointments nationwide in sales/ marketing & support

Academy Graduates Executive Search, Inc.

576 Post Rd., Ste. 210
Darien, Connecticut 06820
Salary Minimum: $33,000
Key Contact: Nathaniel Gallagher

Functions: Most
Industries: Most
Description: A generalist firm, candidates are graduates of U.S. service academies

Accountants

1101 Kermit Dr., Ste. 301
Nashville, Tennessee 37217
Key Contact: Milton H. Ellis

Functions: 08.0 08.1 08.2 08.3 08.4
Description: Full service accounting & finance placements

Accountants On Call

Park 80 W., Plz. II, Garden State Pkwy.
Interstate 80, 9th Fl.
Saddle Brook, New Jersey 07662
Key Contact: Stewart C. Libes
Doris J. Fitzsimmons
Dory Libes
Debbie Buchsbaum
Linda Krutzsch

Functions: 08.0 09.3
Industries: Most
Professional Affiliations: NAPC
Description: Nationwide specialists in the placement of temporary & permanent accounting personnel

Branches:
10929 South St., #204B
Cerritos, California 90701
Key Contact: Norma Constantino

973 N. Grand Ave.
Covina, California 91722

10100 Santa Monica Blvd., #1120
Los Angeles, California 90017
Key Contact: Ira Streitfeld

801 S. Grand Ave., #425
Los Angeles, California 90017
Key Contact: Diane Tice

5000 Birch St., Ste. 550
Newport Beach, California 92660-2132
Key Contact: Kathy Elston

4640 Lankershim Blvd., Ste. 500
North Hollywood, California 91602
Key Contact: Diane O'Meally

7677 Oakport St., #180
Oakland, California 94621
Key Contact: Louis Kruezer

525 University Ave., #23
Palo Alto, California 94301
Key Contact: Gayleen Morris

44 Montgomery St., #840
San Francisco, California 94104
Key Contact: Sara Boyd

2055 Gateway Pl., Ste. 140
San Jose, California 95110
Key Contact: Michael Boyd

23440 Hawthorne Blvd., Ste. 240
Torrance, California 90505
Key Contact: Dennis Defeo

2175 N. California Blvd., Ste. 615
Walnut Creek, California 94596
Key Contact: Kathleen W. Allatore

21800 Oxnard St., Ste. 750
Woodland Hills, California 91367
Key Contact: William DeMario

1650 Spruce St., Ste. 210
Riverside, California 92507
Key Contact: Vic Schneider

100 Howe Ave., Ste. 210N
Sacramento, California 95825
Key Contact: Ron Garner
Ann Garner

100 Constitution Pl., Ste. 957
Hartford, Connecticut 06103
Key Contact: Larry Greenbaum
Marvin Sternlicht

2777 Summer St.
Stamford, Connecticut 06905
Key Contact: Marvin Sternlicht

Christiana Exec. Campus
220 Continental Dr., Ste. 213
Newark, Delaware 19713
Key Contact: Carole Leskin

800 Douglas Entrance
Coral Gables, Florida 33134
Key Contact: Daniel Perron

2699 Lee Rd., Ste. 525
Winter Park, Florida 32789
Key Contact: Don Phillips

200 N. LaSalle St., #2830
Chicago, Illinois 60601
Key Contact: Julianne Weiss

3400 Dundee Rd., Ste. 260
Northbrook, Illinois 60062
Key Contact: Bridget O'Connell

99 Summer St., Ste. 1610
Boston, Massachusetts 02110
Key Contact: Beth LeClaire

161 Worcester Rd.
Framingham, Massachusetts 01701
Key Contact: Beth Herman

6 St. Paul St., Ste. 2204
Baltimore, Maryland 21202
Key Contact: David Mayer

Plaza VII Bldg., 45 S. 7th St., Ste. 2312
Minneapolis, Minnesota 55402
Key Contact: Jan Kruchoski

911 Main St., Ste. 620
Kansas City, Missouri 64105
Key Contact: Jonathan Brandt

515 N. 6th St., Ste. 610
St. Louis, Missouri 63101
Key Contact: Mark Rahe

111 Westport Plz., Ste. 512
Westport Plaza, Missouri 63146
Key Contact: Carol Kennedy

505 Thornall St.
Edison, New Jersey 08837
Key Contact: Sue Ellen Hepworth

354 Eisenhower Pkwy.
Livingston, New Jersey 07039
Key Contact: Rita Silverstein

The Atruim, E. 80 Rte. 4, Ste. 430
Paramus, New Jersey 07652
Key Contact: Neil Lebovits

Princeton Corp. Ctr.
5 Independence Way
Princeton, New Jersey 08540
Key Contact: Sandi Wujack

Evesham Corp. Ctr.
3 Eves Dr., Ste. 302
Marlton, New Jersey 08053
Key Contact: Mark S. Libes

450 Harmon Meadow Blvd., 3rd Fl.
Secaucus, New Jersey 07094
Key Contact: Brad Violette

400 Jericho Tpke., #320
Jericho, New York 11753

535 Fifth Ave.
New York, New York 10606
Key Contact: Bernard M. Simon

50 Main St., 10th Fl.
White Plains, New York 10606
Key Contact: Marvin Sternlicht

250 E. Fifth St., Ste. 1630
Chiquita Ctr.
Cincinnati, Ohio 45202
Key Contact: Gary Merrifield

41 S. High St., Ste. 2490
Huntington Ctr.
Columbus, Ohio 43215
Key Contact: John Marshall
Russell Sheetz

International Branches:
Hertforshire

Accountants On Call
1715 N. Westshore Ave., Ste. 753
Westshore Ctr.
Tampa, Florida 33607
Key Contact: Jeffrey Waldon
Maita Waldon

Accountants On Call
3355 Lenox Rd. NE, Ste. 630
Atlanta, Georgia 30326
Key Contact: Stacy Selbo

Valley Forge Plz., 1150 First Ave., #1005
King of Prussia, Pennsylvania 19406
Key Contact: Mark S. Libes

1600 Market St., #3318
Philadelphia, Pennsylvania 19103
Key Contact: Mark S. Libes

300 Crescent Ct., Ste. 930
The Crescent Bldg.
Dallas, Texas 75201
Key Contact: Sherri Ferris

5520 LBJ Freeway, #150
Dallas, Texas 75240
Key Contact: Brett Schaifer

1980 Post Oak Blvd., Ste. 1300
Houston, Texas 77056
Key Contact: Bea Battistoni

8000 Towers Crescent Dr., Ste. 250
Vienna, Virginia 22182
Key Contact: Michael Parbs

3333 N. Mayfair Rd., Ste. 112
Milwaukee, Wisconsin 53222

P.O. Box 49292
The Bentall Ctr.
Vancouver, British Columbia V7X 1P5
    Canada

40 Dundas St. West, Ste. 225
P.O. Box 75
Toronto, Ontario M5G 2C2 Canada

Functions: 07.1 07.4 08.0 08.1 08.2
Industries: Most + D.E0 D.H0 H.00 I.18 I.19
Description: Temporary & permanent financial
    personnel

Professional Affiliations: AAPC, APA, NAPC
Description: Specializing in accounting &
    finance with temporary & permanent
    placement

Accounting & Computer Personnel

220 Salina Meadows Pkwy., Ste. 220
Syracuse, New York 13212
Salary Minimum: $20,000
Key Contact: William E. Winnewisser

Functions: 01.0 05.4 07.4 08.0 09.0
Industries: Most
Professional Affiliations: APCC, ASM, DPMA, IPCCNY, NAA, NAPC, NFIB
Description: Specialists in placing accounting, financial, computer & MIS management professionals

Accounting Personnel Assoc.

100 First Ave.
Pittsburgh, Pennsylvania 15222
Key Contact: Dennis J. Papciak
Robert H. Pachavis

Functions: 03.1 06.0 07.4 08.0 11.1
Industries: Most
Professional Affiliations: AAFA, AICPA, ASWCPA, DPMA, IIA, NAA, NAPC
Description: Twenty-six years of experience, devoted exclusively to financial recruitment

Accounting Resources Int'l., Inc.

2670 Del Mar Heights Rd., Ste. 213
Del Mar, California 92014
Salary Minimum: $30,000
Key Contact: T. Robert Storevik

Functions: 02.0 08.0 09.0 11.0 11.1
Industries: D.00 D.H0 D.I0 H.00 I.14
Professional Affiliations: AICPA, NAA
Description: Specialize in CPA's, financial executives, management consultants & litigation support pros

Branches:
410 17th St., Ste. 1355
Denver, Colorado 80202
Key Contact: Dan Colwell

88A Elm St.
Hopkinton, Massachusetts 01748
Key Contact: Mike O'Brien

P.O. Box 890063
Houston, Texas 77289
Key Contact: Dan Haller

11 Broadway
New York, New York 10004
Key Contact: Bob Kaufmann

2261 Brookhollow Plaza, Ste. 100
Arlington, Texas 76006
Key Contact: Tom Hinds

Ace Resources

6776 Southwest Fwy., Ste. 150
Houston, Texas 77074
Salary Minimum: $25,000
Key Contact: Peter E. Osagie
Patience Osula
Isoken Osagie

Functions: Most
Industries: D.17 D.18 I.14 I.15 I.16
Professional Affiliations: NAPC, TAPC
Description: The search & placement firm for all medical & healthcare facilities—service & manufacturing

Action Inc.

390 Commercial St.
Boston, Massachusetts 02109
Salary Minimum: $35,000
Key Contact: Proctor A. Coffin

Functions: Most
Industries: Most
Description: Executive search & consulting in organizational problems

AdStaff Personnel, Inc.

201 Rosser Ave., P.O. Box 1085
Waynesboro, Virginia 22980
Key Contact: David D. Gilliam

Functions: Most
Industries: Most
Description: Provide professional recruiting service for executive, technical & administration positions

Arthur Adams & Assoc.

100 E. Wilson Bridge Rd., Ste. 217
Worthington, Ohio 43085
Salary Minimum: $40,000
Key Contact: Arthur Adams

Functions: 05.4
Industries: D.24
Professional Affiliations: NAER
Description: Contingency/retainer search in the computer networking sales/marketing field

The Adams Group

7840 Madison Ave., Ste. 185
Fair Oaks, California 95628
Salary Minimum: $50,000
Key Contact: Bruce W. Adams

Functions: 11.5
Industries: B.10
Professional Affiliations: CAPC, NAPC, NEN
Description: Exclusively hazardous waste search with emphasis on analytical laboratories/remediation

The Addison Consulting Group

P.O. Box 1007
Turnersville, New Jersey 08012
Salary Minimum: $50,000
Key Contact: Sandy Korkuch

Functions: 01.0 02.0 04.0 05.0
Industries: D.17 D.18 D.I0
Description: Dedicated to discerning service combined with extensive industry specific expertise

Additional Technical Support Inc.

1466 Main St.
Waltham, Massachusetts 02254-9018
Salary Minimum: $30,000
Key Contact: Michael Nolan

Functions: 11.3 11.5 11.6
Industries: B.00 B.0W B.10 D.00 D.15
Description: We have supplied industries nationwide with temporary and permanent engineering personnel

Adel Lawrence Assoc., Inc.

142 Hwy. 34
Aberdeen, New Jersey 07747
Salary Minimum: $25,000
Key Contact: Larry Radzely
Allan Adams
Mark Stadnyk

Functions: 01.3 02.0 09.4 11.3 11.6
Industries: D.15 D.18 D.24 D.25 D.H0
Professional Affiliations: MAAPC, NJAPC
Description: Specializing in nationwide placement of engineering, biomedical & technical personnel

Adept Tech Recruiting, Inc.

1 Summit Ave., Ste. 12
White Plains, New York 10606
Salary Minimum: $20,000
Key Contact: Fredrick R. Press

Functions: 02.0 03.0 04.0 09.0 11.3
Industries: D.00 D.E0 D.H0 I.14 I.18
Description: Permanent placement of professional technical personnel

The Adler Group

1560 Broadway, Ste. 905
New York, New York 10036
Salary Minimum: $50,000
Key Contact: Eric Adler

Functions: 01.4 05.4 06.0 06.1 06.2
Industries: Most
Description: Contingency & retained search in human resources—gen. mgmt search includes sales, marketing, MIS

Advanced Corporate Search

3180 Sumac Ridge Rd.
Malibu, California 90265
Salary Minimum: $35,000
Key Contact: Jan Gibson
Lee Davis

Functions: 04.0 05.2 09.4 10.0 11.3
Industries: D.H0 H.I0 J.13 K.10
Professional Affiliations: AFCEA, AOC
Description: Respect from industry executives for honesty, ethics & professionalism

Advanced Information Management

444 Castro St., #320
Mountain View, California 94041
Salary Minimum: $25,000
Key Contact: Linda McKell
Yvonne Boxerman

Professional Affiliations: ALA, CLA, SLA
Description: Library, research & information
    personnel

Branches:
3020 Old Ranch Pky.
Seal Beach, California 90740-2751
Key Contact: Jeanne Spala

Advancement Recruiting Services

P.O. Box 620083
Cleveland, Ohio 44102
Salary Minimum: $30,000
Key Contact: Rudy Socha

Functions: Most + 02.0 04.0 09.0
Industries: B.0W D.00 D.E0 D.H0 D.I0
Professional Affiliations: NAPC
Description: We handle all disciplines &
    industries

John R. Ady & Assoc., Inc.

514 N. Neil St., Ste. A
Champaign, Illinois 61820
Salary Minimum: $35,000
Key Contact: John R. Ady
Sharon L. Ady
Shelly Miles

Functions: Most + 11.0
Industries: D.00 D.10 D.22 E.00 I.14
Professional Affiliations: IPA
Description: Generalist firm serving primarily
    manufacturing organizations in most
    functional areas

Aerospace Technologies, Inc.

3000 Aviation Way
P.O. Box 825
Wallingford, Connecticut 06492
Salary Minimum: $30,000
Key Contact: F.L. Bailey
Evelyn J. Zyzo
Robert Stuart

Functions: 02.0 03.0 04.0 09.0
Industries: D.00 D.E0 D.H0 E.00
Professional Affiliations: ASM, ASMC, IEEE
Description: Concentration in developing
    engineering & manufacturing expertise for
    aerospace industry

Affirmative Action Assoc.

8 Oxford Ave., Ste. 117
North Massapequa, New York 11758
Salary Minimum: $25,000
Key Contact: Melvyn Black

Functions: Most
Industries: Most
Description: Specialize in recruitment of
    minorities, female & the disabled

The Agency- An Employment Consortium

16027 Ventura Blvd., Ste. 503
Encino, California 91436
Salary Minimum: $25,000
Key Contact: Lee Garfield
Amy Haber

Functions: Most + 02.0 10.0 11.5
Industries: Most + B.0W D.00 H.I0 I.14
Professional Affiliations: CAPC, NAPC
Description: Specialize in insurance,
    manufacturing, health, safety,
    environmental & healthcare

Agra Placements, Ltd.

4949 Pleasant St., Ste. 1
West 50th Place III
West Des Moines, Iowa 50265
Salary Minimum: $25,000
Key Contact: Perry M. Schneider
Gary Follmer

Functions: Most
Industries: A.00 B.0W D.00 D.I0 F.00
Professional Affiliations: ASTA, IAPC, NAPC
Description: Recruit managers, sales, &
    technical professionals for agribusiness &
    horticultural companies

Branches:
1104 Keokuk
Lincoln, Illinois 62656
Key Contact: Perry M. Schneider

16 E. 5th St., Berkshire Ct.
Peru, Indiana 46970
Key Contact: Doug Rice

Agri-Personnel
5120 Old Bill Cook Rd.
Atlanta, Georgia 30349
Key Contact: David J. Wicker

Agri-Tech Personnel, Inc.
3113 NE 69th St.
Kansas City, Missouri 64119
Salary Minimum: $20,000
Key Contact: Dale Pickering

Aim Executive Inc.
35000 Chardon Rd.
Willoughby Hills, Ohio 44094
Salary Minimum: $25,000
Key Contact: Thomas Beers
Scott R. De Perro

Aitken & Assoc.
P.O. Box 317
Chadds Ford, Pennsylvania 19317
Salary Minimum: $30,000
Key Contact: Carol Aitken

Alaska Executive Search, Inc.
821 "N" St., Ste. 204
Anchorage, Alaska 99501-6093
Salary Minimum: $24,000
Key Contact: Robert E. Bulmer

Alexander Edward Assoc., Inc.
1218 Chestnut St., Ste. 511
Philadelphia, Pennsylvania 19107
Salary Minimum: $28,000
Key Contact: R. Edwin Alexander
Scott Etter
Ed McGovern

Alexander Enterprises, Inc.
P.O. Box 148
Center Square, Pennsylvania 19422
Salary Minimum: $25,000
Key Contact: Florence D. Young

10800 Lyndale Ave. S., Ste. 214
Minneapolis, Minnesota 55420
Key Contact: Roger Malin

Functions: Most
Industries: A.00 B.0W D.10 D.15 D.I0
Professional Affiliations: ASAC, GAPC, NAPC
Description: Specialists in agribusiness
executive professional & technical search
& plcmt nationwide & worldwide

Functions: Most + 01.0 02.0 03.0 04.0 05.0
Industries: Most + A.00 D.00 D.D0 D.I0 E.00
Description: Worldwide search & placement in
the food & agri-business industries

Functions: Most
Industries: D.19 D.23 E.00
Description: Full human resource consulting
firm

Functions: 01.4 09.3 09.4
Industries: Most
Professional Affiliations: MAAPC, NAPC
Description: MIS recruiter for mid-range and
mainframe clients in PA, NJ & DE

Functions: Most
Industries: B.0W C.00 H.00 I.00 J.13
Description: Executive search & consulting
business specializing in the Alaskan
marketplace

Functions: 09.0 09.1 09.3 09.4 09.7
Industries: D.24 D.H0 I.18 J.13 K.10
Description: Technical recruiting organization
emphasizing the information processing
industry worldwide

Functions: 06.0
Industries: D.17 D.18 D.I0 I.15 I.16
Professional Affiliations: ACA, ASPA, EMA
Description: Specialize in placement of all
pharmaceutical professionals & human
resources professionals

Frank E. Allen & Assoc.

15 James St.
Florham Park, New Jersey 07932
Salary Minimum: $45,000
Key Contact: Frank Allen
Linda Braun
Nancy Danker

Functions: 06.0 06.1 06.2
Industries: C.00 D.00 H.00 H.I0 H.R0
Description: An executive search resource
specializing in employee relations &
human resources

D.S. Allen Assoc.

823 S. Springfield Ave.
Springfield, New Jersey 07081
Salary Minimum: $25,000
Key Contact: Don Allen
Mark Presler

Functions: Most
Industries: B.0W D.00 D.H0 I.00 J.00
Professional Affiliations: IACPR
Description: We are an executive search/
management consulting firm specializing
in hi-tech & consumer products

Branches:
4 Adelante, Ste. 200
Irvine, California 92714
Key Contact: Muriel Levitt

4 Commerce Park Sq.
24200 Chagrin Blvd., Ste. 222
Beachwood, Ohio 44122
Key Contact: John Falk

David Allen Assoc.

Box 8783
Red Bank, New Jersey 07701
Salary Minimum: $25,000
Key Contact: David Ritchings
Mary Stark

Functions: 01.4 05.2 06.0 08.0
Industries: B.00 D.10 D.18 D.H0 H.10
Professional Affiliations: NJAPC
Description: Professionals representing industry
leaders in seven industries nationwide

Pat Allen Assoc. Inc.

P.O. Box Q
Goldens Bridge, New York 10526
Salary Minimum: $30,000
Key Contact: Pat Allen

Functions: 10.0
Industries: H.I0
Professional Affiliations: NAPC
Description: Specialists in insurance safety, IH,
HPR

Allen Barry Assoc.

371 S. Broadway
Tarrytown, New York 10591
Salary Minimum: $40,000
Key Contact: Allen B. Ancowitz
Mary Jane Schaumann

Functions: Most + 02.0 04.0 07.0 11.2 11.3
Industries: B.0W D.00 D.H0 D.I0 I.00
Professional Affiliations: ASHRM, NYBA
Description: Executive & professional search in
R&D, marketing, manufacturing, sales,
finance & administration

Ethan Allen Personnel, Inc.

404 Troy-Schenectady Rd.
Latham, New York 12110
Salary Minimum: $30,000
Key Contact: Harris Metzner
M. James Roarke

Functions: 02.0 06.0 10.0
Industries: H.I0 I.14
Professional Affiliations: DPMA, EMA, NAPC
Description: 23 years of providing specialized
recruiting services

Allen/Assoc.

4555 Lake Forest Dr.
650 Westlake Ctr.
Cincinnati, Ohio 45242
Salary Minimum: $60,000
Key Contact: Michael Allen

Functions: Most
Industries: Most
Professional Affiliations: NAHB, NARI
Description: Exclusively accepts senior level
assignments for building products
manufacturers & distributors

Allied Financial Management Co.

1001 SW 5th Ave., Ste. 1000
Portland, Oregon 97204
Salary Minimum: $40,000
Key Contact: Edward W. Cameron

Functions: 08.0
Industries: Most
Professional Affiliations: FEI
Description: Specialists in fields of accounting
& financial management

Allied Search, Inc.

2030 Union St., Ste. 205
San Francisco, California 94123
Salary Minimum: $20,000
Key Contact: Don May

Functions: 08.0 09.1 11.1
Industries: Most
Professional Affiliations: AICPA, ASWCPA,
CACPA, CAPC, EDPAA, IIA, NABA,
NAPC
Description: Public accounting & industry
positions located nationwide & worldwide

Branches:
8530 Wilshire Blvd., Ste. 404
Beverly Hills, California 90211

Alpine Consulting Group

19372 Sunray Ln., Ste. 204
Huntington Beach, California 92648
Salary Minimum: $25,000
Key Contact: Sharon Lamb

Functions: 02.0 03.0 04.0 05.0 11.1
Industries: D.10
Description: Food industry placements in sales,
marketing, technical & plant operations

The Altco Group

100 Menlo Park
Edison, New Jersey 08837
Salary Minimum: $35,000
Key Contact: R. Alt

Functions: 02.3 02.4 03.4 11.3
Industries: D.10 D.16 D.17 D.18 D.D0
Professional Affiliations: NAPC
Description: Operations & technical positions
for medical device, pharmaceutical & food
industries

Alterna-track

575 Madison Ave., Ste. 1006
New York, New York 10022
Salary Minimum: $50,000
Key Contact: Melinda Heslop
Adrienne Rosenfeld

Functions: Most + 01.0 05.0 06.0 08.0 09.0
Industries: H.00 J.00
Description: Interim placement executive
search firm for part-time professionals

Alzed Real Estate Recruiters

Four Gateway Ctr., Ste. 205
Pittsburgh, Pennsylvania 15222
Salary Minimum: $40,000
Key Contact: David E. Stobbe

Functions: Most
Industries: C.00 H.R0 I.13 K.00
Professional Affiliations: ICSC, NAIOP
Description: Specializing in real estate industry,
as well as non-profits

Amato & Assoc., Inc.

#3 Embarcadero, Ste. 1655
San Francisco, California 94111
Salary Minimum: $20,000
Key Contact: Joseph D. Amato

Functions: 05.2 05.4
Industries: H.I0
Professional Affiliations: RIMS
Description: Commercial line insurance:
underwriting, sales, marketing, producers;
$20,000–$200,000

American Resources Corp.
175 N. Harbor Dr. Ste. 3704
Chicago, Illinois 60601
Salary Minimum: $30,000
Key Contact: Osita Oruche, III.
Gene Mojekwu
Steven Grimes
Nike Oruche
Richard Nixon

Functions: 01.0 02.0 06.0 08.0 09.0
Industries: Most
Description: We specialize in the selection of
management professionals

Ames Assoc. Inc.
6935 Wisconsin Ave., Ste. 300
Chevy Chase, Maryland 20815
Salary Minimum: $50,000
Key Contact: Michael J. Ames
Mildred S. Ames

Functions: 01.0 08.0 11.5
Industries: C.00 H.10 H.R0
Professional Affiliations: IACPR
Description: Mid to upper management
positions-commercial, residential mortgage
construction & property mgmt.

Ames Personnel Consultants
34 Hennessey Ave., P.O. Box 651
Brunswick, Maine 04011
Salary Minimum: $30,000
Key Contact: Philip J. Ames

Functions: Most
Industries: Most + B.00 B.0W D.11 D.13
D.19
Professional Affiliations: NAPC, PIMA, TAPPI
Description: Nationwide recruiting &
placement with specialists covering all
disciplines in most industries

Ames-O'Neill Assoc., Inc.
330 Vanderbilt Motor Pkwy.
Hauppauge, New York 11788
Salary Minimum: $20,000
Key Contact: George C. Ames
John J. O'Neill

Functions: Most + 02.0 03.0 04.0 05.0 06.0
Industries: B.0W D.00 D.E0 D.H0 J.13
Professional Affiliations: IPA
Description: We specialize in the recruitment
of high-technology engineering specialists
& managers

Amherst Personnel Group Inc.
550 Old Country Rd., Ste. 203
Hicksville, New York 11801
Salary Minimum: $20,000
Key Contact: Charles J. Eibeler

Functions: Most
Industries: Most
Professional Affiliations: APCNY, NAPC,
NJAPC
Description: 25th year specializing in sales/
marketing, & retailing management

Branches:
133 S. Main St.
Milltown, New Jersey 08850
Key Contact: Neil Eibeler

Analysts Resources Inc.
75 Maiden Ln.
New York, New York 10038
Salary Minimum: $60,000
Key Contact: Monica L. Smith

Functions: 08.0 08.2
Professional Affiliations: FAF
Description: Executive search firm which
recruits investment professionals

Analytic Recruiting, Inc.
1 East 42nd St., Ste. 1002
New York, New York 10017
Salary Minimum: $30,000
Key Contact: Daniel Raz
Rita Raz

Functions: 03.3 05.3 05.5 08.0 09.0
Industries: D.10 D.18 H.00 I.18 J.10
Professional Affiliations: ASA, NASCP, ORSA, TIMS
Description: Specialize in quantitative/ analytical business positions nationwide-analyst through director lvl

Francis V. Anderson Assoc. Inc.
980 N. Michigan Ave., Ste. 1400
Chicago, Illinois 60611
Salary Minimum: $50,000
Key Contact: Francis V. Anderson, Jr.

Functions: 01.3 02.1 02.4 04.0 11.3
Industries: D.17 D.18 D.I0 I.13 I.16
Professional Affiliations: AAAS, AAPS, ACS, ASM, DIA, PDA
Description: Industries: pharmaceuticals/ biotechnology/university science-based positions

Anderson, Graham & Stewart, Inc.
2109 Allgood Rd.
Marietta, Georgia 30062
Salary Minimum: $50,000
Key Contact: Gregory B. Graham

Functions: 02.3 05.0 05.4 09.2 09.4
Industries: D.24 D.25 D.H0
Description: Sales/marketing positions for mfgrs. of discreet process control factory automation products

Anderson Industrial Assoc., Inc.
P.O. Box 767005
Roswell, Georgia 30076-7005
Salary Minimum: $25,000
Key Contact: Gregory D. Anderson
A. M. Anderson
Lee Baxter

Functions: Most
Industries: Most
Description: Professional recruiting firm placing degreed engineers exclusively

Tryg R. Angell Ltd.
2885 Main St.
Stratford, Connecticut 06497
Key Contact: Tryg Angell

Functions: Most + 01.0 02.0 03.3 04.0 05.0
Industries: Most + B.00 C.00 D.00 D.D0 J.00
Professional Affiliations: NAPC
Description: Industrial sales & marketing expertise oriented toward paper printing & graphics

The Angus Group, Inc.
2337 Victory Pkwy.
Cincinnati, Ohio 45206
Salary Minimum: $25,000
Key Contact: Thomas R. Angus
Cindy Schafer
Dave Hartig
Pete Nadherny

Functions: Most
Industries: Most
Professional Affiliations: NPA
Description: Recruiting services to businesses, most disciplines

John Anthony & Assoc.
P.O. Box 12291
La Jolla, California 92039
Salary Minimum: $50,000
John A. Muller, Jr.

Functions: Most + 01.0 02.0 08.0 11.3 11.5
Industries: Most + B.00 B.0W C.00 D.H0 D.I0
Description: Executive search/recruiting in corporate & professional areas

R.W. Apple & Assoc.
200 Atlantic Ave., Box 200
Manasquan, New Jersey 08736
Salary Minimum: $30,000
Key Contact: Richard W. Apple

Functions: 11.1 11.3 11.5
Industries: B.0W B.10
Professional Affiliations: IACPR, ASPA, SMPS
Description: Provide executive search services to technology based consulting firms

Charles P. Aquavella & Assoc.
5925 Longo Dr.
The Colony, Texas 75056
Salary Minimum: $30,000
Key Contact: Charles P. Aquavella

Functions: 01.0 02.4 03.1 05.4 06.0
Industries: D.12 D.23 D.26 G.00
Description: Specializing in personnel management, all manufacturing, general mgmt & manufactured housing

Arancio Assoc.
542 High Rock St.
Needham, Massachusetts 02192
Salary Minimum: $20,000
Key Contact: N. Joseph Arancio

Functions: Most + 05.2 05.3 05.4 11.3
Industries: D.15 D.18 D.25 D.26 D.I0
Description: Primary focus-capital equipment & process manufacturing for Chem.E's, Chemists & Biologists

Aronow Assoc., Inc.
1 Pennsylvania Plz., Ste. 5114
New York, New York 10119
Salary Minimum: $40,000
Key Contact: Lawrence E. Aronow

Functions: 01.0 05.0 08.0 09.0 10.0
Industries: H.00 H.I0
Description: Management recruiting for the financial services industry

E. J. Ashton & Assoc., Ltd.
3125 N. Wilke Rd., Ste. A
Arlington Heights, Illinois 60004
Salary Minimum: $25,000
Key Contact: Edward J. Ashton

Functions: 01.2 01.3 05.4 08.0 10.0
Industries: H.00 H.10 H.11 H.I0 I.14
Professional Affiliations: INS, NAPC
Description: Executive recruiters/consultants in & for the insurance industry nationwide

Ashton Computer Professionals, Inc.
1090 W. Georgia St., Ste. 1000
Vancouver, British Columbia V6E 3V7
    Canada
Salary Minimum: $30,000
Key Contact: Barbara L. Ashton
Jennifer Rigal
Brooke Allen

Functions: 01.0 01.4 02.3 05.0 09.0
Industries: D.E0 D.H0 I.18 J.13 K.10
Professional Affiliations: NAPC, NPA
Description: Western Canada's leading recruitment firm, serving all areas of advanced technology

Ashway Ltd. Agency
295 Madison Ave.
New York, New York 10017
Salary Minimum: $25,000
Key Contact: Steven King

Functions: Most + 02.0 04.0 10.0 11.3 11.6
Industries: D.15 D.18 D.H0 D.I0 H.I0
Professional Affiliations: AMA
Description: Specialize in science, technology, actuarial & insurance; screened by professionals in the field

Atlantic Search Group, Inc.
30 Myano Ln.
Stamford, Connecticut 06902
Salary Minimum: $30,000
Key Contact: Jim Baker

Functions: 09.3 09.5 09.6 10.0
Industries: Most
Description: A nationwide contingency search firm specializing in technical recruiting

Atlantic Search Group, Inc.
114 State St.
Boston, Massachusetts 02109
Key Contact: John B. Beckvold
Dennis F. Moran
Robert B. Howell
Daniel F. Jones

Functions: 08.0 08.1 08.2 08.3 11.2
Industries: Most
Description: Specialists in accounting, finance, tax, auditing, in all industries

Atlantic West Int'l.
125 Kingston Dr., Ste. 101
Chapel Hill, North Carolina 27514
Salary Minimum: $45,000
Key Contact: Richard W. Valenti

Functions: Most + 01.0 02.0 03.0 04.0 05.0
Industries: D.17 D.18 D.I0 I.16
Description: Primary focus: medical devices, biotechnology, pharmaceuticals, national basis

Branches:
25108 Marguerite Pky., Ste. B6
Mission Viejo, California 92692

6337 S. Highland Dr., Ste. 300
Salt Lake City, Utah 84121
Key Contact: James H. Doddridge

Auden Assoc., Inc.
21 Pennywise Ln., P.O. Box 566
Old Saybrook, Connecticut 06475
Salary Minimum: $30,000
Key Contact: John DeCristoforo

Functions: 01.3 02.2 03.1 05.4 09.3
Industries: D.18 D.22 D.26 D.E0 D.H0
Professional Affiliations: CAPC, NAPC
Description: Engineering, pharmaceutical(drug research), sales/marketing & functional middle management

Austin—Allen Co.
8127 Walnut Grove Rd.
Cordova, Tennessee 38018
Salary Minimum: $30,000
Key Contact: C. A. Cupp

Functions: 02.0 03.0 06.0
Industries: Most
Description: Broad range of assignments in engineering, manufacturing, management & human resources

Automation Technology Search
7309 Del Cielo Way
Modesto, California 95356
Salary Minimum: $30,000
Key Contact: Ralph L. Becker

Functions: Most + 01.0 02.0 03.0 04.0 09.0
Industries: Most + B.0W D.00 D.H0 D.I0 J.00
Description: Recruiters of technical managers & engineers for all industries

Availability Personnel Consultants
169 S. River Rd.
Bedford, New Hampshire 03110-6936
Salary Minimum: $30,000
Key Contact: Walter D. Kilian
Lawrence F. Petre

Functions: 02.0 03.0 04.0 08.0
Industries: D.00 I.19
Professional Affiliations: NPA
Description: Contingency search specialists serving Northern New England with national affiliates

Avery Crafts Assoc., Ltd.
116 John St., Ste. 3100
New York, New York 10038
Salary Minimum: $70,000
Key Contact: Norman E. Crafts
James Carter
Robert J. Dubuque

Functions: Most + 01.0 01.2 01.3 10.0 11.0
Industries: H.00 H.I0
Description: Property/casualty: life insurance, banking & financial institutions

Affiliates/Other Offices:
Richard T. Bergsund Assoc., Sausalito
Dutton Executive Search, London

AviSearch Int'l.

85 Perimeter Rd.
Nashua, New Hampshire 03063
Salary Minimum: $35,000
Key Contact: James A. Willis

Functions: Most
Industries: D.E0 E.00 H.00 I.00 K.10
Description: Executive search & recruitment to
the aerospace & aviation industry

The Ayers Group, Inc.

370 Lexington Ave., 24th Fl.
New York, New York 10017
Salary Minimum: $75,000
Key Contact: William L. Ayers, Jr.
Robert Deissig

Functions: 09.0 09.1 09.3 09.7
Industries: Most
Professional Affiliations: APCNY
Description: Specialists in information systems
placement for contingency & retained
search

BGB Assoc., Inc.

P.O. Box 556
Itasca, Illinois 60143
Salary Minimum: $30,000
Key Contact: Gregory J. Burchill
Barbara E. Burchill

Functions: 02.0 03.0 06.0 08.0 09.3
Industries: Most + D.00 D.D0 D.H0 E.00
Professional Affiliations: APICS, ASQC, CLM,
NAFE
Description: Founder has over 20 years
experience in operations senior
management

BIK Search/Force II

14 Washington Rd.
Princeton Junction, New Jersey 08550
Key Contact: Bette I. Kantor

Functions: Most + 02.0 04.0 05.0 11.2 11.3
Industries: Most + D.00 D.10 D.16 D.17 D.18
Professional Affiliations: MAAPC
Description: Performs contingency & retained
searches geared to specific company
requests

B.P.A. Enterprises, Inc.

19967 James Couzens Hwy.
Detroit, Michigan 48235
Salary Minimum: $40,000
Key Contact: Will E. Atkins

Functions: 01.0 02.0 08.0 09.0
Industries: D.00
Professional Affiliations: MAPC
Description: Professional & executive
recruiting with special emphasis on
minorities & females nationwide

BR & Assoc.

300 Winston Dr., Ste. 3123
Cliffside Park, New Jersey 07010
Salary Minimum: $40,000
Key Contact: Dan Andrews
Bernard Rotsky
Sally Rotsky

Functions: 09.0 09.3
Industries: G.00 I.18
Description: Place professional senior &
midlevel retail management &
administrative technical MIS

Bader Research Corp.

6 E. 45th St.
New York, New York 10017
Salary Minimum: $50,000
Key Contact: Sam Bader
Marguerite B. Filson
James D. Harris
Susan J. Holmes
Geraldine Reich
Leila Redmond
Ruth Miles

Professional Affiliations: APC, NALSC
Description: Recruiting attorneys with superior
credentials for 25 years

Affiliates/Other Offices:
Robert Walters Associates, Amsterdam
Robert Walters Associates, Antwerp
Robert Walters Associates, Birmingham
Robert Walters Associates, Brussels
Robert Walters Associates, London
Robert Walters Associates, Windsor

Keith Bagg Personnel Ltd.

36 Toronto St., Ste. 520
Toronto, Ontario M5C 2C5 Canada
Salary Minimum: $35,000
Key Contact: Keith Bagg
Mary Bagg
Bruce McAlpine

Functions: Most + 01.0 05.0 07.0 08.0 11.0
Industries: D.10 D.15 D.18 D.21
Professional Affiliations: APPAC, NAPC
Description: We extend our clients human
resources function competently &
conscientiously

D.W. Baird & Associates

10751 Falls Rd., Ste. 250
Baltimore, Maryland 21093
Salary Minimum: $40,000
Key Contact: David W. Baird

Functions: 02.1 02.4 03.0 04.0 11.5
Industries: B.0W B.10 D.15 D.18 D.19
Description: Mid-Atlantic specialists in
manufacturing, marketing, technical &
management personnel

Baker Scott & Co.

1259 Rte. 46
Parsippany, New Jersey 07054
Salary Minimum: $40,000
Key Contact: Judy Bouer
David Allen
Dawn Levine
Herb Soffer

Functions: Most + 01.0
Industries: I.11 I.19 J.00 J.12 J.13
Professional Affiliations: NAER, NCTA
Description: Nationwide searches in
telecommunications, cable, accounting &
Wall St.—conducted confidentially

Baldwin & Assoc.

2706 Observatory Ave.
Cincinnati, Ohio 45208
Salary Minimum: $30,000
Key Contact: W. Keith Baldwin
Janice F. Seymour

Functions: Most
Industries: Most
Professional Affiliations: NAER
Description: Personnel acquisition consultants
to client employers

Balfour Assoc.

P.O. Box 173
Lansdowne, Pennsylvania 19050
Salary Minimum: $20,000
Key Contact: John E. Flowers

Functions: Most
Industries: D.14
Description: Recruit personnel at all levels for
the printing industry

Ron Ball & Assoc.

P.O. Box 480391
Kansas City, Missouri 64148
Salary Minimum: $25,000
Key Contact: Ronald D. Ball

Functions: Most
Industries: Most
Description: Although the company is our
client, your resume is welcome

Carol Ball & Co., Inc.

156 Fifth Ave., Ste. 702
New York, New York 10010
Salary Minimum: $35,000
Key Contact: Carol Ball
Loren Spiotta-DiMare

Functions: 01.3 05.1 05.7
Industries: D.10 I.14 I.16 J.10 J.11
Professional Affiliations: PRSA
Description: General & healthcare public
relations recruitment

The Bankers Group
10 S. Riverside Plz.
Chicago, Illinois 60606
Salary Minimum: $60,000
Key Contact: June Borntrager
Peter Chappell
Claire Kluever

Functions: 06.1 08.0 08.2 10.0
Industries: H.00 H.10 H.11 H.I0 I.14
Description: Services exclusively to banks, financial institutions & investment firms

The Bankers Register
500 Fifth Ave., Ste. 330
New York, New York 10110
Key Contact: James Bogart
Gilbert Tucker

Functions: Most
Industries: H.10
Professional Affiliations: NAPC
Description: Specialize in recruitment & placement of banking personnel

The Barack Group, Inc.
885 Third Ave.
New York, New York 10022
Salary Minimum: $45,000
Key Contact: Brianne Barack

Functions: Most + 01.0 05.0 05.1 05.2 05.3
Industries: D.10 D.16 D.18 I.11 J.00
Description: Specializing in promotion & marketing for consumer goods & service companies

Barclay Consultants, Inc.
16 Chestnut Ct., Ste. B
Brielle, New Jersey 08730
Salary Minimum: $30,000
Key Contact: Jules Silverman
Linda Pappas

Functions: 01.2 01.3 05.4 09.4
Industries: D.24 D.H0 I.18
Professional Affiliations: NJAPC
Description: Sales, marketing & technical positions within the data/information processing industries

B.K. Barnes & Associates
7000 Executive Ctr. Dr., Ste. 250
Brentwood, Tennessee 37027
Salary Minimum: $30,000
Key Contact: B.K. Barnes

Functions: 01.0 02.0 08.0 09.0
Industries: Most + D.00 H.00 I.00
Professional Affiliations: TAPC
Description: Accounting, data processing, healthcare/financial, & engineering/manufacturing candidates

Barone Assoc.
57 Green St.
Woodbridge, New Jersey 07095
Salary Minimum: $30,000
Key Contact: L. Donald Rizzo
Noel Cram
James J. Hughes
Mildred Merolla

Functions: Most + 02.0 03.0 05.0 11.6
Industries: Most + B.0W C.00 D.00 D.E0
Description: A firm of " industry professionals" reacting to & positively affecting the search process

Barone-O'Hara Assoc., Inc.
29 Emmons Dr.
Princeton, New Jersey 08540
Salary Minimum: $45,000
Key Contact: Marialice Barone
James J. O'Hara

Functions: Most + 02.0 03.0 04.0 05.0
Industries: Most + D.18 D.I0 I.14
Description: Recruit all functions for manufacturers of health care products & related industries

Peter Barrett Assoc., Inc.
302 N. El Camino Real, Ste. 200
San Clemente, California 92672
Salary Minimum: $40,000
Key Contact: Peter Barrett

Functions: Most + 01.0 05.0 06.0 08.0
Industries: I.10 I.11
Professional Affiliations: AHMA, CRA, NRA
Description: Recruit senior/middle level hospitality executives worldwide, both operations & staff positions

Barrett Partners

6 N. Michigan Ave., Ste. 708
Chicago, Illinois 60602
Salary Minimum: $20,000
Key Contact: Joseph Thielman
Patrick Reda

Functions: Most + 08.0 08.1 08.2 08.3 08.4
Industries: Most + D.00 H.00
Description: Search consultants specializing in accounting/financial & engineering/technical candidates

Bartl & Evins

100 Crossways Park West
Woodbury, New York 11797
Salary Minimum: $35,000
Key Contact: Susan Evins
Frank Bartl

Functions: 08.0
Industries: J.11
Description: All areas of finance and accounting in the Long Island-NYC area

Bartlett, Bunn & Travis, Inc.

6320 LBJ Frwy., Ste. 224
Dallas, Texas 75240
Salary Minimum: $30,000
Key Contact: Edward J. Bunn
Judy K. Bartlett

Functions: 01.2 01.3 01.5 05.2 11.5
Industries: B.0W C.00 I.14 I.17
Professional Affiliations: NAPC
Description: Diverse national firm confidentially recruiting qualified candidates for serious employers

Bast & Assoc., Inc.

11726 San Vicente Blvd., Ste. 200
Los Angeles, California 90049
Salary Minimum: $50,000
Key Contact: Larry C. Bast
Sue E. Bast

Functions: 05.0 05.1 05.2 05.3 05.5
Industries: D.10 D.16 D.19 I.10 I.11
Description: Marketing/advertising management with consumer goods/services firms in West

L. Battalin & Co.

P.O. Box 31815
Palm Beach Gardens, Florida 33410-7815
Salary Minimum: $50,000
Key Contact: Laurence H. Battalin

Functions: 05.0 05.2 05.3 05.4
Industries: D.10
Description: Marketing & sales recruiters in the consumer package goods industry

Battista Assoc., Inc.

P.O. Box 245
Marshfield, Massachusetts 02050
Salary Minimum: $40,000
Key Contact: Gerard E. Battista, Jr.

Functions: 09.0 09.1 09.3 09.4 09.6
Industries: I.18
Professional Affiliations: NAPC
Description: Specialize exclusively in the information systems professional areas

R. Gaines Baty Assoc., Inc.

9400 N. Central Expressway
Ste. 410, LB171
Dallas, Texas 75231
Salary Minimum: $40,000
Key Contact: R. Gaines Baty
Eric Hochfelder

Functions: 01.4 02.0 03.0 09.0 11.1
Industries: Most + D.00 D.H0 F.00 I.18 J.13
Professional Affiliations: SERC
Description: Search for specialized management & consulting professionals: systems, audit, financial, sales

Jim Baum—Executive Search

P.O. Box 10166
Eugene, Oregon 97440
Salary Minimum: $25,000
Key Contact: Jim Baum

Functions: Most + 01.0 02.0 03.0 04.0 05.1
Industries: Most + D.00 D.11 D.12 D.16 F.00
Description: Specializing in apparel, textile, sporting goods industry

Ted Bavly Assoc., Inc.
369 San Miguel Dr., Ste. 160
Prestige House
Newport Beach, California 92660-7878
Key Contact: Ted Bavly

Functions: 01.0 02.0 08.0 09.0 11.1
Industries: D.00 D.H0 H.R0 I.00 J.00
Description: Nationwide services, service fee arrangements, staffed by experienced professionals

Beckwith, Thomas & Fanning
11444 W. Olympic Blvd., 10th Fl.
Los Angeles, California 90064-1544
Salary Minimum: $60,000
Key Contact: Pat Bowers Thomas
Randy Beckwith
Chuck Fanning

Functions: 01.1 01.5 08.4 11.3 11.5
Industries: Most + I.17
Professional Affiliations: CBA, NAER, NALSC
Description: Attorney search & placement for national & international law firms & corporations

Bedford-Orion Group, Inc.
105 College Rd. E.
Princeton, New Jersey 08540
Salary Minimum: $40,000
Key Contact: Alvin I. Silverstein
Jeffrey M. Stark
Andrea Campbell
A. Robert Perez

Functions: Most
Industries: D.15 D.18 H.I0 I.16 J.00
Description: Generalist executive recruiting & human resources consulting firm

Ray N. Bedingfield, Consultant
P.O. Box 1383
Monument, Colorado 80132
Salary Minimum: $60,000
Key Contact: Ray N. Bedingfield

Functions: 02.0 04.0 11.0 11.3 11.5
Industries: B.0W D.00
Description: Eighteen years nationwide search experience. Thorough, confidential, professional

Marcia Beilin, Inc.
230 Park Ave., Ste. 1255
New York, New York 10169
Salary Minimum: $60,000
Key Contact: Marcia Beilin

Functions: 01.5
Industries: Most
Professional Affiliations: NALSC
Description: Founded in 1981 with three years of prior experience in the field-we place lawyers only

Gary S. Bell Assoc., Inc.
55 Harristown Rd.
Glen Rock, New Jersey 07452
Salary Minimum: $50,000
Key Contact: Gary S. Bell

Functions: 01.0 02.0 03.0 05.0 06.2
Industries: D.15 D.D0 D.I0 I.14 I.15
Description: Biomedical industries incl.medical devices, lab product/services, pharmaceutical, biotechnology

Bell Professional Placement
P.O. Box 1429
Skyland, North Carolina 28776
Salary Minimum: $20,000
Key Contact: James W. Bell

Functions: 01.0 02.0 04.0 05.0
Industries: D.11 D.15
Professional Affiliations: AATCC, AATT
Description: Recruit professional level personnel for the fiber, textile & associated industries

Bellon & Assoc., Inc.
1175 Peachtree St., NE
100 Colony Sq., Ste 1920
Atlanta, Georgia 30361
Key Contact: Lee Ann Bellon

Functions: 01.5
Industries: I.17
Description: Specialists in legal search & consulting

Bench Int'l. Search, Inc.
116 N. Robertson Blvd., Ste. 503
Los Angeles, California 90048
Salary Minimum: $50,000
Key Contact: Denise DeMan

Industries: B.10 D.18 D.I0 I.15 I.16
Professional Affiliations: ACT, NALSC, SRA
Description: Recruiting & consulting for the
pharmaceutical, petrochemical, chemcial
agchem & biotech fields

Dotson Benefield & Assoc., Inc.
100 Crescent Center Pkwy., Ste. 300
Atlanta, Georgia 30084
Salary Minimum: $20,000
Key Contact: Dotson Benefield
Conrad Taylor

Functions: Most
Industries: Most + D.11 D.13 E.00 H.10
Description: We specialize in putting good
people & good companies together

Bennett & Curran, Inc.
4155 E. Jewell Ave., Ste. 616
Denver, Colorado 80222
Salary Minimum: $50,000
Key Contact: Jeffrey B. Stephenson
W. L. Curran

Functions: Most
Industries: Most
Professional Affiliations: AMA, CAPC
Description: Generalist firm-nationwide
searches for companies /divisions in
Rocky Mountain Region

Bennett-Munson Inc.
4820 E. University
Odessa, Texas 79762
Salary Minimum: $35,000
Key Contact: Mark Bennett
Craig D. Munson
Marie O. Munson

Functions: Most + 02.2 02.4 11.5 11.6
Industries: B.0W D.15 D.20 I.14 I.15
Description: Search firm specializing in the
medical, petrochemical & energy
industries

Berger & Assoc.
50 California St., Ste. 460
San Francisco, California 94111
Salary Minimum: $30,000
Key Contact: Alan H. Berger

Functions: 01.4 08.0 08.4 09.0 11.1
Industries: Most
Professional Affiliations: NCHRC
Description: Executive search & recruiting in
accounting, finance & data processing

C. Berger and Company
327 E. Gundersen Dr.
Carol Stream, Illinois 60188
Salary Minimum: $30,000
Key Contact: Carol A. Berger
Catherine Bartholomew
Linnea Johnson

Industries: B.00 D.00 H.00 I.00 J.00
Professional Affiliations: NAPC, NATS,
NAWBO
Description: Executive search, specialized
temporaries & consulting for libraries/
information centers

Besen Assoc. Inc.
115 Rte. 46, W., Ste. 21
Mountain, New Jersey 07046
Salary Minimum: $40,000
Key Contact: Douglas Besen

Functions: 01.1 02.2 02.5 04.0 06.0
Industries: D.17 D.18 D.I0 I.15
Professional Affiliations: IACPR, ASPA
Description: Executive recruiting for the
pharmaceutical industry-heavy emphasis
in research & engineering

Binary Search
P.O. Box 1216
Wall, New Jersey 07719
Salary Minimum: $25,000
Key Contact: John P. Everson

Functions: 01.4 09.0 09.2 09.3 09.6
Industries: Most
Professional Affiliations: NJAPC
Description: Specialized placement in software
engineering, development, systems
programming

Charles A. Binswanger Assoc., Inc.

P.O. Box 5325
Baltimore, Maryland 21209
Salary Minimum: $35,000
Key Contact: Ronald W. Nelson

Functions: 09.0 11.3 11.5
Industries: B.0W D.E0 D.H0 J.13
Professional Affiliations: MAPRC, NPA
Description: Recruit engineers nationally for electronics, telecommunications, process & environmental fields

Biotech Sourcing

33 Boston Post Rd. W., Ste. 270
Marlborough, Massachusetts 01721
Salary Minimum: $20,000
Key Contact: Dr. Jack Randall

Functions: Most + 01.2 01.3 02.1 02.5 04.0
Industries: D.15 D.17 D.18 D.I0
Description: Strong biotech/biomed orientation, owner has Ph.D. in chemistry & 6 years recruiting experience

Bioventure Resources, Inc.

5632 SW 88th Terrace
Ft. Lauderdale, Florida 33328
Salary Minimum: $50,000
Key Contact: Franklin A. Heasley

Functions: 02.5 04.0 11.3
Industries: D.15 D.16 D.17 D.18 D.I0
Description: Over 25 years executive experience in diagnostic, pharmaceutical, biotechnical industries

Branches:
466 NW 104th Ave.
Coral Springs, Florida 33071
Key Contact: Michael Gallagher

Blanton & Co.

P.O. Box 94041
Birmingham, Alabama 35220-4041
Salary Minimum: $50,000
Key Contact: Julia Blanton
Thomas Blanton

Functions: Most + 02.0 02.5 05.0 09.0 09.4
Industries: B.0W D.00 D.D0 D.H0 D.I0
Description: United States & Canada

D. R. Blood & Assoc.

P.O. Box 1335
Chandler, Arizona 85244
Salary Minimum: $40,000
Key Contact: Dennis R. Blood
Sue A. Slaviero
Burwood O. Blood

Functions: 01.2 01.4 08.1
Industries: I.11 I.13 I.14 J.12 J.13
Professional Affiliations: NAER
Description: Established client relationships with midwest & west coast companies

The Howard C. Bloom Co.

5000 Quorum Dr., Ste. 160
Dallas, Texas 75240
Salary Minimum: $30,000
Key Contact: Howard Bloom
Joyce Bloom

Functions: 01.0 05.2 07.4
Industries: I.17
Professional Affiliations: NALSC, SERC
Description: Attorney search & placement

Bodner Inc.

372 Fifth Ave., Ste. 9K
New York, New York 10018
Salary Minimum: $25,000
Key Contact: Marilyn S. Bodner

Functions: 08.0 08.1
Industries: Most
Description: Specialize in placement of accounting & financial professionals

Bonifield Assoc.

Greentree Exec. Campus
3003E Lincoln Dr. W
Marlton, New Jersey 08053
Salary Minimum: $50,000
Key Contact: Len Bonifield

Functions: 01.0 05.0 07.0 08.0 10.0
Industries: H.00 H.I0
Professional Affiliations: MAAPC, NAPC,
SAM
Description: Specialist in executive search &
professional staffing for insurance &
banking industries

Gregory L. Borchert, Inc.

1121 E. Main St., Ste. 140
St. Charles, Illinois 60174
Key Contact: Gregory L. Borchert

Functions: Most
Industries: D.22 D.23
Professional Affiliations: AFS
Description: Specializing in metalcasting &
automotive component manufacturing,
nationally

Bornholdt Shivas & Friends

295 Madison Ave., Ste. 1206
New York, New York 10017
Salary Minimum: $40,000
Key Contact: John N. Bornholdt
James M. Shivas

Functions: Most + 01.0 05.0 08.0 09.0 11.0
Industries: Most + D.00 D.H0 D.I0 I.00 J.00
Description: Executive search firm for
advertising, sales, sales promotion,
marketing & broadcasting/cable

Bowersox & Assoc., Inc.

1025 Margret St.
Des Plaines, Illinois 60016
Salary Minimum: $50,000
Key Contact: Thomas L. Bowersox

Functions: Most
Industries: Most

Bowling Executive Registry, Inc.

702 W. Timonium Rd.
Timonium, Maryland 21093
Salary Minimum: $30,000
Key Contact: Richard A. Davis

Functions: 01.0 01.2 01.3 05.2 11.0
Industries: I.11
Professional Affiliations: ACG
Description: Search & placement: middle &
upper level bowling industry executives

Bowman & Marshall

P.O. Box 25503
Overland Park, Kansas 66225
Key Contact: Peter Grassl

Functions: 05.0 08.0
Industries: D.00
Professional Affiliations: NAPC
Description: Financial searches in
manufacturing & sales/marketing for food
companies

Bradford & Galt, Inc.

711 Old Ballas Rd., Ste. 205
Creve Coeur, Missouri 63141
Salary Minimum: $30,000
Key Contact: Bradford Layton
Barbara Layton

Functions: 09.0 09.2 09.4 09.6 11.2
Industries: Most

Charles Bradley Professionals

1900 Ave. of the Stars, Ste. 200
Los Angeles, California 90067
Salary Minimum: $35,000
Key Contact: Harry C. Kraushaar
John B. Jameson

Functions: 01.5 05.2 07.4 08.0 11.1
Industries: D.26 D.H0 I.11 I.17 I.19
Professional Affiliations: AICPA, CBA,
CSCPA, NALSC
Description: Top rated firm based on American
Lawyer surveys

Bradstreet Mgt.
450 Seventh Ave., Ste. 507A
New York, New York 10123
Salary Minimum: $30,000
Key Contact: Lisa Dieli
Carmine Dieli

Functions: Most
Industries: Most
Professional Affiliations: IACPR, NYABE
Description: Generalist type recruiting firm
doing both search & contingency

M.F. Branch Assoc., Inc.
Rte. 1, Box 588
Sylva, North Carolina 28779
Salary Minimum: $45,000
Key Contact: Minnie Branch

Functions: 04.0 05.2 05.4 09.2 09.7
Industries: J.00 J.13
Description: Specializing in search for voice &
network communication clients
nationwide

Brandjes Assoc.
16 S. Calvert, Ste. 500
Baltimore, Maryland 21202
Salary Minimum: $25,000
Key Contact: Michael Brandjes

Functions: Most + 01.2 01.3 06.1 06.2
Industries: H.10 H.I0 I.17
Description: A small, very specialized financial
services recruiting firm- primarily banking
& legal

C.W. Brandon & Assoc., Inc.
34208 Aurora Rd., Ste. 138
Solon, Ohio 44139
Salary Minimum: $25,000
Key Contact: Jacqueline Nagel
Clara Brooks

Functions: Most + 01.2 05.0 05.4 06.0 08.0
Industries: D.24 I.18 J.13
Description: Recruitment for all positions
within telecommunications & computer
industries

Jerold Braun & Assoc.
P.O. Box 67C13
Century City Station
Los Angeles, California 90067
Key Contact: Jerold Braun

Functions: 01.0 05.0 06.0 08.0
Industries: D.11 F.00 G.00
Description: Specialists in retail, wholesale,
apparel manufacturing & television
retailing

The Bren Group
7610 E. McDonald Dr., Ste. B
Scottsdale, Arizona 85250-6047
Salary Minimum: $25,000
Key Contact: Brenda Rowenhorst

Functions: Most
Industries: I.10 I.11
Description: Exclusive data bank of high
quality travel industry personnel

Brennan Assoc.
2775 Villa Creek Dr., Ste. 200
Dallas, Texas 75234
Salary Minimum: $40,000
Key Contact: Jerry Brennan

Functions: Most + 01.0 02.0 05.0 05.4 05.6
Industries: C.00 D.00 D.12 D.22 D.26
Description: Middle/upper management for
industrial, consumer & high technology
companies

Britt Assoc., Inc.
53 W. Jackson Blvd.
Chicago, Illinois 60604
Salary Minimum: $25,000
Key Contact: William E. Lichtenauer

Functions: 02.2 03.0 03.1 03.2 03.3
Industries: Most
Professional Affiliations: APS, CLM, IAPC,
NAPC
Description: Specializing nationally in
placement of distribution & materials
management personnel

Broad Waverly & Assoc.
200 Broad St., P.O. Box 741
Red Bank, New Jersey 07701
Salary Minimum: $25,000
Key Contact: Bill I. Saloukas

Functions: 10.0
Industries: H.10 H.I0 I.17
Professional Affiliations: MAAPC, NAPC, NIRA, NJAPC
Description: Keeping you first

Ira Broadman Assoc.
6701 Rockledge Dr., Ste. 250
Bethesda, Maryland 20817
Key Contact: Ira Broadman
Steve Broadman

Functions: 01.0 04.0 09.0
Industries: D.24 I.18 I.21 K.10
Description: Nationwide searches/contingency placements for info-systems & telecommunications professionals

Dan B. Brockman
P.O. Box 913
Barrington, Illinois 60011
Salary Minimum: $25,000
Key Contact: Dan B. Brockman

Functions: 02.4 02.6 11.5
Industries: Most
Professional Affiliations: AIHA, ASSE, NSC
Description: Specialists in safety engineers, industrial hygienists, ergonomists and environmentalists

J.R. Brody & Assoc., Inc.
P.O. Box 1421
Summit, New Jersey 07902-8421
Salary Minimum: $25,000
Key Contact: James R. Brody

Functions: Most + 01.5 06.0 06.1 06.2
Industries: Most
Professional Affiliations: IAPW, NAER, NJAPC, SHRM
Description: We recruit attorneys & human resource professionals

Brooke Chase Assoc., Inc.
505 N. Lake Shore Dr., Ste. 5507
Chicago, Illinois 60611
Salary Minimum: $30,000
Key Contact: Joseph J. McElmeel

Functions: 01.2 01.3 02.1 03.4 05.0
Industries: D.00 D.12 D.20 D.D0 I.14
Professional Affiliations: IACPR, IAP, NAER
Description: Hardware, plumbing, building materials, consumer electronics, lawn & garden, housewares industries

David F. Brooks & Co., Inc.
4840 Agate Dr.
Alpharetta, Georgia 30202
Key Contact: David F. Brooks

Functions: 05.2 05.3 05.4 09.0 09.1
Description: Computer sales, marketing sales management & technical recruiters

Brooks Executive Personnel
140 Sylvan Ave.
Englewood Cliffs, New Jersey 07632
Salary Minimum: $30,000
Key Contact: Marty Kay

Functions: Most + 01.0 04.0 07.4 08.0 10.0
Industries: Most + D.10 D.15 I.17 I.19 I.21
Professional Affiliations: NAPC, NJAPC
Description: Full-service, highly reputable agency providing search at senior as well as staff levels

Broward-Dobbs, Inc.
1532 Dunwoody Village Pky., Ste. 200
Atlanta, Georgia 30338
Salary Minimum: $35,000
Key Contact: W. Luke Greene, Jr.

Functions: 02.2 02.3 02.4 05.2 11.5
Industries: B.00 B.0W D.13 D.15 D.18
Professional Affiliations: NPA
Description: Engineering, manufacturing, telecommunications, tech. sales, environmental engineers & chemists

Branches:
1811 Haisten Dr., Ste. 100
Dothan, Alabama 36301
Key Contact: Lamar Hendricks

Brown/Bernardy, Inc.
12100 Wilshire Blvd., Ste. M-40
Los Angeles, California 90025
Salary Minimum: $30,000
Key Contact: Buzz Brown
Roger Van Remmen

Functions: 05.1 05.2 05.3 05.5
Industries: Most + E.00 I.10 I.11 J.00
Professional Affiliations: AIEF, DMCG,
   DMCSC, TTRA
Description: Consumer marketing, direct
   marketing & advertising executive &
   creative personnel

Bryant Assoc., Inc.
300 W. Washington St. S-706
Chicago, Illinois 60606-1772
Salary Minimum: $25,000
Key Contact: Richard D. Bryant

Functions: Most
Industries: Most
Professional Affiliations: AMA, NAPC,
   NCPDM, NPA
Description: Middle management recruiting
   firm

Bryant Research
466 Old Hook Rd., Ste. 32
Emerson, New Jersey 07630
Salary Minimum: $50,000
Key Contact: Tom Bryant

Functions: 02.5 04.0 11.3
Industries: D.18 D.I0 I.15 I.16
Description: Specializing in the recruitment of
   pharmaceutical research & development
   executives

Paul J. Burns
5472 Kenilworth Dr., Ste. 200
Huntington Beach, California 92649
Salary Minimum: $30,000
Key Contact: Paul J. Burns
Eugene A. Reitz

Functions: 01.0 02.0 04.0 05.0 11.5
Industries: B.00 D.00 D.E0 D.H0 D.I0
Professional Affiliations: IEEE, ISDE, ISPA,
   SPIE
Description: Place marketing, engineering &
   manufacturing personnel in aerospace &
   high technology companies

W. Bussell & Assoc.
11304 Spotted Oak
Austin, Texas 78759
Salary Minimum: $25,000
Key Contact: Bill Bussell

Industries: H.I0
Description: Recruit data processing and
   administrative professionals for insurance
   industry

The Butlers Co. Insurance Recruiters
2753 State Rd. 580, Ste. 104
Clearwater, Florida 34621
Salary Minimum: $30,000
Key Contact: Kirby B. Butler, Jr.
Martha Butler

Functions: 01.0 05.0 06.0 08.0 10.0
Industries: H.I0
Professional Affiliations: FAPC, NAPC, NIRA
Description: Insurance technical to upper
   mgmt; actuarial, accting, underwriting,
   marketing, claims & sales

The Byrnes Group
149 W. Market St.
York, Pennsylvania 17401
Salary Minimum: $26,500
Key Contact: Randy Byrnes

Functions: 01.0 02.0 08.0 09.0
Industries: D.00 I.15 I.18 I.19
Professional Affiliations: NAPC, NAPR
Description: We're dedicated to assisting our
   clients in custom staffing solutions

Branches:
1863 Charter Ln.
Lancaster, Pennsylvania 17601

C & H Personnel
245 Butler Ave.
Lancaster, Pennsylvania 17601
Salary Minimum: $30,000
Key Contact: Jon A. Singer

CAS Comsearch Inc.
501 Madison Ave., Ste. 406
New York, New York 10022
Salary Minimum: $40,000
Key Contact: Laurie Altman Raiber
Gail Kleinberg Koch

CCI—Career Consultants Int'l.
620 Newport Ctr. Dr., 11th Fl.
Newport Center
Newport Beach, California 92660
Salary Minimum: $25,000
Key Contact: George Vasu
Rex Rolf
Tom Meyer
Clarke Carroll
Mark Rinovato

CDH & Assoc., Inc.
9550 Warner Ave., Ste. 322
Fountain Valley, California 92708
Salary Minimum: $30,000
Key Contact: Cynthia D. Harper

CES
31 Wilson Rd.
Lambertville, New Jersey 08530
Salary Minimum: $30,000
Key Contact: Lindell J. Correll

Branches:
207 Dunkirk Rd.
Baltimore, Maryland 21212
Key Contact: Gregory Dougherty

C.G. & Assoc.
Box 11160
Pittsburgh, Pennsylvania 15237
Salary Minimum: $45,000
Key Contact: Charles C. Groom

395 St. John's Church Rd.
Camp Hill, Pennsylvania 17011-1328

Functions: Most + 02.0 03.3 05.5 08.0 10.0
Industries: Most + D.00 H.00 H.I0 I.00 J.10
Professional Affiliations: PAPC
Description: Serving professionals since 1975, two CPC's on staff

Functions: Most
Industries: D.H0 H.00 H.10 I.12 J.13
Description: Executive search firm specializing in recruitment of sales, mktg. & communication professionals

Functions: 08.0 08.1 08.2 08.3 08.4
Industries: Most
Description: Contingency specialists serving accounting & finance professionals for the S. California area

Functions: 01.0 01.1 01.2 01.3 05.0
Industries: D.24 D.25 D.H0
Description: Marketing & sales/engineers-electronics industry

Functions: 02.0 03.2 05.4 07.1 11.1
Industries: D.00 I1.10 H.I0 I.10 I.14
Professional Affiliations: AMA, APICS, ASM, ASQC, ASTD
Description: Provide experienced mgmt. & systems consultants, OD, systems analysts & industrial engineers

Functions: 08.0 11.0 11.5 11.6
Industries: B.00 C.00 H.R0
Professional Affiliations: IACPR
Description: We specialize in real estate & construction, development, acquisition & property management

CN Associates

21 Tamal Vista Blvd., Ste. 150
Corte Madera, California 94925
Salary Minimum: $40,000
Key Contact: Charles Nicolosi

Functions: 05.0 05.4 09.0 09.4 09.7
Industries: D.24 D.H0 I.18 J.00 J.12
Professional Affiliations: NCHRC
Description: Voice-data-LAN-software; sales,
    marketing & technical/customer support

CPI Technical Services

957-B Russell Ave.
Gaithersburg, Maryland 20879
Key Contact: F. Douglas Damon

Functions: 02.1 09.2 09.3 09.4 09.7
Industries: D.24 D.25 D.H0 I.18 J.13
Professional Affiliations: MAPRC
Description: Ethical employment counseling
    and placement of electronics/data
    processing professionals

C.P.S., Inc.

1 Westbrook Corp. Ctr., Ste. 600
Westchester, Illinois 60154
Key Contact: Lindy Alo
H. Douglas Christiansen
Frank Filippelli
James Gilbert
Don Owens
Bill Carr

Branches:
303 Congress St.
Boston, Massachusetts 02210-1012
Key Contact: Mary O'Connell

Functions: Most + 02.0 11.6
Industries: Most + D.00 D.15 D.D0 I.00 I.17
Professional Affiliations: IAPC, NAPC
Description: Excelling in technical recruiting
    nationwide since 1973

C.R. Assoc.

378 Cambridge Ave., Ste. D
Palo Alto, California 94306
Salary Minimum: $25,000
Key Contact: Harold Stephenson

Industries: H.10
Professional Affiliations: CAPC, NAER
Description: Established 1977, we specialize in
    recruiting for the banking industry

CRI Professional Search

1784 Leimert Blvd.
Oakland, California 94602
Salary Minimum: $20,000
Key Contact: Charles W. Acridge

Industries: I.14
Professional Affiliations: NPA
Description: Professional placement for the
    health care industry, nationwide

CRS Assoc., Inc.

P.O. Box 350453
New York, New York 11235-0008
Salary Minimum: $30,000
Key Contact: Leonard Corwen
Al Davis

Functions: 05.0 05.7 06.0 08.0
Industries: D.00 I.00 J.00 J.10 K.00
Professional Affiliations: ASJA, IABC
Description: 25+ years placing corporate
    communications, PR, advertising,
    financial, marketing & HR personnel

Peter M. Cahill Assoc., Inc.

P.O. Box 816, 207 Maple Ave.
Cheshire, Connecticut 06410
Salary Minimum: $30,000
Key Contact: Peter Cahill

Functions: Most
Industries: Most + D.00 I.00
Description: Specialize in filling key
    management & senior staff positions for
    small to medium firms

Affiliates/Other Offices:
The Charles Ryan Group, Inc., Deerfield Beach

Cambridge & Assoc., Inc.

100 First Ave., NE, Ste. 109
Cedar Rapids, Iowa 52401-1134
Salary Minimum: $20,000
Key Contact Mike Cambridge

Functions: Most
Professional Affiliations: AMS, NAPC
Description: Generalist, Midwest contingency
recruiters

The Cambridge Group Ltd.

830 Post Rd. E.
Westport, Connecticut 06880
Salary Minimum: $40,000
Key Contact: Al Judge
Fern Levine
Mike Salvagno

Functions: 01.2 01.4 03.4 08.0 09.0
Industries: Most
Description: Specialists in information systems,
healthcare, pharmaceutical, finance &
engineering nationwide

J.P. Canon Assoc.

225 Broadway, #3602
New York, New York 10007-3001
Salary Minimum: $30,000
Key Contact: James Rohan
Paula Blumenthal

Functions: 02.0 03.0 03.1 03.3 03.4
Industries: Most
Professional Affiliations: APICS, CLM, IPA,
NAPC
Description: Recruitment services for the
materials management, logistics,
purchasing & systems professions

The Cantor Concern, Inc.

330 W. 58th St., Ste. 216
New York, New York 10019
Salary Minimum: $35,000
Key Contact: Bill Cantor
Robert D. Walsh
Marie T. Raperto

Functions: 05.7
Industries: Most
Professional Affiliations: NIRI, PRSA
Description: National search specializing in
public affairs & relations, corporate/
marketing comm.,IR

Cap, Inc.

P.O. Box 82
Tennent, New Jersey 07763
Salary Minimum: $25,000
Key Contact: Stephen D. Porada

Functions: Most
Industries: C.00 D.00 D.12 D.19 D.20
Description: Recruiting & consulting firm

Capitol Management Consulting, Inc.

114 Hopewell-Lambertville Rd.
Hopewell, New Jersey 08525
Salary Minimum: $30,000
Key Contact: Joseph J. Kowalski

Functions: Most + 01.0 02.0 03.0 04.0
Industries: Most + A.00 D.00 D.IO I.00
Professional Affiliations: IMC, MAAPC
Description: Executive search specializing in
healthcare & industrial manufacturing
firms

Career Advancement

1525 W. 29th St., N.
Wichita, Kansas 67204
Key Contact: Tony Stutey
Ted Gregory

Functions: Most
Industries: Most
Description: Excellence in executive recruiting
since 1980. Guarantee placements for one
year

Career Consulting Group, Inc.

1150 Summer St.
Stamford, Connecticut 06905
Salary Minimum: $30,000
Key Contact: Gerald Kanovsky
Marlene Kanovsky

Functions: 05.1 05.2 05.3 05.5 09.6
Industries: D.10 D.18 I.16 I.17 J.10
Professional Affiliations: CAPC, NAPC
Description: Sales & marketing & legal
divisions primarily serve clients in
metropolitan NYC

Career Guides, Inc.

450 7th Ave., Ste. 507A
New York, New York 10123
Salary Minimum: $30,000
Key Contact: Carmine Dieli
Sy Gellman

Functions: Most
Industries: Most
Professional Affiliations: APCNY
Description: Sales specialists-sales managers,
  sales engineers, salesmen & women

Career Information Services, Inc.

McClure Bldg., Ste. 710
306 W. Main St.
Frankfort, Kentucky 40601
Salary Minimum: $25,000
Key Contact: Ty Hawkins
Greg Hydes

Functions: Most
Industries: Most
Description: Specializing in general
  manufacturing

Career Logic, Inc.

P.O. Box 13487
Atlanta, Georgia 30324
Salary Minimum: $20,000
Key Contact: Mary E. Larsen

Functions: Most + 08.0
Industries: Most
Professional Affiliations: AICPA, GAPC
Description: Atlanta's bookkeeping search
  specialists

Career Management, Inc.

698 Perimeter Dr., Ste. 200
Lexington, Kentucky 40517
Salary Minimum: $25,000
Key Contact: Richard E. Blanchard, Sr.
Rick Blanchard
Dwight Cotton
Ray Davis

Functions: Most + 02.0 03.0 05.0 09.0 11.0
Industries: Most
Professional Affiliations: IMC
Description: Specialist in executive search with
  over 15 years experience, plus
  outplacement & consulting

Career Marketing Assoc.

7100 E. Belleview Ave. #102
Englewood, Colorado 80111-1634
Salary Minimum: $25,000
Key Contact: Jan Sather
Terry Leyden
Chip Doro
Richard Steinman
Susanne Gregg
Deborah L. Viles
Jim Cahoon

Functions: 02.0 05.0 08.0 09.0 11.0
Industries: B.10 D.00 D.H0 H.00 J.00
Professional Affiliations: NAPC, NPA
Description: Professional recruiting & search
  firm since 1968

Career Profiles

44 Market St., P.O. Box 4430
Portsmouth, New Hampshire 03801
Key Contact: Leanne P. Gray
Norman G. Gray

Functions: 05.0 05.4 11.2
Industries: D.00 D.D0 I.00 J.00
Professional Affiliations: NNEAPC
Description: Placing sales, sales management &
  marketing personnel

Career Resource Assoc., Inc.

1627 Main St.
Houston, Texas 77002
Salary Minimum: $25,000
Key Contact: Charles E. Vienn

Functions: 06.2 11.2
Industries: I.10 I.21 J.10
Professional Affiliations: AMA, ASTD, MESA
Description: Founded in 1979, emphasizes
  executive search, professional staffing &
  consulting

Career Search Assoc.
100 Menlo Park, Ste. 301
Edison, New Jersey 08837
Salary Minimum: $18,000
Key Contact: Bruce Rovinsky
Steve Provenzano

Functions: 01.0 03.0 05.0 06.0 07.0
Industries: B.0W E.00 F.00 G.00 I.00
Description: Executive search organization
specializing in retail industry

Career Specialists, Inc.
155-108th Ave., N.E., Ste. 200
Bellevue, Washington 98004
Salary Minimum: $30,000
Key Contact: Pamela Rolfe

Functions: Most
Industries: D.00 I.00
Description: Specializing in management &
highly technical positions

Careers Unlimited
84 Villa Rd., Ste. 610, Henderson Bldg.
P.O. Box 6532
Greenville, South Carolina 29606-6532
Salary Minimum: $35,000
Key Contact: Thomas K. Ninan
H. Cecil Howell

Functions: Most
Industries: Most
Professional Affiliations: GMRA, SCAPS
Description: Professional recruitment:
marketing, sales management, engineering
& computer operations

Careers/Inc.
1919 Banco Popular Ctr.
Hato Rey, Puerto Rico 00918
Salary Minimum: $10,000
Key Contact: J. V. DeMoss
Rupert R. Amy

Functions: Most
Industries: Most
Professional Affiliations: NAPC, NATS, NPA
Description: The largest recruiting firm in the
Caribbean area-all disciplines

Caremarc & Assoc.
9681 Hudson St.
Miramar, Florida 33025
Salary Minimum: $20,000
Key Contact: Curt W. Chittenden

Functions: 11.5 11.6
Industries: B.10 D.I0 I.14
Description: Specializing in career placements
for highly skilled/trained engineering
professionals

Carlden Personnel Services Inc.
107-40 Queens Blvd.
Forest Hills, New York 11375
Salary Minimum: $30,000
Key Contact: Carl Denny
Suzanne Denny
Mark Sussman

Functions: 02.4 03.0 05.4 07.4 08.0
Industries: C.00 D.00 D.13 I.19
Professional Affiliations: NAPC
Description: Specializing in middle to senior
management positions in the Northeast
corridor

The Carlyle Group, Ltd.
401 N. Michigan Ave.
Ste. 1780
Chicago, Illinois 60611
Salary Minimum: $40,000
Key Contact: Max DeZara
Mitchell Berman

Functions: 01.0 01.1 01.2 01.3 06.0
Industries: H.10 H.R0 I.17
Professional Affiliations: NAER, NAIOP,
NALSC, ULI
Description: Specializing in the placement of
commercial real estate, finance, corp.
finance & legal professions

Andrew B. Carr & Assoc.
P.O. Box 5631
San Angelo, Texas 76902
Salary Minimum: $30,000
Key Contact: Andrew B. Caracciolo

Functions: Most
Industries: D.19 D.25 D.E0 D.H0
Description: Specialize in the general aviation
& aerospace industries

K. Carroll & Assoc.
707 Skokie Blvd., Ste. 600
Northbrook, Illinois 60062
Salary Minimum: $35,000
Key Contact: Kathy Carroll

Functions: 09.0 09.3 09.4 09.6
Industries: Most
Description: Professional & executive search
    specializing in information systems

Carter, Lavoie Assocs.
5 Division St., Ste. A
Warwick, Rhode Island 02818
Salary Minimum: $30,000
Key Contact: Leo R. Lavoie

Functions: Most
Industries: Most
Description: Placement of professionals in
    manufacturing, accounting, marketing,
    personnel & banking

Carter McKenzie, Inc.
100 Executive Dr., Ste. 370
West Orange, New Jersey 07052
Salary Minimum: $25,000
Key Contact: Richard Kilcoyne
John Capo

Functions: 01.4 09.0 09.1 09.2 11.2
Industries: J.13
Description: Specializing in exempt level
    information systems recruiting-services all
    industries

Carter-Evdemon & Assoc.
777 S. Harbour Is. Blvd., Ste. 876
1 Harbour Pl.
Tampa, Florida 33602
Key Contact: Jeffrey M. Carter
Michael S. Evdemon, II
James A. Carter

Functions: 10.0
Industries: H.I0 I.17
Professional Affiliations: FAPC, NAPR
Description: Search & placement of insurance
    executives, managers & professional
    personnel

Carver Search Consultants
4942 E. Yale, Ste. 102
Fresno, California 93727
Salary Minimum: $50,000
Key Contact: Michael Cavolina

Functions: Most + 02.0 04.0 08.0 11.3
Industries: Most + B.0W D.00 D.H0 I.14 I.19
Description: Senior management, techncial
    management, scientific, medical &
    engineering recruiting srvcs

Allen Case & Assoc., Inc.
7975 N. Hayden Rd., Ste. D-241
Scottsdale, Arizona 85258
Salary Minimum: $40,000
Key Contact: Allen Case
Frank Fabiano

Functions: 02.0 02.1 08.0 08.3 09.0
Industries: F.00 H.10
Professional Affiliations: ASCA
Description: Clients are nationwide in
    manufacturing, data processing, banking &
    engineering

Case Executive Search
15008 Kercheval Ave.
Grosse Pointe Park, Michigan 48230
Salary Minimum: $30,000
Key Contact: David R. Case

Functions: 01.0 02.0 03.0 04.0 05.0
Industries: D.00 D.19 D.23 D.H0 E.00
Professional Affiliations: EMA, MAPC, SAE,
    SHRM
Description: Automotive, aerospace & machine
    tool-design, manufacturing & quality
    engineering staffing

Casey & Gerrish Assoc., Inc.
209 W. Central St.
Natick, Massachusetts 01760
Salary Minimum: $50,000
Key Contact: Stuart A. Gerrish
Kent A. Long

Functions: Most + 01.0 02.0 04.0 05.0 09.0
Industries: Most + B.0W C.00 D.00 D.E0
    D.H0
Description: Critical mid/senior management
    search with emphasis on speed

Affiliates/Other Offices:
Jeff Bowman Management Services, Langon
P.M.R. Limited, Wadhurst

Cassie & Assoc.
2906 Wm. Penn Hwy.
Easton, Pennsylvania 18042
Salary Minimum: $50,000
Key Contact: Ronald L. Cassie

Functions: Most
Industries: D.I0
Professional Affiliations: ACS, ASPA, DCAT,
   HFMA, PAC, RAPS
Description: Executive recruiting for the
   healthcare industry by experienced
   healthcare executives

Affiliates/Other Offices:
Indermaur Healthcare Int'l. Ltd., London
Lennon/Walck, Pymble

H.O. Catherman Inc.
4900 Parliament Way, Ste. 250
Atlanta, Georgia 30338-5036
Salary Minimum: $30,000
Key Contact: H.O. Catherman

Functions: 05.2 05.4
Industries: D.24
Description: Specialized electrical sales &
   marketing contingency firm

Cemco, Ltd.
Two First Nat'l. Plz., Ste. 610
Chicago, Illinois 60603
Salary Minimum: $35,000
Key Contact: Dillon Hale

Functions: 01.4 06.0 08.0
Industries: H.00 H.R0 I.14
Professional Affiliations: IACPR, ASPA, IAPC,
   ICSC, NAPC
Description: Full service national executive
   search firm

Branches:
2701 N. 16th St., Ste. 101
Phoenix, Arizona 85006
Key Contact: Rose Skladowski

2015 Spring Rd., #250
Oak Brook, Illinois 60521
Key Contact: Dave Gordon

1 S. 450 Summit, #360
Oakbrook Terrace, Illinois 60181
Key Contact: Julia E. Huston

Centaur Int'l.
3303 Harbor Blvd., Ste. D8
Costa Mesa, California 92626
Key Contact: Beverly Froley Kenefick
David Holbrooke

Functions: 11.0
Industries: I.14 I.15
Professional Affiliations: IACPR
Description: Customizes on site health care
   systems worldwide; total systems
   management to recruiting & staffing

The Century Group
9800 La Cienega Blvd., Ste. 904
Inglewood, California 90301
Salary Minimum: $25,000
Key Contact: Harry Boxer
Don Yaeger

Functions: 08.0 08.1 08.2 08.4 09.1
Industries: Most
Description: Specializing in accounting &
   finance in a broad range of industries

Chaloner Assoc.
Box 1097, Back Bay Station
Boston, Massachusetts 02117
Salary Minimum: $35,000
Key Contact: Edward H. Chaloner

Functions: 05.1 05.5 05.7 11.4
Industries: Most + J.10
Professional Affiliations: MPPC, NAPC
Description: Specialist in public relations,
   marketing communications & corporate
   communications

Wayne S. Chamberlain & Assoc.

25835 Narbonne Ave., Ste. 290
Lomita, California 90717
Salary Minimum: $30,000
Key Contact: Wayne Chamberlain

Functions: 02.0
Industries: D.24
Description: Specialists in electronic engineers
(especially connectors) & trust bankers

The Chapman Group, Inc.

7320 E. Butherus Dr., 205-C
Scottsdale, Arizona 85260
Salary Minimum: $45,000
Key Contact: Jeff H. Chapman

Functions: 02.3 05.2 05.4 09.4
Industries: D.25 D.H0
Description: Specializing in factory automation
search

Robert L. Charon

P.O. Box 29405
Minneapolis, Minnesota 55429
Salary Minimum: $30,000
Key Contact: Robert L. Charon

Functions: 02.1 02.2 02.3 02.4 02.5
Industries: D.22 D.23
Description: Specializing in industrial/
manufacturing & design engineering

Chase Waterford Ltd.

1834 Walden Office Sq., Ste. 150
Schaumburg, Illinois 60173
Salary Minimum: $30,000
Key Contact: Paul J. Myer
Earl McDermid

Functions: 01.0 04.0 05.0 06.0 11.0
Industries: I.00 I.10 I.11
Professional Affiliations: NAPC
Description: Placement in hotels, corporate &
property level, on a national basis

Chicago Legal Search, Ltd.

770 N. Halsted, Ste. 107
Chicago, Illinois 60622
Key Contact: Gary A. D'Alessio
Anne M. Violante
M. Chris Percival

Functions: 01.5
Industries: I.17
Professional Affiliations: NALSC
Description: Exclusively attorney & legal
assistant search & placement in Chicago

William J. Christopher Assoc., Inc.

307 N. Walnut St.
West Chester, Pennsylvania 19380
Salary Minimum: $30,000
Key Contact: John Jeffrey Bole

Functions: 01.0 02.0 02.4 05.0 05.4
Industries: D.13 D.24 D.D0 J.11
Description: Search specialist in graphic arts
for sales & manufacturing, general
management

The Christopher Group

P.O. Box 30085
Kansas City, Missouri 64112
Salary Minimum: $40,000
Key Contact: J. Christopher Sprehe

Functions: 08.4 11.0
Industries: H.10 H.I0 H.R0 I.19 I.21
Professional Affiliations: IACPR, AI, ASA,
IAAO, IPT, IREM, NACORE
Description: Specialize in corporate real estate,
appraisal, property tax & property/asset
management

J.F. Church Assoc., Inc.

P.O.Box 6128
Bellevue, Washington 98008-0128
Salary Minimum: $40,000
Key Contact: James F. Church

Functions: 01.0 05.0 09.0
Industries: D.24 D.H0 I.18
Description: Computer industry recruiting,
focal areas: sales, software engineering &
marketing

Cibotti Assoc., Inc.
611 Trapelo Rd.
Waltham, Massachusetts 02154
Salary Minimum: $40,000
Key Contact: Thomas J. Cibotti
Charles F. Mather
Ann M. Williams

Functions: Most + 01.0 05.0 07.0 09.0 11.1
Industries: Most
Description: Over 20 years specializing in the
    data processing industry

Circuit Search
7 Moul Dr.,P.O. Box 218, Ste. 2B
Red Hook, New York 12571
Salary Minimum: $35,000
Key Contact: Kevin M. Stack
Linda Herring

Functions: Most
Industries: D.15 D.19 D.22 D.24
Description: Specialist recruiters in the field of
    electronic circuitry (printed circuits & I.C.)

Clanton & Co.
1095 N. Main St., Ste. M
Orange, California 92667
Salary Minimum: $25,000
Key Contact: Diane Clanton

Functions: 05.4 11.2
Industries: D.00 D.10 D.13 D.D0
Description: Specialize within the institutional,
    packaging & consumer goods industry,
    placement of sales & mktg

Claremont-Branan, Inc.
2150 Parklake Dr., Ste. 212
Atlanta, Georgia 30345
Salary Minimum: $40,000
Key Contact: Phil Collins
Bob Bowers

Functions: 11.5 11.6
Industries: B.0W B.10 C.00
Professional Affiliations: ACA, AJA, ASHE,
    AWWA, FMG, PSMA, SMPS, TAPPI
Description: Professional recruitment for
    consulting engineers, architects & related
    design professionals

Howard Clark Assoc.
P.O. Box 58846
Philadelphia, Pennsylvania 19102
Salary Minimum: $20,000
Key Contact: Howard L. Clark
Jim Anderson

Branches:
231 S. White Horse Pike
Audubon, New Jersey 08106

Functions: Most
Industries: Most
Description: Specialize in recruitment and
    placement of professionals with major
    corporations nationwide

Clark Assoc., Inc.
P.O. Box 459
Statham, Georgia 30666-0459
Salary Minimum: $30,000
Key Contact: Robert E. Clark

Functions: 02.0
Industries: D.00 D.23 D.26
Description: Specialists in recruiting for
    engineering & production management
    positions

Toby Clark Assoc. Inc.
405 E. 54th St.
New York, New York 10022
Salary Minimum: $30,000
Key Contact: Toby Clark
Sharon Davis

Functions: 05.0 05.1 05.7
Description: High caliber recruitment for
    marketing communications, advertising &
    public relations

Clark-Winans, Inc.
707-B Davis Rd., Ste. 203
Elgin, Illinois 60123
Salary Minimum: $35,000
Key Contact: Douglas P. Clark
James E. Winans

Functions: 01.0 05.0 05.3 05.4 05.5
Industries: D.00 D.14 G.00 I.00 J.00
Description: Diversified executive search &
human resources development
organization

John M. Clarke & Assoc.
11855 SW Ridgecrest Dr., Ste. 205
Beaverton, Oregon 97005
Salary Minimum: $40,000
Key Contact: John M. Clarke

Functions: 01.2 01.3 05.4 08.2 09.4
Industries: H.10
Description: Former bankers recruiting bankers
for banking clients

Richard Clarke Assoc., Inc.
9 West 95th St., Ste. C
New York, New York 10025
Salary Minimum: $40,000
Key Contact: Richard Clarke

Functions: Most
Industries: Most
Description: Specialists in minority &
executive recruiting in the private &
public sector

CoEnergy Inc.
5065 Westheimer, Ste. 815 E.
Galleria Financial Ctr.
Houston, Texas 77056
Salary Minimum: $60,000
Key Contact: Luis A. Hernandez, Jr.
Carole Fricks

Functions: 01.0 01.1 01.2 01.3 05.4
Industries: B.00 B.0W
Professional Affiliations: CIPCA, HAAPC,
NAPC
Description: Houston based firm specializing in
independent power industry executive
search

Cochran, Cochran, & Yale, Inc.
955 E. Henrietta Rd.
Rochester, New York 14623
Salary Minimum: $30,000
Key Contact: Gary M. Baker
Walter Y. Critchley

Functions: 02.0 05.3 08.4 09.4 11.6
Industries: D.13 D.18 D.24 D.E0 D.H0
Professional Affiliations: AAFA, ASM, DPMA,
IEEE, NAA, NPA, SHRM
Description: Search with specialized divisions:
finance, software, electronics,
manufacturing & marketing

Malcolm Cole & Assoc.
2604 Elmwood Ave., Ste. 321
Rochester, New York 14618
Salary Minimum: $40,000
Key Contact: Jane E. Hopkins

Functions: 01.2 01.3 02.1 04.0 11.3
Industries: D.17 D.18 D.I0
Professional Affiliations: ABC, ASQC, NAPC,
PS, RAPS
Description: Scientific, technical &
management positions in biotech &
pharmaceutical industries

Coleman Legal Search Consultants
100 S. Broad St., Ste. 1525
Land Title Bldg.
Philadelphia, Pennsylvania 19110
Key Contact: Michael M. Coleman

Functions: 01.5
Industries: I.17
Professional Affiliations: NALSC
Description: Specializes in legal recruiting for
law firms on the East coast & corporations
nationwide

Commonwealth Consultants
4840 Roswell Rd., Ste. C 301
Atlanta, Georgia 30342
Salary Minimum: $35,000
Key Contact: David Aiken
Tim Panetta

Functions: Most
Industries: D.24 I.19 J.13
Professional Affiliations: GAPC
Description: Computers: programmers, systems
    analysts, hardware/software engineers,
    sales in NY/CHI/ATL

Competitive Resources, Inc.
19125 Northcreek Pkwy., Ste. 104
Bothell, Washington 98011-8002
Salary Minimum: $40,000
Key Contact: Marvin E. Smith
James R. Heffernan

Functions: Most + 01.0 02.0 03.0 05.0 08.0
Industries: Most + D.00 D.E0 D.H0 E.00
    G.00
Description: Practice focuses on
    manufacturing/high tech companies
    placing middle & senior management

CompuPro
312 W. Randolph St., Ste. 250
Chicago, Illinois 60606
Salary Minimum: $50,000
Key Contact: Douglas J. Baniqued

Functions: 01.4 09.0 09.1 09.2 09.4
Industries: Most
Description: Specialists in the computer
    industry & related areas

Computer Network Resources
28231 Tinajo
Mission Viejo, California 92692
Salary Minimum: $30,000
Key Contact: Kenneth Miller

Functions: 06.0 08.0 09.0
Industries: D.H0 H.00 H.I0 I.14 I.18
Professional Affiliations: GAPC, NAPC
Description: A national search firm specializing
    in data processing

Branches:
7000 Central Pkwy., Ste. 1010
Atlanta, Georgia 30328

Computer Recruiters, Inc.
22276 Buenaventura St.
Woodland Hills, California 91364-5006
Salary Minimum: $25,000
Key Contact: Bob Moore

Functions: 09.0 09.1 09.3 09.4
Industries: Most
Description: Specialists for IBM mainframe
    personnel & relocations specialists

Computer Security Placement Service, Inc.
One Computer Dr., Box 204-D
Northborough, Massachusetts 01532
Salary Minimum: $30,000
Key Contact: Cameron Carey

Functions: 09.1
Industries: D.00 H.10 H.11
Professional Affiliations: CSA, CSI, ISSA,
    MAPC
Description: The oldest recruiting firm
    specializing in information security

Computer Strategies, Inc.
7454 E. Broadway, Ste. 205
Tucson, Arizona 85710
Salary Minimum: $25,000
Key Contact: Moira Silver

Functions: 09.3
Professional Affiliations: AAPC, NAPC
Description: Placement of programmers
    analysts, systems programmers, DBA's,
    software engineers, ect.

The Comwell Co. Inc.
Bartley Sq., Rte. 206
Flanders, New Jersey 07836
Salary Minimum: $50,000
Key Contact: David Gavin

Functions: Most + 01.0 05.0 06.0 07.0 11.1
Industries: Most + A.00 D.00 I.00
Description: Identify staffing needs-consultants
    in senior & executive management search

Cona Personnel Search
FOA Center, Ste. 504
One N. Old State Capitol Pl.
Springfield, Illinois 62701
Salary Minimum: $30,000
Key Contact: Joseph A. Cona

Functions: Most + 01.3 05.4 08.2 09.3 11.5
Industries: Most + B.0W H.10 H.I0 I.21
Professional Affiliations: IAPC, IBA, NAER, SHRM
Description: Executive search and recruitment for banking, EDP, accounting and management

Conaway Legal Search
16 S. Calvert St., Ste. 1100
Baltimore, Maryland 21202
Salary Minimum: $15,000
Key Contact: Howard H. Conaway, Jr.

Functions: 01.0 06.2
Industries: B.10 H.10 I.14 I.17 J.13
Professional Affiliations: NALSC
Description: Nationwide partner, associate & corporate counsel recruiting; merger consultation

The Connolly Consulting Group
601 Lake Ave., Ste. 300
Racine, Wisconsin 53403
Salary Minimum: $50,000
Key Contact: M. Michael Connolly
Charles Hartwig

Functions: Most
Industries: Most
Professional Affiliations: NAPC, PIRA
Description: We offer management consulting & executive search

The Consortium
One Times Sq., 13th Fl.
New York, New York 10036
Salary Minimum: $30,000
Key Contact: Martin Blaire
Howard Ross

Functions: Most + 01.4 05.4 08.2 08.4 09.3
Industries: Most + H.00 H.10 H.R0 I.17 I.18
Description: Search & consulting services to data processing, legal, bank/finance, tax & sales

Branches:
Village Green, 100 Rte. 46
Budd Lake, New Jersey 07828
Key Contact: Scott W. Ream

277 fairfield Rd.
Fairfield, New Jersey 07004
Key Contact: Barry Meyers

Consult One, Inc.
10291 N. Meridian St., Ste 325
Indianapolis, Indiana 46290
Salary Minimum: $30,000
Key Contact: Ben W. Brown

Functions: Most + 09.0 09.3 09.4
Industries: I.14 I.15
Professional Affiliations: NAPC
Description: Progressive firm growing rapidly in healthcare markets, physicians search field

Consumer Search, Inc.
1 S. 280 Summit Ave., Ct. D
Oakbrook Terrace, Illinois 60181
Salary Minimum: $40,000
Key Contact: Robert S. Ott
Joann Shilt

Functions: 01.0 01.1 01.2 01.3 05.0
Industries: Most + D.00
Description: Consumer package good industry w/heavy emphasis on electronics, telecommunications & mobile cellular

David P. Cordell Assoc.
82 Wall St., Ste. 1105
New York, New York 10005
Salary Minimum: $30,000
Key Contact: David P. Cordell
Pauline Cordell

Functions: 01.3 05.2 08.2 09.6 11.1
Industries: Most
Professional Affiliations: NABE, PF
Description: Specialists for ecommomists, portfolio/treasury operations & corporate/strategic planners

Corporate Advisors Inc.

250 NE. 27th St.
Miami, Florida 33137
Salary Minimum: $40,000
Key Contact: Jerry Kurtzman

Functions: 01.0 01.2 01.3 01.4 06.0
Industries: D.00 H.00 H.10 H.R0
Professional Affiliations: DPMA, IMA
Description: Specializing in finance,
accounting, MIS, banking, real estate,
distribution & manufacturing

Corporate Careers Inc.

188 E. Post Rd.
White Plains, New York 10601
Salary Minimum: $50,000
Key Contact: Richard Birnbaum

Functions: Most + 02.0 05.0 06.0 08.0
Industries: Most + D.00 D.H0 H.00 H.I0 J.00
Professional Affiliations: APCNY, NAPC
Description: Complete staffing service for
major corporate clients

The Corporate Connection, Ltd.

7204 Glen Forest Dr.
Richmond, Virginia 23226
Salary Minimum: $18,000
Key Contact: Marshall W. Rotella, Jr.

Functions: Most + 02.0 05.0 06.0 07.0 08.0
Industries: Most
Professional Affiliations: NAPC
Description: Full service executive recruiting
firm specializing in financial, engineering,
sales

Corporate Consultants Inc.

P.O. Box 16885
Tampa, Florida 33687-6885
Salary Minimum: $35,000
Key Contact: Steve Ring

Functions: 02.0 02.1 02.2 02.4 02.5
Industries: D.00 D.10 D.21 D.22 D.D0

Corporate Management Services Inc.

Foster Plaza V
Pittsburgh, Pennsylvania 15220
Salary Minimum: $30,000
Key Contact: Robert J. Bushee
Dorothea Crass

Functions: Most
Industries: D.19 D.22
Description: We help client companies identify
& employ qualified people

Corporate Personnel, Inc.

1148 Hampton Hall Dr.
Atlanta, Georgia 30319
Salary Minimum: $30,000
Key Contact: A.H. Sautter

Functions: 02.0 02.1 03.0 04.0 06.0
Industries: D.00 D.13 D.15 D.24 D.26
Description: Recruiting key exempt-level
employees for manufacturers since 1950

Corporate Recruiters, Inc.

4351 W. College Ave., Ste 408
Appleton, Wisconsin 54914-3928
Salary Minimum: $50,000
Key Contact: Dan Dieck
Michael S. Mueller

Functions: Most + 01.0 02.0 02.4 05.0 05.4
Industries: D.13 D.14 D.15 D.D0
Professional Affiliations: AMA, PIMA, TAPPI,
WAPC
Description: Paper industry search firm
specialization: technical, management,
sales, marketing & research

Corporate Recruiters Inc.

275 Commerce Dr., Ste. 231
Ft. Washington, Pennsylvania 19034
Salary Minimum: $100,000
Key Contact: Stephen Berlin

Functions: 04.0 11.3
Industries: D.17 D.18 D.I0 I.15 I.16
Description: 26 years successful recruiting for
industry

Corporate Resources Professional Placement

300 S. Hwy. 169, Ste. 480
Minneapolis, Minnesota 55426
Salary Minimum: $35,000
Key Contact: Bill Lanctot
Dean Anderson

Functions: Most + 01.3 02.0 09.0 11.3 11.6
Industries: B.0W D.19 D.E0 D.H0 D.I0
Description: Retained & contingent search for
    engineering, medical & technical
    management

Corporate Suite, Ltd.

507 Merle Hay Tower
Des Moines, Iowa 50310
Salary Minimum: $21,000
Key Contact: Pat Brown

Functions: 01.0 08.0 10.0 11.2
Industries: H.I0
Professional Affiliations: NAPC, NIRA
Description: Over 20 years of actual experience
    in the insurance industry

Cosco Resources Inc.

980 Post Rd.
Darien, Connecticut 06820
Salary Minimum: $40,000
Key Contact: Suzanne F. Cosco
Stuart A. Lohr
Julie Biasotti

Functions: 08.0 11.0
Industries: B.00 H.00 H.10 H.R0 I.20
Description: Diversified financial services
    including corporate finance, commercial
    lending & equipment leasing

Cowin Assoc.

1 Old Country Rd.
Carle Place, New York 11514
Salary Minimum: $40,000
Key Contact: David M. Cowin

Functions: Most + 01.2 01.3 02.0 04.0
Industries: D.22 D.26 D.E0 D.H0
Description: Specialists in the aerospace &
    related high technology industries

The Crawford Group

100 Colony Sq., Box 326
Atlanta, Georgia 30361
Key Contact: Tom Crawford

Functions: 05.0 05.1 05.2 05.5 05.7
Industries: D.10 J.10
Description: Executive search specialists in
    advertising & marketing

Crest Management Search, Inc.

P.O. Box 6118
Louisville, Kentucky 40206
Salary Minimum: $40,000
Key Contact: Don Rupp
John Johnson
Linda Yoffe
Nancy Ann Young

Functions: 01.0 02.0 04.0 05.0
Industries: D.15 D.19 D.D0
Professional Affiliations: ASQC, SPE
Description: Plastics specialists, from resins to
    end-products; experienced in industry
    technology

Crickenberger Assoc.

P.O. Box 8082
Roanoke, Virginia 24014-0082
Salary Minimum: $40,000
Key Contact: Harold P. Crickenberger

Functions: 01.5 11.2
Industries: D.00 H.10 I.10 I.12 I.15
Description: Serve primarily non-union
    companies in filling key positions

The Cris Group., Inc.

274 Madison Ave.
New York, New York 10016
Salary Minimum: $75,000
Key Contact: Jan Cris

Functions: Most
Industries: Most
Description: General management & financial/
    accounting areas for consumer, industrial
    & service businesses

Joseph Crisanti, Inc.
26 Broadway, Ste. 400
New York, New York 10004
Salary Minimum: $50,000
Key Contact: Joseph S. Crisanti

Branches:
960 Holmdel Rd., Ste 5, Bldg. 2
Holmdel, New Jersey 07733

Professional Affiliations: EMA
Description: Specialized in fixed income
    positions for financial services institutions

Crispi, Wagner & Co., Inc.
420 Lexington Ave.
New York, New York 10170
Salary Minimum: $85,000
Key Contact: Nicholas Crispi

Functions: 08.2
Industries: H.00 H.10 H.11 H.12
Description: Executive recruitment & search
    firm specializing in the placement of
    investment professionals

Criterion Executive Search, Inc.
5420 Bay Center Dr., Ste. 101
Tampa, Florida 33609-3402
Key Contact: Richard James

Functions: 08.0 09.0 09.1 10.0
Industries: G.00 H.00 H.I0 I.00 I.14
Professional Affiliations: FAPC, NAPC
Description: Specializes in accounting, banking,
    data processing, healthcare, insurance &
    retail cand.

Cross Country Consultants, Inc.
111 Warren Rd., Ste. 4B
Hunt Valley, Maryland 21030
Salary Minimum: $30,000
Key Contact: Sheldon Gottesfeld

Functions: 02.0 03.0 04.0 05.4 11.3
Industries: D.00 D.D0 D.H0 I.14 I.16
Professional Affiliations: MAPRC, NPA
Description: Specialize in, medical, health care,
    engineering, manufacturing, accounting &
    sales

Timothy D. Crowe, Jr.
26 Higate Rd., Ste. 101
Chelmsford, Massachusetts 01824
Salary Minimum: $30,000
Key Contact: Timothy D. Crowe, Jr.

Functions: Most + 02.0 03.0 04.0 05.0 08.0
Industries: D.00 D.E0 D.H0 D.I0
Description: Our firm is a small consulting
    organization dedicated to providing
    service to a few companies

Crown, Michels & Assoc., Inc.
14002 Palawan Way, Ste. 309
Marina Del Rey, California 90291
Salary Minimum: $25,000
Key Contact: Frank R. Crown

Functions: 08.0 08.1 08.2 08.3 08.4
Industries: Most
Professional Affiliations: CAPC, NAA
Description: Search specializing in locating &
    placing financial & accounting
    professionals

Frank Cuomo & Assoc., Inc.
111 Brook St.
Scarsdale, New York 10583
Salary Minimum: $30,000
Key Contact: Frank Cuomo

Functions: 01.0 02.0 05.0 05.4 11.5
Industries: B.0W B.10 C.00 D.15 D.25
Professional Affiliations: HMCRI, ISA, NAPC,
    WPCF
Description: Provider to manufacturing &
    service companies to include all functions

Curts/Jackson, Inc.
3692 Beach Blvd.
Jacksonville, Florida 32207
Salary Minimum: $25,000
Key Contact: Don Curts
Dave Jackson

Functions: Most + 01.0 05.0 08.0 09.0
Industries: Most + D.13 H.I0 H.R0 I.14 I.19
Description: Consultants to management in the
recruitment & selection of key personnel

DEI Executive Services
P.O. Box 9233
Cincinnati, Ohio 45209
Salary Minimum: $25,000
Key Contact: Jeffrey G. Dorrance

Functions: 02.0 03.0 04.0
Industries: D.22 D.24 D.E0 D.H0 K.10
Professional Affiliations: NAPC
Description: We specialize in serving the Ohio,
Kentucky, Indiana triangle

DLB Assoc.
271 Madison Ave., Ste. 1406
New York, New York 10016
Salary Minimum: $50,000
Key Contact: Lawrence E. Brolin
Dorothy Goodman-Brolin

Functions: 02.1 05.0 11.1 11.2
Industries: D.00 H.10 I.10 I.11 J.00
Description: Marketing, advertising, direct
response, corporate communications for
consumer & service oriented cos

The DLR Group, Inc.
310 Madison Ave., Ste. 320
New York, New York 10017
Salary Minimum: $50,000
Key Contact: Corey C. Roberts

Functions: Most + 01.0 05.0 06.0 08.0
Industries: Most + D.10 D.17 D.18 D.I0 G.00
Description: Middle & senior management for
all industries

D.P. Specialists, Inc.
2041 Rosecrans, Ste. 106
El Segundo, California 90245
Salary Minimum: $40,000
Key Contact: Randy Hinkley
Ed Myers

Functions: 09.3 09.4 09.6 09.7 11.1
Industries: Most
Professional Affiliations: NACCB
Description: Full service recruitment firm
specializing in data processing

Dalton Management Consultants, Ltd.
335 Grove St., Ste. 279
Jersey City, New Jersey 07302
Salary Minimum: $50,000
Key Contact: Evonne Dalton

Functions: 06.0 09.0 09.3
Industries: Most

Dalton-Smith & Assoc., Inc.
564 S. Washington St., Ste. 304
Naperville, Illinois 60540
Salary Minimum: $20,000
Key Contact: Don Smith
Marguerite Smith

Functions: 09.3 09.4 09.5 09.6 09.7
Industries: Most
Description: Specialize in data processing
personnel, in particular, mini-computer,
DEC, HP, etc.

Damon & Assoc., Inc.
7515 Greenville Ave., Ste. 900
Dallas, Texas 75231
Salary Minimum: $25,000
Key Contact: Richard E. Damon
H.M. Hailey

Functions: 05.0 05.4 07.3 09.0 09.4
Industries: Most
Professional Affiliations: FIN, TAPC
Description: Sales management: medical,
consumer, industrial, software/hardware,
furniture, info. technology

Dankowski & Assoc., Inc.

842 Corporate Way, Ste. 820
Cleveland, Ohio 44115
Salary Minimum: $30,000
Key Contact: Ken Dankowski
Tom Dankowski
Paul Juliano

Functions: Most + 06.0 06.1 06.2 08.0
Industries: Most
Professional Affiliations: EMA, NAPC, NPA, SHRM
Description: Specialists in recruitment of personnel, human resource,accounting & financial professionals

Dapexs Consultants, Inc.

One Park Pl.
Syracuse, New York 13202
Salary Minimum: $25,000
Key Contact: Peter J. Leofsky

Functions: 01.0 01.4 02.0 03.2 08.0 09.0
Industries: Most + B.00 D.00 I.00 J.13
Professional Affiliations: ACM, IMA, IPCCNY, NAPC, PEI
Description: Search & placement specialists in data processing, engineering, finance/accounting, medical, sales

The DataFinders Group, Inc.

25 Spring Valley Ave.
Maywood, New Jersey 07607
Salary Minimum: $20,000
Key Contact: Thomas J. Credidio
Peter Warns

Functions: 01.4 05.4 09.3 09.4 09.7
Industries: D.24 D.H0 I.18 I.20 J.13
Description: Providing nationwide search services for the data tele/processing industries .

Datamatics Management Services, Inc.

330 New Brunswick Ave.
Fords, New Jersey 08863
Salary Minimum: $20,000
Key Contact: Norman C. Heinle, Jr.
R. Kevin Heinle
Tony Courtade

Functions: Most
Industries: Most
Description: Service-related industries, general management, personnel, finance, data processing, labor rltns

Datamax Services Inc.

560 Willowbrook Office Pk.
Fairport, New York 14564
Key Contact: Eileen Marticelli
Jodi Campbell
Patricia Maxwell

Functions: 01.4 09.3 09.4
Industries: B.00 D.00 H.10 I.14 J.13
Description: Consulting firm hiring DP professionals to work at local client sites & internal development projects

N. Dean Davic Assoc., Inc.

400 Penn Center Blvd. Ste 900
Pittsburgh, Pennsylvania 15235-5609
Salary Minimum: $40,000
Key Contact: Nicholas D. Davic

Functions: 01.3 02.4 03.0 05.0 06.0
Industries: C.00 D.00 D.D0 I.00 J.00
Description: Search & contingency recruiting in most manufacturing & construction industries

David—Kris Assoc., Inc.

225 Main St., P.O. Box 5051
Westport, Connecticut 06881
Salary Minimum: $40,000
Key Contact: Michael J. Dellacato

Functions: Most + 01.0 01.3 05.4 08.2 08.3
Industries: H.10 I.17 I.20
Professional Affiliations: AAEL
Description: Specializing in executive search for the leasing, banking & commercial finance industry

Davis & James, Inc.
425 N. New Ballas, Ste. 200
St. Louis, Missouri 63141
Salary Minimum: $25,000
Key Contact: Jerry Pate

Functions: Most + 02.0 06.0 08.0 09.3 11.3
Industries: B.00 D.00 D.H0 H.00 I.21
Professional Affiliations: MAPC
Description: Nationwide professional recruiters specializing in engineering, manufacturing & financial positions

Bert Davis Assoc., Inc.
400 Madison Ave.
New York, New York 10017
Salary Minimum: $25,000
Key Contact: Bert Davis
Sarah B. Dougan
Wendy Baker

Functions: 05.1 05.5 05.7
Industries: J.00 J.11
Professional Affiliations: NAPC
Description: The leading executive placement firm specializing in the publishing field

Davis-Smith Medical-Dental Employment Service, Inc.
24725 W. 12 Mile Rd., Ste. 302
Southfield, Michigan 48034
Key Contact: Charles C. Corbett
Diana Watson
Connie Harrison
Karen Hogan

Functions: 01.2 01.3
Industries: I.14 I.15
Professional Affiliations: NAPC, NAPR
Description: A full service human resources firm for the medical profession

DeCorrevont & Assoc.
1901 S. Ashland
Park Ridge, Illinois 60068
Salary Minimum: $30,000
Key Contact: James De Correvont

Functions: Most + 05.0 06.0 11.4
Industries: Most + I.14
Professional Affiliations: EMA, HRMA, SHRM
Description: Recruiting & search: human resources, healthcare, sales & marketing, not for profit

DeLalla—Fried Assoc.
201 E. 69th St., Ste. 4K
New York, New York 10021
Salary Minimum: $45,000
Key Contact: Barbara DeLalla
Ann Fried

Functions: 01.0 05.0 09.0 11.2
Industries: D.00 I.00 J.00
Professional Affiliations: NAER
Description: Consumer packaged goods service industry specialization; full time & consultant

Dean-Wharton Assoc.
P.O. Box 279
Somerville, New Jersey 08876
Salary Minimum: $35,000
Key Contact: James L. Dean
Alfred Dentale
Natalie H. Brooks

Functions: 01.0 02.0 05.0 05.4 06.0
Industries: Most
Professional Affiliations: NPA
Description: Specializing in human resources/ personnel, sales, engineering, marketing & manufacturing operations

Deeco Int'l.
710 Aspen Heights Dr.
P.O. Box 7033
Salt Lake City, Utah 84107
Key Contact: Dee McBride
Patricia Clark
Karen Mollison

Functions: 02.0 05.0 09.0 09.3
Industries: D.18 I.14
Description: Specialize in medical products marketing, sales, engineering, research positions

Deery Geddis & Assoc.

1195 Park Ave., Ste. 201
Emeryville, California 94608
Salary Minimum: $60,000
Key Contact: Peter R. Geddis

Branches:
25 N. Main St.
Cranbury, New Jersey 08512
Key Contact: John R. Deery

Delacore Personnel

101 Park Pl., Ste. 206
Hutchinson, Minnesota 55350
Salary Minimum: $30,000
Key Contact: Verne Meyer

Delta Personnel Services

100 Franklin Square Dr.
Somerset, New Jersey 08873
Salary Minimum: $35,000
Key Contact: Rose Liccardi
Stan Pierce

Delta Personnel Services

2045 Royal Ave., Ste. 221
Simi Valley, California 93065
Key Contact: Norma Brody

Delta Resource Group, Ltd.

1600 Parkwood Cir. NW., Ste 620
Atlanta, Georgia 30339-2116
Salary Minimum: $30,000
Key Contact: Jerry Harmon

Development Resource Group

36 W. 44th St., Ste. 1416
New York, New York 10036
Key Contact: David Edell
Linda Low

Branches:
6253 Hollywood Blvd., Ste.1026
Hollywood, California 90028
Key Contact: Suzanne Medalje

Dillard Executive Search

1617 Hawthorne Park
Columbus, Ohio 43203
Salary Minimum: $30,000
Key Contact: Tom Dillard
G. Hannah Dillard

Functions: Most + 01.0 05.0 06.0 08.0 09.0
Industries: D.24 I.18 J.13
Description: Sharply focused on
  telecommunications industry in all
  functional areas of the business

Functions: 02.0
Industries: I.15
Description: High standards of competence and
  integrity by strictly subscribing to a code
  of ethics

Functions: Most
Industries: Most
Description: Full line management & executive
  search in all types of industry

Functions: 11.5
Industries: D.H0 D.I0 I.11 K.00
Description: We do temporary & permanent
  placements, as well as executive recruiting

Functions: Most + 02.0 05.0 08.0 09.0 09.7
Industries: Most + B.0W D.24 H.00 I.14 J.13
Description: General practice emphasizing
  corporations & degreed professionals
  wishing to relocate to GA

Functions: 05.2 08.2 11.4
Industries: I.12 I.13 K.00
Description: Specialist in search for all not-for-
  profit managers & development specialists

1629 K. St. NW., Ste. 802
Washington, District of Columbia 20006
Key Contact: Anne Morrison

Functions: 01.3 02.0 06.0 09.0 11.2
Industries: D.00 I.00
Professional Affiliations: ASTD
Description: Employment services firm
  specializing in recruiting minorities &
  women

Branches:
P.O. Box 9226
Toledo, Ohio 43697-9226
Key Contact: Morris Lewis

Diversified Placement Int'l., Inc.
3961 MacArthur Blvd., Ste. 112
Newport Beach, California 92660
Salary Minimum: $35,000
Key Contact: William P. Dowell

Functions: Most + 01.0 08.0 08.3 09.0 11.3
Industries: Most + D.24 D.H0 H.00 I.20
Description: National finance placement
specialist, with concentration in
equipment leasing/finance

L.J. Doherty & Assoc.
65 Ford Rd.
Sudbury, Massachusetts 01776
Salary Minimum: $70,000
Key Contact: Leonard J. Doherty

Functions: 01.0 02.0 05.0 09.0
Industries: D.H0
Description: Computer industry focus:
software, communications, & information
technology services

Domenico/Brown Group
2151 Michelson Dr., Ste. 217
Irvine, California 92715
Salary Minimum: $35,000
Key Contact: Alfred J. Domenico
Paul A. Brown

Functions: Most + 01.0 05.0 06.0 08.0 11.0
Industries: I.00 I.10 I.11
Professional Affiliations: CAHMA, CRA, IAHC
Description: Specialists in the hospitality field
providing executive search to management

J P Donnelly Assoc., Inc.
420 Lexington Ave., Ste. 300
New York, New York 10170
Salary Minimum: $40,000
Key Contact: John P. Donnelly

Functions: 01.4 06.0 08.2 09.0 09.6
Industries: H.00 H.10 H.11
Description: Practice divided between
computer related positions & careers on
Wall Street

Double M Executive Placement Service, Inc.
1 Garfield Cir.
Burlington, Massachusetts 01803
Salary Minimum: $25,000
Key Contact: Nancy Harris
Christine K. Hoiriis

Functions: Most + 02.0 03.0 04.0 09.0 11.0
Industries: Most
Professional Affiliations: IPA, MAPC, NAPC
Description: Broad range of clients with
heaviest concentration in engineering,
manufacturing & biotech industries

Downing & Downing
6988 Spinach Ave.
Mentor, Ohio 44060
Salary Minimum: $25,000
Key Contact: Gus Downing
Jacqueline Downing

Industries: G.00
Professional Affiliations: IACPR
Description: Specializing in the loss prevention
(security) & audit industries

Drake & Assoc.
9454 Wilshire Blvd., Ste. 650
Beverly Hills, California 90212
Salary Minimum: $40,000
Key Contact: Mary Ann Schuessler

Functions: Most + 05.0 08.0 09.0 11.1 11.2
Industries: Most + B.0W B.10 D.I0 H.R0 I.00
Description: Nationwide, highly discreet
searches

Dreier Consulting
P.O. Box 356
10 S. Franklin Tpke.
Ramsey, New Jersey 07446
Salary Minimum: $40,000
Key Contact: John S. Dreier

Functions: 02.0 02.1 04.0 09.7 11.3
Industries: D.18 D.24 D.25 D.H0 J.13
Professional Affiliations: NJAPC
Description: Marketing & engineering
specialists for high technology industries

Robert Drexler Assoc., Inc.
210 River St.
Hackensack, New Jersey 07601
Salary Minimum: $50,000
Key Contact: Robert C. Drexler

Functions: 02.3 02.4 11.3 11.6
Industries: B.00 B.0W C.00 D.00 E.00
Description: Engineering management,
    engineering, technical & executive search
    consultants

Drummond Assoc., Inc.
50 Broadway, Ste. 1201
New York, New York 10004
Salary Minimum: $35,000
Key Contact: Chester A. Fienberg

Functions: 01.0 01.2 01.3
Industries: H.00 H.10 H.11 H.12 H.R0
Description: We fill middle/upper level
    positions for NYC financial institutions

J. H. Dugan & Assoc., Inc.
455 E. Illinois St., Ste. 565
Chicago, Illinois 60611
Salary Minimum: $50,000
Key Contact: John H. Dugan
Patrick Murray
Carol Semrad
Jeanette Feldman
Polly Prosser

Branches:
11 Union Wharf
Boston, Massachusetts 02109
Key Contact: Nicholas Fountas

Functions: Most + 01.0 02.0 04.0 05.0
Industries: D.15 D.18 D.19 D.20 D.D0
Professional Affiliations: NAER, SPE, SPI
Description: Plastics industry specialists, all
    functions & markets including commercial
    development

Dumont Moriarty & Assoc.
160 State St.
Boston, Massachusetts 02109
Salary Minimum: $20,000
Key Contact: Robert C. Dumont

Functions: Most + 01.0 02.0 03.0 05.0 06.0
Industries: Most
Description: Professional & managerial
    placement services in the mid-level job
    market

Dunhill Personnel System, Inc.
1000 Woodbury Rd.
Woodbury, New York 11797
Salary Minimum: $25,000
Key Contact: D.A. Coape-Arnold
Howard Scott
Linda Wynne
Richard W. Kean
Kathleen McCollough

Branches:
P.O. Box 2955
Decatur, Alabama 35602

2117 Magnolia Ave., Ste. 210
Birmingham, Alabama 35205

100 Century Pk. S, Ste. 120
Birmingham, Alabama 35226

P.O. Box 6149
Ft. Smith, Arkansas 72906

P.O. Box 1570
Rogers, Arkansas 72756

Functions: Most + 02.0 05.0 08.0 09.0
Industries: I.14
Professional Affiliations: AHRC, ASPA, NAPC,
    NATS
Description: A nationwide network of more
    than 250 recruiting offices specializing in
    many disciplines

4949 Buckley Way, Ste. 203
Bakersfield, California 93389

2192 Myrtle Beach Ln.
Danville, California 94526

220 Montgomery St., Ste. 1085
San Francisco, California 94104

150 N. Wiget Ln., Ste. 100A
Walnut Creek, California 94598

5657 Wilshire Blvd., Ste 200
Los Angeles, California 90048

1060 E. Main St., Ste. A
Santa Paula, California 93060

1790 30th St., Ste. 230
Boulder, Colorado 80301

P.O. Box 440995
Aurora, Colorado 80044

14 Inverness Dr. E, Bldg. H, Ste. 220
Englewood, Colorado 80112

2120 S. College Ave., Ste. 3
Ft. Collins, Colorado 80525

5 Padanaram Rd.
Danbury, Connecticut 06811

270 Farmington Ave., Ste. 134
The Exchange
Farmington, Connecticut 06032

4695 Main St., Commerce Park
Bridgeport, Connecticut 06606

12 Main St.
Norwalk, Connecticut 06851

660 Linton Blvd., Ste. 102
Delray Beach, Florida 33444

1101 Gulf Breeze Pkwy., Ste. 200
Gulf Breeze, Florida 32561

1915 E. Bay Dr., Ste. 3B
Largo, Florida 34641

5053 Ocean Ave., Ste. 59
Sarasota, Florida 34242

2017 Delta Blvd., Ste. 204
Tallahassee, Florida 32303

3270 Pineda Ave.
Melbourne, Florida 32940

3340 Peachtree Rd., NE
Ste. 2570
Atlanta, Georgia 30026

1400 Lake Hearn Dr., Ste. 218
Atlanta, Georgia 30319

801 Broad St., Ste. 412
Trust Company Bank Bldg.
Augusta, Georgia 30901

301 Broome St., Ste. 100
La Grange, Georgia 30240

507 N. Houston Rd., Ste. A-3
Warner Robins, Georgia 31093

119 Third St., NE
121 Professional Park
Cedar Rapids, Iowa 52401

1233 Gilbert Ct., Ste. A
Iowa City, Iowa 52240

P.O. Box 9142
Boise, Idaho 83707

5005 Newport Dr., Ste. 201
Rolling Meadows, Illinois 60008

15475 S. Park Ave.
South Holland, Illinois 60473

230 N. Michigan Ave., 30th Fl.
Chicago, Illinois 60601

5701 N. Sheridan Rd., #9-0
Chicago, Illinois 60660

1111 S. Alpine, Ste. 503
Rockford, Illinois 61108

176 W. Adams, Ste. 1219T
Chicago, Illinois 60603

705 Franklin Sq., Ste. 3
Michigan City, Indiana 46360

7202 N. Shadeland Ave., Ste. 128
Indianapolis, Indiana 46250

4060 25th St.
Columbus, Indiana 47203-3198

9918 Coldwater Rd.
Ft. Wayne, Indiana 46825-2040

P.O. Box 15706
Ft. Wayne, Indiana 46885

P.O. Box 1068
Nashville, Indiana 47448-1068

7460 S. Madison
Indianapolis, Indiana 46227

P.O. Box 23
Claypool, Indiana 46510

9245 Calumet Ave., Ste. 104
Munster, Indiana 46321

7701 College Blvd.
Overland Park, Kansas 66210

150 SW 33rd St.
Topeka, Kansas 66611

425 N. Broadway
Wichita, Kansas 67202

230 Second St., Ste. 412
Citi-Center
Henderson, Kentucky 42420

P.O. Box 469
Crestwood, Kentucky 40014-0469

P.O. Box 128
Gracey, Kentucky 42232-0128

5723 Superior Dr., Ste. B-4
Baton Rouge, Louisiana 70816

P.O. Box 4851
Monroe, Louisiana 71211

3010 Knight St., Ste. 200
Shreveport, Louisiana 71105-2553

32 Hampden St.
Springfield, Massachusetts 01103-1212
Key Contact: Brent Northup
Mal Schneider

414 Hungerford Dr., Ste. 220
Rockville, Maryland 20850

1 Union St.
Portland, Maine 04101

315 N. Main, Ste. 400
Ann Arbor, Michigan 48104

29350 Southfield Rd.
Harvard Plz.
Southfield, Michigan 48076

32985 Hamilton Ct., Ste. 120
Farmington Hills, Michigan 48018

1627 Lake Lansing Rd.
Lansing, Michigan 48912

1014 S. Beacon Blvd.
Grand Haven, Michigan 49417

4406 Elmhurst
Saginaw, Michigan 48603

7500 Market Place Dr.
Eden Prairie, Minnesota 55344

101 W. Burnsville Pkwy.
Ste. 108 F
Burnsville, Minnesota 55337

1750 S. Brentwood Blvd., Ste. 207
St. Louis, Missouri 63144

300 Chesterfield Ctr., Ste. 260
Chesterfield, Missouri 63017

225 S. Meramec, Ste. 408
Clayton, Missouri 63105

916 Walnut, Ste. 604
Ridge Arcade Bldg.
Kansas City, Missouri 64106

400 E. Red Bridge Rd., Ste. 203
Kansas City, Missouri 64131

P.O. Box 1218
Madison, Mississippi 39130-1218

975 Walnut St., Ste. 260
Cary, North Carolina 27511

108-1/2 South Main St.
Kernersville, North Carolina 27284

1040 Kings Hwy. N, Ste. 400
Cherry Hill, New Jersey 08034

303 W. Main St.
Freehold, New Jersey 07728

520 Stokes Rd
The Ironstone Bldg. B-11
Medford, New Jersey 08055

E. 28th Fairview Terr.
Paramus, New Jersey 07652

200 State Hwy. 17, Ste. 208
Mahwah, New Jersey 07430

P.O. Box 246
Rutherford, New Jersey 07070

P.O. Box 528
Pittsford, New York 14534

P.O. Box 85
Yorktown Heights, New York 10598

570 Delaware Ave.
Buffalo, New York 14202-6250

P.O.Box 1347
Port Washington, New York 11050

331 N. Broad St.
Fairborn, Ohio 45324

5461 Southwyck Blvd., #2-J
Toledo, Ohio 43614

11440 Market St.
North Lima, Ohio 44452

1500 W. Broadway
Ardmore, Oklahoma 73401

1320 N. Main St., Ste. 126
Muskogee, Oklahoma 74403

5100 E Skully Dr., Ste. 660
Tulsa, Oklahoma 74135

3801 NW 63rd, Ste. 100
Edgewater Office Complex
Oklahoma City, Oklahoma 73116

1000 W. Wilshire, Ste. 310
Oklahoma City, Oklahoma 73316

1015 Waterwood Pkwy., Ste. E
Edmond, Oklahoma 73034

1500 Chestnut St., Ste. 900
Philadelphia, Pennsylvania 19103

1790 Yardley-Langhorne Rd.
Carriagehouse, Ste. 203
Yardley, Pennsylvania 19067

1801 Lititz Pike
Lancaster, Pennsylvania 17601

736 Ingomar Rd.
Ingomar, Pennsylvania 15127

145 W. Lancaster Ave.
Paoli, Pennsylvania 19301

801 West Street Rd.
Feasterville, Pennsylvania 19047

1012 W. 8th Ave., Ste. 1
King of Prussia, Pennsylvania 19406

P.O. Box 2989
Marina Station
Mayaguez, Puerto Rico 00709

875 Centerville Rd.
Warwick, Rhode Island 02886

33 Villa Rd., B-120
Piedmont Ctr.
Greenville, South Carolina 29615

231F Hampton St.
6 Village Sq.
Greenwood, South Carolina 29646

16 Berryhill Rd., Ste. 120
Interstate Ctr.
Columbia, South Carolina 29210

301 King Den Dr. NW
Cleveland, Tennessee 37311

202 Airways Blvd.
Jackson, Tennessee 38301

5120 Stage Rd., #2
Stage Woods Office Park
Memphis, Tennessee 38134

109 Holiday Ct., A-3
Franklin, Tennessee 37064

1301 S. Bowen Rd., Ste. 370
Arlington, Texas 76013

505 E. Huntland Dr., Ste. 190
Austin, Texas 78752

4950 FM 1960 W., Ste. C313
Houston, Texas 77069

5151 Belt Line Rd., Ste. 420
Dallas, Texas 75240

1320 S. University Dr., Ste. 103
Ft. Worth, Texas 76107

5720 W. Little York, Ste. 322
Houston, Texas 77091

P.O. Box 35806
Houston, Texas 77235

P.O. Box 773136
Houston, Texas 77215-3156

P.O. Box 3114
McAllen, Texas 78502

15102 Jones Maltsoerger, Ste. 101
San Antonio, Texas 78270-0888

15603 Kuykendhal Rd., Ste. 145
Houston, Texas 77090

P.O. Box 836028
Richardson, Texas 75083-6028

314 E. Commerce St., Ste. 710
San Antonio, Texas 78205

3308 Broadway, Ste. 209
San Antonio, Texas 78209

8930 Four Winds Dr., Ste. 101
Windsor Exec. Plaza L
San Antonio, Texas 78239

P.O. Box 380131
San Antonio, Texas 78280

P.O. Box 293371
Lewisville, Texas 75029

P.O. Box 58411
Houston, Texas 77258

502 B. North Main
Weatherford, Texas 76086

14514 Majestic Prince
San Antonio, Texas 78248

1606 Santa Rosa Rd., Ste. 132
Richmond, Virginia 23288

2222 Electric Rd., Ste. 205
Roanoke, Virginia 24018

1446 Kempsville Rd., Ste. 204
Virginia Beach, Virginia 23464

336 S. Jefferson St.
Green Bay, Wisconsin 54301

3 S. Pinckney St., Ste 318
Madison, Wisconsin 53703

P.O. Box 1006
Lewisburg, West Virginia 24901

744 W. Hastings St., Ste. 500
Vancouver, British Columbia V6C 1A5
   Canada

210 Dundas Sr.
London, Ontario N6A-5J3 Canada

3995 Bathurst St., Ste. 102
North York, Ontario M3H 5V3 Canada

Dunhill Professional Search, Inc. of Kearney
3810 Ave. A, Ste. F
Kearney, Nebraska 68847-2498
Key Contact: Charles F. Dummer
Diana L. Steube
Jeffry J. Drummer

Functions: 01.0 02.0 03.0 04.0 05.0
Professional Affiliations: NAPC
Description: We are the outdoor power
   equipment specialists

Dunhill Professional Search of Hawaii
841 Bishop St., Ste. 420
Davies Pacific Ctr.
Honolulu, Hawaii 96813
Key Contact: Ed Kitchen
Joan Kitchen
Nadine Calizo

Functions: Most + 08.0 08.4 09.0
Industries: Most + B.00 B.0W C.00 H.10 I.19
Professional Affiliations: DPMA, SME
Description: Professional recruitment in
   engineering, data processing, construction
   management & accounting

Branches:
80 Pauahi St., Ste. 208
Hilo, Hawaii 96720
Key Contact: Jack Crowther

75-167 Kalani Ct., Ste. 208
Kailua-Kona, Hawaii 96740
Key Contact: Teri Valentine-Hong

Dunhill of Denton, Inc.
P.O. Box 50692
Denton, Texas 76206
Salary Minimum: $40,000
Key Contact: Daniel J. Pajak

Functions: 02.0 03.4 04.0 06.0 11.6
Industries: D.15 D.19
Description: 20 years rubber & plastics;
   executive & technical search/recruiting
   nationwide

Dunhill Professional Search
80 Grand Ave., Ste. 810
Oakland, California 94612
Salary Minimum: $30,000
Key Contact: John F. Tierney

Functions: 01.2 01.3 02.2 02.4 03.4
Industries: B.0W B.10 D.00 D.D0 D.H0

Dunhill of Southeast Fort Worth, Inc.
4000 Old Benbrook Rd.
Ft. Worth, Texas 76116
Salary Minimum: $20,000
Key Contact: Dana S. Oliver

Functions: 02.0 02.2 02.4 02.5 04.0
Industries: D.10 D.15 D.16 D.18
Description: Ten years specialization in food,
   pharmaceuticals, medical device industries

Dunhill of Houston
10303 NW Frwy., Ste. 408
Houston, Texas 77092
Key Contact: Harry R. Coates

Functions: Most
Description: Placement of professional
   administrative personnel in finance,
   health, manufacturing, banking

Dunhill Personnel of Northeast Tulsa, Inc.

10159 E. 11th St., Ste. 370
Tulsa, Oklahoma 74128
Salary Minimum: $40,000
Key Contact: Joy M. Porrello
Judy Norfleet

Functions: 01.0 06.0 08.0 09.0 11.1
Industries: H.00 H.10 I.00 I.18
Professional Affiliations: NAPC
Description: 30 years combined experience in the banking, finance & data processing fields

Dunhill Search of West Atlanta

340 Interstate N., Ste. 140
Atlanta, Georgia 30339
Salary Minimum: $30,000
Key Contact: Jon Harvill

Functions: 01.3 02.0 03.0 06.0
Professional Affiliations: GAPC, NAPC
Description: Close electronic network of 250 offices for fast national searches/marketing

Dunhill of Bradenton, Inc.

4301 32nd St. W., Ste. C-19
Bradenton, Florida 34205
Key Contact: Joan Abrahamson
Jan Proctor
Lori Collins

Industries: I.14
Description: Distinctiveness, professionalism & sensitivity contribute to leadership in nursing mgmt placement

Dunhill of Huntsville, Inc.

2010 Jordan Ln., NW
Huntsville, Alabama 35816
Salary Minimum: $25,000
Key Contact: Jim Fowler
Mike Fowler
Kerry Chatham

Functions: 01.3 02.1 04.0 05.4 11.3
Description: Sales/mktg, production, R&D, tech services in animal health, poultry, seed & related agri indus.

Dunhill of Freehold, Inc.

303 W. Main St.
Freehold, New Jersey 07728
Salary Minimum: $35,000
Key Contact: Gary T. Livingston

Functions: 06.1 08.0 08.1 08.3 08.4
Industries: D.18 D.26 D.E0 I.19 K.10
Professional Affiliations: AGA
Description: Specializing in defense industry & payroll accounting

Dunhill of Manchester Inc.

814 Elm St., Beacon Bldg.
Manchester, New Hampshire 03101
Key Contact: Jack Schoenfeld
Martin Schoenfeld

Functions: 01.0 01.2 01.3 01.5 07.4
Industries: H.10 H.I0 I.14 I.15 I.17
Description: Specialize in banking, legal, insurance, healthcare, office support

Dunhill International Search

250 Sargent Dr., 2nd Fl.
New Haven, Connecticut 06511
Salary Minimum: $30,000
Key Contact: Donald J. Kaiser

Functions: Most + 01.0 05.0 06.0 08.0 09.0
Industries: Most + D.00 D.18 D.H0 I.14 J.13
Description: International recruiting for Europe, Far East & South America since 1978

Dunhill Professional Search

213 Danbury Rd.
Wilton, Connecticut 06897
Salary Minimum: $30,000
Key Contact: Kay Strakosch

Functions: 01.3 05.1 05.2 05.3 05.4
Industries: D.15 D.19 D.20 I.19
Professional Affiliations: NAPC

Dunhill of Greater Akron, Inc.

2675 Oakwood Dr.
Cuyahoga Falls, Ohio 44222-2648
Salary Minimum: $30,000
Key Contact: Charles R. Woodward

Functions: 01.2 02.0 05.2 05.3 11.3
Industries: D.22 D.24 D.25
Description: Placement of engineers & sales

Dunhill Professional Search Inc.

2000 W. Henderson Rd., Ste. 560
Columbus, Ohio 43220
Key Contact: Leo E. Salzman

Functions: 02.3 09.1 11.5
Industries: D.10 D.13 D.15 H.10 H.I0
Description: 26 years experience in recruiting;
auditor, DP, auditors, process control
engineers

Dunhill Professional Search of Kalamazoo

902 S. Westnedge Ave.
Kalamazoo, Michigan 49008
Key Contact: Ronald A. Hill
Kenneth A. Killman

Functions: Most
Description: Data processing, banking, sales &
marketing, accounting & finance &
healthcare professionals

Dunhill Personnel of Milwaukee

735 N. Water St., Ste. 185
Milwaukee, Wisconsin 53202
Key Contact: Bradley Brin

Functions: 02.0 02.1 02.2 10.0
Industries: D.22 D.I0 H.I0 I.14 I.15
Professional Affiliations: NAPR
Description: We place people where they want
to go

Dunhill Professional Search of Wilkes-Barre/Scranton, Inc.

67 Public Sq., Ste. 1214
Northeastern Bank Bldg.
Wilkes-Barre, Pennsylvania 18701
Key Contact: Anthony J. Desiderio

Functions: 01.0 02.0 03.0 04.0 05.0
Industries: B.00 B.0W B.10 D.00 D.H0
Description: Focused on engineering, quality
assurance, technical marketing & sales

Dunhill Personnel Search

47 E. 44th St.
New York, New York 10017
Salary Minimum: $40,000
Key Contact: Robert J. Morris

Functions: 01.3 05.4 09.2
Industries: D.24 I.18
Description: Many of our past placements are
now hiring managers

Dunhill Professional Search

801 E. 20th St., Ste. 1
Joplin, Missouri 64804
Salary Minimum: $30,000
Key Contact: Frank Wattelet

Functions: 02.5 06.1
Industries: D.10 D.15 D.17 D.18 D.19
Description: Top 2 counselors, 30 years
experience, master's degree, manufacturing
background

Dunhill Professional Search Group

11710 Reisterstown Rd., Ste. 210
Cherryvale Plaza
Reisterstown, Maryland 21136
Salary Minimum: $30,000
Key Contact: Ivan W. Smith
Karen Kurland
Fred Geerken
Marcia Bernstein
Judi Summerlin

Industries: D.10 D.18 I.14 I.15
Description: Food & dairy manufacturing &
healthcare specialists

Dunhill Search of Omaha, Inc.

13426 A St., Ste. 12
P.O. Box 37287
Omaha, Nebraska 68137
Salary Minimum: $25,000
Key Contact: Kenneth A. Jaspersen

Functions: Most + 01.2 01.3 08.0 11.5
Industries: B.0W D.15 D.17 D.18 H.10
Description: Search/recruitment of
professionals in environmental & banking
industries

Dunhill Personnel of Tampa

4350 W. Cypress St., Ste. 814
Tampa, Florida 33607
Salary Minimum: $20,000
Key Contact: Donald J. Kramer
Peter Kramer
Mona Kramer

Functions: 09.1
Industries: I.14
Description: We specialize in nurse managers,
hospital techs, hospital administration,
finance & auditing

Dunhill Professional Search Irvine/Newport

9 Executive Cir., Ste. 240, Bldg. 9
Irvine, California 92714
Salary Minimum: $30,000
Key Contact: David B. Vaughan

Functions: 01.0 02.0 05.0 05.4
Industries: D.00 D.18 D.22 D.E0
Description: Specialist sales, mkt, mgmt, in
industrial, medical, aviation, engineering,
sporting goods

Dunhill Professional Search of Ramsey

393 State Rte. 202
Oakland, New Jersey 07436-2644
Salary Minimum: $30,000
Key Contact: Roger Lippincott

Functions: 01.1 02.5 05.3 05.4 06.0
Industries: D.17 D.18 D.24 J.13
Professional Affiliations: ASQC, ASTD
Description: Over 25 years experience in sales,
marketing, training, development &
executive search.

Dussick Management Assoc.

149 Durham Rd.
Madison, Connecticut 06443
Salary Minimum: $45,000
Key Contact: Vince Dussick
Harry Ervin
Evylon Leone

Functions: 01.0 05.0 05.1 05.4 11.2
Industries: D.10 D.16 D.17 D.18 J.10
Professional Affiliations: CAPC
Description: Marketing/marketing research,
sales/sales promo & research positions-
packaged goods & service ind.

Gwen Dycus, Inc.

P.O. Box 5210
Winter Park, Florida 32793
Salary Minimum: $30,000
Key Contact: Gwen Dycus
Frank Hamilton

Functions: 05.1 11.0
Industries: C.00 G.00 H.R0 L.00
Professional Affiliations: ICSC
Description: Specialize in shopping center
industry, retail real estate & construction

G.L. Dykstra Assoc., Inc.

469 E. Bayberry Pt. Dr.
P.O. Box 141546
Grand Rapids, Michigan 49514-1546
Salary Minimum: $40,000
Key Contact: Gene L. Dykstra
Glenda M. Dykstra

Functions: Most + 02.0
Industries: Most
Description: Provides exclusive executive
search function for small to medium sized
companies

Dynamic Search Systems, Inc.

3800 N. Wilke Rd., Ste. 485
Arlington Heights, Illinois 60004
Salary Minimum: $15,000
Key Contact: Michael J. Brindise
Kevin J. Leonard

Functions: 09.0 09.1 09.3 09.4 09.6
Industries: Most
Professional Affiliations: IAPC, NAPC
Description: Placement of MIS professionals
from programming through administrative
levels

The E & K Group

23 Diamond Spring Rd.
Denville, New Jersey 07834
Salary Minimum: $40,000
Key Contact: Frank Brescher

Functions: Most + 01.0 02.0 04.0 06.0 11.6
Industries: Most
Description: Search & recruitment activities in
the national market .

E O Technical

213 Main St.
Danbury, Connecticut 06810
Key Contact: Jeanette Petroski
Gary Petroski

Functions: 02.0 03.0 04.0 06.0 11.3
Industries: Most
Professional Affiliations: CAPC, NAPC
Description: Handling the staffing needs of
local & national businesses since 1987

E T Search Inc.

737 Pearl St., Ste. 202
La Jolla, California 92037
Salary Minimum: $40,000
Key Contact: Kathleen Jennings

Functions: 08.0 08.4
Industries: Most
Professional Affiliations: NAER
Description: Exclusive tax search, serving
major corporations, public accounting
firms, & law firms

EPN, Inc.

P.O. Box 1082
Londonderry, New Hampshire 03053
Salary Minimum: $20,000
Key Contact: Geoffrey N. Eckler

Functions: 09.0 09.3 09.4
Professional Affiliations: NNEAPC
Description: Regionalized search & placement
firm specializing in DP/MIS/software

EXETER 2100

Computer Park
P.O. Box 2120
Hampton, New Hampshire 03842
Salary Minimum: $50,000
Key Contact: Bruce A. Montville

Functions: 01.4 09.0 09.1 09.2 09.3
Industries: Most
Professional Affiliations: DPMA, EMA, NPA
Description: Search exclusively in the
information systems &
telecommunications disciplines

Eastern Executive Assoc.

45 Hamilton Dr. E.
North Caldwell, New Jersey 07006
Key Contact: Madeline G. Jones

Functions: 01.0 02.0 03.0 04.0 09.0
Industries: B.00 B.0W D.00 D.E0 D.H0
Professional Affiliations: ASPA, NEA, NJPEA
Description: We regularly serve these
industries: electronics, aerospace,
pharmaceutical, consumer products, EDP

The Eastridge Group

824 Camino del Rio N., Ste. 374
San Diego, California 92108
Key Contact: Ra Halevi
Susan Daum
Nanci Porter

Functions: 11.3
Industries: B.0W B.10
Description: Environmental search
nationwide—air quality, hazardous & solid
waste, toxicology

Ecco Personnel Svcs.

1 North Broadway
White Plains, New York 10601
Salary Minimum: $30,000
Key Contact: Joanne C. Fiala

Branches:
555 Summer St.
Stamford, Connecticut 06901

Functions: 06.0 07.0 08.0 10.0
Industries: D.00 H.00 H.I0 J.00
Professional Affiliations: APCNY

1880 Commerce St.
Yorktown Heights, New York 10598

Eckert, Enghauser and Partners, Inc.

160 Newport Ctr. Dr., Ste. 260
Newport Beach, California 92660
Salary Minimum: $25,000
Key Contact: Paul D. Enghauser

Functions: Most + 11.5
Industries: B.0W D.00 D.H0 G.00 J.00
Professional Affiliations: NAER
Description: Specialize in marketing, sales,
advertising, real estate, engineering &
environmental

Eden & Assoc., Inc.

Valley Forge Plaza
King of Prussia, Pennsylvania 19406
Salary Minimum: $50,000
Key Contact: Brooks D. Eden
Fred A. Nunziata

Functions: Most + 01.0 02.0 05.0 08.0
Industries: D.10 D.13 D.17 F.00 G.00
Professional Affiliations: FMI
Description: Service food & drug retailers,
distributors, manfctrs., specialty & mass
merchandising retailers

Eggers Consulting Co., Inc.

11272 Elm St.
Omaha, Nebraska 68144-4788
Salary Minimum: $25,000
Key Contact: James W. Eggers
Brad Moore
Dan Barrow
Raymond Hamilius
Dee Miller

Functions: 01.0 02.0 04.0 08.0 09.1
Industries: B.0W D.10 G.00 H.00 H.I0
Professional Affiliations: NAPC
Description: Executive recruiting firm
specializing in banking, engineering, EDP,
accounting & insurance

W. Robert Eissler & Assoc., Inc.

1610 Woodstead Ct., Ste. 230
The Woodlands, Texas 77380
Salary Minimum: $25,000
Key Contact: W. Robert Eissler
Tom Boak
David White
Kirby Mills
Frank Marentez
Larry Patronella
Susan Magarity

Functions: 02.0 05.0 05.4 09.0 11.5
Industries: B.0W D.15 D.19 D.22 D.25
Professional Affiliations: FPS, ISA, SPE,
TAPPI
Description: Recruiters for nationwide senior
& middle level sales, marketing &
technical positions

Ells Personnel Systems Inc.

9900 Bren Rd.
Minneapolis, Minnesota 55343
Key Contact: Tom Gladitsch

Functions: 05.0 05.1 06.0 06.2 08.0
Industries: D.12 D.14 H.00 J.00
Professional Affiliations: NAPC, NPA
Description: Recruiting firm with over 75 years
servicing client companies

Mark Elzweig Co. Ltd.

110 Greene St., Ste. 3S
The Soho Bldg.
New York, New York 10012
Salary Minimum: $75,000
Key Contact: Mark Elzweig
David Turner

Functions: 05.4 10.0
Industries: H.00 H.10 H.11
Description: We specialize in the recruitment
of retail stock, commodity brokers &
actuaries

Emerson & Co.

449 Pleasant Hill Rd., Ste. 315
Lilburn, Georgia 30247
Salary Minimum: $40,000
Key Contact: Harold C. Popham

Functions: 02.0 05.4 05.6 11.3
Industries: D.14 D.18 D.22 D.24 I.14
Description: Middle to upper management
recruitment primarily in manufacturing

The Energists

10260 Westheimer, Ste. 300
Houston, Texas 77042
Salary Minimum: $45,000
Key Contact: Bradford Macurda
Alex Preston

Functions: 01.0 04.0 11.5 11.6
Industries: B.00 B.0W B.10 D.15 D.20
Professional Affiliations: AAPG, API, SPE
Description: Worldwide oil & gas,
environmental, & hazardous waste

Engineering & Scientific Search Assoc.

P.O. Box 14
Fanwood, New Jersey 07023
Salary Minimum: $25,000
Key Contact: Richard H. Skaar
Ralph Skaar
M. Patrick Curry
Edward Monahan

Functions: 02.4 04.0 05.3 05.4 11.6
Industries: D.15 D.19 D.20
Professional Affiliations: ACS, AIC, AICHE,
SPE
Description: Recruit R&D, engineering &
marketing personnel for chemical & allied
industries

Engineering Directions

95 Washington St., Ste. 222
Canton, Massachusetts 02021
Salary Minimum: $20,000
Key Contact: Eric Greenstein

Functions: Most
Industries: Most
Professional Affiliations: IEEE, MPPC
Description: The engineers in the personnel
business

Engineering Resource Group, Inc.

139 South St., Murray Hill Ctr.
Ste. 100
Murray Hill, New Jersey 07974
Salary Minimum: $40,000
Key Contact: Branko A. Terkovich

Functions: 02.1
Industries: D.22 D.23 D.24 D.E0 D.H0
Professional Affiliations: ASME, IEEE, NSPE
Description: Professional recruiting of
mechanical, electrical, electronic &
aerospace engineers

Engineering Search Assoc.

99 Durham Rd.
Madison, Connecticut 06443
Salary Minimum: $30,000
Key Contact: Barry L. Dicker
Geoffrey M. Kerrigan
Donald E. Eckdahl

Functions: 01.2 02.1 03.2 04.0 11.3
Industries: D.24 D.26 J.00 J.13
Description: High tech electronics hardware &
software design & management

Engineering Specialists

3215 W. Lawrence St., Ste. 6
Appleton, Wisconsin 54914-4274
Key Contact: Lynn Sexton
Moonyean Ihde
James Vannoy

Functions: Most
Industries: Most
Professional Affiliations: WAPC
Description: Domestic/international recruiting-
all disciplines

Environmental Professional Assoc.

9454 Wilshire Blvd., Ste. 650
Beverly Hills, California 90212
Salary Minimum: $40,000
Key Contact: Mary Ann Schuessler

Functions: Most + 01.4 01.5 11.1 11.3 11.5
Industries: Most + B.0W B.10 D.00 D.I0 I.17
Description: Knowledgable with personnel
experience dealing with super fund

Environmental Resources Int'l.

4017 Washington Rd., Ste. 6000
McMurray, Pennsylvania 15317-2520
Salary Minimum: $35,000
Key Contact: George A. Armes
Georgean N. Sharp

Functions: 11.3 11.5 11.6
Industries: B.00 B.0W B.10 D.15 D.20
Description: Mid to senior level civil &
environmental search

Allen Etcovitch Assoc. Ltd.

666 Sherbrooke St., W, Ste. 1707
Montreal, Quebec H3A 1E7 Canada
Salary Minimum: $30,000

Functions: Most
Industries: D.00 G.00
Professional Affiliations: APA, BCPA, BPS,
  CPA, CPPQ, OPA
Description: Registered management
  psychologists offering psychological
  consulting services

Branches:
2050 Nelson, Apt. 703
Vancouver, British Columbia V6G 1N6
  Canada
Key Contact: Anna Baron

International Branches:
London

Affiliates/Other Offices:
A. W. Fraser & Assoc., Edmonton
E. H. Scissons & Assoc. Ltd., Saskatoon
Westcott Thomas & Assoc. Ltd., Toronto

Evans & James Assoc., Inc.

1 North Broadway, Ste. 411
White Plains, New York 10601
Salary Minimum: $30,000
Key Contact: Arnold Evans

Functions: 02.4 02.5 03.4 05.2 05.4
Industries: D.13 D.14 D.19 D.D0
Professional Affiliations: IOPP
Description: Contingency search firm placing
  packaging, graphics, paper & plastics
  professionals

Exec 2000

5251 N. 16th St., Ste. 310
Phoenix, Arizona 85016-3289
Salary Minimum: $25,000
Key Contact: Martin Jacobs

Functions: 01.2 01.4 01.5 05.4 09.3
Industries: D.10 D.H0 I.14 I.15 I.17
Professional Affiliations: ASCA, NALSC,
  NAPC
Description: Insurance, attorneys, electronic
  engineering, medical (physicians & admin.
  nurses) nat'l. & int'l.

Execu-Search, Inc.

488 Madison Ave.
New York, New York 10022
Salary Minimum: $30,000
Key Contact: Edward Fleischman
Robert Fligel

Functions: 08.0 08.1 08.2 08.4
Industries: Most
Description: Specialists in the recruitment of
  accounting, financial & tax professionals

ExecuSource Int'l.

4120 Rio Bravo, Ste. 106
El Paso, Texas 79902-1012
Salary Minimum: $25,000
Key Contact: John L. Marshall

Functions: Most + 02.2 03.0 05.0 06.0 08.0
Industries: Most + D.00 D.24 D.H0
Professional Affiliations: SHRM
Description: Small but effective contingency
  search firm with wide clientele

ExecuTech

350 Sagamore Pkwy., Ste. 6
West Lafayette, Indiana 47906
Salary Minimum: $25,000
Key Contact: Thomas P. Fidelle

Functions: 02.0 02.1 04.0 11.3 11.5
Industries: B.10 D.11 D.15 D.18 D.19
Description: Recruiting chemists & chemical
  engineers for the chemical industry

Executive Careers

1801 Ave. of the Stars
Ste. 640
Los Angeles, California 90067
Salary Minimum: $40,000
Key Contact: Annette Segil

Functions: Most + 05.0 06.0 11.2 11.4
Industries: D.11 G.00 I.12 I.21 J.10
Professional Affiliations: CERA, NAER
Description: Search generalist as well as
specialties in retail, direct marketing, &
catalogue

The Executive Consulting Group—N.Y.

215 N. Ocean Ave.
Patchogue, New York 11772
Salary Minimum: $35,000
Key Contact: David Glaser

Functions: 08.4
Industries: Most
Professional Affiliations: APCNY
Description: Tax specialty recruiting-extensive
Big 8 contacts-financial services
concentration

Executive Dynamics, Inc.

Airport Square 19, Ste. 140
1099 Winterson Rd.
Linthicum, Maryland 21090
Salary Minimum: $25,000
Key Contact: David A. Carden

Functions: Most
Industries: D.15 H.10 H.I0 H.R0 I.14
Professional Affiliations: NAA
Description: Search for financial, accounting &
data processing professionals with 2+
years experience

Executive Exchange Corp.

560 Sylvan Ave.
Englewood Cliffs, New Jersey 07632
Key Contact: Elizabeth B. Glosser

Functions: 01.4 05.4 09.0 09.3 09.7
Industries: D.00 D.18 H.10 I.18
Professional Affiliations: NAPC, NJAPC
Description: Data processing & computer
related sales, permanent & temporary
assignments

Branches:
2517 Hwy. 35 G-103
Manasquan, New Jersey 08736

Executive Recruiters, Inc.

P.O. Box 567
Elm Grove, Wisconsin 53122-0567
Salary Minimum: $35,000
Key Contact: Gilbert E. Ormson

Functions: 02.0 04.0 05.0 09.0 11.5
Industries: B.0W D.00 D.22 D.24 D.H0
Description: Technical & management
positions-engineering, manufacturing,
sales/marketing & data processing

Executive Referral Services, Inc.

8745 W. Higgin Rd., Ste. 470
Chicago, Illinois 60631
Salary Minimum: $25,000
Key Contact: Bruce Freier
Linda Herrick
Arthur Gladstone
Sandra Kelly
Mark Gray

Functions: Most + 01.1 01.2 01.3 02.0 06.0
Industries: D.18 G.00 I.10 I.14 I.16
Professional Affiliations: HMAI, IAHA, IRA
Description: Specialists in retail, restaurant,
club, hotel & pharmaceutical industry
recruitment

Executive Register, Inc.

34 Mill Plain Rd.,
Danbury, Connecticut 06811
Salary Minimum: $40,000
Key Contact: J. Scott Williams

Functions: 02.0 03.0 08.0 09.0
Industries: Most + D.00 H.00 H.I0 H.R0
Professional Affiliations: APICS, CAPC,
DPMA, IMA, NAPC, SME
Description: Specialize in data processing,
accounting/finance & engineering/
manufacturing

Executive Resource Inc.

245 Regency Ct., Ste. 100
Waukesha, Wisconsin 53186
Salary Minimum: $25,000
Key Contact: William H. Mitton
Duane Strong

Functions: 02.0 03.0 06.0 08.0 09.0
Industries: Most
Professional Affiliations: NPA
Description: Deal in broad range of functions in most industries

Executive Search of New England, Inc.

Citicorp Park, Foden Rd.
South Portland, Maine 04106
Salary Minimum: $18,000
Key Contact: Robert L. Sloat
Robert T. Thayer
Julia H. Olson
Frank A. DiGiacomo
Reis F. Hagerman
Anne Ritchie

Functions: Most
Industries: Most
Professional Affiliations: NAPC, NPA
Description: Data processing, banking, accounting, sales, retail,environmental engineering, medical

Executives' Personnel Service Inc.

17117 W. Nine Mile Rd., Ste. 605P
Southfield, Michigan 48075
Salary Minimum: $35,000
Key Contact: Frank A. Cowall
Charles S. Brooks

Functions: Most
Industries: Most
Professional Affiliations: MAPC
Description: Executive search & recruiting, nationwide placement—Michigan's oldest agency

eXsource

1802 Bay St.
Beaufort, South Carolina 29902
Salary Minimum: $30,000
Key Contact: Samuel F. Domby

Functions: 01.4 05.2 06.0 08.0 09.0
Industries: D.H0 H.10 I.14 I.18 J.13
Description: Specialists in banking, healthcare, MIS & telecommunications recruiting services

F.L.A.G.

347 Scioto St.
Urbana, Ohio 43078
Salary Minimum: $40,000
Key Contact: Tom S. Warren

Functions: 04.0 05.0
Industries: D.15 D.20
Description: Fuel, lubricant, grease, asphalt, oil field & refinery chemicals

Paul Falcone Assoc., Inc.

14 Ridgedale Ave., Ste. 207
Cedar Knolls, New Jersey 07927
Salary Minimum: $40,000

Functions: 02.0 03.0 05.0 06.0
Industries: D.10 D.16 D.17 D.18 I.16
Description: Specializing in: food, beverage, pharmaceutical & cosmetic industries

Fallstaff Search

111 Warren Rd., Ste. 4B
Hunt Valley, Maryland 21030
Key Contact: Robert Chertkof

Functions: Most
Industries: I.00 I.14
Description: Medical sales, executives, operations

David Farmer & Assoc.

500 Throckmorton, Box 44386
Ft. Worth, Texas 76102
Salary Minimum: $30,000
Key Contact: David W. Farmer

Functions: 01.2 01.3 01.4 06.0 08.0
Industries: D.00 H.00 H.I0 H.R0 I.00
Professional Affiliations: SERC
Description: Specialize in recruitment for banks & human resource professionals

Federal Placement Services

78 Lafayette Ave., Ste. 116
Suffern Plz.
Suffern, New York 10901
Salary Minimum: $20,000
Key Contact: Joan Bialkin
Pam Ericson

Functions: Most
Industries: H.00 H.10
Description: Executive search exclusively for
banking community representing major
banking institutions

A.E. Feldman Assoc.

295 Northern Blvd.
Great Neck, New York 11021
Salary Minimum: $40,000
Key Contact: Abe Feldman
Burt Stern
Len Ziegle
Claudeth Crowe
Charles Ferguson
Robert Rothfeld

Functions: Most
Industries: Most
Description: A boutique recruiting organization
founded in 1967

N. Steven Fells & Co., Inc.

11 Grace Ave., Ste. 200
Great Neck, New York 11021
Salary Minimum: $40,000
Key Contact: Norman Fells

Functions: Most + 01.0 05.2 05.4 09.3 09.4
Industries: D.H0 I.18 I.20
Description: Specialists in the data processing
community-user & vendor

Fergason Assoc., Inc.

1360 Lake Shore Dr., Ste. 1417
Chicago, Illinois 60610
Salary Minimum: $25,000
Key Contact: Loel G. Hahn

Functions: Most + 01.0 02.0 05.0 08.0 09.0
Industries: Most + D.00 D.D0 D.H0 F.00
H.I0
Description: Retained executive search middle
& senior level distribution, manufacturing
& financial

Fernow Assoc.

191 Presidential Blvd., Ste. BN13
Bala Cynwyd, Pennsylvania 19004-1207
Salary Minimum: $30,000
Key Contact: Charles S. Fernow
S. George Goich
William Dransfield
Sidney Aitkens
Mark Dransfield

Functions: 01.0 04.0 05.0 06.0 09.0
Industries: B.0W D.00 D.H0 I.00 K.10
Description: Search consultants to electronic &
computer industries

Ferrari Consulting Group

30799 Pinetree Rd., Ste. 118
Pepper Pike, Ohio 44124
Salary Minimum: $30,000
Key Contact: S. Jay Ferrari
Jerry Salerno
Brenda G. Short

Functions: 01.0 05.2 05.3 06.0 09.0
Industries: B.0W H.00 I.11 I.17 I.19
Professional Affiliations: ASPA, NAPC
Description: Executive search on a proactive
basis serving the financial community on
a national basis

G.A. Field Personnel Consultants

75 Second Ave.
Needham, Massachusetts 02194
Salary Minimum: $50,000
Key Contact: Gloria Adelson Field

Functions: 05.0 05.1 05.2 05.4 05.5
Industries: D.24 J.10 J.11
Description: Computer sales & marketing,
communications, advertising, public
relations & publishing

Jerry Fields Assoc.
353 Lexington Ave., 11th Fl.
New York, New York 10016
Salary Minimum: $18,000
Key Contact: Jerry Fields
Eleanor Fields

Functions: 05.1 05.5 05.7
Industries: J.10 J.11
Professional Affiliations: ACNY, ADC
Description: The largest full-service advertising
& graphic arts contingency search
specialists

Finance & Accounting Search Firm
211 E. Six Forks Rd., Ste. 211
Raleigh, North Carolina 27609
Key Contact: Anne C. Jones

Functions: 08.0
Industries: Most
Professional Affiliations: IMA
Description: Conduct search assignments for
CFOs & their accounting management
staff

Financial Resource Assoc., Inc.
105 W. Orange St.
Altamonte Springs, Florida 32714
Salary Minimum: $30,000
Key Contact: John Cannavino
Terry L. Krick
Joe Satilli

Functions: Most
Industries: H.10
Professional Affiliations: FAPC, NAER, NBN
Description: Mid-sr. mgmt. for mortgage
companies, banks, savings & loans &
other financial institutions

Financial Search Corp.
2720 Des Plaines Ave., Ste. 154
Des Plaines, Illinois 60018
Salary Minimum: $20,000
Key Contact: Robert J. Collins

Functions: 08.0 08.1 08.2 08.3 08.4
Industries: Most
Description: Recruitment, screening and
placement of accounting and financial
professionals

Financial Search Group, Inc.
800 Turnpike St., Ste. 300
North Andover, Massachusetts 01845
Salary Minimum: $40,000
Key Contact: Paul T. Luther

Functions: 01.2 01.3 08.0 08.2
Industries: H.10 H.12 I.20
Professional Affiliations: AAEL
Description: Specializes in investment-based
financial services marketplace

First Search Inc.
9025 Kostner Ave., Ste. D
Skokie, Illinois 60076
Salary Minimum: $35,000
Key Contact: Allen M. Katz
Michael R. Zarnek
Charles A. Szajkovics

Functions: 02.0 04.0 05.0 09.0 09.7
Industries: D.24 D.H0 I.18 J.00
Professional Affiliations: IAPC, IEEE, NAPC
Description: Specialists in executive and
technical recruiting in the
communications/cellular industry

Jack Stuart Fisher Assoc.
328 Poplar St.
Philadelphia, Pennsylvania 19123
Salary Minimum: $45,000
Key Contact: Jack Stuart Fisher

Functions: 04.0 05.2 05.3 05.5 10.0
Industries: D.15 D.18 D.I0 H.I0 I.13
Description: Highly focused scientist searches,
both retainer & exclusive contingency

Fisher-Todd Assoc.
535 Fifth Ave., Ste. 1100
New York, New York 10017
Salary Minimum: $30,000
Key Contact: Philip Fisher
Ronald Franz
Barbara Stoller
Michael Brauth
Cliff Schorr

Functions: 01.0 02.0 05.0 06.0 08.0
Industries: D.00 D.I0 H.00 H.I0 I.00
Description: We recruit at all levels of
management within functional specialties

A.G. Fishkin & Assoc., Inc.

P.O. Box 34413
Bethesda, Maryland 20827
Salary Minimum: $30,000
Key Contact: Anita Fishkin
Paul F. Kallfelz

Functions: 01.0 05.0 09.0 11.1 11.3
Industries: D.24 D.H0 I.18 I.21 J.13
Professional Affiliations: MAPRC, NAPC
Description: High technology clients with emphasis on computer & data communications

James L. Fisk & Assoc.

1921 Buckington Dr.
St. Louis, Missouri 63017
Salary Minimum: $25,000
Key Contact: James L. Fisk

Functions: Most + 01.0 01.4 02.0 04.0 05.0
Industries: Most + B.0W D.18 I.14 I.15 I.16
Description: Hospitals/registered medical practitioners (nurses O.T., pharmacists) medical devices/pharmaceutical

Florapersonnel, Inc.

2180 W. State Rd. 434, Ste. 6152
Longwood, Florida 32779-5008
Key Contact: Robert F. Zahra
Jeffrey S. Brower
Joseph Dalton
Judy Wozny

Functions: Most
Industries: A.00
Professional Affiliations: NAER
Description: International search firm for the ornamental horticulture industry only

Flores & Assoc.

4500 Cameron Valley Pkwy., Ste. 430
Charlotte, North Carolina 28211
Salary Minimum: $25,000
Key Contact: Mario Flores
Robert Harrington

Functions: 01.3 02.0 03.0 05.0 08.0
Industries: D.00 D.E0 F.00 G.00 I.19
Professional Affiliations: ASPA, EMA
Description: Client tailored search, selection & performance appraisal & employee development programs

Flynn, Hannock, Inc.

1216 Farmington Ave.
P.O. Box 7F
West Hartford, Connecticut 06127
Salary Minimum: $50,000
Key Contact: Elwin W. Hannock, III

Branches:
P.O. Box 8027
Stamford, Connecticut 06905
Key Contact: Richard Sandor

Functions: 01.2 01.3 06.0 08.0 10.0
Industries: D.00 H.10 H.I0 I.00
Professional Affiliations: IACPR, SHRM
Description: Executive search with emphasis on banking, insurance, manufacturing

David Fockler & Assoc., Inc.

P.O. Box 251
Barrington, Illinois 60011
Salary Minimum: $30,000
Key Contact: David B. Fockler

Functions: 05.3 05.4 08.0
Industries: C.00 D.10 D.16 D.17
Description: Sales, marketing & financial positions for food/consumer/HABA companies nationally

Focus: HealthCare

129 N. Adams St.
Louisville, Kentucky 40206
Key Contact: Frank Poschinger
Deborah Pennington

Industries: I.14 I.15
Professional Affiliations: NAPR
Description: Management consultants specializing in physician recruitment nationwide

Ford & Assoc., Inc.

534 W. Broadway, Ste. 100
Myrtle Beach, South Carolina 29578
Salary Minimum: $27,000
Key Contact: Travis Ford
Charles Hendrick
Martin B. Ford

Functions: Most + 01.0 02.0 03.0 06.0 11.5
Industries: B.0W D.11 D.15 D.18 D.19
Professional Affiliations: SCAPS
Description: Textile, chemical &
   environmental line/staff recruiting
   specialists since 1980

Ford & Ford

105 Chestnut St., Ste. 34
Needham, Massachusetts 02192
Salary Minimum: $45,000
Key Contact: Bernard H. Ford
Eileen F. Ford

Functions: Most + 05.0 06.0 11.2 11.5
Industries: Most + G.00 I.15
Professional Affiliations: ASTD, MAPC,
   NAPC, NARPC
Description: Retail, direct marketing as
   industry—human resources, dist., apparel,
   all retail occupations

Fortune Personnel Consultants of Sarasota Inc.

3131 Clark Rd., Ste. 201
Sarasota, Florida 34231
Salary Minimum: $30,000
Key Contact: Arthur R. Grindlinger

Functions: 02.0 03.0 03.1 03.2
Industries: D.00 D.E0 D.H0 D.I0
Professional Affiliations: AIIE, AME, APICS,
   ASQC, NAPM
Description: Providing professionals for
   manufacturing companies up through the
   executive level

Fortune Personnel Consultants

505 W. Hollis St., Ste. 208
Nashua, New Hampshire 03062
Salary Minimum: $30,000
Key Contact: Norman J. Oppenheim

Functions: 01.2 01.3 02.5 04.0
Industries: D.17 D.18 D.I0 I.14 I.15
Description: Specialize in healthcare, bio-tech,
   pharmaceutical & medical devices
   industries

Fortune Personnel Consultants of Huntsville, Inc.

3311 Bob Wallace Ave. Ste. 204 4
Huntsville, Alabama 35805
Salary Minimum: $35,000
Key Contact: Robert W. Langford
Lynn Lamb
Kevin O'Neill
Samuel Borden
Michael Martyniak

Functions: 01.0 02.0 03.0 04.0 09.0
Industries: D.18 D.22 D.23 D.24 D.H0
Description: Servicing general management,
   manufacturing, materials, quality,
   engineering & software

Forum Assoc.

Willamette Park Plz.
6420 S.W. Macadam, #206
Portland, Oregon 97201
Salary Minimum: $50,000
Key Contact: Chris Rickford

Functions: 09.2 09.3 09.4 09.7
Industries: D.24 D.H0 J.13
Professional Affiliations: NAPC
Description: High technology—voice/data
   communications, soft/hardware engineers,
   engineering mgrs, mrktg

Foster Assoc.

The Livery, 209 Cooper Ave.
Upper Montclair, New Jersey 07043
Salary Minimum: $60,000
Key Contact: Donald J. Foster

Functions: Most + 01.5 08.0 08.4 09.1 11.1
Industries: Most + D.00 H.10 H.R0 I.17 I.19
Professional Affiliations: AICPA
Description: Highly personalized professional
   srvc.; generalist practice & CPA,
   consulting, legal & financial svcs

The Foster McKay Group

535 Fifth Ave., 32nd Fl.
New York, New York 10017
Salary Minimum: $40,000
Key Contact: Rolfe I. Kopelan
Joseph R. Monaco

Fox-Morris Assoc., Inc.

1617 JFK Blvd., Ste. 210
Philadelphia, Pennsylvania 19103
Salary Minimum: $35,000
Key Contact: Thomas J. Glynn
Harvey Brooks

Branches:
1535 E. Orangewood Ave.
Ste. 106
Anaheim, California 92805
Key Contact: Dave Jatinen

507 N. New York Ave., Ste. 200
Winter Park, Florida 32789
Key Contact: Paul Murphy

47 Perimeter Ctr. East, NE
Ste. 540
Atlanta, Georgia 30346

409 Washington Ave.
Baltimore, Maryland 21204
Key Contact: George Simmons

500 Route 17 S.
Hasbrouck Heights, New Jersey 07604
Key Contact: Larry Keating

9140 Arrowhead Blvd., Ste. 380
Charlotte, North Carolina 28273
Key Contact: Reed Baker
Steve Jesseph

Franchise Recruiters Ltd.

3500 Innsburck
Lincolnshire Country Club
Crete, Illinois 60417
Salary Minimum: $40,000
Key Contact: Jerry C. Wilkerson

Branches:
2201 Wisconsin Ave., NW, Ste. C-120
Washington, District of Columbia 20007

347 Bay St., Ste 1200
Toronto, Ontario M5H 2R7 Canada
Key Contact: Bill Coke
George Kinzie

Functions: 08.0 09.0
Industries: Most
Professional Affiliations: APC
Description: Corp. financial & accounting
specialists, mid & exec. mgmt. investment
banking & capital markets

Functions: Most
Industries: Most + C.00 D.00 E.00 H.I0 I.00
Professional Affiliations: IACPR, IPA, NAPC

4700 Rockside Rd., Ste. 640
Cleveland, Ohio 44131
Key Contact: Bill Yorke

One Gateway Ctr., 18th Fl.
North Wing
Pittsburgh, Pennsylvania 15222
Key Contact: Murray Leety

P.O. Box 10087, Calder Sq.
State College, Pennsylvania 16805-0087
Key Contact: Dick Wilson

14643 Dallas Pkwy., Ste. 775
LB3
Dallas, Texas 75240
Key Contact: Jerry Sewell

Greenwich Ctr., Ste.205
192 Ballard Ct.
Virginia Beach, Virginia 23462
Key Contact: Paul Murphy

Functions: 05.2 07.0
Industries: Most
Professional Affiliations: IFA
Description: Executive search for franchisors
with franchise experienced candidates only

Franchise Search, Inc.
20 Latting Town Rd.
Glen Cove, New York 11542
Salary Minimum: $30,000
Key Contact: Douglas T. Kushell

Functions: 08.0
Industries: B.0W B.10 I.10
Description: The foremost personnel placement
    company servicing the franchise industry
    exclusively

Franklin Int'l. Search, Inc.
4 Franklin Commons
Framingham, Massachusetts 01701
Salary Minimum: $50,000
Key Contact: Stanley L. Shindler

Functions: 01.0 04.0 05.0 05.3 11.3
Industries: D.18 D.25 D.H0 J.13
Description: Specializing in lasers, optics, fiber
    optics, semiconductor materials &
    equipment

Mel Frazer & Assoc.
20350 Chapter Dr.
Woodland Hills, California 91364-5609
Salary Minimum: $40,000
Key Contact: Mel Frazer
Nancy Frazer

Functions: Most + 02.0 04.0 06.0 08.0 09.0
Industries: D.18 D.H0 D.I0 I.14 J.12
Professional Affiliations: CPPA, IEEE, ISA
Description: Middle management medical
    device contingency search

Frey & Conboy Assoc., Inc.
1800 N. Kent St., Ste. 1006
Arlington, Virginia 22209
Key Contact: Florence Frey
Lucy Conboy

Functions: 01.5
Industries: I.17
Professional Affiliations: NALSC
Description: Attorney search specialists

The Fry Group, Inc.
18 E. 41st St.
New York, New York 10017
Salary Minimum: $25,000
Key Contact: John M. Fry

Functions: 05.1 05.5 05.7
Industries: J.10
Professional Affiliations: APCNY, IABC,
    NAPC
Description: Public relations, advertising &
    marketing communications executive
    recruiting

Fuller Search
6433 Devonshire Dr., Ste. 400
Ft. Worth, Texas 76180-8449
Salary Minimum: $40,000
Key Contact: Bill Fuller

Functions: 10.0 11.0
Industries: B.00 B.0W H.I0 I.14 I.15
Professional Affiliations: ASSE, INS, NAER,
    NAPC, NIRA, TAPC
Description: Serving property/casualty
    insurance corporate risk management,
    rehabilitation, healthcare industries

The Furst Group
6085 Strathmoor Dr.
Rockford, Illinois 61107
Salary Minimum: $50,000
Key Contact: Thomas C. Furst
Bradford B. Marion

Functions: Most
Industries: Most
Description: Retained/non-retained recruiting,
    manufacturing and financial markets

Future Sense
68 Shoreline Dr.
Gulf Breeze, Florida 32561
Salary Minimum: $40,000
Key Contact: Ann R. Carlsen
Justin Rallis

Functions: Most + 01.0 05.0 11.2
Industries: J.11 J.12
Description: Mid to upper level management
    positions in cable TV, cellular,
    entertainment & publishing

G.A.M. Executive Search, Inc.
30400 Telegraph Rd., Ste. 358
Bingham Farms, Michigan 48025
Salary Minimum: $15,000
Key Contact: Sally August
Pam Anderson

Functions: Most
Industries: Most
Professional Affiliations: NAPC, MAPC
Description: The good at matching firm that specializes in quality placements

GHK Technical Recruiter
P.O. Box 131
Trumbull, Connecticut 06611
Salary Minimum: $25,000
Key Contact: George Kehoe
Lillian Kehoe

Functions: 02.0 04.0 05.0 11.3
Industries: D.00 D.E0 D.H0 D.I0
Professional Affiliations: ACerS, IEEE, ISHM, SAMPE
Description: Leader in ceramics and glass, materials science; associated technologies and arts

Gabriel & Bowie Assoc., Ltd.
612 Norhurst Way
Baltimore, Maryland 21228
Salary Minimum: $40,000
Key Contact: Andrew Bowie

Functions: 03.3
Industries: E.00
Description: International trade & transportation. Handle searches in all U.S. cities

Gaines & Assoc. Int'l., Inc.
645 N. Michigan Ave., Ste. 800
Chicago, Illinois 60611
Salary Minimum: $20,000
Key Contact: Donna Gaines
Charles L. Roberson

Functions: 01.1 01.2 02.2 11.6
Industries: Most
Description: Management consulting firm specializing in architecture, engineering & general contractors

Galen Giles Group
635 Nut Plains Rd.
Guilford, Connecticut 06437
Salary Minimum: $25,000
Key Contact: David Johnson

Functions: 01.2 01.3 02.0 03.4
Industries: B.0W D.10 D.19 D.22 D.D0
Description: Confidential & thorough matchmaking of worthy candidates and desirable companies

Gallagher & Assoc.
1145 Linn Ridge Rd.
Mount Vernon, Iowa 52314
Salary Minimum: $30,000
Key Contact: Donald Gallagher

Functions: 02.0 04.0 09.4 11.3 11.6
Industries: D.25 D.E0 D.H0 J.13 K.10
Professional Affiliations: IEEE, SHRM, SME
Description: Specializing in recruitment of engineering professionals for companies in the Midwest

Gallin Assoc.
P.O. Box 3120
Princeton, New Jersey 08543
Salary Minimum: $40,000
Key Contact: Lawrence Gallin
Andrea Costello
Mark Richards
John Costello
Jack Costello

Functions: 02.0 04.0 05.0 11.5 11.6
Industries: B.0W D.13 D.15 D.19 D.20
Description: Specialists-chemicals & plastics

Michael Garbi Assoc., Inc.

1351 Washington Blvd.
Stamford, Connecticut 06902
Salary Minimum: $40,000
Key Contact: Michael Caradimitropoulo
Georgia Siomkos

International Branches:
London

Functions: Most
Industries: D.00 F.00 H.00 I.00 J.00
Description: Search for financial/accounting/
MIS/marketing-sales/strategic planning/art
directors

Gardner, Savage Assoc.

Box 430
Boundbrook, New Jersey 08805
Salary Minimum: $20,000
Key Contact: Jack Gardner
Jean Savage

Functions: 01.3 04.0 05.2 05.3 05.4
Industries: D.18 D.I0
Description: Marketing & scientific managers
for medical diagnostics & device
industries

Garrett Assoc. Inc.

P.O. Box 190189
Atlanta, Georgia 31119-0189
Salary Minimum: $30,000
Key Contact: Donald L. Garrett
Linda Garrett
Janis Morrison

Functions: 01.0 06.0 07.0 08.0 09.0
Industries: I.14 I.15
Professional Affiliations: NAPPH
Description: Serving the healthcare industry-
candidates may come from outside health-
care

The Garrison Group

15 Toronto St., Ste. 500
Toronto, Ontario M5C 2E3 Canada
Salary Minimum: $35,000
Key Contact: Ronald J. McGee
Adriana Porretta

Functions: 08.0 08.1 08.2 08.4
Industries: Most
Professional Affiliations: NAPC, NPA

Garrison, McGuigan & Sisson

1050 17th St., N.W., Ste. 301
Washington, District of Columbia 20036
Key Contact: Charles W. Garrison
Martha Ann Sisson
Lori D. Bornstein

Industries: I.17
Description: Attorney search for law firms,
corporations & trade associations

The Garrison Organization

600 5th Ave. Plz.
Des Moines, Iowa 50309
Salary Minimum: $60,000
Key Contact: Ed Garrison

Functions: 05.0 05.4 10.0
Industries: H.I0
Description: An executive search & consulting
intermediary serving the life insurance
industry

Gatti & Assoc.

266 Main St., Ste. 21
Medfield, Massachusetts 02052
Key Contact: Robert D. Gatti
Judith Banker

Functions: 06.0
Industries: Most
Professional Affiliations: ACA, ASTD, HRPS,
HRSP, NCPA, NEHRA, NEHRMG
Description: Specialists in the placement of
human resource professionals-all
industries

Branches:
11 Beacon St. Ste. 915
Boston, Massachusetts 02108

400 Cummings Park W.
Woburn, Massachusetts 01801
Key Contact: Rita Allen

Gaudette & Co.
980 W. Paseo Del Cilantro
Green Valley, Arizona 85614
Salary Minimum: $40,000
Key Contact: Charles L. Gaudette

Functions: 01.2 01.3 05.3 06.1 10.0
Industries: I.14
Description: Eighteen years confidential
specialization in sr management,
insurance & financial institutions

Genesis
P.O. Box 2388
Roseville, California 95746
Salary Minimum: $30,000
Key Contact: Jerry Kleames

Functions: 02.1 02.5 02.6 04.0 11.5
Industries: B.0W D.00 D.10 D.15 D.20
Description: Recruiting chemists, chemical
engineers, civil & structural engineers

Genesis Personnel Service, Inc.
10921 Reed Hartman Hwy., Ste. 226
Cincinnati, Ohio 45242
Salary Minimum: $22,000
Key Contact: Delora Bennett

Functions: Most + 01.0 05.0 08.0 09.0 11.2
Industries: D.00 D.10 D.18 D.19 I.00
Description: Black female solely owned &
operated professional recruiting firm

Delores F. George
269 Hamilton St.
Worcester, Massachusetts 01604
Key Contact: Delores F. George

Functions: Most + 01.0 02.0 05.0 07.0 08.0
Industries: Most + B.0W D.00 H.00 H.I0 I.00
Professional Affiliations: MAPC, NAPC, SBSB
Description: Individual &/or career options
with knowledgeable & friendly service/
personal attention

J. Gifford, Inc.
5310 E. 31st St., Ste.514
Tulsa, Oklahoma 74135
Salary Minimum: $30,000
Key Contact: James R. Gifford

Functions: 02.0 02.1 02.2 02.3 02.4
Industries: B.00 B.0W D.00 D.15 D.20
Professional Affiliations: NPA
Description: Professional engineering staffing in
oil/gas, manufacturing, national network
affiliation

Joe L. Giles & Assoc., Inc.
21700 Northwestern Hwy.
Tower 14, Ste. 1195
Southfield, Michigan 48075
Salary Minimum: $40,000
Key Contact: Joe L. Giles

Functions: Most
Industries: Most
Professional Affiliations: MAPC
Description: Undertakes individuals and/or
multiple recruiting assignments on a
nationwide basis

Alan Glenn & Keener
2744 E. Coast Hwy., Ste. 600
Corona del Mar, California 92625
Salary Minimum: $30,000
Key Contact: James R. Keener

Functions: Most
Industries: B.10 D.00 D.H0 I.15 I.18
Professional Affiliations: CERA
Description: EDP, manufacturing,
environmental/waste mgmt. engineers,
technicians, attornies & physicians

Branches:
638 Arrowhead Dr.
Carson City, Nevada 89706
Key Contact: Brian Dallas

Global Data Services, Inc.

200 Broad Hollow Rd., Ste. 306
Melville, New York 11747
Salary Minimum: $60,000
Key Contact: Garry Silivanch

Functions: 01.0 01.4 05.0 09.0 11.1
Industries: D.00 D.24 D.H0 I.00 I.18
Description: A dynamic experienced firm
    employing professionals whose business
    acumen is unsurpassed

Branches:
601 University Ave., Ste. 150
Sacramento, California 95825
Key Contact: Douglas Razzano

345 Rte. 17
Upper Saddle River, New Jersey 07458
Key Contact: Larry Griffin

W.T. Glover & Assoc., Inc.

2 Gateway Ctr., 18th Fl., E. Wing
Pittsburgh, Pennsylvania 15222
Salary Minimum: $30,000
Key Contact: Terry Glover
John Bobola
William Brundage

Functions: 01.0 02.0 05.0 08.0 09.0
Industries: D.00 H.10 I.14 I.18 I.19
Professional Affiliations: NAA, NAPC, PAPC
Description: Mid to upper level management
    contingency recruiting

Gold Coast Partners

3 Cardinal Ct., Ste. 239
Hilton Head Island, South Carolina 29926
Salary Minimum: $24,000
Key Contact: William Slaughter
Steven Lombardo

Functions: 01.2 05.2 05.3 05.4 09.3
Industries: D.24
Description: Sales & marketing placements for
    point of sale manufacturers

The Goldman Group Inc.

183 Madison Ave., Ste. 1105
New York, New York 10016
Salary Minimum: $40,000
Key Contact: Elaine Goldman
Jim Wills
Daniel J. Relton

Functions: 05.0 05.7
Industries: H.00
Professional Affiliations: IACPR, IABC,
    NAER, PRSA
Description: Specialists in public relations,
    marketing & marketing communications

Goldstein & Assoc.

1136 Alvira St.
Los Angeles, California 90035
Salary Minimum: $35,000
Key Contact: Jack Goldstein

Functions: 01.3 01.4 08.3 11.1 11.3
Industries: I.00 I.14 I.15 I.18 I.21
Description: Place professionals nationally in
    healthcare, technology & finance

The Goodman Group

591 Redwood Highway, Ste. 3210
Mill Valley, California 94941
Salary Minimum: $40,000
Key Contact: Lion Goodman
Thelma Kay-Weiss
Leonard Leinow
Lynda Sheridan
Mark Schneider

Functions: 01.0 04.0 05.0 05.4 09.0
Industries: D.24 I.14 I.18
Professional Affiliations: CAPC, HFMA,
    HIMSS, NAER
Description: Specialists in high technology,
    biotechnology, healthcare & the computer
    industries

Graham Assoc. Inc.

111 Madison Ave., Ste. 100
Morristown, New Jersey 07960
Salary Minimum: $40,000
Key Contact: W. M. Stephenson

Functions: 04.0 05.3 05.4
Industries: D.18 D.I0 I.16
Description: Confidential retained and
    exclusive contingency searches, mid to
    high level executives

Grant, Franks & Assoc.
929 N. Kings Hwy.
Cherry Hill, New Jersey 08034
Salary Minimum: $20,000
Key Contact: Lee Grant

Functions: Most
Industries: Most
Description: Expertise with mid-sized firms in many functions & industries in greater Delaware Valley area

Graphic Search Assoc. Inc.
P.O. Box 373
Newtown Square, Pennsylvania 19073
Salary Minimum: $25,000
Key Contact: Roger W. Linde

Functions: Most
Industries: D.14
Professional Affiliations: NAER, PIA
Description: Recruiters for the graphic arts industry

Gray-Kimball Assoc., Inc.
71 Executive Blvd.
Farmingdale, New York 11735
Salary Minimum: $50,000
Key Contact: Louis Basso, Jr.
Walter Ruina
Barry Shorten

Functions: 01.2 01.3 05.2 11.3
Industries: D.E0 D.H0
Description: Specialty recruitment & placement of engineering & scientific professionals

GreenHall Assoc., Inc.
6420 Richmond Ave., Ste. 658
Houston, Texas 77057
Salary Minimum: $60,000
Key Contact: Anne Hall
L.H. Puccio

Functions: 01.5 11.0
Industries: I.17
Professional Affiliations: ATLA
Description: National search firm specializing in career opportunities for attorneys

Greene & Co.
124 Mt. Auburn St.
University Pl., Ste. 200
Cambridge, Massachusetts 02138
Key Contact: Timothy G. Greene

Functions: 08.0 08.1 08.2 08.3
Industries: H.00 H.10 H.11 H.12 I.00
Description: Experienced search services for banking & financial executives in New England

Greene Personnel Consultants
1009 Fleet Bank Bldg.
Providence, Rhode Island 02903
Salary Minimum: $30,000
Key Contact: Dorcas P. Greene
Fred Raisner
Candice Thomas

Functions: Most + 02.2 05.1 05.3 09.4 11.5
Industries: Most + B.0W B.10 D.10 D.11 G.00
Professional Affiliations: NAPC, NPA
Description: Mktg./advertising/PR/sales/retail/ engineering/finacial/healthcare/consumer & technical

Louis Gregory Assoc., Inc.
7270 Arborwood
Hudson, Ohio 44236
Salary Minimum: $30,000
Key Contact: June Chrzan
Leo Futia

Functions: 08.0
Industries: Most
Professional Affiliations: NAPC, OAPC
Description: Specialists in financial recruitment for firms in Ohio

Gregory Michaels & Assoc., Inc.
625 N. Michigan Ave., Ste. 500
Chicago, Illinois 60611
Salary Minimum: $40,000
Key Contact: Gregory P. Crecos
Tamara J. Lee
Joseph J. Scodius
Kathleen A. Kleffel
Kambrea R. Krohe

Functions: 01.0 08.1 09.1 11.2
Industries: D.00 D.10 D.18 D.26
Description: Executive search for top MBA's in finance/accounting for mid to upper management

Groenekamp & Assoc.
P.O. Box 2308
Beverly Hills, California 90213
Salary Minimum: $30,000
Key Contact: William A. Groenekamp

Functions: Most
Industries: Most
Description: Executive search & professional
   staffing in broad range of industries

J. Gross & Assoc.
2722 Fircrest Ave., Bldg. A
Stafford, Texas 77477
Salary Minimum: $35,000
Key Contact: Jerry Gross
Cheryl Denise

Functions: Most + 01.0 01.1 02.4 06.1 11.2
Industries: D.00 D.H0 I.00 I.10 J.13
Professional Affiliations: DPMA, PIRA,
   SHARP, SHRM
Description: Minority owned 5 person
   recruitment organization supporting all
   industries nationally

Branches:
6730 S. Shore, Ste. 1104
Chicago, Illinois 60649

The Alice-Groves Co., Inc.
225 West 34th St., Ste. 1514
New York, New York 10122
Salary Minimum: $45,000
Key Contact: Raymond J. Leavee
Kenneth S. Leavee

Functions: Most + 01.0
Industries: D.11 G.00
Description: Specializing in retail executive
   search & selection since 1947

Guidarelli Assoc., Inc.
5748 James Dr.
Stevensville, Michigan 49127
Salary Minimum: $50,000
Key Contact: Shelley Guidarelli

Functions: 01.0 01.2 02.1 05.0 05.2
Industries: D.00 D.10 D.16
Description: Consumer package goods
   marketing recruitment specialists

The Gumbinner Co.
254 East 49th St.
New York, New York 10017
Salary Minimum: $50,000
Key Contact: Paul S. Gumbinner

Functions: 05.0 05.1 05.2
Industries: J.00 J.10
Description: Specializing in advertising agency
   account management & client side
   advertising

HLR Consulting
215 Katonah Ave.
Katonah, New York 10536
Salary Minimum: $25,000
Key Contact: Harvey Zuckerman

Functions: 05.4 08.2 08.3
Industries: H.10 L.00
Description: A national executive search firm
   specializing in equipment leasing

HMO Executive Search
8910 Purdue Rd., Ste. 200
Indianapolis, Indiana 46268-1155
Salary Minimum: $30,000
Key Contact: Richard J. Carroll

Functions: Most
Industries: I.14 I.15
Professional Affiliations: IAPC, NAPC
Description: Recruiting specialists for all
   professional level personnel in the HMO
   & managed care industries

Hahn & Assoc., Inc.
7026 Corporate Way, Ste. 212
Dayton, Ohio 45459
Key Contact: Kenneth R. Hahn

Functions: Most + 01.0 02.0 03.0 06.0 08.0
Industries: B.0W D.00
Professional Affiliations: DAPC, EMA, NAPC,
   OAPC, SHRM
Description: Founded 1971-Mr. Hahn in
   private personnel business since 1960

Halbrecht & Co.

P.O. Box 324
Old Greenwich, Connecticut 06870
Salary Minimum: $30,000
Key Contact: Thomas J. Kubiak

Functions: 01.4 02.3 05.0 09.0 11.1
Industries: Most
Professional Affiliations: AAAI, ASA, SIM, TIMS
Description: Specialists in information systems, management science, artificial intelligence, decision support

Branches:
10195 Main St., Ste. L
Fairfax, Virginia 22031
Key Contact: Thomas J. Maltby
Kurt Wilkinson

Robert Half Int'l.

40 Eglinton Ave. E., Ste. 303
Toronto, Ontario M4P 3A2 Canada
Key Contact: Paul McDonald
Cindy Grant

Functions: 08.0 08.1 08.2 08.3 09.0
Industries: Most
Professional Affiliations: APPAC
Description: Specialist recruiters in finance, accounting, & information systems

Hall, Cooper & Bartman, Ltd.

1519 East Ave.
Rochester, New York 14610
Key Contact: Elizabeth Hall
Paul Bartman

Functions: 01.0 04.0 05.0 09.0 11.2
Industries: D.H0 J.13
Description: Provide search services for the domestic & international telecommunications marketplace

Branches:
327 S. La Salle, Ste. 1740-A
Chicago, Illinois 60604
Key Contact: Joyce Stricklin

Hamilton Edwards, Ltd.

1717 W. Northern Ave., Ste. 116
Phoenix, Arizona 85021
Salary Minimum: $40,000
Key Contact: Eileen Edwards

Functions: 01.5
Industries: I.17
Description: Attorney search firm including law firms and corporations as clients

Handwerk & Assoc.

5005 Newport Dr., Ste. 500
Rolling Meadows, Illinois 60008
Salary Minimum: $40,000
Key Contact: Robert Handwerk

Functions: 02.0 02.4 11.3 11.5 11.6
Industries: A.00 B.00 B.0W E.00
Description: Engineering & scientific recruitment, mid level to senior management

W. Hanley & Assoc.

111 High Ridge Plz.
Stamford, Connecticut 06905
Salary Minimum: $50,000
Key Contact: J. Patrick Hanley
Richard T. Hanley

Functions: 06.0 08.0 09.1 10.0 11.1
Industries: Most
Professional Affiliations: AICPA, FEI
Description: Specialists in the recruitment of financial, controllership & tax executives

International Branches:
London

Harrison Moore Inc.
7638 Pierce St.
Omaha, Nebraska 68124
Key Contact: Curt McLey
Jim Hicks

Functions: 01.0 02.0 02.1 04.0 05.0
Industries: D.00 D.22
Professional Affiliations: NAPC
Description: Specialization in the foundry
    industry

The Hart Group
Box 1483
Bellevue, Washington 98009
Salary Minimum: $50,000
Key Contact: Timothy Hart

Functions: 05.2 05.3 05.4 05.5 08.2
Industries: H.10 H.11 H.12 H.I0
Description: Senior sales/marketing personnel
    in investment management/mutual funds
    & financial services

Hartman Personnel Services
150 W. 6th St.
Erie, Pennsylvania 16501
Salary Minimum: $20,000
Key Contact: Glenn Marshall
Kathie Hartman

Functions: Most + 01.0 02.0 05.0 08.0 09.0
Industries: D.00 D.10 D.18 D.19 D.22
Professional Affiliations: IPA, NATS, SPE
Description: Professional recruitment of
    management, technical, manufacturing &
    marketing; networked nationally

Hawkes-Randolph & Assoc., Inc.
The Crystal Pavillion, 805 Third Ave.
New York, New York 10022
Salary Minimum: $60,000
Key Contact: Ted King

Functions: 05.0 05.2 05.3 11.1
Industries: Most
Description: Placing top MBA's into
    investment banking/finance/planning/
    marketing/consulting

Phyllis Hawkins & Assoc.
3550 N. Central Ave., Ste. 1400
Phoenix, Arizona 85012
Salary Minimum: $40,000
Key Contact: Phyllis Hawkins
Barbara Burkholder
Sandy Myers
Denise Timmons
Nancy Newman
Susan Olney

Functions: 01.5
Industries: I.15 I.17
Professional Affiliations: NALSC, NAPR
Description: Specializing in placement of
    attorneys and physicians, law firm mergers

Branches:
31017 Westwood
Farmington Hills, Michigan 48331

Donald P. Hayes Assoc., Inc.
218 Ridgedale Ave.
Cedar Knolls, New Jersey 07927-2103
Salary Minimum: $50,000
Key Contact: J. Robert McCrystal
Grant M. Hanson

Functions: Most
Industries: Most + D.17 D.25 D.H0 H.12 I.16
Description: Executive search consultants to
    the healthcare, pharmaceutical &
    biotechnology industries

Branches:
8061 E. Paseo de Beatriz
Tucson, Arizona 85715
Key Contact: Donald P. Hayes

The Headhunter
6411 Robinhood Ln.
Huntsville, Alabama 35806-1965
Salary Minimum: $35,000
Key Contact: Robert B. Smock

Functions: 04.0
Industries: D.E0 K.10
Description: R & D scientists & managers for
  SDI, missiles & space

Headhunters National, Inc.
5319 S. W. Westgate Dr.
Portland, Oregon 97221
Key Contact: Russ Bachard

Functions: 11.5 11.6
Industries: B.0W
Professional Affiliations: NAPC, OAPC
Description: "Professionals for Professionals"

The Headhunters
3342 E. Cochise Rd.
Phoenix, Arizona 85028
Salary Minimum: $50,000
Key Contact: Elaine M. Davis

Functions: 01.5
Industries: Most + I.17
Professional Affiliations: NALSC
Description: Professional placement of
  attorneys to law firms & private
  corporations locally & nationally

Health Industry Resources, Inc.
GPO Box 2075
New York, New York 10116
Salary Minimum: $40,000
Key Contact: Dov Fobar

Functions: 01.0 01.4 05.0 08.0
Industries: I.12 I.14 K.00
Description: Executive search & management
  consulting in administrative areas of
  healthcare industry

Health Technology, Inc.
7502 S. Willow Cir.
Englewood, Colorado 80112
Salary Minimum: $50,000
Key Contact: Thomas C. Miller
Janet Head

Functions: 01.0 02.0 04.0 05.0 11.1
Industries: D.00 D.H0 D.I0 I.14 I.16
Professional Affiliations: AIUM, ASMS, SPE
Description: Organizations in the medical
  device, biotechnology & pharmaceutical
  industries

Healthcare Resources Group
3000 United Founders Blvd., Ste 225Г
Oklahoma City, Oklahoma 73112
Key Contact: Dan Smith

Functions: 01.3 03.1 05.4 07.4
Industries: D.18 I.14 I.15
Professional Affiliations: FIN
Description: Specializing in medical field of
  licensed, registered, certified professionals

Hedlund Corp.
360 N. Michigan Ave., Ste. 902
Chicago, Illinois 60601
Salary Minimum: $30,000
Key Contact: David Hedlund
Holly Burny
Eve Shapiro
Webb Sexton, Jr.
Kathleen Armstrong
James O'Donnell

Affiliates/Other Offices:
Strategic Executives, Inc., Stamford

Functions: 01.0 06.0 07.0 08.2 09.0
Industries: H.10 H.11 I.10 I.21 J.13
Professional Affiliations: FSN, NAER
Description: National management search firm
  specialized in banking, strategic planning
  & MIS

Kent R. Hedman & Assoc.

P.O. Box 13726
Arlington, Texas 76094-0726
Salary Minimum: $40,000
Key Contact: Kent R. Hedman

Functions: Most
Industries: Most
Professional Affiliations: SERC, SHRM
Description: Confidential; 20+ years recruiting experience; search intensity on contingency basis

Heller Kil Assoc., Inc.

123 Green Heron Ct.
Daytona Beach, Florida 32119
Salary Minimum: $40,000
Key Contact: Phillip Heller

Branches:
4534 Frontier
Kalamazoo, Michigan 49002
Key Contact: Richard Kil

Functions: 01.0 02.0 03.0 04.0 05.0
Industries: D.23 E.00
Description: Automotive & heavy-duty truck components industry specialists

Hemingway Personnel, Inc.

1301 Dove St., Ste. 710
Newport Beach, California 92660
Salary Minimum: $35,000
Key Contact: Arne Beruldsen
Dolores Lara

Functions: 08.0 08.1 08.2 08.3 08.4
Industries: Most
Professional Affiliations: CAPC
Description: Executive search & temporaries serving the accounting & finance professions

Kay Henry, Inc.

Executive Ste. 7
1200 Bustleton Pike
Feasterville, Pennsylvania 19053
Salary Minimum: $25,000
Key Contact: Kay Henry
Rose Gregory

Functions: 05.1 05.2 05.3 05.5 05.7
Industries: A.00 I.16 J.10
Professional Affiliations: AMWA, MAAPC, NAMA
Description: Advertising, public relations, marketing including medical, pharmaceutical, Ag/animal chem.

Heritage Search Group, Inc.

7687 Wyldwood Way, Ste. 100
Port St. Lucie, Florida 34986
Salary Minimum: $40,000
Key Contact: Philip Tripician

Branches:
4675 Main St.
Bridgeport, Connecticut 06606
Key Contact: Fred Hodde

Functions: 05.0 05.1 05.3
Industries: D.10 D.11 D.13 D.15 D.16
Professional Affiliations: CAPC, NAER
Description: Specialize in consumer marketing opportunities with medium & small companies

J. D. Hersey & Assoc.

6099 Riverside Dr., Ste. 104
Dublin, Ohio 43017
Salary Minimum: $30,000
Key Contact: Jeffrey D. Hersey
Ned Neely

Functions: Most + 01.0 02.0 03.4 11.6
Industries: C.00 D.18 D.D0 H.R0 I.00
Professional Affiliations: IOPP, ISPE, NACORE
Description: Specializing in real estate, construction, retail, food, pharmaceutical, medical & packaging areas

Robert Hess & Assoc., Inc.

4585 Hilton Pkwy., Ste. 203
Colorado Springs, Colorado 80907
Salary Minimum: $40,000
Key Contact: Robert W. Hess
John Little
Mark Norquest

Functions: Most
Industries: C.00 D.22 H.R0
Description: National recruiters specializing in
real estate & value manufacturing
industries

Hessel Assoc., Inc.

420 Lexington Ave., Ste. 300
New York, New York 10170
Salary Minimum: $35,000
Key Contact: Jeffrey J. Hessel

Functions: 02.0 08.0
Industries: Most
Professional Affiliations: NAPC
Description: Specializes in the recruitment of
accounting & financial professionals

Hi-Tech Search, Inc.

561 Oak Shade Rd.
Vincentown, New Jersey 08088
Key Contact: Bruce Palmer
Lydia Palmer

Functions: Most
Industries: Most
Description: Technical and executive search
with an emphasis on the electronics
industries

Higbee Assoc., Inc.

112 Rowayton Ave.
Rowayton, Connecticut 06853
Salary Minimum: $50,000
Key Contact: R. W. Higbee

Functions: 01.4 05.2 08.0 09.3 11.1
Industries: H.10 H.I0 H.R0 I.20
Description: Specialize in finance, Wall St.,
commercial banking, management
consulting

High Tech Opportunities, Inc.

P.O. Box 119
North Salem, New Hampshire 03073
Salary Minimum: $30,000
Key Contact: Ron Cooper
Richard Kania

Functions: 09.7
Industries: D.E0 D.H0 J.00 J.12
Professional Affiliations: NAPC, NHAPC
Description: Specializing in
EDA,semiconductor & satellite
communication professionals

High Technology Search Assoc.

55 Prospect St.
Willimantic, Connecticut 06226
Salary Minimum: $40,000
Key Contact: C.K. Rehberger
M.J. Donahue
R.J. Bruno, Jr.

Functions: 01.1 04.0 11.0
Industries: B.00 D.E0 D.I0 J.00
Description: 5 years engineering experience, 15
years high tech search experience

Affiliates/Other Offices:
Management Consulting International, Isernhagen

High-Tech Recruiters

30 High St., Ste 104A
Hartford, Connecticut 06103
Salary Minimum: $30,000
Key Contact: Clement W. Williams

Functions: 01.4 08.0 09.4 09.7 11.2
Industries: D.24 D.H0 H.00 H.I0 J.13
Professional Affiliations: CAPC, NAPC
Description: Data processing/data
communications/engineering/telecomm./
finance/minorities/nationwide affiliates

Hill & Assoc.

300 Valley St., Ste. 201
Sausalito, California 94965
Salary Minimum: $35,000
Key Contact: Tom Hill

Functions: 01.0 01.1 01.2 05.1 05.2
Industries: D.00 D.10 D.18 J.00 J.10
Description: International specialists within the
food & beverage industry dealing with
suppliers

Hill Allyn Assoc.

P.O. Box 15247
San Francisco, California 94115
Salary Minimum: $25,000
Key Contact: Gayle W. Hill

Functions: 08.0 08.1 08.2 08.4 09.1
Industries: Most + D.00 D.H0 G.00 H.00
Description: Recruits CPA's for accounting &
finance in Bay area corporations

Frank P. Hill

Rio Guadalquivir 38-701
Col. Cuauhtemoc
Mexico City, Mexico D.F. 06500 Mexico
Salary Minimum: $25,000
Key Contact: Frank P. Hill
Andrea Garcia Sauer

Functions: Most
Industries: Most
Description: Specializing in upper-level
executive search-all disciplines

Hintz Associates

Box 442
Valhalla, New York 10595
Salary Minimum: $25,000
Key Contact: George Hintz
George Jefferies
D. DiMaggio

Functions: 02.4 02.6 07.0 09.3 11.1
Industries: D.00 H.00 H.I0
Professional Affiliations: AOPA, ASM
Description: Banking, insurance-cost reduction
analysts, methods analysts, internal/
external consultants

Hipp Waters, Inc.

217 Bedford St.
Stamford, Connecticut 06901
Salary Minimum: $25,000
Key Contact: Anthony Townley
Louis M. Hipp, III

Branches:
209 Bedford St.
Stamford, Connecticut 06901

Functions: 08.0
Industries: I.14
Professional Affiliations: NAPC
Description: Established firm specializing in
engineering, data processing, accounting/
finance, insurance & sales

Hitchens & Foster, Inc.

Pines Office Ctr., 1 Pine Ct.
St. Louis, Missouri 63141
Key Contact: Rex Hermsmeyer

Functions: Most
Industries: D.00 I.15
Professional Affiliations: NAPR
Description: Specializing in physician search
and recruitment for medical practices
nationwide

Horizon Assoc.

322 S. Broadway
Redondo Beach, California 90277
Salary Minimum: $30,000
Key Contact: Arnold Zimmerman

Functions: 02.0 04.0
Industries: A.00 D.10 D.I0
Professional Affiliations: IFT, NAER
Description: Executive search to the food,
agriculture & biotechnology industries

Hornberger Management Co., Inc.

1 Commerce Ctr., 7th Fl.
Wilmington, Delaware 19801
Salary Minimum: $75,000
Key Contact: Frederick C. Hornberger

Functions: 01.1 01.2 05.4 11.6
Industries: C.00
Description: Retained executive recruitment
   exclusively for builders & construction
   managers worldwide

Branches:
2102 Business Center Dr.
Irvine, California 92715
Key Contact: Linda Rassenti

618 Rose Hill Rd.
Asheville, North Carolina 28803
Key Contact: G.R. Knight

International Branches:
Montreal

John M. Horton

P.O. Box 891
Wrightsville Beach, North Carolina 28480-
   0891
Salary Minimum: $45,000
Key Contact: John M. Horton

Functions: 05.0 05.1 05.2 05.3
Industries: I.00 I.14 I.16
Description: Specializing in health care
   management: marketing & market
   research

Hoskins, Rees & Smith

Manor Oak Two, Ste. 658
1910 Cochran Rd.
Pittsburgh, Pennsylvania 15220
Salary Minimum: $40,000
Key Contact: David P. Smith
Jeffrey D. Latterell
C.J. Hauser
Kevin G. O'Neill
Carol J. Zurat
John J. Elster

Functions: Most + 01.0 02.0 03.0 05.0 09.0
Industries: Most + D.00 D.22 I.12 I.17 J.13
Description: Management, sales & marketing,
   engineering, automation, composites,
   chemicals, metals

Hospitality Executive Search, Inc.

608 Tremont St.
Boston, Massachusetts 02118-1605
Salary Minimum: $75,000
Key Contact: Jonathan M. Spatt

Functions: 01.1 01.2
Industries: D.10 I.10 I.11 I.12 I.14
Professional Affiliations: CSH, HSMA, NACE
Description: One of the oldest executive firms
   in the U.S.

Hospitality Int'l.

Davis Rd., Box 906
Valley Forge, Pennsylvania 19481
Salary Minimum: $25,000
Key Contact: Ralda F. Adams
Geoffrey L. Goone

Functions: 01.1 01.2 01.3 05.3 05.4
Industries: D.10 I.10 I.11 I.14
Professional Affiliations: AHMA, AIWF,
   IFSEA, NRA
Description: Recruitment & placement of
   management & staff support for
   hospitality & food service industries

Branches:
9 E. 45th St.
New York, New York 10017

P.O. Box 562
Tully, New York 13159

Hospitality Resources Int'l., Ltd.

P.O. Box 364, 5675 Bridge Pointe
Alpharetta, Georgia 30239
Salary Minimum: $35,000
Key Contact: Joan E. Williams

Functions: 01.0 01.1 01.2 01.3 05.4
Industries: I.00 I.10 I.11
Professional Affiliations: ACF, GAPC, HSMA
Description: Service oriented search ideal for
   small to medium sized companies

Affiliates/Other Offices:
Kauffman Hospitality, Inc., Atlanta

George Howard Assoc.
105 S. Narcissus Ave., Ste. 806
West Palm Beach, Florida 33401
Key Contact: George Howard

Functions: 01.5
Industries: Most
Description: Recruit attorneys for Florida law
firms & corporations only

Don Howard Personnel
160 Front St.
New York, New York 10038
Key Contact: Bill Landau

Functions: Most
Industries: D.13 D.19 D.26 D.D0 J.11
Description: Recruitment of professionals at all
levels in graphic arts

Howard-Sloan Assoc.
545 Fifth Ave.
New York, New York 10017
Salary Minimum: $50,000
Key Contact: Edward R. Koller, Jr.

Functions: 05.0 05.1 05.4 05.5 05.7
Industries: J.10 J.11 J.12
Professional Affiliations: APCNY, BPAA,
DMA, IIA, NAER, NAPC, PRSA
Description: Contingency recruiting firm in
magazine publishing, direct marketing, PR
& accounting

Howard-Sloan Legal Search, Inc.
545 Fifth Ave.
New York, New York 10017
Salary Minimum: $40,000
Key Contact: Mitchell L. Berger

Functions: 01.5
Industries: Most
Professional Affiliations: APCNY, NALSC,
NAPC
Description: Attorney recruiting services
exclusively for both law firms &
corporations

C. L. Howe & Co., Inc.
P.O. Box 2233
Darien, Connecticut 06820-0233
Key Contact: Craig Howe

Functions: 11.0
Industries: H.11
Description: We specialize in recruiting quality
retail stockbrokers & branch office
managers

Howie & Assoc., Inc.
875 Old Roswell Rd., F-100
Roswell, Georgia 30076
Key Contact: David W. Howie

Functions: 01.3 01.4 05.4 09.3 09.4
Industries: I.14 I.18
Professional Affiliations: NAPC, NPA
Description: Healthcare sales/sales
management, healthcare administration,
data processing, technical & sales

Hudson Assoc. Inc.
P.O. Box 2502
Anderson, Indiana 46018
Salary Minimum: $30,000
Key Contact: George A. Hudson

Functions: 01.0 05.0 05.4 10.0 11.5
Industries: B.0W B.10 H.00 H.I0
Professional Affiliations: INS
Description: Insurance specialists at home
office, regional, or agency locations

The Hudson Group
P.O. Box 263
Simsbury, Connecticut 06070
Salary Minimum: $35,000
Key Contact: Paul E. Hudson
Judy K. Hudson

Functions: Most + 02.0 04.0 09.0 11.3 11.5
Industries: Most + B.00 B.0W D.00 D.H0
D.I0
Professional Affiliations: NAPC
Description: Engineers, scientists, managers,
marketing, manufacturing: national &
international placement

Hughes & Assoc.
718 Oakwood Trail
Ft. Worth, Texas 76112
Salary Minimum: $30,000
Key Contact: Ken Hughes

Functions: Most + 10.0
Industries: H.I0
Professional Affiliations: SERC, TAPC
Description: Contingency recruiting & retained
search in life/health insurance industries;
nationwide

Human Resource Bureau
P.O. Box 18500-234
Irvine, California 92714
Key Contact: Joyce Newberry
Pat Brogan

Functions: 05.1 05.4
Industries: Most
Description: Nationwide executive search firm
dealing exclusively with franchise sales
executives

The Human Resource Group
600 Fifth Ave. Plz.
Des Moines, Iowa 50309
Salary Minimum: $20,000
Key Contact: Will Canine
Frankie Bruner
Jim Caraccio

Functions: 06.0 11.6
Industries: A.00 C.00
Description: Construction/engineering/
agriculture specialities, also medical claims
specialist

Human Resource Network
2705 Lowell Rd.
Ann Arbor, Michigan 48103
Salary Minimum: $30,000
Key Contact: John Johnson

Functions: Most + 01.0 02.4 06.0 09.0 11.2
Industries: Most + B.0W D.00 D.H0 H.00
J.13
Professional Affiliations: MAPC
Description: Specializes in professional &
management recruiting for all industries

Human Resource Recruiters
P.O. Box 198
Elm Grove, Wisconsin 53122
Salary Minimum: $25,000
Key Contact: Jane A. Seefeld
Anthony J. Katsune

Functions: Most + 02.0 06.0 06.1 08.0 11.6
Industries: Most
Professional Affiliations: PIRA, WAPC
Description: Upper & middle management
recruiting-retainer & contingency, difficult
& unusual assignments

E. F. Humay Assoc.
P.O. Box 173 R
Fairview Village, Pennsylvania 19409
Salary Minimum: $35,000
Key Contact: Gene Humay
Jane Humay

Functions: 01.0 02.0 05.0
Description: Involved with manufacturers and
distributors of construction equipment
(road/bridge/mining/etc.)

Hunt Ltd.
21 W. 38th St.
New York, New York 10018
Salary Minimum: $30,000
Key Contact: Alex Metz
Donald Jacobson

Functions: 02.6 03.0 03.1 03.2 03.3
Industries: D.00 E.00
Professional Affiliations: CLM, NAPC, WERC
Description: Distribution/transportation related areas on a permanent/temporary executive level, nationwide

Hunter Assoc.
181 Park Ave.
West Springfield, Massachusetts 01089
Salary Minimum: $30,000
Key Contact: D.M. Shooshan

Functions: 02.3 03.1 08.0
Industries: D.23 D.24 D.E0 D.H0
Professional Affiliations: IPA
Description: Specialization is contract/subcontract, financial, engineering/environmental professionals nationwide

Hyland Executive Search
16626 N. 61st Way
Scottsdale, Arizona 85254
Salary Minimum: $25,000
Key Contact: Kenneth J. Hyland
Susan L. Hyland

Functions: 11.0
Industries: C.00 H.R0 J.00
Professional Affiliations: CAI, IREM, NAHB
Description: Real estate related searches: asset management, development, property management, marketing

I.S. Consultants, Inc.
22700 Shore Ctr. Dr.
Cleveland, Ohio 44123
Salary Minimum: $30,000
Key Contact: Scott A. Carpenter

Functions: 01.3 02.2 05.4 11.3 11.5
Industries: D.10 D.15 D.22 D.H0 D.I0
Professional Affiliations: ASPA
Description: Engineering, sales/marketing, hotel/restaurant, accts., chemical sales/eng., medical industry

ISOPS Personnel Services, Inc.
105 S. Ave de la Estrella, Ste. 3C
San Clemente, California 92672
Salary Minimum: $50,000
Key Contact: Michael E. Slaby
Eugene R. Slaby

Functions: Most
Industries: B.0W B.10 D.00 D.I0 H.I0
Description: We work exclusively in the environmental industry on recruiting assignments

Impact Executive Search, Inc.
P.O. Box 862368
Marietta, Georgia 30062
Salary Minimum: $30,000
Key Contact: Randall Martens

Functions: 01.3 02.4 02.5 05.4 05.6
Industries: D.10 D.13 D.D0 H.10 I.10
Professional Affiliations: PAPER, TAPPI
Description: Specialists in the paper, packaging, banking, food & food service industries

Individual Employment Services
90-A 6th St., P.O. Box 917
Dover, New Hampshire 03820
Key Contact: James E. Otis

Functions: Most
Industries: H.10 H.I0 H.R0 J.10 J.13
Description: We offer you strict confidentiality at all times, fully referenced high quality candidates

Industrial Recruiters Assoc., Inc.
630 Oakwood Ave., Ste. 318
West Hartford, Connecticut 06110
Salary Minimum: $20,000
Key Contact: Len Baron

Functions: 01.0 02.0 05.0 05.4
Industries: B.0W D.00 D.D0 D.E0 D.H0
Description: Placement in full spectrum marketing, sales, manufacturing, engineering, print & graphics

Industry Consultants, Inc.

P.O. Box 922155
Norcross, Georgia 30092
Salary Minimum: $50,000
Key Contact: Joseph Corey
Gail Marantz

Functions: 02.0 02.1 02.4 02.5 11.3
Industries: D.10 D.16 D.17 D.18 I.00
Professional Affiliations: AIIE
Description: Engineering & operations
    management recruitment for consumer
    packaged goods manufacturers

Information Systems Professionals

5904 Castlebrook Dr.
Raleigh, North Carolina 27604
Key Contact: Brad Moses
Diane Moses

Functions: 01.4 06.0 09.0
Industries: Most
Description: With integrity & a personal touch
    we serve our clients

Intech Summit Group, Inc.

11772 Sorrento Valley Rd., Ste. 101
San Diego, California 92121-1016
Salary Minimum: $40,000
Key Contact: Steven A. Adams
Robert C. Cohen
Michael R. Cohen

Functions: 05.0 06.0 08.0 11.1 11.5
Industries: B.0W D.18 I.14 I.15
Professional Affiliations: CAPC
Description: Professional search at all levels of
    executive recruitment worldwide

Integrated Management Solutions

32 Broadway, Ste. 514
New York, New York 10004
Key Contact: Howard Spindel

Functions: Most + 01.0 07.0 08.0 09.0 11.1
Industries: H.10 H.11 H.12 I.19 I.21
Description: Emphasis on finance, accounting,
    operations, regulatory, sales, research and
    trading

Integrated Professional Services, Inc.

3725 National Dr., Ste. 214
Raleigh, North Carolina 27612
Key Contact: Dick Starling
James Leierzapf
Luanna Spears
Reta McCallum

Functions: 01.4 05.0 09.0
Industries: I.18
Description: Recruiting in the data processing
    and data communication industry vendors
    nationwide

Branches:
426 E. Price St.
Keller, Texas 76248

International Staffing Consultants, Inc.

19762 MacArthur Blvd.
P.O. Box 19688
Irvine, California 92715
Salary Minimum: $25,000
Key Contact: James R. Gettys

Functions: Most + 06.0 11.3 11.5 11.6
Industries: B.00 B.0W C.00 D.15 D.20
Professional Affiliations: NPA
Description: International and US recruitment
    and services for most industries and
    professions

International Branches:
London

Intertech Search Group

170 US Rte. One
Portland, Maine 04105
Key Contact: Hugh D. Olmstead
Carolyn Davidson
Cleo Werner
Bill Hart

Functions: 01.3 05.2 05.3 11.3 11.5
Industries: B.10 D.15 D.19
Professional Affiliations: ACS, HMCRI, SME,
    SPE
Description: Specialize in technical,
    professional & management personnel for
    environmental & chemical industries

IprGroup, Inc.
8097 B Roswell Rd.
Atlanta, Georgia 30350
Salary Minimum: $25,000
Key Contact: Richard C. Gay

Functions: 06.0 06.1 06.2 10.0
Industries: Most
Description: Recruit HRM & insurance/risk
management in all industries

J.D. Limited
881 Bosworth Field
Barrington, Illinois 60010
Key Contact: John DeGiulio

Functions: 01.5 11.5
Industries: I.17
Professional Affiliations: NALSC
Description: Specialize in legal placements
nationwide

JDG Assoc., Ltd.
1700 Research Blvd.
Rockville, Maryland 20850
Salary Minimum: $30,000
Key Contact: Joseph DeGioia

Functions: 01.4 03.3 09.3 09.7 11.1
Industries: D.00 D.E0 D.H0 I.18 K.10
Professional Affiliations: MAPRC
Description: Recruiters serving the disciplines
of computer science, engineering &
management sciences

JM Assoc.
4199 Campus Dr., Ste. 900
Irvine, California 92715
Salary Minimum: $60,000
Key Contact: Merry E. Neitlich

Functions: 01.5 05.2
Industries: I.17
Professional Affiliations: NALSC
Description: Place attorneys in law firms &
corporations in Orange County

J.M. Eagle Partners
10140 N. Port Washington Rd.
Mequon, Wisconsin 53092
Salary Minimum: $50,000
Key Contact: Jerry Moses

Functions: Most
Industries: D.17 D.18 D.24 D.H0 D.I0
Professional Affiliations: ACA
Description: Contingency search in medical
industry with specialization in diagnostic
imaging

JNB Assoc., Inc.
2 Oliver St.
Boston, Massachusetts 02109
Salary Minimum: $50,000
Key Contact: Joseph N. Baker, Jr.

Functions: Most + 01.2 01.3 02.0 06.0 08.0
Industries: D.00 H.00 H.10
Description: Banking & financial specialists—
retainer & contingency

J.P.D. Group
6 Rolling Hills Dr.
Huntington Station, New York 11746
Salary Minimum: $30,000
Key Contact: Judith Spencer
Phil Svendsen

Functions: 07.0 08.0 09.0
Industries: Most
Description: Executive recruiting source for
lower to mid range management personnel

JT Assoc.
89 Comstock Hill Rd.
New Canaan, Connecticut 06840
Salary Minimum: $40,000
Key Contact: Joe Fazio
Mary Ellen Calderone

Functions: 01.0 05.0 06.0 08.0 09.0
Industries: B.00 D.00 H.00 I.18 I.20
Description: Search & recruiting for
professional, technical & executive
disciplines

Jackley Search Consultants

7400 Metro Blvd., Ste. 112
Minneapolis, Minnesota 55439
Salary Minimum: $40,000
Key Contact: Brian Jackley

Functions: 01.3 02.0 02.1 02.2 04.0
Industries: D.18 D.19 D.24 D.H0 D.I0
Description: Technical search: engineers,
scientists, technical managers,
manufacturing managers, technical mktg.

Jacobson Assoc.

150 N. Wacker Dr., Ste. 1120
Chicago, Illinois 60606
Salary Minimum: $20,000
Key Contact: David Jacobson

Functions: 09.0 09.1 10.0
Industries: Most + H.10 H.I0
Description: A national executive recruiting
firm specializing in insurance since 1971

Branches:
1785 The Exchange, Ste. 320
Atlanta, Georgia 30339

440 Public Ledger Bldg.
Philadelphia, Pennsylvania 19106

The James Group

P.O. Box 54061
Hurst, Texas 76054
Key Contact: Jim Blazek

Functions: 08.0 10.0
Industries: H.I0 I.14
Professional Affiliations: HFMA, NAA
Description: Specialize in the healthcare &
insurance industry

R.I. James, Inc.

530 E. 89th St., Ste. 6L
New York, New York 10128
Salary Minimum: $40,000
Key Contact: Rhoda Isaacs

Functions: Most + 01.1 01.2 01.3 03.3
Industries: D.00 D.H0 E.00 F.00 G.00
Professional Affiliations: CLM
Description: Mid-senior level placement; our
client references reflect the highest
standards of excellence

Jefferson-Ross Assoc. Inc.

2 Penn Ctr. Plaza
Philadelphia, Pennsylvania 19102
Salary Minimum: $25,000
Key Contact: Walter Lloyd

Functions: Most
Industries: Most
Description: Recruiting assignments in
technical, dp, marketing & administrative
positions

John-David Assoc., Inc.

150 Broadway, Ste. 1816
New York, New York 10048
Salary Minimum: $20,000
Key Contact: Ben Paige

Functions: 06.0 08.0 08.4
Industries: Most + H.10 H.11
Description: Corporate tax & accounting
specialists-entry level to senior executives

K.E. Johnson Assoc.

4213-187th Place SE.
Issaquah, Washington 98027
Salary Minimum: $50,000
Key Contact: Karl Johnson

Functions: Most + 01.0 02.0 04.0 09.0 11.0
Industries: Most + B.0W D.00 D.H0 D.I0
G.00
Description: Hi-tech, electronic/computer
related, engineering, sales/marketing,
executive management positions

The Johnson Group, Inc.

1 World Trade Ctr., Ste. 4517
New York, New York 10048
Salary Minimum: $46,000
Key Contact: Priscilla Johnson
Steve Collins
Charles Grevious

Functions: Most + 01.0 05.0 06.0 08.0
Industries: Most + D.00 H.00 H.I0 H.R0
Description: Naitonwide executive search for
financial services & consumer products

Kathryn L. Johnson
1212 E. Wayzata Blvd., Ste. 210
Minneapolis, Minnesota 55391
Salary Minimum: $35,000
Key Contact: Kathryn L. Johnson

Functions: Most + 01.0 02.0 03.0 05.0
Industries: Most + D.00 D.10 D.D0 F.00
Description: A full service search firm working
in numerous areas

J. Johnston Group, Inc.
50 E. Shuman Blvd., Ste. 200
Naperville, Illinois 60563
Salary Minimum: $25,000
Key Contact: James E. Johnston

Functions: 09.3
Industries: D.24
Description: Technical search directed toward
data processing & software engineering

E. G. Jones Assoc., Ltd.
54 Scott Adam Rd., Ste. 308
Cockeysville, Maryland 21030
Salary Minimum: $25,000
Key Contact: Edward G. Jones

Functions: Most
Industries: B.0W D.10 H.R0 I.14
Professional Affiliations: ACA, ASM, ASQC,
MAPRC, NAA
Description: Professional search & recruitment
firm

Branches:
1 Church St., Ste. 202
Rockville, Maryland 20850-4158
Key Contact: Bruce Wiggett

Jordon & Jordon, Inc.
101 Greenwood Ave., Ste. LC-10
Jenkintown, Pennsylvania 19046
Salary Minimum: $40,000
Key Contact: Bud Jordon
Carole Bowman

Functions: Most
Industries: D.11 G.00
Professional Affiliations: NAER
Description: International search firm
specializing in retail & venture capital

J.M. Joseph Assoc.
177 W. High St.
Somerville, New Jersey 08876
Salary Minimum: $40,000
Key Contact: C. Russell Ditzel

Functions: Most + 02.0 03.0 04.0 06.0 11.2
Industries: Most + D.00 D.10 D.15 D.18 D.19
Description: Full-service, broad based firm
serving clients nationally

Joslin & Assoc., Ltd.
291 Deer Trail Ct., Ste. C-3
Barrington, Illinois 60010
Salary Minimum: $40,000
Key Contact: Robert S. Joslin

Functions: 04.0 11.3
Industries: D.18
Professional Affiliations: AAPS, ACS, AFPE,
AIC, APS, APhA, CPDG, CRS, PDA
Description: Scientific & technical people &
positions, pharmaceutical industry
exclusively

Jubilee, Inc.
P.O. Box 340
Arlington, Georgia 31713
Salary Minimum: $20,000
Key Contact: William E. Gleaton, Jr.

Functions: 01.0 01.2 02.0 02.4 06.0
Industries: D.00 I.14 I.16 I.18 I.19
Description: International & national finance,
accounting, human resources & key
management

Julian Assoc., Inc.
162 Willard Ave.
Newington, Connecticut 06111
Salary Minimum: $30,000
Key Contact: Julian Brownstein
Joan Brownstein

Functions: 05.1 05.7
Industries: J.10
Description: Specializing in advertising &
public relations, agency & corporate,
account & creative

A.H. Justice & Assoc.

P.O. Box 891552
Houston, Texas 77289-1552
Salary Minimum: $30,000
Key Contact: Arnold Justice

Functions: Most
Industries: Most + D.22 D.23 D.26
Professional Affiliations: CERA
Description: Specialize in petro/chemicals &
  metals industries

K & C Assoc.

290 A Oakhurst Lane
Arcadia, California 91007
Salary Minimum: $25,000
Key Contact: R.G. Kuhnmuench

Functions: Most + 01.0 02.0 03.0 05.0 08.0
Industries: A.00 C.00 D.22 F.00 G.00
Description: Construction, industrial, mining &
  municipal machinery industries-domestic
  & international

Kacevich, Lewis & Brown, Inc.

300 W. Main St., Bldg. B
Northborough, Massachusetts 01532
Salary Minimum: $50,000
Key Contact: Joseph B. Kacevich, Jr.
Maria C. Routh

Functions: 01.0 01.3 04.0 05.0 05.4
Industries: D.H0
Description: Middle mgmt. & senior individual
  contributors in the network &
  communications industry

Richard Kader & Assoc.

16600 Sprague Rd., #440
Cleveland, Ohio 44130
Salary Minimum: $40,000
Key Contact: Richard H. Kader
Shari A. Dahmer
Marilyn Longmore
Vern Sponseller
Alyse Sands
James Balazy
Art Delong

Functions: Most + 01.0 05.4 08.0 09.0 11.5
Industries: Most
Description: Highly technical areas-industrial-
  engineering, EDP, R&D.

Lisa Kalus & Assoc., Inc.

150 Broadway, Ste. 811
New York, New York 10038
Key Contact: Lisa Kalus

Functions: 11.0 11.5 11.6
Industries: C.00 H.R0
Description: Recruitment firm specializing in
  construction, engineering & real estate
  personnel

Kane Ford Karrel & Assoc.

777 Third Avenue
New York, New York 10017
Salary Minimum: $50,000
Key Contact: Richard E. Kane
John Karrel

Functions: 05.0 05.1 05.2 05.3 05.5
Industries: Most
Professional Affiliations: IACPR
Description: Management positions—marketing
  & advertising

Karras Personnel, Inc.

2 Central Ave.
Madison, New Jersey 07940
Salary Minimum: $20,000
Key Contact: Bill Karras

Functions: 06.0
Industries: Most
Professional Affiliations: ASTD, NJAPC
Description: Human resources recruiting

Kauffman Hospitality, Inc.

P.O. Box 53218
Atlanta, Georgia 30305
Salary Minimum: $40,000
Key Contact: Christopher C. Kauffman
Joan F. Williams

Functions: Most
Industries: I.10 I.11
Professional Affiliations: ACF, NAPC
Description: Restaurant, hotel, contract
  feeding, culinary & food service sales
  professionals

Kelley & Keller, Inc.
2518 Key Largo
Ft. Lauderdale, Florida 33312
Salary Minimum: $50,000
Key Contact: Verne Kelley

Functions: 05.0 05.1 05.2 05.3 11.1
Industries: D.10 D.11 D.16 D.24 G.00
Description: Management consultants doing
   executive search for consumer marketing
   management only

Kendall & Davis Co., Inc.
910 N. 11th St., Ste. 2-711
St. Louis, Missouri 63101
Key Contact: James C. Kendall

Functions: 04.0 09.0 09.7
Industries: D.E0 D.H0 I.14 J.00 J.13
Professional Affiliations: NAPC
Description: Specialists in: electronics, defense,
   electro optics, physicians, data processing,
   telecom.

Branches:
One City Ctr., Ste. 110
Bloomington, Indiana 47404
Key Contact: Michael May

Kenmore Executives Inc.
1 S. Ocean Blvd., Ste. 208
Boca Raton, Florida 33432
Salary Minimum: $30,000
Key Contact: Lawrence D. Loprete
Marilyn Orr
Steven LoPrete

Functions: 01.4 02.5 03.2 09.4 11.1
Industries: Most
Professional Affiliations: ASM
Description: Provide experienced management
   consultants to industry & consulting firms

John J. Kennedy Assoc., Inc.
35 Bedford St., Ste. 4
Lexington, Massachusetts 02173
Salary Minimum: $20,000
Key Contact: John J. Kennedy

Functions: Most
Industries: D.15 D.19 D.E0 D.H0 D.I0
Description: Executive search, recruiting
   consultant & specialized outplacement

Jack Kennedy Assoc., Inc.
P.O. Box 14613
Chicago, Illinois 60614-0613
Salary Minimum: $35,000
Key Contact: John J. Kennedy
Noel G. Kennedy

Functions: 05.0 05.1 05.2 05.3 05.4
Industries: J.00 J.10 J.11 J.12
Professional Affiliations: ACG, IESA
Description: All facets of search for marketing,
   advertising & communications

James H. Kennedy
21 Collins Pond Trail
Fitzwilliam, New Hampshire 03447
Salary Minimum: $100,000
Key Contact: James H. Kennedy, III

Description: Contingent referrals in
   management consulting and executive
   search only

The Kennett Group, Inc.
15 W. Third St.
Media, Pennsylvania 19063
Salary Minimum: $35,000
Key Contact: Patrick B. Sweeney
Michael O'Horo

Functions: 01.4 03.2 09.4 11.3
Industries: Most + D.10 D.18 D.24 I.17
Professional Affiliations: NAPC
Description: Executive search services
   specializing in the MIS arena

Branches:
13115 Cross Keys Ct.
Fairfax, Virginia 22033

Kennison & Assoc.

100 Westport Sq., # 210
4200 Pennsylvania
Kansas City, Missouri 64111
Salary Minimum: $18,000
Key Contact: Gary S. Fawkes
Victoria Kennison

Functions: 01.4 09.1 09.3 09.5 09.7
Industries: Most
Professional Affiliations: DPMA, MAPC,
    NAPC
Description: Specialized, experienced &
    provide highest degree of honesty,
    integrity & professionalism

Kensington Int'l.

50 Victoria Ave.
Millbrae, California 94030
Salary Minimum: $60,000
Key Contact: Holland Kensington
Judy Foley Flow
Robert Kennedy
Barbara Fortune
Phyllis Ingmire
Stephen Hessler

Functions: Most + 04.0 05.0 08.0 09.0
Industries: Most + D.00 D.I0 G.00 I.00
Description: Domestic & international; mid-
    senior level; marketing/sales, accounting/
    finance, technical

Kepler & Assoc.

40 Atlantic Ave., Ste. D
Long Beach, California 90802
Salary Minimum: $20,000
Key Contact: Ernie Davis

Functions: Most + 05.4 11.5 11.6
Industries: Most
Professional Affiliations: CAPC, NAPC
Description: Sales placement specialist for
    industrial and commercial environments

Barbara Kerner Consultants

230 Park Ave., Ste. 315
New York, New York 10169
Salary Minimum: $50,000
Key Contact: Barbara Kerner

Functions: 01.5
Industries: I.17
Professional Affiliations: APA, NALSC, NASP,
    NYSBA, SPA
Description: Legal search-attorneys with major
    law firms & corporations worldwide

Blair Kershaw Assoc., Inc.

23 W. 10th Street
Erie, Pennsylvania 16501
Key Contact: Blair Kershaw

Functions: 02.4 02.5
Industries: D.13 D.22 D.26
Professional Affiliations: NAPC, NPA, PAPC
Description: We recruit for manufacturing,
    engineering, insurance, financial &
    management people

Kershner & Co.

4801 Massachusetts Ave., NW
Ste. 400
Washington, District of Columbia 20016
Salary Minimum: $50,000
Key Contact: Bruce Kershner

Functions: 08.0
Industries: C.00 H.10 H.R0
Description: Real estate executive search:
    commercial & corporate, development,
    leasing, finance & mgmt.

Key Employment

1014 Livingston Ave.
North Brunswick, New Jersey 08902
Salary Minimum: $30,000
Key Contact: Gary Silberger
Cliff Koblin

Functions: 02.0 05.4
Industries: B.00 C.00 D.00
Description: National search and recruiting for
    engineering, manufacturing & sales/
    marketing

Key Employment Services

1001 Office Park Rd., #320
West Des Moines, Iowa 50265-2567
Salary Minimum: $25,000
Key Contact: Don Jayne

Functions: 02.0 05.4 08.0 09.0 10.0
Industries: Most
Professional Affiliations: NAPC
Description: Specialists in mid to upper level
mgmt. positions; insurance, accounting,
engineering, D.P. & sales

Key Talent, Inc.

P.O. Box 3342
Annapolis, Maryland 21403-3342
Salary Minimum: $50,000
Key Contact: Robert Kames

Functions: 01.0 05.0 05.4 08.0 09.0
Industries: D.E0 D.H0 J.00
Professional Affiliations: AFCEA
Description: Intelligence, aerospace, software,
telecom, C3I, EW, intel, hi-tech, defense
prof., mktg & sales

Joseph Keyes Assoc.

275 Forest Ave., Ste. 206
Paramus, New Jersey 07653-0745
Salary Minimum: $30,000
Key Contact: Joseph A. Keyes
Edward M. Michaels
Matthew J. Coppola

Functions: 02.0 03.0 06.0 08.0 09.0
Industries: D.00 D.10 D.18 D.22 D.H0
Description: Specialists in manufacturing,
engineering, accounting, data processing &
outplacement

Kiley-Owen Assoc., Inc.

1218 Chestnut St., Ste. 510
Philadelphia, Pennsylvania 19107
Salary Minimum: $25,000
Key Contact: Sheila M. McGovern
Lynne Page
Tom Vandegrift

Functions: 02.0 05.0 09.2 09.4 09.7
Industries: D.10 D.16 D.24 D.E0 J.13
Professional Affiliations: MAAPC, NPC
Description: Search firm recruiting in the
electronics, data communications &
consumer goods industries

Kimmel & Fredericks, Inc.

25 Page Ave.
Asheville, North Carolina 28801
Salary Minimum: $50,000
Key Contact: Joe W. Kimmel
Marcus Hegarty

Functions: 01.1 01.2 05.2 11.5 11.6
Industries: B.0W B.10 C.00 H.R0
Professional Affiliations: NAPC
Description: Aggressive, national recruiting
firm-real estate, construction,
environmental & architectural search

Kinderis & Loercher Group

105 S. Roselle Rd., Ste. 200
Schaumburg, Illinois 60193
Salary Minimum: $20,000
Key Contact: Paul Kinderis

Functions: 10.0
Industries: H.I0
Description: Straight forward, no nonsense
style with a priority on ethics

Michael King Assoc., Inc.

366 Madison Ave.
New York, New York 10017
Key Contact: Michael King
Dolores Bullard

Industries: H.10 H.11
Description: Specialists in matching Wall Street
producers with premier firms

Millie Kipp Assoc., Inc.

P.O. Box 2187
Ocean, New Jersey 07712
Salary Minimum: $25,000
Key Contact: Millie Kipp

Functions: 08.0
Industries: H.I0
Professional Affiliations: NAPC, NJAPC,
NJAWBO
Description: Insurance/accounting/property/
casualty/claims/loss control/underwriting/
reinsurance are specialties

Kiradjieff & Co.
8 Faneuil Hall Marketplace
Boston, Massachusetts 02109
Salary Minimum: $50,000
Key Contact: Edward J. Kiradjieff

Functions: 08.0
Industries: D.00 H.10
Description: Executive search firm specializing in financial accounting searches

Kirkbride Assoc., Inc.
405-114th Ave. SE, Ste. 300
Bellevue, Washington 98004
Salary Minimum: $30,000
Key Contact: Robert Kirkbride
Gregg Patberg

Functions: 02.0 05.4
Industries: D.13 D.15 D.E0
Description: Specializing in sales, marketing, engineering, & management positions

Kirland Search, Inc.
2900 W. Peterson Ave.
Chicago, Illinois 60659
Salary Minimum: $30,000
Key Contact: William J. Kirland
Kerry J. Kirland

Functions: 02.0 05.0 09.0 09.7 11.6
Industries: D.00
Professional Affiliations: CASA, NCGA, SME
Description: Recruit & place advanced technology engineering/marketing personnel

Sanford Kleiner Assoc., Inc.
111 Linden St.
Malverne, New York 11565
Salary Minimum: $30,000
Key Contact: Sanford Kleiner

Functions: Most + 01.0 05.0 06.0 08.0 11.0
Industries: H.00 H.10 I.21
Description: Management recruiting for commercial banks, thrifts & related financial specialties

Kling Personnel Assoc., Inc.
180 Broadway, Ste. 501
New York, New York 10038
Salary Minimum: $25,000
Key Contact: Len Adams
Antonio Vittorioso

Functions: Most + 06.0 07.0 08.0 09.0
Industries: H.00 H.I0 I.14 I.15 I.16
Professional Affiliations: APCNY, NAPC
Description: All positions within financial services industries-banking, finance & insurance

Joyce C. Knauff & Assoc.
P.O. Box 624
Wilmette, Illinois 60091
Salary Minimum: $35,000
Key Contact: Joyce C. Knauff

Functions: 09.0 09.3 09.4
Industries: Most
Professional Affiliations: NAWBO
Description: Search firm specializing in the MIS function of corporations & consulting firms

The Koehler Group
P.O. Box 18156
Philadelphia, Pennsylvania 19116
Salary Minimum: $40,000
Key Contact: Frank R. Koehler

Functions: Most + 01.0 05.0 06.0 08.0
Industries: Most
Description: Search for human resource professionals, accounting, finance, sales & marketing

Kogon Assoc., Inc.
39 King's Pointe Dr.
Lititz, Pennsylvania 17543
Salary Minimum: $30,000
Key Contact: Gary Kogon

Functions: 03.3
Industries: Most + E.00
Professional Affiliations: ASTL, CLM, NAPC, WERC
Description: Traffic/transportation, warehousing, distribution, materials management, customer service-nationwide

Kordus Consulting Group
1470 E. Standish Pl.
Milwaukee, Wisconsin 53217-1958
Salary Minimum: $30,000
Key Contact: Lee Walther Kordus

Functions: Most + 01.0 01.1 05.0 05.1 05.2
Industries: Most + D.00 I.10 I.11 I.12 J.00
Professional Affiliations: AAF, NAPC, WAPC
Description: Specialize in all areas of marketing, advertising, promotions & public relations—nationwide basis

Koren, Rogers Assoc.
370 Lexington Ave., Ste. 2202
New York, New York 10017
Salary Minimum: $40,000
Key Contact: Michael Koren

Functions: 05.5 08.0 08.1 08.2 08.4
Industries: D.00 I.00 I.11 J.00 J.10
Professional Affiliations: NAER, NAPC, NASCP
Description: Professional mid market research oriented-finance & accounting retainer & contingency

Kossuth & Assoc., Inc.
135 Lake St. S., Ste. 255
Kirkland, Washington 98033
Salary Minimum: $50,000
Key Contact: Jane Kossuth
David Kossuth

Functions: Most + 11.2 11.3 11.5
Industries: D.00 D.H0 H.R0 J.00
Description: Retained search in all functional areas above $50,000

Kozlin Assoc., Inc.
9070 Main St.
Clarence, New York 14031
Salary Minimum: $40,000
Key Contact: Jeffrey M. Kozlin

Functions: 01.0 02.0 03.0 06.0
Industries: B.0W D.00 D.15 D.18 D.22
Description: Established in 1972-contingency recruitment & executive search serving manufacturing

Kramer Executive Resources, Inc.
885 Third Ave., Ste. 2900
New York, New York 10022-4082
Salary Minimum: $45,000
Key Contact: Alan L. Kramer
Carol Almour

Functions: 08.0 08.4
Industries: I.19
Description: Recruitment specialists in accounting, tax & financial placement

Krautler Personnel Recruitment
P.O. Box 491
Olney, Maryland 20832-0491
Salary Minimum: $50,000
Key Contact: William H. Krautler

Functions: Most
Industries: Most
Description: Targeted for engineering, management, sales, telecommunications, data processing/programming

Kravitz * Larkin * Silver Assoc.
2020 Broadway, Ste. 200
Santa Monica, California 90404
Salary Minimum: $30,000
Key Contact: Susan B. Silver
Jack Kravitz
James Larkin Jonassen

Functions: Most + 01.4 05.0 08.0 09.0
Industries: Most
Description: Executive search: finance & accounting, audit, tax, sales/marketing, MIS

Kreofsky & Assoc.
8400 Normandale Lake Blvd., Ste. 934
Minneapolis, Minnesota 55437
Salary Minimum: $40,000
Key Contact: Dean Kreofsky

Functions: 05.4 09.2 09.3 09.4
Industries: D.24
Professional Affiliations: FIN, NAPC
Description: Contingency search in computer/ data processing/sales & sales support

Kresin Wingard

333 N. Michigan Ave. #622
Chicago, Illinois 60601
Salary Minimum: $30,000
Key Contact: David Wingard

Functions: 01.1 01.2 01.3 05.1 05.3
Industries: J.00 J.10 J.11
Description: Concentration visual
communications—advertising, graphic
design, marketing communications

Kreuzberger, Fehr & Assoc.

115 Sansome St., Ste. 1204
San Francisco, California 94104
Salary Minimum: $40,000
Key Contact: James K. Fehr
Neil L. Kreuzberger

Functions: 08.0
Industries: Most
Description: Executive search firm specializing
in accounting, finance & tax professionals

Kromenaker & Associates

10230-32nd Ave. N., Ste. 242
Minneapolis, Minnesota 55441
Salary Minimum: $30,000
Key Contact: Robert Kromenaker

Functions: 02.1 02.2 02.3 02.5 02.6
Industries: D.00 D.19 D.22 D.25 D.26
Professional Affiliations: NAPC
Description: Specializes in engineering with
manufacturing clients in the Midwest

Krow Assoc., Inc.

150 Clove Rd.
P.O. Box 201
Little Falls, New Jersey 07424
Salary Minimum: $25,000
Key Contact: Irwin A. Ruderfer
Shellie Caplan

Branches:
175 Strafford Ave., Ste. 1, Bldg. 4
Wayne, Pennsylvania 19087
Key Contact: Dr. Louise H. Greenberg

Functions: 01.0 02.0 04.0 05.0 11.2
Industries: D.17 D.18 D.I0 I.15 I.17
Professional Affiliations: ASA, DIA, NJAPC,
PAC, RAPS
Description: In pharmaceutical recruiting-we
do it all!

Kurtz Pro-Search, Inc.

P.O. Box 4263
Warren, New Jersey 07059-0263
Salary Minimum: $35,000
Key Contact: Sheldon I. Kurtz

Functions: 05.4 09.3 09.4 09.7 11.1
Industries: D.24 D.H0 I.18 I.20 J.13
Description: Placement of sales, marketing &
systems professionals in the computer
industry

Kutt, Inc.

2336 Canyon Blvd.
Boulder, Colorado 80302
Key Contact: Larry Kutt
David Huff

Functions: Most
Industries: D.14
Professional Affiliations: CAPC
Description: Executive search & recruiting firm
serving the printing & medical industries

L & K Assoc.

179 W. Broadway, Ste. 7
P.O. Box 202
Salem, New Jersey 08079
Key Contact: Tom Kay
Gene Lankenau

Industries: Most
Description: Ethical technical recruiters:
specializing in D.P., telecommunications
and patent attorneys

LAS Management Consulting Group, Inc.

21 Kilmer Dr., Ste. F, Bldg. 2
Morganville, New Jersey 07751
Salary Minimum: $40,000
Key Contact: Philip A. Salvatore

Functions: 09.1 09.7
Industries: Most
Professional Affiliations: EDPAA
Description: Fifteen + years, specializing in
EDP audit & financial audit recruiting

LMB Assoc.

1468 Sunnyside Ave.
Highland Park, Illinois 60035
Salary Minimum: $30,000
Key Contact: Lorena M. Blonsky

Functions: 09.0
Industries: Most
Description: Professional and executive search
specializing in information systems

The LaBorde Group

5410 Wilshire Blvd., Ste. 713
Los Angeles, California 90036
Salary Minimum: $50,000
Key Contact: John LaBorde
Jim Kelly
Bob Martin

Description: Broad base executive recruiting
including sales, engineering, human
resource

LaDuke & Assoc., Inc.

1655 Penobscot Bldg.
Detroit, Michigan 48226
Salary Minimum: $50,000
Key Contact: Dan LaDuke
Dorothy Young

Functions: 11.2
Industries: D.00
Description: Executive search in manufacturing

Lacrosse Assoc., Inc.

P.O. Box 3596
Easton, Pennsylvania 18043-3596
Salary Minimum: $50,000
Key Contact: Anthony J. Badway

Functions: Most + 01.0 02.0 03.0 04.0 05.0
Industries: D.10 D.15 D.22 D.24 D.26
Description: A professional search firm with a
proven track record of management
recruiting

Lam Assoc.

Eaton Sq.—P.O. Box 75113
Honolulu, Hawaii 96836-0113
Salary Minimum: $40,000
Key Contact: Pat Lambrecht

Functions: 01.1 01.2 08.0 11.5 11.6
Industries: B.10 C.00 H.10 H.R0 I.15
Professional Affiliations: AIA, NAPC, NAPR,
SHRM
Description: We provide quality executive
search services to Hawaii & mainland
corporate clients

Lambert & Sullivan Assoc.

253 Riverside Ave.
Westport, Connecticut 06880
Salary Minimum: $75,000
Key Contact: Erwin Lambert
Dawn B.H. Sullivan

Functions: 06.0 06.1 06.2
Industries: Most
Description: Executive search consultants,
specializing in personnel/human resources

Lancaster Assoc., Inc.

94 Grove St.
Somerville, New Jersey 08876
Salary Minimum: $40,000
Key Contact: Raymond F. Lancaster
Barbara Swan

Functions: 09.0 09.2 09.3 09.6 09.7
Industries: D.00 D.15 D.17 D.18 D.26
Professional Affiliations: NAPC, NJAPC
Description: Professional data processing
recruiters serving the central & Northern
N.J. metro area

E.J. Lance Management Assoc., Inc.
261 Madison Ave., 2nd Fl.
New York, New York 10016
Salary Minimum: $40,000
Key Contact: Elizabeth Kay
Elliot Webb

Functions: 05.2 08.0 08.2 11.2
Industries: Most + D.00 H.00 H.10 H.I0 J.11
Description: Strong Wall St./banking practice-
also Fortune 1000 NYC metro

Landon-Brookes Executive Search
P.O. Box 5679
Woodland Park, Colorado 80866
Salary Minimum: $30,000
Key Contact: Ron Hubbard

Functions: Most
Industries: H.I0
Professional Affiliations: NIRA
Description: Commercial insurance recruiter

Lange & Assoc., Inc.
107 W. Market St.
Wabash, Indiana 46992
Salary Minimum: $20,000
Key Contact: Jack Lange, Sr.
Jim Lange

Functions: 01.0 02.0 03.0 06.0 08.0
Industries: D.13 D.18 D.19 D.22 D.E0
Description: Recruit all disciplines-specialize in
rubber, plastics, metals & defense
electronics

Langlois & Assoc.
P.O. Box 218
Accord, Massachusetts 02018-0218
Salary Minimum: $35,000
Key Contact: Robert L. Langlois

Functions: 01.0 05.2 06.0 08.0 09.3
Industries: I.14
Professional Affiliations: AHA, NEAIHC
Description: Recruit administrative, financial
& clinical management functions in the
healthcare field

Lanzi & Assoc.
2900 Chamblee-Tucker Rd.
Park Ridge 85, Bldg. 2
Atlanta, Georgia 30341
Salary Minimum: $30,000
Key Contact: Vince Lanzi

Functions: 01.1 01.2 01.3 05.4 11.2
Industries: D.17 D.18 I.14 I.15 I.16
Professional Affiliations: NAPC
Description: Recruiting physicians/healthcare
professionals; medical sales/marketing
management

Lappe & Assoc.
9755 N. 90th St., Ste. 150
Scottsdale, Arizona 85258
Salary Minimum: $40,000
Key Contact: Mark Lappe
Kristi Lappe

Functions: 01.2 01.3 02.0 09.2 09.3
Industries: D.18 D.H0 I.14 K.10
Description: Specialists in defense, medical,
electronics & healthcare

R.H. Larsen & Assoc., Inc.
1401 E. Broward Blvd.
Ft. Lauderdale, Florida 33301
Salary Minimum: $50,000
Key Contact: Robert H. Larsen

Functions: Most
Industries: Most
Professional Affiliations: FAPC
Description: Serving corporate clients
throughout Florida since 1972

Jack B. Larsen & Assoc.
334 West 8th St.
Erie, Pennsylvania 16502
Salary Minimum: $25,000
Key Contact: Jack B. Larsen

Functions: Most + 01.0 02.0 05.0 06.0 08.0
Industries: Most + D.00 D.E0 D.H0 H.00 I.00
Professional Affiliations: NAPC
Description: Full scope recruiting firm with
temporary & contract personnel also

Larson Assoc.

P.O. Box 9005
Brea, California 92621
Salary Minimum: $30,000
Key Contact: Ray Larson

Functions: Most + 01.0 02.4 05.0 09.0
Industries: B.0W D.15 D.24 D.H0 J.13
Professional Affiliations: CAPC, NAPC
Description: Executive & professional search
for chemical, electronics, hi-tech firms

Latham Int'l., Ltd.

568 Broadway, Ste. 1002
New York, New York 10012-3225
Salary Minimum: $50,000
Key Contact: Jennifer Martin
Audrey Lynn

Functions: 05.2 08.2 11.1 11.2
Industries: Most
Description: Consulting, planning, finance,
marketing experience in all industries

Latin America Assoc., S.C.

Paseo de la Reforma, 369-18 P.B.
Col Cuauhtemoc, Mexico DF 06500 Mexico
Salary Minimum: $20,000
Key Contact: Michael Ritz
Chris Miller

Functions: Most
Industries: Most
Professional Affiliations: SHRM
Description: Specialists in recruiting bi-lingual
executives, managers & administrative
staff for Mexico

Branches:
3784 Guess Rd., Ste. 711
Durham, North Carolina 27705
Key Contact: Guy C. Gentry

International Branches:
Veracruz

Jonathan Lawrence Assoc.

2001 Rte. 46
Parsippany, New Jersey 07054
Salary Minimum: $50,000
Key Contact: Don Singel

Functions: 09.0 09.1 09.3 09.4 09.6
Industries: Most
Professional Affiliations: NJAPC
Description: Focus on information systems
professionals

Lawrence Executive Search, Ltd.

85 Old Shore Rd.
Port Washington, New York 11050-2242
Salary Minimum: $35,000
Key Contact: Larry Kamisher
Sylvia Schaffer
Leslie Miller
Valerie Crane
Jennifer Lincoln

Professional Affiliations: DMA, DMCNY,
WDRG, WIP
Description: Specialists in direct response, data
processing, advertising, printing,
publishing & telemarketing

Affiliates/Other Offices:
Bornholdt Shivas & Friends, New York
Ford & Ford, Needham
Media Consultants, Denver

Lawrence-Balakonis & Assoc., Inc.

Dunwoody Village, P.O. Box 888241
Atlanta, Georgia 30356-0241
Salary Minimum: $45,000
Key Contact: Charles L. Balakonis
J. Robert Lawrence

Functions: 01.0 01.2 01.3 05.0 05.4
Industries: D.00 D.10 D.13 D.16 D.18
Description: Consumer packaged goods
industry specialists, focusing on sales &
marketing management

W.R. Lawry, Inc.
6 Wilcox St., P.O. Box 832
Simsbury, Connecticut 06070
Salary Minimum: $40,000
Key Contact: William R. Lawry

Functions: Most + 01.3 02.1 02.5 04.0 11.3
Industries: Most + D.15 D.18 D.19 D.H0 D.I0
Professional Affiliations: ASQC
Description: Technical recruiting firm placing at all levels (contributor & managerial)

The Lawson Group
9100 East D Ave.
Richland, Michigan 49083
Key Contact: James W. Lawson
Kay H. Ishmael
Terry A. Domres
Mike Lentes

Functions: Most + 01.1 02.0 02.1 03.1 05.1
Industries: D.13 D.D0
Professional Affiliations: PIMA, TAPPI
Description: Our staff is committed to making the American industry work efficiently & cost effectively

Reynolds Lebus Assoc.
P.O. Box 9177
Scottsdale, Arizona 85252
Salary Minimum: $30,000
Key Contact: Reynolds Lebus

Functions: 05.3
Industries: D.26
Professional Affiliations: ASCA
Description: Product marketing people for consumer goods companies

Lechner & Assoc., Inc.
7737 Holiday Dr.
Sarasota, Florida 34231
Salary Minimum: $45,000
Key Contact: David B. Lechner
Sue E. Hermanson

Functions: 10.0
Industries: H.I0
Description: Executive search firm with physician & insurance recruiting division in national market

Vincent Lee Assoc.
91 Fallon Ave.
Elmont, New York 11003
Salary Minimum: $20,000
Key Contact: Vincent Lee
Brian Lee
Sheryl Baxter
Linda Monte
Kathy Esposito

Functions: Most + 05.0 06.0 08.0 10.0
Industries: Most + H.00 H.I0 I.19 I.21
Description: Banking, accounting, human resources, finance executive search & management consulting

Lee Associates
106 Greenwood Ave.
Rumford, Rhode Island 02916
Salary Minimum: $50,000
Key Contact: Albert G. Lee

Functions: Most + 02.0 04.0 05.0 08.0 09.0
Description: Finance, MIS, engineering, marketing & medical

Lee Management Group Inc.
12700 Hillcrest, Ste. 172
Dallas, Texas 75230
Salary Minimum: $30,000
Key Contact: Barbara Lee
Glenna Love

Functions: Most
Industries: D.00 D.11
Professional Affiliations: NAPC, SERC
Description: Specialists in all disciplines; strong affiliation with top apparel manufacturers

Legal Placements Inc.
380 N. Broadway, Ste. 301
Jericho, New York 11753
Key Contact: Elizabeth G. Nunemaker

Functions: Most + 01.0 01.5
Industries: I.00 I.17
Professional Affiliations: APCNY, NALSC
Description: Specializes in the placement of attorneys at the partnership & associate level

Brian Leggee & Assoc.
12526 High Bluff Dr., Ste. 300
San Diego, California 92130
Salary Minimum: $18,000
Key Contact: Brian Leggee

Functions: 01.4 02.1 02.2 02.3 09.0
Industries: D.24 D.D0 D.E0 D.H0
Description: Engineering & technical placement

Alan Lerner Assoc.
1300 Park of Commerce Blvd.
Delray Beach, Florida 33445
Salary Minimum: $18,000
Key Contact: Alan Lerner

Functions: Most
Industries: Most
Description: Nationwide retail executive search
& placement

Branches:
3420 Norman Berry Dr., Ste. 509
Hapeville, Georgia 30354
Key Contact: Ormond Curl

209 West St., Ste. 304
Annapolis, Maryland 21401
Key Contact: Thomas Lamm

161 Forbes Rd., Ste 104
Braintree, Massachusetts 02184
Key Contact: Luke Roberts
Gary Belastock

Lakeview Commons, Ste. 400
Gibbsboro, New Jersey 08026
Key Contact: Jeff Senges

The Lighthouse Group
4056 Wetherburn Way, Ste. 101
Norcross, Georgia 30092
Salary Minimum: $30,000
Key Contact: Eric E. Walker

Functions: 01.2 01.3 05.2 05.4
Industries: D.24
Professional Affiliations: NAPC
Description: Sales/marketing nationally &
internationally to LAN, E-Mail & PC
communications manufacturers

Paul Ligon Co.
11241 Rosser Rd.
Dallas, Texas 75229
Salary Minimum: $35,000
Key Contact: T. Paul Ligon

Functions: 01.0 05.0 06.0 08.0
Industries: H.00 H.10 I.00 I.10 J.00
Professional Affiliations: MAPC, TAPC
Description: Executive search in all phases of
the hospitality industry-25 years-11 years
in contingency search

Lindsey & Assoc., Inc.
P.O. Box 1642
Darien, Connecticut 06820-1642
Salary Minimum: $50,000
Key Contact: Lary L. Lindsey

Functions: 01.0 02.0 05.0 07.0 08.0
Industries: D.10
Description: General search—all functions

Lineal Recruiting Services
46 Copper Kettle Rd.
Trumbull, Connecticut 06611
Key Contact: Lisa Lineal

Functions: 02.4 05.4 05.6 11.0 11.3
Industries: E.00 I.20 L.00
Description: Electrical apparatus & systems
industry specialists, emphasizing service &
repair

Link Personnel & Assoc.
2311 Westbury Dr.
Midland, Michigan 48642
Salary Minimum: $25,000
Key Contact: Art Link
Sue Link

Functions: Most + 01.0 02.0 03.0 05.0 06.0
Industries: Most + B.0W D.00 D.15 D.19 J.10
Professional Affiliations: MAPC
Description: Contingency specialists in plastics,
chemicals, auto & metal working
industries

The James Lloyd Group

P.O. Box 3
Ashland, Oregon 97520-0001
Salary Minimum: $30,000
Key Contact: James Lloyd

Functions: 01.2 04.0 09.2 09.3 11.3
Industries: D.24 D.H0 I.11 J.11 J.12
Description: International search specializing in professional television industries: broadcasting & videographic

Locus Inc.

4263 Cambria-Wilson Dr.
Lockport, New York 14094
Salary Minimum: $20,000
Key Contact: Nancy Wainwright

Functions: Most
Industries: B.00 D.00 D.D0 D.H0
Description: Work primarily with engineers offering personalized service emphasizing applicant needs

Loewenstein & Assoc.

5847 San Felipe, Ste. 990
Houston, Texas 77057
Salary Minimum: $40,000
Key Contact: Ron Loewenstein
Paul McEwan, Jr.
Mark O'Brien
Judy Alford
Dean Hunt
Karl Alfeld
Rick Kolke

Functions: 02.3 05.4 11.3 11.5 11.6
Industries: B.10 D.15 D.20 D.24 D.25
Description: Specializes in executive search for technical sales, marketing & engineering professionals

Logistics Management Resources, Inc.

P.O. Box 2204
New City, New York 19056-0588
Salary Minimum: $45,000
Key Contact: Marjorie Slater

Functions: 02.0 02.2 03.0 03.1
Industries: Most + D.00 G.00
Professional Affiliations: CLM, ICSA
Description: Recruiting individuals considering a career change to accelerate their career

Logix, Inc.

1601 Trapelo Rd.
Waltham, Massachusetts 02154
Salary Minimum: $40,000
Key Contact: David M. Zell

Functions: 01.4 04.0 09.3 09.4 09.6
Industries: D.H0 I.18
Description: Dedicated search & consulting services to industry leaders in engineering and data processing

Logue & Rice Inc.

8000 Towers Crescent Dr., Ste. 1295
Vienna, Virginia 22182-2700
Salary Minimum: $35,000
Key Contact: Raymond D. Rice
Kenneth F. Logue

Functions: Most + 01.0 06.0 08.0 09.0 11.1
Industries: Most + D.10 G.00 H.00 H.I0
Description: Primarily financial executive search in Washington D.C., Virginia & Maryland

Lord & Albus Co.

11902 Jones Rd., Ste. L-185
Houston, Texas 77070
Salary Minimum: $25,000
Key Contact: John P. Albus

Functions: 02.0 03.0 04.0 06.0 09.0
Industries: B.0W D.00 D.D0 D.H0 D.I0
Description: Thirteen plus years experience client development & recruiting program

R.E. Lowe Assoc.
8080 Ravines Edge Ct.
Worthington, Ohio 43235
Salary Minimum: $30,000
Key Contact: Robert A. Gammill
Richard E. Lowe
Paul M. Shimp
William R. Taylor
Kevin P. Walter

Functions: Most
Industries: Most + D.00
Professional Affiliations: NAPC
Description: Line, mid management & higher
contingency specialty recruiters

Branches:
7621 Little Ave., Ste. 212
Charlotte, North Carolina 28226
Key Contact: Patrick Perkins

4770 Duke Dr., Ste. 390
Mason, Ohio 45040
Key Contact: Vince Messina

Lowery, Cotter, & Assoc.
2959 Lucerne Dr. SE, Ste. 104
Grand Rapids, Michigan 49546-7173
Salary Minimum: $50,000
Key Contact: Alina A. Cotter
Bruce N. Lowery

Functions: 01.0 02.0 06.0 07.0 08.0
Industries: C.00 D.00 E.00 H.00 I.00
Professional Affiliations: ACA, AICPA
Description: Minority-owned search firm
specializing in middle & upper positions

Lucas & Assoc., Ltd.
1000 Maple Ave., Ste. I-E
Downers Grove, Illinois 60515
Key Contact: J. Curtis Lucas

Functions: Most
Industries: Most
Description: Management recruiting &
consulting in all industries

Ludot Personnel Services, Inc.
3000 Town Ctr.,Ste. 2025
Southfield, Michigan 48075
Salary Minimum: $40,000
Key Contact: Michael J. Morton

Functions: 01.0 02.0 06.0 08.0 11.2
Industries: D.00 D.E0 D.H0 H.00 I.00
Description: Recruitment & placement of well
qualified minorities & females

Fran Luisi Assoc.
P.O. Box 3658
Princeton, New Jersey 08543-3658
Salary Minimum: $40,000
Key Contact: Fran Luisi

Functions: 06.0 06.1 06.2
Industries: Most
Professional Affiliations: ACA, AHRSP, EMA,
SHRM
Description: Firm specializing exclusively in·
human resources on a national basis

Luke, Lincoln, & Brugger
P.O. Box 3891
Erie, Pennsylvania 16508-0891
Salary Minimum: $40,000
Key Contact: Gene William Brugger
Kraig Lincoln
Kevin Luke

Functions: Most + 01.0 02.0 05.0 06.0 08.0
Industries: Most + C.00 D.00 I.00
Description: Firm excels in locating exceptional
talent for difficult assignments

Lunney, Hadden & Assoc.
5750 W. 95th St.
P.O. Box 7790
Overland Park, Kansas 66207-0790
Salary Minimum: $30,000
Key Contact: Richard H. Lunney
Elizabeth Hadden

Functions: 01.2 01.3 02.4 02.5 05.6
Industries: D.13 D.14 D.20 D.D0 J.11
Description: Management consulting/executive
search for printing, packaging, and ink
industries

Lybrook Assoc., Inc.
P.O. Box 572
Newport, Rhode Island 02840
Salary Minimum: $25,000
Key Contact: Karen Lybrook

Functions: 02.1 02.5 04.0 11.3 11.5
Industries: B.0W D.15 D.18 D.19 I.16
Professional Affiliations: ACS, NAPC, NPA, SPE, TAPPI
Description: Recruiting chemistry & related scientists, engineers, & managers nationwide

Arthur Lyle Assoc., Inc.
1 Norwalk W., 40 Richards Ave.
Norwalk, Connecticut 06854
Salary Minimum: $25,000
Key Contact: Arthur L. Tomack

Functions: 08.0 08.1 08.2 08.3 09.0
Industries: Most
Description: Specialists in accounting/financial & data processing placement in NY, NJ and CT

Lyons & Assoc., Inc.
P.O. Box 3633
Oak Brook, Illinois 60522-3633
Salary Minimum: $35,000
Key Contact: Kent T. Lyons

Functions: Most
Industries: D.13 D.14 D.D0
Professional Affiliations: PIA
Description: A graphic arts specialist firm focused on sales, staff & management roles

M H Executive Search Group
P.O. Box 868068
Plano, Texas 75086-8068
Salary Minimum: $35,000
Key Contact: Mike Hochwalt
Lee Walt

Functions: 01.3 02.2 02.4 03.4 05.4
Industries: D.13 D.19 D.D0
Professional Affiliations: IOPP, SERC
Description: Specialize in packaging & graphics industries in sales, marketing, plant & management personnel

M-A Management Assoc., Inc.
6 E. 39th St., Ste. 401
New York, New York 10016
Salary Minimum: $35,000
Key Contact: Mark Altman
Deborah Valchar
Penny Lowy
Ileen Dotson
Jan Dow

Functions: 01.3 01.4 05.3 08.1 08.2
Industries: H.10 H.11 H.12 H.R0 I.20
Description: Specialize in banking, accounting, marketing, foreign exchange sales/trading & data processing

MARBL Consultants, Inc.
11270 W. Park Pl., Ste. 270
Milwaukee, Wisconsin 53224-3624
Salary Minimum: $40,000
Key Contact: Allan G. Adzima
Michael R. Smith
Dennis J. Pradarelli
Patricia G. Cooper

Functions: Most + 01.0 02.0 03.0 06.0 09.0
Industries: D.00 D.H0
Professional Affiliations: NAPC, NPA, WAPC
Description: Over 30 years of successful recruiting/search experience serving diversified clientele

M/ARS
P.O. Box 15037
Arlington, Texas 76016
Salary Minimum: $35,000
Key Contact: Ginger Lindsey

Functions: 01.2 01.3 05.1 05.3 05.7
Industries: G.00 I.10 I.11 J.00 J.10
Description: Marketing, advertising-client side & agency side; packaged goods, fast food, retail & automotive

MB Inc.
505 Fifth Ave.
New York, New York 10024
Salary Minimum: $40,000
Key Contact: Alan M. Levine
Margo Berk-Levine

Professional Affiliations: NAPC, NATS, NPA
Description: Marketing/sales-middle to senior
management; nationally-consumer and
industrial

Affiliates/Other Offices:
Temporarily Yours Personnel Service Inc., New York
Temporarily Yours Personnel Service Inc., Tokyo

mfg/Search, Inc.
The Commerce Center
401 E. Colfax Ave., Ste. 203
South Bend, Indiana 46617
Salary Minimum: $25,000
Key Contact: Howard C. Mueller
Judith Van Es

Functions: 01.0 02.0 03.0 04.0 05.0
Industries: D.00 D.19 D.22 D.23 D.24
Description: Technical recruiting & executive
search for America's manufacturers

Branches:
325 E. Eisenhower Dr., Ste 106
Ann Arbor, Michigan 48108

MJF Assoc.
187 N. Main St., P.O. Box 132
Wallingford, Connecticut 06492
Key Contact: Matt Furman

Functions: 01.0 02.0 05.0 05.4 09.0
Industries: D.00 D.E0 D.H0 J.00
Professional Affiliations: CAPC, NAPC
Description: Do professional, technical,
executive recruitment, sales, marketing,
engineering & management

MKM Search Consultants, Inc.
444 N. Michigan Ave., Ste. 1900
Chicago, Illinois 60611
Salary Minimum: $40,000
Key Contact: Vivian Fabbro

Functions: 01.0 02.0 05.0 06.0 08.0
Industries: Most
Professional Affiliations: IAPW, NAWBO,
SHARP
Description: Specialists in middle/senior
management-environmental, accounting/
finance, sales/marketing

MPI Assoc.
761 W. Birch Ct.
Louisville, Colorado 80027
Salary Minimum: $35,000
Key Contact: Frank E. Welzig

Functions: Most
Industries: D.H0
Description: Specialize in software hardware
engineers, sales & marketing, general
management

MRG Search & Placement
900 Chapel St., Ste. 515
New Haven, Connecticut 06510
Salary Minimum: $25,000
Key Contact: Steve Polak

Functions: Most + 01.4 09.0
Industries: Most + D.17 H.10 I.16
Description: Areas of specialization include
data processing, banking & pharmaceutical
industry.

Alan MacDonald & Assoc.

729 Scott Blvd., Ste. 1
Decatur, Georgia 30030
Salary Minimum: $25,000
Key Contact: Alan MacDonald
Mel Minkin
Mark Gil

Affiliates/Other Offices:
MacDonald, Mitchell & Assoc., Inc., Norcross

Functions: Most + 08.0
Industries: Most
Description: A contingency/retainer firm
    specializing in financial/administrative
    disciplines

Magnum Search

1000 Golfhurst
Mt. Prospect, Illinois 60056
Salary Minimum: $30,000
Key Contact: Arthur N. Kristufek

Functions: Most
Industries: D.00 D.13 D.22 D.23 D.24
Professional Affiliations: SHRM, SHRP
Description: Generalist firm specializing in the
    manufacturing industry

Tom Mahon & Assoc.

1 Starbuck Ln., P.O. Box 1208
Saratoga Springs, New York 12866
Salary Minimum: $25,000
Key Contact: Tom Mahon

Functions: 09.3 09.4 09.7
Industries: D.H0 H.10
Description: Recruit in banking internationally,
    electronic & telecommunications

Mahony & Assoc., Ltd.

6065 Roswell Rd., NE, Ste. 1355
Atlanta, Georgia 30328
Salary Minimum: $25,000
Key Contact: Charles F. Mahony

Functions: Most + 01.0 02.0 04.0 05.0 06.0
Industries: Most + D.00 D.10
Professional Affiliations: IACPR, AMI, NAER
Description: Nationwide executive search for
    the meat industry

Major, Wilson & Africa

325 Pacific Ave.
San Francisco, California 94111
Key Contact: Martha Fay Africa

Functions: 01.5
Industries: I.17
Professional Affiliations: ABA, NALSC
Description: Exclusively attorney search and
    placement of partners, associates,
    corporate counsel

Branches:
2311 M St., NW, Ste. 1004
Washington, District of Columbia 20037
Key Contact: Robert A. Major, Jr.

311 Market St., 2nd Fl., Ste 203
Dallas, Texas 75202
Key Contact: Heidi L. Haring
Robin Elkin

200 N. Dearborn St., Ste. 4502
Chicago, Illinois 60601
Key Contact: Laura J. Hagen
Leslie A. Kase

808 Travis St., Ste 1007
Houston, Texas 77002
Key Contact: James M. Wilson, Jr.

Affiliates/Other Offices:
Hughes-Castell Ltd., Hong Kong
Hughes-Castell Ltd., London

Management Advisors Int'l., Inc.

P.O. Box 3708
Hickory, North Carolina 28603
Key Contact: William J. Castell, Jr.

Functions: 09.3
Industries: D.11 D.15 H.10 H.R0
Description: Executive search/professional
    placement for the real estate finance
    industry

Management Assoc.
9735 Magledt Rd.
Baltimore, Maryland 21234
Salary Minimum: $30,000
Key Contact: Walter J. Sistek
George Hankins
Beverly Hartman
Joyce Ralph Herman
Craig Joseph
William McFaul

Functions: Most
Industries: Most
Professional Affiliations: IACPR, ASPA,
ASTD, NAPC
Description: Consultants to the financial
services industry, generalists to industry

Management Assoc.
2700 Augustine Dr., Ste. 255
Santa Clara, California 95054
Salary Minimum: $60,000
Key Contact: William H. Greenhalgh
Val B. Baldwin

Functions: 01.1 01.3 05.2 09.7
Industries: D.H0 D.I0 J.13
Description: Our commitment to quality in our
search activities opens up opportunities
for successful careers

Management Recruiters
1127 Euclid Ave., Ste. 1400
Cleveland, Ohio 44115-1638
Salary Minimum: $20,000
Key Contact: Alan R. Schonberg
William Aglinsky
Robert A. Angell
Michael F. DiDomenico
Stephen W. Fogelgren
Robert Gandal
Donald L. Goldman
David L. Marth
Louis R. Scott

Professional Affiliations: AHRC, AMA, IFA,
PERC
Description: The search & recruiting
specialists; 413 offices, all mid-
management & professional areas

Branches:
2 Office Park Cir., Ste. 106
Birmingham, Alabama 35223-2578
Key Contact: Glenn E. Estess
J. Peyton McDaniel

801 Executive Park Dr., Ste. 201
Mobile, Alabama 36606
Key Contact: Rufus C. Brock

3322 Memorial Pkwy., SW, Ste. 12
Bldg. 200
Huntsville, Alabama 35801-5335
Key Contact: Barbara W. Jackson

2863 Old Missouri Rd.
Fayetteville, Arkansas 72703-3765
Key Contact: Steven W. Bulla

402 Linwood Dr., Ste. 1
Paragould, Arkansas 72450-4027
Key Contact: Lawanda K. Hooten
Mark S. Woodruff

235 N. Freeport Dr., Ste. 6
Nogales, Arizona 85621-2423
Key Contact: Joseph Garcia

6900 E. Camelback Rd., Ste. 935
Security Pacific Bank Bldg.
Scottsdale, Arizona 85251-2491
Key Contact: Dick Govig
Todd A. Govig

1730 E. River Rd., Ste. 220
Cambric Corporate Ctr.
Tucson, Arizona 85718
Key Contact: Erin Blanchette
Dave Blanchette

1027 S. Santo Antonio Dr., Ste. E
Colton, California 92324-4165
Key Contact: Maurice R. Meyers

940 S. Coast Dr., Ste. 255
Costa Mesa, California 92626
Key Contact: Ralph L. Bunker

16530 Ventura Blvd., Ste. 300
The Atrium
Encino, California 91436
Key Contact: Tony Byrne

300 Corp. Pointe, Ste. 100
Culver City, California 90230-7612
Key Contact: Joe Ruzich

945 Coffee Rd., Ste. 3
Modesto, California 95350
Key Contact: Frank Phillips

4665 MacArthur Ct., Ste. 100-B
Newport Beach, California 92660
Key Contact: James P. Meehan
Trish Ryan

4125 Mohr Ave., Ste. M
Pleasanton, California 94566-4740
Key Contact: Mike Machi
Jerry Annicchero

2316 Bell Executive Ln., Ste. 100
Sacramento, California 95825-3893
Key Contact: Ken McCollum

50 Francisco St., Ste. 495
Francisco Bay Office Pk.
San Francisco, California 94133-2114
Key Contact: Eric C. Wheel

3031 Tisch Way, Ste. 401
San Jose, California 95128-2541
Key Contact: Robert S. Lineback
Tom Davenport

5370 Hollister Ave., Ste. 1
University Professional Bldg.
Santa Barbara, California 93111
Key Contact: Al W. Mehrbrodt

591 Redwood Hwy., Ste. 2225
Mill Valley, California 94941
Key Contact: Eric Wheel
David Lego

400 S. Beverly Dr., Ste. 412
Beverly Hills, California 90212-4406
Key Contact: Peter Wall

3620 W. Hammer Ln., Ste. A
Stockton, California 95209
Key Contact: Charles Blackburn

325 E. Hillcrest Dr., Ste. 160
Bldg. C
Thousand Oaks, California 91360-5828
Key Contact: John L. Dempster
Loren Kaun

32123 Lindero Canyon Rd., Ste. 201
The Landing
Westlake Village, California 91361
Key Contact: Ward A. Fredericks
Peter May

1090 Adams St., Ste. K
Benicia, California 94510
Key Contact: Mark A. Hoffman

11717 Kiowa Ave., Ste. 104
Los Angeles, California 90049-6145
Key Contact: Lonny Kaufman
Marshall Field

22 Seascape Vlg.
Aptos, California 95003
Key Contact: Robert Lineback
Dale E. Henderson

One City Blvd. W. Ste. 710
Orange, California 92668-3157
Key Contact: John Lewis

6020 Commerce Blvd., Ste. 125
Rohnert Park, California 94928-2102
Key Contact: Robert Cary

307 N. Santa Anita Ave.
Arcadia, California 91007
Key Contact: Roger Staebler

3800 Barham Blvd., Ste. 405
Los Angeles, California 90068-1042
Key Contact: Jeffrey Merino

1900 S. Norfolk St., Ste. 318
San Mateo, California 94403-1151
Key Contact: Don Hirschbein

125 Ryan Industriasl Ct., Ste. 201
San Ramon, California 94583-1527
Key Contact: James Napolitano

1727 Mesa Verde Ave., Ste. 203
Ventura, California 93003-6540
Key Contact: Robert Packer
Gail Packer

1401 Walnut St., Ste. 301
P.O. Box 4657
Boulder, Colorado 80306-4657
Key Contact: Sharon Hunter
Janet N. Arnold

6760 Corporate Dr., Ste. 220
Colorado Springs, Colorado 80919
Key Contact: Mark Merriman

3090 S. Jamaica Ct., Ste. 100
Wedgwood Bldg.
Aurora, Colorado 80014-2978
Key Contact: Kent L. Milius
Gregg A. Milius

12600 W. Colfax Ave., Ste. C-440
Lakewood, Colorado 80215-3736
Key Contact: Rodney D. Bonner

10 Boulder Crescent, Ste. 302 B
Colorado Springs, Colorado 80903
Key Contact: Bud Reynolds

1120 Lincoln St., Ste. 709
Denver, Colorado 80203-2137
Key Contact: Pete Neumann
Vicki Neumann

105 Sanford St.
Hamden, Connecticut 06514
Key Contact: Jackson P. Burke

Glastonbury Commons
117 New London Turnpike
Glastonbury, Connecticut 06033
Key Contact: Jack Cirino

15 Bank St., Ste. 204
Stamford, Connecticut 06901
Key Contact: Lynn W. Moore

82 North St.
Danbury, Connecticut 06810-5633
Key Contact: Doug Wright

1660 L St., NW, Ste. 606
Washington, District of Columbia 20036
Key Contact: Frank S. Black, Jr.
Marilyn H. Hingers

911 S. Dupont Hwy., Ste. A
Lotus Plz. Bldg.
Dover, Delaware 19901
Key Contact: Wally Collins

501 Silverside Rd.
Wilmington, Delaware 19809-1317
Key Contact: Eleanor DeMeglio
Nick DeMeglio

2963 Gulf To Bay, Ste. 220
Waters Edge
Clearwater, Florida 34619-4200
Key Contact: Helen Gleason-Fay

1000 Corporate Dr., Ste. 410
Ft. Lauderdale, Florida 33334
Key Contact: Joel Dickstein

3388 NE Sugarhill Ave.
Jensen Beach, Florida 34957-3723
Key Contact: Philip Goodman

6700 S. Florida Ave., Ste. 25
Lakeland, Florida 33813-3312
Key Contact: Terry Evans

2121 Ponce Deleon Blvd., Ste. 220
Miami, Florida 33134
Key Contact: Walt Krysowaty

4500 Biscayne Blvd., Ste. 230
The Heller Bldg.
Miami, Florida 33137
Key Contact: Del Diaz

603-A E. Government St.
Pensacola, Florida 32501
Key Contact: Ken F. Kirchgessner

9500 Koger Blvd., Ste. 203
St. Petersburg, Florida 33702
Key Contact: Robert P. Raffin

7737 Holiday Dr.
Sarasota, Florida 34231
Key Contact: Dr. David B. Lechner

5017 W. Laurel St.
Tampa, Florida 33607-3816
Key Contact: Betty Jo Faulk

One San Jose Pl., Ste. 27
Jacksonville, Florida 32257-7579
Key Contact: Charles Hansen

1117 N. Donnelly St.
Mount Dora, Florida 32757-4259
Key Contact: Roger M. Holloway
Donald J. Braley

3005 26th St.,W.,Ste. C
Bradenton, Florida 34205
Key Contact: Lynn Moore

1775 W. Hibiscus Blvd., Ste. 215
Melbourne, Florida 32901
Key Contact: Larry Cinco

2301 Lucien Way, Ste. 295
Maitland, Florida 32751
Key Contact: Chub Ensminger
John L. Bates

5104 N. OrangeBlossom Tr.
Ste. 109
Orlando, Florida 32810-1013
Key Contact: Kenneth J. Clark

570 SE Port St. Lucie Blvd.
Port St. Lucie, Florida 34984
Key Contact: Meredith Breault
Larry Breault

3228 SW Martin Downs Blvd., Ste. 4
Palm City, Florida 34990-2697
Key Contact: William Hollinger
Lois Hollinger

1406 Hays St., Ste. 7
Tallahassee, Florida 32301-2842
Key Contact: Kittie Carter

3111 W. DeLeon St.
Tampa, Florida 33609-4601
Key Contact: Rudy Koletic

710 Oakfield Dr., Ste. 129
Merchant Bank Bldg.
Brandon, Florida 33511
Key Contact: Terry Wesley
Dave Titus

1777 Tamiami Trail
Port Charlotte, Florida 33948-1051
Key Contact: Michael Cimilluca

8000 Arlington Exwy., Ste. 112
Jacksonville, Florida 32211
Key Contact: Terry E. Piazza

5340 Gulf Dr., Ste. 205
New Port Richey, Florida 34652-3950
Key Contact: Scott Brodey

4020 Park St., Lighthouse Point
St. Petersburg, Florida 33709-4034
Key Contact: Jean Hand

4200 W. Cypress St., Ste. 640
Tampa, Florida 36607
Key Contact: David Peterson

5901-B Peachtree-Dunwoody NE, Ste. 360
Atlanta, Georgia 30328-5342
Key Contact: Jeff Ram
Cliff F. Drown

30 Woodstock St.
Roswell, Georgia 30075-3546
Key Contact: Art E. Katz

640 Village Trace, Ste. 200
Marietta, Georgia 30067
Key Contact: James Hokkanen

6724 Church St., Ste. 5
Riverdale, Georgia 30274
Key Contact: Ronald L. Wise

3228 Cody Rd., Ste. 203
Columbus, Georgia 31907-2110
Key Contact: Michael L. Silverstein

5230 Atlanta Hwy.
Alpharetta, Georgia 30201-2925
Key Contact: Ted F. Ellis

303 Parkway 575, Ste. 303
Bldg. 300
Woodstock, Georgia 30188-3882
Key Contact: David T. Riggs
Lena K. Riggs

1188 Bishop St., Ste.2601
Honolulu, Hawaii 96813
Key Contact: Al Ward

P.O. Box 787
Iowa City, Iowa 52244
Key Contact: John Sims

520 S. Pierce Ave., Ste. 202
Westbrook
Mason City, Iowa 50401
Key Contact: Cheryl L. Plagge

2435 Kimberly Rd., Penthouse
Alpine Centre S.
Bettendorf, Iowa 52722
Key Contact: Jerry Herrmann

P.O. Box 1977
Waterloo, Iowa 50704
Key Contact: Jerry Holbach

290 Bobwhite Ct., Ste. 220
Park Ctr.
Boise, Idaho 83706-3966
Key Contact: Teresa Alexander
Craig A. Alexander

129 S. 4th St.
Albion, Illinois 62806
Key Contact: Lois Christensen
Thomas C. Christensen

220 Campus Ct., Ste. 100
Arlington Heights, Illinois 60004
Key Contact: Steve Briody
John Dowiat

2205 Lakeside Dr.
Bannockburn, Illinois 60015-1287
Key Contact: Dennis Gross

31 W. Downer Pl., Ste. 402
Aurora, Illinois 60506-5134
Key Contact: Karen Hatten
Dick Hatten

211 Landmark Dr., Ste. El
Normal, Illinois 61761
Key Contact: Alan Snedden

2110 N. Market St., Ste. 112
Champaign, Illinois 61821-1306
Key Contact: Kenneth C. Williams

2 N. Riverside Plz., Ste. 1815
Chicago, Illinois 60606-2701
Key Contact: David Baranski
Glenda Baranski

1400 E. Touhy Ave., Ste. 220
Des Plaines, Illinois 60018-3374
Key Contact: Dick Kurz

472 N. McLean Blvd., Ste. 201
Elgin, Illinois 60123
Key Contact: Ron Reeves

1000 Maple Ave., Ste. I-E
Downers Grove, Illinois 60515
Key Contact: J. Curtis Lucas

1740 Bell School Rd.
Point East
Cherry Valley, Illinois 61016-9337
Key Contact: D. Michael Carter

7804 W. College Dr.
College Dr. Office Ctr.
Palos Heights, Illinois 60463-1010
Key Contact: Victor J. Persico

10 E. State Ave.
St. Charles, Illinois 60174
Key Contact: Daniel C. Lasse

9933 Lawler Ave., Ste. 315
Westmoreland Bldg.
Skokie, Illinois 60077-3715
Key Contact: Erik Conley

401 S. Milwaukee Ave., Ste. 220
Wheeling, Illinois 60090
Key Contact: James Wooten

100 Tower Dr., Ste. 224
Burr Ridge, Illinois 60521-5720
Key Contact: Geary L. Dodendorf

101 Court St., Ste. 209
Riverside 1
Evansville, Indiana 47708
Key Contact: Marjorie Caldemeyer

8200 Haverstick Rd., Ste. 240
Haverstick One
Indianapolis, Indiana 46240-2472
Key Contact: George Ceryak
Brenda Patterson

907 Franklin St.
P.O. Box 8576, Canterbury Sq.
Michigan City, Indiana 46360
Key Contact: Roland Cantway
Anita Cantway

2519 E. Main St., Ste. 101
Forest Park Bldg.
Richmond, Indiana 47374-5864
Key Contact: Rande Martin

205 W. Jefferson Blvd.
First Bank Bldg., Ste. 400
South Bend, Indiana 46601-1811
Key Contact: Jeff Spicer

432 Washington, The Alley Ste.
P.O. Box 2234
Columbus, Indiana 47202-2234
Key Contact: J. Michael Percifield

3702-A S. Reed Rd.
Kokomo, Indiana 46902-3817
Key Contact: H. Peter Isenberg

9401 Indian Creek Pkwy., Ste. 1250
Corporate Woods Bldg. 40
Overland Park, Kansas 66210-2098
Key Contact: Danny Buda
Marc E. Wagman

8441 E. 32nd N., Ste. 100
Wichita, Kansas 67226
Key Contact: Tony Wolters
Marvin Reimer

10 E. Cambridge Circle Dr., Ste. 190
10 Cambridge Pl.
Kansas City, Kansas 66103-1312
Key Contact: John Hornbeck

322 N. Lincoln
Liberal, Kansas 67901-2720
Key Contact: Cynthia Kruse

2900 Wanamaker Dr., Ste. E
Topeka, Kansas 66614-4188
Key Contact: Stan Wiechert

105 Citation, Ste. A
Danville, Kentucky 40422-9200
Key Contact: Sue Smith
Mike Smith

P.O. Box 10
Owenton, Kentucky 40359-0010
Key Contact: R. Jan Smith

1711 Ashley Circle, Unit A-6
Bowling Green, Kentucky 42101-3339
Key Contact: Bob A. Toth

2350 Sterlington Rd.
Alumni Office Pk.
Lexington, Kentucky 40502
Key Contact: Judy Simpson
Kent Simpson

1930 Bishop Ln., Ste. 426
Watterson Towers
Louisville, Kentucky 40218-1966
Key Contact: Steven R. Angel

155 South Keeneland Dr.
Richmond, Kentucky 40475-8679
Key Contact: Ron S. Lawson

P.O. Box 3553
Baton Rouge, Louisiana 70821-3553
Key Contact: Cecilia Franklin
Cleve Franklin

P.O. Box 6605
Metairie, Louisiana 70009
Key Contact: Edward C. Ameen

106 Village St., Ste. 2
Slidell, Louisiana 70458
Key Contact: Jack L. Pecot

P.O. Box 894
Boston, Massachusetts 02117-0894
Key Contact: Jack Mohan
Art Greenfield

607 Boylston St.
Boston, Massachusetts 02116
Key Contact: Stan Banner

639 Granite St.
Braintree, Massachusetts 02184
Key Contact: Stephen W. Morse
Stephen G. Marshall

1500 Main St., Ste. 1822
Bay Bank Tower
Springfield, Massachusetts 01115
Key Contact: Jack Mohan

2000 W. Park Dr.
Westborough Office Pk.
Westborough, Massachusetts 01581-3901
Key Contact: Irene Garrity

9515 Deereco Rd., Ste. 801
Baltimore, Maryland 21093
Key Contact: Ken Davis
Linda Burton
Dick Forder

One Church St., Ste. 402
Rockville, Maryland 20850
Key Contact: Tom Hubin

2083 West St., Ste. 5A
Annapolis, Maryland 21401-3030
Key Contact: John Czajkowski

One Bank St., Ste. 220
Gaithersburg, Maryland 20878-1504
Key Contact: John L. Butts, Jr.
Ginnabeth Butts

132 E. Main St., Ste. 300
Salisbury, Maryland 21801-4921
Key Contact: Fred J. Puente

412 Malcolm Dr., Ste. 300
Westminister, Maryland 21157
Key Contact: John J. LaMartina

1344 Ashton Rd., Ste. 102
Hanover, Maryland 21076
Key Contact: Thomas Graff

1505 Dixie Dr., Ste. 2
Monroe, Michigan 48161-2577
Key Contact: Robert Sewell

2929 Plymouth Rd., Ste. 202
The Plymouth Bldg.
Ann Arbor, Michigan 48105-3293
Key Contact: Sameer N. Sarafa

30300 Telegraph Rd., Ste. 285
Bingham Office Pk.
Bingham Farms, Michigan 48025-4509
Key Contact: Fred B. Bawulski

P.O. Box 3
Blissfield, Michigan 49228-0003
Key Contact: Mary W. Snellbaker

8137 W. Grand River, Ste. 5
Woodland Office Ctr.
Brighton, Michigan 48116-9346
Key Contact: John Sass

G-5524 S. Saginaw
Flint, Michigan 48507
Key Contact: David Reed
Spence Wolfe

2876 28th St., SW, Ste. 4
Grandville, Michigan 49418
Key Contact: Ronald Meadley

300 River Pl., Ste. 3000
Detroit, Michigan 48207
Key Contact: Debra Lawson-Niezgocki

4021 W. Main St., Ste. 200
Briarwood Valley Office Plz.
Kalamazoo, Michigan 49007-2746
Key Contact: Dr. M.J. Tessin

2491 Cedar Park Dr.
Holt, Michigan 48842-2184
Key Contact: Priscilla J. Peterson
John A. Peterson

5103 Eastman Pl., Ste. 101
Midland, Michigan 48640
Key Contact: Vicki M. Harris
John L. Harris
Jack L. Harris

3435 Hill St.
St. Joseph, Michigan 49085-3001
Key Contact: Victor F. Palenske

550 Stephenson Hwy., Ste. 407
Troy, Michigan 48083-1152
Key Contact: Ed Moeller

3145 Henry St., Ste. 203
Muskegon, Michigan 49441
Key Contact: John R. Mitchell, Jr.

126 Boardman Ave., Ste. B
Traverse City, Michigan 49684-2502
Key Contact: Robert S. Icard, Sr.
Cheryl A. Valencia-Icard

2 Heritage Oak Lane, Ste. 3
Battle Creek, Michigan 49015-4282
Key Contact: Mary J. Barker

400 N. 136th Ave., Ste. 6, Bldg. 200
Holland, Michigan 49424-1830
Key Contact: Robert Bakker

102 South Main @ Broadway, Ste. 2
Mt. Pleasant, Michigan 48858-2309
Key Contact: Patrick Doyle

7625 Metro Blvd.
Belzer & Brenner Office Bldg.
Minneapolis, Minnesota 55435-3058
Key Contact: Robert Hammer
Lucy Huber

P.O. Box 1197
Camdenton, Missouri 65020-9004
Key Contact: Judy Hodgson
Robert D. Hodgson

Two Pershing Sq.
2300 Main, Ste. 1020
Kansas City, Missouri 64108-2428
Key Contact: Stephen F. Orr
Eileen Mason

3301 Rider Trail S., Ste. 100
St. Louis, Missouri 63045
Key Contact: Robert J. Keymer

11701 Borman Dr., Ste. 250
St. Louis, Missouri 63146
Key Contact: Phil L. Bertsch

200 N. Broadway, Ste. 1520
St. Louis, Missouri 63102-2799
Key Contact: Jim Jackson

200 Fabricator Dr.
Meramec Valley Ctr.
Fenton, Missouri 63026
Key Contact: Edward Travis
Glenwood Alley

1807 E. Edgewood
The Edgewood # B
Springfield, Missouri 65804
Key Contact: Arlyn B. Rudolph

1310 Business 63 South, Ste. 1
Columbia, Missouri 65201
Key Contact: David Dunn

14825 E. 42nd St., Ste. 250
Three Oaks Office Bldg.
Independence, Missouri 64055-4776
Key Contact: William Elam
Kathy S. Howard

1755 Lelia Dr., Ste. 102
Jackson, Mississippi 39216
Key Contact: J.W. Gardner
Ben Barrett

211 South Ctr., Ste. 305
City Center
Statesville, North Carolina 28677
Key Contact: Neil F. Coleman

P.O. Box 6077
Bethlehem, North Carolina 28603-6077
Key Contact: J.D. Liles
Byron King

228 Westinghouse Blvd., Ste. 104
P.O. Box 7483
Charlotte, North Carolina 28241-7483
Key Contact: Gerald E. Orlick
James A. Tuohy

5102 Chapel Hill-Durham Blvd., Ste 216
Durham, North Carolina 27707
Key Contact: Elaine Dibner

951 S. McPherson Church Rd., Ste 105
Fayetteville, North Carolina 28303
Key Contact: John R. Semmes

835 Highland Ave., SE
Hickory, North Carolina 28602-1140
Key Contact: Scott Volz

603-C Eastchester Dr.
High Point, North Carolina 27260
Key Contact: John R. Williams

907 Centergrove Rd.
Kannapolis, North Carolina 28081-8005
Key Contact: Tom Whitley
Thomas Whitley

P.O. Box 8
Louisburg, North Carolina 27549-0008
Key Contact: Darrell Perry

5509 Creedmoor Rd., Ste. 206
Raleigh, North Carolina 27612-6314
Key Contact: Wade Stanley

P.O. Box 17054
Winston-Salem, North Carolina 27116-7054
Key Contact: Mike Jones

324 W. Wendover, Ste. 230
Greensboro, North Carolina 27408
Key Contact: Mitch Oakley

5 Cole Park Plz.
Chapel Hill, North Carolina 27514-9134
Key Contact: Joe McMahon

322 East Center Ave.
Mooresville, North Carolina 28115
Key Contact: Hugh L. Sykes

107 Independence Blvd., Ste. 3
Mount Airy, North Carolina 27030-3589
Key Contact: Ronald A. Ellis

2605 West Roosevelt Blvd. te. 209
Monroe, North Carolina 28110-8409
Key Contact: Diane Patch
Dick Patch

111 NW Railroad St.
Enfield, North Carolina 27823-1334
Key Contact: Maria Snook
Marvin Snook

1319 S. Glenburnie Rd.
New Bern, North Carolina 28562-2605
Key Contact: Fred Eatman

336 Holy Hill Lane
Burlington, North Carolina 27215-5209
Key Contact: Harry Bargholz

210 Gateway, Ste. 434
Greentree Court
Lincoln, Nebraska 68505-2438
Key Contact: Renee A. Elam

7171 W. Mercy Rd., Ste. 252
Omaha, Nebraska 68106-2696
Key Contact: Les Zanotti

116-C South River Rd.
Cold Stream Office Pk.
Bedford, New Hampshire 03110
Key Contact: Frank P. Kace

61 N. Maple Ave., 3rd Fl.
Germaine Bldg.
Ridgewood, New Jersey 07450
Key Contact: Jack S. Osher

65 S. Main St., Bldg. B 301
Pennington, New Jersey 08534
Key Contact: Robert B. White

1325 Paterson Plank Rd.
Secaucus, New Jersey 07094-3707
Key Contact: Ted Prehodka

42 Court St.
Morristown, New Jersey 07960-5154
Key Contact: Susan Young
Wayne T. Young

707 State Rd., Ste. 220
Princeton, New Jersey 08540-1413
Key Contact: Warren Schorr

2 Carnegie Rd.
Lawrenceville, New Jersey 08648
Key Contact: William D. Hogan

1104 Springfield Ave.
Mountainside Crossing
Mountainside, New Jersey 07092
Key Contact: Jim Malfetti
Rosemary Malfetti

10 Anderson Rd., Ste. 7
Bernardsville, New Jersey 07924-2319
Key Contact: Barbara J. O'Brien

750 Hamburg Trnpk., Ste. 203
Pompton Lakes, New Jersey 07442-1418
Key Contact: David Zawicki

191 Woodport Rd., Ste. 201
Sparta, New Jersey 07871-2641
Key Contact: Lance M. Incitti

118 Tamarack Circle
Skillman, New Jersey 08558
Key Contact: Julia Neri

210 Lake Dr., E., Ste. 104
Woodland Falls Corp. Park
Cherry Hill, New Jersey 08002-0110
Key Contact: Roy Kelly
Allen Salikof

Box 54, Olde Lafayette Village
Lafayette, New Jersey 07848-9513
Key Contact: Gary R. Chiusano
David M. Mortimer

830 Bear Tavern Rd., Ste. 301
West Trenton, New Jersey 08628
Key Contact: Robert Bodnar
Beverly Bodnar

163 Route 130, Bldg. 2, Ste. R
Bordentown, New Jersey 08505-2250
Key Contact: Randy Ruschak

108-D Centre Blvd.
Marlton, New Jersey 08053-4132
Key Contact: Fred L. Hollander

520 Stokes Rd., Bldg. C
Ironstone Office
Medford, New Jersey 08055-3007
Key Contact: Norman Talbot

104 Mountain Ct.
Hackettstown, New Jersey 07840-2300
Key Contact: Henry F. Magnusen

540 Marshall St., C-2
Phillipsburg, New Jersey 08865-2658
Key Contact: Hank Dempsey

210 W. Front St.
Red Bank, New Jersey 07701
Key Contact: Mike Unger
Terri L. Sabados

7 Regent St., Ste. 708, 4 Waterloo Rd.
Waterloo Executive Plz.
Livingston, New Jersey 07039-1617
Key Contact: Joanne Jamison
Ted Jamison

8205 Spain Rd. NE, Ste. 201
Albuquerque, New Mexico 87109-3155
Key Contact: Don Smiset

Two Executive Park Dr.
Stuyvesant Plz.
Albany, New York 12203-3707
Key Contact: Bob Mulcahey

76 E. Main St., Ste. 1
Huntington, New York 11743
Key Contact: Sue Goldfarb

350 Fifth Ave., Ste. 2205
New York, New York 10118
Key Contact: Joseph H. Kay

575 Lexington Ave., Ste. 505
New York, New York 10022-6102
Key Contact: Jeffrey A. Heath

305 Madison Ave., Ste. 1146
New York, New York 10165
Key Contact: David Kim

5500 Main St., Ste. 260
The Ctr. of Williamsville
Williamsville, New York 14221-6737
Key Contact: Bob Melone

47 S. Fitzhugh St.
Ebenezer Watts Bldg.
Rochester, New York 14614
Key Contact: Jerry Annesi

Ste. 321, Route 22
Clock Tower Commons
Brewster, New York 10509-9998
Key Contact: Stan Wien

7000-B E. Genesee St.
Lyndon Office Park
Syracuse, New York 13220-2307
Key Contact: Theodore R. Lowe

239 Genesee St., Ste. 101
Mayro Bldg.
Utica, New York 13501-3409
Key Contact: Carl Tardugno
Wayne Corley

100 Crossways Park W.
Plaza Bldg., Ste. 208
Woodbury, New York 11797
Key Contact: Warren E. Kornfeld

One Blue Hill Plz., Ste. 1428
P.O. Box 1603
Pearl River, New York 10965-8603
Key Contact: Tom Malone
Veronica Varian

10 E. Main St., Ste. 204
Victor, New York 14564-1302
Key Contact: Ed Ristau

120 Genesee St., Ste. 602
Auburn, New York 13021-3643
Key Contact: Ed Dunn
Joanne Grimaldi

P.O. Box 386, Route 209
Stone Ridge, New York 12484-0386
Key Contact: Robert A. Mackenzie

P.O. Box 1530
Windermere Ave.
Greenwood Lake, New York 10925-1530
Key Contact: Carolyn A. Chermak
Susan Chermak-Shepis

2 Church St.
P.O. Box 218
Madrid, New York 13660
Key Contact: James A. Infantino
Sharon M. Infantino

147 Bell St.
Chagrin Falls, Ohio 44022-2947
Key Contact: Mike Rosenshein

1375 Kemper Meadow Dr., Ste 6
Cincinnati, Ohio 45240-1635
Key Contact: David Howard

30432 Euclid Ave., Ste 205
Wickliffe, Ohio 44092
Key Contact: Ronald L. Sterling
Cheryl E. Sterling

1900 E. Dublin-Granville, Ste. 110B
Columbus, Ohio 43229-3374
Key Contact: Robert Stoltz

66 S. Miller Rd.
Akron, Ohio 44313-4141
Key Contact: Tom J. Gerst

42 E. Main St., Ste. 200
The Centre
Ashland, Ohio 44805-2358
Key Contact: Edward J. Houska

P.O. Box 2970
North Canton, Ohio 44720-0970
Key Contact: Shirley R. Bascom

7 W. Seventh St., Ste. 1650
The Federated Bldg.
Cincinnati, Ohio 45202-2451
Key Contact: Tony D'Eramo
Joe McCullough

26250 Euclid Ave., Ste. 811
Euclid Office Plz.
Cleveland, Ohio 44132-3674
Key Contact: Terry Wesley

3511 Center Rd., Ste. E-A
P.O. Box 178
Brunswick, Ohio 44212-0178
Key Contact: Robert A. Boal

20950 Center Ridge Rd., Ste. 207
Cleveland, Ohio 44116-4307
Key Contact: Philip P. Minko
Dolores I. Minko

800 East Broad St.
Columbus, Ohio 43205
Key Contact: David D. Oberting

40 W. Fourth St., Ste. 1222
Miami Valley Tower
Dayton, Ohio 45402-1831
Key Contact: Joel L. Noble
Jeffrey M. Noble

347 Scioto St.
Urbana, Ohio 43078
Key Contact: Tom S. Warren

8090 Market St., Ste. 2
Boardman, Ohio 44512-6216
Key Contact: Robert J. Lutsky

34100 Ctr. Ridge Rd., Ste. 110
Liberty Ctr.
North Ridgeville, Ohio 44039-3220
Key Contact: James Spellacy

9700 Rockside Rd., Ste. 490
Cleveland, Ohio 44125-6264
Key Contact: Paul F. Montigny

18472 S. Salem Row
Strongsville, Ohio 44136-7137
Key Contact: Mike Murray

1127 Euclid Ave., Ste. 1010
Statler Office Twr.
Cleveland, Ohio 44115-1602
Key Contact: Barry R. Niemann

6200 SOM Center Rd., Ste. B-20
P.O. Box 39361
Solon, Ohio 44139-2911
Key Contact: Kim Barnett

314 W. Fourth St., Ste. 101
Dover, Ohio 44622-3106
Key Contact: Larry Ice

8505 Tanglewood Sq., Ste. 111
Chagrin Falls, Ohio 44022
Key Contact: Lou Radakovich

676 Enterprise Dr., Ste. B
Westerville, Ohio 43081-8847
Key Contact: Richard Harkins
Margaret Harkins

3441 W. Memorial Rd., Ste. 4
Memport Office Pk.
Oklahoma City, Oklahoma 73134
Key Contact: Gary Roy

2020 Lloyd Ctr.
Portland, Oregon 97232-1376
Key Contact: Larry P. Engelgau
Elvita B. Engelgau

927 Country Club Rd., Ste. 175
Eugene, Oregon 97401-2272
Key Contact: Tom Hirsch

560 S. Prince St.
Lancaster, Pennsylvania 17603
Key Contact: James W. Speitel

49 E. Fourth St., Ste. 205
Williamsport, Pennsylvania 17701-6355
Key Contact: Joel Reid

400 Penn Ctr. Blvd., Ste 224
Pittsburgh, Pennsylvania 15235-5602
Key Contact: Samih M. Paalbaki

100 N. 17th St.
Robert Morris Bldg.
Philadelphia, Pennsylvania 19103
Key Contact: Thomas J. Lucas

125 Seventh St.
Pittsburgh, Pennsylvania 15222-3477
Key Contact: Douglas H. Cain

4840 McKnight Rd.
Pittsburgh, Pennsylvania 15237-3413
Key Contact: Patricia L. Holupka
Gary F. Holupka

300 Weyman Plaza, Ste. 140
Pittsburgh, Pennsylvania 15236
Key Contact: Andy Hallam
Paul R. Rossman

3901 Commerce Ave., Ste. 185
Willow Wood Office Ctr.
Willow Grove, Pennsylvania 19090
Key Contact: Rowland R. Norris, Sr.
John P. Zerkle, Sr.

3333 Street Rd., Ste. 235
One Greenwood Sq.
Bensalem, Pennsylvania 19020-2022
Key Contact: Theodore M. Mashack

701 Main St., Ste. 302
Shearson Lehman Brothers Bldg.
Stroudsburg, Pennsylvania 18360-2010
Key Contact: Margi Depew
Barry Depew

60 W. Broad St., Ste. 301
Bethlehem, Pennsylvania 18018-5721
Key Contact: Fred R. Meyer

950 Haverford Rd., Ste. 107
Bryn Mawr, Pennsylvania 19010-3820
Key Contact: M.A. Bishop

101 Dyer St., Ste. 5-A
Providence, Rhode Island 02903-3904
Key Contact: Stephen W. Morse

P.O. Box 2874
2406 N. Main St., Ste. D
Anderson, South Carolina 29622
Key Contact: Vernon R. Pagan

4 Carriage Ln., Ste. 301
Charleston, South Carolina 29407
Key Contact: Robert L. Bean, Jr.

35 Orleans Plaza, Ste. N
Hilton Head, South Carolina 29938
Key Contact: Gerald I. Wood

518 East Main St., Ste. 8
Lexington, South Carolina 29072-3668
Key Contact: Philip Black
Roy Black

1201 Hampton St., Ste. 2 B
P.O. Box 50785
Columbia, South Carolina 29250-0785
Key Contact: Robert Keen, Jr.

25 Woods Lake Rd., Ste. 306
Green Gate Office Pk.
Greenville, South Carolina 29607
Key Contact: J.C. Ponder

5 Harbour Village
Salem, South Carolina 29676
Key Contact: Jim K. Rice
Ann Rice

2037 St. Matthews Rd.
Orangeburg, South Carolina 29115
Key Contact: Dick Crawford
Ed Chewning

1925 Ebenezer Rd.
Rock Hill, South Carolina 29730
Key Contact: Herman D. Smith

2282 Powdersville Rd., Ste. A
Easley, South Carolina 29642-8921
Key Contact: Dan Rogers
Jane Rogers

P.O. Box 639
907 N. Main St.
Travelers Rest, South Carolina 29690-0639
Key Contact: Guy Carter

2600 S. Minnesota Ave.
Sioux Falls, South Dakota 57105-4731
Key Contact: Bob Good
Dave Good

909 St. Joe, Ste. 555
First Federal Plaza
Rapid City, South Dakota 57709-8321
Key Contact: Deanna Langerud

7405 Shallowford Rd., Ste. 520
Chattanooga, Tennessee 37421
Key Contact: Bill Cooper

9050 Executive Park Dr., Ste. 16
Knoxville, Tennessee 37923-4693
Key Contact: James D. Kline

502 Hickman Rd., Ste. 202
Lenoir City Professional Pk.
Lenoir City, Tennessee 37771-8914
Key Contact: Ray S. Strobo

5495 Winchester Rd., Ste. 5
Memphis, Tennessee 38115-4607
Key Contact: Wally Watson

278 Franklin Rd., Ste. 125 01
Brentwood, Tennessee 37027
Key Contact: Greg Shaw

95 White Bridge Rd., Ste. 415
Nashville, Tennessee 37205-1412
Key Contact: Bill Jameson
Mike Allen

1616 S. Kentucky, Ste. 114
Bldg. A
Amarillo, Texas 79102
Key Contact: Mike Rokey

1221 S. Main St.
Boerne, Texas 78006-2813
Key Contact: G. Jeff Penfield

1250 Capital of Texas Hwy., S.
Ste. 200, 1 Cielo Ctr.
Austin, Texas 78746-2605
Key Contact: Martin L. Hansen

5310 Harvest Hill Rd.
Ste. 110—LB105
Dallas, Texas 75230-5805

8585 Stemmons Frwy., Ste. 535
Twin Towers N.
Dallas, Texas 75247
Key Contact: Frank Roberts

5310 Harvest Hill Rd., Ste. 110-LB105
Dallas, Texas 75230-5805
Key Contact: Robert Lineback

317 S. Friendswood Dr.
Friendswood, Texas 77546
Key Contact: Louis P. Bellview
Sibyl Bellview

1701 River Run Rd., Ste. 610
Ft. Worth, Texas 76107-6530
Key Contact: Bill Anderson

6500 West Freeway, Ste. 720 641
One Ridgmar Centre
Ft. Worth, Texas 76116-2140
Key Contact: Bob Bond
Carole Bond

3200 Broadway, Ste. 420
Garland, Texas 75043-1529
Key Contact: Bob Adcock

801 W. Freeway, Ste. 610
NCNB Bank Tower
Grand Prairie, Texas 75051
Key Contact: Larry Klos

10333 Richmond Ave., #650
Houston, Texas 77042-4116

1360 Post Oak Blvd., Ste. 2110
Cigna Tower
Houston, Texas 77056
Key Contact: Rich Bolls

13111 Westheimer Rd., Ste 111
Houston, Texas 77077-5520
Key Contact: Shay Soll

1660 S. Stemmons, Ste. 460
Brookhollow N.
Lewisville, Texas 75067
Key Contact: Anthony D. Kuehler
Desni C. Kramer

494 S. Seguin
New Braunfels, Texas 78130-7938
Key Contact: Jim K. Rice

101 E. Park Blvd., Ste. 355
Plano, Texas 75074-5445
Key Contact: Robert W. Bassman
Sandra M. Bassman

8700 Crownhill, Ste. 701
San Antonio, Texas 78209
Key Contact: James L. Cornfoot
Denise Carrigan

2203 Timberloch Pl., Ste. 241
The Woodlands, Texas 77380-1102
Key Contact: Marshall S. Croner

6600 South 1100 East, Ste. 420
Salt Lake City, Utah 84121-2400
Key Contact: Dirk Cotterell

4660 Kenmore Ave., Ste. 1018
Seminary Plaza Bldg.
Alexandria, Virginia 22304-1361
Key Contact: Michael Prentiss

901 State St., Ste. 300
Bristol, Virginia 24201-3815
Key Contact: Mike Williams
Marie Williams

4400 Fair Lakes Court, Ste. 103
Fairfax, Virginia 22033
Key Contact: Tony A. Ehrenzeller
Jennie Ehrenzeller

2511 Memorial Ave., Ste. 302
Memorial Professional Bldg.
Lynchburg, Virginia 24501
Key Contact: C. David Blue

1568 Spring Hill Rd. Ste. 301
McLean, Virginia 22102
Howard H. Reitkopp

827 Diligence Dr., Ste. 111 1011-D
Newport News, Virginia 23606-4203
Key Contact: Barry B. Marsh

6620 W. Broad St., Ste. 406
Brookfield Bldg.
Richmond, Virginia 23230
Key Contact: Jay Schwartz
Ed Becker
Rita Becker

6 Pidgeon Hill Dr., Ste. 250
Sterling, Virginia 22170-5617
Key Contact: Carol J. Poltorak

4092 Foxwood Dr., Ste. 102
Virginia Beach, Virginia 23462-4237
Key Contact: James F. Murphey

611 S. Cameron St.
Winchester, Virginia 22601
Key Contact: William L. McKeown
Patricia McKeown

P.O. Box 8084
The Vermont Bldg., Ste. 2-D
Brattleboro, Vermont 05304-8084
Key Contact: Phil Morin
Joyce Morin

11811 Northeast First St., Ste. 304
Eastridge Corporate Ctr.
Bellevue, Washington 98005-3094
Key Contact: Mark Stevens

19125 N. Creek Pkwy., Ste. 127
Bothell, Washington 98011-8002
Key Contact: Ronda G. Clark
Dan Jilka

9725 SE 36th St., Ste. 312
Globe Bldg.
Mercer Island, Washington 98040-3896
Key Contact: James J. Dykeman

2633-A Parkmount Ln., SW, Ste. B
Olympia, Washington 98502
Key Contact: Jim Pitchford

N. 1212 Washington, Ste. 130
Rock Pointe Corporate Ctr.
Spokane, Washington 99201-2434
Key Contact: Larry Smith

1019 Pacific Ave., Ste. 806
The Washington Bldg.
Tacoma, Washington 98402-4403
Key Contact: Ron Westover

601 Main St., Ste. 202
Vancouver, Washington 98660
Key Contact: Steve Fox

911 N. Lynndale Dr.
Appleton, Wisconsin 54914
Key Contact: Russ Hanson

375 Bishops Way, Ste. 150
Corporate Woods
Brookfield, Wisconsin 53005-6200
Key Contact: Peder Medtlie

P.O. Box 1237
104 S. Main St., Ste. 420
Fond du Lac, Wisconsin 54936-1237
Key Contact: Judith L. Berger

444 S. Adams St.
Cadillac Sq.
Green Bay, Wisconsin 54301
Garland Ross

515 Gold St.
Green Lake, Wisconsin 54941-0638
Key Contact: James Beerbaum
Judy Beerbaum

5307 S. 92nd St., Ste. 125
Valley View Ctr.
Hales Corners, Wisconsin 53130
Key Contact: Thomas E. Hurt

4781 Hayes Rd.
Madison, Wisconsin 53704
Key Contact: Paul T. Esser

1222 Washington St.
Manitowoc, Wisconsin 54220
Key Contact: Russ Hanson

P.O. Box 11557
Milwaukee, Wisconsin 53211-0557
Key Contact: Diana L. Fenrich

310 W. Wisconsin Ave.
Federal Plz., Ste. 1150
Milwaukee, Wisconsin 53203-2215
Key Contact: William C. Healy
Vanda K. Healy
Jane Schmidt

601 E. Henry Clay
Milwaukee, Wisconsin 53217-5646
Key Contact: Tim Lawler

435 E. Mill St.
The Mill St. Transfer
Plymouth, Wisconsin 53073-1840
Key Contact: Barry Dukes

222 Main St., Ste. 103
Shoop Office Bldg.
Racine, Wisconsin 53403
Key Contact: John J. Henkel

1547 Strongs Ave.
Stevens Point, Wisconsin 54481
Brad Barick

242 E. Thomas St.
Wausau, Wisconsin 54401-5415
Key Contact: Rebecca J. Knutson

P.O. Box 2870
1008 E. 21st St.
Cheyenne, Wyoming 82003-2898
Key Contact: Verle Meister

Management Recruiters of Little Rock

10816 Executive Center Dr., Ste. 110
Little Rock, Arkansas 72211-4392
Salary Minimum: $30,000
Key Contact: Noel K. Hall
Earl R. Hall

Functions: Most
Industries: D.10 D.23 F.00 I.18 I.19

Management Recruiters—Concord, CA.

1001 Galaxy Way, Ste. 404
Galaxy Office Park
Concord, California 94520-5725
Key Contact: Gordon Soares
Bonnie Holmes

Functions: Most
Industries: I.14
Description: Specialists in the health/medical
field in technical through senior
management positions

Management Recruiters

114 E. Shaw, Ste. 207
Fresno, California 93710
Key Contact: Ron L. Johnson
Mike Cornelison
Kay Lemon
Roben Kennedy

Functions: Most + 02.2 02.4 05.4
Industries: B.00 D.10 D.18 D.22 I.14
Description: 1990 MRII office of the year—13
years in business

Management Recruiters Peninsula

1900 S. Norfolk St., Ste. 318
San Mateo, California 94403
Salary Minimum: $20,000
Key Contact: Don Hirschbein

Functions: Most + 01.0 05.0 09.0
Industries: Most + D.I0 F.00 G.00 I.00 J.00
Description: Rank in top 10% of all offices
nationwide

Management Recruiters of Laguna Hills

23461 S. Pointe Dr., Ste. 390
Laguna Hills, California 92653
Key Contact: Thomas J. Toole

Functions: 02.0 04.0 08.0 09.0 11.5
Industries: B.0W D.15 D.18 D.I0 J.13
Professional Affiliations: CAPC, PIRA
Description: Specialists in biotech,
environmental, chemical, pharmaceutical,
telecommunications, finance

Management Recruiters of Monterey

494 Alvarado St., Ste. F
Monterey, California 93940-2717
Key Contact: Richard J. Kashinsky

Functions: 01.0 02.0 06.0 08.0
Industries: D.10 D.26 H.10 I.14 I.19

Management Recruiters of Oakland

480 Roland Way, Ste. 103
Oakland, California 94621
Key Contact: Tom S. Thrower

Functions: Most + 01.3 02.2 05.4 08.2 09.1
Industries: Most

Management Recruiters

9455 Ridgehaven Ct., Ste. 205
San Diego, California 92123-1632
Key Contact: Harvey J. Baron

Functions: 01.2 01.3 05.4 08.4 09.3
Industries: C.00 D.13 D.24 I.14 I.15
Professional Affiliations: CAPC, NAPC

Management Recruiters

4998 W. Broad St., Ste. 202
Lincoln Bldg.
Columbus, Ohio 43228-1604
Salary Minimum: $30,000
Key Contact: Marilyn Wallace

Functions: Most + 01.1 01.2 01.3
Industries: I.14 I.15
Description: Placement of physicians, nurses, allied health professionals & managers nationwide

Management Recruiters of Greater Bridgeport, Inc.

140 Sherman St.
Fairfield, Connecticut 06430-5849
Salary Minimum: $40,000
Key Contact: R. Rush Oster

Functions: Most + 04.0 11.3 11.5
Industries: B.10 D.10 D.I0 I.14 I.16
Professional Affiliations: IFT
Description: Areas of expertise are science, engineering & materials management

Management Recruiters of Waterbury, Inc.

45 Freight St.
Waterbury, Connecticut 06702-1880
Key Contact: Jack Bourque

Functions: 01.2 01.3 02.1 02.4 11.3
Industries: D.00 D.22 D.25 D.H0 J.13
Professional Affiliations: WAI
Description: Identify, locate & evaluate the top engineering & manufacturing achievers

Management Recruiters of Atlanta Downtown

225 Peachtree St. NE, Ste. 1420
Atlanta, Georgia 30303
Salary Minimum: $35,000
Key Contact: Eugene E. Houchins, Jr.
Elizabeth Thomas

Functions: 02.4 11.3 11.5
Industries: B.0W D.13 D.21 D.22 I.14
Description: Specialize in healthcare & engineering/manufacturing management placement

Management Recruiters of Savannah

2431 Habersham St., 2nd Fl.
Savannah, Georgia 31401
Salary Minimum: $30,000
Key Contact: Ron McElhaney
Tom Wichman
Ron McElhaney, Jr.
Bo Simmons
Carolyn Hawkins

Functions: Most + 02.0 03.0 04.0 08.0
Industries: B.0W D.13 D.15 D.19 D.24
Professional Affiliations: AICHE, TAPPI
Description: In business over 12 years; clients/candidates throughout the United States

Management Recruiters of Redding

7092 Sylvan Ln.
Anderson, California 96007
Salary Minimum: $50,000
Key Contact: Michael R. Connolly

Functions: 01.1 01.2
Industries: H.10 H.11
Description: Equity derivatives sales, bonds, foreign exchange, trades

Management Recruiters of Cedar Rapids, Inc.

150 First Ave. NE Ste. 400
Brenton Financial Ctr., Ste 400
Cedar Rapids, Iowa 52401
Salary Minimum: $25,000
Key Contact: Fritz Weber
Wanda Weber
Cindy Lyness
Marlene Miller
Sara Henton

Functions: 02.0 02.1 02.2 03.0 04.0
Industries: D.00 D.10 D.19 D.22 D.I0
Professional Affiliations: SME
Description: Tenured staff, over 50 years recruiting experience; professional & confidential

Management Recruiters of Topeka, Inc.

3400 SW Van Buren
Topeka, Kansas 66611
Salary Minimum: $25,000
Key Contact: Kirk Hawkins

Functions: Most
Industries: B.0W D.22 H.10 I.14 I.19

Management Recruiters of Frederick, Inc.

201 Thomas Johnson Dr., Ste. 202
Frederick, Maryland 21702
Key Contact: Richard Bates

Functions: 01.1 01.2 05.3 05.4 11.5
Industries: B.0W I.14 I.15 I.16
Description: Specialize in healthcare,
pharmaceutical, biomedical &
environmental industries

Management Recruiters of Dearborn, Inc.

3 Parklane Blvd., Ste. 1224
Parklane Towers West
Dearborn, Michigan 48126
Salary Minimum: $25,000
Key Contact: William J. Tripp

Functions: Most + 07.0 08.0 09.0 10.0 11.5
Industries: B.0W D.00 H.I0 I.18 I.19
Description: Confidential recruitment &
placement of mid. mgmt & professionals
in most functional disciplines

Management Recruiters of North Oakland County, Inc.

1000 W. University Dr., Ste. 303
Rochester, Michigan 48307
Salary Minimum: $20,000
Key Contact: Mark R. Angott
H. L. Westley

Functions: Most
Industries: D.00 D.23 H.10 I.10 I.14 I.19
Professional Affiliations: ASM, ASQC, ESD,
JS, SME
Description: Specialize in the accounting/
financial, banking engineering, medical &
data processing areas

Management Recruiters of Reno

1575 Delucchi Ln., Ste. 205
Meadowood Crown Plz.
Reno, Nevada 89502-6582
Key Contact: Ed Trapp

Functions: 01.4 02.4 03.3 08.2 10.0
Industries: B.0W D.19 D.D0 D.H0 H.I0

Management Recruiters of Middlesex County NJ.

984 Rte. 9, Ste. 5
Parlin, New Jersey 08859
Key Contact: Herbert Hardbrod

Functions: 05.0 05.1 05.2 05.3
Industries: D.18 I.16 J.10
Professional Affiliations: NJAPC
Description: Specializing in pharmaceutical/
healthcare industry, marketing &
advertising

Management Recruiters of Passaic, inc.

1373 Broad St., 2nd Fl.
Sutton Plz.
Clifton, New Jersey 07013-4221
Key Contact: Brian Wittlin

Functions: 04.0 11.0 11.3 11.5 11.6
Industries: B.0W B.10 D.15 D.18 D.I0
Description: Focused technical/professional/
management placement for chemical
engineers & chemists

Management Recruiters of Stanhope Corp.

4 Waterloo Rd.
Waterloo Executive Plz.
Stanhope, New Jersey 07874
Salary Minimum: $25,000
Key Contact: Arthur Young
Janet Joyce

Functions: 01.4 05.0 05.3 09.0 09.1
Industries: G.00 H.I0 I.10 I.18 J.13
Description: Our specialties include: local &
wide area networks SLS & SLS support

Management Recruiters of Nassau, Inc.

77 N. Centre Ave., Ste. 211
Rockville Centre, New York 11570
Key Contact: Thomas Wieder
William Jose

Functions: 01.0 05.3 05.4 08.2 11.5
Industries: B.0W D.18 H.00 I.16
Description: No excuses, no alibis; Just
maximum recruiting performance

Management Recruiters of Ft. Myers, FL.

4100 Center Pointe Dr., Ste. 105
Ft. Myers, Florida 33916-9450
Salary Minimum: $30,000
Key Contact: Calvin Beals
Charlotte Beals
R.J. Lynge

Functions: 01.0 02.0 03.0 08.0 10.0
Industries: B.0W D.12 H.10 H.I0 I.14
Description: Specializing in recruiting on a
national basis & management consulting

Management Recruiters of Hendersonville, inc.

Four Seasons Blvd., Ste. 149
Four Seasons Mall
Hendersonville, North Carolina 28792
Salary Minimum: $30,000
Key Contact: Frank J. Schoff

Functions: 01.4 09.7 11.1
Industries: Most + I.14 J.13
Description: Specializing in end user
telecommunications & healthcare
professionals

Management Recruiters of Kinston

Village Square, Hwy. 258 N.
P.O. Box 219
Kinston, North Carolina 28502-0219
Salary Minimum: $30,000
Key Contact: Bill E. Thomas

Functions: 02.0 03.0 06.0
Industries: D.22 D.23 D.24 H.10 I.14
Description: Recruit engineering,
manufacturing, healthcare & banking
professionals & managers

Management Recruiters of Butler County

4830 Interstate Dr.
Heitman Centre Tri-County
Cincinnati, Ohio 45246-1114
Salary Minimum: $40,000
Key Contact: James J. Cimino
Steve Storer
Terry Cimino

Functions: Most + 01.3 02.1 02.2 02.4 06.0
Description: Nationally recognized in
manufacturing, human resource &
engineering recruitment & placement

Management Recruiters

5801 E. 41st St., Ste. 440
Tulsa, Oklahoma 74135-5614
Salary Minimum: $30,000
Key Contact: Tony Wolters

Functions: Most
Industries: Most + I.14

Management Recruiters

440 E. Swedesford Rd., Ste. 3050
Valley Forge S.
Wayne, Pennsylvania 19087
Key Contact: John P. Zerkle, Sr.

Functions: 01.4 05.0 07.0 10.0 11.5
Industries: Most + H.I0 I.14 I.15 I.18
Description: Specializing in sales, financial,
administrative, technical, insurance &
EDP areas

Management Recruiters

435 Broad St., P.O. Box 69
Sewickley, Pennsylvania 15143
Key Contact: Richard Lampl
Joni Lampl

Industries: Most + B.0W C.00 H.I0 I.14 I.15
Description: Law, data processing,
medical(DRS), medical sales, engineering
designers, construction, insurance

Management Recruiters

529 Reading Ave., Ste. J
Berkshire Plz.
West Reading, Pennsylvania 19611
Salary Minimum: $40,000
Key Contact: Robert E. O'Hayer

Functions: 01.2 02.0 03.0 08.0
Industries: D.11 D.13 D.22 D.26 H.00
Description: Accounting, finance, banking, eng.,
materials management; apparel, paper,
general manufacturing

Management Recruiters

P.O. Box 730
Aiken, South Carolina 29802-0730
Key Contact: Michael Hardwick

Functions: Most
Industries: Most
Description: Nationwide industry specialists for
the industries we serve

Management Recruiters Treasure Coast, Inc.

576 SE Port St. Lucie Blvd.
Magic Plaza Bldg.
Port St. Lucie, Florida 34984
Key Contact: Arthur J. Sheehan
Patricia M. Sheehan

Functions: Most
Industries: I.14 I.16
Description: Our specialty is healthcare
"There's no substitute for knowing your
industry"

Management Recruiters

1009 W. Randol Mill Rd., Ste. 209
Arlington, Texas 76012
Salary Minimum: $30,000
Key Contact: Robert J. Stoessel

Functions: Most
Professional Affiliations: MAPC, TAPC
Description: 18 years experience recruiting
engineering, manufacturing, insurance &
graphic arts

Management Recruiters of Atlanta West, Inc.

685 Thorton Way
Lithia Springs, Georgia 30057-1579
Salary Minimum: $35,000
Key Contact: Gene Brown
Steven W. Kendall

Functions: 01.0 04.0 05.0
Industries: D.15 I.14
Description: We have the largest network of
offices & recruiters

Management Recruiters of Gramercy, Inc.

200 Park Ave. S., Ste. 1510
New York, New York 10003
Key Contact: Stephen D. Schwartz
James K. Harrafan
Jospeh W. Hatcher

Functions: Most + 01.0 01.1 05.0 05.1 08.0
Industries: Most + D.00 D.H0 H.00 I.10 J.00
Description: Consumate professionals,
commited to the pursuit of excellence

Management Recruiters

19109 36th Ave. W., Ste. 208
Alderwood Business Ctr.
Lynnwood, Washington 98036-5767
Salary Minimum: $30,000
Key Contact: Bud Naff

Functions: 01.1 01.2 01.3 11.6
Industries: B.10 I.14
Description: Recruitment & placement of
professionals in the environmental
consulting, eng. & healthcare indus.

Management Recruiters

5007 Carriage Dr. SW
Roanoke, Virginia 24018-2200
Key Contact: Daniel W. Dowdy
Keith Zillifro

Functions: 02.0 02.2 02.4 05.0 05.4
Industries: B.10 D.13 D.15 D.22
Professional Affiliations: TAPPI
Description: Paper industry: technical,
production, management & supplier sales,
service, marketing

Management Recruiters

375 Bishops Way, Ste. 150
Corporate Woods
Brookfield, Wisconsin 53005-6200
Salary Minimum: $35,000
Key Contact: William C. Healy
Peder Medtlie

Functions: Most + 11.3 11.5 11.6
Industries: Most
Description: Specializing in middle
management & professional people; most
industries, including healthcare

Management Recruiters of Charlotte—Southwest

4600 Lebanon Rd., Ste. A
Charlotte, North Carolina 28227
Salary Minimum: $30,000
Key Contact: David K. Camp
Frank A. Quinn

Functions: 01.0 02.0 03.0 05.0 06.0
Industries: B.00 B.0W B.10 D.00 I.14
Description: Nations largest contingency search
firm with access to nationwide referral
system

Management Recruiters of Wilmington

4006 Oleander Dr., Ste. 4-B
Oleander Office Park
Wilmington, North Carolina 28403
Salary Minimum: $30,000
Key Contact: Harry L. Bargholz

Functions: 02.0 02.2 02.4 06.0
Industries: D.00 D.15 D.17 D.18 D.20
Professional Affiliations: SHRM
Description: MRW provides professional
recruiting services directed at individual
needs

Management Recruiters of North Brunswick, Inc.

669 Nassau St., Ste. 5
North Brunswick, New Jersey 08902
Salary Minimum: $30,000
Key Contact: Raymond Sadow

Functions: 01.3 01.4 02.0 08.0 09.3
Industries: Most + D.00 I.18 I.19 J.11
Description: Largest contingency search firm in
U.S.

Management Recruiters of Westchester, Inc.

570 Taxter Rd.
Robert Martin Bldg.
Elmsford, New York 10523
Salary Minimum: $50,000
Key Contact: R.P. Neuffer
Larry Schanbacher
Dennis O'Brian

Functions: 01.3 02.2 04.0 05.3 11.3
Industries: D.10 D.16 D.17 D.18 D.H0
Description: Middle management,
pharmaceuticals, engineering, packaged
goods, manufacturing, international

Management Recruiters

8310 N. Capital of Texas Hwy.
Prominent Pointe, Ste. 400
Austin, Texas 78731-1024
Salary Minimum: $30,000
Key Contact: Lorraine Keller

Industries: D.15 D.19 D.I0 I.14
Professional Affiliations: TAPC
Description: Biomedical research & the petro
chemicals are our specialties.

Management Recruiters

1590 Ponce De Leon, Ste. 112
General Computer Bldg.
Rio Piedras, Puerto Rico 00926-2702
Salary Minimum: $9,600
Key Contact: Carlos R. Rodriguez

Functions: Most + 02.0 03.0 05.0 08.0 09.0
Industries: Most + B.0W D.00 D.H0 F.00
H.00
Professional Affiliations: SME
Description: Bi-lingual, bi-cultural talent for
Puerto Rico, the Caribbean & Latin
America

Management Recruiters of Berkeley

2150 Shattuck Ave., Ste. 610
Berkeley, California 94704-1306
Salary Minimum: $35,000
Key Contact: Richard H. Howard

Functions: Most + 01.3 08.0 09.1
Industries: D.00 H.00 H.10 I.14 I.15
Description: Franchise of industry leading
contingency company

Management Recruiters of El Dorado

5011 Golden Foothill Pkwy., Ste. 2
El Dorado Hills, California 95630-9633
Key Contact: Charles B. Stafford
JoDene Stafford

Functions: 01.3 11.0 11.3 11.5 11.6
Industries: B.0W B.10 L.00
Description: Our account executives are
specialized—leading to in-depth industry
knowledge & mrkt penetration

Management Recruiters

2055 Gateway Place, Ste. 420
San Jose, California 95110
Salary Minimum: $30,000
Key Contact: Ron Whitney

Functions: Most + 03.4 04.0 05.4 08.2 11.3

Management Recruiters of Middlesex

154 West St., Bldg. 3, Unit C
Cromwell, Connecticut 06416-2425
Key Contact: Leslie C. Cole

Functions: 01.3 05.3 05.4
Industries: B.10 D.15 D.16 D.17 D.19
Description: Twelve years experience in
recruiting sales/marketing & management
individuals

Management Recruiters of Tampa North

4012 Gunn Hwy., Ste. 140
Tampa, Florida 33624-4724
Salary Minimum: $30,000
Key Contact: Gary King
Gail King

Functions: 02.5 10.0 11.0 11.1 11.5
Industries: B.0W D.13 D.D0 H.I0 I.14

Management Recruiters of Poughkeepsie, Inc.

2 Summit Ct., Ste. 302
Fishkill, New York 12524-1333
Salary Minimum: $30,000
Key Contact: Michael Gionta

Functions: 05.1 09.2 09.4 09.7
Industries: D.24 I.14 I.18 J.13
Description: Specialize in computer sales,
marketing & healthcare

Management Recruiters of Cincinnati/Sharonville, Inc.

4050 Executive Park Dr., Ste. 125
Cincinnati, Ohio 45241-2020
Salary Minimum: $25,000
Key Contact: William O'Reilly

Functions: Most + 01.0 02.0 02.2 08.0 11.5
Industries: Most + B.0W D.00 D.15 D.19
D.D0
Description: National retained & contingency
executive search firm

Management Recruiters

20600 Chagrin Blvd., Ste. 703
Cleveland, Ohio 44122
Salary Minimum: $40,000
Key Contact: Robert Gandee

Functions: Most + 01.0 05.4 08.0
Industries: D.00 I.14 I.15
Description: Sales/salesmanagement &
healthcare positions throughout the U.S.

Management Recruiters

350 S. Reynolds Rd.
Toledo, Ohio 43615
Salary Minimum: $35,000
Key Contact: John C. Brauninger

Functions: Most
Industries: Most
Description: Full service, part of 600 office
national service

Management Recruiters

3925 Reed Blvd., Ste. 200
Murrysville, Pennsylvania 15668-1852
Salary Minimum: $3,000
Key Contact: Frank Williamson

Functions: 02.1 02.3 04.0 05.4 08.0
Description: Chemical: sales, marketing, tech
support; fluid power: sales, sales mgmt,
marketing, applications

Management Recruiters

1224 W. Evans St., Ste. B
P.O. Box 5320
Florence, South Carolina 29501-3322
Salary Minimum: $35,000
Key Contact: Richard Harrington
JoAn Harrington
Skip Middleton

Functions: 03.0 06.0 11.2 11.6
Professional Affiliations: APICS
Description: MRI offers access to positions
through all 600 offices

Management Recruiters
611 N. Main, Ste. A
Columbia, Tennessee 38401-3303
Key Contact: Roger H. Marriott
Gloria A. Marriott

Functions: 05.4

Management Recruiters
15400 Knoll Trail, Ste. 230
Dallas, Texas 75248-3465
Salary Minimum: $30,000
Key Contact: John Burkholder

Functions: 06.0 10.0
Description: National practice in insurance at
the professional and executive level.

Management Recruiters of Ashville, Inc.
22 S. Pack Sq., Ste. 302
Asheville, North Carolina 28801
Salary Minimum: $25,000
Key Contact: Paul M. Rumson
Barbara A. Rumson

Functions: Most + 02.1 02.3 02.5 04.0 11.3
Industries: Most
Description: Search & recruitment specialists
for upper & middle management
professionals

Management Resource Assoc., Inc.
P.O. Box 3266
Boca Raton, Florida 33427
Salary Minimum: $40,000
Key Contact: Gerald Schneiderman
Sheila Schneiderman

Functions: Most + 02.0 03.0 05.0 08.0 09.0
Industries: Most + D.00 D.E0 D.H0 H.00
Professional Affiliations: FEI, NAER
Description: A dynamic middle to upper
management, management search firm

Management Resources
P.O. Box 243
Bala Cynwyd, Pennsylvania 19004
Salary Minimum: $40,000
Key Contact: Harry L. Dunlavy
Teri O'Brien

Functions: 04.0 05.0 11.3 11.5
Industries: B.0W D.15 D.20
Description: Recruiting in research &
development & marketing

Management Resource Group, Inc.
77 Bleecker St., Ste. 124
New York, New York 10012
Salary Minimum: $40,000
Key Contact: Matthew J. DeLuca
Grace Eremin

Functions: Most
Industries: H.10 H.11 H.12 H.I0
Professional Affiliations: NYPMA, SHRM
Description: Clients primarily major
commercial banks - also recruit for
personnel/human resources

Management Search, Inc.
Jackson Tower Bldg.
806 SW Broadway, Ste 550
Portland, Oregon 97205
Salary Minimum: $25,000
Key Contact: Douglas J. Calder, Jr.

Functions: 02.2 02.4 05.2 05.4 08.0
Industries: D.12 D.13 D.22
Professional Affiliations: NAPC
Description: Experienced professionals in
executive & technical search since 1958

Management Search, Inc.
2800 W. Country Club Dr.
Oklahoma City, Oklahoma 73116
Salary Minimum: $25,000
Key Contact: David L. Orwig

Functions: 01.4 09.2 09.3 09.4 09.7
Industries: A.00
Description: Agriculture technical positions;
also data processing positions

Management Search Int'l.
15375 Barranca Pkwy., Ste. B-205
Irvine, California 92718
Salary Minimum: $40,000
Key Contact: Scott J. Sawyer
Jess J. Lee

Functions: Most + 01.0 05.0 08.0 09.0
Industries: Most + D.00 H.R0 I.00 J.00
Professional Affiliations: NAPC
Description: Low volume, highly personalized
full service firm, finance/accounting
emphasis

Management Search, Inc.
500 N. Michigan Ave., Ste. 1920
Chicago, Illinois 60611
Key Contact: Stefan Levy

Functions: Most + 08.0 09.7 11.5
Industries: Most + D.00 D.24 D.H0 H.I0 J.00
Professional Affiliations: IAPC, NAPC
Description: Reduced cost per hire; recruitment results for select clients

Marcus & Assoc.
345 Kear St.
Yorktown Heights, New York 10598
Salary Minimum: $40,000
Key Contact: Alvin B. Marcus
Catherine McKenna
Brian Sloane
Dean Kaplan
J. Christopher Sherman
Doreen Rosenblatt
Thomas O'Connor

Functions: Most + 01.0 02.0 04.0 05.0 06.0
Industries: D.18 D.H0 D.I0 I.14 I.16
Professional Affiliations: NAER
Description: General firm specializing in recruitment for scientific oriented businesses

Margolin Consultants, Inc.
185 Madison Ave., 5th Fl.
New York, New York 10016
Salary Minimum: $35,000
Key Contact: Efraim Margolin

Functions: Most
Industries: Most
Description: Int'l./nat'l. capabilities for executive search, product development, mkt research & joint ventures

Mariaschin & Co.
150 E. 52nd St.
New York, New York 10022
Salary Minimum: $60,000
Key Contact: Mark A. Mariaschin

Functions: 01.0 01.2 01.3 06.0 06.1
Industries: H.00 H.10 H.11 H.12
Description: Specialty senior management for major banks & investment management firms

Mark III Personnel, Inc.
4801 E. Independence Blvd.
Ste. 604
Charlotte, North Carolina 28212
Salary Minimum: $35,000
Key Contact: Lindsay Allen

Functions: Most
Industries: Most
Professional Affiliations: NCAPC
Description: Specialize in all engineering, research & developement, banking

MarketSearch, Inc.
216 N. Green Bay Rd., Ste. 111
Thiensville, Wisconsin 53092
Salary Minimum: $35,000
Key Contact: Linda Klobasa Barkwill
Randy Banas

Functions: 05.0 05.1 05.2 05.3 05.5
Industries: D.10 D.11 D.13 D.16 D.26
Professional Affiliations: NAPC, WAPC
Description: Executive recruitment-marketing, market research, advertising, sales promotion, public relations

Marketing Recruiters, Inc.
P.O. Box 4098
Asheboro, North Carolina 27204
Salary Minimum: $30,000
Key Contact: Rass Bagley

Functions: Most + 05.2 05.3 05.4
Industries: D.10 D.18 D.22 D.23
Description: We specialize in finding & placing sales & marketing professionals

Marketing Resource
18 North Rd.
Chelmsford, Massachusetts 01824
Salary Minimum: $50,000
Key Contact: Joseph D. Sheedy

Functions: 05.0 05.2 05.3 05.4 05.6
Industries: D.17 D.18 D.25 D.I0
Description: Executive search & placement services for medical marketing or sales

Marley Group Ltd.
216 E. 18th St.
New York, New York 10003
Salary Minimum: $60,000
Key Contact: K.C. Victor

Functions: 01.5
Industries: I.17
Description: Legal executive recruiting-associates, partners, counsel, mergers; contingency & retainer

Karen Marshall Assoc.
6304 Deep Creek Dr.
Prospect, Kentucky 40059
Salary Minimum: $30,000
Key Contact: Karen Marshall
Dennis Marshall

Functions: 01.0 09.0
Industries: Most + D.00 H.I0 I.14
Professional Affiliations: DPMA
Description: Personnel search & placement specializing in MIS professionals & executives

Donovan Martin & Assoc.
1000 Elwell Ct., Ste. 217
Palo Alto, California 94303
Salary Minimum: $50,000
Key Contact: Donovan Martin

Functions: Most + 01.0 02.0 03.0 04.0 05.0
Industries: D.D0 D.H0 D.I0
Description: Executive & professional search services, from large companies to start-ups

Martin Personnel Assoc.
100 W. Mount Pleasant Ave.
Livingston, New Jersey 07039
Salary Minimum: $30,000
Key Contact: Martin Untermeyer

Functions: 01.2 01.3 05.0 05.4
Industries: C.00 D.00 D.18 D.22 D.25
Description: Sales, sales management, marketing, executive search

Masserman & Assoc.
30 Myano Ln., Ste. 36
Stamford, Connecticut 06902
Key Contact: Bruce Masserman

Functions: 01.4 05.5 09.3 09.4
Industries: Most
Description: Specializing in the placement of MIS & marketing professionals

Richard L. Mather & Assoc.
P.O. Box 1183
Glastonbury, Connecticut 06033
Salary Minimum: $35,000
Key Contact: Richard L. Mather

Functions: Most
Industries: B.00 B.0W D.00 D.E0 D.H0
Professional Affiliations: IACPR, NAPC
Description: Specializing in manufacturing & engineering professional & management recruiting

Mathey Services
RR 2 Box 147
Sycamore, Illinois 60178
Salary Minimum: $30,000
Key Contact: Joyce Mathey

Functions: 01.0 02.0 04.0 05.0 05.4
Industries: D.15 D.19 D.D0
Professional Affiliations: IACPR, SPE
Description: Executive recruitment services for the plastics & chemicals industries, nationwide

Matthews Professional Employment Specialists, Inc.
321 Grand Ave.
Waukegan, Illinois 60085
Salary Minimum: $20,000
Key Contact: Charles W. Matthews

Functions: Most
Industries: Most
Professional Affiliations: NAPC, NATS
Description: Contingency professional/technical & support staff search & placement

Branches:
311 E. Park Ave.
Libertyville, Illinois 60048
Key Contact: Jane E. Ross

505 N. Wolf Rd.
Wheeling, Illinois 60090
Key Contact: Debra Semple

Maximum Management Corp.

60 E. 42nd St., Ste. 2226
New York, New York 10165
Key Contact: Melissa Brophy
Nancy Shield

Functions: 06.0 06.1 06.2
Industries: D.18 D.24 J.00 J.13
Professional Affiliations: IACPR, EMA
Description: Human resource consulting,
contract recruiting & search firm

K. Maxin & Assoc.

Allegheny Ctr., Bldg. 10, Ste. 421
Pittsburgh, Pennsylvania 15212
Salary Minimum: $30,000
Key Contact: Keith A. Maxin

Functions: Most
Industries: B.0W C.00 H.00 H.R0
Description: Specializing in the construction &
real estate industries

Mary L. Mayer, Ltd.

641 E. Lake St., Ste. 205
Wayzata, Minnesota 55391
Salary Minimum: $30
Key Contact: Mary L. Mayer

Functions: 05.0 05.4 06.1 10.0
Industries: H.I0 I.14
Description: Property/casualty insurance, risk&
claims mgmt, loss control, marketing &
sales of insurance

The McCormick Group, Inc.

9000-B Crownwood Ct. 10
Burke, Virginia 22015
Salary Minimum: $50,000
Key Contact: William J. McCormick

Functions: 01.5 06.1 09.7 11.5
Industries: Most + B.0W H.I0 I.14 I.17
Professional Affiliations: NAPC
Description: Full service executive search &
placement company

McCracken, Wilcox, Bertoux & Miller

601 University Ave., Ste. 236
Sacramento, California 95825
Salary Minimum: $48,000
Key Contact: Fred T. Wilcox
Larry K. McCracken
Michael P. Bertoux
Diane Miller

Functions: 01.0 01.4 08.0 09.0 11.1
Industries: H.00 I.14 I.17 I.18 I.19
Professional Affiliations: NAER
Description: Executive search firm specializing
in middle & upper administrative &
financial managers

McCulloch Assoc.

346 Main St., P.O. Box 210
Chatham, New Jersey 07928
Salary Minimum: $40,000
Key Contact: John Donovan
William A. McCulloch

Functions: Most + 01.0 02.0 05.0 06.0 09.7
Industries: Most + D.00 D.24 D.H0 I.00
Description: Small firm, primarily focused on
high technology, telecommunications,
information systems

Earl L. McDermid & Assoc.

1834 Walden Office Sq., Ste. 150
Schaumburg, Illinois 60173
Salary Minimum: $25,000
Key Contact: Earl McDermid
W. John McGinnis

Functions: 01.0 04.0 05.0 06.0 08.0
Industries: D.00 D.10 I.00 I.10 I.11
Professional Affiliations: NAMA, SFM
Description: Recruiting for executive &
management positions in the food service
industry

McDermott & Assoc.

P.O. Box 798
Crystal Lake, Illinois 60014-0798
Salary Minimum: $30,000
Key Contact: Tom McDermott

Functions: Most + 02.0 04.0 05.0 11.5 11.6
Industries: Most + B.00 B.0W D.00 D.I0 H.00
Description: General industrial; specialty-
environmental/process capital equipment/
services; banking

Sandi McDonald & Assoc., Inc.

P.O. Box 68
Boystown, Nebraska 68010
Salary Minimum: $35,000
Key Contact: Sandi McDonald
Michele Gorman

Functions: Most + 01.4 02.0 09.0 09.4 09.7
Industries: D.24 D.H0 J.13
Description: Small sophisticated
   telecommunications search firm using
   electronic networking tools

McDonald Ledterman Executive Search

2425 E. Camelback Rd., Ste. 375
Phoenix, Arizona 85016
Salary Minimum: $50,000
Key Contact: John R. McDonald

Functions: Most
Professional Affiliations: NPA
Description: Retainer/partial retainer firm
   specializing in high technology executive
   placement

McGladrey Search Group

400 Locust St., Ste. 690
Des Moines, Iowa 50309
Salary Minimum: $20,000
Key Contact: Thomas Hamilton
Loren Jacobson

Functions: Most
Industries: D.00 H.00 H.I0 I.00
Professional Affiliations: NAER, NAPC
Description: Serving Midwestern clients in
   managerial,sales & technical positions

McGuire Executive Search, Inc.

7575 Dr. Phillips Blvd., Ste. 211
Orlando, Florida 32819
Salary Minimum: $20,000
Key Contact: Harry McGuire

Functions: 01.0 05.0 06.0 08.0 11.0
Industries: I.00 I.10 I.11 I.14 I.19
Description: Management recruiters for hotels,
   resorts, restaurants, clubs conference
   centers & marinas

R. H. McIlwaine & Assoc.

P.O. Box 115
Deerfield, Illinois 60015
Key Contact: Roy H. McIlwaine
Carol Ottemann

Functions: 01.3 05.4 09.3
Industries: D.24
Description: Salesman & sales management &
   sales support recruiting for information
   technology companies

McInturff & Assoc., Inc.

209 G West Central St.
Natick, Massachusetts 01760
Salary Minimum: $35,000
Key Contact: Robert E. McInturff, Jr.

Functions: 02.0 03.0
Industries: D.00 D.H0 E.00
Professional Affiliations: APICS, ASQC, IEEE,
   MPPC, SME
Description: Over 15 years as specialists in
   materials & manufacturing management
   recruiting

The McKee Co.

404 Pharr Rd.
Ste. A-202
Atlanta, Georgia 30305
Salary Minimum: $100,000
Key Contact: Edward F. McKee

Functions: 02.2 02.3 02.5 05.4 11.5
Industries: B.10 D.00 D.H0 J.13
Professional Affiliations: ASME, IEEE, ISA
Description: Recruiters who specialize in
   locating technically qualified persons, job
   design/sales

John McLellan Assoc., Inc.

230 Park Ave., Ste. 1910
New York, New York 10169
Salary Minimum: $50,000
Key Contact: John H. McLellan

Industries: B.00 H.00 H.10 H.11
Description: Specialty recruiter for municipal
   finance & bond investments

McRoberts & Assoc.
24600 Center Ridge Rd., Ste. 125
Cleveland, Ohio 44145
Salary Minimum: $40,000
Key Contact: C.F. McRoberts
Jack Steele

Functions: Most
Industries: Most
Description: Generalists with emphasis on technical searches

Joseph J. McTaggart
P.O. Box 785
Campbell, California 95009
Salary Minimum: $40,000
Key Contact: Joseph J. McTaggart

Functions: Most
Industries: Most
Description: General management-every candidate I have ever moved is better off now

Meads & Assoc.
4420 Orangewood Loop, E.
Lakeland, Florida 33813
Salary Minimum: $35,000
Key Contact: Walter F. Meads

Functions: 05.1
Industries: J.10
Professional Affiliations: NAER
Description: Specialists in executive recruitment for advertising agencies

Medical Executive Search Assoc.
3250 N. Riverbend Cirle E.
Tucson, Arizona 85715
Salary Minimum: $30,000
Key Contact: William L. Piatkiewicz
Mary Lou Piatkiewicz

Functions: 01.0 02.0 03.0 04.0 05.0 11.3
Industries: D.15 D.17 D.18 D.I0 I.16
Description: Eight years of recruitment in the medical device industry with contacts in 1500+ major firms

Medical Sales & Management Specialists
1515 N. Warson Rd., Ste. 257
St. Louis, Missouri 63132
Key Contact: Karen Mendrala
Eric Ivers

Functions: 01.2 01.3 05.4
Industries: D.18 D.I0
Professional Affiliations: NAPC
Description: Lab sales & lab sales management positions

Medquest Assoc.
9250 E. Costilla Ave., Ste. 600
Englewood, Colorado 80112
Salary Minimum: $30,000
Key Contact: Judy Stiles

Functions: 01.0 02.0 03.0 04.0 05.0
Industries: D.00 D.18 D.25 D.H0 D.I0
Description: Nationwide medical device industry recruiting

Medtrac & Assoc.
P.O. Box 309
Tustin, California 92681-0309
Salary Minimum: $50,000
Key Contact: Ed Shipcott

Functions: 01.0 02.0 04.0 05.0 11.0
Industries: D.18 D.I0 I.14 I.16
Description: Executive search consulting-health care industry, most positions

Todd Melon Group
1888 Century Park E., Ste. 1900
Los Angeles, California 90067
Salary Minimum: $60,000
Key Contact: Todd Melon
Brent Tiffany

Functions: 01.0 02.0 04.0 05.0 08.0
Industries: D.00 D.11
Description: Placement mid-upper management manufacturing, marketing, design, apparel related

Mengel & McDonald Ltd.
650 N. Dearborn, Ste. 750
Chicago, Illinois 60610
Salary Minimum: $50,000
Key Contact: Thomas W. McDonald
Nancy R. Mengel

Functions: 05.1
Industries: J.10 J.12
Professional Affiliations: CAC, WACC
Description: National executive search specializing in upper-level advertising professionals

Meridian Personnel Assoc., Inc.
25 W. 43rd St., Ste. 700
New York, New York 10036
Salary Minimum: $50,000
Key Contact: Joel Berger

Functions: 01.5
Industries: I.14 I.15 I.16 I.17
Professional Affiliations: APCNY, NALSC
Description: Attorney recruitment organization
(founded 1936) corporate, law firm; not
for profit

Merlin Int'l. Inc.
P.O. Box 313
Ramsey, New Jersey 07446
Salary Minimum: $50,000
Key Contact: V. James Cinquina
Robert Matheson
Alan Fitzpatrick

Branches:
P.O. Box 549, Van Brunt Station
Brooklyn, New York 11215

Functions: Most + 02.1 02.4 02.5 05.2 11.3
Industries: Most + D.18
Professional Affiliations: NAER
Description: Specialized to pharmaceutical
industry, research, development,
marketing & advertising services

Merrick & Moore
22 Broad St.
Asheville, North Carolina 28801
Salary Minimum: $30,000
Key Contact: Barbara J. Bauman

Functions: 02.1 02.5 03.4 04.0 05.0
Industries: D.00 D.13 D.15 D.D0
Professional Affiliations: NAER
Description: Direct recruiting specialists in
paper, nonwovens & their supplier
industries

Olaf S. Meyer & Co., Ltd.
250 E Hartsdale Ave., Ste. 31
Hartsdale, New York 10530
Salary Minimum: $75,000
Key Contact: Olaf S. Meyer
Stephen A. McCord
Joan C. Levine

Functions: 01.2 01.3 08.2 10.0
Industries: H.10 H.11
Description: Highly respected for performance
& honesty in treasury, capital market &
private banking search

Michael/Merrill
Box 7509
Shawnee Mission, Kansas 66207
Salary Minimum: $25,000
Key Contact: Wilson M. Liggett

Functions: 01.3 01.4 09.3
Industries: D.10 I.15
Description: A full service search firm

Lou Michaels Assoc.
12200 E. Michigan Ave.
Battle Creek, Michigan 49017
Salary Minimum: $25,000
Key Contact: Lou Michaels
Mike Schulz
Kib Snow

Functions: Most
Industries: D.13 D.19 D.22 D.23 D.26
Professional Affiliations: AFS, MAPC, SPE
Description: Engineering & management/metal
machining & fabrication, plastics &
process foundry, die cast

B. Paul Mickey & Assoc.
11 Stanwix St., Ste. 518
6 Gateway Ctr.
Pittsburgh, Pennsylvania 15222
Salary Minimum: $40,000
Key Contact: B. Paul Mickey

Functions: Most + 01.0 06.0 11.1 11.5
Industries: B.0W C.00 D.22 H.R0
Description: Search, recruitment & human
resource consulting practice

Midgette Consultants, Inc.

182 Grand St., Ste. 421
Waterbury, Connecticut 06702
Salary Minimum: $40,000
Key Contact: Earl W. Midgette

Functions: 02.0 03.1 03.2 06.0 08.0
Industries: D.15 D.17 D.18 D.19 D.22
Description: Technical & professional search
and contingency recruiters, 15 years
experience

Midland Consultants

4715 State Rd.
Cleveland, Ohio 44109
Key Contact: David J. Sgro

Functions: Most
Industries: D.14 D.15 D.19 D.22 D.H0
Professional Affiliations: GCAPC, NAPC,
OAPC
Description: Specialists in the rubber, plastic &
adhesive industries

Midwest Medical Consultants

8910 Purdue Rd., Ste. 200
Indianapolis, Indiana 46268-1155
Salary Minimum: $25,000
Key Contact: Richard Carroll

Functions: 07.0
Industries: I.14 I.15
Professional Affiliations: IAPC, NAPC
Description: Nationwide hospital contingency
recruitment firm specializing in
administrative & clinical search

Midwest Medical Recruiters

12935 W. Bayshore Dr., Ste. 450
Traverse City, Michigan 49684
Salary Minimum: $30,000
Key Contact: Kit E. Schroeder
Daniel J. White

Functions: 01.1 06.1 06.2
Industries: I.14 I.15 I.21
Description: Placement of physicians,
healthcare executives & medical ancillary
service staff

Milgram & Assoc.

100 Adelaide St. W., Ste. 502
Toronto, Ontario M5H 1S3 Canada
Salary Minimum: $50,000
Key Contact: David Milgram

Functions: 01.2 01.3 05.4 09.7 10.0
Industries: B.00 G.00 H.I0 I.10 J.13
Professional Affiliations: IACPR
Description: Personalized personality
matchmaking by clinical therapist

Robert E. Mills, FLMI

2319 Smith Ave.
Marietta, Georgia 30064
Salary Minimum: $25,000
Key Contact: Robert E. Mills

Functions: 01.0 05.6 06.0 09.0 10.0
Industries: H.I0 I.18
Description: Professional, management &
executive recruiting for insurance,
financial services industries

Mogul Consultants, Inc.

380 N. Broadway
Jericho, New York 11753
Salary Minimum: $40,000
Key Contact: Gene Mogul

Functions: 02.0 05.2 09.2 09.7 11.3
Industries: D.24 H.10 H.11 J.12 J.13
Professional Affiliations: IEEE
Description: Search & contingency in the
telecommunications industry &
telecommunications users

Diedre Moire Corp., Inc.

579 Cranbury Rd., Ste. C
East Brunswick, New Jersey 08816
Key Contact: Stephen M. Reuning
Todd Kostrub
John Earl
Gregory Foss
Robert Posluzny

Functions: Most + 01.0 02.0 04.0 09.0 11.0
Industries: Most + D.I0
Professional Affiliations: NAPC, NJAPC
Description: "Retainer quality" search without
the retainer

George J. Mollo Assoc.

50 Main St., Ste. 1000
White Plains, New York 10606
Salary Minimum: $30,000
Key Contact: George J. Mollo

Functions: 08.0 08.1 08.2 08.3 08.4
Industries: Most
Professional Affiliations: FEI
Description: Specialize in accounting and financial talent, former Fortune 50 financial executive

Montaigne Assoc., Inc.

83 East Ave., Ste. 115
Norwalk, Connecticut 06851
Salary Minimum: $60,000
Key Contact: Stellan P. Wollmar
Howard S. Levine

Functions: Most
Industries: D.00 H.00 H.10 H.11 H.12
Description: "Niche" firm dealing almost exclusively with banks & investment banks

Networks:
International Search Partners (ISPA)
Barcelona, Dusseldorf, Ecully, Geneve, High Wycombe, Leusden, Milan, Morbio Inferiore, Nesoya, Vienna, Zurich

The Montanye Group

8940 S. Florence Pl.
Tulsa, Oklahoma 74136
Salary Minimum: $40,000
Key Contact: Michael Montanye

Functions: 01.0 02.0 04.0 05.0 11.0
Industries: B.0W D.00 D.H0 I.00
Professional Affiliations: ACS, ISHM, OAPC, SAMPE
Description: Specialities in ceramics, enviromental safety, health, engineering & legal

Montgomery Resources, Inc.

505 Montgomery St., Ste. 660
San Francisco, California 94111
Salary Minimum: $30,000
Key Contact: Roger A. Lee
Thomas K. McAteer

Functions: 08.0
Industries: Most + D.00 G.00 H.00 I.00
Professional Affiliations: AAFA
Description: Recruitment of finance & accounting professionals for middle-management positions

Moore Employment Svs., Inc.

P.O. Box 3882
Oak Brook, Illinois 60522-3882
Salary Minimum: $32,000
Key Contact: Ellie Moore
Tom Moore

Functions: 07.0 07.4 08.0 09.0 11.2
Industries: Most + D.13 D.14 D.17 I.12 I.19
Professional Affiliations: HRA
Description: Highly responsive solution oriented accounting & financial recruitment firm

Tina Morbitzer & Assoc.

668 N. Orlando Ave., Ste. 105
Maitland, Florida 32751
Salary Minimum: $20,000
Key Contact: Tina Morbitzer

Functions: 05.0 05.1
Industries: H.R0
Description: Recruiting real estate professionals for shopping centers & commercial property

Morency Assoc.

72 Holten St.
Danvers, Massachusetts 01923
Salary Minimum: $30,000
Key Contact: Marcia Morency

Functions: 01.4 03.0 05.0 08.0 09.3
Industries: Most
Professional Affiliations: MAPC
Description: Executive search for management professionals, providing very personal service

Morgan-Stampfl, Inc.
6 W. 32nd St., Ste. 909
New York, New York 10001
Salary Minimum: $50,000
Key Contact: David G. Morgan
Eric Stampfl

The Morris Group
40 Morris Ave.
Bryn Mawr, Pennsylvania 19010
Salary Minimum: $25,000
Key Contact: Paul T. Morris
J. A. Hall
Tom Meltser

Functions: 04.0 06.0 09.0 11.2 11.5
Industries: Most
Description: H/R, legal & pharmaceutical
industry R&D, including clinical MDs &
technical specialists

Mortgage & Financial Personnel Services
17071 Ventura Blvd., Ste. 201
Encino, California 91316
Salary Minimum: $25,000
Key Contact: Robert Sherman
Phyllis Shukiar
Doris Loper

Functions: 08.2 08.3 08.4
Industries: H.10 H.R0
Professional Affiliations: MBA
Description: A placement agency dedicated to
mortgage lending & banking industries

The C. B. Mueller Co., Inc.
550 E. Fourth St.
Cincinnati, Ohio 45202
Salary Minimum: $55,000
Key Contact: Clifford B. Mueller

Functions: 01.0 02.0 03.0 04.0 05.0
Industries: D.00 D.D0 H.00 I.00 K.00
Description: Management consultants...search
& recruitment... executive, management,
professional

Multi Processing, Inc.
3 Militia Dr.
Lexington, Massachusetts 02173
Salary Minimum: $40,000
Key Contact: Joseph Vito

Functions: 01.4 04.0 05.2 09.0
Industries: D.24 D.H0 J.00
Description: A complete recruiting and search
organization-emphasis on computer
professionals

Multisearch Recruiters
2851 Geer Rd., Ste. G
Turlock, California 95380
Salary Minimum: $25,000
Key Contact: Dennis Gallagher

Functions: Most + 01.0 02.0 04.0 05.0 11.0
Industries: Most + B.0W D.00 D.10 D.12
D.19
Professional Affiliations: IFT
Description: Generalist firm emphasizing the
food, plastics, building materials &
environmental industries

The Mulvey Group
400 S. Orange Ave.
South Orange, New Jersey 07079
Salary Minimum: $40,000
Key Contact: John J. Mulvey

Professional Affiliations: DPMA, IEEE
Description: Servicing data processing, both
marketing and technical

John H. Munson & Co.
14640 W. Greenfield Ave., Ste. 105
Brookfield, Wisconsin 53005
Salary Minimum: $40,000
Key Contact: John H. Munson

Functions: 01.0 01.2 02.0 02.1 03.0
Industries: D.00 D.10 D.12 D.D0 D.H0
Professional Affiliations: WAPC
Description: Sole proprietor search firm serving
primarily manufacturing & engineering

Murkett Assoc.

P.O. Box 527
Montgomery, Alabama 36101
Salary Minimum: $35,000
Key Contact: Philip T. Murkett, Jr.

Functions: Most
Industries: Most
Description: Corporate recruiters for managers,
professionals & technical personnel
nationally & internationally

Murphy, Symonds & Stowell Search, Inc.

One Centerpointe Dr., Ste. 570
P.O. Box 2429
Lake Oswego, Oregon 97035
Salary Minimum: $50,000
Key Contact: Linda Kozlowski
Andy Wihtol

Functions: 01.0 02.0 05.0 08.0 09.0
Industries: D.00 I.00 K.00
Description: Since 1968, executive search
specialists for the Pacific Northwest region

NPF Assoc. Ltd. Inc.

1999 University Dr., Ste. 405
Coral Springs, Florida 33071-6032
Salary Minimum: $40,000
Key Contact: Nick P. Fischler

Functions: 01.0 01.5 05.0 06.0 08.0
Industries: B.00 D.00 G.00 I.00
Professional Affiliations: IACPR, EMA, SHRM
Description: Executive search firm specializing
in human resources, marketing, financial
& legal

The NRI Group

11921 Rockville Pike, Ste. 500
Rockville, Maryland 20852
Salary Minimum: $20,000
Key Contact: Robert M. McClimans
Leslie A. Meil
Robert D. Mulberger

Functions: Most + 01.5 07.0 08.0 09.4 10.0
Industries: Most
Professional Affiliations: NAPC
Description: Operates in 6 disciplines in the
Metropolitan D.C. area and Richmond,
VA.

Branches:
1899 L St. NW, Ste. 302
Washington, District of Columbia 20036
Key Contact: Jean Allen

5203 Leesburg Pike, Ste. 500
Baileys Crossroads, Virginia 22041

Nachman Biomedical

60 Hickory Dr.
Waltham, Massachusetts 02154
Salary Minimum: $50,000
Key Contact: Philip S. Nachman

Functions: 01.0 02.0 04.0 05.0 11.3
Industries: D.18 D.19 D.25 D.I0
Description: Specialize in medical device,
medical electronics, instrumentation, biotechnology & pharmaceutical

Jerome H. Nagel Assoc.

1 Hanson Pl., Ste. 2001
Brooklyn, New York 11243
Salary Minimum: $20,000
Key Contact: Jerome H. Nagel

Functions: 01.2 01.3 05.1 05.2 05.4
Industries: D.10 D.18 D.22 D.24 D.25
Description: Management consultants in all
personnel areas-selection, training,
recruitment

Nagel Executive Search Inc.

376 John S. Mosby Dr.
Wilmington, North Carolina 28412
Salary Minimum: $25,000
Key Contact: Conrad A. Nagel

Functions: Most
Industries: D.11
Description: Specialists in the textile industry

The Naples Group, Inc.
841 4th Ave. S. P.O. Box 783
Naples, Florida 33939
Salary Minimum: $25,000
Key Contact: Brad Estes

Branches:
P.O. Box 8253
Gainesville, Florida 32605-8253
Key Contact: Patrick Estes

Functions: Most + 05.0 05.4 06.0 08.0
Industries: G.00 J.00 J.12
Description: A nationwide firm which
specializes in cable television

National Corporate Consultants, Inc.
5916 E. State Blvd.
Ft. Wayne, Indiana 46815
Salary Minimum: $35,000
Key Contact: James E. Corya
Steve Frey
Mary Beth Regan
Michael J. Melillo, Jr.
John Hope
Dorinda Heiden

Functions: Most + 02.0 06.0 08.0 09.0
Industries: Most + D.00 D.E0 D.H0
Description: National affiliate specializing in
mid/upper level professional &
management placement

National Executive Consultants, Inc.
8047 Cleveland Pl.
Merrillville, Indiana 46410
Salary Minimum: $35,000
Key Contact: Morris Stilley

Functions: 01.2 02.4 11.6
Industries: D.22
Description: Recruiting for salaried personnel;
maintenance, engineering of metals &
manufacturing

National Health Search, Inc.
9360 Sunset Dr., Ste. 250
Miami, Florida 33173
Salary Minimum: $60,000
Key Contact: Martin H. Osinski

Functions: 11.0
Industries: I.14 I.15
Professional Affiliations: NAPR
Description: A nationwide physician &
healthcare recruitment organization

National Hospitality Assoc., Inc.
P.O. Box 27965
Tempe, Arizona 85285
Salary Minimum: $15,000
Key Contact: Charles E. Steadmon

Industries: I.10
Professional Affiliations: AHMA, HSMA
Description: Training & consulting firm to the
hospitality industry

National Logistics Recruiters, Inc.
3 Whitney Pl.
Princeton Junction, New Jersey 08550
Salary Minimum: $30,000
Key Contact: Larry J. Rappaport

Functions: 02.0 03.0 05.2 05.4 11.0
Industries: Most
Professional Affiliations: ASTL, CLM
Description: Specializing exclusively in
transportation, distribution & materials
management, nation-wide

National Recruiting Service
P.O. Box 218, 1832 Hart St.
Dyer, Indiana 46311
Salary Minimum: $20,000
Key Contact: Stanley M. Hendricks, II
Dennis M. Toms

Functions: 01.2 01.3 02.4 02.5 05.4
Industries: D.19 D.22
Professional Affiliations: NAPC
Description: Specialist in steel tubular
products, basic metals & plastics
industries

National Search, Inc.
P.O. Box 5236
Woolsey Station, New York 11105
Key Contact: George Alexander
Victor Alexander

Functions: Most
Industries: Most
Description: Personalized & confident search
for career opportunities conducted
nationwide

J. Fielding Nelson & Assoc., Inc.
420 E. South Temple, Ste. 364
Salt Lake City, Utah 84111
Salary Minimum: $30,000
Key Contact: J. Fielding Nelson
Randy H. Craig
Stephen W. Swaner

Functions: Most + 01.0 02.0 05.0 08.0 09.0
Industries: Most + D.00 D.H0 H.00 I.00 J.00
Description: Mostly Mountain states-
management, technical, mfg., sales,
marketing, healthcare & finance

Beverly Nelson & Assoc. Inc.
3727 Camino Del Rio S., Ste. 200
San Diego, California 92108
Salary Minimum: $25,000
Key Contact: Beverly M. Nelson

Functions: 10.0
Industries: H.I0
Professional Affiliations: NIRA
Description: Specialty-placement of
management & technical personnel in the
property/casualty insurance area

Nelson Associates
425 California St., Ste. 606
San Francisco, California 94104
Salary Minimum: $25,000
Key Contact: Gary Nelson
Steve Perry
Tyler Yarbrough

Functions: 08.0 09.4
Industries: Most
Description: Executive recruitment in the areas
of finance, accounting, software &
hardware engineering

Nelson-Larson & Assoc. Ltd.
100 Corporate North, Ste. 205
Bannockburn, Illinois 60015-1255
Salary Minimum: $20,000
Key Contact: Bruce Larson

Functions: Most
Industries: Most
Description: Middle management contingency
search firm with a broad range of skill sets

William H. Nenstiel & Assoc.
4430 N. Civic Center Plz., Ste. 202
Scottsdale, Arizona 85251
Salary Minimum: $50,000
Key Contact: Marion S. Nenstiel
William H. Nenstiel

Functions: 01.3 02.4 04.0 05.2 05.4
Industries: D.13 D.14 D.D0
Description: Recruiting primarily for paper,
packaging & forest products industries-
retainer & contingency

The Network Companies
1595 Spring Hill Rd.
Vienna, Virginia 22182
Salary Minimum: $30,000
Key Contact: Theodore A. Bruccoleri

Functions: 01.4 08.0 09.0
Industries: Most
Description: Firm of experienced financial
executives offering career planning &
placement services

Branches:
1625 K St. NW., Ste 735
Washington, District of Columbia 20006
Key Contact: Barry A. Goldstein

New Dimensions in Technology, Inc.
67 Pleasant St., P.O. Box 267
Swampscott, Massachusetts 01907
Salary Minimum: $45,000
Key Contact: Beverly Kahn

Functions: 04.0 09.0 09.2 09.6 11.0
Industries: D.H0
Professional Affiliations: IACPR, MPPC
Description: Specialize in global new high-tech start-up & high technology industry

Newcombe & Cyr Assoc., Inc.
177 Worcester St., Ste. 303
Wellesley Hills, Massachusetts 02181
Salary Minimum: $45,000
Key Contact: Maury N. Cyr
Walter W. Newcombe

Functions: Most + 01.0 02.0 03.0 04.0 05.0
Industries: Most + D.00 D.10 D.11 D.D0 D.I0
Professional Affiliations: IFT, NEDMA
Description: Provide executive selection & consulting services to business & industry

Newton Assoc.
1470 Maria Ln., Ste. 220
Walnut Creek, California 94596
Salary Minimum: $20,000
Key Contact: Nancy C. Nolan

Functions: 08.0 08.1 08.2 08.3 08.4
Industries: Most
Description: Fourteen high quality professionals specializing in accounting & finance—fully computerized

Noble & Assoc., Inc.
420 Madison Ave., Ste. 803
New York, New York 10017
Salary Minimum: $50,000
Key Contact: Donald Noble

Functions: 05.0
Industries: Most
Description: Specialize in marketing, advertising & corporate communications to include all functions

Normyle/Erstling Health Search
Park 80 West, Plaza Two
Saddle Brook, New Jersey 07662
Salary Minimum: $20,000
Key Contact: Robert J. Normyle
Gregory J. Erstling

Functions: 05.2 05.4
Industries: I.14
Description: Exclusive health care recruiters

Ronald Norris & Assoc.
8457 E. Prairie Rd.
Skokie, Illinois 60076
Salary Minimum: $25,000
Key Contact: Ronald Norris

Functions: 01.3 05.4 08.3
Industries: H.10 I.20
Description: Small, professional specialist in the commercial finance field-sales & credit

Northeastern Search, Inc.
879 Fritztown Rd.
Sinking Spring, Pennsylvania 19608
Salary Minimum: $35,000
Key Contact: Stephan J. Aronson
John L. Anderson
Joseph Zarcone
Andy Kreider

Functions: Most + 01.4 05.4 09.0 09.1 09.3
Industries: B.00 D.H0 D.I0 G.00 J.13
Description: Specializing in data processing, sales/marketing, banking/finance, & pharmaceuticals

Branches:
P.O. Box 2466
Princeton, New Jersey 08543-2466

Northland Recruiting Inc.
6465 Wayzata Blvd., Ste. 130
Minneapolis, Minnesota 55426
Key Contact: David R. Gavin

Functions: Most
Description: Full service professional search services

Norton & Assoc.

7 Michigan Ave.
Dundee, Illinois 60118
Salary Minimum: $25,000
Key Contact: Gregory A. Norton

Functions: 01.0 02.0 03.0 05.0 11.3
Industries: D.23 D.25 D.E0 D.H0 K.10
Description: Specialized in advanced
   technology including SMT, ICs, & hybrid
   electronics

Nuance Personnel Search, Inc.

P.O. Box 13113
Charlotte, North Carolina 28270-6993
Salary Minimum: $25,000
Key Contact: Lynn Green

Functions: 01.3 10.0
Industries: H.I0
Professional Affiliations: NIRA
Description: Specialist in loss control,
   commercial underwriting, medical
   malpractice. Technical/mgmt

OSA Partners, Inc.

2 Park Plaza, Ste. 600
Boston, Massachusetts 02116
Salary Minimum: $45,000
Key Contact: Gaye Hazard
Kate Schnabel

Functions: 01.1 01.2 01.3 05.0 11.0
Industries: D.00 D.H0 D.I0 H.00 I.00
Professional Affiliations: NEHRA
Description: Professional & managerial
   recruitment for corporate & healthcare
   divisions

Oldwick Enterprises, Inc.

P.O. Box 22
Basking Ridge, New Jersey 07920
Salary Minimum: $75,000
Key Contact: Eugene F. Kenny
Mary R. Kenny
Eileen Helmer

Functions: 05.4 08.0 11.3 11.5 11.6
Industries: B.00 B.0W E.00 H.00 I.00
Professional Affiliations: AICHE, ANS, ASCE,
   ASME, ASTM, IEEE, SAME
Description: Prof. recruitment & placement for
   architectural, engineering, environmental
   & construction firms

Charles P. Oliver Assoc., Inc.

P.O. Box 367
Huntington Station, New York 11746-0299
Salary Minimum: $25,000
Key Contact: Charles P. Oliver
Melvin Kaufman
Phyllis Sonen

Functions: Most
Industries: D.15 D.18 D.24 D.E0 D.H0
Professional Affiliations: IEEE, NAPC
Description: Communications/electronic/
   chemical technology: engineering (software
   & hardware), manufacturing

Opportunity Knocking, Inc.

37727 Professional Ctr. Dr., Ste. 115
Livonia, Michigan 48154
Key Contact: Calvin F. Weaver

Functions: 01.0 01.1 01.4 09.0
Industries: Most
Professional Affiliations: MAPC, NAPC
Description: Recruiters dedicated to job-seekers
   & employers, ethically & professionally

Jim Oravetz & Assoc., Inc.

20 Meridian Rd.
Rowayton, Connecticut 06853
Salary Minimum: $40,000
Key Contact: Jim Oravetz

Functions: 08.0 08.2
Industries: H.00 H.I0
Description: Over ten years financial services:
   leasing, secured lending, project finance

Orr Executive Search

5125 N. 16th St., B-223
Phoenix, Arizona 85016
Salary Minimum: $40,000
Key Contact: Don W. Orr

Functions: 05.1 05.3 05.5
Industries: D.10 D.16
Professional Affiliations: DMA, PDMC
Description: Recruit in general advertising,
   direct response & sales promotion, market
   research, product managers

Kitty Ossow & Assoc.
160 E. 48th St.
New York, New York 10017
Salary Minimum: $50,000
Key Contact: Kitty Ossow

Functions: Most + 05.0 05.1 05.2 05.3
Industries: D.00 D.10 D.17 D.18 J.00

LaMonte Owens, Inc.
805 E. Willow Grove Ave., Ste 2C
Philadelphia, Pennsylvania 19118
Salary Minimum: $40,000
Key Contact: LaMonte Owens

Functions: Most + 11.2
Industries: Most
Professional Affiliations: MAAPC
Description: Specialist in minority & female
  recruiting

The Oxford Group
1600 Promenade Bank Twr., Ste. 800
Richardson, Texas 75080
Key Contact: M. Jackson

Functions: Most + 01.0 05.0 05.4 09.0
Description: Executive recruiter search firm
  specializing in computer, medical &
  printing industry

The P & L Group
366 N. Broadway, Ste. 228
Jericho, New York 11753
Salary Minimum: $35,000
Key Contact: Hyman Livingston
James Panos

Functions: 02.0 02.5 03.0 03.1 03.3
Industries: Most
Professional Affiliations: AME, APICS, ASME,
  ASQC, NAPM
Description: Manufacturing operations,
  materials management, purchasing, user-
  oriented systems, quality assur.

P R Associates
15775 Hillcrest, Ste. 508
Dallas, Texas 75248
Salary Minimum: $40,000
Key Contact: Nancy Porter

Functions: Most + 01.0 05.0 06.0 08.0
Industries: G.00
Professional Affiliations: MAPC, NAPC, NRF,
  TAPC
Description: Nationwide retail search &
  recruitment for corporate & field
  executives

P R Management Consultants, Inc.
601 Ewing St., C-5
Princeton, New Jersey 08540
Salary Minimum: $50,000
Key Contact: Jerrold Koenig

Functions: 01.0 02.1 02.4 05.0 09.2
Industries: D.11 D.19 D.25 I.16
Description: Recruiters of biomedical, clinical
  & international management & staff

PC Assoc.
602 Park Point Dr., Ste. 208
Golden, Colorado 80401
Salary Minimum: $35,000
Key Contact: Paul T. Cochlan

Functions: Most + 02.0 11.5 11.6
Industries: A.00 B.00 D.00 D.15 D.H0
Description: Specialist in high technology
  executive & technical recruiting

P&IC Assoc.
107 W. Pine Pl.
St. Louis, Missouri 63108
Salary Minimum: $40,000
Key Contact: Eda Franziska Thadeus
Ralph Robert Thadeus

Functions: 02.2 03.0 03.1 03.2 03.3
Industries: D.22 D.23 D.24 D.25 D.E0
Professional Affiliations: APICS, CASA, SME
Description: Materials management
  professionals placing materials
  management professionals

PLRS/Career Connections
12935 W. Bayshore Dr., Ste. 450
Traverse City, Michigan 49684
Salary Minimum: $30,000
Key Contact: Daniel J. White

Functions: Most + 01.2 02.4 08.0
Industries: Most + D.15 D.H0 I.14 I.15 K.00
Professional Affiliations: NAPC, SHRM
Description: A general executive search firm
    located in Northern Michigan

PMC-ParaLegal Management & Consultants
2040 Ave. of the Stars, # 400
Los Angeles, California 90025-4703
Key Contact: Joanne Sliteris

Functions: 01.3 01.4 01.5 06.1 11.5
Industries: Most
Professional Affiliations: NFPA
Description: Paralegal placement consulting on
    utilization & profitability management
    staff

P.R.H. Management, Inc.
2777 Summer St.
Stamford, Connecticut 06905
Salary Minimum: $50,000
Key Contact: Peter R. Hendelman

Functions: 01.0 05.0 06.0 09.7
Industries: D.H0 I.20 J.13
Description: Specializing in
    telecommunications, technology, &
    emerging businesses

PSP Agency
188 Montague St.
Brooklyn, New York 11201
Salary Minimum: $60,000
Key Contact: Iris E. Nunez
Arnold D. Harvey
Cleveland J. Jones

Description: Targeting sales, marketing: finance

Pacific Advisory Service
225 W. Washington St., Ste. 220
Chicago, Illinois 60606
Salary Minimum: $30,000
Key Contact: Hideki Terada

Functions: 01.2 01.3 05.4 08.0 08.4
Industries: D.00 H.00 H.R0 I.19 I.21
Professional Affiliations: JAS
Description: Japanese national involved in
    Asia Pacific for 20 years

Pacific Search Consultants
2377 S. El Camino Real., Ste. 201
San Clemente, California 92672
Salary Minimum: $35,000
Key Contact: Arnold L. Garlick, III
Gary Schlapeter

Functions: 09.2 09.3 09.4
Industries: D.24
Description: Retained & contingent recruiting
    for Unix kernel level engineers & data
    comm. software engineers

Janou Pakter, Inc.
91 Fifth Ave.
New York, New York 10003
Salary Minimum: $20,000
Key Contact: Janou Pakter
Jerry Tavin

Functions: 03.4 05.2 05.3
Industries: G.00 I.16 J.11
Description: Integrated marketing & creative
    talent for national & international
    searches

R. Parker & Assoc., Inc.
551 5th Ave., Ste. 222
New York, New York 10176
Salary Minimum: $40,000
Key Contact: Roberta Parker

Functions: 01.0 01.2 01.3 05.0 05.1
Industries: D.10 D.16 D.21
Description: Consumer marketing & sales

Parker Page Group

12550 Biscayne Blvd., Ste. 209
Miami, Florida 33181
Salary Minimum: $30,000
Key Contact: Harry Harfenist

Functions: 01.0 01.1 01.2 08.0 11.1
Industries: D.H0 H.10 I.10 I.11 I.17
Professional Affiliations: NCA
Description: Specialize in hospitality industry
also medical, banking, finance, engineering

Largent Parks & Partners, Inc.

12770 Coit Rd., Ste. 900
Dallas, Texas 75251
Salary Minimum: $30,000
Key Contact: Charles J. Labarge

Functions: Most + 02.2 02.4 06.2 10.0 11.4
Industries: D.13 H.10 I.14 I.15 I.21
Description: Firm founded in 1977 conducts
retained searches & contingency recruiting

Robert Parrella Assoc.

60 E. 42nd St., Rm. 1446
New York, New York 10165
Salary Minimum: $30,000
Key Contact: Robert Parrella

Industries: Most
Description: Specializing in public relations
recruitment within the private sector

Part Time Resources

One Greenwich Plz.
Greenwich, Connecticut 06830
Key Contact: Nadine Mockler
Laurie Young

Functions: Most + 01.0 04.0 05.0 06.0 07.0
Industries: Most
Professional Affiliations: AWBO, NAFE
Description: Placement of professionals in
permanent part-time positions or projects

Partridge Assoc., Inc.

1200 Providence Hwy.
Sharon, Massachusetts 02067
Salary Minimum: $40,000
Key Contact: Robert J. Partridge

Functions: Most + 01.0 05.0 06.0 08.0
Industries: I.10 I.11 I.14
Professional Affiliations: IACPR, SHRM
Description: Search firm specializing in hotel,
resort & conference center positions

Carolyn Smith Paschal Int'l.

1155 Camino Del Mar, Ste. 506
Del Mar, California 92014
Salary Minimum: $35,000
Key Contact: Carolyn Smith Paschal

Functions: 05.5 05.7 11.4
Industries: Most + D.H0 J.10
Professional Affiliations: IABC, NAHD, NIRI,
NSFRE, PRSA
Description: National search—public relations,
investor relations, marketing
communications, fund raising

Branches:
916 Fourth St. N.
South St. Paul, Minnesota 55075
Key Contact: Louisa Lynn Paschal

Pathway Executive Search, Inc.

60 E. 42nd St., Ste. 858
Lincoln Bldg.
New York, New York 10165
Key Contact: Jay Berger

Functions: 01.4 09.0 09.3 09.4 09.6
Industries: Most
Description: Experts create personal career
development strategies for optimized
professional growth

Patrick Assoc.

750 E. Pecan St.
Hurst, Texas 76053
Salary Minimum: $25,000
Key Contact: Patrick Coyne
J.J. Turner
R.M. Coyne

Branches:
1621 N. Niagra
Burbank, California 91505
Key Contact: Ron Coyne

Functions: 01.0 02.0 05.0 08.0 09.0
Industries: D.00 D.16 D.18 D.24 D.H0
Description: Seasoned search firm able to make significant contribution

Joel H. Paul & Assoc., Inc.

241 W. 30th St., Ste. 500
New York, New York 10001-2801
Key Contact: Joel H. Paul
Linda Griffler
Rose Grazberg

Functions: 05.0 06.0 07.0 11.0 11.4
Industries: I.00 I.13
Description: Executive search specialists for non-profit organization clients

Robert A. Paul & Assoc.

650 N Sam Houston Pkwy E., Ste. 224
Houston, Texas 77060
Salary Minimum: $50,000
Key Contact: L.R. Ritchie
Paul E. Floth

Functions: 01.2 02.4 10.0 11.3 11.5
Industries: B.00 C.00 D.15
Description: Specializing in refining-petrochemicals-engineering & construction

Kevin W. Paul

8 Sibley Pl.
Rochester, New York 14607
Key Contact: Kevin W. Paul

Functions: 01.0 02.0 05.0 08.0
Industries: Most
Description: Administrative recruiters for clients throughout Upstate New York

Paul-Tittle Assoc., Inc.

1485 Chain Bridge Rd., Ste. 304
McLean, Virginia 22101
Salary Minimum: $40,000
Key Contact: David M. Tittle
Burt Heacock

Functions: 01.4 09.3 09.4 09.7 11.5
Industries: B.10 D.H0 I.18 J.13 K.10
Description: Dedicated recruiting & search for info-systems, telecommunications & energy/environmental

Paules Associates

3231 La Loma Place
Fullerton, California 92635
Salary Minimum: $25,000
Key Contact: Paul E. Paules

Functions: 05.3 05.4 05.6 11.3 11.5
Industries: B.0W D.25 D.H0 D.I0
Professional Affiliations: ACS, ISA
Description: Recruits sales, marketing, engineering & service people process, medical & scientific instruments

The Paxton Group, Ltd.

P.O. Box 11313
Norfolk, Virginia 23517
Salary Minimum: $40,000
Key Contact: James W. Paxton
James N. Davis
Samuel W. Hill

Functions: Most
Industries: H.10 I.10 I.14 I.15 I.21
Description: All industries; specialize in healthcare, finance, human resources, & physician recruiting

Paul S. Pelland
1134 Helen Ave.
Lancaster, Pennsylvania 17601
Salary Minimum: $40,000
Key Contact: Paul S. Pelland
Jane A. Taylor

Functions: 01.2 01.3 02.0 02.4 05.0
Industries: D.22 D.23 D.E0
Professional Affiliations: ADPA, AFS, ASM, ASNT, ASQC
Description: Primary metals & secondary finishing operations, engineering, operations, technical & marketing

M.A. Pelle Assoc., Inc.
P.O. Box 476
Huntington, New York 11743
Salary Minimum: $50,000
Key Contact: Michael A. Pelle

Functions: Most + 01.2 04.0 06.0 09.0 11.3
Industries: Most + D.00 D.E0 D.H0 H.00 I.15
Professional Affiliations: ADPA, AOC, SHRM
Description: Human resource management consultants-executive search/technical recruitment

Pencom Systems Inc.
150 Broadway, Ste. 600
New York, New York 10038
Key Contact: Larry Cohen
Stephen Markman

Functions: 01.4 09.2 09.3 09.4 11.0
Industries: Most
Description: Provide full-time & consulting placement for UNIX-affiliated professionals

Branches:
1731 Technology Dr., Ste. 490
San Jose, California 95110
Key Contact: Edgar Saadi

9050 Capital of Texas Hwy., Ste 300
Austin, Texas 78759
Key Contact: Tom Morgan

17 New England Exec. Park
Burlington, Massachusetts 01803
Key Contact: Ralph Hayden

11260 Roger Bacon Dr.
Reston, Virginia 22090
Key Contact: Jim Kenner

Penn Associates
1411 Walnut St., Ste. 200
Philadelphia, Pennsylvania 19102
Salary Minimum: $60,000
Key Contact: Joseph A. Dickerson

Functions: 02.5 06.1 06.2 11.1 11.2
Industries: Most
Professional Affiliations: ACA, SHRM
Description: Search firm specializing in search of human recruitment & research worldwide

M.R. Pennington Co.
65 S. Main St., Bldg. B
Pennington, New Jersey 08534
Key Contact: Robert B. White
Elizabeth Ludlow
Jenny Chin

Functions: 09.7
Industries: J.13
Description: Executive search & consulting firm specializing in radio common carrier/cellular carrier companies

Performance Professionals
P.O. Box 301
Hillside, New Jersey 07205
Salary Minimum: $25,000
Key Contact: Caesar L. Ferrara
Loretta Gadomski

Functions: Most + 01.0 02.0 06.0 08.0
Industries: Most + B.00 D.00 D.E0
Professional Affiliations: AIAA, AMA, ASME
Description: Executive, administrative, finance, engineering & technical positions our major disciplines

Personnel Advisors Int'l. Corp.
201 E. Kennedy Blvd., Ste. 1516
Tampa, Florida 33602
Salary Minimum: $50,000
Key Contact: Mark N. Strom
Jerry E. Mider
Joseph F. Lane

Branches:
29 Bank St.
Stamford, Connecticut 06901
Key Contact: Mae W. Clarkson

Functions: 01.0 02.0 03.0 05.0 06.0
Industries: Most + D.00 I.00
Professional Affiliations: IACPR
Description: Executive search consultants
providing the highest professional level of
support

Personnel Assoc.
23 Maracay
San Clemente, California 92672-6050
Salary Minimum: $25,000
Key Contact: Marjorie Crawford
Edward Wells

Functions: 05.4
Industries: J.11
Description: Recruit editorial, acquisitions,
sales/marketing for medical/college
publishing

Personnel Inc.
516 Equitable Bldg.
Des Moines, Iowa 50309
Key Contact: Jack T. Textor

Functions: Most + 01.0 02.0 05.0 08.0 09.0
Industries: Most + D.00 D.H0 H.00 I.00 I.15
Professional Affiliations: IAPC
Description: Full service personnel consulting
firm

Personnel Management, Inc.
16 Public Sq., Ste. A
Shelbyville, Indiana 46176
Salary Minimum: $25,000
Key Contact: Daniel P. Brown
Eric D. Jones
Don R. Taylor

Functions: 01.0 02.0 03.0 06.0 09.0
Industries: Most + D.00
Description: Emphasis on small/medium sized
firms in the midwest

The Personnel Network, Inc.
1621 Newberry Ave.
Columbia, South Carolina 29212
Salary Minimum: $20,000
Key Contact: Charles L. Larsen
C. Lars Larsen
James K. Larsen
Merlyne T. Larsen

Functions: Most + 01.0 02.0 04.0 11.5 11.6
Industries: Most + B.0W B.10 D.00 I.00
Professional Affiliations: NAPC, SCAPS
Description: Professionals recruited for:
management, marketing industrial,
environmental, hospitality, engin.

Personnel Systems Int'l. Inc.
52 Temple Pl.
Boston, Massachusetts 02111
Salary Minimum: $18,000
Key Contact: Richard H. Green
Gilbert, A. Spack

Functions: 10.0
Industries: C.00 D.I0 H.10 H.11 H.I0
Description: Executives in the areas of finance/
investments, construction, insurance, &
retail stock brokers

Personnel Unlimited/Executive Search
25 W. Nora
Spokane, Washington 99205
Salary Minimum: $18,000
Key Contact: Gary D. Desgrosellier

Functions: Most + 05.4
Industries: Most
Description: Local firm with 10 recruiters to
assist you

Branches:
1285 Rudy, Ste. 101-A
Onalaska, Wisconsin 54650
Key Contact: Mark Ste. Marie
Lynn Ste. Marie

J.R. Peterman Assoc., Inc.

875 N. Easton Rd., Ste. 3
Doylestown, Pennsylvania 18901
Salary Minimum: $50,000
Key Contact: James R. Peterman

Functions: 10.0
Industries: H.I0
Professional Affiliations: PAPC
Description: Specializes in life & health
  insurance-especially group & pension

Petruzzi Assoc.

2 Eton Row
Scotch Plains, New Jersey 07076
Salary Minimum: $40,000
Key Contact: Vincent J. Petruzzi

Functions: 01.0 02.0 03.0 04.0 05.0
Industries: D.00 D.15 D.18 D.D0 D.I0
Description: In search of excellence of hard to
  find individuals

Robert E. Pfaendler & Assoc., Inc.

317 SW Alder, Ste. 1160
Portland, Oregon 97204
Salary Minimum: $40,000
Key Contact: Robert E. Pfaendler

Functions: 01.2 01.3
Industries: H.10 I.14 I.15
Description: Experienced, professional firm
  knowledgeable in the Pacific North West
  market

Phase II Management

25 Stonybrook Rd.
Westport, Connecticut 06880
Salary Minimum: $40,000
Key Contact: Richard P. Fincher

Functions: Most
Industries: D.13 D.14 D.D0
Professional Affiliations: IOPP
Description: All functions for packaging,
  printing & paper industries & packaging
  professionals

Philip Daniels Assoc., Inc.

551 Roosevelt Rd., Ste. 139
Glen Ellyn, Illinois 60137
Salary Minimum: $40,000
Key Contact: Phil Pollard

Functions: 01.2 01.3 05.0 05.4 11.5
Industries: B.0W E.00 H.10 I.00

Phillips Assoc.

P.O. Box 747
Tenafly, New Jersey 07670-0747
Salary Minimum: $20,000
Key Contact: Veronica Phillips

Functions: 05.1 05.5 06.1 08.3 11.5
Industries: Most + B.0W B.10 J.10 J.12
Professional Affiliations: ACA, NJACP
Description: National executive search-
  specialty environment & advertising in all
  related disciplines

Phillips Personnel/Search

1625 Broadway, Ste. 2160
Denver, Colorado 80202
Salary Minimum: $45,000
Key Contact: Phil Heinschel
Bob Junk

Functions: Most + 05.4 06.2 08.2 09.7 11.5
Industries: Most + B.0W D.H0 H.10 J.13
Professional Affiliations: NAPC, NPA
Description: Contingency & retained search-
  banking/finance, sales/marketing,
  enginering & production

Phillips Resource Group

5 Century Dr., Ste. 230
P.O. Box 5664
Greenville, South Carolina 29607
Salary Minimum: $30,000
Key Contact: Sam B. Phillips, Jr.
Albert M. Hicks
Gene Fitzgerald
James E. Bostic

Functions: Most + 02.0 04.0 05.0 09.0
Industries: Most + D.00 D.11 D.13 D.15
Professional Affiliations: NAPC, SCAPS
Description: 10 industry specialists search for
all management & staff levels

Branches:
2031A Carolina Place
Ft. Mill, South Carolina 29715
Key Contact: Joel McIntyre
Sarah Rhodes
Steve Collins
Herbert L. Gibson, Jr.

355 E. Blackstock Rd.
Spartanburg, South Carolina 29301
Key Contact: William P. Conway
Crawford Chavoos

3614 California Ave., SW
Seattle, Washington 98116-0318
Key Contact: Michele Hale
Phyllis Pascal

Physicians Search Assoc. Agency, Inc.

500 N. State College Blvd., Ste 870
Orange, California 92668
Salary Minimum: $50,000
Key Contact: Clifford W. Rauch
Scotty Bell
Bill LeBoeuf
Barbara Cramer
Steven Angustin

Industries: I.14 I.15 I.16
Professional Affiliations: IBA, NAPR
Description: Physician recruiting & practice
sale—locum tenums

Branches:
N. 112 University Rd., Ste. 201
Spokane, Washington 99206
Key Contact: John Gillis, Jr.

The Pickwick Group, Inc.

110 Cedar St.
Wellesley Hills, Massachusetts 02181
Salary Minimum: $30,000
Key Contact: Cecile J. Klavens
Kim L. Sommer

Functions: Most
Industries: Most
Description: Unique agency specializing in
part-time and temporary middle/executive
level staff

Place Mart Personnel Service

5 Elm Row
New Brunswick, New Jersey 08901
Salary Minimum: $20,000
Key Contact: William R. Kuhl
David Winarsky

Functions: 04.0
Industries: D.I0 I.15 I.16
Description: Scientists in quantitative analysis,
statistics, records management & data
automation

Placement Assoc., Inc.

80 Fifth Ave.
New York, New York 10011
Salary Minimum: $20,000
Key Contact: Len Daniels

Functions: Most
Industries: Most
Professional Affiliations: PRSA
Description: Founded in 1967 by Len Daniels-
nationwide recruitment-all areas of public
relations

Placement Solutions
W270 S3979 Heather Dr.
Waukesha, Wisconsin 53188
Salary Minimum: $30,000
Key Contact: Mary Sue Short

Functions: 08.0 08.1 08.2 08.3 08.4
Industries: D.00 D.D0 G.00 I.00 J.13
Professional Affiliations: WAPC
Description: Accounting & finance are
   specialties—most industries—mainly
   midwest

The Placers, Inc.
111 Continental Dr., Ste. 201
Christiana Exec. Campus
Christiana, Delaware 19713
Salary Minimum: $25,000
Key Contact: Alan Burkhard
Jim Rudman
Larry Waters

Functions: 07.0 08.0 09.0
Industries: H.00
Professional Affiliations: IPA, MAAPC, NAPC
Description: Services in financial, banking,
   office services, data processing, healthcare
   & engineering

Plastics Enterprises
683 Ponus Ridge Rd.
New Canaan, Connecticut 06840
Salary Minimum: $50,000
Key Contact: Peter E. Rodts

Functions: Most + 01.0 02.0 04.0 05.0
Industries: D.19 D.D0
Professional Affiliations: ACG, FPA, SPE, SPI
Description: Specializing in the plastics indus.,
   general mgmt. marketing, sales,
   operations, engineering & R&D

Jerry Pollack & Assoc.
2343E Miramonte Cir. W.
Palm Springs, California 92264
Salary Minimum: $40,000
Key Contact: Jerry Pollack

Functions: 01.1 01.2 01.3
Industries: G.00 H.R0 I.19
Professional Affiliations: ICSC, NAER
Description: Specializing in shopping centers
   and chain store retailing

Polytechnic Design Co.
P.O. Box 1327
Fair Lawn, New Jersey 07410-8327
Salary Minimum: $35,000
Key Contact: Walter B. Grossman

Functions: 11.3 11.6
Industries: B.00 C.00
Professional Affiliations: ASCE, ASME, NSPE
Description: Placement specialists for technical,
   engineering & scientific managers &
   personnel

Polytechnical Consultants, Inc.
7213 W. Breen
Niles, Illinois 60648
Salary Minimum: $25,000
Key Contact: Walt Zimmer

Functions: Most + 02.0 02.1 03.0 04.0
Industries: Most + D.00 D.19 D.24 D.H0
   D.I0
Description: Cater especially to engineering &
   technical disciplines

Posse, Inc.
2943 S. 43rd St.
Milwaukee, Wisconsin 53219
Key Contact: Loni Sucharoa

Functions: 05.0 05.1 09.3 09.4
Industries: D.14 I.18 J.00 J.10 J.11
Description: Specialty: placement of computer
   graphics personnel within the prepress
   industry

Norman Powers Assoc., Inc.
P.O. Box 3221
Saxonville, Massachusetts 01701
Salary Minimum: $25,000
Key Contact: Norman S. Powers

Functions: 02.0 05.0 06.0 09.0 09.4
Industries: D.24 D.E0
Professional Affiliations: MPPC
Description: Hitech & computer industry,
   military & commercial professional
   placement since 1964

Precise Legal, Inc.
P.O. Box 1381
Valparaiso, Indiana 46384-1381
Key Contact: David Lelek

Functions: 01.0 01.5
Industries: B.0W C.00 D.00 H.R0 I.17
Professional Affiliations: IAPC
Description: Proven dedication to the
satisfaction of your career objectives

Presley Consultants, Inc.
812 Third St.
Norco, California 91760
Salary Minimum: $50,000
Key Contact: Philip E. Presley
Linda C. Presley
Jason T. Presley

Functions: 01.0 01.2 01.3 05.0 06.0
Industries: I.10
Description: Executive search, recruitment
specifically in hospitality industry,
primarily contingency

Prestige Search Inc.
1121 E. Main St., Ste. 140
St. Charles, Illinois 60174
Salary Minimum: $50,000
Key Contact: James A. Sammons

Functions: Most
Industries: D.00 F.00 G.00
Description: Active recruiting firm, placing
mid-management to executive level
personnel on a nationwide basis

Branches:
404A Merchandise Mart
Chicago, Illinois 60610
Key Contact: John Heavey

P.O. Box 105
LaValle, Wisconsin 53941
Key Contact: Larry Gordon

Preston Robert & Assoc.-Health Care Div.
570 Taxter Rd., Ste. 565
Elmsford, New York 10523-2399
Salary Minimum: $50,000
Key Contact: Robert P. Neuffer

Functions: 01.3 02.2 04.0 05.3 11.5
Industries: D.10 D.16 D.I0 I.16
Description: Mid-upper mgmt. for R&D,
pharmaceutical, biotech., food industries,
international & engineering

Prestonwood Assoc.
266 Main St., Olde Medfield Sq.
Medfield, Massachusetts 02052
Salary Minimum: $50,000
Key Contact: Diane Coletti

Functions: 05.0 05.2 05.3 05.4 05.5
Industries: D.10 D.16 D.24 D.H0 I.21
Professional Affiliations: EMA, IAPW, MPPC,
NEHRA
Description: Marketing & sales, emphasis in
high technology, industrial, consumer
products & marketing info bus

The Primary Group, Inc.
P.O. Box 916160
Longwood, Florida 32791-6160
Salary Minimum: $50,000
Key Contact: Ken Friedman
Jerry Goldsmith

Functions: 01.0 01.5 05.4 06.0 10.0
Industries: H.10 H.11 H.I0 I.17 I.21
Professional Affiliations: IAFP
Description: Executive search for securities,
insurance, employee benefits, banking &
legal

Princeton Executive Search
P.O. Box 7373
Princeton, New Jersey 08543-7373
Salary Minimum: $25,000
Key Contact: Andrew B. Barkocy

Functions: Most + 06.0 08.0
Industries: D.00 H.00 I.00
Professional Affiliations: IACPR, IMA,
MAAPC, NAPC
Description: Executive search & placement-
management level & supporting staff

Princeton Executive Search, Inc.

15 Fishers Rd.
Pittsford, New York 14534
Key Contact: Donald J. Sheehan

Functions: 01.0 02.0 03.0 05.0 08.0
Industries: Most
Professional Affiliations: APCNY
Description: Specialists in finding key
 executives, managers & professionals

Princeton Planning Consultants, Inc.

210 Carnegie Ctr., Ste. 101
Princeton, New Jersey 08540
Salary Minimum: $75,000
Key Contact: Barbara S. Cohen

Functions: 01.5
Industries: Most
Description: Needs & objectives of client &
 candidate are meshed in an efficient &
 confidential search

Pro Counsel

P.O. Box 580
Avila Beach, California 93424
Salary Minimum: $25,000
Key Contact: John Taylor
Cheryl Taylor

Industries: A.00 C.00 D.21 D.22
Professional Affiliations: ACI, NAER
Description: Concrete specialists-all disciplines
 in ready-mixed, precast/prestressed block,
 pipe

Pro, Inc.

4250 Executive Sq., Ste. 440
La Jolla, California 92037-1482
Salary Minimum: $50,000
Key Contact: E. J. Schneekluth
Randy J. Schmidt
Mark J. Schneekluth
Mary K. McMahon

Functions: 06.1 10.0 11.1 11.5
Industries: B.0W H.I0 I.14 I.15 I.17
Description: Specializes in actuarial, employee
 benefits, comp., managed care,
 environmental & healthcare

Pro Travel Personnel

451 W. Lambert Rd., Ste. 216
Brea, California 92621
Key Contact: Vivian McClintock
Rosalie Russell
Cheryl Munding

Functions: 11.0
Industries: I.10 I.11
Description: Specializing in travel industry

ProSearch, Inc.

1100 E. Hector St., Ste. 305
Conshohocken, Pennsylvania 19428
Salary Minimum: $35,000
Key Contact: Suzanne F. Fairlie

Functions: 01.4 09.0
Industries: D.00 D.I0 I.14 I.16 I.18
Professional Affiliations: NAPC, PAPC
Description: Specializing in placements of
 information systems professionals
 throughout the Delaware Valley

ProSearch, Inc.

2550 SOM Ctr. Rd.
Willoughby Hills, Ohio 44094
Salary Minimum: $40,000
Key Contact: Leonard Goldstein
Cary S. Wayne

Functions: Most
Industries: Most
Description: Specializing in accounting,
 finance, engineering, & manufacturing

Probe Technology

P.O. Box 60521
King of Prussia, Pennsylvania 19406
Salary Minimum: $40,000
Key Contact: Thomas F. Belletieri
Nancy Belletieri

Functions: Most + 01.0 02.0 03.0 04.0
Industries: Most + B.0W D.00 D.H0 D.I0
Description: Recruiting and search primarily in
 high-tech industries

Probus Executive Search
4962 El Camino Real, Ste. 126
Los Altos, California 94022
Salary Minimum: $40,000
Key Contact: Jack McNeal
Jim Amato

Functions: 08.0 11.6
Industries: C.00 D.00 D.24 D.H0
Description: Finance & accounting for
manufacturing; civil engineering

Professional Careers
711 Executive Pl., Ste. 302
Fayetteville, North Carolina 28305
Key Contact: Vicki Hayes

Functions: 09.3
Professional Affiliations: NAPC, NCAPC
Description: Specialize in information systems
& technology positions in the Southeast

Professional Medical
1862 Independence Sq., Ste. D
Dunwoody, Georgia 30338
Key Contact: Louise Sawhill
Harry Newberry

Functions: 01.0 05.0 05.4
Industries: I.14 I.15 I.16
Description: Primarily devoted to medical sales
arena, also medical sales mgmt., &
products/marketing managers

Branches:
90 S. Spruce Ave., Ste. S
San Francisco, California 94080
Key Contact: Bill Hubbard

1290 Worcester Rd.
Framingham, Massachusetts 01701
Key Contact: Maureen Duffy

23046 Avenida de la Carlota, Ste. 600
Laguna Hills, California 92653
Key Contact: Edward Rider

501 Office Center Dr., Ste. 2
Ft. Washington, Pennsylvania 19034
Key Contact: Jim Rogers

17 W. 755 Butterfield Rd.
Oakbrook Terrace, Illinois 60181
Key Contact: Marci Batsakis

4514 Cole Ave., Ste. 600
Dallas, Texas 75205
Key Contact: Guy Wilson

Professional Personnel Services
110 Grant St.
Bettendorf, Iowa 52722
Salary Minimum: $30,000
Key Contact: James W. Shetler
Patricia A. Shetler

Functions: 01.0 02.0 03.0 08.0
Industries: B.0W D.00 D.D0 D.H0
Description: Eighteen years experience, full
service screening & interviewing of
candidates

Professional Placement Assoc., Inc.
14 Rye Ridge Plz.
Rye Brook, New York 10573
Key Contact: Laura J. Schachter

Functions: 01.2 01.3 08.0
Industries: D.18 I.14 I.15 I.16
Professional Affiliations: APCNY, NAPC
Description: Intensive quality firm with
focused expertise in the health care
industry

Professional Recruiters
412 Sovran Bank Bldg.
Harrisonburg, Virginia 22801
Salary Minimum: $25,000
Key Contact: Judith Bent
Devin Charles Bent

Functions: 01.4 02.0 02.5 03.0 08.0
Industries: D.10 D.14 D.19 D.22 D.24
Description: Recruitment in manufacturing/
operations management SE, mid-Atlantic

Professional Recruiters Inc.

1 Davis Way
Worcester, Massachusetts 01604
Salary Minimum: $50,000
Key Contact: H.C. Goodwin

Functions: Most + 01.0 02.0 03.0 09.0
Industries: H.10
Professional Affiliations: NAPC
Description: Our consultants are specialists in banking, manufacturing, engineering, finance & EDP

Professional Recruiters Inc.

12751 County Rd., #5, Ste. 107
Burnsville, Minnesota 55337
Salary Minimum: $50,000
Key Contact: Robert Reinitz

Functions: 01.0 02.3 05.0 05.4 11.5
Industries: B.0W B.10 D.25 D.H0
Description: Environmental-mid level mgmt. & up, electrical, electronic, hi-tech equipment-sales/marketing/mgmt

Professional Resources

53 Pecan Valley Dr.
New City, New York 10956
Salary Minimum: $20,000
Key Contact: Irwin J. Feigenbaum

Functions: 03.3 06.0 08.0 09.0
Industries: D.11 G.00
Professional Affiliations: ASPA
Description: Complete scope of retailing & apparel manufacturing

Professional Search Assoc., Inc.

18 E. Lancaster Ave.
Malvern, Pennsylvania 19355
Salary Minimum: $35,000
Key Contact: Edwin J. Thomas

Functions: Most + 01.0 05.0 09.0 10.0
Industries: D.H0 H.I0 I.18
Professional Affiliations: NAPC, PAPC
Description: Experienced professionals placing career oriented sales, marketing & management professionals

Professional Team Search

4050 E. Greenway Rd., Ste. 4
Phoenix, Arizona 85032
Salary Minimum: $50,000
Key Contact: John M. Ledterman
Denise M. O'Brien

Functions: 01.0 05.0 06.0 08.0 09.0
Industries: H.00 H.10 J.00 J.10 J.11
Description: Principals have combined 8 years of experience recruiting on a national level

Professionals in Recruiting Co.

6075 Poplar Ave., Ste. 900
Crescent Ctr.
Memphis, Tennessee 38119
Salary Minimum: $40,000
Key Contact: James O. Murrell
Maxine W. Murrell

Functions: 10.0
Industries: H.I0 I.13 I.14 I.15
Description: We seek highly qualified candidates & send their credentials out only to places approved by them

Professions, Inc.

4665 Cornell Rd., Ste. 204
Cincinnati, Ohio 45241
Salary Minimum: $25,000
Key Contact: Karen Kranak
Carl Coco, Jr.
Samuel N. Cohen

Functions: Most
Industries: D.13 D.18 D.22
Professional Affiliations: NPA
Description: Search and recruiting firm

Professions Unlimited, Inc.

2620-25 St., Ste. 8
Fargo, North Dakota 58103
Salary Minimum: $25,000
Key Contact: Tom Werre

Functions: 01.0 02.0 05.0 08.0 11.6
Industries: Most + D.00 E.00 F.00 G.00 H.00
Description: Dedicated to provide excellent services for candidates & client companies

Promotion Recruiters, Inc.
11 Rectory Ln.
Scarsdale, New York 10583
Key Contact: Howard Burkat

Industries: J.12
Description: Search for experienced television/
radio/cable promotion executives/
producers exclusively

Protocol Inc.
776 E. Green St.
Pasadena, California 91101
Salary Minimum: $40,000
Key Contact: Robert W. Sparks
Kelly J. Lucas

Functions: Most + 06.0 07.0 08.0 09.3
Industries: Most + B.0W D.00 H.00 I.00
Description: Recruiters for accounting,
financial, middle & upper level
management positions

Pursuant Legal Consultants
P.O. Box 1781
Palm Springs, California 92263
Salary Minimum: $50,000
Key Contact: Allen G. Norman
Georgia Reasner

Industries: I.17
Professional Affiliations: AAA
Description: Founded in 1984, exclusively legal
executive search firm

Questor Consultants, Inc.
2515 N. Broad St.
Colmar, Pennsylvania 18915
Salary Minimum: $20,000
Key Contact: Sal Bevivino

Functions: 10.0
Industries: H.I0
Professional Affiliations: NAER, NIRA, PAPC
Description: Specializes in property/casualty
insurance industry recruiting on national
basis

Quickstaff
1745 W. Shaw, Ste. 104
Fresno, California 93711
Key Contact: Cedric Reese
Jeffrey Hayes

Functions: 08.0 09.0
Industries: Most
Description: Central California recruiters
specializing in accounting & computer
programming

RAC International
5020 Campus Dr.
Newport Beach, California 92660
Salary Minimum: $60,000
Key Contact: Robert Racouillat
Marty Sullivan

Functions: Most + 01.0 04.0 05.0 05.4
Industries: D.24 D.H0 D.I0 I.14 I.16
Description: High-tech & general mid-senior
level executives nationwide

RAI Consulting
120 E. Ogden Ave., Ste. 212
Hinsdale, Illinois 60521-3546
Salary Minimum: $50,000
Key Contact: Leonard J. Reszotko

Functions: Most + 01.4 02.0 08.0 09.0 11.1
Industries: Most
Description: Consultative search firm
specializing in strategy, technology and
succession planning issues

RALCO/Richard A. Lucia & Assoc.
1219 Brace Rd.
Cherry Hill, New Jersey 08034
Salary Minimum: $35,000
Key Contact: Richard A. Lucia

Functions: 01.3 01.5 05.4 11.5 11.6
Industries: B.0W B.10 D.25 I.17 I.21
Professional Affiliations: MAAPC
Description: Recruit nationally &
internationally in all specialties

R.A.N. Assoc., Inc.
140 Public Sq., Ste. 804
Cleveland, Ohio 44114
Salary Minimum: $30,000
Key Contact: Norman A. Thomas
Bill Hicks

Functions: Most + 09.0 11.2
Industries: Most + B.0W D.24 D.E0 D.H0
    I.18
Description: Services include all areas of
    professional staffing & E.E.O. consulting

RBR Assoc., Inc.
P.O. Box 602
Silver Spring, Maryland 20901
Salary Minimum: $60,000
Key Contact: R. Brian Ribcke
Lisa Reichardt
Paul Berner

Functions: 01.0 01.1 01.2 05.4 11.5
Industries: B.0W D.15 D.20 I.17
Professional Affiliations: AWWA, HMCRI,
    SMPS, WPCF
Description: Executive search for
    environmental engineering management &
    business development executives

R.G.B. & Assoc., Inc.
575 Copeland Mill Rd., Ste. 2A
Westerville, Ohio 43081
Salary Minimum: $35,000
Key Contact: Nick Rogish
Pete Guthoff

Functions: Most + 05.0 06.0 08.0 10.0
Industries: I.00 I.14
Description: Specialists in healthcare
    professionals & insurance industry
    executives

RGL Assoc., Inc.
440 S. Main St.
Briar Ridge Plz.
Milltown, New Jersey 08850
Salary Minimum: $45,000
Key Contact: Rita G. Levy

Functions: Most + 02.0 05.0 06.0 08.0
Industries: Most + D.00 D.18 D.H0 G.00
Professional Affiliations: APICS, ASWA, PMA
Description: Experienced professionals with
    training in various disciplines from
    finance to manufacturing

RHS Assoc., Inc.
1 Perimeter Park S., Ste. 130 N
Birmingham, Alabama 35243
Salary Minimum: $35,000
Key Contact: Russell H. Stanley
Allan J. Lebow
Bill Munn

Functions: Most + 01.3 01.4 08.0 09.0 10.0
Industries: Most + D.00 F.00 H.00 H.I0 I.00
Professional Affiliations: AMBAE, DPMA,
    NAA
Description: Management & professional
    search, contingency or retained- financial,
    data processing & accounting

RPA Management Consultants, Inc.
P.O. Box 158, Dept. E
Fair Lawn, New Jersey 07410
Salary Minimum: $35,000
Key Contact: Rick Pascal

Functions: 08.0 08.1 08.2 08.3 08.4
Industries: Most
Professional Affiliations: AAA, IMA, NAPC,
    NJAPC, TPF
Description: Strategic planning, business
    development, corporate finance,
    accounting, treasury, financial

RTE Search
100 Executive Plz. P.O. Box 26
Voorhees, New Jersey 08043
Salary Minimum: $25,000
Key Contact: Robert English

Functions: 02.0 04.0 06.0 11.3
Industries: D.00 D.10 D.D0
Professional Affiliations: IFT, NAFBR
Description: Firm recruits research,
    engineering, production, maintenance,
    quality control-food/beverage

Railey & Assoc.

5102 Westerham Pl.
Houston, Texas 77069
Salary Minimum: $75,000
Key Contact: J. Larry Railey

Functions: 01.5
Industries: Most + B.00
Description: Legal only-all levels of practice—
all industries, especially oil & gas

Ranger & Assoc.

500 Sherbrooke W., Ste. 1240
Montreal, Quebec H3A 3C6 Canada
Salary Minimum: $50,000
Key Contact: Jean-Jacques Ranger

Functions: Most + 09.0 11.1 11.3
Industries: Most

Harold L. Rapp Assoc.

80 Hemlock Dr.
Roslyn, New York 11576
Salary Minimum: $35,000
Key Contact: Harold L. Rapp

Industries: F.00 G.00
Description: Personalize & prompt service,
coupled with candidate performance
guarantees

Edward Rast & Co.

220 Montgomery St., Ste. 343
San Francisco, California 94104
Salary Minimum: $40,000

Functions: Most + 01.0 01.2 06.0 08.0 11.2
Industries: Most + D.00 D.H0 D.I0 G.00 I.00
Description: Senior/middle management
primarily CPAs/MBAs, minorities/EEOC,
human resources

Raymond Thomas & Assoc.

407 Wekiva Springs Rd., Ste. 241
Longwood, Florida 32779
Salary Minimum: $50,000
Key Contact: Ray Huegel
Gail Preston

Functions: 01.0 02.0 05.0
Industries: D.22 D.26
Professional Affiliations: RI, SME
Description: Machine tool & factory
automation OEM & user specialization

Real Estate Executive Search, Inc.

120 Montgomery St., Ste. 1390
San Francisco, California 94104
Salary Minimum: $50,000
Key Contact: Erik J. Kempinski
Louise McDonald

Industries: H.R0
Description: Twenty years of service to the real
estate community

Reinecke & Assoc.

612 Harmon Cove Twrs.
P.O. Box 1141
Secaucus, New Jersey 07094
Salary Minimum: $35,000
Key Contact: Robert Schumann
G. Reinecke

Functions: Most + 01.0 03.0 05.0 06.0 07.0
Industries: E.00
Description: Specializing in transportation
executives

Branches:
3037 Grass Valley Hwy.
Ste. 8149
Auburn, California 95603
Key Contact: Richard Bryner

5 Wayne Ct., P.O. Box 185
Merrick, New York 11566
Key Contact: Guenter Haerter

2203 Timberloch Pl., Ste. 220
The Woodlands, Texas 77380
Key Contact: Dieter Ehlers

International Branches:
Dresden, Haiger, Hamburg, Mulheim, Munchen

Remark Assoc. Inc.

P.O. Box 215
Aberdeen, New Jersey 07747-0215
Salary Minimum: $40,000
Key Contact: Gary Leffer
Allan Kreutzer

Functions: 01.2 01.3 02.1 02.4 05.4
Industries: D.15 D.25 D.E0 D.H0 J.13
Professional Affiliations: AICHE, AIP, IEEE, OSA, SPIE
Description: Staffing management, marketing, sales & engineering for hi-tech industries

The Remington Group, Ltd.

555 Pierce Pl., Ste. 215
Itasca, Illinois 60143
Salary Minimum: $50,000
Key Contact: Eleanor Anne Sweet
William Mike Greene
Al Tenneson
Ed Schnabel

Functions: 04.0 05.0 06.0 08.2
Industries: D.10 D.19 H.10
Description: Specialties include consumer products, food, industrial plastics, banking & finance

Repplier & Co.

426 Prospect St.
New Haven, Connecticut 06511
Salary Minimum: $35,000
Key Contact: Marjorie M. Repplier

Functions: Most
Industries: Most + H.10
Description: Generalist with emphasis on banking & health care

Resource Consultants

P.O. Box 921345
Norcross, Georgia 30092
Salary Minimum: $25,000
Key Contact: David Medendorp
Mary C. Van Erp

Functions: 01.2 01.3
Industries: C.00
Description: Professional management supervisory, technical & professional personnel in construction

The Resource Group

P.O. Box 331
Red Bank, New Jersey 07701
Salary Minimum: $50,000
Key Contact: Timothy L. Howe

Functions: 01.2 01.3 02.2 05.2 11.6
Industries: B.00 C.00 D.22 D.24
Description: Our clients sell cogeneration/ power generation & process equipment/ services

Resource Perspectives, Inc.

575 Anton Blvd., 3rd Fl.
Costa Mesa, California 92626
Salary Minimum: $40,000
Key Contact: Donald F. Delany
Steven D. Cherney

Functions: 01.2 02.0 04.0 05.0 11.2
Industries: D.00 D.10 D.13 D.D0 D.I0
Professional Affiliations: ACS, AICE, IFT, NAER, SCC, TAPPI
Description: Serving the consumer packaged goods & related industries

Resource Services, Inc.

20 Crossways Park N.
Woodbury, New York 11797
Salary Minimum: $35,000
Key Contact: Joseph Trainor
Mary Ann Trainor

Functions: Most + 01.4 08.3 08.4
Industries: Most
Professional Affiliations: NPA
Description: Nationwide search specializing in accounting, banking, data processing

Retail Pacesetters, Inc.

479 N. Midland Ave.
Saddle Brook, New Jersey 07662
Salary Minimum: $15,000
Key Contact: Mindy Bell
Carole Thaller

Functions: 01.2 01.3 03.1 05.4
Industries: G.00
Professional Affiliations: NJAPC
Description: Specialize in permanent placements for the retail industry

Retail Placement Assoc.

6110 Executive Blvd., Ste. 835
Rockville, Maryland 20852
Key Contact: Mark J. Suss

Functions: 05.1
Industries: G.00 I.10 J.10 J.11
Professional Affiliations: MAPRC
Description: Retail ind. specialties:
    mechandising/operations/management/
    finance/distribution/loss prevention

Retail Recruiters/Spectra Professional Search

2550 W. Oakland Park Blvd., Ste. 101
Ft. Lauderdale, Florida 33311
Key Contact: Manuel Kaye

Functions: 01.0 01.1 01.2 01.3 01.4
Industries: G.00
Professional Affiliations: FAPC, NAPC

Retail Recruiters of Paramus, Inc.

12 Rte. 17 N., Ste. 113
Paramus, New Jersey 07652-2644
Salary Minimum: $15,000
Key Contact: David Schnitzer

Functions: 01.2 01.3 03.3 05.0 06.0
Industries: G.00 I.10 I.19 I.21
Description: We are staffed with trained,
    experienced placement professionals

Retail Recruiters/Spectrum Consultants, Inc.

One Bala Cynwyd Plz., Ste. 217
Bala Cynwyd, Pennsylvania 19004
Key Contact: Shirlee J. Berman

Functions: Most + 01.0 05.0 06.0 08.0 10.0
Industries: H.10 H.I0 I.10 I.14 I.15
Description: A targeted professional approach
    in executive recruitment; at all levels on a
    national basis

Retail Recruiters of Stamford

999 Summer St., Ste. 200
Stamford, Connecticut 06905
Salary Minimum: $24,000
Key Contact: James N. Trompeter

Functions: Most
Industries: G.00 I.10 I.18 I.19 I.21
Description: We are experienced retailers who
    know the industry; 5+ years as
    experienced recruiters

Rex Assoc., Inc.

157 E. 57th St.
New York, New York 10022
Salary Minimum: $40,000
Key Contact: David R. Hochberg

Functions: 05.1 05.3 05.5
Industries: J.10
Professional Affiliations: DMA, DMCNY,
    WDRG
Description: Primary clients include advertising
    agencies, & other consumer products/
    services companies

S. Reyman & Assoc., Ltd.

20 N. Michigan Ave., Ste. 520
Chicago, Illinois 60602
Salary Minimum: $45,000
Key Contact: Susan Reyman

Functions: Most + 02.0 06.0 06.1 06.2
Industries: Most
Professional Affiliations: IACPR, HRMA
Description: Each consultant works on only
    one assignment at a time

The Reynolds Group, Inc.

2323 Dunwoody Crossing, Ste. E
Atlanta, Georgia 30338
Salary Minimum: $40,000
Key Contact: Jerry Reynolds

Functions: 01.2 01.3 05.3 05.4 09.4
Industries: D.15 D.24 H.I0 I.18 I.19
Professional Affiliations: FIN, SCAPS
Description: Sales, marketing, sales
    management, mid/high level mgmt.,
    nationwide capabilities

Jeff Rich Assoc.

67 Walnut Ave., Ste. 303
Clark, New Jersey 07066
Salary Minimum: $30,000
Key Contact: Richard A. Thunberg
Majorie Fitzgibbon
Kirk Alan Lippincott

Functions: 08.0
Industries: Most
Description: Recruiting financial & accounting
   professionals by experienced financial
   executives

Riotto—Jones Assoc., Inc.

600 Third Ave.
New York, New York 10016
Salary Minimum: $60,000
Key Contact: Anthony P. Riotto

Functions: 01.2 01.3 05.4 08.2
Industries: H.10 H.11
Description: Specializing in investment, trust &
   private banking professionals

Ritta Professional Search Inc.

6 Automation Ln.
Albany, New York 12205
Salary Minimum: $40,000
Key Contact: Arthur E. Hansen
James P. Salfi

Functions: 01.3 04.0 05.2 09.3
Industries: D.E0 D.H0 I.14 I.15 I.18
Description: Aerospace engineering, program
   management, hospital management,
   physicians & software mktg.

Riverside Consultants, Inc.

One Redbud Rd.
Rolling Meadows, Illinois 60008
Salary Minimum: $25,000
Key Contact: Joseph Rosen

Functions: 01.2 01.3 05.4 08.2 10.0
Industries: H.10 H.11 H.I0
Description: Working exclusively on
   assignments related to the property/
   casualty insurance industry

Roberson & Co.

1300 E. Missouri Ave., Ste. D-200
Phoenix, Arizona 85014
Salary Minimum: $30,000
Key Contact: Stephen D. Silvas
Jean Anne Silvas

Functions: Most + 01.0 02.0 03.0 08.0 11.5
Industries: Most + B.10 D.00 D.H0 I.00 J.13
Professional Affiliations: NAPC, NPA
Description: Founded in 1967 a full service
   firm nationally/internationally affiliated

Roberts Assoc.

P.O. Box 748
Highland Lakes, New Jersey 07422
Salary Minimum: $25,000
Key Contact: George R. Roberts
Karen E. Plummer

Functions: 01.2 01.3
Industries: H.10
Description: Recruiting covering total range of
   banking functions

The Robinson Group, D.A., Ltd.

800 E. Northwest Hwy.
Palatine, Illinois 60067
Salary Minimum: $40,000
Key Contact: Donald Alan Robinson

Functions: 01.0 02.0 05.0 08.0 09.0
Industries: D.00 H.00 H.R0 I.00 J.00
Description: Degreed professional consultants
   with Fortune 500 & Big 6 clients

Rockwood Assoc.

144 Prospect St.
Stamford, Connecticut 06901
Salary Minimum: $40,000
Key Contact: Charles R. Bamford

Functions: 03.3 05.0 08.2 09.6
Industries: B.00 D.20 E.00 H.10 H.11
Description: Marketing, trading, analytics,
   finance positions in energy, commodities,
   financial futures

Rocky Mountain Recruiters, Inc.
1801 Broadway, Ste. 810
Denver, Colorado 80202
Salary Minimum: $30,000
Key Contact: Michael Turner
Jack Hulst

Functions: 08.0 08.1 08.4
Industries: A.00 I.19
Professional Affiliations: AAFA, NAA
Description: Colorado's oldest specialty
recruiting firm-handling mostly
accounting/financial nationwide

Rogers & Seymour Inc.
222 Auburn St.
Portland, Maine 04103
Salary Minimum: $18,000
Key Contact: Joseph B. Bergwall

Functions: 05.0 06.0 07.0 08.0 09.0
Industries: Most
Description: We place experienced
professionals in banking, data processing,
accounting, finance & engineering

Romac & Assoc., Inc.
183 Middle St.
P.O. Box 7469 DTS
Portland, Maine 04112
Salary Minimum: $20,000
Key Contact: Ralph E. Struzziero
Donald D. DeCamp

Functions: 08.0 09.0 09.1 09.3 09.7
Industries: H.10
Professional Affiliations: NAPC, PERC
Description: National network of executive
recruiting offices specializing in placing
accounting, banking & DP

Branches:
505 N. 20th St., Ste. 1230
Birmingham, Alabama 35203
Key Contact: John Alvey

500 Summer St., Ste. 302
Stamford, Connecticut 06901
Key Contact: Ron Pascale

One Commerce Ctr.
12th & Orange Sts.
Wilmington, Delaware 19801
Key Contact: Domenic L. Vacca

5900 N. Andrews Ave., Ste. 900
Ft. Lauderdale, Florida 33309
Key Contact: Howard W. Sutter

111 N. Orange Ave., Ste. 1150
Orlando, Florida 32801
Key Contact: Allan Hartley

120 Hyde Park Pl., Ste. 200
Tampa, Florida 33606
Key Contact: David L. Dunkel

20 N. Wacker Dr., Ste. 2420
Chicago, Illinois 60606
Key Contact: Richard M. Cocchiaro
Kenneth P. Kulas

650 Poydras St., Ste. 2523
New Orleans, Louisiana 70130
Key Contact: Richard McCarthy III

125 Summer St., Ste. 1450
Boston, Massachusetts 02110
Key Contact: Brian C. Cuddy

193 Middle St., 3rd Fl.
Portland, Maine 04112
Key Contact: Louis LaPierre

10 S. Fifth St., Ste. 700
Minneapolis, Minnesota 55402
Key Contact: Keith M. Johnson

1001 Craig Rd., Ste. 260
St. Louis, Missouri 63146
Key Contact: Mel Weinberg

P.O. Box 13264
Kansas City, Missouri 64199
Key Contact: James Buenger

3100 Smoketree Ct., Ste. 202
Raleigh, North Carolina 27625
Key Contact: Randy Bye

1700 First Citizens Bank Plz.
128 S. Tryon St.
Charlotte, North Carolina 28202
Key Contact: Walter Kennedy

650 Elm St., Ste. 310
Manchester, New Hampshire 03101
Key Contact: Edmond H. Stone

1200 E. Ridgewood Ave.
Pantzer Plz.
Ridgewood, New Jersey 07451-1210
Key Contact: Harry Sauer

200 Lake Dr., E., Ste. 101
Cherry Hill, New Jersey 08002
Key Contact: Shelly Volta

1200 Stony Brook Ct., Ste. A
Newburgh, New York 12550
Key Contact: Robert J. Vitacco

One Steuben Pl., 2nd Fl.
Albany, New York 12207
Key Contact: William J. LoSasso

840 National City Bank Bldg., Ste. 840
Cleveland, Ohio 44114
Key Contact: Norman L. Benke

111 W. First St., Ste. 420
Dayton, Ohio 45402
Key Contact: Alan C. Scothon

1265 Drummers Ln., Ste. 301
3 Glenhardie Corp. Ctr.
Wayne, Pennsylvania 19087
Key Contact: Edward S. Baumstein

Romac & Assoc.
Three Ravinia Dr., Ste. 1460
Atlanta, Georgia 30346
Salary Minimum: $15,000
Key Contact: Howard J. Cattie

Romac & Assoc.
2000 W. First St., Ste. 701
Winston-Salem, North Carolina 27104
Key Contact: Michael J. LaVallee

Romac & Assoc.
6000 Poplar Ave., Ste. 340
Memphis, Tennessee 38119-3971
Key Contact: Charles G. Haddad

Romac & Assoc. of Dallas
1700 Pacific Ave., Ste. 1650
First City Ctr.
Dallas, Texas 75201
Salary Minimum: $20,000
Key Contact: John E. Mitchell, Jr.

Romac & Assoc.—San Francisco
111 Pine St., Ste. 905
San Francisco, California 94111
Key Contact: John McLaughlin
Steve Reiter

100 Presidential Blvd.
Bala Cynwyd, Pennsylvania 19004
Key Contact: Mary Kay Hamm

1700 Market St., Ste. 2702
Philadelphia, Pennsylvania 19103
Key Contact: Harry J. Sauer

3050 Post Oak Blvd., Ste. 500
Houston, Texas 77056
Key Contact: Jack Mitchell

4350 N. Fairfax Dr., Ste. 400
Arlington, Virginia 22203
Key Contact: John A. Voigt

10900 N.E 4th St., Ste. 600
Bellevue, Washington 98004
Key Contact: Gary Steele

Functions: 08.0 09.0
Industries: H.00 H.I0
Professional Affiliations: GAPC, NAPC
Description: Permanent & temporary services specializing in accounting, banking & data processing

Functions: 09.1 09.2 09.3 09.4 09.7
Description: Contingency search in systems/ data processing

Functions: 01.0 07.0 08.0 09.0
Industries: Most
Professional Affiliations: NAPC, TAPC
Description: Accounting, data processing & banking with concentration in the mid/ south region of USA

Industries: H.00 H.10 H.11 I.19 I.21
Description: Specialty service owned & staffed by CPA's & bankers; match clients & candidates needs

Functions: 01.4 08.0 09.0
Industries: Most
Professional Affiliations: AICPA, IIA, IMA
Description: Specializing in accounting, finance & MIS; consultants have strong technical background

Romano McAvoy Assoc., Inc.
872 Jericho Trnpk.
Nesconset, New York 11767
Salary Minimum: $20,000
Key Contact: Joseph C. Romano
Edward P. McAvoy

Functions: Most
Industries: D.00 D.E0 D.H0 H.00 J.00

Ropella & Assoc.
300 N. State St., Ste. 3929
Chicago, Illinois 60610
Salary Minimum: $50,000
Key Contact: Patrick B. Ropella

Functions: 01.0 02.0 04.0 05.0
Industries: D.15
Professional Affiliations: NAER, NAPC
Description: Mid level to executive level
    recruitment worldwide, strong chemical
    network

Emery A. Rose & Assoc.
110 Newport Center Dr.
Ste. 200
Newport Beach, California 92660
Salary Minimum: $30,000
Key Contact: Emery Rose

Functions: Most + 11.1 11.3
Industries: D.E0 D.H0 I.21 J.13 K.10
Professional Affiliations: AFA, AFCEA, NL
Description: Engineers, sales/mrktg., exec. &
    tech. prsnl. in aerospace, defense,
    electronics, telecommunication

Sanford Rose Assoc.
265 S. Main St.
Akron, Ohio 44308
Salary Minimum: $30,000
Key Contact: Sanford M. Rose
Douglas R. Eilertson
Alexander J. Sussman

Functions: Most
Industries: Most
Professional Affiliations: ACM, ASM, DPMA,
    IEEE, IFA, NAPC, NATS, OAPC, SAE
Description: Retainer & contingency search
    firm conducting only custom recruiting

Branches:
501 N. Golden Circle Dr.
Santa Ana, California 92705
Key Contact: Robert Endres

44 Main St., Ste. 510
Lincoln Bldg.
Champaign, Illinois 61820
Key Contact: Matt M. Gordon

1811 Santa Rita Rd., Ste. 106
Pleasanton, California 94566
Key Contact: Samuel Raber

444 S. Willow, Ste. 11
Effingham, Illinois 62401
Key Contact: Robert A. St. Denis

5910 Cortez Rd. W., Ste. 150
Bradenton, Florida 34210
Key Contact: John F. Faucher

2625 Butterfield Rd., Ste. 107W
Oak Brook, Illinois 60521
Key Contact: James Keogh

N. Dale Mabry Hgwy., Ste. 202
Lutz, Florida 33549
Key Contact: George M. Johnson

527 Park Place Ct. Ste. 100
Mishawaka, Indiana 46545
Key Contact: Warren B. Eichstaedt

394 S. Milledge Ave., Ste. 107
Athens, Georgia 30605
Key Contact: Art Weiner

300 Main St., Ste. 320
Lafayette, Indiana 47901
Key Contact: Richard R. Roe

5446 Peachtree Industrial Blvd.
Atlanta, Georgia 30341
Key Contact: Glenn E. Gordon

805 1/2 Anderson St.
Franklin, Louisiana 70538
Key Contact: Randolph A. LeBlanc

3500 Parkway Ln. NE, Ste. 460
Norcross, Georgia 30092
Key Contact: Donald Patrick

872 Main St.
Osterville, Massachusetts 02655
Key Contact: Alan Donheiser

57 W. Timonium Rd., Ste. 310
Timonium, Maryland 21093
Key Contact: Thomas C. McPoyle, Jr.

1400 N. Woodward Ave., Ste. 101
Bloomfield Hills, Michigan 48304
Key Contact: Steven A. Passon

3816 S. New Hope Rd., Ste. 21
Gastonia, North Carolina 28056
Key Contact: Frederick Halek

3329 Wrightsville Ave., Ste. L.
Wilmington, North Carolina 28403
Key Contact: Edward J. Karchinski

P.O. Box 36099
Raleigh, North Carolina 27606-6099
Key Contact: Marshall E. Molliver

7422 Carmel Executive Park
Charlotte, North Carolina 28226
Key Contact: Bennett Liebstein

2505 Old Monroe Rd.
Matthews, North Carolina 28105
Key Contact: Bruce G. Lindal

1904 South St., Ste. 105
Blair, Nebraska 68008
Key Contact: Deborah K. Best

32 Daniel Webster Hgwy., Ste. 21-21
Merrimack, New Hampshire 03054
Key Contact: Dennis L. Cardon

629 Amboy Ave.
Edison, New Jersey 08837
Key Contact: John Fodor

P.O. Box 725
Englewood, New Jersey 07631
Key Contact: Don Anderson

3100 Princeton Pike, Bldg. 2, Ste. C
Lawrenceville, New Jersey 08648
Key Contact: Melvin R. Hamelsky

125 Wolf Rd., Ste. 102
Albany, New York 12205
Key Contact: Ernest Steinmann

Orchard Park Corporate Park
Fields Ln., Bldg. 1
Brewster, New York 10509
Key Contact: Robert E. Roberts

260 Northern Blvd., Ste. 22
Great Neck, New York 11021
Key Contact: K.E. Nielsen

4211 N. Buffalo St.
Tremont Park Sq.
Orchard Park, New York 14127
Key Contact: John Bos

71 Baker Blvd.
Akron, Ohio 44313
Key Contact: Gary T. Suhay

545 N. Broad St., Ste. 2
Canfield, Ohio 44406-9204
Key Contact: Richard Ellison

4919 Spruce Hill Dr., NW
Canton, Ohio 44718
Key Contact: Robert Richards

614 Superior Ave., NW, Ste. 1404
Cleveland, Ohio 44113
Key Contact: Joseph A. Rutkowski

6100 Channingway Blvd., Ste. 404
Columbus, Ohio 43232
Key Contact: James R. Allen

6500 Poe Ave., Ste. 407
Dayton, Ohio 45414
Key Contact: Mark R. Adams

7071 Corporate Way, Ste. 201
Dayton, Ohio 45459
Key Contact: Hermann Kaiser

482 N. Abbe Rd.
Elyria, Ohio 44035
Key Contact: Don Leedy

26250 Euclid Ave., Ste. 629
Euclid Office Plz.
Euclid, Ohio 44132
Key Contact: Ralph Orkin

P.O. Box 6093
Hudson, Ohio 44236
Key Contact: Harry Cummings

602 Quincy St.
Ironton, Ohio 45638
Key Contact: John Milar

500 S. Depeyster St.
Kent, Ohio 44240
Key Contact: Mark Seaholts

409 Second St.
Marietta, Ohio 45750
Key Contact: Fred C. Tippel

124 Lafayette
Medina, Ohio 44256
Key Contact: John W. Webb

1206 N. Main St., Ste. 112
Peoples Pro Bldg.
North Canton, Ohio 44720
Key Contact: Michael E. Ziarko

20325 Center Ridge Rd., Ste. 622
Rocky River, Ohio 44116
Key Contact: John M. Brunschwig

150 E. Wilson Bridge Rd., Ste. 120
Worthington, Ohio 43085
Key Contact: Roosevelt Tabb

10200 SW Eastridge, Ste. 200
Portland, Oregon 97225-5029
Key Contact: Jack D. Stiles

4150 Washington Rd., Ste. 201
McMurray, Pennsylvania 15317
Key Contact: Donald A. Holtkamp

Newtown Commons Plz., Ste. 113
P.O. Box 554
Newtown, Pennsylvania 18940
Key Contact: L. Paul Weaver

1000 R.I.D.C. Plz., Ste. 102
Pittsburgh, Pennsylvania 15238
Key Contact: Robert P. McKinley

11676 Perry Hwy., Ste. 1200
Wexford Prof. Bldg.
Wexford, Pennsylvania 15090-8755
Key Contact: Edward F. Rogus

1338 Burke Rd.
West Chester, Pennsylvania 19380
Key Contact: Douglas Laster

154 Quicksand Pond Rd.
Little Compton, Rhode Island 02837
Key Contact: Jack Edwards

P.O. Box 4444
Cleveland, Tennessee 37320-4444
Key Contact: John J. Gildee

1000 Northchase, Ste. 207
Goodlettsville, Tennessee 37072
Key Contact: John R. Johnson

10127 Morocco, Ste. 116
San Antonio, Texas 78216
Key Contact: James E. O'Daniel

245 Regency Ct., Ste. 200
Waukesha, Wisconsin 53186
Key Contact: Mark Norlander

Klos Tower, Ste. 500A
Wheeling, West Virginia 26003
Key Contact: Steve S. Heiser

Sanford Rose Assoc.—Santa Barbara
101 E. Victoria St., Ste. 22
Santa Barbara, California 93101
Salary Minimum: $50,000
Key Contact: James S. Myatt, Jr.
Rachael McNaughton

Functions: Most + 01.0 02.0 04.0 05.0 09.0
Industries: Most
Description: Networks with 80 offices throughout the United States thru large database

Sanford Rose Assoc. of Hartford
P.O. Box 567
East Windsor, Connecticut 06088
Salary Minimum: $40,000
Key Contact: J. Kent Lindquist

Functions: Most + 02.3 05.3 05.4 11.3 11.5
Industries: Most + B.00 B.0W D.13 D.25 D.D0
Description: Specialize in technical & scientific personnel for the nuclear power industry

Sanford Rose Assoc. of Wilmington
7460 Lancaster Pike, Ste. 4
Hockessin Mill Plz.
Hockessin, Delaware 19707
Salary Minimum: $45,000
Key Contact: E.M. Hogan

Functions: Most + 02.0 04.0 11.3 11.5 11.6
Industries: Most + B.0W D.00
Description: Chemical & high tech materials industries, composites, environmental & IH

Sanford Rose Assoc.- Woodbury
51 Sherman Hill Rd., Ste A-104C
Cornerstone Prof. Park
Woodbury, Connecticut 06798
Salary Minimum: $50,000
Key Contact: William R. Kuh
Lillian Stolfi

Functions: 01.0 02.0 04.0 05.0 11.3
Description: Practice restricted to medical technology & products

Sanford Rose Assoc.

3206 Mallard Cove Ln.
Ft. Wayne, Indiana 46804
Salary Minimum: $25,000
Key Contact: Robert Hoffman
Linda Hoffman

Functions: 02.0 03.0 04.0 05.0 06.0
Industries: D.00 D.H0
Description: Specializing in the appliance,
HVAC/R & electronics industries

Sanford Rose Assoc.—Rockville

2440 Research Blvd., Ste. 330
Rockville, Maryland 20850
Salary Minimum: $40,000
Key Contact: Ted Schneider

Functions: Most
Industries: I.14 I.15 I.18
Description: Nationwide recruitment of clinical
& administrative healthcare managers

Sanford Rose Assoc. of Binghamton

32 W. State St., Ste. 8
Colonial Plz.
Binghamton, New York 13901
Salary Minimum: $40,000
Key Contact: Frank B. Sommer

Functions: 04.0 11.1 11.3 11.5 11.6
Industries: B.0W D.12 D.15 D.24 D.E0
Professional Affiliations: AWMA
Description: Nationwide network for
exceptional exposure—100% confidential

Sanford Rose Assoc.—Great Neck

260 Northern Blvd., Ste. 22
Great Neck, New York 11021
Key Contact: K.E. Nielsen

Functions: 01.3 01.4 02.2 02.4
Industries: A.00 B.00 B.0W D.15 D.22
Description: Specializing in environmental,
energy, chemical engineering, minning &
data processing

Sanford Rose Assoc.- Brecksville

8221 Brecksville Rd., Bldg. 3, Ste. 2
Brecksville, Ohio 44141
Salary Minimum: $30,000
Key Contact: Steven C. Brandvold
Jan Brandvold

Functions: Most

Sanford Rose Assoc. of Lima

114 1/2 N. West St., Ste. 204
P.O. Box 994
Lima, Ohio 45802
Salary Minimum: $20,000
Key Contact: Thomas Dautenhahn
Joe Hobgood

Functions: Most + 01.3 02.1 02.3 02.4 02.5
Industries: D.19 D.22 D.23 D.24 D.26
Description: We are experienced professionals
from manufacturing industries; we can
help

Sanford Rose Assoc. of Quakertown

93 S. West End Blvd., Ste. 105B
Quakertown, Pennsylvania 18951
Salary Minimum: $30,000
Key Contact: Sharon A. Barr
Charly Barr

Functions: Most + 02.1 02.2 05.3 08.2 08.3
Industries: D.24 D.H0 H.10 J.13
Description: Customized recruiting service
dedicated to the banking &
microelectronics industries

Sanford Rose Assoc.- Suburban Philadelphia

200 Jenkintown Commons
Old York & Wyncote Rds.
Jenkintown, Pennsylvania 19046
Salary Minimum: $40,000
Key Contact: James V. Kehoe

Functions: 02.0 02.1 03.0 04.0 11.3
Industries: D.17 D.18 D.25 D.I0 I.16
Professional Affiliations: AAAS, AAPS, DIA
Description: Professional/technical recruiters in
pharmaceuticals, biotech & medical
diagnostics

Sanford Rose Assoc. of Nashville

313 E. Main St., Ste. 12
Hendersonville, Tennessee 37075
Salary Minimum: $32,000
Key Contact: Richard D. Holtz

Functions: 01.3 02.0 04.0 05.0 11.5
Professional Affiliations: AIHA, ASM, ASNT, SAMPE, SME, SPE
Description: Technical & management recruiting/search in all areas of advanced materials

Sanford Rose Assoc. of Beachwood

26949 Chagrin Blvd., Ste. 203
Beachwood, Ohio 44122
Salary Minimum: $35,000
Key Contact: M.A. Hanna, Jr.
D.W. Grenier
C. Szymanski
R. Herrmann
E. Spiegel

Functions: 01.2 01.3 02.0 05.0 11.6
Industries: C.00 D.00 D.I0 E.00 J.00
Professional Affiliations: SAE
Description: Mid to upper level management search in manufacturing, engineering & sales/marketing

Sanford Rose Assoc.—Virginia Beach

440 Viking Dr., Ste. 110
Virginia Beach, Virginia 23452
Salary Minimum: $30,000
Key Contact: James M. Mulvaney

Functions: Most + 02.0 03.0 04.0 05.0 08.0
Industries: Most + D.00 D.10 D.15 D.22 D.23
Description: Three former senior executives— custom recruiting for manufacturing companies

Sanford Rose Assoc.- Detroit North

29777 Telegraph Rd., Ste. 2450
Southfield, Michigan 48034-7651
Salary Minimum: $50,000
Key Contact: Martin J. Rosenfeld

Functions: 01.0 01.1 02.0 09.0 11.3
Industries: D.00 D.E0 D.H0 I.14 I.15
Professional Affiliations: MAPC, NALSC
Description: Retainer & contingency recruiting of attornneys, engineers & service sector executives

Ross Personnel Consultants, Inc.

161 East Ave., Ste. 105
Norwalk, Connecticut 06851
Salary Minimum: $30,000
Key Contact: Anthony J. Barca
Robert H. Magrath

Functions: 05.1 05.2 05.3 05.4 09.2
Industries: D.24 D.H0 J.13
Description: Sales, marketing, systems, training, field engineering—computers, facsimile, copiers

Roth Young of Boston

One Montvale Ave.
Stoneham, Massachusetts 02180
Key Contact: James M. Ward
Jacques F. Pelletier

Functions: Most
Industries: D.10 D.D0 F.00 G.00 I.10
Description: 25 years executive recruiting experience with emphasis on chemistry as well as credentials

Roth Young Executive Recruiters

4530 W. 77th St., Ste. 250
Minneapolis, Minnesota 55435
Key Contact: Donald B. Spahr

Industries: D.00 D.D0 G.00 I.10 I.16
Professional Affiliations: MAPC, NAPC

Roth Young of Pittsburgh

3087 Carson St.
Murrysville, Pennsylvania 15668
Salary Minimum: $15,000
Key Contact: Len Di Naples

Functions: Most
Industries: I.10 I.14
Description: Specialists in healthcare, supermarket & hospitality industries

Roth Young Seattle

2025–112th Ave. NW, Ste. 301
Bellevue, Washington 90084
Salary Minimum: $30,000
Key Contact: David Salzberg
Dale White

Functions: 02.0 03.0 05.0 06.0 08.0
Industries: D.00 D.10 F.00 G.00 I.10
Professional Affiliations: NAPC, NRA
Description: Committed to excellence in sourcing quality candidates for client companies

Roth Young of Tampa

5201 W. Kennedy Blvd., Ste. 409
Tampa, Florida 33609
Salary Minimum: $20,000
Key Contact: P. Barry Cushing
Joseph V. Tedesco
James R. Krieger

Functions: Most
Industries: D.10 D.18 G.00 I.10 I.15
Description: Currently the only Roth young office in the SE, offering national Roth Young interchange service

Rothrock Assoc.

P.O. Box 1796
Cary, North Carolina 27512-1796
Salary Minimum: $30,000
Key Contact: T. Hardy Rothrock, Jr.

Functions: Most + 02.0 03.0 04.0 06.0 11.3
Industries: D.22 D.23 D.24 D.H0
Professional Affiliations: APICS, NCAPC
Description: Engineers, specialists & managers in engineering, manufacturing & human resources

Louis Rudzinsky Assoc., Inc.

394 Lowell St., Ste. 17
Harrington Park
Lexington, Massachusetts 02173
Salary Minimum: $40,000
Key Contact: Louis Rudzinsky
Howard Rudzinsky
Jeff Rudzinsky
Frank O. Gallagher

Functions: 01.0 02.0 04.0 05.0 11.6
Industries: D.24 D.25 D.E0
Professional Affiliations: EMA, FIPC, MPPC, NEHRA, NPA
Description: Executive & technical recruiters specializing in optics, electronics, electro-optics & fiber optics

John P. Runden & Co., Inc.

1 Bellevue Plz., Box 879
Upper Montclair, New Jersey 07043
Salary Minimum: $50,000
Key Contact: John P. Runden, Jr.

Functions: Most + 01.0 06.0 08.0 09.0
Industries: Most + A.00 D.00 H.10 I.16
Description: Professional personalized service in sensitive areas of recruiting & outplacement

Rushlow & Co.

11486 E. Maid Court
Inverness, Florida 32650
Salary Minimum: $45,000
Key Contact: M.M. Rushlow

Functions: Most + 01.2 02.4 05.2 11.3
Industries: D.E0 D.H0
Professional Affiliations: SAMPE
Description: Retained search in high technology, particularly advanced composite material

Russell Assoc.

9500 Annapolis Rd., Ste. C-4
Lanham, Maryland 20706-2063
Salary Minimum: $35,000
Key Contact: Frank Russell

Functions: 09.0
Industries: B.0W D.H0 D.I0 H.I0
Description: Environmental services, insurance, high tech/elec, biotech/genetic engineering, information tech

Russillo/Gardner

One International Pl., 11th Fl.
100 Oliver St.
Boston, Massachusetts 02110-2633
Salary Minimum: $50,000
Key Contact: Thomas P. Russillo
Richard E. Gardner
Robert J. Spolsino
Anastasia Leotsakos
Richard S. Barnard
Paula J. Cullinane

Functions: 01.2 01.3 09.0 09.4 10.0
Industries: H.I0
Description: Insurance/risk management, data
    processing & software development

Ryan & Assoc.

1700 Montgomery St., Ste. 225
San Francisco, California 94111
Salary Minimum: $30,000
Key Contact: Paul C. Ryan

Functions: Most + 08.0 08.4
Industries: Most
Description: Finance & accounting

A. Ryan Assoc.

110 E. 59th St., 23rd Fl.
New York, New York 10022
Salary Minimum: $30,000
Key Contact: Ann Ryan

Functions: 08.4
Industries: I.17 I.19
Professional Affiliations: APCNY, NAPC
Description: A contingency search firm
    specializing in taxation recruitment &
    placement

Branches:
3 Landmark Sq.
Stamford, Connecticut 06904

The Charles Ryan Group, Inc.

2151 W. Hillsboro Blvd., Ste. 210
Deerfield Beach, Florida 33442
Salary Minimum: $40,000
Key Contact: Norman D. St. Jean
Carol Gregory

Functions: Most + 01.0 02.0 03.0 05.0 06.0
Industries: Most + D.00 D.D0 D.E0 D.H0
Description: A creative nationwide recruiting
    firm providing personalized, results
    oriented service

Branches:
5440 N. Cumberland, Ste. 222
Chicago, Illinois 60656

Affiliates/Other Offices:
Peter M. Cahill Assoc., Inc., Cheshire

Ryerson Tabor Assoc.

150 County Rd.
Tenafly, New Jersey 07670
Salary Minimum: $50,000
Key Contact: Jerry Ryerson
Gary Tabor

Functions: 01.0 05.0 05.1 05.3 05.4
Industries: D.10 D.16 D.18
Description: Specializing in general
    management & marketing at top package
    groups companies

Ryman, Bell, Green & Michaels, Inc.

2401 Fountainview, Ste. 600
Houston, Texas 77057
Salary Minimum: $50,000
Key Contact: Phillip R. Forman

Functions: 01.5 02.0 11.2 11.3 11.5
Industries: Most + B.0W D.00 I.00 I.17
Description: National & international search
    firm representing Fortune 5000

S. P. Assoc.
700 Kenilworth Ave., Box 31335
Charlotte, North Carolina 28231
Salary Minimum: $30,000
Key Contact: A J. Edahl

Functions: Most
Industries: Most
Description: All functions-client oriented, textiles, fibers, paper mills, packaging, metals & pharmaceuticals

S-H-S of Allentown
1401 N. Cedar Crest Blvd., Ste. 56
Allentown, Pennsylvania 18104-2399
Salary Minimum: $25,000
Key Contact: Donald A. Hall

Functions: Most + 01.0 02.0 04.0 05.4
Industries: A.01 D.13 D.15 D.21 D.22
Description: Nationwide coverage of the minerals, explosives & battery industries

STM Assoc.
230 S. 500 East, Suite 500
Salt Lake City, Utah 84102
Salary Minimum: $60,000
Key Contact: Gerald W. Cooke
Robert L. Roylance
Margo Silvester

Functions: Most
Industries: A.00 B.00 B.0W B.10 D.21
Description: Natural resources, national/ international

Saber-Salisbury & Assoc., Inc.
25505 W. 12 Mile Rd., Ste. 4500
Southfield, Michigan 48034
Key Contact: Debra Saber-Salisbury

Industries: I.14 I.15
Professional Affiliations: NAPR
Description: Recruitment of administrative & clinical professionals for the healthcare industry

Robert Sage Recruiting
26586 Windsor Ave.
Elkhart, Indiana 46514
Salary Minimum: $30,000
Key Contact: Frank Alvey
John McGuire
Bill Hudson, Sr.
R.J. Hill
Jean Keyser
Fred Howard
Bob Mandrell

Functions: Most + 02.0 04.0 05.0 06.0 08.0
Industries: B.0W D.00 D.23 F.00 H.00
Description: Auto, truck, recreational vehicle conversions, marine, factory built housing & safety industries

The Salem Group, Executive Recruiters
Westridge #3-267
Advance, North Carolina 27006
Salary Minimum: $50,000
Key Contact: Steven L. Clapham
Barbara Baensch
Tanja Sherden

Functions: 01.4 02.0 08.0 09.0 11.0
Industries: Most
Professional Affiliations: ADAPSO, AIIM, IEEE, IMA
Description: Technologists specializing in data processing, financial services, engineering & sciences

Sales & Management Search, Inc.
10 S. Riverside Plz.
Chicago, Illinois 60606
Salary Minimum: $50,000
Key Contact: C.L. Mulligan

Functions: Most + 01.2 01.3 02.0 05.4 10.0
Industries: D.00 D.22 D.H0 H.I0 I.14
Description: Middle & senior management recruitment in sales & marketing

Sales Consultants
1127 Euclid Ave., Ste. 1400
Cleveland, Ohio 44115-1638
Salary Minimum: $20,000
Key Contact: Alan R. Schonberg
William Aglinsky
Robert A. Angell
Michael F. DiDomenico
Stephen W. Fogelgren
Robert Gandal
Donald L. Goldman
David L. Marth
Louis R. Scott

Functions: Most
Industries: Most
Professional Affiliations: AHRC, AMA, IFA, PERC
Description: Finding sales, sales management talent & marketing talent is our only business,162 offices nationwide

Branches:
2 Office Park Cir., Ste. 106
Birmingham, Alabama 35223-2578
Key Contact: Glenn E. Estess
J. Peyton McDaniel

5111 N. Scottsdale Rd., Ste. 156
Scottsdale, Arizona 85250
Key Contact: Al Britten

310 S. Wilmont Rd., Ste. B-230
Old Adobe Office Pk.
Tucson, Arizona 85711-4030
Key Contact: Jewel Spivack
Marvin Spivack

390 Diablo Rd., Ste. 110
Danville, California 94526-3432
Key Contact: Bob E. Richards

114 E. Shaw, Ste. 207
Fresno, California 93710
Key Contact: Ron L. Johnson

300 Corporate Pointe, Ste. 100
Culver City, California 90230-7612
Key Contact: Michael Bryant

16530 Ventura Blvd., Ste. 300
The Atrium
Encino, California 91436-2006
Key Contact: Tony Byrne

6994 El Camino Real, Ste. 208
La Costa, California 92009

1101 Sylvan Ave., Ste. B-20
Modesto, California 95350
Key Contact: James P. Ortman

1701 Novato Blvd., Ste. 301
City Ctr.
Novato, California 94947-3030
Key Contact: Mark Robbins
Valerie Robbins

480 Roland Way, Ste. 103
Oakland, California 94621-2065
Key Contact: Tom S. Thrower

One City Blvd. W. Ste. 710
Bank of America Twr.
Orange, California 92668-3157
Key Contact: John Lewis

251 S. Lake Ave., Ste. 120
Jacobs Engineering Ctr.
Pasadena, California 91101-3003
Key Contact: Michael Olson

4811 Chippendale Dr., Ste. 701
Sacramento, California 95841
Key Contact: Larry A. Williams

635 Camino de Los Mares
The 635 Bldg., Ste. 210
San Clemente, California 92672
Key Contact: James P. Meehan
Melissa Wainz

9939 Hibert St., Ste. 209
San Diego, California 92131
Key Contact: Deborah Erickson

5850 Oberlin Dr., Ste. 210
San Diego, California 92121
Key Contact: Tom Erickson

2055 Gateway Pl., Ste. 420
San Jose, California 95110
Key Contact: Ron Whitney

1900 S. Norfolk St., Ste. 318
San Mateo, California 94403-1151
Key Contact: Donald Hirschbein

3325 Cochran St., Ste. 100
Simi Valley, California 93063-2528
Key Contact: Donald A. Vezina

43500 Ridge Pk. Dr., Ste. 103
Temecula, California 92390
Key Contact: Scott Little

325 E. Hillcrest Dr., Ste. 160
Bldg. C
Thousand Oaks, California 91360-5828
Key Contact: John L. Dempster
Key Contact: Jim Yager

3033 S. Parker Rd., Ste. 304
One Market Twr.
Aurora, Colorado 80014-2978
Key Contact: Dick Geltz

P.O. Box 658
Rocky Hill, Connecticut 06067-1316
Key Contact: Frederick Raley

1055 Washington Blvd.
Stamford, Connecticut 06901-2204
Key Contact: John R. Wright

55 Walls Dr., Ste 205
Fairfield, Connecticut 06430-5139
Key Contact: Elton M. Fowler

326 W. Main St.
Milford, Connecticut 06460-3044
Key Contact: Ronald L. Fink

1660 L St., NW, Ste. 604
Washington, District of Columbia 20036
Key Contact: Brian Hoffman

1320 S. Dixie, Ste. 941
Coral Gables, Florida 33146
Key Contact: Dennis McCarthy

9471 Baymeadows Rd., Ste. 204
Baymeadows Place
Jacksonville, Florida 32216
Key Contact: Mark Allen
Rita Allen

1057 Maitland Ctr., Ste. 8
Commons
Maitland, Florida 32751
Key Contact: David Peterson
Steve Fox

1390 Main St., Ste 810
Sarasota, Florida 34236
Key Contact: Donald A. Mattran
Rose L. Castellano

259 Corey Ave., Ste. 259
Mercantile Ctr.
St. Petersburg Beach, Florida 33706-1818
Key Contact: William R. Garrett

4200 W. Cypress St., Ste. 640
Tampa, Florida 36607
Key Contact: Jeff Ram

5901-B Peachtree-Dunwoody Rd., Ste. 360
Atlanta, Georgia 30328-5342
Key Contact: Gary Corcoran

33 S. King St., Ste. 160-M
Honolulu, Hawaii 96813-3206
Key Contact: James A. Morse

200 First Ave. NE., Ste. 203
The Roosevelt Bldg.
Cedar Rapids, Iowa 52401-1188
Key Contact: Don Gabriel

290 Bobwhite Ct., Ste. 220
Park Ctr.
Boise, Idaho 83706-3966
Key Contact: Craig A. Alexander
Teresa Alexander

308 N. Main St., Ste. 201
Bloomington, Illinois 61701
Key Contact: Jack O. Edwards

420 N. Wabash
Chicago, Illinois 60611-3539
Key Contact: Bob Bowes

1419 Lake Cook Rd., Ste. 820
Lake Cook Office Ctr.
Deerfield, Illinois 60015-5230
Key Contact: Gary T. Polvere

241 Commerce Dr., Ste 101
Crystal Lake, Illinois 60014-3541
Key Contact: Daniel M. Grant

430 Milwaukee Ave., Ste. 6
Oak Tree Corners
Lincolnshire, Illinois 60069
Key Contact: Steve Briody

1100 Jorie Blvd., Ste. 210
The Corporate Ctr.
Oak Brook, Illinois 60521-2273
Key Contact: Gary L. Miller

1701 E. Woodfield Rd.
One Woodfield Pl., Ste. 415
Schaumburg, Illinois 60173

1540 East Dundee Rd., Ste. 320
Palatine, Illinois 60067-8321
Key Contact: Brian Roberts

101 Court St., Ste. 207
Riverside 1
Evansville, Indiana 47708
Key Contact: Marjorie Caldemeyer

8200 Haverstick Rd., Ste. 240
Haverstick One
Indianapolis, Indiana 46240-2472
Key Contact: George Ceryak

9401 Indian Creek Pkwy., Bldg. 40, Ste. 1250
Corporate Woods
Overland Park, Kansas 66210-2098
Key Contact: Danny Buda

8441 E. 32nd St. N., Ste.100
Wichita, Kansas 67226-3607
Key Contact: Tony Wolters
Marvin Reimer

804C Newtown Cir.
Lexington, Kentucky 40511
Key Contact: Robert F. Mater, Jr.

1930 Bishop Ln., Ste. 426
Watterson Twrs.
Louisville, Kentucky 40218
Key Contact: Steve Angel

5551 Corporate Blvd., Ste. 3-F
Lamar Bldg.
Baton Rouge, Louisiana 70808-2512
Key Contact: Robert G. Stockard
Francine Smerlas

P.O. Box 6605
Metairie, Louisiana 70009
Key Contact: Edward C. Ameen

567 Pleasant St.
Brockton, Massachusetts 02401-2512
Key Contact: Milton M. Feinson

180 Denslow Rd., Ste. 2
East Longmeadow, Massachusetts 01028
Key Contact: William J. Carroll

222 Rosewood Dr., Ste. 1020
The Tower At Northwoods
Danvers, Massachusetts 01923
Peter Martin

180 State Rd., Ste 5-L
P.O. Box 420
Sagamore Beach, Massachusetts 02562-0420
Key Contact: Edward T. Cahan

9515 Deereco Rd., Ste. 801
Baltimore, Maryland 21093
Key Contact: Ken Davis
Dick Forder
Linda Burton

575 S. Charles St., Ste 401
Baltimore, Maryland 21201
Key Contact: Steven R. Braun

5550 Sterrett Pl., Ste. 215
Columbia, Maryland 21044-2626
Key Contact: David S. Rubin
Lynda Rubin

7515 Annapolis Rd., Ste. 404
Hyattsville, Maryland 20784
Key Contact: Thomas F. Hummel

66 Pearl St., Ste 326
Portland, Maine 04101-4107
Key Contact: Harriet B. Cave
Carla J. Akalarian

34405 W. 12 Mile Rd., Ste. 139
Farmington Hills, Michigan 48331
Key Contact: Mary Walsh

900 E. Paris Ave., 301
Grand Rapids, Michigan 49546
Key Contact: Dave Underwood

4021 W. Main St., Ste. 200
Briarwood Valley Office Plz.
Kalamazoo, Michigan 49007-2746
Key Contact: Dr. M.J. Tessin

6500 Centurion Dr., Ste. 265
Lansing, Michigan 48917-9275
Key Contact: Jeffrey A. Yeager

3900 Capital City Blvd., Ste. 103
Lansing, Michigan 48906
Key Contact: Jerry P. Kuper

119 1/2 S. University
Mt. Pleasant, Michigan 48858-2309
Key Contact: Michael Heintz

851 S. Main St.
Plymouth, Michigan 48170-2046
Key Contact: Patricia Redmond

17117 W. Nine Mile Rd., Ste. 1505
N. Park Twr.
Southfield, Michigan 48075
Key Contact: Thomas J. Hoy

550 Stephenson Hwy., Ste. 407
Troy, Michigan 48083-1152
Key Contact: Edward J. Moeller

7550 France Ave. S. Ste. 180
Minneapolis, Minnesota 55435
Key Contact: Lucy Huber

800 W. 47th, Ste. 215
Plaza Center Bldg.
Kansas City, Missouri 64112
Key Contact: Bob Belcher

8000 Maryland Ave., Ste. 610
Clayton Mercantile Ctr.
St. Louis, Missouri 63105-3718
Key Contact: Bob Keymer
Don Borgschulte

3301 Rider Trail S, Ste. 100
St. Louis, Missouri 63045
Key Contact: A.B. Caywood
Bob Keymer

2505 S. Mebane St., Ste. D
Burlington, North Carolina 27215-6235
Key Contact: Deane Adams

5815 Westpark Dr., Ste. 106
Charlotte, North Carolina 28217
Key Contact: Bobby J. Brown
Ev Fuller

254 Church St. NE
Concord, North Carolina 28025-4737
Key Contact: A.B. Pearson
Anna Lee Pearson

438 E. Garrison Blvd., Ste. B
Gastonia, North Carolina 28054-4429
Key Contact: Chuck Deal

3 Centerview Dr., Ste. 112
Hickory Bldg.
Greensboro, North Carolina 27407
Key Contact: Wally Adams
Edward O. Gore

322 E. Ctr. Ave.
Mooresville, North Carolina 28115
Key Contact: Hugh L. Sykes

606 Idol Dr., Ste. 3
High Point, North Carolina 27260-2923
Key Contact: Pervis Greene
Tom Bunton

8025 N. Point Blvd., Ste. 256W
Winston-Salem, North Carolina 27106-3203
Key Contact: Donald R. Hicks

10855 W. Dodge Rd., Ste. 290
Two Old Mill
Omaha, Nebraska 68154

6 Chenell Dr., Ste. 280
Waverly Bldg. One
Concord, New Hampshire 03301-8514
Key Contact: Joel P. White
John J. Cote

360 Rt. 516, Ste. 205
Califon, New Jersey 07830
Key Contact: Linda Mirro

181 Westfield Ave., Ste. 2
Clark, New Jersey 07066-1538
Key Contact: Mark Daly

800 King's Hwy. N, Ste. 402
Cherry Hill, New Jersey 08034-1511
Key Contact: Jere B. Chambers

271 Rte. 46 W., Ste. 205
Bldg. A
Fairfield, New Jersey 07006
Key Contact: Charles Seminerio

41 Middlesex Ave.
Iselin, New Jersey 08830-1745
Key Contact: Craig M. Glickstein
Harris J. Cohen

Two Hudson Pl.
Baker Bldg.
Hoboken, New Jersey 07030-5502
Key Contact: Richard K. Sinay

One Greentree Ctr., Ste. 201
Marlton, New Jersey 08053
Key Contact: Bob Morrison

210 W. Front St., Ste. 102
Red Bank, New Jersey 07701-0871
Key Contact: Mike Unger

70 Sparta Ave., Ste. 105
Sparta, New Jersey 07871-1730
Key Contact: Harvey C. Bass

18 Bank St., Ste. 201
Summit, New Jersey 07901
Key Contact: Remus Klimaski

830 Bear Tavern Rd., Ste. 301
West Trenton, New Jersey 08628
Key Contact: Beverly Bodner
Robert Bodnar

P.O. Box 727
DeWitt, New York 13214
Key Contact: Roderick B. Seabrook
Richard D. Nassar

33 Walt Whitman Rd., Ste. 208
Huntington Station, New York 11746-3627
Key Contact: Bob Levitt

Latham Cir. Mall, Ste. 402-402A
Latham, New York 12110
Key Contact: A.C. Budd Mazurek

363 Hempstead Ave.
Malverne, New York 11565-1297
Key Contact: James F. Jacobs

47 S. Fitzhugh St.
Ebenezer Watts Bldg.
Rochester, New York 14614-2201
Key Contact: Jerry Annesi

8560 Main St., Harris Hill Sq.
Williamsville, New York 14221-9990
Key Contact: Robert Artis

20600 Chagrin Blvd., Ste. 703
Cleveland, Ohio 44122
Key Contact: Bob Gandee

7550 Lucerne Dr., Ste. 205
Islander Office Bldg.
Cleveland, Ohio 44130
Key Contact: Brian Doherty

11311 Cornell Park Dr., Ste. 404
Cincinnati, Ohio 45242
Key Contact: Daniel M. Smith

800 E. Broad St.
Columbus, Ohio 43205
Key Contact: David J. Oberting

7650 Rivers Edge Dr., Ste. 130
Columbus, Ohio 43235-1342
Key Contact: Mark W. Brubach

6525 N. Meridian, Ste. 212
Oklahoma City, Oklahoma 73116
Key Contact: Darla Emig

5801 E. 41st St., Ste. 440
Tulsa, Oklahoma 74135-5610
Key Contact: Tony Wolters

10159 E. 11th St., Ste. 620
Tulsa, Oklahoma 74128-3005
Key Contact: Jane Campbell

5100 SW Macadam Ave., Ste. 208
Portland, Oregon 97201-3621

323 Norristown Rd., Ste. 103
Springhouse Corp. Ctr.
Ambler, Pennsylvania 19002
Key Contact: Horace Luckey
Jan Luckey

3325 Street Rd., Ste. 210
Four Greenwood Sq.
Bensalem, Pennsylvania 19020
Key Contact: Dave Hedstrom

702 Lisburn Rd.
Camp Hill, Pennsylvania 17011-7423
Key Contact: Thomas M. Waite

8 N. Queen St., Penn Sq.
Lancaster, Pennsylvania 17603-3829
Key Contact: Jon Raber
James Landis

9501 Roosevelt Blvd., Ste. 410
Philadelphia, Pennsylvania 19114-1025
Key Contact: Jeff A. Cohen
Gene P. Rice

One Valley Forge Office Colony
P.O. Box 827, Ste. 827
Valley Forge, Pennsylvania 19481-0827
Key Contact: Doug Mitchell

330 Pelham Rd., Ste. 109B
Greenville, South Carolina 29615
Key Contact: Richard C. Brennecke

3506 Medical Dr.
Columbia, South Carolina 29203
Key Contact: William T. Clowney

3252 Landmark Dr., Ste. 141
North Charleston, South Carolina 29418-8487
Key Contact: John G. Dick

7003 Chadwick Dr., Ste. 311
The Bristol Bldg.
Brentwood, Tennessee 37027-5232
Key Contact: Andrew Foster

7405 Shallowford Rd., Ste. 520
Chattanooga, Tennessee 37421
Key Contact: Bill Cooper
Danton Neal

3385 Airways Blvd., Ste. 107
Memphis, Tennessee 38116
Key Contact: Steve Austin

1101 Kermit Dr., Ste. 426
The Oaks Twr.
Nashville, Tennessee 37217-2127
Key Contact: Lou Jumonville

1111 W. Mockingbird Ln., Ste. 1300
Dallas, Texas 75247-5075
Key Contact: Mark Rednick
John Steiner

5075 Westheimer, Ste. 790
Houston, Texas 77056
Key Contact: Steve Rubin

1405 E. 2100 South
Salt Lake City, Utah 84105-3724
Key Contact: Lynn S. Stoker

6620 W. Broad St., Ste. 406
Brookfield Bldg.
Richmond, Virginia 23230-1781
Key Contact: Jay Schwartz
Ed Becker
Rita Becker

4092 Foxwood Dr., Ste. 102
Virginia Beach, Virginia 23462-4237
Key Contact: James F. Murphey

11811 NE First St., Ste. 304
Eastbridge Corporate Ctr.
Bellevue, Washington 98005-3094
Key Contact: Mark L. Stephens

444 S. Adams St.
Cadillac Sq.
Green Bay, Wisconsin 54301
Key Contact: Garland Ross

8338 Coro. Dr., Ste 300
Racine, Wisconsin 53406
Key Contact: John J. Henkel
Thomas E. Hurt

Sales Consultants
111 Pine St., Ste. 1313
San Francisco, California 94111
Key Contact: Tom Thrower
Aubrey Copeland

Sales Consultants of Ft. Lauderdale
500 Fairway Dr., Ste. 203
Deerfield Beach, Florida 33441
Key Contact: Jeffrey A. Taylor
Greg Peterson

Sales Consultants of Savannah, GA.
329 Eisenhower Dr., Ste. B-100
Savannah, Georgia 31406
Key Contact: Cal Bridgett
Gloria Bridgett

Sales Consultants Chicago Southeast
6420 W. 127th St., Ste. 209
Palos Heights, Illinois 60463
Salary Minimum: $30,000
Key Contact: Jack White
Carroll White

Sales Consultants—Bristol County
272 Chauncy St.
Mansfield, Massachusetts 02048
Key Contact: Jim Noyes

Sales Consultants of Wellesley, Inc.
60 William St., Ste. 330
Wellesley Office Park
Wellesley, Massachusetts 02181-3803
Key Contact: Arthur J. Durante

Sales Consultants of Nashua—Manchester
6 Medallion Ctr.
Greeley St. & Rt. 3
Merrimack, New Hampshire 03054
Salary Minimum: $15,000
Key Contact: Sheldon S. Baron

601 E. Henry Clay
Milwaukee, Wisconsin 53217
Key Contact: Tim Lawler
James Luzar

160 Traders Blvd., Ste 111
Traders Exchange
Mississauga, Ontario L4Z-3K7 Canada
Key Contact: Brian Peto

Functions: 05.3 05.4
Industries: D.00 D.D0 D.H0 H.I0 J.00
Description: Specialists in sales, sales
    management & marketing positions

Functions: Most + 05.0
Industries: Most + D.10 D.18 H.10 I.14 I.18
Professional Affiliations: FAPC, PERC
Description: Sales, sales management,
    marketing & executive placement; fees
    paid by employers

Functions: 01.2 01.3 03.4 05.4
Industries: D.13 D.14 D.D0 J.11
Description: Professional contingency search
    firm

Functions: 05.0 05.1 05.2 05.3 05.4
Industries: Most
Description: Specializing in nationwide
    placement of sales, marketing &
    management people

Functions: 01.3 05.0 05.2 05.3 05.4
Industries: D.15 D.19 D.20 D.E0 D.H0
Professional Affiliations: MAPC, NAPC
Description: Marketing, sales, marketing-sales
    management, applications & support
    positions

Functions: 05.1 05.4
Industries: Most
Professional Affiliations: NAPC
Description: We specialize in the placement &
    recruitment of sales & marketing talent

Functions: 05.0 05.1 05.2 05.3 05.4
Industries: H.10
Professional Affiliations: NNEAPC
Description: We specialize in recruiting &
    placing banking, sales, sales management
    & marketing people

Sales Consultants of Northern Jersey, Inc.

139 Harristown Rd.
Glen Rock, New Jersey 07452
Key Contact: Robert A. Bakker
Daniel H. Steenstra

Functions: 05.0 05.1 05.2 05.3 05.4
Description: Placing sales & marketing
   professionals is our only business

Sales Consultants of Morris County, Inc.

364 Parsippany Rd., Ste. 8B
Parsippany, New Jersey 07054
Salary Minimum: $20,000
Key Contact: Ernest Bivona

Functions: 05.0 05.2 05.3 05.4 05.5
Industries: Most + B.0W D.D0 H.I0 I.00 J.00
Professional Affiliations: AHRC, NAPC,
   NJAPC
Description: Office sales specialties include:
   chemicals, environmental, graphics,
   packaging & services

Sales Consultants of Westchester-South, Inc.

Nine Skyline Dr.
Hawthorne, New York 10532-2190
Salary Minimum: $30,000
Key Contact: Robert J. Penney
Ruth Vogel

Functions: 01.3 05.3 05.4 09.7 11.5
Industries: B.0W D.10 D.12 J.13
Description: National search in functions of
   sales, marketing, management & related
   areas

Sales Consultants of Fayetteville, AR.

1111 B Zion Rd.
Fayetteville, Arkansas 72703-5013
Salary Minimum: $45,000
Key Contact: Daniel A. Morris

Functions: 05.2 05.3 05.4
Industries: D.13 D.15 D.22
Professional Affiliations: PIMA, TAPPI
Description: We offer a totally confidential
   service based on your criteria for new
   opportunities

Sales Consultants of Akron, Inc.

3200 W. Market St.
Akron, Ohio 44313
Salary Minimum: $30,000
Key Contact: Sidney Kaufman

Functions: 01.2 05.2 05.4 11.5 11.6
Description: Placement of sales & marketing
   professionals

Sales Consultants of Ft. Myers, Inc.

6325 Presidential Ct., Ste. 3
Ft. Myers, Florida 33919-3515
Salary Minimum: $30,000
Key Contact: Thomas E. Harris

Functions: 05.1 05.3 05.4 05.6 09.7
Industries: D.24 J.13
Professional Affiliations: ITPA, SME
Description: Value added services incl.
   guarantees, relocation discounts, prof.
   relocation coordination

Sales Consultants

125 Seventh St.
Pittsburgh, Pennsylvania 15222-3477
Salary Minimum: $24,000
Key Contact: Douglas A. Cain

Functions: Most
Industries: Most + D.00 F.00 H.00 I.00 J.00
Description: Specialize in sales, consumer,
   medical, services, data processing,
   insurance, chemical & industrial

Sales Consultants of Rhode Island, Inc.

Office Commons 95, 349 Centerville Rd.
Warwick, Rhode Island 02886
Salary Minimum: $20,000
Key Contact: Peter C. Cotton

Functions: 05.0 05.2 05.3 05.4
Industries: Most
Professional Affiliations: PERC
Description: Specializes in sales, sales
   management & marketing search &
   recruitment

Sales Consultants of Fox Valley

150 Houston St., Ste. 305
Batavia, Illinois 60510-1512
Salary Minimum: $25,000
Key Contact: John W. Seebert

Functions: 05.4
Industries: D.18
Description: Specialize in medical &
   pharmaceutical sales & marketing

Sales Consultants Bowling Green

1032 College St., Ste. 102
Bowling Green, Kentucky 42101-2145
Key Contact: Thomas A. Ingala

Functions: 05.4 05.5
Industries: J.10 J.11
Professional Affiliations: CADM
Description: Recruit & place sales, sales
   support & marketing professionals
   nationally

Sales Consultants of Raleigh-Durham-RTP

113 Edinburgh S., Ste. 203
Cary, North Carolina 27511
Salary Minimum: $30,000
Key Contact: David C. Bunce
Louise M. Bunce

Functions: 05.1 05.4 10.0 11.3 11.5
Industries: Most + B.0W D.00 D.D0 H.I0
Description: Medical/pharmaceutical,
   packaging, industrial, instramentation, &
   insurance

Sales Consultants

3490 S. Dixie Hwy.
Dayton, Ohio 45439-2317
Key Contact: C.E. Ford

Functions: 05.0 05.4
Industries: D.00 D.15 D.19 D.20 D.26
Description: Particularly responsive to the
   chemical & packaging sales professionals

Sales Consultants of Fairfax, Inc.

10565 Lee Hwy., Ste. 102
Fairfax, Virginia 22030-3103
Key Contact: David S. Kurke

Functions: 02.5 05.4 11.1 11.5
Industries: Most
Professional Affiliations: ASQC, ASTD
Description: Honest & straight forward in
   working with candidates to meet our
   client needs

Sales Consultants of Madison

7600 Terrace Ave., Ste. 203
Old Middleton Ctr.
Middleton, Wisconsin 53562-3171
Salary Minimum: $20,000
Key Contact: William A. Schultz

Functions: 01.2 05.2 05.4 10.0 11.1
Industries: D.18 D.24 D.D0 H.I0 I.18
Description: Specialize in territory sales & sales
   management positions

Sales Consultants of Andover

17A Rt. 206
Stanhope, New Jersey 07874
Key Contact: Robert P. Ceresi
Carole Ceresi

Functions: 02.2 02.3 03.1 05.2 05.4
Industries: D.24
Professional Affiliations: IEEE
Description: Our firm specializes in the
   electrical industry

Sales Consultants of Newtown

201 Corporate Dr. E.
Luxembourg Corporate Ctr.
Langhorne, Pennsylvania 19047-8099
Salary Minimum: $30,000
Key Contact: James F. Plappert

Functions: 01.2 01.3 05.2 05.3 05.4
Industries: B.0W B.10 D.25 H.I0
Description: Specialists in environmental &
   insurance industry, sales/marketing
   recruiting

Sales Consultants of Austin, Inc.
106 E. 6th St., Ste. 630
The Littlefield Bldg.
Austin, Texas 78701-3696
Key Contact: C. Jay Middlebrook
Linda Middlebrook

Functions: Most + 01.0 02.0 04.0 05.0 11.0
Industries: B.00 B.0W D.00 D.18 I.16
Description: Executive sales/marketing recruitment specializing in medical, HVAC & environmental

Sales Professionals Personnel Services
595 Market St., Ste. 2500
San Francisco, California 94105
Salary Minimum: $25,000
Key Contact: Sheldon Israel

Functions: 05.0 05.1 05.2 05.3 05.4
Industries: Most
Professional Affiliations: NPA, SME
Description: Placement of sales, sales management, & marketing management personnel

Salesworld-Division of Metacor Inc.
10 Fairway Dr., Ste. 303
Deerfield Beach, Florida 33441-1854
Salary Minimum: $30,000
Key Contact: E. Steven Wald
Len Garvin
Richard Harding
Robert Havener

Functions: 05.0 05.1 05.3 05.4 05.5
Industries: D.00 D.D0 D.H0 I.00 J.00
Professional Affiliations: EMA
Description: Company owned contingency executive search firm specializing in sales/marketing

Branches:
One Oak Brook Tower, Ste. 360
Chicago, Illinois 60181

460 Totten Pond Rd., 7th Fl.
Boston, Massachusetts 02154

901 Dulaney Valley Rd.
Ste. 508
Baltimore, Maryland 21204

30100 Telegraph Rd., Ste. 340
Detroit, Michigan 48010

Park 80 West Plaza 1, 3rd Fl.
Saddle Brook, New Jersey 07662

6600 LBJ Freeway, Ste. 4184
Dallas, Texas 75240

Samper Assoc.
15715 SE 34th Cir.
Vancouver, Washington 98684
Salary Minimum: $40,000
Key Contact: Juan M. Samper

Functions: 01.0 03.0 04.0
Industries: D.13 D.24 J.13
Description: Executive recruiting

George D. Sandel Assoc.
P.O. Box 588
Waltham, Massachusetts 02254
Key Contact: Ivan R. Samuels

Functions: Most + 03.0 04.0 05.0 09.0 11.3
Industries: D.24 D.25 D.E0 D.H0
Professional Affiliations: BCS, HFS, IEEE, MPPC
Description: Since 1958-technical & mid to upper management-high technology & DOD

Santangelo Consultants Inc.
60 E. 42nd St., Ste. 1345
New York, New York 10165
Salary Minimum: $60,000
Key Contact: Richard Santangelo

Functions: Most + 02.6 03.1 05.2 08.0 09.0
Industries: H.10 H.I0 I.14 I.18 I.19
Description: Info-systems, operations improvement, healthcare, financial service, financial & strategic planning

Sarver-Garland, Inc.

P.O. Box 1967
Buellton, California 93427
Key Contact: Cathy Sarver

Functions: Most
Industries: Most
Professional Affiliations: NAFE, NAWBO, SHRM
Description: A small human resources consulting firm

Savalli & Assoc., Inc.

77 Hickory Ln.
Battle Creek, Michigan 49017
Salary Minimum: $40,000
Key Contact: Frank Savalli

Functions: 05.0 05.2 05.3
Industries: D.00 D.10 G.00 I.10
Professional Affiliations: MAPC
Description: Specialize in brand management & executive placements in the consumer packaged goods area

David Saxner & Assoc., Inc.

3 First National Plz., Ste. 1400
Chicago, Illinois 60602
Salary Minimum: $50,000
Key Contact: David Saxner
Rikke Vognsen
Carol Atkins-Gottlieb

Functions: 08.0
Industries: H.R0 I.10
Professional Affiliations: ICSC
Description: Specializing in real estate, national practice, personalized service, contingency/retainer

Saxon Morse Assoc.

P.O. Box 177, Northside Plz.
Pomona, New York 10970
Salary Minimum: $50,000
Key Contact: Stan Case

Functions: 01.2 01.3 02.1 05.0 06.2
Industries: D.24 D.H0 I.11 J.12 J.13
Description: Specialist recruiter: consumer electronics, office products, POS, watch/jewelry industries

Scan Management Inc.

Drawer 4835
Gettysburg, Pennsylvania 17325-4835
Salary Minimum: $75,000
Key Contact: Diana Hallberg

Functions: 01.0 07.4 08.0
Industries: H.00 H.10 H.11 I.17
Description: An independent consulting firm providing services to the commodity & financial futures industry

Schattle Personnel Consultants, Inc.

1130 Ten Rod Rd., B-207
North Kingstown, Rhode Island 02852
Salary Minimum: $50,000
Key Contact: Donald J. Schattle
Edmond J. Duquette

Functions: 02.0 06.0 08.0 11.5 11.6
Industries: B.00 D.00 D.19 H.00 H.10
Professional Affiliations: NPA
Description: Bank/finance/manufacturing/engineering specialists for Northeast & U.S.

Schenck & Assoc. SC

Box 1739
Appleton, Wisconsin 54913
Salary Minimum: $35,000
Key Contact: Patrick J. Egan

Functions: Most + 01.2 02.2 02.4 05.4 08.2
Industries: Most + C.00 D.00 D.D0 H.10 I.14
Description: Professionalism, ethical & long lasting relationships, confidentiality & thoroughness

Schreuder Randall Corp.

5 Mallard Dr.
Huntington, New York 11743
Salary Minimum: $45,000
Key Contact: A. Leo Schreuder
J.E. Randall

Functions: Most + 05.0 11.3 11.5 11.6
Industries: B.00 B.0W B.10 C.00 E.00
Professional Affiliations: NWWA
Description: Serving infra-structure, power & environmental consulting engineering/remediation firms

Devin Scott Assoc.
2125 Center Ave., Ste. 402
Ft. Lee, New Jersey 07024
Salary Minimum: $50,000
Key Contact: Rocco M. Fedele

Functions: Most + 01.2 01.3 05.0 06.0
Industries: G.00 I.00 I.10 I.21
Professional Affiliations: NAER
Description: Personalized, professional &
    results oriented searches handled only by
    the president

Scott Kappele & Gnodde
211 W. Chicago Ave., Ste. 116
Hinsdale, Illinois 60521
Salary Minimum: $40,000
Key Contact: R. Dirk Gnodde

Functions: 08.0 08.1 08.2 08.3 09.0
Industries: H.00 H.10 H.11 H.I0 H.R0
Description: All professionals have prior
    financial services industry experience.
    Search nationally

Scott-Wayne Assoc., Inc.
Prudential Tower, 19th Fl.
Boston, Massachusetts 02199
Salary Minimum: $20,000
Key Contact: R. Steven Dow

Functions: 01.4 08.0 09.0
Industries: Most
Description: Specialists in placement of
    accounting, financial MIS & temporary
    personnel

Search & Recruit Int'l.
4455 South Blvd.
Virginia Beach, Virginia 23452
Salary Minimum: $25,000
Key Contact: William N. Graves

Functions: 02.0 09.0 09.4
Professional Affiliations: EMA, VAPS
Description: Recruiting at all levels of high
    technology

Search Assoc., Inc.
4827 Sepulveda, Ste. 410
Sherman Oaks, California 91403-1991
Key Contact: Lee Woodward
Bernard Sharf

Functions: Most + 05.5 08.0 08.4 10.0 11.5
Industries: Most
Description: Contingency/retainer-major
    emphasis on insurance, accounting,
    environmental, marketing & healthcare

Search Assoc., Inc.
18 Bank St.
Summit, New Jersey 07901
Key Contact: Trina R. Lawson
George A. Richner

Functions: Most
Industries: Most
Description: Diversified disciplines recruited
    for a broad range of clients

Search Bureau Int'l.
P.O. Box 377608
Chicago, Illinois 60637
Salary Minimum: $25,000
Key Contact: Reginald M. Hudson

Functions: 01.4 06.0 08.0 09.0 11.2
Industries: D.00
Description: We are a group of professionals
    specializing in finance/accounting/human
    resource management

The Search Center Inc.
1155 Dairy Ashford, Ste. 704
Houston, Texas 77079-3011
Salary Minimum: $60,000
Key Contact: Linda L. Center
Susan M. Magnani

Functions: 03.3 11.0
Industries: B.00 D.00 D.15 D.20 H.11
Description: Retainer/contingency search for
    trading/marketing petroleum products &
    petrochemical professionals

Search Consultants Int'l., Inc.
4545 Post Oak Place, Ste. 208
Houston, Texas 77027
Salary Minimum: $50,000
Key Contact: S. Joseph Baker

Functions: 01.2 01.3 11.5 11.6
Industries: Most + B.00 D.15 D.H0
Professional Affiliations: AWMA, NAPC,
  TAPC
Description: Specialized technical expertise in
  environmental engineering/hazardous
  waste & cogeneration

Search Dynamics, Inc.
9420 W. Foster Ave., Ste. 200
Chicago, Illinois 60656
Salary Minimum: $30,000
Key Contact: George Apostle
James C. Pappas

Functions: 02.0 02.1 02.2 02.3 04.0
Industries: Most
Description: Specialize in technical, engineering
  & management, concentrating in the Mid-
  West

Search Enterprises, Inc.
520 Quail Ridge Dr.
Westmont, Illinois 60559
Salary Minimum: $30,000
Key Contact: Frank Polacek

Functions: 02.0 03.0 04.0 06.0 11.0
Industries: B.00 B.0W D.00 D.D0 D.I0
Description: Engineering, manufacturing
  management & environmental
  professionals

Branches:
10100 W. Sample Rd.
Coral Springs, Florida 33065
Key Contact: Gary K. Runge

The Search Firm Inc.
595 Market St., Ste. 1400
San Francisco, California 94105
Key Contact: Peter Jozwik
Jim Schneider

Functions: 09.0 09.3 09.4 09.6 09.7
Industries: Most
Description: Data processing, software
  engineering recruiting & consulting

Search Group
1328 Sierra Alta Way
Los Angeles, California 90069
Salary Minimum: $25,000
Key Contact: Yardena Keren

Functions: 01.4 02.1 02.2 05.0 09.0
Industries: B.10 D.19 D.E0 D.H0 J.13
Description: Employer paid executive search/
  tech recruitment firm, specializing in
  engineering

Search Leader, Inc.
5695 Cherokee Rd.
Lyndhurst, Ohio 44124
Salary Minimum: $25,000
Key Contact: John J. Selvaggio

Functions: 08.3 09.1 09.3
Industries: Most + H.10
Description: Mid and upper level positions
  primarily in the financial service &
  computer industry

Search Masters
188 Industrial Dr., Ste. 108
Elmhurst, Illinois 60126
Key Contact: Glenn Kubat
John Volpe

Functions: 02.0 03.1 03.4 05.0
Industries: B.0W D.00 D.D0 D.I0 I.16
Description: Specializing in technical sales &
  marketing in the process industries

Search Masters Int'l.
500 Foothills Dr., Ste. 2
Sedona, Arizona 86336
Salary Minimum: $50,000
Key Contact: David G. Jensen

Functions: 04.0
Industries: Most + D.00 D.17 D.18
Description: Engineering, life sciences &
  biomedical search

The Search Network
5752 Oberlin Dr., Ste. 100
San Diego, California 92121
Salary Minimum: $30,000
Key Contact: Liz Henderson

Functions: 01.0 02.0 02.5 03.0 11.3
Professional Affiliations: CAPC
Description: Specializing in technical positions within hi-tech electronics industry in San Diego

Search North America, Inc.
620 SW Fifth, Ste. 925
Portland, Oregon 97204
Salary Minimum: $35,000
Key Contact: Carl Jansen

Functions: Most
Industries: A.00 B.00 B.10 D.12 D.13
Professional Affiliations: AIIE, ASME, ASSE, FPRS, ISA, NAPC, NAPM, TAPPI
Description: Professional recruiters for firms throughout North America

Search Northwest Assoc.
4505 N. Channel
Portland, Oregon 97217
Salary Minimum: $30,000
Key Contact: Douglas L. Jansen

Functions: 02.0 02.3 04.0 11.3 11.5
Industries: D.12 D.15 D.22 D.H0
Professional Affiliations: ICPA, NAPC, OAPC
Description: Over ten years of successful nationwide recruitment & placement

Search Solutions, Inc.
4540 Woodland Ave.
Western Springs, Illinois 60558
Salary Minimum: $50,000
Key Contact: Robert C. Khoury
Susan Khoury

Functions: 01.0 02.0 02.1 02.4 05.0
Industries: D.00 F.00 G.00
Description: Specializing in housewares, hardware, sporting goods & office products

Search West, Inc.
1875 Century Park E., Ste. 1350
Los Angeles, California 90067
Salary Minimum: $25,000
Key Contact: Robert A. Cowan
Lawrence G. Cowan

Functions: Most
Industries: D.00 D.H0 H.00 H.I0 I.00
Professional Affiliations: CAPC
Description: California's largest contingency search firm—all disciplines & industries

Branches:
16133 Ventura Blvd., Ste. 900
Encino, California 91436-2446
Key Contact: Jeff Weiss

353 Sacramento St., Ste. 1360
San Francisco, California 94111
Key Contact: Ellen Williams

750 City Dr. S., Ste. 100
Orange, California 92668
Key Contact: Phil Lowitz

340 West Lake Blvd., Ste. 200
Westlake Village, California 91362
Key Contact: Mike Begun

3401 Centrelake Dr., Ste. 600
Ontario, California 91764
Key Contact: David Roller

Selected Executives, Inc.
959 Park Sq. Bldg.
Boston, Massachusetts 02116
Salary Minimum: $30,000
Key Contact: Lee R. Sanborn, Jr.
K. Jane Lewis
Suzanne S. Martin
Kenneth T. Dinklage

Functions: Most + 11.2 11.3 11.4 11.5 11.6
Industries: Most
Description: Specializing in minority & women professionals since 1970

Selective Management Services, Inc.

319 S. Sixteenth St.
Philadelphia, Pennsylvania 19102
Salary Minimum: $25,000
Key Contact: Alan M. Schwartz
Mark D. Steel

Functions: Most + 01.0 02.0 03.4 05.0 10.0
Industries: D.13 D.14 D.18 D.D0 H.I0
Description: Company fee paid service specializing in packaging & insurance industries

Selective Staffing

4905 N. West Ave., Ste. 118
Fresno, California 93710
Salary Minimum: $25,000
Key Contact: Jane Small

Functions: Most + 02.0 02.4 06.0 06.1 10.0
Industries: C.00 H.I0
Description: Co. started May 1987; owners in recruiting total of ten years; specialty is insurance recruiting

Stephen Sellers Assoc.

805 Augusta Ave.
Elgin, Illinois 60120
Salary Minimum: $25,000
Key Contact: Stephen E. Sellers

Functions: 01.0 02.1 02.3 02.4 04.0
Industries: D.23 D.24 D.25 D.H0
Professional Affiliations: IAPC, ISHM, NAPC, SMTA
Description: Microelectronic recruiting including thick & thin film, hybrid SMT, PCBs

Jules Seltzer Assoc.

P.O. Box 279
Otis, Massachusetts 01253
Salary Minimum: $60,000
Key Contact: Jules Seltzer

Functions: 01.2 02.0 04.0 05.0 11.3
Industries: D.15 D.17 D.18 D.I0
Description: Recruitment of senior managers for the bio-tech, pharmaceutical, medical device & chemical industry

Setford-Shaw-Najarian Assoc., Ltd.

111 Broadway, 10th Fl.
New York, New York 10006
Salary Minimum: $20,000
Key Contact: Jeffrey C. Najarian
George A. Setford
Edward L. Shaw
Jonathan Toder
Stephen Tracy
Mark Arzoomanian
Aster Davis
Paula Lerner
Judy Sherman
Robert Weiner
Jim Hughes
Ben Calabrese

Functions: 01.4 06.0 06.1 09.0
Industries: Most
Description: Specialists in data processing search & consultation-greater Metropolitan area

Shannahan & Co., Inc.

655 Redwood Hwy., Ste. 133
Mill Valley, California 94941
Salary Minimum: $50,000
Key Contact: Peter Shannahan

Functions: 01.2 01.3 05.4 08.2 09.0
Industries: D.H0 H.00 H.10 H.11 J.13
Description: Handle financial services area

Sharrow & Assoc., Inc.

24735 Van Dyke
Centerline, Michigan 48015
Key Contact: Douglas Sharrow
Mike Johnson

Functions: 01.3 01.5 02.1 02.2 02.4
Industries: C.00 D.19 D.23 I.14 I.17
Professional Affiliations: MAPC
Description: 80% contingency, 20% retainer; various specialty areas; national recruitment

Branches:
199 S. Main, Box 5430
Plymouth, Michigan 48170
Key Contact: Beth Sharrow

644 Linn St., Ste. 236
Cincinnati, Ohio 45203
Key Contact: James W. Cole

Scott Sibley Assoc.

24 Bent Oak Tree
Fairport, New York 14450
Salary Minimum: $25,000
Key Contact: Scott S. McElhearn

Functions: 01.0 05.0 06.0 08.0
Industries: H.10 I.14 I.15 I.19 I.21
Professional Affiliations: SHRM
Description: We take a personal interest in our
clients & candidates

RitaSue Siegel Assoc., Inc.

18 E. 48th St.
New York, New York 10017
Salary Minimum: $20,000
Key Contact: Yvonne Shultis
RitaSue Siegel
Shari Grossman
Emily Dupras
Jack Odette

Functions: 02.1 05.0 05.2 05.3 11.6
Industries: D.24 D.D0 J.00 J.11
Professional Affiliations: ACNY, AIGA, AMA,
DMI, IDSA, SEGD
Description: Design/marketing management &
staff in industrial, graphic, interior design
& architecture

Marvin L. Silcott & Assoc., Inc.

7557 Rambler Rd., Ste. 1336
Dallas, Texas 75231
Salary Minimum: $50,000
Key Contact: Marvin L. Silcott

Industries: B.00 B.0W D.00 D.I0 H.00
Description: Executives, corporate & patent
attorneys, financial, engineering
management & scientists

L. A. Silver Assoc., Inc.

463 Worcester Rd.
Framingham, Massachusetts 01701
Salary Minimum: $60,000
Key Contact: Lee Silver

Functions: Most + 01.2 02.0 04.0 05.0 08.0
Industries: Most + D.00 D.H0 H.00 I.00 J.00
Description: Senior multinational recruitment:
all functions/disciplines, international &
U.S.

SilverCrest Search

P.O. Box 1568
Largo, Florida 34649
Salary Minimum: $40,000
Key Contact: David R. Anderson
Susan T. Anderson

Functions: 01.0 02.0 04.0 05.0 08.0
Industries: D.10 D.13 D.18 D.19 D.D0
Description: Search consultants specializing in
packaging personnel in food,
pharmaceutical & general mfg.

The Simmons Group

951-2 Old County Rd., Ste. 136
Belmont, California 94002
Salary Minimum: $50,000
Key Contact: Noel A. Simmons

Functions: Most
Industries: D.E0 D.H0 K.10
Professional Affiliations: NCHRC, PATCA,
SCVPA, SHRM
Description: Specialize in semiconductor
capital equipment, microwave components
& defense electronics

Simpson Assoc.

106 Central Park South
New York, New York 10019
Salary Minimum: $50,000
Key Contact: Terre Simpson
Trudy Weingarten

Functions: 05.1 05.5 06.0 08.0
Industries: D.11 F.00 G.00
Professional Affiliations: IFG, NAFE, NRF,
UC
Description: Middle/senior management for
department stores, specialty stores &
apparel manufacturers

Simpson Nance & Graham, Inc.

2200 Century Pkwy NE, Ste. 525
Atlanta, Georgia 30345-3203
Salary Minimum: $25,000
Key Contact: Lee Simpson

Functions: Most
Industries: Most
Description: General & staff management, with
emphasis in accounting & finance

Sloan & Assoc., Inc.

1761 Jamestown Rd.
Williamsburg, Virginia 23185-2324
Salary Minimum: $50,000
Key Contact: Michael Sloan
Gail Warren
Donald J. Hughes
John H. Holland
Mickey Anas

Functions: 05.0 05.1 05.4 06.1 11.1
Industries: D.10 D.13 D.16 D.I0
Description: Executive recruiters to the grocery
industry nationwide

James F. Smith & Assoc.

4651 Roswell Rd., NE, Ste. B102
Atlanta, Georgia 30342
Salary Minimum: $30,000
Key Contact: Howard T. Smith
James F. Smith

Functions: Most
Industries: Most
Professional Affiliations: APA
Description: Consulting psychologists who
provide executive search/recruiting svcs.
to their corporate clients

Raymond James Smith & Assoc.

Cary Oaks Executive Building
8807 Cary-Algonquin Rd.
Cary, Illinois 60013
Salary Minimum: $20,000
Key Contact: Raymond J. Smith

Functions: Most + 01.5
Industries: Most + I.17
Description: Nationwide attorney recruitment/
placement & search for law firms &
corporate legal departments

Ralph Smith & Assoc.

15219 Sunset Blvd., #205
Pacific Palisades, California 90272
Salary Minimum: $50,000
Key Contact: Ralph E. Smith

Functions: Most
Industries: Most
Description: General search practice, all
functional areas, most industries,
specialize in Southern CA

Smith, Anderson & Co.

163 Oldfield Road
Fairfield, Connecticut 06430
Salary Minimum: $60,000
Key Contact: Henry B. Smith

Functions: 01.0 05.4 08.2
Industries: H.00 H.R0 I.17
Description: Executive search for broad range
of financial service specialties/functions

Abbott Smith Assoc., Inc.

P.O. Box 318, Franklin Ave.
Millbrook, New York 12545
Salary Minimum: $40,000
Key Contact: David W. Brinkerhoff

Functions: Most + 06.0
Industries: Most
Professional Affiliations: AM, ASTD, EMA,
HRPS, ODN, SHRM
Description: Specialists in the recruitment of
human resource professionals

Branches:
P.O. Box 84111
Los Angeles, California 90073
Key Contact: William Dewhurst

1308 N. Astor St.
Chicago, Illinois 60610
Key Contact: David D. Dalenberg
David D. Franzone

International Branches:
London

J. Harrington Smith Assoc.

P.O. Box 90065
Indianapolis, Indiana 46290
Salary Minimum: $60,000
Key Contact: James H. Smith

Functions: Most + 01.0 02.0 03.0 05.0 06.0
Industries: Most + D.00 E.00 I.21
Description: Human resource consultant to
management

Smith, Beaty, Barlow Assoc., Inc.

P.O. Box 956069
Duluth, Georgia 30136-4647
Key Contact: Tom Smith
Mark Barlow

Functions: 05.0 05.2 05.4
Industries: Most + D.00 D.10 I.10
Professional Affiliations: GAPC, NAPC
Description: Food related industries, including
supermarkets, wholesale & food service

Smith Bradley & Assoc.

Box 25094, Corporate Woods
Overland Park, Kansas 66225
Salary Minimum: $40,000
Key Contact: Renea A. Bradley

Functions: Most + 01.2
Industries: H.00 H.10 I.14 I.16 I.21
Professional Affiliations: AHA, NAPC
Description: National & regional executive
search to banking & healthcare industries

Smith Hanley Assoc., Inc.

99 Park Ave.
New York, New York 10016
Salary Minimum: $40,000
Key Contact: Thomas A. Hanley, Jr.

Functions: 01.3 04.0 05.3 09.6 11.3
Industries: D.10 D.18 H.10 I.19 J.10
Professional Affiliations: AMA, ASA, ORSA,
TIMS
Description: Primarily oriented towards the
financial services, consumer products &
consulting industries

Branches:
203 N.LaSalle
Chicago, Illinois 60601
Key Contact: Linda Burtek

Snelling Personnel Services

203 Carondelet St., Ste. 530
Latter & Blum Bldg.
New Orleans, Louisiana 70130
Salary Minimum: $30,000
Key Contact: Julie Kent

Functions: 01.4 02.0 05.0 09.0 11.5
Industries: B.00 B.0W D.00 E.00 I.00
Description: Specializing in data processing,
sales & engineering positions on a
national basis

Phyllis Solomon Executive Search, Inc.

120 Sylvan Ave.
Englewood Cliffs, New Jersey 07632
Salary Minimum: $25,000
Key Contact: Phyllis Solomon

Functions: 01.1 01.2 01.3 01.5 05.1
Industries: D.18 H.00 I.10 I.19
Professional Affiliations: NJAPC
Description: Expertise with pharmaceuticals &
legal

Stephen M. Sonis Assoc.

463 Worcester Rd., 2nd. Fl.
Framingham, Massachusetts 01701-5354
Salary Minimum: $30,000
Key Contact: Stephen M. Sonis

Functions: Most + 01.0 03.0 05.0 06.0 08.0
Industries: F.00 G.00 H.00 I.00 J.00
Professional Affiliations: MPPC
Description: National & international retail &
human resources executive search

Source EDP

4545 Fuller Dr., Ste. 100
Irving, Texas 75038
Key Contact: Dennis Klembara

Branches:
4722 N. 24th St, #42D
Phoenix, Arizona 85016
Key Contact: Bob Rich

One Park Plz.
Irvine, California 92714
Key Contact: Bob Gennawey

4510 Executive Dr.
San Diego, California 92121
Key Contact: Mark Malone

345 California St.
San Francisco, California 94104
Key Contact: Jim Kosturos

2350 Mission College Blvd.
Santa Clara, California 95054
Key Contact: Maurice Stokes

15260 Ventura Blvd., Ste. 220
Sherman Oaks, California 91403
Key Contact: Vicki Girdziunas

970 W. 190th St., Ste. 560
Torrance, California 90502
Key Contact: Joe Gendron

1990 N. California Blvd.
Walnut Creek, California 94596
Key Contact: Trish Murphy

7730 E. Belleview Ave.
Englewood, Colorado 80111
Key Contact: Tom Conner

111 Founders Plz.
East Hartford, Connecticut 06108
Key Contact: Ray Anselmi

2777 Summer St.
Stamford, Connecticut 06905
Mark Polansky

Merritt 8 Corporate Pk.
99 Hawley Lane, Ste. 1101
Stratford, Connecticut 06497
Key Contact: Bob Macaluso

1800 K St., NW
Washington, District of Columbia 20006
Key Contact: Paul Villella

1201 N. Market St.
Wilmington, Delaware 19801
Key Contact: John Carney

Functions: 09.0 09.3 09.4
Industries: Most
Description: Computer recruiting specialists

7205 N.W. 19th St.
Miami, Florida 33126
Key Contact: Jim Scimone

1511 N. Westshore Blvd., Ste. 640
Tampa, Florida 33607
Key Contact: Buster Long

4170 Ashford Dunwoody Rd., NE
Atlanta, Georgia 30319
Key Contact: Tom Freeh

150 S. Wacker Dr., Ste. 400
Chicago, Illinois 60606
Key Contact: Larry Stanczak

One TransAm Plz., Ste 410
Oakbrook Terrace, Illinois 60181
Key Contact: Dennis Ortman

3701 Algonquin Rd., Ste. 380
Rolling Meadows, Illinois 60008
Key Contact: Jerry Lump

135 N. Pennsylvania Ave., Ste. 1770
Indianapolis, Indiana 46204
Key Contact: Randy Emerson

10300 W. 103rd St., Ste. 101
Overland Park, Kansas 66214
Key Contact: Dan Sudeikis

7804 E. Funston
Wichita, Kansas 67207
Key Contact: Dwight Ensminger

3110 First National Twr.
Louisville, Kentucky 40202
Key Contact: Kathy Mattingly

155 Federal St., Ste. 410
Boston, Massachusetts 02110
Key Contact: Steve McMahan

60 Mall Rd.
Burlington, Massachusetts 01803
Key Contact: Jim Mazzeo

1500 W. Park Dr.
Westborough, Massachusetts 01581
Key Contact: Gary Zegel

7 St. Paul St., Ste. 1660
Baltimore, Maryland 21202
Key Contact: Mike Bogdan

161 Ottawa N.W., Ste. 409D
Grand Rapids, Michigan 49503
Key Contact: Tom Combs

2000 Town Ctr., Ste. 350
Southfield, Michigan 48075
Key Contact: George Corser

8400 Normandale Lake Blvd.
Bloomington, Minnesota 55437
Key Contact: Chuck Lodge

150 S. Fifth St.
Minneapolis, Minnesota 55402
Key Contact: Steve Wolf

6 W. 5th St.
St. Paul, Minnesota 55102
Key Contact: Bob Hartzler

15 W. 10th St., 6th Fl.
Kansas City, Missouri 64105
Key Contact: J.B. Blocher

12312 Olive Blvd.
St. Louis, Missouri 63141
Key Contact: Nancy Riehl

71 Spit Brook Rd.
Nashua, New Hampshire 03060
Key Contact: Doug Hartwick

379 Thornall St.
Edison, New Jersey 08837
Key Contact: Gerry Gonyo

15 Essex Rd.
Paramus, New Jersey 07652
Key Contact: Tom Peressini

One Gatehall Dr.
Parsippany, New Jersey 07054
Key Contact: Joe Eiseman

101 Carnegie Ctr.
Princeton, New Jersey 08540
Key Contact: Jerry Goodman

120 Broadway
New York, New York 10271
Key Contact: Jack Schwartz

1200-C Scottsville Rd.
Rochester, New York 14624
Key Contact: Leigh Virkus

3280 Sunrise Hwy., Ste. 160
Wantagh, New York 11793
Key Contact: Jack Schwartz

925 Westchester Ave.
White Plains, New York 10604
Key Contact: Mark Polansky

3 Summit Park Dr., Ste.510
Cleveland, Ohio 44131
Key Contact: David Fell

525 Vine St., Ste.1070
Cincinnati, Ohio 45202
Key Contact: Greg Johnson

1105 Schrock Rd., Ste 510
Columbus, Ohio 43229
Key Contact: Chuck Rothenbush

One South Main St., Ste 410
Dayton, Ohio 45402
Key Contact: Bruce Rockwell

100 W. Fifth St.
Tulsa, Oklahoma 74103
Key Contact: Stacey Martin

Crown Plz. Bldg.
1500 SW First Ave., Ste 1140
Portland, Oregon 97201
Key Contact: George Bartosh

Walnut Hill Plz.
150 S. Warner Rd.
King of Prussia, Pennsylvania 19406
Key Contact: Rich Strimel

1800 John F. Kennedy Blvd.
Philadelphia, Pennsylvania 19103
Key Contact: Pamela Ciccantelli

Foster Plz. Bldg. VI
681 Andersen Dr., 2nd Fl.
Pittsburgh, Pennsylvania 15220
Key Contact: Leslie Finkel

6606 LBJ Feeway
Dallas, Texas 75240
Key Contact: Mike Varrichio

2515 McKinney Ave.
Dallas, Texas 75201
Key Contact: Davis Palmer

1800 W. Loop S.
Houston, Texas 77027
Key Contact: Lorna Henderson

7918 Jones Branch Dr.
McLean, Virginia 22102
Key Contact: Marty Grolnic

411 108th Ave. NE
Bellevue, Washington 98004
Key Contact: Blaine Millet

2129 S. Oneida St.
Green Bay, Wisconsin 54304-4612
Key Contact: Tom Hilgenberg

1233 N. Mayfair Rd.
Milwaukee, Wisconsin 53226
Key Contact: Dave Youngberg

Four Robert Speck Pkwy., Ste. 1180
Mississauga, Ontario L4Z 1S1 Canada
Key Contact: Dianne King

Source Engineering
4545 Fuller Dr., Ste 100
Irving, Texas 75038

Branches:
1290 Oakmead Pkwy., Ste. 318
Sunnyvale, California 94086
Key Contact: David Pregeant

60 Mall Rd.
Burlington, Massachusetts 01803
Key Contact: Jim Twomey

1500 W. Park Dr.
Westborough, Massachusetts 01581
Key Contact: Michael Neece

71 Spit Brook Rd.
Nashua, New Hampshire 03060
Key Contact: Peter Baranowski

Source Finance
4545 Fuller Dr., Ste 100
Irving, Texas 75038
Key Contact: Jack Causa
Howard Honig

Branches:
4722 N. 24th St.
Phoenix, Arizona 85016
Key Contact: John Kuzmick

One Park Plz.
Irvine, California 92714
Key Contact: Bob Kyle

345 California St.
San Francisco, California 94104
Key Contact: Bob Mensik

2350 Mission College Blvd.
Santa Clara, California 95054
Key Contact: Kurt Byer

15260 Ventura Blvd.
Sherman Oaks, California 91403
Key Contact: Rich Barrett

1990 N. California Blvd.
Walnut Creek, California 94596

970 W. 190th St.
Torrance, California 90502
Key Contact: John Cooney

40 King St. W., Ste. 3514
Toronto, Ontario M5H 3Y2 Canada
Key Contact: Susan Banting

251 Consumers Rd., Ste. 328
Willowdale, Ontario M2J 4R3 Canada
Key Contact: Les Nagy

Functions: 01.0 02.0 09.0 11.6
Industries: Most
Description: Engineering recruiting specialists

1500 SW First Ave., Crown Plaza Building
Portland, Oregon 97201
Key Contact: George Bartosh

6606 LBJ Freeway
Dallas, Texas 75240
Key Contact: Mike Varrichio

791B Jones Branch Dr.
McLean, Virginia 22102
Key Contact: Bill Boczany

411 108th Ave N.E.
Bellevue, Washington 98004

Functions: 01.0 08.0
Industries: Most
Description: Accounting & financial recruiting
  specialists

7730 E. Belleview Ave.
Englewood, Colorado 80111
Key Contact: Brad Francis

111 Founders Plz.
East Hartford, Connecticut 06108

2777 Summer St.
Stamford, Connecticut 06905
Key Contact: Warren Ladenheim

1667 K St. NW
Washington, District of Columbia 20006
Key Contact: Jay Schneider

7205 N.W. 19th St., #300
Miami, Florida 33126
Key Contact: Dave Semple

1511 N. Westshore Blvd., #640
Tampa, Florida 33607
Key Contact: Mike Carney

4170 Ashford-Dunwoody Rd. NE, #475
Atlanta, Georgia 30319
Key Contact: Gail Coutcher-Hughes

150 S. Wacker Dr.
Chicago, Illinois 60606
Key Contact: Paul Zellner

1 TransAm Pl., Ste. 410
Oakbrook Terrace, Illinois 60181

135 N. Pennsylvania
Indianapolis, Indiana 46204

10300 W. 103rd St.
Overland Park, Kansas 66214
Key Contact: Dan Cummings

7804 E. Funston
Wichita, Kansas 67207

155 Federal St.
Boston, Massachusetts 02110
Key Contact: Matt Karpacz

7 St. Paul St.
Baltimore, Maryland 21202
Key Contact: Chad Houck

161 Ottawa NW, Waters Bldg.
Grand Rapids, Michigan 49503
Key Contact: Mike Trewhella

2000 Town Ctr.
Southfield, Michigan 48075
Key Contact: Bill Swanner

8400 Normandale Lake Blvd.
Bloomington, Minnesota 55437

15 W. 10th St., 6th Fl.
Kansas City, Missouri 64105

150 S. Fifth St.
Minneapolis, Minnesota 55402
Key Contact: Evan Keene

6 W. 5th St.
St. Paul, Minnesota 55102

12312 Olive Blvd.
St. Louis, Missouri 63141
Key Contact: Marv Smiley

11212 Davenport St.
Omaha, Nebraska 68154
Key Contact: Tony Nemec

71 Spit Brook Rd.
Nashua, New Hampshire 03060
Key Contact: Joseph Reardon

399 Thornall St.
Edison, New Jersey 08837
Key Contact: Rich Singer

15 Essex Rd.
Paramus, New Jersey 07652
Key Contact: Matt Burgay

1 Gatehall Dr.
Parsippany, New Jersey 07054
Key Contact: Mike Lowenbraun

101 Carnegie Ctr.
Princeton, New Jersey 08540
Key Contact: Phil Ahn

195 Broadway
New York, New York 10007
Key Contact: Phil Bank

925 Westchester Ave.
White Plains, New York 10604
Key Contact: Frank Riniti

3867 W. Market St.
Akron, Ohio 44333
Key Contact: Vic Meles

525 Vine St.
Cincinnati, Ohio 45202
Key Contact: Greg Johnson

1375 E. 9th St.
Cleveland, Ohio 44114
Key Contact: Randy Samsel

1105 Schrock Rd.
Columbus, Ohio 43229
Key Contact: John Williamson

3 Summit Park Dr.
Independence, Ohio 44131
Key Contact: Tim Smith

100 W. 5th St.
Tulsa, Oklahoma 74103
Key Contact: Rick St. Thomas

1500 SW 1st Ave.
Portland, Oregon 97201
Key Contact: Jeff Johnson

150 S. Warner Rd.
Walnut Hill Plz.
King of Prussia, Pennsylvania 19406
Key Contact: Mark Taplinger

1800 John F. Kennedy Blvd.
Philadelphia, Pennsylvania 19103
Key Contact: Rob Cohen

681 Anderson Dr., 2nd Fl., Foster Pl. VI
Pittsburgh, Pennsylvania 15220
Key Contact: Bill Puckett

2515 McKinney Ave.
Dallas, Texas 75201
Key Contact: Robert DeVoe

777 Main St., Continental Plz.
Ft. Worth, Texas 76102
Key Contact: Charlie Pillow

1800 W. Loop S.
Houston, Texas 77027
Key Contact: Dan Luce

7918 Jones Branch Dr.
McLean, Virginia 22102
Key Contact: Sam Russell

Southwest Search Inc.
4500 S. Lakeshore Dr., Ste. 520
Tempe, Arizona 85282
Key Contact: Marilyn McDannel

411 108th Ave. NE
Bellevue, Washington 98004
Key Contact: Deena Eber

1233 N. Mayfair Rd.
Milwaukee, Wisconsin 53226
Key Contact: Chris Scherrer

40 King St. W.
Toronto, Ontario M5H 3Y2 Canada
Key Contact: Peter Britton

Functions: 09.0 09.3 09.4
Industries: Most
Description: AS400/IBM mainframe specialists
emphasizing applications & systems
programming nationwide

Specialized Search Assoc.
15200 Carter Rd.
Delray Beach, Florida 33446
Salary Minimum: $40,000
Key Contact: Leonard Morris

Functions: 01.3 05.2 05.4 11.5 11.6
Industries: B.0W B.10 C.00
Professional Affiliations: AGC, ITE, SAME,
SMPS
Description: Serving architecture, construction
& consulting engineering firms

Specialty Consultants, Inc.
Gateway Towers, Ste. 2710
Pittsburgh, Pennsylvania 15222
Salary Minimum: $40,000
Key Contact: Glenn Schreiber
Charles J. Abbott
Joseph R. DiSanti

Functions: Most
Industries: C.00 G.00 H.00 H.R0
Professional Affiliations: BOMA, ICSC, IREM,
MBA, NACORE, NAIOP, NMHC, RESSI
Description: Executive search-real estate &
construction industries

Spectra West
333 Twin Dolphin Dr., Ste. 145
Redwood City, California 94065
Salary Minimum: $50,000
Key Contact: Fred Arredondo

Functions: 05.4 09.2 09.3 09.4 09.7
Industries: D.24 D.H0 G.00 I.18
Professional Affiliations: IEEE
Description: High technology search for
computer engineers & sales professionals

Spectrum Consultants
12707 High Bluff Dr., Ste. 120
San Diego, California 92130-2036
Salary Minimum: $50,000
Key Contact: Stanley Bass
G.W. Christiansen

Branches:
6879 E. Dorado Ct.
Tucson, Arizona 85715-4753
Key Contact: Aram Tootelian

Functions: Most + 01.0 02.0 04.0 05.0 09.0
Industries: Most + B.00 D.E0 D.H0 D.I0 I.00
Description: Aerospace, hi-tech, engineering,
scientists, advanced materials, general
management, marketing

Spring Executive Search, Inc.

10 East 23rd St.
New York, New York 10010
Salary Minimum: $50,000
Key Contact: Dennis Spring

Functions: 01.0 05.0 05.7 11.1 11.2
Industries: J.10
Professional Affiliations: IABC, PRSA
Description: Specializing in the public
relations, marketing, advertising & sales
promotion fields

St. James And DeDominic

5900 Wilshire Blvd., 4th Fl.
Los Angeles, California 90036
Salary Minimum: $60,000
Key Contact: J. Baumgart

Functions: Most + 11.0
Industries: Most + B.0W D.00 I.00 K.00
Description: Search for senior executives in
corporate, government & non-profit
sectors

St. Lawrence Int'l., Inc.

219 Lamson St.
Syracuse, New York 13206
Salary Minimum: $30,000
Key Contact: Kathi Rodgers

Functions: Most
Industries: Most
Professional Affiliations: NAFE, NAPC
Description: Permanent, interim management
in manufacturing

International Branches:
Worchester

Staffing Consultants

P.O. Box 86, 15477 Smith Rd.
Summitville, Ohio 43962
Salary Minimum: $30,000
Key Contact: Jerry Muck
Sandi Shaffer

Functions: Most
Industries: Most
Professional Affiliations: AISI, AMA
Description: Specializes in the iron, steel &
nonferrous metals industry

Staffing Solutions

15466 Los Gatos Blvd. 109-373
Los Gatos, California 95031
Key Contact: Mike Gore

Functions: 01.4 04.0 06.1 09.2 09.4
Description: We unbundle the search process &
sell the pieces

Stanewick, Hart & Assoc., Inc.

3501 Turkey Run Ln.
Tallahassee, Florida 32312
Salary Minimum: $30,000
Key Contact: David Hunter
B. David Stanewick

Functions: 01.4 09.3 09.4 09.6 09.7
Industries: D.24 H.10 I.18
Professional Affiliations: ASM, DPMA
Description: Telecommunications and M.I.S.
recruiting for the banking &
manufacturing industry

Stanton/Schoen Professionals, Inc.

1800 St. James Pl., Ste. 303
Houston, Texas 77056
Key Contact: Richard N. Fiore

Functions: 11.3 11.5
Industries: B.0W
Professional Affiliations: NAPC
Description: Contingency & retained-search for
high level environmental professionals

Steeple Associates, Inc.

25 Notch Rd., P.O. Box 353
Little Falls, New Jersey 07424
Salary Minimum: $25,000
Key Contact: Sam Fusco

Functions: 08.0 08.1 08.2 08.3 08.4
Industries: H.00 H.10 H.11 H.12
Professional Affiliations: NAPC, NJAPC
Description: Accounting & financial
recruitment specialist since 1974

Steinbach & Co.

1 Pleasant St.
Maynard, Massachusetts 01754
Salary Minimum: $80,000
Key Contact: David M. Steinbach
Daniel E. Steinbach

Functions: 01.1 01.2 01.3 04.0 09.2
Industries: D.H0
Professional Affiliations: ACM, IEEE, NAPC
Description: Research, applied research &
advanced development in computer
software technologies

John R. Stephens & Assoc.

7007 Gulf Frwy., Ste. 202
Houston, Texas 77087
Salary Minimum: $35,000
Key Contact: John R. Stephens

Industries: C.00 D.13 D.15
Professional Affiliations: HAAPC, HESS, IEEE,
ISA, NAPC, NSPE, TAPC, TAPPI, TSPE
Description: 18 years-process industries,
engineering, construction, paper, pulp &
converting

Peter Sterling & Co.

One Riverway, Ste. 1700
Houston, Texas 77056
Salary Minimum: $40,000
Key Contact: Peter D. Sterling

Functions: Most
Industries: H.10
Description: Former banker specializing in
recruitment for financial institutions

Daniel Stern & Assoc.

211 N. Whitfield St., Ste. 240
The Medical Ctr. E.
Pittsburgh, Pennsylvania 15206
Salary Minimum: $50,000
Key Contact: Daniel Stern
John Dempster
David Marks

Functions: Most
Industries: I.14 I.15
Professional Affiliations: AHA, NAPR
Description: Specialized medical staff recruiting
& consulting services

Branches:
20 Merrill St.
Hingham, Massachusetts 02043
Key Contact: Steve Matson

Ron Stevens & Assoc., Inc.

P.O. Box 941251
Atlanta, Georgia 30341-0251
Salary Minimum: $35,000
Key Contact: Ron Stevens

Functions: 02.1 02.4 05.4 11.3 11.5
Industries: B.00 B.0W D.13 D.15 D.19
Professional Affiliations: TAPPI
Description: Chemical process/pulp & paper/
petro-chemical/utilities/agriculture/
plastics/metals/mining/envrn

The Stevens Group, Inc.

P.O. Box 367
Woodland Hills, California 91365
Salary Minimum: $40,000
Key Contact: Martha Stevens

Functions: 01.0 02.0 05.0 06.0 08.0
Industries: Most
Description: Executive search consultants
specializing in accounting, finance,
marketing & human resources

Affiliates/Other Offices:
The DLR Group, Inc., New York

Stewart Assoc.

245 Butler Ave., The Executive Offices
Lancaster, Pennsylvania 17601
Salary Minimum: $35,000
Key Contact: Walter S. Poyck

Functions: Most + 02.0 03.0 04.0 06.0 08.0
Industries: D.00 D.D0 D.E0 D.H0 E.00
Description: Recruiting specialists servicing the
commercial & defense manufacturing
sectors

Charles Stickler Assoc.
P.O. Box 5312C
Lancaster, Pennsylvania 17601
Salary Minimum: $35,000
Key Contact: Charles W. Stickler, III

Functions: Most + 01.0 02.0 03.0 04.0 05.0
Industries: D.22
Description: Recruiting specialists for the
metals & metal distribution industries

The Stoddard Co.
P.O. Box 329
Portland, Maine 04112
Salary Minimum: $30,000
Key Contact: Dean Stoddard
John Cobleigh

Branches:
P.O. Box 13681
Spokane, Washington 99213
Key Contact: Dorothy Stoddard

Functions: Most + 02.4 02.5 03.0
Industries: Most + D.22
Description: Engineering & manufacturing
search concentration on metal removal
industry

Stone Enterprises Ltd.
405 N. Wabash St., Ste. 1702
Chicago, Illinois 60611
Salary Minimum: $30,000
Key Contact: Susan L. Stone

Functions: 01.4 09.1 09.3 09.4 09.7
Description: Successful Chicago-based firm
assisting Fortune 20 to small, privately
held firms in most industries

Stoneburner Assoc., Inc.
10000 W. 75th St., Ste. 102
King's Cove
Shawnee Mission, Kansas 66204
Salary Minimum: $25,000
Key Contact: Dwight T. Stoneburner

Functions: Most + 02.4 02.5 04.0 11.3 11.5
Industries: Most
Description: Generalist with emphasis on high
tech industries and professionals

Storfer & Assoc.
1200 Broadway, Ste. 7D
New York, New York 10001
Salary Minimum: $30,000
Key Contact: Herbert F. Storfer
Nancy I. Johnson
Paul D. Storfer

Functions: 03.1 03.4 05.2 05.4 11.3
Industries: D.16 D.17 D.18 D.D0 I.16
Professional Affiliations: NAER, NAPC, PI
Description: A highly professional, specialized
executive search firm offering focussed,
personalized

Storti Assoc., Inc.
4060 Post Rd.
Warwick, Rhode Island 02886
Salary Minimum: $50,000
Key Contact: Michael A. Storti

Functions: Most
Industries: I.10 I.16 I.18 I.20 J.13

Phyllis Stovall Assoc., Inc.
32675 Woodside Dr.
Evergreen, Colorado 80439
Salary Minimum: $30,000
Key Contact: Phyllis Stovall

Functions: 09.0 11.1
Industries: I.14 I.18
Description: Over 25 years as MIS specialist

Straight & Co.
636 W. Jackson Ave.
Bridgeport, Connecticut 06604
Salary Minimum: $75,000
Key Contact: Gary R. Straight

Functions: 01.0 08.0 08.2 10.0
Industries: H.00 H.10 H.I0 H.R0
Description: Executive search & consulting to
management within the financial services
industry

Strategic Assoc., Inc.

9442 Capital of Texas Hwy.
Plz. I, Ste. 790
Austin, Texas 78759
Salary Minimum: $40,000
Key Contact: Michael L. Goldman
Jeff Browning
John Williams
Jeff Vise
Teresa Page
Sue Hargraves
John Poff
Bill Miles

Functions: 01.0 02.0 03.0 06.0 11.1
Industries: D.00 D.D0 D.H0 D.I0 E.00
Professional Affiliations: APICS, CLM, NAPC,
 NAPM, TAPC
Description: Executive recruitment firm
 specializing in manufacturing professionals
 nationwide

Strategic Executives, Inc.

6 Landmark Sq., 4th Fl.
Stamford, Connecticut 06901
Salary Minimum: $65,000
Key Contact: Randolph S. Gulian

Functions: 01.0 08.0 09.0 11.1
Industries: Most
Description: A resource for management
 consultants & strategic planning/
 development professionals

Branches:
980 N. Michigan Ave., Ste. 1400
Chicago, Illinois 60611

Strategic Search Group

P.O. Box 39472, 32533 Jefferson
Cleveland, Ohio 44139
Salary Minimum: $20,000
Key Contact: Barry Saxon
Ruth Sutton

Functions: 01.0 02.0 05.0 05.4 09.0
Industries: D.24 I.19 J.00
Professional Affiliations: OAPC
Description: Fifty plus years of business
 experience provide a commitment to
 personal service

Strategy 2000

P.O. Box 1824
Warsaw, Indiana 46581-1824
Key Contact: Kenneth P. Kelley

Functions: Most + 02.0 03.0 04.0 05.0 11.2
Industries: Most
Professional Affiliations: NAPC
Description: Cross-cultural training, targeted
 placement, technical, management,
 executive search

Strauss Personnel Service

Fifth & Smithfield St., Ste. 1523
Park Bldg.
Pittsburgh, Pennsylvania 15222
Key Contact: Jay Jarrell
Robert Stern
John O'Neill
Peter Glassner

Functions: Most
Industries: Most
Professional Affiliations: NALSC, NPA
Description: Pittsburgh area clients chiefly
 small/medium sized firms seeking an
 infusion of professional talent

Sturm, Burrows & Co.

P.O. Box 393
Flourtown, Pennsylvania 19031-9998
Salary Minimum: $50,000
Key Contact: Frederick C. Sturm, Jr.

Functions: Most + 01.0 05.0 06.0 08.0
Industries: Most + H.00 I.00
Description: Satisfying clients by giving the
 ultimate in service since 1954

S. Tyler Sullivan & Assoc., Inc.
85 Oak Knoll Dr.
Berwyn, Pennsylvania 19312
Salary Minimum: $40,000
Key Contact: Susan T. Sullivan

Functions: Most + 02.0 02.1 02.5 04.0 11.3
Industries: D.17 D.18 D.25 I.16
Description: Executive search for professionals in the pharmaceutical & biotechnology industries

Branches:
4350 Brownsboro Rd., Ste. 110
Louisville, Kentucky 40207
Key Contact: Robert J. Butler

Summerfield Assoc., Inc.
6555 Quince Rd., Ste. 105, The Koger Ctr.
The Koger Ctr.
Memphis, Tennessee 38119
Salary Minimum: $25,000
Key Contact: Dotty Summerfield-Beall

Functions: 01.4 01.5 02.0 06.0 09.0
Industries: Most
Professional Affiliations: DPMA, TAPC
Description: Offering 25+ years professional services to technical & managerial professionals

Summit Executive Search Consultants, Inc.
420 Lincoln Rd., Ste. 437
Miami Beach, Florida 33139
Salary Minimum: $25,000
Key Contact: Alfred J. Holzman

Functions: 02.0 02.2 11.2 11.5 11.6
Industries: B.10 D.23 D.26 K.00 L.00
Description: Handles retainer & contingency based assignments

Sumrall Personnel Consultants, Inc.
2915 LBJ Freeway, Ste. 107
Dallas, Texas 75234
Salary Minimum: $35,000
Key Contact: Virginia Sumrall

Functions: Most + 08.0 09.0
Industries: I.14 I.15
Description: Offers accounting, financial, data processing & engineering recruiting & search services

Ron Sunshine & Assoc.
1 First Missouri Ctr.
St. Louis, Missouri 63141
Salary Minimum: $50,000
Key Contact: Ron Sunshine
Scott Frazier
Barbara Blake

Functions: 01.0 02.0 03.0 04.0 06.0
Industries: D.10 D.22 D.23 D.26
Description: Specialization in manufacturing disciplines - metals, plastics & consumer goods

Supreme Assoc.
622 Taco Ave.
Westwood, New Jersey 07675
Salary Minimum: $35,000
Key Contact: Albert F. Chestone

Functions: Most + 11.0
Industries: Most
Professional Affiliations: NJAPC
Description: We are the specialist in executive security directors

Donna Svei Assoc.
1111 Third Ave., Ste. 2500
Seattle, Washington 98101
Salary Minimum: $25,000
Key Contact: Donna Svei

Functions: 08.0 08.1 08.2 08.3 08.4
Industries: Most
Description: Specializes in the recruitment of accountants & other financial management professionals

Systems Careers
211 Sutter St., Ste. 607
San Francisco, California 94108
Salary Minimum: $50,000
A. Wayne Sarchett

Functions: 05.6 09.0
Industries: Most + D.H0 I.18
Professional Affiliations: ASM
Description: Placement of computer systems, consultants, technical support, marketing & software engineers

Systems One Ltd.
1100 E. Woodfield Rd.
Schaumburg, Illinois 60173
Salary Minimum: $50,000
Key Contact: John Dahl

Functions: 01.4 09.0 09.3 09.6 09.7
Industries: Most
Professional Affiliations: NAER, NAPC
Description: Confidential service with established specialists in the emerging technology fields

The Talley Group
102 MacTanly Pl., Ste. A
Staunton, Virginia 24401
Salary Minimum: $30,000
Key Contact: E.H. Talley
E.G. Souder

Functions: 02.0 03.0 06.0 08.0 11.5
Industries: B.0W D.00 G.00 H.00
Professional Affiliations: ACA, SHRM
Description: Conducts searches for human resources, engineering accounting professionals

Tanzi Executive Search
3577 Fourth Ave.
San Diego, California 92103
Salary Minimum: $35,000
Key Contact: Vito A. Tanzi

Functions: 01.0 05.0
Industries: Most
Professional Affiliations: CONRO
Description: Specialists in management recruiting, marketing & general management

Branches:
110 Sutter, Ste. 414
San Francisco, California 94104
Key Contact: Richard Meyerhoff

Tatum & Assoc., Inc.
P.O. Box 1409
Gulf Breeze, Florida 32562-1409
Salary Minimum: $50,000
Key Contact: Philip M. Tatum, Sr.

Industries: I.15
Description: Physician search for hospitals & other health organizations specializing in Florida & Southeast

Branches:
P.O. Box 725049
Atlanta, Georgia 30339
Key Contact: Philip M. Tatum, Jr.

M. L. Tawney & Assoc.
P.O. Box 630573
Houston, Texas 77263-0573
Salary Minimum: $40,000
Key Contact: Mel Tawney

Functions: Most
Industries: B.00 B.0W C.00 D.H0 H.00
Professional Affiliations: TSCPA
Description: Executive search, mergers & acquisitions, new venture financing

Peter R. Taylor Assoc., Inc.
43 Orchard Dr.
East Williston, New York 11596
Salary Minimum: $40,000
Key Contact: Peter R. Taylor

Industries: H.R0
Professional Affiliations: ICSC, NACORE
Description: Corporate real estate executive search

Tech Consulting
50 S. Belcher Rd., Ste. 113
Clearwater, Florida 34625
Salary Minimum: $40,000
Key Contact: Mark Bavli

Functions: 04.0 05.2 09.2 09.7 11.3
Industries: D.24 D.25 D.E0 D.H0 J.13
Description: Recruiting senior staff &
   management in engineering, R&D,
   computers & telecommunications

Tech International
P.O. Box 297
Hope Valley, Rhode Island 02832
Salary Minimum: $25,000
Key Contact: Howard A. Smith
Helen M. Smith

Functions: Most + 02.0 04.0 05.0 09.2 11.3
Industries: Most + B.0W D.00 D.E0 D.H0
   D.I0
Professional Affiliations: ISA, OSA, SPIE
Description: Scientists/engineers, technical
   sales/management for instrumentation,
   electro-optics, biotechnology

Tech Vision Co.
30 Stonewyck, Ste. 1100
Chatham, New Jersey 07928
Salary Minimum: $60,000
Key Contact: Robert A. Molnar

Functions: Most + 01.4 08.0 09.0 09.3 09.7
Industries: Most
Description: Specializing in data processing,
   engineering, telecommunications, finance
   & human resources

Techcon Co.
3 Old Farm Rd.
Warren, New Jersey 07059
Salary Minimum: $35,000
Key Contact: John Pittman

Functions: 01.2 01.3 02.2 03.2 05.4
Industries: D.18 D.22 D.24 D.25 D.H0
Professional Affiliations: APICS, DPMA, IEEE
Description: Sales, marketing & technical
   personnel for electronic test &
   measurement, ATE, & computers

Technical Employment Consultants
P.O. Box 11643
Philadelphia, Pennsylvania 19116
Salary Minimum: $25,000
Key Contact: Carl Richards
Maureen Richards
James Orlando
Ann Organ

Professional Affiliations: ASQC, IEEE
Description: Technical employment consultants
   specializing in the aerospace, avionics &
   manufacturing industries

Technical Engineering Consultants
P.O. Box 825
Barnes Industrial Park
Wallingford, Connecticut 06492
Salary Minimum: $25,000
Key Contact: Paul Rooney
Bill Walsh

Functions: 01.0 02.0 03.0 04.0 09.0
Industries: D.00 D.18 D.23 D.E0 D.H0
Professional Affiliations: IEEE, NPA
Description: Specialist in advanced
   technologies as applied to manufacturing,
   aerospace, mechanical & electronics

Technical Recruiting Services
6100 Channingway Blvd., Ste. 506
Columbus, Ohio 43232
Salary Minimum: $35,000
Key Contact: Nick Lang

Functions: Most + 01.0 02.0 05.0 05.4
Industries: D.00 D.15 D.19 D.22 D.H0
Description: Search in high-tech metals,
   materials, and power transmission
   industries

Technical Recruiting Consultants
215 N. Arlington Heights Rd.
Ste. 102
Arlington Heights, Illinois 60004
Key Contact: Dick Latimer

Functions: 01.4 09.3 09.4
Industries: Most
Description: Specialists in information systems,
   engineering & manufacturing positions

Technical Staffing Assoc.
2712 Route 9
Ballston Spa, New York 12020
Key Contact: Donald Munger

Functions: 01.0 05.2 11.3 11.5 11.6
Industries: B.00 B.0W B.10 C.00 E.00
Description: Specializing in contruct
management (all areas), consulting
engineering (civil, environmental)

Technitrac, Inc.
P.O. Box 653
Long Valley, New Jersey 07853-0653
Salary Minimum: $35,000
Key Contact: Alvin S. Gustafson

Functions: 01.2 02.1 03.1 04.0 05.3
Industries: B.00 D.22 D.25 D.E0 D.I0
Description: Manufacturing, marketing &
engineering for the heavy rotating
machinery industries

Techno-Trac Systems, Inc.
251 Central Park W.
New York, New York 10024
Salary Minimum: $20,000
Key Contact: Mort Trachtenberg

Functions: 09.0 09.2 09.3 09.4 09.7
Industries: H.00 H.10 H.11 I.18 I.19
Description: Data processing, banking &
financial placement, from director to
programmer

Techsearch Services Inc.
1500 Broadway #2203
New York, New York 10036
Salary Minimum: $30,000
Key Contact: David G. Taft
Patrick Gorman
Alan Hunter

Functions: 01.4 09.3 09.5 09.6
Industries: H.00 H.10 H.11 I.00
Professional Affiliations: NAER
Description: Executive recruitment of data
processing professionals for Fortune 100
companies

Tecmark Assoc. Inc.
P.O. Box 545
Port Washington, New York 11050
Salary Minimum: $30,000
Key Contact: Donald K. Valentine
Douglas K. Hess
Bradford M. Kennedy

Functions: Most + 01.0 05.0 09.4
Industries: D.24 D.25 D.H0 J.00
Description: Electronics industry & related
high technology search/recruiting both
nationwide & international

Branches:
10675 S. DeAnza Blvd.
Cupertino, California 95014
Key Contact: Bradley Wilkinson

636 Great Rd.
Stow, Massachusetts 01775
Key Contact: James M. Farley

TeleSearch, Inc.
268 U.S. Hwy. 206, Bldg. D
Bartley Sq.
Flanders, New Jersey 07836
Salary Minimum: $30,000
Key Contact: Debra A. Sola-Furnari
Polly McDonald

Functions: 05.4 09.7 11.6
Industries: D.H0 J.00 J.13
Professional Affiliations: NAPC
Description: Specializing in the placement of
management personnel within the
telecommunications industry

Telem Adhesive Search Corp.
104 Church Ln., Ste. 202
Baltimore, Maryland 21208
Salary Minimum: $40,000
Key Contact: Peter B. Telem

Functions: 02.2 02.4 04.0 05.0 11.3
Industries: D.13 D.14 D.15 D.20
Professional Affiliations: IPA, NAER
Description: Technical, sales & marketing
professionals for adhesives, coatings &
polymer industries

Telemarketing Search, Inc.
55 E. Washington St.
Chicago, Illinois 60602
Salary Minimum: $25,000
Key Contact: Joseph J. Culotta

Functions: 05.5 05.6
Industries: Most
Professional Affiliations: ATA, DMA
Description: Professional recruiting,
    specializing in both telemarketing &
    customer service

Tell/Com Recruiters
306 Corporate Dr. E.
Langhorne, Pennsylvania 19047
Salary Minimum: $30,000
Key Contact: Dennis F. Young

Functions: 02.1 05.4 09.7
Industries: J.13
Description: Placing sales, marketing &
    management telecommunications
    professionals

Thomas, Whelan Assoc., Inc.
2000 K St. NW., Ste. 444
Washington, District of Columbia 20006
Salary Minimum: $25,000
Key Contact: Cheryl Molliver Ross
Kerry Baker
Susan Provyn
James Reo

Functions: 08.0 08.1 08.4
Industries: Most
Description: Specialize in the placement of
    accounting & financial professionals

Judy Thompson & Assoc., Inc.
3727 Camino Del Rio S., Ste. 200
San Diego, California 92108
Salary Minimum: $25,000
Key Contact: Judy Thompson

Functions: 08.0 08.1 08.2 08.3 08.4
Industries: Most
Professional Affiliations: IMA
Description: Specialize in experienced, degreed
    accounting/financial professionals in San
    Diego County

Thornton Assoc.
9800 McKnight Rd., Ste. 300A
Pittsburgh, Pennsylvania 15237
Salary Minimum: $30,000
Key Contact: John C. Thornton

Functions: Most + 11.2 11.4
Industries: H.10
Professional Affiliations: NAPC, PAPC
Description: Firm specializes in financial
    institutions & marketing

Thoroughbred Executive Search
9616 Reisterstown Rd., Ste. 462
Owings Mills, Maryland 21117
Salary Minimum: $30,000
Key Contact: Susan J. Sellers

Functions: Most + 11.1
Industries: Most
Description: Int'l recruitment of management
    consultants specializing in productivity/
    profit improvement

The Tibbetts Group Ltd.
22930 Crenshaw Blvd., Ste. B2
Torrance, California 90505
Salary Minimum: $25,000
Key Contact: Charles A. Tibbetts

Functions: 01.0 02.0 03.0 04.0 06.0
Industries: C.00 D.00 D.D0 E.00 I.00
Professional Affiliations: APICS
Description: Providing honest search &
    consulting for improved profitability

Tidewater Group Inc.
66 Crescent St.
Stamford, Connecticut 06906
Salary Minimum: $40,000
Key Contact: John Kalas

Functions: Most
Industries: Most
Description: Nationwide recruiting primarily
    for Fortune 1000 clients

Topaz Int'l., Inc.
383 Northfield Ave.
West Orange, New Jersey 07052
Salary Minimum: $50,000
Key Contact: Ronni L. Gaines
Stewart Michaels

Functions: 01.5
Industries: Most + I.17
Professional Affiliations: ACG, NALSC,
  NAPC, NATS
Description: Attorney recruitment:
  multinational corporations & law firms,
  emphasizing client/candidate needs

Tower Consultants, Ltd.
250 W. Lancaster Ave., Ste. 265
Paoli, Pennsylvania 19301
Key Contact: Donna L. Friedman

Functions: 01.3 06.1 06.2 10.0 11.2
Industries: Most + H.I0 I.14
Professional Affiliations: ACA, ASTD,
  ORTHO, RR, SHRM
Description: Nationwide search: benefits &
  compensation, human resources, health
  care, managed care

Jay Tracey Assoc.
P.O. Box 371
Jamestown, Rhode Island 02835
Salary Minimum: $25,000

Functions: 02.2 02.3 05.4
Industries: B.00 D.13 D.19 D.24
Description: Sales, application & project
  engineers for drives, PLC'S, factory
  automation & process control

TransAmerica Network
215 Jack Boot Way
Monument, Colorado 80132
Salary Minimum: $38,000
Key Contact: Don Wunder
Nancy Wunder

Functions: Most + 04.0 09.0
Industries: Most + B.0W
Description: Professional placement, all
  industries, all functions-nationally

Travel Executive Search
5 Rose Ave.
Great Neck, New York 11021
Salary Minimum: $30,000
Key Contact: Karen Rubin

Functions: Most
Industries: E.00 I.10 I.11
Description: Executive recruitment specialists
  for the travel industry

Traynor Confidential, Ltd.
10 Gibbs St., Ste. 400
Rochester, New York 14604
Salary Minimum: $20,000
Key Contact: Thomas H. Traynor
Margaret Baxter
Rachel Cornell
Frank Mandicott

Functions: 01.4 02.0 06.0 08.0 09.0
Industries: C.00 D.00 D.H0 H.00 J.13
Professional Affiliations: NAER, NAPC
Description: Practice limited to upstate NY &
  companies with $5 million & above

Triangle Assoc.
P.O. Box 506
Warrington, Pennsylvania 18976
Salary Minimum: $30,000
Key Contact: Stephen R. Ostroff

Functions: 01.3 02.2 02.4 11.6
Industries: D.15 D.16 D.18 D.19 D.20
Description: Engineering & technical
  management positions for the process &
  manufacturing industries

Triangle Consulting Group
23 Fifer Lane
Lexington, Massachusetts 02173
Salary Minimum: $40,000
Key Contact: James A. Bricker
Baxter Baer
J. Cohen

Functions: 01.0 02.0 05.0
Industries: D.00 D.H0 I.00
Description: Specialists working with start-ups,
  troubled companies & growth situations

Trilogy Enterprises, Inc.

1919 Midwest Rd., Ste. 108
Oak Brook, Illinois 60521
Salary Minimum: $35,000
Key Contact: Eric K. Schuller
Bonita Mae

Functions: Most + 01.4 02.0 08.0 09.0
Industries: Most
Description: Our practice is geared to satisfy
   client requirements & needs

Peter C. Tumminelli & Assoc.

P.O. Box 645
Folsom, California 95630
Key Contact: Peter C. Tumminelli

Functions: 05.0 05.1 05.2 05.3 05.4
Industries: D.10 D.18
Description: Specialists in all facets of medical
   sales & marketing

J.Q. Turner & Assoc., Inc.

11940 E. Bates Cir., Suite 200
Aurora, Colorado 80014-3105
Salary Minimum: $35,000
Key Contact: Jim Turner

Functions: 02.0 03.0 04.0 09.0 11.3
Industries: B.0W D.00 D.H0 D.I0 J.00
Professional Affiliations: CAPC
Description: Technical professionals-research/
   development/manufacturers/process/
   quality/test/plant/project

U.S. Search

7921 Jones Branch Dr., Ste. 411
McLean, Virginia 22102
Salary Minimum: $30,000
Key Contact: Arnie Hiller
Alan Fedder

Functions: 03.0 03.4
Industries: D.15 D.19 D.D0
Description: Established national recruitment
   & search firm with specialization by
   industry

USA Medical Placement Inc.

3604 Date Palm
McAllen, Texas 78501
Salary Minimum: $50,000
Key Contact: Patricia Tracy

Functions: 04.0 07.0 10.0
Industries: I.14 I.15
Description: A medical search firm, working all
   areas in the medical field strictly on
   contingency

Unisearch

814 Morena Blvd., Ste. 302
San Diego, California 92110
Salary Minimum: $30,000
Key Contact: Robert H. Begalke

Functions: Most + 01.0 02.0 04.0 11.3 11.5
Industries: B.0W B.10 D.I0 H.00 H.10
Description: Executive search concentration is
   in the banking, bio-tech & environmental
   disciplines

The Urban Placement Service

2211 Norfolk, Ste. 816
Houston, Texas 77098-4044
Salary Minimum: $20,000
Key Contact: Willie S. Bright

Functions: Most + 02.0 05.4 08.0 11.2 11.6
Industries: Most + D.00 D.10 D.15 D.18
   D.E0
Description: Professional search-minority
   recruitment

Valentine & Assoc.

One Woodfield Lake, Ste. 117
Schaumburg, Illinois 60173
Salary Minimum: $25,000
Key Contact: Linda S. Valentine
James P. Valentine

Functions: 02.0 03.0 09.3
Industries: D.00 D.D0 E.00
Professional Affiliations: APICS, NIIA
Description: Small, owner operated firm
   handling only materials management
   professionals

Vento Assoc.

7 Cadmus Ct.
West Orange, New Jersey 07052
Salary Minimum: $40,000
Key Contact: Joseph P. Vento

Functions: 01.0 02.3 05.4 09.2 09.4
Industries: D.18 D.24 D.25 D.H0 D.I0
Description: Dedicated to industrial
automation, CIM, process & analytical
instrumentation & biotechnology markets

Vezan Assoc.

1000 Farmington Ave.
West Hartford, Connecticut 06107
Key Contact: Henry D. Vezan

Functions: 05.0 06.0 07.0 08.0 11.0
Industries: D.H0 H.10 H.I0 I.14 I.16
Description: Specialized recruiting for New
England companies

Vick & Assoc.

3325 Landershire Ln., Ste.1001
Plano, Texas 75023
Salary Minimum: $50,000
Key Contact: Bill Vick

Functions: 05.0 05.1 05.2 05.3 05.4
Industries: D.24 D.H0 G.00 J.13
Professional Affiliations: NPA, TAPC
Description: Executive search in
microcomputer industry with focus on
sales & marketing

Video Interview Professionals, Inc.

919 Orange Ave., Ste. 202
Winter Park, Florida 32789
Salary Minimum: $30,000
Key Contact: Lynn M. Walbright
Ross Miller

Functions: Most + 04.0 11.3 11.5
Industries: B.0W D.18 D.I0
Professional Affiliations: AAPG, ACS, AIPG,
BPS
Description: Scientific recruiting, including
environmental

Darryl Vincent & Assoc.

12651 Briar Forest, Ste. 165
Houston, Texas 77077
Salary Minimum: $30,000
Key Contact: Darryl Vincent

Functions: 05.1 05.3 05.4
Industries: D.10 D.11 D.13 D.16
Description: Recruiting consumer package good
sales managers -first through third line

C. J. Vincent Assoc., Inc.

2000 Century Plz.
Columbia, Maryland 21044
Salary Minimum: $30,000
Key Contact: Vincent J. Cucuzzella

Functions: 05.2 05.3 05.4
Industries: D.24
Professional Affiliations: MAPRC
Description: Professional recruitment for sales
& marketing in the computer industry

Vogel Assoc.

P.O. Box 269R
Huntingdon Valley, Pennsylvania 19006-0269
Salary Minimum: $25,000
Key Contact: Michael S. Vogel

Functions: 06.0 06.1 06.2
Industries: Most
Professional Affiliations: ACA, ASTD, CPC,
EMA, IAPW, NAPC, NPA, ODN, SHRM
Description: Professional recruiting & search
specializing exclusively in human
resources nationwide

WBS Network Professional & Executive Search

P.O. Box 346
Citrus Heights, California 95611-0346
Salary Minimum: $35,000
Key Contact: W. Barry Spiller

Functions: Most
Industries: Most
Description: Specialize in professional,
technical & executive search/recruiting
nationwide

Gordon Wahls Co.
797 Harrison Rd.
Villanova, Pennsylvania 19085
Salary Minimum: $50,000
Key Contact: David Cochran

Functions: 01.0 02.0 05.0 09.0
Industries: D.13 D.14 D.D0 J.13
Professional Affiliations: IACPR, NAPC
Description: We specialize in publishing, printing, graphic arts & paper industries

Waldorf Associates, Inc.
11911 San Vicente Blvd., Ste. 240
Los Angeles, California 90049-5086
Key Contact: Michael Waldorf, Esq.

Functions: 01.5 11.0
Industries: I.17
Professional Affiliations: NALSC
Description: Attorney search & placement, in California & nationally

Wallace Assoc.
193 Grand St., Ste. 416
P.O. Box 9354
Waterbury, Connecticut 06724
Salary Minimum: $30,000
Key Contact: Gregory Gordon

Functions: 01.0 02.0 03.0 04.0 09.0
Industries: B.0W D.00 D.D0 D.H0 D.I0
Professional Affiliations: APICS, ASM, ASQC, IEEE, SME, SPE
Description: Engineering & manufacturing support up to & including executive level

Denis P. Walsh & Assoc., Inc.
5402 Bent Bough
Houston, Texas 77088
Salary Minimum: $40,000
Key Contact: Denis P. Walsh, Jr.

Functions: Most
Industries: B.00 C.00
Description: Most functions; heavy in engineering, construction industries, refining & petrochemicals

Frank X. Walsh & Co., Inc.
5325 W. Burleigh St.
Milwaukee, Wisconsin 53210
Salary Minimum: $30,000
Key Contact: Richard E. Boeck
Charles N. Wallens

Functions: Most + 02.0 03.0 05.0 08.0 09.0
Industries: Most + B.0W D.00 D.H0 H.00 I.00
Description: Service to management wanting to hire "the very best" - all fields

Martha Ward Assoc., Inc.
15 E. 40th St., Ste. 1100
New York, New York 10016
Salary Minimum: $50,000
Key Contact: Martha Ward
Nat Lane

Functions: 05.0 05.1 05.2 05.3 05.5
Industries: D.00 H.00 I.00
Professional Affiliations: EMA
Description: Specialize in consumer marketing, marketing services, package goods & financial services

M.K. Wasse & Assoc., Inc.
84 Villa Rd., B-7
Greenville, South Carolina 29615
Salary Minimum: $30,000
Key Contact: Mary K. Wasse

Functions: Most + 01.3 02.1 06.2 11.2 11.3
Description: Assist client organizations identify, appraise & employ middle & top management executives

Water Street Assoc.
130 Water St., Ste 12C
New York, New York 10005
Key Contact: Stephen Flynn
Joseph Logan

Functions: 06.0 08.0 10.0
Industries: D.00 H.00 H.I0
Description: We are a specialized recruiting firm committed to professionalism & integrity

Waterford, Inc.
4200 Northside Pkwy., NW
11 N. Pkwy. Sq.
Atlanta, Georgia 30327
Salary Minimum: $35,000
Key Contact: Mark Alexander
B. M. DuBose, III

Functions: Most
Industries: H.10
Description: Executive recruitment for financial
institutions with offices in the Southeast

Wayne Assoc., Inc.
2628 Barrett St.
Virginia Beach, Virginia 23452
Salary Minimum: $40,000
Key Contact: Robert W. Cozzens

Functions: 01.0 04.0 05.0 05.4 10.0
Industries: B.0W C.00 D.13 D.15 H.10
Professional Affiliations: NAPC, NEN
Description: Specialized by industry-successful
in chemicals & hazardous waste

Weatherby Healthcare
25 Van Zant St.
Norwalk, Connecticut 06855
Salary Minimum: $40,000
Key Contact: Joseph Pendergast
Lawrence D. Stewart

Functions: Most + 11.0
Industries: D.00 D.H0 I.14 I.15
Professional Affiliations: AHA, AMA, HFMA,
MGMA, NAER, NAPR
Description: Healthcare executive search &
physician recruitment; general
management

Branches:
3200 Commercial Blvd., W.
Ft. Lauderdale, Florida 33309

D.L. Weaver & Assoc.
6 Hutton Ctr. Dr., Ste. 650
Santa Ana, California 92707-5707
Salary Minimum: $20,000
Key Contact: Doris Weaver

Functions: Most + 01.0 07.0 08.0 09.0
Industries: Most
Professional Affiliations: IACPR, BIA, NAA
Description: Generalists with focus on real
estate, finance, accounting &
environmental industries

Weeks & Assoc.
921 Cottage Hill Ave.
Mobile, Alabama 36693
Salary Minimum: $30,000
Key Contact: Mercon A. Weeks

Functions: 01.2 01.3 02.2 02.4 02.6
Industries: D.22 D.23
Description: Recruitment of management
personnel for the shipbuilding industry

Wegner & Assoc.
11270 W. Park Pl., Ste. 310
One Park Plz.
Milwaukee, Wisconsin 53224
Salary Minimum: $25,000
Key Contact: Carl Wegner
John Sweet
Bob Schultz

Functions: 01.0 02.0 05.0 08.0 09.0
Industries: Most
Professional Affiliations: EDPAA, HFMA, IIA
Description: Specialization in general
management, financial & MIS recruiting

Weinman & Assoc.
P.O. Box 31336
Phoenix, Arizona 85046
Salary Minimum: $30,000
Key Contact: Mary Weinman

Functions: 07.4
Industries: I.10
Professional Affiliations: ASPA, VIA
Description: Executive search specializing in
the hospitality & food service industry

Weinpel & Co.
20 Hamburg Tpke.
Riverdale, New Jersey 07457
Salary Minimum: $50,000
Key Contact: Leon Seldin
Bernd Stecker
Charles J. Weinpel

Functions: Most + 02.0 04.0 05.0 11.0 11.3
Industries: D.00 D.E0 D.H0
Description: Specialize in recruitment for high
technology, aerospace & engineering
management—est. 1950

Weiss & Assoc., Inc.
P.O. Box 915656
Longwood, Florida 32791-5656
Key Contact: Terry M. Weiss

Functions: 01.5 08.4
Industries: D.20 I.17
Professional Affiliations: FAPC, NALSC,
NAPC
Description: Specialize with experienced
attorneys & tax professionals nationwide

Weliver & Assoc.
37727 Professional Center Dr., Ste. 115D
Livonia, Michigan 48154
Key Contact: Edward A. Weliver

Industries: Most
Professional Affiliations: HRA, MAPC, NAPC
Description: Specialize in H.P. & mainframe-
directors to programmers

Henry Welker & Assoc.
24901 Northwestern, Ste. 305
Southfield, Michigan 48075-2203
Salary Minimum: $40,000
Key Contact: Henry A. Welker

Functions: Most + 01.3 02.1 02.2 02.5 11.5
Industries: Most + D.22 D.23 D.25 D.26
D.H0
Description: Recruiting/search in management,
engineering & data processing

Wellington Thomas Ltd.
9887 Gandy Blvd. N., Ste. 233
St. Petersburg, Florida 33702
Key Contact: Jean M. De Mange

Functions: 11.0
Industries: I.14
Professional Affiliations: AOTA, APTA, NHIF
Description: Our focus is on healthcare
professionals in rehab settings

Wells, Bradley & Assoc.
7582 Currell Blvd., # 207
St. Paul, Minnesota 55125
Salary Minimum: $30,000
Key Contact: Sandy Bradley

Functions: Most
Industries: H.00 H.10 H.R0
Professional Affiliations: NBNS
Description: Executive search concentrating on
banking, savings & loan associations &
investment firms

R.A. Wells Co.
P.O. Box 723-232
Atlanta, Georgia 30339
Salary Minimum: $30,000
Key Contact: Robert A. Wells

Functions: 01.2 02.1 02.4 03.4 05.4
Industries: D.10 D.19 D.22 D.D0 D.H0
Description: Search specialist in engineering/
management in plastic & metal packaging
industry

Werbin Assoc. Executive Search, Inc.
521 Fifth Ave., Ste. 1749
New York, New York 10175
Key Contact: Susan Werbin

Functions: 01.4 05.2 05.3 08.0 09.0
Industries: Most + D.00 H.00 I.00 J.00
Professional Affiliations: AWC, TIMS
Description: Oriented towards assisting the
computer, research & mgmt science
professionals tech mgmt-all levels

Wesson, Taylor, Wells & Assoc.
P.O. Box 23587
Columbia, South Carolina 29224
Salary Minimum: $25,000
Key Contact: Paul Clifton

Branches:
P.O. Box 72137
Atlanta, Georgia 30007-2137
Key Contact: Tom Hesson

P.O. Box 3046
Valley Forge, Pennsylvania 19404-3046
Key Contact: Bob Thomas

Functions: 01.4 09.3 09.4 09.7 11.3
Industries: D.15 D.26 D.E0 D.H0 J.00
Description: Specialize in placement of
   contract programming & analysis data
   processing professionals

P.O. Box 12274
Research Triangle Pk., North Carolina 27709-
2274
Key Contact: Skip Marsh

WestCare Executive Search
11535 Eaglesview Ct., Ste. 2E
San Diego, California 92127-2037
Salary Minimum: $40,000
Key Contact: Lisa West
   Nicholas Warrillow

Functions: Most + 11.0
Industries: I.00 I.14 I.15
Description: Specializing in healthcare
   professionals for acute care, managed care
   & alternative systems

Bob Westerfield & Assoc., Inc.
5150 S. Florida Ave.
Lakeland, Florida 33813
Key Contact: Robert H. Westerfield
   Portia P. Westerfield
   Richard D. May
   Kathryn C. Henry

Functions: 05.1
Industries: J.10
Description: Specialists in recruiting creative
   people for advertising agencies

Western Personnel Assoc., Inc.
316 E. Flower
Phoenix, Arizona 85012
Salary Minimum: $30,000
Key Contact: Richard A. Fishel
   Gregory A. Gee

Functions: Most
Industries: Most
Professional Affiliations: EMA, NAPC, NPA,
   SHRM
Description: Full service, nationwide,
   contingency firm- H.R., engineering, sales,
   management & technical

Western Search Assoc.
800 Silverado, Ste. 301
La Jolla, California 92037
Salary Minimum: $35,000
Key Contact: Karen Green

Functions: Most
Industries: D.24 D.26 D.E0 H.R0
Description: Specializing in hi-tech, bio-tech &
   environmental industries in San Diego &
   Southern California

S.J. Wexler Assoc., Inc.
522 Fifth Ave.
New York, New York 10036
Salary Minimum: $65,000
Key Contact: Suzanne Wexler

Functions: 01.4 06.0 08.0 09.0
Industries: Most
Professional Affiliations: IACPR, HRPS
Description: Specializing in placing executives
   at the mid & senior management level

E.T. Wharton Assoc., Inc.
2698 Glen Plz., Rte. 516
Old Bridge, New Jersey 08857
Salary Minimum: $30,000
Key Contact: Bob Jones

Functions: 01.0 02.4 02.5 03.4 11.6
Industries: Most
Professional Affiliations: IIE, NJAPC, PI
Description: Primarily specializing in
   engineering & manufacturing management

Wheeler Assoc.

P.O. Box 6589
Incline Village, Nevada 89450
Salary Minimum: $40,000
Key Contact: Janelle M. Feliciano
Robert W. Wheeler

Functions: 08.4
Industries: Most
Description: Tax professionals for public
  accounting firms & major corporations

Wheelless Group

49 E. Elm St.
Chicago, Illinois 60611
Key Contact: Pat Wheelless

Functions: 05.1 05.2 05.3 05.4 05.5
Professional Affiliations: CADM, DMA,
  WDRG
Description: Retained search firm serving the
  direct marketing community

Whitaker, Fellows & Assoc.

820 Gessner, Ste. 1500
Houston, Texas 77024
Salary Minimum: $40,000
Key Contact: Bruce Whitaker
William Fellows

Functions: Most
Industries: D.15 D.19 I.15 I.17
Professional Affiliations: HAAPC, NALSC,
  NAPC, TAPC
Description: Executive search & recruiting firm
  with legal, healthcare & engineering
  specialties

Whitbeck & Assoc.

701 Fourth Ave., S, Ste. 500
Minneapolis, Minnesota 55415
Salary Minimum: $50,000
Key Contact: Elizabeth C. Whitbeck

Functions: 01.5
Industries: I.17
Description: Legal search

David J. White & Assoc., Inc.

809 Ridge Rd., Ste. 200
Wilmette, Illinois 60091
Salary Minimum: $50,000
Key Contact: David J. White

Functions: Most
Industries: Most
Description: Consultants to law firms &
  corporate legal depts.; attorney & general
  recruitment & placement

White-Ridgely & Assoc., Inc.

2201 Old Court Rd.
Rockland Grist Mill
Baltimore, Maryland 21208
Salary Minimum: $40,000
Charles R. White, Jr.

Functions: 01.0 05.0 06.0 08.0
Industries: D.00 H.00 H.I0 H.R0
Description: Search consultants in financial
  services, banking, marketing & human
  resources

Whitehead & Assoc., Inc.

330 Palisades Dr.
Lake Ozark, Missouri 65049
Key Contact: Robert S. Whitehead
Elizabeth S. Whitehead

Functions: Most
Industries: Most
Description: Engineering, manufacturing,
  industrial/design engineers to upper
  management

Whittaker & Assoc., Inc.

2675 Cumberland Pkwy., Ste. 263
Atlanta, Georgia 30339
Salary Minimum: $30,000
Key Contact: Millie A. Boatman
Arnold G. Whittaker
Brad Winkler

Functions: 01.0 02.0 04.0 05.0 06.0
Industries: D.10 D.D0
Professional Affiliations: GAPC, NAPC
Description: Specializes in the search &
  placement of food executives nationwide

Whittlesey & Assoc., Inc.

300 S. High St.
West Chester, Pennsylvania 19380
Salary Minimum: $40,000
Key Contact: James G. Hogg, Jr.
Elizabeth B. H. Landreth
Robert M. Linneman
Barbara Lyons

Functions: 01.0 02.0 05.0 06.0 11.2
Industries: D.00 D.10 D.13 D.15 D.18
Professional Affiliations: IACPR, AMA, ASTD,
    HRPS, PIMA, TAPPI
Description: Focus on assignments with
    organizations committed to excellence

Joel H. Wilensky Assoc., Inc.

22 Union Ave.
P.O. Box 155
Sudbury, Massachusetts 01776
Salary Minimum: $40,000
Key Contact: Joel H. Wilensky

Functions: Most + 01.1 01.2 01.4 08.0 09.0
Industries: G.00
Professional Affiliations: NPA
Description: One person contingency recruiting
    firm specializing in retail chain placement

Wilkinson Boyd

199 Elm St.
New Canaan, Connecticut 06840
Salary Minimum: $50,000
Key Contact: Frank M. Wilkinson
Michael J. Boyd
Marya Hahn

Functions: 08.2
Industries: H.10 H.11
Professional Affiliations: ICI
Description: Specialize in investment advisory
    firms & fixed income securities dealers

The Wilkinson Group

470 Starlight Crest Dr.
La Canada, California 91011
Salary Minimum: $30,000
Key Contact: Burton F. Wilkinson, Jr.
Charles Wilkinson

Functions: 11.1 11.2
Industries: H.I0 H.R0
Description: Executive search & consulting for
    financial institutions & real estate

Williams, Adley & Co.

130 Sutter St., Ste. 706
San Francisco, California 94104
Salary Minimum: $25,000
Key Contact: Steven M. Price

Functions: 08.0 11.2
Industries: Most + H.00
Professional Affiliations: CERA
Description: Specialize in recruiting & placing
    accounting, banking & finance
    professionals

Branches:
1330 Broadway St., Ste. 1825
Oakland, California 94612

C. J. Williams Human Resource Group, Inc.

24591 Del Prado, Ste. 201
Dana Point, California 92629
Salary Minimum: $30,000
Key Contact: Carolyn J. Williams
Daniel J. Antonczak

Professional Affiliations: CAPC, NAPC
Description: Female owned, retained firm,
    nationwide, high tech professionals.
    Member: NAPC, ASPC, CAPC

Willmott & Assoc.

594 Marrett Rd.
Lexington, Massachusetts 02173
Salary Minimum: $20,000
Key Contact: D. Clark Willmott
David Tomaras
Francine Sparks

Functions: 06.0 06.1 06.2
Industries: Most
Professional Affiliations: IAPW, NEHRA
Description: We specialize in the search &
    placement of human resource
    professionals

N. Willner & Co., Inc.
P.O. Box 746
Matawan, New Jersey 07747
Salary Minimum: $45,000
Key Contact: Nathaniel Willner

Functions: 05.0 05.1 05.2 05.3 05.4
Industries: Most
Description: Specializing in all areas of
consumer & industrial marketing

The Windham Group
288 Littleton Rd.
Westford, Massachusetts 01886
Key Contact: Gregory Gostanian

Functions: 06.1 06.2
Industries: Most
Description: Committed to the right candidate
for the right position nationwide

Windward Executive Search, Inc.
298 Juliet Ln., Ste. A
Marietta, Georgia 30063-3263
Salary Minimum: $35,000
Key Contact: Tom Arnette

Functions: 02.0 02.4 05.4 06.0 06.1
Industries: D.13
Professional Affiliations: GAPC, NAPC, TAPPI
Description: Specialize in engineers, sales
managers & HR staff for paper mills

Winfield Assoc.
53 Winter St.
Weymouth, Massachusetts 02189
Salary Minimum: $25,000
Key Contact: Carl W. Siegel
Joseph M. Baldanza
Randa Fawaz

Functions: 01.0 02.0 04.0 05.0 11.0
Industries: D.17 D.18 D.I0 I.14 I.16
Professional Affiliations: RAPS
Description: Provides recruiting services for
manufacturers of medical products

Wing Tips & Pumps, Inc.
P.O. Box 99580
Troy, Michigan 48099
Salary Minimum: $20,000
Key Contact: Verba Lee Edwards

Functions: Most + 01.4 02.0 06.0 08.0 09.0
Industries: B.0W D.00 D.15 D.H0 H.00
Description: A minority-owned corp.
emphasizing world class service to
corporate America; from $20K to $200K

Winship Assoc.
110 Sutter St., Ste. 615
San Francisco, California 94104-4011
Salary Minimum: $50,000
Key Contact: Carol Winship

Functions: 01.5
Industries: I.17
Professional Affiliations: NALSC
Description: Positions in major law firms &
corporate legal departments; mergers

Winston Rooney & Green
201 N. Wells, Ste. 1410
Chicago, Illinois 60606
Salary Minimum: $50,000
Key Contact: David G. Winston
Michael F. Rooney
Larry A. Green

Functions: 11.0
Industries: Most + I.17
Professional Affiliations: NALSC
Description: Attorney search for law firms &
corporate legal departments

Winter, Wyman & Co.
950 Winter St.
Waltham, Massachusetts 02154
Salary Minimum: $25,000
Key Contact: Kevin Steele

Functions: 01.4 06.0 08.0 09.0
Industries: Most
Professional Affiliations: MPPC
Description: Founded in 1972, we are one of
the largest professional placement firms in
New England

Woehr Assoc.

38 Haddon Ave.
Haddonfield, New Jersey 08033
Salary Minimum: $50,000
Key Contact: Harry J. Woehr, Ph.D.
Mindell S. Woehr
Michael Bowers

Functions: Most + 01.0 02.0 05.0 06.0 08.0
Industries: Most + G.00
Professional Affiliations: APA
Description: 35 years human resource
    consulting experience

Jim Woodson & Assoc., Inc.

2600 Insurance Center Dr.
Jackson, Mississippi 39216
Salary Minimum: $25,000
Key Contact: Jim Woodson

Functions: 02.0 03.0 06.0 08.0
Industries: D.22 D.23 D.24 D.25 I.19
Professional Affiliations: MAPC, NAPC
Description: Recruit nationally for
    predominantly mid-South client base

Worlco Computer Resources, Inc.

901 Rte 38
Cherry Hill, New Jersey 08002
Salary Minimum: $25,000
Key Contact: Frank Parisi

Functions: 01.4 05.4 09.0 09.3 09.4
Industries: Most
Professional Affiliations: MAAPC, NAPC,
    PAPC
Description: Leading computer industry career
    planning & staffing specialists in
    Philadelphia

World Search

4130 Linden Ave., Ste. 105
Dayton, Ohio 45432
Salary Minimum: $40,000
Key Contact: Robert W. Rushbrook
Ruth L. Bell

Functions: 01.0 02.0 03.0 04.0 05.0
Industries: B.0W D.00 D.22
Professional Affiliations: NAPC
Description: Specific search for technical,
    manufacturing, sales/marketing & finance/
    accounting positions

Worldwide Anesthesia Assoc., Inc.

617 S. State
Ukiah, California 95487
Key Contact: John Paju

Industries: I.00 I.14 I.15
Professional Affiliations: NAPR
Description: Consultant & specialist in
    anesthesia personnel recruitment since
    1969

Nola Worley & Assoc., Inc.

510 S.W. 3rd Ave., Ste. 400
Portland, Oregon 97204
Salary Minimum: $50,000
Key Contact: Nola Jeli

Functions: 01.0 01.2 05.0 08.0 11.2
Industries: H.00 H.I0 H.R0 I.19
Professional Affiliations: APC
Description: Succession planning & executive
    search-primary industry, finance &
    accounting

John W. Worsham & Assoc., Inc.

River Oaks Bank Twr.
2001 Kirby Dr., Ste. 505
Houston, Texas 77019-6033
Key Contact: John W. Worsham

Functions: Most + 01.2 01.3
Industries: H.10
Description: Serving the banking profession in
    Southwest at the officer level

J.D. Wright & Assoc., Inc.

1301 Margate Ct.
Naperville, Illinois 60540
Key Contact: James Wright
Marilyn Wright
Donald Halenza

Functions: 01.0 05.0 09.0
Industries: Most
Description: Data processing specialist with
    emphasis in sales, manufacturing, banking
    & IBM

The Wright Group

5902 Windmier Ct.
Dallas, Texas 75252
Salary Minimum: $25,000
Key Contact: Jay Wright
Leslie A. Root

Functions: Most + 02.1 05.2 05.3 09.6
Industries: Most
Professional Affiliations: AMA
Description: Nationwide executive recruiting specializing in marketing, marketing research & direct response

The Wright Group

P.O. Box 690206
Houston, Texas 77269
Salary Minimum: $40,000
Key Contact: Louis C. Caston
M.L. Wright

Functions: Most
Industries: D.00 D.11 D.12 F.00 G.00
Description: Professional search firm focusing on individual executives & professionals

John Wylie Assoc., Inc.

1727 E. 71st
Tulsa, Oklahoma 74136
Salary Minimum: $25,000
Key Contact: John L. Wylie

Functions: Most + 01.0 02.0 03.0 11.3 11.5
Industries: B.00 D.15 D.19 D.20 D.22
Description: Contingency recruitment of technical & managerial talents in the Southwest

Dennis Wynn Assoc., Inc.

2201 Fourth St., N.
St. Petersburg, Florida 33704
Salary Minimum: $20,000
Key Contact: Dennis N. Wynn
Jean Wynn

Functions: 01.4 09.0 09.3 09.4 09.6
Industries: Most
Professional Affiliations: ASM, DPMA
Description: Data processing recruitment specialist

Xavier Assoc., Inc.

1350 Belmont St.
Williamsburg Sq.
Brockton, Massachusetts 02401-4430
Salary Minimum: $25,000
Key Contact: Frank X. McCarthy

Functions: Most + 11.2
Industries: D.15 D.17 D.24 H.I0
Professional Affiliations: MPPC, NAPC
Description: Specialize in minority recruiting, executive search, MIS, database & research projects

The Yaiser Group

904 Riverview Dr.
Brielle, New Jersey 08730-1635
Salary Minimum: $40,000
Key Contact: Richard A. Yaiser
Tom Coghan

Functions: 01.0 02.0 03.4 04.0 11.3
Industries: D.10 D.15 D.18 D.19 D.D0
Description: The successful candidate will not be seeking a change, but will be recruited from another company

Yake & Assoc.

P.O. Box 42
Kennebunk, Maine 04043
Salary Minimum: $30,000
Key Contact: Tom Yake

Functions: 09.1 10.0
Industries: G.00 H.12
Description: Specialize in retail security, loss prevention executives, internal auditors & finance

Yannelli, Randolph & Co.

994 Old Eagle School Rd., Ste. 1020
Wayne, Pennsylvania 19087
Salary Minimum: $65,000
Key Contact: Albert Yannelli
Bonnie Randolph
Patricia Mensack

Industries: I.15
Professional Affiliations: NAPR
Description: Specializing in physician search

Zaccaria Group, Inc.
52 Forest Ave.
Paramus, New Jersey 07652
Key Contact: Frances Zaccaria
Jack Zaccaria

Functions: Most
Industries: G.00 I.14 I.15 I.16
Professional Affiliations: DIA, NAPC, NAPR, NJAPC
Description: Consultants are thoroughly trained & experienced in their respective fields-retail/healthcare

Affiliates/Other Offices:
The Professional Resource Inc., Paramus

Zachary & Sanders, Inc.
82 N. Broadway, Ste. 102
Hicksville, New York 11801-2921
Salary Minimum: $45,000
Key Contact: Jasmine Andrews
Richard Todd
Richard W. Zachary

Functions: Most
Industries: D.13 D.14 D.D0 J.10 J.11
Description: Recruiters personally experienced in specialty; combined years of experience: 75

Zackrison Assoc., Inc.
88 Beach Rd.
Fairfield, Connecticut 06430
Salary Minimum: $25,000
Key Contact: Walter J. Zackrison

Functions: Most
Industries: Most + D.00 I.15 I.16
Professional Affiliations: NAPC, NAPR
Description: Specialists in banking/financing, data processing, engineering, marketing, personnel & health care

Zeiger Technical Careers, Inc.
20969 Ventura Blvd., Ste. 217
Woodland Hills, California 91364
Salary Minimum: $45,000
Key Contact: Stephen A. Zeiger
David Barkin Zeiger

Functions: Most + 01.0 01.1 01.2 02.1 11.3
Industries: D.E0 D.H0 J.00 J.13 K.10
Professional Affiliations: NAPC
Description: Design, manufacturing, project, R&D, engineering & engineering mgmt & executive tech. management

P.D. Zier Assoc.
14 Ascolese Rd.
Trumbull, Connecticut 06611
Salary Minimum: $25,000
Key Contact: Patricia D. Zier

Functions: 01.4 09.0 09.1 09.2 11.3
Industries: Most
Professional Affiliations: BIC, CBIA, DPMA, NAFE
Description: Professional, experienced, knowledgeable & successful high technology recruiters

Contingency Firm Indexes

Retainer Indexes begin after the Retainer Section, page 331.

Basis of "Functions" Classification

The kernel of this coding system was developed by several parties including Jerome H. Fuchs, Glenn Van Doren and Kennedy Publications.

00.0 **MOST**

01.0 **GENERAL MANAGEMENT**
01.1 Directors
01.2 Senior management
01.3 Middle management
01.4 MIS-Management information systems
01.5 Legal

02.0 **MANUFACTURING**
02.1 Product development
02.2 Production engineering, planning, scheduling & control
02.3 Automation, robotics
02.4 Plant management
02.5 Quality
02.6 Productivity

03.0 **MATERIALS MANAGEMENT**
03.1 Purchasing, inventory management
03.2 Materials & requirement planning
03.3 Physical distribution, traffic & transportation, logistics
03.4 Packaging

04.0 **RESEARCH & DEVELOPMENT**

05.0 **MARKETING**
05.1 Advertising, sales promotion
05.2 Marketing strategy & organization
05.3 Marketing & product research, consumer marketing
05.4 Sales, sales management, sales training
05.5 Direct mail, marketing, telemarketing
05.6 Customer service
05.7 Public relations

06.0 **HUMAN RESOURCE MANAGEMENT**
06.1 Benefits, compensation planning
06.2 Personnel selection, placement & records

07.0 **ADMINISTRATIVE SERVICES**
07.1 Clerical work measurement, records retention & management
07.2 Forms design, order processing & fulfillment, systems & procedures
07.3 Office layout, space planning
07.4 Office management

08.0 **FINANCE & ACCOUNTING**
08.1 Budgeting, cost controls
08.2 Cash management, financing & management of funds, portfolios
08.3 Credit & collection
08.4 Taxes

09.0 **INFORMATION TECHNOLOGY**
09.1 Computer security, disaster recovery, EDP audit
09.2 Specific technologies, e.g. AI, image, fiber-optics
09.3 Systems analysis & design, development, implementation, training & support
09.4 Systems integration, including hardware/software services, evaluation & selection
09.5 Expert systems
09.6 Decision support
09.7 Telecommunications

10.0 **INSURANCE/RISK MANAGEMENT**

11.0 **SPECIALIZED SERVICES**
11.1 Management consultants
11.2 Minorities
11.3 Scientific/technical
11.4 Fund-raisers & other non-profit services
11.5 Environmental
11.6 Architectural/engineering

Contingency Cross-Index by Functions

00.0 MOST

A. D. & Assoc.
AJS Assoc.
APA Search, Inc.
Academy Graduates Executive Search, Inc.
Ace Resources
Action Inc.
AdStaff Personnel, Inc.
Advancement Recruiting Services
John R. Ady & Assoc., Inc.
Affirmative Action Assoc.
The Agency- An Employment Consortium
Agra Placements, Ltd.
Agri-Personnel
Agri-Tech Personnel, Inc.
Aim Executive Inc.
Alaska Executive Search, Inc.
D.S. Allen Assoc.
Allen Barry Assoc.
Allen/Assoc.
Alterna-track
Alzed Real Estate Recruiters
Ames Personnel Consultants
Ames-O'Neill Assoc., Inc.
Amherst Personnel Group Inc.
Anderson Industrial Assoc., Inc.
Tryg R. Angell Ltd.
The Angus Group, Inc.
John Anthony & Assoc.
Arancio Assoc.
Ashway Ltd. Agency
Atlantic West Int'l.
Automation Technology Search
Avery Crafts Assoc., Ltd.
AviSearch Int'l.
BIK Search/Force II
Keith Bagg Personnel Ltd.
Baker Scott & Co.
Baldwin & Assoc.
Balfour Assoc.
Ron Ball & Assoc.
The Bankers Register
The Barack Group, Inc.
Barone Assoc.
Barone-O'Hara Assoc., Inc.
Peter Barrett Assoc., Inc.
Barrett Partners
Jim Baum - Executive Search
Bedford-Orion Group, Inc.

Dotson Benefield & Assoc., Inc.
Bennett & Curran, Inc.
Bennett-Munson Inc.
Biotech Sourcing
Blanton & Co.
Gregory L. Borchert, Inc.
Bornholdt Shivas & Friends
Bowersox & Assoc., Inc.
Bradstreet Mgt.
Brandjes Assoc.
C.W. Brandon & Assoc., Inc.
The Bren Group
Brennan Assoc.
J.R. Brody & Assoc., Inc.
Brooks Executive Personnel
Bryant Assoc., Inc.
C & H Personnel
CAS Comsearch Inc.
C.P.S., Inc.
Peter M. Cahill Assoc., Inc.
Cambridge & Assoc., Inc.
Cap, Inc.
Capitol Management Consulting, Inc.
Career Advancement
Career Guides, Inc.
Career Information Services, Inc.
Career Logic, Inc.
Career Management, Inc.
Career Specialists, Inc.
Careers Unlimited
Careers/Inc.
Andrew B. Carr & Assoc.
Carter, Lavoie Assocs.
Carver Search Consultants
Casey & Gerrish Assoc., Inc.
Cassie & Assoc.
Cibotti Assoc., Inc.
Circuit Search
Howard Clark Assoc.
Richard Clarke Assoc., Inc.
Commonwealth Consultants
Competitive Resources, Inc.
The Comwell Co. Inc.
Cona Personnel Search
The Connolly Consulting Group
The Consortium
Consult One, Inc.
Corporate Careers Inc.
The Corporate Connection, Ltd.

00.0 MOST (Cont'd)

Corporate Management Services Inc.
Corporate Recruiters, Inc.
Corporate Resources Professional Placement
Cowin Assoc.
The Cris Group., Inc.
Timothy D. Crowe, Jr.
Curts/Jackson, Inc.
The DLR Group, Inc.
Dankowski & Assoc., Inc.
Datamatics Management Services, Inc.
David - Kris Assoc., Inc.
Davis & James, Inc.
DeCorrevont & Assoc.
Deery Geddis & Assoc.
Delta Personnel Services
Delta Resource Group, Ltd.
Diversified Placement Int'l., Inc.
Domenico/Brown Group
Double M Executive Placement Service, Inc.
Drake & Assoc.
J. H. Dugan & Assoc., Inc.
Dumont Moriarty & Assoc.
Dunhill Personnel System, Inc.
Dunhill of Houston
Dunhill Search of Omaha, Inc.
Dunhill Professional Search of Kalamazoo
Dunhill Professional Search of Hawaii
Dunhill International Search
G.L. Dykstra Assoc., Inc.
The E & K Group
Eckert, Enghauser and Partners, Inc.
Eden & Assoc., Inc.
Engineering Directions
Engineering Specialists
Environmental Professional Assoc.
Allen Etcovitch Assoc. Ltd.
ExecuSource Int'l.
Executive Careers
Executive Dynamics, Inc.
Executive Referral Services, Inc.
Executive Search of New England, Inc.
Executives' Personnel Service Inc.
Fallstaff Search
Federal Placement Services
A.E. Feldman Assoc.
N. Steven Fells & Co., Inc.
Fergason Assoc., Inc.
Financial Resource Assoc., Inc.
James L. Fisk & Assoc.
Florapersonnel, Inc.
Ford & Assoc., Inc.
Ford & Ford
Foster Assoc.
Fox-Morris Assoc., Inc.
Mel Frazer & Assoc.
The Furst Group
Future Sense
G.A.M. Executive Search, Inc.
Michael Garbi Assoc., Inc.
Genesis Personnel Service, Inc.
Delores F. George

Joe L. Giles & Assoc., Inc.
Alan Glenn & Keener
Grant, Franks & Assoc.
Graphic Search Assoc. Inc.
Greene Personnel Consultants
Groenekamp & Assoc.
J. Gross & Assoc.
The Alice-Groves Co., Inc.
HMO Executive Search
Hahn & Assoc., Inc.
Hartman Personnel Services
Donald P. Hayes Assoc., Inc.
Kent R. Hedman & Assoc.
J. D. Hersey & Assoc.
Robert Hess & Assoc., Inc.
Hi-Tech Search, Inc.
Frank P. Hill
Hitchens & Foster, Inc.
Hoskins, Rees & Smith
Don Howard Personnel
The Hudson Group
Hughes & Assoc.
Human Resource Network
Human Resource Recruiters
ISOPS Personnel Services, Inc.
Individual Employment Services
Integrated Management Solutions
International Staffing Consultants, Inc.
J.M. Eagle Partners
JNB Assoc., Inc.
R.I. James, Inc.
Jefferson-Ross Assoc. Inc.
K.E. Johnson Assoc.
The Johnson Group, Inc.
Kathryn L. Johnson
E. G. Jones Assoc., Ltd.
Jordon & Jordon, Inc.
J.M. Joseph Assoc.
A.H. Justice & Assoc.
K & C Assoc.
Richard Kader & Assoc.
Kauffman Hospitality, Inc.
John J. Kennedy Assoc., Inc.
Kensington Int'l.
Kepler & Assoc.
Sanford Kleiner Assoc., Inc.
Kling Personnel Assoc., Inc.
The Koehler Group
Kordus Consulting Group
Kossuth & Assoc., Inc.
Krautler Personnel Recruitment
Kravitz * Larkin * Silver Assoc.
Kutt, Inc.
Lacrosse Assoc., Inc.
Landon-Brookes Executive Search
R.H. Larsen & Assoc., Inc.
Jack B. Larsen & Assoc.
Larson Assoc.
Latin America Assoc., S.C.
W.R. Lawry, Inc.
The Lawson Group
Vincent Lee Assoc.
Lee Associates

0.00 MOST (Cont'd)

Lee Management Group Inc.
Legal Placements Inc.
Alan Lerner Assoc.
Link Personnel & Assoc.
Locus Inc.
Logue & Rice Inc.
R.E. Lowe Assoc.
Lucas & Assoc., Ltd.
Luke, Lincoln, & Brugger
Lyons & Assoc., Inc.
MARBL Consultants, Inc.
MPI Assoc.
MRG Search & Placement
Alan MacDonald & Assoc.
Magnum Search
Mahony & Assoc., Ltd.
Management Assoc.
Management Recruiters of Savannah
Management Recruiters of Dearborn, Inc.
Management Recruiters of Gramercy, Inc.
Management Recruiters
Management Recruiters of Cincinnati/
   Sharonville, Inc.
Management Recruiters of Greater Bridgeport,
   Inc.
Management Recruiters
Management Recruiters
Management Recruiters
Management Recruiters
Management Recruiters
Management Recruiters
Management Recruiters
Management Recruiters of Butler County
Management Recruiters of Little Rock
Management Recruiters of Berkeley
Management Recruiters - Concord, CA.
Management Recruiters
Management Recruiters of Oakland
Management Recruiters
Management Recruiters Peninsula
Management Recruiters Treasure Coast, Inc.
Management Recruiters of Topeka, Inc.
Management Recruiters of North Oakland
   County, Inc.
Management Recruiters of Ashville, Inc.
Management Resource Group, Inc.
Management Resource Assoc., Inc.
Management Search, Inc.
Management Search Int'l.
Marcus & Assoc.
Margolin Consultants, Inc.
Mark III Personnel, Inc.
Marketing Recruiters, Inc.
Donovan Martin & Assoc.
Richard L. Mather & Assoc.
Matthews Professional Employment
   Specialists, Inc.
K. Maxin & Assoc.
McCulloch Assoc.
McDermott & Assoc.
Sandi McDonald & Assoc., Inc.

McDonald Ledterman Executive Search
McGladrey Search Group
McRoberts & Assoc.
Joseph J. McTaggart
Merlin Int'l. Inc.
Lou Michaels Assoc.
B. Paul Mickey & Assoc.
Midland Consultants
Diedre Moire Corp., Inc.
Montaigne Assoc., Inc.
Multisearch Recruiters
Murkett Assoc.
The NRI Group
Nagel Executive Search Inc.
The Naples Group, Inc.
National Corporate Consultants, Inc.
National Search, Inc.
J. Fielding Nelson & Assoc., Inc.
Nelson-Larson & Assoc. Ltd.
Newcombe & Cyr Assoc., Inc.
Northeastern Search, Inc.
Northland Recruiting Inc.
Charles P. Oliver Assoc., Inc.
Kitty Ossow & Assoc.
LaMonte Owens, Inc.
The Oxford Group
P R Associates
PC Assoc.
PLRS/Career Connections
Largent Parks & Partners, Inc.
Part Time Resources
Partridge Assoc., Inc.
The Paxton Group, Ltd.
M.A. Pelle Assoc., Inc.
Performance Professionals
Personnel Inc.
The Personnel Network, Inc.
Personnel Unlimited/Executive Search
Phase II Management
Phillips Personnel/Search
Phillips Resource Group
The Pickwick Group, Inc.
Placement Assoc., Inc.
Plastics Enterprises
Polytechnical Consultants, Inc.
Prestige Search Inc.
Princeton Executive Search
ProSearch, Inc.
Probe Technology
Professional Recruiters Inc.
Professional Search Assoc., Inc.
Professions, Inc.
Protocol Inc.
RAC International
RAI Consulting
R.A.N. Assoc., Inc.
R.G.B. & Assoc., Inc.
RGL Assoc., Inc.
RHS Assoc., Inc.
Ranger & Assoc.
Edward Rast & Co.
Reinecke & Assoc.
Repplier & Co.

0.00 MOST (Cont'd)

Resource Services, Inc.
Retail Recruiters/Spectrum Consultants, Inc.
Retail Recruiters of Stamford
S. Reyman & Assoc., Ltd.
Roberson & Co.
Romano McAvoy Assoc., Inc.
Emery A. Rose & Assoc.
Sanford Rose Assoc.
Sanford Rose Assoc. of Lima
Sanford Rose Assoc. - Santa Barbara
Sanford Rose Assoc. of Hartford
Sanford Rose Assoc. of Wilmington
Sanford Rose Assoc. - Rockville
Sanford Rose Assoc.- Brecksville
Sanford Rose Assoc. of Quakertown
Sanford Rose Assoc. - Virginia Beach
Roth Young of Tampa
Roth Young of Boston
Roth Young of Pittsburgh
Rothrock Assoc.
John P. Runden & Co., Inc.
Rushlow & Co.
Ryan & Assoc.
The Charles Ryan Group, Inc.
S. P. Assoc.
S-H-S of Allentown
STM Assoc.
Robert Sage Recruiting
Sales & Management Search, Inc.
Sales Consultants
Sales Consultants of Austin, Inc.
Sales Consultants
Sales Consultants of Ft. Lauderdale
George D. Sandel Assoc.
Santangelo Consultants Inc.
Sarver-Garland, Inc.
Schenck & Assoc. SC
Schreuder Randall Corp.
Devin Scott Assoc.
Search Assoc., Inc.
Search Assoc., Inc.
Search North America, Inc.
Search West, Inc.
Selected Executives, Inc.
Selective Management Services, Inc.
Selective Staffing
L. A. Silver Assoc., Inc.
The Simmons Group
Simpson Nance & Graham, Inc.
James F. Smith & Assoc.
Ralph Smith & Assoc.
Raymond James Smith & Assoc.
Abbott Smith Assoc., Inc.
J. Harrington Smith Assoc.
Smith Bradley & Assoc.
Stephen M. Sonis Assoc.
Specialty Consultants, Inc.
Spectrum Consultants
St. James And DeDominic
St. Lawrence Int'l., Inc.
Staffing Consultants

Peter Sterling & Co.
Daniel Stern & Assoc.
Stewart Assoc.
Charles Stickler Assoc.
The Stoddard Co.
Stoneburner Assoc., Inc.
Storti Assoc., Inc.
Strategy 2000
Strauss Personnel Service
Sturm, Burrows & Co.
S. Tyler Sullivan & Assoc., Inc.
Sumrall Personnel Consultants, Inc.
Supreme Assoc.
M. L. Tawney & Assoc.
Tech International
Tech Vision Co.
Technical Recruiting Services
Tecmark Assoc. Inc.
Thornton Assoc.
Thoroughbred Executive Search
Tidewater Group Inc.
TransAmerica Network
Travel Executive Search
Trilogy Enterprises, Inc.
Unisearch
The Urban Placement Service
Video Interview Professionals, Inc.
WBS Network Professional & Executive
  Search
Denis P. Walsh & Assoc., Inc.
Frank X. Walsh & Co., Inc.
M.K. Wasse & Assoc., Inc.
Waterford, Inc.
Weatherby Healthcare
D.L. Weaver & Assoc.
Weinpel & Co.
Henry Welker & Assoc.
Wells, Bradley & Assoc.
WestCare Executive Search
Western Personnel Assoc., Inc.
Western Search Assoc.
Whitaker, Fellows & Assoc.
David J. White & Assoc., Inc.
Whitehead & Assoc., Inc.
Joel H. Wilensky Assoc., Inc.
Wing Tips & Pumps, Inc.
Woehr Assoc.
John W. Worsham & Assoc., Inc.
The Wright Group
The Wright Group
John Wylie Assoc., Inc.
Xavier Assoc., Inc.
Zaccaria Group, Inc.
Zachary & Sanders, Inc.
Zackrison Assoc., Inc.
Zeiger Technical Careers, Inc.

01.0 GENERAL MANAGEMENT

AGRI-associates
A.M.C.R., Inc.
ARJay & Assoc.
Accounting & Computer Personnel

01.0 GENERAL MANAGEMENT (Cont'd)

The Addison Consulting Group
Agri-Tech Personnel, Inc.
Alterna-track
American Resources Corp.
Ames Assoc. Inc.
Tryg R. Angell Ltd.
John Anthony & Assoc.
Charles P. Aquavella & Assoc.
Aronow Assoc., Inc.
Ashton Computer Professionals, Inc.
Atlantic West Int'l.
Automation Technology Search
Avery Crafts Assoc., Ltd.
B.P.A. Enterprises, Inc.
Keith Bagg Personnel Ltd.
Baker Scott & Co.
The Barack Group, Inc.
B.K. Barnes & Associates
Peter Barrett Assoc., Inc.
Jim Baum - Executive Search
Ted Bavly Assoc., Inc.
Gary S. Bell Assoc., Inc.
Bell Professional Placement
The Howard C. Bloom Co.
Bonifield Assoc.
Bornholdt Shivas & Friends
Bowling Executive Registry, Inc.
Jerold Braun & Assoc.
Brennan Assoc.
Ira Broadman Assoc.
Brooks Executive Personnel
Paul J. Burns
The Butlers Co. Insurance Recruiters
The Byrnes Group
CDH & Assoc., Inc.
Capitol Management Consulting, Inc.
Career Search Assoc.
The Carlyle Group, Ltd.
Case Executive Search
Casey & Gerrish Assoc., Inc.
Chase Waterford Ltd.
William J. Christopher Assoc., Inc.
J.F. Church Assoc., Inc.
Cibotti Assoc., Inc.
Clark-Winans, Inc.
CoEnergy Inc.
Competitive Resources, Inc.
The Comwell Co. Inc.
Conaway Legal Search
Consumer Search, Inc.
Corporate Advisors Inc.
Corporate Recruiters, Inc.
Corporate Suite, Ltd.
Crest Management Search, Inc.
Frank Cuomo & Assoc., Inc.
Curts/Jackson, Inc.
The DLR Group, Inc.
Dapexs Consultants, Inc.
David - Kris Assoc., Inc.
DeLalla - Fried Assoc.

Dean-Wharton Assoc.
Deery Geddis & Assoc.
Diversified Placement Int'l., Inc.
L.J. Doherty & Assoc.
Domenico/Brown Group
Drummond Assoc., Inc.
J. H. Dugan & Assoc., Inc.
Dumont Moriarty & Assoc.
Dunhill Professional Search, Inc. of Kearney
Dunhill Professional Search of Wilkes-Barre/ Scranton, Inc.
Dunhill Personnel of Northeast Tulsa, Inc.
Dunhill of Manchester Inc.
Dunhill International Search
Dunhill Professional Search Irvine/Newport
Dussick Management Assoc.
The E & K Group
Eastern Executive Assoc.
Eden & Assoc., Inc.
Eggers Consulting Co., Inc.
The Energists
N. Steven Fells & Co., Inc.
Fergason Assoc., Inc.
Fernow Assoc.
Ferrari Consulting Group
Fisher-Todd Assoc.
A.G. Fishkin & Assoc., Inc.
James L. Fisk & Assoc.
Ford & Assoc., Inc.
Fortune Personnel Consultants of Huntsville, Inc.
Franklin Int'l. Search, Inc.
Future Sense
Garrett Assoc. Inc.
Genesis Personnel Service, Inc.
Delores F. George
Global Data Services, Inc.
W.T. Glover & Assoc., Inc.
The Goodman Group
Gregory Michaels & Assoc., Inc.
J. Gross & Assoc.
The Alice-Groves Co., Inc.
Guidarelli Assoc., Inc.
Hahn & Assoc., Inc.
Hall, Cooper & Bartman, Ltd.
Harrison Moore Inc.
Hartman Personnel Services
Health Industry Resources, Inc.
Health Technology, Inc.
Hedlund Corp.
Heller Kil Assoc., Inc.
J. D. Hersey & Assoc.
Hill & Assoc.
Hoskins, Rees & Smith
Hospitality Resources Int'l., Ltd.
Hudson Assoc. Inc.
Human Resource Network
E. F. Humay Assoc.
Industrial Recruiters Assoc., Inc.
Integrated Management Solutions
JT Assoc.
K.E. Johnson Assoc.
The Johnson Group, Inc.

01.0 GENERAL MANAGEMENT (Cont'd)

Kathryn L. Johnson
Jubilee, Inc.
K & C Assoc.
Kacevich, Lewis & Brown, Inc.
Richard Kader & Assoc.
Key Talent, Inc.
Sanford Kleiner Assoc., Inc.
The Koehler Group
Kordus Consulting Group
Kozlin Assoc., Inc.
Krow Assoc., Inc.
Lacrosse Assoc., Inc.
Lange & Assoc., Inc.
Langlois & Assoc.
Jack B. Larsen & Assoc.
Larson Assoc.
Lawrence-Balakonis & Assoc., Inc.
Legal Placements Inc.
Paul Ligon Co.
Lindsey & Assoc., Inc.
Link Personnel & Assoc.
Logue & Rice Inc.
Lowery, Cotter, & Assoc.
Ludot Personnel Services, Inc.
Luke, Lincoln, & Brugger
MARBL Consultants, Inc.
mfg/Search, Inc.
MJF Assoc.
MKM Search Consultants, Inc.
Mahony & Assoc., Ltd.
Management Recruiters of Gramercy, Inc.
Management Recruiters
Management Recruiters of Cincinnati/
  Sharonville, Inc.
Management Recruiters of Ft. Myers, FL.
Management Recruiters of Monterey
Management Recruiters Peninsula
Management Recruiters of Atlanta West, Inc.
Management Recruiters of Nassau, Inc.
Management Recruiters of Charlotte -
  Southwest
Management Search Int'l.
Marcus & Assoc.
Mariaschin & Co.
Karen Marshall Assoc.
Donovan Martin & Assoc.
Mathey Services
McCracken, Wilcox, Bertoux & Miller
McCulloch Assoc.
Earl L. McDermid & Assoc.
McGuire Executive Search, Inc.
Medical Executive Search Assoc.
Medquest Assoc.
Medtrac & Assoc.
Todd Melon Group
B. Paul Mickey & Assoc.
Robert E. Mills, FLMI
Diedre Moire Corp., Inc.
The Montanye Group
The C. B. Mueller Co., Inc.

Multisearch Recruiters
John H. Munson & Co.
Murphy, Symonds & Stowell Search, Inc.
NPF Assoc. Ltd. Inc.
Nachman Biomedical
J. Fielding Nelson & Assoc., Inc.
Newcombe & Cyr Assoc., Inc.
Norton & Assoc.
Opportunity Knocking, Inc.
The Oxford Group
P R Associates
P R Management Consultants, Inc.
P.R.H. Management, Inc.
R. Parker & Assoc., Inc.
Parker Page Group
Part Time Resources
Partridge Assoc., Inc.
Patrick Assoc.
Kevin W. Paul
Performance Professionals
Personnel Advisors Int'l. Corp.
Personnel Inc.
Personnel Management, Inc.
The Personnel Network, Inc.
Petruzzi Assoc.
Plastics Enterprises
Precise Legal, Inc.
Presley Consultants, Inc.
The Primary Group, Inc.
Princeton Executive Search, Inc.
Probe Technology
Professional Medical
Professional Personnel Services
Professional Recruiters Inc.
Professional Recruiters Inc.
Professional Search Assoc., Inc.
Professional Team Search
Professions Unlimited, Inc.
RAC International
RBR Assoc., Inc.
Edward Rast & Co.
Raymond Thomas & Assoc.
Reinecke & Assoc.
Retail Recruiters/Spectrum Consultants, Inc.
Retail Recruiters/Spectra Professional Search
Roberson & Co.
The Robinson Group, D.A., Ltd.
Romac & Assoc.
Ropella & Assoc.
Sanford Rose Assoc. - Santa Barbara
Sanford Rose Assoc.- Woodbury
Sanford Rose Assoc.- Detroit North
Louis Rudzinsky Assoc., Inc.
John P. Runden & Co., Inc.
The Charles Ryan Group, Inc.
Ryerson Tabor Assoc.
S-H-S of Allentown
Sales Consultants of Austin, Inc.
Samper Assoc.
Scan Management Inc.
The Search Network
Search Solutions, Inc.
Selective Management Services, Inc.

01.0 GENERAL MANAGEMENT (Cont'd)

Stephen Sellers Assoc.
Scott Sibley Assoc.
SilverCrest Search
Smith, Anderson & Co.
J. Harrington Smith Assoc.
Stephen M. Sonis Assoc.
Source Engineering
Source Finance
Spectrum Consultants
Spring Executive Search, Inc.
The Stevens Group, Inc.
Charles Stickler Assoc.
Straight & Co.
Strategic Assoc., Inc.
Strategic Executives, Inc.
Strategic Search Group
Sturm, Burrows & Co.
Ron Sunshine & Assoc.
Tanzi Executive Search
Technical Engineering Consultants
Technical Recruiting Services
Technical Staffing Assoc.
Tecmark Assoc. Inc.
The Tibbetts Group Ltd.
Triangle Consulting Group
Unisearch
Vento Assoc.
Gordon Wahls Co.
Wallace Assoc.
Wayne Assoc., Inc.
D.L. Weaver & Assoc.
Wegner & Assoc.
E.T. Wharton Assoc., Inc.
White-Ridgely & Assoc., Inc.
Whittaker & Assoc., Inc.
Whittlesey & Assoc., Inc.
Winfield Assoc.
Woehr Assoc.
World Search
Nola Worley & Assoc., Inc.
J.D. Wright & Assoc., Inc.
John Wylie Assoc., Inc.
The Yaiser Group
Zeiger Technical Careers, Inc.

01.1 DIRECTORS

ACC Consultants, Inc.
Beckwith, Thomas & Fanning
Besen Assoc. Inc.
CDH & Assoc., Inc.
The Carlyle Group, Ltd.
CoEnergy Inc.
Consumer Search, Inc.
Dunhill Professional Search of Ramsey
Executive Referral Services, Inc.
Gaines & Assoc. Int'l., Inc.
J. Gross & Assoc.
High Technology Search Assoc.
Hill & Assoc.
Hornberger Management Co., Inc.

Hospitality Executive Search, Inc.
Hospitality Int'l.
Hospitality Resources Int'l., Ltd.
R.I. James, Inc.
Kimmel & Fredericks, Inc.
Kordus Consulting Group
Kresin Wingard
Lam Assoc.
Lanzi & Assoc.
The Lawson Group
Management Assoc.
Management Recruiters of Frederick, Inc.'
Management Recruiters of Gramercy, Inc.
Management Recruiters
Management Recruiters
Management Recruiters of Redding
Midwest Medical Recruiters
OSA Partners, Inc.
Opportunity Knocking, Inc.
Parker Page Group
Jerry Pollack & Assoc.
RBR Assoc., Inc.
Retail Recruiters/Spectra Professional Search
Sanford Rose Assoc.- Detroit North
Phyllis Solomon Executive Search, Inc.
Steinbach & Co.
Joel H. Wilensky Assoc., Inc.
Zeiger Technical Careers, Inc.

01.2 SENIOR MANAGEMENT

ACC Consultants, Inc.
E. J. Ashton & Assoc., Ltd.
Avery Crafts Assoc., Ltd.
Barclay Consultants, Inc.
Bartlett, Bunn & Travis, Inc.
Biotech Sourcing
D. R. Blood & Assoc.
Bowling Executive Registry, Inc.
Brandjes Assoc.
C.W. Brandon & Assoc., Inc.
Brooke Chase Assoc., Inc.
CDH & Assoc., Inc.
The Cambridge Group Ltd.
The Carlyle Group, Ltd.
John M. Clarke & Assoc.
CoEnergy Inc.
Malcolm Cole & Assoc.
Consumer Search, Inc.
Corporate Advisors Inc.
Cowin Assoc.
Davis-Smith Medical-Dental Employment Service, Inc.
Drummond Assoc., Inc.
Dunhill of Greater Akron, Inc.
Dunhill of Manchester Inc.
Dunhill Search of Omaha, Inc.
Dunhill Professional Search
Engineering Search Assoc.
Exec 2000
Executive Referral Services, Inc.
David Farmer & Assoc.
Financial Search Group, Inc.

01.2 SENIOR MANAGEMENT (Cont'd)

Flynn, Hannock, Inc.
Fortune Personnel Consultants
Gaines & Assoc. Int'l., Inc.
Galen Giles Group
Gaudette & Co.
Gold Coast Partners
Gray-Kimball Assoc., Inc.
Guidarelli Assoc., Inc.
Hill & Assoc.
Hornberger Management Co., Inc.
Hospitality Executive Search, Inc.
Hospitality Int'l.
Hospitality Resources Int'l., Ltd.
JNB Assoc., Inc.
R.I. James, Inc.
Jubilee, Inc.
Kimmel & Fredericks, Inc.
Kresin Wingard
Lam Assoc.
Lanzi & Assoc.
Lappe & Assoc.
Lawrence-Balakonis & Assoc., Inc.
The Lighthouse Group
The James Lloyd Group
Lunney, Hadden & Assoc.
M/ARS
Management Recruiters of Frederick, Inc.'
Management Recruiters
Management Recruiters
Management Recruiters
Management Recruiters of Redding
Management Recruiters
Management Recruiters of Waterbury, Inc.
Mariaschin & Co.
Martin Personnel Assoc.
Medical Sales & Management Specialists
Olaf S. Meyer & Co., Ltd.
Milgram & Assoc.
John H. Munson & Co.
Jerome H. Nagel Assoc.
National Executive Consultants, Inc.
National Recruiting Service
OSA Partners, Inc.
PLRS/Career Connections
Pacific Advisory Service
R. Parker & Assoc., Inc.
Parker Page Group
Robert A. Paul & Assoc.
Paul S. Pelland
M.A. Pelle Assoc., Inc.
Robert E. Pfaendler & Assoc., Inc.
Philip Daniels Assoc., Inc.
Jerry Pollack & Assoc.
Presley Consultants, Inc.
Professional Placement Assoc., Inc.
RBR Assoc., Inc.
Edward Rast & Co.
Remark Assoc. Inc.
Resource Consultants
The Resource Group

Resource Perspectives, Inc.
Retail Pacesetters, Inc.
Retail Recruiters of Paramus, Inc.
Retail Recruiters/Spectra Professional Search
The Reynolds Group, Inc.
Riotto - Jones Assoc., Inc.
Riverside Consultants, Inc.
Roberts Assoc.
Sanford Rose Assoc. of Beachwood
Rushlow & Co.
Russillo/Gardner
Sales & Management Search, Inc.
Sales Consultants of Madison
Sales Consultants of Newtown
Sales Consultants of Akron, Inc.
Sales Consultants of Savannah, GA.
Saxon Morse Assoc.
Schenck & Assoc. SC
Devin Scott Assoc.
Search Consultants Int'l., Inc.
Jules Seltzer Assoc.
Shannahan & Co., Inc.
L. A. Silver Assoc., Inc.
Smith Bradley & Assoc.
Phyllis Solomon Executive Search, Inc.
Steinbach & Co.
Techcon Co.
Technitrac, Inc.
Weeks & Assoc.
R.A. Wells Co.
Joel H. Wilensky Assoc., Inc.
Nola Worley & Assoc., Inc.
John W. Worsham & Assoc., Inc.
Zeiger Technical Careers, Inc.

01.3 MIDDLE MANAGEMENT

ACC Consultants, Inc.
Aberdeen Assoc.
Adel Lawrence Assoc., Inc.
Francis V. Anderson Assoc. Inc.
E. J. Ashton & Assoc., Ltd.
Auden Assoc., Inc.
Avery Crafts Assoc., Ltd.
Carol Ball & Co., Inc.
Barclay Consultants, Inc.
Bartlett, Bunn & Travis, Inc.
Biotech Sourcing
Bowling Executive Registry, Inc.
Brandjes Assoc.
Brooke Chase Assoc., Inc.
CDH & Assoc., Inc.
The Carlyle Group, Ltd.
John M. Clarke & Assoc.
CoEnergy Inc.
Malcolm Cole & Assoc.
Cona Personnel Search
Consumer Search, Inc.
David P. Cordell Assoc.
Corporate Advisors Inc.
Corporate Resources Professional Placement
Cowin Assoc.
N. Dean Davic Assoc., Inc.

01.3 MIDDLE MANAGEMENT
(Cont'd)
David - Kris Assoc., Inc.
Davis-Smith Medical-Dental Employment
  Service, Inc.
Dillard Executive Search
Drummond Assoc., Inc.
Dunhill Professional Search
Dunhill of Huntsville, Inc.
Dunhill Personnel Search
Dunhill of Manchester Inc.
Dunhill Search of Omaha, Inc.
Dunhill Search of West Atlanta
Dunhill Professional Search
Executive Referral Services, Inc.
David Farmer & Assoc.
Financial Search Group, Inc.
Flores & Assoc.
Flynn, Hannock, Inc.
Fortune Personnel Consultants
Galen Giles Group
Gardner, Savage Assoc.
Gaudette & Co.
Goldstein & Assoc.
Gray-Kimball Assoc., Inc.
Healthcare Resources Group
Hospitality Int'l.
Hospitality Resources Int'l., Ltd.
Howie & Assoc., Inc.
I.S. Consultants, Inc.
Impact Executive Search, Inc.
Intertech Search Group
JNB Assoc., Inc.
Jackley Search Consultants
R.I. James, Inc.
Kacevich, Lewis & Brown, Inc.
Kresin Wingard
Lanzi & Assoc.
Lappe & Assoc.
Lawrence-Balakonis & Assoc., Inc.
W.R. Lawry, Inc.
The Lighthouse Group
Lunney, Hadden & Assoc.
M H Executive Search Group
M-A Management Assoc., Inc.
M/ARS
Management Assoc.
Management Recruiters
Management Recruiters
Management Recruiters of Butler County
Management Recruiters of Berkeley
Management Recruiters of El Dorado
Management Recruiters of Oakland
Management Recruiters
Management Recruiters of Middlesex
Management Recruiters of Waterbury, Inc.
Management Recruiters of North Brunswick,
  Inc.
Management Recruiters of Westchester, Inc.
Mariaschin & Co.
Martin Personnel Assoc.
R. H. McIlwaine & Assoc.

Medical Sales & Management Specialists
Olaf S. Meyer & Co., Ltd.
Michael/Merrill
Milgram & Assoc.
Jerome H. Nagel Assoc.
National Recruiting Service
William H. Nenstiel & Assoc.
Ronald Norris & Assoc.
Nuance Personnel Search, Inc.
OSA Partners, Inc.
PMC-ParaLegal Management & Consultants
Pacific Advisory Service
R. Parker & Assoc., Inc.
Paul S. Pelland
Robert E. Pfaendler & Assoc., Inc.
Philip Daniels Assoc., Inc.
Jerry Pollack & Assoc.
Presley Consultants, Inc.
Preston Robert & Assoc.-Health Care Div.
Professional Placement Assoc., Inc.
RALCO/Richard A. Lucia & Assoc.
RHS Assoc., Inc.
Remark Assoc. Inc.
Resource Consultants
The Resource Group
Retail Pacesetters, Inc.
Retail Recruiters of Paramus, Inc.
Retail Recruiters/Spectra Professional Search
The Reynolds Group, Inc.
Riotto - Jones Assoc., Inc.
Ritta Professional Search Inc.
Riverside Consultants, Inc.
Roberts Assoc.
Sanford Rose Assoc. of Lima
Sanford Rose Assoc. - Great Neck
Sanford Rose Assoc. of Beachwood
Sanford Rose Assoc. of Nashville
Russillo/Gardner
Sales & Management Search, Inc.
Sales Consultants of Newtown
Sales Consultants of Westchester-South, Inc.
Sales Consultants - Bristol County
Sales Consultants of Savannah, GA.
Saxon Morse Assoc.
Devin Scott Assoc.
Search Consultants Int'l., Inc.
Shannahan & Co., Inc.
Sharrow & Assoc., Inc.
Smith Hanley Assoc., Inc.
Phyllis Solomon Executive Search, Inc.
Specialized Search Assoc.
Steinbach & Co.
Techcon Co.
Tower Consultants, Ltd.
Triangle Assoc.
M.K. Wasse & Assoc., Inc.
Weeks & Assoc.
Henry Welker & Assoc.
John W. Worsham & Assoc., Inc.

01.4 MIS-MANAGEMENT
INFORMATION SYSTEMS
AJS Assoc.
Abacus Consultants

01.4 MIS-MANAGEMENT INFORMATION SYSTEMS (Cont'd)

The Adler Group
Aitken & Assoc.
David Allen Assoc.
Ashton Computer Professionals, Inc.
R. Gaines Baty Assoc., Inc.
Berger & Assoc.
Binary Search
D. R. Blood & Assoc.
The Cambridge Group Ltd.
Carter McKenzie, Inc.
Cemco, Ltd.
CompuPro
The Consortium
Corporate Advisors Inc.
Dapexs Consultants, Inc.
The DataFinders Group, Inc.
Datamax Services Inc.
J P Donnelly Assoc., Inc.
EXETER 2100
Environmental Professional Assoc.
Exec 2000
Executive Exchange Corp.
eXsource
David Farmer & Assoc.
James L. Fisk & Assoc.
Global Data Services, Inc.
Goldstein & Assoc.
Halbrecht & Co.
Health Industry Resources, Inc.
Higbee Assoc., Inc.
High-Tech Recruiters
Howie & Assoc., Inc.
Information Systems Professionals
Integrated Professional Services, Inc.
JDG Assoc., Ltd.
Kenmore Executives Inc.
The Kennett Group, Inc.
Kennison & Assoc.
Kravitz * Larkin * Silver Assoc.
Brian Leggee & Assoc.
Logix, Inc.
M-A Management Assoc., Inc.
MRG Search & Placement
Management Recruiters
Management Recruiters of Hendersonville, inc.
Management Recruiters of Reno
Management Recruiters of Stanhope Corp.
Management Recruiters of North Brunswick, Inc.
Management Search, Inc.
Masserman & Assoc.
McCracken, Wilcox, Bertoux & Miller
Sandi McDonald & Assoc., Inc.
Michael/Merrill
Morency Assoc.
Multi Processing, Inc.
The Network Companies
Northeastern Search, Inc.
Opportunity Knocking, Inc.
PMC-ParaLegal Management & Consultants

Pathway Executive Search, Inc.
Paul-Tittle Assoc., Inc.
Pencom Systems Inc.
ProSearch, Inc.
Professional Recruiters
RAI Consulting
RHS Assoc., Inc.
Resource Services, Inc.
Retail Recruiters/Spectra Professional Search
Romac & Assoc. - San Francisco
Sanford Rose Assoc. - Great Neck
The Salem Group, Executive Recruiters
Scott-Wayne Assoc., Inc.
Search Bureau Int'l.
Search Group
Setford-Shaw-Najarian Assoc., Ltd.
Snelling Personnel Services
Staffing Solutions
Stanewick, Hart & Assoc., Inc.
Stone Enterprises Ltd.
Summerfield Assoc., Inc.
Systems One Ltd.
Tech Vision Co.
Technical Recruiting Consultants
Techsearch Services Inc.
Traynor Confidential, Ltd.
Trilogy Enterprises, Inc.
Werbin Assoc. Executive Search, Inc.
Wesson, Taylor, Wells & Assoc.
S.J. Wexler Assoc., Inc.
Joel H. Wilensky Assoc., Inc.
Wing Tips & Pumps, Inc.
Winter, Wyman & Co.
Worlco Computer Resources, Inc.
Dennis Wynn Assoc., Inc.
P.D. Zier Assoc.
W.F. Richer Assoc., Inc.

01.5 LEGAL

Bartlett, Bunn & Travis, Inc.
Beckwith, Thomas & Fanning
Marcia Beilin, Inc.
Bellon & Assoc., Inc.
Charles Bradley Professionals
J.R. Brody & Assoc., Inc.
Chicago Legal Search, Ltd.
Coleman Legal Search Consultants
Crickenberger Assoc.
Dunhill of Manchester Inc.
Environmental Professional Assoc.
Exec 2000
Foster Assoc.
Frey & Conboy Assoc., Inc.
GreenHall Assoc., Inc.
Hamilton Edwards, Ltd.
Phyllis Hawkins & Assoc.
The Headhunters
George Howard Assoc.
Howard-Sloan Legal Search, Inc.
J.D. Limited
JM Assoc.
Barbara Kerner Consultants

01.5 LEGAL

Legal Placements Inc.
Major, Wilson & Africa
Marley Group Ltd.
The McCormick Group, Inc.
Meridian Personnel Assoc., Inc.
NPF Assoc. Ltd. Inc.
The NRI Group
PMC-ParaLegal Management & Consultants
Precise Legal, Inc.
The Primary Group, Inc.
Princeton Planning Consultants, Inc.
RALCO/Richard A. Lucia & Assoc.
Railey & Assoc.
Ryman, Bell, Green & Michaels, Inc.
Sharrow & Assoc., Inc.
Raymond James Smith & Assoc.
Phyllis Solomon Executive Search, Inc.
Summerfield Assoc., Inc.
Topaz Int'l., Inc.
Waldorf Associates, Inc.
Weiss & Assoc., Inc.
Whitbeck & Assoc.
Winship Assoc.

02.0 MANUFACTURING

AGRI-associates
A.M.C.R., Inc.
APA Search, Inc.
ARJay & Assoc.
Accounting Resources Int'l., Inc.
The Addison Consulting Group
Adel Lawrence Assoc., Inc.
Adept Tech Recruiting, Inc.
Advancement Recruiting Services
Aerospace Technologies, Inc.
The Agency- An Employment Consortium
Agri-Tech Personnel, Inc.
Allen Barry Assoc.
Ethan Allen Personnel, Inc.
Alpine Consulting Group
American Resources Corp.
Ames-O'Neill Assoc., Inc.
Tryg R. Angell Ltd.
John Anthony & Assoc.
Ashway Ltd. Agency
Atlantic West Int'l.
Austin - Allen Co.
Automation Technology Search
Availability Personnel Consultants
BGB Assoc., Inc.
BIK Search/Force II
B.P.A. Enterprises, Inc.
B.K. Barnes & Associates
Barone Assoc.
Barone-O'Hara Assoc., Inc.
R. Gaines Baty Assoc., Inc.
Jim Baum - Executive Search
Ted Bavly Assoc., Inc.
Ray N. Bedingfield, Consultant
Gary S. Bell Assoc., Inc.
Bell Professional Placement

Blanton & Co.
Brennan Assoc.
Paul J. Burns
The Byrnes Group
C & H Personnel
CES
C.P.S., Inc.
J.P. Canon Assoc.
Capitol Management Consulting, Inc.
Career Management, Inc.
Career Marketing Assoc.
Carver Search Consultants
Allen Case & Assoc., Inc.
Case Executive Search
Casey & Gerrish Assoc., Inc.
Wayne S. Chamberlain & Assoc.
William J. Christopher Assoc., Inc.
Clark Assoc., Inc.
Cochran, Cochran, & Yale, Inc.
Competitive Resources, Inc.
Corporate Careers Inc.
The Corporate Connection, Ltd.
Corporate Consultants Inc.
Corporate Personnel, Inc.
Corporate Recruiters, Inc.
Corporate Resources Professional Placement
Cowin Assoc.
Crest Management Search, Inc.
Cross Country Consultants, Inc.
Timothy D. Crowe, Jr.
Frank Cuomo & Assoc., Inc.
DEI Executive Services
Dapexs Consultants, Inc.
Davis & James, Inc.
Dean-Wharton Assoc.
Deeco Int'l.
Delacore Personnel
Delta Resource Group, Ltd.
Dillard Executive Search
L.J. Doherty & Assoc.
Double M Executive Placement Service, Inc.
Dreier Consulting
J. H. Dugan & Assoc., Inc.
Dumont Moriarty & Assoc.
Dunhill Personnel System, Inc.
Dunhill Personnel of Milwaukee
Dunhill Professional Search, Inc. of Kearney
Dunhill of Southeast Fort Worth, Inc.
Dunhill of Denton, Inc.
Dunhill Professional Search of Wilkes-Barre/
    Scranton, Inc.
Dunhill of Greater Akron, Inc.
Dunhill Search of West Atlanta
Dunhill Professional Search Irvine/Newport
G.L. Dykstra Assoc., Inc.
The E & K Group
E O Technical
Eastern Executive Assoc.
Eden & Assoc., Inc.
Eggers Consulting Co., Inc.
W. Robert Eissler & Assoc., Inc.
Emerson & Co.
ExecuTech

02.0 MANUFACTURING (Cont'd)

Executive Recruiters, Inc.
Executive Referral Services, Inc.
Executive Register, Inc.
Executive Resource Inc.
Paul Falcone Assoc., Inc.
Fergason Assoc., Inc.
First Search Inc.
Fisher-Todd Assoc.
James L. Fisk & Assoc.
Flores & Assoc.
Ford & Assoc., Inc.
Fortune Personnel Consultants of Huntsville, Inc.
Fortune Personnel Consultants of Sarasota Inc.
Mel Frazer & Assoc.
GHK Technical Recruiter
Galen Giles Group
Gallagher & Assoc.
Gallin Assoc.
Delores F. George
J. Gifford, Inc.
W.T. Glover & Assoc., Inc.
Hahn & Assoc., Inc.
Handwerk & Assoc.
Harrison Moore Inc.
Hartman Personnel Services
Health Technology, Inc.
Heller Kil Assoc., Inc.
J. D. Hersey & Assoc.
Hessel Assoc., Inc.
Horizon Assoc.
Hoskins, Rees & Smith
The Hudson Group
Human Resource Recruiters
E. F. Humay Assoc.
Industrial Recruiters Assoc., Inc.
Industry Consultants, Inc.
JNB Assoc., Inc.
Jackley Search Consultants
K.E. Johnson Assoc.
Kathryn L. Johnson
J.M. Joseph Assoc.
Jubilee, Inc.
K & C Assoc.
Key Employment Services
Joseph Keyes Assoc.
Kiley-Owen Assoc., Inc
Kirkbride Assoc., Inc.
Kirland Search, Inc.
Kozlin Assoc., Inc.
Krow Assoc., Inc.
Lacrosse Assoc., Inc.
Lange & Assoc., Inc.
Lappe & Assoc.
Jack B. Larsen & Assoc.
The Lawson Group
Lee Associates
Lindsey & Assoc., Inc.
Link Personnel & Assoc.
Logistics Management Resources, Inc.
Lord & Albus Co.

Lowery, Cotter, & Assoc.
Ludot Personnel Services, Inc.
Luke, Lincoln, & Brugger
MARBL Consultants, Inc.
mfg/Search, Inc.
MJF Assoc.
MKM Search Consultants, Inc.
Mahony & Assoc., Ltd.
Management Recruiters of Savannah
Management Recruiters of Cedar Rapids, Inc.
Management Recruiters of Wilmington
Management Recruiters of Cincinnati/ Sharonville, Inc.
Management Recruiters
Management Recruiters
Management Recruiters
Management Recruiters of Kinston
Management Recruiters of Ft. Myers, FL.
Management Recruiters of Laguna Hills
Management Recruiters of Monterey
Management Recruiters of North Brunswick, Inc.
Management Recruiters of Charlotte - Southwest
Management Resource Assoc., Inc.
Marcus & Assoc.
Donovan Martin & Assoc.
Mathey Services
McCulloch Assoc.
McDermott & Assoc.
Sandi McDonald & Assoc., Inc.
McInturff & Assoc., Inc.
Medical Executive Search Assoc.
Medquest Assoc.
Medtrac & Assoc.
Todd Melon Group
Midgette Consultants, Inc.
Mogul Consultants, Inc.
Diedre Moire Corp., Inc.
The Montanye Group
The C. B. Mueller Co., Inc.
Multisearch Recruiters
John H. Munson & Co.
Murphy, Symonds & Stowell Search, Inc.
Nachman Biomedical
National Corporate Consultants, Inc.
National Logistics Recruiters, Inc.
J. Fielding Nelson & Assoc., Inc.
Newcombe & Cyr Assoc., Inc.
Norton & Assoc.
The P & L Group
PC Assoc.
Patrick Assoc.
Kevin W. Paul
Paul S. Pelland
Performance Professionals
Personnel Advisors Int'l. Corp.
Personnel Inc.
Personnel Management, Inc.
The Personnel Network, Inc.
Petruzzi Assoc.
Phillips Resource Group
Plastics Enterprises

02.0 MANUFACTURING (Cont'd)

Polytechnical Consultants, Inc.
Norman Powers Assoc., Inc.
Princeton Executive Search, Inc.
Probe Technology
Professional Personnel Services
Professional Recruiters
Professional Recruiters Inc.
Professions Unlimited, Inc.
RAI Consulting
RGL Assoc., Inc.
RTE Search
Raymond Thomas & Assoc.
Resource Perspectives, Inc.
S. Reyman & Assoc., Ltd.
Roberson & Co.
The Robinson Group, D.A., Ltd.
Ropella & Assoc.
Sanford Rose Assoc.- Woodbury
Sanford Rose Assoc.
Sanford Rose Assoc. - Santa Barbara
Sanford Rose Assoc. of Wilmington
Sanford Rose Assoc.- Detroit North
Sanford Rose Assoc. of Beachwood
Sanford Rose Assoc.- Suburban Philadelphia
Sanford Rose Assoc. of Nashville
Sanford Rose Assoc. - Virginia Beach
Roth Young Seattle
Rothrock Assoc.
Louis Rudzinsky Assoc., Inc.
The Charles Ryan Group, Inc.
Ryman, Bell, Green & Michaels, Inc.
S-H-S of Allentown
Robert Sage Recruiting
The Salem Group, Executive Recruiters
Sales & Management Search, Inc.
Sales Consultants of Austin, Inc.
Schattle Personnel Consultants, Inc.
Search & Recruit Int'l.
Search Dynamics, Inc.
Search Enterprises, Inc.
Search Masters
The Search Network
Search Northwest Assoc.
Search Solutions, Inc.
Selective Management Services, Inc.
Selective Staffing
Jules Seltzer Assoc.
L. A. Silver Assoc., Inc.
SilverCrest Search
J. Harrington Smith Assoc.
Snelling Personnel Services
Source Engineering
Spectrum Consultants
The Stevens Group, Inc.
Stewart Assoc.
Charles Stickler Assoc.
Strategic Assoc., Inc.
Strategic Search Group
Strategy 2000
S. Tyler Sullivan & Assoc., Inc.
Summerfield Assoc., Inc.

Summit Executive Search Consultants, Inc.
Ron Sunshine & Assoc.
The Talley Group
Tech International
Technical Engineering Consultants
Technical Recruiting Services
The Tibbetts Group Ltd.
Traynor Confidential, Ltd.
Triangle Consulting Group
Trilogy Enterprises, Inc.
J.Q. Turner & Assoc., Inc.
Key Employment
Unisearch
The Urban Placement Service
Valentine & Assoc.
Gordon Wahls Co.
Wallace Assoc.
Frank X. Walsh & Co., Inc.
Wegner & Assoc.
Weinpel & Co.
Whittaker & Assoc., Inc.
Whittlesey & Assoc., Inc.
Windward Executive Search, Inc.
Winfield Assoc.
Wing Tips & Pumps, Inc.
Woehr Assoc.
Jim Woodson & Assoc., Inc.
World Search
John Wylie Assoc., Inc.
The Yaiser Group

02.1 PRODUCT DEVELOPMENT

Francis V. Anderson Assoc. Inc.
D.W. Baird & Associates
Biotech Sourcing
Brooke Chase Assoc., Inc.
CPI Technical Services
Allen Case & Assoc., Inc.
Robert L. Charon
Malcolm Cole & Assoc.
Corporate Consultants Inc.
Corporate Personnel, Inc.
DLB Assoc.
Dreier Consulting
Dunhill Personnel of Milwaukee
Dunhill of Huntsville, Inc.
Engineering Resource Group, Inc.
Engineering Search Assoc.
ExecuTech
Genesis
J. Gifford, Inc.
Guidarelli Assoc., Inc.
Harrison Moore Inc.
Industry Consultants, Inc.
Jackley Search Consultants
Kromenaker & Associates
W.R. Lawry, Inc.
The Lawson Group
Brian Leggee & Assoc.
Lybrook Assoc., Inc.
Management Recruiters of Cedar Rapids, Inc.
Management Recruiters

02.1 PRODUCT DEVELOPMENT (Cont'd)

Management Recruiters of Butler County
Management Recruiters of Waterbury, Inc.
Management Recruiters of Ashville, Inc.
Merlin Int'l. Inc.
Merrick & Moore
John H. Munson & Co.
P R Management Consultants, Inc.
Polytechnical Consultants, Inc.
Remark Assoc. Inc.
Sanford Rose Assoc. of Lima
Sanford Rose Assoc.- Suburban Philadelphia
Sanford Rose Assoc. of Quakertown
Saxon Morse Assoc.
Search Dynamics, Inc.
Search Group
Search Solutions, Inc.
Stephen Sellers Assoc.
Sharrow & Assoc., Inc.
RitaSue Siegel Assoc., Inc.
Ron Stevens & Assoc., Inc.
S. Tyler Sullivan & Assoc., Inc.
Technitrac, Inc.
Tell/Com Recruiters
M.K. Wasse & Assoc., Inc.
Henry Welker & Assoc.
R.A. Wells Co.
The Wright Group
Zeiger Technical Careers, Inc.

02.2 PRODUCTION ENGINEERING, PLANNING, SCHEDULING & CONTROL

APA Search, Inc.
Auden Assoc., Inc.
Bennett-Munson Inc.
Besen Assoc. Inc.
Britt Assoc., Inc.
Broward-Dobbs, Inc.
Robert L. Charon
Corporate Consultants Inc.
Dunhill Personnel of Milwaukee
Dunhill of Southeast Fort Worth, Inc.
Dunhill Professional Search
ExecuSource Int'l.
Gaines & Assoc. Int'l., Inc.
J. Gifford, Inc.
Greene Personnel Consultants
I.S. Consultants, Inc.
Jackley Search Consultants
Kromenaker & Associates
Brian Leggee & Assoc.
Logistics Management Resources, Inc.
M H Executive Search Group
Management Recruiters of Cedar Rapids, Inc.
Management Recruiters of Wilmington
Management Recruiters of Cincinnati/ Sharonville, Inc.
Management Recruiters
Management Recruiters of Butler County
Management Recruiters

Management Recruiters of Oakland
Management Recruiters of Westchester, Inc.
Management Search, Inc.
The McKee Co.
P&IC Assoc.
Largent Parks & Partners, Inc.
Preston Robert & Assoc.-Health Care Div.
The Resource Group
Sanford Rose Assoc. - Great Neck
Sanford Rose Assoc. of Quakertown
Sales Consultants of Andover
Schenck & Assoc. SC
Search Dynamics, Inc.
Search Group
Sharrow & Assoc., Inc.
Summit Executive Search Consultants, Inc.
Techcon Co.
Telem Adhesive Search Corp.
Jay Tracey Assoc.
Triangle Assoc.
Weeks & Assoc.
Henry Welker & Assoc.

02.3 AUTOMATION, ROBOTICS

Aberdeen Assoc.
The Altco Group
Anderson, Graham & Stewart, Inc.
Ashton Computer Professionals, Inc.
Broward-Dobbs, Inc.
The Chapman Group, Inc.
Robert L. Charon
Robert Drexler Assoc., Inc.
Dunhill Professional Search Inc.
J. Gifford, Inc.
Halbrecht & Co.
Hunter Assoc.
Kromenaker & Associates
Brian Leggee & Assoc.
Loewenstein & Assoc.
Management Recruiters
Management Recruiters of Ashville, Inc.
The McKee Co.
Professional Recruiters Inc.
Sanford Rose Assoc. of Lima
Sanford Rose Assoc. of Hartford
Sales Consultants of Andover
Search Dynamics, Inc.
Search Northwest Assoc.
Stephen Sellers Assoc.
Jay Tracey Assoc.
Vento Assoc.

02.4 PLANT MANAGEMENT

The Altco Group
Francis V. Anderson Assoc. Inc.
Charles P. Aquavella & Assoc.
D.W. Baird & Associates
Bennett-Munson Inc.
Dan B. Brockman
Broward-Dobbs, Inc.
Carlden Personnel Services Inc.
Robert L. Charon

02.4 PLANT MANAGEMENT (Cont'd)

William J. Christopher Assoc., Inc.
Corporate Consultants Inc.
Corporate Recruiters, Inc.
N. Dean Davic Assoc., Inc.
Robert Drexler Assoc., Inc.
Dunhill of Southeast Fort Worth, Inc.
Dunhill Professional Search
Engineering & Scientific Search Assoc.
Evans & James Assoc., Inc.
J. Gifford, Inc.
J. Gross & Assoc.
Handwerk & Assoc.
Hintz Associates
Human Resource Network
Impact Executive Search, Inc.
Industry Consultants, Inc.
Jubilee, Inc.
Blair Kershaw Assoc., Inc.
Larson Assoc.
Lineal Recruiting Services
Lunney, Hadden & Assoc.
M H Executive Search Group
Management Recruiters of Wilmington
Management Recruiters
Management Recruiters of Butler County
Management Recruiters
Management Recruiters of Waterbury, Inc.
Management Recruiters of Atlanta Downtown
Management Recruiters of Reno
Management Search, Inc.
Merlin Int'l. Inc.
National Executive Consultants, Inc.
National Recruiting Service
William H. Nenstiel & Assoc.
P R Management Consultants, Inc.
PLRS/Career Connections
Largent Parks & Partners, Inc.
Robert A. Paul & Assoc.
Paul S. Pelland
Remark Assoc. Inc.
Sanford Rose Assoc. of Lima
Sanford Rose Assoc. - Great Neck
Rushlow & Co.
Schenck & Assoc. SC
Search Solutions, Inc.
Selective Staffing
Stephen Sellers Assoc.
Sharrow & Assoc., Inc.
Ron Stevens & Assoc., Inc.
The Stoddard Co.
Stoneburner Assoc., Inc.
Telem Adhesive Search Corp.
Triangle Assoc.
Weeks & Assoc.
R.A. Wells Co.
E.T. Wharton Assoc., Inc.
Windward Executive Search, Inc.

02.5 QUALITY

Besen Assoc. Inc.
Biotech Sourcing

Bioventure Resources, Inc.
Blanton & Co.
Bryant Research
Robert L. Charon
Corporate Consultants Inc.
Dunhill of Southeast Fort Worth, Inc.
Dunhill Professional Search of Ramsey
Dunhill Professional Search
Evans & James Assoc., Inc.
Fortune Personnel Consultants
Genesis
Impact Executive Search, Inc.
Industry Consultants, Inc.
Kenmore Executives Inc.
Blair Kershaw Assoc., Inc.
Kromenaker & Associates
W.R. Lawry, Inc.
Lunney, Hadden & Assoc.
Lybrook Assoc., Inc.
Management Recruiters of Tampa North
Management Recruiters of Ashville, Inc.
The McKee Co.
Merlin Int'l. Inc.
Merrick & Moore
National Recruiting Service
The P & L Group
Penn Associates
Professional Recruiters
Sanford Rose Assoc. of Lima
Sales Consultants of Fairfax, Inc.
The Search Network
The Stoddard Co.
Stoneburner Assoc., Inc.
S. Tyler Sullivan & Assoc., Inc.
Henry Welker & Assoc.
E.T. Wharton Assoc., Inc.

02.6 PRODUCTIVITY

Dan B. Brockman
Genesis
Hintz Associates
Hunt Ltd.
Kromenaker & Associates
Santangelo Consultants Inc.
Weeks & Assoc.

03.0 MATERIALS MANAGEMENT

APA Search, Inc.
ARJay & Assoc.
Adept Tech Recruiting, Inc.
Aerospace Technologies, Inc.
Agri-Tech Personnel, Inc.
Alpine Consulting Group
Ames-O'Neill Assoc., Inc.
Atlantic West Int'l.
Austin - Allen Co.
Automation Technology Search
Availability Personnel Consultants
BGB Assoc., Inc.
D.W. Baird & Associates
Barone Assoc.
Barone-O'Hara Assoc., Inc.

624 / DIRECTORY OF EXECUTIVE RECRUITERS

03.0 MATERIALS MANAGEMENT (Cont'd)

R. Gaines Baty Assoc., Inc.
Jim Baum - Executive Search
Gary S. Bell Assoc., Inc.
Britt Assoc., Inc.
J.P. Canon Assoc.
Capitol Management Consulting, Inc.
Career Management, Inc.
Career Search Assoc.
Carlden Personnel Services Inc.
Case Executive Search
Competitive Resources, Inc.
Corporate Personnel, Inc.
Cross Country Consultants, Inc.
Timothy D. Crowe, Jr.
DEI Executive Services
N. Dean Davic Assoc., Inc.
Double M Executive Placement Service, Inc.
Dumont Moriarty & Assoc.
Dunhill Professional Search, Inc. of Kearney
Dunhill Professional Search of Wilkes-Barre/ Scranton, Inc.
Dunhill Search of West Atlanta
E O Technical
Eastern Executive Assoc.
ExecuSource Int'l.
Executive Register, Inc.
Executive Resource Inc.
Paul Falcone Assoc., Inc.
Flores & Assoc.
Ford & Assoc., Inc.
Fortune Personnel Consultants of Huntsville, Inc.
Fortune Personnel Consultants of Sarasota Inc.
Hahn & Assoc., Inc.
Heller Kil Assoc., Inc.
Hoskins, Rees & Smith
Hunt Ltd.
Kathryn L. Johnson
J.M. Joseph Assoc.
K & C Assoc.
Joseph Keyes Assoc.
Kozlin Assoc., Inc.
Lacrosse Assoc., Inc.
Lange & Assoc., Inc.
Link Personnel & Assoc.
Logistics Management Resources, Inc.
Lord & Albus Co.
MARBL Consultants, Inc.
mfg/Search, Inc.
Management Recruiters of Savannah
Management Recruiters of Cedar Rapids, Inc.
Management Recruiters
Management Recruiters
Management Recruiters
Management Recruiters of Kinston
Management Recruiters of Ft. Myers, FL.
Management Recruiters of Charlotte - Southwest
Management Resource Assoc., Inc.
Donovan Martin & Assoc.

McInturff & Assoc., Inc.
Medical Executive Search Assoc.
Medquest Assoc.
Morency Assoc.
The C. B. Mueller Co., Inc.
John H. Munson & Co.
National Logistics Recruiters, Inc.
Newcombe & Cyr Assoc., Inc.
Norton & Assoc.
The P & L Group
P&IC Assoc.
Personnel Advisors Int'l. Corp.
Personnel Management, Inc.
Petruzzi Assoc.
Polytechnical Consultants, Inc.
Princeton Executive Search, Inc.
Probe Technology
Professional Personnel Services
Professional Recruiters
Professional Recruiters Inc.
Reinecke & Assoc.
Roberson & Co.
Sanford Rose Assoc.
Sanford Rose Assoc.- Suburban Philadelphia
Sanford Rose Assoc. - Virginia Beach
Roth Young Seattle
Rothrock Assoc.
The Charles Ryan Group, Inc.
Samper Assoc.
George D. Sandel Assoc.
Search Enterprises, Inc.
The Search Network
J. Harrington Smith Assoc.
Stephen M. Sonis Assoc.
Stewart Assoc.
Charles Stickler Assoc.
The Stoddard Co.
Strategic Assoc., Inc.
Strategy 2000
Ron Sunshine & Assoc.
The Talley Group
Technical Engineering Consultants
The Tibbetts Group Ltd.
J.Q. Turner & Assoc., Inc.
U.S. Search
Valentine & Assoc.
Wallace Assoc.
Frank X. Walsh & Co., Inc.
Jim Woodson & Assoc., Inc.
World Search
John Wylie Assoc., Inc.

03.1 PURCHASING, INVENTORY MANAGEMENT

APA Search, Inc.
Accounting Personnel Assoc.
Charles P. Aquavella & Assoc.
Auden Assoc., Inc.
Britt Assoc., Inc.
J.P. Canon Assoc.
Fortune Personnel Consultants of Sarasota Inc.
Healthcare Resources Group

03.1 PURCHASING, INVENTORY MANAGEMENT (Cont'd)

Hunt Ltd.
Hunter Assoc.
The Lawson Group
Logistics Management Resources, Inc.
Midgette Consultants, Inc.
The P & L Group
P&IC Assoc.
Retail Pacesetters, Inc.
Sales Consultants of Andover
Santangelo Consultants Inc.
Search Masters
Storfer & Assoc.
Technitrac, Inc.

03.2 MATERIALS & REQUIREMENT PLANNING

Britt Assoc., Inc.
CES
Dapexs Consultants, Inc.
Engineering Search Assoc.
Fortune Personnel Consultants of Sarasota Inc.
Hunt Ltd.
Kenmore Executives Inc.
The Kennett Group, Inc.
Midgette Consultants, Inc.
P&IC Assoc.
Techcon Co.

03.3 PHYSICAL DISTRIBUTION, TRAFFIC & TRANSPORTATION, LOGISTICS

Analytic Recruiting, Inc.
Tryg R. Angell Ltd.
Britt Assoc., Inc.
C & H Personnel
J.P. Canon Assoc.
Gabriel & Bowie Assoc., Ltd.
Hunt Ltd.
JDG Assoc., Ltd.
R.I. James, Inc.
Kogon Assoc., Inc.
Management Recruiters of Reno
The P & L Group
P&IC Assoc.
Professional Resources
Retail Recruiters of Paramus, Inc.
Rockwood Assoc.
The Search Center Inc.

03.4 PACKAGING

The Altco Group
Brooke Chase Assoc., Inc.
The Cambridge Group Ltd.
J.P. Canon Assoc.
Dunhill of Denton, Inc.
Dunhill Professional Search
Evans & James Assoc., Inc.
Galen Giles Group
J. D. Hersey & Assoc.

M H Executive Search Group
Management Recruiters
Merrick & Moore
Janou Pakter, Inc.
Sales Consultants of Savannah, GA.
Search Masters
Selective Management Services, Inc.
Storfer & Assoc.
U.S. Search
R.A. Wells Co.
E.T. Wharton Assoc., Inc.
The Yaiser Group

04.0 RESEARCH & DEVELOPMENT

ACR Assoc.
AGRI-associates
A.M.C.R., Inc.
ARJay & Assoc.
The Addison Consulting Group
Adept Tech Recruiting, Inc.
Advanced Corporate Search
Advancement Recruiting Services
Aerospace Technologies, Inc.
Agri-Tech Personnel, Inc.
Allen Barry Assoc.
Alpine Consulting Group
Ames-O'Neill Assoc., Inc.
Francis V. Anderson Assoc. Inc.
Tryg R. Angell Ltd.
Ashway Ltd. Agency
Atlantic West Int'l.
Automation Technology Search
Availability Personnel Consultants
BIK Search/Force II
D.W. Baird & Associates
Barone-O'Hara Assoc., Inc.
Jim Baum - Executive Search
Ray N. Bedingfield, Consultant
Bell Professional Placement
Besen Assoc. Inc.
Biotech Sourcing
Bioventure Resources, Inc.
M.F. Branch Assoc., Inc.
Ira Broadman Assoc.
Brooks Executive Personnel
Bryant Research
Paul J. Burns
Capitol Management Consulting, Inc.
Carver Search Consultants
Case Executive Search
Casey & Gerrish Assoc., Inc.
Chase Waterford Ltd.
Malcolm Cole & Assoc.
Corporate Personnel, Inc.
Corporate Recruiters Inc.
Cowin Assoc.
Crest Management Search, Inc.
Cross Country Consultants, Inc.
Timothy D. Crowe, Jr.
DEI Executive Services
Double M Executive Placement Service, Inc.
Dreier Consulting

04.0 RESEARCH & DEVELOPMENT (Cont'd)

J. H. Dugan & Assoc., Inc.
Dunhill Professional Search, Inc. of Kearney
Dunhill of Huntsville, Inc.
Dunhill of Southeast Fort Worth, Inc.
Dunhill of Denton, Inc.
Dunhill Professional Search of Wilkes-Barre/ Scranton, Inc.
The E & K Group
E O Technical
Eastern Executive Assoc.
Eggers Consulting Co., Inc.
The Energists
Engineering & Scientific Search Assoc.
Engineering Search Assoc.
ExecuTech
Executive Recruiters, Inc.
F.L.A.G.
Fernow Assoc.
First Search Inc.
Jack Stuart Fisher Assoc.
James L. Fisk & Assoc.
Fortune Personnel Consultants of Huntsville, Inc.
Fortune Personnel Consultants
Franklin Int'l. Search, Inc.
Mel Frazer & Assoc.
GHK Technical Recruiter
Gallagher & Assoc.
Gallin Assoc.
Gardner, Savage Assoc.
Genesis
The Goodman Group
Graham Assoc. Inc.
Hall, Cooper & Bartman, Ltd.
Harrison Moore Inc.
The Headhunter
Health Technology, Inc.
Heller Kil Assoc., Inc.
High Technology Search Assoc.
Horizon Assoc.
The Hudson Group
Jackley Search Consultants
K.E. Johnson Assoc.
J.M. Joseph Assoc.
Joslin & Assoc., Ltd.
Kacevich, Lewis & Brown, Inc.
Kendall & Davis Co., Inc.
Kensington Int'l.
Krow Assoc., Inc.
Lacrosse Assoc., Inc.
W.R. Lawry, Inc.
Lee Associates
The James Lloyd Group
Logix, Inc.
Lord & Albus Co.
Lybrook Assoc., Inc.
mfg/Search, Inc.
Mahony & Assoc., Ltd.
Management Recruiters of Ashville, Inc.
Management Recruiters of Savannah

Management Recruiters of Cedar Rapids, Inc.
Management Recruiters of Greater Bridgeport, Inc.
Management Recruiters
Management Recruiters of Laguna Hills
Management Recruiters
Management Recruiters of Atlanta West, Inc.
Management Recruiters of Passaic, inc.
Management Recruiters of Westchester, Inc.
Management Resources
Marcus & Assoc.
Donovan Martin & Assoc.
Mathey Services
Earl L. McDermid & Assoc.
McDermott & Assoc.
Medical Executive Search Assoc.
Medquest Assoc.
Medtrac & Assoc.
Todd Melon Group
Merrick & Moore
Diedre Moire Corp., Inc.
The Montanye Group
The Morris Group
The C. B. Mueller Co., Inc.
Multi Processing, Inc.
Multisearch Recruiters
Nachman Biomedical
William H. Nenstiel & Assoc.
New Dimensions in Technology, Inc.
Newcombe & Cyr Assoc., Inc.
Part Time Resources
M.A. Pelle Assoc., Inc.
The Personnel Network, Inc.
Petruzzi Assoc.
Phillips Resource Group
Place Mart Personnel Service
Plastics Enterprises
Polytechnical Consultants, Inc.
Preston Robert & Assoc.-Health Care Div.
Probe Technology
RAC International
RTE Search
The Remington Group, Ltd.
Resource Perspectives, Inc.
Ritta Professional Search Inc.
Ropella & Assoc.
Sanford Rose Assoc.- Woodbury
Sanford Rose Assoc.
Sanford Rose Assoc. - Santa Barbara
Sanford Rose Assoc. of Wilmington
Sanford Rose Assoc. of Binghamton
Sanford Rose Assoc.- Suburban Philadelphia
Sanford Rose Assoc. of Nashville
Sanford Rose Assoc. - Virginia Beach
Rothrock Assoc.
Louis Rudzinsky Assoc., Inc.
S-H-S of Allentown
Robert Sage Recruiting
Sales Consultants of Austin, Inc.
Samper Assoc.
George D. Sandel Assoc.
Search Dynamics, Inc.
Search Enterprises, Inc.

04.0 RESEARCH & DEVELOPMENT (Cont'd)

Search Masters Int'l.
Search Northwest Assoc.
Stephen Sellers Assoc.
Jules Seltzer Assoc.
L. A. Silver Assoc., Inc.
SilverCrest Search
Smith Hanley Assoc., Inc.
Spectrum Consultants
Staffing Solutions
Steinbach & Co.
Stewart Assoc.
Charles Stickler Assoc.
Stoneburner Assoc., Inc.
Strategy 2000
S. Tyler Sullivan & Assoc., Inc.
Ron Sunshine & Assoc.
Tech Consulting
Tech International
Technical Engineering Consultants
Technitrac, Inc.
Telem Adhesive Search Corp.
The Tibbetts Group Ltd.
TransAmerica Network
J.Q. Turner & Assoc., Inc.
USA Medical Placement Inc.
Unisearch
Video Interview Professionals, Inc.
Wallace Assoc.
Wayne Assoc., Inc.
Weinpel & Co.
Whittaker & Assoc., Inc.
Winfield Assoc.
World Search
The Yaiser Group

05.0 MARKETING

A. D. & Assoc.
A.M.C.R., Inc.
APA Search, Inc.
ARJay & Assoc.
Abraham & London Ltd.
The Addison Consulting Group
Agri-Tech Personnel, Inc.
Alpine Consulting Group
Alterna-track
Ames-O'Neill Assoc., Inc.
Anderson, Graham & Stewart, Inc.
Tryg R. Angell Ltd.
Aronow Assoc., Inc.
Ashton Computer Professionals, Inc.
Atlantic West Int'l.
BIK Search/Force II
Keith Bagg Personnel Ltd.
The Barack Group, Inc.
Barone Assoc.
Barone-O'Hara Assoc., Inc.
Peter Barrett Assoc., Inc.
Bast & Assoc., Inc.
L. Battalin & Co.
Gary S. Bell Assoc., Inc.

Bell Professional Placement
Blanton & Co.
Bonifield Assoc.
Bornholdt Shivas & Friends
Bowman & Marshall
C.W. Brandon & Assoc., Inc.
Jerold Braun & Assoc.
Brennan Assoc.
Brooke Chase Assoc., Inc.
Paul J. Burns
The Butlers Co. Insurance Recruiters
CDH & Assoc., Inc.
CN Associates
CRS Assoc., Inc.
Career Management, Inc.
Career Marketing Assoc.
Career Profiles
Career Search Assoc.
Case Executive Search
Casey & Gerrish Assoc., Inc.
Chase Waterford Ltd.
William J. Christopher Assoc., Inc.
J.F. Church Assoc., Inc.
Cibotti Assoc., Inc.
Toby Clark Assoc. Inc.
Clark-Winans, Inc.
Competitive Resources, Inc.
The Comwell Co. Inc.
Consumer Search, Inc.
Corporate Careers Inc.
The Corporate Connection, Ltd.
Corporate Recruiters, Inc.
The Crawford Group
Crest Management Search, Inc.
Timothy D. Crowe, Jr.
Frank Cuomo & Assoc., Inc.
Curts/Jackson, Inc.
DLB Assoc.
The DLR Group, Inc.
Damon & Assoc., Inc.
N. Dean Davic Assoc., Inc.
DeCorrevont & Assoc.
DeLalla - Fried Assoc.
Dean-Wharton Assoc.
Deeco Int'l.
Deery Geddis & Assoc.
Delta Resource Group, Ltd.
L.J. Doherty & Assoc.
Domenico/Brown Group
Drake & Assoc.
J. H. Dugan & Assoc., Inc.
Dumont Moriarty & Assoc.
Dunhill Personnel System, Inc.
Dunhill Professional Search, Inc. of Kearney
Dunhill Professional Search of Wilkes-Barre/Scranton, Inc.
Dunhill International Search
Dunhill Professional Search Irvine/Newport
Dussick Management Assoc.
Eden & Assoc., Inc.
W. Robert Eissler & Assoc., Inc.
Ells Personnel Systems Inc.
ExecuSource Int'l.

05.0 MARKETING (Cont'd)

Executive Careers
Executive Recruiters, Inc.
F.L.A.G.
Paul Falcone Assoc., Inc.
Fergason Assoc., Inc.
Fernow Assoc.
G.A. Field Personnel Consultants
First Search Inc.
Fisher-Todd Assoc.
A.G. Fishkin & Assoc., Inc.
James L. Fisk & Assoc.
Flores & Assoc.
Ford & Ford
Franklin Int'l. Search, Inc.
Future Sense
GHK Technical Recruiter
Gallin Assoc.
The Garrison Organization
Genesis Personnel Service, Inc.
Delores F. George
Global Data Services, Inc.
W.T. Glover & Assoc., Inc.
The Goldman Group Inc.
The Goodman Group
Guidarelli Assoc., Inc.
The Gumbinner Co.
Halbrecht & Co.
Hall, Cooper & Bartman, Ltd.
Harrison Moore Inc.
Hartman Personnel Services
Hawkes-Randolph & Assoc., Inc.
Health Industry Resources, Inc.
Health Technology, Inc.
Heller Kil Assoc., Inc.
Heritage Search Group, Inc.
John M. Horton
Hoskins, Rees & Smith
Howard-Sloan Assoc.
Hudson Assoc. Inc.
E. F. Humay Assoc.
Industrial Recruiters Assoc., Inc.
Intech Summit Group, Inc.
Integrated Professional Services, Inc.
JT Assoc.
The Johnson Group, Inc.
Kathryn L. Johnson
K & C Assoc.
Kacevich, Lewis & Brown, Inc.
Kane Ford Karrel & Assoc.
Kelley & Keller, Inc.
Jack Kennedy Assoc., Inc.
Kensington Int'l.
Key Talent, Inc.
Kiley-Owen Assoc., Inc.
Kirland Search, Inc.
Sanford Kleiner Assoc., Inc.
The Koehler Group
Kordus Consulting Group
Kravitz * Larkin * Silver Assoc.
Krow Assoc., Inc.
Lacrosse Assoc., Inc.

Jack B. Larsen & Assoc.
Larson Assoc.
Lawrence-Balakonis & Assoc., Inc.
Vincent Lee Assoc.
Lee Associates
Paul Ligon Co.
Lindsey & Assoc., Inc.
Link Personnel & Assoc.
Luke, Lincoln, & Brugger
mfg/Search, Inc.
MJF Assoc.
MKM Search Consultants, Inc.
Mahony & Assoc., Ltd.
Management Recruiters of Middlesex County NJ.
Management Recruiters of Gramercy, Inc.
Management Recruiters
Management Recruiters
Management Recruiters
Management Recruiters Peninsula
Management Recruiters of Atlanta West, Inc.
Management Recruiters of Stanhope Corp.
Management Recruiters of Charlotte - Southwest
Management Resource Assoc., Inc.
Management Resources
Management Search Int'l.
Marcus & Assoc.
MarketSearch, Inc.
Marketing Resource
Donovan Martin & Assoc.
Martin Personnel Assoc.
Mathey Services
Mary L. Mayer, Ltd.
McCulloch Assoc.
Earl L. McDermid & Assoc.
McDermott & Assoc.
McGuire Executive Search, Inc.
Medical Executive Search Assoc.
Medquest Assoc.
Medtrac & Assoc.
Todd Melon Group
Merrick & Moore
The Montanye Group
Tina Morbitzer & Assoc.
Morency Assoc.
The C. B. Mueller Co., Inc.
Multisearch Recruiters
Murphy, Symonds & Stowell Search, Inc.
NPF Assoc. Ltd. Inc.
Nachman Biomedical
The Naples Group, Inc.
J. Fielding Nelson & Assoc., Inc.
Newcombe & Cyr Assoc., Inc.
Noble & Assoc., Inc.
Norton & Assoc.
OSA Partners, Inc.
Kitty Ossow & Assoc.
The Oxford Group
P R Associates
P R Management Consultants, Inc.
P.R.H. Management, Inc.
R. Parker & Assoc., Inc.

05.0 MARKETING (Cont'd)

Part Time Resources
Partridge Assoc., Inc.
Patrick Assoc.
Joel H. Paul & Assoc., Inc.
Kevin W. Paul
Paul S. Pelland
Personnel Advisors Int'l. Corp.
Personnel Inc.
Petruzzi Assoc.
Philip Daniels Assoc., Inc.
Phillips Resource Group
Plastics Enterprises
Posse, Inc.
Norman Powers Assoc., Inc.
Presley Consultants, Inc.
Prestonwood Assoc.
Princeton Executive Search, Inc.
Professional Medical
Professional Recruiters Inc.
Professional Search Assoc., Inc.
Professional Team Search
Professions Unlimited, Inc.
RAC International
R.G.B. & Assoc., Inc.
RGL Assoc., Inc.
Raymond Thomas & Assoc.
Reinecke & Assoc.
The Remington Group, Ltd.
Resource Perspectives, Inc.
Retail Recruiters/Spectrum Consultants, Inc.
Retail Recruiters of Paramus, Inc.
The Robinson Group, D.A., Ltd.
Rockwood Assoc.
Rogers & Seymour Inc.
Ropella & Assoc.
Sanford Rose Assoc.- Woodbury
Sanford Rose Assoc.
Sanford Rose Assoc. - Santa Barbara
Sanford Rose Assoc. of Beachwood
Sanford Rose Assoc. of Nashville
Sanford Rose Assoc. - Virginia Beach
Roth Young Seattle
Louis Rudzinsky Assoc., Inc.
The Charles Ryan Group, Inc.
Ryerson Tabor Assoc.
Robert Sage Recruiting
Sales Consultants of Austin, Inc.
Sales Consultants of Rhode Island, Inc.
Sales Consultants
Sales Consultants of Morris County, Inc.
Sales Consultants of Northern Jersey, Inc.
Sales Consultants of Nashua - Manchester
Sales Consultants - Bristol County
Sales Consultants Chicago Southeast
Sales Consultants of Ft. Lauderdale
Sales Professionals Personnel Services
Salesworld-Division of Metacor Inc.
George D. Sandel Assoc.
Savalli & Assoc., Inc.
Saxon Morse Assoc.
Schreuder Randall Corp.

Devin Scott Assoc.
Search Group
Search Masters
Search Solutions, Inc.
Selective Management Services, Inc.
Jules Seltzer Assoc.
Scott Sibley Assoc.
RitaSue Siegel Assoc., Inc.
L. A. Silver Assoc., Inc.
SilverCrest Search
Sloan & Assoc., Inc.
J. Harrington Smith Assoc.
Smith, Beaty, Barlow Assoc., Inc.
Snelling Personnel Services
Stephen M. Sonis Assoc.
Spectrum Consultants
Spring Executive Search, Inc.
The Stevens Group, Inc.
Charles Stickler Assoc.
Strategic Search Group
Strategy 2000
Sturm, Burrows & Co.
Tanzi Executive Search
Tech International
Technical Recruiting Services
Tecmark Assoc. Inc.
Telem Adhesive Search Corp.
Triangle Consulting Group
Peter C. Tumminelli & Assoc.
Vezan Assoc.
Vick & Assoc.
Gordon Wahls Co.
Frank X. Walsh & Co., Inc.
Martha Ward Assoc., Inc.
Wayne Assoc., Inc.
Wegner & Assoc.
Weinpel & Co.
White-Ridgely & Assoc., Inc.
Whittaker & Assoc., Inc.
Whittlesey & Assoc., Inc.
N. Willner & Co., Inc.
Winfield Assoc.
Woehr Assoc.
World Search
Nola Worley & Assoc., Inc.
J.D. Wright & Assoc., Inc.

05.1 ADVERTISING, SALES PROMOTION

Carol Ball & Co., Inc.
The Barack Group, Inc.
Bast & Assoc., Inc.
Jim Baum - Executive Search
Brown/Bernardy, Inc.
Career Consulting Group, Inc.
Chaloner Assoc.
Toby Clark Assoc. Inc.
The Crawford Group
Bert Davis Assoc., Inc.
Dunhill Professional Search
Dussick Management Assoc.
Gwen Dycus, Inc.

05.1 ADVERTISING, SALES PROMOTION (Cont'd)

Ells Personnel Systems Inc.
G.A. Field Personnel Consultants
Jerry Fields Assoc.
The Fry Group, Inc.
Greene Personnel Consultants
The Gumbinner Co.
Kay Henry, Inc.
Heritage Search Group, Inc.
Hill & Assoc.
John M. Horton
Howard-Sloan Assoc.
Human Resource Bureau
Julian Assoc., Inc.
Kane Ford Karrel & Assoc.
Kelley & Keller, Inc.
Jack Kennedy Assoc., Inc.
Kordus Consulting Group
Kresin Wingard
The Lawson Group
M/ARS
Management Recruiters of Middlesex County NJ.
Management Recruiters of Gramercy, Inc.
Management Recruiters of Poughkeepsie, Inc.
MarketSearch, Inc.
Meads & Assoc.
Mengel & McDonald Ltd.
Tina Morbitzer & Assoc.
Jerome H. Nagel Assoc.
Orr Executive Search
Kitty Ossow & Assoc.
R. Parker & Assoc., Inc.
Phillips Assoc.
Posse, Inc.
Retail Placement Assoc.
Rex Assoc., Inc.
Ross Personnel Consultants, Inc.
Ryerson Tabor Assoc.
Sales Consultants of Rraleigh - Durham - RTP
Sales Consultants of Northern Jersey, Inc.
Sales Consultants of Nashua - Manchester
Sales Consultants of Wellesley, Inc.
Sales Consultants Chicago Southeast
Sales Consultants of Ft. Myers, Inc.
Sales Professionals Personnel Services
Salesworld-Division of Metacor Inc.
Simpson Assoc.
Sloan & Assoc., Inc.
Phyllis Solomon Executive Search, Inc.
Peter C. Tumminelli & Assoc.
Vick & Assoc.
Darryl Vincent & Assoc.
Martha Ward Assoc., Inc.
Bob Westerfield & Assoc., Inc.
Wheelless Group
N. Willner & Co., Inc.

05.2 MARKETING STRATEGY & ORGANIZATION

Advanced Corporate Search
David Allen Assoc.

Amato & Assoc., Inc.
Arancio Assoc.
The Barack Group, Inc.
Bartlett, Bunn & Travis, Inc.
Bast & Assoc., Inc.
L. Battalin & Co.
The Howard C. Bloom Co.
Bowling Executive Registry, Inc.
Charles Bradley Professionals
M.F. Branch Assoc., Inc.
David F. Brooks & Co., Inc.
Broward-Dobbs, Inc.
Brown/Bernardy, Inc.
Career Consulting Group, Inc.
H.O. Catherman Inc.
The Chapman Group, Inc.
David P. Cordell Assoc.
The Crawford Group
Development Resource Group
Dunhill Professional Search
Dunhill of Greater Akron, Inc.
Evans & James Assoc., Inc.
eXsource
N. Steven Fells & Co., Inc.
Ferrari Consulting Group
G.A. Field Personnel Consultants
Jack Stuart Fisher Assoc.
Franchise Recruiters Ltd.
Gardner, Savage Assoc.
Gold Coast Partners
Gray-Kimball Assoc., Inc.
Guidarelli Assoc., Inc.
The Gumbinner Co.
The Hart Group
Hawkes-Randolph & Assoc., Inc.
Kay Henry, Inc.
Higbee Assoc., Inc.
Hill & Assoc.
John M. Horton
Intertech Search Group
JM Assoc.
Kane Ford Karrel & Assoc.
Kelley & Keller, Inc.
Jack Kennedy Assoc., Inc.
Kimmel & Fredericks, Inc.
Kordus Consulting Group
E.J. Lance Management Assoc., Inc.
Langlois & Assoc.
Latham Int'l., Ltd.
The Lighthouse Group
Management Assoc.
Management Recruiters of Middlesex County NJ.
Management Search, Inc.
MarketSearch, Inc.
Marketing Recruiters, Inc.
Marketing Resource
Merlin Int'l. Inc.
Mogul Consultants, Inc.
Multi Processing, Inc.
Jerome H. Nagel Assoc.
National Logistics Recruiters, Inc.
William H. Nenstiel & Assoc.

05.2 MARKETING STRATEGY & ORGANIZATION (Cont'd)

Normyle/Erstling Health Search
Kitty Ossow & Assoc.
Janou Pakter, Inc.
Prestonwood Assoc.
The Resource Group
Ritta Professional Search Inc.
Ross Personnel Consultants, Inc.
Rushlow & Co.
Sales Consultants of Madison
Sales Consultants of Rhode Island, Inc.
Sales Consultants of Newtown
Sales Consultants of Akron, Inc.
Sales Consultants of Andover
Sales Consultants of Morris County, Inc.
Sales Consultants of Northern Jersey, Inc.
Sales Consultants of Nashua - Manchester
Sales Consultants - Bristol County
Sales Consultants Chicago Southeast
Sales Consultants of Fayetteville, AR.
Sales Professionals Personnel Services
Santangelo Consultants Inc.
Savalli & Assoc., Inc.
RitaSue Siegel Assoc., Inc.
Smith, Beaty, Barlow Assoc., Inc.
Specialized Search Assoc.
Storfer & Assoc.
Tech Consulting
Technical Staffing Assoc.
Peter C. Tumminelli & Assoc.
Vick & Assoc.
C. J. Vincent Assoc., Inc.
Martha Ward Assoc., Inc.
Werbin Assoc. Executive Search, Inc.
Wheelless Group
N. Willner & Co., Inc.
The Wright Group

05.3 MARKETING & PRODUCT RESEARCH, CONSUMER MARKETING

Analytic Recruiting, Inc.
Arancio Assoc.
The Barack Group, Inc.
Bast & Assoc., Inc.
L. Battalin & Co.
David F. Brooks & Co., Inc.
Brown/Bernardy, Inc.
Career Consulting Group, Inc.
Clark-Winans, Inc.
Cochran, Cochran, & Yale, Inc.
Dunhill Professional Search
Dunhill of Greater Akron, Inc.
Dunhill Professional Search of Ramsey
Engineering & Scientific Search Assoc.
Ferrari Consulting Group
Jack Stuart Fisher Assoc.
David Fockler & Assoc., Inc.
Franklin Int'l. Search, Inc.
Gardner, Savage Assoc.
Gaudette & Co.

Gold Coast Partners
Graham Assoc. Inc.
Greene Personnel Consultants
The Hart Group
Hawkes-Randolph & Assoc., Inc.
Kay Henry, Inc.
Heritage Search Group, Inc.
John M. Horton
Hospitality Int'l.
Intertech Search Group
Kane Ford Karrel & Assoc.
Kelley & Keller, Inc.
Jack Kennedy Assoc., Inc.
Kresin Wingard
Reynolds Lebus Assoc.
M-A Management Assoc., Inc.
M/ARS
Management Recruiters of Frederick, Inc.
Management Recruiters of Middlesex County NJ.
Management Recruiters of Middlesex
Management Recruiters of Stanhope Corp.
Management Recruiters of Westchester, Inc.
Management Recruiters of Nassau, Inc.
MarketSearch, Inc.
Marketing Recruiters, Inc.
Marketing Resource
Orr Executive Search
Kitty Ossow & Assoc.
Janou Pakter, Inc.
Paules Associates
Preston Robert & Assoc.-Health Care Div.
Prestonwood Assoc.
Rex Assoc., Inc.
The Reynolds Group, Inc.
Sanford Rose Assoc. of Hartford
Sanford Rose Assoc. of Quakertown
Ross Personnel Consultants, Inc.
Ryerson Tabor Assoc.
Sales Consultants of Rhode Island, Inc.
Sales Consultants of Newtown
Sales Consultants of Westchester-South, Inc.
Sales Consultants of Morris County, Inc.
Sales Consultants of Northern Jersey, Inc.
Sales Consultants of Nashua - Manchester
Sales Consultants - Bristol County
Sales Consultants Chicago Southeast
Sales Consultants of Ft. Myers, Inc.
Sales Consultants
Sales Consultants of Fayetteville, AR.
Sales Professionals Personnel Services
Salesworld-Division of Metacor Inc.
Savalli & Assoc., Inc.
RitaSue Siegel Assoc., Inc.
Smith Hanley Assoc., Inc.
Technitrac, Inc.
Peter C. Tumminelli & Assoc.
Vick & Assoc.
Darryl Vincent & Assoc.
C. J. Vincent Assoc., Inc.
Martha Ward Assoc., Inc.
Werbin Assoc. Executive Search, Inc.
Wheelless Group

05.3 MARKETING & PRODUCT RESEARCH, CONSUMER MARKETING (Cont'd)

N. Willner & Co., Inc.
The Wright Group

05.4 SALES, SALES MANAGEMENT, SALES TRAINING

A. D. & Assoc.
Aberdeen Assoc.
Accounting & Computer Personnel
Arthur Adams & Assoc.
The Adler Group
Amato & Assoc., Inc.
Anderson, Graham & Stewart, Inc.
Charles P. Aquavella & Assoc.
Arancio Assoc.
E. J. Ashton & Assoc., Ltd.
Auden Assoc., Inc.
Barclay Consultants, Inc.
L. Battalin & Co.
M.F. Branch Assoc., Inc.
C.W. Brandon & Assoc., Inc.
Brennan Assoc.
David F. Brooks & Co., Inc.
CES
CN Associates
Career Profiles
Carlden Personnel Services Inc.
H.O. Catherman Inc.
The Chapman Group, Inc.
William J. Christopher Assoc., Inc.
Clanton & Co.
Clark-Winans, Inc.
John M. Clarke & Assoc.
CoEnergy Inc.
Cona Personnel Search
The Consortium
Corporate Recruiters, Inc.
Cross Country Consultants, Inc.
Frank Cuomo & Assoc., Inc.
Damon & Assoc., Inc.
The DataFinders Group, Inc.
David - Kris Assoc., Inc.
Dean-Wharton Assoc.
Dunhill Professional Search
Dunhill of Huntsville, Inc.
Dunhill Personnel Search
Dunhill Professional Search of Ramsey
Dunhill Professional Search Irvine/Newport
Dussick Management Assoc.
W. Robert Eissler & Assoc., Inc.
Mark Elzweig Co. Ltd.
Emerson & Co.
Engineering & Scientific Search Assoc.
Evans & James Assoc., Inc.
Exec 2000
Executive Exchange Corp.
N. Steven Fells & Co., Inc.
G.A. Field Personnel Consultants
David Fockler & Assoc., Inc.
Gardner, Savage Assoc.

The Garrison Organization
Gold Coast Partners
The Goodman Group
Graham Assoc. Inc.
HLR Consulting
The Hart Group
Healthcare Resources Group
Hornberger Management Co., Inc.
Hospitality Int'l.
Hospitality Resources Int'l., Ltd.
Howard-Sloan Assoc.
Howie & Assoc., Inc.
Hudson Assoc. Inc.
Human Resource Bureau
I.S. Consultants, Inc.
Impact Executive Search, Inc.
Industrial Recruiters Assoc., Inc.
Kacevich, Lewis & Brown, Inc.
Richard Kader & Assoc.
Jack Kennedy Assoc., Inc.
Kepler & Assoc.
Key Employment Services
Key Talent, Inc.
Kirkbride Assoc., Inc.
Kreofsky & Assoc.
Kurtz Pro-Search, Inc.
Lanzi & Assoc.
Lawrence-Balakonis & Assoc., Inc.
The Lighthouse Group
Lineal Recruiting Services
Loewenstein & Assoc.
M H Executive Search Group
MJF Assoc.
Management Recruiters of Frederick, Inc.
Management Recruiters
Management Recruiters
Management Recruiters
Management Recruiters
Management Recruiters
Management Recruiters of Oakland
Management Recruiters
Management Recruiters
Management Recruiters of Middlesex
Management Recruiters of Nassau, Inc.
Management Search, Inc.
Marketing Recruiters, Inc.
Marketing Resource
Martin Personnel Assoc.
Mathey Services
Mary L. Mayer, Ltd.
R. H. McIlwaine & Assoc.
The McKee Co.
Medical Sales & Management Specialists
Milgram & Assoc.
Jerome H. Nagel Assoc.
The Naples Group, Inc.
National Logistics Recruiters, Inc.
National Recruiting Service
William H. Nenstiel & Assoc.
Normyle/Erstling Health Search
Ronald Norris & Assoc.
Northeastern Search, Inc.
Oldwick Enterprises, Inc.

05.4 SALES, SALES MANAGEMENT, SALES TRAINING (Cont'd)

The Oxford Group
Pacific Advisory Service
Paules Associates
Personnel Assoc.
Personnel Unlimited/Executive Search
Philip Daniels Assoc., Inc.
Phillips Personnel/Search
Prestonwood Assoc.
The Primary Group, Inc.
Professional Medical
Professional Recruiters Inc.
RAC International
RALCO/Richard A. Lucia & Assoc.
RBR Assoc., Inc.
Remark Assoc. Inc.
Retail Pacesetters, Inc.
The Reynolds Group, Inc.
Riotto - Jones Assoc., Inc.
Riverside Consultants, Inc.
Sanford Rose Assoc. of Hartford
Ross Personnel Consultants, Inc.
Ryerson Tabor Assoc.
S-H-S of Allentown
Sales & Management Search, Inc.
Sales Consultants of Madison
Sales Consultants of Fairfax, Inc.
Sales Consultants of Rhode Island, Inc.
Sales Consultants of Newtown
Sales Consultants
Sales Consultants of Akron, Inc.
Sales Consultants of Rraleigh - Durham - RTP
Sales Consultants of Westchester-South, Inc.
Sales Consultants of Andover
Sales Consultants of Morris County, Inc.
Sales Consultants of Northern Jersey, Inc.
Sales Consultants of Nashua - Manchester
Sales Consultants of Wellesley, Inc.
Sales Consultants - Bristol County
Sales Consultants Bowling Green
Sales Consultants Chicago Southeast
Sales Consultants of Fox Valley
Sales Consultants of Savannah, GA.
Sales Consultants of Ft. Myers, Inc.
Sales Consultants
Sales Consultants of Fayetteville, AR.
Sales Professionals Personnel Services
Salesworld-Division of Metacor Inc.
Schenck & Assoc. SC
Shannahan & Co., Inc.
Sloan & Assoc., Inc.
Smith, Anderson & Co.
Smith, Beaty, Barlow Assoc., Inc.
Specialized Search Assoc.
Spectra West
Ron Stevens & Assoc., Inc.
Storfer & Assoc.
Strategic Search Group
Techcon Co.
Technical Recruiting Services
TeleSearch, Inc.

Tell/Com Recruiters
Jay Tracey Assoc.
Peter C. Tumminelli & Assoc.
Key Employment
The Urban Placement Service
Vento Assoc.
Vick & Assoc.
Darryl Vincent & Assoc.
C. J. Vincent Assoc., Inc.
Wayne Assoc., Inc.
R.A. Wells Co.
Wheelless Group
N. Willner & Co., Inc.
Windward Executive Search, Inc.
Worlco Computer Resources, Inc.

05.5 DIRECT MAIL, MARKETING, TELEMARKETING

Analytic Recruiting, Inc.
Bast & Assoc., Inc.
Brown/Bernardy, Inc.
C & H Personnel
Career Consulting Group, Inc.
Chaloner Assoc.
Clark-Winans, Inc.
The Crawford Group
Bert Davis Assoc., Inc.
G.A. Field Personnel Consultants
Jerry Fields Assoc.
Jack Stuart Fisher Assoc.
The Fry Group, Inc.
The Hart Group
Kay Henry, Inc.
Howard-Sloan Assoc.
Kane Ford Karrel & Assoc.
Koren, Rogers Assoc.
MarketSearch, Inc.
Masserman & Assoc.
Orr Executive Search
Carolyn Smith Paschal Int'l.
Phillips Assoc.
Prestonwood Assoc.
Rex Assoc., Inc.
Sales Consultants of Morris County, Inc.
Sales Consultants Bowling Green
Salesworld-Division of Metacor Inc.
Search Assoc., Inc.
Simpson Assoc.
Telemarketing Search, Inc.
Martha Ward Assoc., Inc.
Wheelless Group

05.6 CUSTOMER SERVICE

Brennan Assoc.
Emerson & Co.
Impact Executive Search, Inc.
Lineal Recruiting Services
Lunney, Hadden & Assoc.
Marketing Resource
Robert E. Mills, FLMI
Paules Associates
Sales Consultants of Ft. Myers, Inc.

05.6 CUSTOMER SERVICE (Cont'd)

Systems Careers
Telemarketing Search, Inc.

05.7 PUBLIC RELATIONS

Carol Ball & Co., Inc.
CRS Assoc., Inc.
The Cantor Concern, Inc.
Chaloner Assoc.
Toby Clark Assoc. Inc.
The Crawford Group
Bert Davis Assoc., Inc.
Jerry Fields Assoc.
The Fry Group, Inc.
The Goldman Group Inc.
Kay Henry, Inc.
Howard-Sloan Assoc.
Julian Assoc., Inc.
M/ARS
Carolyn Smith Paschal Int'l.
Spring Executive Search, Inc.

06.0 HUMAN RESOURCE MANAGEMENT

AGRI-associates
A.M.C.R., Inc.
Accounting Personnel Assoc.
The Adler Group
Alexander Enterprises, Inc.
Frank E. Allen & Assoc.
David Allen Assoc.
Ethan Allen Personnel, Inc.
Alterna-track
American Resources Corp.
Ames-O'Neill Assoc., Inc.
Charles P. Aquavella & Assoc.
Austin - Allen Co.
BGB Assoc., Inc.
Peter Barrett Assoc., Inc.
Besen Assoc. Inc.
C.W. Brandon & Assoc., Inc.
Jerold Braun & Assoc.
J.R. Brody & Assoc., Inc.
The Butlers Co. Insurance Recruiters
CRS Assoc., Inc.
Career Search Assoc.
The Carlyle Group, Ltd.
Cemco, Ltd.
Chase Waterford Ltd.
Computer Network Resources
The Comwell Co. Inc.
Corporate Advisors Inc.
Corporate Careers Inc.
The Corporate Connection, Ltd.
Corporate Personnel, Inc.
The DLR Group, Inc.
Dalton Management Consultants, Ltd.
Dankowski & Assoc., Inc.
N. Dean Davic Assoc., Inc.
Davis & James, Inc.
DeCorrevont & Assoc.
Dean-Wharton Assoc.

Deery Geddis & Assoc.
Dillard Executive Search
Domenico/Brown Group
J P Donnelly Assoc., Inc.
Dumont Moriarty & Assoc.
Dunhill of Denton, Inc.
Dunhill Personnel of Northeast Tulsa, Inc.
Dunhill Professional Search of Ramsey
Dunhill Search of West Atlanta
Dunhill International Search
The E & K Group
E O Technical
Ecco Personnel Svs.
Ells Personnel Systems Inc.
ExecuSource Int'l.
Executive Careers
Executive Referral Services, Inc.
Executive Resource Inc.
eXsource
Paul Falcone Assoc., Inc.
David Farmer & Assoc.
Fernow Assoc.
Ferrari Consulting Group
Fisher-Todd Assoc.
Flynn, Hannock, Inc.
Ford & Assoc., Inc.
Ford & Ford
Mel Frazer & Assoc.
Garrett Assoc. Inc.
Gatti & Assoc.
Hahn & Assoc., Inc.
W. Hanley & Assoc.
Hedlund Corp.
The Human Resource Group
Human Resource Network
Human Resource Recruiters
Information Systems Professionals
Intech Summit Group, Inc.
International Staffing Consultants, Inc.
IprGroup, Inc.
JNB Assoc., Inc.
JT Assoc.
John-David Assoc., Inc.
The Johnson Group, Inc.
J.M. Joseph Assoc.
Jubilee, Inc.
Karras Personnel, Inc.
Joseph Keyes Assoc.
Sanford Kleiner Assoc., Inc.
Kling Personnel Assoc., Inc.
The Koehler Group
Kozlin Assoc., Inc.
Lambert & Sullivan Assoc.
Lange & Assoc., Inc.
Langlois & Assoc.
Jack B. Larsen & Assoc.
Vincent Lee Assoc.
Paul Ligon Co.
Link Personnel & Assoc.
Logue & Rice Inc.
Lord & Albus Co.
Lowery, Cotter, & Assoc.
Ludot Personnel Services, Inc.

06.1 BENEFITS, COMPENSATION PLANNING (Cont'd)

Tower Consultants, Ltd.
Vogel Assoc.
Willmott & Assoc.
The Windham Group
Windward Executive Search, Inc.

06.2 PERSONNEL SELECTION, PLACEMENT & RECORDS

The Adler Group
Frank E. Allen & Assoc.
Gary S. Bell Assoc., Inc.
Brandjes Assoc.
J.R. Brody & Assoc., Inc.
Career Resource Assoc., Inc.
Conaway Legal Search
Dankowski & Assoc., Inc.
Ells Personnel Systems Inc.
IprGroup, Inc.
Lambert & Sullivan Assoc.
Fran Luisi Assoc.
Maximum Management Corp.
Midwest Medical Recruiters
Largent Parks & Partners, Inc.
Penn Associates
Phillips Personnel/Search
S. Reyman & Assoc., Ltd.
Saxon Morse Assoc.
Tower Consultants, Ltd.
Vogel Assoc.
M.K. Wasse & Assoc., Inc.
Willmott & Assoc.
The Windham Group

07.0 ADMINISTRATIVE SERVICES

AGRI-associates
Allen Barry Assoc.
Keith Bagg Personnel Ltd.
Bonifield Assoc.
Career Search Assoc.
Cibotti Assoc., Inc.
The Comwell Co. Inc.
The Corporate Connection, Ltd.
Ecco Personnel Svs.
Franchise Recruiters Ltd.
Garrett Assoc. Inc.
Delores F. George
Hedlund Corp.
Hintz Associates
Integrated Management Solutions
J.P.D. Group
Kling Personnel Assoc., Inc.
Lindsey & Assoc., Inc.
Lowery, Cotter, & Assoc.
Management Recruiters of Dearborn, Inc.
Management Recruiters
Midwest Medical Consultants
Moore Employment Svs., Inc.
The NRI Group
Part Time Resources
Joel H. Paul & Assoc., Inc.

The Placers, Inc.
Protocol Inc.
Reinecke & Assoc.
Rogers & Seymour Inc.
Romac & Assoc.
USA Medical Placement Inc.
Vezan Assoc.
D.L. Weaver & Assoc.

07.1 CLERICAL WORK MEASUREMENT, RECORDS RETENTION & MANAGEMENT

Accountants On Call
CES

07.3 OFFICE LAYOUT, SPACE PLANNING

Damon & Assoc., Inc.

07.4 OFFICE MANAGEMENT

Accountants On Call
Accounting & Computer Personnel
Accounting Personnel Assoc.
The Howard C. Bloom Co.
Charles Bradley Professionals
Brooks Executive Personnel
Carlden Personnel Services Inc.
Dunhill of Manchester Inc.
Healthcare Resources Group
Moore Employment Svs., Inc.
Scan Management Inc.
Weinman & Assoc.

08.0 FINANCE & ACCOUNTING

A. D. & Assoc.
Accountants
Accountants On Call
Accountants On Call
Accounting & Computer Personnel
Accounting Personnel Assoc.
Accounting Resources Int'l., Inc.
David Allen Assoc.
Allied Financial Management Co.
Allied Search, Inc.
Alterna-track
American Resources Corp.
Ames Assoc. Inc.
Analysts Resources Inc.
Analytic Recruiting, Inc.
John Anthony & Assoc.
Aronow Assoc., Inc.
E. J. Ashton & Assoc., Ltd.
Atlantic Search Group, Inc.
Availability Personnel Consultants
BGB Assoc., Inc.
B.P.A. Enterprises, Inc.
Keith Bagg Personnel Ltd.
The Bankers Group
B.K. Barnes & Associates
Peter Barrett Assoc., Inc.
Barrett Partners
Bartl & Evins

08.0 FINANCE & ACCOUNTING (Cont'd)

Ted Bavly Assoc., Inc.
Berger & Assoc.
Bodner Inc.
Bonifield Assoc.
Bornholdt Shivas & Friends
Bowman & Marshall
Charles Bradley Professionals
C.W. Brandon & Assoc., Inc.
Jerold Braun & Assoc.
Brooks Executive Personnel
The Butlers Co. Insurance Recruiters
The Byrnes Group
C & H Personnel
CCI - Career Consultants Int'l.
C.G. & Assoc.
CRS Assoc., Inc.
The Cambridge Group Ltd.
Career Logic, Inc.
Career Marketing Assoc.
Carlden Personnel Services Inc.
Carver Search Consultants
Allen Case & Assoc., Inc.
Cemco, Ltd.
The Century Group
Competitive Resources, Inc.
Computer Network Resources
Corporate Careers Inc.
The Corporate Connection, Ltd.
Corporate Suite, Ltd.
Cosco Resources Inc.
Criterion Executive Search, Inc.
Timothy D. Crowe, Jr.
Crown, Michels & Assoc., Inc.
Curts/Jackson, Inc.
The DLR Group, Inc.
Dankowski & Assoc., Inc.
Dapexs Consultants, Inc.
Davis & James, Inc.
Deery Geddis & Assoc.
Delta Resource Group, Ltd.
Diversified Placement Int'l., Inc.
Domenico/Brown Group
Drake & Assoc.
Dunhill Personnel System, Inc.
Dunhill of Freehold, Inc.
Dunhill Personnel of Northeast Tulsa, Inc.
Dunhill Search of Omaha, Inc.
Dunhill Professional Search of Hawaii
Dunhill International Search
E T Search Inc.
Ecco Personnel Svs.
Eden & Assoc., Inc.
Eggers Consulting Co., Inc.
Ells Personnel Systems Inc.
Execu-Search, Inc.
ExecuSource Int'l.
Executive Register, Inc.
Executive Resource Inc.
eXsource
David Farmer & Assoc.

Fergason Assoc., Inc.
Finance & Accounting Search Firm
Financial Search Group, Inc.
Financial Search Corp.
Fisher-Todd Assoc.
Flores & Assoc.
Flynn, Hannock, Inc.
David Fockler & Assoc., Inc.
Foster Assoc.
The Foster McKay Group
Franchise Search, Inc.
Mel Frazer & Assoc.
Garrett Assoc. Inc.
The Garrison Group
Genesis Personnel Service, Inc.
Delores F. George
W.T. Glover & Assoc., Inc.
Greene & Co.
Louis Gregory Assoc., Inc.
Hahn & Assoc., Inc.
Robert Half Int'l.
W. Hanley & Assoc.
Hartman Personnel Services
Health Industry Resources, Inc.
Hemingway Personnel, Inc.
Hessel Assoc., Inc.
Higbee Assoc., Inc.
High-Tech Recruiters
Hill Allyn Assoc.
Hipp Waters, Inc.
Human Resource Recruiters
Hunter Assoc.
Intech Summit Group, Inc.
Integrated Management Solutions
JNB Assoc., Inc.
J.P.D. Group
JT Assoc.
The James Group
John-David Assoc., Inc.
The Johnson Group, Inc.
K & C Assoc.
Richard Kader & Assoc.
Kensington Int'l.
Kershner & Co.
Key Employment Services
Key Talent, Inc.
Joseph Keyes Assoc.
Millie Kipp Assoc., Inc.
Kiradjieff & Co.
Sanford Kleiner Assoc., Inc.
Kling Personnel Assoc., Inc.
The Koehler Group
Koren, Rogers Assoc.
Kramer Executive Resources, Inc.
Kravitz * Larkin * Silver Assoc.
Kreuzberger, Fehr & Assoc.
Lam Assoc.
E.J. Lance Management Assoc., Inc.
Lange & Assoc., Inc.
Langlois & Assoc.
Jack B. Larsen & Assoc.
Vincent Lee Assoc.
Lee Associates

08.0 FINANCE & ACCOUNTING (Cont'd)

Paul Ligon Co.
Lindsey & Assoc., Inc.
Logue & Rice Inc.
Lowery, Cotter, & Assoc.
Ludot Personnel Services, Inc.
Luke, Lincoln, & Brugger
Arthur Lyle Assoc., Inc.
MKM Search Consultants, Inc.
Alan MacDonald & Assoc.
Management Recruiters of Savannah
Management Recruiters of Dearborn, Inc.
Management Recruiters of Gramercy, Inc.
Management Recruiters
Management Recruiters of Cincinnati/ Sharonville, Inc.
Management Recruiters
Management Recruiters
Management Recruiters
Management Recruiters of Berkeley
Management Recruiters of Ft. Myers, FL.
Management Recruiters of Laguna Hills
Management Recruiters of Monterey
Management Recruiters of North Brunswick, Inc.
Management Resource Assoc., Inc.
Management Search, Inc.
Management Search Int'l.
Management Search, Inc.
McCracken, Wilcox, Bertoux & Miller
Earl L. McDermid & Assoc.
McGuire Executive Search, Inc.
Todd Melon Group
Midgette Consultants, Inc.
George J. Mollo Assoc.
Montgomery Resources, Inc.
Moore Employment Svs., Inc.
Morency Assoc.
Murphy, Symonds & Stowell Search, Inc.
NPF Assoc. Ltd. Inc.
The NRI Group
The Naples Group, Inc.
National Corporate Consultants, Inc.
J. Fielding Nelson & Assoc., Inc.
Nelson Associates
The Network Companies
Newton Assoc.
Oldwick Enterprises, Inc.
Jim Oravetz & Assoc., Inc.
P R Associates
PLRS/Career Connections
Pacific Advisory Service
Parker Page Group
Partridge Assoc., Inc.
Patrick Assoc.
Kevin W. Paul
Performance Professionals
Personnel Inc.
Placement Solutions
The Placers, Inc.
Princeton Executive Search, Inc.

Princeton Executive Search
Probus Executive Search
Professional Personnel Services
Professional Placement Assoc., Inc.
Professional Recruiters
Professional Resources
Professional Team Search
Professions Unlimited, Inc.
Protocol Inc.
Quickstaff
RAI Consulting
R.G.B. & Assoc., Inc.
RGL Assoc., Inc.
RHS Assoc., Inc.
RPA Management Consultants, Inc.
Edward Rast & Co.
Retail Recruiters/Spectrum Consultants, Inc.
Jeff Rich Assoc.
Roberson & Co.
The Robinson Group, D.A., Ltd.
Rocky Mountain Recruiters, Inc.
Rogers & Seymour Inc.
Romac & Assoc.
Romac & Assoc.
Romac & Assoc. - San Francisco
Romac & Assoc., Inc.
Sanford Rose Assoc. - Virginia Beach
Roth Young Seattle
John P. Runden & Co., Inc.
Ryan & Assoc.
Robert Sage Recruiting
The Salem Group, Executive Recruiters
Santangelo Consultants Inc.
David Saxner & Assoc., Inc.
Scan Management Inc.
Schattle Personnel Consultants, Inc.
Scott Kappele & Gnodde
Scott-Wayne Assoc., Inc.
Search Assoc., Inc.
Search Bureau Int'l.
Scott Sibley Assoc.
L. A. Silver Assoc., Inc.
SilverCrest Search
Simpson Assoc.
Stephen M. Sonis Assoc.
Source Finance
Steeple Associates, Inc.
The Stevens Group, Inc.
Stewart Assoc.
Straight & Co.
Strategic Executives, Inc.
Sturm, Burrows & Co.
Sumrall Personnel Consultants, Inc.
Donna Svei Assoc.
The Talley Group
Tech Vision Co.
Thomas, Whelan Assoc., Inc.
Judy Thompson & Assoc., Inc.
Traynor Confidential, Ltd.
Trilogy Enterprises, Inc.
The Urban Placement Service
Vezan Assoc.
Frank X. Walsh & Co., Inc.

08.3 CREDIT & COLLECTION (Cont'd)

Diversified Placement Int'l., Inc.
Dunhill of Freehold, Inc.
Financial Search Corp.
Goldstein & Assoc.
Greene & Co.
HLR Consulting
Robert Half Int'l.
Hemingway Personnel, Inc.
Arthur Lyle Assoc., Inc.
George J. Mollo Assoc.
Mortgage & Financial Personnel Services
Newton Assoc.
Ronald Norris & Assoc.
Phillips Assoc.
Placement Solutions
RPA Management Consultants, Inc.
Resource Services, Inc.
Sanford Rose Assoc. of Quakertown
Scott Kappele & Gnodde
Search Leader, Inc.
Steeple Associates, Inc.
Donna Svei Assoc.
Judy Thompson & Assoc., Inc.

08.4 TAXES

Accountants
Barrett Partners
Beckwith, Thomas & Fanning
Berger & Assoc.
CCI - Career Consultants Int'l.
The Century Group
The Christopher Group
Cochran, Cochran, & Yale, Inc.
The Consortium
Crown, Michels & Assoc., Inc.
Dunhill of Freehold, Inc.
Dunhill Professional Search of Hawaii
E T Search Inc.
Execu-Search, Inc.
The Executive Consulting Group -N.Y.
Financial Search Corp.
Foster Assoc.
The Garrison Group
Hemingway Personnel, Inc.
Hill Allyn Assoc.
John-David Assoc., Inc.
Koren, Rogers Assoc.
Kramer Executive Resources, Inc.
Management Recruiters
George J. Mollo Assoc.
Mortgage & Financial Personnel Services
Newton Assoc.
Pacific Advisory Service
Placement Solutions
RPA Management Consultants, Inc.
Resource Services, Inc.
Rocky Mountain Recruiters, Inc.
Ryan & Assoc.
A. Ryan Assoc.
Search Assoc., Inc.

Steeple Associates, Inc.
Donna Svei Assoc.
Thomas, Whelan Assoc., Inc.
Judy Thompson & Assoc., Inc.
Weiss & Assoc., Inc.
Wheeler Assoc.

09.0 INFORMATION TECHNOLOGY

A. D. & Assoc.
AJS Assoc.
Accounting & Computer Personnel
Accounting Resources Int'l., Inc.
Adept Tech Recruiting, Inc.
Advancement Recruiting Services
Aerospace Technologies, Inc.
Alexander Edward Assoc., Inc.
Alterna-track
American Resources Corp.
Analytic Recruiting, Inc.
Aronow Assoc., Inc.
Ashton Computer Professionals, Inc.
Automation Technology Search
The Ayers Group, Inc.
B.P.A. Enterprises, Inc.
BR & Assoc.
B.K. Barnes & Associates
Battista Assoc., Inc.
R. Gaines Baty Assoc., Inc.
Ted Bavly Assoc., Inc.
Berger & Assoc.
Binary Search
Charles A. Binswanger Assoc., Inc.
Blanton & Co.
Bornholdt Shivas & Friends
Bradford & Galt, Inc.
Ira Broadman Assoc.
David F. Brooks & Co., Inc.
The Byrnes Group
CN Associates
The Cambridge Group Ltd.
Career Management, Inc.
Career Marketing Assoc.
K. Carroll & Assoc.
Carter McKenzie, Inc.
Allen Case & Assoc., Inc.
Casey & Gerrish Assoc., Inc.
J.F. Church Assoc., Inc.
Cibotti Assoc., Inc.
CompuPro
Computer Network Resources
Computer Recruiters, Inc.
Consult One, Inc.
Corporate Resources Professional Placement
Criterion Executive Search, Inc.
Curts/Jackson, Inc.
Dalton Management Consultants, Ltd.
Damon & Assoc., Inc.
Dapexs Consultants, Inc.
DeLalla - Fried Assoc.
Deeco Int'l.
Deery Geddis & Assoc.
Delta Resource Group, Ltd.

09.0 INFORMATION TECHNOLOGY (Cont'd)

The Salem Group, Executive Recruiters
George D. Sandel Assoc.
Santangelo Consultants Inc.
Scott Kappele & Gnodde
Scott-Wayne Assoc., Inc.
Search & Recruit Int'l.
Search Bureau Int'l.
The Search Firm Inc.
Search Group
Setford-Shaw-Najarian Assoc., Ltd.
Shannahan & Co., Inc.
Snelling Personnel Services
Source EDP
Source Engineering
Southwest Search Inc.
Spectrum Consultants
Phyllis Stovall Assoc., Inc.
Strategic Executives, Inc.
Strategic Search Group
Summerfield Assoc., Inc.
Sumrall Personnel Consultants, Inc.
Systems Careers
Systems One Ltd.
Tech Vision Co.
Technical Engineering Consultants
Techno-Trac Systems, Inc.
TransAmerica Network
Traynor Confidential, Ltd.
Trilogy Enterprises, Inc.
J.Q. Turner & Assoc., Inc.
Gordon Wahls Co.
Wallace Assoc.
Frank X. Walsh & Co., Inc.
D.L. Weaver & Assoc.
Wegner & Assoc.
Werbin Assoc. Executive Search, Inc.
S.J. Wexler Assoc., Inc.
Joel H. Wilensky Assoc., Inc.
Wing Tips & Pumps, Inc.
Winter, Wyman & Co.
Worlco Computer Resources, Inc.
J.D. Wright & Assoc., Inc.
Dennis Wynn Assoc., Inc.
P.D. Zier Assoc.

09.1 COMPUTER SECURITY, DISASTER RECOVERY, EDP AUDIT

Abacus Consultants
Alexander Edward Assoc., Inc.
Allied Search, Inc.
The Ayers Group, Inc.
Battista Assoc., Inc.
David F. Brooks & Co., Inc.
Carter McKenzie, Inc.
The Century Group
CompuPro
Computer Recruiters, Inc.
Computer Security Placement Service, Inc.
Criterion Executive Search, Inc.
Dunhill Professional Search Inc.

Dunhill Personnel of Tampa
Dynamic Search Systems, Inc.
EXETER 2100
Eggers Consulting Co., Inc.
Foster Assoc.
Gregory Michaels & Assoc., Inc.
W. Hanley & Assoc.
Hill Allyn Assoc.
Jacobson Assoc.
Kennison & Assoc.
LAS Management Consulting Group, Inc.
Jonathan Lawrence Assoc.
Management Recruiters of Berkeley
Management Recruiters of Oakland
Management Recruiters of Stanhope Corp.
Northeastern Search, Inc.
Romac & Assoc.
Romac & Assoc., Inc.
Search Leader, Inc.
Stone Enterprises Ltd.
Yake & Assoc.
P.D. Zier Assoc.

09.2 SPECIFIC TECHNOLOGIES, E.G. AI, IMAGE, FIBER-OPTICS

Abbott, James & Oliver
Abraham & London Ltd.
Anderson, Graham & Stewart, Inc.
Binary Search
Bradford & Galt, Inc.
M.F. Branch Assoc., Inc.
CPI Technical Services
Carter McKenzie, Inc.
CompuPro
Dunhill Personnel Search
EXETER 2100
Forum Assoc.
Kiley-Owen Assoc., Inc.
Kreofsky & Assoc.
Lancaster Assoc., Inc.
Lappe & Assoc.
The James Lloyd Group
Management Recruiters of Poughkeepsie, Inc.
Management Search, Inc.
Mogul Consultants, Inc.
New Dimensions in Technology, Inc.
P R Management Consultants, Inc.
Pacific Search Consultants
Pencom Systems Inc.
Romac & Assoc.
Ross Personnel Consultants, Inc.
Spectra West
Staffing Solutions
Steinbach & Co.
Tech Consulting
Tech International
Techno-Trac Systems, Inc.
Vento Assoc.
P.D. Zier Assoc.
W.F. Richer Assoc., Inc.

09.4 SYSTEMS INTEGRATION, INCLUDING HARDWARE/ SOFTWARE SERVICES, EVALUATION (Cont'd)

N. Steven Fells & Co., Inc.
Forum Assoc.
Gallagher & Assoc.
Greene Personnel Consultants
High-Tech Recruiters
Howie & Assoc., Inc.
Kenmore Executives Inc.
The Kennett Group, Inc.
Kiley-Owen Assoc., Inc.
Joyce C. Knauff & Assoc.
Kreofsky & Assoc.
Kurtz Pro-Search, Inc.
Jonathan Lawrence Assoc.
Logix, Inc.
Tom Mahon & Assoc.
Management Recruiters of Poughkeepsie, Inc.
Management Search, Inc.
Masserman & Assoc.
Sandi McDonald & Assoc., Inc.
The NRI Group
Nelson Associates
Pacific Search Consultants
Pathway Executive Search, Inc.
Paul-Tittle Assoc., Inc.
Pencom Systems Inc.
Posse, Inc.
Norman Powers Assoc., Inc.
The Reynolds Group, Inc.
Romac & Assoc.
Russillo/Gardner
Search & Recruit Int'l.
The Search Firm Inc.
Source EDP
Southwest Search Inc.
Spectra West
Staffing Solutions
Stanewick, Hart & Assoc., Inc.
Stone Enterprises Ltd.
Technical Recruiting Consultants
Techno-Trac Systems, Inc.
Tecmark Assoc. Inc.
Vento Assoc.
Wesson, Taylor, Wells & Assoc.
Worlco Computer Resources, Inc.
Dennis Wynn Assoc., Inc.
W.F. Richer Assoc., Inc.

09.5 EXPERT SYSTEMS

Atlantic Search Group, Inc.
Dalton-Smith & Assoc., Inc.
Kennison & Assoc.
Techsearch Services Inc.

09.6 DECISION SUPPORT

Atlantic Search Group, Inc.
Battista Assoc., Inc.
Binary Search
Bradford & Galt, Inc.

Career Consulting Group, Inc.
K. Carroll & Assoc.
David P. Cordell Assoc.
D.P. Specialists, Inc.
Dalton-Smith & Assoc., Inc.
J P Donnelly Assoc., Inc.
Dynamic Search Systems, Inc.
Lancaster Assoc., Inc.
Jonathan Lawrence Assoc.
Logix, Inc.
New Dimensions in Technology, Inc.
Pathway Executive Search, Inc.
Rockwood Assoc.
The Search Firm Inc.
Smith Hanley Assoc., Inc.
Stanewick, Hart & Assoc., Inc.
Systems One Ltd.
Techsearch Services Inc.
The Wright Group
Dennis Wynn Assoc., Inc.
W.F. Richer Assoc., Inc.

09.7 TELECOMMUNICATIONS

A. D. & Assoc.
Abacus Consultants
Abbott, James & Oliver
Abraham & London Ltd.
Alexander Edward Assoc., Inc.
The Ayers Group, Inc.
M.F. Branch Assoc., Inc.
CN Associates
CPI Technical Services
D.P. Specialists, Inc.
Dalton-Smith & Assoc., Inc.
The DataFinders Group, Inc.
Delta Resource Group, Ltd.
Dreier Consulting
Executive Exchange Corp.
First Search Inc.
Forum Assoc.
High Tech Opportunities, Inc.
High-Tech Recruiters
JDG Assoc., Ltd.
Kendall & Davis Co., Inc.
Kennison & Assoc.
Kiley-Owen Assoc., Inc.
Kirland Search, Inc.
Kurtz Pro-Search, Inc.
LAS Management Consulting Group, Inc.
Lancaster Assoc., Inc.
Tom Mahon & Assoc.
Management Assoc.
Management Recruiters of Hendersonville, inc.
Management Recruiters of Poughkeepsie, Inc.
Management Search, Inc.
Management Search, Inc.
The McCormick Group, Inc.
McCulloch Assoc.
Sandi McDonald & Assoc., Inc.
Milgram & Assoc.
Mogul Consultants, Inc.
P.R.H. Management, Inc.

09.7 TELECOMMUNICATIONS (Cont'd)

Paul-Tittle Assoc., Inc.
M.R. Pennington Co.
Phillips Personnel/Search
Romac & Assoc.
Romac & Assoc., Inc.
Sales Consultants of Westchester-South, Inc.
Sales Consultants of Ft. Myers, Inc.
The Search Firm Inc.
Spectra West
Stanewick, Hart & Assoc., Inc.
Stone Enterprises Ltd.
Systems One Ltd.
Tech Consulting
Tech Vision Co.
Techno-Trac Systems, Inc.
TeleSearch, Inc.
Tell/Com Recruiters
Wesson, Taylor, Wells & Assoc.

10.0 INSURANCE/RISK MANAGEMENT

Advanced Corporate Search
The Agency- An Employment Consortium
Pat Allen Assoc. Inc.
Ethan Allen Personnel, Inc.
Aronow Assoc., Inc.
E. J. Ashton & Assoc., Ltd.
Ashway Ltd. Agency
Atlantic Search Group, Inc.
Avery Crafts Assoc., Ltd.
The Bankers Group
Bonifield Assoc.
Broad Waverly & Assoc.
Brooks Executive Personnel
The Butlers Co. Insurance Recruiters
C & H Personnel
Carter-Evdemon & Assoc.
Corporate Suite, Ltd.
Criterion Executive Search, Inc.
Dunhill Personnel of Milwaukee
Ecco Personnel Svs.
Mark Elzweig Co. Ltd.
Jack Stuart Fisher Assoc.
Flynn, Hannock, Inc.
Fuller Search
The Garrison Organization
Gaudette & Co.
W. Hanley & Assoc.
Hudson Assoc. Inc.
Hughes & Assoc.
IprGroup, Inc.
Jacobson Assoc.
The James Group
Key Employment Services
Kinderis & Loercher Group
Lechner & Assoc., Inc.
Vincent Lee Assoc.
Management Recruiters of Dearborn, Inc.
Management Recruiters
Management Recruiters

Management Recruiters of Ft. Myers, FL.
Management Recruiters of Tampa North
Management Recruiters of Reno
Mary L. Mayer, Ltd.
Olaf S. Meyer & Co., Ltd.
Milgram & Assoc.
Robert E. Mills, FLMI
The NRI Group
Beverly Nelson & Assoc. Inc.
Nuance Personnel Search, Inc.
Largent Parks & Partners, Inc.
Robert A. Paul & Assoc.
Personnel Systems Int'l. Inc.
J.R. Peterman Assoc., Inc.
The Primary Group, Inc.
Pro, Inc.
Professional Search Assoc., Inc.
Professionals in Recruiting Co.
Questor Consultants, Inc.
R.G.B. & Assoc., Inc.
RHS Assoc., Inc.
Retail Recruiters/Spectrum Consultants, Inc.
Riverside Consultants, Inc.
Russillo/Gardner
Sales & Management Search, Inc.
Sales Consultants of Madison
Sales Consultants of Rraleigh - Durham - RTP
Search Assoc., Inc.
Selective Management Services, Inc.
Selective Staffing
Straight & Co.
Tower Consultants, Ltd.
USA Medical Placement Inc.
Water Street Assoc.
Wayne Assoc., Inc.
Yake & Assoc.

11.0 SPECIALIZED SERVICES

Accounting Resources Int'l., Inc.
John R. Ady & Assoc., Inc.
Avery Crafts Assoc., Ltd.
Keith Bagg Personnel Ltd.
Ray N. Bedingfield, Consultant
Bornholdt Shivas & Friends
Bowling Executive Registry, Inc.
C.G. & Assoc.
Career Management, Inc.
Career Marketing Assoc.
Centaur Int'l.
Chase Waterford Ltd.
The Christopher Group
Cosco Resources Inc.
Domenico/Brown Group
Double M Executive Placement Service, Inc.
Gwen Dycus, Inc.
Fuller Search
GreenHall Assoc., Inc.
High Technology Search Assoc.
C. L. Howe & Co., Inc.
Hyland Executive Search
K.E. Johnson Assoc.
Lisa Kalus & Assoc., Inc.

11.0 SPECIALIZED SERVICES (Cont'd)

Sanford Kleiner Assoc., Inc.
Lineal Recruiting Services
Management Recruiters of El Dorado
Management Recruiters of Tampa North
Management Recruiters of Passaic, inc.
McGuire Executive Search, Inc.
Medtrac & Assoc.
Diedre Moire Corp., Inc.
The Montanye Group
Multisearch Recruiters
National Health Search, Inc.
National Logistics Recruiters, Inc.
New Dimensions in Technology, Inc.
OSA Partners, Inc.
Joel H. Paul & Assoc., Inc.
Pencom Systems Inc.
Pro Travel Personnel
The Salem Group, Executive Recruiters
Sales Consultants of Austin, Inc.
The Search Center Inc.
Search Enterprises, Inc.
St. James And DeDominic
Supreme Assoc.
Vezan Assoc.
Waldorf Associates, Inc.
Weatherby Healthcare
Weinpel & Co.
Wellington Thomas Ltd.
WestCare Executive Search
Winfield Assoc.
Winston Rooney & Green

11.1 MANAGEMENT CONSULTANTS

Accounting Personnel Assoc.
Accounting Resources Int'l., Inc.
Allied Search, Inc.
Alpine Consulting Group
R.W. Apple & Assoc.
R. Gaines Baty Assoc., Inc.
Ted Bavly Assoc., Inc.
Berger & Assoc.
Charles Bradley Professionals
CES
Cibotti Assoc., Inc.
The Comwell Co. Inc.
David P. Cordell Assoc.
DLB Assoc.
D.P. Specialists, Inc.
Drake & Assoc.
Dunhill Personnel of Northeast Tulsa, Inc.
Environmental Professional Assoc.
A.G. Fishkin & Assoc., Inc.
Foster Assoc.
Global Data Services, Inc.
Goldstein & Assoc.
Halbrecht & Co.
W. Hanley & Assoc.
Hawkes-Randolph & Assoc., Inc.
Health Technology, Inc.

Higbee Assoc., Inc.
Hintz Associates
Intech Summit Group, Inc.
Integrated Management Solutions
JDG Assoc., Ltd.
Kelley & Keller, Inc.
Kenmore Executives Inc.
Kurtz Pro-Search, Inc.
Latham Int'l., Ltd.
Logue & Rice Inc.
Management Recruiters of Hendersonville, inc.
Management Recruiters of Tampa North
McCracken, Wilcox, Bertoux & Miller
B. Paul Mickey & Assoc.
Parker Page Group
Penn Associates
Pro, Inc.
RAI Consulting
Ranger & Assoc.
Emery A. Rose & Assoc.
Sanford Rose Assoc. of Binghamton
Sales Consultants of Madison
Sales Consultants of Fairfax, Inc.
Sloan & Assoc., Inc.
Spring Executive Search, Inc.
Phyllis Stovall Assoc., Inc.
Strategic Assoc., Inc.
Strategic Executives, Inc.
Thoroughbred Executive Search
The Wilkinson Group

11.2 MINORITIES

Allen Barry Assoc.
Atlantic Search Group, Inc.
BIK Search/Force II
Bradford & Galt, Inc.
Career Profiles
Career Resource Assoc., Inc.
Carter McKenzie, Inc.
Clanton & Co.
Corporate Suite, Ltd.
Crickenberger Assoc.
DLB Assoc.
DeLalla - Fried Assoc.
Dillard Executive Search
Drake & Assoc.
Dussick Management Assoc.
Executive Careers
Ford & Ford
Future Sense
Genesis Personnel Service, Inc.
Gregory Michaels & Assoc., Inc.
J. Gross & Assoc.
Hall, Cooper & Bartman, Ltd.
High-Tech Recruiters
Human Resource Network
J.M. Joseph Assoc.
Kossuth & Assoc., Inc.
Krow Assoc., Inc.
LaDuke & Assoc., Inc.
E.J. Lance Management Assoc., Inc.
Lanzi & Assoc.

11.2 MINORITIES (Cont'd)

Latham Int'l., Ltd.
Ludot Personnel Services, Inc.
Management Recruiters
Moore Employment Svs., Inc.
The Morris Group
LaMonte Owens, Inc.
Penn Associates
R.A.N. Assoc., Inc.
Edward Rast & Co.
Resource Perspectives, Inc.
Ryman, Bell, Green & Michaels, Inc.
Search Bureau Int'l.
Selected Executives, Inc.
Spring Executive Search, Inc.
Strategy 2000
Summit Executive Search Consultants, Inc.
Thornton Assoc.
Tower Consultants, Ltd.
The Urban Placement Service
M.K. Wasse & Assoc., Inc.
Whittlesey & Assoc., Inc.
The Wilkinson Group
Williams, Adley & Co.
Nola Worley & Assoc., Inc.
Xavier Assoc., Inc.

11.3 SCIENTIFIC/TECHNICAL

ACR Assoc.
Additional Technical Support Inc.
Adel Lawrence Assoc., Inc.
Adept Tech Recruiting, Inc.
Advanced Corporate Search
Allen Barry Assoc.
The Altco Group
Francis V. Anderson Assoc. Inc.
John Anthony & Assoc.
R.W. Apple & Assoc.
Arancio Assoc.
Ashway Ltd. Agency
BIK Search/Force II
Beckwith, Thomas & Fanning
Ray N. Bedingfield, Consultant
Charles A. Binswanger Assoc., Inc.
Bioventure Resources, Inc.
Bryant Research
Carver Search Consultants
Malcolm Cole & Assoc.
Corporate Recruiters Inc.
Corporate Resources Professional Placement
Cross Country Consultants, Inc.
Davis & James, Inc.
Diversified Placement Int'l., Inc.
Dreier Consulting
Robert Drexler Assoc., Inc.
Dunhill of Huntsville, Inc.
Dunhill of Greater Akron, Inc.
E O Technical
The Eastridge Group
Emerson & Co.
Engineering Search Assoc.
Environmental Professional Assoc.

Environmental Resources Int'l.
ExecuTech
A.G. Fishkin & Assoc., Inc.
Franklin Int'l. Search, Inc.
GHK Technical Recruiter
Gallagher & Assoc.
Goldstein & Assoc.
Gray-Kimball Assoc., Inc.
Handwerk & Assoc.
The Hudson Group
I.S. Consultants, Inc.
Industry Consultants, Inc.
International Staffing Consultants, Inc.
Intertech Search Group
Joslin & Assoc., Ltd.
The Kennett Group, Inc.
Kossuth & Assoc., Inc.
W.R. Lawry, Inc.
Lineal Recruiting Services
The James Lloyd Group
Loewenstein & Assoc.
Lybrook Assoc., Inc.
Management Recruiters of Greater Bridgeport, Inc.
Management Recruiters
Management Recruiters of El Dorado
Management Recruiters
Management Recruiters of Waterbury, Inc.
Management Recruiters of Atlanta Downtown
Management Recruiters of Passaic, inc.
Management Recruiters of Westchester, Inc.
Management Recruiters of Ashville, Inc.
Management Resources
Medical Executive Search Assoc.
Merlin Int'l. Inc.
Mogul Consultants, Inc.
Nachman Biomedical
Norton & Assoc.
Oldwick Enterprises, Inc.
Robert A. Paul & Assoc.
Paules Associates
M.A. Pelle Assoc., Inc.
Polytechnic Design Co.
RTE Search
Ranger & Assoc.
Emery A. Rose & Assoc.
Sanford Rose Assoc.- Woodbury
Sanford Rose Assoc. of Hartford
Sanford Rose Assoc. of Wilmington
Sanford Rose Assoc.- Detroit North
Sanford Rose Assoc. of Binghamton
Sanford Rose Assoc.- Suburban Philadelphia
Rothrock Assoc.
Rushlow & Co.
Ryman, Bell, Green & Michaels, Inc.
Sales Consultants of Rraleigh - Durham - RTP
George D. Sandel Assoc.
Schreuder Randall Corp.
The Search Network
Search Northwest Assoc.
Selected Executives, Inc.
Jules Seltzer Assoc.
Smith Hanley Assoc., Inc.

11.3 SCIENTIFIC/TECHNICAL (Cont'd)

Stanton/Schoen Professionals, Inc.
Ron Stevens & Assoc., Inc.
Stoneburner Assoc., Inc.
Storfer & Assoc.
S. Tyler Sullivan & Assoc., Inc.
Tech Consulting
Tech International
Technical Staffing Assoc.
Telem Adhesive Search Corp.
J.Q. Turner & Assoc., Inc.
Unisearch
Video Interview Professionals, Inc.
M.K. Wasse & Assoc., Inc.
Weinpel & Co.
Wesson, Taylor, Wells & Assoc.
John Wylie Assoc., Inc.
The Yaiser Group
Zeiger Technical Careers, Inc.
P.D. Zier Assoc.

11.4 FUND-RAISERS & OTHER NON-PROFIT SERVICES

Chaloner Assoc.
DeCorrevont & Assoc.
Development Resource Group
Executive Careers
Largent Parks & Partners, Inc.
Carolyn Smith Paschal Int'l.
Joel H. Paul & Assoc., Inc.
Selected Executives, Inc.
Thornton Assoc.

11.5 ENVIRONMENTAL

ACC Consultants, Inc.
The Adams Group
Additional Technical Support Inc.
The Agency- An Employment Consortium
Ames Assoc. Inc.
John Anthony & Assoc.
R.W. Apple & Assoc.
D.W. Baird & Associates
Bartlett, Bunn & Travis, Inc.
Beckwith, Thomas & Fanning
Ray N. Bedingfield, Consultant
Bennett-Munson Inc.
Charles A. Binswanger Assoc., Inc.
Dan B. Brockman
Broward-Dobbs, Inc.
Paul J. Burns
C.G. & Assoc.
Caremarc & Assoc.
Claremont-Branan, Inc.
Cona Personnel Search
Frank Cuomo & Assoc., Inc.
Delta Personnel Services
Dunhill Professional Search Inc.
Dunhill Search of Omaha, Inc.
Eckert, Enghauser and Partners, Inc.
W. Robert Eissler & Assoc., Inc.
The Energists

Environmental Professional Assoc.
Environmental Resources Int'l.
ExecuTech
Executive Recruiters, Inc.
Ford & Assoc., Inc.
Ford & Ford
Gallin Assoc.
Genesis
Greene Personnel Consultants
Handwerk & Assoc.
Headhunters National, Inc.
Hudson Assoc. Inc.
The Hudson Group
I.S. Consultants, Inc.
Intech Summit Group, Inc.
International Staffing Consultants, Inc.
Intertech Search Group
J.D. Limited
Richard Kader & Assoc.
Lisa Kalus & Assoc., Inc.
Kepler & Assoc.
Kimmel & Fredericks, Inc.
Kossuth & Assoc., Inc.
Lam Assoc.
Loewenstein & Assoc.
Lybrook Assoc., Inc.
Management Recruiters of Laguna Hills
Management Recruiters of Frederick, Inc.
Management Recruiters of Dearborn, Inc.
Management Recruiters of Cincinnati/ Sharonville, Inc.
Management Recruiters of Greater Bridgeport, Inc.
Management Recruiters
Management Recruiters
Management Recruiters of El Dorado
Management Recruiters of Tampa North
Management Recruiters of Atlanta Downtown
Management Recruiters of Passaic, inc.
Management Recruiters of Nassau, Inc.
Management Resources
Management Search, Inc.
The McCormick Group, Inc.
McDermott & Assoc.
The McKee Co.
B. Paul Mickey & Assoc.
The Morris Group
Oldwick Enterprises, Inc.
PC Assoc.
PMC-ParaLegal Management & Consultants
Robert A. Paul & Assoc.
Paul-Tittle Assoc., Inc.
Paules Associates
The Personnel Network, Inc.
Philip Daniels Assoc., Inc.
Phillips Assoc.
Phillips Personnel/Search
Preston Robert & Assoc.-Health Care Div.
Pro, Inc.
Professional Recruiters Inc.
RALCO/Richard A. Lucia & Assoc.
RBR Assoc., Inc.
Roberson & Co.

Basis of "Industries" Classification

This classification system is based on the U.S. Government's SIC code but has been customized and updated by Kennedy Publications to suit our users' needs.

0.00 **MOST**

A.00 **AGRICULTURE, FORESTRY, FISHING & MINING**
A.01 Specific:

B.00 **ENERGY/UTILITIES**

B.0W **ENVIRONMENTAL SERVICES**
B.10 Hazardous waste, study, clean up

C.00 **CONSTRUCTION**

D.00 **MANUFACTURING**
D.10 Food, beverage, tobacco & kindred products
D.11 Textile, apparel, related products
D.12 Lumber, wood, furniture & fixtures
D.13 Paper & allied products
D.14 Printing & allied industry
D.15 Chemicals & allied products
D.16 Soap, perfume, cosmetics
D.17 Drugs
D.18 Pharmaceuticals, medical manufacturers
D.19 Plastics, rubber products
D.20 Paints, allied products, petroleum products
D.21 Leather, stone, glass, concrete, clay products
D.22 Primary metal industry, fabricated metal products, machinery, general industrial machinery & appliances
D.23 Transportation equipment including automobiles & other motor vehicles
D.24 Office machinery, computers, computer products, software, electronic & electrical equipment & components
D.25 Measuring/analyzing & controlling instruments & optical goods
D.26 Miscellaneous manufacturing industries

D.D0	**PACKAGING**
D.E0	**AEROSPACE**
D.H0	**HIGH TECH/ELECTRONICS**
D.I0	**BIOTECH/GENETIC ENGINEERING**
E.00	**TRANSPORTATION**
F.00	**WHOLESALE TRADE**
G.00	**RETAIL TRADE**
H.00	**FINANCE**
H.10	Banking, financial institutions, credit agencies
H.11	Securities & commodities brokers
H.12	Venture capital
H.I0	**INSURANCE**
H.R0	**REAL ESTATE**
I.00	**SERVICES**
I.10	Hospitality-including hotels, resorts, clubs, restaurants, food & beverage services
I.11	Entertainment, leisure, amusement, recreation, sports, travel
I.12	Museums, galleries, music/arts, libraries & information services, membership & other non-profits
I.13	Higher Education
I.14	Healthcare (except physicians; see I.15) to include administrators & practitioners-hospitals, nursing/ personal care, clinics
I.15	Physicians
I.16	Pharmaceutical (other than manufacturing)
I.17	Legal
I.18	Computer Services
I.19	Accounting & miscellaneous business services
I.20	Equipment services, including leasing
I.21	Management & personnel services
J.00	**COMMUNICATIONS**
J.10	Advertising/public relations
J.11	Publishing, print media
J.12	TV, cable, motion pictures, video, radio
J.13	Telephone, telecommunications
K.00	**PUBLIC ADMINISTRATION/GOVERNMENT**
K.10	Defense
L.00	**NON-CLASSIFIABLE INDUSTRIES**

Contingency Cross-Index by Industries

0.00 MOST

A. D. & Assoc.
AJS Assoc.
A.M.C.R., Inc.
Academy Graduates Executive Search, Inc.
Accountants On Call
Accountants On Call
Accounting & Computer Personnel
Accounting Personnel Assoc.
Action Inc.
AdStaff Personnel, Inc.
The Adler Group
Affirmative Action Assoc.
The Agency- An Employment Consortium
Agri-Tech Personnel, Inc.
Aitken & Assoc.
Allen/Assoc.
Allied Financial Management Co.
Allied Search, Inc.
American Resources Corp.
Ames Personnel Consultants
Amherst Personnel Group Inc.
Anderson Industrial Assoc., Inc.
Tryg R. Angell Ltd.
The Angus Group, Inc.
John Anthony & Assoc.
Atlantic Search Group, Inc.
Atlantic Search Group, Inc.
Austin - Allen Co.
Automation Technology Search
The Ayers Group, Inc.
BGB Assoc., Inc.
BIK Search/Force II
Baldwin & Assoc.
Ron Ball & Assoc.
B.K. Barnes & Associates
Barone Assoc.
Barone-O'Hara Assoc., Inc.
Barrett Partners
R. Gaines Baty Assoc., Inc.
Jim Baum - Executive Search
Beckwith, Thomas & Fanning
Marcia Beilin, Inc.
Dotson Benefield & Assoc., Inc.
Bennett & Curran, Inc.
Berger & Assoc.
Binary Search
Bodner Inc.
Bornholdt Shivas & Friends

Bowersox & Assoc., Inc.
Bradford & Galt, Inc.
Bradstreet Mgt.
Britt Assoc., Inc.
Dan B. Brockman
J.R. Brody & Assoc., Inc.
Brooks Executive Personnel
Brown/Bernardy, Inc.
Bryant Assoc., Inc.
C & H Personnel
CCI - Career Consultants Int'l.
C.P.S., Inc.
Peter M. Cahill Assoc., Inc.
The Cambridge Group Ltd.
J.P. Canon Assoc.
The Cantor Concern, Inc.
Capitol Management Consulting, Inc.
Career Advancement
Career Guides, Inc.
Career Information Services, Inc.
Career Logic, Inc.
Career Management, Inc.
Careers Unlimited
Careers/Inc.
K. Carroll & Assoc.
Carter, Lavoie Assocs.
Carver Search Consultants
Casey & Gerrish Assoc., Inc.
The Century Group
Chaloner Assoc.
Cibotti Assoc., Inc.
Howard Clark Assoc.
Richard Clarke Assoc., Inc.
Competitive Resources, Inc.
CompuPro
Computer Recruiters, Inc.
The Comwell Co. Inc.
Cona Personnel Search
The Connolly Consulting Group
The Consortium
Consumer Search, Inc.
David P. Cordell Assoc.
Corporate Careers Inc.
The Corporate Connection, Ltd.
The Cris Group, Inc.
Crown, Michels & Assoc., Inc.
Curts/Jackson, Inc.
The DLR Group, Inc.
D.P. Specialists, Inc.

0.00 MOST (Cont'd)

Dalton Management Consultants, Ltd.
Dalton-Smith & Assoc., Inc.
Damon & Assoc., Inc.
Dankowski & Assoc., Inc.
Dapexs Consultants, Inc.
Datamatics Management Services, Inc.
DeCorrevont & Assoc.
Dean-Wharton Assoc.
Delta Personnel Services
Delta Resource Group, Ltd.
Diversified Placement Int'l., Inc.
Double M Executive Placement Service, Inc.
Drake & Assoc.
Dumont Moriarty & Assoc.
Dunhill Professional Search of Hawaii
Dunhill International Search
G.L. Dykstra Assoc., Inc.
Dynamic Search Systems, Inc.
The E & K Group
E O Technical
E T Search Inc.
EXETER 2100
Engineering Directions
Engineering Specialists
Environmental Professional Assoc.
Execu-Search, Inc.
ExecuSource Int'l.
The Executive Consulting Group -N.Y.
Executive Register, Inc.
Executive Resource Inc.
Executive Search of New England, Inc.
Executives' Personnel Service Inc.
A.E. Feldman Assoc.
Fergason Assoc., Inc.
Finance & Accounting Search Firm
Financial Search Corp.
James L. Fisk & Assoc.
Ford & Ford
Foster Assoc.
The Foster McKay Group
Fox-Morris Assoc., Inc.
Franchise Recruiters Ltd.
The Furst Group
G.A.M. Executive Search, Inc.
Gaines & Assoc. Int'l., Inc.
The Garrison Group
Gatti & Assoc.
Delores F. George
Joe L. Giles & Assoc., Inc.
Grant, Franks & Assoc.
Greene Personnel Consultants
Louis Gregory Assoc., Inc.
Groenekamp & Assoc.
Halbrecht & Co.
Robert Half Int'l.
W. Hanley & Assoc.
Hawkes-Randolph & Assoc., Inc.
Donald P. Hayes Assoc., Inc.
The Headhunters
Kent R. Hedman & Assoc.
Hemingway Personnel, Inc.

Hessel Assoc., Inc.
Hi-Tech Search, Inc.
Hill Allyn Assoc.
Frank P. Hill
Hoskins, Rees & Smith
George Howard Assoc.
Howard-Sloan Legal Search, Inc.
The Hudson Group
Human Resource Bureau
Human Resource Network
Human Resource Recruiters
Information Systems Professionals
IprGroup, Inc.
J.P.D. Group
Jacobson Assoc.
Jefferson-Ross Assoc. Inc.
John-David Assoc., Inc.
K.E. Johnson Assoc.
The Johnson Group, Inc.
Kathryn L. Johnson
J.M. Joseph Assoc.
A.H. Justice & Assoc.
Richard Kader & Assoc.
Kane Ford Karrel & Assoc.
Karras Personnel, Inc.
Kenmore Executives Inc.
The Kennett Group, Inc.
Kennison & Assoc.
Kensington Int'l.
Kepler & Assoc.
Key Employment Services
Joyce C. Knauff & Assoc.
The Koehler Group
Kogon Assoc., Inc.
Kordus Consulting Group
Krautler Personnel Recruitment
Kravitz * Larkin * Silver Assoc.
Kreuzberger, Fehr & Assoc.
L & K Assoc.
LAS Management Consulting Group, Inc.
LMB Assoc.
Lambert & Sullivan Assoc.
E.J. Lance Management Assoc., Inc.
Jack B. Larsen & Assoc.
R.H. Larsen & Assoc., Inc.
Latham Int'l., Ltd.
Latin America Assoc., S.C.
Jonathan Lawrence Assoc.
W.R. Lawry, Inc.
Vincent Lee Assoc.
Alan Lerner Assoc.
Link Personnel & Assoc.
Logistics Management Resources, Inc.
Logue & Rice Inc.
R.E. Lowe Assoc.
Lucas & Assoc., Ltd.
Fran Luisi Assoc.
Luke, Lincoln, & Brugger
Arthur Lyle Assoc., Inc.
MKM Search Consultants, Inc.
MRG Search & Placement
Alan MacDonald & Assoc.
Mahony & Assoc., Ltd.

0.00 MOST (Cont'd)

Management Assoc.
Management Recruiters of Gramercy, Inc.
Management Recruiters of Cincinnati/
  Sharonville, Inc.
Management Recruiters
Management Recruiters
Management Recruiters
Management Recruiters
Management Recruiters
Management Recruiters
Management Recruiters
Management Recruiters of Hendersonville, inc.
Management Recruiters of Oakland
Management Recruiters Peninsula
Management Recruiters of North Brunswick,
  Inc.
Management Recruiters of Ashville, Inc.
Management Resource Assoc., Inc.
Management Search, Inc.
Management Search Int'l.
Margolin Consultants, Inc.
Mark III Personnel, Inc.
Karen Marshall Assoc.
Masserman & Assoc.
Matthews Professional Employment
  Specialists, Inc.
The McCormick Group, Inc.
McCulloch Assoc.
McDermott & Assoc.
McRoberts & Assoc.
Joseph J. McTaggart
Merlin Int'l. Inc.
Diedre Moire Corp., Inc.
George J. Mollo Assoc.
Montgomery Resources, Inc.
Moore Employment Svs., Inc.
Morency Assoc.
The Morris Group
Multisearch Recruiters
Murkett Assoc.
The NRI Group
National Corporate Consultants, Inc.
National Logistics Recruiters, Inc.
National Search, Inc.
J. Fielding Nelson & Assoc., Inc.
Nelson Associates
Nelson-Larson & Assoc. Ltd.
The Network Companies
Newcombe & Cyr Assoc., Inc.
Newton Assoc.
Noble & Assoc., Inc.
Opportunity Knocking, Inc.
LaMonte Owens, Inc.
The P & L Group
PLRS/Career Connections
PMC-ParaLegal Management & Consultants
Robert Parrella Assoc.
Part Time Resources
Carolyn Smith Paschal Int'l.
Pathway Executive Search, Inc.
Kevin W. Paul

M.A. Pelle Assoc., Inc.
Pencom Systems Inc.
Penn Associates
Performance Professionals
Personnel Advisors Int'l. Corp.
Personnel Inc.
Personnel Management, Inc.
The Personnel Network, Inc.
Personnel Unlimited/Executive Search
Phillips Assoc.
Phillips Personnel/Search
Phillips Resource Group
The Pickwick Group, Inc.
Placement Assoc., Inc.
Polytechnical Consultants, Inc.
Princeton Executive Search, Inc.
Princeton Planning Consultants, Inc.
ProSearch, Inc.
Probe Technology
Professions Unlimited, Inc.
Protocol Inc.
Quickstaff
RAI Consulting
R.A.N. Assoc., Inc.
RGL Assoc., Inc.
RHS Assoc., Inc.
RPA Management Consultants, Inc.
Railey & Assoc.
Ranger & Assoc.
Edward Rast & Co.
Repplier & Co.
Resource Services, Inc.
S. Reyman & Assoc., Ltd.
Jeff Rich Assoc.
Roberson & Co.
Rogers & Seymour Inc.
Romac & Assoc.
Romac & Assoc. - San Francisco
Sanford Rose Assoc.
Sanford Rose Assoc. - Santa Barbara
Sanford Rose Assoc. of Hartford
Sanford Rose Assoc. of Wilmington
Sanford Rose Assoc. - Virginia Beach
John P. Runden & Co., Inc.
Ryan & Assoc.
The Charles Ryan Group, Inc.
Ryman, Bell, Green & Michaels, Inc.
S. P. Assoc.
The Salem Group, Executive Recruiters
Sales Consultants
Sales Consultants of Fairfax, Inc.
Sales Consultants of Rhode Island, Inc.
Sales Consultants
Sales Consultants of Rraleigh - Durham - RTP
Sales Consultants of Morris County, Inc.
Sales Consultants of Wellesley, Inc.
Sales Consultants Chicago Southeast
Sales Consultants of Ft. Lauderdale
Sales Professionals Personnel Services
Sarver-Garland, Inc.
Schenck & Assoc. SC
Scott-Wayne Assoc., Inc.
Search Assoc., Inc.

0.00 MOST (Cont'd)

Search Assoc., Inc.
Search Consultants Int'l., Inc.
Search Dynamics, Inc.
The Search Firm Inc.
Search Leader, Inc.
Search Masters Int'l.
Selected Executives, Inc.
Setford-Shaw-Najarian Assoc., Ltd.
L. A. Silver Assoc., Inc.
Simpson Nance & Graham, Inc.
James F. Smith & Assoc.
Raymond James Smith & Assoc.
Ralph Smith & Assoc.
Abbott Smith Assoc., Inc.
J. Harrington Smith Assoc.
Smith, Beaty, Barlow Assoc., Inc.
Source EDP
Source Engineering
Source Finance
Southwest Search Inc.
Spectrum Consultants
St. James And DeDominic
St. Lawrence Int'l., Inc.
Staffing Consultants
The Stevens Group, Inc.
The Stoddard Co.
Stoneburner Assoc., Inc.
Strategic Executives, Inc.
Strategy 2000
Strauss Personnel Service
Sturm, Burrows & Co.
Summerfield Assoc., Inc.
Supreme Assoc.
Donna Svei Assoc.
Systems Careers
Systems One Ltd.
Tanzi Executive Search
Tech International
Tech Vision Co.
Technical Recruiting Consultants
Telemarketing Search, Inc.
Thomas, Whelan Assoc., Inc.
Judy Thompson & Assoc., Inc.
Thoroughbred Executive Search
Tidewater Group Inc.
Topaz Int'l., Inc.
Tower Consultants, Ltd.
TransAmerica Network
Trilogy Enterprises, Inc.
The Urban Placement Service
Vogel Assoc.
WBS Network Professional & Executive
    Search
Frank X. Walsh & Co., Inc.
D.L. Weaver & Assoc.
Wegner & Assoc.
Weliver & Assoc.
Henry Welker & Assoc.
Werbin Assoc. Executive Search, Inc.
Western Personnel Assoc., Inc.
S.J. Wexler Assoc., Inc.

E.T. Wharton Assoc., Inc.
Wheeler Assoc.
David J. White & Assoc., Inc.
Whitehead & Assoc., Inc.
Williams, Adley & Co.
Willmott & Assoc.
N. Willner & Co., Inc.
The Windham Group
Winston Rooney & Green
Winter, Wyman & Co.
Woehr Assoc.
Worlco Computer Resources, Inc.
J.D. Wright & Assoc., Inc.
The Wright Group
Dennis Wynn Assoc., Inc.
Zackrison Assoc., Inc.
P.D. Zier Assoc.

A.00 AGRICULTURE, FORESTRY, FISHING & MINING

ACC Consultants, Inc.
AGRI-associates
Agra Placements, Ltd.
Agri-Personnel
Agri-Tech Personnel, Inc.
Capitol Management Consulting, Inc.
The Comwell Co. Inc.
Florapersonnel, Inc.
Handwerk & Assoc.
Kay Henry, Inc.
Horizon Assoc.
The Human Resource Group
K & C Assoc.
Management Search, Inc.
PC Assoc.
Pro Counsel
Rocky Mountain Recruiters, Inc.
Sanford Rose Assoc. - Great Neck
John P. Runden & Co., Inc.
STM Assoc.
Search North America, Inc.

A.01 SPECIFIC:

S-H-S of Allentown

B.00 ENERGY/UTILITIES

ARJay & Assoc.
Aberdeen Assoc.
Additional Technical Support Inc.
David Allen Assoc.
Ames Personnel Consultants
Tryg R. Angell Ltd.
John Anthony & Assoc.
C. Berger and Company
Broward-Dobbs, Inc.
Paul J. Burns
C.G. & Assoc.
CoEnergy Inc.
Cosco Resources Inc.
Dapexs Consultants, Inc.
Datamax Services Inc.
Davis & James, Inc.

B.00 ENERGY/UTILITIES (Cont'd)

Robert Drexler Assoc., Inc.
Dunhill Professional Search of Wilkes-Barre/
    Scranton, Inc.
Dunhill Professional Search of Hawaii
Eastern Executive Assoc.
The Energists
Environmental Resources Int'l.
Fuller Search
J. Gifford, Inc.
Handwerk & Assoc.
High Technology Search Assoc.
The Hudson Group
International Staffing Consultants, Inc.
JT Assoc.
Locus Inc.
Management Recruiters
Management Recruiters of Charlotte -
    Southwest
Richard L. Mather & Assoc.
McDermott & Assoc.
John McLellan Assoc., Inc.
Milgram & Assoc.
NPF Assoc. Ltd. Inc.
Northeastern Search, Inc.
Oldwick Enterprises, Inc.
PC Assoc.
Robert A. Paul & Assoc.
Performance Professionals
Polytechnic Design Co.
Railey & Assoc.
The Resource Group
Rockwood Assoc.
Sanford Rose Assoc. of Hartford
Sanford Rose Assoc. - Great Neck
STM Assoc.
Sales Consultants of Austin, Inc.
Schattle Personnel Consultants, Inc.
Schreuder Randall Corp.
The Search Center Inc.
Search Consultants Int'l., Inc.
Search Enterprises, Inc.
Search North America, Inc.
Marvin L. Silcott & Assoc., Inc.
Snelling Personnel Services
Spectrum Consultants
Ron Stevens & Assoc., Inc.
M. L. Tawney & Assoc.
Technical Staffing Assoc.
Technitrac, Inc.
Jay Tracey Assoc.
Key Employment
Denis P. Walsh & Assoc., Inc.
John Wylie Assoc., Inc.

B.0W ENVIRONMENTAL SERVICES

ACC Consultants, Inc.
Additional Technical Support Inc.
Advancement Recruiting Services
The Agency- An Employment Consortium
Agra Placements, Ltd.
Agri-Personnel

Alaska Executive Search, Inc.
D.S. Allen Assoc.
Allen Barry Assoc.
Ames Personnel Consultants
Ames-O'Neill Assoc., Inc.
John Anthony & Assoc.
R.W. Apple & Assoc.
Automation Technology Search
D.W. Baird & Associates
Barone Assoc.
Bartlett, Bunn & Travis, Inc.
Ray N. Bedingfield, Consultant
Bennett-Munson Inc.
Charles A. Binswanger Assoc., Inc.
Blanton & Co.
Broward-Dobbs, Inc.
Career Search Assoc.
Carver Search Consultants
Casey & Gerrish Assoc., Inc.
Claremont-Branan, Inc.
CoEnergy Inc.
Cona Personnel Search
Corporate Resources Professional Placement
Frank Cuomo & Assoc., Inc.
Delta Resource Group, Ltd.
Drake & Assoc.
Robert Drexler Assoc., Inc.
Dunhill Professional Search of Wilkes-Barre/
    Scranton, Inc.
Dunhill Search of Omaha, Inc.
Dunhill Professional Search of Hawaii
Dunhill Professional Search
Eastern Executive Assoc.
The Eastridge Group
Eckert, Enghauser and Partners, Inc.
Eggers Consulting Co., Inc.
W. Robert Eissler & Assoc., Inc.
The Energists
Environmental Professional Assoc.
Environmental Resources Int'l.
Executive Recruiters, Inc.
Fernow Assoc.
Ferrari Consulting Group
James L. Fisk & Assoc.
Ford & Assoc., Inc.
Franchise Search, Inc.
Fuller Search
Galen Giles Group
Gallin Assoc.
Genesis
Delores F. George
J. Gifford, Inc.
Greene Personnel Consultants
Hahn & Assoc., Inc.
Handwerk & Assoc.
Headhunters National, Inc.
Hudson Assoc. Inc.
The Hudson Group
Human Resource Network
ISOPS Personnel Services, Inc.
Industrial Recruiters Assoc., Inc.
Intech Summit Group, Inc.
International Staffing Consultants, Inc.

B.0W ENVIRONMENTAL SERVICES (Cont'd)

K.E. Johnson Assoc.
E. G. Jones Assoc., Ltd.
Kimmel & Fredericks, Inc.
Kozlin Assoc., Inc.
Larson Assoc.
Link Personnel & Assoc.
Lord & Albus Co.
Lybrook Assoc., Inc.
Management Recruiters of Tampa North
Management Recruiters of Savannah
Management Recruiters of Frederick, Inc.
Management Recruiters of Dearborn, Inc.
Management Recruiters of Cincinnati/
   Sharonville, Inc.
Management Recruiters
Management Recruiters
Management Recruiters of El Dorado
Management Recruiters of Ft. Myers, FL.
Management Recruiters of Laguna Hills
Management Recruiters of Atlanta Downtown
Management Recruiters of Topeka, Inc.
Management Recruiters of Reno
Management Recruiters of Passaic, inc.
Management Recruiters of Nassau, Inc.
Management Recruiters of Charlotte -
   Southwest
Management Resources
Richard L. Mather & Assoc.
K. Maxin & Assoc.
The McCormick Group, Inc.
McDermott & Assoc.
B. Paul Mickey & Assoc.
The Montanye Group
Multisearch Recruiters
Oldwick Enterprises, Inc.
Paules Associates
The Personnel Network, Inc.
Philip Daniels Assoc., Inc.
Phillips Assoc.
Phillips Personnel/Search
Precise Legal, Inc.
Pro, Inc.
Probe Technology
Professional Personnel Services
Professional Recruiters Inc.
Protocol Inc.
RALCO/Richard A. Lucia & Assoc.
R.A.N. Assoc., Inc.
RBR Assoc., Inc.
Sanford Rose Assoc. of Hartford
Sanford Rose Assoc. of Wilmington
Sanford Rose Assoc. of Binghamton
Sanford Rose Assoc. - Great Neck
Russell Assoc.
Ryman, Bell, Green & Michaels, Inc.
STM Assoc.
Robert Sage Recruiting
Sales Consultants of Austin, Inc.
Sales Consultants of Newtown
Sales Consultants of Rraleigh - Durham - RTP

Sales Consultants of Westchester-South, Inc.
Sales Consultants of Morris County, Inc.
Schreuder Randall Corp.
Search Enterprises, Inc.
Search Masters
Marvin L. Silcott & Assoc., Inc.
Snelling Personnel Services
Specialized Search Assoc.
St. James And DeDominic
Stanton/Schoen Professionals, Inc.
Ron Stevens & Assoc., Inc.
The Talley Group
M. L. Tawney & Assoc.
Tech International
Technical Staffing Assoc.
TransAmerica Network
J.Q. Turner & Assoc., Inc.
Unisearch
Video Interview Professionals, Inc.
Wallace Assoc.
Frank X. Walsh & Co., Inc.
Wayne Assoc., Inc.
Wing Tips & Pumps, Inc.
World Search

B.10 HAZARDOUS WASTE, STUDY, CLEAN UP

ACC Consultants, Inc.
The Adams Group
Additional Technical Support Inc.
R.W. Apple & Assoc.
D.W. Baird & Associates
Bench Int'l. Search, Inc.
Career Marketing Assoc.
Caremarc & Assoc.
Claremont-Branan, Inc.
Conaway Legal Search
Frank Cuomo & Assoc., Inc.
Drake & Assoc.
Dunhill Professional Search of Wilkes-Barre/
   Scranton, Inc.
Dunhill Professional Search
The Eastridge Group
The Energists
Environmental Professional Assoc.
Environmental Resources Int'l.
ExecuTech
Franchise Search, Inc.
Alan Glenn & Keener
Greene Personnel Consultants
Hudson Assoc. Inc.
ISOPS Personnel Services, Inc.
Intertech Search Group
Kimmel & Fredericks, Inc.
Lam Assoc.
Loewenstein & Assoc.
Management Recruiters of Greater Bridgeport,
   Inc.
Management Recruiters
Management Recruiters
Management Recruiters of El Dorado
Management Recruiters of Middlesex

B.10 HAZARDOUS WASTE, STUDY, CLEAN UP (Cont'd)

Management Recruiters of Passaic, inc.
Management Recruiters of Charlotte - Southwest
The McKee Co.
Paul-Tittle Assoc., Inc.
The Personnel Network, Inc.
Phillips Assoc.
Professional Recruiters Inc.
RALCO/Richard A. Lucia & Assoc.
Roberson & Co.
STM Assoc.
Sales Consultants of Newtown
Schreuder Randall Corp.
Search Group
Search North America, Inc.
Specialized Search Assoc.
Summit Executive Search Consultants, Inc.
Technical Staffing Assoc.
Unisearch

C.00 CONSTRUCTION

Aberdeen Assoc.
Alaska Executive Search, Inc.
Frank E. Allen & Assoc.
Alzed Real Estate Recruiters
Ames Assoc. Inc.
Tryg R. Angell Ltd.
John Anthony & Assoc.
Barone Assoc.
Bartlett, Bunn & Travis, Inc.
Brennan Assoc.
C.G. & Assoc.
Cap, Inc.
Carlden Personnel Services Inc.
Casey & Gerrish Assoc., Inc.
Claremont-Branan, Inc.
Frank Cuomo & Assoc., Inc.
N. Dean Davic Assoc., Inc.
Robert Drexler Assoc., Inc.
Dunhill Professional Search of Hawaii
Gwen Dycus, Inc.
David Fockler & Assoc., Inc.
Fox-Morris Assoc., Inc.
J. D. Hersey & Assoc.
Robert Hess & Assoc., Inc.
Hornberger Management Co., Inc.
The Human Resource Group
Hyland Executive Search
International Staffing Consultants, Inc.
K & C Assoc.
Lisa Kalus & Assoc., Inc.
Kershner & Co.
Kimmel & Fredericks, Inc.
Lam Assoc.
Lowery, Cotter, & Assoc.
Luke, Lincoln, & Brugger
Management Recruiters
Management Recruiters
Martin Personnel Assoc.
K. Maxin & Assoc.

B. Paul Mickey & Assoc.
Robert A. Paul & Assoc.
Personnel Systems Int'l. Inc.
Polytechnic Design Co.
Precise Legal, Inc.
Pro Counsel
Probus Executive Search
Resource Consultants
The Resource Group
Sanford Rose Assoc. of Beachwood
Schenck & Assoc. SC
Schreuder Randall Corp.
Selective Staffing
Sharrow & Assoc., Inc.
Specialized Search Assoc.
Specialty Consultants, Inc.
John R. Stephens & Assoc.
M. L. Tawney & Assoc.
Technical Staffing Assoc.
The Tibbetts Group Ltd.
Traynor Confidential, Ltd.
Key Employment
Denis P. Walsh & Assoc., Inc.
Wayne Assoc., Inc.

D.00 MANUFACTURING

AJS Assoc.
A.M.C.R., Inc.
APA Search, Inc.
Abacus Consultants
Accounting Resources Int'l., Inc.
Additional Technical Support Inc.
Adept Tech Recruiting, Inc.
Advancement Recruiting Services
John R. Ady & Assoc., Inc.
Aerospace Technologies, Inc.
The Agency- An Employment Consortium
Agra Placements, Ltd.
Agri-Tech Personnel, Inc.
Frank E. Allen & Assoc.
D.S. Allen Assoc.
Allen Barry Assoc.
Ames-O'Neill Assoc., Inc.
Tryg R. Angell Ltd.
Automation Technology Search
Availability Personnel Consultants
BGB Assoc., Inc.
BIK Search/Force II
B.P.A. Enterprises, Inc.
B.K. Barnes & Associates
Barone Assoc.
Barrett Partners
R. Gaines Baty Assoc., Inc.
Jim Baum - Executive Search
Ted Bavly Assoc., Inc.
Ray N. Bedingfield, Consultant
C. Berger and Company
Blanton & Co.
Bornholdt Shivas & Friends
Bowman & Marshall
Brennan Assoc.
Brooke Chase Assoc., Inc.

D.00 MANUFACTURING (Cont'd)

Paul J. Burns
The Byrnes Group
C & H Personnel
CES
C.P.S., Inc.
CRS Assoc., Inc.
Peter M. Cahill Assoc., Inc.
Cap, Inc.
Capitol Management Consulting, Inc.
Career Marketing Assoc.
Career Profiles
Career Specialists, Inc.
Carlden Personnel Services Inc.
Carver Search Consultants
Case Executive Search
Casey & Gerrish Assoc., Inc.
Clanton & Co.
Clark Assoc., Inc.
Clark-Winans, Inc.
Competitive Resources, Inc.
Computer Security Placement Service, Inc.
The Comwell Co. Inc.
Consumer Search, Inc.
Corporate Advisors Inc.
Corporate Careers Inc.
Corporate Consultants Inc.
Corporate Personnel, Inc.
Crickenberger Assoc.
Cross Country Consultants, Inc.
Timothy D. Crowe, Jr.
DLB Assoc.
Dapexs Consultants, Inc.
Datamax Services Inc.
N. Dean Davic Assoc., Inc.
Davis & James, Inc.
DeLalla - Fried Assoc.
Dillard Executive Search
Robert Drexler Assoc., Inc.
Dunhill Professional Search of Wilkes-Barre/ Scranton, Inc.
Dunhill International Search
Dunhill Professional Search
Dunhill Professional Search Irvine/Newport
Eastern Executive Assoc.
Ecco Personnel Svs.
Eckert, Enghauser and Partners, Inc.
Environmental Professional Assoc.
Allen Etcovitch Assoc. Ltd.
ExecuSource Int'l.
Executive Exchange Corp.
Executive Recruiters, Inc.
Executive Register, Inc.
David Farmer & Assoc.
Fergason Assoc., Inc.
Fernow Assoc.
Fisher-Todd Assoc.
Flores & Assoc.
Flynn, Hannock, Inc.
Fortune Personnel Consultants of Sarasota Inc.
Foster Assoc.
Fox-Morris Assoc., Inc.

GHK Technical Recruiter
Michael Garbi Assoc., Inc.
Genesis
Genesis Personnel Service, Inc.
Delores F. George
J. Gifford, Inc.
Alan Glenn & Keener
Global Data Services, Inc.
W.T. Glover & Assoc., Inc.
Gregory Michaels & Assoc., Inc.
J. Gross & Assoc.
Guidarelli Assoc., Inc.
Hahn & Assoc., Inc.
Harrison Moore Inc.
Hartman Personnel Services
Health Technology, Inc.
Hill & Assoc.
Hill Allyn Assoc.
Hintz Associates
Hitchens & Foster, Inc.
Hoskins, Rees & Smith
The Hudson Group
Human Resource Network
Hunt Ltd.
ISOPS Personnel Services, Inc.
Industrial Recruiters Assoc., Inc.
JDG Assoc., Ltd.
JNB Assoc., Inc.
JT Assoc.
R.I. James, Inc.
K.E. Johnson Assoc.
The Johnson Group, Inc.
Kathryn L. Johnson
J.M. Joseph Assoc.
Jubilee, Inc.
Kensington Int'l.
Joseph Keyes Assoc.
Kiradjieff & Co.
Kirland Search, Inc.
Kordus Consulting Group
Koren, Rogers Assoc.
Kossuth & Assoc., Inc.
Kozlin Assoc., Inc.
Kromenaker & Associates
LaDuke & Assoc., Inc.
Lancaster Assoc., Inc.
E.J. Lance Management Assoc., Inc.
Jack B. Larsen & Assoc.
Lawrence-Balakonis & Assoc., Inc.
Lee Management Group Inc.
Link Personnel & Assoc.
Locus Inc.
Logistics Management Resources, Inc.
Lord & Albus Co.
R.E. Lowe Assoc.
Lowery, Cotter, & Assoc.
Ludot Personnel Services, Inc.
Luke, Lincoln, & Brugger
MARBL Consultants, Inc.
mfg/Search, Inc.
MJF Assoc.
Magnum Search
Mahony & Assoc., Ltd.

D.00 MANUFACTURING (Cont'd)

Management Recruiters of Cedar Rapids, Inc.
Management Recruiters of Dearborn, Inc.
Management Recruiters of Wilmington
Management Recruiters of Gramercy, Inc.
Management Recruiters
Management Recruiters of Cincinnati/
Sharonville, Inc.
Management Recruiters
Management Recruiters of Berkeley
Management Recruiters of Waterbury, Inc.
Management Recruiters of North Oakland
County, Inc.
Management Recruiters of North Brunswick,
Inc.
Management Recruiters of Charlotte -
Southwest
Management Resource Assoc., Inc.
Management Search, Inc.
Management Search Int'l.
Karen Marshall Assoc.
Martin Personnel Assoc.
Richard L. Mather & Assoc.
McCulloch Assoc.
Earl L. McDermid & Assoc.
McDermott & Assoc.
McGladrey Search Group
McInturff & Assoc., Inc.
The McKee Co.
Medquest Assoc.
Todd Melon Group
Merrick & Moore
Montaigne Assoc., Inc.
The Montanye Group
Montgomery Resources, Inc.
The C. B. Mueller Co., Inc.
Multisearch Recruiters
John H. Munson & Co.
Murphy, Symonds & Stowell Search, Inc.
NPF Assoc. Ltd. Inc.
National Corporate Consultants, Inc.
J. Fielding Nelson & Assoc., Inc.
Newcombe & Cyr Assoc., Inc.
OSA Partners, Inc.
Kitty Ossow & Assoc.
PC Assoc.
Pacific Advisory Service
Patrick Assoc.
M.A. Pelle Assoc., Inc.
Performance Professionals
Personnel Advisors Int'l. Corp.
Personnel Inc.
Personnel Management, Inc.
The Personnel Network, Inc.
Petruzzi Assoc.
Phillips Resource Group
Placement Solutions
Polytechnical Consultants, Inc.
Precise Legal, Inc.
Prestige Search Inc.
Princeton Executive Search
ProSearch, Inc.

Probe Technology
Probus Executive Search
Professional Personnel Services
Professions Unlimited, Inc.
Protocol Inc.
RGL Assoc., Inc.
RHS Assoc., Inc.
RTE Search
Edward Rast & Co.
Resource Perspectives, Inc.
Roberson & Co.
The Robinson Group, D.A., Ltd.
Romano McAvoy Assoc., Inc.
Sanford Rose Assoc.
Sanford Rose Assoc. of Wilmington
Sanford Rose Assoc.- Detroit North
Sanford Rose Assoc. of Beachwood
Sanford Rose Assoc. - Virginia Beach
Roth Young Executive Recruiters
Roth Young Seattle
John P. Runden & Co., Inc.
The Charles Ryan Group, Inc.
Ryman, Bell, Green & Michaels, Inc.
Robert Sage Recruiting
Sales & Management Search, Inc.
Sales Consultants of Austin, Inc.
Sales Consultants
Sales Consultants
Sales Consultants of Rraleigh - Durham - RTP
Sales Consultants
Salesworld-Division of Metacor Inc.
Savalli & Assoc., Inc.
Schattle Personnel Consultants, Inc.
Schenck & Assoc. SC
Search Bureau Int'l.
The Search Center Inc.
Search Enterprises, Inc.
Search Masters
Search Masters Int'l.
Search Solutions, Inc.
Search West, Inc.
Marvin L. Silcott & Assoc., Inc.
L. A. Silver Assoc., Inc.
J. Harrington Smith Assoc.
Smith, Beaty, Barlow Assoc., Inc.
Snelling Personnel Services
St. James And DeDominic
Stewart Assoc.
Strategic Assoc., Inc.
The Talley Group
Tech International
Technical Engineering Consultants
Technical Recruiting Services
The Tibbetts Group Ltd.
Traynor Confidential, Ltd.
Triangle Consulting Group
J.Q. Turner & Assoc., Inc.
Key Employment
The Urban Placement Service
Valentine & Assoc.
Wallace Assoc.
Frank X. Walsh & Co., Inc.
Martha Ward Assoc., Inc.

D.00 MANUFACTURING (Cont'd)

Water Street Assoc.
Weatherby Healthcare
Weinpel & Co.
Werbin Assoc. Executive Search, Inc.
White-Ridgely & Assoc., Inc.
Whittlesey & Assoc., Inc.
Wing Tips & Pumps, Inc.
World Search
The Wright Group
Zackrison Assoc., Inc.

D.10 FOOD, BEVERAGE, TOBACCO & KINDRED PRODUCTS

ACR Assoc.
John R. Ady & Assoc., Inc.
Agri-Personnel
David Allen Assoc.
Alpine Consulting Group
The Altco Group
Analytic Recruiting, Inc.
BIK Search/Force II
Keith Bagg Personnel Ltd.
Carol Ball & Co., Inc.
The Barack Group, Inc.
Bast & Assoc., Inc.
L. Battalin & Co.
Brooks Executive Personnel
Career Consulting Group, Inc.
Clanton & Co.
Corporate Consultants Inc.
The Crawford Group
The DLR Group, Inc.
Dunhill of Southeast Fort Worth, Inc.
Dunhill Professional Search Inc.
Dunhill Professional Search
Dunhill Professional Search Group
Dussick Management Assoc.
Eden & Assoc., Inc.
Eggers Consulting Co., Inc.
Exec 2000
Paul Falcone Assoc., Inc.
David Fockler & Assoc., Inc.
Galen Giles Group
Genesis
Genesis Personnel Service, Inc.
Greene Personnel Consultants
Gregory Michaels & Assoc., Inc.
Guidarelli Assoc., Inc.
Hartman Personnel Services
Heritage Search Group, Inc.
Hill & Assoc.
Horizon Assoc.
Hospitality Executive Search, Inc.
Hospitality Int'l.
I.S. Consultants, Inc.
Impact Executive Search, Inc.
Industry Consultants, Inc.
Kathryn L. Johnson
E. G. Jones Assoc., Ltd.
J.M. Joseph Assoc.
Kelley & Keller, Inc.

The Kennett Group, Inc.
Joseph Keyes Assoc.
Kiley-Owen Assoc., Inc.
Lacrosse Assoc., Inc.
Lawrence-Balakonis & Assoc., Inc.
Lindsey & Assoc., Inc.
Logue & Rice Inc.
Mahony & Assoc., Ltd.
Management Recruiters of Cedar Rapids, Inc.
Management Recruiters of Greater Bridgeport, Inc.
Management Recruiters of Little Rock
Management Recruiters
Management Recruiters of Monterey
Management Recruiters of Westchester, Inc.
MarketSearch, Inc.
Marketing Recruiters, Inc.
Earl L. McDermid & Assoc.
Michael/Merrill
Multisearch Recruiters
John H. Munson & Co.
Jerome H. Nagel Assoc.
Newcombe & Cyr Assoc., Inc.
Orr Executive Search
Kitty Ossow & Assoc.
R. Parker & Assoc., Inc.
Preston Robert & Assoc.-Health Care Div.
Prestonwood Assoc.
Professional Recruiters
RTE Search
The Remington Group, Ltd.
Resource Perspectives, Inc.
Sanford Rose Assoc. - Virginia Beach
Roth Young of Tampa
Roth Young of Boston
Roth Young Seattle
Ryerson Tabor Assoc.
Sales Consultants of Westchester-South, Inc.
Sales Consultants of Ft. Lauderdale
Savalli & Assoc., Inc.
SilverCrest Search
Sloan & Assoc., Inc.
Smith, Beaty, Barlow Assoc., Inc.
Smith Hanley Assoc., Inc.
Ron Sunshine & Assoc.
Peter C. Tumminelli & Assoc.
The Urban Placement Service
Darryl Vincent & Assoc.
R.A. Wells Co.
Whittaker & Assoc., Inc.
Whittlesey & Assoc., Inc.
The Yaiser Group

D.11 TEXTILE, APPAREL, RELATED PRODUCTS

Ames Personnel Consultants
Jim Baum - Executive Search
Bell Professional Placement
Dotson Benefield & Assoc., Inc.
Jerold Braun & Assoc.
ExecuTech
Executive Careers

D.11 TEXTILE, APPAREL, RELATED PRODUCTS (Cont'd)

Ford & Assoc., Inc.
Greene Personnel Consultants
The Alice-Groves Co., Inc.
Heritage Search Group, Inc.
Jordon & Jordon, Inc.
Kelley & Keller, Inc.
Lee Management Group Inc.
Management Advisors Int'l., Inc.
Management Recruiters
MarketSearch, Inc.
Todd Melon Group
Nagel Executive Search Inc.
Newcombe & Cyr Assoc., Inc.
P R Management Consultants, Inc.
Phillips Resource Group
Professional Resources
Simpson Assoc.
Darryl Vincent & Assoc.
The Wright Group

D.12 LUMBER, WOOD, FURNITURE & FIXTURES

Charles P. Aquavella & Assoc.
Jim Baum - Executive Search
Brennan Assoc.
Brooke Chase Assoc., Inc.
Cap, Inc.
Ells Personnel Systems Inc.
Management Recruiters of Ft. Myers, FL.
Management Search, Inc.
Multisearch Recruiters
John H. Munson & Co.
Sanford Rose Assoc. of Binghamton
Sales Consultants of Westchester-South, Inc.
Search North America, Inc.
Search Northwest Assoc.
The Wright Group

D.13 PAPER & ALLIED PRODUCTS

Ames Personnel Consultants
Dotson Benefield & Assoc., Inc.
Broward-Dobbs, Inc.
Carlden Personnel Services Inc.
William J. Christopher Assoc., Inc.
Clanton & Co.
Cochran, Cochran, & Yale, Inc.
Corporate Personnel, Inc.
Corporate Recruiters, Inc.
Curts/Jackson, Inc.
Dunhill Professional Search Inc.
Eden & Assoc., Inc.
Evans & James Assoc., Inc.
Gallin Assoc.
Heritage Search Group, Inc.
Don Howard Personnel
Impact Executive Search, Inc.
Blair Kershaw Assoc., Inc.
Kirkbride Assoc., Inc.
Lange & Assoc., Inc.
Lawrence-Balakonis & Assoc., Inc.

The Lawson Group
Lunney, Hadden & Assoc.
Lyons & Assoc., Inc.
M H Executive Search Group
Magnum Search
Management Recruiters of Tampa North
Management Recruiters of Savannah
Management Recruiters
Management Recruiters
Management Recruiters
Management Recruiters of Atlanta Downtown
Management Search, Inc.
MarketSearch, Inc.
Merrick & Moore
Lou Michaels Assoc.
Moore Employment Svs., Inc.
William H. Nenstiel & Assoc.
Largent Parks & Partners, Inc.
Phase II Management
Phillips Resource Group
Professions, Inc.
Resource Perspectives, Inc.
Sanford Rose Assoc. of Hartford
S-H-S of Allentown
Sales Consultants of Savannah, GA.
Sales Consultants of Fayetteville, AR.
Samper Assoc.
Search North America, Inc.
Selective Management Services, Inc.
SilverCrest Search
Sloan & Assoc., Inc.
John R. Stephens & Assoc.
Ron Stevens & Assoc., Inc.
Telem Adhesive Search Corp.
Jay Tracey Assoc.
Darryl Vincent & Assoc.
Gordon Wahls Co.
Wayne Assoc., Inc.
Whittlesey & Assoc., Inc.
Windward Executive Search, Inc.
Zachary & Sanders, Inc.

D.14 PRINTING & ALLIED INDUSTRY

Balfour Assoc.
Clark-Winans, Inc.
Corporate Recruiters, Inc.
Ells Personnel Systems Inc.
Emerson & Co.
Evans & James Assoc., Inc.
Graphic Search Assoc. Inc.
Kutt, Inc.
Lunney, Hadden & Assoc.
Lyons & Assoc., Inc.
Midland Consultants
Moore Employment Svs., Inc.
William H. Nenstiel & Assoc.
Phase II Management
Posse, Inc.
Professional Recruiters
Sales Consultants of Savannah, GA.
Selective Management Services, Inc.

D.14 PRINTING & ALLIED INDUSTRY (Cont'd)

Telem Adhesive Search Corp.
Gordon Wahls Co.
Zachary & Sanders, Inc.

D.15 CHEMICALS & ALLIED PRODUCTS

Additional Technical Support Inc.
Adel Lawrence Assoc., Inc.
Agri-Personnel
Arancio Assoc.
Ashway Ltd. Agency
Keith Bagg Personnel Ltd.
D.W. Baird & Associates
Bedford-Orion Group, Inc.
Gary S. Bell Assoc., Inc.
Bell Professional Placement
Bennett-Munson Inc.
Biotech Sourcing
Bioventure Resources, Inc.
Brooks Executive Personnel
Broward-Dobbs, Inc.
C.P.S., Inc.
Circuit Search
Corporate Personnel, Inc.
Corporate Recruiters, Inc.
Crest Management Search, Inc.
Frank Cuomo & Assoc., Inc.
J. H. Dugan & Assoc., Inc.
Dunhill Professional Search
Dunhill of Southeast Fort Worth, Inc.
Dunhill of Denton, Inc.
Dunhill Professional Search Inc.
Dunhill Search of Omaha, Inc.
Dunhill Professional Search
W. Robert Eissler & Assoc., Inc.
The Energists
Engineering & Scientific Search Assoc.
Environmental Resources Int'l.
ExecuTech
Executive Dynamics, Inc.
F.L.A.G.
Jack Stuart Fisher Assoc.
Ford & Assoc., Inc.
Gallin Assoc.
Genesis
J. Gifford, Inc.
Heritage Search Group, Inc.
I.S. Consultants, Inc.
International Staffing Consultants, Inc.
Intertech Search Group
J.M. Joseph Assoc.
John J. Kennedy Assoc., Inc.
Kirkbride Assoc., Inc.
Kozlin Assoc., Inc.
Lacrosse Assoc., Inc.
Lancaster Assoc., Inc.
Larson Assoc.
W.R. Lawry, Inc.
Link Personnel & Assoc.
Loewenstein & Assoc.

Lybrook Assoc., Inc.
Management Advisors Int'l., Inc.
Management Recruiters of Savannah
Management Recruiters of Wilmington
Management Recruiters of Cincinnati/
  Sharonville, Inc.
Management Recruiters
Management Recruiters
Management Recruiters of Laguna Hills
Management Recruiters of Middlesex
Management Recruiters of Atlanta West, Inc.
Management Recruiters of Passaic, inc.
Management Resources
Mathey Services
Medical Executive Search Assoc.
Merrick & Moore
Midgette Consultants, Inc.
Midland Consultants
Charles P. Oliver Assoc., Inc.
PC Assoc.
PLRS/Career Connections
Robert A. Paul & Assoc.
Petruzzi Assoc.
Phillips Resource Group
RBR Assoc., Inc.
Remark Assoc. Inc.
The Reynolds Group, Inc.
Ropella & Assoc.
Sanford Rose Assoc. of Binghamton
Sanford Rose Assoc. - Great Neck
Sanford Rose Assoc. - Virginia Beach
S-H-S of Allentown
Sales Consultants
Sales Consultants - Bristol County
Sales Consultants of Fayetteville, AR.
The Search Center Inc.
Search Consultants Int'l., Inc.
Search Northwest Assoc.
Jules Seltzer Assoc.
John R. Stephens & Assoc.
Ron Stevens & Assoc., Inc.
Technical Recruiting Services
Telem Adhesive Search Corp.
Triangle Assoc.
U.S. Search
The Urban Placement Service
Wayne Assoc., Inc.
Wesson, Taylor, Wells & Assoc.
Whitaker, Fellows & Assoc.
Whittlesey & Assoc., Inc.
Wing Tips & Pumps, Inc.
John Wylie Assoc., Inc.
Xavier Assoc., Inc.
The Yaiser Group

D.16 SOAP, PERFUME, COSMETICS

A.M.C.R., Inc.
The Altco Group
BIK Search/Force II
The Barack Group, Inc.
Bast & Assoc., Inc.
Jim Baum - Executive Search

D.16 SOAP, PERFUME, COSMETICS (Cont'd)

Bioventure Resources, Inc.
Dunhill of Southeast Fort Worth, Inc.
Dussick Management Assoc.
Paul Falcone Assoc., Inc.
David Fockler & Assoc., Inc.
Guidarelli Assoc., Inc.
Heritage Search Group, Inc.
Industry Consultants, Inc.
Kelley & Keller, Inc.
Kiley-Owen Assoc., Inc.
Lawrence-Balakonis & Assoc., Inc.
Management Recruiters of Middlesex
Management Recruiters of Westchester, Inc.
MarketSearch, Inc.
Orr Executive Search
R. Parker & Assoc., Inc.
Patrick Assoc.
Preston Robert & Assoc.-Health Care Div.
Prestonwood Assoc.
Ryerson Tabor Assoc.
Sloan & Assoc., Inc.
Storfer & Assoc.
Triangle Assoc.
Darryl Vincent & Assoc.

D.17 DRUGS

Ace Resources
The Addison Consulting Group
Alexander Enterprises, Inc.
The Altco Group
Francis V. Anderson Assoc. Inc.
Atlantic West Int'l.
BIK Search/Force II
Besen Assoc. Inc.
Biotech Sourcing
Bioventure Resources, Inc.
Malcolm Cole & Assoc.
Corporate Recruiters Inc.
The DLR Group, Inc.
Dunhill Professional Search of Ramsey
Dunhill Search of Omaha, Inc.
Dunhill Professional Search
Dussick Management Assoc.
Eden & Assoc., Inc.
Paul Falcone Assoc., Inc.
David Fockler & Assoc., Inc.
Fortune Personnel Consultants
Donald P. Hayes Assoc., Inc.
Industry Consultants, Inc.
J.M. Eagle Partners
Krow Assoc., Inc.
Lancaster Assoc., Inc.
Lanzi & Assoc.
MRG Search & Placement
Management Recruiters of Middlesex
Management Recruiters of Wilmington
Management Recruiters of Westchester, Inc.
Marketing Resource
Medical Executive Search Assoc.
Midgette Consultants, Inc.

Moore Employment Svs., Inc.
Kitty Ossow & Assoc.
Sanford Rose Assoc.- Suburban Philadelphia
Search Masters Int'l.
Jules Seltzer Assoc.
Storfer & Assoc.
S. Tyler Sullivan & Assoc., Inc.
Winfield Assoc.
Xavier Assoc., Inc.

D.18 PHARMACEUTICALS, MEDICAL MANUFACTURERS

Abraham & London Ltd.
Ace Resources
The Addison Consulting Group
Adel Lawrence Assoc., Inc.
Alexander Enterprises, Inc.
David Allen Assoc.
The Altco Group
Analytic Recruiting, Inc.
Francis V. Anderson Assoc. Inc.
Arancio Assoc.
Ashway Ltd. Agency
Atlantic West Int'l.
Auden Assoc., Inc.
BIK Search/Force II
Keith Bagg Personnel Ltd.
D.W. Baird & Associates
The Barack Group, Inc.
Barone-O'Hara Assoc., Inc.
Bedford-Orion Group, Inc.
Bench Int'l. Search, Inc.
Besen Assoc. Inc.
Biotech Sourcing
Bioventure Resources, Inc.
Broward-Dobbs, Inc.
Bryant Research
Career Consulting Group, Inc.
Cochran, Cochran, & Yale, Inc.
Malcolm Cole & Assoc.
Corporate Recruiters Inc.
The DLR Group, Inc.
Deeco Int'l.
Dreier Consulting
J. H. Dugan & Assoc., Inc.
Dunhill of Freehold, Inc.
Dunhill of Southeast Fort Worth, Inc.
Dunhill Professional Search of Ramsey
Dunhill Search of Omaha, Inc.
Dunhill Professional Search
Dunhill Professional Search Group
Dunhill International Search
Dunhill Professional Search Irvine/Newport
Dussick Management Assoc.
Emerson & Co.
ExecuTech
Executive Exchange Corp.
Executive Referral Services, Inc.
Paul Falcone Assoc., Inc.
Jack Stuart Fisher Assoc.
James L. Fisk & Assoc.
Ford & Assoc., Inc.

D.18 PHARMACEUTICALS, MEDICAL MANUFACTURERS (Cont'd)

Fortune Personnel Consultants of Huntsville, Inc.
Fortune Personnel Consultants
Franklin Int'l. Search, Inc.
Mel Frazer & Assoc.
Gardner, Savage Assoc.
Genesis Personnel Service, Inc.
Graham Assoc. Inc.
Gregory Michaels & Assoc., Inc.
Hartman Personnel Services
Healthcare Resources Group
J. D. Hersey & Assoc.
Hill & Assoc.
Industry Consultants, Inc.
Intech Summit Group, Inc.
J.M. Eagle Partners
Jackley Search Consultants
J.M. Joseph Assoc.
Joslin & Assoc., Ltd.
The Kennett Group, Inc.
Joseph Keyes Assoc.
Kozlin Assoc., Inc.
Krow Assoc., Inc.
Lancaster Assoc., Inc.
Lange & Assoc., Inc.
Lanzi & Assoc.
Lappe & Assoc.
Lawrence-Balakonis & Assoc., Inc.
W.R. Lawry, Inc.
Lybrook Assoc., Inc.
Management Recruiters of Wilmington
Management Recruiters of Middlesex County NJ.
Management Recruiters
Management Recruiters of Laguna Hills
Management Recruiters of Passaic, inc.
Management Recruiters of Westchester, Inc.
Management Recruiters of Nassau, Inc.
Marcus & Assoc.
Marketing Recruiters, Inc.
Marketing Resource
Martin Personnel Assoc.
Maximum Management Corp.
Medical Executive Search Assoc.
Medical Sales & Management Specialists
Medquest Assoc.
Medtrac & Assoc.
Merlin Int'l. Inc.
Midgette Consultants, Inc.
Nachman Biomedical
Jerome H. Nagel Assoc.
Charles P. Oliver Assoc., Inc.
Kitty Ossow & Assoc.
Patrick Assoc.
Petruzzi Assoc.
Professional Placement Assoc., Inc.
Professions, Inc.
RGL Assoc., Inc.
Sanford Rose Assoc.- Suburban Philadelphia

Roth Young of Tampa
Ryerson Tabor Assoc.
Sales Consultants of Austin, Inc.
Sales Consultants of Madison
Sales Consultants of Fox Valley
Sales Consultants of Ft. Lauderdale
Search Masters Int'l.
Selective Management Services, Inc.
Jules Seltzer Assoc.
SilverCrest Search
Smith Hanley Assoc., Inc.
Phyllis Solomon Executive Search, Inc.
Storfer & Assoc.
S. Tyler Sullivan & Assoc., Inc.
Techcon Co.
Technical Engineering Consultants
Triangle Assoc.
Peter C. Tumminelli & Assoc.
The Urban Placement Service
Vento Assoc.
Video Interview Professionals, Inc.
Whittlesey & Assoc., Inc.
Winfield Assoc.
The Yaiser Group

D.19 PLASTICS, RUBBER PRODUCTS

A.M.C.R., Inc.
Aim Executive Inc.
Ames Personnel Consultants
D.W. Baird & Associates
Bast & Assoc., Inc.
Cap, Inc.
Andrew B. Carr & Assoc.
Case Executive Search
Circuit Search
Corporate Management Services Inc.
Corporate Resources Professional Placement
Crest Management Search, Inc.
J. H. Dugan & Assoc., Inc.
Dunhill Professional Search
Dunhill of Denton, Inc.
Dunhill Professional Search
W. Robert Eissler & Assoc., Inc.
Engineering & Scientific Search Assoc.
Evans & James Assoc., Inc.
ExecuTech
Ford & Assoc., Inc.
Galen Giles Group
Gallin Assoc.
Genesis Personnel Service, Inc.
Hartman Personnel Services
Don Howard Personnel
Intertech Search Group
Jackley Search Consultants
J.M. Joseph Assoc.
John J. Kennedy Assoc., Inc.
Kromenaker & Associates
Lange & Assoc., Inc.
W.R. Lawry, Inc.
Link Personnel & Assoc.
Lybrook Assoc., Inc.

D.19 PLASTICS, RUBBER PRODUCTS (Cont'd)

M H Executive Search Group
mfg/Search, Inc.
Management Recruiters of Savannah
Management Recruiters of Cedar Rapids, Inc.
Management Recruiters of Cincinnati/
  Sharonville, Inc.
Management Recruiters
Management Recruiters of Middlesex
Management Recruiters of Reno
Mathey Services
Lou Michaels Assoc.
Midgette Consultants, Inc.
Midland Consultants
Multisearch Recruiters
Nachman Biomedical
National Recruiting Service
P R Management Consultants, Inc.
Plastics Enterprises
Polytechnical Consultants, Inc.
Professional Recruiters
The Remington Group, Ltd.
Sanford Rose Assoc. of Lima
Sales Consultants
Sales Consultants - Bristol County
Schattle Personnel Consultants, Inc.
Search Group
Sharrow & Assoc., Inc.
SilverCrest Search
Ron Stevens & Assoc., Inc.
Technical Recruiting Services
Jay Tracey Assoc.
Triangle Assoc.
U.S. Search
R.A. Wells Co.
Whitaker, Fellows & Assoc.
John Wylie Assoc., Inc.
The Yaiser Group

D.20 PAINTS, ALLIED PRODUCTS, PETROLEUM PRODUCTS

APA Search, Inc.
Bennett-Munson Inc.
Brooke Chase Assoc., Inc.
Cap, Inc.
J. H. Dugan & Assoc., Inc.
Dunhill Professional Search
The Energists
Engineering & Scientific Search Assoc.
Environmental Resources Int'l.
F.L.A.G.
Gallin Assoc.
Genesis
J. Gifford, Inc.
International Staffing Consultants, Inc.
Loewenstein & Assoc.
Lunney, Hadden & Assoc.
Management Recruiters of Wilmington
Management Resources
RBR Assoc., Inc.
Rockwood Assoc.

Sales Consultants
Sales Consultants - Bristol County
The Search Center Inc.
Telem Adhesive Search Corp.
Triangle Assoc.
Weiss & Assoc., Inc.
John Wylie Assoc., Inc.

D.21 LEATHER, STONE, GLASS, CONCRETE, CLAY PRODUCTS

Keith Bagg Personnel Ltd.
Corporate Consultants Inc.
Management Recruiters of Atlanta Downtown
R. Parker & Assoc., Inc.
Pro Counsel
S-H-S of Allentown
STM Assoc.

D.22 PRIMARY METAL INDUSTRY, FABRICATED METAL PRODUCTS, MACHINERY, GENERAL

APA Search, Inc.
ARJay & Assoc.
John R. Ady & Assoc., Inc.
Auden Assoc., Inc.
Gregory L. Borchert, Inc.
Brennan Assoc.
Robert L. Charon
Circuit Search
Corporate Consultants Inc.
Corporate Management Services Inc.
Cowin Assoc.
DEI Executive Services
Dunhill Personnel of Milwaukee
Dunhill of Greater Akron, Inc.
Dunhill Professional Search Irvine/Newport
W. Robert Eissler & Assoc., Inc.
Emerson & Co.
Engineering Resource Group, Inc.
Executive Recruiters, Inc.
Fortune Personnel Consultants of Huntsville,
  Inc.
Galen Giles Group
Harrison Moore Inc.
Hartman Personnel Services
Robert Hess & Assoc., Inc.
Hoskins, Rees & Smith
I.S. Consultants, Inc.
A.H. Justice & Assoc.
K & C Assoc.
Blair Kershaw Assoc., Inc.
Joseph Keyes Assoc.
Kozlin Assoc., Inc.
Kromenaker & Associates
Lacrosse Assoc., Inc.
Lange & Assoc., Inc.
mfg/Search, Inc.
Magnum Search
Management Recruiters of Cedar Rapids, Inc.
Management Recruiters
Management Recruiters
Management Recruiters of Kinston

D.22 PRIMARY METAL INDUSTRY, FABRICATED METAL PRODUCTS, MACHINERY, GENERAL (Cont'd)

Management Recruiters
Management Recruiters of Waterbury, Inc.
Management Recruiters of Atlanta Downtown
Management Recruiters of Topeka, Inc.
Management Search, Inc.
Marketing Recruiters, Inc.
Martin Personnel Assoc.
Lou Michaels Assoc.
B. Paul Mickey & Assoc.
Midgette Consultants, Inc.
Midland Consultants
Jerome H. Nagel Assoc.
National Executive Consultants, Inc.
National Recruiting Service
P&IC Assoc.
Paul S. Pelland
Pro Counsel
Professional Recruiters
Professions, Inc.
Raymond Thomas & Assoc.
The Resource Group
Sanford Rose Assoc. of Lima
Sanford Rose Assoc. - Great Neck
Sanford Rose Assoc. - Virginia Beach
Rothrock Assoc.
S-H-S of Allentown
Sales & Management Search, Inc.
Sales Consultants of Fayetteville, AR.
Search Northwest Assoc.
Charles Stickler Assoc.
The Stoddard Co.
Ron Sunshine & Assoc.
Techcon Co.
Technical Recruiting Services
Technitrac, Inc.
Weeks & Assoc.
Henry Welker & Assoc.
R.A. Wells Co.
Jim Woodson & Assoc., Inc.
World Search
John Wylie Assoc., Inc.

D.23 TRANSPORTATION EQUIPMENT INCLUDING AUTOMOBILES & OTHER MOTOR VEHICLES

Aim Executive Inc.
Charles P. Aquavella & Assoc.
Gregory L. Borchert, Inc.
Case Executive Search
Robert L. Charon
Clark Assoc., Inc.
Engineering Resource Group, Inc.
Fortune Personnel Consultants of Huntsville, Inc.
Heller Kil Assoc., Inc.
Hunter Assoc.
A.H. Justice & Assoc.

mfg/Search, Inc.
Magnum Search
Management Recruiters of Kinston
Management Recruiters of Little Rock
Management Recruiters of North Oakland County, Inc.
Marketing Recruiters, Inc.
Lou Michaels Assoc.
Norton & Assoc.
P&IC Assoc.
Paul S. Pelland
Sanford Rose Assoc. of Lima
Sanford Rose Assoc. - Virginia Beach
Rothrock Assoc.
Robert Sage Recruiting
Stephen Sellers Assoc.
Sharrow & Assoc., Inc.
Summit Executive Search Consultants, Inc.
Ron Sunshine & Assoc.
Technical Engineering Consultants
Weeks & Assoc.
Henry Welker & Assoc.
Jim Woodson & Assoc., Inc.

D.24 OFFICE MACHINERY, COMPUTERS, COMPUTER PRODUCTS, SOFTWARE, ELECTRONIC &

ARJay & Assoc.
Arthur Adams & Assoc.
Adel Lawrence Assoc., Inc.
Alexander Edward Assoc., Inc.
Anderson, Graham & Stewart, Inc.
Barclay Consultants, Inc.
C.W. Brandon & Assoc., Inc.
Ira Broadman Assoc.
CDH & Assoc., Inc.
CN Associates
CPI Technical Services
H.O. Catherman Inc.
Wayne S. Chamberlain & Assoc.
William J. Christopher Assoc., Inc.
J.F. Church Assoc., Inc.
Circuit Search
Cochran, Cochran, & Yale, Inc.
Commonwealth Consultants
Corporate Personnel, Inc.
DEI Executive Services
The DataFinders Group, Inc.
Deery Geddis & Assoc.
Delta Resource Group, Ltd.
Diversified Placement Int'l., Inc.
Dreier Consulting
Dunhill of Greater Akron, Inc.
Dunhill Personnel Search
Dunhill Professional Search of Ramsey
Emerson & Co.
Engineering Resource Group, Inc.
Engineering Search Assoc.
ExecuSource Int'l.
Executive Recruiters, Inc.
G.A. Field Personnel Consultants

D.24 OFFICE MACHINERY, COMPUTERS, COMPUTER PRODUCTS, SOFTWARE, ELECTRONIC & (Cont'd)

First Search Inc.
A.G. Fishkin & Assoc., Inc.
Fortune Personnel Consultants of Huntsville, Inc.
Forum Assoc.
Global Data Services, Inc.
Gold Coast Partners
The Goodman Group
High-Tech Recruiters
Hunter Assoc.
J.M. Eagle Partners
Jackley Search Consultants
J. Johnston Group, Inc.
Kelley & Keller, Inc.
The Kennett Group, Inc.
Kiley-Owen Assoc., Inc.
Kreofsky & Assoc.
Kurtz Pro-Search, Inc.
Lacrosse Assoc., Inc.
Larson Assoc.
Brian Leggee & Assoc.
The Lighthouse Group
The James Lloyd Group
Loewenstein & Assoc.
mfg/Search, Inc.
Magnum Search
Management Recruiters of Savannah
Management Recruiters of Kinston
Management Recruiters
Management Recruiters of Poughkeepsie, Inc.
Management Search, Inc.
Maximum Management Corp.
McCulloch Assoc.
Sandi McDonald & Assoc., Inc.
R. H. McIlwaine & Assoc.
Mogul Consultants, Inc.
Multi Processing, Inc.
Jerome H. Nagel Assoc.
Charles P. Oliver Assoc., Inc.
P&IC Assoc.
Pacific Search Consultants
Patrick Assoc.
Polytechnical Consultants, Inc.
Norman Powers Assoc., Inc.
Prestonwood Assoc.
Probus Executive Search
Professional Recruiters
RAC International
R.A.N. Assoc., Inc.
The Resource Group
The Reynolds Group, Inc.
Sanford Rose Assoc. of Lima
Sanford Rose Assoc. of Binghamton
Sanford Rose Assoc. of Quakertown
Ross Personnel Consultants, Inc.
Rothrock Assoc.
Louis Rudzinsky Assoc., Inc.
Sales Consultants of Madison

Sales Consultants of Andover
Sales Consultants of Ft. Myers, Inc.
Samper Assoc.
George D. Sandel Assoc.
Saxon Morse Assoc.
Stephen Sellers Assoc.
RitaSue Siegel Assoc., Inc.
Spectra West
Stanewick, Hart & Assoc., Inc.
Strategic Search Group
Tech Consulting
Techcon Co.
Tecmark Assoc. Inc.
Jay Tracey Assoc.
Vento Assoc.
Vick & Assoc.
C. J. Vincent Assoc., Inc.
Western Search Assoc.
Jim Woodson & Assoc., Inc.
Xavier Assoc., Inc.

D.25 MEASURING/ANALYZING & CONTROLLING INSTRUMENTS & OPTICAL GOODS

Aberdeen Assoc.
Adel Lawrence Assoc., Inc.
Anderson, Graham & Stewart, Inc.
Arancio Assoc.
CDH & Assoc., Inc.
CPI Technical Services
Andrew B. Carr & Assoc.
The Chapman Group, Inc.
Frank Cuomo & Assoc., Inc.
Dreier Consulting
Dunhill of Greater Akron, Inc.
W. Robert Eissler & Assoc., Inc.
Franklin Int'l. Search, Inc.
Gallagher & Assoc.
Donald P. Hayes Assoc., Inc.
Kromenaker & Associates
Loewenstein & Assoc.
Management Recruiters of Waterbury, Inc.
Marketing Resource
Martin Personnel Assoc.
Medquest Assoc.
Nachman Biomedical
Jerome H. Nagel Assoc.
Norton & Assoc.
P R Management Consultants, Inc.
P&IC Assoc.
Paules Associates
Professional Recruiters Inc.
RALCO/Richard A. Lucia & Assoc.
Remark Assoc. Inc.
Sanford Rose Assoc. of Hartford
Sanford Rose Assoc.- Suburban Philadelphia
Louis Rudzinsky Assoc., Inc.
Sales Consultants of Newtown
George D. Sandel Assoc.
Stephen Sellers Assoc.
S. Tyler Sullivan & Assoc., Inc.
Tech Consulting

D.25 MEASURING/ANALYZING & CONTROLLING INSTRUMENTS & OPTICAL GOODS (Cont'd)

Techcon Co.
Technitrac, Inc.
Tecmark Assoc. Inc.
Vento Assoc.
Henry Welker & Assoc.
Jim Woodson & Assoc., Inc.

D.26 MISCELLANEOUS MANUFACTURING INDUSTRIES

Charles P. Aquavella & Assoc.
Arancio Assoc.
Auden Assoc., Inc.
Charles Bradley Professionals
Brennan Assoc.
Clark Assoc., Inc.
Corporate Personnel, Inc.
Cowin Assoc.
Dunhill of Freehold, Inc.
Engineering Search Assoc.
Gregory Michaels & Assoc., Inc.
Don Howard Personnel
A.H. Justice & Assoc.
Blair Kershaw Assoc., Inc.
Kromenaker & Associates
Lacrosse Assoc., Inc.
Lancaster Assoc., Inc.
Reynolds Lebus Assoc.
Management Recruiters
Management Recruiters of Monterey
MarketSearch, Inc.
Lou Michaels Assoc.
Raymond Thomas & Assoc.
Sanford Rose Assoc. of Lima
Sales Consultants
Summit Executive Search Consultants, Inc.
Ron Sunshine & Assoc.
Henry Welker & Assoc.
Wesson, Taylor, Wells & Assoc.
Western Search Assoc.

D.D0 PACKAGING

A.M.C.R., Inc.
Agri-Tech Personnel, Inc.
The Altco Group
Tryg R. Angell Ltd.
BGB Assoc., Inc.
Gary S. Bell Assoc., Inc.
Blanton & Co.
Brooke Chase Assoc., Inc.
C.P.S., Inc.
Career Profiles
William J. Christopher Assoc., Inc.
Clanton & Co.
Corporate Consultants Inc.
Corporate Recruiters, Inc.
Crest Management Search, Inc.
Cross Country Consultants, Inc.
N. Dean Davic Assoc., Inc.
J. H. Dugan & Assoc., Inc.

Dunhill Professional Search
Evans & James Assoc., Inc.
Fergason Assoc., Inc.
Galen Giles Group
J. D. Hersey & Assoc.
Don Howard Personnel
Impact Executive Search, Inc.
Industrial Recruiters Assoc., Inc.
Kathryn L. Johnson
The Lawson Group
Brian Leggee & Assoc.
Locus Inc.
Lord & Albus Co.
Lunney, Hadden & Assoc.
Lyons & Assoc., Inc.
M H Executive Search Group
Management Recruiters of Tampa North
Management Recruiters of Cincinnati/
  Sharonville, Inc.
Management Recruiters of Reno
Donovan Martin & Assoc.
Mathey Services
Merrick & Moore
The C. B. Mueller Co., Inc.
John H. Munson & Co.
William H. Nenstiel & Assoc.
Newcombe & Cyr Assoc., Inc.
Petruzzi Assoc.
Phase II Management
Placement Solutions
Plastics Enterprises
Professional Personnel Services
RTE Search
Resource Perspectives, Inc.
Sanford Rose Assoc. of Hartford
Roth Young of Boston
Roth Young Executive Recruiters
The Charles Ryan Group, Inc.
Sales Consultants of Madison
Sales Consultants of Raleigh - Durham - RTP
Sales Consultants of Morris County, Inc.
Sales Consultants of Savannah, GA.
Sales Consultants
Salesworld-Division of Metacor Inc.
Schenck & Assoc. SC
Search Enterprises, Inc.
Search Masters
Selective Management Services, Inc.
RitaSue Siegel Assoc., Inc.
SilverCrest Search
Stewart Assoc.
Storfer & Assoc.
Strategic Assoc., Inc.
The Tibbetts Group Ltd.
U.S. Search
Valentine & Assoc.
Gordon Wahls Co.
Wallace Assoc.
R.A. Wells Co.
Whittaker & Assoc., Inc.
The Yaiser Group
Zachary & Sanders, Inc.

D.H0 HIGH TECH/ELECTRONICS (Cont'd)

J.F. Church Assoc., Inc.
Cochran, Cochran, & Yale, Inc.
Competitive Resources, Inc.
Computer Network Resources
Corporate Careers Inc.
Corporate Resources Professional Placement
Cowin Assoc.
Cross Country Consultants, Inc.
Timothy D. Crowe, Jr.
DEI Executive Services
The DataFinders Group, Inc.
Davis & James, Inc.
Delta Personnel Services
Diversified Placement Int'l., Inc.
L.J. Doherty & Assoc.
Dreier Consulting
Dunhill Professional Search of Wilkes-Barre/Scranton, Inc.
Dunhill International Search
Dunhill Professional Search
Eastern Executive Assoc.
Eckert, Enghauser and Partners, Inc.
Engineering Resource Group, Inc.
Exec 2000
ExecuSource Int'l.
Executive Recruiters, Inc.
eXsource
N. Steven Fells & Co., Inc.
Fergason Assoc., Inc.
Fernow Assoc.
First Search Inc.
A.G. Fishkin & Assoc., Inc.
Fortune Personnel Consultants of Huntsville, Inc.
Fortune Personnel Consultants of Sarasota Inc.
Forum Assoc.
Franklin Int'l. Search, Inc.
Mel Frazer & Assoc.
GHK Technical Recruiter
Gallagher & Assoc.
Alan Glenn & Keener
Global Data Services, Inc.
Gray-Kimball Assoc., Inc.
J. Gross & Assoc.
Hall, Cooper & Bartman, Ltd.
Donald P. Hayes Assoc., Inc.
Health Technology, Inc.
High Tech Opportunities, Inc.
High-Tech Recruiters
Hill Allyn Assoc.
The Hudson Group
Human Resource Network
Hunter Assoc.
I.S. Consultants, Inc.
Industrial Recruiters Assoc., Inc.
JDG Assoc., Ltd.
J.M. Eagle Partners
Jackley Search Consultants
R.I. James, Inc.
K.E. Johnson Assoc.

Kacevich, Lewis & Brown, Inc.
Kendall & Davis Co., Inc.
John J. Kennedy Assoc., Inc.
Key Talent, Inc.
Joseph Keyes Assoc.
Kossuth & Assoc., Inc.
Kurtz Pro-Search, Inc.
Lappe & Assoc.
Jack B. Larsen & Assoc.
Larson Assoc.
W.R. Lawry, Inc.
Brian Leggee & Assoc.
The James Lloyd Group
Locus Inc.
Logix, Inc.
Lord & Albus Co.
Ludot Personnel Services, Inc.
MARBL Consultants, Inc.
MJF Assoc.
MPI Assoc.
Tom Mahon & Assoc.
Management Assoc.
Management Recruiters of Gramercy, Inc.
Management Recruiters
Management Recruiters of Waterbury, Inc.
Management Recruiters of Reno
Management Recruiters of Westchester, Inc.
Management Resource Assoc., Inc.
Management Search, Inc.
Marcus & Assoc.
Donovan Martin & Assoc.
Richard L. Mather & Assoc.
McCulloch Assoc.
Sandi McDonald & Assoc., Inc.
McInturff & Assoc., Inc.
The McKee Co.
Medquest Assoc.
Midland Consultants
The Montanye Group
Multi Processing, Inc.
John H. Munson & Co.
National Corporate Consultants, Inc.
J. Fielding Nelson & Assoc., Inc.
New Dimensions in Technology, Inc.
Northeastern Search, Inc.
Norton & Assoc.
OSA Partners, Inc.
Charles P. Oliver Assoc., Inc.
PC Assoc.
PLRS/Career Connections
P.R.H. Management, Inc.
Parker Page Group
Carolyn Smith Paschal Int'l.
Patrick Assoc.
Paul-Tittle Assoc., Inc.
Paules Associates
M.A. Pelle Assoc., Inc.
Personnel Inc.
Phillips Personnel/Search
Polytechnical Consultants, Inc.
Prestonwood Assoc.
Probe Technology
Probus Executive Search

D.H0 HIGH TECH/ELECTRONICS (Cont'd)

Professional Personnel Services
Professional Recruiters Inc.
Professional Search Assoc., Inc.
RAC International
R.A.N. Assoc., Inc.
RGL Assoc., Inc.
Edward Rast & Co.
Remark Assoc. Inc.
Ritta Professional Search Inc.
Roberson & Co.
Romano McAvoy Assoc., Inc.
Emery A. Rose & Assoc.
Sanford Rose Assoc.
Sanford Rose Assoc.- Detroit North
Sanford Rose Assoc. of Quakertown
Ross Personnel Consultants, Inc.
Rothrock Assoc.
Rushlow & Co.
Russell Assoc.
The Charles Ryan Group, Inc.
Sales & Management Search, Inc.
Sales Consultants - Bristol County
Sales Consultants
Salesworld-Division of Metacor Inc.
George D. Sandel Assoc.
Saxon Morse Assoc.
Search Consultants Int'l., Inc.
Search Group
Search Northwest Assoc.
Search West, Inc.
Stephen Sellers Assoc.
Shannahan & Co., Inc.
L. A. Silver Assoc., Inc.
The Simmons Group
Spectra West
Spectrum Consultants
Steinbach & Co.
Stewart Assoc.
Strategic Assoc., Inc.
Systems Careers
M. L. Tawney & Assoc.
Tech Consulting
Tech International
Techcon Co.
Technical Engineering Consultants
Technical Recruiting Services
Tecmark Assoc. Inc.
TeleSearch, Inc.
Traynor Confidential, Ltd.
Triangle Consulting Group
J.Q. Turner & Assoc., Inc.
Vento Assoc.
Vezan Assoc.
Vick & Assoc.
Wallace Assoc.
Frank X. Walsh & Co., Inc.
Weatherby Healthcare
Weinpel & Co.
Henry Welker & Assoc.
R.A. Wells Co.

Wesson, Taylor, Wells & Assoc.
Wing Tips & Pumps, Inc.
Zeiger Technical Careers, Inc.
W.F. Richer Assoc., Inc.

D.I0 BIOTECH/GENETIC ENGINEERING

Abraham & London Ltd.
Accounting Resources Int'l., Inc.
The Addison Consulting Group
Advancement Recruiting Services
Agra Placements, Ltd.
Agri-Personnel
Agri-Tech Personnel, Inc.
Alexander Enterprises, Inc.
Allen Barry Assoc.
Francis V. Anderson Assoc. Inc.
John Anthony & Assoc.
Arancio Assoc.
Ashway Ltd. Agency
Atlantic West Int'l.
Automation Technology Search
Barone-O'Hara Assoc., Inc.
Gary S. Bell Assoc., Inc.
Bench Int'l. Search, Inc.
Besen Assoc. Inc.
Biotech Sourcing
Bioventure Resources, Inc.
Blanton & Co.
Bornholdt Shivas & Friends
Bryant Research
Paul J. Burns
Capitol Management Consulting, Inc.
Caremarc & Assoc.
Cassie & Assoc.
Malcolm Cole & Assoc.
Corporate Recruiters Inc.
Corporate Resources Professional Placement
Timothy D. Crowe, Jr.
The DLR Group, Inc.
Delta Personnel Services
Drake & Assoc.
Dunhill Personnel of Milwaukee
Environmental Professional Assoc.
Jack Stuart Fisher Assoc.
Fisher-Todd Assoc.
Fortune Personnel Consultants of Sarasota Inc.
Fortune Personnel Consultants
Mel Frazer & Assoc.
GHK Technical Recruiter
Gardner, Savage Assoc.
Graham Assoc. Inc.
Health Technology, Inc.
High Technology Search Assoc.
Horizon Assoc.
The Hudson Group
I.S. Consultants, Inc.
ISOPS Personnel Services, Inc.
J.M. Eagle Partners
Jackley Search Consultants
K.E. Johnson Assoc.
John J. Kennedy Assoc., Inc.

D.l0 BIOTECH/GENETIC ENGINEERING (Cont'd)

Kensington Int'l.
Krow Assoc., Inc.
W.R. Lawry, Inc.
Lord & Albus Co.
Management Assoc.
Management Recruiters of Laguna Hills
Management Recruiters of Cedar Rapids, Inc.
Management Recruiters
Management Recruiters of Greater Bridgeport, Inc.
Management Recruiters Peninsula
Management Recruiters of Passaic, inc.
Marcus & Assoc.
Marketing Resource
Donovan Martin & Assoc.
McDermott & Assoc.
Medical Executive Search Assoc.
Medical Sales & Management Specialists
Medquest Assoc.
Medtrac & Assoc.
Diedre Moire Corp., Inc.
Nachman Biomedical
Newcombe & Cyr Assoc., Inc.
Northeastern Search, Inc.
OSA Partners, Inc.
Paules Associates
Personnel Systems Int'l. Inc.
Petruzzi Assoc.
Place Mart Personnel Service
Polytechnical Consultants, Inc.
Preston Robert & Assoc.-Health Care Div.
ProSearch, Inc.
Probe Technology
RAC International
Edward Rast & Co.
Resource Perspectives, Inc.
Sanford Rose Assoc. of Beachwood
Sanford Rose Assoc.- Suburban Philadelphia
Russell Assoc.
Search Enterprises, Inc.
Search Masters
Jules Seltzer Assoc.
Marvin L. Silcott & Assoc., Inc.
Sloan & Assoc., Inc.
Spectrum Consultants
Strategic Assoc., Inc.
Tech International
Technitrac, Inc.
J.Q. Turner & Assoc., Inc.
Unisearch
Vento Assoc.
Video Interview Professionals, Inc.
Wallace Assoc.
Winfield Assoc.

E.00 TRANSPORTATION

APA Search, Inc.
John R. Ady & Assoc., Inc.
Aerospace Technologies, Inc.
Agri-Tech Personnel, Inc.

Aim Executive Inc.
AviSearch Int'l.
BGB Assoc., Inc.
Dotson Benefield & Assoc., Inc.
Brown/Bernardy, Inc.
Career Search Assoc.
Case Executive Search
Competitive Resources, Inc.
Robert Drexler Assoc., Inc.
Fox-Morris Assoc., Inc.
Gabriel & Bowie Assoc., Ltd.
Handwerk & Assoc.
Heller Kil Assoc., Inc.
Hunt Ltd.
R.I. James, Inc.
Kogon Assoc., Inc.
Lineal Recruiting Services
Lowery, Cotter, & Assoc.
McInturff & Assoc., Inc.
Oldwick Enterprises, Inc.
Philip Daniels Assoc., Inc.
Professions Unlimited, Inc.
Reinecke & Assoc.
Rockwood Assoc.
Sanford Rose Assoc. of Beachwood
Schreuder Randall Corp.
J. Harrington Smith Assoc.
Snelling Personnel Services
Stewart Assoc.
Strategic Assoc., Inc.
Technical Staffing Assoc.
The Tibbetts Group Ltd.
Travel Executive Search
Valentine & Assoc.

F.00 WHOLESALE TRADE

Agra Placements, Ltd.
R. Gaines Baty Assoc., Inc.
Jim Baum - Executive Search
Jerold Braun & Assoc.
Career Search Assoc.
Allen Case & Assoc., Inc.
Eden & Assoc., Inc.
Fergason Assoc., Inc.
Flores & Assoc.
Michael Garbi Assoc., Inc.
R.I. James, Inc.
Kathryn L. Johnson
K & C Assoc.
Management Recruiters
Management Recruiters of Little Rock
Management Recruiters Peninsula
Prestige Search Inc.
Professions Unlimited, Inc.
RHS Assoc., Inc.
Harold L. Rapp Assoc.
Roth Young of Boston
Roth Young Seattle
Robert Sage Recruiting
Sales Consultants
Search Solutions, Inc.
Simpson Assoc.

H.00 FINANCE (Cont'd)

Greene & Co.
High-Tech Recruiters
Hill Allyn Assoc.
Hintz Associates
Hudson Assoc. Inc.
Human Resource Network
JNB Assoc., Inc.
JT Assoc.
The Johnson Group, Inc.
Sanford Kleiner Assoc., Inc.
Kling Personnel Assoc., Inc.
E.J. Lance Management Assoc., Inc.
Jack B. Larsen & Assoc.
Vincent Lee Assoc.
Paul Ligon Co.
Logue & Rice Inc.
Lowery, Cotter, & Assoc.
Ludot Personnel Services, Inc.
Tom Mahon & Assoc.
Management Recruiters of Gramercy, Inc.
Management Recruiters
Management Recruiters
Management Recruiters of Berkeley
Management Recruiters of Nassau, Inc.
Management Resource Assoc., Inc.
Mariaschin & Co.
K. Maxin & Assoc.
McCracken, Wilcox, Bertoux & Miller
McDermott & Assoc.
McGladrey Search Group
John McLellan Assoc., Inc.
Montaigne Assoc., Inc.
Montgomery Resources, Inc.
The C. B. Mueller Co., Inc.
J. Fielding Nelson & Assoc., Inc.
OSA Partners, Inc.
Oldwick Enterprises, Inc.
Jim Oravetz & Assoc., Inc.
Pacific Advisory Service
M.A. Pelle Assoc., Inc.
Personnel Inc.
The Placers, Inc.
Princeton Executive Search
Professional Team Search
Professions Unlimited, Inc.
Protocol Inc.
RHS Assoc., Inc.
The Robinson Group, D.A., Ltd.
Romac & Assoc.
Romac & Assoc. of Dallas
Romano McAvoy Assoc., Inc.
Robert Sage Recruiting
Sales Consultants
Scan Management Inc.
Schattle Personnel Consultants, Inc.
Scott Kappele & Gnodde
Search West, Inc.
Shannahan & Co., Inc.
Marvin L. Silcott & Assoc., Inc.
L. A. Silver Assoc., Inc.
Smith, Anderson & Co.

Smith Bradley & Assoc.
Phyllis Solomon Executive Search, Inc.
Stephen M. Sonis Assoc.
Specialty Consultants, Inc.
Steeple Associates, Inc.
Straight & Co.
Sturm, Burrows & Co.
The Talley Group
M. L. Tawney & Assoc.
Techno-Trac Systems, Inc.
Techsearch Services Inc.
Traynor Confidential, Ltd.
Unisearch
Frank X. Walsh & Co., Inc.
Martha Ward Assoc., Inc.
Water Street Assoc.
Wells, Bradley & Assoc.
Werbin Assoc. Executive Search, Inc.
White-Ridgely & Assoc., Inc.
Williams, Adley & Co.
Wing Tips & Pumps, Inc.
Nola Worley & Assoc., Inc.

H.10 BANKING, FINANCIAL INSTITUTIONS, CREDIT AGENCIES

A.L.S. Group
David Allen Assoc.
Ames Assoc. Inc.
E. J. Ashton & Assoc., Ltd.
The Bankers Group
The Bankers Register
Dotson Benefield & Assoc., Inc.
Brandjes Assoc.
Broad Waverly & Assoc.
CAS Comsearch Inc.
CES
C.R. Assoc.
The Carlyle Group, Ltd.
Allen Case & Assoc., Inc.
The Christopher Group
John M. Clarke & Assoc.
Computer Security Placement Service, Inc.
Cona Personnel Search
Conaway Legal Search
The Consortium
Corporate Advisors Inc.
Cosco Resources Inc.
Crickenberger Assoc.
Crispi, Wagner & Co., Inc.
DLB Assoc.
Datamax Services Inc.
David - Kris Assoc., Inc.
J P Donnelly Assoc., Inc.
Drummond Assoc., Inc.
Dunhill Personnel of Northeast Tulsa, Inc.
Dunhill Professional Search Inc.
Dunhill of Manchester Inc.
Dunhill Search of Omaha, Inc.
Dunhill Professional Search of Hawaii
Mark Elzweig Co. Ltd.
Executive Dynamics, Inc.
Executive Exchange Corp.

H.10 BANKING, FINANCIAL INSTITUTIONS, CREDIT AGENCIES (Cont'd)

eXsource
Federal Placement Services
Financial Resource Assoc., Inc.
Financial Search Group, Inc.
Flynn, Hannock, Inc.
Foster Assoc.
W.T. Glover & Assoc., Inc.
Greene & Co.
HLR Consulting
The Hart Group
Hedlund Corp.
Higbee Assoc., Inc.
Impact Executive Search, Inc.
Individual Employment Services
Integrated Management Solutions
JNB Assoc., Inc.
Jacobson Assoc.
John-David Assoc., Inc.
Kershner & Co.
Michael King Assoc., Inc.
Kiradjieff & Co.
Sanford Kleiner Assoc., Inc.
Lam Assoc.
E.J. Lance Management Assoc., Inc.
Paul Ligon Co.
M-A Management Assoc., Inc.
MRG Search & Placement
Tom Mahon & Assoc.
Management Advisors Int'l., Inc.
Management Recruiters of Kinston
Management Recruiters of Redding
Management Recruiters of Berkeley
Management Recruiters of Ft. Myers, FL.
Management Recruiters of Monterey
Management Recruiters of Topeka, Inc.
Management Recruiters of North Oakland
  County, Inc.
Management Resource Group, Inc.
Mariaschin & Co.
John McLellan Assoc., Inc.
Olaf S. Meyer & Co., Ltd.
Mogul Consultants, Inc.
Montaigne Assoc., Inc.
Mortgage & Financial Personnel Services
Ronald Norris & Assoc.
Parker Page Group
Largent Parks & Partners, Inc.
The Paxton Group, Ltd.
Personnel Systems Int'l. Inc.
Robert E. Pfaendler & Assoc., Inc.
Philip Daniels Assoc., Inc.
Phillips Personnel/Search
The Primary Group, Inc.
Professional Recruiters Inc.
Professional Team Search
The Remington Group, Ltd.
Repplier & Co.
Retail Recruiters/Spectrum Consultants, Inc.
Riotto - Jones Assoc., Inc.

Riverside Consultants, Inc.
Roberts Assoc.
Rockwood Assoc.
Romac & Assoc. of Dallas
Romac & Assoc., Inc.
Sanford Rose Assoc. of Quakertown
John P. Runden & Co., Inc.
Sales Consultants of Nashua - Manchester
Sales Consultants of Ft. Lauderdale
Santangelo Consultants Inc.
Scan Management Inc.
Schattle Personnel Consultants, Inc.
Schenck & Assoc. SC
Scott Kappele & Gnodde
Search Leader, Inc.
Shannahan & Co., Inc.
Scott Sibley Assoc.
Smith Bradley & Assoc.
Smith Hanley Assoc., Inc.
Stanewick, Hart & Assoc., Inc.
Steeple Associates, Inc.
Peter Sterling & Co.
Straight & Co.
Techno-Trac Systems, Inc.
Techsearch Services Inc.
Thornton Assoc.
Unisearch
Vezan Assoc.
Waterford, Inc.
Wayne Assoc., Inc.
Wells, Bradley & Assoc.
Wilkinson Boyd
John W. Worsham & Assoc., Inc.
W.F. Richer Assoc., Inc.

H.11 SECURITIES & COMMODITIES BROKERS

A.L.S. Group
E. J. Ashton & Assoc., Ltd.
The Bankers Group
Computer Security Placement Service, Inc.
Crispi, Wagner & Co., Inc.
J P Donnelly Assoc., Inc.
Drummond Assoc., Inc.
Mark Elzweig Co. Ltd.
Greene & Co.
The Hart Group
Hedlund Corp.
C. L. Howe & Co., Inc.
Integrated Management Solutions
John-David Assoc., Inc.
Michael King Assoc., Inc.
M-A Management Assoc., Inc.
Management Recruiters of Redding
Management Resource Group, Inc.
Mariaschin & Co.
John McLellan Assoc., Inc.
Olaf S. Meyer & Co., Ltd.
Mogul Consultants, Inc.
Montaigne Assoc., Inc.
Personnel Systems Int'l. Inc.
The Primary Group, Inc.

678 / DIRECTORY OF EXECUTIVE RECRUITERS

H.11 SECURITIES & COMMODITIES BROKERS (Cont'd)

Riotto - Jones Assoc., Inc.
Riverside Consultants, Inc.
Rockwood Assoc.
Romac & Assoc. of Dallas
Scan Management Inc.
Scott Kappele & Gnodde
The Search Center Inc.
Shannahan & Co., Inc.
Steeple Associates, Inc.
Techno-Trac Systems, Inc.
Techsearch Services Inc.
Wilkinson Boyd
W.F. Richer Assoc., Inc.

H.12 VENTURE CAPITAL

A.L.S. Group
Crispi, Wagner & Co., Inc.
Drummond Assoc., Inc.
Financial Search Group, Inc.
Greene & Co.
The Hart Group
Donald P. Hayes Assoc., Inc.
Integrated Management Solutions
M-A Management Assoc., Inc.
Management Resource Group, Inc.
Mariaschin & Co.
Montaigne Assoc., Inc.
Steeple Associates, Inc.
Yake & Assoc.

H.I0 INSURANCE

Abacus Consultants
Advanced Corporate Search
The Agency- An Employment Consortium
Frank E. Allen & Assoc.
Pat Allen Assoc. Inc.
Ethan Allen Personnel, Inc.
Amato & Assoc., Inc.
Aronow Assoc., Inc.
E. J. Ashton & Assoc., Ltd.
Ashway Ltd. Agency
Avery Crafts Assoc., Ltd.
The Bankers Group
Bedford-Orion Group, Inc.
Bonifield Assoc.
Brandjes Assoc.
Broad Waverly & Assoc.
W. Bussell & Assoc.
The Butlers Co. Insurance Recruiters
C & H Personnel
CES
Carter-Evdemon & Assoc.
The Christopher Group
Computer Network Resources
Cona Personnel Search
Corporate Careers Inc.
Corporate Suite, Ltd.
Criterion Executive Search, Inc.
Curts/Jackson, Inc.
Dunhill Professional Search Inc.

Dunhill Personnel of Milwaukee
Dunhill of Manchester Inc.
Ecco Personnel Svs.
Eggers Consulting Co., Inc.
Executive Dynamics, Inc.
Executive Register, Inc.
David Farmer & Assoc.
Fergason Assoc., Inc.
Jack Stuart Fisher Assoc.
Fisher-Todd Assoc.
Flynn, Hannock, Inc.
Fox-Morris Assoc., Inc.
Fuller Search
The Garrison Organization
Delores F. George
The Hart Group
Higbee Assoc., Inc.
High-Tech Recruiters
Hintz Associates
Hudson Assoc. Inc.
Hughes & Assoc.
ISOPS Personnel Services, Inc.
Individual Employment Services
Jacobson Assoc.
The James Group
The Johnson Group, Inc.
Kinderis & Loercher Group
Millie Kipp Assoc., Inc.
Kling Personnel Assoc., Inc.
E.J. Lance Management Assoc., Inc.
Landon-Brookes Executive Search
Lechner & Assoc., Inc.
Vincent Lee Assoc.
Logue & Rice Inc.
Management Recruiters of Tampa North
Management Recruiters of Dearborn, Inc.
Management Recruiters
Management Recruiters
Management Recruiters of Ft. Myers, FL.
Management Recruiters of Reno
Management Recruiters of Stanhope Corp.
Management Resource Group, Inc.
Management Search, Inc.
Karen Marshall Assoc.
Mary L. Mayer, Ltd.
The McCormick Group, Inc.
McGladrey Search Group
Milgram & Assoc.
Robert E. Mills, FLMI
Beverly Nelson & Assoc. Inc.
Nuance Personnel Search, Inc.
Jim Oravetz & Assoc., Inc.
Personnel Systems Int'l. Inc.
J.R. Peterman Assoc., Inc.
The Primary Group, Inc.
Pro, Inc.
Professional Search Assoc., Inc.
Professionals in Recruiting Co.
Questor Consultants, Inc.
RHS Assoc., Inc.
Retail Recruiters/Spectrum Consultants, Inc.
The Reynolds Group, Inc.
Riverside Consultants, Inc.

H.I0 INSURANCE (Cont'd)

Romac & Assoc.
Russell Assoc.
Russillo/Gardner
Sales & Management Search, Inc.
Sales Consultants of Madison
Sales Consultants of Newtown
Sales Consultants of Rraleigh - Durham - RTP
Sales Consultants of Morris County, Inc.
Sales Consultants
Santangelo Consultants Inc.
Scott Kappele & Gnodde
Search West, Inc.
Selective Management Services, Inc.
Selective Staffing
Straight & Co.
Tower Consultants, Ltd.
Vezan Assoc.
Water Street Assoc.
White-Ridgely & Assoc., Inc.
The Wilkinson Group
Nola Worley & Assoc., Inc.
Xavier Assoc., Inc.
W.F. Richer Assoc., Inc.

H.R0 REAL ESTATE

A.L.S. Group
Frank E. Allen & Assoc.
Alzed Real Estate Recruiters
Ames Assoc. Inc.
Ted Bavly Assoc., Inc.
C.G. & Assoc.
The Carlyle Group, Ltd.
Cemco, Ltd.
The Christopher Group
The Consortium
Corporate Advisors Inc.
Cosco Resources Inc.
Curts/Jackson, Inc.
Drake & Assoc.
Drummond Assoc., Inc.
Gwen Dycus, Inc.
Executive Dynamics, Inc.
Executive Register, Inc.
David Farmer & Assoc.
Foster Assoc.
J. D. Hersey & Assoc.
Robert Hess & Assoc., Inc.
Higbee Assoc., Inc.
Hyland Executive Search
Individual Employment Services
The Johnson Group, Inc.
E. G. Jones Assoc., Ltd.
Lisa Kalus & Assoc., Inc.
Kershner & Co.
Kimmel & Fredericks, Inc.
Kossuth & Assoc., Inc.
Lam Assoc.
M-A Management Assoc., Inc.
Management Advisors Int'l., Inc.
Management Search Int'l.
K. Maxin & Assoc.

B. Paul Mickey & Assoc.
Tina Morbitzer & Assoc.
Mortgage & Financial Personnel Services
Pacific Advisory Service
Jerry Pollack & Assoc.
Precise Legal, Inc.
Real Estate Executive Search, Inc.
The Robinson Group, D.A., Ltd.
David Saxner & Assoc., Inc.
Scott Kappele & Gnodde
Smith, Anderson & Co.
Specialty Consultants, Inc.
Straight & Co.
Peter R. Taylor Assoc., Inc.
Wells, Bradley & Assoc.
Western Search Assoc.
White-Ridgely & Assoc., Inc.
The Wilkinson Group
Nola Worley & Assoc., Inc.

I.00 SERVICES

A. D. & Assoc.
AJS Assoc.
Alaska Executive Search, Inc.
D.S. Allen Assoc.
Allen Barry Assoc.
AviSearch Int'l.
B.K. Barnes & Associates
Ted Bavly Assoc., Inc.
C. Berger and Company
Bornholdt Shivas & Friends
C & H Personnel
C.P.S., Inc.
CRS Assoc., Inc.
Peter M. Cahill Assoc., Inc.
Capitol Management Consulting, Inc.
Career Profiles
Career Search Assoc.
Career Specialists, Inc.
Chase Waterford Ltd.
Clark-Winans, Inc.
The Comwell Co. Inc.
Criterion Executive Search, Inc.
Dapexs Consultants, Inc.
N. Dean Davic Assoc., Inc.
DeLalla - Fried Assoc.
Dillard Executive Search
Domenico/Brown Group
Drake & Assoc.
Dunhill Personnel of Northeast Tulsa, Inc.
Fallstaff Search
David Farmer & Assoc.
Fernow Assoc.
Fisher-Todd Assoc.
Flynn, Hannock, Inc.
Fox-Morris Assoc., Inc.
Michael Garbi Assoc., Inc.
Genesis Personnel Service, Inc.
Delores F. George
Global Data Services, Inc.
Goldstein & Assoc.
Greene & Co.

I.00 SERVICES (Cont'd)

J. Gross & Assoc.
J. D. Hersey & Assoc.
John M. Horton
Hospitality Resources Int'l., Ltd.
Industry Consultants, Inc.
Kensington Int'l.
Koren, Rogers Assoc.
Jack B. Larsen & Assoc.
Legal Placements Inc.
Paul Ligon Co.
Lowery, Cotter, & Assoc.
Ludot Personnel Services, Inc.
Luke, Lincoln, & Brugger
Management Recruiters Peninsula
Management Search Int'l.
McCulloch Assoc.
Earl L. McDermid & Assoc.
McGladrey Search Group
McGuire Executive Search, Inc.
The Montanye Group
Montgomery Resources, Inc.
The C. B. Mueller Co., Inc.
Murphy, Symonds & Stowell Search, Inc.
NPF Assoc. Ltd. Inc.
J. Fielding Nelson & Assoc., Inc.
OSA Partners, Inc.
Oldwick Enterprises, Inc.
Joel H. Paul & Assoc., Inc.
Personnel Advisors Int'l. Corp.
Personnel Inc.
The Personnel Network, Inc.
Philip Daniels Assoc., Inc.
Placement Solutions
Princeton Executive Search
Protocol Inc.
R.G.B. & Assoc., Inc.
RHS Assoc., Inc.
Edward Rast & Co.
Roberson & Co.
The Robinson Group, D.A., Ltd.
Ryman, Bell, Green & Michaels, Inc.
Sales Consultants
Sales Consultants of Morris County, Inc.
Salesworld-Division of Metacor Inc.
Devin Scott Assoc.
Search West, Inc.
L. A. Silver Assoc., Inc.
Snelling Personnel Services
Stephen M. Sonis Assoc.
Spectrum Consultants
St. James And DeDominic
Sturm, Burrows & Co.
Techsearch Services Inc.
The Tibbetts Group Ltd.
Triangle Consulting Group
Frank X. Walsh & Co., Inc.
Martha Ward Assoc., Inc.
Werbin Assoc. Executive Search, Inc.
WestCare Executive Search
Worldwide Anesthesia Assoc., Inc.

I.10 HOSPITALITY-INCLUDING HOTELS, RESORTS, CLUBS, RESTAURANTS, FOOD & BEVE

ACC Consultants, Inc.
Peter Barrett Assoc., Inc.
Bast & Assoc., Inc.
The Bren Group
Brown/Bernardy, Inc.
CES
Career Resource Assoc., Inc.
Chase Waterford Ltd.
Crickenberger Assoc.
DLB Assoc.
Domenico/Brown Group
Executive Referral Services, Inc.
Franchise Search, Inc.
J. Gross & Assoc.
Hedlund Corp.
Hospitality Executive Search, Inc.
Hospitality Int'l.
Hospitality Resources Int'l., Ltd.
Impact Executive Search, Inc.
Kauffman Hospitality, Inc.
Kordus Consulting Group
Paul Ligon Co.
M/ARS
Management Recruiters of Gramercy, Inc.
Management Recruiters of North Oakland County, Inc.
Management Recruiters of Stanhope Corp.
Earl L. McDermid & Assoc.
McGuire Executive Search, Inc.
Milgram & Assoc.
National Hospitality Assoc., Inc.
Parker Page Group
Partridge Assoc., Inc.
The Paxton Group, Ltd.
Presley Consultants, Inc.
Pro Travel Personnel
Retail Placement Assoc.
Retail Recruiters/Spectrum Consultants, Inc.
Retail Recruiters of Paramus, Inc.
Retail Recruiters of Stamford
Roth Young of Pittsburgh
Roth Young of Tampa
Roth Young of Boston
Roth Young Executive Recruiters
Roth Young Seattle
Savalli & Assoc., Inc.
David Saxner & Assoc., Inc.
Devin Scott Assoc.
Smith, Beaty, Barlow Assoc., Inc.
Phyllis Solomon Executive Search, Inc.
Storti Assoc., Inc.
Travel Executive Search
Weinman & Assoc.

I.11 ENTERTAINMENT, LEISURE, AMUSEMENT, RECREATION, SPORTS, TRAVEL

Baker Scott & Co.
The Barack Group, Inc.

I.11 ENTERTAINMENT, LEISURE, AMUSEMENT, RECREATION, SPORTS, TRAVEL (Cont'd)

Peter Barrett Assoc., Inc.
Bast & Assoc., Inc.
D. R. Blood & Assoc.
Bowling Executive Registry, Inc.
Charles Bradley Professionals
The Bren Group
Brown/Bernardy, Inc.
Chase Waterford Ltd.
DLB Assoc.
Delta Personnel Services
Domenico/Brown Group
Ferrari Consulting Group
Hospitality Executive Search, Inc.
Hospitality Int'l.
Hospitality Resources Int'l., Ltd.
Kauffman Hospitality, Inc.
Kordus Consulting Group
Koren, Rogers Assoc.
The James Lloyd Group
M/ARS
Earl L. McDermid & Assoc.
McGuire Executive Search, Inc.
Parker Page Group
Partridge Assoc., Inc.
Pro Travel Personnel
Saxon Morse Assoc.
Travel Executive Search

I.12 MUSEUMS, GALLERIES, MUSIC/ARTS, LIBRARIES & INFORMATION SERVICES, MEMB

CAS Comsearch Inc.
Crickenberger Assoc.
Development Resource Group
Executive Careers
Health Industry Resources, Inc.
Hoskins, Rees & Smith
Hospitality Executive Search, Inc.
Kordus Consulting Group
Moore Employment Svs., Inc.

I.13 HIGHER EDUCATION

Alzed Real Estate Recruiters
Francis V. Anderson Assoc. Inc.
D. R. Blood & Assoc.
Development Resource Group
Jack Stuart Fisher Assoc.
Joel H. Paul & Assoc., Inc.
Professionals in Recruiting Co.

I.14 HEALTHCARE (EXCEPT PHYSICIANS; SEE I.15) TO INCLUDE ADMINISTRATORS & P

Accounting Resources Int'l., Inc.
Ace Resources
Adept Tech Recruiting, Inc.
John R. Ady & Assoc., Inc.
The Agency- An Employment Consortium
Ethan Allen Personnel, Inc.
E. J. Ashton & Assoc., Ltd.
Carol Ball & Co., Inc.
The Bankers Group
Barone-O'Hara Assoc., Inc.
Bartlett, Bunn & Travis, Inc.
Gary S. Bell Assoc., Inc.
Bennett-Munson Inc.
D. R. Blood & Assoc.
Brooke Chase Assoc., Inc.
CES
CRI Professional Search
Caremarc & Assoc.
Carver Search Consultants
Cemco, Ltd.
Centaur Int'l.
Computer Network Resources
Conaway Legal Search
Consult One, Inc.
Criterion Executive Search, Inc.
Cross Country Consultants, Inc.
Curts/Jackson, Inc.
Datamax Services Inc.
Davis-Smith Medical-Dental Employment Service, Inc.
DeCorrevont & Assoc.
Deeco Int'l.
Delta Resource Group, Ltd.
Dunhill Personnel System, Inc.
Dunhill Personnel of Milwaukee
Dunhill of Bradenton, Inc.
Dunhill of Manchester Inc.
Dunhill Professional Search Group
Dunhill Personnel of Tampa
Dunhill International Search
Emerson & Co.
Exec 2000
Executive Dynamics, Inc.
Executive Referral Services, Inc.
eXsource
Fallstaff Search
James L. Fisk & Assoc.
Focus: HealthCare
Fortune Personnel Consultants
Mel Frazer & Assoc.
Fuller Search
Garrett Assoc. Inc.
Gaudette & Co.
W.T. Glover & Assoc., Inc.
Goldstein & Assoc.
The Goodman Group
HMO Executive Search
Health Industry Resources, Inc.
Health Technology, Inc.
Healthcare Resources Group
Hipp Waters, Inc.
John M. Horton
Hospitality Executive Search, Inc.
Hospitality Int'l.
Howie & Assoc., Inc.
Intech Summit Group, Inc.
The James Group
E. G. Jones Assoc., Ltd.

I.14 HEALTHCARE (EXCEPT PHYSICIANS; SEE I.15) TO INCLUDE ADMINISTRATORS & P (Cont'd)

Jubilee, Inc.
Kendall & Davis Co., Inc.
Kling Personnel Assoc., Inc.
Langlois & Assoc.
Lanzi & Assoc.
Lappe & Assoc.
Management Recruiters of Tampa North
Management Recruiters of Frederick, Inc.
Management Recruiters
Management Recruiters
Management Recruiters
Management Recruiters of Greater Bridgeport, Inc.
Management Recruiters
Management Recruiters
Management Recruiters
Management Recruiters
Management Recruiters of Kinston
Management Recruiters of Hendersonville, inc.
Management Recruiters of Berkeley
Management Recruiters - Concord, CA.
Management Recruiters of Ft. Myers, FL.
Management Recruiters
Management Recruiters of Monterey
Management Recruiters
Management Recruiters Treasure Coast, Inc.
Management Recruiters of Atlanta Downtown
Management Recruiters of Atlanta West, Inc.
Management Recruiters of Topeka, Inc.
Management Recruiters of North Oakland County, Inc.
Management Recruiters of Poughkeepsie, Inc.
Management Recruiters of Charlotte - Southwest
Marcus & Assoc.
Karen Marshall Assoc.
Mary L. Mayer, Ltd.
The McCormick Group, Inc.
McCracken, Wilcox, Bertoux & Miller
McGuire Executive Search, Inc.
Medtrac & Assoc.
Meridian Personnel Assoc., Inc.
Midwest Medical Consultants
Midwest Medical Recruiters
National Health Search, Inc.
Normyle/Erstling Health Search
PLRS/Career Connections
Largent Parks & Partners, Inc.
Partridge Assoc., Inc.
The Paxton Group, Ltd.
Robert E. Pfaendler & Assoc., Inc.
Physicians Search Assoc. Agency, Inc.
Pro, Inc.
ProSearch, Inc.
Professional Medical
Professional Placement Assoc., Inc.
Professionals in Recruiting Co.
RAC International

R.G.B. & Assoc., Inc.
Retail Recruiters/Spectrum Consultants, Inc.
Ritta Professional Search Inc.
Sanford Rose Assoc. - Rockville
Sanford Rose Assoc.- Detroit North
Roth Young of Pittsburgh
Saber-Salisbury & Assoc., Inc.
Sales & Management Search, Inc.
Sales Consultants of Ft. Lauderdale
Santangelo Consultants Inc.
Schenck & Assoc. SC
Sharrow & Assoc., Inc.
Scott Sibley Assoc.
Smith Bradley & Assoc.
Daniel Stern & Assoc.
Phyllis Stovall Assoc., Inc.
Sumrall Personnel Consultants, Inc.
Tower Consultants, Ltd.
USA Medical Placement Inc.
Vezan Assoc.
Weatherby Healthcare
Wellington Thomas Ltd.
WestCare Executive Search
Winfield Assoc.
Worldwide Anesthesia Assoc., Inc.
Zaccaria Group, Inc.

I.15 PHYSICIANS

Ace Resources
Alexander Enterprises, Inc.
Gary S. Bell Assoc., Inc.
Bench Int'l. Search, Inc.
Bennett-Munson Inc.
Besen Assoc. Inc.
Bryant Research
The Byrnes Group
Centaur Int'l.
Consult One, Inc.
Corporate Recruiters Inc.
Crickenberger Assoc.
Davis-Smith Medical-Dental Employment Service, Inc.
Delacore Personnel
Dunhill Personnel of Milwaukee
Dunhill of Manchester Inc.
Dunhill Professional Search Group
Exec 2000
James L. Fisk & Assoc.
Focus: HealthCare
Ford & Ford
Fortune Personnel Consultants
Fuller Search
Garrett Assoc. Inc.
Alan Glenn & Keener
Goldstein & Assoc.
HMO Executive Search
Phyllis Hawkins & Assoc.
Healthcare Resources Group
Hitchens & Foster, Inc.
Intech Summit Group, Inc.
Kling Personnel Assoc., Inc.
Krow Assoc., Inc.

I.15 PHYSICIANS (Cont'd)

Lam Assoc.
Lanzi & Assoc.
Management Recruiters of Frederick, Inc.
Management Recruiters
Management Recruiters
Management Recruiters
Management Recruiters
Management Recruiters of Berkeley
Management Recruiters
Meridian Personnel Assoc., Inc.
Michael/Merrill
Midwest Medical Consultants
Midwest Medical Recruiters
National Health Search, Inc.
PLRS/Career Connections
Largent Parks & Partners, Inc.
The Paxton Group, Ltd.
M.A. Pelle Assoc., Inc.
Personnel Inc.
Robert E. Pfaendler & Assoc., Inc.
Physicians Search Assoc. Agency, Inc.
Place Mart Personnel Service
Pro, Inc.
Professional Medical
Professional Placement Assoc., Inc.
Professionals in Recruiting Co.
Retail Recruiters/Spectrum Consultants, Inc.
Ritta Professional Search Inc.
Sanford Rose Assoc. - Rockville
Sanford Rose Assoc.- Detroit North
Roth Young of Tampa
Saber-Salisbury & Assoc., Inc.
Scott Sibley Assoc.
Daniel Stern & Assoc.
Sumrall Personnel Consultants, Inc.
Tatum & Assoc., Inc.
USA Medical Placement Inc.
Weatherby Healthcare
WestCare Executive Search
Whitaker, Fellows & Assoc.
Worldwide Anesthesia Assoc., Inc.
Yannelli, Randolph & Co.
Zaccaria Group, Inc.
Zackrison Assoc., Inc.

I.16 PHARMACEUTICAL (OTHER THAN MANUFACTURING)

ACR Assoc.
Ace Resources
Alexander Enterprises, Inc.
Francis V. Anderson Assoc. Inc.
Atlantic West Int'l.
Carol Ball & Co., Inc.
Bedford-Orion Group, Inc.
Bench Int'l. Search, Inc.
Bryant Research
Career Consulting Group, Inc.
Corporate Recruiters Inc.
Cross Country Consultants, Inc.
Executive Referral Services, Inc.
Paul Falcone Assoc., Inc.

James L. Fisk & Assoc.
Graham Assoc. Inc.
Donald P. Hayes Assoc., Inc.
Health Technology, Inc.
Kay Henry, Inc.
John M. Horton
Jubilee, Inc.
Kling Personnel Assoc., Inc.
Lanzi & Assoc.
Lybrook Assoc., Inc.
MRG Search & Placement
Management Recruiters of Frederick, Inc.
Management Recruiters of Middlesex County NJ.
Management Recruiters of Greater Bridgeport, Inc.
Management Recruiters Treasure Coast, Inc.
Management Recruiters of Nassau, Inc.
Marcus & Assoc.
Medical Executive Search Assoc.
Medtrac & Assoc.
Meridian Personnel Assoc., Inc.
P R Management Consultants, Inc.
Janou Pakter, Inc.
Physicians Search Assoc. Agency, Inc.
Place Mart Personnel Service
Preston Robert & Assoc.-Health Care Div.
ProSearch, Inc.
Professional Medical
Professional Placement Assoc., Inc.
RAC International
Sanford Rose Assoc.- Suburban Philadelphia
Roth Young Executive Recruiters
John P. Runden & Co., Inc.
Sales Consultants of Austin, Inc.
Search Masters
Smith Bradley & Assoc.
Storfer & Assoc.
Storti Assoc., Inc.
S. Tyler Sullivan & Assoc., Inc.
Vezan Assoc.
Winfield Assoc.
Zaccaria Group, Inc.
Zackrison Assoc., Inc.

I.17 LEGAL

Bartlett, Bunn & Travis, Inc.
Beckwith, Thomas & Fanning
Bellon & Assoc., Inc.
The Howard C. Bloom Co.
Charles Bradley Professionals
Brandjes Assoc.
Broad Waverly & Assoc.
Brooks Executive Personnel
C.P.S., Inc.
Career Consulting Group, Inc.
The Carlyle Group, Ltd.
Carter-Evdemon & Assoc.
Chicago Legal Search, Ltd.
Coleman Legal Search Consultants
Conaway Legal Search
The Consortium

I.17 LEGAL (Cont'd)

David - Kris Assoc., Inc.
Dunhill of Manchester Inc.
Environmental Professional Assoc.
Exec 2000
Ferrari Consulting Group
Foster Assoc.
Frey & Conboy Assoc., Inc.
Garrison, McGuigan & Sisson
GreenHall Assoc., Inc.
Hamilton Edwards, Ltd.
Phyllis Hawkins & Assoc.
The Headhunters
Hoskins, Rees & Smith
J.D. Limited
JM Assoc.
The Kennett Group, Inc.
Barbara Kerner Consultants
Krow Assoc., Inc.
Legal Placements Inc.
Major, Wilson & Africa
Marley Group Ltd.
The McCormick Group, Inc.
McCracken, Wilcox, Bertoux & Miller
Meridian Personnel Assoc., Inc.
Parker Page Group
Precise Legal, Inc.
The Primary Group, Inc.
Pro, Inc.
Pursuant Legal Consultants
RALCO/Richard A. Lucia & Assoc.
RBR Assoc., Inc.
A. Ryan Assoc.
Ryman, Bell, Green & Michaels, Inc.
Scan Management Inc.
Sharrow & Assoc., Inc.
Raymond James Smith & Assoc.
Smith, Anderson & Co.
Topaz Int'l., Inc.
Waldorf Associates, Inc.
Weiss & Assoc., Inc.
Whitaker, Fellows & Assoc.
Whitbeck & Assoc.
Winship Assoc.
Winston Rooney & Green

I.18 COMPUTER SERVICES

Abacus Consultants
Abraham & London Ltd.
Accountants On Call
Adept Tech Recruiting, Inc.
Alexander Edward Assoc., Inc.
Analytic Recruiting, Inc.
Ashton Computer Professionals, Inc.
BR & Assoc.
Barclay Consultants, Inc.
Battista Assoc., Inc.
R. Gaines Baty Assoc., Inc.
C.W. Brandon & Assoc., Inc.
Ira Broadman Assoc.
The Byrnes Group
CN Associates

CPI Technical Services
J.F. Church Assoc., Inc.
Computer Network Resources
The Consortium
The DataFinders Group, Inc.
Deery Geddis & Assoc.
Dunhill Personnel of Northeast Tulsa, Inc.
Dunhill Personnel Search
Executive Exchange Corp.
eXsource
N. Steven Fells & Co., Inc.
First Search Inc.
A.G. Fishkin & Assoc., Inc.
Alan Glenn & Keener
Global Data Services, Inc.
W.T. Glover & Assoc., Inc.
Goldstein & Assoc.
The Goodman Group
Howie & Assoc., Inc.
Integrated Professional Services, Inc.
JDG Assoc., Ltd.
JT Assoc.
Jubilee, Inc.
Kurtz Pro-Search, Inc.
Logix, Inc.
Management Recruiters of Dearborn, Inc.
Management Recruiters
Management Recruiters of Little Rock
Management Recruiters of Stanhope Corp.
Management Recruiters of North Brunswick, Inc.
Management Recruiters of Poughkeepsie, Inc.
McCracken, Wilcox, Bertoux & Miller
Robert E. Mills, FLMI
Paul-Tittle Assoc., Inc.
Posse, Inc.
ProSearch, Inc.
Professional Search Assoc., Inc.
R.A.N. Assoc., Inc.
Retail Recruiters of Stamford
The Reynolds Group, Inc.
Ritta Professional Search Inc.
Sanford Rose Assoc. - Rockville
Sales Consultants of Madison
Sales Consultants of Ft. Lauderdale
Santangelo Consultants Inc.
Spectra West
Stanewick, Hart & Assoc., Inc.
Storti Assoc., Inc.
Phyllis Stovall Assoc., Inc.
Systems Careers
Techno-Trac Systems, Inc.
W.F. Richer Assoc., Inc.

I.19 ACCOUNTING & MISCELLANEOUS BUSINESS SERVICES

A. D. & Assoc.
Accountants On Call
Availability Personnel Consultants
Baker Scott & Co.
Charles Bradley Professionals

J.00 COMMUNICATIONS (Cont'd)

Engineering Search Assoc.
First Search Inc.
Michael Garbi Assoc., Inc.
The Gumbinner Co.
High Tech Opportunities, Inc.
High Technology Search Assoc.
Hill & Assoc.
Hyland Executive Search
Kendall & Davis Co., Inc.
Jack Kennedy Assoc., Inc.
Key Talent, Inc.
Kordus Consulting Group
Koren, Rogers Assoc.
Kossuth & Assoc., Inc.
Kresin Wingard
Paul Ligon Co.
M/ARS
MJF Assoc.
Management Recruiters of Gramercy, Inc.
Management Recruiters Peninsula
Management Search, Inc.
Management Search Int'l.
Maximum Management Corp.
Multi Processing, Inc.
The Naples Group, Inc.
J. Fielding Nelson & Assoc., Inc.
Kitty Ossow & Assoc.
Posse, Inc.
Professional Team Search
The Robinson Group, D.A., Ltd.
Romano McAvoy Assoc., Inc.
Sanford Rose Assoc. of Beachwood
Sales Consultants
Sales Consultants of Morris County, Inc.
Sales Consultants
Salesworld-Division of Metacor Inc.
RitaSue Siegel Assoc., Inc.
L. A. Silver Assoc., Inc.
Stephen M. Sonis Assoc.
Strategic Search Group
Tecmark Assoc. Inc.
TeleSearch, Inc.
J.Q. Turner & Assoc., Inc.
Werbin Assoc. Executive Search, Inc.
Wesson, Taylor, Wells & Assoc.
Zeiger Technical Careers, Inc.

J.10 ADVERTISING/PUBLIC RELATIONS

Analytic Recruiting, Inc.
Carol Ball & Co., Inc.
C & H Personnel
CRS Assoc., Inc.
Career Consulting Group, Inc.
Career Resource Assoc., Inc.
Chaloner Assoc.
The Crawford Group
Dussick Management Assoc.
Executive Careers
G.A. Field Personnel Consultants
Jerry Fields Assoc.

The Fry Group, Inc.
The Gumbinner Co.
Kay Henry, Inc.
Hill & Assoc.
Howard-Sloan Assoc.
Individual Employment Services
Julian Assoc., Inc.
Jack Kennedy Assoc., Inc.
Koren, Rogers Assoc.
Kresin Wingard
Link Personnel & Assoc.
M/ARS
Management Recruiters of Middlesex County NJ.
Meads & Assoc.
Mengel & McDonald Ltd.
Carolyn Smith Paschal Int'l.
Phillips Assoc.
Posse, Inc.
Professional Team Search
Retail Placement Assoc.
Rex Assoc., Inc.
Sales Consultants Bowling Green
Smith Hanley Assoc., Inc.
Spring Executive Search, Inc.
Bob Westerfield & Assoc., Inc.
Zachary & Sanders, Inc.

J.11 PUBLISHING, PRINT MEDIA

Carol Ball & Co., Inc.
Bartl & Evins
William J. Christopher Assoc., Inc.
Bert Davis Assoc., Inc.
G.A. Field Personnel Consultants
Jerry Fields Assoc.
Future Sense
Don Howard Personnel
Howard-Sloan Assoc.
Jack Kennedy Assoc., Inc.
Kresin Wingard
E.J. Lance Management Assoc., Inc.
The James Lloyd Group
Lunney, Hadden & Assoc.
Management Recruiters of North Brunswick, Inc.
Janou Pakter, Inc.
Personnel Assoc.
Posse, Inc.
Professional Team Search
Retail Placement Assoc.
Sales Consultants Bowling Green
Sales Consultants of Savannah, GA.
RitaSue Siegel Assoc., Inc.
Zachary & Sanders, Inc.

J.12 TV, CABLE, MOTION PICTURES, VIDEO, RADIO

Baker Scott & Co.
D. R. Blood & Assoc.
CN Associates
Mel Frazer & Assoc.
Future Sense

J.12 TV, CABLE, MOTION PICTURES, VIDEO, RADIO (Cont'd)

High Tech Opportunities, Inc.
Howard-Sloan Assoc.
Jack Kennedy Assoc., Inc.
The James Lloyd Group
Mengel & McDonald Ltd.
Mogul Consultants, Inc.
The Naples Group, Inc.
Phillips Assoc.
Promotion Recruiters, Inc.
Saxon Morse Assoc.

J.13 TELEPHONE, TELECOMMUNICATIONS

A. D. & Assoc.
Abraham & London Ltd.
Advanced Corporate Search
Alaska Executive Search, Inc.
Alexander Edward Assoc., Inc.
Ames-O'Neill Assoc., Inc.
Ashton Computer Professionals, Inc.
Baker Scott & Co.
R. Gaines Baty Assoc., Inc.
Charles A. Binswanger Assoc., Inc.
D. R. Blood & Assoc.
M.F. Branch Assoc., Inc.
C.W. Brandon & Assoc., Inc.
CAS Comsearch Inc.
CPI Technical Services
Carter McKenzie, Inc.
Commonwealth Consultants
Conaway Legal Search
Dapexs Consultants, Inc.
The DataFinders Group, Inc.
Datamax Services Inc.
Deery Geddis & Assoc.
Delta Resource Group, Ltd.
Dreier Consulting
Dunhill Professional Search of Ramsey
Dunhill International Search
Engineering Search Assoc.
eXsource
A.G. Fishkin & Assoc., Inc.
Forum Assoc.
Franklin Int'l. Search, Inc.
Gallagher & Assoc.
J. Gross & Assoc.
Hall, Cooper & Bartman, Ltd.
Hedlund Corp.
High-Tech Recruiters
Hoskins, Rees & Smith
Human Resource Network
Individual Employment Services
Kendall & Davis Co., Inc.
Kiley-Owen Assoc., Inc.
Kurtz Pro-Search, Inc.
Larson Assoc.
Management Assoc.
Management Recruiters of Hendersonville, inc.
Management Recruiters of Laguna Hills
Management Recruiters of Waterbury, Inc.

Management Recruiters of Stanhope Corp.
Management Recruiters of Poughkeepsie, Inc.
Maximum Management Corp.
Sandi McDonald & Assoc., Inc.
The McKee Co.
Milgram & Assoc.
Mogul Consultants, Inc.
Northeastern Search, Inc.
P.R.H. Management, Inc.
Paul-Tittle Assoc., Inc.
M.R. Pennington Co.
Phillips Personnel/Search
Placement Solutions
Remark Assoc. Inc.
Roberson & Co.
Emery A. Rose & Assoc.
Sanford Rose Assoc. of Quakertown
Ross Personnel Consultants, Inc.
Sales Consultants of Westchester-South, Inc.
Sales Consultants of Ft. Myers, Inc.
Samper Assoc.
Saxon Morse Assoc.
Search Group
Shannahan & Co., Inc.
Storti Assoc., Inc.
Tech Consulting
TeleSearch, Inc.
Tell/Com Recruiters
Traynor Confidential, Ltd.
Vick & Assoc.
Gordon Wahls Co.
Zeiger Technical Careers, Inc.

K.00 PUBLIC ADMINISTRATION/ GOVERNMENT

Alzed Real Estate Recruiters
CRS Assoc., Inc.
Delta Personnel Services
Development Resource Group
Health Industry Resources, Inc.
The C. B. Mueller Co., Inc.
Murphy, Symonds & Stowell Search, Inc.
PLRS/Career Connections
St. James And DeDominic
Summit Executive Search Consultants, Inc.

K.10 DEFENSE

Advanced Corporate Search
Alexander Edward Assoc., Inc.
Ashton Computer Professionals, Inc.
AviSearch Int'l.
Ira Broadman Assoc.
DEI Executive Services
Dunhill of Freehold, Inc.
Fernow Assoc.
Gallagher & Assoc.
The Headhunter
JDG Assoc., Ltd.
Lappe & Assoc.
Norton & Assoc.
Paul-Tittle Assoc., Inc.
Emery A. Rose & Assoc.

K.10 DEFENSE (Cont'd)
The Simmons Group
Zeiger Technical Careers, Inc.

L.00 NON-CLASSIFIABLE INDUSTRIES
Gwen Dycus, Inc.
HLR Consulting
Lineal Recruiting Services
Management Recruiters of El Dorado
Summit Executive Search Consultants, Inc.

Retainer and Contingency Geographical Cross-Index

USA alphabetical by state, followed by Canada and Mexico.
Firms with an (R) are from the Retainer Firms Section.

ALABAMA

Birmingham
Blanton & Co.
Dunhill Personnel System, Inc.
Dunhill Personnel System, Inc.
Management Recruiters
RHS Assoc., Inc.
Romac & Assoc., Inc.
Sales Consultants

Decatur
Dunhill Personnel System, Inc.

Dothan
Broward-Dobbs, Inc.

Huntsville
Dunhill of Huntsville, Inc.
Fortune Personnel Consultants of
Huntsville, Inc.
The Headhunter
Management Recruiters

Mobile
Management Recruiters
Weeks & Assoc.

Montgomery
Locke & Assoc. (R)
Murkett Assoc.

ALASKA

Anchorage
Alaska Executive Search, Inc.

ARIZONA

Chandler
D. R. Blood & Assoc.

Green Valley
Gaudette & Co.
Paul C. Green & Assoc. Ltd. (R)

Nogales
Management Recruiters

Phoenix
Barton Sans Int'l. (R)
CSI Inc. (R)
Cemco, Ltd.
Exec 2000
Hamilton Edwards, Ltd.
Hans & Assoc., Inc. (R)
Phyllis Hawkins & Assoc.
The Headhunters
McDonald Ledterman Executive Search
Richard E. Nosky & Assoc. (R)
Orr Executive Search
Professional Team Search
Roberson & Co.
SS & A Executive Search Consultants (R)
Source EDP
Source Finance
Tirocchi, Wright, Inc. (R)
Weinman & Assoc.
Western Personnel Assoc., Inc.
Donald Williams Assoc., Inc. (R)

Scottsdale
The Bren Group
Allen Case & Assoc., Inc.
The Chapman Group, Inc.
Halden & Assoc. (R)
Hyland Executive Search
Kearney Executive Search (R)
Lappe & Assoc.

Reynolds Lebus Assoc.
Management Recruiters
McMahon & Dee, Inc. (R)
William H. Nenstiel & Assoc.
Sales Consultants

Sedona
Search Masters Int'l.

Tempe
National Hospitality Assoc., Inc.
Southwest Search Inc.

Tucson
Computer Strategies, Inc.
Donald P. Hayes Assoc., Inc.
Management Recruiters
Medical Executive Search Assoc.
Sales Consultants
Spectrum Consultants

ARKANSAS

Fayetteville
Management Recruiters
Sales Consultants of Fayetteville, AR.

Ft. Smith
Dunhill Personnel System, Inc.

Little Rock
Management Recruiters of Little Rock

Paragould
Management Recruiters

Rogers
Dunhill Personnel System, Inc.

CALIFORNIA

Agoura Hills
F. B. Schmidt Intl. (R)

Alameda
Deborah Bishop & Assoc. (R)

Anaheim
Fox-Morris Assoc., Inc.

Anaheim Hills
Warring & Assoc. (R)

Anderson
Management Recruiters of Redding

Apple Valley
Studwell Assoc. (R)

Aptos
Management Recruiters

Arcadia
K & C Assoc.
Management Recruiters

Atherton
Tirocchi, Wright, Inc. (R)

Auburn
Reinecke & Assoc.

Avila Beach
Pro Counsel

Bakersfield
Dunhill Personnel System, Inc.

Belmont
The Simmons Group

Belvedere
Belvedere Partners (R)

Benicia
Management Recruiters

Berkeley
Management Recruiters of Berkeley

Beverly Hills
Allied Search, Inc.
Drake & Assoc.
Environmental Professional Assoc.
Groenekamp & Assoc.
Management Recruiters
The Stevenson Group/SES (R)

Brea
Larson Assoc.
Pro Travel Personnel

Buellton
Sarver-Garland, Inc.

Burbank
Patrick Assoc.

Calabasas
Furlong - Gates, Inc. (R)
Montenido Assoc. (R)
Trout & Assoc., Inc. (R)

Hermosa Beach
Hergenrather & Co. (R)

Hollywood
Development Resource Group

Huntington Beach
Alpine Consulting Group
Paul J. Burns

Inglewood
The Century Group

Irvine
D.S. Allen Assoc.
Deven Assoc., Int'l., Inc. (R)
Domenico/Brown Group
Dunhill Professional Search Irvine/Newport
Hornberger Management Co., Inc.
Human Resource Bureau
International Staffing Consultants, Inc.
JM Assoc.
John Kurosky & Assoc. (R)
Management Search Int'l.
Source EDP
Source Finance
D. L. Weiss & Assoc. (R)
Witt Assoc. Inc. (R)

La Canada
The Wilkinson Group

La Costa
Sales Consultants

La Jolla
John Anthony & Assoc.
CEO'S Only (R)
Alfred Daniels & Assoc. (R)
E T Search Inc.
Pro, Inc.
Western Search Assoc.

La Quinta
William C. Houze & Co. (R)

Laguna Hills
Management Recruiters of Laguna Hills
Professional Medical

Lomita
Wayne S. Chamberlain & Assoc.

Long Beach
Houze, Shourds & Montgomery, Inc. (R)
Kepler & Assoc.
Korn/Ferry Int'l. (R)
Personnel Assoc. (R)

Los Altos
Busch Int'l. (R)
Johnson & Assoc., Inc. (R)
Probus Executive Search
Dick Wray & Consultants (R)

Los Angeles
Accountants On Call
Accountants On Call
BDO Seidman (R)
Bast & Assoc., Inc.
Beckwith, Thomas & Fanning
Bench Int'l. Search, Inc.
Billington & Assoc., Inc. (R)
Charles Bradley Professionals
Jerold Braun & Assoc.
Brentwood Int'l. (R)
Brown/Bernardy, Inc.
Robert Caldwell & Assoc. (R)
Chrisman & Co., Inc. (R)
Conex Inc. (R)
The Corrigan Group (R)
DHR Int'l., Inc. (R)
Dunhill Personnel System, Inc.
Executive Careers
N.W. Gibson Int'l. (R)
Goldstein & Assoc.
Jack Groban & Assoc. (R)
The Hawkins Co. (R)
Heidrick and Struggles, Inc. (R)
Ronald S. Johnson Assoc., Inc. (R)
Kearney Executive Search (R)
Korn/Ferry Int'l. (R)
Korn/Ferry Int'l. (R)
The LaBorde Group
Marvin Laba & Assoc. (R)
Management Recruiters
Management Recruiters
Brad Marks Int'l. (R)
Marlar Int'l. Inc. (R)
J. Martin & Assoc. (R)
Todd Melon Group
Mitchell, Larsen & Zilliacus (R)
Ober & Company (R)
The Odessa Group (R)
PMC-ParaLegal Management & Consultants
Poirier, Hoevel & Co. (R)
Paul R. Ray & Co., Inc. (R)
Russell Reynolds Assoc., Inc. (R)
Norman Roberts & Assoc., Inc. (R)
Search Group
Search West, Inc.
Abbott Smith Assoc., Inc.
SpencerStuart (R)
St. James And DeDominic
Thomas Mangum Co. (R)
Waldorf Associates, Inc.
Ward Howell Int'l. Inc. (R)
Egon Zehnder Int'l. Inc. (R)

Los Gatos
Abbott, James & Oliver
Boyden Int'l., Inc. (R)

Deane, Howard & Simon, Inc. (R)
Splaine & Assoc., Inc. (R)
Staffing Solutions

Malibu
Advanced Corporate Search
Career Plus Executive Search (R)
Kremple & Meade, Inc. (R)

Manhattan Beach
Fisher Personnel Management Services (R)
Hauft Mark Assoc., Inc. (R)

Marina Del Rey
Crown, Michels & Assoc., Inc.

Menlo Park
Ames & Ames (R)
Bartholdi & Co. (R)
Heidrick and Struggles, Inc. (R)
Hockett Assoc., Inc. (R)
Levin & Assoc. (R)
SpencerStuart (R)
Strategic Alternatives (R)
The Ultimate Source (R)
Winguth & Company (R)

Mill Valley
Block & Assoc. (R)
The Goodman Group
M.J. Hughes Int'l., Inc. (R)
Maly & Assoc. (R)
Management Recruiters
Shannahan & Co., Inc.
Yelverton & Co. (R)

Millbrae
Kensington Int'l.

Mission Viejo
Atlantic West Int'l.
Computer Network Resources

Modesto
Automation Technology Search
Management Recruiters
Sales Consultants

Monterey
Gibson & Co., Inc. (R)
Management Recruiters of Monterey

Moraga
Predictor Systems Corp. (R)

Moss Beach
Ballantyne & Assoc. (R)

Mountain View
Advanced Information Management

Newport Beach
Accountants On Call
Ted Bavly Assoc., Inc.
CCI - Career Consultants Int'l.
Diversified Placement Int'l., Inc.
Eckert, Enghauser and Partners, Inc.
The Gobbell Co. (R)
Hemingway Personnel, Inc.
Korn/Ferry Int'l. (R)
Lynch & Co. (R)
Management Recruiters
Marlar Int'l. Inc. (R)
O'Shea, Divine & Co. (R)
Robert Ottke Assoc. (R)
Pflueger & Company (R)
RAC International
Emery A. Rose & Assoc.
W. Shryock & Co. (R)
Vista Resource Group (R)
Vlcek & Co., Inc. (R)

Norco
Presley Consultants, Inc.

North Hollywood
Accountants On Call

Novato
Sales Consultants

Oakland
Accountants On Call
CRI Professional Search
Dunhill Professional Search
Management Recruiters of Oakland
Personnel Assoc. (R)
Sales Consultants
Williams, Adley & Co.

Ojai
Henning & Assoc. (R)

Ontario
Search West, Inc.

Orange
Clanton & Co.
Kieffer, Ford, & Hadelman, Ltd. (R)
Lynch & Co. (R)
Management Recruiters
Frank Parillo & Assoc. (R)
Physicians Search Assoc. Agency, Inc.
Sales Consultants
Search West, Inc.

Pacific Palisades
Ralph Smith & Assoc.

Palm Desert
Tech Mark Group (R)

Palm Springs
Jerry Pollack & Assoc.
Pursuant Legal Consultants
Thomas Mangum Co. (R)

Palo Alto
Accountants On Call
C.R. Assoc.
Furlong - Gates, Inc. (R)
Geneva Group Int'l (R)
Haley Assoc., Inc. (R)
Hamlin Assoc. (R)
Howe-Lewis Int'l. (R)
Korn/Ferry Int'l. (R)
Donovan Martin & Assoc.
Rusher & Loscacio (R)
TASA Executive Search (R)

Palos Verdes Estates
Finnegan Assoc. (R)

Pasadena
J. Kevin Coleman & Assoc., Inc. (R)
R. H. Horton Assoc., Inc. (R)
Gary Kaplan & Assoc. (R)
Ira W. Krinsky & Assoc. (R)
Morris & Berger (R)
Ott & Hansen, Inc. (R)
Protocol Inc.
L. J. Quinn & Assoc., Inc. (R)
Redden & Assoc. (R)
The Repovich - Reynolds Group (R)
Sales Consultants

Pleasanton
Management Recruiters
Sanford Rose Assoc.

Rancho Palos Verdes
The Baxter Group (R)

Redondo Beach
Horizon Assoc.

Redwood City
L.L. Carey & Assoc., Inc. (R)
Kearney Executive Search (R)
Spectra West

Riverside
Accountants On Call

Rohnert Park
Management Recruiters

Roseville
DeHayes Consulting Group (R)
Genesis

Ross
A. William Smyth, Inc. (R)

Sacramento
Accountants On Call
Global Data Services, Inc.
Management Recruiters
McCracken, Wilcox, Bertoux & Miller
Sales Consultants

San Clemente
Peter Barrett Assoc., Inc.
ISOPS Personnel Services, Inc.
Pacific Search Consultants
Personnel Assoc.
Sales Consultants

San Diego
The Eastridge Group
Executive Management Systems, Inc. (R)
GSW Consulting Group, Inc. (R)
Global Resources Group (R)
Intech Summit Group, Inc.
Lansky Assoc. (R)
Brian Leggee & Assoc.
Management Recruiters
Beverly Nelson & Assoc. Inc.
Phillips Group of Companies (R)
Sales Consultants
Sales Consultants
The Search Network
Source EDP
Spectrum Consultants
Lee Stephens & Assoc. (R)
Tanzi Executive Search
Judy Thompson & Assoc., Inc.
Unisearch
WestCare Executive Search

San Francisco
Accountants On Call
Jeffrey C. Adams & Co., Inc. (R)
Allied Search, Inc.
Amato & Assoc., Inc.
Berger & Assoc.
BioQuest Inc. (R)
Boyden Int'l., Inc. (R)
Bullis & Co., Inc. (R)
Chartwell Partners Int'l., Inc. (R)
Colton Bernard Inc. (R)
The Domann Organization (R)
Dunhill Personnel System, Inc.
Leon A. Farley Assoc. (R)
Geneva Group Int'l. (R)
Harreus & Assoc., Inc. (R)
Heidrick and Struggles, Inc. (R)
Hill Allyn Assoc.
Korn/Ferry Int'l. (R)
Kreuzberger, Fehr & Assoc.
Larkin & Co. (R)
Major, Wilson & Africa
Management Recruiters

McFeely Wackerle Shulman (R)
Montgomery Resources, Inc.
Nelson Associates
Professional Medical
Edward Rast & Co.
Real Estate Executive Search, Inc.
Russell Reynolds Assoc., Inc. (R)
Romac & Assoc. - San Francisco
Rusher, Loscavio & Lo Presto (R)
Ryan & Assoc.
Sales Consultants
Sales Professionals Personnel Services
The Search Firm Inc.
Search West, Inc.
Seitchik, Corwin & Seitchik Inc. (R)
M.B. Shattuck & Assoc., Inc. (R)
Smith, Goerss & Ferneborg, Inc. (R)
Source EDP
Source Finance
SpencerStuart (R)
Systems Careers
Tanzi Executive Search
Theobald & Assoc. (R)
Wilkinson & Ives (R)
Williams, Adley & Co.
Winship Assoc.
The Zivic Group, Inc. (R)

San Jose
Accountants On Call
American Executive Search Services, Inc.
 (R)
Coopers & Lybrand, Management
 Consulting Services (R)
Management Recruiters
Management Recruiters
Pencom Systems Inc.
Sales Consultants
C.W. Sink & Co., Inc. (R)

San Juan Capistrano
Larson & Stephanian (R)

San Marcos
The Niemond Corp. (R)

San Mateo
Coelyn Miller Phillip & Assoc. (R)
The Corporate Staff (R)
Howard Karr & Assoc., Inc. (R)
Management Recruiters Peninsula
Management Recruiterss
Sales Consultants
Venture Resources, Inc. (R)
The Winchester Group (R)

San Pedro
The Wentworth Co., Inc. (R)

San Ramon
Management Recruiters

Santa Ana
Sanford Rose Assoc.
D.L. Weaver & Assoc.

Santa Barbara
Garland Assoc. (R)
Management Recruiters
Sanford Rose Assoc. - Santa Barbara

Santa Clara
Holland, McFadzean & Assoc., Inc. (R)
Management Assoc.
Nadzam, Lusk & Assoc., Inc. (R)
Source EDP
Source Finance
John Velcamp & Assoc. (R)

Santa Monica
Ast/Bryant (R)
Greger Assoc. (R)
Kravitz * Larkin * Silver Assoc.

Santa Paula
Dunhill Personnel System, Inc.

Saratoga
Pinsker & Co., Inc. (R)

Sausalito
Richard T. Bergsund Assoc. (R)
Bialla & Assoc., Inc. (R)
Hill & Assoc.
Torretto & Assoc., Inc. (R)

Scotts Valley
Blanchard, Zufall & Assoc. (R)

Seal Beach
Advanced Information Management

Sherman Oaks
Deven Assoc., Int'l., Inc. (R)
Search Assoc., Inc.
Source EDP
Source Finance

Simi Valley
Delta Personnel Services
Sales Consultants

Solvang
Hergenrather & Co. (R)

Stockton
Management Recruiters

Sunnyvale
Christian & Timbers, Inc. (R)
Source Engineering

Temecula
Sales Consultants

Thousand Oaks
Management Recruiters
Sales Consultants

Tiburon
Holt Pearson & Caldwell, Inc. (R)

Torrance
Accountants On Call
William C. Houze & Co. (R)
Interim Management (R)
Meng, Finseth & Assoc., Inc. (R)
Source EDP
Source Finance
The Tibbetts Group Ltd.

Turlock
Multisearch Recruiters

Tustin
Medtrac & Assoc.

Ukiah
Worldwide Anesthesia Assoc., Inc.

Van Nuys
Fred J. Goldsmith Assoc. (R)
Pocrass Assoc. (R)

Ventura
Management Recruiters
Shaffer Consulting Group (R)

Walnut Creek
Accountants On Call
Dunhill Personnel System, Inc.
The Martin Group (R)
Newton Assoc.
Source EDP
Source Finance

West Covina
Lund & Assoc., Inc. (R)

Westlake Village
Byron Leonard Int'l., Inc. (R)
D E G Co., Inc. (R)
Robert W. Dingman Co., Inc. (R)
Management Recruiters
Predictor Systems Corp. (R)
Schenkel & Company (R)
Search West, Inc.
Tech Mark Group (R)

Woodland Hills
Accountants On Call
Computer Recruiters, Inc.

Raymond L. Extract & Assoc. (R)
Mel Frazer & Assoc.
Paul Norsell & Assoc., Inc. (R)
M.H. Springer & Assoc. (R)
The Stevens Group, Inc.
Zeiger Technical Careers, Inc.

Woodside
David Powell, Inc. (R)
Venture Management (R)

COLORADO

Aurora
Comann Assoc., Inc. (R)
D'Aries Five Enterprises (R)
Dunhill Personnel System, Inc.
First Colorado Consulting Group, Inc. (R)
Hughes & Assoc., Inc. (R)
Management Recruiters
Sales Consultants
J.Q. Turner & Assoc., Inc.

Avon
Bartholdi & Co. (R)

Boulder
Dunhill Personnel System, Inc.
Kutt, Inc.
Management Recruiters
Sigma Group Inc. (R)

Colorado Springs
Excelsior Service Group, Inc. (R)
Robert Hess & Assoc., Inc.
Management Recruiters
Management Recruiters

Denver
Abacus Consultants
Accounting Resources Int'l., Inc.
William B. Arnold Assoc., Inc. (R)
Bennett & Curran, Inc.
DiMarchi Partners (R)
EFL Assoc. (R)
Human Resource Services, Inc. (R)
Karam Group Int'l. (R)
Kearney Executive Search (R)
Lee & Burgess Assoc., Inc. (R)
Lovejoy & Lovejoy (R)
Management Recruiters
Phillips Personnel/Search
R.L. Plimpton Assoc. (R)
Rocky Mountain Recruiters, Inc.
Sigma Group Inc. (R)

Englewood
Career Marketing Assoc.
Dunhill Personnel System, Inc.

Health Industry Consultants, Inc. (R)
Health Technology, Inc.
Medquest Assoc.
Source EDP
Source Finance

Evergreen
Phyllis Stovall Assoc., Inc.

Ft. Collins
Dunhill Personnel Systems, Inc.
McDonald Assoc. (R)

Golden
PC Assoc.

Lakewood
The Human Resource Consulting Group, Inc. (R)
Management Recruiters

Louisville
MPI Assoc.

Monument
Ray N. Bedingfield, Consultant
TransAmerica Network

Parker
Euromedica USA (R)

Woodland Park
Landon-Brookes Executive Search

CONNECTICUT

Avon
R. H. Horton Int'l. (R)

Bridgeport
Curran Partners (R)
Dunhill Personnel System, Inc.
Heritage Search Group, Inc.
Straight & Co.

Cheshire
Peter M. Cahill Assoc., Inc.

Cos Cob
The Hyde Group, Inc. (R)

Cromwell
Management Recruiters of Middlesex

Danbury
Abraham & London Ltd.
Argus National, Inc. (R)
Dunhill Personnel System, Inc.
E O Technical
Executive Register, Inc.
Management Recruiters

Darien
Academy Graduates Executive Search, Inc.
Cosco Resources Inc.
C. L. Howe & Co., Inc.
Lindsey & Assoc., Inc.
W.D. Nolte & Company (R)
Walter Raleigh & Assoc. (R)

East Hartford
Source EDP
Source Finance

East Haven
Marge Dana Assoc. (R)

East Windsor
Sanford Rose Assoc. of Hartford

Fairfield
J.R. Akin & Co. (R)
C. A. Durakis Assoc., Inc. (R)
B. Goodwin, Ltd. (R)
K/N Int'l. (R)
Management Recruiters of Greater Bridgeport, Inc.
Sales Consultants
Smith, Anderson & Co.
Zackrison Assoc., Inc.

Farmington
Dunhill Personnel System, Inc.

Glastonbury
R. C. Handel Assoc. Inc. (R)
Management Recruiters
Richard L. Mather & Assoc.
The Stamford Group Inc. (R)

Green Farms
Claveloux, McCaffrey, McInerney, Inc. (R)

Greenwich
Blackshaw, Olmstead & Atwood (R)
Erlanger Assoc. (R)
Heidrick and Struggles, Inc. (R)
Inside Management Assoc. (R)
Matte & Company, Inc. (R)
Part Time Resources
Von Storch Assoc. (R)
William Willis Worldwide, Inc. (R)

Guilford
Galen Giles Group

Hamden
Management Recruiters

Hartford
Accountants On Call
Deane, Howard & Simon, Inc. (R)
High-Tech Recruiters
Pierce Assoc. (R)
Howard W. Smith Assoc. (R)

Madison
Dussick Management Assoc.
Engineering Search Assoc.

Milford
Sales Consultants

New Canaan
Ast/Bryant (R)
Baldwin Associates, Inc. (R)
Danforth Group (R)
Emmons Assoc., Inc. (R)
JT Assoc.
Plastics Enterprises
Stack Assoc. (R)
J.D. Walsh & Co. (R)
Wilkinson Boyd

New Haven
Dunhill International Search
MRG Search & Placement
Repplier & Co.

Newington
Julian Assoc., Inc.

Norwalk
Dunhill Personnel System, Inc.
Fairfaxx Management Assoc. (R)
The Goodrich & Sherwood Co. (R)
Harris Heery & Assoc., Inc. (R)
Arthur Lyle Assoc., Inc.
Marks & Co., Inc. (R)
Montaigne Assoc., Inc.
Barry Persky & Co., Inc. (R)
Ross Personnel Consultants, Inc.
Weatherby Healthcare

Old Greenwich
Halbrecht & Co.

Old Saybrook
Auden Assoc., Inc.

Oxford
Hunter Int'l., Inc. (R)

Ridgefield
P.J. Lynch Assoc. (R)
Maiorino & Weston Assoc., Inc. (R)

Rocky Hill
Sales Consultants

Rowayton
Higbee Assoc., Inc.
Jim Oravetz & Assoc., Inc.

Simsbury
The Hudson Group
W.R. Lawry, Inc.
People Management Northeast, Inc. (R)

Southport
Alwyn Assoc., Inc. (R)
John O'Keefe & Assoc., Inc. (R)

Stamford
Accountants On Call
Atlantic Search Group, Inc.
Boyden Int'l., Inc. (R)
Brissenden, McFarland, Wagoner &
   Fuccella, Inc. (R)
Career Consulting Group, Inc.
Earley Kielty & Assoc., Inc. (R)
Fleming Energy Group (R)
Flynn, Hannock, Kennan, Inc.
D.E. Foster & Partners, L.P. (R)
Michael Garbi Assoc., Inc.
Halbrecht Lieberman Assoc., Inc. (R)
W. Hanley & Assoc.
Stanley Herz & Co. (R)
Hipp Waters, Inc.
Hipp Waters, Inc.
Interim Managment Corp. (R)
Kearney Executive Search (R)
Kensington Management Consultants, Inc.
   (R)
Korn/Ferry Int'l. (R)
M/P Lotufo Assoc. Inc. (R)
Management Recruiters
Martin Mirtz Morice, Inc. (R)
Masserman & Assoc.
Robert E. McGrath & Assoc. (R)
Norman Broadbent Int'l. (R)
P.R.H. Management, Inc.
Personnel Advisors Int'l. Corp.
The Personnel Laboratory (R)
Plummer & Assoc., Inc. (R)
Retail Recruiters of Stamford
Russell Reynolds Assoc., Inc. (R)
Rockwood Assoc.
Romac & Assoc., Inc.
A. Ryan Assoc.
SRH Resource Group (R)
Sales Consultants
Source EDP
Source Finance

SpencerStuart (R)
Strategic Executives, Inc.
Sullivan-Murphy Assoc. (R)
Tidewater Group Inc.
Ward Howell Int'l. Inc. (R)
Westfield Recruiters

Stratford
Tryg R. Angell Ltd.
Source EDP

Trumbull
GHK Technical Recruiter
Lineal Recruiting Services
P.D. Zier Assoc.

Wallingford
Aerospace Technologies, Inc.
MJF Assoc.
Technical Engineering Consultants

Waterbury
Management Recruiters of Waterbury, Inc.
Midgette Consultants, Inc.
Wallace Assoc.

West Hartford
Flynn, Hannock, Inc.
Industrial Recruiters Assoc., Inc.
The Stevenson Group/SES (R)
Vezan Assoc.

West Haven
Harvard Aimes Group (R)

Westport
Atlantic Search (R)
The Cambridge Group Ltd.
Cambridge Group Ltd.-Exec. Search Div. (R)
David - Kris Assoc., Inc.
DeHayes Consulting Group (R)
Lambert & Sullivan Assoc.
James Mead & Co. (R)
Phase II Management
VideoFields, Ltd. (R)
Ward Liebelt Assoc. Inc. (R)

Willimantic
High Technology Search Assoc.

Wilton
Dunhill Professional Search
Knapp Consultants (R)

Woodbury
Sanford Rose Assoc.- Woodbury

DELAWARE

Christiana
The Placers, Inc.

Dover
Management Recruiters

Hockessin
Sanford Rose Assoc. of Wilmington

Newark
Accountants On Call

Wilmington
Gilbert Tweed Assoc. (R)
Hornberger Management Co., Inc.
Management Recruiters
Romac & Assoc., Inc.
Source EDP

DISTRICT OF COLUMBIA

Washington
Beall & Co., Inc. (R)
Blake, Hansen & Nye, Ltd. (R)
The Corporate Source Group (R)
Development Resource Group
Financial Placement Network
D.E. Foster & Partners, L.P. (R)
Franchise Recruiters Ltd.
Garrison, McGuigan & Sisson
Heidrick and Struggles, Inc. (R)
The Interface Group, Ltd. (R)
Isaacson, Miller, Gilvar & Boulware (R)
Kershner & Co.
Korn/Ferry Int'l. (R)
Major, Wilson & Africa
Management Recruiters
McBride Assoc., Inc. (R)
The NRI Group
R. H. Perry & Assoc., Inc. (R)
Russell Reynolds Assoc., Inc. (R)
Rurak & Assoc., Inc (R)
Sales Consultants
Savoy Partners, Ltd. (R)
Robert Sellery Assoc., Ltd. (R)
Source EDP
Source Finance
Thomas, Whelan Assoc., Inc.

FLORIDA

Altamonte Springs
Financial Resource Assoc., Inc.

Boca Raton
The Curtiss Group, Inc. (R)
Dahl-Morrow Int'l. (R)
Kenmore Executives Inc.
Management Resource Assoc., Inc.
Daniel A. Silverstein Assoc. Inc. (R)

Bradenton
Dunhill of Bradenton, Inc.
Management Recruiters
Sanford Rose Assoc.

Brandon
Management Recruiters

Clearwater
The Butlers Co. Insurance Recruiters
Management Recruiters
Tech Consulting

Coral Gables
Accountants On Call
Mark Stanley & Co. (R)
Sales Consultants

Coral Springs
Bioventure Resources, Inc.
NPF Assoc. Ltd. Inc.
Search Enterprises, Inc.

Daytona Beach
Heller Kil Assoc., Inc.

Deerfield Beach
The Charles Ryan Group, Inc.
Sales Consultants of Ft. Lauderdale
Salesworld-Division of Metacor Inc.

Delray Beach
Dunhill Personnel System, Inc.
Alan Lerner Assoc.
Specialized Search Assoc.

Englewood
Hansen Group, Ltd. (R)

Ft. Lauderdale
Actuaries & Assoc. (R)
Bioventure Resources, Inc.
DHR Int'l, Inc. (R)
Executive Manning Corp. (R)
Kelley & Keller, Inc.
Kirby & Assoc. (R)
R.H. Larsen & Assoc., Inc.
Lasher Assoc. (R)
Management Recruiters
Retail Recruiters/Spectra Professional Search
Romac & Assoc., Inc.
Ropes Assoc., Inc. (R)
Weatherby Healthcare

Ft. Myers
Management Recruiters of Ft. Myers, FL.
Sales Consultants of Ft. Myers, Inc.

Gainesville
The Naples Group, Inc.

Gulf Breeze
Dunhill Personnel System, Inc.
Future Sense
Tatum & Assoc., Inc.

Inverness
Rushlow & Co.

Jacksonville
Curts/Jackson, Inc.
Heidrick and Struggles, Inc. (R)
Management Recruiters
Management Recruiters
RIC Corp. (R)
Sales Consultants

Jensen Beach
Management Recruiters

Lakeland
Management Recruiters
Meads & Assoc.
Jim Parham & Assoc., Inc. (R)
Bob Westerfield & Assoc., Inc.

Largo
Dunhill Personnel System, Inc.
SilverCrest Search

Longwood
Fiordalis Assoc., Inc. (R)
Florapersonnel, Inc.
R.J. Maglio & Assoc., Inc. (R)
The Primary Group, Inc.
Raymond Thomas & Assoc.
Weiss & Assoc., Inc.

Lutz
Sanford Rose Assoc.

Maitland
Management Recruiters
Tina Morbitzer & Assoc.
Sales Consultants

Margate
Staples Consulting Inc. (R)

Melbourne
Dunhill Personnel System, Inc.
Management Recruiters

Miami
Bowker, Brown & Co. (R)
Corporate Advisors Inc.
Griffith & Werner, Inc. (R)
Kearney Executive Search (R)
MD Resources, Inc. (R)
Management Recruiters
Management Recruiters
Messett Assoc., Inc. (R)
National Health Search, Inc.
Parker Page Group
Source EDP
Source Finance

Miami Beach
Summit Executive Search Consultants, Inc.

Miramar
Caremarc & Assoc.

Mount Dora
Management Recruiters

Naples
Bennett Search & Consulting Co. (R)
The Naples Group, Inc.

New Port Richey
Management Recruiters

North Palm Beach
RIC Corp. (R)

Orlando
Management Recruiters
McGuire Executive Search, Inc.
Romac & Assoc., Inc.

Palm Beach Gardens
L. Battalin & Co.

Palm City
Management Recruiters
RIC Corp. (R)

Pensacola
Management Recruiters

Ponte Vedra Beach
Kellogg Consulting Group (R)

Port Charlotte
Management Recruiters

Port St. Lucie
Heritage Search Group, Inc.
Management Recruiters Treasure Coast, Inc.
Management Recruiters

Safety Harbor
Jim Just & Assoc. (R)

Sarasota
Dunhill Personnel System , Inc.
Fortune Personnel Consultants of Sarasota
Inc.
Lechner & Assoc., Inc.
Management Recruiters
Sales Consultants
TASA/Fleming (R)

St. Petersburg
Management Recruiters
Management Recruiters
Wellington Thomas Ltd.
Dennis Wynn Assoc., Inc.

St. Petersburg Beach
Sales Consultants

Tallahassee
Dunhill Personnel System, Inc.
Management Recruiters
Stanewick, Hart & Assoc., Inc.

Tampa
Accountants On Call
Carter-Evdemon & Assoc.
Corporate Consultants Inc.
The Corporate Source Group (R)
Criterion Executive Search, Inc.
Dunhill Personnel of Tampa
Gynn Assoc., Inc. (R)
Lamalie Assoc., Inc. (R)
Management Recruiters of Tampa North
Management Recruiters
Management Recruiters
Management Recruiters
Personnel Advisors Int'l. Corp.
Physician Executive Management Center (R)
Romac & Assoc., Inc.
Roth Young of Tampa
Sales Consultants
Source EDP
Source Finance
Sweeney Shepherd Bueschel Provus Harbert
& Mummert, Inc. (R)

Vero Beach
The Brand Co., Inc. (R)

West Palm Beach
Erlanger Assoc. Inc. (R)
Executive Quest (R)
George Howard Assoc.

Winter Park
Accountants On Call
Gwen Dycus, Inc.
Fox-Morris Assoc., Inc.

Video Interview Professionals, Inc.

GEORGIA

Alpharetta
David F. Brooks & Co., Inc.
Hospitality Resources Int'l., Ltd.
Management Recruiters

Arlington
Jubilee, Inc.

Athens
Sanford Rose Assoc.

Atlanta
A. D. & Assoc.
Accountants On Call
Agri-Personnel
Bellon & Assoc., Inc.
Dotson Benefield & Assoc., Inc.
The Berman Consulting Group (R)
Blackshaw, Olmstead & Atwood (R)
Broward-Dobbs, Inc.
Career Logic, Inc.
M.L. Carter & Assoc., Inc. (R)
H.O. Catherman Inc.
Claremont-Branan, Inc.
Commonwealth Consultants
Computer Network Resources
Corporate Personnel, Inc.
The Crawford Group
Delta Resource Group, Ltd.
Dunhill Search of West Atlanta
Dunhill Personnel System, Inc.
Dunhill Personnel System, Inc.
Eastman & Beaudine, Inc. (R)
Eggleston Consulting Int'l. (R)
Fox-Morris Assoc., Inc.
GKR Int'l. (R)
Garrett Assoc. Inc.
Genovese & Co. (R)
W.L. Handler & Assoc. (R)
Heidrick and Struggles, Inc. (R)
Robert Howe & Assoc. (R)
IprGroup, Inc.
Jackson & Coker (R)
Jacobson Assoc.
Kauffman Hospitality, Inc.
Kearney Executive Search (R)
Korn/Ferry Int'l. (R)
Lamalie Assoc., Inc. (R)
Lanzi & Assoc.
Lawrence-Balakonis & Assoc., Inc.
Mahony & Assoc., Ltd.
Management Recruiters of Atlanta
   Downtown
Management Recruiters
The McKee Co.

McMahon & Dee, Inc. (R)
Jon McRae & Assoc., Inc. (R)
The Mercer Group, Inc. (R)
People Management, Inc. (R)
Richard Peterson & Assoc., Inc. (R)
QVS Int'l. (R)
Paul R. Ray & Co., Inc. (R)
Reddick and Co., Int'l. (R)
Russell Reynolds Assoc., Inc. (R)
The Reynolds Group, Inc.
Romac & Assoc.
Sanford Rose Assoc.
Sales Consultants
Schuyler, Frye & Baker, Inc. (R)
Shoemaker & Assoc. (R)
Simpson Nance & Graham, Inc.
James F. Smith & Assoc.
Source EDP
Source Finance
SpencerStuart (R)
Ron Stevens & Assoc., Inc.
Tatum & Assoc., Inc.
Thalatta Corp. (R)
The Brand Co., Inc. (R)
Thomas-Pond Enterprises (R)
Tyler & Co. (R)
Ward Howell Int'l. Inc. (R)
Waterford, Inc.
R.A. Wells Co.
Wesson, Taylor, Wells & Assoc.
Whittaker & Assoc., Inc.
Zay & Company (R)
Egon Zehnder Int'l. Inc. (R)

Augusta
Dunhill Personnel System, Inc.

Columbus
Management Recruiters

Decatur
Alan MacDonald & Assoc.

Duluth
Smith, Beaty, Barlow Assoc., Inc.

Dunwoody
Professional Medical

Hapeville
Alan Lerner Assoc.

La Grange
Dunhill Personnel System, Inc.

Lawrenceville
Business Search America (R)

Lilburn
Emerson & Co.

Lithia Springs
Management Recruiters of Atlanta West,
Inc.

Marietta
Anderson, Graham & Stewart, Inc.
Impact Executive Search, Inc.
Lowderman & Haney, Inc. (R)
Management Recruiters
Robert E. Mills, FLMI
The Regis Group, Ltd. (R)
Windward Executive Search, Inc.

Norcross
Industry Consultants, Inc.
Michael James & Co., Inc. (R)
The Lighthouse Group
Resource Consultants
Sanford Rose Assoc.

Riverdale
Management Recruiters

Roswell
Anderson Industrial Assoc., Inc.
Beall & Co., Inc. (R)
Howie & Assoc., Inc.
Management Recruiters
Norton & Assoc., Inc. (R)

Savannah
Management Recruiters of Savannah
Sales Consultants of Savannah, GA.

Statham
Clark Assoc., Inc.

Warner Robins
Dunhill Personnel System, Inc.

Woodstock
Management Recruiters

HAWAII

Hilo
Dunhill Professional Search of Hawaii

Honolulu
Dunhill Professional Search of Hawaii
Lam Assoc.
Management Recruiters
Sales Consultants

Kailua-Kona
Dunhill Professional Search of Hawaii

IDAHO

Boise
Dunhill Personnel System, Inc.
Management Recruiters
O'Rourke Co., Inc. (R)
Sales Consultants

ILLINOIS

Albion
Management Recruiters

Arlington Heights
E. J. Ashton & Assoc., Ltd.
Dynamic Search Systems, Inc.
Management Recruiters
Menzel, Robinson, Baldwin, Inc. (R)
Technical Recruiting Consultants

Aurora
Management Recruiters

Bannockburn
Management Recruiters
Mitchell/Wolfson, Assoc. (R)
Nelson-Larson & Assoc. Ltd.

Barrington
Adams & Assoc. Int'l (R)
Dan B. Brockman
David Fockler & Assoc., Inc.
Howe-Weaver, Inc. (R)
J.D. Limited
Joslin & Assoc., Ltd.
L. E. Justice Consulting Assoc. (R)
The Lumsden Co., Inc. (R)
Ward Howell Int'l. Inc. (R)
Wilkins & Co. (R)

Barrington Hills
Richard Beers & Assoc., Ltd. (R)

Batavia
Sales Consultants of Fox Valley

Bloomingdale
Gaffney Management Consultants (R)

Bloomington
James Russell, Inc. (R)
Sales Consultants

Burr Ridge
Management Recruiters
Quigley Assoc., Inc. (R)

Carol Stream
C. Berger and Company

Cary
Raymond James Smith & Assoc.

Champaign
John R. Ady & Assoc., Inc.
Management Recruiters
Sanford Rose Assoc.

Cherry Valley
Management Recruiters

Chicago
Accountants On Call
Allerton Heneghan & O'Neill (R)
American Resources Corp.
Francis V. Anderson Assoc. Inc.
The Bankers Group
Barrett Partners
Billington, Fox & Ellis, Inc. (R)
The Blackman Kallick Search Division (R)
Boyden Int'l., Inc. (R)
Bricker & Assoc., Inc. (R)
Britt Assoc., Inc.
Brooke Chase Assoc., Inc.
Bryant Assoc., Inc.
Robert Campbell & Assoc. (R)
The Carlyle Group, Ltd.
Carpenter, Shackleton & Co. (R)
Cemco, Ltd.
Chicago Legal Search, Ltd.
Compass Group Ltd. (R)
CompuPro
Joseph Conley & Assoc., Inc. (R)
Coopers & Lybrand, Management
  Consulting Services (R)
DHR Int'l., Inc. (R)
Dieckmann & Assoc., Ltd. (R)
Donahue/Bales Assoc. (R)
J. H. Dugan & Assoc., Inc.
Dunhill Personnel System, Inc.
Dunhill Personnel System, Inc.
Dunhill Personnel System, Inc.
Bert H. Early Assoc., Inc. (R)
Elliott, Pfisterer, Chinetti Assoc., Inc. (R)
Executive Referral Services, Inc.
George Fee Assoc., Inc. (R)
Fergason Assoc., Inc.
GKR Int'l. (R)
Gaines & Assoc. Int'l., Inc.
Gregory Michaels & Assoc., Inc.
J. Gross & Assoc.
Hall, Cooper & Bartman, Ltd.
Hedlund Corp.
Hegarty & Co. (R)

The Heidrick Partners, Inc. (R)
Heidrick and Struggles, Inc. (R)
Holland Rusk & Assoc. (R)
The Hollins Group, Inc. (R)
Dieckmann & Associates (R)
Jacobson Assoc.
James, Layton Int'l., Inc. (R)
John H. Johnson & Assoc., Inc. (R)
A.T. Kearney Executive Search (R)
Kennedy & Co. (R)
Jack Kennedy Assoc., Inc.
Kirland Search, Inc.
Kittleman & Assoc. (R)
Korn/Ferry Int'l. (R)
Kresin Wingard
Kuehne & Co., Inc. (R)
Lamalie Assoc., Inc. (R)
Lauer Consulting Services, Inc. (R)
Lauer, Sbarbaro Assoc., Inc. (R)
Lynch Miller Moore, Inc. (R)
MKM Search Consultants, Inc.
Major, Wilson & Africa
Management Recruiters
Management Search, Inc.
C.R. Martin & Assoc. (R)
McFeely Wackerle Shulman (R)
Mengel & McDonald Ltd.
Moriarty/Fox, Inc. (R)
Nordeman Grimm, Inc. (R)
C. J. Noty & Assoc. (R)
Pacific Advisory Service
Prestige Search Inc.
Quaintance Assoc., Inc. (R)
Paul R. Ray & Co., Inc. (R)
S. Reyman & Assoc., Ltd.
Russell Reynolds Assoc., Inc. (R)
Ridenour & Assoc. (R)
Robertson, Spoerlein & Wengert (R)
Romac & Assoc., Inc.
Ropella & Assoc.
The Ryan Charles Group, Inc.
Sales & Management Search, Inc.
Sales Consultants
Salesworld-Division of Metacor Inc.
David Saxner & Assoc., Inc.
Search Bureau Int'l.
Search Dynamics, Inc.
Sheridan Search (R)
John Sibbald Assoc., Inc. (R)
Slayton Int'l., Inc. (R)
Abbott Smith Assoc., Inc.
Smith Hanley Assoc.
Source EDP
Source Finance
SpencerStuart (R)
Stone Enterprises Ltd.
Strategic Executives., Inc.
Strategic Search Corp. (R)
Sweeney Shepherd Bueschel Provus Harbert
  & Mummert, Inc. (R)
Synergistics Assoc. Ltd. (R)
Taylor Search Assoc., Inc. (R)
Telemarketing Search, Inc.

Tesar-Reynes, Inc. (R)
Universal Executive Search, Inc. (R)
Ward Howell Int'l. Inc. (R)
Westcott Associates, Inc. (R)
Wheelless Group
Donald Williams Assoc., Inc. (R)
Williams, Roth & Krueger, Inc. (R)
Winston Rooney & Green
Wood/Sprau/Tannura, Inc. (R)
Wytmar & Co., Inc. (R)
Egon Zehnder Int'l. Inc. (R)

Crete
Franchise Recruiters Ltd.

Crystal Lake
Corporate Environment Ltd. (R)
McDermott & Assoc.
Sales Consultants

Darien
Strategic Staffing Concepts, Inc. (R)

Deerfield
The Elson Group, Inc. (R)
Higgins Assoc., Inc. (R)
R. H. McIlwaine & Assoc.
Meder & Assoc. (R)
Sales Consultants

Des Plaines
Bowersox & Assoc., Inc.
Financial Search Corp.
Human Resource Technologies, Inc. (R)
The Lockridge Group, Inc. (R)
Management Recruiters

Downers Grove
Lucas & Assoc., Ltd.
Studwell Assoc. (R)

Dundee
Norton & Assoc.

Effingham
Sanford Rose Assoc.

Elgin
Clark-Winans, Inc.
Management Recruiters
Stephen Sellers Assoc.

Elk Grove Village
Gutreuter & Assoc. (R)

Elmhurst
Michael Assoc. (R)
Search Masters

Geneva
Oberlander & Co., Inc. (R)
Xagas & Assoc. (R)

Glen Ellyn
Michael S. Dunford, Inc. (R)
Parsons Assoc. Inc. (R)
Philip Daniels Assoc., Inc.

Glenview
John C. Boone & Co. (R)
Spriggs & Co., Inc. (R)

Granite City
Search Source, Inc. (R)

Highland Park
LMB Assoc.

Hinsdale
Philip Conway Management (R)
De Funiak & Edwards (R)
RAI Consulting
David Rowe & Assoc., Inc. (R)
Scott Kappele & Gnodde

Inverness
William Hetzel Assoc., Inc. (R)

Itasca
BGB Assoc., Inc.
The Remington Group, Ltd.
VanMaldegiam Assoc., Inc. (R)

La Grange
Joseph Chandler & Assoc., Inc. (R)

Lake Bluff
The PAR Group - Paul A. Reaume, Ltd. (R)

Lake Forest
Chicago Research Group, Inc. (R)
McDonald Assoc. (R)

Libertyville
Matthews Professional Employment
Specialists, Inc.

Lincoln
Agra Placements, Ltd.

Lincolnshire
Sales Consultants

Lincolnwood
Pre-Search, Inc. (R)

Lisle
Benton Schneider & Assoc. (R)
Peterson Consulting/W.P., Inc. (R)
Verkamp-Joyce Assoc., Inc. (R)

McHenry
Stephen Fox Assoc. Inc. (R)

Mt. Prospect
Hansen Management Search Co. (R)
Magnum Search

Naperville
Dalton-Smith & Assoc., Inc.
Jender & Company (R)
J. Johnston Group, Inc.
Stephen R. Smith & Co., Inc. (R)
J.D. Wright & Assoc., Inc.

Niles
Polytechnical Consultants, Inc.

Normal
Management Recruiters

Northbrook
Accountants On Call
K. Carroll & Assoc.
Jack Clarey Assoc., Inc. (R)
The Crosby Group, Inc. (R)
Hersher Assoc., Ltd. (R)
Voigt Assoc. (R)

Northfield
James Feerst & Assoc., Inc. (R)

Oak Brook
Callan Assoc., Ltd. (R)
Cemco Syetems
Erwin Assoc. (R)
Executive Appointments Ltd., Int'l. (R)
Robert Grossberg & Assoc. (R)
Kieffer, Ford, & Hadelman, Ltd. (R)
Kolden & Assoc., Ltd. (R)
Kunzer Assoc., Ltd. (R)
Lyons & Assoc., Inc.
M/J/A Partners (R)
Moore Employment Svs., Inc.
Newpher & Co., Inc. (R)
John Paisios Ltd. (R)
Pasini & Co. (R)
Sanford Rose Assoc.
Sales Consultants
Trilogy Enterprises, Inc.
Witt Assoc. Inc. (R)

Oak Park
O'Toole & Company (R)
Research Alternatives, Inc. (R)

Oakbrook Terrace
Cemco Medical
Consumer Search, Inc.
Professional Medical
Source EDP
Source Finance

Orland Park
McSherry & Assoc. (R)
Nicholaou & Co. (R)

Palatine
The Robinson Group, D.A., Ltd.
Sales Consultants

Palos Heights
Management Recruiters
Sales Consultants Chicago Southeast

Park Ridge
DeCorrevont & Assoc.

Rockford
Dunhill Personnel System, Inc.
Effective Search, Inc. (R)
The Furst Group

Rolling Meadows
Computer Professionals (R)
Dunhill Personnel System, Inc.
Effective Search, Inc. (R)
Handwerk & Assoc.
John Imber Assoc., Ltd. (R)
Riverside Consultants, Inc.
Source EDP

Rosemont
Bertrand, Ross & Assoc., Inc. (R)
Paul J. Biestek Assoc., Inc. (R)
Hodge-Cronin & Assoc., Inc. (R)
International Management Services Inc. (R)

Schaumburg
Chase Waterford Ltd.
Henry Michaels & Assoc. (R)
Kinderis & Loercher Group
Earl L. McDermid & Assoc.
National Restaurant Search, Inc. (R)
Sales Consultants
Systems One Ltd.
Valentine & Assoc.

Skokie
First Search Inc.
Management Recruiters
Ronald Norris & Assoc.

South Holland
Dunhill Personnel System, Inc.

Spring Grove
Tully & Birch, Inc. (R)

Springfield
Cona Personnel Search

St. Charles
Gregory L. Borchert, Inc.
Management Recrutiers
Prestige Search Inc.

Sycamore
Mathey Services

Waukegan
Matthews Professional Employment
Specialists, Inc.

Westchester
C.P.S., Inc.

Western Springs
Chandler & Rozner Assoc. (R)
Search Solutions, Inc.

Westmont
Search Enterprises, Inc.

Wheeling
Management Recruiters
Matthews Professional Employment
Specialists, Inc.

Wilmette
Joyce C. Knauff & Assoc.
David J. White & Assoc., Inc.

Winnetka
Harold Webb Assoc., Ltd. (R)

INDIANA

Anderson
Hudson Assoc. Inc.

Bloomington
Kendall & Davis Co., Inc.

Claypool
Dunhill Personnel System, Inc.

Columbus
Dunhill Personnel System, Inc.
Management Recruiters
TASA/Fleming (R)

Dyer
National Recruiting Service

Elkhart
Robert Sage Recruiting

Evansville
Management Recruiters
Sales Consultants

Ft. Wayne
Dunhill Personnel System, Inc.
Dunhill Personnel System, Inc.
National Corporate Consultants, Inc.
Sanford Rose Assoc.

Indianapolis
Consult One, Inc.
Dunhill Personnel System, Inc.
Dunhill Personnel System, Inc.
HMO Executive Search
Management Recruiters
Midwest Medical Consultants
Resource Network Inc. (R)
Sales Consultants
J. Harrington Smith Assoc.
Source EDP
Source Finance

Kokomo
Management Recruiters

Lafayette
Sanford Rose Assoc.

Merrillville
National Executive Consultants, Inc.

Michigan City
Dunhill Personnel System, Inc.
Management Recruiters

Mishawaka
Sanford Rose Assoc.

Munster
Dunhill Personnel System, Inc.

Nashville
Dunhill Personnel System, Inc.

Peru
Agra Placements, Ltd.

Richmond
Management Recruiters

Shelbyville
Personnel Management, Inc.

South Bend
mfg/Search, Inc.
Management Recruiters

Valparaiso
Precise Legal, Inc.

Wabash
Lange & Assoc., Inc.

Warsaw
Strategy 2000

West Layfayette
ExecuTech

IOWA

Bettendorf
Management Recruiters
Professional Personnel Services

Cedar Rapids
Cambridge & Assoc., Inc.
Dunhill Personnel System, Inc.
Management Recruiters of Cedar Rapids,
Inc.
Sales Consultants

Des Moines
Corporate Suite, Ltd.
The Garrison Organization
The Human Resource Group
McGladrey Search Group
Personnel Inc.

Iowa City
Dunhill Personnel System, Inc.
Management Recruiters

Mason City
Management Recruiters

Mount Vernon
Gallagher & Assoc.

Waterloo
Management Recruiters

West Des Moines
Agra Placements, Ltd.
Francis & Assoc. (R)
Key Employment Services

KANSAS

Kansas City
Management Recruiters

Leawood
Lee & Burgess Assoc., Inc. (R)

Lenexa
Gleason & Assoc. (R)

Liberal
Management Recruiters

Overland Park
Bowman & Marshall
Dunhill Personnel System, Inc.
EFL Assoc. (R)
Lunney, Hadden & Assoc.
Management Recruiters
Charles Russ Assoc. (R)
Sales Consultants
Michael Shirley Assoc. (R)
Smith Bradley & Assoc.
Source EDP
Source Finance
Wood-Glavin, Inc. (R)

Shawnee Mission
Michael/Merrill
Stoneburner Assoc., Inc.

Topeka
Dunhill Personnel System, Inc.
Management Recruiters of Topeka, Inc.
Management Recruiters

Wichita
Career Advancement
Dunhill Personnel System, Inc.
Management Recruiters
Sales Consultants
Source EDP
Source Finance

KENTUCKY

Bowling Green
Management Recruiters
Sales Consultants Bowling Green

Crestwood
Dunhill Personnel System, Inc.

Danville
Management Recruiters

Frankfort
Career Information Services, Inc.

Gracey
Dunhill Personnel System, Inc.

Henderson
Dunhill Personnel System, Inc.

Lexington
Career Management, Inc.
Management Recruiters
Sales Consultants

Louisville
Crest Management Search, Inc.
Focus: HealthCare
The Hindman Co. (R)
Management Recruiters
Physician Services of America (R)
Sales Consultants
Smith Roth & Squires (R)
Source EDP
TASA/Fleming (R)

Owenton
Management Recruiters

Prospect
Karen Marshall Assoc.

Richmond
Management Recruiters

LOUISIANA

Baton Rouge
Dunhill Personnel System, Inc.
Management Recruiters
Sales Consultants

Franklin
Sanford Rose Assoc.

Metairie
Management Recruiters
Sales Consultants

Monroe
Dunhill Personnel System, Inc.

New Orleans
Romac & Assoc., Inc.
Snelling Personnel Services

Shreveport
Dunhill Personnel System, Inc.

Slidell
Management Recruiters

MAINE

Brunswick
Ames Personnel Consultants

Cape Elizabeth
Executive Resource Group (R)

Hampden
Northern Consultants Inc. (R)

Kennebunk
Yake & Assoc.

Portland
Elliott J. Berv & Assoc. (R)
Dunhill Personnel System, Inc.
Intertech Search Group
Rogers & Seymour Inc.
Romac & Assoc., Inc.
Romac & Assoc., Inc.
Sales Consultants
The Stoddard Co.

South Portland
Executive Search of New England, Inc.

MARYLAND

Annapolis
The Abbott Group (R)
Inmark Executive Search (R)
Key Talent, Inc.
Alan Lerner Assoc.
Management Recruiters
Marlar Int'l. Inc. (R)

Baltimore
Accountants On Call
Babson, Moore & Wilcox (R)
D.W. Baird & Associates
Charles A. Binswanger Assoc., Inc.
Brandjes Assoc.
CES
Conaway Legal Search
Walter V. Connor Int'l., Inc. (R)
Fox-Morris Assoc., Inc.
Gabriel & Bowie Assoc., Ltd.
A.T. Kearney Executive Svs. (R)

Kostmayer Assoc., Inc. (R)
Management Assoc.
Management Recruiters
Sales Consultants
Sales Consultants
Salesworld-Division of Metacor Inc.
Source EDP
Source Finance
Telem Adhesive Search Corp.
White-Ridgely & Assoc., Inc.

Bethesda
Ira Broadman Assoc.
A.G. Fishkin & Assoc., Inc.
Larsen & Lee, Inc. (R)
Larsen Int'l., Inc. (R)
Craig Williamson, Inc. (R)
Witt Assoc. Inc. (R)

Calverton
C.A. Durakis Assoc., Inc. (R)

Chevy Chase
Ames Assoc. Inc.
Krauthamer & Assoc. (R)

Cockeysville
E. G. Jones Assoc., Ltd.

Columbia
Gleason & Assoc. (R)
Sales Consultants
C. J. Vincent Assoc., Inc.

Frederick
Management Recruiters of Frederick, Inc.

Gaithersburg
CPI Technical Services
Management Recruiters

Germantown
James L. Walsh & Assoc., Inc. (R)

Hanover
Management Recruiters

Hunt Valley
Cross Country Consultants, Inc.
Fallstaff Search

Hyattsville
Sales Consultants

Lanham
Russell Assoc.

Linthicum
Annapolis Consulting Group (R)
Executive Dynamics, Inc.
Roberts Ryan & Bentley (R)

Olney
Krautler Personnel Recruitment

Owings Mills
Thoroughbred Executive Search

Reisterstown
Dunhill Professional Search Group

Rockville
Dunhill Personnel System, Inc.
JDG Assoc., Ltd.
E. G. Jones Assoc., Ltd.
Management Recruiters
The NRI Group
Retail Placement Assoc.
Sanford Rose Assoc. - Rockville

Salisbury
Management Recruiters

Silver Spring
Excelsior Services Group Inc. (R)
RBR Assoc., Inc.

Stevensville
Studwell Assoc. (R)

Timonium
Bowling Executive Registry, Inc.
Sanford Rose Assoc.

Westminister
Management Recruiters

MASSACHUSETTS

Accord
Langlois & Assoc.

Acton
Stimmel Search Division (R)

Andover
Kishbaugh Associates (R)
Straube Assoc., Inc. (R)

Belmont
Auerbach Assoc. (R)

Boston

Aberdeen Assoc.
Accountants On Call
Action Inc.
Ashworth Consultants, Inc. (R)
Atlantic Search Group, Inc.
Nathan Barry Assoc., Inc. (R)
Elliott J. Berv & Assoc. (R)
C.P.S., Inc.
Canny, Bowen Inc. (R)
Chaloner Assoc.
Dean M. Coe Assoc. (R)
M.J. Curran & Assoc., Inc. (R)
J.H. Dugan & Assoc., Inc.
Dumont Moriarty & Assoc.
Gardiner Stone Hunter Int'l., Inc. (R)
Gatti & Assoc.
Hayden Group, Inc. (R)
Heidrick and Struggles, Inc. (R)
Hospitality Executive Search, Inc.
Isaacson, Miller, Inc. (R)
JNB Assoc., Inc.
Kiradjieff & Co.
Korn/Ferry Int'l. (R)
Management Recruiters
Management Recruiters
Mercedes & Co., Inc. (R)
OSA Partners, Inc.
Organization Resources Inc. (R)
P.A.R. Assoc., Inc. (R)
Parker, Sholl & Gordon, Inc. (R)
Personnel Systems Int'l. Inc.
Russell Reynolds Assoc., Inc. (R)
Robsham & Assoc. (R)
Romac & Assoc., Inc.
Russillo/Gardner
Salesworld-Division of Metacor Inc.
J. Robert Scott (R)
Scott-Wayne Assoc., Inc.
Selected Executives, Inc.
Source EDP
Source Finance

Braintree

Alan Lerner Assoc.
Management Recruiters

Brockton

Sales Consultants
Xavier Assoc., Inc.

Burlington

Double M Executive Placement Service, Inc.
Pencom Systems Inc.
C.W. Sink & Co., Inc. (R)
Source EDP
Source Engineering

Cambridge

Greene & Co.
The Viscusi Group, Inc. (R)

Canton

Engineering Directions

Chelmsford

Timothy D. Crowe, Jr.
Marketing Resource

Concord

Blaney Executive Search (R)
Haddad Assoc. (R)
Human Resource Research Inc. (R)

Danvers

Morency Assoc.
Sales Consultants

East Longmeadow

Sales Consultants

Framingham

Accountants On Call
Franklin Int'l. Search, Inc.
Professional Medical
L. A. Silver Assoc., Inc.
Stephen M. Sonis Assoc.

Hingham

The PAR Group - Paul A. Reaume, Ltd. (R)
Kimball Shaw Assoc. (R)
Daniel Stern & Assoc.

Hopkinton

Accounting Resources Int'l., Inc.

Lexington

Lee Calhoon & Co., Inc. (R)
The Corporate Source Group (R)
Fenwick Partners (R)
Human Resource Consulting Group, Inc. (R)
John J. Kennedy Assoc., Inc.
Multi Processing, Inc.
Louis Rudzinsky Assoc., Inc.
Triangle Consulting Group
Willmott & Assoc.

Mansfield

Sales Consultants - Bristol County

Marblehead

J. H. Folger Company (R)

Marlborough

Biotech Sourcing
Gilbert Tweed Assoc., Inc. (R)

Marshfield

Battista Assoc., Inc.

Maynard
Steinbach & Co.

Medfield
Gatti & Assoc.
Prestonwood Assoc.

Nantucket
Educational Management Network (R)

Natick
Casey & Gerrish Assoc., Inc.
The Kinlin Co., Inc. (R)
McInturff & Assoc., Inc.

Needham
Arancio Assoc.
Edwin Mruk & Partners (R)
G.A. Field Personnel Consultants
Ford & Ford
Glou Int'l., Inc. (R)

Newton
Keane Assoc. (R)
Charles Zabriskie Assoc., Inc. (R)

Newton Lower Falls
Gustin Partners, Ltd. (R)

Newton Upper Falls
The Yorkshire Group, Ltd. (R)

North Andover
Financial Search Group, Inc.

Northborough
Computer Security Placement Service, Inc.
Kacevich, Lewis & Brown, Inc.

Norwood
Heffelfinger Assoc., Inc. (R)

Osterville
Sanford Rose Assoc.

Otis
Jules Seltzer Assoc.

Sagamore Beach
Sales Consultants

Salem
American Executive Management, Inc. (R)

Sandwich
Dean M. Coe Assoc. (R)

Saxonville
Norman Powers Assoc., Inc.

Sharon
Partridge Assoc., Inc.

Springfield
Dunhill Personnel System, Inc.
Management Recruiters
Rand Assoc. (R)

Stoneham
Roth Young of Boston

Stow
Tecmark/Massachusetts Inc.

Sudbury
L.J. Doherty & Assoc.
Travis & Co., Inc. (R)
Joel H. Wilensky Assoc., Inc.

Swampscott
New Dimensions in Technology, Inc.

Waltham
Additional Technical Support Inc.
Aubin Int'l. Inc. (R)
Cibotti Assoc., Inc.
Logix, Inc.
Nachman Biomedical
George D. Sandel Assoc.
Winter, Wyman & Co.

Wellesley
Bartholdi & Co. (R)
Boyden(Onstott Group) (R)
Christian & Timbers, Inc. (R)
Dromeshauser Assoc. (R)
The Marlow Group (R)
The Onstott Group (R)
D.P. Parker & Assoc., Inc. (R)
Rafey & Company (R)
Sales Consultants of Wellesley, Inc.

Wellesley Hills
Chestnut Hill Partners, Inc. (R)
Mazza & Riley, Inc. (R)
Nagler & Co., Inc. (R)
Newcombe & Cyr Assoc., Inc.
The Pickwick Group, Inc.
Trowbridge & Co., Inc. (R)

West Springfield
Hunter Assoc.

Westborough
Management Recruiters
Source EDP
Source Engineering

Westford
The Windham Group

Weston
F. L. Mannix & Co., Inc. (R)
Weston Consultants, Inc. (R)

Weymouth
Winfield Assoc.

Woburn
The Elliott Company (R)
Gatti & Assoc.
Zurick, Davis & Co. (R)

Worcester
Delores F. George
Professional Recruiters Inc.

MICHIGAN

Ann Arbor
Davis & Company (R)
Charles E. Day & Assoc., Inc. (R)
Dunhill Personnel System, Inc.
Elwell & Assoc., Inc. (R)
Human Resource Network
L.J. Johnson & Co. (R)
Management Recruiters
Gayle L. Mattson & Assoc. (R)
mfg/Search

Battle Creek
Management Recruiters
Lou Michaels Assoc.
Savalli & Assoc., Inc.

Bingham Farms
G.A.M. Executive Search, Inc.
Management Recruiters

Birmingham
Compass Group Ltd. (R)
Crowder & Company (R)
Duane I. Wilson Assoc., Inc. (R)

Blissfield
Management Recruiters

Bloomfield Hills
The Blunt Co., Inc. (R)
S.R. Dunlap & Assoc., Inc. (R)
Gundersen Brenner, Inc. (R)
M. Scott Kemp & Assoc., Inc. (R)
Sanford Rose Assoc.

Brighton
Management Recruiters

Centerline
Sharrow & Assoc., Inc.

Dearborn
Management Recruiters of Dearborn, Inc.

Detroit
B.P.A. Enterprises, Inc.
Coopers & Lybrand, Management
Consulting Services (R)
LaDuke & Assoc., Inc.
Management Recruiters
Salesworld-Division of Metacor Inc.

Farmington Hills
Dunhill Personnel System, Inc.
Phyllis Hawkins & Assoc., Inc.
Sales Consultants

Fenton
Dupuis & Ryden, P.C. (R)

Flint
Dupuis & Ryden, P.C. (R)
Management Recruiters

Grand Haven
Dunhill Personnel System, Inc.

Grand Rapids
Advanced Executive Resources (R)
BDO Seidam (R)
G.L. Dykstra Assoc., Inc.
Lowery, Cotter, & Assoc.
Sales Consultants
Source EDP
Source Finance

Grandville
The Clayton Edward Group, Inc.

Grosse Pointe Farms
Michael W. Parres & Assoc. (R)

Grosse Pointe Park
Case Executive Search

Holland
Management Recruiters
The Viscusi Group, Inc. (R)

Holt
Management Recruiters

Kalamazoo
Dunhill Professional Search of Kalamazoo
Heller Kil Assoc., Inc.
Management Recruiters
Sales Consultants

Lansing
Dunhill Personnel System, Inc.
Sales Consultants
Sales Consultants

Lapeer
J. E. Lessner Assoc., Inc. (R)

Livonia
Opportunity Knocking, Inc.
Weliver & Assoc.

Midland
Link Personnel & Assoc.
Management Recruiters

Monroe
Management Recruiters

Mt. Pleasant
Management Recruiters
Sales Consultants

Muskegon
Management Recruiters

Northville
NDI Services (R)

Plymouth
Sales Consultants
Sharrow & Assoc., Inc.

Richland
The Lawson Group

Rochester
Management Recruiters of North Oakland
County, Inc.

Saginaw
Dunhill Personnel System, Inc.

Southfield
Davis-Smith Medical-Dental Employment
Service, Inc.
Dunhill Personnel System, Inc.
Executives' Personnel Service Inc.
Joe L. Giles & Assoc., Inc.
Ludot Personnel Services, Inc.
Sanford Rose Assoc.- Detroit North
Saber-Salisbury & Assoc., Inc.
Sales Consultants
Source EDP
Source Finance
Henry Welker & Assoc.

St. Joseph
Management Recruiters

Stevensville
Guidarelli Assoc., Inc.

Traverse City
Management Recruiters
Midwest Medical Recruiters
PLRS/Career Connections

Troy
Dupuis & Ryden, P.C. (R)
Harvey Hohauser & Assoc. (R)
Management Recruiters
Sales Consultants
Wing Tips & Pumps, Inc.

West Bloomfield
Geneva Group Int'l. (R)

MINNESOTA

Bloomington
Source EDP
Source Finance

Burnsville
Dunhill Personnel System, Inc.
Professional Recruiters Inc.

Eden Prairie
Dunhill Personnel System, Inc.

Hutchinson
Delacore Personnel

Minneapolis
Accountants On Call
Agra Placements, Ltd.
Andcor Human Resources (R)
Robert L. Charon
Robert Connelly & Assoc., Inc. (R)
Corporate Resources Professional Placement
Ells Personnel Systems Inc.
Mary R. Erickson & Assoc. (R)
Executive Search Inc. (R)
D.E. Foster & Partners, L.P. (R)
Jackley Search Consultants
Kathryn L. Johnson
Kearney Executive Search (R)
Korn/Ferry Int'l. (R)
Kreofsky & Assoc.
Kromenaker & Associates
Management Recruiters
Northland Recruiting Inc.
People Management, Inc. (R)
Polson & Co., Inc. (R)
Russell Reynolds Assoc., Inc. (R)
Romac & Assoc., Inc.
Roth Young Executive Recruiters

Sales Consultants
Sathe & Assoc., Inc. (R)
Schalekamp & Assoc., Inc. (R)
Source EDP
Source Finance
Stewart, Stein & Scott, Ltd. (R)
Stone, Murphy & Olson (R)
Walker Group, Inc. (R)
Whitbeck & Assoc.
Wood, Franchot Inc. (R)
Steven Yungerberg Assoc., Inc. (R)

South St. Paul
Carolyn Smith Paschal Intl.

St. Paul
Development Search Specialists (R)
Sievers & Assoc. (R)
Source EDP
Source Finance
Wells, Bradley & Assoc.

Wayzata
James Bangert & Assoc., Inc. (R)
Mary L. Mayer, Ltd.
The Mazzitelli Group, Ltd. (R)
Peter Van Leer & Assoc. (R)

MISSISSIPPI

Bolton
Buzhardt Assoc. (R)

Jackson
Management Recruiters
Jim Woodson & Assoc., Inc.

Madison
Dunhill Personnel System, Inc.

MISSOURI

Camdenton
Management Recruiters

Chesterfield
Dunhill Personnel System, Inc.

Clayton
Dunhill Personnel System, Inc.
Annie Gray Assoc., Inc. (R)

Columbia
Management Recruiters

Creve Coeur
Bradford & Galt, Inc.

Fenton
Management Recruiters

Independence
Management Recruiters
Management Science Assoc. (R)

Joplin
Dunhill Professional Search

Kansas City
AGRI-associates
Accountants On Call
Agri-Tech Personnel, Inc.
Ron Ball & Assoc.
The Christopher Group
Dunhill Personnel System, Inc.
Dunhill Personnel System, Inc.
Kennison & Assoc.
Lawrence-Leiter & Co. (R)
Management Recruiters
Romac & Assoc., Inc.
Sales Consultants
Source EDP
Source Finance

Lake Ozark
Whitehead & Assoc., Inc.

Springfield
Management Recruiters

St. Louis
Accountants On Call
Cejka & Co. (R)
Challenger & Hunt (R)
Grant Cooper & Assoc., Inc. (R)
Davis & James, Inc.
Dunhill Personnel System, Inc.
James L. Fisk & Assoc.
Gleason & Assoc. (R)
Hitchens & Foster, Inc.
Holohan Group, Ltd. (R)
John & Powers, Inc. (R)
Kendall & Davis Co., Inc.
Kensington Management Consultants (R)
Michael Latas & Assoc., Inc. (R)
Lee & Burgess Assoc., Inc. (R)
The Logan Group, Inc. (R)
Management Recruiters
Management Recruiters
Management Recruiters
Medical Sales & Management Specialists
R.C. Morton & Assoc. Inc. (R)
R. F. Mulvaney & Assoc., Inc. (R)
P&IC Assoc.
Rieser & Assoc., Inc. (R)
Romac & Assoc., Inc.

Sales Consultants
Sales Consultants
Source EDP
Source Finance
Ron Sunshine & Assoc.
Thomure Medsearch, Inc. (R)

St. Peters
Huxtable Assoc., Inc. (R)

Westport Plaza
Accountants On Call

NEBRASKA

Blair
Sanford Rose Assoc.

Boystown
Sandi McDonald & Assoc., Inc.

Kearney
Dunhill Professional Search, Inc. of Kearney

Lincoln
Blau Kaptain Schroeder (R)
William J. Elam & Assoc. (R)
Management Recruiters

Omaha
Dunhill Search of Omaha, Inc.
Eggers Consulting Co., Inc.
Harrison Moore Inc.
Management Recruiters
Sales Consultants
Source Finance

NEVADA

Carson City
Alan Glenn & Keener

Incline Village
Wheeler Assoc.

Reno
Management Recruiters of Reno

NEW HAMPSHIRE

Bedford
Availability Personnel Consultants
Elliott J. Berv & Assoc. (R)

Management Recruiters

Concord
Barger & Sargeant, Inc. (R)
Sales Consultants

Dover
Individual Employment Services

Fitzwilliam
James H. Kennedy

Hampton
EXETER 2100

Londonderry
EPN, Inc.

Manchester
Dunhill of Manchester Inc.
Romac & Assoc., Inc.

Merrimack
Sanford Rose Assoc.
Sales Consultants of Nashua - Manchester

Nashua
AviSearch Int'l.
Conard Assoc., Inc. (R)
Fortune Personnel Consultants
Source EDP
Source Engineering
Source Finance

North Hampton
McDonald Assoc. (R)

North Salem
High Tech Opportunities, Inc.

Portsmouth
Career Profiles

NEW JERSEY

Aberdeen
Adel Lawrence Assoc., Inc.
Remark Assoc. Inc.

Andover
Carris, Jackowitz Assoc. (R)

Audubon
Howard Clark Assoc.

Basking Ridge
Oldwick Enterprises, Inc.

Beach Haven
Maschal/Connors Inc. (R)

Bernardsville
Management Recruiters

Bordentown
Management Recruiters

Boundbrook
Gardner, Savage Assoc.

Bridgewater
Brissenden, McFarland, Wagoner &
Fuccella, Inc. (R)

Brielle
Barclay Consultants, Inc.
The Yaiser Group

Budd Lake
The Consortium

Califon
Sales Consultants

Cedar Knolls
Paul Falcone Assoc., Inc.
Donald P. Hayes Assoc., Inc.

Chatham
Christenson & Hutchison (R)
Koontz, Jeffries & Assoc., Inc. (R)
McCulloch Assoc.
Tech Vision Co.

Cherry Hill
Dunhill Personnel System, Inc.
Allan Gardner & Assoc., Inc. (R)
Grant, Franks & Assoc.
Management Recruiters
RALCO/Richard A. Lucia & Assoc.
Ramming & Assoc., Inc. (R)
Romac & Assoc., Inc.
Romeo-Hudgins & Assoc. Ltd. (R)
Sales Consultants
Worlco Computer Resources, Inc.

Clark
HRD Consultants, Inc. (R)
Jeff Rich Assoc.
Sales Consultants

Cliffside Park
BR & Assoc.

Clifton
Management Recruiters of Passaic, inc.

Colonia
Sherbrooke Assoc., Inc. (R)

Cranbury
Deery, Geddis & Assoc.

Cranford
McCullough Assoc. (R)

Cresskill
JDavid Assoc., Inc. (R)

Denville
The E & K Group

East Brunswick
Diedre Moire Corp., Inc.

Edison
Accountants On Call
The Altco Group
Career Search Assoc.
Sanford Rose Assoc.
Source EDP
Source Finance

Emerson
Bryant Research

Englewood
Sanford Rose Assoc.

Englewood Cliffs
Brooks Executive Personnel
Executive Exchange Corp.
Phyllis Solomon Executive Search, Inc.
The Stevenson Group/SES (R)

Englishtown
Stewart/Laurence Assoc., Inc. (R)

Fair Lawn
Polytechnic Design Co.
RPA Management Consultants, Inc.

Fairfield
The Consortium
Sales Consultants

Fanwood
Engineering & Scientific Search Assoc.
Peeney Assoc., Inc. (R)

Flanders
The Comwell Co. Inc.
TeleSearch, Inc.

Florham Park
Frank E. Allen & Assoc.

Fords
Datamatics Management Services, Inc.

Freehold
Dunhill of Freehold, Inc.
Dunhill Personnel System, Inc.

Ft. Lee
Devin Scott Assoc.

Gibbsboro
Alan Lerner Assoc.

Glen Rock
Gary S. Bell Assoc., Inc.
Sales Consultants of Northern Jersey, Inc.

Green Brook
Trac One (R)

Hackensack
Robert Drexler Assoc., Inc.

Hackettstown
MCC Assoc. (R)
Management Recruiters

Haddonfield
Woehr Assoc.

Hasbrouck Heights
Fox-Morris Assoc., Inc.

Highland Lakes
Roberts Assoc.

Highlands
Hartman, Barnette & Assoc. (R)

Hillside
Performance Professionals

Hoboken
Sales Consultants

Holmdel
Joseph Crisanti, Inc.

Hopewell
Capitol Management Consulting, Inc.

Howell Twp.
D.M. Rein & Co., Inc. (R)

Iselin
A. Davis Grant & Co. (R)
META/MAT, Ltd. (R)
Sales Consultants

Jersey City
Dalton Management Consultants, Ltd.

Lafayette
Management Recruiters

Lambertville
CES

Lawrenceville
Management Recruiters
Sanford Rose Assoc.

Liberty Corner
Paul Ray & Carre Orban Int'l (R)

Little Falls
Krow Assoc., Inc.
Steeple Associates, Inc.

Little Silver
Graham & Co. (R)

Livingston
Accountants On Call
Management Recruiters
Martin Personnel Assoc.

Long Valley
Technitrac, Inc.

Madison
Joseph R. Burns & Assoc., Inc. (R)
Karras Personnel, Inc.

Mahwah
Dunhill Personnel System, Inc.

Manasquan
R.W. Apple & Assoc.
Executive Exchange Corp.
The Mulshine Co., Inc. (R)

Marlton
Accountants On Call
Bonifield Assoc.
Management Recruiters
Sales Consultants

Matawan
N. Willner & Co., Inc.

Maywood
The DataFinders Group, Inc.

Medford
Dunhill Personnel System, Inc.
Management Recruiters
Munroe, Curry & Bond Assoc. (R)

Milford
A.L.S. Group

Millburn
Marra/Pizzi Assoc., Inc. (R)

Milltown
Amherst Personnel Group Inc.
Curry, Telleri Group, Inc. (R)
RGL Assoc., Inc.

Montclair
Drew Assoc. Int'l. (R)

Morganville
LAS Management Consulting Group, Inc.

Morris Plains
Ballos & Co., Inc. (R)
Thomas-Pond (R)

Morristown
Boyden Int'l., Inc. (R)
Graham Assoc. Inc.
Jahrling & Co. (R)
Management Recruiters

Mountain
Besen Assoc. Inc.

Mountain Lakes
J.B. Gilbert Assoc., Inc. (R)
Orion Consulting, Inc. (R)

Mountainside
Management Recruiters

Murray Hill
Engineering Resource Group, Inc.

New Brunswick
Place Mart Personnel Service

North Bergen
Allan Karson Assoc., Inc. (R)

North Branch
T. J. Koellhoffer & Assoc. (R)

North Brunswick
Management Recruiters of North Brunswick, Inc.
Key Employment

North Caldwell
Eastern Executive Assoc.
McMahon & Dee, Inc. (R)
K. L. Whitney & Co., Inc. (R)

Oakland
Dunhill Professional Search of Ramsey

Ocean
Millie Kipp Assoc., Inc.

Ocean City
Huff Assoc. (R)

Old Bridge
E.T. Wharton Assoc., Inc.

Paramus
Accountants On Call
Dunhill Personnel System, Inc.
Joseph Keyes Assoc.
Retail Recruiters of Paramus, Inc.
Source EDP
Source Finance
Zaccaria Group, Inc.

Parlin
Management Recruiters of Middlesex County NJ.

Parsippany
Baker Scott & Co.
The Goodrich & Sherwood Co. (R)
Jonathan Lawrence Assoc.
Sales Consultants of Morris County, Inc.
Source EDP
Source Finance

Pennington
Management Recruiters
Palmer Assoc., Inc. (R)
M.R. Pennington Co.

Phillipsburg
Management Recruiters

Pompton Lakes
Management Recruiters

Princeton
Accountants On Call
Barone-O'Hara Assoc., Inc.
Bedford-Orion Group, Inc.
Blau Kaptain Schroeder (R)
Burke, O'Brien & Bishop Assoc., Inc. (R)
China Human Resources Group (R)
Gallin Assoc.
The Goodrich & Sherwood Co. (R)
Kostmayer Assoc., Inc. (R)
L O R Personnel Div. (R)

Fran Luisi Assoc.
Management Advisors of Princeton, Inc. (R)
Management Recruiters
Northeastern Search, Inc.
P R Management Consultants, Inc.
Princeton Executive Search
Princeton Planning Consultants, Inc.
Source EDP
Source Finance
Tucker Assoc. (R)
Michael D. Zinn & Assoc., Inc. (R)

Princeton Junction
BIK Search/Force II
National Logistics Recruiters, Inc.

Ramsey
Dreier Consulting
Merlin Int'l. Inc.

Randolph
Paul Kull & Co. (R)

Red Bank
David Allen Assoc.
Broad Waverly & Assoc.
Management Recruiters
The Resource Group
Sales Consultants

Ridgewood
Management Recruiters
McCooe & Assoc., Inc. (R)
Romac & Assoc., Inc.

Riverdale
Weinpel & Co.

Roseland
Warring & Assoc. (R)

Rutherford
Dunhill Personnel System, Inc.
The Macdonald Group, Inc. (R)
Skott/Edwards Consultants (R)

Saddle Brook
Accountants On Call
Normyle/Erstling Health Search
Retail Pacesetters, Inc.
Salesworld-Division of Metacor Inc.

Salem
L & K Assoc.

Scotch Plains
Petruzzi Assoc.

Secaucus
Accountants On Call
Management Recruiters
Reinecke & Assoc.

Ship Bottom
Management Catalysts (R)

Short Hills
Cole Human Resource Services (R)
John J. Davis & Assoc., Inc. (R)

Skillman
Management Recruiters

Somerset
Delta Personnel Services

Somerville
Dean-Wharton Assoc.
J.M. Joseph Assoc.
Lancaster Assoc., Inc.

South Orange
The Mulvey Group

Sparta
Management Recruiters
Sales Consultants

Springfield
D.S. Allen Assoc.
Tarnow Int'l. (R)

Stanhope
Management Recruiters of Stanhope Corp.
Sales Consultants of Andover

Summit
J.R. Brody & Assoc., Inc.
Cornell Int'l. (R)
Sales Consultants
Search Assoc., Inc.

Tenafly
Phillips Assoc.
Ryerson Tabor Assoc.

Tennent
Cap, Inc.

Turnersville
The Addison Consulting Group

Union
RG International (R)

Upper Montclair
DHR Int'l., Inc. (R)
Foster Assoc.
John P. Runden & Co., Inc.
Sampson, Neill & Wilkins Inc. (R)

Upper Saddle River
Global Data Services, Inc.

Verona
Deven Assoc., Int'l., Inc. (R)

Vincentown
Hi-Tech Search, Inc.

Voorhees
RTE Search

Wall
Binary Search

Warren
Kurtz Pro-Search, Inc.
Techcon Co.

West Orange
Carter McKenzie, Inc.
Gilbert Tweed Assoc., Inc. (R)
Topaz Int'l., Inc.
Vento Assoc.

West Trenton
Management Recruiters
Sales Consultants

Westfield
W.N. Garbarini & Assoc. (R)

Westwood
Executive Appointments Ltd., Int'l. (R)
Supreme Assoc.

Woodbridge
Barone Assoc.

Woodcliff Lake
Stuart, Wood Inc. (R)

Wyckoff
Edmond J. Corry & Co., Inc. (R)

NEW MEXICO

Albuquerque
ACC Consultants, Inc.
Management Recruiters

Santa Fe
DCS Assoc., Inc. (R)

NEW YORK

Albany
Lee Calhoon & Co., Inc. (R)
Management Recruiters
Ritta Professional Search Inc.
Romac & Assoc., Inc.
Sanford Rose Assoc.

Auburn
Management Recruiters

Babylon
Inside Management Assoc. (R)

Ballston Spa
Technical Staffing Assoc.

Belle Harbor
Hutchinson Resources International (R)

Binghamton
Richard D. Holbrook Assoc. (R)
Sanford Rose Assoc. of Binghamton

Brewster
Management Recruiters
Sanford Rose Assoc.

Brooklyn
Merlin Int'l. Inc.
Jerome H. Nagel Assoc.
PSP Agency

Buffalo
Dunhill Personnel System, Inc.

Carle Place
Cowin Assoc.

Centerport
Boardroom Planning & Consulting Group
(R)

Clarence
Kozlin Assoc., Inc.

DeWitt
Sales Consultants

East Williston
Peter R. Taylor Assoc., Inc.

Elmont
Vincent Lee Assoc.

Elmsford
Management Recruiters of Westchester, Inc.
Preston Robert & Assoc.-Health Care Div.

Fairport
Datamax Services Inc.
Scott Sibley Assoc.

Farmingdale
Gray-Kimball Assoc., Inc.

Fishkill
Management Recruiters of Poughkeepsie,
Inc.

Forest Hills
Carlden Personnel Services Inc.

Ft. Montgomery
The Gedge Group (R)

Ft. Plain
T.J. Koellhoffer & Assoc. (R)

Glen Cove
Franchise Search, Inc.

Goldens Bridge
Pat Allen Assoc. Inc.

Great Neck
A.E. Feldman Assoc.
N. Steven Fells & Co., Inc.
Barry Nathanson Assoc. (R)
Sanford Rose Assoc. - Great Neck
Sanford Rose Assoc. - Great Neck
Travel Executive Search
Hilton N. Wasserman & Assoc. Inc. (R)

Greenwood Lake
Management Recruiters

Hartsdale
Olaf S. Meyer & Co., Ltd.

Hauppauge
Ames-O'Neill Assoc., Inc.

Hawthorne
Boyden World Corp. (R)
Sales Consultants of Westchester-South, Inc.

Hicksville
Amherst Personnel Group Inc.
Zachary & Sanders, Inc.

Huntington
J. Krauss Assoc. (R)
Management Recruiters
M.A. Pelle Assoc., Inc.
The Romark Group, Ltd. (R)
Schreuder Randall Corp.
Weber Executive Search (R)

Huntington Station
J.P.D. Group
Charles P. Oliver Assoc., Inc.
Sales Consultants

Jericho
Accountants On Call
Legal Placements Inc.
Mogul Consultants, Inc.
The P & L Group

Johnson City
Valletta Ritson & Co. (R)

Katonah
HLR Consulting

Larchmont
E.J. Michaels, Ltd. (R)
Dennis P. O'Toole & Assoc. Inc. (R)

Latham
Ethan Allen Personnel, Inc.
Sales Consultants

Lockport
Locus Inc.

Madrid
Management Recruiters

Malverne
Sanford Kleiner Assoc., Inc.
Sales Consultants

Massapequa
Morgan/Webber (R)

Melville
Global Data Services, Inc.

Merrick
Reinecke & Assoc.

Millbrook
Abbott Smith Assoc., Inc.

Nesconset
Romano McAvoy Assoc., Inc.

New City
Jakobs & Assoc. Int'l. (R)
Logistics Management Resources, Inc.
Professional Resources

New Rochelle
Newell Assoc. (R)

New York
APA Search, Inc.
Accountants On Call
Accounting Resources Int'l., Inc.
The Adler Group
Alexander Ross Inc. (R)
Alterna-track
American Group Practice, Inc. (R)
Analysts Resources Inc.
Analytic Recruiting, Inc.
Aronow Assoc., Inc.
Ashway Ltd. Agency
Avery Crafts Assoc., Ltd.
The Ayers Group, Inc.
BDO Seidman (R)
Bader Research Corp.
Carol Ball & Co., Inc.
The Bankers Register
The Barack Group, Inc.
Barton Sans Int'l. (R)
Battalia Winston Int'l., Inc. (R)
Martin H. Bauman Assoc., Inc. (R)
The Beam Group (R)
Marcia Beilin, Inc.
Nelson Bell & Partners Inc. (R)
Bialecki Inc. (R)
Bishop Assoc. (R)
Blake, Hansen & Nye, Ltd. (R)
Marc-Paul Bloome Ltd. (R)
Bodner Inc.
Bornholdt Shivas & Friends
Dr. Will G. Bowman, Inc. (R)
Boyden World Corp. (R)
Bradstreet Mgt.
Brady Assoc. Int'l., Inc. (R)
Charles Buck & Assoc., Inc. (R)
Butterfass/Pepe Assoc., Inc. (R)
T. Byrnes & Co., Inc. (R)
CAS Comsearch Inc.
CRS Assoc., Inc.
Canny, Bowen Inc. (R)
J.P. Canon Assoc.
The Cantor Concern, Inc.
Career Guides, Inc.
Carris, Jackowitz Assoc. (R)
Catalyx Group, Inc. (R)
David Chambers & Assoc., Inc. (R)
Chanko-Ward, Ltd. (R)
Toby Clark Assoc. Inc.
Richard Clarke Assoc., Inc.
W. Hoyt Colton Assoc., Inc. (R)
Colton Bernard Inc. (R)
The Communications Search Group (R)
Conex Inc. (R)

The Consortium
David P. Cordell Assoc.
The Cris Group., Inc.
Joseph Crisanti, Inc.
Crispi, Wagner & Co., Inc.
Peter Cusack & Partners, Inc. (R)
DHR Int'l., Inc. (R)
DLB Assoc.
The DLR Group, Inc. (R)
The DLR Group, Inc.
The Dartmouth Group (R)
Bert Davis Assoc., Inc.
DeLalla - Fried Assoc.
Thorndike Deland Assoc. (R)
Development Resource Group
Deven Assoc., Int'l., Inc. (R)
J P Donnelly Assoc., Inc.
Drummond Assoc., Inc.
The Duncan Group Inc. (R)
Dunhill Personnel Search
Dwyer Consulting Group, Inc. (R)
ESP Management Services, Inc. (R)
Earley Kielty & Assoc., Inc. (R)
David M. Ellner Assoc. (R)
Mark Elzweig Co. Ltd.
Execu-Search, Inc.
Farrell & Phin, Inc. (R)
Jerry Fields Assoc.
Fisher-Todd Assoc.
D.E. Foster & Partners, L.P. (R)
The Foster McKay Group
Foy, Schneid & Daniel, Inc. (R)
Gerald Frisch Assoc., Inc. (R)
The Fry Group, Inc.
The Furman Group, Ltd. (R)
GKR Int'l. (R)
Jay Gaines & Co. (R)
Gardiner Stone Hunter Int'l., Inc. (R)
Gardner-Ross Assoc., Inc. (R)
Gilbert & Van Campen Int'l. (R)
Gilbert Tweed Assoc., Inc. (R)
The Goldman Group Inc.
The Goodrich & Sherwood Co. (R)
Gossage Regan Assoc. (R)
Gould & McCoy, Inc. (R)
The Alice-Groves Co., Inc.
The Gumbinner Co.
Gundersen Brenner, Inc. (R)
Hackett & Co. (R)
Hadley Lockwood, Inc. (R)
Handy HRM (R)
Hanzel & Co., Inc. (R)
Hawkes-Randolph & Assoc., Inc.
Health Industry Resources, Inc.
F. P. Healy & Co., Inc. (R)
Heath/Norton Assoc., Inc. (R)
Heidrick and Struggles, Inc. (R)
Hessel Assoc., Inc.
Higdon, Joys & Mingle, Inc. (R)
J.B. Homer Assoc. Inc. (R)
Hospitality Int'l., Inc.
Don Howard Personnel
Howard-Sloan Assoc.

Howard-Sloan Communications Search (R)
Howard-Sloan Legal Search, Inc.
Howe-Lewis Int'l., Inc. (R)
Arnold Huberman Assoc., Inc. (R)
The Hunt Co. (R)
Hunt Ltd.
Ingram, Inc. (R)
Innkeeper's Management Corp. (R)
Inside Management Assoc. (R)
Integrated Management Solutions
The Interim Management Corp.(IMCOR)
    (R)
International Management Advisors, Inc.
    (R)
Pendleton James & Assoc., Inc. (R)
R.I. James, Inc.
John-David Assoc., Inc.
The Johnson Group, Inc.
Johnson Smith & Knisely Inc. (R)
Inge Judd Assoc. (R)
Lisa Kalus & Assoc., Inc.
Kane Ford Karrel & Assoc.
Martin Kartin & Co., Inc. (R)
Kearney Executive Search (R)
Kenny, Kindler, Hunt & Howe (R)
Barbara Kerner Consultants
Michael King Assoc., Inc.
Richard Kinser & Assoc. (R)
Jonah Kleinstein Assoc., Inc. (R)
Kline Consulting, Inc. (R)
Kling Personnel Assoc., Inc.
Koren, Rogers Assoc.
Korn/Ferry Int'l. (R)
Kramer Executive Resources, Inc.
Laguzza Assoc., Ltd. (R)
Lamalie Assoc., Inc. (R)
E.J. Lance Management Assoc., Inc.
Lawrence L. Lapham, Inc. (R)
Latham Int'l., Ltd.
The Lieberman Group (R)
J.P. Logan & Co., Inc. (R)
H.M. Long Int'l., Ltd. (R)
The John Lucht Consultancy Inc. (R)
M-A Management Assoc., Inc.
MB Inc.
META/MAT, Ltd. (R)
Robert Madigan Assoc., Inc. (R)
The Madison Group (R)
Management Recruiters of Gramercy, Inc.
Management Recruiters
Management Recruiters
Management Recruiters
Management Resources Int'l. (R)
Management Resource Group, Inc.
Margolin Consultants, Inc.
Mariaschin & Co.
Marlar Int'l. Inc. (R)
Marley Group Ltd.
Marshall Consultants, Inc. (R)
Maximum Management Corp.
John McLellan Assoc., Inc.
McManners Assoc., Inc. (R)
Martin H. Meisel Assoc., Inc. (R)

Meridian Personnel Assoc., Inc.
The Neil Michael Group, Inc. (R)
Herbert Mines Assoc., Inc. (R)
Jay Mitchell & Co. (R)
Mitchell, Larsen & Zilliacus (R)
Morgan-Stampfl, Inc.
Edwin Mruk & Partners (R)
Robert Murphy Assoc. (R)
Nicholson & Assoc., Inc. (R)
Noble & Assoc., Inc.
Nordeman Grimm, Inc. (R)
Norman Broadbent Int'l., Inc. (R)
The Ogdon Partnership (R)
Oliver & Rozner Assoc., Inc. (R)
Robert Olivier & Assoc., Inc. (R)
Oppedisano & Co., Inc. (R)
Kitty Ossow & Assoc.
Janou Pakter, Inc.
Kirk Palmer & Assoc., Inc. (R)
R. Parker & Assoc., Inc.
Robert Parrella Assoc.
Pathway Executive Search, Inc.
Joel H. Paul & Assoc., Inc.
The Peck Consultancy (R)
Pencom Systems Inc.
Picard & Co., Inc. (R)
Placement Assoc., Inc.
Rene Plessner Assoc., Inc. (R)
L. J. Quinn & Assoc., Inc. (R)
Raines Int'l. Inc. (R)
Randell-Heiken, Inc. (R)
Paul R. Ray & Co., Inc. (R)
Rex Assoc., Inc.
Russell Reynolds Assoc., Inc. (R)
Sydney Reynolds Assoc., Inc. (R)
E.J. Rhodes Assoc. (R)
Riotto - Jones Assoc., Inc.
Roberts-Lund Assoc., Ltd. (R)
Bruce Robinson Assoc. (R)
James J. Rust Executive Search (R)
A. Ryan Assoc.
Sage/Walters Ltd. (R)
Santangelo Consultants Inc.
Allan Sarn Assoc., Inc. (R)
The Schmitt Tolette Group (R)
The Michael Scott Consulting Co., Inc. (R)
Seiden Assoc., Inc. (R)
Seitchik, Corwin & Seitchik Inc. (R)
Setford-Shaw-Najarian Assoc., Ltd.
RitaSue Siegel Assoc., Inc.
Simpson Assoc.
Robert L. Smith & Co., Inc. (R)
Smith Hanley Assoc., Inc.
Smith, Roth & Squires (R)
Source EDP
Source Finance
SpencerStuart (R)
Spring Executive Search, Inc.
Staub, Warmbold & Barkauskas, Inc. (R)
Stern & Watson, Inc. (R)
Stonehill Management Consultants, Inc. (R)
Storfer & Assoc.
W. R. Strathmann Assoc. (R)

Stricker & Zagor (R)
Sullivan & Co. (R)
TASA, Inc. (R)
Tama Lucas Ltd. (R)
Techno-Trac Systems, Inc.
Techsearch Services Inc.
Thorne, Brieger Assoc., Inc. (R)
The Viscusi Group, Inc. (R)
WTW Assoc., Inc. (R)
Martha Ward Assoc., Inc.
Ward Howell Int'l. Inc. (R)
Water Street Assoc.
Webb, Johnson & Klemmer, Inc. (R)
C. Weiss Assoc., Inc. (R)
Werbin Assoc. Executive Search, Inc.
Werner Int'l., Inc. (R)
Wesley Brown & Bartle Co., Inc. (R)
S.J. Wexler Assoc., Inc.
K. L. Whitney & Co., Inc. (R)
The Whitney Group (R)
S. R. Wolman Assoc., Inc. (R)
Egon Zehnder Int'l. Inc. (R)
W.F. Richer Assoc., Inc.

Newburgh
Romac & Assoc., Inc.

North Massapequa
Affirmative Action Assoc.

Orchard Park
Sanford Rose Assoc.

Ossining-on-Hudson
Ramsey & Beirne Assoc., Inc. (R)

Patchogue
The Executive Consulting Group -N.Y.

Pearl River
Management Recruiters

Pelham
Blendow, Crowley & Oliver, Inc. (R)

Pittsford
Dunhill Personnel System, Inc.
Princeton Executive Search, Inc.

Pomona
Saxon Morse Assoc.

Port Washington
Dunhill Personnel System, Inc.
Lawrence Executive Search, Ltd.
Tecmark Assoc. Inc.

Red Hook
Circuit Search

Rochester
Cochran, Cochran, & Yale, Inc.
Malcolm Cole & Assoc.
The Goodrich & Sherwood Co. (R)
Hall, Cooper & Bartman, Ltd.
Management Recruiters
Kevin W. Paul
Sales Consultants
Source EDP
Traynor Confidential, Ltd.
Valletta Ritson & Co. (R)
VanReypen Enterprises, Ltd. (R)

Rockville Centre
Management Recruiters of Nassau, Inc.

Roslyn
Harold L. Rapp Assoc.

Rye
H.C. Smith Ltd. (R)

Rye Brook
Professional Placement Assoc., Inc.

Saratoga Springs
Tom Mahon & Assoc.

Scarsdale
Frank Cuomo & Assoc., Inc.
McDonald/Long Assoc., Inc. (R)
Promotion Recruiters, Inc.
Redden & McGrath Assoc., Inc. (R)

Southampton
H.M. Long Int'l., Ltd. (R)

Southold
Joe Sullivan & Assoc., Inc. (R)

Stone Ridge
Management Recruiters

Suffern
Federal Placement Services

Syracuse
Accounting & Computer Personnel
Dapexs Consultants, Inc.
Management Recruiters
St. Lawrence Int'l., Inc.

Tarrytown
Allen Barry Assoc.

Tully
Hospitality Int'l., Inc.

Utica
Management Recruiters

Valhalla
Hintz Associates

Victor
Management Recruiters

Wantagh
Source EDP

White Plains
Accountants On Call
Adept Tech Recruiting, Inc.
Corporate Careers Inc.
Ecco Personnel Svs.
Evans & James Assoc., Inc.
Langer Assoc., Inc. (R)
George J. Mollo Assoc.
Wilbur M. Sachtjen Assoc., Inc. (R)
Source EDP
Source Finance

Williamsville
Management Recruiters
Sales Consultants

Woodbury
Bartl & Evins
Dunhill Personnel System, Inc.
Management Recruiters
Resource Services, Inc.

Woodmere
Fred Koffler Assoc. (R)

Woodstock
Sloane, Sloane & Mayne (R)

Woolsey Station
National Search, Inc.

Yorktown Heights
Dunhill Personnel System, Inc.
Marcus & Assoc.
Westfield Recruiters

NORTH CAROLINA

Advance
The Salem Group, Executive Recruiters

Asheboro
Marketing Recruiters, Inc.

Asheville
The Borton Wallace Co. (R)
Hornberger Management Co., Inc.
Kimmel & Fredericks, Inc.
Management Recruiters of Ashville, Inc.
Merrick & Moore

Bethlehem
Management Recruiters

Burlington
Management Recruiters
Sales Consultants

Cary
ARJay & Assoc.
Dunhill Personnel System, Inc.
Rothrock Assoc.
Sales Consultants of Raleigh-Durham-RTP

Chapel Hill
Atlantic West Int'l.
Grantham & Co., Inc. (R)
Management Recruiters

Charlotte
Coleman Lew & Assoc., Inc. (R)
Flores & Assoc.
Fox-Morris Assoc., Inc.
The Halyburton Co., Inc. (R)
Locke & Assoc. (R)
R.E. Lowe Assoc.
Management Recruiters of Charlotte - Southwest
Management Recruiters
Mark III Personnel, Inc.
Nuance Personnel Search, Inc.
Patton, Perry & Sproull Inc. (R)
Robison & McAulay (R)
Romac & Assoc., Inc.
Sanford Rose Assoc.
S. P. Assoc.
Sales Consultants
Schwab-Carrese Assoc. (R)
Sockwell & Anderson (R)

Concord
Sales Consultants

Durham
Bruce Edwards & Associates, Inc. (R)
Management Recruiters

Enfield
Management Recruiters

Fayetteville
Management Recruiters
Professional Careers

Gastonia
Sanford Rose Assoc.
Sales Consultants

Greensboro
Ariail & Assoc. (R)
Management Recruiters
Sales Consultants

Hendersonville
Management Recruiters of Hendersonville,
inc.

Hickory
Management Advisors Int'l., Inc.
Management Recruiters

High Point
Management Recruiters
Sales Consultants

Kannapolis
Management Recruiters

Kernersville
Dunhill Personnel System, Inc.

Kinston
Management Recruiters of Kinston

Louisburg
Management Recruiters

Matthews
Sanford Rose Assoc.

Monroe
Management Recruiters

Mooresville
Management Recruiters
Sales Consultants

Mount Airy
Management Recruiters

New Bern
Management Recruiters

Raleigh
Finance & Accounting Search Firm
Information Systems Professionals
Integrated Professional Services, Inc.
Management Recruiters
Paul Mueller & Assoc., Inc. (R)
Romac & Assoc., Inc.
Sanford Rose assoc.

Research Triangle Pk.
Wesson, Taylor, Wells & Assoc.

Skyland
Bell Professional Placement

Statesville
Management Recruiters

Sylva
M.F. Branch Assoc., Inc.

Wilmington
Management Recruiters of Wilmington
Nagel Executive Search Inc.
Sanford Rose Assoc.

Winston-Salem
Management Recruiters
Romac & Assoc.
Sales Consultants

Wrightsville Beach
John M. Horton

NORTH DAKOTA

Fargo
Professions Unlimited, Inc.

OHIO

Akron
A.M.C.R., Inc.
Management Recruiters
Sanford Rose Assoc.
Sanford Rose Assoc.
Sales Consultants of Akron, Inc.
Source Finance

Ashland
Management Recruiters

Bath
The Revere Assoc., Inc. (R)
Western Reserve Search Assoc. (R)

Beachwood
D.S. Allen Assoc.
Christopher-Patrick & Assoc. (R)
Howard Gilmore & Assoc. (R)
Sanford Rose Assoc. of Beachwood

Boardman
Management Recruiters

Brecksville
Sanford Rose Assoc.- Brecksville

Brunswick
Management Recruiters

Canfield
Sanford Rose Assoc.

Canton
Sanford Rose Assoc.

Chagrin Falls
Clemo, Evans & Co., Inc. (R)
Hogan Assoc. (R)
Management Recruiters
Management Recruiters

Cincinnati
Accountants On Call
Allen/Assoc.
The Angus Group, Inc.
Baldwin & Assoc.
Bason Assoc., Inc. (R)
DEI Executive Services
Genesis Personnel Service, Inc.
Management Recruiters of Butler County
Management Recruiters
Management Recruiters
Management Recruiters of Cincinnati/
    Sharonville, Inc.
Million & Assoc., Inc. (R)
The C. B. Mueller Co., Inc.
Professions, Inc.
Sales Consultants
Sharrow & Assoc., Inc.
Source EDP
Source Finance
S. K. Stewart & Assoc. (R)

Cleveland
Advancement Recruiting Services
Anders Incorporated (R)
Artgo, Inc. (R)
Bowden & Co., Inc. (R)
Cardwell Group (R)
Christian & Timbers, Inc. (R)
Dankowski & Assoc., Inc.
Fox-Morris Assoc., Inc.
Heidrick and Struggles, Inc. (R)
Hite Executive Search (R)
I.S. Consultants, Inc.
Richard Kader & Assoc.
Kearney Executive Search (R)
Korn/Ferry Int'l. (R)
Lamalie Assoc., Inc. (R)
Management Recruiters
Management Recruiters

Management Recruiters
Management Recruiters
Management Recruiters
Management Recruiters
McRoberts & Assoc.
Midland Consultants
O'Brien & Co., Inc. (R)
R.A.N. Assoc., Inc.
Romac & Assoc., Inc.
Sanford Rose Assoc.
Sales Consultants
Sales Consultants
Sales Consultants
Search Express (R)
H.C. Smith Ltd. (R)
Source EDP
Source Finance
Strategic Search Group
Valletta Ritson & Co. (R)

Columbus
Accountants On Call
Dillard Executive Search
Dunhill Professional Search Inc.
G.W. Henn & Co. (R)
January Management Group (R)
Melvin Kent & Assoc., Inc. (R)
Management Recruiters
Management Recruiters
Management Recruiters
Sanford Rose Assoc.
Sales Consultants
Sales Consultants
Source EDP
Source Finance
Stephens Assoc. Ltd. (R)
Technical Recruiting Services

Cuyahoga Falls
Dunhill of Greater Akron, Inc.

Dayton
H. L. Goehring & Assoc., Inc. (R)
Hahn & Assoc., Inc.
Management Recruiters
Romac & Assoc., Inc.
Sanford Rose Assoc.
Sanford Rose Assoc.
Sales Consultants
Source EDP
World Search

Dover
Management Recruiters

Dublin
J. D. Hersey & Assoc.
Marling Inc. (R)

Elyria
Sanford Rose Assoc.

Euclid
Sanford Rose Assoc.

Fairborn
Dunhill Personnel System, Inc.

Hudson
Louis Gregory Assoc., Inc.
Sanford Rose Assoc.
The Zammataro Co. (R)

Independence
Source Finance

Ironton
Sanford Rose Assoc.

Kent
Sanford Rose Assoc.

Lima
Sanford Rose Assoc. of Lima

Lyndhurst
Search Leader, Inc.

Marietta
Sanford Rose Assoc.

Mason
R.E. Lowe Assoc.

Medina
Sanford Rose Assoc.

Mentor
Downing & Downing

North Canton
Management Recruiters
Sanford Rose Assoc.

North Lima
Dunhill Personnel System, Inc.

North Ridgeville
Management Recruiters

Pepper Pike
Ferrari Consulting Group

Reynoldsburg
J.W. Barleycorn & Assoc. (R)

Rocky River
Sanford Rose Assoc.

Sandusky
William N. Davis & Assoc., Inc. (R)

Solon
AJS Assoc.
C.W. Brandon & Assoc., Inc.
Management Recruiters

Strongsville
Management Recruiters

Summitville
Staffing Consultants

Toledo
Aim Executive Consulting Services (R)
Counsel Search Co. (R)
Dillard Execuative Search of Toledo
Dunhill Personnel System, Inc.
Management Recruiters

Troy
Granger, Counts & Assoc. (R)

Urbana
F.L.A.G.

Westerville
Management Recruiters
R.G.B. & Assoc., Inc.

Wickliffe
Management Recruiters

Willoughby Hills
Aim Executive Consulting Services (R)
Aim Executive Inc.
ProSearch, Inc.

Worthington
Arthur Adams & Assoc.
Grover & Assoc. (R)
R.E. Lowe Assoc.
Sanford Rose Assoc.

Youngstown
Michael Latas & Assoc., Inc. (R)

OKLAHOMA

Ardmore
Dunhill Personnel System, Inc.

Edmond
Dunhill Personnel System, Inc.

Muskogee
Dunhill Personnel System, Inc.

Oklahoma City
Joy Reed Belt & Assoc., Inc. (R)
Dunhill Personnel System, Inc.
Dunhill Personnel System, Inc.
James Farris Assoc. (R)
Healthcare Resources Group
Management Recruiters
Management Search, Inc.
Sales Consultants

Owasso
F.J. Bruckner & Co. (R)

Tulsa
Dunhill Personnel System, Inc.
Dunhill Personnel of Northeast Tulsa, Inc.
J. Gifford, Inc.
Management Recruiters
The Montanye Group
Sales Consultants
Sales Consultants
Source EDP
Source Finance
Villareal & Assoc., Inc. (R)
John Wylie Assoc., Inc.

OREGON

Ashland
The James Lloyd Group

Beaverton
John M. Clarke & Assoc.

Eugene
Jim Baum - Executive Search
Management Recruiters

Lake Oswego
Murphy, Symonds & Stowell Search, Inc.

Portland
Allied Financial Management Co.
Cascadia Group Int'l. (R)
Forum Assoc.
Headhunters National, Inc.
Management Recruiters
Management Search, Inc.
Robert E. Pfaendler & Assoc., Inc.
Prior Martech Assoc. (R)
Sanford Rose Assoc.
Sales Consultants
Search North America, Inc.
Search Northwest Assoc.
Source EDP

Source Engineering
Source Finance
Nola Worley & Assoc., Inc.

Salem
Richard Winn & Co. (R)

PENNSYLVANIA

Allentown
S-H-S of Allentown

Allison Park
Becker, Norton & Co. (R)
Gleason & Assoc. (R)

Ambler
Sales Consultants

Ardmore
Garofolo, Curtiss, Lambert & MacLean (R)

Bala Cynwyd
Fernow Assoc.
Management Resources
Retail Recruiters/Spectrum Consultants, Inc.
Romac & Assoc., Inc.

Bensalem
Management Recruiters
Sales Consultants

Berwyn
Empire International (R)
S. Tyler Sullivan & Assoc., Inc.

Bethlehem
Management Recruiters

Birchrunville
Lee Calhoon & Co., Inc. (R)

Bryn Mawr
Management Recruiters
The Morris Group

Camp Hill
The Byrnes Group
Sales Consultants

Center Square
Alexander Enterprises, Inc.

Chadds Ford
Aitken & Assoc.

Colmar
Questor Consultants, Inc.

Conshohocken
ProSearch, Inc.

Doylestown
Corporate Staffing Group (R)
George R. Martin (R)
J.R. Peterman Assoc., Inc.

Easton
Cassie & Assoc.
Lacrosse Assoc., Inc.

Erie
Hartman Personnel Services
Blair Kershaw Assoc., Inc.
Jack B. Larsen & Assoc.
Luke, Lincoln, & Brugger

Fairview Village
E. F. Humay Assoc.

Feasterville
Dunhill Personnel System, Inc.
Kay Henry, Inc.

Flourtown
Sturm, Burrows & Co.

Ft. Washington
Corporate Recruiters Inc.
Professional Medical

Gettysburg
Scan Management Inc.

Glen Rock
Peter Newell Bowen (R)

Hanover
Studwell Assoc. (R)

Haverford
Quinn Bailey & Morgan (R)

Huntingdon Valley
Vogel Assoc.

Ingomar
Dunhill Personnel System, Inc.

Jenkintown
Jordon & Jordon, Inc.
Sanford Rose Assoc.- Suburban Philadelphia

King of Prussia
Accountants On Call
The Andre Group, Inc. (R)
Dunhill Personnel System, Inc.
Eden & Assoc., Inc.
Probe Technology
Source EDP
Source Finance
K. W. Tunnell Co., Inc. (R)

Lancaster
The Byrnes Group
C & H Personnel
Dunhill Personnel System, Inc.
Management Recruiters
Paul S. Pelland
Sales Consultants
Stewart Assoc.
Charles Stickler Assoc.

Langhorne
Sales Consultants of Newtown
Tell/Com Recruiters

Lansdowne
Balfour Assoc.

Ligonier
Fagan & Co. (R)

Lititz
Kogon Assoc., Inc.

Malvern
Professional Search Assoc., Inc.

McMurray
Environmental Resources Int'l.
Sanford Rose Assoc.

Media
The Kennett Group, Inc.

Monroeville
John D. Gibbons & Assoc., Inc. (R)

Murrysville
Management Recruiters
Roth Young of Pittsburgh

Newtown
Sanford Rose Assoc.
Albert J. Walsh & Assoc. (R)

Newtown Square
Graphic Search Assoc. Inc.

Paoli
Dunhill Personnel System, Inc.
Tower Consultants, Ltd.

Philadelphia
Accountants On Call
Alexander Edward Assoc., Inc.
The Beam Group (R)
Chase-Owens Assoc., Inc. (R)
Howard Clark Assoc.
Cole, Warren & Long, Inc. (R)
Coleman Legal Search Consultants
Diversified Health Search (R)
Diversified Search, Inc. (R)
Dunhill Personnel System, Inc.
Effective Search, Inc. (R)
Howard Fischer Assoc., Inc. (R)
Jack Stuart Fisher Assoc.
Fox-Morris Assoc., Inc.
Gordon/Tyler (R)
Jacobson Assoc.
Jefferson-Ross Assoc. Inc.
D. F. Kerry & Assoc. (R)
Kiley-Owen Assoc., Inc.
The Koehler Group
D.A. Kreuter Assoc., Inc. (R)
Management Recruiters
McNichol Assoc. (R)
Nuessle, Kurdziel & Weiss, Inc. (R)
LaMonte Owens, Inc.
Penn Associates
Romac & Assoc., Inc.
Sales Consultants
Selective Management Services, Inc.
Source EDP
Source Finance
SpencerStuart (R)
Technical Employment Consultants
Wellington Management Group (R)

Pittsburgh
Accounting Personnel Assoc.
Alzed Real Estate Recruiters
Boyden Int'l., Inc. (R)
C.G. & Assoc.
Corporate Management Services Inc.
N. Dean Davic Assoc., Inc.
Denney & Co., Inc. (R)
Fox-Morris Assoc., Inc.
W.T. Glover & Assoc., Inc.
Hoskins, Rees & Smith
The J. Kovach Group, Inc. (R)
Management Recruiters
Management Recruiters
Management Recruiters
Management Recruiters
K. Maxin & Assoc.
B. Paul Mickey & Assoc.
O'Connor, O'Connor, Lordi, Ltd. (R)
Resources for Management (R)
Sanford Rose Assoc.
Sales Consultants

Source EDP
Source Finance
Specialty Consultants, Inc.
Daniel Stern & Assoc.
Strauss Personnel Service
Thornton Assoc.
The WalCar Partnership (R)

Plymouth Meeting
Fulton, Longshore & Assoc., Inc. (R)

Quakertown
Sanford Rose Assoc. of Quakertown

Radnor
Howe, McMahon & Assoc., Inc. (R)
Soltis Management Services (R)

Sewickley
Management Recruiters

Sinking Spring
Northeastern Search, Inc.

St. Peters
Lee Calhoon & Co., Inc. (R)

State College
Fox-Morris Assoc., Inc.

Stroudsburg
Management Recruiters

Valley Forge
Hospitality Int'l.
Sales Consultants
Wesson, Taylor, Wells & Assoc.

Villanova
Gordon Wahls Co.

Warrington
Triangle Assoc.

Wayne
JM & Co. (R)
Krow Assoc., Inc.
Management Recruiters
Romac & Assoc., Inc.
Yannelli, Randolph & Co.

West Chester
Brandywine Consulting Group (R)
William J. Christopher Assoc., Inc.
Nursing Technomics (R)
Sanford Rose Assoc.
Whittlesey & Assoc., Inc.

West Reading
Management Recruiters

Wexford
Reese Assoc. (R)
Sanford Rose Assoc.

Wilkes-Barre
Dunhill Professional Search of Wilkes-Barre/
Scranton, Inc.
Tierney Assoc., Inc. (R)

Williamsport
Management Recruiters

Willow Grove
Management Recruiters

Wynnewood
PCD Partners (R)

Yardley
Dunhill Personnel System, Inc.

York
The Byrnes Group

PUERTO RICO

Hato Rey
Careers/Inc.

Mayaguez
Dunhill Personnel System, Inc.

Rio Piedras
Management Recruiters

RHODE ISLAND

Charlestown
Marshall Rice Assoc. (R)

Hope Valley
Tech International

Jamestown
Jay Tracey Assoc.

Little Compton
Sanford Rose Assoc.

Newport
Robert Graham Assoc., Inc. (R)
Lybrook Assoc., Inc.

North Kingstown
Schattle Personnel Consultants, Inc.

Providence
Greene Personnel Consultants
Human Resources, Inc. (R)
Management Recruiters

Rumford
Lee Associates

Warwick
Carter, Lavoie Assocs.
Dunhill Personnel System, Inc.
Sales Consultants of Rhode Island, Inc.
Storti Assoc., Inc.

SOUTH CAROLINA

Aiken
Management Recruiters

Anderson
Management Recruiters

Beaufort
eXsource

Charleston
Management Recruiters

Columbia
Dunhill Personnel System, Inc.
Management Recruiters
The Personnel Network, Inc.
Sales Consultants
Wesson, Taylor, Wells & Assoc.

Easley
Management Recruiters

Florence
Management Recruiters

Ft. Mill
Phillips Resource Group

Greenville
Careers Unlimited
Dunhill Personnel System, Inc.
Management Recruiters
Phillips Resource Group
Sales Consultants

M.K. Wasse & Assoc., Inc.

Greenwood
Dunhill Personnel System, Inc.

Hilton Head
Management Recruiters
WDI, Int'l. (R)

Hilton Head Island
Gold Coast Partners

Lexington
Management Recruiters

Myrtle Beach
Ford & Assoc., Inc.

North Charleston
Sales Consultants

Orangeburg
Management Recruiters

Rock Hill
Management Recruiters

Salem
Management Recruiters

Spartanburg
Phillips Resource Group

Travelers Rest
Management Recruiters

SOUTH DAKOTA

Rapid City
Management Recruiters

Sioux Falls
Management Recruiters

TENNESSEE

Brentwood
B.K. Barnes & Associates
Management Recruiters
Russell, Montgomery & Assoc. (R)
Sales Consultants

Chattanooga
Management Recruiters
Sales Consultants

Cleveland
Dunhill Personnel System, Inc.
Sanford Rose Assoc.

Columbia
Management Recruiters

Cordova
Austin - Allen Co.

Franklin
Dunhill Personnel System, Inc.

Goodlettsville
Sanford Rose Assoc.

Hendersonville
Sanford Rose Assoc. of Nashville

Jackson
Dunhill Personnel System, Inc.

Knoxville
Management Recruiters
Russell, Montgomery & Assoc. (R)

Lenoir City
Management Recruiters

Memphis
Dunhill Personnel System, Inc.
Randall Howard & Assoc., Inc. (R)
Management Recruiters
Professionals in Recruiting Co.
Romac & Assoc.
Sales Consultants
Summerfield Assoc., Inc.

Nashville
Accountants
Helfer Executive Consultants (R)
George Kaludis Assoc., Inc. (R)
Management Recruiters
Sales Consultants

TEXAS

Allen
DeHayes Consulting Group (R)

Amarillo
Management Recruiters

Arlington
Accounting Resources Int'l., Inc.
Dunhill Personnel System, Inc.
Hill Fallon & Assoc. (R)
Kent R. Hedman & Assoc.
Kieffer, Ford, & Hadelman, Ltd. (R)
M/ARS
Management Recruiters
Thomas R. Moore Executive Search (R)
Martin Pierce Inc. (R)

Austin
W. Bussell & Assoc.
Dunhill Personnel System, Inc.
R. W. Hebel Assoc. (R)
Houtz, Strawn Assoc. (R)
Management Recruiters
Management Recruiters
Pencom Systems Inc.
Pierce & Assoc., Inc. (R)
Sales Consultants of Austin, Inc.
Strategic Assoc., Inc.
Zingaro & Co. (R)

Boerne
Management Recruiters

Dallas
Accountants On Call
Accountants On Call
Peter W. Ambler Co. (R)
Bartlett, Bunn & Travis, Inc.
R. Gaines Baty Assoc., Inc.
The Howard C. Bloom Co.
Brennan Assoc.
Robert Connelly & Assoc., Inc. (R)
Damon & Assoc., Inc.
R. J. Dishaw & Assoc. (R)
Dunhill Personnel System, Inc.
Eastman & Beaudine, Inc. (R)
D.E. Foster & Partners, L.P. (R)
Fox-Morris Assoc., Inc.
Halstead & Assoc. (R)
Hayman & Co. (R)
Heidrick and Struggles, Inc. (R)
Hyde Danforth & Co. (R)
Jablo Partners (R)
Kearney Executive Search (R)
Korn/Ferry Int'l. (R)
Lamalie Assoc., Inc. (R)
Lee Management Group Inc.
Paul Ligon Co.
Robert Lowell Int'l. (R)
Major, Wilson & Africa
Management Recruiters
Management Recruiters
Management Recruiters
Management Recruiters
P R Associates
G.S. Page Inc. (R)
Page-Wheatcroft & Co. Ltd. (R)
Largent Parks & Partners, Inc.

Professional Medical
Paul R. Ray & Co., Inc. (R)
Russell Reynolds Assoc., Inc. (R)
Romac & Assoc. of Dallas
Sales Consultants
Salesworld-Division of Metacor Inc.
Sandhurst Assoc. (R)
Marvin L. Silcott & Assoc., Inc.
C.W. Sink & Co., Inc. (R)
Slater & Assoc. (R)
Source EDP
Source EDP
Source Engineering
Source Finance
SpencerStuart (R)
Sumrall Personnel Consultants, Inc.
Carl J. Taylor & Co. (R)
Michael Tucker Assoc. (R)
Tuttle, Neidhart, Semyan, Inc. (R)
Ward Howell Int'l. Inc. (R)
Wheeler, Moore & Elam Co. (R)
Witt Assoc. Inc. (R)
The Wright Group
Youngs & Co. (R)

Denton
Dunhill of Denton, Inc.

El Paso
ExecuSource Int'l.

Friendswood
Management Recruiters

Ft. Worth
Dunhill Personnel System, Inc.
Dunhill of Southeast Fort Worth, Inc.
David Farmer & Assoc.
Fuller Search
Hughes & Assoc.
Management Recruiters
Management Recruiters
O'Rourke Co., Inc. (R)
Paul Ray & Carre Orban Int'l. (R)
Paul Ray & Carre Orban Int'l (R)
Source Finance

Garland
Management Recruiters

Grand Prairie
Management Recruiters

Houston
Accountants On Call
Accounting Resources Int'l., Inc.
Ace Resources
Anderson Bradshaw Assoc., Inc. (R)
Barton Raben, Inc. (R)
Career Resource Assoc., Inc.
CoEnergy Inc.

Dougan-McKinley-Strain (R)
Dougan-McKinley-Strain (R)
Dunhill Personnel System, Inc.
Dunhill Personnel System, Inc.
Dunhill Personnel System, Inc.
Dunhill Personnel System, Inc.
Dunhill Personnel System, Inc.
Dunhill Personnel System, Inc.
Dunhill of Houston
The Energists
Goss & Assoc., Inc. (R)
GreenHall Assoc., Inc.
A.H. Justice & Assoc.
Kearney Executive Search (R)
Korn/Ferry Int'l. (R)
Kors Montgomery Int'l. (R)
Lamalie Assoc., Inc. (R)
Loewenstein & Assoc.
Lord & Albus Co.
Major, Wilson & Assoc.
Management Recruiters
Management Recruiters
Management Recruiters
Robert A. Paul & Assoc.
Preng & Assoc., Inc. (R)
Railey & Assoc.
Paul R. Ray & Co., Inc. (R)
Russell Reynolds Assoc., Inc. (R)
Romac & Assoc., Inc.
Ryman, Bell, Green & Michaels, Inc.
Saber Consultants, Inc. (R)
Sales Consultants
The Search Center Inc.
Search Consultants Int'l., Inc.
Source EDP
Source Finance
SpencerStuart (R)
Stanton/Schoen Professionals, Inc.
John R. Stephens & Assoc.
Peter Sterling & Co.
M. L. Tawney & Assoc.
Thomas, Richardson, Runden & Co. Inc.
 (R)
The Urban Placement Service
Darryl Vincent & Assoc.
Denis P. Walsh & Assoc., Inc.
Ward Howell Int'l. Inc. (R)
Warring & Assoc. (R)
Whitaker, Fellows & Assoc.
John W. Worsham & Assoc., Inc.
The Wright Group

Humble
Guidry, East, Barnes & Bono, Inc. (R)

Hurst
The James Group
Patrick Assoc.

Irving
Benton Schneider & Assoc. (R)
DHR Int'l, Inc (R)

Source EDP
Source Engineering
Source Finance

Keller
Starling & Assoc., Inc.

Lewisville
Dunhill Personnel System, Inc.
Management Recruiters

McAllen
Dunhill Personnel System, Inc.
USA Medical Placement Inc.

New Braunfels
Management Recruiters

Odessa
Bennett-Munson Inc.

Plano
Jack Hurst & Assoc., Inc. (R)
M H Executive Search Group
Management Recruiters
Vick & Assoc.

Richardson
Dunhill Personnel System, Inc.
McKeen Melancon & Co. (R)
The Oxford Group

San Angelo
Andrew B. Carr & Assoc.

San Antonio
Dunhill Personnel System, Inc.
Dunhill Personnel System, Inc.
Dunhill Personnel System, Inc.
Dunhill Personnel System, Inc.
Dunhill Personnel System, Inc.
Dunhill Personnel System, Inc.
Jordan-Sitter Assoc. (R)
Management Recruiters
Sanford Rose Assoc.

Stafford
J. Gross & Assoc.

The Colony
Charles P. Aquavella & Assoc.

The Woodlands
W, Robert Eissler & Assoc., Inc.
Management Recruiters
Reinecke & Assoc.

Weatherford
Dunhill Personnel System, Inc.

UTAH

Salt Lake City
Atlantic West Int'l.
Deeco Int'l.
Management Recruiters
J. Fielding Nelson & Assoc., Inc.
STM Assoc.
Sales Consultants
Harold Webb Assoc., Ltd. (R)

VERMONT

Brattleboro
Management Recruiters

Pittsford
Gilbert Tweed Assoc., Inc. (R)

VIRGINIA

Alexandria
Jeffrey Irving Assoc., Inc. (R)
Kearney Executive Search (R)
Management Recruiters

Arlington
Frey & Conboy Assoc., Inc.
Romac & Assoc., Inc.

Baileys Crossroads
The NRI Group

Bristol
Management Recruiters

Burke
The McCormick Group, Inc.

Charlottesville
Hartman, Barnette & Assoc. (R)

Earleysville
Tierney Assoc., Inc. (R)

Fairfax
Halbrecht & Co.
The Kennett Group, Inc.
Management Recruiters
Sales Consultants of Fairfax, Inc.

Harrisonburg
Professional Recruiters

Herndon
MD Resources, Inc. (R)

Lynchburg
Management Recruiters

Manassas
Gleason & Asaoc. (R)

McLean
Management Recruiters
Paul-Tittle Assoc., Inc.
Source EDP
Source Engineering
Source Finance
U.S. Search

Newport News
Management Recruiters

Norfolk
The Paxton Group, Ltd.

Reston
Brault & Assoc., Ltd. (R)
Dahl-Morrow Int'l. (R)
Pencom System Inc.

Richmond
The Corporate Connection, Ltd.
Dunhill Personnel System, Inc.
Management Recruiters
Sales Consultants

Roanoke
Crickenberger Assoc.
Dunhill Personnel System, Inc.
Management Recruiters

Staunton
The Talley Group

Sterling
Management Recruiters

Vienna
Accountants On Call
De Funiak & Edwards (R)
FGI (R)
The Hamilton Group (R)
Kincannon & Reed (R)
Kirkman & Searing (R)
Logue & Rice Inc.
The Network Companies
P. T. Unger Assoc. (R)

Virginia Beach
A la Carte Int'l., Inc. (R)
Dunhill Personnel System, Inc.
Fox-Morris Assoc., Inc.
Management Recruiters
Sanford Rose Assoc. - Virginia Beach
Sales Consultants
Search & Recruit Int'l.
Wayne Assoc., Inc.

Waynesboro
AdStaff Personnel, Inc.

Williamsburg
Sloan & Assoc., Inc.

Winchester
Management Recruiters

WASHINGTON

Bellevue
Career Specialists, Inc.
J.F. Church Assoc., Inc.
L.W. Foote Co. (R)
The Hart Group
Kirkbride Assoc., Inc.
Management Recruiters
John O'Keefe & Assoc., Inc. (R)
Prior Martech Assoc. (R)
Romac & Assoc., Inc.
Roth Young Seattle
Sales Consultants
Source EDP
Source Engineering
Source Finance

Bothell
Competitive Resources, Inc.
Management Recruiters

Issaquah
K.E. Johnson Assoc.

Kirkland
Kossuth & Assoc., Inc.

Lynnwood
Management Recruiters

Mercer Island
Management Recruiters

Olympia
Management Recruiters

Seattle
Korn/Ferry Int'l. (R)
MD Resources, Inc. (R)
Marshall Consultants, Inc. (R)
Phillips Resource Group
Donna Svei Assoc.

Spokane
Management Recruiters
Personnel Unlimited/Executive Search
Physicians Search Assoc. Agency, Inc.
The Stoddard Co.

Tacoma
Management Recruiters

Vancouver
Management Recruiters
Samper Assoc.

WEST VIRGINIA

Lewisburg
Dunhill Personnel System, Inc.

Wheeling
Sanford Rose Assoc.

WISCONSIN

Appleton
Corporate Recruiters, Inc.
Engineering Specialists
Management Recruiters
Schenck & Assoc. SC

Brookfield
Boettcher Assoc. (R)
Fogec Consultants (R)
Maglio & Co., Inc. (R)
Management Recruiters
Management Recruiters
John H. Munson & Co.
Stanislaw & Assoc., Inc. (R)
Jude M. Werra & Assoc. (R)

Delafield
The Cooper Executive Search Group, Inc. (R)

Elm Grove
Executive Recruiters, Inc.
Human Resource Recruiters
Koehler & Co. (R)

Fond du Lac
Management Recruiters

Green Bay
Dunhill Personnel System, Inc.
Management Recruiters
Sales Consultants
Source EDP

Green Lake
Management Recruiters

Hales Corners
John Kuhn & Assoc. (R)
Management Recruiters

Hartland
Conley Assoc., Inc. (R)

LaValle
Prestige Search Inc.

Lake Geneva
The Rankin Group, Ltd. (R)

Madison
Dunhill Personnel System, Inc.
Management Recruiters
Wojdula & Assoc. (R)

Manitowoc
Management Recruiters

Mequon
J.M. Eagle Partners
Kendro & Assoc. (R)
Overton Group (R)

Middleton
Sales Consultants of Madison

Milwaukee
Accountants On Call
BDO Seidam (R)
Barnes, Walters & Assoc., Inc. (R)
Caswell/Winters & Assoc., Inc. (R)
Dunhill Personnel of Milwaukee
Kordus Consulting Group
MARBL Consultants, Inc.
Management Recruiters
Management Recruiters
Management Recruiters
P. J. Murphy & Assoc., Inc. (R)
Posse, Inc.
Sales Consultants
Source EDP
Source Finance
Sullivan-Murphy Assoc. (R)
Frank X. Walsh & Co., Inc.
Wegner & Assoc.

Nashotah
Blum & Co. (R)

Oconomowoc
TEMCO - The Executive Mgmt. Cons. Org.
(R)

Onalaska
Personnel Unlimited/Executive Search

Plymouth
Management Recruiters

Racine
The Connolly Consulting Group
Management Recruiters
Sales Consultants

Stevens Point
Management Recruiters

Thiensville
MarketSearch, Inc.

Waukesha
Executive Resource Inc.
Fox Hill Assoc., Ltd. (R)
Placement Solutions
Sanford Rose Assoc.
Wargo & Co., Inc. (R)

Wausau
Management Recruiters

West Bend
Egan & Assoc. (R)
Gibson & Co., Inc. (R)

WYOMING

Cheyenne
Management Recruiters

CANADA

ALBERTA

Calgary
The Caldwell Partners Int'l. (R)
Coopers & Lybrand Consulting Group (R)

O'Callaghan, Honey & Assoc., Inc. (R)
Peat Marwick Stevenson & Kellogg (R)

Edmonton
Peat Marwick Stevenson & Kellogg (R)

BRITISH COLUMBIA

Vancouver
Accountants On Call
Ashton Computer Professionals, Inc.
The Caldwell Partners Int'l. (R)
Coopers & Lybrand Consulting Group (R)
Dunhill Personnel System, Inc.
Allen Etcovitch Assoc. Ltd.
Peat Marwick Stevenson & Kellogg (R)
Tanton/Mitchell Group (R)

MANITOBA

Winnipeg
Peat Marwick Stevenson & Kellogg (R)

NEWFOUNDLAND

St. John's
Peat Marwick Stevenson & Kellogg (R)

NOVA SCOTIA

Halifax
Peat Marwick Stevenson & Kellogg (R)
Robertson-Surrette Ltd. (R)

ONTARIO

Kitchener
Peat Marwick Stevenson & Kellogg (R)

London
Dunhill Personnel System, Inc.
Peat Marwick Stevenson & Kellogg (R)

Mississauga
CanMed Consultants Inc. (R)
William Humphreys & Assoc., Inc. (R)
Sales Consultants

Source EDP

North York
Dunhill Personnel System, Inc.

Ottawa
Peat Marwick Stevenson & Kellogg (R)
Phillips Group of Companies (R)

Toronto
Accountants On Call
Armitage Assoc. (R)
Keith Bagg Personnel Ltd.
Beech Preger & Partners, Ltd. (R)
Botrie Assoc. (R)
Boyden Int'l., Inc. (R)
Bryce, Haultain & Assoc. (R)
The Caldwell Partners Int'l. (R)
Cambridge Management Planning (R)
Michael J. Cavanaugh & Assoc. (R)
Chase Partners (R)
Coopers & Lybrand Consulting Group (R)
Deven Assoc., Inc. (R)
George Enns Partners Inc. (R)
ExecuCounsel Management Consultants Inc.
  (R)
Executive Profiles Inc. (R)
Leon A. Farley Assoc. (R)
Franchise Recruiters Ltd.
The Garrison Group
Robert Half Int'l.
Heidrick and Struggles, Inc. (R)
Kearney Executive Search (R)
Korn/Ferry Int'l. (R)
The Landmark Consulting Group Inc. (R)
Bruce Massey & Partners Inc. (R)
Milgram & Assoc.
Parker Page Group
Peat Marwick Stevenson & Kellogg (R)
Phillips Group of Companies (R)
Rourke, Bourbonnais Assoc., Ltd. (R)
Saley Partners Int'l. (R)
E.L. Shore & Assoc. Corp. (R)
Herman Smith Transearch Inc. (R)
Source EDP
Source Finance
Michael Stern Assoc. Inc. (R)
Stoneham Assoc. (R)
Ward Howell Int'l. Inc. (R)
Weir Executive Search Assoc., Inc. (R)
Egon Zehnder Int'l., Inc. (R)

Willowdale
Hyman, Mackenzie & Partners, Inc. (R)
Source EDP

QUEBEC

Montreal
The Caldwell Partners Int'l. (R)
Coopers & Lybrand Consulting Group (R)

Deven Assoc., Inc. (R)
Allen Etcovitch Assoc. Ltd.
Heidrick and Struggles, Inc. (R)
Peat Marwick Stevenson & Kellogg (R)
Phillips Group of Companies (R)
Ranger & Assoc.
Rourke, Bourbonnais Assoc., Ltd. (R)
Gilles Tremblay & Assoc. (R)
Egon Zehnder Int'l., Inc. (R)

SASKATCHEWAN

Regina
Peat Marwick Stevenson & Kellogg (R)

MEXICO

JALISCO

Guadalajara
Smith, Gaxiola y Asociados (R)

MEXICO

Mexico City
Boyden Latin America S.A. de C.V. (R)
Boyden Latin America S.A. de C.V. (R)
Conrey Interamericana (R)
Frank P. Hill
Korn/Ferry, Int'l., S.A. de C.V. (R)
Korn/Ferry Int'l. (R)
RZL Y Asociados, S.C. (R)
Smith Search, S.A. (R)
Ward Howell Int'l. Inc. (R)
Egon Zehnder Int'l. Inc. (R)

NUEVO LEON

Garza Garcia
RZL Y Asociados, S.C. (R)

Monterrey
Korn/Ferry, Int'l., S.A. de C.V. (R)
Korn/Ferry Int'l. (R)

QUERETARO

Queretaro
RZL Y Asociados, S.C. (R)

Retainer and Contingency Key Principals Index

Names with an (R) are from the Retainer Firms Section.

Abbott, Charles J.—Specialty Consultants, Inc.
Abbott, Peter Darby—The Abbott Group (R)
Abrahamsen, Marcia—John Velcamp & Assoc. (R)
Abrahamson, Joan—Dunhill of Bradenton, Inc.
Acridge, Charles W.—CRI Professional Search
Adams, Allan—Adel Lawrence Assoc., Inc.
Adams, Arthur—Arthur Adams & Assoc.
Adams, Bruce W.—The Adams Group
Adams, Deane—Sales Consultants
Adams, Jeffrey C.—Jeffrey C. Adams & Co., Inc. (R)
Adams, Len—Kling Personnel Assoc., Inc.
Adams, Mark R.—Sanford Rose Assoc.
Adams, Ralda F.—Hospitality Int'l.
Adams, Steven A.—Intech Summit Group, Inc.
Adams, Wally—Sales Consultants
Adcock, Bob—Management Recruiters
Adin, Sarah—Battalia Winston Int'l., Inc. (R)
Adkisson, Billy D.—James Russell, Inc. (R)
Adler, Eric—The Adler Group
Adler, Jack—D.M. Rein & Co., Inc. (R)
Ady, John R.—John R. Ady & Assoc., Inc.
Ady, Sharon L.—John R. Ady & Assoc., Inc.
Adzima, Allan G.—MARBL Consultants, Inc.
Africa, Martha Fay—Major, Wilson & Africa
Aglinsky, William—Management Recruiters
Aglinsky, William—Sales Consultants
Ahn, Phil—Source Finance
Aiken, David—Commonwealth Consultants
Aitken, Carol—Aitken & Assoc.
Aitkens, Sidney—Fernow Assoc.
Akalarian, Carla J.—Sales Consultants
Akin, J.R.—J.R. Akin & Co. (R)
Albus, John P.—Lord & Albus Co.
Alders, Timothy C.—Gary Kaplan & Assoc. (R)
Alexander, Craig A.—Management Recruiters
Alexander, Craig A.—Sales Consultants
Alexander, George—National Search, Inc.

Alexander, Mark—Waterford, Inc.
Alexander, R. Edwin—Alexander Edward Assoc., Inc.
Alexander, Teresa—Management Recruiters
Alexander, Teresa—Sales Consultants
Alexander, Victor—National Search, Inc.
Alfeld, Karl—Loewenstein & Assoc.
Alford, Judy—Loewenstein & Assoc.
Allatore, Kathleen W.—Accountants On Call
Allen, Brooke—Ashton Computer Professionals, Inc.
Allen, David—Baker Scott & Co.
Allen, Don—D.S. Allen Assoc.
Allen, Elizabeth—Garofolo, Curtiss, Lambert & MacLean (R)
Allen, Frank—Frank E. Allen & Assoc.
Allen, James R.—Sanford Rose Assoc.
Allen, Jean—The NRI Group
Allen, Lindsay—Mark III Personnel, Inc.
Allen, Mark—Sales Consultants
Allen, Michael—Allen/Assoc.
Allen, Mike—Management Recruiters
Allen, Pat—Pat Allen Assoc. Inc.
Allen, Rita—Sales Consultants
Allen, Rita—Gatti & Assoc.
Allen, Robert—Hegarty & Co. (R)
Aller, Joan—L O R Personnel Div. (R)
Allerton, Donald—Allerton Heneghan & O'Neill (R)
Alley, Glenwood—Management Recruiters
Almour, Carol—Kramer Executive Resources, Inc.
Alo, Lindy—C.P.S., Inc.
Alt, R.—The Altco Group
Altman, Mark—M-A Management Assoc., Inc.
Alves, Manuel J.—M/J/A Partners (R)
Alvey, Frank—Robert Sage Recruiting
Alvey, John—Romac & Assoc., Inc.
Amato, Jim—Probus Executive Search

Amato, Joseph D.–Amato & Assoc., Inc.

Ambler, Peter W.–Peter W. Ambler Co. (R)

Ambruster, David L.–Tierney Assoc., Inc. (R)

Ameen, Edward C.–Management Recruiters

Ameen, Edward C.–Sales Consultants

Ames, Andrew P.–Ames & Ames (R)

Ames, George C.–Ames-O'Neill Assoc., Inc.

Ames, Michael J.–Ames Assoc. Inc.

Ames, Mildred S.–Ames Assoc. Inc.

Ames, Philip J.–Ames Personnel Consultants

Amy, Rupert R.–Careers/Inc.

Anas, Mickey–Sloan & Assoc., Inc.

Ancowitz, Allen B.–Allen Barry Assoc.

Andersen, Carol–Stimmel Search Division (R)

Anderson, A. M.–Anderson Industrial Assoc., Inc.

Anderson, Bill–Management Recruiters

Anderson, Chris A.–Effective Search, Inc. (R)

Anderson, David C.–SpencerStuart (R)

Anderson, David R.–SilverCrest Search

Anderson, Dean–Corporate Resources Professional Placement

Anderson, Dennis–Andcor Human Resources (R)

Anderson, Don–Sanford Rose Assoc.

Anderson, Douglas K.–Sockwell & Anderson (R)

Anderson, Jr., Francis V.–Francis V. Anderson Assoc. Inc.

Anderson, Gregory D.–Anderson Industrial Assoc., Inc.

Anderson, James L.–R.L. Plimpton Assoc. (R)

Anderson, Jim–Howard Clark Assoc.

Anderson, John L.–Northeastern Search, Inc.

Anderson, Kenneth J.–Anders Incorporated (R)

Anderson, Kristine M.–Gary Kaplan & Assoc. (R)

Anderson, Pam–G.A.M. Executive Search, Inc.

Anderson, Robert T.–Hanzel & Co., Inc. (R)

Anderson, Robert W.–Anderson Bradshaw Assoc., Inc. (R)

Anderson, Roger J.–BioQuest Inc. (R)

Anderson, Susan T.–SilverCrest Search

Andre, Jacques P.–Paul R. Ray & Co., Inc. (R)

Andre, Richard–The Andre Group, Inc. (R)

Andrews, Dan–BR & Assoc.

Andrews, J. Douglas–Jack Clarey Assoc., Inc. (R)

Andrews, Jasmine–Zachary & Sanders, Inc.

Angel, Steve–Sales Consultants

Angel, Steven R.–Management Recruiters

Angell, Robert A.–Management Recruiters

Angell, Robert A.–Sales Consultants

Angell, Tryg–Tryg R. Angell Ltd.

Angott, Mark R.–Management Recruiters of North Oakland County, Inc.

Angus, Thomas R.–The Angus Group, Inc.

Angustin, Steven–Physicians Search Assoc. Agency, Inc.

Ankerson, Robert W.–Ward Howell Int'l. Inc. (R)

Annesi, Jerry–Management Recruiters

Annesi, Jerry–Sales Consultants

Annicchero, Jerry–Management Recruiters

Anselmi, Ray–Source EDP

Anthony, Charles H.–Anthony Executive Search

Antonczak, Daniel J.–C. J. Williams Human Resource Group, Inc.

Anwar, Tarin–Jay Gaines & Co. (R)

Apostle, George–Search Dynamics, Inc.

Apple, Richard W.–R.W. Apple & Assoc.

Aquavella, Charles P.–Charles P. Aquavella & Assoc.

Arancio, N. Joseph–Arancio Assoc.

Archer-Martin, Nancy–Educational Management Network (R)

Ariail, Randolph C.–Ariail & Assoc. (R)

Armes, George A.–Environmental Resources Int'l.

Armitage, John D.–Armitage Assoc. (R)

Armstrong, Kathleen–Hedlund Corp.

Arnette, Tom–Windward Executive Search, Inc.

Arnold, David–SpencerStuart (R)

Arnold, Janet N.–Management Recruiters

Arnold, Sheridan J.–William B. Arnold Assoc., Inc. (R)

Arnold, William B.–William B. Arnold Assoc., Inc. (R)

Aronow, Lawrence E.–Aronow Assoc., Inc.

Aronson, Stephan J.–Northeastern Search, Inc.

Arredondo, Fred–Spectra West

Artis, Robert–Sales Consultants

Arzoomanian, Mark–Setford-Shaw-Najarian Assoc., Ltd.

Ash, Robert I.–Ashworth Consultants, Inc. (R)

Ashton, Barbara L.–Ashton Computer Professionals, Inc.

Ashton, Edward J.–E. J. Ashton & Assoc., Ltd.

Aslaksen, James G.–James, Layton Int'l., Inc. (R)

Ast, Steven T.–Ast/Bryant (R)

Atkeson, George G.–Ward Howell Int'l. Inc. (R)

Atkins, Laurie–Battalia Winston Int'l., Inc. (R)

Atkins, Will E.–B.P.A. Enterprises, Inc.

Atkins-Gottlieb, Carol–David Saxner & Assoc., Inc.

Atwood, Calvin W.–Blackshaw, Olmstead & Atwood (R)

Aubin, Richard E.–Aubin Int'l. Inc. (R)

Auerbach, Judith A.–Auerbach Assoc. (R)

August, Sally–G.A.M. Executive Search, Inc.

Auster, A. Marc–Tarnow Int'l. (R)
Austin, Peter T.–Organization Resources Inc. (R)
Austin, Steve–Sales Consultants
Aydelotte, G. Thomas–Ingram, Inc. (R)
Ayers, Jr., William L.–The Ayers Group, Inc.
Baalbaki, Samih M.–Management Recruiters
Bachard, Russ–Headhunters National, Inc.
Bader, Sam–Bader Research Corp.
Badger, Fred–The Badger Group (R)
Badway, Anthony J.–Lacrosse Assoc., Inc.
Baensch, Barbara–The Salem Group, Executive Recruiters
Baer, Baxter–Triangle Consulting Group
Bagg, Keith–Keith Bagg Personnel Ltd.
Bagg, Mary–Keith Bagg Personnel Ltd.
Bagileo, Jean–David Powell, Inc. (R)
Bagley, Rass–Marketing Recruiters, Inc.
Bailey, F.L.–Aerospace Technologies, Inc.
Baird, David W.–D.W. Baird & Associates
Baitler, Simon C.–The Stevenson Group/SES (R)
Baker, C.D.–Corporate Staffing Group (R)
Baker, Gary M.–Cochran, Cochran, & Yale, Inc.
Baker, Jerry H.–Schuyler, Frye & Baker, Inc. (R)
Baker, Jim–Atlantic Search Group, Inc.
Baker, Jon L.–Studwell Assoc. (R)
Baker, Jr., Joseph N.–JNB Assoc., Inc.
Baker, Kerry–Thomas, Whelan Assoc., Inc.
Baker, Reed–Fox-Morris Assoc., Inc.
Baker, S. Joseph–Search Consultants Int'l., Inc.
Baker, Wendy–Bert Davis Assoc., Inc.
Bakker, Robert–Management Recruiters
Bakker, Robert A.–Sales Consultants of Northern Jersey, Inc.
Balakonis, Charles L.–Lawrence-Balakonis & Assoc., Inc.
Balazy, James–Richard Kader & Assoc.
Baldanza, Joseph M.–Winfield Assoc.
Baldwin, II, Arthur D.–Artgo, Inc. (R)
Baldwin, Keith R.–Menzel, Robinson, Baldwin, Inc. (R)
Baldwin, Max M.–Baldwin Associates, Inc. (R)
Baldwin, Val B.–Management Assoc.
Baldwin, W. Keith–Baldwin & Assoc.
Bales, L. Patrick–Donahue/Bales Assoc. (R)
Ball, Carol–Carol Ball & Co., Inc.
Ball, Ronald D.–Ron Ball & Assoc.
Ballantyne, Tom–Ballantyne & Assoc. (R)
Ballein, Kathleen–Witt Assoc. Inc. (R)
Ballos, Constantine J.–Ballos & Co., Inc. (R)
Ballos, H.P.–Ballos & Co., Inc. (R)
Bamford, Charles R.–Rockwood Assoc.

Banas, Randy–MarketSearch, Inc.
Bangert, James–James Bangert & Assoc., Inc. (R)
Baniqued, Douglas J.–CompuPro
Bank, Phil–Source Finance
Banker, Judith–Gatti & Assoc.
Banner, Stan–Management Recruiters
Bannon, Rainette–DHR Int'l., Inc. (R)
Banting, Susan–Source EDP
Barack, Brianne–The Barack Group, Inc.
Baranowski, Peter–Source Engineering
Baranski, David–Management Recruiters
Baranski, Glenda–Management Recruiters
Barbosa, Franklin J.–Boyden Int'l., Inc. (R)
Barca, Anthony J.–Ross Personnel Consultants, Inc.
Barger, H. Carter–Barger & Sargeant, Inc. (R)
Bargholz, Harry–Management Recruiters
Bargholz, Harry L.–Management Recruiters of Wilmington
Barick, Brad–Management Recruiters
Barkauskas, Richard–Staub, Warmbold & Barkauskas, Inc. (R)
Barker, Mary J.–Management Recruiters
Barkin, Herbert L.–B. Goodwin, Ltd. (R)
Barkocy, Andrew B.–Princeton Executive Search
Barleycorn, James M.–J.W. Barleycorn & Assoc. (R)
Barlow, Mark–Smith, Beaty, Barlow Assoc., Inc.
Barnard, Richard S.–Russillo/Gardner
Barnes, B.K.–B.K. Barnes & Associates
Barnes, Greg–Guidry, East, Barnes & Bono, Inc. (R)
Barnes, Karen S.–EFL Assoc. (R)
Barnes, Richard E.–Barnes, Walters & Assoc., Inc. (R)
Barnett, Kim–Management Recruiters
Barnette, Fred A.–Hartman, Barnette & Assoc. (R)
Barnum, Toni M.–Stone, Murphy & Olson (R)
Baron, Anna–Allen Etcovitch Assoc. Ltd.
Baron, Harvey J.–Management Recruiters
Baron, Len–Industrial Recruiters Assoc., Inc.
Baron, Sheldon S.–Sales Consultants of Nashua - Manchester
Barone, Marialice–Barone-O'Hara Assoc., Inc.
Barr, Barbara–Vista Resource Group (R)
Barr, Charly–Sanford Rose Assoc. of Quakertown
Barr, Sharon A.–Sanford Rose Assoc. of Quakertown
Barrett, Ben–Management Recruiters
Barrett, Peter–Peter Barrett Assoc., Inc.
Barrett, Rich–Source Finance

Barrow, Dan—Eggers Consulting Co., Inc.

Barry, James P.—International Management Services Inc. (R)

Barry, Nathan—Nathan Barry Assoc., Inc. (R)

Bartholdi, Sr., Theodore G.—Bartholdi & Co. (R)

Bartholdi, Jr., Theodore G.—Bartholdi & Co. (R)

Bartholomew, Catherine—C. Berger and Company

Bartl, Frank—Bartl & Evins

Bartle, Tom—Wesley Brown & Bartle Co., Inc. (R)

Bartlett, Judy K.—Bartlett, Bunn & Travis, Inc.

Bartman, Paul—Hall, Cooper & Bartman, Ltd.

Barton, Creighton E.—Leon A. Farley Assoc. (R)

Barton, Gary—Barton Raben, Inc. (R)

Bartosh, George—Source Engineering

Bartosh, George—Source EDP

Barz, James M.—International Management Services Inc. (R)

Bascom, Shirley R.—Management Recruiters

Bason, Maurice L.—Bason Assoc., Inc. (R)

Bass, Harvey C.—Sales Consultants

Bass, Stanley—Spectrum Consultants

Bassin, Craig—Geneva Group Int'l. (R)

Bassman, Robert W.—Management Recruiters

Bassman, Sandra M.—Management Recruiters

Basso, Jr., Louis—Gray-Kimball Assoc., Inc.

Bast, Larry C.—Bast & Assoc., Inc.

Bast, Sue E.—Bast & Assoc., Inc.

Bastoky, Bruce M.—January Management Group (R)

Batchelder, Gale—Auerbach Assoc. (R)

Bates, John L.—Management Recruiters

Bates, Richard—Management Recruiters of Frederick, Inc.

Batsakis, Marci—Professional Medical

Battalia, O. William—Battalia Winston Int'l., Inc. (R)

Battalin, Laurence H.—L. Battalin & Co.

Battani, Kenneth J.—Barnes, Walters & Assoc., Inc. (R)

Battista, Jr., Gerard E.—Battista Assoc., Inc.

Battistoni, Bea—Accountants On Call

Battles, Thomas E.—Gilbert Tweed Assoc., Inc. (R)

Baty, R. Gaines—R. Gaines Baty Assoc., Inc.

Baum, Jim—Jim Baum - Executive Search

Bauman, Barbara J.—Merrick & Moore

Bauman, Martin H.—Martin H. Bauman Assoc., Inc. (R)

Baumgart, J.—St. James And DeDominic

Baumstein, Edward S.—Romac & Assoc., Inc.

Bavli, Mark—Tech Consulting

Bavly, Ted—Ted Bavly Assoc., Inc.

Bawulski, Fred B.—Management Recruiters

Baxter, Lee—Anderson Industrial Assoc., Inc.

Baxter, Margaret—Traynor Confidential, Ltd.

Baxter, Sheryl—Vincent Lee Assoc.

Bayliss, Chet—The Baxter Group (R)

Beall, Charles P.—Beall & Co., Inc. (R)

Beals, Calvin—Management Recruiters of Ft. Myers, FL.

Beals, Charlotte—Management Recruiters of Ft. Myers, FL.

Bean, Jr., Robert L.—Management Recruiters

Bearman, Linda—Grant Cooper & Assoc., Inc. (R)

Beatty, Richard H.—Brandywine Consulting Group (R)

Beatty, Robert L.—The Curtiss Group, Inc. (R)

Beaudine, Frank R.—Eastman & Beaudine, Inc. (R)

Beaudine, Jr., Frank R.—Eastman & Beaudine, Inc. (R)

Beaudine, Robert E.—Eastman & Beaudine, Inc. (R)

Beaupre, Joseph M. B.—The Caldwell Partners Int'l. (R)

Beaver, Bentley H.—J. Robert Scott (R)

Becker, Ed—Management Recruiters

Becker, Ed—Sales Consultants

Becker, Ralph L.—Automation Technology Search

Becker, Rita—Management Recruiters

Becker, Rita—Sales Consultants

Becker, Robert C.—Becker, Norton & Co. (R)

Beckvold, John B.—Atlantic Search Group, Inc.

Beckwith, Randy—Beckwith, Thomas & Fanning

Bedingfield, Ray N.—Ray N. Bedingfield, Consultant

Beech, Lisa M.—Beech Preger & Partners, Ltd. (R)

Beerbaum, James—Management Recruiters

Beerbaum, Judy—Management Recruiters

Beers, Richard W.—Richard Beers & Assoc., Ltd. (R)

Beers, Thomas—Aim Executive Inc.

Beeson, Wm B.—Lawrence-Leiter & Co. (R)

Begalke, Robert H.—Unisearch

Begun, Mike—Search West, Inc.

Behringer, W. Neail—Inside Management Assoc. (R)

Beilin, Marcia—Marcia Beilin, Inc.

Beirne, David M.—Ramsey & Beirne Assoc., Inc. (R)

Belastock, Gary—Alan Lerner Assoc.

Belcher, Bob—Sales Consultants

Bell, Gary S.—Gary S. Bell Assoc., Inc.

Bell, James W.—Bell Professional Placement

Bell, Jeffrey G.—Norman Broadbent Int'l., Inc. (R)
Bell, Mindy—Retail Pacesetters, Inc.
Bell, Nelson C.—Nelson Bell & Partners Inc. (R)
Bell, Ruth L.—World Search
Bell, Scotty—Physicians Search Assoc. Agency, Inc.
Belletieri, Nancy—Probe Technology
Belletieri, Thomas F.—Probe Technology
Bellon, Lee Ann—Bellon & Assoc., Inc.
Bellview, Louis P.—Management Recruiters
Bellview, Sibyl—Management Recruiters
Belt, Joy Reed—Joy Reed Belt & Assoc., Inc. (R)
Bender, Alan—S. R. Wolman Assoc., Inc. (R)
Benefield, Dotson—Dotson Benefield & Assoc., Inc.
Benke, Norman L.—Romac & Assoc., Inc.
Bennett, Delora—Genesis Personnel Service, Inc.
Bennett, Jr., Godfrey G.—Schwab-Carrese Assoc. (R)
Bennett, Jo—Battalia Winston Int'l., Inc. (R)
Bennett, Marilyn—Brentwood Int'l. (R)
Bennett, Mark—Bennett-Munson Inc.
Bennett, Richard T.—The PAR Group - Paul A. Reaume, Ltd. (R)
Bennett, Jr., Robert C.—Bennett Search & Consulting Co. (R)
Benson, Robert L.—SpencerStuart (R)
Bent, Devin Charles—Professional Recruiters
Bent, Judith—Professional Recruiters
Berger, Alan H.—Berger & Assoc.
Berger, Carol A.—C. Berger and Company
Berger, Jay—Pathway Executive Search, Inc.
Berger, Jay V.—Morris & Berger (R)
Berger, Jerry—ACC Consultants, Inc.
Berger, Joel—Meridian Personnel Assoc., Inc.
Berger, Judith E.—MD Resources, Inc. (R)
Berger, Judith L.—Management Recruiters
Berger, Mitchell L.—Howard-Sloan Legal Search, Inc.
Bergsund, Joan R.—Richard T. Bergsund Assoc. (R)
Bergsund, Richard T.—Richard T. Bergsund Assoc. (R)
Bergwall, Joseph B.—Rogers & Seymour Inc.
Berk-Levine, Margo—MB Inc.
Berlet, William—Peat Marwick Stevenson & Kellogg (R)
Berlin, Stephen—Corporate Recruiters Inc.
Berman, Fred—The Berman Consulting Group (R)
Berman, Mitchell—The Carlyle Group, Ltd.

Berman, Robert—The Berman Consulting Group (R)
Berman, Shirlee J.—Retail Recruiters/Spectrum Consultants, Inc.
Bernard, Gary D.—Byron Leonard Int'l., Inc. (R)
Bernard, Harry—Colton Bernard Inc. (R)
Berner, Paul—RBR Assoc., Inc.
Bernstein, Marcia—Dunhill Professional Search Group
Berry, Harold B.—The Hindman Co. (R)
Berry, John R.—The Heidrick Partners, Inc. (R)
Bertoux, Michael P.—McCracken, Wilcox, Bertoux & Miller
Bertrand, Thomas R.—Bertrand, Ross & Assoc., Inc. (R)
Bertsch, Phil L.—Management Recruiters
Beruldsen, Arne—Hemingway Personnel, Inc.
Berv, Elliott J.—Elliott J. Berv & Assoc. (R)
Besen, Douglas—Besen Assoc. Inc.
Best, Deborah K.—Sanford Rose Assoc.
Bevivino, Sal—Questor Consultants, Inc.
Bialecki, Linda—Bialecki Inc. (R)
Bialkin, Joan—Federal Placement Services
Bialla, Vito—Bialla & Assoc., Inc. (R)
Biasotti, Julie—Cosco Resources Inc.
Bidaman, K. Michael—Robert Howe & Assoc. (R)
Biestek, Paul J.—Paul J. Biestek Assoc., Inc. (R)
Bignell, Lynn Tendler—Gilbert Tweed Assoc., Inc. (R)
Billingsly, Dorothy M.—DHR Int'l, Inc (R)
Billington, Brian J.—Billington & Assoc., Inc. (R)
Billington, W. H.—Billington, Fox & Ellis, Inc. (R)
Birch, John—Tully & Birch, Inc. (R)
Birch, Thomas B.—Lynch & Co. (R)
Birnbaum, Richard—Corporate Careers Inc.
Bishop, Deborah—Deborah Bishop & Assoc. (R)
Bishop, James F.—Burke, O'Brien & Bishop Assoc., Inc. (R)
Bishop, M.A.—Management Recruiters
Bishop, Susan K.—Bishop Assoc. (R)
Bissell, John—Gundersen Brenner, Inc. (R)
Bitar, Edward—Larsen Int'l., Inc. (R)
Bivona, Ernest—Sales Consultants of Morris County, Inc.
Black, Jr., Frank S.—Management Recruiters
Black, Melvyn—Affirmative Action Assoc.
Black, Philip—Management Recruiters
Black, Roy—Management Recruiters
Blackburn, Charles—Management Recruiters
Blackshaw, Brian—Blackshaw, Olmstead & Atwood (R)

Blackwell, Ann E.—Smith, Goerss & Ferneborg, Inc. (R)

Blair, Kelly A.—The Caldwell Partners Int'l. (R)

Blaire, Martin—The Consortium

Blake, Barbara—Ron Sunshine & Assoc.

Blanchard, Sr., Richard E.—Career Management, Inc.

Blanchard, Rick—Career Management, Inc.

Blanchard, Ross L.—Blanchard, Zufall & Assoc. (R)

Blanchette, Dave—Management Recruiters

Blanchette, Erin—Management Recruiters

Blaney, John A.—Blaney Executive Search (R)

Blanton, Julia—Blanton & Co.

Blanton, Thomas—Blanton & Co.

Blazek, Jim—The James Group

Blazek, Susan M.—Executive Appointments Ltd., Int'l. (R)

Bleau, Donn E.—Global Resources Group (R)

Blecksmith, Ed—Korn/Ferry Int'l. (R)

Blocher, J.B.—Source EDP

Block, Randall T.—Block & Assoc. (R)

Blonsky, Lorena M.—LMB Assoc.

Blood, Burwood O.—D. R. Blood & Assoc.

Blood, Dennis R.—D. R. Blood & Assoc.

Bloom, Howard—The Howard C. Bloom Co.

Bloom, Joyce—The Howard C. Bloom Co.

Bloome, Marc—Marc-Paul Bloome Ltd. (R)

Blount, K. Michael—Ward Howell Int'l. Inc. (R)

Blue, C. David—Management Recruiters

Blum, D. L. Buzz—Blum & Co. (R)

Blumenfeld, Myron I.—Colton Bernard Inc. (R)

Blumenthal, Paula—J.P. Canon Assoc.

Blunt, John W.—The Blunt Co., Inc. (R)

Blunt, Miles—The Blunt Co., Inc. (R)

Boak, Tom—W. Robert Eissler & Assoc., Inc.

Boal, Robert A.—Management Recruiters

Boatman, Millie A.—Whittaker & Assoc., Inc.

Bobola, John—W.T. Glover & Assoc., Inc.

Boczany, Bill—Source Engineering

Bodnar, Beverly—Management Recruiters

Bodnar, Robert—Management Recruiters

Bodnar, Robert—Sales Consultants

Bodner, Beverly—Sales Consultants

Bodner, Marilyn S.—Bodner Inc.

Boeck, Richard E.—Frank X. Walsh & Co., Inc.

Boettcher, Jack W.—Boettcher Assoc. (R)

Bogar, Erika—Walter V. Connor Int'l., Inc. (R)

Bogart, James—The Bankers Register

Bogdan, Mike—Source EDP

Boguski, Ronald T.—The Hamilton Group (R)

Bole, John Jeffrey—William J. Christopher Assoc., Inc.

Bolls, Rich—Management Recruiters

Bond, Bob—Management Recruiters

Bond, Carole—Management Recruiters

Bondur, John M.—Handy HRM (R)

Bonifield, Len—Bonifield Assoc.

Bonner, Rodney D.—Management Recruiters

Bonnot, Wyche—Larsen Int'l., Inc. (R)

Bono, Susan—Guidry, East, Barnes & Bono, Inc. (R)

Boone, John C.—John C. Boone & Co. (R)

Borchert, Gregory L.—Gregory L. Borchert, Inc.

Borden, Samuel—Fortune Personnel Consultants of Huntsville, Inc.

Borenstine, Alvin J.—Synergistics Assoc. Ltd. (R)

Borgschulte, Don—Sales Consultants

Borkin, Andrew—META/MAT, Ltd. (R)

Bornholdt, John N.—Bornholdt Shivas & Friends

Bornstein, Lori D.—Garrison, McGuigan & Sisson

Borntrager, June—The Bankers Group

Bos, John—Sanford Rose Assoc.

Bosch, Eric—John O'Keefe & Assoc., Inc. (R)

Bostic, James E.—Phillips Resource Group

Botrie, James—Botrie Assoc. (R)

Bouer, Judy—Baker Scott & Co.

Boulvd, Eric—Egon Zehnder Int'l., Inc. (R)

Bourque, Jack—Management Recruiters of Waterbury, Inc.

Bouzan, Paul X.—Executive Management Systems, Inc. (R)

Bova, Barry—E.J. Rhodes Assoc. (R)

Bowden, II, Otis H.—Bowden & Co., Inc. (R)

Bowen, Barbara—Studwell Assoc. (R)

Bowen, Peter Newell—Peter Newell Bowen (R)

Bowen, William—Abraham & London Ltd.

Bowers, Bob—Claremont-Branan, Inc.

Bowers, Michael—Woehr Assoc.

Bowersox, Thomas L.—Bowersox & Assoc., Inc.

Bowes, Bob—Sales Consultants

Bowie, Andrew—Gabriel & Bowie Assoc., Ltd.

Bowker, Gordon R.—Bowker, Brown & Co. (R)

Bowman, Carole—Jordon & Jordon, Inc.

Bowman, Will G.—Dr. Will G. Bowman, Inc. (R)

Boxberger, Michael—Korn/Ferry Int'l. (R)

Boxer, Harry—The Century Group

Boxerman, Yvonne—Advanced Information Management

Boyd, Michael—Accountants On Call

Boyd, Michael J.—Wilkinson Boyd

Boyd, N.O.—Management Catalysts (R)

Boyd, Sara—Accountants On Call

Boyer, Dennis—SpencerStuart (R)

Boyer, Heath C.—SpencerStuart (R)

Boyer, Mark—M. Scott Kemp & Assoc., Inc. (R)

Bradbury, Jr., Paul W.—The Bradbury Management Group (R)

Bradley, Mark—Ramsey & Beirne Assoc., Inc. (R)

Bradley, Renea A.—Smith Bradley & Assoc.

Bradley, Sandy—Wells, Bradley & Assoc.

Bradshaw, John W.—Anderson Bradshaw Assoc., Inc. (R)

Brady, Colin S.—GKR Int'l. (R)

Brady, Robert E.—Brady Assoc. Int'l., Inc. (R)

Bragg, Amy F.—Canny, Bowen Inc. (R)

Braley, Donald J.—Management Recruiters

Branch, Minnie—M.F. Branch Assoc., Inc.

Brandjes, Michael—Brandjes Assoc.

Brandon, Irwin—Hadley Lockwood, Inc. (R)

Brandt, Jonathan—Accountants On Call

Brandvold, Jan—Sanford Rose Assoc.- Brecksville

Brandvold, Steven C.—Sanford Rose Assoc.- Brecksville

Brannan, Harold D.—EFL Assoc. (R)

Brassey, Andrew L.—O'Rourke Co., Inc. (R)

Brassey, Chrystine Eiguren—O'Rourke Co., Inc. (R)

Bratches, Howard—Thorndike Deland Assoc. (R)

Brault, J-P.—Brault & Assoc., Ltd. (R)

Braun, Jerold—Jerold Braun & Assoc.

Braun, Linda—Frank E. Allen & Assoc.

Braun, Steven R.—Sales Consultants

Brauninger, John C.—Management Recruiters

Brauth, Michael—Fisher-Todd Assoc.

Breault, Larry—Management Recruiters

Breault, Meredith—Management Recruiters

Breder, C.M.—RIC Corp. (R)

Brennan, Jerry—Brennan Assoc.

Brennan, Patrick—Handy HRM (R)

Brennecke, Richard C.—Sales Consultants

Brenner, Roberta—Gundersen Brenner, Inc. (R)

Brescher, Frank—The E & K Group

Bricker, Deborah A.—Bricker & Assoc., Inc. (R)

Bricker, James A.—Triangle Consulting Group

Bridgett, Cal—Sales Consultants of Savannah, GA.

Bridgett, Gloria—Sales Consultants of Savannah, GA.

Brieger, Steven M.—Thorne, Brieger Assoc., Inc. (R)

Bright, Willie S.—The Urban Placement Service

Brimeger, Jim—Sathe & Assoc., Inc. (R)

Brin, Bradley—Dunhill Personnel of Milwaukee

Brindise, Michael J.—Dynamic Search Systems, Inc.

Brinkerhoff, David W.—Abbott Smith Assoc., Inc.

Briody, Steve—Management Recruiters

Briody, Steve—Sales Consultants

Brissenden, Hoke—Brissenden, McFarland, Wagoner & Fuccella, Inc. (R)

Britcher, Janet—Keane Assoc. (R)

Britten, Al—Sales Consultants

Britton, Peter—Source Finance

Broadman, Ira—Ira Broadman Assoc.

Broadman, Steve—Ira Broadman Assoc.

Brocard, Vivian C.—Gustin Partners, Ltd. (R)

Brock, Rufus C.—Management Recruiters

Brockman, Dan B.—Dan B. Brockman

Brodey, Scott—Management Recruiters

Brody, James R.—J.R. Brody & Assoc., Inc.

Brody, Norma—Delta Personnel Services

Broe, Laurence—Gary Kaplan & Assoc. (R)

Brogan, Pat—Human Resource Bureau

Brolin, Lawrence E.—DLB Assoc.

Bronder, Stephanie L.—Fagan & Co. (R)

Brooks, Bernard E.—Edwin Mruk & Partners (R)

Brooks, Charles S.—Executives' Personnel Service Inc.

Brooks, Clara—C.W. Brandon & Assoc., Inc.

Brooks, David F.—David F. Brooks & Co., Inc.

Brooks, Harvey—Fox-Morris Assoc., Inc.

Brooks, Natalie H.—Dean-Wharton Assoc.

Brophy, Melissa—Maximum Management Corp.

Brower, Jeffrey S.—Florapersonnel, Inc.

Brown, Alta C.—Northern Consultants Inc. (R)

Brown, Ben W.—Consult One, Inc.

Brown, Bobby J.—Sales Consultants

Brown, Buzz—Brown/Bernardy, Inc.

Brown, Chris—Babson, Moore & Wilcox (R)

Brown, Daniel P.—Personnel Management, Inc.

Brown, Franklin Key—Handy HRM (R)

Brown, Gene—Management Recruiters of Atlanta West, Inc.

Brown, Jr., Hobson—Russell Reynolds Assoc., Inc. (R)

Brown, James D.—Northern Consultants Inc. (R)

Brown, Jerome J.—Venture Resources, Inc. (R)

Brown, Pat—Corporate Suite, Ltd.

Brown, Paul A.—Domenico/Brown Group

Brown, Richard E.—O'Connor, O'Connor, Lordi, Ltd. (R)

Brown, S. Ross—Egon Zehnder Int'l. Inc. (R)

Browning, Jeff—Strategic Assoc., Inc.

Brownson, Bruce F.—Kearney Executive Search (R)

Brownstein, Joan—Julian Assoc., Inc.
Brownstein, Julian—Julian Assoc., Inc.
Brubach, Mark W.—Sales Consultants
Bruccoleri, Theodore A.—The Network Companies
Bruckner, Frank—F.J. Bruckner & Co. (R)
Brudno, Robert J.—Savoy Partners, Ltd. (R)
Brugger, Gene William—Luke, Lincoln, & Brugger
Brundage, William—W.T. Glover & Assoc., Inc.
Brunelle, Francis W. H.—The Caldwell Partners Int'l. (R)
Bruner, Frankie—The Human Resource Group
Bruno, Jr., R.J.—High Technology Search Assoc.
Brunschwig, John M.—Sanford Rose Assoc.
Bryant, Christopher P.—Ast/Bryant (R)
Bryant, Michael—Sales Consultants
Bryant, Richard D.—Bryant Assoc., Inc.
Bryant, Tom—Bryant Research
Bryner, Richard—Reinecke & Assoc.
Bryza, Robert M.—Robert Lowell Int'l. (R)
Buchsbaum, Debbie—Accountants On Call
Buck, Jr., Charles A.—Charles Buck & Assoc., Inc. (R)
Buda, Danny—Management Recruiters
Buda, Danny—Sales Consultants
Buenger, James—Romac & Assoc., Inc.
Bueschel, David A.—Sweeney Shepherd Bueschel Provus Harbert & Mummert, Inc. (R)
Bulla, Steven W.—Management Recruiters
Bullard, Dolores—Michael King Assoc., Inc.
Bullis, Richard J.—Bullis & Co., Inc. (R)
Bulmer, Robert E.—Alaska Executive Search, Inc.
Bump, Gerald J.—SpencerStuart (R)
Bunce, David C.—Sales Consultants of Raleigh-Durham-RTP
Bunce, Louise M.—Sales Consultants of Raleigh-Durham-RTP
Bunker, Ralph L.—Management Recruiters
Bunn, Edward J.—Bartlett, Bunn & Travis, Inc.
Bunton, Tom—Sales Consultants
Burbach, Vicki—Maglio & Co., Inc. (R)
Burchill, Barbara E.—BGB Assoc., Inc.
Burchill, Gregory J.—BGB Assoc., Inc.
Burfield, Elaine—Marra/Pizzi Assoc., Inc. (R)
Burgay, Matt—Source Finance
Burkat, Howard—Promotion Recruiters, Inc.
Burke, Jackson P.—Management Recruiters
Burke, Markey—The Kinlin Co., Inc. (R)
Burke, Tom—The Communications Search Group (R)
Burkhard, Alan—The Placers, Inc.
Burkholder, Barbara—Phyllis Hawkins & Assoc.

Burkholder, John—Management Recruiters
Burkland, Skott B.—Skott/Edwards Consultants (R)
Burnett, Brendan G.—Sullivan & Co. (R)
Burnett, Louis C.—Chartwell Partners Int'l., Inc. (R)
Burnham, Thomas—Thomas Burnham Co. (R)
Burns, Alan—George Enns Partners Inc. (R)
Burns, Claire—Bishop Assoc. (R)
Burns, Francis J.—Handy HRM (R)
Burns, John—Quinn Bailey & Morgan (R)
Burns, Joseph R.—Joseph R. Burns & Assoc., Inc. (R)
Burns, Paul J.—Paul J. Burns
Burns, Terence N.—Dieckmann & Assoc., Ltd. (R)
Burny, Holly—Hedlund Corp.
Burr, Jr., Robert L.—Fleming Energy Group (R)
Burris, James C.—Boyden Int'l., Inc. (R)
Burtek, Linda—Smith Hanley Assoc.
Burton, Linda—Management Recruiters
Burton, Linda—Sales Consultants
Busch, Jack—Busch Int'l. (R)
Bush, Nancy Tilley—Howard Karr & Assoc., Inc. (R)
Bushee, Robert J.—Corporate Management Services Inc.
Bussell, Bill—W. Bussell & Assoc.
Buster, Robert—R. J. Dishaw & Assoc. (R)
Butler, Jr., Kirby B.—The Butlers Co. Insurance Recruiters
Butler, Martha—The Butlers Co. Insurance Recruiters
Butler, Robert J.—Smith Roth & Squires (R)
Butterfass, Stanley W.—Butterfass/Pepe Assoc., Inc. (R)
Butts, Ginnabeth—Management Recruiters
Butts, Jr., John L.—Management Recruiters
Buzhardt, J.F.—Buzhardt Assoc. (R)
Bye, Randy—Romac & Assoc., Inc.
Byer, Kurt—Source Finance
Byrne, Tony—Management Recruiters
Byrne, Tony—Sales Consultants
Byrnes, Barbara—T. Byrnes & Co., Inc. (R)
Byrnes, Philip L.—JM & Co. (R)
Byrnes, Randy—The Byrnes Group
Cahan, Edward T.—Sales Consultants
Cahill, Peter—Peter M. Cahill Assoc., Inc.
Cahoon, Jim—Career Marketing Assoc.
Cain, Douglas A.—Sales Consultants
Cain, Douglas H.—Management Recruiters
Cain, John A.—Effective Search, Inc. (R)

Calabrese, Ben—Setford-Shaw-Najarian Assoc., Ltd.

Caldemeyer, Marjorie—Management Recruiters

Caldemeyer, Marjorie—Sales Consultants

Calder, Jr., Douglas J.—Management Search, Inc.

Calderone, Mary Ellen—JT Assoc.

Caldwell, C. Douglas—The Caldwell Partners Int'l. (R)

Caldwell, Randall S.—A.M.C.R., Inc.

Caldwell, Robert—Robert Caldwell & Assoc. (R)

Caldwell, William R.—Holt Pearson & Caldwell, Inc. (R)

Caleo, Victor A.—The Michael Scott Consulting Co., Inc. (R)

Calhoon, Lee—Lee Calhoon & Co., Inc. (R)

Calhoon, Pat—Lee Calhoon & Co., Inc. (R)

Calizo, Nadine—Dunhill Professional Search of Hawaii

Callahan, Cy—L. J. Quinn & Assoc., Inc. (R)

Callan, Robert M.—Callan Assoc., Ltd. (R)

Callan Beaudin, Elizabeth—Callan Assoc., Ltd. (R)

Callan Ray, Marianne—Callan Assoc., Ltd. (R)

Callen, Jr., John H.—Ward Howell Int'l. Inc. (R)

Caloca, Gab.—Gilles Tremblay & Assoc. (R)

Camastra, John—Gleason & Asaoc. (R)

Cambridge, Mike—Cambridge & Assoc., Inc.

Cameron, Edward W.—Allied Financial Management Co.

Camp, David K.—Management Recruiters of Charlotte - Southwest

Campa, Carl—Cambridge Management Planning (R)

Campbell, Andrea—Bedford-Orion Group, Inc.

Campbell, Jane—Sales Consultants

Campbell, Jodi—Datamax Services Inc.

Campbell, Patricia A.—The Onstott Group (R)

Campbell, Robert—Robert Campbell & Assoc. (R)

Campbell, Robert Scott—Wellington Management Group (R)

Canine, Will—The Human Resource Group

Cannavino, John—Financial Resource Assoc., Inc.

Cantor, Bill—The Cantor Concern, Inc.

Cantor, Daniel D.—Human Resource Consulting Group, Inc. (R)

Cantway, Anita—Management Recruiters

Cantway, Roland—Management Recruiters

Capizzi, Monica—William N. Davis & Assoc., Inc. (R)

Caplan, Shellie—Krow Assoc., Inc.

Capo, John—Carter McKenzie, Inc.

Cappe, Richard R.—Roberts Ryan & Bentley (R)

Carabelli, Paula—Ira W. Krinsky & Assoc. (R)

Caraccio, Jim—The Human Resource Group

Caracciolo, Andrew B.—Andrew B. Carr & Assoc.

Caradimitropoulo, Michael—Michael Garbi Assoc., Inc.

Carden, David A.—Executive Dynamics, Inc.

Cardon, Dennis L.—Sanford Rose Assoc.

Cardwell, James W.—Cardwell Group (R)

Carey, Cameron—Computer Security Placement Service, Inc.

Carey, Dennis C.—SpencerStuart (R)

Carey, L. B.—Corporate Staffing Group (R)

Carey, Linda L.—L.L. Carey & Assoc., Inc. (R)

Carideo, J.—Thorndike Deland Assoc. (R)

Carlsen, Ann R.—Future Sense

Carmichael, Wayne F.—Beall & Co., Inc. (R)

Carney, John—Source EDP

Carney, Mike—Source Finance

Carpenter, Eric G.—Carpenter, Shackleton & Co. (R)

Carpenter, Scott A.—I.S. Consultants, Inc.

Carr, Bill—C.P.S., Inc.

Carr, Sarah—Euromedica USA (R)

Carrick, Jr., Kenneth D.—Coleman Lew & Assoc., Inc. (R)

Carrigan, Denise—Management Recruiters

Carrillo, Jose G.—RZL Y Asociados, S.C. (R)

Carris, S. Joseph—Carris, Jackowitz Assoc. (R)

Carroll, Clarke—CCI - Career Consultants Int'l.

Carroll, Kathy—K. Carroll & Assoc.

Carroll, Richard—Midwest Medical Consultants

Carroll, Richard J.—HMO Executive Search

Carroll, William J.—Sales Consultants

Carrott, Gregory T.—Egon Zehnder Int'l. Inc. (R)

Carson, Joe—Jackson & Coker (R)

Carter, Carolyn—Thomas Mangum Co. (R)

Carter, D. Michael—Management Recruiters

Carter, Guy—Management Recruiters

Carter, James—Avery Crafts Assoc., Ltd.

Carter, James A.—Carter-Evdemon & Assoc.

Carter, Jeffrey M.—Carter-Evdemon & Assoc.

Carter, Kittie—Management Recruiters

Carter, Minor L.—M.L. Carter & Assoc., Inc. (R)

Cartoon, June M.—Rurak & Assoc., Inc (R)

Carver, Graham—Cambridge Management Planning (R)

Cary, Robert—Management Recruiters

Casati, Christine—China Human Resources Group (R)

Case, Allen—Allen Case & Assoc., Inc.

Case, David R.—Case Executive Search

Case, Stan—Saxon Morse Assoc.

Cashen, Anthony B.—Lamalie Assoc., Inc. (R)

Cassie, Ronald L.—Cassie & Assoc.

Castell, Jr., William J.—Management Advisors Int'l., Inc.

Castellani, John A.—Raines Int'l. Inc. (R)

Castellano, Rose L.—Sales Consultants

Castine, Michael—SpencerStuart (R)

Caston, Louis C.—The Wright Group

Caswell, David G.—Caswell/Winters & Assoc., Inc. (R)

Catherman, H.O.—H.O. Catherman Inc.

Cattie, Howard J.—Romac & Assoc.

Caulfield, Jean M.—Garofolo, Curtiss, Lambert & MacLean (R)

Causa, Jack—Source Finance

Cavanaugh, Michael—Michael J. Cavanaugh & Assoc. (R)

Cave, Harriet B.—Sales Consultants

Cavolina, Michael—Carver Search Consultants

Caywood, A.B.—Sales Consultants

Cejka, Susan—Cejka & Co. (R)

Celmainis, Andy—Coopers & Lybrand Consulting Group (R)

Center, Linda L.—The Search Center Inc.

Ceresi, Carole—Sales Consultants of Andover

Ceresi, Robert P.—Sales Consultants of Andover

Ceryak, George—Management Recruiters

Ceryak, George—Sales Consultants

Chadick, Susan L.—Gould & McCoy, Inc. (R)

Chagnon, Roger E.—The Regis Group, Ltd. (R)

Chalk, Charles J.—GKR Int'l. (R)

Chaloner, Edward H.—Chaloner Assoc.

Chamberlain, John W.—Egon Zehnder Int'l. Inc.

Chamberlain, Wayne—Wayne S. Chamberlain & Assoc.

Chambers, David E.—David Chambers & Assoc., Inc. (R)

Chambers, Jere B.—Sales Consultants

Chandler, Joseph J.—Joseph Chandler & Assoc., Inc. (R)

Chanko, Jim—Chanko-Ward, Ltd. (R)

Chant, Richard—People Management, Inc. (R)

Chapman, Jeff H.—The Chapman Group, Inc.

Chappell, Peter—The Bankers Group

Charles, Ronald D.—The Caldwell Partners Int'l. (R)

Charon, Robert L.—Robert L. Charon

Chatham, Kerry—Dunhill of Huntsville, Inc.

Chauvin, Ralph A.—The Caldwell Partners Int'l. (R)

Chavoos, Crawford—Phillips Resource Group

Check, Andrew D.—Tierney Assoc., Inc. (R)

Chermak, Carolyn A.—Management Recruiters

Chermak-Shepis, Susan—Management Recruiters

Cherney, Steven D.—Resource Perspectives, Inc.

Chertkof, Robert—Fallstaff Search

Chestone, Albert F.—Supreme Assoc.

Chewning, Ed—Management Recruiters

Chin, Jenny—M.R. Pennington Co.

Chinetti, Peter J.—Elliott, Pfisterer, Chinetti Assoc., Inc. (R)

Chittenden, Curt W.—Caremarc & Assoc.

Chitvanni, John W.—National Restaurant Search, Inc. (R)

Chiusano, Gary R.—Management Recruiters

Chornan, Marilyn A.—Hite Executive Search (R)

Chrisman, Timothy—Chrisman & Co., Inc. (R)

Christensen, Lois—Management Recruiters

Christensen, Thomas C.—Management Recruiters

Christenson, H. Alan—Christenson & Hutchison (R)

Christian, Jeffrey E.—Christian & Timbers, Inc. (R)

Christiansen, G.W.—Spectrum Consultants

Christiansen, H. Douglas—C.P.S., Inc.

Christo, Jordan V.—Beall & Co., Inc. (R)

Christy, Jill—Robert Campbell & Assoc. (R)

Chrzan, June—Louis Gregory Assoc., Inc.

Church, James F.—J.F. Church Assoc., Inc.

Cibotti, Thomas J.—Cibotti Assoc., Inc.

Ciccantelli, Pamela—Source EDP

Cimilluca, Michael—Management Recruiters

Cimino, James J.—Management Recruiters of Butler County

Cimino, Terry—Management Recruiters of Butler County

Cinco, Larry—Management Recruiters

Cinquina, V. James—Merlin Int'l. Inc.

Cirino, Jack—Management Recruiters

Cizek, John T.—Erwin Assoc. (R)

Cizek, Marti J.—Richard E. Nosky & Assoc. (R)

Clanton, Diane—Clanton & Co.

Clapham, Steven L.—The Salem Group, Executive Recruiters

Clapp, Arlene—Sathe & Assoc., Inc. (R)

Clarey, Jack R.—Jack Clarey Assoc., Inc. (R)

Clarey, II, William A.—Lamalie Assoc., Inc. (R)

Clark, Bruce M.—Interim Managment Corp. (R)

Clark, Douglas P.—Clark-Winans, Inc.

Clark, Howard L.—Howard Clark Assoc.

Clark, Kenneth J.—Management Recruiters

Clark, Kenneth M.—Paul Ray & Carre Orban Int'l (R)

Clark, Jr., Leonard J.—Boyden World Corp. (R)
Clark, Patricia—Deeco Int'l.
Clark, Ricki—Robert Campbell & Assoc. (R)
Clark, Robert E.—Clark Assoc., Inc.
Clark, Ronda G.—Management Recruiters
Clark, Toby—Toby Clark Assoc. Inc.
Clarke, John M.—John M. Clarke & Assoc.
Clarke, Richard—Richard Clarke Assoc., Inc.
Clarkson, Mae W.—Personnel Advisors Int'l. Corp.
Claveloux, Denis—Claveloux, McCaffrey, McInerney, Inc. (R)
Clayton, Fred J.—Ward Howell Int'l. Inc. (R)
Clemens, Jeannette—Kremple & Meade, Inc. (R)
Clemens, Jr., William B.—Norman Broadbent Int'l., Inc. (R)
Clemo, James A.—Clemo, Evans & Co., Inc. (R)
Clifton, Paul—Wesson, Taylor, Wells & Assoc.
Close, Jr., E. Wade—Boyden Int'l., Inc. (R)
Cloutier, E. J.—American Executive Management, Inc. (R)
Clovis, Jr., James R.—Handy HRM (R)
Clowney, William T.—Sales Consultants
Coape-Arnold, D.A.—Dunhill Personnel System, Inc.
Coates, Harry R.—Dunhill of Houston
Cobleigh, John—The Stoddard Co.
Cocchiaro, Richard M.—Romac & Assoc., Inc.
Cochlan, Paul T.—PC Assoc.
Cochran, David—Gordon Wahls Co.
Cochran, David M.—Barry Persky & Co., Inc. (R)
Coco, Jr., Carl—Professions, Inc.
Coe, Dean M—Dean M. Coe Assoc. (R)
Coe, M.D., K. C.—O'Callaghan, Honey & Assoc., Inc. (R)
Coelyn, Ronald H.—Coelyn Miller Phillip & Assoc. (R)
Coffin, Proctor A.—Action Inc.
Coffou, Jim—DHR Int'l., Inc. (R)
Coghan, Tom—The Yaiser Group
Cohen, Barbara S.—Princeton Planning Consultants, Inc.
Cohen, Harris J.—Sales Consultants
Cohen, J.—Triangle Consulting Group
Cohen, Jeff A.—Sales Consultants
Cohen, Jeri—K. L. Whitney & Co., Inc. (R)
Cohen, Larry—Pencom Systems Inc.
Cohen, Michael R.—Intech Summit Group, Inc.
Cohen, Rob—Source Finance
Cohen, Robert C.—Intech Summit Group, Inc.
Cohen, Samuel N.—Professions, Inc.
Coke, Bill—Franchise Recruiters Ltd.

Cole, Charlotte L.—Cole Human Resource Services (R)
Cole, James W.—Sharrow & Assoc., Inc.
Cole, Leslie C.—Management Recruiters of Middlesex
Cole, Ronald—Cole, Warren & Long, Inc. (R)
Cole, T. David—Munroe, Curry & Bond Assoc. (R)
Cole-Hill, Susan—Brentwood Int'l. (R)
Coleman, J. Kevin—J. Kevin Coleman & Assoc., Inc. (R)
Coleman, John A.—Canny, Bowen Inc. (R)
Coleman, Michael M.—Coleman Legal Search Consultants
Coleman, Neil F.—Management Recruiters
Coletti, Diane—Prestonwood Assoc.
Collard, Joseph A.—SpencerStuart (R)
Collins, H. Richard—The Heidrick Partners, Inc. (R)
Collins, Lori—Dunhill of Bradenton, Inc.
Collins, Mollie Paul—Belvedere Partners (R)
Collins, Phil—Claremont-Branan, Inc.
Collins, Robert J.—Financial Search Corp.
Collins, Steve—Phillips Resource Group
Collins, Steve—The Johnson Group, Inc.
Collins, Wally—Management Recruiters
Colton, Roy C.—Colton Bernard Inc. (R)
Colton, W. Hoyt—W. Hoyt Colton Assoc., Inc. (R)
Colucci, Bart A.—Blendow & Johnson Inc. (R)
Colwell, Dan—Accounting Resources Int'l., Inc.
Comann, R. Kent—Comann Assoc., Inc. (R)
Combe, II, Charles V.—Empire International (R)
Combs, Tom—Source EDP
Compton, Jo Ann—Coopers & Lybrand Consulting Group (R)
Cona, Joseph A.—Cona Personnel Search
Conard, Rodney J.—Conard Assoc., Inc. (R)
Conaway, Jr., Howard H.—Conaway Legal Search
Conboy, Lucy—Frey & Conboy Assoc., Inc.
Conboy, Mary Rose—Canny, Bowen Inc. (R)
Conley, Erik—Management Recruiters
Conley, Joseph R.—Joseph Conley & Assoc., Inc. (R)
Connelly, Heather—Peat Marwick Stevenson & Kellogg (R)
Conner, Tom—Source EDP
Connolly, M. Michael—The Connolly Consulting Group
Connolly, Michael R.—Management Recruiters of Redding
Constantino, Norma—Accountants On Call
Contorinis, Byron G.—Byron Leonard Int'l., Inc. (R)

Conway, Philip A.—Philip Conway Management (R)

Conway, William P.—Phillips Resource Group

Cook, Jane—Management Science Assoc. (R)

Cook, Patricia S.—Kearney Executive Search (R)

Cook, R. Lynn—Physician Services of America (R)

Cook, Thomas—Robert Murphy Assoc. (R)

Cooke, Gerald W.—STM Assoc.

Coon, Michael—Drew Assoc. Int'l. (R)

Coonam, Bruce—Lee & Burgess Assoc., Inc. (R)

Cooney, John—Source Finance

Cooper, B. V.—QVS Int'l. (R)

Cooper, Bill—Management Recruiters

Cooper, Bill—Sales Consultants

Cooper, Glenn—Stimmel Search Division (R)

Cooper, Patricia G.—MARBL Consultants, Inc.

Cooper, Robert M.—The Cooper Executive Search Group, Inc. (R)

Cooper, Ron—High Tech Opportunities, Inc.

Copeland, Aubrey—Sales Consultants

Coppola, Matthew J.—Joseph Keyes Assoc.

Corbani, John F.—C. A. Durakis Assoc., Inc. (R)

Corbett, Charles C.—Davis-Smith Medical-Dental Employment Service, Inc.

Corcoran, Gary—Sales Consultants

Cordell, David P.—David P. Cordell Assoc.

Cordell, Pauline—David P. Cordell Assoc.

Corey, Joseph—Industry Consultants, Inc.

Corley, Wayne—Management Recruiters

Cornelison, Mike—Management Recruiters

Cornell, H. Arthur—Cornell Int'l. (R)

Cornell, Marcia H.—Cornell Int'l. (R)

Cornell, Rachel—Traynor Confidential, Ltd.

Cornfoot, James L.—Management Recruiters

Correia, Linda Mercedes—Mercedes & Co., Inc. (R)

Correll, Lindell J.—CES

Corrigan, George T.—JM & Co. (R)

Corrigan, Gerald F.—The Corrigan Group (R)

Corry, Edmond J.—Edmond J. Corry & Co., Inc. (R)

Corser, George—Source EDP

Corwen, Leonard—CRS Assoc., Inc.

Corwin, Blade—Seitchik, Corwin & Seitchik Inc. (R)

Corya, James E.—National Corporate Consultants, Inc.

Cosco, Suzanne F.—Cosco Resources Inc.

Costa, Frances—Gilbert Tweed Assoc., Inc. (R)

Costello, Andrea—Gallin Assoc.

Costello, Jack—Gallin Assoc.

Costello, John—Gallin Assoc.

Costick, Kathryn J.—John Sibbald Assoc., Inc. (R)

Costikyan, Wendy W.—Egon Zehnder Int'l. Inc. (R)

Cote, John J.—Sales Consultants

Cotter, Alina A.—Lowery, Cotter, & Assoc.

Cotter, Chuck—AJS Assoc.

Cotterell, Dirk—Management Recruiters

Cotton, Dwight—Career Management, Inc.

Cotton, Peter C.—Sales Consultants of Rhode Island, Inc.

Couch, Ellen K.—Kline Consulting, Inc. (R)

Coulter, Thomas H.—Wytmar & Co., Inc. (R)

Counts, Robert L.—Granger, Counts & Assoc. (R)

Courtade, Tony—Datamatics Management Services, Inc.

Coutcher-Hughes, Gail—Source Finance

Cowall, Frank A.—Executives' Personnel Service Inc.

Cowan, Lawrence G.—Search West, Inc.

Cowan, Robert A.—Search West, Inc.

Cowell, Roy A.—Wood/Sprau/Tannura, Inc. (R)

Cowin, David M.—Cowin Assoc.

Cox, Mark M.—Witt Assoc. Inc. (R)

Cox, Patti—O'Rourke Co., Inc. (R)

Coyne, Patrick—Patrick Assoc.

Coyne, R.M.—Patrick Assoc.

Coyne, Ron—Patrick Assoc.

Cozzens, Robert W.—Wayne Assoc., Inc.

Crafts, Norman E.—Avery Crafts Assoc., Ltd.

Craig, Randy H.—J. Fielding Nelson & Assoc., Inc.

Cram, Noel—Barone Assoc.

Cramer, Barbara—Physicians Search Assoc. Agency, Inc.

Crane, Valerie—Lawrence Executive Search, Ltd.

Crass, Dorothea—Corporate Management Services Inc.

Crawford, Dick—Management Recruiters

Crawford, Marjorie—Personnel Assoc.

Crawford, Tom—The Crawford Group

Crecos, Gregory P.—Gregory Michaels & Assoc., Inc.

Credidio, Thomas J.—The DataFinders Group, Inc.

Crickenberger, Harold P.—Crickenberger Assoc.

Cris, Jan—The Cris Group., Inc.

Crisanti, Joseph S.—Joseph Crisanti, Inc.

Crispi, Nicholas—Crispi, Wagner & Co., Inc.

Crist, Peter D.—Russell Reynolds Assoc., Inc. (R)

Critchell, Nancy—Educational Management Network (R)

Davis, Ernie—Kepler & Assoc.

Davis, Evelyn C.—EFL Assoc. (R)

Davis, Frank—Bertrand, Ross & Assoc., Inc. (R)

Davis, Frank—International Management Services Inc. (R)

Davis, G. Gordon—Davis & Company (R)

Davis, J. Richard—D.E. Foster & Partners, L.P. (R)

Davis, James N.—The Paxton Group, Ltd.

Davis, John J.—John J. Davis & Assoc., Inc. (R)

Davis, Ken—Management Recruiters

Davis, Ken—Sales Consultants

Davis, Kim—Aim Executive Consulting Services (R)

Davis, Lee—Advanced Corporate Search

Davis, Peter E.—Zurick, Davis & Co. (R)

Davis, Ray—Career Management, Inc.

Davis, Richard A.—Bowling Executive Registry, Inc.

Davis, Sharon—Toby Clark Assoc. Inc.

Davis, Timothy—Atlantic Search (R)

Davis, Timothy J.—VideoFields, Ltd. (R)

Davis, William N.—William N. Davis & Assoc., Inc. (R)

Day, Charles E.—Charles E. Day & Assoc., Inc. (R)

Day-Berry, Charlotte—Joy Reed Belt & Assoc., Inc. (R)

De Correvont, James—DeCorrevont & Assoc.

De Funiak, William S.—De Funiak & Edwards (R)

De Hayes, A. James—DeHayes Consulting Group (R)

De Mange, Jean M.—Wellington Thomas Ltd.

De Perro, Scott R.—Aim Executive Inc.

De Vries, A.—DHR Int'l., Inc. (R)

DeCamp, Donald D.—Romac & Assoc., Inc.

DeCristoforo, John—Auden Assoc., Inc.

DeGioia, Joseph—JDG Assoc., Ltd.

DeGiulio, John—J.D. Limited

DeKesel, Herman—TASA Executive Search (R)

DeLalla, Barbara—DeLalla - Fried Assoc.

DeLuca, Matthew J.—Management Resource Group, Inc.

DeMan, Denise—Bench Int'l. Search, Inc.

DeMario, William—Accountants On Call

DeMay, P.—DHR Int'l., Inc. (R)

DeMeglio, Eleanor—Management Recruiters

DeMeglio, Nick—Management Recruiters

DeMoss, J. V.—Careers/Inc.

DeVoe, Robert—Source Finance

de Vries, Peter J.M.—Ward Howell Int'l. Inc. (R)

deWilde, David M.—Chartwell Partners Int'l., Inc. (R)

DeZara, Max—The Carlyle Group, Ltd.

Deal, Chuck—Sales Consultants

Dean, James L.—Dean-Wharton Assoc.

Dearwent, Donald E.—M.L. Carter & Assoc., Inc. (R)

Dee, William Vincent—McMahon & Dee, Inc. (R)

Deery, John R.—Deery, Geddis & Assoc.

Defeo, Dennis—Accountants On Call

Deignan, Rebecca M.—Mercedes & Co., Inc. (R)

Deissig, Robert—The Ayers Group, Inc.

Deland, Thorndike—Thorndike Deland Assoc. (R)

Delaney, George P.—The Caldwell Partners Int'l. (R)

Delany, Donald F.—Resource Perspectives, Inc.

Dellacato, Michael J.—David - Kris Assoc., Inc.

Delong, Art—Richard Kader & Assoc.

Demchak, James P.—Sandhurst Assoc. (R)

Dempsey, Hank—Management Recruiters

Dempster, John—Daniel Stern & Assoc.

Dempster, John L.—Management Recruiters

Dempster, John L.—Sales Consultants

Dempster, Kathy—Peat Marwick Stevenson & Kellogg (R)

Denise, Cheryl—J. Gross & Assoc.

Denney, Thomas L.—Denney & Co., Inc. (R)

Dennis, Jessie—Venture Resources, Inc. (R)

Denny, Carl—Carlden Personnel Services Inc.

Denny, Suzanne—Carlden Personnel Services Inc.

Dentale, Alfred—Dean-Wharton Assoc.

Depew, Barry—Management Recruiters

Depew, Margi—Management Recruiters

Derning, John P.—Egon Zehnder Int'l. Inc. (R)

Desgrosellier, Gary D.—Personnel Unlimited/ Executive Search

Desiderio, Anthony J.—Dunhill Professional Search of Wilkes-Barre/Scranton, Inc.

Desmond, Dennis A.—Beall & Co., Inc. (R)

Detore, Robert R.—Drew Assoc. Int'l. (R)

Devere, Dennis—Thorndike Deland Assoc. (R)

Devoir, Philip W.—Effective Search, Inc. (R)

Dewhurst, William—Abbott Smith Assoc., Inc.

DiCamillo, Ron—Sydney Reynolds Assoc., Inc. (R)

DiDomenico, Michael F.—Management Recruiters

DiDomenico, Michael F.—Sales Consultants

DiGiacomo, Frank A.—Executive Search of New England, Inc.

DiMaggio, D.—Hintz Associates

DiMarchi, Paul—DiMarchi Partners (R)

DiSanti, Joseph R.—Specialty Consultants, Inc.

DiVenuto, John P.—Deven Assoc., Int'l., Inc. (R)

Diaz, Del—Management Recruiters
Dibner, Elaine—Management Recruiters
Dick, John G.—Sales Consultants
Dicker, Barry L.—Engineering Search Assoc.
Dickerson, Joseph A.—Penn Associates
Dickey, Chester W.—Bowden & Co., Inc. (R)
Dickstein, Joel—Management Recruiters
Dieck, Dan—Corporate Recruiters, Inc.
Dieckmann, Ralph E.—Dieckmann & Assoc., Ltd. (R)
Dieli, Carmine—Bradstreet Mgt.
Dieli, Carmine—Career Guides, Inc.
Dieli, Lisa—Bradstreet Mgt.
Dillard, G. Hannah—Dillard Executive Search
Dillard, Tom—Dillard Executive Search
Dillon, Larry A.—Predictor Systems Corp. (R)
Dingman, Bruce—Robert W. Dingman Co., Inc. (R)
Dingman, Robert W.—Robert W. Dingman Co., Inc. (R)
Dinklage, Kenneth T.—Selected Executives, Inc.
Dishaw, Raymond J.—R. J. Dishaw & Assoc. (R)
Ditter, Bernie—John Velcamp & Assoc. (R)
Ditzel, C. Russell—J.M. Joseph Assoc.
Divine, Robert S.—O'Shea, Divine & Co. (R)
Dobbins, Barbara—J.R. Akin & Co. (R)
Doddridge, James H.—Atlantic West Int'l.
Dodendorf, Geary L.—Management Recruiters
Doherty, Brian—Sales Consultants
Doherty, Leonard J.—L.J. Doherty & Assoc.
Domann, Jr., William A.—The Domann Organization (R)
Dombeck, Diane—Kennedy & Co. (R)
Domby, Samuel F.—eXsource
Domenico, Alfred J.—Domenico/Brown Group
Domres, Terry A.—The Lawson Group
Domres, Terry A.—The Lawson Group
Doms, Keith—Gossage Regan Assoc. (R)
Donahue, E.M.—Donahue/Bales Assoc. (R)
Donahue, M.J.—High Technology Search Assoc.
Donahue, Patrick D.—Winguth & Company (R)
Donaldson, Marianne—Rourke, Bourbonnais Assoc., Ltd. (R)
Donheiser, Alan—Sanford Rose Assoc.
Donnelly, George J.—Ward Howell Int'l. Inc. (R)
Donnelly, John P.—J P Donnelly Assoc., Inc.
Donnelly, John R.—Christopher-Patrick & Assoc. (R)
Donohue, Tim—Thomure Medsearch, Inc. (R)
Donovan, John—McCulloch Assoc.
Doody, Michael F.—Kieffer, Ford, & Hadelman, Ltd. (R)

Dorfman, Ellen S.—Krauthamer & Assoc. (R)
Doro, Chip—Career Marketing Assoc.
Dorrance, Jeffrey G.—DEI Executive Services
Dotson, Ileen—M-A Management Assoc., Inc.
Dougan, David W.—Dougan-McKinley-Strain (R)
Dougan, Sarah B.—Bert Davis Assoc., Inc.
Dougherty, Gregory—CES
Dow, Jan—M-A Management Assoc., Inc.
Dow, R. Steven—Scott-Wayne Assoc., Inc.
Dowdy, Daniel W.—Management Recruiters
Dowell, William P.—Diversified Placement Int'l., Inc.
Dowiat, John—Management Recruiters
Downing, Gus—Downing & Downing
Downing, Jacqueline—Downing & Downing
Doyle, Patrick—Management Recruiters
Dransfield, Mark—Fernow Assoc.
Dransfield, William—Fernow Assoc.
Dreier, John S.—Dreier Consulting
Drexler, Robert C.—Robert Drexler Assoc., Inc.
Dreyfus, Rita—Robert Murphy Assoc. (R)
Dromeshauser, Peter—Dromeshauser Assoc. (R)
Dromsky, James V.—Orion Consulting, Inc. (R)
Drost, Dee—Stonehill Management Consultants, Inc. (R)
Drown, Cliff F.—Management Recruiters
Drummer, Jeffry J.—Dunhill Professional Search, Inc. of Kearney
Drummond-Hay, Peter—Russell Reynolds Assoc., Inc. (R)
Drury, III, James J.—SpencerStuart (R)
DuBose, III, B. M.—Waterford, Inc.
Dubbs, Bill—Sathe & Assoc., Inc. (R)
Dubuque, Robert J.—Avery Crafts Assoc., Ltd.
Dudley, Craig J.—Conrey Interamericana (R)
Duffy, Ken—International Management Services Inc. (R)
Duffy, Maureen—Professional Medical
Dugan, John H.—J. H. Dugan & Assoc., Inc.
Duggan, Edward J.—Duggan & Company (R)
Dukes, Barry—Management Recruiters
Dulhanty, Ronald—Peat Marwick Stevenson & Kellogg (R)
Dummer, Charles F.—Dunhill Professional Search, Inc. of Kearney
Dumont, Robert C.—Dumont Moriarty & Assoc.
Duncan, Melba J.—The Duncan Group Inc. (R)
Duncan-Powell, Roxanne—Stern & Watson, Inc. (R)
Dunford, Michael S.—Michael S. Dunford, Inc. (R)
Dunkel, David L.—Romac & Assoc., Inc.

Dunlap, Stanley R.—S.R. Dunlap & Assoc., Inc. (R)

Dunlavy, Harry L.—Management Resources

Dunn, David—Management Recruiters

Dunn, Ed—Management Recruiters

Dupman, Violetta—Michael Latas & Assoc., Inc. (R)

Dupras, Emily—RitaSue Siegel Assoc., Inc.

Duquette, Edmond J.—Schattle Personnel Consultants, Inc.

Durakis, Jr., Charles—C. A. Durakis Assoc., Inc. (R)

Durakis, Sr., Charles A.—C. A. Durakis Assoc., Inc. (R)

Durante, Arthur J.—Sales Consultants of Wellesley, Inc.

Dussick, Vince—Dussick Management Assoc.

Dwigans, Lynn—Lynn Dwigans & Co. (R)

Dworsky, Sherry—Wesley Brown & Bartle Co., Inc. (R)

Dwyer, Gilbert E.—Dwyer Consulting Group, Inc. (R)

Dycus, Gwen—Gwen Dycus, Inc.

Dykeman, James J.—Management Recruiters

Dykstra, Gene L.—G.L. Dykstra Assoc., Inc.

Dykstra, Glenda M.—G.L. Dykstra Assoc., Inc.

Earl, John—Diedre Moire Corp., Inc.

Earle, Paul W.—SpencerStuart (R)

Early, Bert—Bert H. Early Assoc., Inc. (R)

East, Robert G.—Guidry, East, Barnes & Bono, Inc. (R)

Eastham, Marvene M.—Kieffer, Ford, & Hadelman, Ltd. (R)

Eastman, Phillip—The Odessa Group (R)

Eatman, Fred—Management Recruiters

Ebbert, Duane—Ebbert Assoc. (R)

Ebeling, John A.—Gilbert Tweed Assoc., Inc. (R)

Eber, Deena—Source Finance

Eckdahl, Donald E.—Engineering Search Assoc.

Eckler, Geoffrey N.—EPN, Inc.

Edahl, A J.—S. P. Assoc.

Edell, David—Development Resource Group

Eden, Brooks D.—Eden & Assoc., Inc.

Edwards, Bruce—Bruce Edwards & Associates, Inc. (R)

Edwards, Douglas W.—Egon Zehnder Int'l. Inc. (R)

Edwards, Eileen—Hamilton Edwards, Ltd.

Edwards, Jack—Sanford Rose Assoc.

Edwards, Jack O.—Sales Consultants

Edwards, Randolph J.—De Funiak & Edwards (R)

Edwards, Verba Lee—Wing Tips & Pumps, Inc.

Egan, Daniel K.—Egan & Assoc. (R)

Egan, Patrick J.—Schenck & Assoc. SC

Eggers, James W.—Eggers Consulting Co., Inc.

Eggleston, G. Dudley—Eggleston Consulting Int'l. (R)

Ehlers, Dieter—Reinecke & Assoc.

Ehrenzeller, Jennie—Management Recruiters

Ehrenzeller, Tony A.—Management Recruiters

Eibeler, Charles J.—Amherst Personnel Group Inc.

Eibeler, Neil—Amherst Personnel Group Inc.

Eichstaedt, Warren B.—Sanford Rose Assoc.

Eidenberg, Joyce—W.F. Richer Assoc., Inc.

Eilenberg, Phoebe—Seiden Assoc., Inc. (R)

Eilertson, Douglas R.—Sanford Rose Assoc.

Eiseman, Joe—Source EDP

Eisenbach, Earl E.—The Stevenson Group/SES (R)

Eissler, W. Robert—W. Robert Eissler & Assoc., Inc.

Elam, Renee A.—Management Recruiters

Elam, Robert W.—Wheeler, Moore & Elam Co. (R)

Elam, William—Management Recruiters

Elam, Jr., William J.—William J. Elam & Assoc. (R)

Elhart, Robert D.—The Caldwell Partners Int'l. (R)

Elkin, Robin—Major, Wilson & Africa

Elliott, John G.—Elliott, Pfisterer, Chinetti Assoc., Inc. (R)

Elliott, Roger S.—The Elliott Company (R)

Ellis, Milton H.—Accountants

Ellis, Ronald A.—Management Recruiters

Ellis, Ted F.—Management Recruiters

Ellis, Ted K.—The Hindman Co. (R)

Ellison, Richard—Sanford Rose Assoc.

Ellner, David M.—David M. Ellner Assoc. (R)

Elsom, Jr., Kendall A.—Johnson Smith & Knisely Inc. (R)

Elson, John B.—The Elson Group, Inc. (R)

Elster, John J.—Hoskins, Rees & Smith

Elston, Kathy—Accountants On Call

Elwell, Richard F.—Elwell & Assoc., Inc. (R)

Elzweig, Mark—Mark Elzweig Co. Ltd.

Emerson, Randy—Source EDP

Emig, Darla—Sales Consultants

Emmons, William F.—Emmons Assoc., Inc. (R)

Emmons, Jr., William F.—Handy HRM (R)

Endres, Robert—Sanford Rose Assoc.

Engelgau, Elvita B.—Management Recruiters

Engelgau, Larry P.—Management Recruiters

Enghauser, Paul D.—Eckert, Enghauser and Partners, Inc.

English, Edna—The Baxter Group (R)

English, Robert—RTE Search

Enns, George—George Enns Partners Inc. (R)

Ensminger, Chub—Management Recruiters

Ensminger, Dwight—Source EDP

Erder, Debbie—Johnson Smith & Knisely Inc. (R)

Eremin, Grace—Management Resource Group, Inc.

Erickson, Deborah—Sales Consultants

Erickson, Mary R.—Mary R. Erickson & Assoc. (R)

Erickson, Tom—Sales Consultants

Ericson, Pam—Federal Placement Services

Erikson, Theodore J.—Canny, Bowen Inc. (R)

Erlanger, Richard A.—Erlanger Assoc. (R)

Erstling, Gregory J.—Normyle/Erstling Health Search

Ervin, Harry—Dussick Management Assoc.

Erwin, Ronald R.—Erwin Assoc. (R)

Erwin, Susan—J.W. Barleycorn & Assoc. (R)

Esposito, Kathy—Vincent Lee Assoc.

Esser, Paul T.—Management Recruiters

Estes, Brad—The Naples Group, Inc.

Estes, Patrick—The Naples Group, Inc.

Estess, Glenn E.—Management Recruiters

Estess, Glenn E.—Sales Consultants

Etter, Scott—Alexander Edward Assoc., Inc.

Evans, Arnold—Evans & James Assoc., Inc.

Evans, Lois—Richard Kinser & Assoc. (R)

Evans, Martha—The Caldwell Partners Int'l. (R)

Evans, Rick—The Beam Group (R)

Evans, Robert M.—TASA/Fleming (R)

Evans, Ronald R.—Sigma Group Inc. (R)

Evans, Terry—Management Recruiters

Evdemon, II, Michael S.—Carter-Evdemon & Assoc.

Everson, John P.—Binary Search

Evins, Susan—Bartl & Evins

Extract, Raymond L.—Raymond L. Extract & Assoc. (R)

Fabbro, Vivian—MKM Search Consultants, Inc.

Faber, Jill S.—Kearney Executive Search (R)

Fabian, G. Leslie—Ward Howell Int'l. Inc. (R)

Fabiano, Frank—Allen Case & Assoc., Inc.

Fagan, III, Charles A.—Fagan & Co. (R)

Fairlie, Suzanne F.—ProSearch, Inc.

Falk, John—D.S. Allen Assoc.

Faller, Laura McGrath—Redden & McGrath Assoc., Inc. (R)

Fallon, Hillman O.—Hill Fallon & Assoc. (R)

Falvey, William M.—Counsel Search Co. (R)

Fancher, Robert L.—Bason Assoc., Inc. (R)

Fanning, Chuck—Beckwith, Thomas & Fanning

Farago, Richard A.—Conex Inc. (R)

Farley, James M.—Tecmark/Massachusetts Inc.

Farley, Leon A.—Leon A. Farley Assoc. (R)

Farmer, David W.—David Farmer & Assoc.

Farnsworth, John A.—Holt Pearson & Caldwell, Inc. (R)

Farrell, Jr., Frank J.—Farrell & Phin, Inc. (R)

Farrell, James N.—Sandhurst Assoc. (R)

Farrell, John A.—The Curtiss Group, Inc. (R)

Farrell, Joseph T.—Challenger & Hunt (R)

Farrington, Jr., Robert J. M.—Webb, Johnson & Klemmer, Inc. (R)

Farris, James W.—James Farris Assoc. (R)

Farrow, Jerry M.—McCormack & Farrow (R)

Faubion, John G.—The Zivic Group, Inc. (R)

Faucher, John F.—Sanford Rose Assoc.

Faught, Thomas F.—Boyden Int'l., Inc. (R)

Faulk, Betty Jo—Management Recruiters

Faure, Nicole—The Caldwell Partners Int'l. (R)

Fawaz, Randa—Winfield Assoc.

Fawcett, Anne M.—The Caldwell Partners Int'l. (R)

Fawkes, Gary S.—Kennison & Assoc.

Fazio, Joe—JT Assoc.

Fedder, Alan—U.S. Search

Fedele, Rocco M.—Devin Scott Assoc.

Fee, J. Curtis—SpencerStuart (R)

Feerst, James E.—James Feerst & Assoc., Inc. (R)

Fehr, James K.—Kreuzberger, Fehr & Assoc.

Feigenbaum, Irwin J.—Professional Resources

Fein, Susan E.—Stern & Watson, Inc. (R)

Feinson, Milton M.—Sales Consultants

Felactu, Odessa J.—The Odessa Group (R)

Feldman, Abe—A.E. Feldman Assoc.

Feldman, Jeanette—J. H. Dugan & Assoc., Inc.

Feliciano, Janelle M.—Wheeler Assoc.

Fell, David—Source EDP

Fellows, William—Whitaker, Fellows & Assoc.

Fells, Norman—N. Steven Fells & Co., Inc.

Felt, D. Kyle—Ingram, Inc. (R)

Fenrich, Diana L.—Management Recruiters

Ferguson, Charles—A.E. Feldman Assoc.

Ferneborg, John R.—Smith, Goerss & Ferneborg, Inc. (R)

Fernow, Charles S.—Fernow Assoc.

Ferrara, Caesar L.—Performance Professionals

Ferrari, S. Jay—Ferrari Consulting Group

Ferris, Sherri—Accountants On Call

Ferry, Richard M.—Korn/Ferry Int'l. (R)

Fiala, Joanne C.—Ecco Personnel Svs.

Fidelle, Thomas P.—ExecuTech

Field, Gloria Adelson—G.A. Field Personnel Consultants

Field, Marshall—Management Recruiters

Fields, Eleanor—Jerry Fields Assoc.

Fields, Jerry—Jerry Fields Assoc.

Fienberg, Chester A.—Drummond Assoc., Inc.

Fifield, George C.—Egon Zehnder Int'l. Inc. (R)

Filipkowski, Donna—BDO Seidman (R)

Filippelli, Frank—C.P.S., Inc.

Filo, Jeanne M.—P. J. Murphy & Assoc., Inc. (R)

Filson, Marguerite B.—Bader Research Corp.

Fimmano, Ann M.—Kensington Management Consultants, Inc. (R)

Fimmano, Gerald—Kensington Management Consultants (R)

Fincher, Richard P.—Phase II Management

Fink, Jay M.—Executive Appointments Ltd., Int'l. (R)

Fink, Ronald L.—Sales Consultants

Finkel, Leslie—Source EDP

Finlay, Ross—Bryce, Haultain & Assoc. (R)

Finnegan, Richard—Finnegan Assoc. (R)

Finseth, Carl L.—Meng, Finseth & Assoc., Inc. (R)

Fiordalis, Stuart Clark—Fiordalis Assoc., Inc. (R)

Fiore, Richard N.—Stanton/Schoen Professionals, Inc.

Fischer, Howard M.—Howard Fischer Assoc., Inc. (R)

Fischer, Janet L.—Boyden Int'l., Inc. (R)

Fischer, John C.—R. H. Horton Int'l. (R)

Fischler, Nick P.—NPF Assoc. Ltd. Inc.

Fishel, Richard A.—Western Personnel Assoc., Inc.

Fisher, Jack Stuart—Jack Stuart Fisher Assoc.

Fisher, Neal—Fisher Personnel Management Services (R)

Fisher, Philip—Fisher-Todd Assoc.

Fishkin, Anita—A.G. Fishkin & Assoc., Inc.

Fisk, James L.—James L. Fisk & Assoc.

Fitzgerald, Gene—Phillips Resource Group

Fitzgerald, Geoffrey—Lee Calhoon & Co., Inc. (R)

Fitzgerald, Jack—The Communications Search Group (R)

Fitzgerald, Jon K.—Health Industry Consultants, Inc. (R)

Fitzgibbon, Majorie—Jeff Rich Assoc.

Fitzpatrick, Alan—Merlin Int'l. Inc.

Fitzsimmons, Doris J.—Accountants On Call

Flannery, Thomas T.—Resources for Management (R)

Fleischauer, Alan—DCS Assoc., Inc. (R)

Fleischman, Edward—Execu-Search, Inc.

Fleming, Richard L.—TASA/Fleming (R)

Flemister, Jr., William M.—Kellogg Consulting Group (R)

Fligel, Robert—Execu-Search, Inc.

Flohr, Robert A.—Picard & Co., Inc. (R)

Flores, Mario—Flores & Assoc.

Floth, Paul E.—Robert A. Paul & Assoc.

Flow, Judy Foley—Kensington Int'l.

Flowers, John E.—Balfour Assoc.

Flynn, Stephen—Water Street Assoc.

Fobar, Dov—Health Industry Resources, Inc.

Fockler, David B.—David Fockler & Assoc., Inc.

Fodor, John—Sanford Rose Assoc.

Foehl, John—ESP Management Services, Inc. (R)

Fogec, Thomas G.—Fogec Consultants (R)

Fogelgren, Stephen W.—Management Recruiters

Fogelgren, Stephen W.—Sales Consultants

Folger, J.H.—J. H. Folger Company (R)

Follett, Michael R.—Peat Marwick Stevenson & Kellogg (R)

Folliard, Kieran—Andcor Human Resources (R)

Follmer, Gary—Agra Placements, Ltd.

Folsom, Karen—SpencerStuart (R)

Foote, Lee—L.W. Foote Co. (R)

Foote, Jr., Ray P.—Heidrick and Struggles, Inc. (R)

Ford, Bernard H.—Ford & Ford

Ford, C.E.—Sales Consultants

Ford, Eileen F.—Ford & Ford

Ford, J. Daniel—Kieffer, Ford, & Hadelman, Ltd. (R)

Ford, Martin B.—Ford & Assoc., Inc.

Ford, Travis—Ford & Assoc., Inc.

Forder, Dick—Management Recruiters

Forder, Dick—Sales Consultants

Fordyce, Donald M.—GKR Int'l. (R)

Forman, Phillip R.—Ryman, Bell, Green & Michaels, Inc.

Fortune, Barbara—Kensington Int'l.

Foss, Gregory—Diedre Moire Corp., Inc.

Foster, Andrew—Sales Consultants

Foster, Byron R.—Allerton Heneghan & O'Neill

Foster, Donald J.—Foster Assoc.

Foster, Dwight E.—D.E. Foster & Partners, L.P. (R)

Foster, John M.—Brissenden, McFarland, Wagoner & Fuccella, Inc. (R)

Garfield, Lee—The Agency- An Employment Consortium

Garfinkle, Steven M.—Chestnut Hill Partners, Inc. (R)

Gargalli, Claire W.—Diversified Health Search (R)

Gargalli, Claire W.—Diversified Search, Inc. (R)

Garland, R. Darryl—Garland Assoc. (R)

Garlick, III, Arnold L.—Pacific Search Consultants

Garner, Ann—Accountants On Call

Garner, Ron—Accountants On Call

Garofolo, Frank—Garofolo, Curtiss, Lambert & MacLean (R)

Garoufalis, Byron T.—International Management Services Inc. (R)

Garrett, Donald L.—Garrett Assoc. Inc.

Garrett, Linda—Garrett Assoc. Inc.

Garrett, William R.—Sales Consultants

Garrison, Charles W.—Garrison, McGuigan & Sisson

Garrison, Ed—The Garrison Organization

Garrity, Irene—Management Recruiters

Garvin, Len—Salesworld-Division of Metacor Inc.

Gates, Edward—Furlong - Gates, Inc. (R)

Gatti, Robert D.—Gatti & Assoc.

Gaudette, Charles L.—Gaudette & Co.

Gauss, James W.—Witt Assoc. Inc. (R)

Gavin, David—The Comwell Co. Inc.

Gavin, David R.—Northland Recruiting Inc.

Gaxiola, Alejendro—Smith, Gaxiola y Asociados (R)

Gay, Richard C.—IprGroup, Inc.

Geddis, Peter R.—Deery Geddis & Assoc.

Gedge, Albert C.—The Gedge Group (R)

Gee, Gregory A.—Western Personnel Assoc., Inc.

Geerken, Fred—Dunhill Professional Search Group

Geller, Allen A.—Raines Int'l. Inc. (R)

Gellman, Sy—Career Guides, Inc.

Geltz, Dick—Sales Consultants

Gendron, Joe—Source EDP

Gennawey, Bob—Source EDP

Genovese, Donald P.—Genovese & Co. (R)

Gentry, Guy C.—Latin America Assoc.

George, Dave—Jim Parham & Assoc., Inc. (R)

George, Delores F.—Delores F. George

Germaine, Deb—Gilbert Tweed Assoc., Inc. (R)

Gerrish, Stuart A.—Casey & Gerrish Assoc., Inc.

Gerson, Russ D.—The Whitney Group (R)

Gerst, Tom J.—Management Recruiters

Gerstl, Ronald—DHR Int'l, Inc. (R)

Gesing, Rand W.—Rand Assoc. (R)

Gettys, James R.—International Staffing Consultants, Inc.

Gibbons, John—John D. Gibbons & Assoc., Inc. (R)

Gibson, Bruce—Gibson & Co., Inc. (R)

Gibson, Jr., Herbert L.—Phillips Resource Group

Gibson, Jan—Advanced Corporate Search

Gibson, Johanna—N.W. Gibson Int'l. (R)

Gibson, Nelson W.—N.W. Gibson Int'l. (R)

Gifford, James R.—J. Gifford, Inc.

Gil, Mark—Alan MacDonald & Assoc.

Gilbert, Elaine—Herbert Mines Assoc., Inc. (R)

Gilbert, James—C.P.S., Inc.

Gilbert, Jerry—Gilbert & Van Campen Int'l. (R)

Gildee, John J.—Sanford Rose Assoc.

Giles, Joe L.—Joe L. Giles & Assoc., Inc.

Gilliam, David D.—AdStaff Personnel, Inc.

Gillis, Austin P.—Pierce Assoc. (R)

Gillis, Jr., John—Physicians Search Assoc. Agency, Inc.

Gillum, Jack A.—McDonald Assoc. (R)

Gilmore, David A.—Elwell & Assoc., Inc. (R)

Gilmore, Howard A.—Howard Gilmore & Assoc. (R)

Gilmore, John P.—Inside Management Assoc. (R)

Gilmore, Nancy—Pocrass Assoc. (R)

Ginty, Brian—The Beam Group (R)

Gionta, Michael—Management Recruiters of Poughkeepsie, Inc.

Giordano, Louis P.—Gilbert Tweed Assoc., Inc. (R)

Girdziunas, Vicki—Source EDP

Gladitsch, Tom—Ells Personnel Systems Inc.

Gladstone, Arthur—Executive Referral Services, Inc.

Glaser, David—The Executive Consulting Group - N.Y.

Glassner, Peter—Strauss Personnel Service

Glatman, Marcia—HRD Consultants, Inc. (R)

Glavin, James E.—Wood-Glavin, Inc. (R)

Glazer, Howard—The Neil Michael Group, Inc. (R)

Gleason, Kenneth R.—Gleason & Assoc. (R)

Gleason-Fay, Helen—Management Recruiters

Gleaton, Jr., William E.—Jubilee, Inc.

Glicksman, Russell A.—The Beam Group (R)

Glickstein, Craig M.—Sales Consultants

Gloss, Fred C.—FGI (R)

Glosser, Elizabeth B.—Executive Exchange Corp.

Glou, Alan—Glou Int'l., Inc. (R)

Glover, Terry—W.T. Glover & Assoc., Inc.

Glynn, Thomas J.—Fox-Morris Assoc., Inc.

Gnall, John—Gleason & Assoc. (R)
Gnodde, R. Dirk—Scott Kappele & Gnodde
Goar, Duane R.—Sandhurst Assoc. (R)
Gobbell, John J.—The Gobbell Co. (R)
Goehring, Hal—H. L. Goehring & Assoc., Inc. (R)
Goerss, Ronald G.—Smith, Goerss & Ferneborg, Inc. (R)
Goich, S. George—Fernow Assoc.
Goldfarb, Sue—Management Recruiters
Golding, Michael S.—Michael Assoc. (R)
Golding, Robert L.—R. W. Hebel Assoc. (R)
Goldman, Donald L.—Management Recruiters
Goldman, Donald L.—Sales Consultants
Goldman, Elaine—The Goldman Group Inc.
Goldman, Michael L.—Strategic Assoc., Inc.
Goldsmith, Jerry—The Primary Group, Inc.
Goldstein, Barry A.—Financial Placement Network
Goldstein, Gary S.—The Whitney Group (R)
Goldstein, Jack—Goldstein & Assoc.
Goldstein, Leonard—ProSearch, Inc.
Gombrecht, Peter P.—Bartholdi & Co. (R)
Gonye, Peter K.—Egon Zehnder Int'l. Inc. (R)
Gonyo, Gerry—Source EDP
Good, Bob—Management Recruiters
Good, Dave—Management Recruiters
Goodman, Jerry—Source EDP
Goodman, Lion—The Goodman Group
Goodman, Michael—Coopers & Lybrand Consulting Group (R)
Goodman, Philip—Management Recruiters
Goodman, Susan—Johnson Smith & Knisely Inc. (R)
Goodman, IV, William E.—Boyden World Corp. (R)
Goodman-Brolin, Dorothy—DLB Assoc.
Goodwin, H.C.—Professional Recruiters Inc.
Goodwin, Tom—Isaacson, Miller, Gilvar & Boulware (R)
Goone, Geoffrey L.—Hospitality Int'l.
Gordon, Dave—Cemco Syetems
Gordon, Elliot—Korn/Ferry Int'l. (R)
Gordon, Glenn E.—Sanford Rose Assoc.
Gordon, Gregory—Wallace Assoc.
Gordon, Karen L.—Tarnow Int'l. (R)
Gordon, Larry—Prestige Search Inc.
Gordon, Lowell A.—Stephens Assoc. Ltd. (R)
Gordon, Matt M.—Sanford Rose Assoc.
Gordon, Raymond C.—Parker, Sholl & Gordon, Inc. (R)
Gordon, Trina D.—Boyden Int'l., Inc. (R)
Gore, Edward O.—Sales Consultants

Gore, Mike—Staffing Solutions
Gorman, Michele—Sandi McDonald & Assoc., Inc.
Gorman, Patrick—Techsearch Services Inc.
Goss, Stanley B.—Goss & Assoc., Inc. (R)
Gossage, Wayne—Gossage Regan Assoc. (R)
Gostanian, Gregory—The Windham Group
Gottenberg, Norbert A.—Norman Broadbent Int'l., Inc. (R)
Gottesfeld, Sheldon—Cross Country Consultants, Inc.
Gould, Kathryn C.—Venture Management (R)
Gould, William E.—Gould & McCoy, Inc. (R)
Gouran, Marc S.—The DLR Group, Inc. (R)
Goushas, Frank D.—Robert Lowell Int'l. (R)
Goveia, Steve—Coopers & Lybrand, Management Consulting Services (R)
Govig, Dick—Management Recruiters
Govig, Todd A.—Management Recruiters
Graff, Thomas—Management Recruiters
Graham, Gregory B.—Anderson, Graham & Stewart, Inc.
Graham, Kevin—Munroe, Curry & Bond Assoc. (R)
Graham, Robert—Cambridge Management Planning (R)
Graham, Robert F.—CSI Inc. (R)
Graham, Robert W.—Robert Graham Assoc., Inc. (R)
Grand, III, Gordon—Russell Reynolds Assoc., Inc. (R)
Grant, Cindy—Robert Half Int'l.
Grant, Daniel M.—Sales Consultants
Grant, Kristin—Kellogg Consulting Group (R)
Grant, Lee—Grant, Franks & Assoc.
Grantham, John D.—Grantham & Co., Inc. (R)
Grassl, Peter—Bowman & Marshall
Graves, William N.—Search & Recruit Int'l.
Gray, Annie—Annie Gray Assoc., Inc. (R)
Gray, James—Graham & Co. (R)
Gray, Leanne P.—Career Profiles
Gray, Mark—Executive Referral Services, Inc.
Gray, Norman G.—Career Profiles
Gray, William K.—Becker, Norton & Co. (R)
Grayson, E.C.—SpencerStuart (R)
Grazberg, Rose—Joel H. Paul & Assoc., Inc.
Grebenschikoff, Jennifer R.—Physician Executive Management Center (R)
Green, Carole J.—Paul C. Green & Assoc. Ltd. (R)
Green, John—R. F. Mulvaney & Assoc., Inc. (R)
Green, Karen—Western Search Assoc.
Green, Larry A.—Winston Rooney & Green
Green, Lynn—Nuance Personnel Search, Inc.

Green, Normand W.—Boyden Int'l., Inc. (R)
Green, Paul C.—Paul C. Green & Assoc. Ltd. (R)
Green, Richard H.—Personnel Systems Int'l. Inc.
Greenbaum, Larry—Accountants On Call
Greenberg, Louise H.—Krow Assoc., Inc.
Greene, Dorcas P.—Greene Personnel Consultants
Greene, Frederick J.—Boyden Int'l., Inc. (R)
Greene, Luke—Thomas-Pond Enterprises (R)
Greene, Pervis—Sales Consultants
Greene, Timothy G.—Greene & Co.
Greene, Jr., W. Luke—Broward-Dobbs, Inc.
Greene, William Mike—The Remington Group, Ltd.
Greener, Alan L.—Marshall Rice Assoc. (R)
Greenfield, Art—Management Recruiters
Greenhalgh, William H.—Management Assoc.
Greenstein, Eric—Engineering Directions
Greenwald, Jane K.—Gilbert Tweed Assoc., Inc. (R)
Greger, Kenneth R.—Greger Assoc. (R)
Gregg, Arthur W.—Denney & Co., Inc. (R)
Gregg, Susanne—Career Marketing Assoc.
Gregory, Carol—The Charles Ryan Group, Inc.
Gregory, Rose—Kay Henry, Inc.
Gregory, Ted—Career Advancement
Greiff, Robert—Management Advisors of Princeton, Inc. (R)
Grenier, D.W.—Sanford Rose Assoc. of Beachwood
Gresham, James G.—Executive Search Inc. (R)
Grevious, Charles—The Johnson Group, Inc.
Griesedieck, Jr., Joseph E.—SpencerStuart (R)
Griffin, Al—Gardner-Ross Assoc., Inc. (R)
Griffin, Gerald—Korn/Ferry Int'l. (R)
Griffin, John A.—SpencerStuart (R)
Griffin, Larry—Global Data Services, Inc.
Griffith, III, Warland—Griffith & Werner, Inc. (R)
Griffler, Linda—Joel H. Paul & Assoc., Inc.
Grimaldi, Joanne—Management Recruiters
Grimes, Steven—American Resources Corp.
Grimm, Peter G.—Nordeman Grimm, Inc. (R)
Grindlinger, Arthur R.—Fortune Personnel Consultants of Sarasota Inc.
Groban, Jack L.—Jack Groban & Assoc. (R)
Groenekamp, William A.—Groenekamp & Assoc.
Grolnic, Marty—Source EDP
Gronet, Mark A.—Robert Olivier & Assoc., Inc. (R)
Groom, Charles C.—C.G. & Assoc.
Gross, Alan H.—Heath/Norton Assoc., Inc. (R)
Gross, Dennis—Management Recruiters

Gross, Howard—Herbert Mines Assoc., Inc. (R)
Gross, James M.—Boyden Int'l., Inc. (R)
Gross, Jerry—J. Gross & Assoc.
Grossberg, Robert M.—Robert Grossberg & Assoc. (R)
Grossman, Allan D.—A. Davis Grant & Co. (R)
Grossman, Shari—RitaSue Siegel Assoc., Inc.
Grossman, Walter B.—Polytechnic Design Co.
Grover, James R.—Grover & Assoc. (R)
Gruen, Constance—Argus National, Inc. (R)
Grumney, David E.—D E G Co., Inc. (R)
Gude, John S.—Boyden Int'l., Inc. (R)
Guidarelli, Shelley—Guidarelli Assoc., Inc.
Guido, Ronald J—Argus National, Inc. (R)
Guidry, Jim—Guidry, East, Barnes & Bono, Inc. (R)
Gulian, Randolph S.—Strategic Executives, Inc.
Gumbinner, Paul S.—The Gumbinner Co.
Gundersen, Steven G.—Gundersen Brenner, Inc. (R)
Gunther, James J.—Harvard Aimes Group (R)
Gustafson, Alvin S.—Technitrac, Inc.
Guthoff, Pete—R.G.B. & Assoc., Inc.
Gutreuter, William E.—Gutreuter & Assoc. (R)
Guy, C. William—William Guy & Assoc., Inc. (R)
Gynn, Margaret A.—Gynn Assoc., Inc. (R)
Gynn, Walter T.—Gynn Assoc., Inc. (R)
Habelmann, Jerry—Coopers & Lybrand, Management Consulting Services (R)
Haber, Amy—The Agency- An Employment Consortium
Haberman, Joseph C.—A.T. Kearney Executive Svs. (R)
Hackett, K.J.—Hackett & Co. (R)
Haddad, Charles G.—Romac & Assoc.
Haddad, Ronald J.—Haddad Assoc. (R)
Hadden, Elizabeth—Lunney, Hadden & Assoc.
Hadelman, Jordan M.—Kieffer, Ford, & Hadelman, Ltd. (R)
Haerter, Guenter—Reinecke & Assoc.
Hagen, Laura J.—Major, Wilson & Africa
Hagerman, Reis F.—Executive Search of New England, Inc.
Hagerthy, Michael J.—Interim Management (R)
Hahn, Kenneth R.—Hahn & Assoc., Inc.
Hahn, Loel G.—Fergason Assoc., Inc.
Hahn, Marya—Wilkinson Boyd
Hailey, H.M.—Damon & Assoc., Inc.
Haines, Chuck—Babson, Moore & Wilcox (R)
Haladyna, Stanley R.—SRH Resource Group (R)
Halbrecht, Herb—Halbrecht Lieberman Assoc., Inc. (R)

Halden, Kermit W.—Halden & Assoc. (R)
Hale, Dillon—Cemco, Ltd.
Hale, Michele—Phillips Resource Group
Halek, Frederick—Sanford Rose Assoc.
Halenza, Donald—J.D. Wright & Assoc., Inc.
Halerz, James K.—Strategic Staffing Concepts, Inc. (R)
Halevi, Ra—The Eastridge Group
Haley, George H.—Ward Howell Int'l. Inc. (R)
Haley, Timothy—Haley Assoc., Inc. (R)
Hall, Anne—GreenHall Assoc., Inc.
Hall, Donald A.—S-H-S of Allentown
Hall, Earl R.—Management Recruiters of Little Rock
Hall, Elizabeth—Hall, Cooper & Bartman, Ltd.
Hall, Gretta—SRH Resource Group (R)
Hall, J. A.—The Morris Group
Hall, Noel K.—Management Recruiters of Little Rock
Hall, Peter V.—Chartwell Partners Int'l., Inc. (R)
Hall, Tom—Korn/Ferry Int'l. (R)
Hallagan, Robert E.—Heidrick and Struggles, Inc. (R)
Hallagan, Robert E.—Heidrick and Struggles, Inc. (R)
Hallam, Andy—Management Recruiters
Hallberg, Diana—Scan Management Inc.
Haller, Dan—Accounting Resources Int'l., Inc.
Halstead, Frederick A.—Halstead & Assoc. (R)
Halvorsen, Jeanne M.—Kittleman & Assoc. (R)
Halyburton, Robert R.—The Halyburton Co., Inc. (R)
Hamelsky, Melvin R.—Sanford Rose Assoc.
Hamer, Thurston R.—Korn/Ferry, Int'l., S.A. de C.V. (R)
Hamilius, Raymond—Eggers Consulting Co., Inc.
Hamill, Robert W.—Robert Howe & Assoc. (R)
Hamilton, Frank—Gwen Dycus, Inc.
Hamilton, Thomas—McGladrey Search Group
Hamlin, Harry—Hamlin Assoc. (R)
Hamm, Mary Kay—Romac & Assoc., Inc.
Hammer, Robert—Management Recruiters
Hanawalt, Robert C.—Larsen Int'l., Inc. (R)
Hand, Jean—Management Recruiters
Handel, Jr., Richard C.—R. C. Handel Assoc. Inc. (R)
Handler, William L.—W.L. Handler & Assoc. (R)
Handwerk, Robert—Handwerk & Assoc.
Haney, J. Don—Lowderman & Haney, Inc. (R)
Hankins, George—Management Assoc.
Hanley, Alan P.—Kennedy & Co. (R)
Hanley, J. Patrick—W. Hanley & Assoc.

Hanley, Richard T.—W. Hanley & Assoc.
Hanley, Jr., Thomas A.—Smith Hanley Assoc., Inc.
Hanna, Jr., M.A.—Sanford Rose Assoc. of Beachwood
Hannock, III, Elwin W.—Flynn, Hannock, Inc.
Hansen, Arthur E.—Ritta Professional Search Inc.
Hansen, Charles—Management Recruiters
Hansen, David G.—Ott & Hansen, Inc. (R)
Hansen, H. Jack—Hansen Management Search Co. (R)
Hansen, Joan D.—Hansen Management Search Co. (R)
Hansen, Martin L.—Management Recruiters
Hansen, Ty E.—Hansen Group, Ltd. (R)
Hanson, Grant M.—Donald P. Hayes Assoc., Inc.
Hanson, Russ—Management Recruiters
Hanson, Russ—Management Recruiters
Hanzel, Bruce S.—Hanzel & Co., Inc. (R)
Haragan, Patrick W.—SpencerStuart (R)
Harbaugh, Jr., Paul J.—International Management Advisors, Inc. (R)
Harbers, Susan E.—Brady Assoc. Int'l., Inc. (R)
Harbert, David O.—Sweeney Shepherd Bueschel Provus Harbert & Mummert, Inc. (R)
Hardbrod, Herbert—Management Recruiters of Middlesex County NJ.
Hardie, Jennifer C.—Boyden Int'l., Inc. (R)
Harding, Richard—Salesworld-Division of Metacor Inc.
Hardison, Richard—Korn/Ferry Int'l. (R)
Hardwick, Michael—Management Recruiters
Hardy, Robert—Cejka & Co. (R)
Hardy, Thomas G.—SpencerStuart (R)
Harfenist, Harry—Parker Page Group
Hargraves, Sue—Strategic Assoc., Inc.
Haring, Heidi L.—Major, Wilson & Africa
Harkins, Margaret—Management Recruiters
Harkins, Michael P.—Munroe, Curry & Bond Assoc. (R)
Harkins, Richard—Management Recruiters
Harmon, Jerry—Delta Resource Group, Ltd.
Harms, Fred D.—Billington, Fox & Ellis, Inc. (R)
Harper, Cynthia D.—CDH & Assoc., Inc.
Harrafan, James K.—Management Recruiters of Gramercy, Inc.
Harreus, Charles F.—Harreus & Assoc., Inc. (R)
Harrington, JoAn—Management Recruiters
Harrington, Richard—Management Recruiters
Harrington, Robert—Flores & Assoc.
Harris, Andrew S.—Harris Heery & Assoc., Inc. (R)

Harris, Jack L.—Management Recruiters

Harris, James D.—Bader Research Corp.

Harris, John L.—Management Recruiters

Harris, Nancy—Double M Executive Placement Service, Inc.

Harris, Thomas E.—Sales Consultants of Ft. Myers, Inc.

Harris, Vicki M.—Management Recruiters

Harrison, Connie—Davis-Smith Medical-Dental Employment Service, Inc.

Harrison, Joel—D.A. Kreuter Assoc., Inc. (R)

Harrison, John S.—Chase Partners (R)

Harshman, Donald—The Stevenson Group/SES (R)

Hart, Bill—Intertech Search Group

Hart, David—Hadley Lockwood, Inc. (R)

Hart, Susan—SpencerStuart (R)

Hart, Timothy—The Hart Group

Hartig, Dave—The Angus Group, Inc.

Hartley, Allan—Romac & Assoc., Inc.

Hartman, Beverly—Management Assoc.

Hartman, Kathie—Hartman Personnel Services

Hartman, Robert J.—Hartman, Barnette & Assoc. (R)

Hartwick, Doug—Source EDP

Hartwig, Charles—The Connolly Consulting Group

Hartzler, Bob—Source EDP

Harvey, Arnold D.—PSP Agency

Harvey, Michael D.—Advanced Executive Resources (R)

Harvill, Jon—Dunhill Search of West Atlanta

Hatcher, Jospeh W.—Management Recruiters of Gramercy, Inc.

Hatten, Dick—Management Recruiters

Hatten, Karen—Management Recruiters

Hauft, Neil E.—Hauft Mark Assoc., Inc. (R)

Haughton, Michael C.—Lee & Burgess Assoc., Inc. (R)

Hauser, C.J.—Hoskins, Rees & Smith

Hauser, Marth—Tyler & Co. (R)

Hausheer, Ph.D., W. Jeff—ACR Assoc.

Havener, D. Clarke—The Abbott Group (R)

Havener, Robert—Salesworld-Division of Metacor Inc.

Hawkins, Carolyn—Management Recruiters of Savannah

Hawkins, Kirk—Management Recruiters of Topeka, Inc.

Hawkins, Phyllis—Phyllis Hawkins & Assoc.

Hawkins, Ty—Career Information Services, Inc.

Hawkins, W. Davis—SpencerStuart (R)

Hawkins, William D.—The Hawkins Co. (R)

Hawksworth, A. Dwight—A. D. & Assoc.

Hawley, Robert E.—Hayden Group, Inc. (R)

Hayden, James A.—Hayden Group, Inc. (R)

Hayden, Ralph—Pencom Systems Inc.

Hayes, Donald P.—Donald P. Hayes Assoc., Inc.

Hayes, Jeffrey—Quickstaff

Hayes, Vicki—Professional Careers

Hayman, Thomas C.—Hayman & Co. (R)

Hazard, Gaye—OSA Partners, Inc.

Heacock, Burt—Paul-Tittle Assoc., Inc.

Head, Janet—Health Technology, Inc.

Headrick, Glenn—Stoneham Assoc. (R)

Heald, William H.—The Goodrich & Sherwood Co. (R)

Healy, Frank P.—F. P. Healy & Co., Inc. (R)

Healy, Vanda K.—Management Recruiters

Healy, William C.—Management Recruiters

Healy, William C.—Management Recruiters

Heasley, Franklin A.—Bioventure Resources, Inc.

Heath, Jeffrey A.—Management Recruiters

Heavey, John—Prestige Search Inc.

Hebel, Robert W.—R. W. Hebel Assoc. (R)

Hedlund, David—Hedlund Corp.

Hedman, Kent R.—Kent R. Hedman & Assoc.

Hedstrom, Dave—Sales Consultants

Heery, William J.—Harris Heery & Assoc., Inc. (R)

Heffelfinger, Thomas V.—Heffelfinger Assoc., Inc. (R)

Heffernan, James R.—Competitive Resources, Inc.

Hegarty, Marcus—Kimmel & Fredericks, Inc.

Hegarty, Robert J.—Hegarty & Co. (R)

Heiden, Dorinda—National Corporate Consultants, Inc.

Heidrick, Gardner W.—The Heidrick Partners, Inc. (R)

Heidrick, Robert L.—The Heidrick Partners, Inc. (R)

Heiken, Barbara E.—Randell-Heiken, Inc. (R)

Heinle, Jr., Norman C.—Datamatics Management Services, Inc.

Heinle, R. Kevin—Datamatics Management Services, Inc.

Heinschel, Phil—Phillips Personnel/Search

Heintz, Michael—Sales Consultants

Heiser, Steve S.—Sanford Rose Assoc.

Heissan, Arlene—P.J. Lynch Assoc. (R)

Helfer, Frederick W.—Helfer Executive Consultants (R)

Helft, Michael—Korn/Ferry Int'l. (R)

Heller, Jim—BDO Seidam (R)

Heller, Phillip—Heller Kil Assoc., Inc.

Hite, III, William A.—Hite Executive Search (R)

Hobbs, Adriana—Conrey Interamericana (R)

Hobbs, Robert B.—JM & Co. (R)

Hobgood, Joe—Sanford Rose Assoc. of Lima

Hochberg, David R.—Rex Assoc., Inc.

Hochfelder, Eric—R. Gaines Baty Assoc., Inc.

Hochwalt, Mike—M H Executive Search Group

Hockett, Bill—Hockett Assoc., Inc. (R)

Hodde, Fred—Heritage Search Group, Inc.

Hodge, Jeffrey W.—SpencerStuart (R)

Hodges, Linda B.—Hersher Assoc., Ltd. (R)

Hodges, Robert J.—Sampson, Neill & Wilkins Inc. (R)

Hodgson, Judy—Management Recruiters

Hodgson, Robert D.—Management Recruiters

Hoevel, Michael J.—Poirier, Hoevel & Co. (R)

Hoffman, Brian—Sales Consultants

Hoffman, Linda—Sanford Rose Assoc.

Hoffman, Mark A.—Management Recruiters

Hoffman, Robert—Sanford Rose Assoc.

Hoffmann, David H.—DHR Int'l., Inc. (R)

Hoffmeir, Patricia—Gilbert Tweed Assoc. (R)

Hogan, E.M.—Sanford Rose Assoc. of Wilmington

Hogan, Karen—Davis-Smith Medical-Dental Employment Service, Inc.

Hogan, Kevin—Computer Professionals (R)

Hogan, Lawrence—Hogan Assoc. (R)

Hogan, William D.—Management Recruiters

Hogg, Jr., James G.—Whittlesey & Assoc., Inc.

Hohauser, Harvey—Harvey Hohauser & Assoc. (R)

Hoiriis, Christine K.—Double M Executive Placement Service, Inc.

Hokkanen, James—Management Recruiters

Holbach, Jerry—Management Recruiters

Holbrook, Richard D.—Richard D. Holbrook Assoc. (R)

Holbrooke, David—Centaur Int'l.

Holland, John H.—Sloan & Assoc., Inc.

Holland, Susan R.—Holland Rusk & Assoc. (R)

Hollander, Fred L.—Management Recruiters

Hollinger, Lois—Management Recruiters

Hollinger, William—Management Recruiters

Hollingsworth, Leslie—Brad Marks Int'l. (R)

Hollins, Lawrence I.—The Hollins Group, Inc. (R)

Holloway, Linda—Dupuis & Ryden, P.C. (R)

Holloway, Roger M.—Management Recruiters

Holmes, Bonnie—Management Recruiters - Concord, CA.

Holmes, Susan J.—Bader Research Corp.

Holodnak, William A.—J. Robert Scott (R)

Holohan, Jr., Barth A.—Holohan Group, Ltd. (R)

Holohan, Marie Falbo—Holohan Group, Ltd. (R)

Holt, Buddy—Kellogg Consulting Group (R)

Holtkamp, Donald A.—Sanford Rose Assoc.

Holtz, Richard D.—Sanford Rose Assoc. of Nashville

Holupka, Gary F.—Management Recruiters

Holupka, Patricia L.—Management Recruiters

Holzman, Alfred J.—Summit Executive Search Consultants, Inc.

Homer, Judy B.—J.B. Homer Assoc. Inc. (R)

Hone, Stanley B.—Charles E. Day & Assoc., Inc. (R)

Honey, W. M. M.—O'Callaghan, Honey & Assoc., Inc. (R)

Honig, Howard—Source Finance

Hooten, Lawanda K.—Management Recruiters

Hope, John—National Corporate Consultants, Inc.

Hopkins, Chester A.—Handy HRM (R)

Hopkins, Jane E.—Malcolm Cole & Assoc.

Hornady, Caroline S.—A.T. Kearney Executive Svs. (R)

Hornbeck, John—Management Recruiters

Hornberger, Frederick C.—Hornberger Management Co., Inc.

Horton, John M.—John M. Horton

Horton, Robert H.—R. H. Horton Int'l. (R)

Hoskins, Charles R.—Heidrick and Struggles, Inc. (R)

Houchins, Jr., Eugene E.—Management Recruiters of Atlanta Downtown

Houck, Chad—Source Finance

Housfeld, Gordon—Conley Assoc., Inc. (R)

Houska, Edward J.—Management Recruiters

Houston, Christine—TASA, Inc. (R)

Houtz, Kenneth H.—Houtz, Strawn Assoc. (R)

Houze, Geoffry—William C. Houze & Co. (R)

Houze, William C.—William C. Houze & Co. (R)

Hovey, Delese—C.W. Sink & Co., Inc. (R)

Howard, David—Management Recruiters

Howard, Fred—Robert Sage Recruiting

Howard, George—George Howard Assoc.

Howard, Kathy S.—Management Recruiters

Howard, Randall C.—Randall Howard & Assoc., Inc. (R)

Howard, Richard H.—Management Recruiters of Berkeley

Howe, Craig—C. L. Howe & Co., Inc.

Howe, Jr., Edward R.—Howe, McMahon & Assoc., Inc. (R)

Howe, Timothy L.—The Resource Group

Howe, Vance A.—Ward Howell Int'l. Inc. (R)

Howe, W. Lawrence—Howe-Weaver, Inc. (R)
Howe, William S.—Kenny, Kindler, Hunt & Howe (R)
Howe-Waxman, Anita—Howe-Lewis Int'l., Inc. (R)
Howell, H. Cecil—Careers Unlimited
Howell, Robert B.—Atlantic Search Group, Inc.
Howie, David W.—Howie & Assoc., Inc.
Hoy, Thomas J.—Sales Consultants
Hoyda, L.—Thorndike Deland Assoc. (R)
Hubbard, Bill—Professional Medical
Hubbard, Kenneth A.H.—Peat Marwick Stevenson & Kellogg (R)
Hubbard, Ron—Landon-Brookes Executive Search
Huber, Lucy—Management Recruiters
Huber, Lucy—Sales Consultants
Huberman, Arnold—Arnold Huberman Assoc., Inc. (R)
Hubin, Tom—Management Recruiters
Hucko, Donald—Barnes, Walters & Assoc., Inc. (R)
Hudson, Sr., Bill—Robert Sage Recruiting
Hudson, George A.—Hudson Assoc. Inc.
Hudson, Judy K.—The Hudson Group
Hudson, Paul E.—The Hudson Group
Hudson, Reginald M.—Search Bureau Int'l.
Hudson, Sue Ann—Babson, Moore & Wilcox (R)
Huegel, Ray—Raymond Thomas & Assoc.
Huette, H.—DHR Int'l., Inc. (R)
Huff, David—Kutt, Inc.
Huff, Margaret L.—Huff Assoc. (R)
Huff, William Z.—Huff Assoc. (R)
Hughes, A.J. Bud—Hughes & Assoc., Inc. (R)
Hughes, Donald J.—Sloan & Assoc., Inc.
Hughes, James J.—Barone Assoc.
Hughes, Jim—Setford-Shaw-Najarian Assoc., Ltd.
Hughes, Ken—Hughes & Assoc.
Hughes, Michele J.—M.J. Hughes Int'l., Inc. (R)
Hulst, Jack—Rocky Mountain Recruiters, Inc.
Humay, Gene—E. F. Humay Assoc.
Humay, Jane—E. F. Humay Assoc.
Hummel, Thomas F.—Sales Consultants
Humphrey, H. H.—SpencerStuart (R)
Humphreys, Scott W.—William Humphreys & Assoc., Inc. (R)
Humphreys, Sid—Korn/Ferry Int'l. (R)
Humphreys, William M.—William Humphreys & Assoc., Inc. (R)
Humphry, III, James—Gossage Regan Assoc. (R)
Hunt, Bridgford H.—The Hunt Co. (R)
Hunt, Dean—Loewenstein & Assoc.
Hunt, James E.—Kenny, Kindler, Hunt & Howe (R)

Hunter, Alan—Techsearch Services Inc.
Hunter, David—Stanewick, Hart & Assoc., Inc.
Hunter, Durant A.—Gardiner Stone Hunter Int'l., Inc. (R)
Hunter, Jr., John B.—John Sibbald Assoc., Inc. (R)
Hunter, Sharon—Management Recruiters
Hurd, Jane—Korn/Ferry Int'l. (R)
Hurst, Jack K.—Jack Hurst & Assoc., Inc. (R)
Hurst, Kenneth N.—Jack Hurst & Assoc., Inc. (R)
Hurt, Thomas E.—Management Recruiters
Hurt, Thomas E.—Sales Consultants
Huskin, John—Studwell Assoc. (R)
Huskin, John—Studwell Assoc. (R)
Huston, Julia E.—Cemco Medical
Hutchinson, Loretta M.—Hutchinson Resources International (R)
Hutchison, William K.—Christenson & Hutchison (R)
Huxtable, Carroll G.—Huxtable Assoc., Inc. (R)
Huxtable, Fulton L.—Huxtable Assoc., Inc. (R)
Hyde, Anne P.—The Hyde Group, Inc. (R)
Hyde, W. Jerry—Hyde Danforth & Co. (R)
Hydes, Greg—Career Information Services, Inc.
Hykes, Don A.—Kearney Executive Search (R)
Hyland, Kenneth J.—Hyland Executive Search
Hyland, Susan L.—Hyland Executive Search
Hyman, Curtis D.—Hyman, Mackenzie & Partners, Inc. (R)
Hypes, Jr., Richard G.—Lynch Miller Moore, Inc. (R)
Ibarra, Marco Antonio—Ward Howell Int'l. Inc. (R)
Icard, Sr., Robert S.—Management Recruiters
Ice, Larry—Management Recruiters
Ihde, Moonyean—Engineering Specialists
Ikle, A. Donald—Ward Howell Int'l. Inc. (R)
Illsley, Hugh G.—Ward Howell Int'l. Inc. (R)
Imber, John—John Imber Assoc., Ltd. (R)
Incitti, Lance M.—Management Recruiters
Infantino, James A.—Management Recruiters
Infantino, Sharon M.—Management Recruiters
Infinger, Ronald E.—Robison & McAulay (R)
Ingala, Thomas A.—Sales Consultants Bowling Green
Ingmire, Phyllis—Kensington Int'l.
Ingram, D. John—Ingram, Inc. (R)
Ingram, Dan—Challenger & Hunt (R)
Irving, Jeffrey J.—Jeffrey Irving Assoc., Inc. (R)
Isaacs, Rhoda—R.I. James, Inc.
Isaacson, John—Isaacson, Miller, Inc. (R)
Isenberg, H. Peter—Management Recruiters

Iserson, Michael P.—Roberts-Lund Assoc., Ltd. (R)
Ishmael, Kay H.—The Lawson Group
Ishmael, Kay H.—The Lawson Group
Israel, Sheldon—Sales Professionals Personnel Services
Ivers, Eric—Medical Sales & Management Specialists
Jablo, Steven A.—Jablo Partners (R)
Jack, III, Charles E.—Fox Hill Assoc., Ltd. (R)
Jackley, Brian—Jackley Search Consultants
Jackowitz, Ronald N.—Carris, Jackowitz Assoc. (R)
Jackson, Barbara W.—Management Recruiters
Jackson, Clarke H.—The Caldwell Partners Int'l. (R)
Jackson, Dave—Curts/Jackson, Inc.
Jackson, Jim—Management Recruiters
Jackson, M.—The Oxford Group
Jacobs, James F.—Sales Consultants
Jacobs, Klaus—TASA, Inc. (R)
Jacobs, Martin—Exec 2000
Jacobs, Mike—Thorne, Brieger Assoc., Inc. (R)
Jacobs, Ph.D., Phillip E.—E.J. Michaels, Ltd. (R)
Jacobson, Allan—Peat Marwick Stevenson & Kellogg (R)
Jacobson, David—Jacobson Assoc.
Jacobson, Donald—Hunt Ltd.
Jacobson, Loren—McGladrey Search Group
Jahrling, Walter F.—Jahrling & Co. (R)
Jakobs, Frederick H.—Jakobs & Assoc. Int'l. (R)
Jakobs, Nancy M.—Jakobs & Assoc. Int'l. (R)
James, E. Pendleton—Pendleton James & Assoc., Inc. (R)
James, Richard—Criterion Executive Search, Inc.
Jameson, Bill—Management Recruiters
Jameson, John B.—Charles Bradley Professionals
Jamison, Joanne—Management Recruiters
Jamison, Ted—Management Recruiters
Jansen, Carl—Search North America, Inc.
Jansen, Douglas L.—Search Northwest Assoc.
Jarrell, Jay—Strauss Personnel Service
Jaspersen, Kenneth A.—Dunhill Search of Omaha, Inc.
Jatinen, Dave—Fox-Morris Assoc., Inc.
Jay, John C.—Organization Resources Inc. (R)
Jayne, Don—Key Employment Services
Jeanes, Marshall M.—The Interim Management Corp.(IMCOR) (R)
Jefferies, George—Hintz Associates
Jeffers, Carol S.—John Sibbald Assoc., Inc. (R)
Jeli, Nola—Nola Worley & Assoc., Inc.

Jender, Jesse—Jender & Company (R)
Jenkins, Reginald K.—Drew Assoc. Int'l. (R)
Jennings, Kathleen—E T Search Inc.
Jensen, David G.—Search Masters Int'l.
Jerman, Virginia—Martin H. Bauman Assoc., Inc. (R)
Jesberg, Gary—Michael Latas & Assoc., Inc. (R)
Jesseph, Steve—Fox-Morris Assoc., Inc.
Jilka, Dan—Management Recruiters
John, Harold A.—John & Powers, Inc. (R)
Johnson, Alan M.—GKR Int'l. (R)
Johnson, Carl A.—Bertrand, Ross & Assoc., Inc. (R)
Johnson, Carl A.—International Management Services Inc. (R)
Johnson, Cheri—Johnson & Assoc., Inc. (R)
Johnson, David—Galen Giles Group
Johnson, David S.—McManners Assoc., Inc. (R)
Johnson, George M.—Sanford Rose Assoc.
Johnson, Greg—Source Finance
Johnson, Greg—Source EDP
Johnson, Jeff—Source Finance
Johnson, John—Crest Management Search, Inc.
Johnson, John—Human Resource Network
Johnson, John F.—Lamalie Assoc., Inc. (R)
Johnson, John F.—Lamalie Assoc., Inc. (R)
Johnson, John H.—John H. Johnson & Assoc., Inc. (R)
Johnson, John R.—Sanford Rose Assoc.
Johnson, Jr., John W.—Webb, Johnson & Klemmer, Inc. (R)
Johnson, Karl—K.E. Johnson Assoc.
Johnson, Kathryn L.—Kathryn L. Johnson
Johnson, Keith M.—Romac & Assoc., Inc.
Johnson, L.J.—L.J. Johnson & Co. (R)
Johnson, Linnea—C. Berger and Company
Johnson, Mike—Sharrow & Assoc., Inc.
Johnson, Nancy I.—Storfer & Assoc.
Johnson, Nancy I.—The Dartmouth Group (R)
Johnson, Priscilla—The Johnson Group, Inc.
Johnson, Rocky—Kearney Executive Search (R)
Johnson, Ron L.—Management Recruiters
Johnson, Ron L.—Sales Consultants
Johnson, Ronald S.—Ronald S. Johnson Assoc., Inc. (R)
Johnson, S. Hope—The Interface Group, Ltd. (R)
Johnston, James E.—J. Johnston Group, Inc.
Johnston, James R.—The Stevenson Group/SES (R)
Jones, Anne C.—Finance & Accounting Search Firm
Jones, Bob—E.T. Wharton Assoc., Inc.

Kehoe, George—GHK Technical Recruiter

Kehoe, James V.—Sanford Rose Assoc.- Suburban Philadelphia

Kehoe, Lillian—GHK Technical Recruiter

Keider, Norman B.—Kearney Executive Search (R)

Keith-Murray, Marnie—Executive Profiles Inc. (R)

Kelleher, Maureen—Johnson Smith & Knisely Inc. (R)

Keller, Lorraine—Management Recruiters

Kelley, Kathy—Straube Assoc., Inc. (R)

Kelley, Kenneth P.—Strategy 2000

Kelley, Verne—Kelley & Keller, Inc.

Kelly, Claudia L.—Norman Broadbent Int'l., Inc. (R)

Kelly, Jim—The LaBorde Group

Kelly, Ron—Hunter Int'l., Inc. (R)

Kelly, Roy—Management Recruiters

Kelly, Sandra—Executive Referral Services, Inc.

Kemp, Scott—M. Scott Kemp & Assoc., Inc. (R)

Kempinski, Erik J.—Real Estate Executive Search, Inc.

Kendall, James C.—Kendall & Davis Co., Inc.

Kendall, Steven W.—Management Recruiters of Atlanta West, Inc.

Kendro, Barbara A.—Kendro & Assoc. (R)

Kendro, Richard J.—Kendro & Assoc. (R)

Kenefick, Beverly Froley—Centaur Int'l.

Kennedy, Bradford M.—Tecmark Assoc. Inc.

Kennedy, Carol—Accountants On Call

Kennedy, J. Michael—Geneva Group Int'l (R)

Kennedy, III, James H.—James H. Kennedy

Kennedy, John J.—Jack Kennedy Assoc., Inc.

Kennedy, John J.—John J. Kennedy Assoc., Inc.

Kennedy, Noel G.—Jack Kennedy Assoc., Inc.

Kennedy, Roben—Management Recruiters

Kennedy, Robert—Kensington Int'l.

Kennedy, Walter—Romac & Assoc., Inc.

Kenner, Jim—Pencom System Inc.

Kennison, Victoria—Kennison & Assoc.

Kenny, Eugene F.—Oldwick Enterprises, Inc.

Kenny, J. Thomas—Billington, Fox & Ellis, Inc. (R)

Kenny, Mary R.—Oldwick Enterprises, Inc.

Kenny, Roger M.—Kenny, Kindler, Hunt & Howe (R)

Kensington, Holland—Kensington Int'l.

Kent, Julie—Snelling Personnel Services

Kent, Melvin—Melvin Kent & Assoc., Inc. (R)

Kent, Pat—McManners Assoc., Inc. (R)

Keogh, James—Sanford Rose Assoc.

Kepler, Charles W.—Russell Reynolds Assoc., Inc. (R)

Keren, Yardena—Search Group

Kerner, Barbara—Barbara Kerner Consultants

Kerrigan, Geoffrey M.—Engineering Search Assoc.

Kerrs, James—The Michael Scott Consulting Co., Inc. (R)

Kerry, Donald F.—D. F. Kerry & Assoc. (R)

Kershaw, Blair—Blair Kershaw Assoc., Inc.

Kershner, Bruce—Kershner & Co.

Kerstein, Daniel J.—First Colorado Consulting Group, Inc. (R)

Kesten, Howard—APA Search, Inc.

Keyes, Joseph A.—Joseph Keyes Assoc.

Keymer, Bob—Sales Consultants

Keymer, Bob—Sales Consultants

Keymer, Robert J.—Management Recruiters

Keyser, Jean—Robert Sage Recruiting

Khoury, Robert C.—Search Solutions, Inc.

Khoury, Susan—Search Solutions, Inc.

Khoury, Susan C.—Dieckmann & Assoc., Ltd. (R)

Kieffer, Michael C.—Kieffer, Ford, & Hadelman, Ltd. (R)

Kielty, III, John L.—Earley Kielty & Assoc., Inc. (R)

Kil, Richard—Heller Kil Assoc., Inc.

Kilcoyne, Richard—Carter McKenzie, Inc.

Kilcullen, Brian A.—D.A. Kreuter Assoc., Inc. (R)

Kilian, Walter D.—Availability Personnel Consultants

Killman, Kenneth A.—Dunhill Professional Search of Kalamazoo

Kim, David—Management Recruiters

Kimmel, Joe W.—Kimmel & Fredericks, Inc.

Kincannon, Kelly—Kincannon & Reed (R)

Kinderis, Paul—Kinderis & Loercher Group

Kindler, Peter A.—Kenny, Kindler, Hunt & Howe (R)

King, Byron—Management Recruiters

King, Dianne—Source EDP

King, Gail—Management Recruiters of Tampa North

King, Gary—Management Recruiters of Tampa North

King, James B.—Ingram, Inc. (R)

King, Michael—Michael King Assoc., Inc.

King, Richard M.—Kittleman & Assoc. (R)

King, Steven—Ashway Ltd. Agency

King, Ted—Hawkes-Randolph & Assoc., Inc.

Kinlin, Ellen C.—The Kinlin Co., Inc. (R)

Kinser, Richard—Richard Kinser & Assoc. (R)

Kinzie, George—Franchise Recruiters Ltd.

Kipp, Millie—Millie Kipp Assoc., Inc.

Kiradjieff, Edward J.—Kiradjieff & Co.

Kirby, Richard L.—Kirby & Assoc. (R)
Kirchgessner, Ken F.—Management Recruiters
Kirkbride, Robert—Kirkbride Assoc., Inc.
Kirkman, J. Michael—Kirkman & Searing (R)
Kirkpatrick, Robert L.—Boyden Int'l., Inc. (R)
Kirland, Kerry J.—Kirland Search, Inc.
Kirland, William J.—Kirland Search, Inc.
Kirschman, David R.—Physician Executive Management Center (R)
Kirschner, Stephan W.—The Regis Group, Ltd. (R)
Kishbaugh, Herbert S.—Kishbaugh Associates (R)
Kitchen, Ed—Dunhill Professional Search of Hawaii
Kitchen, Joan—Dunhill Professional Search of Hawaii
Kittleman, James M.—Kittleman & Assoc. (R)
Kixmiller, David B.—Heidrick and Struggles, Inc. (R)
Klages, Constance W.—International Management Advisors, Inc. (R)
Klauck, James J.—R. H. Horton Int'l. (R)
Klavens, Cecile J.—The Pickwick Group, Inc.
Kleames, Jerry—Genesis
Kleffel, Kathleen A.—Gregory Michaels & Assoc., Inc.
Klein, Gary I.—Johnson Smith & Knisely Inc. (R)
Klein, Shelley—Stewart/Laurence Assoc., Inc. (R)
Kleiner, Sanford—Sanford Kleiner Assoc., Inc.
Kleinman, Robert—Heath/Norton Assoc., Inc. (R)
Kleinstein, Jonah A.—Jonah Kleinstein Assoc., Inc. (R)
Klembara, Dennis—Source EDP
Klemmer, Raymond J.—Webb, Johnson & Klemmer, Inc. (R)
Klimaski, Remus—Sales Consultants
Kline, James D.—Management Recruiters
Kline, Linda—Kline Consulting, Inc. (R)
Klobasa Barkwill, Linda—MarketSearch, Inc.
Klos, Larry—Management Recruiters
Kluever, Claire—The Bankers Group
Knapp, Carl—RIC Corp. (R)
Knapp, Ronald A.—Knapp Consultants (R)
Knauff, Joyce C.—Joyce C. Knauff & Assoc.
Knight, G.R.—Hornberger Management Co., Inc.
Knipper, Carol—Rafey & Company (R)
Knisely, Gary—Johnson Smith & Knisely Inc. (R)
Knotts, Jerry E.—Tech Mark Group (R)
Knutson, Rebecca J.—Management Recruiters
Kobleutz, Joel M.—Egon Zehnder Int'l. Inc. (R)
Koblin, Cliff—Key Employment
Koch, Gail Kleinberg—CAS Comsearch Inc.

Kocmond, H. Michael—Henry Michaels & Assoc. (R)
Koehler, Frank R.—The Koehler Group
Koehler, Jack—Koehler & Co. (R)
Koellhoffer, Thomas J.—T. J. Koellhoffer & Assoc. (R)
Koenig, Jerrold—P R Management Consultants, Inc.
Koffler, Fred—Fred Koffler Assoc. (R)
Kogon, Gary—Kogon Assoc., Inc.
Kohn, Adam—Search Express (R)
Kolden, John A.—Kolden & Assoc., Ltd. (R)
Koletic, Rudy—Management Recruiters
Kolke, Rick—Loewenstein & Assoc.
Koller, Jr., Edward R.—Howard-Sloan Assoc.
Koller, Jr., Edward R.—Howard-Sloan Communications Search (R)
Konetzki, Alan—Maglio & Co., Inc. (R)
Konker, David N.—Russell Reynolds Assoc., Inc.
Koontz, Donald N.—Koontz, Jeffries & Assoc., Inc. (R)
Kopelan, Rolfe I.—The Foster McKay Group
Kopff, Fred—META/MAT, Ltd. (R)
Kopsick, Joseph—SpencerStuart (R)
Kordus, Lee Walther—Kordus Consulting Group
Koren, Michael—Koren, Rogers Assoc.
Korkuch, Sandy—The Addison Consulting Group
Kornfeld, Warren E.—Management Recruiters
Kors, R. Paul—Kors Montgomery Int'l. (R)
Kossuth, David—Kossuth & Assoc., Inc.
Kossuth, Jane—Kossuth & Assoc., Inc.
Kosteva, David—NDI Services (R)
Kostka, Pamela—Fenwick Partners (R)
Kostmayer, Roger—Kostmayer Assoc., Inc. (R)
Kostmayer, Roger C.—Kostmayer Assoc., Inc. (R)
Kostrub, Todd—Diedre Moire Corp., Inc.
Kosturos, Jim—Source EDP
Kovach, Jerry—The J. Kovach Group, Inc. (R)
Kowalski, Joseph J.—Capitol Management Consulting, Inc.
Kowalski, Robert—Research Alternatives, Inc. (R)
Kozlin, Jeffrey M.—Kozlin Assoc., Inc.
Kozlowski, Linda—Murphy, Symonds & Stowell Search, Inc.
Kraemer, Kathy—Busch Int'l. (R)
Krafski, Charlene R.—Howe-Weaver, Inc. (R)
Kramer, Alan L.—Kramer Executive Resources, Inc.
Kramer, Desni C.—Management Recruiters
Kramer, Donald J.—Dunhill Personnel of Tampa
Kramer, Kim—Million & Assoc., Inc. (R)

Kramer, Mona—Dunhill Personnel of Tampa
Kramer, Peter—Dunhill Personnel of Tampa
Kranak, Karen—Professions, Inc.
Krauser, H. James—SpencerStuart (R)
Kraushaar, Harry C.—Charles Bradley
  Professionals
Krauss, Jack—J. Krauss Assoc. (R)
Krauthamer, Gary L.—Krauthamer & Assoc. (R)
Krautler, William H.—Krautler Personnel
  Recruitment
Kravitz, Jack—Kravitz * Larkin * Silver Assoc.
Kreider, Andy—Northeastern Search, Inc.
Kreofsky, Dean—Kreofsky & Assoc.
Kreuter, Daniel A.—D.A. Kreuter Assoc., Inc. (R)
Kreutzer, Allan—Remark Assoc. Inc.
Kreuzberger, Neil L.—Kreuzberger, Fehr & Assoc.
Krick, Terry L.—Financial Resource Assoc., Inc.
Krieger, James R.—Roth Young of Tampa
Kring, Kenneth L.—SpencerStuart (R)
Krinsky, Ira W.—Ira W. Krinsky & Assoc. (R)
Kris, John R.—Organization Resources Inc. (R)
Kriste, Pat—Ronald S. Johnson Assoc., Inc. (R)
Kristufek, Arthur N.—Magnum Search
Krohe, Kambrea R.—Gregory Michaels & Assoc.,
  Inc.
Kromenaker, Robert—Kromenaker & Associates
Kruchoski, Jan—Accountants On Call
Krueger, Clarence F.—Williams, Roth & Krueger,
  Inc. (R)
Kruezer, Louis—Accountants On Call
Kruse, Cynthia—Management Recruiters
Krutzsch, Linda—Accountants On Call
Krysowaty, Walt—Management Recruiters
Kubat, Glenn—Search Masters
Kubiak, Thomas J.—Halbrecht & Co.
Kucherepa, Sharon—The Caldwell Partners Int'l.
  (R)
Kuehler, Anthony D.—Management Recruiters
Kuehne, Kenneth H.—Kuehne & Co., Inc. (R)
Kuh, William R.—Sanford Rose Assoc.- Woodbury
Kuhl, William R.—Place Mart Personnel Service
Kuhn, John J.—John Kuhn & Assoc. (R)
Kuhn, John J.—Egan & Assoc. (R)
Kuhnmuench, R.G.—K & C Assoc.
Kukoy, Sandra M.—Abacus Consultants
Kukoy, Stephen J.—Abacus Consultants
Kulas, Kenneth P.—Romac & Assoc., Inc.
Kull, Paul—Paul Kull & Co. (R)
Kunzer, Diane S.—Kunzer Assoc., Ltd. (R)
Kunzer, William J.—Kunzer Assoc., Ltd. (R)
Kuper, Jerry P.—Sales Consultants

Kurdziel, John F.—Nuessle, Kurdziel & Weiss,
  Inc. (R)
Kurke, David S.—Sales Consultants of Fairfax, Inc.
Kurland, Karen—Dunhill Professional Search
  Group
Kurosky, John—John Kurosky & Assoc. (R)
Kurtz, Michael E.—MD Resources, Inc. (R)
Kurtz, Sheldon I.—Kurtz Pro-Search, Inc.
Kurtzman, Jerry—Corporate Advisors Inc.
Kurz, Dick—Management Recruiters
Kushell, Douglas T.—Franchise Search, Inc.
Kutt, Larry—Kutt, Inc.
Kuzma, Edward J.—K/N Int'l. (R)
Kuzmick, John—Source Finance
Kyle, Bob—Source Finance
LaBorde, John—The LaBorde Group
LaDuke, Dan—LaDuke & Assoc., Inc.
LaGreca, Alfred J.—Organization Resources Inc.
  (R)
LaMartina, John J.—Management Recruiters
LaPierre, Louis—Romac & Assoc., Inc.
LaVallee, Michael J.—Romac & Assoc.
Laba, Marvin—Marvin Laba & Assoc. (R)
Labarge, Charles J.—Largent Parks & Partners,
  Inc.
Lacey, Jean—M. Scott Kemp & Assoc., Inc. (R)
Lachance, Roger—Rourke, Bourbonnais Assoc.,
  Ltd. (R)
Ladenheim, Warren—Source Finance
Laguna, Jose Luis—RZL Y Asociados, S.C. (R)
Laguzza, John—Laguzza Assoc., Ltd. (R)
Lamb, Lynn—Fortune Personnel Consultants of
  Huntsville, Inc.
Lamb, Sharon—Alpine Consulting Group
Lambert, Craig—BioQuest Inc. (R)
Lambert, David H.—Garofolo, Curtiss, Lambert &
  MacLean (R)
Lambert, Erwin—Lambert & Sullivan Assoc.
Lambrecht, Pat—Lam Assoc.
Lamm, Thomas—Alan Lerner Assoc.
Lampl, Joni—Management Recruiters
Lampl, Richard—Management Recruiters
Lancaster, Raymond F.—Lancaster Assoc., Inc.
Lance, Alice R.—Executive Quest (R)
Lance, David—Executive Quest (R)
Lanctot, Bill—Corporate Resources Professional
  Placement
Landau, Bill—Don Howard Personnel
Landes, Michael S.—PCD Partners (R)
Landis, James—Sales Consultants
Landreth, Elizabeth B. H.—Whittlesey & Assoc.,
  Inc.

Lane, Andrew J.—James, Layton Int'l., Inc. (R)
Lane, Joseph F.—Personnel Advisors Int'l. Corp.
Lane, Nat—Martha Ward Assoc., Inc.
Lang, Nick—Technical Recruiting Services
Lang, Peter D.—The Bradbury Management Group (R)
Langan, Elizabeth—The Crosby Group, Inc. (R)
Lange, Sr., Jack—Lange & Assoc., Inc.
Lange, Jim—Lange & Assoc., Inc.
Langer, Joel A.—Langer Assoc., Inc. (R)
Langerud, Deanna—Management Recruiters
Langford, Robert W.—Fortune Personnel Consultants of Huntsville, Inc.
Langlois, Robert L.—Langlois & Assoc.
Langstaff, E. Kennedy—Ward Howell Int'l. Inc. (R)
Lankenau, Gene—L & K Assoc.
Lansing, Margot S.—Auerbach Assoc. (R)
Lansky, Loren—Lansky Assoc. (R)
Lantis, Cindy—Venture Resources, Inc. (R)
Lanzi, Vince—Lanzi & Assoc.
Lapham, Lawrence L.—Lawrence L. Lapham, Inc. (R)
Lappe, Kristi—Lappe & Assoc.
Lappe, Mark—Lappe & Assoc.
Lara, Dolores—Hemingway Personnel, Inc.
Larkin, Dick—Larkin & Co. (R)
Larkin Jonassen, James—Kravitz * Larkin * Silver Assoc.
Larsen, C. Lars—The Personnel Network, Inc.
Larsen, Charles L.—The Personnel Network, Inc.
Larsen, Jack B.—Jack B. Larsen & Assoc.
Larsen, James K.—The Personnel Network, Inc.
Larsen, Mary E.—Career Logic, Inc.
Larsen, Merlyne T.—The Personnel Network, Inc.
Larsen, Richard F.—Mitchell, Larsen & Zilliacus (R)
Larsen, Robert H.—R.H. Larsen & Assoc., Inc.
Larson, Bruce—Nelson-Larson & Assoc. Ltd.
Larson, Paul W.—Larson & Stephanian (R)
Larson, Ray—Larson Assoc.
Lasher, Charles M.—Lasher Assoc. (R)
Lasse, Daniel C.—Management Recrutiers
Laster, Douglas—Sanford Rose Assoc.
Latas, Michael—Michael Latas & Assoc., Inc. (R)
Latas, Richard—Michael Latas & Assoc., Inc. (R)
Latimer, Dick—Technical Recruiting Consultants
Latterell, Jeffrey D.—Hoskins, Rees & Smith
Laubitz, Christopher J.—The Caldwell Partners Int'l. (R)
Lauchiere, Linda—W.N. Garbarini & Assoc. (R)

Lauer, Peter H.—Lauer Consulting Services, Inc. (R)
Lauer, Therese A.—Lauer Consulting Services, Inc. (R)
Lauerman, Fred J.—Development Search Specialists (R)
Laughlin, Alexander M.—Denney & Co., Inc. (R)
Lavender, Steven M.—Morgan/Webber (R)
Lavoie, Leo R.—Carter, Lavoie Assocs.
Lawler, Tim—Management Recruiters
Lawler, Tim—Sales Consultants
Lawrence, J. Robert—Lawrence-Balakonis & Assoc., Inc.
Lawrence, James B.—The Hamilton Group (R)
Lawry, William R.—W.R. Lawry, Inc.
Lawson, James W.—The Lawson Group
Lawson, Ron S.—Management Recruiters
Lawson, Trina R.—Search Assoc., Inc.
Lawson-Niezgocki, Debra—Management Recruiters
Layton, Barbara—Bradford & Galt, Inc.
Layton, Bernard L.—James, Layton Int'l., Inc. (R)
Layton, Bradford—Bradford & Galt, Inc.
Lazaro, Alicia C.—The Whitney Group (R)
LeBlanc, Randolph A.—Sanford Rose Assoc.
LeBoeuf, Bill—Physicians Search Assoc. Agency, Inc.
LeClaire, Beth—Accountants On Call
LeMay, Steven E.—Saber Consultants, Inc. (R)
Leavee, Kenneth S.—The Alice-Groves Co., Inc.
Leavee, Raymond J.—The Alice-Groves Co., Inc.
Lebovits, Neil—Accountants On Call
Lebow, Allan J.—RHS Assoc., Inc.
Lebus, Reynolds—Reynolds Lebus Assoc.
Lechner, David B.—Management Recruiters
Lechner, David B.—Lechner & Assoc., Inc.
Ledterman, John M.—Professional Team Search
Lee, Albert G.—Lee Associates
Lee, Barbara—Lee Management Group Inc.
Lee, Brian—Vincent Lee Assoc.
Lee, Conrad P.—The Curtiss Group, Inc. (R)
Lee, Jess J.—Management Search Int'l.
Lee, Jospeh J.—Larsen & Lee, Inc. (R)
Lee, Kenneth D.—The Regis Group, Ltd. (R)
Lee, Roger A.—Montgomery Resources, Inc.
Lee, Tamara J.—Gregory Michaels & Assoc., Inc.
Lee, Vincent—Vincent Lee Assoc.
Leedy, Don—Sanford Rose Assoc.
Leety, Murray—Fox-Morris Assoc., Inc.
Lefebure, Pierre—Phillips Group of Companies (R)
Leffer, Gary—Remark Assoc. Inc.

Leggee, Brian—Brian Leggee & Assoc.

Lego, David—Management Recruiters

Leierzapf, James—Integrated Professional Services, Inc.

Leighton, Alan—Cole Human Resource Services (R)

Leinow, Leonard—The Goodman Group

Lelek, David—Precise Legal, Inc.

Lemke, Peter K.—EFL Assoc. (R)

Lemon, Kay—Management Recruiters

Lengeling, Renee A.—William J. Elam & Assoc. (R)

Lenkaitis, Lewis F.—Kearney Executive Search (R)

Lennon, Finian I.—Edwin Mruk & Partners (R)

Lentes, Mike—The Lawson Group

Leofsky, Peter J.—Dapexs Consultants, Inc.

Leonard, Kevin J.—Dynamic Search Systems, Inc.

Leonard, Linda—Harris Heery & Assoc., Inc. (R)

Leone, Evylon—Dussick Management Assoc.

Leone, Pamela S.—Lee Calhoon & Co., Inc. (R)

Leonhart, Lee—O'Rourke Co., Inc. (R)

Leotsakos, Anastasia—Russillo/Gardner

Lerner, Alan—Alan Lerner Assoc.

Lerner, Paula—Setford-Shaw-Najarian Assoc., Ltd.

Lesama, Luis—Conrey Interamericana (R)

Lesher, John—Korn/Ferry Int'l. (R)

Leskin, Carole—Accountants On Call

Lessner, Jack—J. E. Lessner Assoc., Inc. (R)

Lessner, Mary Ann—J. E. Lessner Assoc., Inc. (R)

Leubert, Ann—Barton Sans Int'l. (R)

Levasseur, Marc—Gilles Tremblay & Assoc. (R)

Levin, Becky—Levin & Assoc. (R)

Levine, Alan M.—MB Inc.

Levine, Dawn—Baker Scott & Co.

Levine, Fern—The Cambridge Group Ltd.

Levine, Howard S.—Montaigne Assoc., Inc.

Levine, Joan C.—Olaf S. Meyer & Co., Ltd.

Levine, Martin R.—Earley Kielty & Assoc., Inc. (R)

Levitt, Bob—Sales Consultants

Levitt, Muriel—D.S. Allen Assoc.

Levy, Rita G.—RGL Assoc., Inc.

Levy, Stefan—Management Search, Inc.

Levy, William M.—Sherbrooke Assoc., Inc. (R)

Lew, Charles E.—Coleman Lew & Assoc., Inc. (R)

Lewis, Daphne—Howe-Lewis Int'l. (R)

Lewis, E. Theodore—The Stevenson Group/SES (R)

Lewis, John—Management Recruiters

Lewis, John—Sales Consultants

Lewis, K. Jane—Selected Executives, Inc.

Lewis, Lynn—A. Davis Grant & Co. (R)

Lewis, Marc D.—Handy HRM (R)

Lewis, Morris—Dillard Executive Search of Toledo

Lewke, Reynold H.—Egon Zehnder Int'l. Inc. (R)

Leyden, Terry—Career Marketing Assoc.

Libes, Dory—Accountants On Call

Libes, Mark S.—Accountants On Call

Libes, Stewart C.—Accountants On Call

Liccardi, Rose—Delta Personnel Services

Lichtenauer, William E.—Britt Assoc., Inc.

Lichtenstein, Ben—Alexander Ross Inc. (R)

Lichtenstein, Georgina—Picard & Co., Inc. (R)

Liebelt, Albert J.—Ward Liebelt Assoc. Inc. (R)

Lieberman, Beverly—Halbrecht Lieberman Assoc., Inc. (R)

Lieberman, Carole S.—The Lieberman Group (R)

Liebesny, Claudia B.—Human Resource Research Inc. (R)

Liebstein, Bennett—Sanford Rose Assoc.

Liggett, Wilson M.—Michael/Merrill

Light, Paul—Ward Howell Int'l. Inc. (R)

Ligon, T. Paul—Paul Ligon Co.

Liles, J.D.—Management Recruiters

Lincoln, Jennifer—Lawrence Executive Search, Ltd.

Lincoln, Kraig—Luke, Lincoln, & Brugger

Lincoln, Thomas C.—Oppedisano & Co., Inc. (R)

Lindal, Bruce G.—Sanford Rose Assoc.

Linde, Richard E.—The Ogdon Partnership (R)

Linde, Roger W.—Graphic Search Assoc. Inc.

Lindholst, Kai—Egon Zehnder Int'l. Inc. (R)

Lindner, Ronald J.—Annapolis Consulting Group (R)

Lindquist, J. Kent—Sanford Rose Assoc. of Hartford

Lindquist, Sheryl—Personnel Assoc. (R)

Lindsay, M. Evan—SpencerStuart (R)

Lindsey, Ginger—M/ARS

Lindsey, Lary L.—Lindsey & Assoc., Inc.

Lineal, Lisa—Lineal Recruiting Services

Lineback, Robert—Management Recruiters

Lineback, Robert—Management Recruiters

Lineback, Robert S.—Management Recruiters

Link, Art—Link Personnel & Assoc.

Link, Sue—Link Personnel & Assoc.

Linneman, Robert M.—Whittlesey & Assoc., Inc.

Linton, Leonard M.—Byron Leonard Int'l., Inc. (R)

Linton, Linda—Hartman, Barnette & Assoc. (R)

Lipe, Jerold L.—Compass Group Ltd. (R)

Lippincott, Kirk Alan—Jeff Rich Assoc.

Lynch, III, John P.—Blackshaw, Olmstead & Atwood (R)

Lynch, John W.—Lynch & Co. (R)

Lynch, Michael C.—Lynch Miller Moore, Inc. (R)

Lynch, Patrick J.—P.J. Lynch Assoc. (R)

Lynch, Theodore P.—Lynch & Co. (R)

Lyness, Cindy—Management Recruiters of Cedar Rapids, Inc.

Lynge, R.J.—Management Recruiters of Ft. Myers, FL.

Lyngen, Robert—D.E. Foster & Partners, L.P. (R)

Lynn, Audrey—Latham Int'l., Ltd.

Lyons, Barbara—Whittlesey & Assoc., Inc.

Lyons, Denis B.K.—SpencerStuart (R)

Lyons, James C.—The PAR Group - Paul A. Reaume, Ltd. (R)

Lyons, Kent T.—Lyons & Assoc., Inc.

Lyons, M. Don—L O R Personnel Div. (R)

Lysenko, Lisa—A.L.S. Group

Lysenko, Scott—A.L.S. Group

MacCallan, Deirdre—Butterfass/Pepe Assoc., Inc. (R)

MacDonald, Alan—Alan MacDonald & Assoc.

MacGregor, Angus Putgorney—Robert Campbell & Assoc. (R)

MacGregor, Malcolm—Boyden Int'l., Inc. (R)

MacKenzie, William D.—RG International (R)

MacLean, Burton A.—Garofolo, Curtiss, Lambert & MacLean (R)

Macaluso, Bob—Source EDP

Macdonald, G. William—The Macdonald Group, Inc. (R)

Machi, Mike—Management Recruiters

Mackenzie, Robert A.—Management Recruiters

Macurda, Bradford—The Energists

Madden, Francis J.—Ward Howell Int'l. Inc. (R)

Maddin, Leslie—SpencerStuart (R)

Madigan, Robert M.—Robert Madigan Assoc., Inc. (R)

Mady, Johan—Egon Zehnder Int'l., Inc. (R)

Mae, Bonita—Trilogy Enterprises, Inc.

Magarity, Susan—W. Robert Eissler & Assoc., Inc.

Magee, Harrison R.—Bowden & Co., Inc. (R)

Maglio, Charles J.—Maglio & Co., Inc. (R)

Maglio, Dick—R.J. Maglio & Assoc., Inc. (R)

Magnani, Susan M.—The Search Center Inc.

Magnusen, Henry F.—Management Recruiters

Magrath, Robert H.—Ross Personnel Consultants, Inc.

Maher, Peter T.—Deven Assoc., Int'l., Inc. (R)

Maher, William—Johnson Smith & Knisely Inc. (R)

Mahon, Tom—Tom Mahon & Assoc.

Mahony, Charles F.—Mahony & Assoc., Ltd.

Main, Bart L.—The Winchester Group (R)

Maiorino, Robert V.—Maiorino & Weston Assoc., Inc. (R)

Major, Jr., Robert A.—Major, Wilson & Africa

Makrianes, Jr., James K.—Ward Howell Int'l. Inc. (R)

Malcom, John W.—Johnson Smith & Knisely Inc. (R)

Malfetti, Jim—Management Recruiters

Malfetti, Rosemary—Management Recruiters

Malin, Roger—Agra Placements, Ltd.

Mallon III, Hugh A.—Walter V. Connor Int'l., Inc. (R)

Malone, George V.—Boyden Int'l., Inc. (R)

Malone, Mark—Source EDP

Malone, Tom—Management Recruiters

Maltby, Thomas J.—Halbrecht & Co.

Maly, Anna Mae—Maly & Assoc. (R)

Mamikonian, Steve—Benton Schneider & Assoc. (R)

Manassero, Henri J.P.—International Management Advisors, Inc. (R)

Mancini, Jennifer—Maschal/Connors Inc. (R)

Mancino, Gene—Blau Kaptain Schroeder (R)

Mandicott, Frank—Traynor Confidential, Ltd.

Mandrell, Bob—Robert Sage Recruiting

Mangum, Maria—Thomas Mangum Co. (R)

Mangum, William T.—Thomas Mangum Co. (R)

Mannix, Francis L.—F. L. Mannix & Co., Inc. (R)

Manthey, Merv—Peat Marwick Stevenson & Kellogg (R)

Manuso, James—The Neil Michael Group, Inc. (R)

Marantz, Gail—Industry Consultants, Inc.

Marcus, Alvin B.—Marcus & Assoc.

Marentez, Frank—W. Robert Eissler & Assoc., Inc.

Margolin, Efraim—Margolin Consultants, Inc.

Margolis, Arlene M.—Universal Executive Search, Inc. (R)

Mariaschin, Mark A.—Mariaschin & Co.

Marino, Jory J.—Sullivan & Co. (R)

Marion, Bradford B.—The Furst Group

Mark, John L.—Hauft Mark Assoc., Inc. (R)

Markman, Stephen—Pencom Systems Inc.

Marks, Brad—Brad Marks Int'l. (R)

Marks, David—Daniel Stern & Assoc.

Marks, Ira M.—Strategic Alternatives (R)

Marks, Marjorie J.—Gilbert Tweed Assoc., Inc. (R)

Marks, Paula—Alexander Ross Inc. (R)

Marks, Jr., Russell—Webb, Johnson & Klemmer, Inc. (R)

Marks, Sharon—Marks & Co., Inc. (R)

Marling, Richard A.—Marling Inc. (R)

Marlow, Bill—Straube Assoc., Inc. (R)

Marmur, Michael J.—Weir Executive Search Assoc., Inc. (R)

Marra, Jr., John V.—Marra/Pizzi Assoc., Inc. (R)

Marriott, Gloria A.—Management Recruiters

Marriott, Roger H.—Management Recruiters

Marroquin, Josue P.—RZL Y Asociados, S.C. (R)

Marsh, Barry B.—Management Recruiters

Marsh, Skip—Wesson, Taylor, Wells & Assoc.

Marshall, Deborah—Chicago Research Group, Inc. (R)

Marshall, Dennis—Karen Marshall Assoc.

Marshall, Glenn—Hartman Personnel Services

Marshall, John—Accountants On Call

Marshall, John C.—JM & Co. (R)

Marshall, John L.—ExecuSource Int'l.

Marshall, Karen—Karen Marshall Assoc.

Marshall, Larry—Marshall Consultants, Inc. (R)

Marshall, Stephen G.—Management Recruiters

Martens, Maxine—Rene Plessner Assoc., Inc. (R)

Martens, Randall—Impact Executive Search, Inc.

Marth, David L.—Management Recruiters

Marth, David L.—Sales Consultants

Marticelli, Eileen—Datamax Services Inc.

Martin, Bob—The LaBorde Group

Martin, C. Robert—C.R. Martin & Assoc. (R)

Martin, Donovan—Donovan Martin & Assoc.

Martin, George R.—George R. Martin (R)

Martin, Henry—Raines Int'l. Inc. (R)

Martin, Jean M.—The Ultimate Source (R)

Martin, Jennifer—Latham Int'l., Ltd.

Martin, Judy R.—J. Martin & Assoc. (R)

Martin, Lois G.—The Martin Group (R)

Martin, Lynne Koll—Boyden Int'l., Inc. (R)

Martin, Peter—Sales Consultants

Martin, Rande—Management Recruiters

Martin, Robert—SRH Resource Group (R)

Martin, Robert F.—Martin Mirtz Morice, Inc. (R)

Martin, Stacey—Source EDP

Martin, Suzanne S.—Selected Executives, Inc.

Martin, Ted—Nordeman Grimm, Inc. (R)

Martin, Timothy P.—The Martin Group (R)

Martinez, Stephen A.—Stephens Assoc. Ltd. (R)

Marting, Leeda P.—Boyden World Corp. (R)

Martinolich, Michael—Martin H. Bauman Assoc., Inc. (R)

Martwick, Gail—Cascadia Group Int'l. (R)

Marty, Dick—ExecuCounsel Management Consultants Inc. (R)

Martyniak, Michael—Fortune Personnel Consultants of Huntsville, Inc.

Marumoto, William H.—The Interface Group, Ltd. (R)

Maschal, Chuck—Maschal/Connors Inc. (R)

Mashack, Theodore M.—Management Recruiters

Maslan, Neal L.—Ward Howell Int'l. Inc. (R)

Mason, Eileen—Management Recruiters

Masquelier, Sibyl—Executive Resource Group (R)

Massar, Joy V.—Egan & Assoc. (R)

Masse, Laurence R.—Ward Howell Int'l. Inc. (R)

Masserman, Bruce—Masserman & Assoc.

Massey, Jr., Harold—W.L. Handler & Assoc. (R)

Massey, R. Bruce—Bruce Massey & Partners Inc. (R)

Masson, Thomas E.—TEMCO - The Executive Mgmt. Cons. Org. (R)

Mater, Jr., Robert F.—Sales Consultants

Mather, Charles F.—Cibotti Assoc., Inc.

Mather, Richard L.—Richard L. Mather & Assoc.

Matheson, Robert—Merlin Int'l. Inc.

Mathey, Joyce—Mathey Services

Matson, Steve—Daniel Stern & Assoc.

Matte, Norman E.—Matte & Company, Inc. (R)

Matthews, Charles W.—Matthews Professional Employment Specialists, Inc.

Matthews, Mary E.—Bishop Assoc. (R)

Mattingly, Kathy—Source EDP

Mattran, Donald A.—Sales Consultants

Mattson, Gayle L.—Gayle L. Mattson & Assoc. (R)

Maxin, Keith A.—K. Maxin & Assoc.

Maxwell, Patricia—Datamax Services Inc.

May, Don—Allied Search, Inc.

May, Michael—Kendall & Davis Co., Inc.

May, Peter—Management Recruiters

May, Richard D.—Bob Westerfield & Assoc., Inc.

Mayer, David—Accountants On Call

Mayer, Mary L.—Mary L. Mayer, Ltd.

Mayer, Robert A.—Lauer, Sbarbaro Assoc., Inc. (R)

Mayes, Abby—Lee Calhoon & Co., Inc. (R)

Mazurek, A.C. Budd—Sales Consultants

Mazza, David B.—Mazza & Riley, Inc. (R)

Mazzeo, Jim—Source EDP

Mazzitelli, Teresa—The Mazzitelli Group, Ltd. (R)

McAlister, W. Juan—Excelsior Services Group Inc. (R)

McAlpine, Bruce—Keith Bagg Personnel Ltd.

McAteer, Thomas K.—Montgomery Resources, Inc.
McAulay, Jr., A.L.—Robison & McAulay (R)
McAvoy, Edward P.—Romano McAvoy Assoc., Inc.
McBride, Dee—Deeco Int'l.
McBride, Jonathan E.—McBride Assoc., Inc. (R)
McBurney, Kevin R.—The Caldwell Partners Int'l. (R)
McCabe, Tara—Lee Calhoon & Co., Inc. (R)
McCall, Judith—Sandhurst Assoc. (R)
McCallister, Richard A.—Boyden Int'l., Inc. (R)
McCallum, Reta—Integrated Professional Services, Inc.
McCandless, Hugh—Marshall Consultants, Inc. (R)
McCann, III, Joseph E.—Egon Zehnder Int'l. Inc. (R)
McCann, III, Joseph H.—The Whitney Group (R)
McCarthy, David R.—SpencerStuart (R)
McCarthy, Dennis—Sales Consultants
McCarthy, Frank X.—Xavier Assoc., Inc.
McCarthy III, Richard—Romac & Assoc., Inc.
McClimans, Robert M.—The NRI Group
McClintock, Vivian—Pro Travel Personnel
McCloskey, Karen—Lee Calhoon & Co., Inc. (R)
McCollough, Kathleen—Dunhill Personnel System, Inc.
McCollum, Ken—Management Recruiters
McConnell, Daniel P.—MCC Assoc. (R)
McCooe, John J.—McCooe & Assoc., Inc. (R)
McCooe, Sean J.—McCooe & Assoc., Inc. (R)
McCord, Stephen A.—Olaf S. Meyer & Co., Ltd.
McCormack, Joseph A.—McCormack & Farrow (R)
McCormick, William J.—The McCormick Group, Inc.
McCoy, Horacio—Korn/Ferry Int'l. (R)
McCoy, Horacio—Korn/Ferry, Int'l., S.A. de C.V. (R)
McCoy, Millington F.—Gould & McCoy, Inc. (R)
McCracken, Larry K.—McCracken, Wilcox, Bertoux & Miller
McCrea, Joan I.—Nursing Technomics (R)
McCrystal, J. Robert—Donald P. Hayes Assoc., Inc.
McCulloch, William A.—McCulloch Assoc.
McCullough, Joe—Management Recruiters
McCullough, Kenneth D.—McCullough Assoc. (R)
McDaniel, J. Peyton—Management Recruiters
McDaniel, J. Peyton—Sales Consultants
McDannel, Marilyn—Southwest Search Inc.
McDermid, Earl—Chase Waterford Ltd.

McDermid, Earl—Earl L. McDermid & Assoc.
McDermott, Tom—McDermott & Assoc.
McDermott, Tom—Corporate Environment Ltd. (R)
McDonald, Edwin C.—McDonald/Long Assoc., Inc. (R)
McDonald, John R.—McDonald Ledterman Executive Search
McDonald, Louise—Real Estate Executive Search, Inc.
McDonald, Pamela G.—Gleason & Assoc. (R)
McDonald, Paul—Robert Half Int'l.
McDonald, Polly—TeleSearch, Inc.
McDonald, Sandi—Sandi McDonald & Assoc., Inc.
McDonald, Scott A.—McDonald Assoc. (R)
McDonald, Stanleigh B.—McDonald Assoc. (R)
McDonald, Thomas W.—Mengel & McDonald Ltd.
McDowell, Sally A.—Schuyler, Frye & Baker, Inc. (R)
McElhaney, Jr., Ron—Management Recruiters of Savannah
McElhaney, Ron—Management Recruiters of Savannah
McElhearn, Scott S.—Scott Sibley Assoc.
McElmeel, Joseph J.—Brooke Chase Assoc., Inc.
McEwan, Jr., Paul—Loewenstein & Assoc.
McFadden, George—The Abbott Group (R)
McFadzean, James A.—Holland, McFadzean & Assoc., Inc. (R)
McFarland, Richard M.—Brissenden, McFarland, Wagoner & Fuccella, Inc. (R)
McFaul, William—Management Assoc.
McFeely, Clarence E.—McFeely Wackerle Shulman (R)
McGavern, David O.—The Yorkshire Group, Ltd. (R)
McGee, Ronald J.—The Garrison Group
McGeehan, Thomas—Tierney Assoc., Inc. (R)
McGinnis, A. Ashley—Kirby & Assoc. (R)
McGinnis, W. John—Earl L. McDermid & Assoc.
McGovern, Ed—Alexander Edward Assoc., Inc.
McGovern, Sheila M.—Kiley-Owen Assoc., Inc.
McGrath, Robert E.—Robert E. McGrath & Assoc. (R)
McGuire, Harry—McGuire Executive Search, Inc.
McGuire, John—Robert Sage Recruiting
McIlwaine, Roy H.—R. H. McIlwaine & Assoc.
McInerney, Ellen—Claveloux, McCaffrey, McInerney, Inc. (R)
McInturff, Jr., Robert E.—McInturff & Assoc., Inc.

Methven, W. Allan—Peat Marwick Stevenson & Kellogg (R)

Metz, Alex—Hunt Ltd.

Metzger, Norman—Martin H. Meisel Assoc., Inc. (R)

Metzner, Harris—Ethan Allen Personnel, Inc.

Meyer, Fred R.—Management Recruiters

Meyer, Olaf S.—Olaf S. Meyer & Co., Ltd.

Meyer, Paul R.—Prior Martech Assoc. (R)

Meyer, Tom—CCI - Career Consultants Int'l.

Meyer, Verne—Delacore Personnel

Meyerhoff, Richard—Tanzi Executive Search

Meyers, Barry—The Consortium

Meyers, Maurice R.—Management Recruiters

Michaelis, Paul—Heidrick and Struggles, Inc. (R)

Michaels, Edward M.—Joseph Keyes Assoc.

Michaels, Kenneth—K. L. Whitney & Co., Inc. (R)

Michaels, Lou—Lou Michaels Assoc.

Michaels, Stewart—Topaz Int'l., Inc.

Mickey, B. Paul—B. Paul Mickey & Assoc.

Middlebrook, C. Jay—Sales Consultants of Austin, Inc.

Middlebrook, Linda—Sales Consultants of Austin, Inc.

Middleton, Alfred—The Neil Michael Group, Inc. (R)

Middleton, Skip—Management Recruiters

Mider, Jerry E.—Personnel Advisors Int'l. Corp.

Midgette, Earl W.—Midgette Consultants, Inc.

Mikula, Linda—Mercedes & Co., Inc. (R)

Milar, John—Sanford Rose Assoc.

Miles, Bill—Strategic Assoc., Inc.

Miles, Ruth—Bader Research Corp.

Miles, Shelly—John R. Ady & Assoc., Inc.

Milgram, David—Milgram & Assoc.

Milius, Gregg A.—Management Recruiters

Milius, Kent L.—Management Recruiters

Miller, Arnie—Isaacson, Miller, Inc. (R)

Miller, Dee—Eggers Consulting Co., Inc.

Miller, Diane—McCracken, Wilcox, Bertoux & Miller

Miller, Gary L.—Sales Consultants

Miller, George M.—Christopher-Patrick & Assoc. (R)

Miller, Irene M.—Human Resource Research Inc. (R)

Miller, Joanna B.—R. H. Horton Int'l. (R)

Miller, Jon P.—Walter V. Connor Int'l., Inc. (R)

Miller, Kathleen M.—Dieckmann & Assoc., Ltd. (R)

Miller, Kenneth—Computer Network Resources

Miller, Leslie—Lawrence Executive Search, Ltd.

Miller, Marlene—Management Recruiters of Cedar Rapids, Inc.

Miller, Michael R.—Lynch Miller Moore, Inc. (R)

Miller, Ross—Video Interview Professionals, Inc.

Miller, Roy—George Enns Partners Inc. (R)

Miller, Russell E.—ARJay & Assoc.

Miller, Ph.D., Stephen J.—Compass Group Ltd. (R)

Miller, Thomas C.—Health Technology, Inc.

Millet, Blaine—Source EDP

Million, Ken—Million & Assoc., Inc. (R)

Millonzi, M.D., Joel—Johnson Smith & Knisely Inc. (R)

Mills, Kirby—W. Robert Eissler & Assoc., Inc.

Mills, Robert E.—Robert E. Mills, FLMI

Milnes, Louise M.—Munroe, Curry & Bond Assoc. (R)

Mindlin, Freda—Johnson Smith & Knisely Inc. (R)

Miners, Richard A.—The Goodrich & Sherwood Co. (R)

Mines, Herbert—Herbert Mines Assoc., Inc. (R)

Mingle, Larry D.—Higdon, Joys & Mingle, Inc. (R)

Minkin, Mel—Alan MacDonald & Assoc.

Minko, Dolores I.—Management Recruiters

Minko, Philip P.—Management Recruiters

Mirro, Linda—Sales Consultants

Mirtz, P. John—Martin Mirtz Morice, Inc. (R)

Mitchell, Doug—Sales Consultants

Mitchell, E. Thomas—Andcor Human Resources (R)

Mitchell, Jack—Romac & Assoc., Inc.

Mitchell, Jr., John E.—Romac & Assoc. of Dallas

Mitchell, Jr., John R.—Management Recruiters

Mitchell, Kyle—Tanton/Mitchell Group (R)

Mitchell, Michael—Jay Mitchell & Co. (R)

Mitchell, Norman F.—Kearney Executive Search (R)

Mitchell, Sue—M/J/A Partners (R)

Mitchell, Thomas M.—Heidrick and Struggles, Inc. (R)

Mitton, William H.—Executive Resource Inc.

Mockler, Nadine—Part Time Resources

Moeller, Ed—Management Recruiters

Moeller, Edward J.—Sales Consultants

Mogul, Gene—Mogul Consultants, Inc.

Mohan, Jack—Management Recruiters

Mohan, Jack—Management Recruiters

Mojekwu, Gene—American Resources Corp.

Mollison, Karen—Deeco Int'l.

Molliver, Marshall E.—Sanford Rose assoc.

Mollo, George J.—George J. Mollo Assoc.

Molnar, Robert A.—Tech Vision Co.

Monaco, Joseph R.—The Foster McKay Group

Monahan, Edward—Engineering & Scientific Search Assoc.

Montagna, Christine—Gary Kaplan & Assoc. (R)

Montanye, Michael—The Montanye Group

Monte, Linda—Vincent Lee Assoc.

Montgomery, James—Houze, Shourds & Montgomery, Inc. (R)

Montgomery, John—GKR Int'l. (R)

Montgomery, William S.—Russell, Montgomery & Assoc. (R)

Montigny, Paul F.—Management Recruiters

Montville, Bruce A.—EXETER 2100

Monych, Bonnie—Goss & Assoc., Inc. (R)

Mooney, Bryan E.—Babson, Moore & Wilcox (R)

Moore, Anne—Peat Marwick Stevenson & Kellogg (R)

Moore, Bob—Computer Recruiters, Inc.

Moore, Brad—Eggers Consulting Co., Inc.

Moore, David S.—Lynch Miller Moore, Inc. (R)

Moore, Ellie—Moore Employment Svs., Inc.

Moore, John—Babson, Moore & Wilcox (R)

Moore, Lynn—Management Recruiters

Moore, Lynn W.—Management Recruiters

Moore, Ph.D., Mark H.—Wheeler, Moore & Elam Co. (R)

Moore, Thomas R.—Thomas R. Moore Executive Search (R)

Moore, Tom—Moore Employment Svs., Inc.

Moore, Vickie—The Abbott Group (R)

Moore, W. J.—The Hawkins Co. (R)

Moorhead, W. Allen—Canny, Bowen Inc. (R)

Moran, Dennis F.—Atlantic Search Group, Inc.

Moran, Thomas J.—Kennedy & Co. (R)

Morbitzer, Tina—Tina Morbitzer & Assoc.

Morency, Marcia—Morency Assoc.

Morgan, David G.—Morgan-Stampfl, Inc.

Morgan, J. David—Ward Howell Int'l. Inc. (R)

Morgan, Tom—Pencom Systems Inc.

Morgan, Vincent S.—Johnson Smith & Knisely Inc. (R)

Moriarty, Philip S.J.—Moriarty/Fox, Inc. (R)

Morice, James L.—Martin Mirtz Morice, Inc. (R)

Morin, Joyce—Management Recruiters

Morin, Phil—Management Recruiters

Morin-Tutsch, Camille—Phillips Group of Companies (R)

Morris, Daniel A.—Sales Consultants of Fayetteville, AR.

Morris, David A.—Russell Reynolds Assoc., Inc. (R)

Morris, David W.—WTW Assoc., Inc. (R)

Morris, Gayleen—Accountants On Call

Morris, Kristine A.—Morris & Berger (R)

Morris, Leonard—Specialized Search Assoc.

Morris, Paul T.—The Morris Group

Morris, Robert J.—Dunhill Personnel Search

Morrison, Anne—Development Resource Group

Morrison, Bob—Sales Consultants

Morrison, Janis—Garrett Assoc. Inc.

Morse, James A.—Sales Consultants

Morse, Mary K.—J. Robert Scott (R)

Morse, Stephen W.—Management Recruiters

Morse, Stephen W.—Management Recruiters

Mortimer, David M.—Management Recruiters

Morton, Michael J.—Ludot Personnel Services, Inc.

Morton, R. C.—R.C. Morton & Assoc. Inc. (R)

Moses, Brad—Information Systems Professionals

Moses, Diane—Information Systems Professionals

Moses, Jerry—J.M. Eagle Partners

Moss, Kenneth L.—Executive Appointments Ltd., Int'l. (R)

Mruk, Edwin S.—Edwin Mruk & Partners (R)

Muck, Jerry—Staffing Consultants

Mueller, Clifford B.—The C. B. Mueller Co., Inc.

Mueller, Howard C.—mfg/Search, Inc.

Mueller, Michael S.—Corporate Recruiters, Inc.

Mueller, Paul M.—Paul Mueller & Assoc., Inc. (R)

Mueller-Maerki, Fortunat F.—Egon Zehnder Int'l. Inc. (R)

Muendel, H. Edward—Marlar Int'l. Inc. (R)

Mulberger, Robert D.—The NRI Group

Mulcahey, Bob—Management Recruiters

Muller, Jr., John A.—John Anthony & Assoc.

Mulligan, C.L.—Sales & Management Search, Inc.

Mulligan, Margaret B.—James, Layton Int'l., Inc. (R)

Mulligan, Robert P.—William Willis Worldwide, Inc. (R)

Mulshine, Michael A.—The Mulshine Co., Inc. (R)

Mulshine, Michael G.—The Mulshine Co., Inc. (R)

Mulvaney, James M.—Sanford Rose Assoc. - Virginia Beach

Mulvaney, Ronald F.—R. F. Mulvaney & Assoc., Inc. (R)

Mulvey, John J.—The Mulvey Group

Mummert, Dennis D.—Sweeney Shepherd Bueschel Provus Harbert & Mummert, Inc. (R)

Munding, Cheryl–Pro Travel Personnel
Munger, Donald–Technical Staffing Assoc.
Munn, Bill–RHS Assoc., Inc.
Munoz, Vicki–DeHayes Consulting Group (R)
Munson, Craig D.–Bennett-Munson Inc.
Munson, John H.–John H. Munson & Co.
Munson, Marie O.–Bennett-Munson Inc.
Murkett, Jr., Philip T.–Murkett Assoc.
Murnane, Harold–Graham & Co. (R)
Murphey, James F.–Management Recruiters
Murphey, James F.–Sales Consultants
Murphy, Arthur E.–K. W. Tunnell Co., Inc. (R)
Murphy, Barbara–Chandler & Rozner Assoc. (R)
Murphy, Bob–Coopers & Lybrand, Management
  Consulting Services (R)
Murphy, Cornelius J.–The Goodrich & Sherwood
  Co. (R)
Murphy, Gary J.–Stone, Murphy & Olson (R)
Murphy, Lisa–Bialla & Assoc., Inc. (R)
Murphy, Marsha–Michael Tucker Assoc. (R)
Murphy, Patrick J.–P. J. Murphy & Assoc., Inc.
  (R)
Murphy, Paul–Fox-Morris Assoc., Inc.
Murphy, Paul–Fox-Morris Assoc., Inc.
Murphy, Peter–David Chambers & Assoc., Inc.
  (R)
Murphy, R. Blair–Sullivan-Murphy Assoc. (R)
Murphy, Robert–Robert Murphy Assoc. (R)
Murphy, Trish–Source EDP
Murray, John–Robert Murphy Assoc. (R)
Murray, Mike–Management Recruiters
Murray, Patrick–J. H. Dugan & Assoc., Inc.
Murrell, James O.–Professionals in Recruiting
  Co.
Murrell, Maxine W.–Professionals in Recruiting
  Co.
Myatt, Jr., James S.–Sanford Rose Assoc. - Santa
  Barbara
Myer, Paul J.–Chase Waterford Ltd.
Myers, Ed–D.P. Specialists, Inc.
Myers, Sandy–Phyllis Hawkins & Assoc.
Myers, Thomas–Career Plus Executive Search (R)
Nachman, Philip S.–Nachman Biomedical
Nadherny, Christopher C.–SpencerStuart (R)
Nadherny, F.–Russell Reynolds Assoc., Inc. (R)
Nadherny, Pete–The Angus Group, Inc.
Nadzam, Richard J.–Nadzam, Lusk & Assoc.,
  Inc. (R)
Naff, Bud–Management Recruiters
Nagel, Conrad A.–Nagel Executive Search Inc.
Nagel, Jacqueline–C.W. Brandon & Assoc., Inc.
Nagel, Jerome H.–Jerome H. Nagel Assoc.

Nagle, Walter M.–Barry Persky & Co., Inc. (R)
Nagler, Leon G.–Nagler & Co., Inc. (R)
Naglieri, Thomas J.–Barry Persky & Co., Inc. (R)
Nagy, Les–Source EDP
Nahas, Robert E.–Ward Howell Int'l. Inc. (R)
Najarian, Jeffrey C.–Setford-Shaw-Najarian
  Assoc., Ltd.
Napier, Ginger L.–Preng & Assoc., Inc. (R)
Naples, Len Di–Roth Young of Pittsburgh
Napolitano, James–Management Recruiters
Nassar, Richard D.–Sales Consultants
Nathanson, Barry F.–Barry Nathanson Assoc. (R)
Neal, Danton–Sales Consultants
Neal, Gregory R.–M.H. Springer & Assoc. (R)
Neece, Michael–Source Engineering
Neely, Ned–J. D. Hersey & Assoc.
Neff, Thomas J.–SpencerStuart (R)
Neidhart, Craig C.–Tuttle, Neidhart, Semyan, Inc.
  (R)
Neill, Wellden C.–Sampson, Neill & Wilkins Inc.
  (R)
Nein, Lawrence F.–Nordeman Grimm, Inc. (R)
Neitlich, Merry E.–JM Assoc.
Nelson, Barbara–Herman Smith Transearch Inc.
  (R)
Nelson, Beverly M.–Beverly Nelson & Assoc. Inc.
Nelson, Gary–Nelson Associates
Nelson, J. Fielding–J. Fielding Nelson & Assoc.,
  Inc.
Nelson, Ronald W.–Charles A. Binswanger
  Assoc., Inc.
Nemec, Tony–Source Finance
Nenstiel, Marion S.–William H. Nenstiel &
  Assoc.
Nenstiel, William H.–William H. Nenstiel &
  Assoc.
Neri, Julia–Management Recruiters
Neri, Steve D.–Empire International (R)
Neuberth, Jeffrey G.–Canny, Bowen Inc. (R)
Neuffer, R.P.–Management Recruiters of
  Westchester, Inc.
Neuffer, Robert P.–Preston Robert & Assoc.-
  Health Care Div.
Neumann, Pete–Management Recruiters
Neumann, Vicki–Management Recruiters
Newberry, Harry–Professional Medical
Newberry, Joyce–Human Resource Bureau
Newcombe, Walter W.–Newcombe & Cyr Assoc.,
  Inc.
Newell, Carlyle–Koontz, Jeffries & Assoc., Inc.
  (R)
Newell, Donald Pierce–Newell Assoc. (R)
Newman, Arthur–Lamalie Assoc., Inc. (R)

Newman, Edgar F.—K/N Int'l. (R)
Newman, Nancy—Phyllis Hawkins & Assoc.
Newman, Richard J.—Stricker & Zagor (R)
Newpher, James A.—Newpher & Co., Inc. (R)
Nicholaou, Jean—Nicholaou & Co. (R)
Nicholsen, Richard E.—C. J. Noty & Assoc. (R)
Nicholson, Constantine—Nicholson & Assoc., Inc. (R)
Nicolosi, Charles—CN Associates
Nielsen, K.E.—Sanford Rose Assoc. - Great Neck
Nielsen, K.E.—Sanford Rose Assoc. - Great Neck
Nielsen, Robert—Herbert Mines Assoc., Inc. (R)
Niemann, Barry R.—Management Recruiters
Niemond, Nancy A.—The Niemond Corp. (R)
Niemond, Wesley E.—The Niemond Corp. (R)
Ninan, Thomas K.—Careers Unlimited
Nitchke, Howard D.—Deane, Howard & Simon, Inc. (R)
Nixon, Richard—American Resources Corp.
Noble, Donald—Noble & Assoc., Inc.
Noble, Jeffrey M.—Management Recruiters
Noble, Joel L.—Management Recruiters
Nolan, Michael—Additional Technical Support Inc.
Nolan, Nancy C.—Newton Assoc.
Noll, Robert J.—The Hindman Co. (R)
Nolte, Jr., William D.—W.D. Nolte & Company (R)
Nordeman, Jacques C.—Nordeman Grimm, Inc. (R)
Norfleet, Judy—Dunhill Personnel of Northeast Tulsa, Inc.
Norlander, Mark—Sanford Rose Assoc.
Norman, Allen G.—Pursuant Legal Consultants
Norman, Paul W.—Wood/Sprau/Tannura, Inc. (R)
Norman, Shirley S.—Polson & Co., Inc. (R)
Normyle, Robert J.—Normyle/Erstling Health Search
Norquest, Mark—Robert Hess & Assoc., Inc.
Norris, Ronald—Ronald Norris & Assoc.
Norris, Sr., Rowland R.—Management Recruiters
Norsell, Paul E.—Paul Norsell & Assoc., Inc. (R)
Northup, Brent—Dunhill Personnel System, Inc.
Norton, Gregory A.—Norton & Assoc.
Norton, III, James B.—Norton & Assoc., Inc. (R)
Nosky, Richard E.—Richard E. Nosky & Assoc. (R)
Nothnagel, Marcie R.—P.A.R. Assoc., Inc. (R)
Noty, Charles—C. J. Noty & Assoc. (R)
Noyes, Jim—Sales Consultants - Bristol County
Nuessle, Warren G.—Nuessle, Kurdziel & Weiss, Inc. (R)

Nunemaker, Elizabeth G.—Legal Placements Inc.
Nunez, Iris E.—PSP Agency
Nunziata, Fred A.—Eden & Assoc., Inc.
Nye, David S.—Blake, Hansen & Nye, Ltd. (R)
Nyvall, S. L.—McKeen Melancon & Co. (R)
O'Brian, Dennis—Management Recruiters of Westchester, Inc.
O'Brien, Barbara J.—Management Recruiters
O'Brien, Denise M.—Professional Team Search
O'Brien, Mark—Loewenstein & Assoc.
O'Brien, Mike—Accounting Resources Int'l., Inc.
O'Brien, Teri—Management Resources
O'Brien, Tim—O'Brien & Co., Inc. (R)
O'Callaghan, Patrick—The Caldwell Partners Int'l. (R)
O'Callaghan, T. K.—O'Callaghan, Honey & Assoc., Inc. (R)
O'Connell, Bridget—Accountants On Call
O'Connell, Mary—C.P.S., Inc.
O'Connor, Daniel J.—International Management Advisors, Inc. (R)
O'Connor, Thomas—Marcus & Assoc.
O'Connor, Thomas F.—O'Connor, O'Connor, Lordi, Ltd. (R)
O'Daniel, James E.—Sanford Rose Assoc.
O'Donnell, James—Hedlund Corp.
O'Donnell, Timothy W.—James, Layton Int'l., Inc. (R)
O'Hara, Daniel M.—Lynch Miller Moore, Inc. (R)
O'Hara, James J.—Barone-O'Hara Assoc., Inc.
O'Hayer, Robert E.—Management Recruiters
O'Horo, Michael—The Kennett Group, Inc.
O'Keefe, Jack—John O'Keefe & Assoc., Inc. (R)
O'Keefe, John—John O'Keefe & Assoc., Inc. (R)
O'Keefe, Kathy—John O'Keefe & Assoc., Inc. (R)
O'Leary, Michael P.—Saber Consultants, Inc. (R)
O'Meally, Diane—Accountants On Call
O'Neill, James P.—Allerton Heneghan & O'Neill (R)
O'Neill, John—Strauss Personnel Service
O'Neill, John J.—Ames-O'Neill Assoc., Inc.
O'Neill, Kathleen A.—RIC Corp. (R)
O'Neill, Kevin—Fortune Personnel Consultants of Huntsville, Inc.
O'Neill, Kevin G.—Hoskins, Rees & Smith
O'Neill, Mary—The Caldwell Partners Int'l. (R)
O'Reilly, William—Management Recruiters of Cincinnati/Sharonville, Inc.
O'Rourke, Dennis M.—O'Rourke Co., Inc. (R)
O'Shea, Timothy J.—O'Shea, Divine & Co. (R)
O'Toole, Dennis P.—Dennis P. O'Toole & Assoc. Inc. (R)

O'Toole, William R.—O'Toole & Company (R)

Oakley, Mitch—Management Recruiters

Ober, Lynn W.—Ober & Company (R)

Oberlander, Howard I.—Oberlander & Co., Inc. (R)

Oberting, David D.—Management Recruiters

Oberting, David J.—Sales Consultants

Ochota, A.—DHR Int'l., Inc. (R)

Odette, Jack—RitaSue Siegel Assoc., Inc.

Ogden, Dayton—SpencerStuart (R)

Ogdon, Thomas H.—The Ogdon Partnership (R)

Okun, S. K.—American Executive Management, Inc. (R)

Oliver, Charles P.—Charles P. Oliver Assoc., Inc.

Oliver, Dana S.—Dunhill of Southeast Fort Worth, Inc.

Oliver, Ronald H.—Blendow, Crowley & Oliver, Inc. (R)

Olmstead, George T.—Blackshaw, Olmstead & Atwood (R)

Olmstead, Hugh D.—Intertech Search Group

Olney, Susan—Phyllis Hawkins & Assoc.

Olsen, Carl—Kearney Executive Search (R)

Olsen, Robert F.—Robert Connelly & Assoc., Inc. (R)

Olson, B. Tucker—Bert H. Early Assoc., Inc. (R)

Olson, Julia H.—Executive Search of New England, Inc.

Olson, Michael—Sales Consultants

Onstott, Joseph E.—The Onstott Group (R)

Oppedisano, Edward A.—Oppedisano & Co., Inc. (R)

Oppenheim, Norman J.—Fortune Personnel Consultants

Oravetz, Jim—Jim Oravetz & Assoc., Inc.

Organ, Ann—Technical Employment Consultants

Orgelman, George H.—J.R. Akin & Co. (R)

Orkin, Ralph—Sanford Rose Assoc.

Orlando, James—Technical Employment Consultants

Orlick, Gerald E.—Management Recruiters

Ormson, Gilbert E.—Executive Recruiters, Inc.

Orr, Don W.—Orr Executive Search

Orr, Marilyn—Kenmore Executives Inc.

Orr, Stephen F.—Management Recruiters

Ortman, Dennis—Source EDP

Ortman, James P.—Sales Consultants

Oruche, Nike—American Resources Corp.

Oruche, III., Osita—American Resources Corp.

Orwig, David L.—Management Search, Inc.

Osagie, Isoken—Ace Resources

Osagie, Peter E.—Ace Resources

Osher, Jack S.—Management Recruiters

Osinski, Martin H.—MD Resources, Inc. (R)

Osinski, Martin H.—National Health Search, Inc.

Ossow, Kitty—Kitty Ossow & Assoc.

Oster, R. Rush—Management Recruiters of Greater Bridgeport, Inc.

Ostroff, Stephen R.—Triangle Assoc.

Osula, Patience—Ace Resources

Otero, Cony Gutierrez—Smith Search, S.A. (R)

Otis, James E.—Individual Employment Services

Ott, George W.—Ott & Hansen, Inc. (R)

Ott, Robert S.—Consumer Search, Inc.

Ottemann, Carol—R. H. McIlwaine & Assoc.

Ottke, Robert C.—Robert Ottke Assoc. (R)

Owen, Marie—Callan Assoc., Ltd. (R)

Owen, Ralph—Chase-Owens Assoc., Inc. (R)

Owens, Don—C.P.S., Inc.

Owens, LaMonte—LaMonte Owens, Inc.

Pachavis, Robert H.—Accounting Personnel Assoc.

Pacini, Lauren R.—Hite Executive Search (R)

Packer, Gail—Management Recruiters

Packer, Robert—Management Recruiters

Pagan, Vernon R.—Management Recruiters

Page, Lynne—Kiley-Owen Assoc., Inc.

Page, Schuyler—G.S. Page Inc. (R)

Page, Stephen J. L.—Page-Wheatcroft & Co. Ltd. (R)

Page, Teresa—Strategic Assoc., Inc.

Paige, Ben—John-David Assoc., Inc.

Paine, Theresa—The Caldwell Partners Int'l. (R)

Paisios, John P.—John Paisios Ltd. (R)

Pajak, Daniel J.—Dunhill of Denton, Inc.

Paju, John—Worldwide Anesthesia Assoc., Inc.

Pakter, Janou—Janou Pakter, Inc.

Palenske, Victor F.—Management Recruiters

Palmer, Bruce—Hi-Tech Search, Inc.

Palmer, Carleton A.—Beall & Co., Inc. (R)

Palmer, Davis—Source EDP

Palmer, John C.—Palmer Assoc., Inc. (R)

Palmer, Kirk—Kirk Palmer & Assoc., Inc. (R)

Palmer, Lydia—Hi-Tech Search, Inc.

Palmer, Margot E.—Palmer Assoc., Inc. (R)

Panetta, Tim—Commonwealth Consultants

Panos, James—The P & L Group

Papanek, Paul J.—Ward Howell Int'l. Inc. (R)

Papayanopulos, Manuel—Korn/Ferry, Int'l., S.A. de C.V. (R)

Papciak, Dennis J.—Accounting Personnel Assoc.

Pappas, James—PCD Partners (R)

Pappas, James C.—Search Dynamics, Inc.

Pappas, Linda—Barclay Consultants, Inc.

Pappas, Timothy—Barnes, Walters & Assoc., Inc. (R)
Parbs, Michael—Accountants On Call
Pardo, Maria Elena—Smith Search, S.A. (R)
Parham, Jim—Jim Parham & Assoc., Inc. (R)
Parillo, Frank—Frank Parillo & Assoc. (R)
Parisi, Frank—Worlco Computer Resources, Inc.
Parker, David P.—D.P. Parker & Assoc., Inc. (R)
Parker, Donald E.—Marlar Int'l. Inc. (R)
Parker, Murray B.—The Borton Wallace Co. (R)
Parker, Raymond A.—Mark Stanley & Co. (R)
Parker, Roberta—R. Parker & Assoc., Inc.
Parker, Stephen B.—Russell Reynolds Assoc., Inc. (R)
Parmenter, Allen E.—Mitchell, Larsen & Zilliacus (R)
Parr, James A.—Peat Marwick Stevenson & Kellogg (R)
Parrella, Robert—Robert Parrella Assoc.
Parres, Mike—Michael W. Parres & Assoc. (R)
Parsons, Sue N.—Parsons Assoc. Inc. (R)
Partridge, Robert J.—Partridge Assoc., Inc.
Pascal, Phyllis—Phillips Resource Group
Pascal, Rick—RPA Management Consultants, Inc.
Pascale, Ron—Romac & Assoc., Inc.
Paschal, Carolyn Smith—Carolyn Smith Paschal Int'l.
Paschal, Louisa Lynn—Carolyn Smith Paschal Intl.
Pasini, Raymond J.—Pasini & Co. (R)
Passon, Steven A.—Sanford Rose Assoc.
Patberg, Gregg—Kirkbride Assoc., Inc.
Patch, Diane—Management Recruiters
Patch, Dick—Management Recruiters
Pate, Jerry—Davis & James, Inc.
Patrick, Donald—Sanford Rose Assoc.
Patronella, Larry—W. Robert Eissler & Assoc., Inc.
Patterson, Brenda—Management Recruiters
Patterson, Jamie—Brentwood Int'l. (R)
Patton, Mitchell—Patton, Perry & Sproull Inc. (R)
Paul, Joel H.—Joel H. Paul & Assoc., Inc.
Paul, Kevin W.—Kevin W. Paul
Paules, Paul E.—Paules Associates
Pautler, Margaret O.—Holohan Group, Ltd. (R)
Paxton, James W.—The Paxton Group, Ltd.
Payette, Pierre—Egon Zehnder Int'l., Inc. (R)
Peaks, Lynne—L.L. Carey & Assoc., Inc. (R)
Pearle, Laura—Gilbert & Van Campen Int'l. (R)
Pearlman, Emanuel—Robert Lowell Int'l. (R)
Pearson, A.B.—Sales Consultants
Pearson, Anna Lee—Sales Consultants

Pearson, John R.—Holt Pearson & Caldwell, Inc. (R)
Pearson, Robert L.—Lamalie Assoc., Inc. (R)
Pearson, Robert L.—Lamalie Assoc., Inc. (R)
Peasback, David R.—Canny, Bowen Inc. (R)
Peck, Jr., David W.—The Peck Consultancy (R)
Peck, Douglas C.—Rafey & Company (R)
Peckenpaugh, Ann—Schweichler Assoc., Inc. (R)
Pecot, Jack L.—Management Recruiters
Pedalino, Michael D.—International Management Advisors, Inc. (R)
Pedroza, Art—Rusher & Loscacio (R)
Peeney, James D.—Peeney Assoc., Inc. (R)
Pelland, Paul S.—Paul S. Pelland
Pelle, Michael A.—M.A. Pelle Assoc., Inc.
Pelletier, Jacques F.—Roth Young of Boston
Pelton, Margaret—The Caldwell Partners Int'l. (R)
Pendergast, Joseph—Weatherby Healthcare
Penfield, G. Jeff—Management Recruiters
Penney, Robert J.—Sales Consultants of Westchester-South, Inc.
Pennington, Deborah—Focus: HealthCare
Peoples, Denice—The Stamford Group Inc. (R)
Peoples, William—The Stamford Group Inc. (R)
Pepe, Leonida R.—Butterfass/Pepe Assoc., Inc. (R)
Percifield, J. Michael—Management Recruiters
Percival, M. Chris—Chicago Legal Search, Ltd.
Peressini, Tom—Source EDP
Perez, A. Robert—Bedford-Orion Group, Inc.
Pergal, Donald—Resource Network Inc. (R)
Perkins, Patrick—R.E. Lowe Assoc.
Perron, Daniel—Accountants On Call
Perry, Achilles—Gilbert Tweed Assoc., Inc. (R)
Perry, Darrell—Management Recruiters
Perry, Len—Perry-D'Amico & Assoc. (R)
Perry, R. H.—R. H. Perry & Assoc., Inc. (R)
Perry, Robin—Patton, Perry & Sproull Inc. (R)
Perry, Steve—Nelson Associates
Perry, Wayne B.—Bruce Massey & Partners Inc. (R)
Persico, Victor J.—Management Recruiters
Persky, Barry—Barry Persky & Co., Inc. (R)
Person, Glenn J.—AGRI-associates
Pert, Kevin—Venture Resources, Inc. (R)
Peterman, James R.—J.R. Peterman Assoc., Inc.
Peters, Erwin H.—Holohan Group, Ltd. (R)
Peters, James W.—Wargo & Co., Inc. (R)
Peterson, David—Management Recruiters
Peterson, David—Sales Consultants
Peterson, Don—Peterson Consulting/W.P., Inc. (R)

Peterson, Eric—Aim Executive Consulting Services (R)
Peterson, Greg—Sales Consultants of Ft. Lauderdale
Peterson, John A.—Management Recruiters
Peterson, Mike—Peterson Consulting/W.P., Inc. (R)
Peterson, Pat—Peterson Consulting/W.P., Inc. (R)
Peterson, Priscilla J.—Management Recruiters
Peterson, Richard A.—Richard Peterson & Assoc., Inc. (R)
Peterson, Thomas—Kennedy & Co. (R)
Peto, Brian—Sales Consultants
Petre, Lawrence F.—Availability Personnel Consultants
Petrie, Chris—R.J. Maglio & Assoc., Inc. (R)
Petroski, Gary—E O Technical
Petroski, Jeanette—E O Technical
Petruzzi, Vincent J.—Petruzzi Assoc.
Pettibone, Linda—Herbert Mines Assoc., Inc. (R)
Pettigrew, Reece—Paul Ray & Carre Orban Int'l. (R)
Pettway, Samuel H.—Egon Zehnder Int'l. Inc. (R)
Pfaendler, Robert E.—Robert E. Pfaendler & Assoc., Inc.
Pfannkuche, Anthony—SpencerStuart (R)
Pfister, Annette—Howe-Lewis Int'l., Inc. (R)
Pflueger, Andrew P.—Pflueger & Company (R)
Phaneuf, Don—Bryce, Haultain & Assoc. (R)
Phelps, Laura P.—Ward Howell Int'l. Inc. (R)
Phillip, John R.—Coelyn Miller Phillip & Assoc. (R)
Phillips, Don—Accountants On Call
Phillips, Frank—Management Recruiters
Phillips, Richard K.—Handy HRM (R)
Phillips, Jr., Sam B.—Phillips Resource Group
Phillips, Veronica—Phillips Assoc.
Phillips, Wendell—Excelsior Service Group, Inc. (R)
Phillips, Will—Excelsior Services Group Inc. (R)
Phin, Jane G.—Farrell & Phin, Inc. (R)
Pianin, Sheila—Thorndike Deland Assoc. (R)
Piatkiewicz, Mary Lou—Medical Executive Search Assoc.
Piatkiewicz, William L.—Medical Executive Search Assoc.
Piazza, Terry E.—Management Recruiters
Picard, Daniel A.—Picard & Co., Inc. (R)
Pickens, Barbara—Johnson Smith & Knisely Inc. (R)
Pickering, Dale—Agri-Tech Personnel, Inc.
Pickford, Stephen T.—The Corporate Staff (R)
Pierce, Douglas F.—Pierce & Assoc., Inc. (R)

Pierce, Martin J.—Martin Pierce Inc. (R)
Pierce, Richard—Pierce Assoc. (R)
Pierce, Stan—Delta Personnel Services
Pierce, William C.—Martin Pierce Inc. (R)
Piers, Robert L.—TASA/Fleming (R)
Pillow, Charlie—Source Finance
Pilz, Alfred N.—Fagan & Co. (R)
Pinsker, Richard J.—Pinsker & Co., Inc. (R)
Pinson, Stephanie—Gilbert Tweed Assoc., Inc. (R)
Pister, M. Claire—Rusher, Loscavio & Lo Presto (R)
Pitchford, Jim—Management Recruiters
Pittard, Patrick S.—Heidrick and Struggles, Inc. (R)
Pittman, John—Techcon Co.
Pizzariello, Ann Marie—Conex Inc. (R)
Pizzi, Don—Marra/Pizzi Assoc., Inc. (R)
Plagge, Cheryl L.—Management Recruiters
Plappert, James F.—Sales Consultants of Newtown
Plazza, R.C.—Hackett & Co. (R)
Plessner, Rene—Rene Plessner Assoc., Inc. (R)
Plimpton, Ralph L.—R.L. Plimpton Assoc. (R)
Plock, Gerald R.—The PAR Group - Paul A. Reaume, Ltd. (R)
Plummer, John—Plummer & Assoc., Inc. (R)
Plummer, Karen E.—Roberts Assoc.
Pocrass, Richard D.—Pocrass Assoc. (R)
Podgorski, Robert P.—Benton Schneider & Assoc. (R)
Poff, John—Strategic Assoc., Inc.
Poirier, Roland L.—Poirier, Hoevel & Co. (R)
Pokart, Lorna—Herbert Mines Assoc., Inc. (R)
Polacek, Frank—Search Enterprises, Inc.
Polak, Steve—MRG Search & Placement
Polan, Marilyn B.—Jablo Partners (R)
Polansky, Mark—Source EDP
Polansky, Mark—Source EDP
Polaski, Fern—Gordon/Tyler (R)
Pollack, Jerry—Jerry Pollack & Assoc.
Pollard, Phil—Philip Daniels Assoc., Inc.
Polson, Christopher C.—Polson & Co., Inc. (R)
Poltorak, Carol J.—Management Recruiters
Polvere, Gary T.—Sales Consultants
Polz, Laddie J.—Benton Schneider & Assoc. (R)
Pomeroy, II, T. Lee—Egon Zehnder Int'l. Inc. (R)
Pond, K. James—Abbott, James & Oliver
Ponder, J.C.—Management Recruiters
Poore, Larry—Ward Howell Int'l. Inc. (R)
Popham, Harold C.—Emerson & Co.

Ramsey, John H.—Mark Stanley & Co. (R)
Randall, J.E.—Schreuder Randall Corp.
Randall, Jack—Biotech Sourcing
Randall, Julia B.—Robert Sellery Assoc., Ltd. (R)
Randell, Jr., James W.—Randell-Heiken, Inc. (R)
Randolph, Bonnie—Yannelli, Randolph & Co.
Ranger, Jean-Jacques—Ranger & Assoc.
Rankin, Jeffrey A.—The Rankin Group, Ltd. (R)
Rankin, M. J.—The Rankin Group, Ltd. (R)
Raperto, Marie T.—The Cantor Concern, Inc.
Rapp, Harold L.—Harold L. Rapp Assoc.
Rappaport, Larry J.—National Logistics Recruiters, Inc.
Rassenti, Linda—Hornberger Management Co., Inc.
Ratts, K. Wayne—Holohan Group, Ltd. (R)
Rauch, Clifford W.—Physicians Search Assoc. Agency, Inc.
Rawson, Robert—Barton Sans Int'l. (R)
Ray, Breck—Paul Ray & Carre Orban Int'l (R)
Ray, Sr., Paul R.—Paul Ray & Carre Orban Int'l. (R)
Ray, Jr., Paul R.—Paul Ray & Carre Orban Int'l. (R)
Raymond, Allan—Korn/Ferry Int'l. (R)
Raymond, Christopher—Benton Schneider & Assoc. (R)
Raymond, Jean—The Caldwell Partners Int'l. (R)
Raynolds, Eleanor H.—Ward Howell Int'l. Inc. (R)
Raz, Daniel—Analytic Recruiting, Inc.
Raz, Rita—Analytic Recruiting, Inc.
Razzano, Douglas—Global Data Services, Inc.
Reagan, Richard C.—Egon Zehnder Int'l. Inc. (R)
Ream, Scott W.—The Consortium
Reardon, Joseph—Source Finance
Reasner, Georgia—Pursuant Legal Consultants
Reaume, Paul A.—The PAR Group - Paul A. Reaume, Ltd. (R)
Reda, Patrick—Barrett Partners
Redden, Daniel J.—Redden & Assoc. (R)
Redden, Mary—Redden & McGrath Assoc., Inc. (R)
Reddick, David C.—Reddick and Co., Int'l. (R)
Redmond, Leila—Bader Research Corp.
Redmond, Patricia—Sales Consultants
Rednick, Mark—Sales Consultants
Reed, David—Management Recruiters
Reeder, Michael S.—Lamalie Assoc., Inc. (R)
Reese, Cedric—Quickstaff
Reese, Jr., Charles D.—Reese Assoc. (R)
Reese, Whitney—Marks & Co., Inc. (R)
Reeves, Ron—Management Recruiters

Reeves, William B.—SpencerStuart (R)
Regan, Mary Beth—National Corporate Consultants, Inc.
Regan, Muriel—Gossage Regan Assoc. (R)
Regehly, Herbert—Innkeeper's Management Corp. (R)
Rehberger, C.K.—High Technology Search Assoc.
Reich, Geraldine—Bader Research Corp.
Reichardt, Lisa—RBR Assoc., Inc.
Reid, Garry—Peat Marwick Stevenson & Kellogg (R)
Reid, Jack L.—The Hindman Co. (R)
Reid, Joel—Management Recruiters
Reimer, Marvin—Management Recruiters
Reimer, Marvin—Sales Consultants
Rein, David—D.M. Rein & Co., Inc. (R)
Reinecke, G.—Reinecke & Assoc.
Reinitz, Robert—Professional Recruiters Inc.
Reisfeld, Lynn Scullion—Alfred Daniels & Assoc. (R)
Reisinger, George L.—Sigma Group Inc. (R)
Reiter, Steve—Romac & Assoc. - San Francisco
Reitkopp, Howard H.—Management Recruiters
Reitz, Eugene A.—Paul J. Burns
Rekedal, Steve—DeHayes Consulting Group (R)
Relton, Daniel J.—The Goldman Group Inc.
Reo, James—Thomas, Whelan Assoc., Inc.
Repplier, Marjorie M.—Repplier & Co.
Reszotko, Leonard J.—RAI Consulting
Reuning, Stephen M.—Diedre Moire Corp., Inc.
Rexrode, Kathleen E.—The Odessa Group (R)
Reyman, Susan—S. Reyman & Assoc., Ltd.
Reynes, Tony—Tesar-Reynes, Inc. (R)
Reynolds, Bud—Management Recruiters
Reynolds, Jerry—The Reynolds Group, Inc.
Reynolds, John R.—Brissenden, McFarland, Wagoner & Fuccella, Inc. (R)
Reynolds, Juli Ann—Aubin Int'l. Inc. (R)
Reynolds, Jr., Russell S.—Russell Reynolds Assoc., Inc. (R)
Reynolds, Smooch S.—The Repovich - Reynolds Group (R)
Reynolds, Sydney—Sydney Reynolds Assoc., Inc. (R)
Rhodes, Sarah—Phillips Resource Group
Ribcke, R. Brian—RBR Assoc., Inc.
Rice, Ann—Management Recruiters
Rice, Doug—Agra Placements, Ltd.
Rice, Gene P.—Sales Consultants
Rice, Jim K.—Management Recruiters
Rice, Jim K.—Management Recruiters
Rice, Marshall T.—Marshall Rice Assoc. (R)

Rice, Raymond D.—Logue & Rice Inc.
Rich, Bob—Source EDP
Richard, Jr., Albert L.—Human Resources, Inc. (R)
Richards, Bob E.—Sales Consultants
Richards, Carl—Technical Employment Consultants
Richards, Lance J.—Norton & Assoc., Inc. (R)
Richards, Mark—Gallin Assoc.
Richards, Maureen—Technical Employment Consultants
Richards, Robert—Sanford Rose Assoc.
Richardson, Colleen J.—Schweichler Assoc., Inc. (R)
Richardson, David M—DHR Int'l., Inc. (R)
Richardson, Paul C.—Boyden Int'l., Inc. (R)
Richardson, Rick—SpencerStuart (R)
Richer, William F.—W.F. Richer Assoc., Inc.
Richmond, Theodore P.—Lee & Burgess Assoc., Inc. (R)
Richner, George A.—Search Assoc., Inc.
Rickford, Chris—Forum Assoc.
Rico, Frank—J.R. Akin & Co. (R)
Ridenour, Suzanne S.—Ridenour & Assoc. (R)
Rider, Edward—Professional Medical
Rieger, Louis J.—SpencerStuart (R)
Riehl, Nancy—Source EDP
Rieser, John D.—Rieser & Assoc., Inc. (R)
Rigal, Jennifer—Ashton Computer Professionals, Inc.
Riggs, David T.—Management Recruiters
Riggs, Lena K.—Management Recruiters
Rijke, R. Fred—TASA, Inc. (R)
Riley, Elizabeth—Mazza & Riley, Inc. (R)
Riley, Jeffrey K.—EFL Assoc. (R)
Ring, Steve—Corporate Consultants Inc.
Riniti, Frank—Source Finance
Rinovato, Mark—CCI - Career Consultants Int'l.
Riotto, Anthony P.—Riotto - Jones Assoc., Inc.
Ristau, Ed—Management Recruiters
Ritchie, Anne—Executive Search of New England, Inc.
Ritchie, L.R.—Robert A. Paul & Assoc.
Ritchings, David—David Allen Assoc.
Ritson, Steve—Valletta Ritson & Co. (R)
Ritz, Robert W.—T.J. Koellhoffer & Assoc. (R)
Rivas, Alberto—Boyden Latin America S.A. de C.V. (R)
Rivas, Alberto—Boyden Latin America S.A. de C.V. (R)
Rizzo, L. Donald—Barone Assoc.
Roarke, M. James—Ethan Allen Personnel, Inc.

Robbins, Mark—Sales Consultants
Robbins, Valerie—Sales Consultants
Roberson, Charles L.—Gaines & Assoc. Int'l., Inc.
Roberts, Brian—Sales Consultants
Roberts, Corey C.—The DLR Group, Inc.
Roberts, Daniel Lee—The DLR Group, Inc. (R)
Roberts, Donald J.—Gilbert Tweed Assoc. (R)
Roberts, Frank—Management Recruiters
Roberts, George R.—Roberts Assoc.
Roberts, Luke—Alan Lerner Assoc.
Roberts, Norman C.—Norman Roberts & Assoc., Inc. (R)
Roberts, Rick—Coopers & Lybrand Consulting Group (R)
Roberts, Robert E.—Sanford Rose Assoc.
Robertson, Bruce J.—Norman Broadbent Int'l., Inc. (R)
Robertson, Darrell G.—Western Reserve Search Assoc. (R)
Robertson, George O.—Robertson, Spoerlein & Wengert (R)
Robertson, Ronald W.—Robertson-Surrette Ltd. (R)
Robertson, William R.—Ward Howell Int'l. Inc. (R)
Robinson, Bruce—Bruce Robinson Assoc. (R)
Robinson, Donald Alan—The Robinson Group, D.A., Ltd.
Robison, IV, John H.—Robison & McAulay (R)
Robison, John H.—Robison & McAulay (R)
Robison, Margaret H.—William Humphreys & Assoc., Inc. (R)
Robsham, Beverly H.—Robsham & Assoc. (R)
Roche, Gerard R.—Heidrick and Struggles, Inc. (R)
Roche, Rachel L.—Allerton Heneghan & O'Neill (R)
Rockwell, Bruce—Source EDP
Rodgers, Kathi—St. Lawrence Int'l., Inc.
Rodriguez, Carlos R.—Management Recruiters
Rodriguez, Louise—Carpenter, Shackleton & Co. (R)
Rodts, Peter E.—Plastics Enterprises
Roe, Richard R.—Sanford Rose Assoc.
Roffwarg, Betty—Sydney Reynolds Assoc., Inc. (R)
Rogers, Dan—Management Recruiters
Rogers, Jane—Management Recruiters
Rogers, Jim—Professional Medical
Rogers, V. G.—L O R Personnel Div. (R)
Rogish, Nick—R.G.B. & Assoc., Inc.
Rogus, Edward F.—Sanford Rose Assoc.
Rohan, James—J.P. Canon Assoc.
Rojas, Carlos A.—RZL Y Asociados, S.C. (R)

792 / DIRECTORY OF EXECUTIVE RECRUITERS

Rokey, Mike—Management Recruiters
Rolf, Rex—CCI - Career Consultants Int'l.
Rolfe, Pamela—Career Specialists, Inc.
Roller, David—Search West, Inc.
Rollo, Bob—Korn/Ferry Int'l. (R)
Romanchek, Walter R.—Wellington Management Group (R)
Romaniw, Michael—A la Carte Int'l., Inc. (R)
Romano, Joseph C.—Romano McAvoy Assoc., Inc.
Romeo, Paul C.—Romeo-Hudgins & Assoc. Ltd. (R)
Rooney, Michael F.—Winston Rooney & Green
Rooney, Paul—Technical Engineering Consultants
Root, Leslie A.—The Wright Group
Ropella, Patrick B.—Ropella & Assoc.
Ropes, John—Ropes Assoc., Inc. (R)
Rose, Emery—Emery A. Rose & Assoc.
Rose, Sanford M.—Sanford Rose Assoc.
Rosen, Joseph—Riverside Consultants, Inc.
Rosenblatt, Doreen—Marcus & Assoc.
Rosenfeld, Adrienne—Alterna-track
Rosenfeld, Martin J.—Sanford Rose Assoc.-Detroit North
Rosenow, Richard—Heath/Norton Assoc., Inc. (R)
Rosenshein, Mike—Management Recruiters
Rosevear, Nancy—Dupuis & Ryden, P.C. (R)
Ross, Cheryl Molliver—Thomas, Whelan Assoc., Inc.
Ross, Elsa—Gardner-Ross Assoc., Inc. (R)
Ross, Garland—Management Recruiters
Ross, Garland—Sales Consultants
Ross, Howard—The Consortium
Ross, Jane E.—Matthews Professional Employment Specialists, Inc.
Ross, Karen M.—William Hetzel Assoc., Inc. (R)
Ross, Martin B.—Ward Howell Int'l. Inc. (R)
Ross, Robert—Chicago Research Group, Inc. (R)
Ross, Robert F.—Bertrand, Ross & Assoc., Inc. (R)
Rossman, Paul R.—Management Recruiters
Rotella, Jr., Marshall W.—The Corporate Connection, Ltd.
Roth, Robert J.—Williams, Roth & Krueger, Inc. (R)
Roth, Ronald P.—Smith, Roth & Squires (R)
Rothenbush, Chuck—Source EDP
Rothfeld, Robert—A.E. Feldman Assoc.
Rothrock, Jr., T. Hardy—Rothrock Assoc.
Rotsky, Bernard—BR & Assoc.
Rotsky, Sally—BR & Assoc.
Rottblatt, Michael—Korn/Ferry Int'l. (R)
Rotundo, F. J.—Management Resources Int'l. (R)

Rourke, Patrick W.—Rourke, Bourbonnais Assoc., Ltd. (R)
Routh, Maria C.—Kacevich, Lewis & Brown, Inc.
Rovinsky, Bruce—Career Search Assoc.
Rowe, David E.—David Rowe & Assoc., Inc. (R)
Rowenhorst, Brenda—The Bren Group
Roy, G. Charles—D.E. Foster & Partners, L.P. (R)
Roy, Gary—Management Recruiters
Roy, Raymond—Egon Zehnder Int'l., Inc. (R)
Roylance, Robert L.—STM Assoc.
Rozenboom, Carol E.—David Rowe & Assoc., Inc. (R)
Rozner, Burton L.—Oliver & Rozner Assoc., Inc. (R)
Rozner, Daniel J.—Chandler & Rozner Assoc. (R)
Rozner, John—Chandler & Rozner Assoc. (R)
Ruben, Rebecca—H.C. Smith Ltd. (R)
Rubenstein, Martin H.—Werner Int'l., Inc. (R)
Rubin, David S.—Sales Consultants
Rubin, Karen—Travel Executive Search
Rubin, Lynda—Sales Consultants
Rubin, Steve—Sales Consultants
Rucker-Eatherly, Rebecca M.—Boyden Int'l., Inc. (R)
Ruderfer, Irwin A.—Krow Assoc., Inc.
Rudman, Jim—The Placers, Inc.
Rudolph, Arlyn B.—Management Recruiters
Rudzinsky, Howard—Louis Rudzinsky Assoc., Inc.
Rudzinsky, Jeff—Louis Rudzinsky Assoc., Inc.
Rudzinsky, Louis—Louis Rudzinsky Assoc., Inc.
Ruello, Brenda L.—Heidrick and Struggles, Inc. (R)
Ruina, Walter—Gray-Kimball Assoc., Inc.
Rumson, Barbara A.—Management Recruiters of Ashville, Inc.
Rumson, Paul M.—Management Recruiters of Ashville, Inc.
Runden, Jr., John P.—John P. Runden & Co., Inc.
Runge, Gary K.—Search Enterprises, Inc.
Rupp, Don—Crest Management Search, Inc.
Rurak, Zbigniew T.—Rurak & Assoc., Inc (R)
Ruschak, Randy—Management Recruiters
Rushbrook, Robert W.—World Search
Rusher, Jr., William H.—Rusher, Loscavio & Lo Presto (R)
Rushlow, M.M.—Rushlow & Co.
Rusnov, Samuel—Michael Latas & Assoc., Inc. (R)
Russ, Jr., Charles F.—Charles Russ Assoc. (R)
Russell, Dennis M.—Russell, Montgomery & Assoc. (R)
Russell, Frank—Russell Assoc.
Russell, Rosalie—Pro Travel Personnel

Russell, Sam—Source Finance
Russillo, Thomas P.—Russillo/Gardner
Rust, James J.—James J. Rust Executive Search (R)
Rustad, Binth—Educational Management Network (R)
Rutkowski, Joseph A.—Sanford Rose Assoc.
Rutledge, William A.—The Stevenson Group/SES (R)
Ruzich, Joe—Management Recruiters
Ryan, Ann—A. Ryan Assoc.
Ryan, Bernard J.—BDO Seidman (R)
Ryan, Brian—The Logan Group, Inc. (R)
Ryan, J. Barry—The Winchester Group (R)
Ryan, Paul C.—Ryan & Assoc.
Ryan, Trish—Management Recruiters
Ryan, William—Hunter Int'l., Inc. (R)
Ryer, Ed—Lee & Burgess Assoc., Inc. (R)
Ryerson, Jerry—Ryerson Tabor Assoc.
Saadi, Edgar—Pencom Systems Inc.
Sabados, Terri L.—Management Recruiters
Saber-Salisbury, Debra—Saber-Salisbury & Assoc., Inc.
Sachtjen, Wilbur M.—Wilbur M. Sachtjen Assoc., Inc. (R)
Sadick, Stuart H.—Chartwell Partners Int'l., Inc. (R)
Sadow, Raymond—Management Recruiters of North Brunswick, Inc.
Safford, Mark W.—Actuaries & Assoc. (R)
Sage, Fred—Sage/Walters Ltd. (R)
Salerno, Jerry—Ferrari Consulting Group
Salerno, Roberta Vaccaro—The Romark Group, Ltd. (R)
Salese, Irene—The Personnel Laboratory (R)
Salfi, James P.—Ritta Professional Search Inc.
Salikof, Allen—Management Recruiters
Salottolo, Alexander A.—Strategic Alternatives (R)
Saloukas, Bill I.—Broad Waverly & Assoc.
Salvagno, Mike—The Cambridge Group Ltd.
Salvangwo, Michael—Cambridge Group Ltd.-Exec. Search Div. (R)
Salvatore, Philip A.—LAS Management Consulting Group, Inc.
Salzberg, David—Roth Young Seattle
Salzman, Leo E.—Dunhill Professional Search Inc.
Sammons, James A.—Prestige Search Inc.
Samper, Juan M.—Samper Assoc.
Sampson, M.D., Martin C.—Sampson, Neill & Wilkins Inc. (R)
Samsel, Randy—Source Finance
Samuels, Ivan R.—George D. Sandel Assoc.

Sanborn, Jr., Lee R.—Selected Executives, Inc.
Sanders, Spencer H.—Battalia Winston Int'l., Inc. (R)
Sanderson, Richard—Charles Russ Assoc. (R)
Sandor, Richard—Flynn, Hannock, Kennan, Inc.
Sands, Alyse—Richard Kader & Assoc.
Sans, Gerard—Barton Sans Int'l. (R)
Santangelo, Richard—Santangelo Consultants Inc.
Sarafa, Sameer N.—Management Recruiters
Sarchett, A. Wayne—Systems Careers
Sargent, Robert A.—JM & Co. (R)
Sargis, Scott R.—Strategic Search Corp. (R)
Sarn, Allan G.—Allan Sarn Assoc., Inc. (R)
Sarver, Cathy—Sarver-Garland, Inc.
Sasenick, Joseph A.—Vista Resource Group (R)
Sass, John—Management Recruiters
Sathe, Mark—Sathe & Assoc., Inc. (R)
Sather, Jan—Career Marketing Assoc.
Satilli, Joe—Financial Resource Assoc., Inc.
Satoh, Yoshiaki—Carpenter, Shackleton & Co. (R)
Sauer, Andrea Garcia—Frank P. Hill
Sauer, Harry—Romac & Assoc., Inc.
Sauer, Harry J.—Romac & Assoc., Inc.
Sautter, A.H.—Corporate Personnel, Inc.
Savage, Edward J.—Marlar Int'l. Inc. (R)
Savage, Jean—Gardner, Savage Assoc.
Savalli, Frank—Savalli & Assoc., Inc.
Sawhill, Louise—Professional Medical
Sawyer, Patricia L.—Robert L. Smith & Co., Inc. (R)
Sawyer, Scott J.—Management Search Int'l.
Saxner, David—David Saxner & Assoc., Inc.
Saxon, Barry—Strategic Search Group
Sbarbaro, Richard D.—Lauer, Sbarbaro Assoc., Inc. (R)
Scanlon, James D.—Sherbrooke Assoc., Inc. (R)
Scaturro, Mary Ellen—Drew Assoc. Int'l. (R)
Schachter, Laura J.—Professional Placement Assoc., Inc.
Schacke, Hans R.—Hans & Assoc., Inc. (R)
Schafer, Cindy—The Angus Group, Inc.
Schaffer, Sylvia—Lawrence Executive Search, Ltd.
Schaifer, Brett—Accountants On Call
Schalekamp, Paul D.—Schalekamp & Assoc., Inc. (R)
Schanbacher, Larry—Management Recruiters of Westchester, Inc.
Schappell, Marc P.—Egon Zehnder Int'l. Inc. (R)
Scharringhausen, Michael C.—Saber Consultants, Inc. (R)
Schattle, Donald J.—Schattle Personnel Consultants, Inc.

Schaumann, Mary Jane—Allen Barry Assoc.

Schenkel, Donald D.—Schenkel & Company (R)

Scherck, Henry J.—Gardiner Stone Hunter Int'l., Inc. (R)

Scherrer, Chris—Source Finance

Schlapeter, Gary—Pacific Search Consultants

Schmidt, Frank B.—F. B. Schmidt Intl. (R)

Schmidt, James—Cejka & Co. (R)

Schmidt, Jane—Management Recruiters

Schmidt, Jeri E.—Blake, Hansen & Nye, Ltd. (R)

Schmidt, Paul W.—A.T. Kearney Executive Search (R)

Schmidt, Peter R.—Boyden Int'l., Inc. (R)

Schmidt, Randy J.—Pro, Inc.

Schmitt, Thomas G.—The Schmitt Tolette Group (R)

Schnabel, Ed—The Remington Group, Ltd.

Schnabel, Kate—OSA Partners, Inc.

Schneekluth, E. J.—Pro, Inc.

Schneekluth, Mark J.—Pro, Inc.

Schneider, Jay—Source Finance

Schneider, Jim—The Search Firm Inc.

Schneider, Mal—Dunhill Personnel System, Inc.

Schneider, Mark—The Goodman Group

Schneider, Perry M.—Agra Placements, Ltd.

Schneider, Perry M.—Agra Placements, Ltd.

Schneider, Ted—Sanford Rose Assoc. - Rockville

Schneider, Thomas—Gilbert & Van Campen Int'l. (R)

Schneider, Vic—Accountants On Call

Schneider, Wallace—Stuart, Wood Inc. (R)

Schneiderman, Gerald—Management Resource Assoc., Inc.

Schneiderman, Sheila—Management Resource Assoc., Inc.

Schnitzer, David—Retail Recruiters of Paramus, Inc.

Schoales, J. Michael—Herman Smith Transearch Inc. (R)

Schoen, Stephen G.—MD Resources, Inc. (R)

Schoenfeld, Jack—Dunhill of Manchester Inc.

Schoenfeld, Martin—Dunhill of Manchester Inc.

Schoff, Frank J.—Management Recruiters of Hendersonville, inc.

Schonberg, Alan R.—Management Recruiters

Schonberg, Alan R.—Sales Consultants

Schorr, Cliff—Fisher-Todd Assoc.

Schorr, Warren—Management Recruiters

Schreiber, Glenn—Specialty Consultants, Inc.

Schreiber, Stuart M.—Heidrick and Struggles, Inc. (R)

Schreuder, A. Leo—Schreuder Randall Corp.

Schroeder, John W.—SpencerStuart (R)

Schroeder, Kit E.—Midwest Medical Recruiters

Schroeder, Lee—Blau Kaptain Schroeder (R)

Schuessler, Mary Ann—Drake & Assoc.

Schuessler, Mary Ann—Environmental Professional Assoc.

Schuller, Eric K.—Trilogy Enterprises, Inc.

Schulte, Buzz—Korn/Ferry Int'l. (R)

Schulte, Fred—Stricker & Zagor (R)

Schultz, Bob—Wegner & Assoc.

Schultz, Helen—Predictor Systems Corp. (R)

Schultz, William A.—Sales Consultants of Madison

Schulz, Mike—Lou Michaels Assoc.

Schumann, Robert—Reinecke & Assoc.

Schuyler, Jr., Lambert—Schuyler, Frye & Baker, Inc. (R)

Schwab, James—Conex Inc. (R)

Schwab, James K.—Schwab-Carrese Assoc. (R)

Schwartz, Alan M.—Selective Management Services, Inc.

Schwartz, Jack—Source EDP

Schwartz, Jack—Source EDP

Schwartz, Jay—Management Recruiters

Schwartz, Jay—Sales Consultants

Schwartz, Stephen D.—Management Recruiters of Gramercy, Inc.

Schwartz, Vincent P.—Slayton Int'l., Inc. (R)

Schweichler, Lee—Schweichler Assoc., Inc. (R)

Scimone, Jim—Source EDP

Scodius, Joseph J.—Gregory Michaels & Assoc., Inc.

Scofield, Oscar—DeHayes Consulting Group (R)

Scothon, Alan C.—Romac & Assoc., Inc.

Scott, Harold—Graham & Co. (R)

Scott, Howard—Dunhill Personnel System, Inc.

Scott, Karen R.—Stewart, Stein & Scott, Ltd. (R)

Scott, Louis R.—Management Recruiters

Scott, Louis R.—Sales Consultants

Scott, Mike—David Powell, Inc. (R)

Scott, Todd—Abraham & London Ltd.

Seabrook, Roderick B.—Sales Consultants

Seager, Helen—Educational Management Network (R)

Seaholts, Mark—Sanford Rose Assoc.

Searing, James M.—Kirkman & Searing (R)

Seaver, Christine—David Powell, Inc. (R)

Seebert, John W.—Sales Consultants of Fox Valley

Seefeld, Jane A.—Human Resource Recruiters

Segil, Annette—Executive Careers

Seiden, Steven A.—Seiden Assoc., Inc. (R)

Seiler, Alan B.—Ramsey & Beirne Assoc., Inc. (R)

Short, Mary Sue—Placement Solutions

Shorten, Barry—Gray-Kimball Assoc., Inc.

Shotland, David R.—The Shotland Group (R)

Shourds, Mary—Houze, Shourds & Montgomery, Inc. (R)

Shryock, William—W. Shryock & Co. (R)

Shukiar, Phyllis—Mortgage & Financial Personnel Services

Shulman, Mel—McFeely Wackerle Shulman (R)

Shultis, Yvonne—RitaSue Siegel Assoc., Inc.

Shultz, Susan F.—SS & A Executive Search Consultants (R)

Sibbald, John R.—John Sibbald Assoc., Inc. (R)

Siegel, Carl W.—Winfield Assoc.

Siegel, Fred—Conex Inc. (R)

Siegel, RitaSue—RitaSue Siegel Assoc., Inc.

Siemandel, Marjorie K.—Newpher & Co., Inc. (R)

Sievers, III, Carl R.—Sievers & Assoc. (R)

Silberger, Gary—Key Employment

Silcott, Marvin L.—Marvin L. Silcott & Assoc., Inc.

Silivanch, Garry—Global Data Services, Inc.

Sill, Igor M.—Geneva Group Int'l. (R)

Silvas, Jean Anne—Roberson & Co.

Silvas, Stephen D.—Roberson & Co.

Silver, David—DCS Assoc., Inc. (R)

Silver, Lee—L. A. Silver Assoc., Inc.

Silver, Moira—Computer Strategies, Inc.

Silver, Susan B.—Kravitz * Larkin * Silver Assoc.

Silverman, Jules—Barclay Consultants, Inc.

Silverstein, Alvin I.—Bedford-Orion Group, Inc.

Silverstein, Daniel A.—Daniel A. Silverstein Assoc. Inc. (R)

Silverstein, Michael L.—Management Recruiters

Silverstein, Rita—Accountants On Call

Silvester, Margo—STM Assoc.

Simmons, Bo—Management Recruiters of Savannah

Simmons, George—Fox-Morris Assoc., Inc.

Simmons, J. Gerald—Handy HRM (R)

Simmons, Noel A.—The Simmons Group

Simon, Bernard M.—Accountants On Call

Simon, John D.—John J. Davis & Assoc., Inc. (R)

Simon, Robert A.—Deane, Howard & Simon, Inc. (R)

Simpson, Judy—Management Recruiters

Simpson, Kent—Management Recruiters

Simpson, Lee—Simpson Nance & Graham, Inc.

Simpson, Terre—Simpson Assoc.

Sims, John—Management Recruiters

Sinay, Richard K.—Sales Consultants

Sinclair, John—Peat Marwick Stevenson & Kellogg (R)

Sindeband, Seymour J.—Kensington Management Consultants, Inc. (R)

Singel, Don—Jonathan Lawrence Assoc.

Singer, Jon A.—C & H Personnel

Singer, Rich—Source Finance

Sink, Clifton W.—C.W. Sink & Co., Inc. (R)

Siomkos, Georgia—Michael Garbi Assoc., Inc.

Sisson, Martha Ann—Garrison, McGuigan & Sisson

Sistek, Walter J.—Management Assoc.

Sitter, William P.—Jordan-Sitter Assoc. (R)

Sivertsen, Gordon—Peat Marwick Stevenson & Kellogg (R)

Skaar, Ralph—Engineering & Scientific Search Assoc.

Skaar, Richard H.—Engineering & Scientific Search Assoc.

Skladowski, Rose—Cemco, Ltd.

Skunda, Donna M.—DHR Int'l., Inc. (R)

Slaby, Eugene R.—ISOPS Personnel Services, Inc.

Slaby, Michael E.—ISOPS Personnel Services, Inc.

Slater, Marjorie—Logistics Management Resources, Inc.

Slater, Robert W.—Slater & Assoc. (R)

Slaughter, William—Gold Coast Partners

Slauter, Larry T.—Overton Group (R)

Slaviero, Sue A.—D. R. Blood & Assoc.

Slayden, Kay—Jackson & Coker (R)

Slayton, Richard C.—Slayton Int'l., Inc. (R)

Slayton, Richard S.—Slayton Int'l., Inc. (R)

Sliteris, Joanne—PMC-ParaLegal Management & Consultants

Sloan, Michael—Sloan & Assoc., Inc.

Sloane, Brian—Marcus & Assoc.

Sloane, William G.—Sloane, Sloane & Mayne (R)

Sloat, Robert L.—Executive Search of New England, Inc.

Slowik, Edward C.—SpencerStuart (R)

Small, Alan—Peat Marwick Stevenson & Kellogg (R)

Small, Jane—Selective Staffing

Smerlas, Francine—Sales Consultants

Smiley, Marv—Source Finance

Smiset, Don—Management Recruiters

Smith, Dale E.—R. H. Horton Int'l. (R)

Smith, Dan—Healthcare Resources Group

Smith, Daniel M.—Sales Consultants

Smith, David P.—Hoskins, Rees & Smith

Smith, Don—Dalton-Smith & Assoc., Inc.

Smith, Douglas M.—Ward Howell Int'l. Inc. (R)

Smith, Emma—Business Search America (R)
Smith, F. Clawson—Johnson Smith & Knisely Inc. (R)
Smith, Helen M.—Tech International
Smith, Henry B.—Smith, Anderson & Co.
Smith, Herbert C.—H.C. Smith Ltd. (R)
Smith, Herman D.—Management Recruiters
Smith, Herman M.—Herman Smith Transearch Inc. (R)
Smith, Howard A.—Tech International
Smith, Howard T.—James F. Smith & Assoc.
Smith, Howard W.—Howard W. Smith Assoc. (R)
Smith, Ivan W.—Dunhill Professional Search Group
Smith, James F.—James F. Smith & Assoc.
Smith, James H.—J. Harrington Smith Assoc.
Smith, Jr., John E.—Smith Search, S.A. (R)
Smith, Larry—Management Recruiters
Smith, Marguerite—Dalton-Smith & Assoc., Inc.
Smith, Martin—Business Search America (R)
Smith, Marvin E.—Competitive Resources, Inc.
Smith, Michael R.—MARBL Consultants, Inc.
Smith, Mike—Management Recruiters
Smith, Monica L.—Analysts Resources Inc.
Smith, R. Jan—Management Recruiters
Smith, Ralph E.—Ralph Smith & Assoc.
Smith, Raymond J.—Raymond James Smith & Assoc.
Smith, Richard A.—AJS Assoc.
Smith, Robert L.—Robert L. Smith & Co., Inc. (R)
Smith, S.—American Executive Management, Inc. (R)
Smith, Stephen R.—Stephen R. Smith & Co., Inc. (R)
Smith, Steven L.—Smith, Roth & Squires (R)
Smith, Sue—Management Recruiters
Smith, Tim—Source Finance
Smith, Tom—Smith, Beaty, Barlow Assoc., Inc.
Smith, Toni S.—SpencerStuart (R)
Smith, Wiley C.—Cejka & Co. (R)
Smock, Robert B.—The Headhunter
Smyth, William—A. William Smyth, Inc. (R)
Snedden, Alan—Management Recruiters
Snediker, Gretchen K.—Stephens Assoc. Ltd. (R)
Snellbaker, Mary W.—Management Recruiters
Snook, Maria—Management Recruiters
Snook, Marvin—Management Recruiters
Snow, Kib—Lou Michaels Assoc.
Snyder, C. Edward—R. H. Horton Int'l. (R)
Snyder, C. Edward—R. H. Horton Assoc., Inc. (R)
Snyder, Suzanne—Wilkinson & Ives (R)

Soares, Gordon—Management Recruiters - Concord, CA.
Socha, Rudy—Advancement Recruiting Services
Sockwell, III, J. Edgar—Sockwell & Anderson (R)
Soffer, Herb—Baker Scott & Co.
Sola-Furnari, Debra A.—TeleSearch, Inc.
Soll, Shay—Management Recruiters
Solomon, Neil M.—The Neil Michael Group, Inc. (R)
Solomon, Phyllis—Phyllis Solomon Executive Search, Inc.
Soloway, David—The Madison Group (R)
Soltis, Charles W.—Soltis Management Services (R)
Sommer, Frank B.—Sanford Rose Assoc. of Binghamton
Sommer, Kim L.—The Pickwick Group, Inc.
Sondhi, Rick—Human Resource Technologies, Inc.
Sonen, Phyllis—Charles P. Oliver Assoc., Inc.
Sonis, Stephen M.—Stephen M. Sonis Assoc.
Souder, E.G.—The Talley Group
Souder, Elizabeth W.—Slayton Int'l., Inc. (R)
Southerland, Keith—Witt Assoc. Inc. (R)
Southwell, Robert G.—John Sibbald Assoc., Inc. (R)
Soutouras, M. James—Michael James & Co., Inc. (R)
Sowa, Larry—Peat Marwick Stevenson & Kellogg (R)
Spack, Gilbert, A.—Personnel Systems Int'l. Inc.
Spahr, Donald B.—Roth Young Executive Recruiters
Spala, Jeanne—Advanced Information Management
Spangenberg, J. Brand—The Brand Co., Inc. (R)
Spangler, Lloyd W.—Cole, Warren & Long, Inc. (R)
Spann, Richard E.—The Goodrich & Sherwood Co. (R)
Sparks, Francine—Willmott & Assoc.
Sparks, Robert W.—Protocol Inc.
Spatt, Jonathan M.—Hospitality Executive Search, Inc.
Spears, Luanna—Integrated Professional Services, Inc.
Speitel, James W.—Management Recruiters
Spellacy, James—Management Recruiters
Spence, Jr., Joseph T.—Russell Reynolds Assoc., Inc. (R)
Spencer, Judith—J.P.D. Group
Spicer, Jeff—Management Recruiters
Spiegel, E.—Sanford Rose Assoc. of Beachwood

Spiller, W. Barry—WBS Network Professional & Executive Search

Spindel, Howard—Integrated Management Solutions

Spinks, Robert L.—Joy Reed Belt & Assoc., Inc. (R)

Spiotta-DiMare, Loren—Carol Ball & Co., Inc.

Spitz, L. Grant—The Caldwell Partners Int'l. (R)

Spivack, Jewel—Sales Consultants

Spivack, Marvin—Sales Consultants

Splaine, Charles—Boyden Int'l., Inc. (R)

Splaine, Charles—Splaine & Assoc., Inc. (R)

Spoerlein, Kent—Robertson, Spoerlein & Wengert (R)

Spolsino, Robert J.—Russillo/Gardner

Sponseller, Vern—Richard Kader & Assoc.

Sprague, David—Michael Stern Assoc. Inc. (R)

Sprehe, J. Christopher—The Christopher Group

Spriggs, Robert D.—Spriggs & Co., Inc. (R)

Spring, Dennis—Spring Executive Search, Inc.

Springer, Mark H.—M.H. Springer & Assoc. (R)

Sproull, J. William—Patton, Perry & Sproull Inc. (R)

Squires, R. James—Smith, Roth & Squires (R)

St. Denis, Robert A.—Sanford Rose Assoc.

St. Jean, Norman D.—The Charles Ryan Group, Inc.

St. Thomas, Rick—Source Finance

Stack, Jr., J. William—Stack Assoc. (R)

Stack, Kevin M.—Circuit Search

Stadnyk, Mark—Adel Lawrence Assoc., Inc.

Staebler, Roger—Management Recruiters

Stafford, Charles B.—Management Recruiters of El Dorado

Stafford, JoDene—Management Recruiters of El Dorado

Stampfl, Eric—Morgan-Stampfl, Inc.

Stanczak, Larry—Source EDP

Stanewick, B. David—Stanewick, Hart & Assoc., Inc.

Stanford, M.J.—Empire International (R)

Stanislaw, Robert—Stanislaw & Assoc., Inc. (R)

Stanley, Russell H.—RHS Assoc., Inc.

Stanley, Wade—Management Recruiters

Staples, Arthur B.—Staples Consulting Inc. (R)

Stark, Jeffrey M.—Bedford-Orion Group, Inc.

Stark, Mary—David Allen Assoc.

Starling, Dick—Integrated Professional Services, Inc.

Staub, Robert A.—Staub, Warmbold & Barkauskas, Inc. (R)

Ste. Marie, Lynn—Personnel Unlimited/Executive Search

Ste. Marie, Mark—Personnel Unlimited/Executive Search

Ste. Marie, Stephen B.—Egon Zehnder Int'l. Inc. (R)

Steadmon, Charles E.—National Hospitality Assoc., Inc.

Stearn, Edward A.—Lynch & Co. (R)

Stecker, Bernd—Weinpel & Co.

Steel, Mark D.—Selective Management Services, Inc.

Steele, Gary—Romac & Assoc., Inc.

Steele, Jack—McRoberts & Assoc.

Steele, Kevin—Winter, Wyman & Co.

Steenstra, Daniel H.—Sales Consultants of Northern Jersey, Inc.

Stehr, Dana—Michael J. Cavanaugh & Assoc. (R)

Stein, Neil A.—R. H. Perry & Assoc., Inc. (R)

Stein, Terry W.—Stewart, Stein & Scott, Ltd. (R)

Steinbach, Daniel E.—Steinbach & Co.

Steinbach, David M.—Steinbach & Co.

Steinberg, Joanna—The Personnel Laboratory (R)

Steinberg, Paul D.—Inside Management Assoc. (R)

Steinem, Barbara—Dahl-Morrow Int'l. (R)

Steiner, John—Sales Consultants

Steinman, Richard—Career Marketing Assoc.

Steinman, Stephen M.—The Stevenson Group/SES (R)

Steinmann, Ernest—Sanford Rose Assoc.

Stelika, Kit—Dahl-Morrow Int'l. (R)

Stenholm, Gilbert R.—SpencerStuart (R)

Stephanian, Armand—Larson & Stephanian (R)

Stephens, Frederick H.—The Onstott Group (R)

Stephens, John R.—John R. Stephens & Assoc.

Stephens, Lee—Lee Stephens & Assoc. (R)

Stephens, Mark L.—Sales Consultants

Stephenson, Harold—C.R. Assoc.

Stephenson, Jeffrey B.—Bennett & Curran, Inc.

Stephenson, W. M.—Graham Assoc. Inc.

Sterling, Cheryl E.—Management Recruiters

Sterling, Peter D.—Peter Sterling & Co.

Sterling, Ronald L.—Management Recruiters

Stern, Burt—A.E. Feldman Assoc.

Stern, Daniel—Daniel Stern & Assoc.

Stern, Leslie W.—Stern & Watson, Inc. (R)

Stern, Michael—Michael Stern Assoc. Inc. (R)

Stern, Robert—Strauss Personnel Service

Sternlicht, Marvin—Accountants On Call

Sternlicht, Marvin—Accountants On Call

Sternlicht, Marvin—Accountants On Call

Steube, Diana L.—Dunhill Professional Search, Inc. of Kearney

Stevens, Gary J.—Stonehill Management
Consultants, Inc. (R)
Stevens, Mark—Management Recruiters
Stevens, Martha—The Stevens Group, Inc.
Stevens, Ron—Ron Stevens & Assoc., Inc.
Stevenson, Robert—People Management, Inc. (R)
Stewart, Jan J.—Egon Zehnder Int'l., Inc. (R)
Stewart, Jeffrey O.—Stewart, Stein & Scott, Ltd.
(R)
Stewart, Lawrence D.—Weatherby Healthcare
Stewart, Mel—Stewart/Laurence Assoc., Inc. (R)
Stewart, Stephen K.—S. K. Stewart & Assoc. (R)
Stewart, W.C.—Saley Partners Int'l. (R)
Stickler, III, Charles W.—Charles Stickler Assoc.
Stiles, Jack D.—Sanford Rose Assoc.
Stiles, Judy—Medquest Assoc.
Stiles, Linford E.—Ward Howell Int'l. Inc. (R)
Stilley, Morris—National Executive Consultants,
Inc.
Stimmel, A. Craig—Stimmel Search Division (R)
Stimmel, Carol F.—Stimmel Search Division (R)
Stirling, Jay—Earley Kielty & Assoc., Inc. (R)
Stirn, Brad—SpencerStuart (R)
Stobbe, David E.—Alzed Real Estate Recruiters
Stoch, Mary—Torretto & Assoc., Inc. (R)
Stockard, Robert G.—Sales Consultants
Stockton, J.R.—Management Catalysts (R)
Stoddard, Dean—The Stoddard Co.
Stoddard, Dorothy—The Stoddard Co.
Stoessel, Robert J.—Management Recruiters
Stoker, Lynn S.—Sales Consultants
Stokes, Maurice—Source EDP
Stolfi, Lillian—Sanford Rose Assoc.- Woodbury
Stoller, Barbara—Fisher-Todd Assoc.
Stoller, Richard S.—Heath/Norton Assoc., Inc. (R)
Stoltz, Robert—Management Recruiters
Stone, Edmond H.—Romac & Assoc., Inc.
Stone, Robert—Gardiner Stone Hunter Int'l., Inc.
(R)
Stone, Susan L.—Stone Enterprises Ltd.
Stoneburner, Dwight T.—Stoneburner Assoc., Inc.
Stoneham, Herbert E. C.—Stoneham Assoc. (R)
Storer, Steve—Management Recruiters of Butler
County
Storevik, T. Robert—Accounting Resources Int'l.,
Inc.
Storfer, Herbert F.—Storfer & Assoc.
Storfer, Herbert F.—The Dartmouth Group (R)
Storfer, Paul D.—Storfer & Assoc.
Storm, Danelle—Levin & Assoc. (R)
Storti, Michael A.—Storti Assoc., Inc.

Stovall, Phyllis—Phyllis Stovall Assoc., Inc.
Straight, Gary R.—Straight & Co.
Strain, Lee—Dougan-McKinley-Strain (R)
Strain, Stephen—SpencerStuart (R)
Strakosch, Kay—Dunhill Professional Search
Strathmann, Winfried R.—W. R. Strathmann
Assoc. (R)
Straube, Stan—Straube Assoc., Inc. (R)
Strawn, William M.—Houtz, Strawn Assoc. (R)
Streitfeld, Ira—Accountants On Call
Stricker, Jr., Sidney G.—Stricker & Zagor (R)
Strickland, Frank D.—Reddick and Co., Int'l. (R)
Stricklin, Joyce—Hall, Cooper & Bartman, Ltd.
Strimel, Rich—Source EDP
Stringer, Dann P.—D.E. Foster & Partners, L.P.
(R)
Strobo, Ray S.—Management Recruiters
Strom, Justin V.—Overton Group (R)
Strom, Mark N.—Personnel Advisors Int'l. Corp.
Strong, Duane—Executive Resource Inc.
Struzziero, Ralph E.—Romac & Assoc., Inc.
Stuart, Robert—Aerospace Technologies, Inc.
Sturm, Jr., Frederick C.—Sturm, Burrows & Co.
Stutey, Tony—Career Advancement
Sucharoa, Loni—Posse, Inc.
Sudeikis, Dan—Source EDP
Suhay, Gary T.—Sanford Rose Assoc.
Sulcer, Gordon T.—Boyden Int'l., Inc. (R)
Sullivan, Brian M.—Sullivan & Co. (R)
Sullivan, Dawn B.H.—Lambert & Sullivan Assoc.
Sullivan, Gene—John O'Keefe & Assoc., Inc. (R)
Sullivan, John—Korn/Ferry Int'l. (R)
Sullivan, John—BDO Seidam (R)
Sullivan, Jr., Joseph J.—Joe Sullivan & Assoc.,
Inc. (R)
Sullivan, Marty—RAC International
Sullivan, Robert C.—Sullivan-Murphy Assoc. (R)
Sullivan, Susan T.—S. Tyler Sullivan & Assoc.,
Inc.
Summerfield-Beall, Dotty—Summerfield Assoc.,
Inc.
Summerlin, Judi—Dunhill Professional Search
Group
Sumrall, Virginia—Sumrall Personnel Consultants,
Inc.
Sunshine, Ron—Ron Sunshine & Assoc.
Sur, William K.—Canny, Bowen Inc. (R)
Surrette, Mark J.—Robertson-Surrette Ltd. (R)
Suss, Mark J.—Retail Placement Assoc.
Sussman, Alexander J.—Sanford Rose Assoc.
Sussman, Mark—Carlden Personnel Services Inc.
Sutter, Howard W.—Romac & Assoc., Inc.

Sutton, Gary—CEO'S Only (R)
Sutton, Robert—The Caldwell Partners Int'l. (R)
Sutton, Ruth—Strategic Search Group
Svei, Donna—Donna Svei Assoc.
Svendsen, Phil—J.P.D. Group
Swan, Barbara—Lancaster Assoc., Inc.
Swan, Richard A.—Kieffer, Ford, & Hadelman, Ltd. (R)
Swaner, Stephen W.—J. Fielding Nelson & Assoc., Inc.
Swann, Al—The Beam Group (R)
Swanner, Bill—Source Finance
Swartz, Edward R.—TASA/Fleming (R)
Sweeney, Diane—John O'Keefe & Assoc., Inc. (R)
Sweeney, James W.—Sweeney Shepherd Bueschel Provus Harbert & Mummert, Inc. (R)
Sweeney, Patrick B.—The Kennett Group, Inc.
Sweet, Charles W.—A.T. Kearney Executive Search (R)
Sweet, Eleanor Anne—The Remington Group, Ltd.
Sweet, John—Wegner & Assoc.
Sweet, Robert J.—McMahon & Dee, Inc. (R)
Swidler, J. Robert—Egon Zehnder Int'l., Inc. (R)
Sykes, Hugh L.—Management Recruiters
Sykes, Hugh L.—Sales Consultants
Szajkovics, Charles A.—First Search Inc.
Szymanski, C.—Sanford Rose Assoc. of Beachwood
Tabb, Roosevelt—Sanford Rose Assoc.
Tabor, Gary—Ryerson Tabor Assoc.
Taft, David G.—Techsearch Services Inc.
Takacs, Carl—The WalCar Partnership (R)
Takacs, Gloria—Gilbert & Van Campen Int'l. (R)
Talabisco, Barbara—Gilbert Tweed Assoc., Inc. (R)
Talbot, Norman—Management Recruiters
Talley, E.H.—The Talley Group
Tama, Phyllis E.—Tama Lucas Ltd. (R)
Tannenbaum, David—The Lockridge Group, Inc. (R)
Tanton, John—Tanton/Mitchell Group (R)
Tanzi, Vito A.—Tanzi Executive Search
Taplinger, Mark—Source Finance
Tappan, Michael A.—Ward Howell Int'l. Inc. (R)
Tardugno, Carl—Management Recruiters
Tate, Gene M.—David Chambers & Assoc., Inc. (R)
Tatum, Sr., Philip M.—Tatum & Assoc., Inc.
Tatum, Jr., Philip M.—Tatum & Assoc., Inc.
Tavin, Jerry—Janou Pakter, Inc.
Tawney, Mel—M. L. Tawney & Assoc.
Taylor, Carl J.—Carl J. Taylor & Co. (R)

Taylor, Cheryl—Pro Counsel
Taylor, Conrad—Dotson Benefield & Assoc., Inc.
Taylor, Don R.—Personnel Management, Inc.
Taylor, Ernest A.—Ward Howell Int'l. Inc. (R)
Taylor, Gary C.—Stoneham Assoc. (R)
Taylor, Jane A.—Paul S. Pelland
Taylor, Jeffrey A.—Sales Consultants of Ft. Lauderdale
Taylor, John—Pro Counsel
Taylor, John C.—Howe-Lewis Int'l. (R)
Taylor, Kenneth W.—Egon Zehnder Int'l. Inc. (R)
Taylor, M. Kent—Taylor Search Assoc., Inc. (R)
Taylor, Michael—Cejka & Co. (R)
Taylor, Mike—People Management, Inc. (R)
Taylor, Peter R.—Peter R. Taylor Assoc., Inc.
Taylor, William R.—R.E. Lowe Assoc.
Tedesco, Joseph V.—Roth Young of Tampa
Telem, Peter B.—Telem Adhesive Search Corp.
Telleri, Frank C.—Curry, Telleri Group, Inc. (R)
Tello, Fernando—Korn/Ferry, Int'l., S.A. de C.V. (R)
Templin, Robert E.—Gilbert Tweed Assoc. (R)
Tenneson, Al—The Remington Group, Ltd.
Terada, Hideki—Pacific Advisory Service
Terkovich, Branko A.—Engineering Resource Group, Inc.
Terry, Marilyn M.—Ward Howell Int'l. Inc. (R)
Tesar, Bob—Tesar-Reynes, Inc. (R)
Tessin, M.J.—Management Recruiters
Tessin, M.J.—Sales Consultants
Textor, Jack T.—Personnel Inc.
Thadeus, Eda Franziska—P&IC Assoc.
Thadeus, Ralph Robert—P&IC Assoc.
Thaller, Carole—Retail Pacesetters, Inc.
Thayer, Robert T.—Executive Search of New England, Inc.
Theobald, David B.—Theobald & Assoc. (R)
Theodore, James—Johnson Smith & Knisely Inc. (R)
Thielman, Joseph—Barrett Partners
Thomas, Bill E.—Management Recruiters of Kinston
Thomas, Bob—Wesson, Taylor, Wells & Assoc.
Thomas, Candice—Greene Personnel Consultants
Thomas, Edwin J.—Professional Search Assoc., Inc.
Thomas, Elizabeth—Management Recruiters of Atlanta Downtown
Thomas, Jeffrey—Fairfaxx Management Assoc. (R)
Thomas, John T.—Ward Howell Int'l. Inc. (R)
Thomas, Lori—J. E. Lessner Assoc., Inc. (R)
Thomas, Lorraine M.—Thomas-Pond (R)

Thomas, M. Donald—Harold Webb Assoc., Ltd. (R)

Thomas, Norman A.—R.A.N. Assoc., Inc.

Thomas, Pat Bowers—Beckwith, Thomas & Fanning

Thomas, III, W. H.—Thomas, Richardson, Runden & Co. Inc. (R)

Thomas, William G.—Tech Mark Group (R)

Thompson, Carlton W.—SpencerStuart (R)

Thompson, John A.—The Interim Management Corp.(IMCOR) (R)

Thompson, Joshua C.—Garofolo, Curtiss, Lambert & MacLean (R)

Thompson, Judy—Judy Thompson & Assoc., Inc.

Thompson, Justin—Boardroom Planning & Consulting Group (R)

Thomson, H. Scott—Bialla & Assoc., Inc. (R)

Thomure, Joseph E.—Thomure Medsearch, Inc. (R)

Thornton, John—Aim Executive Consulting Services (R)

Thornton, John C.—Thornton Assoc.

Thornton, John W.—Denney & Co., Inc. (R)

Thorpe, David L.—Interim Managment Corp. (R)

Thrower, Tom—Sales Consultants

Thrower, Tom S.—Management Recruiters of Oakland

Thrower, Tom S.—Sales Consultants

Thunberg, Richard A.—Jeff Rich Assoc.

Tibbetts, Charles A.—The Tibbetts Group Ltd.

Tice, Diane—Accountants On Call

Tierney, George F.—Tierney Assoc., Inc. (R)

Tierney, John F.—Dunhill Professional Search

Tiffany, Brent—Todd Melon Group

Timmons, Denise—Phyllis Hawkins & Assoc.

Tippel, Fred C.—Sanford Rose Assoc.

Tirocchi, Fred—Tirocchi, Wright, Inc. (R)

Tischer, Donald F.—American Executive Search Services, Inc. (R)

Tischio, Lesley C.—META/MAT, Ltd. (R)

Tittle, David M.—Paul-Tittle Assoc., Inc.

Titus, Dave—Management Recruiters

Todd, Richard—Zachary & Sanders, Inc.

Toder, Jonathan—Setford-Shaw-Najarian Assoc., Ltd.

Toedtman, Craig—Effective Search, Inc. (R)

Tolette, I.G. Skip—The Schmitt Tolette Group (R)

Tomack, Arthur L.—Arthur Lyle Assoc., Inc.

Tomaras, David—Willmott & Assoc.

Tomlinson, Betsy S.—Bricker & Assoc., Inc. (R)

Toms, Dennis M.—National Recruiting Service

Toole, Thomas J.—Management Recruiters of Laguna Hills

Tootelian, Aram—Spectrum Consultants

Tornesello, Michael P.—The Yorkshire Group, Ltd. (R)

Torretto, Richard—Torretto & Assoc., Inc. (R)

Toth, Bob A.—Management Recruiters

Townley, Anthony—Hipp Waters, Inc.

Townsend, John W.—The Whitney Group (R)

Trachtenberg, Mort—Techno-Trac Systems, Inc.

Tracy, Patricia—USA Medical Placement Inc.

Tracy, Ronald O.—Egon Zehnder Int'l. Inc. (R)

Tracy, Stephen—Setford-Shaw-Najarian Assoc., Ltd.

Trainor, Joseph—Resource Services, Inc.

Trainor, Mary Ann—Resource Services, Inc.

Trapp, Ed—Management Recruiters of Reno

Trautvetter, Lee G.—Western Reserve Search Assoc. (R)

Travis, Edward—Management Recruiters

Travis, John A.—Travis & Co., Inc. (R)

Traynor, Thomas H.—Traynor Confidential, Ltd.

Tremblay, Gilles—Gilles Tremblay & Assoc. (R)

Trewhella, Mike—Source Finance

Tripician, Philip—Heritage Search Group, Inc.

Tripp, William J.—Management Recruiters of Dearborn, Inc.

Trompeter, James N.—Retail Recruiters of Stamford

Trout, Thomas L.—Trout & Assoc., Inc. (R)

Trowbridge, Robert L.—Trowbridge & Co., Inc. (R)

Troy, Helen O.—Theobald & Assoc. (R)

Truex, John F.—R.C. Morton & Assoc. Inc. (R)

Tsivitis, James—Boardroom Planning & Consulting Group (R)

Tucker, Barbara—Wesley Brown & Bartle Co., Inc. (R)

Tucker, Gilbert—The Bankers Register

Tucker, John J.—Tucker Assoc. (R)

Tucker, Merlene K.—Tucker Assoc. (R)

Tucker, Michael—Michael Tucker Assoc. (R)

Tucker, Thomas A.—The Thomas Tucker Co. (R)

Tully, James—Tully & Birch, Inc. (R)

Tumminelli, Peter C.—Peter C. Tumminelli & Assoc.

Tunney, William—Grant Cooper & Assoc., Inc. (R)

Tuohy, James A.—Management Recruiters

Turbak, Beverly L.—Carpenter, Shackleton & Co. (R)

Turner, David—Mark Elzweig Co. Ltd.

Turner, J.J.—Patrick Assoc.

Turner, Jim—J.Q. Turner & Assoc., Inc.

Turner, Michael—Rocky Mountain Recruiters, Inc.

Turner, R. Bronson—Inmark Executive Search (R)

Turnquist, Nancy J.—Crowder & Company (R)

Tuschman, Joe D.—JDavid Assoc., Inc. (R)

Tuttle, Donald E.—Tuttle, Neidhart, Semyan, Inc. (R)

Tweed, Janet—Gilbert Tweed Assoc., Inc. (R)

Twomey, Jim—Source Engineering

Tyler, J. Larry—Tyler & Co. (R)

Tyler, Ralph S.—H.C. Smith Ltd. (R)

Ulrich, Max M.—Ward Howell Int'l. Inc. (R)

Underwood, Dave—Sales Consultants

Underwood, Kenneth—Harold Webb Assoc., Ltd. (R)

Unger, Mike—Management Recruiters

Unger, Mike—Sales Consultants

Unger, Paul T.—P. T. Unger Assoc. (R)

Unger, Stephen—SpencerStuart (R)

Untermeyer, Martin—Martin Personnel Assoc.

Usher, Harry L.—Russell Reynolds Assoc., Inc. (R)

Utroska, Donald R.—SpencerStuart (R)

Vacca, Domenic L.—Romac & Assoc., Inc.

Vaccaro, George—The Advisory Group, Inc. (R)

Valchar, Deborah—M-A Management Assoc., Inc.

Valdez, Maria Elena—Korn/Ferry, Int'l., S.A. de C.V. (R)

Valencia-Icard, Cheryl A.—Management Recruiters

Valenti, Richard W.—Atlantic West Int'l.

Valentine, Donald K.—Tecmark Assoc. Inc.

Valentine, James P.—Valentine & Assoc.

Valentine, Linda S.—Valentine & Assoc.

Valentine-Hong, Teri—Dunhill Professional Search of Hawaii

Valletta, Frank L.—Valletta Ritson & Co. (R)

Valley, David—Phillips Group of Companies (R)

Van Berkel, Thomas—The Yorkshire Group, Ltd. (R)

Van Campen, Stephen B.—Gilbert & Van Campen Int'l. (R)

Van Dyke, Roger W.—Higgins Assoc., Inc. (R)

Van Erp, Mary C.—Resource Consultants

Van Es, Judith—mfg/Search, Inc.

Van Leer, Peter—Peter Van Leer & Assoc. (R)

Van Olst, Robert—H.M. Long Int'l., Ltd. (R)

Van Remmen, Roger—Brown/Bernardy, Inc.

Van Valkenburg, Arlene—Martin H. Bauman Assoc., Inc. (R)

VanMaldegiam, Norman E.—VanMaldegiam Assoc., Inc. (R)

VanReypen, Robert D.—VanReypen Enterprises, Ltd. (R)

VanReypen, Shirley—VanReypen Enterprises, Ltd. (R)

Vandegrift, Tom—Kiley-Owen Assoc., Inc.

Vanderploeg, Roger—SS & A Executive Search Consultants (R)

Vannoy, James—Engineering Specialists

Varian, Veronica—Management Recruiters

Varrichio, Mike—Source Engineering

Varrichio, Mike—Source EDP

Vasu, George—CCI - Career Consultants Int'l.

Vaughan, David B.—Dunhill Professional Search Irvine/Newport

Velcamp, John—John Velcamp & Assoc. (R)

Vento, Joseph P.—Vento Assoc.

Vergari, Jane—Herbert Mines Assoc., Inc. (R)

Verkamp, J. Frank—Verkamp-Joyce Assoc., Inc. (R)

Vernon, Jack H.—Russell Reynolds Assoc., Inc. (R)

Verstraete, Paul A.—Deven Assoc., Int'l., Inc. (R)

Verstraete, Paul A.—Deven Assoc., Int'l., Inc. (R)

Vevier, Charles—Drew Assoc. Int'l. (R)

Vezan, Henry D.—Vezan Assoc.

Vezina, Donald A.—Sales Consultants

Vick, Bill—Vick & Assoc.

Victor, K.C.—Marley Group Ltd.

Vienn, Charles E.—Career Resource Assoc., Inc.

Viglino, Victor P.—DHR Int'l, Inc. (R)

Viles, Deborah L.—Career Marketing Assoc.

Villa, Joe—DeHayes Consulting Group (R)

Villareal, Morey—Villareal & Assoc., Inc. (R)

Villella, Paul—Source EDP

Vincent, Darryl—Darryl Vincent & Assoc.

Violante, Anne M.—Chicago Legal Search, Ltd.

Violette, Brad—Accountants On Call

Virkler, Kim—Dupuis & Ryden, P.C. (R)

Virkus, Leigh—Source EDP

Viscusi, Stephen P.—The Viscusi Group, Inc. (R)

Vise, Jeff—Strategic Assoc., Inc.

Visnich, L. Christine—Bason Assoc., Inc. (R)

Vitacco, Robert J.—Romac & Assoc., Inc.

Vito, Joseph—Multi Processing, Inc.

Vittorioso, Antonio—Kling Personnel Assoc., Inc.

Vlcek, Thomas J.—Vlcek & Co., Inc. (R)

Vogel, Emil—Tarnow Int'l. (R)

Vogel, Michael S.—Vogel Assoc.

Vogel, Ruth—Sales Consultants of Westchester-South, Inc.

Vognsen, Rikke—David Saxner & Assoc., Inc.

Voigt, John A.—Romac & Assoc., Inc.

Voigt, Raymond R.—Voigt Assoc. (R)

Volpe, John—Search Masters

Volta, Shelly—Romac & Assoc., Inc.

Volz, Scott—Management Recruiters

Von Seldeneck, Judith M.—Diversified Health Search (R)

Von Seldeneck, Judith M.—Diversified Search, Inc. (R)

Von Seldeneck, Jr., L. Wood—Diversified Health Search (R)

Von Seldeneck, Jr., L. Wood—Diversified Search, Inc. (R)

Von Storch, Peter—Von Storch Assoc. (R)

Voros, Sharon—Paul Ray & Carre Orban Int'l. (R)

Wacholz, Rick—Gilbert Tweed Assoc., Inc. (R)

Wackerle, Frederick W.—McFeely Wackerle Shulman (R)

Waggoner, Leland T.—Warring & Assoc. (R)

Wagman, Marc E.—Management Recruiters

Wagoner, Robert E.—Brissenden, McFarland, Wagoner & Fuccella, Inc. (R)

Wainwright, Nancy—Locus Inc.

Wainz, Melissa—Sales Consultants

Waite, Thomas M.—Sales Consultants

Wakefield, J. Alvin—Gilbert Tweed Assoc., Inc. (R)

Walbright, Lynn M.—Video Interview Professionals, Inc.

Wald, E. Steven—Salesworld-Division of Metacor Inc.

Waldon, Jeffrey—Accountants On Call

Waldon, Maita—Accountants On Call

Waldorf, Esq., Michael—Waldorf Associates, Inc.

Waldron, James P.—Boardroom Planning & Consulting Group (R)

Walker, Donald R.—Prior Martech Assoc. (R)

Walker, Douglas G.—Kishbaugh Associates (R)

Walker, Eric E.—The Lighthouse Group

Walker, Robin—Tyler & Co. (R)

Walker, Ron—Korn/Ferry Int'l. (R)

Walker, Walter G.—Walker Group, Inc. (R)

Wall, Pat—MD Resources, Inc. (R)

Wall, Peter—Management Recruiters

Wallace, Jr., Charles E.—Lamalie Assoc., Inc. (R)

Wallace, Marilyn—Management Recruiters

Wallens, Charles N.—Frank X. Walsh & Co., Inc.

Waller, Susan—Goss & Assoc., Inc. (R)

Wallskog, Alan G.—Jude M. Werra & Assoc. (R)

Walsh, Albert J.—Albert J. Walsh & Assoc. (R)

Walsh, Bill—Technical Engineering Consultants

Walsh, Jr., Denis P.—Denis P. Walsh & Assoc., Inc.

Walsh, Edmund J.—Weston Consultants, Inc. (R)

Walsh, James L.—James L. Walsh & Assoc., Inc. (R)

Walsh, Mary—Sales Consultants

Walsh, Robert D.—The Cantor Concern, Inc.

Walt, Lee—M H Executive Search Group

Walter, Kevin P.—R.E. Lowe Assoc.

Walters, William F.—Barnes, Walters & Assoc., Inc. (R)

Walton, Lee H.—Picard & Co., Inc. (R)

Ward, Al—Management Recruiters

Ward, Anthony C.—Ward Liebelt Assoc. Inc. (R)

Ward, Bruce F. G.—Heidrick and Struggles, Inc. (R)

Ward, Dick—Chanko-Ward, Ltd. (R)

Ward, James M.—Roth Young of Boston

Ward, Lincoln R.—Executive Management Systems, Inc. (R)

Ward, Martha—Martha Ward Assoc., Inc.

Ward, Ted—Korn/Ferry Int'l. (R)

Ware, John—SpencerStuart (R)

Warmbold, Herman P.—Staub, Warmbold & Barkauskas, Inc. (R)

Warns, Peter—The DataFinders Group, Inc.

Warren, Gail—Sloan & Assoc., Inc.

Warren, Richard—Cole, Warren & Long, Inc. (R)

Warren, Tom S.—F.L.A.G.

Warrillow, Nicholas—WestCare Executive Search

Warring, J. T.—Warring & Assoc. (R)

Wasp, Jr., Warren T.—WTW Assoc., Inc. (R)

Wasse, Mary K.—M.K. Wasse & Assoc., Inc.

Wasserman, Hilton N.—Hilton N. Wasserman & Assoc. Inc. (R)

Wasson, Thomas W.—SpencerStuart (R)

Watanabe, Kunihiko—The Whitney Group (R)

Watern, Susan—Goss & Assoc., Inc. (R)

Waters, G.E.—WDI, Int'l. (R)

Waters, Larry—The Placers, Inc.

Watkins, Mitchell—Holland Rusk & Assoc. (R)

Watson, Diana—Davis-Smith Medical-Dental Employment Service, Inc.

Watson, Hanan S.—Stern & Watson, Inc. (R)

Watson, Wally—Management Recruiters

Wattelet, Frank—Dunhill Professional Search

Wayne, Cary S.—ProSearch, Inc.

Weaver, Calvin F.—Opportunity Knocking, Inc.

Weaver, Doris—D.L. Weaver & Assoc.

Weaver, John T.—Howe-Weaver, Inc. (R)

Weaver, L. Paul—Sanford Rose Assoc.

Webb, Elliot—E.J. Lance Management Assoc., Inc.

Webb, Jr., George H.—Webb, Johnson & Klemmer, Inc. (R)

Webb, J.S.—N.W. Gibson Int'l. (R)

Webb, John W.—Sanford Rose Assoc.

Webb, Wallace G.—Thalatta Corp. (R)

Weber, Fritz—Management Recruiters of Cedar Rapids, Inc.

Weber, H. Jurgen—BioQuest Inc. (R)

Weber, Ronald R.—Weber Executive Search (R)

Weber, Wanda—Management Recruiters of Cedar Rapids, Inc.

Weber, Zenia—Gilbert Tweed Assoc., Inc. (R)

Weeks, Mercon A.—Weeks & Assoc.

Wegner, Carl—Wegner & Assoc.

Weidener, Andrew E.—Paul R. Ray & Co., Inc. (R)

Weinberg, Mel—Romac & Assoc., Inc.

Weiner, Art—Sanford Rose Assoc.

Weiner, Paula—Johnson Smith & Knisely Inc. (R)

Weiner, Robert—Setford-Shaw-Najarian Assoc., Ltd.

Weingarten, Trudy—Simpson Assoc.

Weinman, Mary—Weinman & Assoc.

Weinpel, Charles J.—Weinpel & Co.

Weir, Douglas S.—Weir Executive Search Assoc., Inc. (R)

Weiss, Cathy—C. Weiss Assoc., Inc. (R)

Weiss, David L.—D. L. Weiss & Assoc. (R)

Weiss, Gerald E.—Nuessle, Kurdziel & Weiss, Inc. (R)

Weiss, Jeff—Search West, Inc.

Weiss, Julianne—Accountants On Call

Weiss, Terry M.—Weiss & Assoc., Inc.

Welch, R. Thomas—RIC Corp. (R)

Weliver, Edward A.—Weliver & Assoc.

Welker, Henry A.—Henry Welker & Assoc.

Weller, Jr., Paul S.—Mark Stanley & Co. (R)

Wells, David—Sheridan Search (R)

Wells, Edward—Personnel Assoc.

Wells, Robert A.—R.A. Wells Co.

Welzig, Frank E.—MPI Assoc.

Wentworth, John—The Wentworth Co., Inc. (R)

Werbin, Susan—Werbin Assoc. Executive Search, Inc.

Werner, Cleo—Intertech Search Group

Werra, Jude M.—Jude M. Werra & Assoc. (R)

Werre, Tom—Professions Unlimited, Inc.

Wesley, Terry—Management Recruiters

Wesley, Terry—Management Recruiters

West, Lisa—WestCare Executive Search

Westberry, David M.—Ward Howell Int'l. Inc. (R)

Westcott, Robert F.—Westcott Associates, Inc. (R)

Westerfield, Portia P.—Bob Westerfield & Assoc., Inc.

Westerfield, Putney—Boyden Int'l., Inc. (R)

Westerfield, Robert H.—Bob Westerfield & Assoc., Inc.

Westley, H. L.—Management Recruiters of North Oakland County, Inc.

Westover, Ron—Management Recruiters

Westwater, John C.—SpencerStuart (R)

Wexler, Suzanne—S.J. Wexler Assoc., Inc.

Wheel, Eric—Management Recruiters

Wheel, Eric C.—Management Recruiters

Wheeler, Robert W.—Wheeler Assoc.

Wheeler, Thomas E.—Blendow, Crowley & Oliver, Inc. (R)

Wheeler, William A.—Wheeler, Moore & Elam Co. (R)

Wheelless, Pat—Wheelless Group

Whisenant, Rachel—O'Rourke Co., Inc. (R)

Whitaker, Bruce—Whitaker, Fellows & Assoc.

Whitbeck, Elizabeth C.—Whitbeck & Assoc.

White, Carroll—Sales Consultants Chicago Southeast

White, Jr., Charles R.—White-Ridgely & Assoc., Inc.

White, Dale—Roth Young Seattle

White, Daniel J.—PLRS/Career Connections

White, Daniel J.—Midwest Medical Recruiters

White, David—W. Robert Eissler & Assoc., Inc.

White, David J.—David J. White & Assoc., Inc.

White, Jack—Sales Consultants Chicago Southeast

White, Joel P.—Sales Consultants

White, Michael—Kellogg Consulting Group (R)

White, Richard B.—SpencerStuart (R)

White, Robert B.—Management Recruiters

White, Robert B.—M.R. Pennington Co.

Whitehead, Elizabeth S.—Whitehead & Assoc., Inc.

Whitehead, Robert S.—Whitehead & Assoc., Inc.

Whitley, Thomas—Management Recruiters

Whitley, Tom—Management Recruiters

Whitlock, Ann N.—Coleman Lew & Assoc., Inc. (R)

Whitney, Jr., Kenneth L.—K. L. Whitney & Co., Inc. (R)

Whitney, Jr., King—The Personnel Laboratory (R)

Whitney, Ron—Sales Consultants

Whitney, Ron—Management Recruiters

Whittaker, Arnold G.—Whittaker & Assoc., Inc.

Whittaker, Cynthia—Brentwood Int'l. (R)

Whittinghill, David—Brentwood Int'l. (R)

Wichman, Tom—Management Recruiters of Savannah

Wicker, David J.—Agri-Personnel

Wolfis, William—William N. Davis & Assoc., Inc. (R)

Wolfson, Gary M.—The Blackman Kallick Search Division (R)

Wolfson, Robert H.—Mitchell/Wolfson, Assoc. (R)

Wolkensperg, G. Michael—Phillips Group of Companies (R)

Wollmar, Stellan P.—Montaigne Assoc., Inc.

Wolman, Steve—S. R. Wolman Assoc., Inc. (R)

Wolters, Tony—Management Recruiters

Wolters, Tony—Management Recruiters

Wolters, Tony—Sales Consultants

Wolters, Tony—Sales Consultants

Wong, Walter—Busch Int'l. (R)

Wood, Gerald I.—Management Recruiters

Wood, Karen—Armitage Assoc. (R)

Wood, Michael D.—Wood, Franchot Inc. (R)

Wood, Milton M.—Wood/Sprau/Tannura, Inc. (R)

Wood, Thomas C.—Trac One (R)

Wood, William M.—Wood-Glavin, Inc. (R)

Woodruff, Mark S.—Management Recruiters

Woodson, Benjamin N.—Warring & Assoc. (R)

Woodson, Jim—Jim Woodson & Assoc., Inc.

Woodward, Charles R.—Dunhill of Greater Akron, Inc.

Woodward, Lee—Search Assoc., Inc.

Woodworth, Gail L.—Cascadia Group Int'l. (R)

Wooten, James—Management Recruiters

Worsham, John W.—John W. Worsham & Assoc., Inc.

Wozny, Judy—Florapersonnel, Inc.

Wraith, Bill—David Powell, Inc. (R)

Wray, Dick—Dick Wray & Consultants (R)

Wright, Don—Bialla & Assoc., Inc. (R)

Wright, Doug—Management Recruiters

Wright, James—J.D. Wright & Assoc., Inc.

Wright, Janet—The Landmark Consulting Group Inc. (R)

Wright, Jay—The Wright Group

Wright, John R.—Sales Consultants

Wright, M.L.—The Wright Group

Wright, Marilyn—J.D. Wright & Assoc., Inc.

Wright, Michael W.—Challenger & Hunt (R)

Wright, Paula G.—Tirocchi, Wright, Inc. (R)

Wright, Ralph—McMahon & Dee, Inc. (R)

Wujack, Sandi—Accountants On Call

Wunder, Don—TransAmerica Network

Wunder, Nancy—TransAmerica Network

Wylie, John L.—John Wylie Assoc., Inc.

Wynn, Dennis N.—Dennis Wynn Assoc., Inc.

Wynn, Jean—Dennis Wynn Assoc., Inc.

Wynne, Linda—Dunhill Personnel System, Inc.

Wytmar, R.J.—Wytmar & Co., Inc. (R)

Wyton, Mary—P.J. Lynch Assoc. (R)

Xagas, Steve—Xagas & Assoc. (R)

Yacullo, William J.—Lauer, Sbarbaro Assoc., Inc. (R)

Yaeger, Don—The Century Group

Yager, Jim—Sales Consultants

Yaiser, Richard A.—The Yaiser Group

Yake, Tom—Yake & Assoc.

Yamamoto, Ronald T.—Boyden Int'l., Inc. (R)

Yannelli, Albert—Yannelli, Randolph & Co.

Yarbrough, Tyler—Nelson Associates

Yaseen, Joel—Pre-Search, Inc. (R)

Yeager, Jeffrey A.—Sales Consultants

Yeisley, Larry—Gaffney Management Consultants (R)

Yelverton, Jack R.—Yelverton & Co. (R)

Yin, Ernest—The Caldwell Partners Int'l. (R)

Yoelin, Andrew S.—Ridenour & Assoc. (R)

Yoffe, Linda—Crest Management Search, Inc.

Yorke, Bill—Fox-Morris Assoc., Inc.

Young, Alexander—Messett Assoc., Inc. (R)

Young, Arthur—Management Recruiters of Stanhope Corp.

Young, Dennis F.—Tell/Com Recruiters

Young, Dorothy—LaDuke & Assoc., Inc.

Young, Edith Lord—Jay Mitchell & Co. (R)

Young, Florence D.—Alexander Enterprises, Inc.

Young, Laurie—Part Time Resources

Young, Louise M.—Raines Int'l. Inc. (R)

Young, Mimi—Educational Management Network (R)

Young, Nancy Ann—Crest Management Search, Inc.

Young, Nicholas S.—SpencerStuart (R)

Young, Susan—Management Recruiters

Young, W. M.—Sigma Group Inc. (R)

Young, Wayne T.—Management Recruiters

Youngberg, Dave—Source EDP

Youngs, Donald L.—Youngs & Co. (R)

Youngs, Judith A.—Youngs & Co. (R)

Yungerberg, Steven A.—Steven Yungerberg Assoc., Inc. (R)

Zabinski, Michael J.—First Colorado Consulting Group, Inc. (R)

Zabriskie, Jr., Charles—Charles Zabriskie Assoc., Inc. (R)

Zaccaria, Frances—Zaccaria Group, Inc.

Zaccaria, Jack—Zaccaria Group, Inc.

Zaccaro, Joseph L.—The Human Resource Consulting Group, Inc. (R)

Appendix

The Job and Career Library

The best books in the field, available through Consultants Bookstore. (See ordering information, page 819.)

General Guides to Job-Changing

WHAT COLOR IS YOUR PARACHUTE?
The "keystone" book, with classic advice on the "how-to-find-your-way-and-get-the-right-job" field. Since '72, the most popular job-hunting book, revised annually . . . includes "Quick Job-Hunting Map." (Ten Speed Press)
. . . by Richard Nelson Bolles/426pp/1992/paperback **$12.95**

BEST OF THE NATIONAL BUSINESS EMPLOYMENT WEEKLY
These booklets zero in on job hunting issues & treat them with substance & style—8 articles per topic. Choose from **On-the-Job Strategies, Before the Job Search, Resume & Letter Writing, Networking, Interviewing, Third-Party Sources, Job Change Fundamentals, Psychological Factors, Barriers to Employment, Negotiation, Relocation, Entrepreneurism & Small Business Issues.** (Dow Jones)
. . . Each booklet: **$5.00 ppd** *. . . Set of 12:* **$60.00 ppd**

THE COMPLETE JOB-SEARCH HANDBOOK
Shows how to look for career opportunities every day. Focuses on 20 life skills in self-assessment, detective work, communication skills & selling yourself. Includes skill-building exercises. (Henry Holt & Co.)
. . . by Howard Figler/366pp/1988/paperback **$12.95**

JOB SEARCH: THE TOTAL SYSTEM

A thorough guide that shows how to link networking/resume writing/interviewing/references/follow-up letters to land that job . . . How to use the right words to push "hot buttons," select the right search firm and negotiate value . . . 30 resumes included . . . Complete package includes hardcover book, 6 cassettes with 9 hours of motivational material, workbook and study guide for action plan and skill-building, companion planner & organizer for job-campaign materials. (John Wiley & Sons, Inc.)
. . . *by Kenneth Dawson & Sheryl Dawson/244pp/1988/paperback*
. . . **Book only: $14.95** . . . **Complete package: $199.95**

HOW TO SEEK A NEW AND BETTER JOB

A good thing in a small package, packed with information on cover letters/resumes/mailings . . . includes a penetrating self-analysis & 56 questions asked by interviewers . . . many useful forms & lists. (Kennedy Publications)
. . . *by William Gerraughty/64pp/1987/paperback* **$5.95**

THE JOB SEARCH ORGANIZER

A job-search manual & workbook in one. Read the text for the basics of goal setting/resume writing/networking/interviewing, then fill in the work sheets with information on job prospects/telephone contacts/mailings. (Miranda Associates)
. . . *100pp/1990/paperback* **$14.95**

WINNING AT JOB HUNTING

This comprehensive video/workbook approaches job hunting as a total system that anyone can master with practice. Schnapper builds on a detailed Accomplishments Form & links that to the "how will it benefit the employer?" acid test. Working with several job hunters, he drives home his points by critiquing resumes & interview responses, offering more powerful alternatives. (Successful Job Hunting, Inc.)
. . . *by Mel Schnapper, Ph.D./1-hr video (VHS) & 53pp manual* **$59.95**

RITES OF PASSAGE AT $100,000+

Though written for high-level job-changers, this book has 6 revealing chapters on dealing with recruiters: interesting to see the kind of advice they're armed with (most of it pretty solid!). (Viceroy Press)
. . . *by John Lucht/547pp/1991/hardcover* **$29.95**

SMART MOVES
Take charge of your career before it takes charge of you! The key is finding the corporate culture that fits your needs & values . . . not a "how to" book so much as a perceptive study of the factors that make for meaningful management careers. (Basil Blackwell)
. . . by Godfrey Golzen and Andrew Garner/228pp/1990 hardcover **$29.95**

STAYING EMPLOYED
An important preventive-maintenance manual, geared toward planning ahead for the day your services are no longer needed, with detailed strategies for keeping yourself marketable & coping with financial matters when you're between jobs. (D.C. Heath and Company)
. . . by Tom Daoust/226pp/1990/paperback **$11.95**

WHAT YOUR BOSS CAN'T TELL YOU
Solid advice on assessing your career by evaluating your job & how you perform, your relationship with your boss & fellow workers, the company & its markets . . . and, the key question: Do you fit? (American Management Association)
. . . by Kent Straat/280pp/1988/paperback **$14.95**

Advice on Your Career

DO IT! LET'S GET OFF OUR BUTS
This brassy batch of inspiration—quoting everyone from Carl Jung to Erica Jong—will jolt even utter sloths onto the right career path. A pop-cultured, gimmicky but accurate map of modern life's rocky, raucous roads. (Prelude Press)
. . . by John-Roger & Peter McWilliams/496pp/1991/ hardcover **$20.00**

CAREERING AND RE-CAREERING FOR THE 1990's
A unique overview that details trends in the marketplace, how to identify opportunities, how to retrain for them & how to land the position you want . . . plus a chapter on starting your own business. (Impact Publications)
. . . by Ronald Krannich/314pp/1989/paperback **$13.95**

GET A BETTER JOB!
Real-world strategies for carving out a better niche for yourself in the job market. Supportive & upbeat, with a welcome touch of irreverence. (Peterson's Guides)
. . . by Ed Rushlow/216pp/1990/paperback **$11.95**

SHIFTING GEARS
Job shifting (& the angst that goes with it) has become a way of life for millions of Americans. Hyatt examines the social/psychological implications of change & offers hope for those who want to face the next transition with aplomb. (Simon & Schuster)
. . . by Carole Hyatt/271pp/1990/hardcover **$18.95**

CONDUCT EXPECTED
These "Unwritten Rules for a Successful Business Career" are hard-nosed, cynical, even bitter, but they are laced with honesty & realism! And they tell you how to turn the unwritten rules to your advantage. (New Century Publishers)
. . . by William Lareau/198pp/1985/paperback **$12.95**

Q: HOW DO I FIND THE RIGHT JOB?
A: ASK THE EXPERTS
Based on candidate interviews with human resource directors at Fortune 500 companies . . . covers a broad range of job-hunting material in an original Q-and-A format. (John Wiley & Sons, Inc.)
. . . by David Bowman & Ronald Kweskin/225pp/1990/ paperback **$10.95**

Making Contact

---

200 LETTERS FOR JOB HUNTERS
A terrific resource for rusty or uninspired letter writers. Samples cover dozens of possible situations & purposes, from approaching the company of your dreams to expressing regret after a turndown. (Ten Speed Press)
. . . by William S. Frank/345pp/1990/paperback **$14.95**

THE PERFECT JOB REFERENCE
Step-by-step methods for securing those all-important words of recommendation, whether you need a letter of introduction, a telephone reference, or a follow-up call made on your behalf. (John Wiley & Sons, Inc.)
. . . by Jeffrey G. Allen/192pp/1990/paperback **$9.95**

NETWORK YOUR WAY TO JOB & CAREER SUCCESS
In-depth practical advice covering everything you need to know to identify, build & use contacts to advance your career. (Impact Publications)
. . . by Ronald L. Krannich & Caryl R. Krannich/147pp/1989/ paperback **$11.95**

Interviewing to Win

THE PERFECT INTERVIEW
How not to hang yourself during those crucial 30 minutes or so, with useful skill-building exercises & tips on psyching yourself up/ framing good questions/following through/negotiating salary. (AMACOM)
. . . by John D. Drake/189pp/1991/paperback **$17.95**

THE FIVE-MINUTE INTERVIEW
Assertive intervention techniques for taking control of the interview & positioning yourself as the best candidate. Scores of sample interview questions are a real bonus. (John Wiley & Sons, Inc.)
. . . by Richard Beatty/201pp/1986/paperback **$10.95**

SWEATY PALMS:
THE NEGLECTED ART OF BEING INTERVIEWED
A guide for several types of interviews, including stress & group sessions . . . how to build confidence, cut tension & handle tough questions . . . perceptive, up-to-date . . . examples ring with realism. (Ten Speed Press)
. . . by H. Anthony Medley/190pp/1984/paperback **$8.95**

KNOCK 'EM DEAD

Good advice on how to win interviews & prepare for them, all as a build-up for "Great Answers to Tough Questions," especially the really nasty ones . . . includes several nifty "finishing touches." (Bob Adams, Inc.)

. . . by Martin John Yate/155pp/1991/paperback **$7.95**

THE JOB INTERVIEW

Solid interviewing tips on two cassettes . . . perfect for a refresher in the car on the way to the interview . . . a short but substantive booklet rounds out the package. (Sullivan/Lee Industries, Inc.)

. . . Two 45-minute cassettes & 20pp booklet/1989 **$19.95**

JOB INTERVIEWS: HOW TO WIN THE OFFER

Succinct practical advice in a no-frills format . . . especially valuable on questions to expect & appropriate responses. (Sun Features)

. . . by Joyce Lain Kennedy/32pp booklet/1990 **$5.00**

Preparing Your Resume

RESUMES: THE NITTY GRITTY

Short and to-the-point: 16 steps to developing a resume, with examples of resumes that sell. (Sun Features)

. . . by Joyce Lain Kennedy/28pp booklet/1987 **$5.00**

THE EXECUTIVE RESUME BOOK

An interview bell-ringer that positions the resume as a strategic tool & demonstrates clearly what to do & how to do it . . . steps into the employer's shoes to show turn-ons & turn-offs . . . self-assessment, telemarketing . . . loaded with sample letters & resumes. (John Wiley & Sons, Inc.)

. . . by Loretta Foxman/210pp/1989/paperback **$12.95**

THE OVERNIGHT RESUME

A results-oriented, nuts-and-bolts guide to resume writing, packed with original tips from a pro. We've seen dozens of books on the subject, & this one really stands out in a crowd. (Ten Speed Press)

. . . by Donald Asher/112pp/1991/paperback **$6.95**

INDIVIDUAL'S RESUME MAKER
A tool for the personal computer user, this multipurpose software package formats your resume automatically once you've entered in your personal data . . . also keeps track of correspondence, appointments & other job-related activities. (Individual Software, Inc.)

. . . IBM PC & PC compatible version requires 512K & DOS 2.0 or higher & includes both 3½" & 5¼" disks **$49.95**
. . . Macintosh version includes 3½" disk **$49.95**

Special Situations

JOB-BRIDGE: AN OUTPLACEMENT AND CAREER TRANSITION PROGRAM
Great multimedia kit includes: text, with job search/marketing plan; workbook with many forms/resumes/cover letters; calendar/ planner, including tax-deductible expense advice; training video with interview strategies & negotiating techniques; information network linking participants with executive search firms. (Wilson & McLaren Inc.)

. . . by Robert Wilson/1988 **$275.00**

HOW TO LEAVE YOUR JOB & BUY A BUSINESS OF YOUR OWN
A basic "buy-or-start-your-own-business" book, but with advice on how to do it while still employed . . . including strategies for leaving your job . . . weak on developing a business plan, strong on finding/valuing/financing a business. (McGraw-Hill)

. . . by C.D. Peterson/207pp/1988/hardbound **$22.95**

MID-CAREER JOB HUNTING
OFFICIAL HANDBOOK OF THE 40+ CLUB
Approaches job search as business problem-solving activity . . . good advice on emotional & practical aspects of searching & interviewing . . . shows how to match second career to self-image. (Prentice-Hall, Inc.)

. . . by E. Patricia Birsner/250pp/1991/paperback **$14.00**

GETTING A JOB AFTER 50
Realistic, age-specific advice for redirecting your career or resuming it after retirement. Strong sections on age discrimination & myths/realities. (Liberty Hall Press)

. . . by John S. Morgan/264pp/1990/paperback **$14.95**

THE RELOCATING SPOUSE'S GUIDE TO EMPLOYMENT
A comprehensive job-hunting resource for the uprooted, military or otherwise. Includes 51 case studies & 3 useful appendices listing associations, publications & federal job information/testing centers. (Woodley Publications)
. . . by Frances Bastress/258pp/1989/paperback **$12.95**

International Careers

THE COMPLETE GUIDE TO INTERNATIONAL JOBS & CAREERS
A valuable resource for anyone contemplating international employment. Combines solid job-hunting advice with nitty-gritty info on major companies, organizations, agencies & consulting firms that hire international specialists. (Impact Publications)
. . . by Ronald L. Krannich and Caryl R. Krannich/320pp/1990/ paperback **$13.95**

KEY EUROPEAN EXECUTIVE SEARCH FIRMS AND THEIR U.S. LINKS
First compilation of its kind. Identifies linkages—from both directions—of more than 500 search offices in U.S. & 23 European countries. Useful in evaluating competitiveness & selecting affiliates. (Kennedy Publications)
. . . 210pp/1991/paperback **$39.00 ppd**

THE EUROPEAN EMPLOYMENT DIRECTORY
Profiles 100 of Europe's largest companies, including home office, operating units, summary size/industry information: complete addresses, phone, key contacts. Same for 125 U.S. companies operating in Europe. Helpful text on nuances of interviews & appropriate behavior. (Docker Research Group)
. . . 96pp/1991/jumbo paperback **$95.00**

Landing on Your Feet

FIRED FOR SUCCESS
Another on the theme of making lemonade from lemons . . . focuses on discovering your unique qualities & communicating them effectively, while coaching you to eliminate barriers to success. (Warner Books)
. . . by Judith A. Dubin & Melanie R. Keveles/233pp/1990/ paperback **$12.95**

CONGRATULATIONS! YOU'VE BEEN FIRED
Savvy, highly readable advice from a woman who learned the hard way . . . loaded with practical tips & tactics for salvaging self-esteem . . . covers everything from what to do "the mourning after" to landing a more gratifying job. (Fawcett Columbine)
. . . by Emily Koltnow & Lynne S. Dumas/260pp/1990/
paperback **$8.95**

Working with Search Firms

THE HEADHUNTERS
Reads like historical novel about high-level search . . . great for down time between interviews . . . case histories loaded with insight, despite Byrne's apparent bias against search. (Macmillan)
. . . by John Byrne/280pp/1986/hardcover **$19.95**

HOW TO GET A HEADHUNTER TO CALL
Heavily anecdoted & delivered in bite-sized pieces, this gee-whiz treatment is factual & informative while coated with candor & humor. (John Wiley)
. . . by Howard Freedman/165pp/1986/paperback **$12.95**

EXECUTIVE MUSICAL CHAIRS
A smorgasbord of practical ideas & insights for recruiters, their clients & candidates . . . spiced with wit, leavened with common sense . . . even veterans of the process can learn a lot from it. (Warrington & Co.)
. . . by William Wilkinson/208pp/1983/hardbound **$15.00**

THE CAREER MAKERS
Fascinating 2-page profiles of "Top 100" individual recruiters, plus industry/functional cross-index including 100 more. Has 80 pages of text on working with recruiters, including a few war stories. (Harper & Row)
. . . by John Sibbald/384pp/1990/hardbound **$22.95**

EXECUTIVE TEMPORARY PLACEMENT FIRMS
First-of-its kind list of firms placing executives in temporary positions . . . profiles market & key players, lists 82 firms, with specialties/address/phone/key contact . . . updated October 1991. (Kennedy Publications)
. . . 14pp report **$10.00 ppd**

HOW TO ANSWER A HEADHUNTER'S CALL
Good roundup of search basics, with solid & practical advice on resumes/interviewing/job campaign/reference-checking/offers, etc . . . by Washington solo (AMACOM)

. . . by Robert Perry/249pp/1984/paperback **$9.95**

THE DIRECTORY OF EXECUTIVE RECRUITERS
Famous Red Book: paperback edition published since '71 for job changers. Lists 3600 offices of over 2000 search firms in U.S./ Canada/Mexico. Indexes management functions, industries, geography and 5500 individuals, plus 100pp of useful text on conducting a successful job search. (Kennedy Publications)

THE CORPORATE EDITION
Jumbo hardcover edition of the above paperback for clients/users of search firms with more detailed information on each firm: revenues, staff sizes, phone numbers, plus 100pp of text on using executive recruiters. (Kennedy Publications)

*. . . **Paperback edition** 800pp/21st ed./1992* **$39.95 ppd**
*. . . **Hardbound edition** 872pp/2nd ed./1991-92* **$79.00 ppd**

50 LEADING RETAINED EXECUTIVE SEARCH FIRMS IN NORTH AMERICA
Special Report from Executive Recruiter News lists top retainer firms large & small in the U.S., Canada & Mexico, with profiles & key contact info on each. (Kennedy Publications)

. . . 8pp report **$10.00 ppd**

40 LARGEST RETAINED EXECUTIVE SEARCH FIRMS, U.S. & WORLD
Special Report detailing revenues/staff size/offices/key contact info for 40 largest retained search firms in the U.S. & world. (Kennedy Publications)

. . . 8pp report **$10.00 ppd**

CUSTOMIZED LABELS AND BREAKOUT REPORTS
Addresses of search firms from The Directory of Executive Recruiters, printed on labels for mailing to groups of firms you select—by industry and function specialties and geographic location. Helps executives approach the search firms most likely to be sources of job leads. Call Consultants Bookstore for details on options and pricing.

DOZENS OF OTHER BOOKS AVAILABLE

We've listed above primarily books of interest to job seekers and career changers, but there are many others available for corporate users of both executive search and management consulting services. Send for our free executive recruiting and management consulting catalogs or call for more information.

KENNEDY PUBLICATIONS

Consultant's Bookstore Ordering Information

Prices subject to change due to publishers' increases.

Postage/Handling	U.S.	Canada
Up to $25.00	+ $4.	+ $7.
$25.01 to $50.00	+ $5.	+ $9.
$50.01 to $75.00	+ $6.	+ $11.
$75.01 to $100.00	+ $7.	+ $13.
$100.01 to $150.00	+ $8.	+ $15.
Over $150.00	+ $9.	+ $17.

For your convenience we accept MasterCard, VISA and American Express or check.

Send to:
  Consultants Bookstore
  Kennedy Publications
  Templeton Road
  Fitzwilliam, NH 03447

Call:
  603/585-6544
  FAX 603/585-9555

All the listings in this directory now available on pressure sensitive labels . . .

_____ $150 for the **Retainer** section of recruiter addresses on self-stick labels

☐ alphabetically sorted

☐ zip code sorted

_____ $175 for the **Contingency** section of recruiter addresses on self-stick labels

☐ alphabetically sorted

☐ zip code sorted

_____ $325 for **ALL** the recruiter addresses on self-stick labels

☐ alphabetically sorted

☐ zip code sorted

Customized Labels and Breakout Reports

Specialized labels may be selected by functions (up to 10) OR industry codes (up to 10) . . . see lists of codes at rear of book or at beginning of indexes. There is a minimum handling charge for up to 50 labels, then a per label charge. Please phone us to determine the number of labels in your category selection and the cost.

Familiarity with the classification system referenced above and found in the book would allow swifter handling of your order.

Special Label Department
Direct line (603) 585-3001

- *Labels come in the same alphabetical sequence as the Directory or sorted by zip code, grouped also in Retainer and Contingency sections.*
- *Saves addressing costs and eliminates errors.*
- *Convenient, inexpensive: lift off and stick on your own envelopes.*

Labels MUST be pre-paid by check, money order, MasterCard, Visa or American Express. Label orders are processed within one week of receipt of order and sent via UPS.

Send orders to:
    Kennedy Publications
    Templeton Road
    Fitzwilliam, N.H. 03447
Call: 603/585-3001 or **FAX:** 603/585-9221

Name _____

Address _____

City _____ State _____ Zip _____

Phone _____

☐ check enclosed   ☐ charge my MasterCard/Visa/American Express

Card # _____ Exp. date _____

Name as it appears on your card _____

Signature _____

Prices guaranteed through December, 1992.

COMMERCIAL USE SPECIFICALLY PROHIBITED. The prices of this directory and its labels are purposely kept as low as possible as a service to executives seeking a change (and organizations seeking to hire an executive search firm). Companies with something to sell to executive recruiters fall within the copyright restriction and must obtain permission and pay a fee for use of all or part of the list.

Basis of "Functions" Classification

Detach and use this convenient card to identify the Function and Industry codes in the recruiter listings.

00.0 **MOST**

01.0 **GENERAL MANAGEMENT**
01.1 Directors
01.2 Senior management
01.3 Middle management
01.4 MIS-Management information systems
01.5 Legal

02.0 **MANUFACTURING**
02.1 Product development
02.2 Production engineering, planning, scheduling & control
02.3 Automation, robotics
02.4 Plant management
02.5 Quality
02.6 Productivity

03.0 **MATERIALS MANAGEMENT**
03.1 Purchasing, inventory management
03.2 Materials & requirement planning
03.3 Physical distribution, traffic & transportation, logistics
03.4 Packaging

04.0 **RESEARCH & DEVELOPMENT**

05.0 **MARKETING**
05.1 Advertising, sales promotion
05.2 Marketing strategy & organization
05.3 Marketing & product research, consumer marketing
05.4 Sales, sales management, sales training
05.5 Direct mail, marketing, telemarketing
05.6 Customer service
05.7 Public relations

06.0 **HUMAN RESOURCE MANAGEMENT**
06.1 Benefits, compensation planning
06.2 Personnel selection, placement & records

07.0 **ADMINISTRATIVE SERVICES**
07.1 Clerical work measurement, records retention & management
07.2 Forms design, order processing & fulfillment, systems & procedures
07.3 Office layout, space planning
07.4 Office management

08.0 **FINANCE & ACCOUNTING**
08.1 Budgeting, cost controls
08.2 Cash management, financing & management of funds, portfolios
08.3 Credit & collection
08.4 Taxes

09.0 **INFORMATION TECHNOLOGY**
09.1 Computer security, disaster recovery, EDP audit
09.2 Specific technologies, e.g. AI, image, fiber-optics
09.3 Systems analysis & design, development, implementation, training & support
09.4 Systems integration, including hardware/software services, evaluation & selection
09.5 Expert systems
09.6 Decision support
09.7 Telecommunications

10.0 **INSURANCE/RISK MANAGEMENT**

11.0 **SPECIALIZED SERVICES**
11.1 Management consultants
11.2 Minorities
11.3 Scientific/technical
11.4 Fund-raisers & other non-profit services
11.5 Environmental
11.6 Architectural/engineering

THE DIRECTORY OF EXECUTIVE RECRUITERS/KENNEDY PUBLICATIONS
Templeton Road, Fitzwilliam, NH 03447/603-585-6544

Basis of "Industries" Classification

0.00 **MOST**	F.00 **WHOLESALE TRADE**
A.00 **AGRICULTURE, FORESTRY, FISHING & MINING**	G.00 **RETAIL TRADE**
A.01 Specific:	H.00 **FINANCE**
	H.10 Banking, financial institutions, credit agencies
B.00 **ENERGY/UTILITIES**	H.11 Securities & commodities brokers
	H.12 Venture capital
B.0W **ENVIRONMENTAL SERVICES**	
B.10 Hazardous waste, study, clean up	H.I0 **INSURANCE**
C.00 **CONSTRUCTION**	H.R0 **REAL ESTATE**
D.00 **MANUFACTURING**	I.00 **SERVICES**
D.10 Food, beverage, tobacco & kindred products	I.10 Hospitality-including hotels, resorts, clubs, restaurants, food & beverage services
D.11 Textile, apparel, related products	I.11 Entertainment, leisure, amusement, recreation, sports, travel
D.12 Lumber, wood, furniture & fixtures	I.12 Museums, galleries, music/arts, libraries & information services, membership & other non-profits
D.13 Paper & allied products	
D.14 Printing & allied industry	
D.15 Chemicals & allied products	I.13 Higher Education
D.16 Soap, perfume, cosmetics	I.14 Healthcare (except physicians; see I.15) to include administrators & practitioners-hospitals, nursing/ personal care, clinics
D.17 Drugs	
D.18 Pharmaceuticals, medical manufacturers	
D.19 Plastics, rubber products	I.15 Physicians
D.20 Paints, allied products, petroleum products	I.16 Pharmaceutical (other than manufacturing)
D.21 Leather, stone, glass, concrete, clay products	I.17 Legal
	I.18 Computer Services
D.22 Primary metal industry, fabricated metal products, machinery, general industrial machinery & appliances	I.19 Accounting & miscellaneous business services
D.23 Transportation equipment including automobiles & other motor vehicles	I.20 Equipment services, including leasing
	I.21 Management & personnel services
D.24 Office machinery, computers, computer products, software, electronic & electrical equipment & components	J.00 **COMMUNICATIONS**
	J.10 Advertising/public relations
	J.11 Publishing, print media
D.25 Measuring/analyzing & controlling instruments & optical goods	J.12 TV, cable, motion pictures, video, radio
D.26 Miscellaneous manufacturing industries	J.13 Telephone, telecommunications
D.D0 **PACKAGING**	K.00 **PUBLIC ADMINISTRATION/ GOVERNMENT**
D.E0 **AEROSPACE**	K.10 Defense
D.H0' **HIGH TECH/ELECTRONICS**	L.00 **NON-CLASSIFIABLE INDUSTRIES**
D.I0 **BIOTECH/GENETIC ENGINEERING**	
E.00 **TRANSPORTATION**	

THE DIRECTORY OF EXECUTIVE RECRUITERS/KENNEDY PUBLICATIONS
Templeton Road, Fitzwilliam, NH 03447/603-585-6544